Neuropsychological Assessment

Neuropsychological Assessment

Second Edition

MURIEL DEUTSCH LEZAK

Oregon Health Sciences University
and
Veterans Administration Hospital
Portland, Oregon

New York   Oxford
OXFORD UNIVERSITY PRESS
1983

Library of Congress Cataloging in Publication Data
Lezak, Muriel Deutsch.
    Neuropsychological assessment.
    Bibliography: p.   Includes index.
    1. Neuropsychology. 2. Psychodiagnostics.
I. Title. [DNLM: 1. Neurophysiology.
2. Psychological tests. 3. Psychophysiology.
WM 145 L686n]
QP360.L52   1983   616.8'0475   82-7937
ISBN 0-19-503039-7   AACR2

Printing (last digit): 9 8 7 6 5 4 3

Printed in the United States of America

To Sidney

Foreword

Although neuropsychological assessment has a long history, its growth during the past two decades has been particularly rapid. In addition to the development of new testing methods to meet special needs in diagnostic evaluation, there has been a steadily increasing utilization of neuropsychological assessment techniques in neurology and psychiatry and an expansion of their scope of application into other fields such as education, behavioral medicine, and gerontology.

It is within this context of rapid growth that the first edition of Dr. Muriel Lezak's book on neuropsychological assessment appeared in 1976. Its immediate success was due to a number of reasons. It was clearly written. It covered the major aspects of neuropsychological assessment in detail and with uncommon insight. Written by a neuropsychologist of wide experience, it was clinically relevant. Above all, as explicitly stated in the preface of the book, it argued for a flexible approach to the assessment of the individual patient if the questions leading to his referral for examination are to be answered adequately.

No wonder then that Dr. Lezak's book was so warmly received. It met a long-standing need and it fulfilled its promise. The advances in the field since the publication of *Neuropsychological Assessment* made it inevitable that an updated edition would soon be required. The revision has now been completed and the result is a textbook of enhanced value to workers in the field. A comparison of the first and second editions makes it clear that Dr. Lezak has devoted a very considerable amount of time, effort, and thought to the task of revision. We are grateful to her.

Arthur L. Benton

Preface

While this revision of *Neuropsychological Assessment* differs from its predecessor in many ways, the goals that guided its preparation were essentially the same as with the first edition. My attempt to achieve these goals in the midst of the explosive growth of the neurosciences and of every clinical domain associated with them has resulted in a somewhat parallel growth of this book.

Updating accounts for only part of this edition's larger size. A number of areas have undergone such rapid development or radical change as to warrant much fuller treatment than they received in the first edition. For example, the discussions of aging and of cerebral lateralization and handedness have more than doubled in length. The presentation of mental status examinations and other observational assessment techniques has been expanded into a chapter (19) on observational methods. The section on assessment of motor functions has also been expanded and incorporated into a new chapter (16) concerning the evaluation of executive functions. An additional chapter (7) reviews the major disorders that affect brain function, covering their nature, pathogenesis, and neuropsychological consequences.

Writing this second edition was much more challenging than I had anticipated. Research in anthropology, psychiatry, education, and cognitive psychology has centered increasingly on the brain. Many theories and techniques emerging from this research can be advantageously applied to neuropsychological assessment. I have therefore included some of the relevant material from these and other fields of study not obviously concerned with neuropsychology or assessment.

A more frustrating challenge has been simply to keep up with the voluminous outpouring of literature in all relevant domains while working through the book chapter by chapter. Often I finished a topic, thinking it would be a closed subject for a while, only to discover some weeks or months later that a critical new issue had been raised or a once seemingly basic tenet or stable finding had come under serious question. In many instances, the new material required an elaboration or even a complete reorganization of what had already been rewritten. The almost daily appearance of new findings and restatements of old theories has made it inevitable that by the time this

PREFACE

book is published, sections will be out of date. One can never really "catch up" in neuropsychology.

Writing this book has also given me much pleasure, particularly in extending my contacts with fellow neuropsychologists and colleagues in the behavioral sciences throughout the world. Many have been generous with their knowledge and skills; all have been encouraging. Lacking the space to acknowledge each of them individually, I hope that each will accept my thanks and appreciation for his or her contribution.

Chief among those whose support and assistance contributed to this book is Arthur L. Benton. Professor Benton was involved with the book from its inception, and has continued as mentor, technical advisor, and a graciously helpful and wise friend.

Proximity placed a number of persons where I could make more than ordinary requests of them. For their extraordinary assistance, I want to thank Laurence M. Binder, Alan E. Brooker, D. Neil Brooks, John M. Ehrfurth, Christine Glenn, Lee Anne Golper, Diane B. Howieson, David Margolin, Oscar S. Marin, Ruth G. Matarazzo, Robert B. Rafal, Marie T. Rau, and Kevin W. Walsh.

Students and trainees have continued to be a source of stimulation and provided a candid sounding board for many ideas. Material prepared by Lowell Coutant for an examination paper has been included in the text.

Like the first edition, this work too has received library and other technical support from the Portland Veterans Administration Medical Center and the Oregon Health Sciences University. The editorial assistance of Brenda Jones and help from Sue Ferguson in preparing the references and indices is gratefully appreciated.

I feel particularly fortunate in having had the continuing benefit of a close working relationship with my editor, Jeffrey House.

My largest measure of gratitude goes to my husband for his pertinent suggestions, his good-humored patience, and his encouragement and support.

Portland, Oregon   M.D.L.
September 1982

Contents

CONTENTS

CONTENTS

CONTENTS

xiv

CONTENTS

CONTENTS

Neuropsychological Assessment

I

The Theory and Practice
of Neuropsychological Assessment

Introduction

Like every other discipline, neuropsychology is a child of its time and place. In this country it began to disengage from its parent disciplines of neurology and psychology and develop an identity of its own in the 1940's (see Aita, Armitage et al., 1947; Hebb, 1949; Klebanoff, 1945; and Teuber, 1948). At that time psychology's looser constructs were undergoing reexamination in the cold light of operationalism and the "intuitive" *modus operandi* of the earlier armchair and couch theoreticians were giving way to more rigorous-appearing *actuarial* (statistical probability) techniques (Meehl, 1954).

Since American neuropsychology evolved mainly out of psychology, it is not surprising that from the beginning some approaches to neuropsychological assessment reflected psychology's new operational/statistical affirmations. These approaches rely on statistical techniques for defining such constructs as "organic impairment" and "failure;" and assign diagnoses on actuarial bases (see Fletcher et al., 1978; Reitan, 1955). In strict applications of some actuarial approaches, the neuropsychologist need not even see the patient but draws his or her conclusions from scores obtained by a technician trained in highly standardized testing procedures. In the strictest applications of this approach, the diagnostic possibilities are generated by a computer (see K.M. Adams et al., 1975; Moses and Golden, 1979; E.W. Russell et al., 1970; Swiercinsky, 1978).

Contemporaneous with these American developments has been the evolution of a clinical-theoretical approach in Russian neuropsychology under the leadership of A.R. Luria, whose training had been in neurology and psychoanalysis. Given Luria's background, it is not surprising that in the Soviet Union neuropsychological assessment developed out of single case studies and emphasized careful, intensive observations. Along with many brilliant theoretical insights and clinical inferences, Luria's contribution to neuropsychological assessment consists of a rich store of sensitive qualitative behavioral descriptions, of reproductions of patients' writings and drawings that capture common patterns of distortion while exemplifying the uniqueness of each patient's behavioral product, of techniques for eliciting behaviors that are relevant to the understanding of brain function and the treatment of neuropsychological prob-

3

lems, and an approach based on the generalization and testing of hypotheses to guide clinical exploration, diagnosis, and treatment (e.g., Luria, 1966, 1970b, 1973b). Although his methodological approach has been systematized, his chief expositor (Christensen, 1979a) has tried to preserve its exploratory and qualitative, hypothesis-testing nature while providing an orderly basis for making observations and drawing inferences (see pp. 567–568).

In their purest forms, actuarial and clinical-theoretical approaches can be thought of as extremes on a continuum of quantification. Actuarial systems that rely exclusively on statistical evaluations of scores based on the number of correct or erroneous responses or on performance time and derived from the universal application of a single procedural format may be located at the quantitative end of the continuum. At the qualitative end are assessment approaches built on sensitive and detailed observations of responses with particular attention paid to the manner in which responses are defective but which lack objective standardization.

However, to do justice to a field of inquiry as complex as brain-behavior relationships in adult human beings, an adaptable assessment methodology that incorporates the strengths of both quantitative and qualitative approaches is required. Standardized procedures eliciting behavior that can be measured along empirically defined and scaled dimensions provide objectivity and the potential to make fine distinctions and comparisons which would be unattainable by clinical observation alone. Still, examinations cannot be adequately conducted nor can test scores be properly interpreted in a psychological or social vacuum. The uniqueness of each patient's capacity, disability, needs, and situation calls for discriminating, flexible, and imaginative use of examination techniques. Judicious interpretation of examination data takes into account the patient's history, present circumstances, attitudes and expectation regarding self and the examination, and the quality of the patient's test responses and behavior in the examination. Of necessity, a reliable examination and valid conclusions depend on intensive examiner contact with the patient. Thus, the assessment approach offered here is best represented by the middle of the quantitative-qualitative continuum, for it seeks to draw upon and integrate the techniques and theoretical contributions from each side.

The nature of its subject matter makes an integrated approach to neuropsychological assessment a complex undertaking. A competent practitioner must have the interviewing and counseling skills, the appreciation of social and cultural variables, and the psychodiagnostic acumen of a clinical psychologist; the statistical sophistication and test familiarity of a psychometrician; and a fairly comprehensive understanding of the human nervous system and its pathologies, at least at a level comparable to that of a general medical practitioner. Regardless of whether the basic training of an aspiring neuropsychologist was in clinical or experimental psychology, neurology or psychiatry, or a related field such as speech pathology, the amount of additional knowledge that must be absorbed and the variety of additional clinical skills that must be learned and polished preclude any quick acquisition of neuropsychological expertise.

A full discussion of the theoretical and clinical foundations of neuropsychological assessment is obviously beyond the scope of a single volume. However, in keeping with my thesis that the neuropsychological examination cannot be properly conducted or interpreted in either a vacuum or a mechanical manner (i.e., as an isolated, impersonal examination procedure, like drawing a blood sample or taking a chest x-ray), the first part of this book touches upon the chief disciplines in which the clinician needs to be knowledgeable in order to conduct responsible neuropsychological assessment. Thus, the first eight chapters deal with behavior in terms of both psychological constructs and neuroanatomical correlates; behavioral measurement from theoretical, statistical, and clinical standpoints; recommendations for conducting a neuropsychological examination; common patterns of neuropsychological deficit; and significant problems in interpreting neuropsychological findings. These chapters should inform the reader of the scope and central issues of neuropsychological assessment and its parent and supporting disciplines. The references will direct the reader into the literature should he or she wish to pursue a topic further.

1

The Practice of Neuropsychology

Clinical neuropsychology is an applied science concerned with the behavioral expression of brain dysfunction. Its rapid evolution in recent years reflects a growing sensitivity among clinicians to the practical problems of identification, assessment, and rehabilitation of brain damaged patients.

The need for screening and diagnosis of brain injured and behaviorally disturbed soldiers during wartime and for their rehabilitation afterwards created the first large-scale demands for neuropsychology programs. Now many psychologists, psychiatrists, and counselors ask for neuropsychological assistance in identifying those candidates for their services who may have underlying neurological disorders. Neurologists and neurosurgeons are increasing their requests for behavioral evaluations to aid in diagnosis and to document the course of brain disorders or the effects of treatment. A fruitful interaction is taking place between neuropsychology and gerontology that enhances the knowledge and clinical applications of each discipline. Child neuropsychology has been developing hand in hand with advances in the study of mental retardation, learning disabilities, and children's behavior problems[1] (Reitan and Davison, 1974, *passim;* E. M. Taylor, 1959; Benton and Pearl, 1978; Filskov and Boll, 1981).

Much of the emphasis in clinical neuropsychology has been on *assessing* behavioral change. In part this has occurred because so much of the demand on neuropsychology has been for assistance with diagnostic problems. Moreover, patients seen by neuropsychologists are often limited in their capacity to benefit from training programs and counseling. Then, too, as one of the clinical sciences, neuropsychology may be evolving naturally, for assessment tends to play a predominant role while these sciences are relatively young. Treatment techniques develop as diagnostic categories and etiological relationships are defined and clarified.

---

[1]The assessment of children and the consideration of brain disorders presenting prior to maturity have their own conceptual framework, methods, and data, which are outside the scope of this book.

Any of three different purposes may prompt a neuropsychological examination: diagnosis, patient care—including questions about treatment and planning, and research. Each purpose calls for some differences in assessment strategies.

1. Diagnosis. Of the many practical applications of neuropsychological assessment, its diagnostic efficacy has probably received the most recognition. Neuropsychological assessment has proven useful in discriminating between psychiatric and neurological symptoms, in identifying a possible neurological disorder in a nonpsychiatric patient, in helping to distinguish between different neurological conditions, and in providing behavioral data for localizing the site—or at least the hemisphere side—of a lesion. However, in many cases today, accurate diagnosis, including localization of a lesion, is achieved by means of the neurologist's examination and laboratory tools. Neuropsychology's diagnostic role has correspondingly diminished as its contributions to patient care and to research have grown.

More than any other advance in techniques for the diagnosis and localization of pathological conditions of the brain, *computerized tomography (CT scan)*[1] has reduced the number of cases in which neuropsychological assessment, along with most other older diagnostic procedures, may make a definitive contribution to the diagnostic process (Bigler and Steinman, 1981; Mazzochi and Vignolo, 1979; Weisberg, 1979). Still, there are many conditions in which CT scans and other laboratory data are not diagnostically helpful and the neuropsychological findings can be diagnostically crucial. Neuropsychological techniques will continue to be an essential part of the neurodiagnostic armamentarium (Fox et al., 1979; L. Jacobs et al., 1976; Masdeu et al., 1977; Weisberg, 1979).

2. Patient care. Some patients referred for neuropsychological assessment are obviously brain damaged. If scars or disfiguration of the face or skull, or a telltale weakness or loss of use of the limbs of one side of the body do not make their problems apparent, histories of convulsive disorder, prolonged unconsciousness following head injury or fever, or slow deterioration of cognitive abilities make their condition evident. Many patients come with definitive diagnoses; others who are clearly brain damaged present such confusing, unfamiliar, or equivocal symptom pictures as to defy any system of discrete categorization. When such patients are referred, it is usually to obtain a detailed description of their intellectual status and personality characteristics—often with questions about their adjustment to their disabilities—so that they and the people responsible for their well-being may know how the neurological condition has affected their behavior.

Descriptive evaluations may be employed in many ways for the care and treatment of the brain injured patient. Precise descriptive information about intellectual and emotional status is essential for careful management of many neurological disorders.

---

[1]Sometimes called *CAT scan*, for *computerized axial tomography*, or *CTT scan*, for *computerized transaxial tomography*: a neuroradiological technique that provides images of the different densities of internal structures, thereby permitting visualization of intracranial anatomy.

Rational planning usually depends on an understanding of the patient's capabilities, limitations, the kinds of psychological changes he is undergoing, and the impact of these changes on his experience of himself and on his behavior.

Neuropsychological data are likely to provide the most sensitive indices of the extent to which medications enhance or compromise a patient's mental efficiency. In many cases the neuropsychological examination can answer questions concerning the patient's capacity for self-care, his reliability in following a therapeutic regimen, his ability not merely to drive a car but to handle traffic emergencies, or his appreciation of money and of his own financial situation. When all the data of the neuropsychological examination—the patient's history and background, the qualitative observations, and the quantitative scores—are taken together, the examiner will know how the patient can best compensate for deficits, how he reacts to them, and whether and how retraining could be profitably undertaken (R. K. Heaton and Pendleton, 1981).

The relative sensitivity and precision of neuropsychological measurements make them well suited for following the course of many neurological diseases. Data from successive neuropsychological examinations repeated at regular intervals can provide reliable indications of whether the underlying neurological condition is changing, and if so, how rapidly and in what ways. Repeated testing may also be used to measure the effects of surgical procedures, medical treatment, or retraining.

A single 27-year-old highly skilled logger with no history of psychiatric disturbance underwent surgical removal of a right frontotemporal subdural hematoma resulting from a car accident. Twenty months later his mother brought him, protesting but docile, to the hospital. This alert, oriented, but poorly groomed man complained of voices that came from his teeth, explaining that he received radio waves and could "communicate to their source." He was emotionally unexpressive with sparse speech and frequent 20–30-second response latencies that occasionally disrupted his train of thought. He denied depression and sleeping or eating disturbances. He also denied delusions or hallucinations, but during one interview pointed out Ichabod Crane's headless horseman while looking at some buildings across the hospital lawn. As he became comfortable, he talked more freely and revealed that he was continually troubled by delusional ideation. His mother complained that he was almost completely reclusive, without initiative, and indifferent to his surroundings. He had some concern about being watched, and once she had heard him muttering, "I would like my mind back."

Most of his neuropsychological test scores were below those he had obtained when examined six-and-one-half months after the injury. His only *above average* scores were on two tests of well-learned verbal material: background information and reading vocabulary. He received scores in the *low average* to *borderline defective* ranges on oral arithmetic, visuomotor tracking, and all visual reasoning and visuo-constructive—including drawing—tests. Although his verbal learning curve was considerably *below average*, immediate verbal span and verbal retention were all within the *average* range. Immediate recall of designs was *defective*.

Shortly after he was hospitalized and had completed the 20-month examination, he was put on trifluoperazine (Stelazine), 15 mg. h.s., continuing this treatment for a month while remaining under hospital observation. He was then reexamined.

9

The patient was still poorly groomed, alert, and oriented. His reaction times were well within normal limits. Speech and thinking were unremarkable. While not expressing strong emotions, he smiled, complained, and displayed irritation appropriately. He reported what hallucinating had been like and related the content of some of his hallucinations. He talked about arranging for a physical activities program when he returned home but felt he was not yet ready to work.

His test scores 21 months after the injury were mostly in the *high average* to *superior* ranges. Much of his gain came from faster response times that enabled him to get full rather than partial or no credit on timed items he had completed perfectly but slowly the previous month. Although puzzle constructions (both geometric designs and objects) were performed at the *high average* level, his drawing continued to be of *low average* quality (but better than at 20 months). All verbal memory tests were performed at *average* to *high average* levels; the visual memory test was performed without error, gaining him a *superior* rating. He did simple visuomotor tracking tasks without error and at an *average* rate of speed; his score on a complex visuomotor tracking task was at the 90th percentile.

In this case, repeated testing provided documentation of both the cognitive repercussions of his psychiatric disturbance and the effects of psychotropic medication on his intellectual functioning. This case demonstrates the value of repeated testing, particularly when one or another aspect of the patient's behavior appears to be in flux. Had testing been done only at the time of the second or third examination, a very distorted impression of the patient's cognitive status would have been gained. Fortunately, since the patient was in a research project, the first examination data were available to cast doubt on the validity of the second and third set of test performances, and therefore the fourth examination was given as well.

The brain damaged patient too must have factual information about his functioning if he is to understand himself and set realistic goals, yet his need for information about himself is often overlooked. Most people who sustain brain injury experience changes in their intellectual and emotional functioning, but because they are on the inside, so to speak, they may have difficulty appreciating how their behavior has changed and what about them is still the same. These misperceptions tend to heighten what mental confusion may already be present as a result of altered patterns of neural activity.

Distrust of their experiences, particularly their memory and perceptions, is another problem shared by many brain damaged persons, probably as a result of even very slight disruptions and alterations of the exceedingly complex neural pathways that mediate the intellectual functions. This distrust seems to arise from the feelings of strangeness and confusion accompanying previously familiar habits, thoughts, and sensations that are now experienced differently. The self-doubt of the brain injured person is usually distinguishable from neurotic self-doubts about life goals, values, principles, and so on, but can be just as painful and emotionally crippling. Careful reporting and explanation of psychological findings can do much to allay the patient's anxieties and dispel confusion.

The following case exemplifies patients' needs for information about their psychological status.

An attractive, unmarried 24-year-old bank teller sustained a brain concussion in a car accident while skiing in Europe. She appeared to make an uneventful and practically complete recovery, with only a little residual facial numbness. When she came home, she returned to her old job but was unable to perform acceptably although she seemed capable of doing each part of it well. She lost interest in outdoor sports although her coordination and strength were essentially unimpaired. She became socially withdrawn, moody, morose, and dependent. A psychiatric consultant diagnosed depression, and when her unhappiness was not diminished by counseling or antidepressant drugs, he administered shock treatment which gave only temporary relief.

While waiting to begin a second course of shock treatment, she was given a neuropsychological examination at the request of the foreign magistrate who was responsible for awarding monetary compensation for her injuries. This examination demonstrated a small but definite impairment of immediate memory, concentration, and conceptual tracking. The patient reported a pervasive sense of unsureness which she expressed in hesitancy and doubt about almost everything she did. These feelings of doubt had undermined the young woman's trust in many of her previously automatic responses, destroying a lively spontaneity that was once a very appealing feature of her personality. Further, like many postconcussion patients, she had compounded the problem by interpreting her inner uneasiness as symptomatic of "mental illness," and psychiatric opinion confirmed her fears. Thus, while her intellectual impairment was not an obstacle to rehabilitation, her bewildered experience of it led to disastrous changes in her personal life. A clear explanation of her actual limitations and their implications brought immediate relief of anxiety and set the stage for sound counseling.

The concerned family also needs to know the patient's psychological condition in order to deal with him appropriately. Family members need to understand the patient's new, often puzzling, mental changes, how they affect his cognitive status and what may be their psychosocial repercussions. Even quite subtle defects in motivation, in abilities to plan, organize, and carry out activities, and in self-monitoring can compromise a patient's capacity to earn a living and may render him socially dependent as well (Lezak, 1982a). Moreover, many brain damaged patients no longer fit easily into family life as their irritability, self-centeredness, impulsivity, or apathy create awesome emotional burdens on family members, generate conflicts between family members and with the patient, and strain family ties, often beyond endurance (Malone, 1977; Oddy et al., 1978a; Rosenbaum and Najenson, 1976). The more information families have about their neurologically impaired member, the better able they will be to cope with both his problems and theirs (Bardach, 1969; Lezak, 1978a).

In many cases, other persons share responsibility for the brain damaged patient's care, such as physiatrists, speech pathologists, rehabilitation counselors, occupational and physical therapists, and visiting nurses. They need current appraisals of the patient's psychological functioning so that they can adapt their program and goals to the patient's changing needs and capacities. Neuropsychological assessment of the patient's defective behavior can provide the rehabilitation therapist with a description of the patient's mental capabilities. In addition, it can give an often more important analysis of *how* the patient fails that will tell the therapist how the patient might improve his performance in a problem area (e.g., Hoyle and Haaland, 1978). Ways in which the results of detailed neuropsychological analyses of behavioral deficits may be applied to rehabilitation problems have been effectively demonstrated by Leonard Diller and his group (1974; Diller and Weinberg, 1977; Institute of Rehabilitation Medicine, 1980, 1981, 1982). Such analyses may also indicate whether a patient can benefit from psychotherapy, particular behavioral training techniques, and generally accepted counseling approaches (e.g., Luria, 1972).

A 57-year-old superintendent of security in a large educational complex lost consciousness at work and was immediately hospitalized with cardiac arrythmia. Although he also had a left-sided paralysis that disappeared within weeks, the physician in charge only told the patient and family that he had had a heart attack.

During the next two years, the now physically competent patient was hired for and fired from 16 different jobs, his formerly satisfying marriage deteriorated badly, he tended to be hostile and irritable, and his spouse complained that this once responsible, caring man had become childishly self-centered, demanding, dependent, and financially irresponsible. In seeking psychiatric help, the family reported the physician's diagnosis. On the basis of the wife's complaints and a brief psychiatric intake examination, the patient was given a provisional diagnosis of "cardiac neurotic." He was admitted to a behaviorally oriented treatment unit that provides patients with chronic illnesses training in resocialization techniques, redirects their activities and interests, and involves the patients in some group psychotherapy and marital counseling.

The patient appeared to benefit from the highly structured program each of the three five-day weeks he participated, in that his activity level rose considerably and he seemed happier. However, he disappointed his therapists by returning to the hospital each Monday with no apparent gains maintained. He was discharged at the end of three weeks and referred to a family therapist who, having had intensive training in neuropsychology, began by asking his wife for a detailed account of the "heart attack." When the family therapist heard that the patient had had left-sided weakness, she referred him for neuropsychological assessment.

On testing the patient achieved high scores on most verbal tests, demonstrated some mild constructional impairment, and did poorly on all tasks requiring integration of details and learning. His relatively low scores on constructional tasks and defective learning and integrating abilities contrasted markedly with his *high average* and better verbal test performances. This pattern of deficit is typically found in persons with right anterior brain lesions and is in accord with the wife's report of left-sided weakness. It was now apparent that the patient could not benefit enough from psychotherapy to make further work with him a practical venture. The focus of treatment shifted to helping his wife understand and cope with his mental and emotional disabilities and to placing the patient in a community-based activity program that could give him the daily structured activities and social stimulation he needed and that his wife alone could not provide.

3. *Research.* Neuropsychological assessment has been used to study the organization of brain activity and its translation into behavior and in investigations of specific brain disorders and behavioral disabilities. Research with neuropsychological assessment techniques also involves their development, standardization, and evaluation. The precision and sensitivity of neuropsychological measurement techniques make them valuable tools for investigating small, sometimes quite subtle behavioral alterations, such as those that may follow certain neurosurgical procedures or metabolic changes.

Neuropsychological research has had a very direct influence on the practice of clinical neuropsychology. Many of the tests used in neuropsychological evaluations—such as arithmetic tests or tests for visual memory and learning—were originally developed for the examination of normal intellectual functioning and were recalibrated for neuropsychological use in the course of research on brain dysfunction. Other assessment techniques—as for instance, certain tests of tactile identification or concept formation—were designed specifically for studies of brain dysfunction. Their often rapid incorporation into clinical use attests to the very lively exchange between research and practice. This exchange works expecially well in neuropsychology because clinician and researcher are so often one and the same.

Usually neuropsychological studies serve more than one purpose. Even though the examination may be initially undertaken to answer a single question—often, a diagnostic issue—the neuropsychologist may uncover vocational or family problems, or patient care needs that have been overlooked, or the patient may prove to be a suitable candidate for research. Integral to all psychological assessment procedures is an evaluation of the patient's needs and circumstances from a psychological viewpoint. When indicated, the neuropsychologist will redirect the scope of his inquiry to include problems he has defined as well as those stated in the referral.

When a single examination is undertaken to serve all three purposes—diagnosis, patient care, and research—a great deal of data may be collected about the patient and then applied selectively. For example, the examination of a patient complaining of immediate memory problems can be conducted to answer various questions. A diagnostic determination of whether his immediate memory is impaired may only require finding out if he remembers significantly fewer words of a list and numbers of a series than the slowest normal adult. To understand *how* he is affected by his memory dysfunction, it is important to know the number of words he can remember and under what conditions, the nature of his errors, his sensitivity and reactions to his performance, and the effect of his disability on his day-to-day activities. Research might involve studying his immediate memory in conjunction with blood sugar levels or brain wave tests, or comparing his performance to that of patients with other kinds of memory complaints.

The ways in which neuropsychological assessment has been employed in legal proceedings illustrate the usefulness of multipurpose studies. It has become quite commonplace in personal injury actions, in which monetary compensation is sought for claims of bodily injury and loss of function, for lawyers to request neuropsychological examinations of the claimant. In such cases, the neuropsychologist usually examines the claimant to evaluate the type and amount of behavioral impairment sustained and to estimate the claimant's rehabilitation potential and the extent of his need for future care. Occasionally, the request for compensation may hinge on the neuropsychologist's report.

In criminal cases, a neuropsychologist may assess a defendant when there is reason to suspect that brain dysfunction contributed to his misbehavior or when there is a question about his mental capacity to stand trial. The case of the murderer of President Kennedy's alleged assailant is perhaps the most famous instance in which a psychologist determined that the defendant's capacity for judgment and self-control was impaired by brain dysfunction (J. Kaplan and Waltz, 1965). Interestingly, the possibility that the defendant, Jack Ruby, had psychomotor epilepsy was first raised by Dr. Roy Schafer's interpretation of the psychological test results and was subsequently confirmed by *electroencephalographic* (EEG) (brain wave) studies. At the sentencing stage of a criminal proceeding, the neuropsychologist may also be asked for his opinion about treatment of a convicted defendant or his potential for rehabilitation.

The clinical neuropsychologist regularly deals with a variety of questions, a wide range of behaviors, and the very disparate capacities of his patients. This diversity of problems and persons presents an unending challenge to the examiner who wants to satisfy all the purposes for which the examination was undertaken and still test the patient at levels suited to his capacities and limitations. Moreover, in so new, complex, and broad-ranging a field few facts or principles can be taken for granted, there are few techniques that cannot benefit from modifications, and few rules of procedure will not be bent or broken as knowledge and experience accumulate. The practice of neuropsychology calls for flexibility, curiosity, and inventiveness even in the most routine work. But even the routine work of the neuropsychologist holds the promise of new insights into the workings of the brain and the excitement of discovery.

14

2
Basic Concepts

Examining the Brain

Direct observation of the fully integrated functioning of living human brains will probably always be impossible. The advances of neurosurgery and sophisticated electrical stimulation techniques permit observations of some circumscribed aspects of brain functioning when discrete structures or areas of the brain are electrically aroused (Fedio and Van Buren, 1975; Ojemann and Whitaker, 1978; Ojemann and Mateer, 1979; Penfield and Rasmussen, 1950). However, the extrinsic, isolated, and functionally irrelevant (if not frankly noxious) nature of the stimulus, the restricted range of response permitted a surgical patient in an operating theater, the already diseased or damaged condition of the brains studied by these direct stimulation techniques, and the inconceivability of opening up or puncturing a human cranium without very serious medical reason necessarily limit the scope of these investigations and the generalizations that can be drawn from them.

Thus, neuroscientists have had to rely for much of their knowledge of the state and functioning of living human brains on indirect methods of examination. Among the most useful of these are neuroradiographic techniques that can visualize the structural spaces within and surrounding the brain *(pneumoencephalography)*, the blood vessels of the brain *(angiography, arteriography, venography)*, and the different densities of internal structures reconstructed into shadow pictures of the intracranial anatomy (CAT scan, see note, p. 8), as well as traditional skull x-rays.

The brain can also be examined indirectly through the study of its functions, such as its electrical activity as manifested in brain waves *(electroencephalography)* or in discrete firing patterns of single cells or cell clusters *(evoked potential techniques)*. The usual clinical approach to the study of brain functions remains the neurological examination, which includes *extensive* study of the brain's chief product—behavior. The neurologist examines the strength, efficiency, reactivity, and appropriateness of the patient's responses to commands, questions, discrete stimulation of particular neural subsystems, and challenges to specific muscle groups and motor patterns. The neurologist also examines body structures, looking for such evidence of brain dysfunction as swelling of the retina or shriveled muscles due to insufficient neural stimulation. In the neurological examination of behavior, the clinician reviews behavior patterns generated by neuroanatomical subsystems, measuring patients' responses in relatively coarse gradations or noting their absence.

Neuropsychological assessment is another method of examining the brain by studying its behavioral product. Since the subject matter of neuropsychological assessment is behavior, it relies on many of the same techniques, assumptions, and theories as does psychological assessment (Cleeland, 1976). Also like psychological assessment, neuropsychological assessment involves the *intensive* study of behavior by means of interviews and standardized scaled tests and questionnaires that provide relatively precise and sensitive indices of behavior. The distinctive character of neuropsychological assessment lies in a conceptual frame of reference that takes brain function as its point of departure. Regardless of whether a behavioral study is undertaken for clinical or research purposes, it is neuropsychological so long as the questions that prompted it, the central issues, the findings, or the inferences drawn from them ultimately relate to brain function.

Brain Damage And Organicity

Old concepts die hard. Physicians, for instance, are still taught that brain concussion rarely has permanent effects (e.g., Åstrom and Vander Eecken, 1977; see pp. 169–174 for a discussion of the sequelae of concussion). Thus, some of the earliest neuropsychological concepts are still with us though the naively crude observations and methods that produced these simplistic explanations have long since been supplanted.

Throughout the 1930s and 40s and well into the 50s, most clinicians treated brain damage as if it were a unitary phenomenon—"organicity." It was certainly well recognized that brain damage resulted from many different conditions and had different effects (Babcock; 1930; Klebanoff, 1945) and that certain specific brain–behavior correlates, such as the role of the left hemisphere in language functions, appeared with predictable regularity. Yet much of the work with brain damaged patients was based on the assumption that organicity was characterized by one central and therefore universal behavioral defect (K. Goldstein, 1939; Yates, 1954). Even so thoughtful an observer as Teuber could say in 1948 that "Multiple-factor hypotheses are not necessarily preferable to an equally tentative, heuristic formulation of a general factor—the assumption of a fundamental disturbance ... which appears with different specifications in each cerebral region. In fact, the assumption of a fundamental disturbance may have definite advantages at the present state of knowledge" (pp. 45–46).

The early formulations of brain damage as a unitary condition that is either present or absent were reflected in the proliferation of single function tests of "organicity" that were evaluated, in turn, solely in terms of how well they distinguished "organics" from psychiatric patients or normal control subjects (e.g., Klebanoff, 1945; Spreen and Benton, 1965; Yates, 1954). The "fundamental disturbance" of brain damage, however, turned out to be exasperatingly elusive. Despite many ingenious efforts to devise

16

a test or examination technique that would be sensitive to organicity per se—a neuropsychological litmus paper, so to speak—no one behavioral phenomenon could be found that was shared by all brain injured persons but by no one else. This one-dimensional approach to neuropsychological assessment continues to show up occasionally in the literature and in clinical assumptions.

In its next evolutionary stage, brain damage was still treated as a unitary phenomenon, but was given measurable extension. The theoretical basis for this position had been provided by Karl Lashley in his Law of Mass Action and Principle of Equipotentiality (1929). Lashley knew that even in rats certain functions, such as visual discrimination, were predictably compromised by lesions involving well-defined *cortical* areas of the brain (see pp. 49–50). However, his experiments with rats led him to conclude that by and large there was a direct correlation between the effectiveness of an animal's behavior and the extent to which its cortex was intact, regardless of the site of damage, and that the contributions of different parts of the cortex were interchangeable.

In their now classical paper, Chapman and Wolff (1959) reviewed the literature on localization of function, presented data on their patients, and concluded with Lashley, that sheer extent of cortical loss played a greater role in determining the amount of cognitive impairment than did the site of the lesion.[1] "Brain damage" (or "organicity," or "organic impairment"—the terms varied from author to author but the meaning was essentially the same) took on a one-dimensionality and lack of specificity similar to that of the concept "sick" (Logue, 1975). Neither "brain damage" or "sickness" has etiological implications, neither implies the presence or absence of any particular symptoms or signs, nor can predictions or prescriptions be made on the basis of either term. Still, "brain damage" as a unitary but measurable condition remains a vigorous concept, reflected in the many test and battery indices, ratios, and quotients that purport to represent some quantity or relative degree of "organicity."

Current thinking in neuropsychology recognizes brain damage as a measurable multidimensional phenomenon that requires a multidimensional examination approach (e.g., G. Goldstein and Shelly, 1973; Goodglass and Kaplan, 1979; A. Smith, 1975). The behavioral repercussions of brain damage vary with the nature, extent, location, and duration of the lesion; with the age, sex, physical condition, and psychosocial background and status of the patient; and with individual neuroanatomical and physiological differences (see pp. 102–104 and Chapter 8). Not only is the pattern of deficits displayed by one brain damaged person likely to differ from the pattern displayed by another with damage involving anatomically and functionally different areas, but impairment patterns of patients with similar lesions may also differ (Ajuriaguerra and Hécaen, 1960; Luria, 1970b; Wepman, 1968). Thus, although brain damage is useful as an organizing concept for a broad range of behavioral disorders,

---

[1] In evaluating the Chapman and Wolff paper, it should be noted that subjects with language impairments had been systematically culled from the patient population. Moreover, the author's estimates of cognitive impairment came from summed Wechsler test scores [i.e., "IQ" scores; see pp. 22–23], thus obscuring subtest score discrepancies that may have differentiated their variously brain injured subjects.

when dealing with individual patients the concept of brain damage only becomes meaningful in terms of specific behavioral dysfunctions and their implications regarding underlying brain pathology.

Dimensions of Behavior

Behavior may be conceptualized in terms of three functional systems: (1) *intellect*, which is the information-handling aspect of behavior; (2) *emotionality*, which concerns feelings and motivation; and (3) *control*, which has to do with how behavior is expressed. Components of each of these three sets of functions are as integral to every bit of behavior as are length and breadth and height to the shape of any object. Moreover, like the dimensions of space, each one can be conceptualized and treated separately. The early Greek philosophers were the first to conceive of a tripartite division of behavior, postulating that different principles of the "soul" governed the rational, appetitive, and animating aspects of behavior. Present-day research in the behavioral sciences tends to support the philosophers' intuitive insights into how the totality of behavior is organized. These classical and scientifically meaningful functional systems lend themselves well to the practical observation, measurement, and description of behavior and constitute a framework for organizing behavioral data generally.

In neuropsychology, the intellectual functions have received more attention than the emotional and control systems. This is partly because the intellectual defects of organically impaired patients can figure so prominently in their symptomatology, partly because they can be so readily conceptualized, measured, and correlated with neuroanatomically identifiable systems, and partly because the structured nature of most medical and psychological examinations does not provide much opportunity for subtle emotional and control deficits to become evident.

However, brain damage rarely affects just one of these systems. Rather, the disruptive effects of most brain lesions, regardless of their size or location, usually involve all three systems.

For example, Korsakoff's psychosis, a condition most commonly associated with severe chronic alcoholism, is typically described only in terms of intellectual dysfunctions; e.g., "The characteristic feature of Korsakow's syndrome is a certain type of amnesia. The patient has a gross defect of memory for recent events so that he has no recollection of what has happened even half an hour previously. He is disoriented in space and time and he fills the gaps in his memory by confabulation, that is, by giving imaginary accounts of his activities" (Walton, 1977. See also, American Psychiatric Association, 1980; Hécaen and Albert, 1978). Yet, chronic Korsakoff patients also exhibit profound changes in affect and executive, or control functions that may be more crippling and more representative of the psychological devastations of this disease than the memory impairments. Patients with this condition tend to be emotionally flat, lack the impulse to initiate activity, and, if given a goal requiring more than an immediate one- or two-step response, they cannot organize, set into motion, and carry through a plan of action to reach it (e.g., Biber et al., 1981). Everyday frustrations, sad events, or worrisome problems, when brought to their attention, will arouse a somewhat appropriate affective response, as will a pleasant happening or a treat; but the arousal is only transitory, subsiding with a change in topic or distraction such as someone entering the room. When not stimulated from outside or by physiological urges, these responsive, comprehending, often well-spoken and well-mannered patients sit quite comfortably doing nothing, not even attending to a TV or nearby conversation. When they have the urge to move, they walk about aimlessly. Even those who talk about wanting to visit a relative, for instance, or call a lawyer, make no effort to do so, although doors are unlocked and the public telephone is in full view.

The behavioral defects characteristic of many patients with right hemisphere damage also reflect the involvement of all three systems. It is well known that these patients are especially likely to show impairments in such cognitive activities as spatial organization, integration of visual and spatial stimuli, and comprehension and manipulation of percepts that do not readily lend themselves to verbal analysis (see pp. 55–58). Right hemisphere damaged patients may also experience characteristic emotional dysfunctions such as an *indifference reaction* (ignoring, playing down, or being unaware of mental and physical disabilities and situational problems), uncalled-for optimism or even euphoria, inappropriate emotional responses and insensitivity to the feelings of others, and loss of the self-perspective needed for accurate self-criticism, appreciation of limitations, or making constructive changes in behavior or attitudes (Gainotti, 1972; E. Valenstein and Heilman, 1979). Furthermore, despite strong, well-expressed motivations and demonstrated knowledgeability and capability, impairments in the capacity to plan and organize complex activities immobilize many of the same right hemisphere damaged patients who have difficulty performing visuospatial tasks (Lezak, 1979a).

Behavior problems may also become more acute and the symptom picture more complex as secondary reactions to the specific problems created by the organic defect further involve each system. Additional repercussions and reactions may then occur as the patient attempts to cope with succeeding sets of reactions and the problems they bring.

The following case of a man who sustained relatively minor brain injuries demonstrates some typical interactions between impairments in different psychological systems.

A middle-aged clerk, the father of teenaged children, incurred a left-sided head injury in a car accident and was unconscious for several days. When examined three months after the accident, his principal complaint was fatigue. His intelligence test scores were consistently *high average* (between the 75th and 90th percentiles). The only cognitive difficulty demonstrated in the psychological examination was a slight impairment of verbal fluency exhibited by a few word-use errors on a sentence-building task. This verbal fluency problem did not seem grave, but it had serious implications for the patient's adjustment.

Because he could no longer produce fluent speech automatically, the patient had to exercise constant vigilance and conscious effort to talk as well as he did. This effort was a continuous drain on his energy so that he fatigued easily. Verbal fluency tended to deteriorate when he grew tired, giving rise to a vicious cycle in which he put out more effort when he was tired, further sapping his energy at the times he needed it the most. He felt worn out and became discouraged, irritable, and depressed. Emotional control too was no longer as automatic or effective as before the accident, and it was poorest when he was tired. He "blew up" frequently with little provocation. His children did not hide their annoyance with their grouchy, sullen father, and his wife became protective and overly solicitous. The patient perceived his family's behavior as further proof of his inadequacy and hopelessness. His depression deepened, he became more self-conscious about his speech, and fluency continued to be a problem.

Intellectual Functions

There are four major classes of intellectual, or cognitive, functions: (1) *receptive functions*, which involve the abilities to acquire, process, classify, and integrate information; (2) *memory and learning*, by means of which information is stored and recalled; (3) *thinking*, which concerns the mental organization and reorganization of information; and (4) *expressive functions*, through which information is communicated or acted upon. Each functional class comprises many discrete activities—such as immediate memory for spoken words, or color recognition. Although each function constitutes a distinct class of behavior, normally they work in close, interdependent concert.

Generally speaking, within each class of intellectual functions, a division may be made between those functions that mediate verbal/symbolic information and those that deal with data that cannot be communicated in words or symbols, such as complex visual or sound patterns. These subclasses of functions differ from one another in their neuroanatomical organization and in their behavioral expression while sharing other basic neuroanatomical and psychometric relationships within the functional system.

The identification of discrete functions within each class of intellectual functions varies with the perspective and techniques of the investigator (Poeck, 1969; Teuber, 1962). Examiners using simple tests that elicit discrete responses can study highly specific functions. Multidimensional tests call forth complex responses and thus measure broader and more complex functions. Verbal functions enter into verbal test responses. Motor functions are demonstrated on tests involving motor behavior. When practical considerations of time and equipment limit the functions that can be studied or when relevant tests are not administered, the examiner may remain ignorant of the untested functions or how their impairment contributes to a patient's deficits. However, even though different investigators may identify or define some of the narrower subclasses of functions differently, they agree on the major functional systems and the large subdivisions.

The Concept of Intelligence

Intellectual behavior was originally attributed to a single intellectual function, *intelligence*. Early investigators treated the concept of intelligence as if it were a unitary variable, which, like physical strength, increased at a regular rate in the course of normal childhood development (Binet and Simon, 1908; Terman, 1916) and decreased with the amount of brain tissue lost through accident or disease (Chapman and Wolff, 1959; Lashley, 1938). As refinements in testing and data-handling techniques have afforded greater precision and control over observations of intellectual behavior, it has become evident that much of the behavior that tests measure is directly referrable to specific intellectual functions.

NEUROPSYCHOLOGY AND THE CONCEPT OF INTELLIGENCE

Neuropsychological research has contributed significantly to the redefinition of the nature of intelligence. One of neuropsychology's earliest findings was that the overall scores (i.e., IQ scores) on standard intelligence tests do not bear a predictably direct relationship with the size of brain lesions (Hebb, 1949; Maher, 1963). When a discrete brain lesion produces deficits over a broad range of intellectual functions, these functions may be affected in different ways. Abilities most directly served by the damaged tissue may be destroyed; associated or dependent abilities may be depressed or distorted, while some others may appear to be heightened or enhanced (e.g., see p. 58). Lesions involving a portion of the cerebral cortex usually impair some functions while sparing others (A. Smith, 1966b; Teuber, 1955; K.W. Walsh, 1978b).

A similar unevenness is typically seen in the effects of deteriorating brain disease on psychological functions generally. Not only are some functions disrupted in the early stages while others may remain relatively intact for years, but the affected functions also deteriorate at different rates (see pp. 179–192). Differential deterioration of diverse psychological functions also occurs in aging (see pp. 216–219). In sum, neuropsychological studies have demonstrated that there is no general intellectual function, but rather many discrete ones that work together so smoothly when the brain is intact that the intellect is experienced as a single, seamless attribute.

The following case shows how very specific organic impairment can be.

A brilliant research scientist was struck on the right side of his head by falling rock while mountain climbing. He was unconscious for several hours and then confused for several days, but was able to return to a full research and writing schedule shortly thereafter. On psychological tests taken six weeks after the injury, he achieved scores within the top 1–5% range on all tests of both verbal and visuoconstructive skills, with the single exception of a picture-arranging test requiring serial organization of cartoons into stories. On this test his score, at approximately the bottom tenth percentile, was almost in the *borderline defective* ability range. He was then given a serial reasoning test involving letter and number patterns which he answered correctly, but only after taking about 25 minutes to do what most

21

bright adults can finish in 5. He reported that his previous high level of work performance was unchanged except for difficulty with sequential organization when writing research papers.

Because of the multiplicity of intellectual functions, "intelligence quotients" (i.e., IQ scores) are not useful in describing the intellectual performance of brain damaged persons. "IQ" refers to a derived score used in many tests designed to measure general ability, i.e., "intelligence tests." "IQ" scores obtained from such tests represent a composite of performances on different kinds of items. While such composite scores are good predictors of academic performance, they represent so many different kinds of functions that they become meaningless in the presence of a neuropsychological disorder.

> Omnibus IQs are aggregate and often unreliable indices of organic intellectual deterioration. Specific defects restricted to certain test modalities, for example, may give a totally erroneous indication of severe intellectual impairment when actually intellectual functions may be relatively intact and lower total scores are a reflection of impairment of test modalities. Conversely, IQs may obscure selective defects in specific subtests (A. Smith, 1966b, p. 56).

In fact, any derived score based on a combination of scores from two or more measures of different abilities results in loss of data. Should the levels of performance for the combined measures differ, the composite score—which will be somewhere between the highest and the lowest of the combined measures—will be misleading. It is for this reason that composite scores of any kind have little place in neuropsychological assessment (see pp. 131–132).

Intelligence, however, remains a meaningful concept when it refers to a tendency shared by most individuals to perform many different intellectual tasks at about the same level of proficiency. Spiker and McCandless (1954) called this tendency "the transituational consistency of intellectual behavior." This consistency has been demonstrated repeatedly in statistical analyses of the interrelationships of performances on tests measuring different intellectual functions (factor analytic studies). The inevitably positive correlations between the different abilities always yield a factor **g**, the general mental ability factor, which is a measure of the extent to which the various abilities under consideration are associated. This general mental ability factor represents the positive association between all intellectual activities (Spearman, 1927).

> The earliest fundamental observation made was that the inter-test correlations, although widely varying in magnitude, were at least regularly positive in sign. On behalf of the old and charitable view, that a person's inferiority in one kind of performance is likely to be compensated by superiority in another, there was found no support whatever. On the contrary, it appeared that any failure in anything is rather a bad than a good augury for all other things (Spearman and Jones, 1950, p. 7).

Thus, from a neuropsychological perspective, Piercy defined intelligence as "a tendency for cerebral regions subserving different intellectual functions to be proportionately developed in any one individual. According to this notion, people with good verbal ability will tend also to have good non-verbal ability, in much the same way as people with big hands tend to have big feet" (1964, p. 341).

The performance of most adults on tests of intellectual ability reflects both the tendency for test scores generally to converge at the same level and for some test scores to differ in small, usually insignificant degrees from others (R. W. Payne, 1961; Vernon, 1950). In normal adults, specialization of interests and activities and singular experiences contribute to intraindividual differences. Social limitations, emotional disturbance, physical illness or handicaps, and brain dysfunction tend to magnify intraindividual test differences to significant proportions.

In neuropsychological assessment, the concept of intelligence has limited application. When attempting to assess the extent of impairment sustained by a patient, the examiner can use the level of the patient's best educational or vocational achievement or test performance as a general standard against which to compare current activities, observations, and test performances (see pp. 94–96). The concept of intelligence provides the justification for this practice.

Classes of Intellectual Functions

As more is learned about how the brain processes information, it becomes more difficult to make theoretically acceptable distinctions between the different functions involved in human information processing. In the laboratory, precise discriminations between sensation and perception may depend upon whether incoming information is processed by analysis of superficial physical and sensory characteristics or at deeper levels involving pattern recognition and meaningful associations (*level of encoding.*) The fluidity of theoretical models of perception and memory in particular becomes apparent in Craik's (1973) definition of primary memory as "continued internal reperception," in Baddeley's (1976) assumption of the "continuity between . . . perceptual phenomenon and memory storage," and in Massaro's (1973) hypothesis that "thinking, imagination, and perception probably lie on a continuum of perceptual functioning." Moreover, it has become increasingly difficult to define one's terms in this area with any sense of assurance for, as Shiffrin noted in 1973 when presenting a fairly radical revision of his 1969 theory of memory, there seem to be "exactly as many models of short-term memory as there are researchers who have published their theoretical views."

Rather than entering theoretical battlegrounds on ticklish issues that are not material to most practical applications in neuropsychology, I shall discuss the intellectual functions within a conceptual framework that has proven useful in psychological assessment generally and in neuropsychological assessment particularly.

RECEPTIVE FUNCTIONS

Entry of information into the central processing system proceeds from sensory stimulation, i.e., *sensation* (visual, auditory, tactile, etc.), through *perception*, which concerns the integration of sensory impressions into psychologically meaningful data, into memory. Thus, light on the retina creates a visual *sensation; perception* involves encoding the impulses transmitted by the aroused retina into a pattern of hues, shades, and intensities recognized as a daffodil in bloom.

Strictly speaking, sensory reception is not so much an intellectual function as it is an arousal process that triggers central registering, analyzing, encoding, and integrating activities. The organism receives sensation passively, shutting it out only, for instance, by holding the nose to avoid a stench. Even in soundest slumber, a stomachache or a loud noise will rouse the sleeper. Perception, on the other hand, involves active processing of the continuous torrent of sensation from all the sense modalities. This processing comprises many levels of analysis (Craik and Lockhart, 1972). Those that deal with such simple physical or sensory characteristics as color, shape, or tone come first both in the processing sequence and serve as foundations for the more complex, or "deeper" levels of semantic or cognitive processing that integrate sensory stimuli with one another at each moment, successively, and with the organism's past experience.

Normal perception in the healthy organism is a complex process engaging many different aspects of brain functioning. Like other intellectual functions, the extensive cortical distribution and complexity of perceptual activities make them highly vulnerable to brain injury. Organic perceptual defects can occur indirectly through loss of a primary sensory input such as vision or smell and directly through impairment of specific integrative processes. Although it may be difficult to separate the sensory from the perceptual components of a behavioral defect in some severely brain damaged patients, sensation and perception each has its own functional integrity. This can be seen clearly when perceptual organization is maintained despite very severe sensory defects or when perceptual functions are markedly disrupted in patients with little or no sensory deficit. The nearly deaf person can readily understand speech patterns when the sound is sufficiently amplified, whereas some brain damaged persons with keen auditory acuity cannot make sense out of what they hear.

The perceptual functions include such activities as awareness, recognition, discrimination, patterning, and orientation. Impairments in perceptual integration appear as disorders of recognition, the *agnosias* (literally, no knowledge). Denny-Brown (1962) points out that "*true agnosia* . . . relates to the whole perceptual field, whether right or left" in contrast to unilateral imperception phenomena where the patient is unaware of sensations or events on only one side (see pp. 66, 72–73). Since a disturbance in any one perceptual activity may affect any of the sensory modalities as well as different aspects of each one, a catalogue of discrete perceptual disturbances can be quite lengthy. Reviewing auditory, visual, and *somatosensory* (body sensation) modalities, M. Williams (1970a) lists 17 different kinds of specific *agnosias*. This list could be expanded, for within most of these categories of perceptual defect there are functionally discrete subcategories (Frederiks, 1969a). For instance, loss of the ability to recognize faces (*prosopagnosia*), one of the visual agnosias, may be manifested in at least two different forms: inability to recognize familiar faces and inability to recognize unfamiliar faces, which usually do not occur together (Benton, Hamsher et al., 1983; Benton and Van Allen, 1968; Warrington and James, 1967b).

MEMORY

Central to all intellectual functions and probably to all that is characteristically human in a person's behavior is the capacity for memory and learning. Memory frees the individual from dependency on physiological urges or situational happenstance for pleasure seeking; dread and despair do not occur in a memory vacuum. Severely impaired memory isolates the patient from emotionally or practically meaningful contact with the world about him and deprives him of a sense of personal continuity, rendering him passive and helplessly dependent. Mildly to moderately impaired memory has a disorienting effect.

A review of the current literature on memory suggests that theory-making may be the most popular sport of investigators using normal subjects (Craik, 1979). In the early 1970s, theoretical issues seemed pretty much settled by Atkinson and Shiffrin's (1968) three-stage model of memory (Craik, 1977a). More recently, the emergence of one-stage theories (Wickelgren, 1975b) and two-stage theories (Baddeley, 1976; Craik, 1973) has shown how much disagreement still exists about the nature and dimensions of memory. However, clinicians who deal with the memory problems associated with brain damage find that a three-stage or elaborated two-stage model provides a suitable framework for conceptualizing and understanding dysfunctional memory (Erickson, 1978; Shallice, 1979; Squire, 1975) (see Table 2-1).

Clinically, three kinds of memory are distinguishable. Two are succeeding stages of *short-term storage* and the third is *long-term storage*.

1. *Registration* holds large amounts of incoming information briefly (1 or 2 seconds at most) in *sensory store* (Joynt, 1975; Loftus and Loftus, 1976). It is neither strictly a memory function nor a perceptual function but rather a selecting and recording process by which perceptions enter the memory system. Registration has been called a "valve determining which memories are stored" (Nauta, 1966). It involves the programming of acquired sensory response patterns (perceptual tendencies) in the recording and memorizing center of the brain (Nauta, 1964). The affective, *set* (perceptual and response predisposition), and attention-focusing components of perception play an integral role in the registration process (Brain, 1969; Pribram, 1969). Information in the registration process is either transferred to short-term memory or it quickly decays.

2a. *Immediate memory*, the first stage of short-term memory storage, concerns the fixation of the information selected for retention by the registration process. It has been aptly called the "working memory" as well as "primary memory." This first stage of the short-term storage system occurs as neuronal activation (Doty, 1979). It serves "as a limited capacity store from which information is transferred to a more

Table 2-1 Memory and Learning Terminology

Psychological process	Duration	Clinical concept	Site of pathology	Neuropsychological deficit
REGISTRATION	Decays in milliseconds	Consciousness	RETICULAR ACTIVATING SYSTEM (RAS)	Decreased alertness, stupor, coma
SHORT-TERM STORAGE (STS); PRIMARY MEMORY	Approximately 30 seconds to one hour	IMMEDIATE ⎫ ACTIVE ⎬ MEMORY WORKING ⎭	LIMBIC SYSTEM	Reduced memory span
REHEARSAL	Hours			

All of the above processes depend primarily on electrochemical activation at the synapses.

All of the processes below involve semipermanent changes in cell structure or chemistry (protein synthesis).

Psychological process	Duration	Clinical concept	Site of pathology	Neuropsychological deficit
CONSOLIDATION	May take place in seconds or continue for years	LEARNING	HIPPOCAMPUS and perhaps other LIMBIC SYSTEM sites	Defective information storage
	From onset of condition to present	RECENT MEMORY	Same as LEARNING	ANTEROGRADE AMNESIA Defective personal history due to defective recall of ongoing events since onset of condition Impaired or lost skills, information, memories, or functions
LONG-TERM STORAGE (LTS); SECONDARY MEMORY	As short as time needed for consolidation; as long as lifetime	REMOTE MEMORY	CORTEX	Defective spontaneous recall although memory and new learning demonstrable by special techniques
RETRIEVAL		RECALL	THALAMUS and perhaps other LIMBIC SYSTEM sites	
FORGETTING		AMNESIA	Various sites	RETROGRADE AMNESIA Defective knowledge of ongoing events dating from onset of condition back in time

permanent store" and also "as a limited capacity retrieval system" (Watkins, 1974. See also Baddeley and Hitch, 1974). Its contents are in conscious awareness (Craik and Lockhart, 1972). Immediate memory is of sufficient duration to enable a person to respond to ongoing events when more enduring forms of memory have been lost (Talland, 1965a; Victor et al., 1971). It lasts from about 30 seconds up to several minutes unless it is sustained by *rehearsal*.

The preponderant evidence suggests that information in immediate memory is temporarily maintained in *reverberating neural circuits* (self-contained neural networks that sustain a nerve impulse by channeling it repeatedly through the same network) (Doty, 1979; Rosenzweig and Leiman, 1968; Thatcher and John, 1977). It appears that, if not converted into a more stable biochemical organization for longer lasting storage, the electrochemical activities that constitute the immediate memory trace spontaneously dissipate and the memory is not retained. For example, only the rare reader with a "photographic" memory will be able to recall verbatim the first sentence on the preceding page although almost everyone who has read this far will have just seen it.

2b. *Rehearsal* is any repetitive mental process that serves to lengthen the duration of a memory trace. With rehearsal, a memory trace may be maintained for hours. Rehearsal also increases the likelihood that a given bit of information will be permanently stored (Schachter, 1980).

2c. Another kind of short-term memory may be distinguished from immediate memory in that it lasts from an hour or so to one or two days—longer than a reverberating circuit could be maintained by even the most conscientious rehearsal efforts, but not yet permanently fixed as learned material in long-term storage (Barondes, 1975; Rosenzweig and Leiman, 1968). These longer impermanent memories have been observed to occur as prolongations of the effects of training. In contrast to primary memory, they may involve an intermediate holding mechanism of a biochemical rather than electrophysiological nature (Doty, 1979; Thatcher and John, 1977). There may be some question as to whether this short-term memory is simply information transferred to long-term memory but so newly laid down as to be relatively vulnerable to interference effects, thus lacking the stability usually associated with long-term memory.

3. *Long-term memory*, sometimes called "secondary memory" (Craik, 1977a) or learning, refers to the organism's ability to store information. The process of storing information as long-term memory, *consolidation*, begins as soon as one-half second after information enters short-term storage and may continue as long as information remains there (Baddeley, 1976; Squire, 1975). Much of the information in the long-term storage system appears to be organized on the basis of meaning, whereas in the short-term storage system it is organized in terms of contiguity or of sensory properties such as similar sounds, shapes, or colors (Broadbent, 1970; Craik and Lockhart, 1972). However, Baddeley (1978) reminds us that rote repetition and association built on superficial, relatively meaningless stimulus characteristics can lead to learning too.

Long-term memory storage appears to be a biochemical process involving protein synthesis in nerve cells (Barondes, 1975; Hydén, 1970; Sokolov, 1977). These transformations, possibly in conjunction with the budding of new cell contact points (Lund, 1978; Rosenzweig et al., 1972; Rutledge, 1976), create the transmission patterns between cells that constitute the long-term memory trace (Rose et al., 1976). There does not appear to be a local storage site for stored memories; instead, memories seem to involve neuronal contributions from many cortical and subcortical centers (Penfield, 1968; Thatcher and John, 1977; R.F. Thompson et al., 1972). Storage and retrieval of information in the memory system appear to take place according to principles of association (Wickelgren, 1981). Breakdown in the capacity to store or retrieve material on the basis of its associative characteristics results in distinctive memory disorders (e.g., see pp. 172–174, 189, 190, 196–197, 201).

Recent and *remote* memory are clinical terms that refer, respectively, to memories stored within the last few hours, days, weeks, or even months and to older memories dating from early childhood (Brierley, 1966; Hécaen and Albert, 1978). In normal persons it is virtually impossible to determine where recent memory ends and remote memory begins, for there are no major discontinuities in memory from the present to early wisps of infantile recollection. Recent memory and remote memory become meaningful concepts when dealing with problems of *amnesia* (literally, no memory), periods for which there is no recall, in contrast to memory impairments that may involve specific deficits.

When registration or storage processes are impaired by disease or accident, acquisition of new information may range from spotty to nonexistent (Barbizet, 1970; Brierley, 1966; Hirst, 1982; also see pp. 75–77). Temporary disruption of these processes, which often follows head injury or electroconvulsive therapy (ECT) for psychiatric conditions, obliterates memory for the period of impairment (Whitty and Zangwill, 1977; M. Williams, 1977). Destruction of these capacities results in a permanent memory vacuum from the time of onset of the disorder. The inability or impaired ability to remember one's life events beginning with the onset of a condition is called *anterograde amnesia*. Patients with *anterograde amnesia* are, for most practical purposes, unable to learn and have defective recent memory, the kind and severity of memory defect varying somewhat with the nature of the disorder (Butters et al., in press; Wetzel and Squire, 1980). Loss of memory for events preceding the onset of brain damage, whether by trauma or disease, is called *retrograde amnesia*. It rarely extends beyond 30 minutes preceding a head injury. When retrograde amnesia occurs with brain disease, loss of one's own history and events may go back years and even decades (M.S. Albert et al., 1979, 1981b; Butters and Cermak, 1976; Wallack, 1976). The dissociation of anterograde and retrograde memory problems in patients with memory disorders suggests that the anatomical structures involved in new learning and in retrieval of old memories are different (M.S. Albert et al., 1980).

The most recent of the remote memories may indicate the approximate time of onset of the memorization problem, since all later events will be very poorly remembered, if at all (Barbizet, 1970; Brain, 1969). When an amnestic period results from an accident or illness, memories stored after memorizing abilities return may be considered recent in contrast to the remote memories antedating the accident or illness.

Following certain kinds of brain injury or disease, bits and chunks of remote memory may be lost (R.D. Adams et al., 1961; Goodglass, 1973). The retention of learned material in long-term storage depends upon the integrity of the cortical areas that subserve the functions involved (Whitty et al., 1977; Barbizet, 1970). Only extensive cortical damage ordinarily disrupts long ingrained memories and habits (Brain, 1969). A global loss of remote memory rarely occurs without some alteration in level of consciousness as well (Ojemann, 1966; Whitty and Lishman, 1966).

From a practical viewpoint, *learning* (the acquisition of new information) and *retention* (storing it beyond the limits of working memory or rehearsal) may appear to be indistinguishable. However, these activities can be readily differentiated by measuring retention of newly learned material both upon completion of the learning task and at varying time intervals thereafter (Erickson and Scott, 1977).

The effectiveness of the memory system also depends on how readily and completely information can be retrieved. Information retrieval is *remembering*, which may occur through *recall* involving an active, complex search process (McCormack, 1972). The question, "What is the capital of Oregon?" tests the recall function. When a like stimulus triggers awareness, remembering takes place through *recognition*. The question, "Which of the following is the capital of Oregon: Albany, Portland, or Salem?" tests the recognition function. Retrieval by recognition is much easier than retrieval by recall for normal persons as well as brain damaged patients. On superficial examination, retrieval problems can be mistaken for learning or retention problems, but the nature of an apparent learning problem can be determined by appropriate testing techniques (see pp. 472ff).

The dimensions of memory function become apparent in pathological conditions of the brain. Besides the overriding distinctions between short-term and long-term memory, patients may display deficits that are specific to the nature of the information to be learned, i.e., *material specific*. Such deficits are specific to either verbal or nonverbalizable information (Butters et al., 1973; Rozin, 1976), or to motor skill learning (Corkin, 1968), cutting across sensory modalities. Mental processes and behavioral activities are also learned, remembered, and subject to forgetting or to extinction by brain damage. Visceral responses, rules and procedures, speech patterns, and conceptual relationships can be lost through defects of memory too. Brain disease affects these different kinds of memories in long-term storage differentially so that a motor speech habit, such as organizing certain sounds into a word, may be wholly retained while rules for organizing words into meaningful speech are lost (Geschwind, 1970). Stored memories involving different sensory modalities and output mechanisms are also differentially affected by brain disease (E.D. Ross, 1982). For example, recognition of printed words or numbers may be severely impaired while speech comprehension and picture recognition remain relatively intact. Still another distinction can be made between *episodic* or *event memory*, and *semantic memory* or skill-dependent knowledge (Schachter and Tulving, 1982; Wood et al., 1982). (see also pp. 469ff). The former refers to memories of one's own experiences and is therefore unique and localizable in time and space. Semantic memory, i.e., what is learned as knowledge, is "timeless and spaceless," as, for instance, the alphabet or historical data unrelated to a person's life. The meaningfulness of this distinction becomes evident in patients whose posttraumatic or post encephalitic (see pp. 173, 199–200) retrograde amnesia may extend back weeks and even years although their fund of information, language usage, and practical knowledge may be quite intact.

THINKING

Thinking may be defined as any mental operation that relates two or more bits of information explicitly (as in making an arithmetic computation) or implicitly (as in judging that *this* is bad, i.e., relative to *that*). A host of complex cognitive functions is subsumed under the rubric of thinking, such as computation, reasoning and judgment, concept formation, abstracting and generalizing, ordering, organizing, and planning.

The nature of the information being mentally manipulated (e.g., numbers, design concepts, words) and the operation (e.g., comparing, compounding, abstracting, ordering) define the category of thinking. Thus, "verbal reasoning" comprises several operations done with words; it generally includes ordering and comparing, sometimes analyzing and synthesizing. "Computation" may involve operations of ordering and compounding done with numbers, and distance judgment involves abstracting and comparing ideas of spatial extension.

The concept of "higher" and "lower" mental processes originated with the ancient Greek and Roman philosophers. This concept figures in the hierarchical theories of brain functions and mental ability factors in which "higher" refers to the more complex mental operations and "lower" to the simpler ones. Thinking is at the high end of this scale. The degree to which a concept is *abstract* or *concrete* also determines its place on the scale. For example, the abstract idea, "a living organism," is presumed to represent a higher level of thinking than the more concrete idea, "my cat Pansy"; the abstract rule, "file specific topics under general topics" is likewise considered to be at a higher level of thinking than the instructions, "file 'fir' under 'conifer,' file 'conifer' under 'tree'." It is interesting to note that the higher intellectual functions have traditionally been equated with "intelligence."

The higher intellectual functions of abstraction, reasoning, judgment, analysis, and synthesis tend to be relatively sensitive to diffuse brain injury even when most specific receptive, expressive, or memory functions remain essentially intact (Goodglass and Kaplan, 1979). They may also be disrupted by any one of a number of lesions in functionally discrete areas of the brain at lower levels of the hierarchy. Thus the higher intellectual functions tend to be more "fragile" than the lower, more discrete functions. Conversely, higher cognitive abilities may remain relatively unaffected in the presence of specific receptive, expressive, and memory dysfunctions (Blakemore et al., 1972; Teuber et al., 1951; Wepman, 1976).

Unlike other intellectual functions, thinking is not tied to specific neuroanatomical systems, although the disruption of feedback, regulatory, and integrating mechanisms can affect thinking more profoundly than other cognitive functions (Luria, 1966). "There is no . . . anatomy [of the higher cerebral functions] in the strict sense of the word. . . . Thinking is regarded as a function of the entire brain that defies localization" (Gloning and Hoff, 1969).

30

As with other kinds of intellectual functions, the quality of any higher cognitive operation will depend in part on the extent to which its sensory and motor components are intact at the central integrative (cortical) level. For example, patients with specific somatosensory perceptual defects tend to do poorly on reasoning tasks involving visuospatial concepts (Teuber, 1959); patients with perceptual disabilities that involve the visual system are more likely to have difficulty solving problems involving visual concepts (Milner, 1954). Verbal defects tend to have more obvious and widespread cognitive consequences than defects in other functional systems because task instructions are frequently verbal, self-regulating and self-critiquing mechanisms are typically verbal, and ideational systems—even for nonverbal material—are usually verbal (Luria, 1973).

EXPRESSIVE FUNCTIONS

Expressive functions, such as speaking, drawing or writing, manipulating, physical gestures, facial expressions, or movements, make up the sum of observable behavior. All other mental activity is inferred from them.

Apraxia.   Disturbances of purposeful expressive functions are known as *apraxias* (literally, no work). The apraxias typically involve impairment of learned voluntary acts despite adequate motor innervation of capable muscles, adequate sensorimotor coordination for complex acts carried out without conscious intent (e.g., articulating isolated spontaneous words or phrases clearly when volitional speech is blocked, brushing crumbs or fiddling with objects when intentional hand movements cannot be performed), and comprehension of the elements and goals of the desired activity. Apraxic behavior occurs when there has been a breakdown in motor integration and executive functions integral to the performance of complex learned acts (Hécaen and Albert, 1978; Luria, 1966, 1973). Thus, when asked to show how he would use a pencil, an apraxic patient who has adequate strength and full use of his muscles may be unable to organize finger and hand movements relative to the pencil sufficiently well to manipulate it appropriately. He may even be unable to relate the instructions to hand movements although he understands the nature of the task (Geschwind, 1975; Heilman, 1979; M. Williams, 1970a). "(T)he hallmark of apraxia is the appearance of well-executed but incorrect movements" (Bogen, 1979).

Like perceptual dysfunctions, apraxias tend to occur in clusters of disabilities that are associated with some specific sensory impairment and share a common anatomical pattern of brain damage (Benton, 1979; Critchley, 1953). For example, apraxias involving impaired ability to perform skilled tasks on command or imitatively and to use objects appropriately and at will are commonly associated with lesions near or overlapping speech centers and typically appear concomitantly with communication disabilities (Dee et al., 1970; Geschwind, 1975; Heilman, 1979; see also pp. 71, 528 f.).

Different investigators define and use such terms as ideational apraxia, ideomotor apraxia, and ideokinetic apraxia in confusingly different ways (compare, for example, Bogen, 1979; Hécaen and Albert, 1977; Heilman, 1979; K.W. Walsh, 1978b; and M. Williams, 1970a). Kimura and Archibald (1974) note that the forms of apraxia that have been called "ideational, ideomotor, ideokinetic, and so on" do not relate to "behaviorally different phenomena, but [to] disturbances at different points in a hypothetical sequence of cognitive events involved in making a movement." Rather than attempt to reconcile the many disparities in the use of these terms and their definitions, I will sidestep these terminological and definitional issues and call these disturbances simply, apraxias. In distinguishing particular forms of apraxia, I recommend the example set by Dee and his co-workers (1970) who use descriptive (e.g., "apraxia of symbolic actions, apraxia of utilization [of objects]") rather than theoretical terminology.

Constructional disorders. Constructional disorders, often classified as apraxias, are actually not apraxias in the strict sense of the concept. Rather, they are disturbances "in formulative activities such as assembling, building, drawing, in which the spatial form of the product proves to be unsuccessful without there being an apraxia of single movements" (Benton, 1969a). They are more often associated with lesions of the non-speech hemisphere of the brain than with lesions of the hemisphere that is dominant for speech and may accompany defects of spatial perception. Benton (1969a) distinguished two different kinds of constructional impairments that often but not always occur together, one having to do with difficulties in making two-dimensional constructions and the other concerned with three-dimensional building tasks.

Aphasia. Defects of symbol formulation, the *aphasias* and *dysphasias* (literally, no speech and impaired speech) were traditionally considered to be apraxias, for the end product of every kind of aphasic or language disturbance is defective or absent speech or defective symbol production (F.L. Darley, 1967). The historical classification of aphasic disorders defined auditory and visual agnosias for symbolic material as *receptive* aphasias and defined verbal apraxias as *expressive* aphasias. With expansion and refinements in the systematic observation and treatment of aphasic disturbances, this simplistic two-part classification has lost its usefulness. Today most investigators identify at least five (Wepman, 1976) and usually more types of aphasia (e.g., Benson, 1979; Goodglass and Kaplan, 1972; Hécaen, 1979; Kertesz and McCabe, 1977; Marin and Gordon, 1979). Some investigators describe a variety of subtypes as well (e.g., Hécaen and Albert, 1978; Luria, 1973) (see Table 2-2).

Analysis of the discrete patterns of defective language processing that can occur with circumscribed brain lesions have identified component processes necessary for normal speech and suggest a regularity in their neuroanatomical correlates (Caramazza and Berndt, 1978). Broad patterns of correlation between types of language dysfunction and neuroanatomical correlates also appear with sufficient regularity to warrant the development of aphasia typologies (Benson, 1977; Blumstein, 1981). However, the presentation of aphasic symptoms also varies enough from patient to patient that clear distinctions do not hold up in many cases. Thus, it is not surprising that the identification of aphasia *syndromes* (sets of symptoms that occur together with sufficient frequency as to "suggest the presence of a specific disease" or site of damage [Geschwind and Strub, 1975]) is complicated both by differences of opinion as to what constitutes an aphasia syndrome, and differences in the labels given those

Table 2-2 Aphasia Nomenclature

Salient features of classification:	EXPRESSIVE defects (dysfluency) with relatively intact comprehension	MEMORY/RETRIEVAL problems with relatively intact comprehension	PROGRAMMING SEQUENCES repetition defects, some garbled words, intact comprehension	COMPREHENSION defects with fluent, garbled "jargon" speech	GLOBAL expressive and comprehension defects in all modalities
Investigators					
Benson, 1979; Goodglass and Kaplan, 1972	Broca's	Anomic	Conduction	Wernicke's, fluent	Global
Hécaen and Albert, 1978	Motor	Amnesic	Conduction	Sensory	
Kertesz and McCabe, 1977	Broca's (motor)	Anomic	Conduction (central)	Wernicke's (sensory)	Global
Luria, 1966, 1970	Efferent motor	Semantic	Afferent motor	Sensory or acoustic	
Wepman, 1976; Wepman and Jones, 1967	Syntactic	Semantic		Jargon, pragmatic	Global

symptom constellations that have been conceptualized as syndromes (Benson, 1979). Major subdivisions agreed upon by most investigators are presented in Table 2-2 with the names given them in five commonly used classification systems. (This table was not meant to be exhaustive, merely illustrative; for a more detailed classification table, see Benson, 1979, p. 28.)

Like other kinds of intellectual defects, language disturbances usually appear in clusters of related dysfunctions. "Impairment of any of the cerebral systems essential to language processes is usually reflected in more than one language modality; conversely impairment of any modality often reflects involvement of more than one process" (Schuell, 1955, p. 308). Thus, *agraphia* (literally, no writing) and *alexia*[1] (literally, no reading) only rarely occur alone. They are most often found together and in association with other language disturbances, typically appearing as impairment (dysgraphia, dyslexia) rather than total loss of function (M.L. Albert, 1979; Marcie and Hécaen, 1979; Piercy, 1964). Not surprisingly, the active modalities of speaking and writing tend to be affected more often and more severely than reading and speech comprehension (A. Smith, 1971). Language disturbances may also occur in confusional states arising from metabolic or toxic disorders rather than a focal brain lesion (Chédru and Geschwind, 1972).

MENTAL ACTIVITY VARIABLES

These are behavior characteristics that concern the efficiency of mental processes. They are intimately involved in intellectual operations but do not constitute intellectual functions as they do not have a unique behavioral end product. They can be classified roughly into three categories, *attentional activities, level of consciousness,* and *activity rate.*

1. *Attentional activities* include *attention, concentration,* and *conceptual tracking.* Disorders of attention may arise from lesions involving any point in the perceptual system (Worden, 1966). Attention refers to the capacity for selective perception (J. Allison et al., 1968; Mirsky, 1978). Concentration is an effortful, usually deliberate, and heightened state of attention in which irrelevant stimuli are selectively excluded from conscious awareness, i.e., *inhibited* (W.R. Russell, 1975). Tracking involves attentively following or tracing a stimulus, e.g., visual tracking or concentrating on a directed train of thought (e.g., *conceptual tracking*) over a period of time. Complex conceptual tracking, which involves the ability to entertain two or more ideas or stimulus patterns simultaneously and sequentially without confusing or losing them, is necessary to solve problems requiring chained associations, such as computing compound interest, interweaving the threads of a complicated story, or figuring distances from a road map (R.W. Gardner et al., 1960). Impairment of attention and concentration functions may result in a shortened attention span, distractibility, susceptibility to confusion, and unpredictable performance (Schulman et al., 1965).

In neuropsychology, the concept of attention includes the three components

---

[1] *Alexia* refers to reading disability of adult onset; *dyslexia* is the name given to developmental reading disorders.

34

defined by Posner and Boies (1971): (1) a readiness to respond called forth by a specific warning event. (Posner calls this *alertness* but it is distinguishable from alertness in a general organismic state [see below]); (2) selectivity, which involves the focusing aspect of attention; and (3) a limited processing capacity. Brain damage affecting these components can result in slowed reaction times, inattentiveness or difficulty screening out impinging stimuli, and restricted range of awareness. Generally, defects in attention will involve all three components although only one may be noticeably impaired.

Impaired attention and concentration are among the most common mental problems associated with brain damage (Lezak, 1978b; Reitan and Kløve, 1959). Not infrequently, such impairments are the only behavioral remnants of a brain disease or trauma (Gronwall and Sampson, 1974). In such cases, although all the intellectual functions may be intact and the person may even be capable of better than average performance, overall intellectual productivity suffers from inattentiveness, faulty concentration, and consequent fatigue.

2. The concept of *consciousness* has eluded a universally acceptable definition (Frederiks, 1969b; Natsoulas, 1978). For neuropsychological assessment purposes, Plum's (1972) definition of consciousness as "psychological awareness of the self and the environment" is satisfactory. *Level of consciousness*, an organismic state, ranges over a continuum from full alertness through drowsiness, somnolence, and stupor, to coma (M.L. Albert et al., 1976; Strub and Black, 1977). Even slight depressions of the alert state may significantly affect a person's mental efficiency, making him tired, inattentive, or slowed. Although disturbances of consciousness may accompany a functional disorder, they usually reflect pathological conditions of the brain (Lishman, 1978).

3. *Activity rate* refers to both the speed at which mental activities are performed and motor response speed. Behavioral slowing is a common characteristic of brain damage (Hicks and Birren, 1970). Motor response slowing is readily observable and may be associated with weakness or poor coordination. Slowing of mental activity shows up most clearly in delayed reaction times and in longer than average total performance times in the absence of a specific motor disability.

Nonintellectual Functions

Personality characteristics, emotionality, and control are aspects of behavior that contribute significantly to a person's general effectiveness. Like intellectual functions, these capacities and characteristics may also be altered by brain dysfunction.

Personality/Emotionality Variables

Some personality or emotional change usually follows brain damage. Some changes tend to occur as fairly characteristic behavior patterns that relate to specific anatomical sites (Botez, 1974; Diller, 1968; Gainotti, 1972; Lishman, 1978). The most common direct effects of brain injury on personality are emotional dulling, disinhibition, diminution of anxiety with associated emotional blandness or mild euphoria, and decreased social sensitivity. Heightened anxiety, depressed moods, and hypersensitivity in interpersonal interactions may also occur (Blumer and Benson, 1975; Folstein et al., 1977; K. Goldstein, 1939; Goodwin et al., 1979).

Many persons suffer profound personality changes following brain injury or concomitant with brain disease, which seem to be not so much a direct product of their illness as a reaction to their experiences of loss, chronic frustration, and radical changes in life-style. As a result, depression is probably the most common single emotional characteristic of brain damaged patients generally, with pervasive anxiety following closely behind (Lezak, 1978b). Some other common behavior problems of brain injured people are irritability, restlessness, low frustration tolerance, and apathy (Kostlan and Van Couvering, 1972; Oddy et al., 1978a; Ota, 1969).

Few brain damaged patients experience personality changes that are plainly either direct consequences of a brain injury or secondary reactions to impairment and loss. For the most part, the personality changes, emotional distress, and behavior problems of a brain damaged patient are the product of extremely complex interactions involving his neurological disabilities, present social demands, previously established behavior patterns, and his ongoing reactions to all of these.

Some brain injured patients display emotional instability characterized by rapid, ofter exaggerated affective swings, a condition called *emotional lability*. Three kinds of lability associated with brain damage can be distinguished.

(1) The emotional ups and downs of some labile patients result from weakened controls and lowered frustration tolerance. This is often most pronounced in the acute stages of their illness and when they are fatigued or stressed. Their emotional expression and their feelings are congruent and their sensitivity and capacity for emotional response are intact. However, emotional reactions, particularly under conditions of stress or fatigue, will be stronger and may last longer than was usual for them premorbidly (Fowler and Fordyce, 1974).

(2) A second group of labile patients have lost emotional sensitivity and the capacity for modulating emotionally charged behavior. They tend to overreact emotionally to whatever external stimulation impinges on them. Their emotional reactivity can generally be brought out in an interview by abruptly changing the subject from a pleasant topic to an unpleasant one and back again, for these patients will beam or cloud up with each topic change. When left alone and physically comfortable, they typically seem emotionless.

(3) A third group of labile patients differ from the others in that their feelings are generally appropriate, but brief episodes of strong affective *expression*—usually tearful crying, sometimes laughter—can be triggered by even quite mild stimulation. This is the *pseudobulbar* state (Horenstein, 1970; Lieberman and Benson, 1977). It results from structural lesions involving the frontal cortex and connecting pathways to lower brain structures (see pp. 79–81 for a discussion of frontal lobe functions). The feeling of patients with this condition is frequently not congruent with their appearance, and they generally can report the discrepancy. Because they tend to cry with every emotionally arousing event, even happy or exciting ones, their family and vis-

itors see them crying much of the time and often misinterpret the tears as evidence of depression. Sometimes the bewildered patient comes to the same mistaken conclusion as well and then really does become depressed. These patients can be identified by the frequency, intensity, and irrelevancy of their tears or guffaws, the rapidity with which the emotional reaction subsides, and the dissociation between their appearance and their stated feelings (B. W. Black, 1982).

Although most brain injured persons tend to undergo adverse emotional changes, brain damage seems to make life more pleasant for a few. This can be most striking in those emotionally constricted, anxious, overly responsible people who become more easygoing and relaxed as a result of a pathological brain condition. However, their families may suffer instead. The following case illustrates this kind of personality change.

> A young Viet Nam veteran lost the entire right frontal portion of his brain in a land mine explosion. His mother and wife described him as having been a quietly pleasant, conscientious, and diligent sawmill worker before entering the service. When he returned home, all of his speech functions and most of his thinking abilities were intact. He was completely free of anxiety and thus without a worry in the world. He had also become very easygoing, self-indulgent, and lacking in general drive and sensitivity to others. His wife was unable to get him to share her concerns when the baby had a fever or the rent was due. Not only did she have to handle all the finances, carry all the family and home responsibilities, and do all the planning, but she also had to see that her husband went to work on time and that he didn't drink up his paycheck or spend it in a foolish shopping spree before getting home on Friday night. For several years it was touch and go as to whether the wife could stand the strain of a truly carefree husband much longer. She finally left him after he had stopped working altogether and begun a pattern of monthly drinking binges that left little of his rather considerable compensation checks.

One significant personality change that is rarely discussed but is a relatively common concomitant of brain injury is a changed sexual drive level (Boller and Frank, 1981; M.W. Buck, 1968). A married man or woman who has settled into a comfortable sexual activity pattern of intercourse two or three times a week may begin demanding sex two and three times a day from the bewildered spouse. More frequently, the patient's loss of sexual interest leaves the spouse feeling unsatisfied and unloved (Lezak, 1978a). Sometimes brain damaged men are unable to achieve or sustain an erection, or they may have ejaculatory problems secondary to nervous tissue damage, which, in turn, add to their emotional disturbance and marital distress (Bray et al., 1981). Patients who become crude, boorish, or childlike as a result of brain damage no longer are welcome bed partners and may be bewildered and upset when rejected by their once affectionate spouses. Although some sexual problems diminish in time, for many patients they seriously complicate the problems of readjusting to new limitations and handicaps by adding another strange set of frustrations, impulses, and reactions.

Executive Functions

The executive functions consist of those capacities that enable a person to engage in independent, purposive, self-serving behavior successfully. They differ from cognitive functions in a number of ways. Questions about executive functions ask *how* or *whether* a person goes about doing something (e.g., Will he do it and, if so, how?); questions about cognitive functions are generally phrased in terms of *what* or *how much* (e.g., How much does he know? What can he do?). So long as the executive functions are intact, a person can sustain considerable cognitive loss and still continue to be independent, constructively self-serving, and productive. When executive functions are impaired, the individual may no longer be capable of satisfactory self-care, of performing remunerative or useful work on his own, or of maintaining normal social relationships regardless of how well preserved are his cognitive capacities—or how high his scores on tests of skills, knowledge, and abilities. Moreover, cognitive deficits usually involve specific functions or functional areas; impairment in executive functions tend to show up globally, affecting all aspects of behavior.

For example, a young woman who survived a head-on collision displayed the same lack of motivation and inability to initiate behavior with respect to eating and drinking, leisure activities, and social interactions as she did about housework, getting a job, sewing (which she had once done well), or reading (which she can still do with comprehension). Her cognitive losses, however, are relatively circumscribed in that verbal skills and much of her background knowledge and capacity to retrieve old information are fairly intact although new learning ability is virtually nonexistent and her constructional abilities are significantly impaired.

Many of the behavior problems arising from impaired executive functions are apparent even to casual or naive observers. For experienced clinicians, these problems can serve as hallmarks of brain damage. Among these are signs of a defective capacity for self-control or self-direction such as emotional lability or flattening, a heightened tendency to irritability and excitability, impulsivity, erratic carelessness, rigidity, and difficulty in making shifts in attention and ongoing behavior. Deterioration in personal grooming and cleanliness may also distinguish these patients.

Other defects in executive functions, however, are not so obvious. The problems they occasion may be missed or not recognized as neuropsychological ones by examiners who only see patients in the well-structured inpatient and clinic settings in which psychiatry and neurology patients are ordinarily observed. Perhaps the most serious of these problems, from a psychosocial standpoint, are impaired capacity to initiate activity, decreased or absent motivation (*anergia*), and defects in planning and carrying out the activity sequences that make up goal-directed behaviors (Hécaen and Albert, 1975; Lezak, 1981, in press; Luria, 1966; K.W. Walsh, 1978a). Patients without significant impairment of receptive or expressive functions who suffer primarily from these kinds of control defects are often mistakenly judged to be malingering, lazy or spoiled, psychiatrically disturbed, or—if this kind of defect appears following a legally compensable brain injury—exhibiting a "compensation neurosis" that some interested persons may believe will disappear when the patient's legal claim has been settled.

How crippling can defects of executive functions be is vividly demonstrated by the case of a hand surgeon who had had a hypoxic (*hypoxia:* insufficient oxygen) episode during a cardiac arrest that occurred in the course of minor facial surgery. His cognitive functions, for the most part, were not significantly affected, but initiating, self-correcting, and self-regulating behaviors were severely compromised. He also displayed some difficulty with new learning—not so much that he lost track of the date or could not follow sporting events from week to week, but enough to render his memory unreliable for most practical purposes.

One year after the anoxic episode, the patient's scores on a standard "intelligence" test ranged from *high average* (75th percentile) to *very superior* (99th percentile) except on a timed symbol substitution task that he performed without error but at a rate of speed that placed him low in the *average* score range. He performed another visual tracking task within normal limits and demonstrated good verbal fluency and visual discrimination abilities—all in keeping with his highest educational and professional achievements. On the basis of a psychologist's conclusion that these high test scores indicated "no clear evidence of organicity," and a psychiatric diagnosis of "traumatic depressive neurosis," the patient's insurance company denied his claim (pressed by his brother who is his guardian) for disability payments. Retesting six years later, again at the request of the brother, produced the same pattern of scores.

The patient's exceptionally good test performance belied his actual adjustment capacity. Seven years after the hypoxic episode, this now 45-year-old man who used to have his own successful private practice, was working for his brother as a delivery truck driver. He was a youthful-looking, nicely groomed man who explained, on questioning, that his niece bought all of his clothing and even selected his wardrobe for important occasions such as a neuropsychological examination. He did not know where she bought his clothes, how much they cost, or where the money came from to buy them, and he did not seem to appreciate that his ignorance was unusual. He was well mannered, pleasantly responsive to questions, but volunteered nothing spontaneously and asked no questions in an hour-and-a-half interview. He spoke in a matter-of-fact, humorless manner that remained unchanged regardless of the topic.

When asked, the patient reported that his practice had been sold but he did not know to whom, for how much, or who had the money. This once briefly married man who had enjoyed years of affluent independence had no questions or complaints about living in his brother's home. He had no idea how much his room and board cost or where the money came from for his support, nor did he exhibit any curiosity or interest in this topic. He said he liked doing deliveries for his brother because, "I get to talk to people." He had enjoyed surgery and said he would like to return to it but thought he was too slow now. When asked what plans he had, his reply was, "None." Not only was he unquestioning of his situation, but the possibility of change seemed not to have occurred to him.

His sister-in-law reported that it took several years of rigorous rule-setting to get the patient to bathe and change his underclothes each morning. He still changes his outer clothing only when instructed. He eats when hungry without planning or accommodating himself to the family's plans. If left home alone for a day or so he may not eat at all although he fixes himself coffee. In seven years he has not brought home or asked for any food, yet he enjoys his meals. He spends most of his leisure time in front of the TV. Though once an active sports enthusiast he now sits in the bar watching TV when taken to ski areas. He has made no plans to hunt or fish in seven years, but enjoys these sports when taken by relatives.

The patient's brother is able to keep the patient employed because he runs his own business. He explained that he can give his brother only routine assignments that require no judgment, and these only one at a time. As the patient finishes each assignment, he calls into his brother's office for the next one. Although he knows that his brother is his guardian, he has never questioned or complained about his legal status.

When the brother reinstituted suit for the patient's disability insurance, the company again denied the claim in the belief that the high test scores showed he was capable of returning to his profession. It was only when the insurance adjustor was reminded of the inappropriateness of the patient's life-style and the unlikelihood that an experienced, competent surgeon would contentedly remain a legal dependent in his brother's household for seven years that the adjustor could appreciate the psychological devastation the surgeon had suffered.

3

The Behavioral Geography
of the Brain

This chapter presents a brief (and necessarily superficial) sketch of some of the structural arrangements in the human central nervous system that are intimately connected with behavioral function. This is followed by a review of anatomical and functional interrelationships that appear with enough regularity to have psychologically meaningful predictive value.

More detailed information regarding neuroanatomy and its behavioral correlates is available in such standard neuroanatomy references as Barr (1979), Brodal (1981), Chusid (1979), Gilman and Winans (1982) or Mitchell and Mayer (1977). An excellent discussion of brain anatomy and physiology that is both detailed and concise is given by M. T. O'Brien and Pallett in their book on care of stroke patients (1978). Kevin Walsh's book, *Neuropsychology* (1978), provides a general review of the neuroanatomical foundations of neuropsychology, basic principles of neurology, and brain-behavior relationship. Kolb and Wishaw's *Fundamentals of human neuropsychology* (1980) offers an extensive overview of the field at an introductory level. E. Miller (1972) gives a more abbreviated review of of brain-behavior relationships from a neuropsychological viewpoint.

The role of physiological and biochemical events in behavioral expression adds another important dimension to neuropsychological phenomena. Most of the work in these areas is beyond the scope of this book. Readers wishing to get some idea of how biochemistry and neurophysiology relate to behavioral phenomena can consult Bechtereva (1978), Eliasson et al. (1978, *passim*); *Scientific American* (1979, *passim*); or Watts (1975).

Brain Pathology and Psychological Functions

The relationship between brain and behavior is exceedingly intricate, frequently puzzling, yet usually taken for granted. Our understanding of this fundamental relationship is still very limited, but the broad outlines and many details of the correlations between brain and behavior have been sufficiently well explained to be clinically useful.

Brain activity underlying any behavior is not limited to one or a few neuroanatomical structures or neural circuits. Recent electrical stimulation studies have demonstrated precisely delimited particularities of function of certain brain areas (Ojemann, 1978; Ojemann and Mateer, 1979), brain cell groupings (Mountcastle, 1978; Pollen, 1975, Hubel and Wiesel, 1979), and even single nerve cells (Ellenberger, 1978; Hubel, 1979). They give us a beginning insight into the functional building blocks of behavior. By themselves, however, they cannot provide an understanding of human activity, for organized behavior involves the whole brain. Complex acts, such as swatting a fly or reading this page, are the product of countless neural interactions involving many, often far-flung sites in the neural network; their neuroanatomical correlates are not confined to any local area of the brain (Luria, 1966; Moscovitch, 1979b; Sherrington, 1955).

However, discrete psychological activities such as the perception of a pure tone or the movement of a finger can be disrupted by *lesions* (localized abnormal tissue changes) involving approximately the same anatomical area in most human brains. This disruption of complex behavior by brain lesions also occurs with enough anatomical regularity that inability to understand speech, to recall recent events, or to copy a design, for example, can often be predicted when the site of the lesion is known (Blakemore et al., 1972; Geschwind, 1979; Laurence and Stein, 1978; Luria, 1970a; Piercy, 1964). Knowledge of the *localization of dysfunction*, as this correlation between damaged neuroanatomical structures and behavioral functions may be called, also enables neuropsychologists and neurologists to make educated guesses about the site of a lesion on the basis of abnormal patterns of behavior (McFie, 1961; V. Meyer, 1961; A. Smith, 1975).

Localization of dysfunction does not imply a "push-button" relationship between local brain sites and specific behaviors (Critchley, 1969; Poeck, 1969). Lesions at many different brain sites may alter or extinguish a single complex act (Luria, 1966, 1973b; Ojemann and Whitaker, 1978; Whitaker and Ojemann, 1977), as can lesions interrupting the neural pathways connecting areas of the brain involved in the act (Geschwind, 1965; Poeck, 1969). E. Miller (1972) reminds us that,

> It is tempting to conclude that if by removing a particular part of the brain we can produce a deficit in behavior, e.g., a difficulty in verbal learning following removal of the left temporal lobe in man, then that part of the brain must be responsible for the impaired function. . . . [T]his conclusion does not necessarily follow from the evidence as can be seen from the following analogy. If we were to remove the fuel tank from a car we would not be surprised to find that the car was incapable of moving itself forward. Nevertheless, it would be very misleading to infer that the function of the fuel tank is to propel the car (pp. 19–20).

The Cellular Substrate

The nervous system carries out communication functions for the organism. It is involved in the reception, processing, storage, and transmission of information within the organism and in the organism's exchanges with the outside world. It is a dynamic system in that its activity modifies its performance, its internal relationships, and its capacity to mediate stimuli from the outside.

Recent estimates of the number of nerve cells *(neurons)* in the brain have risen to 100 billion (Stevens, 1979). When well-nourished and adequately stimulated, tiny receptive organs at the neuronal tips proliferate abundantly, providing the human nervous system with an astronomical multiplicity of points of interaction between nerve cells, the *synapses*. The vast number of these interaction sites is sufficient to provide a structural neural potential for the variability and flexibility of human behavior. Alterations in spatial and temporal excitation patterns in the brain's circuitry can add considerably more to its dynamic potential.

Cells of the mature central nervous system differ from all other cells of the body in that they do not divide, multiply, or in any way replenish themselves. Once such a nerve cell is dead, connective tissue may fill its place or surrounding neurons may close in on the space left behind. New nerve cells cannot replace old ones.

When a nerve cell is injured or diseased, it may stop functioning and the circuits to which it contributed will then be disrupted. Some circuits may eventually reactivate as damaged cells resume functioning or alternative patterns involving different cell populations take over. When a circuit loses a sufficiently great number of neurons, the broken circuit can neither be reactivated nor replaced. Correlative behavioral alterations may indicate the locus and magnitude of the damage.

The Structure of the Brain

The brain is an intricately patterned complex of small and delicate structures. Its bulk is composed of nerve cell bodies, fibers *(axons* and *dendrites)* that extend from the nerve cell bodies and are their transmission organs, and supporting cells *(glia)*. In addition, an elaborate network of very fine blood vessels maintains a rich supply of nutrients to the extremely oxygen-dependent brain tissue.

The brain consists of the complex neural structures that grow out of the front end of the embryonic neural tube. The hind (lower, in humans) portion of the neural tube is the spinal cord. The brain stem and spinal cord serve as the throughway for communications between the brain and the rest of the body.

The neural tube develops a series of pouches, or *ventricles*, through which *cerebrospinal fluid (CSF)* flows. The most prominent of the pouches, the lateral ventricles, are a pair of horn-shaped reservoirs that are situated inside the cerebral hemispheres, running from front to back and curving around into the temporal lobe (see Fig. 3-10). The third and fourth ventricles are small bulges in the neural tube within the brain stem. Cerebrospinal fluid is produced by specialized tissues within all of the ventricles, but mostly in the lateral ventricles. The cerebrospinal fluid serves as a shock absorber and helps to maintain the shape of the soft nervous tissue of the brain. Obstruction of the flow of cerebrospinal fluid in adults can create the condition known as *normal pressure hydrocephalus (NPH)* in which brain tissue surrounding the ventricles gradually erodes to accommodate the accumulating fluid within the ventricular

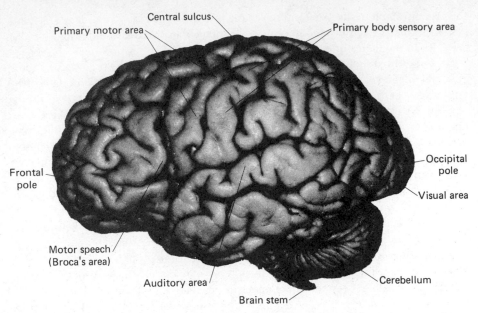

Central sulcus

Primary motor area

Primary body sensory area

Frontal pole

Occipital pole

Visual area

Motor speech (Broca's area)

Auditory area

Brain stem

Cerebellum

Fig. 3-1. Lateral view of the cerebrum, cerebellum, and part of the brain stem. (From DeArmond, Fusco, and Dewey, 1976)

system (see pp. 189–190). In conditions in which brain substance deteriorates, the ventricles enlarge to fill in the void. Thus, the size of the ventricles can be an important indicator of the brain's status.

Three major anatomical divisions of the brain succeed one another along the brain stem: the *hindbrain*, the *midbrain*, and the *forebrain* (see Fig. 3-2). Structurally, the brain centers that are lowest (farthest back) on the neural tube are the most simply organized. In the brain's forward development there is a pronounced tendency for increased anatomical complexity and diversity culminating in huge, elaborate structures at the front end of the neural tube. The functional organization of the brain has a similar pattern of increasing complexity from the lower brain stem up through its succeeding parts. By and large, the lower brain centers mediate the simpler, more primitive functions while the forward part of the brain mediates the highest functions.

The Hindbrain

THE MEDULLA OBLONGATA

The lowest part of the brain stem is the hindbrain, and its lowest section is the *medulla oblongata* or *bulb* (see Fig. 3-2). It is the site of such basic life-maintaining centers as those for nervous control of respiration, blood pressure, and heart beat. Significant injury to the bulb generally results in death.

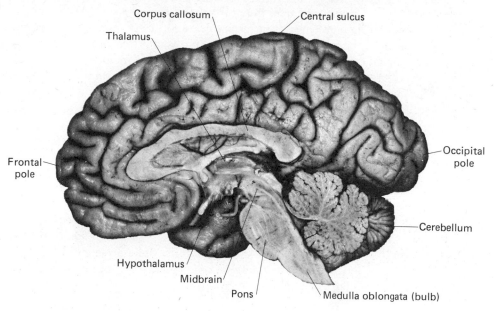

Fig. 3-2. Medial view of the brain. (From DeArmond, Fusco, and Dewey, 1976)

THE RETICULAR FORMATION

Running through the bulb from the upper cord to the *diencephalon* (see pp. 46–47) is the *reticular formation,* a network of intertwined and interconnecting nerve cell bodies and fibers that enter into or connect with all major neural tracts going to and from the brain. The reticular formation is not a single functional unit but contains many nerve centers or *nuclei* (clusters of functionally related nerve cells). These nerve centers mediate important and complex postural reflexes, contribute to the smoothness of muscle activity, and maintain muscle tone.

The reticular formation, from about the level of the lower third of the pons up to and including diencephalic structures, is also the site of the *reticular activating system* (RAS). The reticular activating system controls wakefulness and alerting mechanisms that ready the individual to react. The latter are a precondition for conscious behavior since they arouse the sleeping or inattentive organisms. Brain stem lesions involving the reticular activating system give rise to global disorders of consciousness—such as drowsiness, somnolence, stupor, or coma—which affect the organism's overall responsivity.

THE PONS and CEREBELLUM

The *pons* and the *cerebellum* are structures high in the hindbrain (see Figs. 3-1 and 3-2). Together they correlate postural and *kinesthetic* (muscle movement sense) information, refining and regulating motor impulses relayed from the cerebrum at the top of the brain stem. The pons contains major pathways for fibers running between the cerebral cortex and the cerebellum. The cerebellum is attached to the brain stem. Cerebellar damage is commonly reflected in problems of fine motor control, coordination, and postural regulation. Enough evidence exists to suggest that the cerebellum may also be involved in some aspects of sensory processing, perceptual discrimination, motor learning, and emotionally toned responses (P. J. Watson, 1978).

The Midbrain

The *midbrain*, a small area just forward of the hindbrain includes the major portion of the reticular activating system and contains both sensory and motor correlation centers (see Fig. 3-2). The sensory correlations that take place in midbrain nuclei contribute to the integration of reflex and automatic responses involving the visual and auditory systems. Motor nuclei play a role in the smooth integration of muscle movements and in the patterning of automatic posture. Midbrain lesions have been associated with specific movement disabilities such as certain types of tremor, rigidity, and extraneous movements of local muscle groups.

The Forebrain

The forwardmost part of the brain has two subdivisions. The *diencephalon* ("between-brain") comprises a set of structures, including correlation and relay centers, that evolved at the anterior, or most forward, part of the brain stem. These structures are almost completely embedded within the two halves of the *front* or *end* brain, the *telencephalon* (see Figs. 3-2 and 3-9).

The Diencephalon

From a neuropsychological viewpoint, the most important of the diencephalic structures are the *thalamus* and the *hypothalamus*. The thalamus is a small paired structure lying along the right and left sides of the bulge made by the third ventricle at the forward end of the neural tube. Each half of the thalamus consists of eleven nuclei, matched approximately in size, shape, and position to corresponding nuclei in the other half. Most of the anatomic interconnections formed by these nuclei and many of their functional contributions are known, but enough uncertainty remains to allow for speculation and require caution when interpreting research findings (J. W. Brown, 1975a).

The thalamus serves as a major sensory correlation center and participates in most of the exchanges between higher and lower brain structures, between sensory and motor or regulatory components at the same structural level, and between centers at the highest level of processing—the *cerebral cortex* (see pp. 49–50 ff.). It is the way station for all sensory pathways to the cerebral cortex, contributing significantly to the conscious experience of sensation (Brodal, 1981). It appears to play a role in regulating cortical activity (Mohr et al., 1975), both in focussing and shifting attention (McGhie, 1969) in general as well as in modality-specific alerting functions (Jurko and Andy, 1977; Ojemann, 1974; 1980). It also contributes to memory functions, probably by making accurate and ready retrieval possible (Butters, 1979; Fedio, 1976). That portion of the thalamus which enters into the *limbic system* (see pp. 75–76) also appears to be involved in emotional experience.

Differences in how the two halves of the brain process data, so pronounced at the highest—cortical—level, first appear in thalamic processing of sensory information (Vilkki, 1978). In its lateral asymmetry, thalamic organization parallels cortical organization in that left thalamic structures are implicated in verbal activity and right thalamic structures in nonverbal aspects of cognitive performance (see pp. 53–55). For example, patients with left thalamic lesions or undergoing left thalamic electrostimulation have not lost the capacity for verbal communication but may experience decreased verbal fluency and spontaneity of speech (Botez and Barbeau, 1971; McFarling et al., 1982; Riklan and Cooper, 1975, 1977; Vilkki and Laitinen, 1976), verbal memory and learning disorders (Fedio and Van Buren, 1975; Ojemann et al., 1971), and lower scores on verbal tests (Krayenbühl et al., 1965; McFie, 1961) that do not occur in patients whose thalamic damage is limited to the right side. Patients with right thalamic lesions or undergoing electrostimulation of the right thalamus, on the other hand, can have difficulty with face or pattern recognition and pattern matching (Fedio and Van Buren, 1975; Vilkki and Laitinen, 1976), maze tracing (Meier and Story, 1967), and with design reconstruction (Riklan and Diller, 1961) that is not associated with left thalamic lesions. R. T. Watson and Heilman (1979) describe three patients with right thalamic lesions who displayed denial, emotional flattening, and left-sided neglect characteristic of patients with right-sided—particularly right posterior—cortical lesions (see pp. 60–62, 72–73). The extent to which these symptoms reflected thalamic damage per se or disruption of pathways to the cortex remains unclear. (See also R. T. Watson et al., 1981.)

Bilateral thalamic lesions and thalamic degenerative disease may give rise to intellectual impairment associated with altered activation and arousal (Riklan and Levita, 1969) and some loss of intellectual ability generally (M. L. Albert, 1978). Pronounced damage to certain thalamic nuclei can result in gross memory defects (see pp. 193, 196–197) along with emotional apathy and impaired ability to initiate activity and to plan ahead. Another behavioral feature observed in thalamic degeneration is a "withering" of the language mechanism with initial loss of spontaneous speech and, ultimately, mutism. Apathy, disorientation, and confusion characterize this behavior pattern (J. W. Brown, 1974; Riklan and Cooper, 1975).

The *hypothalamus* regulates such physiologically based drives as appetite, sexual arousal, and thirst. Behavior patterns having to do with physical protection, such as rage and fear reactions, are also regulated by hypothalamic centers. The hypothalamus is part of the *autonomic* subdivision of the nervous system that controls automatic visceral functions. Lesions to hypothalamic nuclei can result in a variety of symptoms including obesity, disorders of temperature control, and changes in drive state and behavior. Mood states may also be affected by hypothalamic lesions.

The Cerebrum

The cerebrum, the most recently evolved, most elaborated, and by far the largest brain structure, has two hemispheres that are almost but not quite identical mirror images of each other (see Figs. 3-1, 3-2, 3-6 and 3-9). Within each cerebral hemisphere, at its base, are situated a number of nuclear masses known as the *basal ganglia* (ganglion is another term for nucleus). The largest is the *corpus striatum* (literally, striped body) consisting of several complex motor correlation centers that modulate both voluntary movements and autonomic reactions. "Figuratively speaking, the neostriatum (structures within the corpus striatum) can be considered as a part of the system which translates cognition into action" (Divac, 1977; see also Marsden, 1982).

The effects of injury to the corpus striatum vary with the specific site of injury, but lesions in this area may result in movement disorders (Delong and Georgopoulus, 1979). *Parkinsonism*, a disease associated with degeneration of basal ganglia structures, is usually considered to be a movement disorder because of muscular rigidity, motor slowing, and tremor that are its most obviously common symptoms. These symptoms suggest that the basal ganglia contribute to the programming of motor behavior. Moreover, it has become clear that patients with parkinsonism also suffer defects in cognitive functioning that show up particularly in short-term memory, concept formation, and mental flexibility defects (see pp. 185–187). It is interesting to note that difficulties in starting activities and in altering the course of ongoing activities characterize both motor and mental aspects of this disease. This cluster of behavioral deficits is akin to those exhibited by patients with lesions in the dorsolateral regions (the convexity) of the frontal lobes (see pp. 79–83) and in patients with degenerative diseases involving the pathways that connect structures within the basal ganglia to the frontal lobe integration centers (Cohn and Neumann, 1978).

Another prominent nuclear mass lying within each of the cerebral hemispheres is the *amygdala,* which has direct connections with the primitive centers involving the sense of smell. Semiautomatic visceral activities, particularly those concerned with feeding (e.g., chewing, salivating, licking, and gagging) and with the visceral components of the fear reactions, are affected by stimulation or ablation of the amygdala. Seizure activity and experimental stimulation of the amygdala provoke visceral responses associated with fright as well as mouth movements involved in feeding. Removal of the amygdala from both hemispheres may have a "taming" effect on animals and humans alike. Amygdalectomized humans become apathetic showing little spontaneity, creativity, or affective expression. Cognitively they are slow to acquire a mind set, but once it is established it becomes hard to dislodge; yet performance on standard measures of intellectual ability (e.g., WAIS subtests) remains essentially unchanged (Andersen, 1978). Material learned by amygdalectomized patients tends to be retained, but they become more dependent on context and external structure for learning new material, for retrieval generally, and in maintaining directed attention and tracking than prior to surgery.

The internal white matter of the cerebral hemispheres consists of densely packed

48

conduction fibers that transmit neural impulses between cortical points within a hemisphere (*association* fibers), between the hemispheres (*commissural* fibers), or between the cerebral cortex and lower centers (*projection* fibers). The *corpus callosum* is the great band of commissural fibers connecting the two hemispheres. Other interhemispheric connections are provided by some smaller bands of fibers. The corpus callosum is organized with a great deal of regularity. Fibers from the frontal cortex make up its anterior portion. The posterior portion consists of fibers originating in posterior cortex. Midcallosal areas contain a mixture of fibers coming from both anterior and more posterior regions. Fibers from the visual cortex at the posterior pole of the cerebrum occupy the posterior end portion of the callosum. The rapid and effective interhemispheric communication maintained by the corpus callosum and other commissural fibers enforces integration of cerebral activity between the two hemispheres (Berlucchi, 1978; Ellenberg and Sperry, 1980).

Section of the corpus callosum cuts off direct interhemispheric communication (A. D. Milner and Jeeves, 1979). When examined by special neuropsychological techniques, patients who have undergone section of commissural fibers *(commissurotomy)* exhibit profound behavioral discontinuities between perception, comprehension, and response, which reflect significant functional differences between the hemispheres (see pp. 54–55). Probably because direct communication between two cortical points occurs far less frequently than indirect communication relayed through lower brain centers, particularly the thalamus and the corpus striatum, these patients generally manage to perform everyday activities quite well. Moreover, patients with *agenesis of the corpus callosum* (a rare congenital condition in which the corpus callosum is insufficiently developed or absent altogether) are identified only when some other condition brings them to a neurologist's attention. Like patients with surgically separated cerebral hemispheres, these persons, whose cerebral hemispheres developed separately, normally display no neurological or neuropsychological defects (Bogen, 1979; Van der Vlugt, 1979) other than slowed motor performances, particularly of bimanual tasks. The functional disconnection between hemispheres can be demonstrated by the testing techniques devised to study the effects of surgical hemispheric disconnection (Berlucchi, 1978; J. N. Walton, 1977; A. D. Milner and Jeeves, 1979).

The cortex of the cerebral hemispheres, the convoluted outer layer of gray matter composed of nerve cell bodies and their synaptic connections, is the most highly organized correlation center of the brain (see Figs. 3-1 and 3-2). Although cortical function has been traced down to the activity of single neurons, the complex activities that require cortical involvement depend on the integrated action of multitudes of cells organized both anatomically and functionally into systems (Hécaen and Albert, 1978; Schmitt, 1978). The specificity of cortical structures in mediating behavior is neither clear-cut nor circumscribed. Predictably established relationships between cortical areas and behavior reflect the systematic organization of the cortex and its interconnections, yet most cortical areas are involved to some degree in the mediation of any complex behavior (Gloning and Hoff, 1969). The boundaries of functionally definable cortical areas, or zones, are vague. Cells subserving a specific function are highly concentrated in the primary area of a zone, thin out, and overlap with other zones as the perimeter of the zone is approached (Polyakov, 1966). Cortical activity at every level, from cellular to integrated system, is maintained and modulated by complex feedback loops that in themselves constitute major subsystems. Moreover, even those functions that are subserved by cells located within relatively well-defined cortical areas have a significant number of components distributed outside the local cortical center. For instance, of the cortical cells subserving voluntary movement (the primary motor cells), only 40% are located in the primary motor area whereas 10–20% are situated in the primary sensory area (Brodal, 1981; Luria, 1965); in turn, there is significant representation of primary sensory cells in what is known as the primary motor area (Penfield, 1958). Thus, it seems appropriate to refer to these areas as "sensorimotor zones with varying degrees of dominance" (Hécaen and Albert, 1978).

The Cerebral Cortex and Behavior

"We do not know exactly what the cortex does." G. von Bonin (1962b)

The patterns of functional localization in the cerebral cortex are broadly organized along two spatial planes. The *lateral plane* cuts through *homologous* (in the corresponding position) areas of the right and left hemispheres. The *longitudinal plane* runs from the front to the back of the cortex, with a relatively sharp demarcation between functions that are primarily localized in the forward portion of the cortex and those whose primary localization is behind the *central sulcus* or *fissure of Rolando.*

Lateral Organization

LATERAL SYMMETRY

The primary sensory and motor centers are homologously positioned within the cerebral cortex of each hemisphere in a mirror-image relationship. With certain exceptions, such as the visual and auditory systems, the centers in each cerebral hemisphere mediate the activities of the *contralateral* (other side) half of the body (see Fig. 3-3). Thus, an injury to the primary *somesthetic* or *somatosensory* (body feeling) area of the right hemisphere results in decreased or absent sensation in the corresponding left-sided body part; an injury affecting the left motor strip results in a right-sided weakness or paralysis *(hemiplegia).*

Point-to-point representation on the cortex.   The organization of both the primary sensory and primary motor areas of the cortex provides for a point-to-point representation of the body. The amount of cortex identified with each body portion or organ

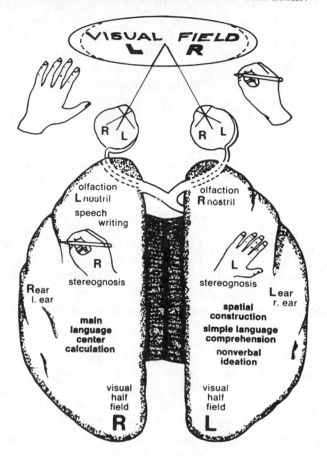

Fig. 3-3. Schematic diagram of visual fields, optic tracts, and associated brain areas, showing left and right lateralization in man (Sperry, 1970).

is proportional to the number of sensory or motor nerve endings in that part of the body rather than to its size. For example, the area concerned with sensation and movement of the tongue or fingers is much more extensive than the area representing the elbow or back.

The visual system is also organized on a contralateral plan, but it is one-half of each *visual field* (the entire view encompassed by the eye), which is projected onto the contralateral visual cortex (see Fig. 3-3). Fibers originating in the right half of each retina, which registers stimuli in the left visual field, project to the right visual cortex; fibers from the left half of the retina convey the right visual field image to the left visual cortex. Thus, destruction of either eye leaves both halves of the visual field intact. Destruction of the right or the left primary visual cortex or of all the fibers leading to either side results in blindness in each eye for that side of the visual field

51

(homonymous hemianopsia.) Lesions involving a portion of the visual projection fibers or visual cortex result in circumscribed *field defects,* such as areas of blindness *(scotoma;* pl. *scotomata)* within the visual field of one or both eyes, depending on whether the lesion involves the visual pathway before or after its fibers cross on their route from the retina of the eye to the visual cortex. The precise point-to-point arrangement of projection fibers from the retina to the visual cortex permits especially accurate localization of lesions within the primary visual system.

A majority of the nerve fibers transmitting auditory stimulation from each ear are projected to the primary auditory centers in the opposite hemisphere; the remaining fibers go to the *ipsilateral* (same side) auditory cortex. Thus, the contralateral pattern is preserved to some degree in the auditory system too. As a result of this mixed projection pattern, destruction of one of the primary auditory centers does not result in loss of hearing in the contralateral ear. A point-to-point relationship between sense receptors and cortical cells is also laid out on the primary auditory cortex, with cortical representation arranged according to pitch, from high tones to low ones.

Destruction of a primary cortical sensory or motor area results in specific sensory or motor deficits but generally has little effect on the higher cortical functions. For instance, an adult onset lesion limited to the primary visual cortex causes cortical blindness while reasoning ability, emotional control, and even the ability for visual conceptualization may remain intact.

Association areas of the cortex.   Cortical representation of sensory or motor nerve endings in the body takes place on a direct point-to-point basis, but stimulation of the primary cortical area gives rise only to meaningless sensations or nonfunctional movements (Gloning and Hoff, 1969; Luria, 1966). Modified and complex functions involve the cortex adjacent to primary sensory and motor centers. These secondary cortical areas and overlap zones are called *association areas.* Neurons in secondary areas integrate and refine raw percepts or simple motor responses. Overlap zones are areas peripheral to functional centers where the neuronal components of two or more different functions are interspersed, providing for integration of the functions mediated by them. Unlike damage to primary cortical areas, a lesion involving association areas and overlap zones typically does not result in specific sensory or motor defects; rather, the behavioral effects of such damage will more likely appear as a pattern of deficits running through related functions or as impairment of a general capacity. Thus, certain lesions that are implicated in drawing distortions also tend to affect the ability to do computations on paper; lesions of the auditory association cortex do not interfere with hearing acuity per se, but with the appreciation of patterned sounds.

ASYMMETRY BETWEEN THE HEMISPHERES

A second kind of organization across the lateral plane differentiates the two hemispheres with respect to the localization of primary cognitive functions and to significant qualitative aspects of behavior processed by each of the hemispheres. These differences appear to have structural foundation (Galaburda et al., 1978). The left hemisphere of most right-handed persons is somewhat larger and heavier than the right (von Bonin, 1962a), the size differential being greatest in those areas that mediate language functions (Geschwind, 1974a; Witelson, 1980). Other cortical areas, such as those involved in visuospatial transformations, tend to be larger on the right than their corresponding areas on the left (Blinkov and Glezer, 1968; Geschwind, 1979; Rubens, 1977). These differences may have a genetic, and possibly evolutionary, foundation for they appear early in human fetal development (Chi et al., 1977; Teszner et al., 1972; Wada et al., 1975) and have even been found in primates (Nottebohm, 1979; Rubens, 1977).

The next logical step toward understanding lateralization of brain structure would seem to be the investigation of cerebral differences at the level of cellular organization. As early as 1963, Hécaen and Angelergues, on careful review of the neuropsychological symptoms associated with lesions of the right or left hemisphere, speculated that neural organization might be more close knit and integrated on the left, more diffuse on the right. In accounting for findings that the spatial performance of right hemisphere damaged patients is adversely affected by lesions occuring over a fairly wide area while only those left hemisphere damaged patients with relatively severe damage to a well-defined area show impaired performance on spatial tasks, De Renzi and Faglione (1967), too, hypothesized more diffuse representation of functions in the right hemisphere, more focal representation in the left. Semmes (1968) came to a similar conclusion based on her findings that patients with right hemisphere damage tended to have a reduced capacity for tactile discrimination in both hands while those with left hemisphere damage experienced impaired tactile discrimination only in the contralateral hand. Additional data supporting an hypothesis that the right hemisphere is more diffusely organized than the left have been provided by a recent study suggesting that visuospatial and constructional disabilities of patients with right hemisphere damage do not differ significantly regardless of the extensiveness of damage (Kertesz and Dobrowolski, 1981). Hammond (1982) reports that damage to the left hemisphere tends to reduce acuity of time discrimination more than right-sided damage, suggesting that the left hemisphere has a capacity for finer temporal resolution than the right. Right organization may also be discrete (Fried et al., 1982).

The most obvious functional difference between the hemispheres is that the left hemisphere in most people is *dominant* for speech (i.e., language functions are primarily mediated in the left hemisphere) and the right hemisphere predominates in mediating complex, nonverbal stimuli. Absence of words does not make a stimulus "nonverbal." Pictorial, diagrammatic, or design stimuli, sounds, sensations of touch and taste, etc., may be more or less susceptible to verbal labeling depending on their meaningfulness, complexity, familiarity, potential for affective arousal, and other characteristics such as patterning or number. Thus, when classifying a wordless stimulus as verbal or nonverbal, it is important to take into account how readily it can be verbalized (Buffery, 1974). (For example, the 7/24 test layout pictured on p. 457 will be processed as a nonverbal stimulus by most patients. A bright, very verbal subject, however, can translate the pattern into a verbal code, such as "2-5, 3-6, 1-3, 1," in the ten-second exposure time.) The right hemisphere has also been called the "minor" or "silent" hemisphere because the often subtle character of right hemisphere disorders had led observers to believe until quite recently that it played no specialized role in intellectual behavior.[1]

The prominence of visuospatial defects among the disabilities that accompany right hemisphere lesions and the verbal nature of left hemisphere symptoms led some early theorists to hold that differences in hemisphere function were primarily related to modality differences, the left hemisphere having to do with auditory, the right with visual stimuli. Studies since then have repeatedly demonstrated that each hemisphere mediates stimuli entering through all sensory channels. Hemisphere specialization is *supramodal* in that it is organized on the basis of the capacity to process verbal or configurational material rather than in terms of sensory modalities.

Until the early 1960s when the technique of commissurotomy was developed to relieve certain kinds of epilepsy, the activities of the two hemispheres had to be studied indirectly through observations of behavioral impairments arising from lateralized lesions. The study of the behavior of patients with intact but surgically separated hemispheres has confirmed earlier observations on the different functions subserved by each hemisphere (Bogen, 1979; Gazzaniga, 1970; Levy, 1974; Levy-Agresti and Sperry, 1968; Nebes, 1974, 1978; Sperry et al., 1969). These findings have also been supported by data obtained from examinations of intact subjects. Studies of hemisphere function in normal persons have used such investigational techniques as reaction time to stimuli directed to the right or left visual field (Moscovitch, 1973); *dichotic* (both ears) studies involving simultaneous presentation of different stimuli to each ear (Gordon, 1974; King and Kimura, 1972); tachistoscopic presentation of visual material to either visual field (Dimond and Beaumont, 1974; Edguer et al., 1982; Kimura and Durnford, 1974; Leehey and Cahn, 1979); task-related electroencephalographic (EEG) asymmetries (Doyle et al, 1974; Ehrlichman and Wiener, 1979; Ornstein et al., 1979); *averaged evoked potentials* (the electrical activity of the brain elicited by discrete stimulation) (G. R. Marsh, 1978; A. E. Davis and Wada, 1977; John et al., 1977); and cerebral blood flow (Larsen et al., 1978; Shakhnovich et al., 1980). Ojemann (1978, 1980) and his colleagues (Ojemann and Mateer, 1979; Whitaker and Ojemann, 1977) have studied the effects of direct thalamic and cortical stimulation on ongoing speech and language in patients undergoing brain surgery.

These studies show that the left hemisphere is the primary mediator of verbal functions including reading and writing, understanding and speaking, verbal ideation, verbal memory, and even comprehension of verbal symbols traced on the skin. The left hemisphere also mediates the numerical symbol system. Moreover, left hemisphere lateralization of verbal functions extends to the musculature of speech, which appears to be under its sole control even though bilateral structures are involved. Left

---

[1]Because the left hemisphere is usually dominant for speech in both right and left-handed persons, it became customary to refer to it as the "dominant" hemisphere before the role of the right hemisphere was appreciated. Nowadays, each hemisphere is regarded as dominant for those functions it performs best. Today's custom is to associate the left and right hemispheres with verbal and nonverbal functions, respectively, despite exceptions to this rule (see pp. 221–22). This custom will be followed here.

hemisphere involvement in tactile and somatosensory perception, however, is limited to the right side of the body. The left hemisphere is less efficient than the right in the perception of shapes, textures, and patterns, whether by sight, sound, or touch, in dealing with spatial relationships, in using visual imagery, and in copying and drawing nonverbal figures.

The right hemisphere dominates the processing of information that does not readily lend itself to verbalization. This includes the processing and storage of visual data, tactile and visual recognition of shapes and forms, perception of spatial orientation and perspective, and copying and drawing geometric and representational designs and pictures. Arithmetic calculations (involving spatial organization of the problem elements as distinct from left hemisphere-mediated linear arithmetic problems involving, for instance, stories or equations with an $a + b = c$ form) have a significant right hemisphere component. Many aspects of musical ability are also localized on the right as are abilities to recognize and discriminate nonverbal sounds. The right hemisphere has bilateral involvement in somatosensory sensitivity and discrimination. In a series of studies, Heilman and Van Den Abell (1979, 1980) have reported that reaction times mediated by the right hemisphere are faster than those mediated by the left, and that the right hemisphere is activated equally by stimuli from either side in contrast to greater left hemisphere activation to right-sided than left-sided events. These findings were interpreted as reflecting a right hemisphere dominance for attention.

Although the right hemisphere appears to have virtually no capacity to generate verbalizations and a limited capacity to comprehend verbal material (Zaidel, 1978b), its active concern with the tone quality and rhythm of speech (Barbizet, 1974b; Marin et al., 1979; Searleman, 1977; Weintraub et al., 1981) is reflected in the poorly modulated, often monotonic speech peculiar to many patients with right hemisphere damage. Many of the reported studies on hemisphere specialization for verbal functions have employed single letters or words as the stimulus material. When the task has involved meaningful material, such as complex sentences (Eisenson, 1962) or stories (Ornstein et al., 1979; Rivers and Love, 1980); or humorous material (Wapner et al., 1981), a right hemisphere contribution to comprehension is suggested (E. D. Ross et al., 1981).

Exceptions to the general patterns are proving as interesting as the finding of lateral asymmetry. In intact persons, processing styles (Bryden, 1979b; P. Ross and Turkewitz, 1981), response set (expectations) (Hécaen, 1978), and the effects of training (Bever and Chiarello, 1974) can override the natural tendencies for involvement of one hemisphere or the other (see also Mazziota et al., 1982).

The study of patients with lateralized brain lesions demonstrates what happens when a part of one hemisphere is functioning badly or not at all (Benton, 1980; De Renzi, 1978; Gazzaniga, 1979, *passim;* Hécaen and Albert, 1978; Heilman and Valenstein, 1979, *passim;* Luria, 1970b). Time-bound relationships of sequence and order characterize many of the functions that are vulnerable to left hemisphere lesions. The intellectual defects commonly associated with left hemisphere damage include aphasia, verbal memory or verbal fluency deficits, concrete thinking, specific impairments in reading or writing, and impaired arithmetic ability characterized by defects or loss of basic mathematical concepts of operations and even of number. Patients with left hemisphere damage may make defective constructions because of tendencies toward simplification and difficulties in drawing angles. Their ability to perform complex manual—as well as oral—motor sequences may also be impaired (De Renzi et al., 1980; Kimura and Archibald, 1974; Tognola and Vignolo, 1980).

Patients with right hemisphere damage may be quite fluent, even verbose (Brookshire, 1978; Lezak and Newman, 1979) but illogical and given to loose generalizations and bad judgment. They are apt to have difficulty ordering, organizing, and making sense out of complex stimuli or situations, even when presented verbally, as in jokes (Wapner et al., 1981). They too display arithmetic deficits that become most apparent in written calculations requiring spatial organization of the problem's elements. These patients tend to have difficulty copying designs, making constructions, matching or discriminating patterns or faces, seeing stereoscopically, or processing the components of music. They may have particular problems with spatial orientation and visuospatial memory such that they get lost, even in familiar surroundings, and can be slow to learn their way around a new area. Their constructional disabilities reflect their spatial disorientation and defective capacity for perceptual or conceptual organization. Their reaction times are slowed.

> The painful efforts of a right hemisphere stroke patient to arrange plain and diagonally colored blocks according to a pictured pattern (Fig. 3-4a) illustrate the kind of solutions available to a person in whom only the left hemisphere is fully intact. This glib 51-year-old retired salesman constructed several simple 2 × 2 block design patterns correctly by verbalizing the relationships: "The red one (block) on the right goes above the white one; there's another red one to the left of the white one." This method worked so long as the relationships of each block to the others in the pattern remained obvious. When the diagonality of a design obscured the relative placement of the blocks, he could neither perceive how each block fit into the design nor guide himself with verbal cues. He continued to use verbal cues, but at this level of complexity his verbalizations only served to confuse him further. He attempted to reproduce diagonally oriented designs by lining up the blocks diagonally (e.g., "to the side," "in back of") without regard for the squared (2 × 2 or 3 × 3) format. He could not orient any one block to more than another single block at a time, and he was unable to maintain a center of focus to the design he was constructing.
>
> On the same task, a 31-year-old mildly dysphasic former logger who had had left hemisphere surgery involving the visual association area had no difficulty on this task until he came to the first 3 × 3 design, the only one of the four nine-block designs that lends itself readily to verbal analysis. On this design, he reproduced the overall pattern immediately but oriented one corner block erroneously. He attempted to reorient it but then turned a correctly oriented block into a 180° error. Though dissatisfied with this solution, he was unable to localize his error or define the simple angulation pattern (Fig. 3-4b).

These differences in hemisphere functioning reflect very basic processing differences between the hemispheres (Bogen, 1969a, b; Kinsbourne, 1978, *passim*, 1982; Krashen, 1977; Levy, 1974; Moscovitch, 1979b). Nebes (1974) characterizes these differences by referring to the left hemisphere as the "analyzer," the right as the "synthesizer." Another way is to think of these processes as "linear" and "configurational," respectively. The left hemisphere best handles time-related material that comes in linear sequences, such as verbal statements, mathematical propositions, and the programming of rapid motor sequences. The right hemisphere is superior when the material cannot be described adequately in words or strings of symbols, such as in recognizing faces or appreciating three-dimensional relationships.

As illustrated in Figure 3-4, the distinctive processing qualities of each hemisphere

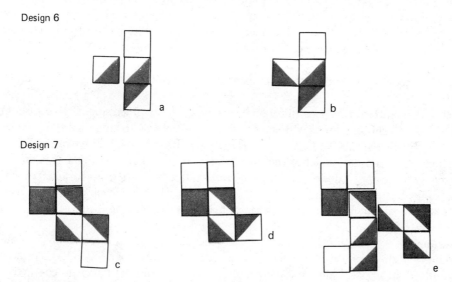

Fig. 3-4a. Attempts of a 51-year-old right hemisphere stroke patient to copy pictured designs with colored blocks. (a) First stage in the construction of a 2 × 2 chevron design. (b) Second stage: the patient does not see the 2 × 2 format and gives up after four minutes. (c) First stage in construction of 3 × 3 pinwheel pattern (see below). (d) Second stage. (e) Third and final stage.

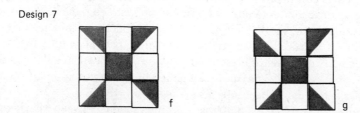

Fig. 3-4b. Attempts of a 31-year-old patient with a surgical lesion of the left visual association area to copy a 3 × 3 pictured pinwheel design with colored blocks. (f) Initial solution: 180° rotation of upper left corner block. (g) "Corrected" solution: upper left corner block rotated to correct position and lower right corner rotated 180° to incorrect position.

become evident in the mediation of spatial relationships. Left hemisphere processing tends to break the visual percept into details that can be identified and conceptualized verbally in terms of number or length of lines, size and direction of angles, etc. In the right hemisphere the tendency is to deal with the same visual stimuli as spatially related wholes. Thus, for most people, the ability to perform such complex visual tasks as the formation of complete impressions from fragmented percepts (the *closure* function), the appreciation of differences in patterns, and the recognition and remembering of faces, depends on the functioning of the right hemisphere. Together the two processing systems provide recognition, storage, and comprehension of discrete and continuous, serial and simultaneous, detailed and holistic aspects of experience across at least the major sensory modalities of vision, audition, and touch. Neither hemisphere appears to have priority over modality presentation, but rather, the dominance of each relative to any given task depends on the nature of the task and the kind of processing best suited for it (Lechelt, 1980; Milner, 1974; Safer and Leventhal, 1977).

The demonstration of two different kinds of cerebral processing of two distinct aspects of information fits in with long-standing conjectures about a duality in modes of thought (Bogen, 1969b; Critchley, 1972; Denny-Brown, 1962; Zangwill, 1974). It supports a conceptual model of the duality of brain functions in which "reason" as formal logic, science-mindedness, or no-nonsense attention to details characterizes left hemisphere thinking; "intuition" as nonverbal perceptiveness, inspirational hunches, and uncritical imagination typifies right hemisphere thinking (Levy-Agresti and Sperry, 1968).

Although oversimplified, this model has clinical value. Loss of tissue in a hemisphere tends to impair its particular processing capacity. When a lesion has rendered lateralized areas essentially nonfunctional, the intact hemisphere may process activities normally handled by the damaged hemisphere (Buffery, 1974; Hécaen, 1979). Fig. 3-4a is an example of this phenomenon). Moreover, a diminished functional capacity in one hemisphere may be accompanied by augmented or exaggerated activity of the intact hemisphere. This phenomenon appears in the verbosity and overwriting of many right hemisphere damaged patients (Babinski and Joltrain, 1924; Dordain et al., 1971; Lezak and Newman, 1979) (see Fig. 3-5b). It may account for improvements shown by psychiatric patients receiving electroconvulsive shock therapy (ECT) to the right hemisphere in performing a task involving the processing of sequential time-dependent stimuli (Knox Cube Imitation Test, see p. 454) (Strauss et al., 1979). These examples suggest that left hemisphere functioning is enhanced when the right hemisphere is impaired. In an analogous manner, patients with left hemisphere damage tend to reproduce the essential configuration but leave out details when copying drawings (see Fig. 3-5a) and they generally perform some perceptual (visual) closure tasks better than intact subjects (Wasserstein, 1980).

These observations support speculation that the interaction between the hemispheres involves a mutually inhibiting effect in the intact state (Broadbent, 1974; Kinsbourne, 1974a,b; Lezak, 1982c; Moscovitch, 1979b). Interaction between the hemispheres also has important mutually enhancing effects as demonstrated, for example,

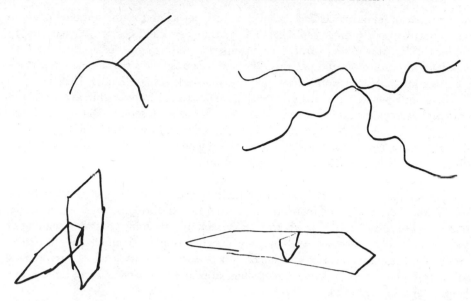

Fig. 3-5a. Simplification and distortions of four Bender-Gestalt designs by a 45-year-old assembly line worker with a high school education. These drawings were made four years after he had incurred left frontal damage in an industrial accident.

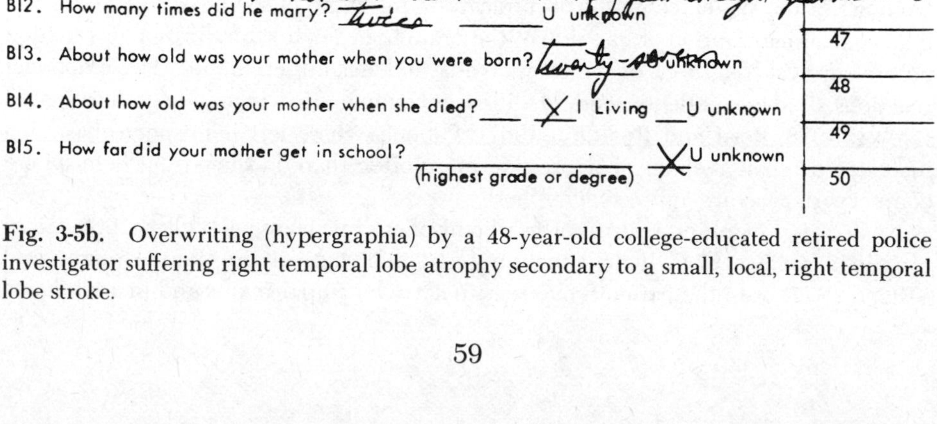

B8. About how old was your father when you were born? _don't forty two_ U unknown

B9. About how old was your father when he died? _about eighty two_ Living __ U unknown | 43

B10. How far did your father get in school? _third grade - used to_ U unknown | 44
B11. _talk / brag about talking_ (highest grade or degree)
What is (was) his usual line of work? _to U.S. Congress out of Eighteen million dolle_ | 45
Railroad Engineer — retired from the Great U unknown
Northern Railroad w/ Fifty Years an Eight years service

B12. How many times did he marry? _three_ _____ U unknown | 47

B13. About how old was your mother when you were born? _twenty-two_ unknown | 48

B14. About how old was your mother when she died? ___ X I Living ___ U unknown | 49

B15. How far did your mother get in school? _____ . X U unknown | 50
(highest grade or degree) X

Fig. 3-5b. Overwriting (hypergraphia) by a 48-year-old college-educated retired police investigator suffering right temporal lobe atrophy secondary to a small, local, right temporal lobe stroke.

59

in the superior memorizing and retrieval of both verbal and configurational material when simultaneously processed (encoded) by the verbal and configurational systems (Milner, 1978; Moscovitch, 1977); and in superior performances of a visual memory task by commissurotomized patients when both hemispheres participate (free-vision condition) than when vision is restricted to either hemisphere (Zaidel, 1979).

The complementary modes of processing that distinguish the cognitive activities of the two hemispheres extend to emotional behavior as well (see pp. 56 to 58; Moscovitch, 1979b; Nebes, 1978; Sackeim et al., 1978; Safer and Leventhal, 1977). The configurational processing of the right hemisphere lends itself most readily to the handling of the multidimensional and alogical stimuli that convey *emotional tone*, such as facial expressions and voice quality (Blumstein and Cooper, 1974; Ley and Bryden, 1982; Sugarman et al, 1980). The analytic, bit-by-bit processing of the left hemisphere, then, deals with the *words* of emotion. A face distorted by fear and the exclamation, "I'm scared to death," both convey affective meaning, but the meaning of each is normally processed well by only one hemisphere (Hansch and Pirozzolo, 1980). Yet the characteristics associated with personal identity, such as preferences, social awareness, and affective associations, appear to be very similar for the two hemispheres (Sperry et al., 1979).

Thus, patients with right hemisphere damage tend to experience relative difficulty in discerning the emotional characteristics of stimuli with corresponding diminution in their emotional responsivity (Morrow et al., 1981). For example, one study showed that patients with right hemisphere damage were deficient in their appreciation of the emotional import of both facial expressions and descriptive phrases (e.g., "A man sinking in quicksand.") (Cicone et al., 1980). Frontal leucotomy patients exhibited overall an even greater degree of emotional incomprehension than the group with right hemisphere damage. Patients with left hemisphere lesions had less difficulty than the other patient groups appreciating facial expressions but were on a par with the right hemisphere group when the stimulus was verbal. In another study, patients with right-sided lesions and unilateral neglect had difficulty comprehending the affective quality of speech, but fluent aphasics with left hemisphere lesions did not (Heilman et al., 1975).

Hemispheric differences also appear in the emotional changes that may accompany brain injury (Diller, 1968; Sackeim et al., 1982; Galin, 1974; E. Valenstein and Heilman, 1979). What can be considered an experimental model of these changes stems from use of the Wada technique of intracarotid injections of sodium amytal for pharmacological inactivation of one side of the brain to evaluate lateralization of function before surgical treatment of epilepsy (Wada and Rasmussen, 1960). The emotional reactions of these patients tend to differ depending on which side is inactivated (Nebes, 1978; Rossi and Rosadini, 1967). Patients whose left hemisphere has been inactivated report feelings of depression more often than do their right hemisphere counterparts who are apt to feel euphoric.

Anxiety is a common feature of left hemisphere involvement (Diller, 1968; Gainotti, 1972; Galin, 1974). It may show up as undue cautiousness (Jones-Gotman and Milner, 1977) or in the patient's oversensitivity to his impairments and in a tendency to exaggerate his disabilities. It is frequently compounded by depression (M. W. Buck, 1968), particularly among patients whose speech difficulties primarily involve expression rather than comprehension (R. G. Robinson and Benson, 1981). Patients with comprehension defects are more likely to appear unaware of their disability or, if disturbed, exhibit paranoid behavior (Benson, 1973). Patients with left hemisphere lesions are more likely than those with right-sided brain damage to exhibit a *catastrophic reaction* (extreme and disruptive transient emotional disturbance). The catastrophic reaction may appear as acute, often disorganizing anxiety, agitation, or tearfulness disrupting the activity that provoked it. Typically, it occurs when patients are confronted with their limitations, as when taking a test. They tend to regain their composure as soon as the source of frustration is removed. Yet, despite tendencies to be overly sensitive to their disabilities, patients with left hemisphere lesions may ultimately compensate for them well enough to make a satisfactory adjustment to their disabilities and living situations.

In contrast, patients whose injuries involve the right hemisphere are less likely to be dissatisfied with themselves or their performances than are those with left hemisphere lesions, and they are less likely to be aware of their mistakes (Hécaen et al., 1951). At least in the acute or early stages of their condition, they may display an *indifference reaction*, tending to deny or make light of the extent of their disabilities (Denny-Brown et al, 1952; Gainotti, 1972; Lezak, 1979a). In extreme cases, patients are unaware of such seemingly obvious defects as crippling left-sided paralysis or slurred and poorly articulated speech (see p. 73).

An indifference reaction, or related behavioral phenomena typically symptomatic of right hemisphere dysfunction, may be manifested by patients with predominant left hemisphere damage in the early days or weeks of their illness when associated physiological disturbances tend to disrupt the normal functioning of all brain regions (Plum and Posner, 1980). These typically right-brain phenomena tend to dissipate when—or soon after—other neurological signs reflecting right hemisphere dysfunction disappear. Moreover, head traumas, hemorrhages, and many tumors may directly involve both hemispheres but with different degrees of severity so that such obvious symptoms as paralysis are referrable only to one hemisphere. Thus, damage that is actually bilateral damage may be classified as unilateral. These two circumstances probably account for most of the reported instances in which patients with predominantly left hemisphere disease have displayed the indifference phenomenon, and certainly raise questions about psychodynamic interpretations of the indifference reaction (e.g., E. A. Weinstein and Kahn, 1955; E. A. Weinstein et al., 1964) as well as explanations that do not distinguish between left and right hemisphere phenomena (e.g., Cutting, 1978).

Relatively few patients with right hemisphere lesions are depressed during their hospitalization (Gainotti, 1972). However, a number become depressed later. In some depressed patients with right hemisphere involvement, the emotional disturbance does not seem to arise from awareness of defects so much as from the secondary effects of the patient's diminished self-awareness. Those patients with right hemisphere lesions who do not appreciate the nature or extent of their disability tend to set unrealistic goals for themselves, or to maintain their previous goals without taking their new limitations into account. As a result, they frequently fail to live up to their goals. Also, their diminished capacity for self-awareness tends to reduce their sensitivity to others so that they become more difficult to live with and thus are more likely to be rejected by family and friends than are patients with left hemisphere lesions. Depression in patients with right-sided cortical damage often takes longer to develop than it does in patients with left hemisphere involvement since it is less likely to be a reaction to immediately perceived disabilities than to their secondary consequences. When it does develop, however, it is apt to be more chronic, more debilitating, and more resistive to intervention.

In light of their difficulties processing the subtleties of facial expressions, voice tone and speech rhythms, postural and gestural nuances that make up much of our emotional communication, it is not surprising that right hemisphere damaged patients may appear to be emotionally insensitive and even lacking normal affective capacity (Gasparrini et al., 1978; Heilman et al., 1975; Daniel M. Tucker et al., 1976,1977). However, right hemisphere damaged patients do not experience emotions any more weakly than other people. Rather, their experience of emotional communications and capacity to transmit the nuances and subtleties of their own feeling states differs from normal affective processing (Barbizet, 1974b; Morrow et al., 1981; E. D. Ross and Mesulam, 1979; E. D. Ross and Rush, 1981), leaving them out of joint with those around them and often difficult to live with (Lezak, 1979a).

These descriptions of differences in the emotional behavior of right and left hemisphere damaged patients reflect observed tendencies that are not necessary consequences of unilateral brain disease. Neither are the emotional reactions reported here only associated with unilateral brain lesions. Mourning reactions naturally follow the experience of personal loss of a capacity whether it be due to brain injury, a lesion lower down in the nervous system, or amputation of a body part. Inappropriate euphoria and self-satisfaction may accompany lesions involving other than right hemisphere areas of the cortex. Further, premorbid personality colors the quality of the patient's response to his disabilities (see p. 225). Thus, the clinician should not be tempted to predict the side of damage from the patient's mood alone.

While knowledge of the asymmetrical pattern of cerebral organization adds to the understanding of many cognitive and emotional phenomena associated with unilateral lesions or demonstrated in laboratory studies of normal subjects or commissurotomized patients, it is inappropriate to generalize these findings to the behavior of persons whose brains are intact. In normal persons, the functioning of the two hemispheres is tightly yoked by the corpus callosum so that neither hemisphere can be engaged without significant activation of the other hemisphere (Lezak, 1982c). Moreover, as much as cognitive styles and personal tastes and habits might seem to reflect the processing characteristics of one or the other hemisphere, these qualities appear to be integral to both hemispheres (Arndt and Berger, 1978; Sperry et al., 1979). "In the normal intact state, the conscious activity is typically a unified and coherent bilateral process that spans both hemispheres through the commissures" (Sperry, 1976; See also Chiarello et al., 1982; D. N. Robinson, 1982; E. D. Ross et al., 1981).

The bilateral integration of cerebral function is most clearly exhibited by creative artists who typically enjoy intact brains. Excepting singing, harmonica playing, and the small repertoire of piano pieces written for one hand, making music is a two-handed activity. Moreover, for instruments such as guitars and the entire violin family, the right hand performs those aspects of the music that are mediated predominantly by the right hemisphere, such as expression, rhythm, and tonality, while the left hand interprets the linear sequence of notes best deciphered by the left hemisphere. Right-handed artists do their drawing, painting, sculpting, and modeling with the right hand, with perhaps an occasional assist from the left. Thus, by its very nature, the artist's performance involves the smoothly integrated activity of both hemispheres. The contributions of each hemisphere are indistinguishable and inseparable as the artist's two eyes and two ears guide the two hands or the bisymmetrical speech and singing structures that together render the artistic production.

Longitudinal Organization

Although no two human brains are exactly alike in their structure, all normally developed brains share the same major distinguishing features (see Fig. 3-6). The external surface of each half of the cerebral cortex is wrinkled into a complex of ridges or convolutions called *gyri* (sing., gyrus), which are separated by two deep *fissures* and many shallow clefts called *sulci* (sing., *sulcus*). The two prominent fissures and certain of the major sulci divide each hemisphere into four *lobes*, the *occipital, parietal, tem-*

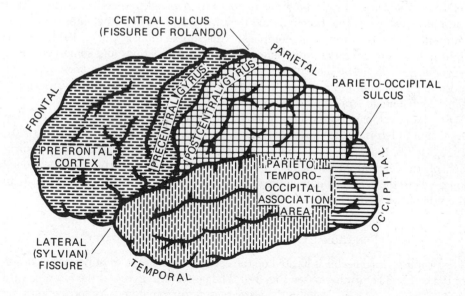

Fig. 3-6. The lobes and landmark structures of the cerebral cortex.

poral, and *frontal* lobes. These lobes received their anatomical delineations by virtue of the visual prominence of their identifying cerebral landmarks rather than from intrinsic functional or structural characteristics.

The *central sulcus* divides the cerebral hemispheres into anterior and posterior regions. Immediately in front of the central sulcus lies the precentral gyrus, which contains much of the *primary motor* or *motor projection* area. The entire frontal area forward of the central sulcus is also called the *precentral* or *prerolandic* area. The bulk of the *primary somesthetic* or *sensory projection* area is located in the gyrus just behind the central sulcus. The area behind the central sulcus is also known as the *retrorolandic* or *postcentral* area.

Certain functional systems have primary or significant representation on the cerebral cortex with sufficient regularity that the lobes do provide a useful anatomical frame of reference for functional localization, much as a continent provides a geographical frame of reference for a country. But, because the lobes were originally defined solely on the basis of their gross appearance, some functionally definable areas overlap two and even three lobes. For example, the boundary between the parietal and occipital lobes is arbitrarily defined by a minor sulcus, the *parieto-occipital sulcus,* lying in what is now known to be an overlap zone for visual and spatial functions.

The two-dimensional organization of cortical functions lends itself to a schema that offers a framework for conceptualizing cortical organization. The anterior and posterior cortical regions may be roughly characterized as having to do with motor/response and sensory/perceptual functions, respectively. Certain left frontal areas mediate various aspects of verbal expression; right frontal regions mediate activities involving the organizing, planning, and carrying out of complex or multifaceted activities. The left and right posterior regions are involved, respectively, with verbal and nonverbal perceptual functions and their integration. The actual interweaving of different functional components complicates this simple model (Milner, 1974), for the right hemisphere has some involvement with verbal functions and some nonverbal behavior is mediated by the left cortex. There is also a considerable motor component in the behavior complexes served by posterior cortical areas, just as sensory components contribute to frontal lobe activity.

For the most part, behavioral changes in cortically damaged patients are best explained in terms of the functional patterning of the cerebral cortex (Luria, 1970a, 1973; McFie, 1969; Talland, 1963). However, a strict pattern of functional organization of the cerebral cortex has not been clearly defined for portions of the frontal lobes where the extent of damage may have a more obvious effect on behavior than the side of the lesion (Hécaen, 1969; Piercy, 1964) (see pp. 79–83).

FUNCTIONAL ORGANIZATION of the POSTERIOR CORTEX

The primary visual cortex is located on the occipital lobe at the most posterior portion of the cerebral hemispheres (see Fig. 3-6). The postcentral gyrus, at the most forward part of the parietal lobe, contains the primary sensory (somatosensory) projection area. The primary auditory cortex is located on the uppermost fold of the temporal lobe close to where it joins the parietal lobe. Kinesthetic and vestibular functions are mediated by areas low on the parietal lobe near the occipital and temporal lobe boundary regions.

There are no clear-cut demarcations among any of the functions localized on the posterior cortex. Rather, although the primary centers of the major functions served by the posterior cerebral regions are relatively distant from one another, their secondary association areas gradually fade into tertiary overlap zones in which visual and body-sensing components intermingle.

As a general rule, the character of the defects arising from lesions of the association areas of the posterior cortex varies according to the extent to which the lesion involves each of the sense modalities. Any disorder with a visual component, for example, may implicate some occipital lobe involvement. If a patient with visual agnosia also has difficulty estimating close distances or feels confused in familiar surroundings, then parietal lobe areas serving spatially related kinesthetic and vestibular functions may also be affected. Knowledge of the sites of the primary sensory centers and of the behavioral correlates of lesions to these sites and to the intermediate association areas enables the clinician to infer the approximate location of a lesion from the patient's behavioral symptoms.

Occipital lobe disorders.   Isolated lesions of the primary visual cortex result in discrete blind spots in the corresponding parts of the visual fields but do not alter the comprehension of visual stimuli or the ability to make a proper response to what is seen.

The nature of the blindness that accompanies total loss of function of the primary visual cortex, and the patient's response to it, vary with the extent of involvement of subcortical or associated cortical areas. Although it is rare for damage or dysfunction to be restricted to the primary visual cortex, when this does occur the patient appears to have lost the capacity to distinguish forms or patterns while remaining responsive to light and dark, a condition called *cortical blindness* (Luria, 1966). Recent research suggests that some visual discrimination may take place at the thalamic level, while the cortex is necessary for the conscious experience of visual phenomena (Hécaen and Albert, 1978; Weiskrantz, 1974). Total blindness due to brain damage appears to require at least destruction of thalamic areas as well as visual cortex or the pathways leading to it (Teuber, 1975). In *denial of blindness* due to brain damage *(visual anosognosia)*, the patient lacks appreciation that he is blind and attempts to behave as if sighted, making elaborate explanations and rationalizations for his difficulties in getting around, handling objects, etc. (Redlich and Dorsey, 1945; K. W. Walsh, 1978b). Denial of blindness, sometimes called *Anton's syndrome*, appears to be associated with disruption of corticothalamic connections and breakdown of sensory feedback loops.

Lesions involving the visual association areas of the occipital lobes give rise to visual agnosias or visual distortions (Gloning et al., 1968). Only rarely do visual perceptual disturbances result from lesions of other lobes or subcortical structures without occipital cortical damage as well. More often, impaired visual awareness or visual recognition is associated with disturbances of other perceptual modalities when lesions in other cortical regions extend to the occipital lobe, as occurs in disorders of visuospatial functions (e.g., Fisher, 1982) (see pp. 68, 71, 72).

Visual agnosia refers to a variety of visual disturbances that generally do not appear in a pure form (Frederiks, 1969a; Hécaen and Albert, 1979; Luria, 1965; Howieson et al.,1981). In *apperceptive visual agnosia,* the patient cannot synthesize what he sees. He may indicate awareness of discrete parts of a word or a phrase, or recognize elements of an object without organizing the discrete percepts into a perceptual whole. Drawings by such patients are fragmented: bits and pieces are recognizable but are not put together. These patients often display general intellectual deterioration as well (Rubens, 1979). According to Luria (1965), patients with *associative visual agnosia* can perceive the whole of a visual stimulus, such as a familiar face or a personal possession, but cannot recognize it. Some investigators limit the definition of associative visual agnosia to the inability to recognize objects and pictures, and report patients with this condition who can copy drawings, read, and recognize faces (Mack and Boller, 1977; Rubens, 1979). *Simultaneous agnosia,* or *simultanagnosia*— also known as Balint's syndrome—appears as an inability to perceive more than one object or point in space at a time. Luria attributes the problem to difficulty in shifting visual attention from one point in the visual field to another, but M. Williams (1970a) discusses it in terms of time needed to form a percept of a second object in the field. *Color agnosia,* the inability to appreciate differences between colors or to relate colors to objects in the presence of intact color vision, is usually found in association with other visual agnosias (Gloning et al., 1968).

Visual inattention associated with occipital lobe damage is similar to simultaneous agnosia in that the patient spontaneously perceives only one object in the field at a time. It differs from simultaneous agnosia in that the patient will see more than one object if others are pointed out to him; this is not the case in a true simultaneous agnosia. Visual inattention also refers to imperception of stimuli. Material in one visual field—usually the left—can be seen but remains unnoticed unless the patient's attention is drawn to it (see Fig. 3-7). This form of visual inattention, also known as *unilateral spatial neglect,* typically occurs only when there is right parietal lobe involvement as well as occipital lobe damage (see p. 72–73).

Visual agnosias are most likely to occur with bilateral occipital lesions. However, some kinds are particularly associated with right or left-sided damage. Patients with lesions in the left occipital cortex and its subcortical connections may have a reading problem that stems from defects of visual recognition, organization, and scanning rather than from defective comprehension of written material, which usually occurs only with parietal damage or from aphasia (Benson, 1977; Damasio, 1977). Agnosia for colors frequently accompanies this kind of reading disability and is also typically associated with damage to the left occipital lobe or to underlying white matter containing visual system pathways (Damasio et al., 1979; Hécaen and Angelergues, 1963). Geschwind (1979) reports that another kind of visual agnosia, *prosopagnosia* (inability to recognize faces), occurs only when the cortex on the undersides of the occipital and temporal lobes is damaged bilaterally, although other investigators have observed

Copy these designs in the space to the right.

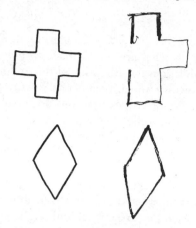

Fig. 3-7. Example of inattention to the left visual field by a 57-year-old college graduate with a right parieto-occipital lesion.

this phenomenon when the damage is predominantly in the right hemisphere (see p. 73). Writing defects associated with occipital lobe lesions may result from inability to recall the visual image of the required symbol or the sequence of the discrete symbols that make up a number or word, or from faulty scanning. One form of *acalculia* (literally, no counting), a disorder that Grewel (1952) considered a primary type of impaired arithmetic ability in which the calculation process itself is affected, may result from visual disturbances of symbol perception associated with left occipital cortex lesions. Right occipital lesions are more likely to give rise to impaired object perception.

The posterior association cortex.   Association areas in the parieto-temporo-occipital region are situated just in front of the visual association areas and behind the primary sensory strip. They run from the *longitudinal fissure* (the deep cleft separating the two hemispheres) laterally to the areas adjacent to and just above the temporal lobe where temporal, occipital, and parietal elements commingle. These association areas include much of the parietal and occipital lobes and some temporal association areas. Functionally they are the site of cortical mediation for all behavior involving vision, touch, body awareness, verbal comprehension, spatial localization, and for abstract and complex intellectual functions of mathematical reasoning and the formulation of logical propositions that have their conceptual roots in basic visuospatial experiences such as "inside," "bigger," "and," or "instead of." It is within these areas that intermodal sensory integration takes place, making this region "an association area of association areas" (Geschwind, 1965).

A variety of apraxias and agnosias have been ascribed to parieto-temporo-occipital lesions. Most of them have to do with verbal or with nonverbal stimuli but not with both and thus are asymmetrically localized (McFie and Zangwill, 1960). A few occur with lesions in either hemisphere.

The posterior association cortex: (a) defects arising from lesions on either hemisphere.   Constructional disorders are among the few predominantly parietal lobe disabilities that appear with lesions on either side of the midline (Black and Strub, 1976; De Renzi, 1978). They involve impairment of the "capacity to draw or construct two or three dimensional figures or shapes from one and two dimensional units" (Strub and Black, 1977). They seem to be closely associated with perceptual defects (Dee, 1970; Pillon, 1981a, b). Constructional disorders take different forms depending on the hemispheric side of the lesion (Consoli, 1979). Left-sided lesions are apt to disrupt the programming or ordering of movements necessary for constructional activity (Hécaen and Assal, 1970). Visuospatial defects tend to underlie right hemisphere constructional disorders (Blakemore et al., 1972). Diagonality in a design or construction can be particularly disorienting to patients with right hemisphere lesions (Milner, 1971; Warrington et al., 1966). Defects in copying designs appear in the drawings of patients with left hemisphere lesions as simplification and difficulty in making angles, and in the drawings of patients with right-sided involvement as a tendency to a counterclockwise tilt (rotation), fragmented percepts, irrelevant overelaborativeness, and neglect of the left half of the page or the left half of elements on the page (Diller and Weinberg, 1965; Piercy et al., 1960; Warrington et al., 1966). (See Fig. 3-8a, b for freehand drawings of left and right hemisphere damaged patients showing typical hemispheric defects.) Puzzle construction in two- and three-dimensional space may be affected by both right and left hemisphere lesions.

Some studies have not shown any difference in the frequency with which left and right hemisphere damaged patients have constructional disorders (e.g., Arena and Gainotti, 1978; Dee et al., 1970); others (Belleza et al., 1979; Benton, 1973; Black and Strub, 1976) have shown more constructional disabilities among right brain damaged patients. Although Arena and Gainotti attribute these differences in findings to the number of aphasic patients included in the left hemisphere damaged samples, other differences between the studies may also account for the apparently conflicting findings (Benton, 1979). For example, Benton (1973) used a difficult three-dimensional construction task while Arena and Gainotti had their patients copy relatively simple geometric designs.

Hécaen (1969) associates difficulties in serial ordering with impairment of the parieto-temporo-occipital area of both the left and right hemispheres. Perception of the temporal order in which stimuli are presented is much more likely to be impaired by left than right hemisphere lesions involving the posterior association areas (Carmon and Nachson, 1971) except when the stimulus array also includes complex spatial configurations, for then the patients with right hemsphere lesions do worse than those with left-sided lesions (Carmon, 1978). Disruption of the sequential organization of speech associated with left hemisphere lesions may result in the language formulation defects of aphasia. Right-sided lesions of the parieto-temporo-occipital area appear to interfere with the comprehension of order and sequence so that the patient has dif-

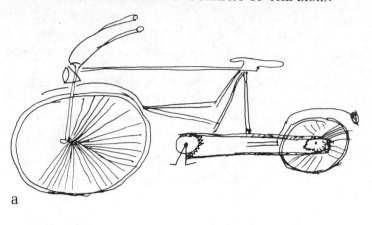

a

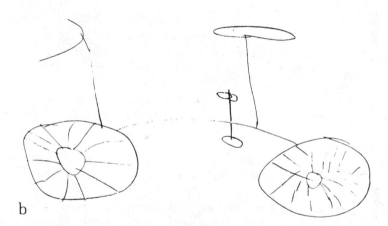

b

Fig. 3-8a. This bicycle was drawn by the same 51-year-old retired salesman who constructed the block designs of Fig. 3-4 (a-e). This drawing demonstrates that neglect of the left visual field is not due to carelessness, for the patient painstakingly drew in the many details and was very pleased with his performance. **b.** This bicycle was drawn by a 24-year-old college graduate almost a year after receiving a severe injury to the left side of his head. He originally drew the bike without pedals, adding them when asked, "How do you make it go?"

ficulty seeing or dealing with temporal relationships and is unable to make plans (Lezak, 1979a; Milberg et al., 1979).

Lesions in either hemisphere involving the sensory association areas posterior to the postcentral gyrus can produce a *tactile agnosia* or *astereognosis* (inability to identify an object by touch) to the body side opposite the lesion. Semmes' (1968) findings that right hemisphere lesions may be associated with impairment of shape perception in both hands have received support (e.g., Boll, 1974), but a high incidence of bilateral sensory defect has also been noted among patients with unilateral lesions of either hemisphere (Milner, 1975).

Recent studies have indicated that difficulty in recognizing unfamiliar faces may accompany left as well as right hemisphere lesions (Benton, 1980; Hamsher et al., 1979). It is less frequent among patients with left hemisphere damage, affecting only aphasic patients who have comprehension defects at about the same rate as all patients with right hemisphere damage. Capitani and his colleagues (1978) report that patients with parietal rather than occipital lobe involvement were significantly error prone on a color discrimination task, with the right-lesioned patients making almost twice as many errors as those whose lesions were on the left.

Historically, the inability to recognize familiar faces (*prosopagnosia*) was attributed to posterior lesions in the right hemisphere. Recent work, however, has demonstrated that bilateral lesions involving the occipitotemporal regions of both hemispheres are necessary for this phenomenon to occur (A. R. Damasio et al., 1982). Moreover, this defect does not appear to be peculiar to faces, but may show up whenever these patients must use vision to make a specific identification of an item in a category of objects or creatures (e.g., "a bird watcher no longer able to identify birds or a farmer no longer able to recognize his cows"). The documentation of the general nature of this problem with visual identification is a good example of how knowledge depends upon the appropriateness of the questions asked: it was not until patients suffering prosopagnosia were asked to perform tasks of identification in categories other than faces that the widespread character of the defect became apparent.

The posterior association cortex: (b) defects arising from left hemisphere lesions. The posterior language areas are situated at the juncture of the temporal and parietal lobes. Direct cortical stimulation studies have implicated the region surrounding this language area in short-term verbal memory (Ojemann, 1978).

When they occur, aphasia and related symbol-processing disabilities are generally the most prominent symptoms of left parieto-temporo-occipital lesions. Fluent aphasia, usually characterized by incomprehension, jargon speech, and apparent lack of awareness of the communication disability commonly follows cortical damage within this area where "the great afferent systems" of audition, vision, and body sensation overlap. W. R. Russell (1963) points out that even very small cortical lesions in this area can have widespread and devastating consequences for verbal behavior.

Communication disabilities arising from lesions in the left parieto-temporo-occipital region tend to involve impaired or absent recognition or comprehension of symbolic stimuli, e.g., word deafness or word blindness. Lesions overlapping both the parietal and occipital cortex may give rise to reading defects. Writing disabilities can occur with lesions limited to either the temporal or parietal lobe, but are more likely when there is damage to any one of the other three lobes as well. The nature of the writing defect depends upon the site and extent of the lesion; in many cases the defects of written language reflect the defects of a concomitant aphasia (Marcie and Hécaen, 1979; Luria, 1970b).

Apraxias characterized by disturbances of nonverbal symbolization, such as gestural defects or inability to demonstrate an activity in pantomine (see pp. 31, 528f.), are usually associated with lesions involving language comprehension areas and the over-lap zone for kinesthetic and visual areas of the left hemisphere, occurring less often with anterior lesions (Heilman, 1979; L.N. Peterson and Kirshner, 1981; Kimura, 1979). Defective ability to comprehend gestures has been specifically associated with impaired reading comprehension. Oral apraxias, in which the ability to imitate simple oral gestures is impaired, may also be associated with more anterior lesions (Tognola and Vignolo, 1980). Apraxias often occur with aphasia and may be obscured by or confused with the language disorder (De Renzi et al., 1980, 1982).

Acalculia and agraphia generally appear in association with other communication disabilities (Hécaen, 1962; Raghaven, 1961). When they occur with left–right spatial disorientation and an inability to identify one's own fingers, to orient oneself to one's own fingers, to recognize or to name them (*finger agnosia*), the symptom cluster is known as Gerstmann's syndrome (Fogel, 1962; Gerstmann, 1940, 1957), and the lesion is likely to involve the left parieto-occipital region. Acalculia associated with finger agnosia typically disrupts such relatively simple arithmetic operations as counting or ordering numbers. The frequency with which these individual symptoms occur together certainly reflects an underlying cortical organization in which components involved in the different impaired acts are in close anatomical proximity. Whether there exists a functional unity between these seemingly disparate activities remains a speculative issue (Benton, 1961; Geschwind and Strub, 1975; Hécaen and Albert, 1978; Orgogozo, 1976). Counting and the appreciation of magnitude may remain intact while knowledge of arithmetic operations has been impaired by left hemi-sphere damage (Warrington, 1982).

Agnosias arising from left hemisphere lesions just anterior to the visual association area tend to appear as disorientation of either extrapersonal or of personal space. The spatial disorientation of left hemisphere lesions generally reflects impaired left-right directional sense and may involve a somatosensory defect as well (Denny-Brown et al., 1952). However, visuospatial perception tends to remain accurate (Belleza et al., 1979). Impaired appreciation of pain has also been associated with left parietal lesions (Pirozzola, 1978).

Disabilities arising from left hemisphere lesions tend to be more severe when the patient is also aphasic. Although all of these disturbances can occur in the absence of aphasia, it is rare for any of them to appear as the sole defect.

The great importance of the left hemisphere for certain intellectual activities becomes apparent when reviewing the behavioral disturbances that can accompany a left parietal lobe lesion even when speech does not appear to be significantly affected or when the task seems to be essentially nonverbal. For example, patients with left parietal lesions did less well than those with right-sided involvement on a formboard memory task (De Renzi, 1968) and another group of left parietal patients displayed impairment on both visual and auditory learning tests (Butters et al., 1970), apparently because these patients had reduced recourse to verbal memory aids.

The posterior association cortex: (c) defects arising from right hemisphere lesions. The most commonly seen disorder associated with the right parietal lobe is impaired constructional ability. Patients with posterior right hemisphere lesions may also have vestibular and oculomotor disorders. In these cases, defective spatial disorientation or impaired visual scanning contribute to the constructional disability. A right hemisphere *dyscalculia* shows up on written calculations as an inability to manipulate numbers in spatial relationships, such as using decimal places or "carrying," although the patient still retains mathematical concepts and the ability to do problems "in his head" (Grewel, 1952). For instance, the 57-yrear-old college graduate with a right parieto-occipital mass lesion (see Fig. 3-7) gave correct answers to relatively complex oral multiplication problems, but when given a written column of five two-place numbers to add, he could not integrate the sum of the right-hand column with the sum of the left-hand one nor could he do written multiplication problems (see Fig. 3-9). *Apraxia for dressing,* in which the patient has difficulty relating to and organizing parts of his body to parts of his clothing, may accompany right-sided parietal lesions. Some performance disabilities of patients with right parietal lobe involvement are clearly the product of a perceptual disorder such as impaired ability to localize objects in the left hemi-space (Hécaen et al., 1951). For example, the chief complaint of a middle-aged rancher with a right parieto-occipital lesion was difficulty in eating because his hand frequently missed when he put it out to reach the cup, or his fork overshot his plate. Others, such as spatial dyscalculia or dressing apraxia, seem to follow from more general impairments of spatial orientation or organization.

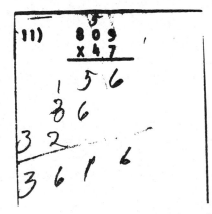

Fig. 3-9. Example of spatial dyscalculia by the patient whose design copies are shown in Fig. 3-7.

Many of the perceptual disorders arising from lesions of the right posterior association cortex are related to the phenomenon of *inattention*, the tendency for decreased or absent awareness of events presented to the half of the body contralateral to the hemispheric side of the lesion (see p. 66). A few left hemisphere damaged patients experience this problem, usually during the acute stages of their illness (Colombo et al., 1976; Welman, 1969). However, it is much more common among patients with right hemisphere lesions (A. S. Schwartz et al., 1977; S. Weinstein, 1964). Inattention may be manifested in a number of ways. It may occur as a relatively discrete and subtle disorder apparent only to the examiner. When stimulated bilaterally with a light touch to both cheeks or fingers wiggled in the outside periphery of each visual field, the inattentive patient consistently ignores the stimulus on the left when both stimuli are presented simultaneously *(double simultaneous stimulation)*, although he has no apparent difficulty noticing the stimulus when it is presented alone. This form of inattention has been variously called *sensory inattention, sensory extinction, sensory suppression,* or *perceptual rivalry* (K. W. Walsh, 1978b). Kertesz and Dobrowolski (1981) have observed left-sided neglect occurring more prominently among patients whose lesions involve the area around the central sulcus (including posterior frontal and some temporal lobe tissue) than among patients whose lesions were confined to the parietal lobe. Auditory inattention is associated with lesions in the right posterior temporal lobe.

In its more severe forms, inattention arising from right parietal lobe lesions may amount to a complete agnosia for the left half of space or for the left half of the patient's body *(hemisomatagnosia)*. Mild inattention to one's own body may appear as simple negligence: the patient rarely uses his left hand spontaneously, may bump into objects on his left, or may not use left side pockets. In more extreme cases in which the patient usually has a left hemiplegia as well, he may appear completely unaware of the left half of his body, even to the point of denying his left-sided disabilities *(anosognosia)* or being unable to recognize that his paralyzed limbs belong to him. One or more of these perceptual disorders generally accompany an apraxia for dressing in which the patient may put clothes on backwards or consistently misbutton his shirt.

In left visual inattention, not only may the patient not attend to stimuli in the left half of space, but he may also fail to draw or copy all of the left side of a figure or design and tend to flatten or otherwise diminish the left side of complete figures (see Fig. 3-7). When copying written material, the patient with unilateral inattention may omit words or numbers on the left side of the model, even though the copy makes less than good sense (see Fig. 11-1, p. 339). Increasing the complexity of the drawing task increases the likelihood of eliciting the inattention phenomenon (Pillon, 1981a). This form of visual imperception, which is a kind of unilateral spatial neglect, typically occurs only when the right parietal damage extends to occipital association areas. Left visual inattention is frequently, but not necessarily, accompanied by left visual field defects, most usually a left homonymous hemianopsia. Some patients with obvious left-sided inattention, particularly those with visual inattention, display a gaze defect such that they do not spontaneously scan the left side of space, even when spoken to from the left. These are the patients who begin reading in the middle of a line of print when asked to read, and seem unaware that the words out of context of the left half of the line make no sense. Most such right hemisphere damaged patients stop reading on their own, explaining that they have "lost interest," although they can still read with understanding when their gaze is guided.

Other perceptual problems associated with lesions of the parieto-occipital cortex include visuospatial disturbances, such as impairment of topographical or spatial thought. These latter problems may involve perceptual fragmentation (Denny-Brown, 1962). A severely left hemiparetic political historian, for instance, when shown photographs of famous people he had known, named bits and pieces correctly, e.g., "This is a mouth . . . this is an eye," but was unable to organize the discrete features into recognizable faces. Warrington and Taylor (1973) also relate difficulties in *perceptual classification*, specifically, the inability to recognize an object from an unfamiliar perspective, to right parietal lesions.

Temporal lobe defects.   The primary auditory cortex is, for the most part, located within the fold between the temporal and the frontal lobe, an area called the *insula* (island). Much of the temporal lobe cortex is concerned with hearing and related functions, such as auditory memory storage and complex perceptual organization. Since the comprehension of most auditory stimuli involves processing along the time dimension, it is not surprising that temporal lobe damage can result in sequencing deficits (Horowitz and Cohen, 1968; Milberg et al., 1979). Left-right asymmetry follows the verbal-nonverbal pattern of the posterior cortex.

Cortical association areas of the left temporal lobe mediate the perception of such verbal material as word and number and even voice recognition (Milner, 1971). The farther back a lesion occurs on the temporal lobe, the more likely it is to produce alexia and verbal apraxias. *Auditory agnosia*, in which the ability to discriminate and comprehend speech sounds is impaired, is associated with lesions in the auditory association cortex (Wernicke's area), located in the topmost (superior) temporal gyrus of the posterior third of the lobe (see Fig. 3-6). Severe auditory agnosia appears only rarely in sufficient isolation to be distinguishable from more global forms of communication disabilities. Perhaps the most crippling of the communication disorders is Wernicke's aphasia (also called sensory, fluent, or jargon aphasia, see Table 2-2, p. 34) since these patients can understand little of what they hear, although motor production of speech remains intact. Many such patients prattle grammatically and syntactically correct nonsense. The auditory incomprehension of patients with lesions in Wernicke's area does not extend to nonverbal sounds for they can respond appropriately to sirens, squealing brakes, and the like. Lesions lower down and farther forward on the left temporal lobe may involve verbal memory, giving rise to difficulties in recalling words, which, when severe, can seriously disrupt fluent speech *(dysnomia)*. These patients find it hard to remember or comprehend long lists, sentences, or complex verbal material, and their ability for new verbal learning may be greatly diminished or even abolished. Although they may no longer be able to perform any but simple, one-step mental operations, they can still do arithmetic on paper, handle abstract concepts, and, if the lesion is not too close to the juncture with the occipital cortex, some of them may also be able to read.

Patients with cortical lesions of the right temporal lobe are unlikely to have language disabilities; rather, they tend to experience comparable problems with nonverbal sound discrimination, recognition, and comprehension (Vignolo, 1969). Spatial disorientation problems. difficulties in recognizing complex, fragmented, or incomplete visual stimuli (Lansdell, 1970) and in making fine visual discriminations (Milner, 1954) have also been associated with right temporal lobe lesions. These patients may have trouble organizing complex data or formulating multifaceted plans.

Temporal lobe damage may result in some form of *amusia* (literally, no music), particularly involving receptive aspects of musicianship such as abilities to distinguish tones, tonal patterns, beats, or timbre, often but not necessarily with resulting inability to enjoy music or to sing or hum a tune or rhythmical pattern (Alajouanine, 1948; Benton, 1977a; Botez et al., 1979). Although damage to the right temporal lobe has been specifically implicated in receptive amusia (Hécaen and Albert, 1978; Shankweiler, 1966), the tendency for similar disturbances in musical appreciation and tone and rhythm recognition to accompany aphasia suggests bilateral contributions to the perceptual components of music (Mazziota et al., 1982; Rubens, 1979; B. E. Shapiro et al., 1981).

The temporal lobes and the limbic system.   Memory deficits with temporal lobe lesions also differ according to the side of the lesion (Delaney, Rosen, et al., 1980; Milner, 1972). Impaired verbal memory appears with surgical resection of the left temporal lobe and visual memory disturbances accompany right temporal lobe resection. Anterior portions of the temporal cortex appear to be involved in the storage of new information; posterior regions are implicated in retrieval. Cortical stimulation of the anterior left temporal cortex interferes with verbal learning without affecting speech while stimulation of the posterior left temporal cortex is more likely to result in retrieval (word finding) problems and *anomia* (literally, no words) (Fedio and Van Buren, 1974; Ojemann, 1978). Ojemann (1978) reported that problems in storage and retrieval of visual stimuli presented in a nonverbal (not necessarily nonverbalizable) format also accompanied direct stimulation of anterior and posterior areas, respectively, of the right temporal cortex. The cortex of the temporal lobe also appears to be the most common site of triggering mechanisms for recall of memories. Awake patients undergoing brain surgery report vivid auditory and visual recall of previously experienced scenes and episodes upon electrical stimulation of the exposed temporal lobe cortex (Penfield and Perot, 1963). Nauta (1964) speculated that these memories involve widespread neural mechanisms and that the temporal and, to a lesser extent, the occipital cortex play a role in organizing the discrete components of memory for orderly and complete recall.

A major component of the memory system, the *hippocampus*, runs within the inside fold of each temporal lobe for much of its length (see Fig. 3-10). It is one of several bodies of gray matter within the temporal lobes that are part of the *limbic system* (Livingston and Escobar, 1972; Watts, 1975). This system has its components

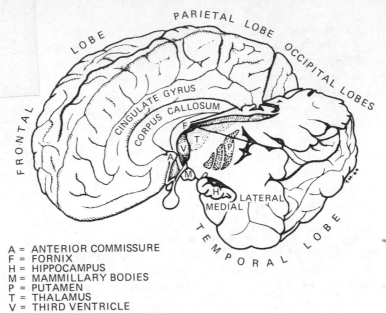

A = ANTERIOR COMMISSURE
F = FORNIX
H = HIPPOCAMPUS
M = MAMMILLARY BODIES
P = PUTAMEN
T = THALAMUS
V = THIRD VENTRICLE

Fig. 3-10. Cutaway perspective drawing of a human brain, showing the spatial relationships of most of the regions and structures thought to be related to general memory function. (The putamen is shown only as a landmark for readers familiar with the brain.) (Ojemann, 1966.)

in the temporal lobe, in the subcortical forebrain, and in midbrain areas. They form an anatomically linked circle of structures that appear to work together as a system (Barbizet, 1963) (see Fig. 3-10). Limbic system structures mediate both memory and emotional behavior (Brain, 1969). They may be involved in those affect-laden and general behavioral attitudes that direct the focus of attention and thereby determine what is screened out of the perceptual field and what is selected for registration (Drachman and Arbit, 1966; J. D. Green, 1964). The hippocampus has been identified as one site of interaction between the perception and the memory systems.

Other limbic system structures that have been specifically implicated in impairment of the recording and consolidation processes of memory are various portions of the thalamus, the mammillary bodies, and the fornix (Brodal, 1981). Massive *antero-grade amnesia* (impaired ability for new learning, including difficulty in remembering events after the onset of the amnesia) and some *retrograde amnesia* (difficulty in remembering events prior to the onset of the amnesia) result from diffuse lesions involving the mammillary bodies (Brion and Mikol, 1978) and the thalamus as well as from bilateral excision of the hippocampal structures. Recording of ongoing events may be mildly impaired by lesions of the *fornix* (Ojemann, 1966), a central forebrain structure that links the hippocampal and the mammillothalamic areas of the limbic system. When the fornix is cut or absent from birth, however, there appears to be no effect on memory function.

Little if any learning takes place after bilateral hippocampal destruction through disease or surgery, with the exception of some motor skills (Corkin, 1968) and conditioning of autonomic reflexes (which latter may not actually qualify as learning in the sense of information or acts for which the subject can have conscious awareness). Cuing does not aid recall; there seems to be nothing to cue. Yet much that was learned prior to surgical loss of functional hippocampus is remembered and may be appropriately retrieved with relative ease. Patients who have lost hippocampal structures through an inflammatory disease process that typically damages surrounding tissue as well show poor recall for information learned before their illness and after; they too do not profit from cuing but can figure out sequential relationships in a conceptual learning task (e.g., Lhermitte et Signoret, 1972). In contrast, although Korsakoff patients have a great deal of difficulty recalling information to which they were first exposed after they became amnesic, and many display difficulties in recalling premorbidly learned material and experiences in an orderly manner, with cuing they demonstrate retention of much that they learned both pre-and postmorbidly. However, the Korsakoff patients fail the sequential relationships task. These finding support the view that the hippocampus is of primary importance in the recording of new information into long-term storage (R. F. Thompson, 1976) and that thalamic structures are necessary for *efficient* information storage and retrieval. "The hippocampus appears to contain a mechanism capable of emitting a signal amounting to a 'Now Print!' message without which no recording can take place. This 'Print!' message could be related to 'affective color or emotional tone' " (R. B. Livingston, quoted in Nauta, 1964, p. 19). In a sense, the thalamic memory structures appear to serve a filing system function.

In unilateral destruction of the hippocampus, hemispheric differences persist. Loss of the left hippocampus impairs verbal memory in all of its modalities and destruction of the right hippocampus results in defective recognition and recall of "complex visual and auditory patterns to which a name cannot readily be assigned" (Milner, 1970, p. 30; Jones-Gotman and Milner, 1978).

Information storage is not confined to any single cortical area or brain structure. Rather, information involving each modality appears to be stored in the association cortex adjacent to its primary sensory cortex (Arnold, 1974; Samuels et al., 1972; R. F. Thompson et al., 1972). Thus, retrieval of visual information is impaired by lesions of the visual association cortex of the occipital lobe, impaired retrieval of auditory information follows lesions of the auditory association cortex of the temporal lobe, and so on. Frontal lobe motor association areas appear to provide the site for programming motor responses.

Disturbances in emotional behavior occur in association with seizure activity involving the hippocampus as well as the amygdala and *uncus* (the small hooked front end of the inner temporal lobe fold in which the hippocampus lies) (Pincus and Tucker, 1978). Abnormal electrical activity of the brain associated with *temporal lobe epilepsy* typically originates within the temporal lobe. This may give rise to a variety of transient behavior disturbances, such as changes in subjective feelings, behavioral automatisms, and bizarre posturing. Specific problems associated with temporal lobe epilepsy include alterations of mood, obsessional thinking, changes in consciousness, hallucinations and perceptual distortions in all sensory modalities including pain, and stereotyped, often repetitive and meaningless motor behavior that may comprise quite complex activities. Other names for these disturbances are *psychomotor epilepsy, psychomotor or partial complex seizures.*

The *interictal* (between seizures) behavior of these patients tends toward emotional and attitudinal extremes. As a group, these patients are prone to have a variety of unpleasant personality characteristics (Bear et al., 1982). Among these are irritability, outbursts of anger, obsessional traits, religiosity, humorlessness, verbosity, hypergraphia, and a quality in interpersonal exchanges variously called viscosity or stickiness. The latter quality is more readily appreciated through experience than description: it involves a slow ponderousness of speech and response, concrete and obsessional overattention to details, and difficulty in shifting set or topic or in leaving a conversation, a room, or a person (Blumer and Benson, 1975; E. Valenstein and Heilman, 1979; A. E. Walker and Blumer, 1977). Some relationship between trait clusters and side of epileptic focus has been suggested by Bear and Fedio (1977). Bear and Fedio found that while both right and left temporal epileptics share many of the same dour, dependent, and obsessional characteristics, those with a seizure focus on the right side tend to exhibit more denial and report more elation and socially approved behavior, while patients with left foci are more likely to display catastrophic reactions, ideational thinking, and self-criticism by both report and observation. However, these differences were not found in patients with temporal lobe epilepsy who have frank psychiatric disorders (Mungas, 1982).

Although psychiatric disorders are not necessarily associated with temporal lobe seizures, there is some tendency for patients subject to epilepsy, and particularly temporal lobe epilepsy, to display a schizophrenic-like psychosis (Pincus and Tucker, 1978). Mulder and Daly (1952) relate such psychic symptoms as anxiety, depression, and schizoid behavior either "specifically to a discharge focus in the temporal lobe . . . (or to) a reaction of the total personality to impairment of cerebral function" (p. 176). Hyposexuality (Boller and Frank, 1981; Lishman, 1978; Pincus and Tucker, 1978) and hypersexuality (G. W. Harris et al., 1969) may occur with both temporal lobe seizures and surgical removal of temporal lobe limbic structures.

THE PRECENTRAL (ANTERIOR) CORTEX: FRONTAL LOBE DISORDERS

In the course of the brain's evolution, the frontal lobes developed most recently to become the largest structures of the human brain. It was only natural for early students of brain function to conclude that the frontal lobes must therefore be the seat of the highest cognitive functions.

Thus, when Hebb reported in 1939 that a small series of patients who had undergone surgical removal of frontal lobe tissue showed no loss in IQ score on a standard intelligence test, he provoked a controversy. In his comprehensive review of the literature on the psychological consequences of frontal lobe lesions, Klebanoff (1945) noted the seemingly unresolvable discrepancies between studies reporting on the intellectual status of patients with frontal lobe lesions. He found that since Fritsch and Hitzig ([1870] 1969) first reported intellectual deterioration in patients with traumatic frontal lesions, more authors described intellectual deficits in patients with frontal lobe damage than denied the presence of such deficits in their patients.

The high incidence of World War II missile wounds and the popularity of psychosurgery on the frontal lobes for treatment of psychiatric disorders in the 1940s and 1950s ultimately provided enough cases of frontal brain damage to eliminate speculative misconceptions about frontal lobe functions. We know now that the ability to perform many different cognitive functions may be disrupted by frontal lobe damage. Hebb's observations were limited both by his use of structured tests that primarily measured old learning and well-established skills rather than abilities to solve unfamiliar problems or exercise judgment, for example, and by his choice of summed IQ scores for his comparison criteria rather than subtest scores or qualitative aspects of the patient's performance.

The cortex and underlying white matter of the frontal lobes is the site of interconnections and feedback loops between the major sensory and the major motor systems, linking and integrating all components of behavior at the highest level (Luria, 1966, 1973; Nauta, 1971). Pathways carrying information about the external environment from the posterior cortex and information about internal states from the limbic system converge in the anterior portions of the frontal lobes, the *prefrontal* cortex. Thus, the frontal lobes are where already correlated incoming information from all sources— external and internal, conscious and unconscious, memory storage and visceral arousal centers—is integrated and enters ongoing activity. "The frontal lobes regulate the 'active state' of the organism, control the essential elements of the subject's intentions, program complex forms of activity, and constantly monitor all aspects of activity" (Hécaen and Albert, 1975).

Lesions of the frontal lobe tend not to disrupt cognitive functions as obviously as do postcentral lesions. Rather, frontal lobe damage may be conceptualized as disrupting reciprocal relationships between the major functional systems—the sensory system of the posterior cortex, the limbic-memory system with its interconnections to subcortical regions involved in arousal, affective, and motivational states, and the effector mechanisms of the motor system. Nauta has characterized frontal lobe disorders as "derangement of behavioral programming" (1971). Frontal lobe disorders involve *how* a person responds, which can certainly affect the *what*, the content of the response. Frontal lobe patients' failures on test items are more likely to result from their approach to problems than from lack of knowledge or perceptual or language incapacities *per se*. For example, patients with frontal lobe damage (almost always involving the right frontal lobe) occasionally will call item one on the Hooper Visual Organization Test "a duck" (see pp. 357–358), and demonstrate that they understand the instructions (to figure out what the cut-up drawings would represent if put together) by answering items two and three correctly. In such cases, the completed "flying duck" shape of the top piece in item one appears to be a stronger stimulus than the directions to combine the pieces. These patients demonstrate accurate perception and facility and accuracy in naming or writing, but get stalled in carrying out all of an intentional performance, in this case by one strong feature of a complex stimulus. Others (e.g., Luria, 1966; K. W. Walsh, 1978a) have called attention to the dissociation between what these patients say or appear to see or comprehend and what they do or seem to feel.

Defects in the control, regulation, and integration of cognitive activities tend to predominate in patients with *dorsolateral* lesions, i.e., when the lesion is on the top or outer sides—the convexity—of the frontal lobes. *Orbitomedial* lesions on the sides of the lobes between the hemispheres or subcortical lesions that involve pathways connecting the cortex between and just under the hemispheres with the drive and affective integration centers in the diencephalon are most apt to affect emotional and social adjustment (E. S. Valenstein, 1973). K. W. Walsh (personal communication, 1980) further distinguishes between the importance of the medial frontal cortex in purposeful initiation and maintenance of activity and the key role played by the orbital, or *basal*, frontal cortex in impulse control and the regulation of ongoing behavior. However, frontal lobe disturbances tend to have repercussions throughout the behavioral repertoire (Luria, 1973a).

The motor and motor association areas just forward of the central sulcus were correctly identified in the late nineteenth century when Fritsch and Hitzig studied the effects of direct electrical stimulation of the cerebral cortex in dogs. Most of the *motor strip* or primary motor cortex lies on the first two ridges in front of the central sulcus, and the *premotor cortex* or secondary motor association area is in the adjacent forward area. Lesions in premotor association areas disrupt the integration of the motor components of complex acts, resulting in discontinuous or incoordinated movements and impaired motor skills.

In the left hemisphere, for example, lesions in the portion of the motor association area that mediates the motor organization and patterning of speech may result in a motor pattern apraxia of speech (Luria, 1965a; 1970b). Patients with this condition display disturbances in organizing the muscles of the speech apparatus to form sounds or in patterning groups of sounds into words. This may leave them incapable of fluent speech production, although their ability to comprehend language is not necessarily impaired. The anterior language center, Broca's area, is lower on the lateral slope of the prefrontal cortex (see Fig. 3-1). It receives information from both the posterior language area and the temporal lobe and serves as "the final common path for the generation of speech impulses" (Luria, 1970b, p. 197). Lesions to this area give rise to Broca's, or efferent, motor aphasia (see Table 2-2), which involves defective symbol formulation as well as a breakdown in the orderly production of speech. Lesions in corresponding areas on the right may contribute to fragmented or piecemeal *modus operandi*, reflected most clearly in impairments of perceptual organization and of planning (see example, p. 57). *Expressive amusia* or *avocalia* (inability to sing) has been seen with lesions of either frontal lobe but occurs most often in association with aphasia when lesions are on the left (Benton, 1977a), whereas an impaired capacity to process such musical elements as pitch, rhythm, and phrasing tends to occur with right-sided anterior lesions (B. E. Shapiro et al., 1980, 1981).

Behavior problems associated with prefrontal damage tend to be supramodal. Similar problems may also occur with lesions involving other areas of the brain, but in these instances they are apt to be associated with specific intellectual, sensory, or motor disabilities. The behavioral disturbances associated with frontal lobe damage can be roughly classified in five general groups with considerable overlap.

1. *Problems of starting* appear in decreased spontaneity, decreased productivity, decreased rate at which behavior is emitted, or decreased or lost initiative. In its milder forms, patients lack initiative and ambition, but may be able to carry through normal activities quite adequately, particularly if these activities are familiar, well structured, or guided (K. Goldstein, 1944). More severely affected patients are apt to do little beyond routine self-care and home activities. To a casual or naive observer, and often to their family and close associates, these patients appear to be lazy. Many can "talk a good game" about plans and projects, but are actually unable to transform their words into deeds. An extreme dissociation between words and deeds has been called *pathological inertia,* and can be seen when a frontal lobe patient describes the correct response to a task but never acts it out (e.g., Luria, 1966; Milner, 1964). Severe problems of starting appear as apathy, unresponsiveness, or mutism. Laterality differences have shown up in fluency studies, which examine productivity. Patients with left frontal lesions tend to have a greatly diminished verbal output (see p. 329f.); right frontal lesions are associated with reduced production of nonsense designs (Jones-Gotman and Milner, 1977).

2. *Difficulties in making mental or behavioral shifts,* whether they are shifts in attention, changes in movement, or flexibility in attitude, come under the heading of *perseveration* or *rigidity.* Perseveration refers specifically to repetitive prolongation or continuation of an act or activity sequence, or repetition of the same or a similar response to various questions, tasks, or situations. In this latter sense it may be described as sterotypy of behavior. Perseveration may also occur with lesions of other lobes, but then it typically appears only in conjunction with the patient's specific cognitive deficits (E. Goldberg and Tucker, 1979; K. W. Walsh, 1978a). In frontal lobe patients, perseveration tends to be *supramodal*—to occur in a variety of situations and on a variety of tasks. Perseveration may sometimes be seen as difficulty in suppressing ongoing activities or attention to prior stimulation. On intellectual tasks it may be expressed in repetitive and uncritical perpetuation of a response that was once correct but becomes an uncorrected error under changed circumstances or in continuation of a response beyond its proper end point. Frontal lobe patients may exhibit rigidity without perseveration. Since behavioral and attitudinal patterns of rigidity characterize some neurologically intact people, rigidity alone does not give sufficient grounds for suspecting frontal lobe damage.

3. *Problems in stopping*—in braking or modulating ongoing behavior—show up in impulsivity, overreactivity, disinhibition, and difficulties in holding back a wrong or unwanted response, particularly when it may either have a strong association value or be part of an already ongoing response chain. These problems frequently come under the heading of "loss of control" and these patients are often described as having "control problems."

4. *Deficient self-awareness* results in an inability to perceive performance errors, to appreciate the impact one makes on others, or to size up a social situation appropriately. Defective self-criticism is associated with tendencies of some frontal lobe

patients to be euphoric and self-satisfied, to experience little or no anxiety, and to be impulsive and unconcerned about social conventions.

5. *A concrete attitude* is also common among patients with frontal lobe damage. This appears in an inability to dissociate oneself from one's immediate surrounds and in a literal attitude in which objects, experiences, and behavior are all taken at their most obvious face value (K. Goldstein, 1944, 1948). The patient becomes incapable of planning and foresight or of sustaining goal-directed behavior. This defect, which is also identified as loss or impairment of abstract attitude, is not the same as impaired ability to form or use abstract concepts. Although many patients with frontal lobe lesions do have difficulty handling abstract concepts and spontaneously generate only concrete ones, others retain high-level conceptual abilities despite a day-to-day literal-mindedness and loss of perspective.

The phenomenon of *frontal amnesia* is interesting both because it is not a true amnesia and because it demonstrates how inertia and rigidity in particular can inter-fere with cognitive processes (K. W. Walsh, 1978a). Patients with frontal amnesia, when read a story or a list of words, may seem able to recall only a little if any of what they heard and steadfastly assert they cannot remember. Yet, when prompted or given indirect questions (such as, "What was the story about?" rather than "Begin at the beginning and tell me everything you can remember"), they may produce some responses, even quite full ones, once started. These same patients may be unable to give their age although they know the date, their year of birth, and can do formally presented subtraction problems. What they cannot do, in each of these examples, is spontaneously undertake the activity that will provide the answer—in the first case, selecting the requested information from memory, and in the second case, identifying a solution set for the question and acting on it.

Patients with subcortical lesions in the medial basal white matter of the frontal lobes may also exhibit an amnestic condition, but in these cases it is pronounced and may be characterized by spontaneous and florid confabulation. One 60-year-old retired teacher who had had a stroke involving this subcortical region of her left fron-tal lobe complained of back pain due to lifting a cow onto a barn roof. Five days later she reported having piloted a 200-passenger plane the previous day (Howieson, 1980a).

Intellectual impairment associated with loss or disconnection of frontal lobe tissue usually does not appear as a loss of specific skills, information, or even reasoning or problem-solving ability (Landis, 1952; Teuber, 1964). In fact, patients with frontal lobe lesions often do not do poorly on those formal intelligence tests in which another person directs the examination, sets the pace, starts and stops the activity, and makes all the discretionary decisions (see Teuber et al., 1951). The closed-ended questions of common fact and familiar situations and the well-structured puzzles with concrete solutions that make up standard tests of intellectual ability are not likely to present special problems for many patients with frontal lobe injuries. Perseveration or care-lessness may lower a patient's scores somewhat but usually not enough to depress them significantly. Cognitive defects associated with frontal lobe damage tend to show up most clearly in the course of daily living and are more often observed by relatives and co-workers than by a medical or psychological examiner in a standard interview.

Common complaints about such patients concern apathy, carelessness, poor or unreliable judgment, poor adaptability to new situations, and blunted social sensibility (Bonner et al., 1953; Lezak, 1978a).

Some specific cognitive defects may be ascribed to frontal lobe lesions. Difficulty in suppressing response tendencies may interfere with learning new associations to stimuli for which the patient has already learned associations or with performing tasks requiring delayed responses (Milner, 1971). Defective abstract thinking and trouble in making response shifts result in impaired mental efficiency (Tow, 1955). These two defects can contribute to *stimulus-boundedness* which, in its milder forms, appears as sluggishness in shifting attention from one element in the environment to another, particularly from a strong stimulus source to a weak or subtle or complex one, or from a well-defined external stimulus to an internal or psychological event. Patients who are severely stimulus-bound may have difficulty directing their gaze or manipulating objects; when the condition is extreme, the patient may handle or look at whatever his attention has fixed upon as if his hands or eyes were stuck to it, and literally pulling them away with difficulty. There appears to be a tendency for a dissociation to occur between language behaviors and ongoing activity so that the patient is less apt to use verbal cues (usually subvocalization) to direct, guide, or organize his ongoing behavior with resultant perseveration, fragmentation, or premature termination of a response (K. Goldstein, 1948; Luria and Homskaya, 1964; Tow, 1955). Visual scanning defects appear as response slowing and inefficiency in the plan of search (Teuber, 1964). Patients with frontal lobe lesions show little of the imagination or innovative thinking that is essential to creativity (Zangwill, 1966). Impaired registration of incoming stimuli resulting in a decreased short-term memory capacity has been associated with frontal lobe damage (Lewinsohn et al., 1972). The frontal lobes have also been implicated in defects of time sense, both with respect to recency and time-span judgments and, in patients with bilateral frontal lobe damage, to orientation in time (Benton, 1968a).

Lateralization of cognitive functions appears to be less marked in the frontal lobes, although some of the distinctions between left and right hemisphere functions obtain here too. As noted above, decreased verbal fluency and impoverishment of spontaneous speech tends to be associated with left frontal lobe lesions, although mildly depressed verbal fluency also occurs with right frontal lobe lesions. Constructional deficits have been noted in patients with right frontal lobe lesions who have difficulty with the motor rather than the perceptual components of the task (Benton, 1968a). Heilman and Valenstein (1972) and A. R. Damasio and his co-workers (1980) describe left visual inattention in patients with right frontal lesions. Some of the difficulties in making response shifts that appear following loss of either right or left frontal lobe tissue tend to be transient in right hemisphere patients who can learn to direct their behavior with verbal cues.

Clinical Limitations of Functional Localization

A well-grounded understanding of functional localization strengthens the clinician's diagnostic capabilities so long as the limitations of its applicability in the individual case are taken into account. Common patterns of behavioral impairment associated with such well-understood neurological conditions as certain kinds of cerebrovascular accidents tend to involve the same anatomical structures with predictable regularity. For example, stroke patients with right arm paralysis due to a lesion involving the left motor projection area of the frontal cortex will generally have an associated Broca's (motor) aphasia. Yet, the clinician will sometimes find behavioral disparities between patients with cortical lesions of apparently similar location and size: some ambulatory stroke victims whose right arms are paralyzed are practically mute; others have successfully returned to highly verbal occupations (M. W. Buck, 1968). In line with these clinical observations, cortical mapping of speech areas of the left hemisphere by electrode stimulation (Ojemann, 1979) and observations of residual speech capacity with left hemisphere inactivation by intracarotid injection of amobarbitol (Kinsbourne, 1974b) have demonstrated a great deal of variability in the location of specific language areas of the left hemisphere and in verbal capacities of the right hemisphere.

Other apparent discontinuities between the patient's behavior and his neurological status may occur when a pattern of behavioral impairment develops spontaneously and without physical evidence of neurological disease. In such cases, "hard" neurological findings (e.g., such positive physical changes on neurological examination as primitive reflexes, unilateral weakness, or spasticity) or abnormal laboratory results (e.g., protein in the spinal fluid, brain wave abnormalities, or radiological anomalies) may appear in time, for instance, as a tumor grows or as arteriosclerotic changes block more blood vessels. Occasionally a suspected brain abnormality may be demonstrated only on postmortem examination, and even then correlative tissue changes may not always be found (Sklar, 1963; A. Smith, 1962a).

The uncertain relation between brain activity and human behavior obligates the clinician to exercise care in observation and caution in prediction, and to take nothing for granted when applying the principles of functional localization to diagnostic problems. However, this uncertain relation does not negate the dominant tendencies to regularity in the functional organization of brain tissue. Knowledge of the regularity with which brain-behavior correlations occur enables the clinician to determine whether a patient's behavioral symptoms make anatomical sense, to know what subtle or unobstrusive changes may accompany the more obvious ones, and to guide the neurosurgeon or neuroradiologist in further diagnostic procedures.

4

The Rationale of Deficit
Measurement

Neuropsychological assessment is similar to conventional psychological evaluation but with an important difference. In the usual psychological examination, the examiner studies a patient's intellectual performance, his personality characteristics, and his emotional state. He may also attempt to explain the patient's behavior in the light of common behavioral patterns and what he knows of the patient's history and his current life situation. Finally, the examining psychologist may draw a diagnostic conclusion for the purpose of facilitating treatment planning or other decision making.

The neuropsychological examination proceeds in much the same manner. The neuropsychologist attends to the same aspects of behavior, relies on similar explanatory assumptions. and pursues the same kind of treatment or decision-making goals. The distinguishing characteristic of neuropsychological assessment is its emphasis on the identification and measurement of psychological deficits, for it is primarily in deficiencies of intellect, emotionality, and control that brain damage is manifested behaviorally.

Brain damage always implies behavioral impairment. Even when psychological changes after head injury or concomitant with brain disease are viewed as improvement rather than impairment, as when there is a welcome increase in sociability or relief from neurotic anxiety, a careful assessment will probably reveal an underlying loss.

A 47-year-old postal clerk with a bachelor's degree in education boasted of having recently become an "extrovert" after having been painfully shy and socially uncomfortable most of his life. His wife brought him to the neurologist with complaints of deteriorating judgment, childishness, untidiness, and negligence of personal hygiene. The patient reported no notable behavioral changes other than his newfound ability to approach and talk with people.

On psychological testing, although his performance of many intellectual functions was at a *superior* level, in accord with his academic achievement and his wife's reports of his prior functioning, the patient also did poorly on tests involving immediate memory, new learning, and attention and concentration. The discrepancy between his best and poorest performances suggested that this patient had already sustained intellectual losses.

In some cases the loss, or deficit, may be subtle, becoming apparent only on complex judgmental tasks or under emotionally charged conditions. In other cases the direct behavioral effects of the impairment may be so slight or ill-defined as to be unobservable under ordinary conditions; the patient reports vague, unaccustomed, and unexpected frustrations or uneasiness while his family and friends are puzzled by his depression or heightened irritability or decreased frustration tolerance.

A physician's wife in her early 40s underwent a radical behavior change, from an active, socially well-adjusted, and apparently quite contented woman with many interests to a restless, dissatisfied, and irritable alcoholic, constantly embroiled in bitter fights with her husband and theatrical crises with her psychiatrist. Her problems were originally diagnosed as functional; but on psychological examination, a significant discrepancy between *superior* verbal functioning and *low average* constructional abilities was discovered, raising the suspicion of brain damage. On questioning, she reported that just before the behavior change she had received a head injury in a car accident. Since routine x-ray and neurological examination were negative, neither she nor her husband had thought anything more about it.

Before the accident, she had done much creative needlework, deriving personal satisfaction from as well as obtaining attention and praise for her talent for sewing. After the injury, she lost interest in any kind of handcraft and stopped sewing altogether. She was unable to develop any compensatory activities as she had difficulty making plans or getting organized. She suddenly had a lot of time on her hands and lacked a significant source of self-esteem. She never associated her disinterest in sewing with the head injury and was not aware, until examined psychologically, that she suffered serious impairment of abilities involving visuospatial organization. Depression following the injury only compounded her self-doubt and bewilderment. She resisted treatment until her intellectual disability was discovered and a rational approach to her problems could be undertaken.

Although the effects of brain damage are rarely confined to a single behavioral dimension or functional system, the assessment of psychological deficit has focused on intellectual impairment for a number of reasons. First, some degree of intellectual impairment accompanies almost all brain dysfunction and is a diagnostically significant feature of many neurological disorders. Moreover, many of the common intellectual defects—aphasias, failures of judgment, lapses of memory, etc.—are likely to be noticed by the casual observer and to interfere most obviously with the patient's capacity to function independently.

In addition, psychologists are better able to measure intellectual behavior than any other kind, except perhaps simple psychophysical reactions and sensorimotor responses. Certainly, intellectual behavior has been systematically scrutinized more times in more permutations and combinations and with more replications and controls than has any other behavior. Out of all these data have evolved numerous reliable and well-standardized techniques for identifying, defining, grading, measuring, and comparing the spectrum of intellectual behaviors. Intelligence and educational testing has provided the neuropsychologist with a ready-made set of operations and a well-defined frame of reference that have been fruitfully applied to deficit measurement. The deficit measurement paradigm can be applied to other kinds of behavioral impairments, such as personality change, decreased intellectual efficiency, or a defective capacity for self-control. However, personality measurement, particularly of brain damaged individuals, has not yet achieved the community of agreement, nor the levels of reliability or predictability, that are now taken for granted when measuring cognitive functions (see chapter 20). Furthermore, in the clinical setting, impairments in efficiency and self-control are usually evaluated on the basis of their effect on specific intellectual functions or personality characteristics rather than studied in their own right.

Comparison Standards for Deficit Measurement

The concept of behavioral deficit presupposes some ideal, normal, or prior level of functioning against which the patient's performance may be measured. This level, the, *comparison standard,* may be *normative* (derived from an appropriate population) or *individual* (derived from the patient's history or present characteristics), depending on the patient, the kind of behavior being evaluated, and the purpose of the assessment. Neuropsychological assessment uses both normative and individual comparison standards for measuring deficit, as appropriate for the function or activity being examined and the purpose of the examination.

Normative Comparison Standards

THE POPULATION AVERAGE

The normative comparison standard may be an *average.* For adults, the normative standard, or "norm," for many measurable psychological functions and characteristics is a score representing the average performance of some more or less well-defined population, such as white women or college graduates over 40. For many intellectual functions, variables of age and education or vocational achievement may significantly affect test performance and therefore are often taken into account in developing test norms. The measurement of children's behavior is concerned with abilities and traits that change with age, so the normative standard may be the average age or grade at which a given trait or function appears or reaches some criterion level of performance. Because of the differential rate of development for boys and girls, children's norms are likely to be given separately for each sex.

Normative standards based on either average performance level or average age of performance are available for a broad range of intellectual behaviors, from simple visuomotor reaction time or verbal mimicry to the most complex activities involving higher mathematics, visuospatial conceptualization, or sophisticated social judgments. Norms based on averages have also been derived for social behaviors, such as frequency of church attendance or age for participation in team play; for vocational interests, such as medicine or truck driving; or for personality traits, such as assertiveness or hypochondria.

In neuropsychological assessment, population norms are most useful in evaluating functions that develop throughout childhood but are not closely tied to general intellectual ability. These functions are largely mediated by subcortical structures. Memory, learning, and attention fall into this category. The normal adult range for immediate memory span, paragraph or design recall, or visuomotor tracking tasks, for example, is relatively narrow and little affected by education or intellectual prowess. Functions most suited to evaluation by population norms also tend to be most age-dependent, particularly from the middle years onward, necessitating the use of age-graded norms (see pp. 142, 217–219).

SPECIES-WIDE PERFORMANCE EXPECTATIONS

The norms for some psychological functions and traits serve as species-wide performance expectations for adults, although they may be age or grade averages for infants or children. This is the case for all intellectual functions that follow a common course of development, that are usually fully developed long before adulthood, and that are taken for granted as part and parcel of the normal adult behavioral repertory. Speech is a good example. The average two-year-old child can talk in two- and three-word phrases. The ability to communicate most needs and thoughts by means of speech is expected of four and five year olds. Seventh- and eighth-grade children can utter and comprehend word groupings in all the basic grammatical forms and their elaborations. Subsequent speech development mainly involves more variety, elegance, abstractness, or complexity of verbal expression. Thus, the adult norm for speech is the intact ability to speak, and all but a few adults function at the normative level. Some other mental abilities that are expected to be fully functional in adults are counting change, drawing a recognizable person, basic map reading, and using a hammer and saw or cooking utensils. Each of these skills is learned, improves with practice, has a common developmental history for most adults, and is sufficiently simple that its mastery or potential mastery is taken for granted. Anything less than an acceptable performance in an adult raises the suspicion of impairment.

Some species-wide capacities, although not present at birth, are manifested relatively early and similarly in all intact persons. Their development appears to be essentially maturational and relatively independent of social learning, although training may enhance their expression and aging may dull it. These include capacities involving motor and visuomotor control and coordination; basic perceptual discriminations—e.g., of color, pattern, and form; of pitch, tone, and loudness; and orientation to personal and extrapersonal space. Everyday life rarely calls upon the pure expression of these capacities. Rather, they are integral to the complex behaviors that make up the normal activities of children and adults alike. Thus, in themselves these capacities are usually observed only by deliberate examination.

Other species-wide normative standards involve components of behavior so rudimentary that they are not generally thought of as psychological functions or abilities. Binaural hearing, or the ability to localize a touch on the skin or to discriminate between noxious and pleasant stimuli, are capacities that are an expected part of the endowment of each human organism, present at birth or shortly thereafter. These capacities are not learned in the usual sense, nor, except when impaired by accident or disease, do they change over time and with experience. Some of these species-wide functions, such as fine tactile discrimination, which is typically among those tested in the neurological examination, appear either as intact or as severely impaired, suggesting an all-or-none pattern of function/dysfunction for many rudimentary capacities (E. W. Russell, 1980b).

Neuropsychological assessment procedures that test the psychological functions all intact adults are capable of performing usually focus on discrete acts or responses and thus are valuable for identifying the defective components of impaired cognitive behavior. However, examinations limited to discrete components of complex functions and functional systems provide little information about how well the patient can perform the complex behaviors involving component defects. Moreover, when the behavioral concomitants of brain damage are mild or subtle, particularly when associated with widespread or diffuse rather than well-localized, "clean" lesions, few if any of these rudimentary components of cognitive behavior will be demonstrably impaired on the basis of species-wide norms.

CUSTOMARY STANDARDS

A number of assumed normative standards have been arbitrarily set, usually by custom. Probably the most familiar of these is the visual acuity standard: 20–20 vision does not represent an average but an arbitrary ideal, which is met or surpassed by different proportions of the population, depending on age. Among the few customary standards of interest in neuropsychological assessment is verbal response latency—the amount of time a person takes to answer a question—which has normative values of one or two seconds for informal conversation in our culture.

APPLICATIONS AND LIMITATIONS OF NORMATIVE STANDARDS

For most psychological purposes, including the description of intellectual status for both children and adults, educational and vocational planning, and personality assessment, normative comparison standards are useful. In the assessment of persons with known or suspected brain pathology of adult onset, however, as a general rule normative standards are only appropriate when the function or skill or capacity that is being measured is well within the capability of all intact adults and does not vary greatly with either education or general intellectual ability. Or, to turn the rule around, normative standards are applicable when the function, skill, or capacity under examination is not normally distributed in the adult population. Thus, for neuropsychological assessment purposes, the capacity for meaningful verbal communication is evaluated on the basis of population norms; but vocabulary level, which is normally distributed, needs an individual comparison standard.

When it is known or suspected that the patient has suffered a decline in cognitive abilities that are normally distributed in the adult population, a description of his functioning in terms of population norms (i.e., by standard test scores) will, in itself, shed no light on either the pattern or the extent of the patient's intellectual impairment. Comparisons with population averages will not add significantly to the information conveyed by the test scores alone, for most test scores are themselves numerical comparisons with population norms. When examining for adult-onset deficits, only by comparing the patient's present with his prior functioning can the examiner assess the individual patient's real losses.

Thus, a first step in measuring intellectual deficit in an adult is to establish—or estimate, when direct information is not available—the patient's premorbid performance level for all of the functions and abilities being assessed. For those functions with species-wide norms, this task is easy. Any adult who can no longer name objects or copy a simple design or who appears unaware of one side of his body has an obvious deficit.

On the other hand, for all those normally distributed functions and abilities for which the normative standard is an average, only an individual comparison provides a meaningful basis for assessing deficit. A population average is not an appropriate comparison standard since it will not necessarily apply to the individual patient. By definition, one-half of the subjects achieve a score within the average range on any well-constructed psychological test; the remainder perform at many different levels both above and below the average. Although the average score may be, statistically, the most likely score a person will receive, statistical likelihood is a far cry from the individual case.

Individual Comparison Standards

As a general rule, *individual comparison standards* are called for whenever a psychological trait or function is evaluated for change. This rule applies both to deficit measurement and the measurement of behavioral change generally. Only on initial examination, and then only when dealing with functions for which there are species-wide or customary norms—such as finger-tapping rate or accuracy of auditory discrimination—are normative standards appropriate for deficit measurement. And even for these functions, the results of repeated examinations will be compared to those of prior examinations of the same individual rather than to the normative standards.

The use of individual comparison standards is probably most clearly exemplified in rate of change studies which depend solely on intraindividual comparisons. Here the same battery of tests is administered three times or more at spaced intervals, and the differences between chronologically sequential pairs of test scores are compared.

The measurement of rate of change is important in child psychology as a method of demonstrating the rate of development. The rate of change approach also has very broad applications in neuropsychology. Knowledge of the rate at which the patient's performance is deteriorating can contribute to the accuracy of predictions of the course of a deteriorating disease. For purposes of rehabilitation, the rate at which intellectual functions improve following cerebral insult may not only aid in predicting the patient's ultimate level of intellectual function, but also provide information about the effectiveness of rehabilitative efforts. Rate of change studies are also important in research on the long-range effects of injury to the brain on intellectual functioning since continuing changes have been reported months and even years after the injury occurred (Kertesz and McCabe, 1977; Lezak, 1979b; A. Smith, 1964).

The Measurement of Deficit

Direct Measurement of Deficit

Deficit can be assessed directly when there are normative comparison standards for the behavior in question. Inability to copy a simple drawing or to follow a sequence of three verbal instructions is obvious evidence of deficit in an adult. The extent of the discrepancy between the level of performance expected for an adult and the level of the patient's performance (which may be given in terms of the age at which the average child performs in a comparable manner) provides one measure of the amount of deficit the patient has sustained.

Direct deficit measurement using individual comparison standards may appear to be a simple, straightforward operation: the examiner compares premorbid and current samples of the behavior he wishes to study and evaluates the discrepancies. Canter's study (1951) of intellectual impairment in multiple sclerosis illustrates this procedure well. He compared the scores that veterans with multiple sclerosis received on the Army General Classification Test (AGCT) at the time of their induction into service with scores obtained on the same test battery after their illness was diagnosed. The results of this direct comparison provided clear-cut, unequivocal answers to questions of behavioral change over time. However, the direct method using individual comparison standards presupposes the availability of premorbid test scores or school grades or other relevant observational data, and these may be either nonexistent or difficult to obtain. Without full documentation of a patient's premorbid intellectual status, there is no direct comparison standard for each and every intellectual function or skill being examined. Therefore, more often than not the examiner must use *indirect* methods of deficit assessment in which the individual comparison standard has been inferred.

Indirect Measurement of Deficit

In indirect measurement, the examiner compares the patient's present performance with an *estimate* of his original ability level. The estimates may be made from a variety of sources. It is the examiner's task to find defensible and meaningful estimates of the original (pretraumatic or premorbid) ability level to serve as comparison standards for each patient.

METHODS OF INDIRECT MEASUREMENT

Different methods of inferring the comparison standard for each patient have been applied with varying degrees of success, depending on the examiner's sophistication and the individual patient's peculiar set of circumstances. Historical and observational data are obvious sources of information, and estimates of premorbid ability may be drawn from them directly. Estimates based on these sources will be more or less satisfactory depending upon how much is known of the patient's past, and whether what is known or can be observed is sufficiently characteristic to distinguish this particular patient from other people. For example, if all that an examiner knows about a brain injured, intellectually impaired patient is that he was a logger with a ninth-grade education and his observed vocabulary and interests seem appropriate to his occupation and education, then the examiner can only estimate a fairly low ability level as the comparison standard. If the patient had been brighter than average, if he could reason exceptionally well, tell stories cleverly, had been due for a promotion to supervisor, this information would probably not be available to the examiner who would then have no way of knowing from history and observations alone just how intelligent this particular logger had been.

Because premorbid ability estimates inferred from historical and observational data may be unpredictably low, indirect assessment of intellectual deficit is usually performed with current psychological test results. A number of different techniques have been developed for measuring intellectual deficit from test data. A common feature of all these techniques is that the premorbid ability level is estimated from the test data themselves.

For many years the most common method for estimating the premorbid ability level from test performance used a vocabulary score as the single best indicator of original intellectual endowment (Yates, 1954). This method was based on observations that many patients suffering various kinds of organic deterioration retained old, well-established verbal skills long after recent memory, reasoning, arithmetic ability, and other intellectual functions had deteriorated badly. A well-known example of this method is the Shipley Institute of Living Scale (Shipley and Burlingame, 1941), which contains both vocabulary and verbal abstraction items (see pp. 573f.). It was expected that mentally deteriorated persons would show large discrepancies between their vocabulary and their reasoning scores. Wechsler and others used the same principle to devise "deterioration" ratios, which were mostly based on the comparison of vocabulary and other verbal skill scores with scores on timed tests involving visuomotor activities (see pp. 248, 250–251).

More recently, McFie (1975) presented a schematic technique for representing deficit diagrammatically. It, too, is based on the assumption that certain kinds of cognitive skills are relatively impervious to organic impairment and therefore scores on tests of those skills will hold up for most brain damaged persons. For McFie, the sturdiest tests are the Wechsler Vocabulary and Picture Completion subtests, both involving verbal skills; the average of their scores, or the highest score of the two should one of the two be markedly depressed, provides the standard against which other Wechsler subtest scores are compared. Nelson (Nelson, no date; Nelson and O'Connell, 1978), in attempting to improve on vocabulary-based methods of estimating the intellectual deterioration of patients with diffusely dementing conditions, has proposed that reading test scores be used to estimate the comparison standard.

Vocabulary and related verbal skill scores sometimes do provide the best estimates of the general premorbid intellectual ability level. However, the vocabulary scores of many patients tend to be more vulnerable to brain damage than the scores of other verbal tests (E. W. Russell, 1972b). Further, a significant proportion of patients with left hemisphere lesions suffer deterioration of verbal skills that shows up in relatively lower scores on more than one test of verbal function. This is well demonstrated in several of McFie's cases (1975, pp. 58, 61, and 92) in which scores on Vocabulary, Picture Completion, and one other verbal subtest are three or more points below the highest score. Aphasic patients have the most obvious verbal disabilities; some are unable to use verbal symbols at all. Some patients with left hemisphere lesions are not technically aphasic, but their verbal fluency is sufficiently depressed that vocabulary scores do not provide good comparison standards (Lansdell, 1968). Even among normal control subjects, vocabulary scores alone may not provide a good estimate of general ability level except in those persons who have superior verbal skills (Jarvie, 1960).

A conceptually simple but somewhat more elaborate method to carry out uses the normalized (z-score) test score median to describe the "individual performance level" for each subject (Birri and Perret, 1980). This procedure provides individualized comparison standards that are likely to be fairly good estimates of premorbid ability when the patient's deficits are circumscribed. However, where damage is widespread or diffuse, leaving only few functions relatively spared, the comparison standard generated by this method will be spuriously low.

Other techniques have been devised for estimating the comparison standard (Thorp and Mahrer, 1959). For instance, one method compares the *variance* (a statistical measure of variability) of all the subtest scores (except the immediate memory subtest) obtained on the verbal section of the Wechsler test battery with the average of these scores, under the assumption that the wider the spread between the subtest scores (i.e., the higher the variance), the higher the estimate of original ability relative to the average of the obtained scores. Another method weights the three highest subtest scores obtained on the Wechsler subtests to provide an "intellectual altitude score." Thorp and Mahrer recommend "testing the limits" after the standard examination has been completed. For example, a patient who failed in his attempt to do arithmetic problems mentally may do them correctly if given paper and pencil. The estimate of original ability will then be based on the better arithmetic performance, although the lower score obtained for the mental calculations still reflects the patient's present functioning in that area. The discrepancy between the two scores indicates the amount of deficit.

In questioning the use of test score formulas for predicting premorbid intelligence (specifically, WAIS IQ score), Wilson and his colleagues (1979) devised a different kind of formula using the demographic variables of age, sex, race, education, and occupation. This formula produced somewhat more accurate estimates than Wechsler's test-based formula (see p. 250). Still, more than a quarter of the estimates made from demographic data alone were inaccurate. This study does show, however, the value of extratest data and the limitations of restricting one's access to any particular kind of data when seeking the most suitable comparison standards for a cognitively impaired patient.

THE BEST PERFORMANCE METHOD

A simpler method utilizes test scores as well as other observations and historical data. This is the *best performance method,* in which the level of the best performance—whether it be the highest score or set of scores, nonscorable behavior not necessarily observed in a formal testing situation, or evidence of premorbid achievement—serves as the best estimate of premorbid ability. Once the highest score or highest level of functioning has been identified, it becomes the standard against which all other aspects of the patient's current performance are compared.

The *best performance method* rests on a number of assumptions that guide the examiner in its practical applications. Basic to this method is the assumption that *each person has an original intellectual potential inherent in and limited by his neural structures and metabolic efficiency* (Maher, 1963). Hebb (1949) spells this out in his conceptualization of endowed capacity as "intelligence A," the underlying potential out of which develops "intelligence B," the manifested abilities.

A second basic assumption is that *given reasonably normal conditions of physical and mental development, there is one intellectual performance level that best represents each person's intellectual abilities generally.* This assumption follows from the well-documented phenomenon of the transituational consistency of intellectual behavior, which is sometimes represented as the general ability factor g (see pp. 22–23). According to this assumption, the performance level of most normally developed, healthy persons on any single test of an intellectual function or skill probably provides a reasonable estimate of their performance level on all other kinds of intellectual tasks. It is this assumption that allows the examiner to estimate a cognitively impaired patient's premorbid general ability level from one or several current test scores. A corollary assumption is that *marked discrepancies between the levels at which a person performs different intellectual functions or skills are evidence of disease, devel-*

opmental anomalies, cultural deprivation, emotional disturbance, or some other condition that has interfered with the full expression of that person's intellectual potential.

Another assumption is that intellectual potential or capacity can either be realized or reduced by external influences; it is not possible to perform at a higher level than one's biological capacity will permit. Brain injury—or cultural deprivation, poor work habits, or anxiety—can only depress intellectual functioning (Rey, 1964). An important corolllary to this assumption is that, for intellectually impaired persons, the least depressed abilities are the best remaining behavioral representatives of the original intellectual potential (Jastak, 1949).

The phenomenon of overachievement (people performing better than their general intelligence would seem to warrant) appears to contradict this assumption, but in fact overachievers do not exceed their biological limitations. Rather, they expend an inordinate amount of energy and effort on developing one or two special skills, usually to the neglect of others. Overachievers generally know their material mostly by rote and cannot handle the complex intellectual operations or highly abstract concepts expected of people at their specialization level.

A related assumption is that no person functions at his endowed maximum potential, for everyone's intellectual effectiveness has been compromised a little here by a childhood illness, a little there by educational deficiencies, or understimulation in infancy, or impulsivity, or a bump on the head, or test anxiety, and so on (Cutter, 1957). A person's performance of any task, no matter how good it might be, only indicates the floor, not the ceiling, of his level of abilities involved in that task.

Another related assumption is that within the limits of chance variations, a person's ability to perform a task is at least as high as his level of performance of that task. It cannot be less. This assumption may not seem to be so obvious when a psychologist is attempting to estimate premorbid intelligence from remnants of abilities or knowledge. In the face of a generally shabby performance, the psychologist may be reluctant to extrapolate an estimate of superior intelligence from one or two indicators of superiority, such as a demonstration of how to use a complicated machine, or the apt use of several abstract or uncommon words, unless he accepts the assumption that prerequisite to knowledge or the development of any skill is the ability to learn or perform it. A patient who names "Washington, Jefferson, Adams, and Nixon" as four presidents since 1900 (approximately 95% of all adults can answer the question correctly) but then identifies correctly a relatively obscure religious book that fewer than 10% of American adults know is demonstrating a significantly higher level of prior intellectual achievement than he maintains. His poor response does not negate his good one; the difference between them represents the extent to which he has suffered intellectual deterioration.

It is also assumed that a patient's premorbid ability level can be reconstructed or estimated from many different kinds of behavioral observations or historical facts. Estimates of original intellectual potential may be based on interview impressions, reports from family and friends, test scores, prior academic or employment level, school grades, army rating, or an intellectual product such as a letter or an invention.

Information that a patient is a physicist or that he designed and built his own canti-levered house is all that is needed to make an estimate of *very superior* premorbid intelligence, regardless of his present mental incapabilities. Except in the most obvious cases of unequivocal high achievement, the estimates should be based on a wide range of information from as many sources as possible to minimize the likelihood that significant data have been overlooked and the patient's premorbid ability level has been underestimated. For instance, verbal fluency can be masked by shyness or a highly developed graphic design talent lost to a motor paralysis. Such achievements might remain unknown without painstaking inquiry or testing.

The value of this method depends on the appropriateness of the data on which estimates of premorbid ability are based. The best performance method places on the examiner the responsibility for making an adequate survey of the patient's accomplishments and residual abilities. This requires sensitive observation with particular attention to qualitative aspects of the patient's test performance; good history-taking, including contacting family, friends, and other likely sources of information about the patient, such as schools and employers; and enough testing to obtain an overview of the patient's cognitive status in each major functional domain (see pp. 107–109).

The best performance method has very practical advantages. Perhaps most important is that a broad range of the patient's abilities are taken into account in identifying a comparison standard for evaluating deficit. By looking to the whole range of cognitive functions and skills for a comparison standard, the examiner is least likely to bias his evaluation of any specific group of patients, such as those with depressed verbal functions. Moreover, the examiner is not bound to one battery of tests but can take his estimate from any test score or cluster of test scores, and from nontest behavior and behavioral reports as well. Thus, if a patient's general functioning is too low or too spotty for him to take a standard adult test, or if he suffers specific sensory or motor defects, many children's tests or tests of specific skills or intellectual functions provide opportunities for him to demonstrate residual intellectual abilities.

There are two circumstances in which the examiner should not rely on a single high test score for his estimate of premorbid ability. One, which was referred to above, involves the overachiever whose highest scores are generally on vocabulary, general information, or arithmetic tests as these are the skills most commonly inflated by parental or school pressure on an ordinary student. The overachiever frequently has high memory scores too. He does not do as well on tests of reasoning, judgment, original thinking, and problem-solving, whether or not they involve words. A single high score on a memory test should not be used for estimating premorbid ability level since, of all the cognitive functions, memory is the least reliable indicator of general intellectual ability. Dull people can have very good memories; some extremely bright people have been notoriously absent-minded.

It is rare to find only one outstandingly high score in a complete neuropsychological examination. Usually even severely impaired patients produce a cluster of relatively higher scores in their least damaged area of functioning so that the likelihood of over-estimating the premorbid ability level from a single, spuriously high score is very slight. The examiner is much more likely to err by underestimating the original ability level of the severely brain injured patient who is unable to perform well on any task.

The Deficit Measurement Paradigm

Once the examiner has determined the comparison standard, whether directly from population norms, premorbid test data, or historical information, or indirectly from current test results and observation, he may assess deficit. To do so, he compares the level of the patient's present intellectual performance with the expected level, the comparison standard. Discrepancies between the expected level and the patient's present functioning are then evaluated for statistical significance (see Chapter 6, *passim*). A statistically significant discrepancy between expected and observed performance levels for any intellectual function or activity represents an intellectual deficit. (See pp. 138–140 for evaluating the significance of a discrepancy.)

This comparison is made for each test score. For each comparison where premorbid test scores are not available, the comparison standard is the estimate of original ability. By chance alone, a certain amount of variation *(scatter)* between test scores can be expected for even the most normal persons. However, chance variations tend to be small (Cronbach, 1970). If significant discrepancies occur for more than one test score, a *pattern* of deficit may emerge. By comparing any given pattern of deficit with patterns known to be associated with specific neurological or psychological conditions, the examiner may be able to identify etiological and remedial possibilities for the patient's problems. When differences between expected and observed performance levels are not statistically significant, deficit cannot be inferred.

For example, it is statistically unlikely that a person whose premorbid ability level was decidedly better than average cannot solve fourth- or fifth-grade arithmetic problems on paper or put together blocks to form any but the simplest patterns. If a patient whose original ability is estimated at the *high average* level produces this pattern of performance, then an assessment of impairment of certain arithmetic and constructional functions can be made with confidence. If the same patient performs at an *average* level on tests of verbal reasoning and learning, then the discrepancy is not significant even though his performance is somewhat lower than expected. His slightly lowered scores on these latter two functions need to be considered in any overall evaluation in which significant impairment has been found in other areas. However, when taken by themselves, *average* scores obtained by patients of *high average* endowment do not indicate impairment, since they may be due to normal score fluctuations. On the other hand, just *average* verbal reasoning and learning scores achieved by persons of estimated original *very superior* endowment represent a statistically significant discrepancy so that in exceptionally bright persons, *average* scores indicate deficit.

Identifiable patterns of intellectual impairment can be demonstrated by the deficit assessment method. Although this discussion has focused on assessment of deficit where there is known or suspected neurological disease, this method can be used to evaluate the intellectual functioning of psychiatrically disabled or educationally or culturally deprived persons as well. The evaluation of children's intellectual disorders follows the same model (E. M. Taylor, 1959). It is of use not only as an aid to neurological or psychiatric diagnosis, but in educational and rehabilitation planning too.

5

The Neuropsychological
Examination: Procedures

There can be no hard and fast rules for conducting a neuropsychological examination. The enormous variety of neurological conditions, patient capacities, and examination purposes necessitates a flexible, open, and imaginative approach. General guidelines for the examination can be summed up in the injunction: *tailor the examination to the patients's needs, abilities, and limitations.* By adapting the examination to the patient rather than the other way around, the examiner can answer the examination questions most fully at the least cost and with the greatest benefit to the patient.

The neuropsychological examination can be individually tailored in two ways. The examiner can select tests and examination techniques for their appropriateness for the patient and for their relevancy to those diagnostic or planning questions that prompted the examination and that arise during its course. He can also apply these assessment tools in a sensitive and resourceful manner by adapting them to suit the patient's condition and enlarging upon them to gain a full measure of information.

The Conceptual Framework of the Examination

Purposes of the Examination

Neuropsychological examinations may be conducted for any of a number of purposes: to aid in diagnosis; to help with management, care, and planning; to evaluate the effectiveness of a treatment technique; to provide information for a legal matter; or for research. In many cases, an examination may be undertaken for more than one purpose. In order to know what kind of information should be obtained in the examination, the examiner must have a clear idea of the reasons for which the patient is being seen.

Although the reason for referral usually is the chief purpose for examining the patient, the examiner needs to evaluate its appropriateness. Since most referrals for neuropsychological assessment come from persons who do not have expertise in neuropsychology, it is not surprising that many of their questions are poorly formulated or beside the point. Thus, the referral may ask for an evaluation of the patient's capacity to return to work after a stroke or head injury when the patient's actual need is for a rehabilitation program and an evaluation of his competency to handle his funds. Frequently, the neuropsychological assessment should address several issues, each important to the patient's welfare, although the referral may have been concerned with only one. Moreover, few referrals are explicit enough to suggest a focus for the examination or are sufficiently broad to define its scope. A request for differential diagnosis between organic and functional behavior disorders, for example, would rarely ask the examiner to give tests sensitive to frontal lobe dysfunction. The need to give such tests has to be determined from the history, the interview, and the patient's performance in the course of the examination. In the final analysis, the content and direction of any neuropsychological examination that is adapted to the patient's needs and capacities must be decided by the examiner.

Examination Questions

The overall thrust of the examination and the general questions that need to be asked will be determined by its purpose. The examiner will probably also raise specific questions about the level of performance of a particular skill or what impaired functions may account for the defective performance of a complex activity.

Examination questions fall into one of two categories. *Diagnostic questions* concern the *nature* of the patient's symptoms and complaints in terms of their etiology and prognosis; i.e., they ask *what* is the patient's problem. *Descriptive* questions inquire into the *characteristics* of the patient's condition; i.e., they ask *how* the patient's problem is expressed. Within these two large categories are specific questions which may each be best answered through somewhat different approaches.

DIAGNOSTIC QUESTIONS

Questions concerning the nature of the patient's condition are always questions of differential diagnosis. Whether implied or directly stated, these questions ask which of two or more diagnostic pigeonholes suits the patient's behavior best. In neuropsychology, diagnostic categorization can consist of coarse screening to differentiate the probably "organic" from "not organic" or "psychiatrically disturbed" patients, fine discrimination between a *presenile dementia* (early onset condition of intellectual deterioration) and mental deterioration associated with a tumor, or the even finer discrimination between the behavioral effects of a parietal lobe lesion and the effects of a lesion involving another part of the brain.

In looking for neuropsychological evidence of organic brain disease, the examiner may need to determine whether the patient's current level of functioning has deteriorated. Thus, one kind of diagnostic question will ask how good was the patient when he was at his best. Differential diagnosis can sometimes hinge on data from the personal history, the nature of the onset of the condition, and the circumstances surrounding the onset. Thus, a second set of diagnostic questions has to do with such issues as whether anyone in the family had a condition similar to the patient's, how fast the condition is progressing, and the patient's mental attitude and personal circumstances at the time the complaints began. Another important diagnostic question asks whether the pattern of deficits exhibited by the patient fits a known or reasonable pattern of organic brain disease—or fits one pattern better than another. More specific diagnostic questions will ask which particular brain functions are compromised, which are intact, and how the specific deficits might account for the patient's condition.

The neuropsychologist cannot make a neurological diagnosis, but he may provide data and diagnostic formulations that contribute to the diagnostic conclusions. Neuropsychological findings assume particular diagnostic importance when neither a neurological nor a psychiatric evaluation can account for behavioral aberrations that fit a neuropsychologically meaningful pattern (Tunks, 1976).

Descriptive Questions

Many kinds of questions call for behavioral description. Questions about specific capacities frequently arise in the course of vocational and educational planning. They become particularly important when planning involves withdrawal or return of normal adult rights and privileges, such as a driving license or legal competency. In these cases, the neuropsychological examination may not be extensive, but rather will focus on the relevant skills and functions.

Longitudinal studies involving repeated measures over time are conducted when there are questions of deterioration or improvement. In such studies, a broad range of functions usually comes under regular neuropsychological review. The initial examination, in which there is a full-scale assessment of each of the major functions in a variety of input and output modalities, is sometimes called a *baseline study* for it provides the standard set of data against which the findings of later examinations will be compared. Regularly repeated full-scale assessments give information about the rate and extent of improvement or deterioration, and about relative rates of change between functions.

Most examinations share one or more questions concerning the presence of organic damage, the estimation of an original potential or premorbid level of functioning, and the identification of a present level of general intellectual functioning. Many examinations also generate one or two questions peculiar to the specific case. There should be few examinations in which the questions and procedures are exactly identical. An examiner who does much the same thing with almost every patient he sees may not be attending to the implicit part of a referral question, to the patient's needs, or to the aberrations that point to specific defects and particular problems.

Hypothesis Testing

When the analytic procedure involved in reaching a diagnostic conclusion or a descriptive generalization is analyzed, its kinship with the experimental method

100

becomes evident (M. B. Shapiro, 1951). The neuropsychological examination can be viewed as a series of experiments that generate explanatory hypotheses in the course of testing them.

DIAGNOSTIC PURPOSES

In essence, the diagnostic process involves the successive elimination of alternative diagnostic possibilities. The examiner formulates the first set of hypotheses on the basis of the referral question, information obtained from the history or informants, and the initial impression of the patient. As the examination proceeds, the examiner can progressively refine general hypotheses (e.g., that the patient is suffering from an organic brain disorder) into increasingly specific hypotheses (e.g., that the disorder most likely stems from a focal or a diffuse brain condition; that this diffuse disorder is more likely to be an Alzheimer's type of dementia, multi-infarct dementia, or normal pressure hydrocephalus [see pp. 180–185, 189–190]). Each diagnostic hypothesis is tested by comparing what is known of the patient's condition (history, appearance, interview behavior, test performance) with what is expected for that particular diagnostic classification.

DESCRIPTIVE PURPOSES

The identification of specific deficits also proceeds by means of hypothesis testing. Since most neuropsychological examination techniques in clinical use elicit complex behavior, the determination of the specific impairments that underlie any given lowered performance becomes an important part of many neuropsychological evaluations. This is usually done by setting up a general hypothesis and testing it in each particular condition. If, for example, the examiner hypothesized that a patient's slowed performance on the Block Design subtest of the Wechsler Adult Intelligence Scale (WAIS, see pp. 276–281) was due to a general slowing, he would examine all other timed performances to see if the hypothesis held up. A finding that the patient was also slowed on all other speed tests would give strong support to the hypothesis. It would not, however, answer the question of whether other deficits also contributed to the low Block Design score.

To find out just what defective functions or capacities enter into an impaired performance requires additional analyses. The investigator must test whether a particular impaired function or capacity (e.g., response slowing) is the effective component in a multivariate phenomenon (e.g., a slowed Block Design performance). This is done by looking for other impaired functions (e.g., a constructional disorder) that might be contributing to the phenomenon of interest in other parts of the patient's performance (e.g., house drawing, design copying) in which the variable under examination plays no role and other component variables (e.g., perceptual accuracy, fine motor coordination) have been shown to be intact. When the patient does well on the task used to examine the alternative variable, the hypothesis that the alternative variable also contributes to the phenomenon of interest can be rejected. If the patient performs poorly on the second task as well as the first, then the hypothesis that poor performance on the first task is multiply determined cannot be rejected.

101

These are the conceptual procedures that can lead to diagnostic conclusions and to the identification of specific deficits. In clinical practice, examiners typically do not formalize these procedures or spell them out in detail, but will apply them intuitively. Yet, whether used wittingly or unwittingly, this conceptual framework underlies much of the diagnostic enterprise and behavioral analysis in individualized neuropsychological assessment.

Conduct of the Examination

Foundations

THE EXAMINER'S BACKGROUND

A strong background in neuropathology (including familiarity with neuroanatomy and neurophysiological principles) and in clinical psychology (including knowledge of psychiatric syndromes and of test theory and practice) is necessary if the examiner is to know what questions to ask, how particular hypotheses can be tested, or what clues or hunches to pursue. Even to know what constitutes a neuropsychologically adequate review of the patient's mental status requires a broad understanding of brain function and its neuroanatomical correlates. Moreover, the examiner must have had enough clinical training and supervised "hands on" experience to know what extratest data (e.g., personal and medical history items, school grades and reports) are needed to make sense out of any given set of observations and test scores, to weigh all of the data appropriately, and to integrate them in a theoretically meaningful and practically usable manner.

THE PATIENT'S BACKGROUND

In neuropsychological assessment, few if any single bits of information about a patient are meaningful in themselves. A test score, for example, only takes on diagnostic significance when compared with other test scores, with academic or vocational accomplishments, or with the patient's interview behavior. Even when the examination has been undertaken for descriptive purposes only, as after a head injury, it is important to distinguish a low test score that is as good as the patient has ever done from a similarly low score when it represents a significant loss from a much higher premorbid performance level. Thus, in order to interpret the examination data properly, each bit of data must be evaluated within a suitable context (Lezak, in press; Luria, 1966). What that context is will vary for different patients and different aspects of the examination. Usually, therefore, the examiner will want to become informed about many aspects of the patient's life. Some of this information can be obtained from the referral source, from records, from hospital personnel working with the patient, or from family, friends, or people with whom the patient works. Patients who can give their own history and discuss their problems reasonably well will be able to provide much of the needed information. Having a broad base of data about the patient will not guarantee accurate judgments, but it can reduce errors greatly. Moreover, the greater the examiner's knowledge about the patient prior to the examination, the better prepared the examiner will be to ask relevant questions and give those tests most likely to elicit information germane to the patient's problems.

A context for interpreting the examination findings may come from any of four aspects of the patient's background: (1) social history, (2) present life circumstances, (3) medical history and current medical status, and (4) circumstances surrounding the examination. Sometimes the examiner only has information about two or three of these aspects of the patient's life. The Korsakoff patient, for example, cannot give a social history or tell much about his current living situation. However, with the aid of informants and records as necessary, the examiner should inquire into each of these categories of background information.

1. Social history. Knowledge of the socioeconomic status of the patient's family of origin as well as current socioeconomic status is valuable for interpreting cognitive test scores, particularly those measuring verbal skills, which tend to reflect, to some extent, social class and academic achievement (see pp. 259 and 271). In the case of an older, retired, or brain damaged adult, the examiner should find out the highest socioeconomic status the patient had attained or the predominant adult socioeconomic status. The examiner should also ask about the patient's school and work history and the occupational level and education of parents, siblings, and other important family members.

The examiner needs to know the patient's marital history, including the obvious questions of number of spouses (or companions), length of relationship, and the nature of the dissolution of each significant alliance. The patient's marital history may tell a lot about the patient's long-term emotional stability, social adjustment, and judgment. It may also contain historical landmarks reflecting significant changes in social or emotional behavior.

Information about the present spouse's health, socioeconomic background, current activity pattern, and understanding of the patient's condition is frequently useful for understanding the patient's behavior (e.g., anxiety, dependency) and is imperative for planning and guidance. These same questions need to be asked about whoever is the most significant person in an unmarried patient's life. An appreciation of the patient's marital—or current living—situation and of the spouse's or responsible relative's condition is necessary both for understanding the patient's mood and concerns—or lack of concern—about his condition and the examination, and for gauging the reliability of the most important informant about the patient.

When reviewing educational and work history, attention should be paid to how work and school performance relate to the medical history and other aspects of the social history. Information about the patient's educational and work experiences is often doubly useful. It may be the best source of data about the patient's original intellectual potential. It may also reflect mental or behavioral changes that had not been appreciated by the patient or his family and were overlooked in cursory examinations.

Military service history may contain important information too. Some blue-collar workers had their only opportunity to display their natural talents in the service. A discussion of military service experiences may also unearth a head trauma or illness that the patient had not thought to mention to a less experienced or less thorough examiner.

Other areas should also be reviewed. Should antisocial behavior be suspected, the examiner will want to inquire about confrontations with the law. A review of family history is obviously important when a hereditary condition is suspected. Moreover, awareness of family experiences with illness and family attitudes about being sick may clarify many of the patient's symptoms, complaints, and preoccupations.

If historical data are the bricks, then chronology is the mortar needed to reconstruct the patient's history meaningfully. For example, the fact that the patient has had a series of unfortunate marriages is open to a variety of interpretations. In contrast, a chronology-based history of one marriage that lasted for two decades, dissolved more than a year after the patient was in coma for several days as a result of a car accident, and then followed by a decade filled with several brief marriages and liaisons, suggests that the patient may have sustained a personality change secondary to the head injury. Additional information that the patient had been a steady workman prior to the accident but since has been unable to hold a job for long gives additional support to that hypothesis. As another example, an elderly patient's complaint of recent mental slowing suggests a number of diagnostic possibilities; that the slowing followed the close occurrence of widowhood, retirement, and change of domicile should alert the diagnostician to the likelihood of depression.

2. Present life circumstances. When inquiring about the patient's current life, the examiner should go beyond factual questions about occupation, income and indebtedness, family statistics, and leisure-time activities to find out how the patient views and feels about these aspects of his situation. The examiner needs to know how long the patient has held his present job, what changes have taken place or are expected at work, whether he likes what he does, and whether there are problems on the job. The examiner should attempt to get an understanding of the quality of the patient's family life and find out whether there are family concerns such as troublesome in-laws, acting-out adolescents, illness or substance abuse among family members. New sexual problems can appear as a result of brain disease or old ones may complicate the patient's symptom picture and adjustment to his condition. Family concerns, marital discord, and sexual dysfunction can generate so much tension that the patient's symptoms may be exacerbated or his test performance adversely affected.

3. Medical history and current medical status. Information about the patient's medical history will usually come from the referring physician, a review of medical charts when possible, and reports of prior examinations as well as the patient's reports. When enough information is available to integrate the medical history with the social history, the examiner can often get a good idea of the nature of the condition and the kinds of problems created by it. Discrepancies between the patient's reports of his health history and his current medical condition or what medical records or physicians have reported may give a clue to the nature of the patient's complaints or the presence of a neuropsychological disorder.

Some aspects of the patient's health status that are apt to be overlooked in the usual medical examination may have considerable importance in making a neuropsychological evaluation. These include visual and auditory defects that may not be documented or even examined, particularly when the patient is old or has other sensory deficits, motor disabilities, or mental changes. In addition, sleeping and eating habits also may be overlooked in a medical examination, although impaired sleep and poor eating habits can be important symptoms of depression; increased sleep, childish or very limited food preferences, or an insatiable appetite may accompany organic brain disease.

4. Circumstances surrounding the examination. The test performance can only be evaluated accurately in the light of the reasons for referral and the relevance of the examination to the patient. For example, does the patient stand to gain money or lose a custody battle as a result of the examination? May his job or hope for early retirement be jeopardized by the findings? Only by knowing what the patient thinks he may gain or lose as a result of the neuropsychological evaluation can the examiner appreciate how the patient perceives the examination.

Procedures

Initial Planning

The neuropsychological examination proceeds in stages. In the first stage, the examiner plans an overall approach to the problem. The hypotheses to be tested and the techniques used to test them will depend upon the examiner's initial understanding and evaluation of the referral questions and the accompanying information about the patient.

Preparatory Interview

The initial interview and assessment make up the second stage. At this stage the examiner tentatively determines the range of functions to be examined, the extent to which psychosocial issues or emotional and personality factors should be explored, the level—of sophistication, complexity, abstraction, etc.—at which the examination should be conducted, and the limitations set by the patient's handicaps.

The first 15–20 minutes of examination time are usually used to evaluate the patient's capacity to take tests and to ascertain his understanding of the purpose of the examination. The examiner also needs time to prepare the patient for the tests. Occasionally, it is necessary to take longer, particularly with anxious or slow patients or with patients who have a confusing history or those whose misconceptions might compromise their intelligent cooperation. The examiner may spend the entire first session preparing a patient who fatigues rapidly and comprehends slowly, reserving testing for the subsequent days when he is no longer a stranger to the patient, and the patient is refreshed.

There are at least seven topics that must be covered with the competent patient before testing begins, if the examiner wants to be assured of the patient's best cooperation. (1) *The purpose of the examination:* Does the patient know why he was referred, and does he have questions of his own he would like answered? (2) *The nature of the examination:* Does the patient understand that the examination will be primarily concerned with his intellectual functioning and that being examined by a psychologist does not mean he is crazy? (3) *The use to which examination information will be put:* The patient must have a clear idea of who will receive the report and how it may be used. (4) *Confidentiality:* The competent patient must be reassured not only about the confidentiality of the examination, but also of his control over his privacy. (5) *Feedback to the patient:* The patient should know before he begins who will report the test findings to him, and if possible, when he will get this information. (6) A *brief explanation of the test procedures:* Many patients are very reassured by a few words about the tests they'll be taking, such as,

> I'll be asking you to do a number of different kinds of tasks. Some will remind you of school, because I'll be asking questions about things you've already learned, or I'll give you arithmetic or memory problems to do, just like a teacher. Others will be different kinds of puzzles and games. You may find that some things I ask you to do are fun and some seem silly; some of the tests will be very easy and some may be so difficult you won't even know what I'm talking about or showing you; but all of them will help me to understand better how your brain is working, what you are doing well and what kinds of difficulties you are having, and how you might be helped.

(7) *How the patient feels about taking the tests:* This can be the most important topic of all, for unless the patient feels that taking the tests is not shameful, not degrading, not a sign of weakness or childishness, not threatening to his job or his legal status or to whatever else he may be worrying about, he cannot meaningfully or wholeheartedly cooperate on his own behalf. Sometimes the threat is real, when the patient's job or his competency, or custody of his children is at stake. It is then incumbent upon the examiner to give the patient a clear understanding of the possible consequences of his noncooperation as well as his full cooperation so that he can make a realistic choice.

The examiner can also conduct a brief mental status examination (see Chapter 19 for a detailed description) in this preliminary interview. The patient's contribution to the discussion will give the examiner a fairly good idea of the level at which he will have to conduct the examination. When beginning the examination with the WAIS or any number of other published tests, the examiner can ask the patient to answer the questions of date, place, birthdate, education, and occupation on the answer

106

sheets, thereby getting information about the patient's orientation and personal awareness while doing the necessary record keeping.

It is often useful to learn the patient's view of his condition, for although his inner experiences are not observable, this kind of self-report can offer important clues to disabilities the neuropsychologist will want to investigate. The patient should be asked to give a history of his condition, for this too will aid the examiner in knowing what to look for and how to proceed. Administrative issues, such as fees, referrals, formal reports to other persons or agencies, should also be discussed at this time.

Patients who are not competent may be unable to appreciate all of the initial discussion. However, the examiner should make some effort to see that each topic is covered within the limits of the patient's comprehension and that the patient has had an opportunity to share his feelings about and understanding of the examination, and that he feels free to ask questions.

TEST SELECTION

Along with the examination questions, the patient's capacities and the examiner's test repertory determine what tests and assessment techniques will be used. In an individualized examination, the examiner rarely knows exactly which tests he is going to give before he begins working with the patient. He usually starts with a basic battery that touches upon the major dimensions of intellectual behavior and makes many of his choices as he proceeds. The patient's strengths and limitations and specific handicaps will determine how he uses the tests in the battery, which he must discard, and which require modifications to suit the patient's capabilities. As he raises and tests hypotheses regarding possible diagnoses, areas of intellectual dysfunction, and psychosocial or emotional contributions to the total behavioral picture, he may need to go outside the basic battery and use techniques relevant to *this* patient at *this* time.

A basic test battery.   With the battery of tests listed below the examiner can review the major functions in the auditory and visual receptive modalities and the spoken, written, graphic, and constructional response modalities. This battery can be used to ascertain baselines and to make longitudinal comparisons in the major areas of intellectual activity. It is limited by the availability of tests in all modalities that are sufficiently well standardized or frequently used to provide reliable comparison standards.

This basic battery contains both individually administered tests and paper and pencil tests the patient can take by himself. The individually administered tests take two and one-half to three hours. Unless there is some compelling reason for doing them all at once, they should be given in two sittings, preferably on two different days if the patient fatigues easily.

The following tests comprise the individually administered part of my battery:

1. The Wechsler Adult Intelligence Scale (WAIS or WAIS-R): Information, Comprehension, Arithmetic, Similarities, Digit Span, Picture Completion, Block Design, Picture Arrangement, and Object Assembly subtests (see Chapter 9).

2. The Symbol Digit Modalities Test (SDMT) (instead of the WAIS Digit Symbol subtest, since the SDMT provides an opportunity to compare spoken and written responses to a symbol substitution test and allows patients with motor slowing or motor handicaps to be tested by this technique) (see pp. 554–555).
3. The Rey Auditory-Verbal Learning Test (see pp. 422–429).
4. A paragraph learning test such as the Babcock Story Recall Test (see pp. 437–439), the Logical Memory subtest of the Wechsler Memory Scale (see pp. 435–437), or other meaningful prose passage containing 20 to 25 content units (see pp. 438–439).
5. Subtracting Serial Sevens (SSS) test (see pp. 552–553).
6. Draw a house or bicycle (pp. 405–406).
7. The Complex Figure Test (see pp. 395–402 and 444–447).
8. The Purdue Pegboard Test or Finger Tapping Test (pp. 529–532) or tests of *"dynamic organization of the motor act"* (Christensen, 1979) involving coordination and motor regulation of each hand and alternating movements (see p. 527).
10. Wisconsin Card Sorting Test (see pp. 487–491).
11. The Trail Making Test (see pp. 556–559).

The paper and pencil tests may be given by clerical or nursing staff. Patients generally take from three to six hours or more to complete them, depending on the extent to which the patient is motorically or mentally slowed and the amount of structuring, reassurance, or prodding he needs. Although some of the tests in this battery were developed as timed tests, none are timed in this administration. The person giving the test notes when the patient takes an unusual amount of time. Responsible patients who are fairly intact can often take the paper and pencil materials home and mail them back or return them at a later appointment. Irresponsible, immature, easily confused, or disoriented and poorly motivated patients should be given the paper and pencil tests under supervision, as should patients whose families tend to be protective or overly helpful.

The paper and pencil testing sessions should also be broken up. A patient may spend an hour or two doing paper and pencil tests and an hour or two with the examiner taking individually administered tests on the same day. If such a testing schedule is interrupted by coffee breaks and lunch, much of the testing can be accomplished in one day without tiring most patients to the point that their performance suffers.

My paper and pencil neuropsychological test packet includes:

1. The Self-Administered Battery (SAB). This is a collection of intellectual and personality tests and test samples suitable for adult patients generally. The SAB we currently use contains (a) 20 Wechsler-type information questions plus two common sense reasoning questions; (b) ten Wechsler-type arithmetic story problems; (c) a page of ten arithmetic calculation problems; (d) three proverbs with instructions to "Write what each of these sayings means" (pp. 476–477) and three verbal reasoning questions involving relationships (EAS p. 302); (e) Picture Absurdity 1d, "man and woman sitting in the rain," of the Stanford-Binet (Form L-M) with instructions to write "What is odd about this picture?" (p. 498); (f) 25 mul-

tiple-choice vocabulary items from the Gates-MacGinitie Reading Tests (pp. 335–336); (g) three designs to copy; (h) a set of 27 sentence completion stems; (i) one card from the Thematic Apperception Test (TAT) with instructions to write a story (see pp. 606–607); (j) the Draw-a-Person Test (DAP) with written instructions (pp. 309f., 404f.); (k) one Rorschach card with instructions to write three associations (pp. 360ff., 601ff.); (l) two simple geometric forms to copy and two to draw from memory; (m) Sentence Building I or II of the Stanford-Binet (Form M), depending on the patient's apparent verbal skill level (p. 341); and (n) Minkus Completion of the Stanford-Binet (p. 337).

2. The Calculations subtest of the Psycho-Educational Battery (p. 499).
3. Raven's Progressive Matrices (RPM), Standard or Coloured Form, depending on the patient's apparent capabilities (pp. 502–506).
4. The Hooper Visual Organization Test (VOT) (pp. 357–358).
5. Vocabulary and Comprehension subtests of the Gates-MacGinitie Reading Tests (usually Form F, but lower level forms can be substituted as needed) (pp. 335–336).
6. The Personal History Inventory, a multiple-choice and fill-in biographical questionnaire (Lezak, 1968).

The tests in this battery screen for organicity at a relatively efficient rate. In many cases, information obtained from the battery alone will reflect the gross outlines of mental impairment patterns with enough clarity to permit the examiner to form a diagnostic impression. Moreover, the examiner can usually determine what areas need further exploration from the data provided by the basic examination.

Like any other group of tests designed to provide a review of functions, this set of tests is not all-inclusive. A patient may have significant deficits that will not be identified if he performs adequately on these tests and is not given any others. This is most likely to occur with patients who have mild right hemisphere or frontal damage whose impairments are apt to be subtle or to go unnoticed in a highly structured clinical examination (Teuber, 1962; Walsh, 1978b). It is important to keep in mind that a *negative* (i.e., within normal limits, not abnormal) performance does not rule out brain pathology; it only demonstrates which functions are at least reasonably intact. On the other hand, an examiner whose patient's test and interview behavior are within normal limits cannot continue looking indefinitely for evidence of a lesion that may not be there. Rather, a good history, keen observation, a well-founded understanding of patterns of neurological and psychiatric dysfunction, and common sense should tell him when to stop—or to keep looking.

Of course, when following a research protocol, the examiner is not free to exercise the flexibility and inventiveness that characterize the selection and presentation of test materials in the clinical situation. For research purposes, the prime consideration in selecting examination techniques is whether they will effectively test the hypotheses. Other important issues in putting together a research battery include practicality, time, and the appropriateness of the instruments for the population under consideration. Since the research investigator cannot change instruments or procedures in midstream without losing or confounding data, selection of a research battery requires a great deal of care.

A note on the use of ready-made batteries. The popularity of ready-made batteries attests to the need for neuropsychological testing and to a general lack of knowledge about how to do it. The most popular batteries extend the scope of the examination beyond the barely minimal neuropsychological examination (which, in many places, consists of a WAIS and a drawing test of some kind). They offer reliable scoring methods for gross diagnostic screening (see Chapter 16). Ready-made batteries can be invaluable in research programs requiring well-standardized tests.

When batteries are used as directed, most patients undergo more testing than is necessary but not enough to satisfy the examination questions specific to their problems. Also, like most psychological tests, ready-made batteries are not geared to the patient's handicaps. The patient with a significant perceptual or motor disability may not be able to perform major portions of the prescribed tests, in which case the functions normally measured by the unusable test items remain unexamined. However, batteries do acquaint the inexperienced examiner with a variety of tests and with the importance of evaluating many different kinds of behaviors when doing neuropsychological testing. They can provide a good starting place for some newcomers to the field, who may then expand their test repertory and introduce variations into their administration procedures as they gain experience and develop their own point of view.

HYPOTHESIS TESTING

This stage of the examination usually has many steps. It begins as the data of the initial examination answer initial questions, raise new ones, and shift the focus from one kind of question to another or from one set of impaired functions that at first appeared to be of critical importance in understanding the patient's complaints to another, perhaps, antecedent, set of functions. This stage may also involve changes in approach, in the level of pace at which the examination is conducted, and in techniques used. The examiner may continue to make more changes in the procedures and shifts in the focus of the examination as he goes along. At any stage of the examination the examiner may decide that more medical or social information about the patient is needed, or that it would be more appropriate to observe rather than test the patient, or that he needs to interview another person, such as a complaining spouse or an intact sibling, for adequate understanding of the patient's condition. This flexible approach enables the examiner to generate multistage, serial hypotheses for identifying subtle or discrete dysfunctions or to make fine diagnostic or etiologic discriminations.

Selection of additional tests. The addition of specialized tests depends on continuing formulation and reformulation of hypotheses as new data answer some questions and raise others. Hypotheses involving differentiation of learning from retrieval, for instance, will dictate the use of techniques for assessing learning when retrieval is impaired. Finer-grained hypotheses concerning the content of the material to be learned—e.g., meaningful versus meaningless or concrete versus abstract or the

110

modality in which it is presented—will require different tests or the innovative use of relevant materials in an appropriate test format, and so on. As with memory, every other function can be examined across modalities and in systematically varied formats. In each case the examiner can best determine what particular combinations of modality, content, and format are needed to test the pertinent hypotheses.

Concluding the Examination

The final stage, of course, has to do with concluding the examination as hypotheses are supported or rejected, and the examiner answers the salient diagnostic and descriptive questions or explains why they cannot be answered (e.g., at this time, by this means). The conclusions should also lead to recommendations for improving or at least making the most of the patient's condition and his situation, and for whatever follow-up contacts may be needed.

An Aid to Test Selection: A Compendium of Tests and Assessment Techniques, Chapters 9 through 20

In the last 12 chapters of this book, most tests of intellectual function and personality in common use, and many relatively uncommon tests, are reviewed. These are tests and assessment techniques that are particularly well suited for *clinical* neuropsychological examination. Clinical examiners can employ the assessment techniques presented in these chapters for most neuropsychological assessment purposes in most kinds of work settings. Most of these tests have been standardized or have been used experimentally so that reports of the performances of control subjects are available. However, the normative populations and control groups for many of these tests may differ from patients on critical variables such as age or education, requiring caution and a good deal of "test wiseness" on the part of the examiner who attempts to extrapolate from unsuitable norms (see p. 117 and pp. 141–143).

Procedural Considerations in Neuropsychological Assessment

Testing Issues

Selecting Tests for Patients with Sensory or Motor Handicaps

Examination of a handicapped patient presents the problem of testing a variety of functions in as many modalities as possible with a more or less restricted test repertory. This is a relatively common problem for neuropsychological assessment, as many patients suffer perceptual or motor disabilities and a few are severely handicapped intellectually; all such patients require special tests for adequate evaluation.

Almost all psychological tests have been constructed with physically able persons in mind. When patients are handicapped, the examiner often has to find reasonable alternatives to the standard tests the patient cannot use, or he has to juggle test norms, improvise, or in the last resort, do without.

Although the examination of patients with sensory or motor disabilities is necessarily limited insofar as the affected input or output modality is concerned, the disability should not preclude at least some test evaluation of any intellectual function not immediately dependent on the affected modality. Of course, a blind patient cannot be tested for his ability to organize visual percepts, nor can a patient with profound facial paralysis be tested for verbal fluency; but both can be tested for memory and learning, arithmetic, vocabulary, abstract reasoning, comprehension of spatial relationships, a multitude of verbal skills, and so on.

Ready-made tests that can be substituted for the standard ones are available for most general functions. Deaf patients can be given written forms of tests of verbal functions; blind patients can take orally administered forms. For verbal and mathematical functions, there are a number of written and orally administered tests of arithmetic skills, vocabulary, and abstract reasoning in particular that have comparable norms. Other common tests of verbal functions, such as tests of background information, common sense reasoning and judgment, and verbal (reading) comprehension, do not have fully standardized counterparts in the other modality, whether it be visual or auditory. For some of these, similar kinds of alternative tests can be found although formats or standardization populations may differ. For others, the examiner may have to devise alternate forms on the spot. For instance, a test of background information that has been standardized for oral administration can be typed as a paper and pencil questionnaire; or a standardized reading comprehension test can be given orally, if the patient's level of verbal comprehension per se is under consideration.

There are fewer ready-made substitutes for tests involving pictures or designs although some test parallels can be found, and the clinician may be able to invent others. The *haptic* (touch) modality lends itself most readily as a substitute for visually presented tests of nonverbal functions (e.g., Fuld, 1980). For example, to assess concept formation of blind patients, size, shape, and texture provide testable dimensions. To test pattern learning or searching behavior, tactile mazes may be used in place of visual mazes. Three-dimensional block constructions will test constructional functions of patients who cannot see painted designs or printed patterns. Modeling in clay can be a substitute for human figure drawings. Even so, it is difficult to find a suitable nonvisual alternative for perceptual organization tests such as the Rorschach or Picture Arrangement series, or for a visuoconstructive task such as drawing a house or a bicycle, or for many others in the standard neuropsychological repertory.

The patient with a movement disorder presents similar challenges. Visual perceptual functions in these patients can be relatively easily tested since most tests of these functions lend themselves to spoken answers or pointing. However, drawing tasks requiring relatively fine motor coordination cannot be satisfactorily evaluated when the patient's preferred hand is paralyzed or spastic. Even when only the nonpreferred hand is involved, some inefficiency and slowing on other construction tasks will result from the patient's inability to anchor a piece of paper with his nonpreferred hand or to turn blocks or manipulate parts of a puzzle with two-handed efficiency.

Some tests have been devised specifically for physically handicapped people. Most of them are listed in test catalogues or can be located through local rehabilitation services. One problem that these substitute tests present is normative comparability, but since this is a problem in any substitute or alternative version of a standard test, it should not dissuade the examiner if the procedure appears to test the relevant functions. Another problem is that alternative forms usually test many fewer and sometimes different functions than the original test. For example, multiple choice forms of design copying tests obviously do not measure constructional abilities. What may be less obvious is the loss of the data about the patient's ability to organize, plan, and order his responses. Unless the examiner is fully aware of all that is missing in his alternative battery, some important functions may be overlooked.

Selecting Tests for the Severely Brain Damaged Patient

With few exceptions, tests developed for adults have neither items nor norms for grading the performance of severely mentally impaired adults. On adult tests, the bottom 1 or 2% of the noninstitutionalized adult population can usually pass the simplest items. These items leave a relatively wide range of behaviors unexamined and are too few to allow for meaningful performance gradations. Yet it is as important to know about the impairment pattern, the rate and extent of improvement or deterioration, and the relative strengths and weaknesses of the severely brain damaged patient as it is for the less afflicted patient.

For very defective patients, one solution is to use children's tests. There are tests of all functions in every modality for children, as well as special children's norms for some tests originally developed for adults (see, for example, F. M. Taylor, 1959; Koppitz, 1964). When given to retarded adults, children's tests require little or no change in wording or procedure. (See Chapter 6 for the application of children's test norms to adult patients.) At the lowest performance levels, the examiner may have to evaluate observations of the patient by means of developmental scales (see Chapter 19).

Some simple tests and tests of discrete functions were devised for use with severely impaired adults. Tests for elderly patients suspected of having deteriorating brain diseases are generally applicable to very defective adults of all ages (Fuld, 1978; Mattis, 1976). Christensen's systematization of Luria's neuropsychological investigation techniques (1979a) give detailed instructions for examining many of the perceptual, motor, and narrowly defined cognitive functions basic to complex intellectual and adaptive behavior. These techniques are particularly well suited for patients who are too impaired to respond meaningfully to graded tests of intellectual prowess, but whose residual capacities need assessment for rehabilitation or management. Their clinical value lies in their flexibility, their focus on qualitative aspects of the data they elicit, and their facilitation of useful behavioral description of the individual patient. Observations made by means of Luria's techniques or by means of the developmental scales and simple tests that enable the examiner to discern and discriminate functions at low performance levels cannot be reduced to numbers and arithmetic operations without losing the very sensitivity that examination of these functions and good neuropsychological practice requires.

113

Occasionally a patient presents an assessment problem for which no well-standardized alternative test is suitable. Improvising appropriate testing techniques can then tax the imagination and ingenuity of any conscientious examiner. He may find a suitable test among the many new and often experimental techniques reported in the literature. A number of them are reviewed in this book. Many of these experimental techniques are inadequately standardized. Some of them may not test the functions they purport to test. Others may be so subject to chance error as to be undependable. Still others may have spurious norms. However, these experimental and relatively unproven tests may be useful in themselves or as a source of ideas for further innovations. Rarely can an examiner evaluate an unfamiliar test's standardization methodically, but with experience he can learn to judge reports and manuals of new tests well enough to know whether the tasks, the author's interpretation, the statistical norms, and the test's reliability are reasonably suitable for his purpose. It should go without saying that when making this kind of evaluation of a relatively untried test, clinical standards need not be as strict as research standards.

ORDER OF PRESENTATION OF THE TESTS

The order of presentation of tests in a battery has not been shown to have appreciable effects on performance (Carter and Bowles, 1948; Cassel, 1962; Quereshi, 1968). Neuger and his colleagues (1981) noted a single exception to this rule when they gave a battery containing many different kinds of tests. A slight slowing occurred on a test of manual speed (Finger Tapping, see p. 529) administered later in the day. The examiner who is accustomed to one or another presentation sequence may feel somewhat uncomfortable and less efficient if it is varied. In an examination tailored to the patient's needs, the examiner varies presentation of the tests to ensure the patient's maximum productivity. For example, he may give those tests he knows will be difficult at the beginning of a testing session when the patient is least fatigued; or he may follow a test that has taxed or discouraged the patient with one on which the patient can relax or recover his pride. The new format of the Wechsler Adult Intelligence Scale (WAIS-R; Wechsler, 1981) alternates verbal tests with visual perceptual or construction tests as a standard procedure. This increases, the likelihood that a test that is easy for the patient follows one that was difficult so that the patient need not experience one failure after another.

TESTING THE LIMITS

Knowledge of the patient's capacities can be extended by going beyond the limits of the test set by the standard procedures. Arithmetic questions provide a good example. When a patient fails the more difficult items on an orally administered arithmetic test because of an immediate memory, concentration, or conceptual tracking problem, the examiner still does not know whether the patient understands the problem, can perform the calculations correctly, or knows what operations are called for. If the examiner stops at the point at which the patient fails the requisite number of items

114

without exploring these questions further, any conclusion he draws about the patient's ability to do arithmetic is questionable. In a case like this, the patient's arithmetic ability can easily be tested further by giving him pencil and paper and repeating the failed items. Some patients can do the problems once they have written the elements down, and still others do not perform any better with paper than without it.

Testing the limits does not affect the standard test procedures or scoring. It is done only after the test or test item in question has been completed according to standard test instructions. This method not only preserves the statistical and normative meaning of the test scores, but it can also afford interesting and often important information about the patient's functioning. For example, a patient who achieves an arithmetic score in the *borderline defective* ability range on the standard presentation of the test and who solves all the problems quickly and correctly at a *superior* level of functioning when he can jot down the elements of a problem, demonstrates a severely crippling immediate memory problem but a continued capacity to handle quite complex computational problems as long as they are written down. From his test score alone, one might conclude that his competency to handle his own funds is questionable; on the basis of the more complete examination of his arithmetic ability, he might be encouraged to continue ordinary bookkeeping activities.

Testing the limits can be done with any test. The examiner should test the limits whenever he suspects that an impairment of some function other than the one under consideration is interfering with an adequate demonstration of that function. Imaginative and careful testing the limits can provide a better understanding of the extent to which a function or functional system is impaired and the impact this impairment may have on related functional systems. Much of the special testing done with handicapped patients is a form of testing the limits.

PRACTICE EFFECTS

The effects of repeated examinations have been studied in both normal subjects and brain damaged patients. In the former and many of the latter, an overall pattern of test susceptibility to practice effects emerges. By and large, tests that have a large speed component, require an unfamiliar or infrequently practiced mode of response, or have a single solution—particularly if it can be easily conceptualized once it is attained—are more likely to show significant practice effects (Dodrill and Troupin, 1975; Quereshi, 1968).

H. E. Lehmann, Ban and Kral (1968) found a positive association between the extent of cognitive impairment (by virtue of psychopathology, duration of institutionalization, and age) in their geriatric population and higher scores on repeated tests. This finding accords with my observations that many brain damaged patients will do much better on a second or third trial of a test such as memorizing a word list or on later items of a novel task than on their initial attempts, even when it increases in difficulty. This response pattern is typical when patients are slow to achieve a new set in an unfamiliar task or even when the task is familiar but follows another to which the patient has become accustomed. It is therefore not surprising to find that the

115

greater the likelihood of brain impairment the more evident is this kind of improvement with repetition of the test. This latter phenomenon should be distinguished from the improvements control subjects make on speeded tests and tests, such as Wechsler's Object Assembly subtest (see pp. 284–285) or Halstead's Category Test (p. 480f.), which have specific solutions that can be easily verbalized or conceptualized visually.

However, when brain damage renders a test, such as Block Design, difficult to conceptualize, the patient is unlikely to improve with practice alone (Diller et al., 1974) Mandleberg (1976) found no improvement in IQ scores when retesting traumatically brain injured subjects 18 months after their third test. Without further study, it is not possible to conclude whether his finding relates to the large amount of time elapsed between the third and fourth tests or to the impracticability of attempting to measure practice effects with summed IQ scores since not all subtests contributing to these scores typically show practice effects. Reviewing the literature on practice effects on the performance of brain damaged patients, Shatz (1981) concluded that improvements attributable to practice tend to be minimal, but this varies with the nature, site, and severity of the lesion and the patient's age.

Among normal persons, large changes between test and retest are not common (Lezak, 1982d). Matarazzo and his co-workers (1980) found the WAIS subtests to be quite robust. They reported that only ten percent of the individual test scores obtained by 29 normal young adults changed more than two scaled score points in either direction on retest after a 20-week interval. Yet relatively large changes of three or more points occurred with sufficient frequency, even on this very reliable and well-standardized test, to lead the authors to caution against making inferences on the basis of any single score change *"in isolation."* The younger the subjects, the more likely it is that their test performances will show practice effects (Shatz, 1981). Thus, retest improvements attributable to practice are observed among normal elderly subjects but tend to be so small as to be virtually inconsequential.

SOME PRACTICAL SUGGESTIONS

With few exceptions, the examiner will communicate best by keeping his language simple. Almost all of the concepts that professionals tend to communicate in technical language can be conveyed in everyday words. It may initially take some effort to substitute "find out about your problem" for "differential diagnosis," or "the part of your brain that normally receives messages from the left half of each of your eyes" for "left homonymous hemianopsia," or "difficulty thinking in terms of ideas" for "abstract conceptualization." However, the examiner may find that forcing himself to word these concepts in his native tongue may add to his understanding as well. My exceptions to this rule are those brain damaged patients who were originally well endowed and highly accomplished, for whom complex ideation and an extensive vocabulary came naturally, and who need recognition of their premorbid status and reassurance of residual intellectual strengths. Talking at their educational level conveys this reassurance and acknowledges their intellectual achievements implicitly and thereby even more forcefully than telling them.

Now for some don'ts. Don't "invite" the patient to be examined, or to take a particular test, or, for that matter, to do anything he needs to do. If you invite him to do something or ask if he would care to do it, he can say "no" as well as "yes." Once he has refused—he does not want to be examined, he would not like to play with these silly blocks, he will not wait around while you finish a phone call or set up test material—you have no choice but to go along with his decision since you had given him the opportunity of making one. You certainly cannot very well retract the invitation simply because you do not like his answer and still expect to maintain a relationship based upon mutual respect as a retraction tells him you do not respect his decision. Therefore, when a patient must do something, tell him what it is he needs to do as simply and as directly as you can.

I have a personal distaste for using expressions such as "I would like you to. . . ." or "I want you to. . . ." when asking patients to do something. I feel it is important for the patient to undertake for his own sake whatever it is the clinician asks or recommends, and that he not do it merely or even additionally to please the clinician. Thus, I tell the patient what he needs to do using such expressions as, "I'm going to show you some pictures and your job is to. . . ." or "When I say, 'Go,' you are to. . . ."

My last "don't" also concerns a personal distaste, and that is for the use of the first person plural when asking the patient to do something: "Let's try these puzzles"; "Let's take a few minutes' rest." The essential model for this plural construction is the kindergarten teacher's directive, "Let's go to the bathroom." The reason for it is usually reluctance to appear bossy or rude. Because it smacks of the kindergarten and is inherently incorrect (the examiner is not going to take the test nor does he need a rest from the testing), a sensitive patient may feel he is being demeaned.

When Special Procedures May Be Needed

EXAMINING ELDERLY PERSONS

Psychological studies of elderly people have shown that, with some psychometrically important exceptions, healthy and active people in their seventies and eighties do not differ greatly in skills or abilities from the generations following them (see pp. 216–219). However, the diminished sensory acuity, motor strength and speed, and particularly flexibility and adaptability that accompany advancing age can affect the elderly person's test performance adversely. These age-related handicaps can result in spuriously low scores and incorrect conclusions about the intellectual capacity of older persons (Birren and Schaie, 1977, *passim;* Botwinick, 1978, 1981; Schonfield, 1974). Krauss (1980) has drawn up a set of guidelines for evaluating the older worker's capacity to continue employment that can apply to neuropsychological assessment of the elderly as well. Among them are recommendations that print be large and high contrast; that answer sheets, which typically add a visual search dimension to whatever else is being tested, be eliminated; that tests have as high face validity as possible; and that norms be appropriate.

When examining elderly people, the clinician needs to determine whether their auditory and visual acuity is adequate for the tests they will be taking and, if not, make every effort to correct the deficit or assist them in compensating for it. We keep a set of reading glasses with our test material and sometimes speak very loudly.

General slowing with advanced age requires age norms for all timed tests. If such norms are not available, the scores of these tests are not interpretable for persons over 60 years of age (see pp. 142, 216ff.). If the examiner is interested in *how* an elderly patient performs a given timed task, administering it without timing, although not standardized procedure, will provide the qualitative information about whether the patient can do the task at all, what kind of errors he makes, how well he corrects them, etc. This approach will probably answer satisfactorily most of the examination questions that prompted use of the timed test.

Often the most important factor in examining elderly persons is their cooperation (Wisotsky and Friedman, 1965). With no school requirements to be met, no jobs to prepare for, and usually little previous experience with psychological tests, a retired person may very reasonably not want to go through a lot of fatiguing mental gymnastics that may well make him look stupid to the youngster in the white coat sitting across the table. Particularly if they are not feeling well or are concerned about diminishing mental acuity, elderly persons may view a test as a nuisance or an unwarranted intrusion into their privacy. (For a discussion of problems encountered when giving the WAIS to elderly subjects, see Savage et al., 1973, and pp. 254–255). Thus, explaining to elderly persons the need for the examination and introducing them to the testing situation will often require more time than with younger people. When the patient is ill or convalescing, the examiner needs to be especially alert to signs of fatigue and sensitive to testing problems created by unusually short attention span and increased distractibility (see pp. 125–126). It has been suggested that some of these problems can be avoided by examining elderly people with familiar materials such as playing cards and designing tasks that are obviously meaningful and nonthreatening (Krauss, 1980).

Examining the Severely Handicapped Patient

When mental or physical handicaps greatly limit the patient's range of response, it may first be necessary to determine whether he has enough verbal comprehension for formal testing procedures. A set of questions and commands calling for one-word answers and simple gestures will quickly give the needed information. Those that are simplest and most likely to be answered are given first to increase the likelihood of initial success. Questions calling for "yes" or "no" answers should be avoided since many patients with impaired speech cannot sound out the difference between "uh-huh" and "uh-uh" clearly; nor is it easy for a weak or tremulous patient to nod or waggle his head with distinct precision.

A patient with no speech impediment might be asked the following kinds of questions:

> What is your name?
> What is your age?

Where are you now?

What do you call this (hand, thumb, article of patient's clothing, coin, button, or safety pin)?

What do you do with a (pen, comb, matches, key)?

What color is (your tie, my dress, etc.)?

How many fingers can you see? (Two or three trials.)

How many coins in my hand? (Two or three trials.)

Say the alphabet; count from one to 20.

Patients who do not speak well enough to be understood can be examined for verbal comprehension and ability to follow directions.

Show me your (hand, thumb, a button, your nose).

Give me your (left, right—the nonparalyzed) hand.

Put your (nonparalyzed) hand on your (other) elbow.

Place several small objects (button, coin, etc.) in front of the patient and ask him to

Show me the button (or key, coin, etc.)

Show me what opens doors. How do you use it?

Show me what you use to write. How do you use it?

Do what I do (salute; touch nose, ear opposite hand, chin in succession).

Place several coins in front of the patient.

Show me the quarter (nickel, dime, etc.).

Show me the smallest coin.

Give me (3, 2, 5) coins.

Patients who can handle a pencil may be asked to write their name, age, where they live, and to answer simple questions calling for "yes" or "no" or short word and simple number answers, and to write the alphabet and the first 20 numbers. Patients who cannot write may be asked to draw a circle, copy a circle drawn by the examiner, copy a vertical line drawn by the examiner, draw a square, and imitate the examiner's gestures and patterns of tapping with a pencil. Word recognition can be tested by asking the patient to point to the one of the several words printed on a word card or piece of paper that is the same as a spoken word (e.g., "cat": cat, dog, hat), or that answers a question (e.g., "Which do you wear on your head?"). Reading comprehension can be tested by printing the question as well as the answers, or by giving the patient a card with printed instructions such as, "If you are a man (or "if it is morning"), hand this card back to me; but if you are a woman (or "if it is afternoon"), set it down."

Patients who respond to most of these questions correctly are able to comprehend and cooperate well enough for formal testing. Patients unable to answer more than two or three questions probably cannot be tested reliably. Their behavior is best evaluated by rating scales (see Chapter 19).

Maximizing the Patient's Level of Performance

"The goal of testing is always to obtain the best performance the patient is capable of producing." (S. R. Heaton and R. K. Heaton, 1981).

It is not very difficult to get a patient to do poorly on a psychological examination. This is especially true of brain damaged patients, for the quality of their performance can be exceedingly vulnerable to external influences or changes in their internal states. All an examiner need do is tire the patient, make him anxious, or subject him to any one of a number of distractions most people ordinarily do not even notice, and his test scores will plummet. In neuropsychological assessment, the difficult task is enabling the patient to perform as well as possible.

Eliciting the patient's maximum output is necessary for a valid behavioral assessment. Interpretation of test scores and of test behavior is predicated on the assumption that the demonstrated behavior is a representative sample of the patient's true capacity in that area. Of course, it is unlikely that all of a person's ability to do something can ever be demonstrated; for this reason many psychologists distinguish between a patient's level of test performance and an estimated ability level. The practical goal is to help the patient do his best so that the difference between what he can and what he does do is negligible.

Optimal versus Standard Conditions

In the ideal testing situation, both *optimal* and *standard* conditions prevail. Optimal conditions are those that enable the patient to do his best on the tests. They differ from patient to patient, but for most brain injured patients, they include freedom from distractions, a nonthreatening emotional climate, and prevention of fatigue.

Standard conditions are prescribed by the test-maker to ensure that each administration of the test is as much like every other administration as possible, so that scores obtained on different test administrations can be compared. To this end, many test-makers give detailed directions on the presentation of their test, including specific instructions on word usage, handling the material, etc. Highly standardized test administration is necessary when using norms of tests that have a fine-graded and statistically well-standardized scoring system, such as the Wechsler Intelligence Tests. By exposing each patient to nearly identical situations, the standardization of testing procedures also enables the examiner to discover the individual characteristics of each patient's responses.

Normally, there need be no conflict between optimal and standard conditions. When brain damaged patients are tested, however, a number will be unable to perform well within the confines of the standard instructions.

For some patients, the difficulty may be in understanding the standard instructions. The Arithmetic subtest of the WAIS provides a good example. A problem similar to the third one of that subtest is, "How much is five dollars and three dollars?" Few talking patients cannot do this problem correctly. However, a number of mathematically adept and verbally competent but very concrete-minded brain injured patients will answer with a note of surprise in their voices that "five dollars and three dollars is five dollars and three dollars!" for the phrasing of the question does not specifically tell them to add. The examiner is then faced with a dilemma: whether to score the problem as failed, although the failure was on the basis of impaired abstract thinking and not a mathematical disability; or to repeat, and if need be, rephrase the question in order to test the patient's ability to add two one-place numbers. Should the patient pass the rephrased question, the examiner must next decide whether to give him credit. (In a case like this, the examiner can maintain a dual scoring system. Scoring strictly, he will obtain an estimate of the level of the patient's day-to-day performance on problems requiring mathematical skills as it is affected by his concrete thinking. Allowing for nonconformity to the standardization requirements produces another—higher—score, which is his estimated arithmetic ability level.)

Memory tests are another kind of test on which instructional problems can occur with concrete-minded or poorly inhibited brain injured patients. When given a list of numbers or words, some patients are apt to begin reciting the items one right after the other as the examiner is still reading the list. Here too, additional instructions must be given if the patient is to do the test as originally conceived and standardized. In this case, a patient's immediate repetition may spoil the ready-made word or number series. When giving these kinds of memory tests, it is helpful to have a substitute list handy, particularly if the examiner does not plan to see the patient at a later date. Otherwise, the identical list can be repeated later in the examination, with the necessary embellishments to the standard instructions.

To provide additional information on immediate memory and allow the examiner to test the patient's comprehension of test questions, the examiner can ask the patient to repeat the question when he gives an erroneous response that sounds as if he forgot or misheard elements of the question. It is particularly important to find out what the patient understood or retained when the patient's original response is so wide of the mark that it is doubtful he was answering the question the examiner asked. In such cases, subtle attention, memory, or hearing defects may emerge; or, if the wrong answer was due to a chance mishearing of the question, the patient has an opportunity to correct the error and gain the credit due him.

Many other comprehension problems of these kinds are peculiar to brain injured patients. A little more flexibility and looseness in interpreting the standard procedures are required on the examiner's part if he is to make the most of the test and elicit the patient's best performance. "The same words do not necessarily mean the same thing to different people and it is the meaning of the instructions which should be the same for all people rather than the wording" (M. Williams, 1965, p. xvii).

Other problems may arise from a patient's short attention span, fatigability, and distractibility (Lezak, 1978b). Occasionally, patients cannot remember enough of a lengthy question to formulate a response. This may reflect an unduly limited span of attention or the slow rate at which the patient must process what he hears (Walsh, 1978b). Because of the possibility that a patient cannot absorb new material at a normal rate, the examiner may need to slow his rate of presentation when the patient seems to be having difficulty in grasping all that he hears. Aphasic patients have difficulty with tape-recorded material, doing significantly better when the same material is presented in direct speech (E. Green and Boller, 1974).

Some patients can only work for brief periods of time. Their examination may continue over days and even a week or two if their performance begins to suffer noticeably after 10 to 15 minutes of concentrated effort, necessitating a recess. On occasion, a patient's fatigue may require the examiner to stop testing in the middle of a subtest in which items are graduated in difficulty or arranged to produce a learning effect. When the test is resumed in a day or two, the examiner must decide whether to start from the beginning and risk overlearning, or pick up where he left off, taking a chance that the patient will have lost the response set or forgotten what he had learned on the first few items.

Should the patient not answer a question for 30 seconds or more, the examiner can ask him to repeat the question, thus finding out if lack of response is due to inattention, forgetting, slow thinking, uncertainty, or unwillingness to admit failure. When the patient has demonstrated a serious defect of attention, immediate memory, or capacity to make generalizations, it is necessary to repeat the format each time one of a series of similar questions is asked. For example, if the patient's vocabulary is being tested, the examiner must ask what the word means with every new word, for the subject may not remember how to respond without prompting at each question.

Scoring questions also arise when the patient gives two or more responses to questions that have only one correct or one best response. When one of the patient's answers is correct, the examiner should invite the patient to decide which of his answers he prefers and then score accordingly.

Timing presents even greater and more common standardization problems than incomprehension in that both brain damaged and elderly patients are likely to do timed tests slowly and lose credit for good performances. Many timing problems can be handled by testing the limits. With a brain damaged population and with older patients (Kramer and Jarvik, 1979), many timed tests should yield two scores: the score for the patient's response within the time limit and another for his performance regardless of time.

Street noises, a telephone's ring, or a door slamming down the hall can easily break an ongoing train of thought in many brain damaged patients. If this occurs in the middle of a timed test, the examiner must decide whether to repeat the item, count the full time taken, including the interruption and recovery, count the time minus the interruption and recovery time, do the item over using an alternate form if possible, skip that item and prorate the score, or repeat the test again another day. Should there not be another testing day, then an alternate form is the next best choice and an estimate of time taken without the interruption is a third choice. A prorated score is also acceptable.

A record of the effects of interruptions due to distractibility on timed tasks gives valuable information about the patient's efficiency. Comparisons between his *efficiency* (performance under standard conditions) and his *capacity* (performance under optimal conditions) are important for rehabilitation and vocational planning. In some cases they may be used as indices of recovery or deterioration (e.g., Gronwall, 1980; Gronwall and Sampson, 1974). The actual effect of the distraction, whether it be in terms of increased response time, lowered productivity within the allotted time, or more errors, should also be noted and reported. Moreover, Nemec's (1978) identification of differences in susceptibility to auditory-verbal or visual pattern distractors in left and right hemisphere damaged patients, respectively, has practical implications in testing in terms of the kinds of distractors most likely to disturb a particular patient.

Nowhere is the conflict between optimal and standard conditions so pronounced or so unnecessary as in the issue of emotional support and reassurance of the test-taking patient. For many examiners, standard conditions have come to mean that they have to maintain an emotionless, standoffish attitude toward their patients when they are testing them. The stern admonitions of test-makers to adhere to the wording of the test manual and not tell the patient whether he passed any single item have probably contributed to the practice of coldly mechanical test administration.

From the viewpoint of any but the most severely regressed or socially insensitive patient, this kind of test experience is very anxiety-producing. Almost every patient approaches psychological testing with a great deal of apprehension. Brain injured patients and persons suspected of harboring a brain tumor or some insidious degenerative disease are often frankly frightened. When such a patient is then confronted with an examiner who maintains an impassive expression on his face and an emotionally toneless voice, who never smiles, and who responds only briefly and curtly to the patient's questions or efforts at conversation, the patient generally assumes that he is doing something wrong—failing, or displeasing the examiner—and his anxiety soars. The impact of such a threatening situation on intellectual performance can be seriously crippling. High anxiety levels may result in such mental efficiency problems as slowing, scrambled or blocked thought and words, and memory failure (Mueller, 1979; G. D. King et al., 1978; Wrightsman, 1962); they certainly will not be conducive to a representative performance.

Fear of appearing stupid may also prevent an impaired patient from showing what he can do. In working with patients who have memory disorders, Howieson has found that many of them say they cannot remember not only when they cannot remember but also when they can make a response but are unsure of its correctness in order to save face. When the examiner gently and encouragingly "pushes them in a way that makes them feel more comfortable," most patients who at first denied any recall of test material demonstrated at least some memory (personal communication, 1980).

Although standard conditions do require that the examiner adhere to the instructions in the test manual and give no hint regarding the correctness of a response, these requirements can easily be met without creating a climate of fear and discomfort. A sensitive examination calls for the same techniques the psychologist uses to put a patient at ease in an interview and to establish a good working relationship. Conversational patter is appropriate and can be very anxiety-reducing. The examiner can maintain a relaxed conversational flow with the patient throughout the entire test session without permitting it to interrupt the administration of any single item or task.

The examiner can give continual support and encouragement to the patient without indicating success or failure by smiling and rewarding the patient's *efforts* with words such as "Good," "Fine," and "You're doing well" or "You're really trying hard!" If the examiner takes care to distribute praise randomly, and not just following correct responses, he is no more giving away answers than if he remains stonily silent throughout (M. B. Shapiro, 1951). However, the patient feels comforted, reassured that he is doing something right and that he is pleasing—or at least not displeasing—the examiner.

When the examiner has established this kind of warmly supportive atmosphere, he can discuss with the patient his strengths and weaknesses and problems as they appear in the course of the examination. The interested, comfortable patient will be able to provide the examiner with information about his functioning that he might otherwise have forgotten or be unwilling to share. He will also be receptive to the examiner's explanations and recommendations regarding the specific difficulties he is encountering and which he and the examiner are exploring together. The examination will have been a mutual learning and sharing experience.

Special Problems of the Brain Damaged Patient

SENSORY DEFICITS

Many brain damaged patients with lateralized lesions will have reduced vision or hearing on the side opposite the lesion, with little awareness that they have such a problem. This is particularly true for patients who have *homonymous field cuts* (loss of vision in the same part of the field of each eye) or in whom nerve damage has reduced auditory acuity or auditory discrimination functions in one ear only. Their normal conversational behavior typically gives no hint of the deficit; yet presentation of test material to the affected side makes their task more difficult.

The neuropsychologist is often not able to find out quickly and reliably whether the patient's sight or hearing has suffered impairment. Therefore, when the patient is known to have a lateralized lesion, it is a good testing practice for the examiner to position himself either across from the patient or to the side least likely to be affected. The examiner must take care that the patient can see all of the visually presented material and the examiner should speak to the ear on the side of the lesion. Patients with right-sided lesions, in particular, may have reduced awareness of stimuli in the left half of space (see pp. 72–73) so that all material must be presented to their right side. Use of vertical arrays for presenting visual stimuli to these patients should be considered (see p. 343).

A visual problem that can occur after a head injury, stroke, or other abrupt insult to the brain, or that may be symptomatic of a degenerative disease of the central nervous system, is eye muscle imbalance resulting in double vision (*diplopia*). The patient may not see double at all angles or in all areas of the visual field. He may experience only slight discomfort or confusion when his head is tilted a certain way, or the diplopia may compromise his ability to read, write, draw, or solve intricate visual puzzles altogether. Young, well-motivated patients with diplopia frequently learn to suppress one set of images and, within one to three years, become relatively untroubled by the problem. Other patients report that they have been handicapped for years by what may appear on examination to be a minor disability. Should the patient complain of diplopia, the examiner may want a neurological or ophthalmological opinion on the actual extent of the problem before determining whether he can proceed with tests requiring visual acuity. He will also want to take into account the patient's attitude toward being examined, toward expending effort, and toward rehabilitation when making his determination.

MOTOR DEFICITS

Motor deficits do not present as great an obstacle to standardized and comprehensive testing as sensory deficits since most all but constructional abilities can be examined when a patient is unable to use either hand. Many brain injured patients with lateralized lesions will have use of only one hand and that may not be the preferred hand. One-handed performances on construction or drawing tests tend to be a little slowed, particularly when performed by the nonpreferred hand (Briggs, 1960). However, neurologically intact subjects using the nonpreferred hand in drawing tasks tend to make no more errors than with the preferred hand, although left-handed distortion errors are notably greater than those made by the right hand (Dee and Fontenot, 1969).

DISTRACTIBILITY

A common concomitant of brain damage is distractibility; the patient has difficulty shutting out or ignoring extraneous stimulation, be it noise outside the testing room, test material scattered on the examination table, or a brightly colored tie or flashy earrings on the examiner (Lezak, 1978b). This difficulty may exacerbate problems in attention and concentration, interfere with learning, and increase the likelihood of fatigue and frustration. The examiner may not realize how his clothing or the location of the examining room or its furnishings are adding to the patient's difficulties, for the normal person screens out extraneous stimuli so automatically that most people are unaware that this problem exists for others.

To reduce the likelihood of interference from unnecessary distractions, the examination should be conducted in what is sometimes referred to as a *sterile environment*. The examining room should be relatively soundproof and decorated in quiet colors, with no bright or distracting objects in sight. The examiner's clothing too can be an unwitting source of distraction. Drab colors and quiet patterns or a lab coat are recommended apparel for testing.

The examining table should be kept bare except for materials needed for the test at hand. When one test is completed, the materials should be cleared away and placed out of the patient's sight before the next materials are brought out. Clocks and ticking sounds can be bothersome. Clocks should be quiet and out of sight, even when test instructions include references to timing. A wall or desk clock with an easily readable second indicator, placed out of the patient's line of sight, is an excellent substitute for a stopwatch and frees the examiner's hands for note taking and manipulation of test materials.

An efficient way to use a watch or regular clock for unobtrusive timing is to pay attention only to the second marker, noting in seconds the times at which a task was begun and completed. Minutes are marked with a slash. Total time is then 60 seconds for each slash, plus the number of seconds between the two times. For example, $53 // 18 = ([60 - 53] + 18) + 120 = 145$ seconds. The examiner can count times under 30 seconds with a fair degree of of accuracy by making a dot on the answer sheet every 5 seconds.

FATIGUE

Brain damaged patients tend to fatigue easily, particularly when the condition is of relatively recent onset (Lezak, 1978b). Easy fatigability can also be a chronic problem, and many brain damaged persons are fatigued most of the time. Once fatigued, they take longer to recuperate than do normal persons.

Many patients will tell the examiner when they are tired, but others may not be aware themselves, or they may be unwilling to admit fatigue. Therefore, the examiner must be alert to such signs as slurring of speech, an increased droop on the paralyzed side of the patient's face, motor slowing, or restlessness.

Brain damaged patients, particularly those whose condition is of recent origin, are most apt to be rested and energized in the early morning and will perform at their best at this time. Even the seemingly restful interlude of lunch may require considerable effort of the patient and fatigue him. Physical or occupational therapy is exhausting for many patients. Therefore, in arranging test time, the patient's daily activity must be considered if the effects of fatigue are to be kept minimal. When necessary, the examiner may insist that the patient take a nap before being tested. If the patient must be examined late in the day, in addition to requesting that he rest beforehand, the examiner should recommend that he also have a snack.

MOTIVATIONAL DEFECTS

A not uncommon characteristic of brain damaged patients, particularly those with damage to the limbic system or prefrontal areas, is loss of motivation. This condition often reflects the patient's inability to formulate meaningful goals or to initiate and carry out plans. Behaviorally, motivational defects appear as more or less pervasive and crippling apathy (Lezak, in press; Walsh, 1978b). Because of their general lack of involvement and what Lishman (1973) calls "sluggishness," they may perform significantly below their capacities unless cajoled or goaded or somehow stimulated to perform.

DEPRESSION AND FRUSTRATION

Depression and frustration are often intimately related to fatigue in brain damaged patients, and the pernicious interplay between them can seriously compromise the patient's performance (Lezak, 1978b). The patient who fatigues easily rarely performs well and may experience even relatively intact functions as more impaired than they actually are. He stumbles more when walking, speaking, and thinking and is more frustrated, which in turn drains his energies and increases his fatigue. This results in a greater likelihood of failure and leads to more frustration and eventual despair. Repeated failure in exercising previously accomplished skills, difficulty in solving once easy problems, and the need for effort to coordinate previously automatic responses further contribute to the depression that commonly accompanies brain damage, particularly in the first year. After a while, the patient may give up trying. Such discouragement will usually carry over into a patient's test performance and may obscure his intellectual strengths from himself as well as his examiner.

When examining a brain damaged patient, it is important to deal with the problems of motivation and depression. Encouragement is useful. The examiner can deliberately ensure that the patient will have some success, no matter how extensive his impairments. Frequently the neuropsychologist may be the first person to help the patient share his feelings and particularly to reassure him that his depression is natural and common to people with his condition and that it will probably dissipate in time. Many patients experience a great deal of relief and even some lifting of their depression by this kind of informational reassurance.

When a patient is depressed, it is important for the examiner to form a clear picture of his state at the time of testing. If the examiner cannot allay his patient's depression or engage his interested cooperation, then he not only must report this but he must take these problems into account in interpreting the test protocol.

Constructive Assessment

Every psychological examination can be a personally useful experience for the patient. Each patient should leave the examination feeling he gained something for his efforts, whether it was an increased sense of dignity or self-worth, insight into his behavior, or constructive appreciation of his problems or limitations.

When the patient feels better at the end of the examination than he did at the beginning, the examiner knows that he has probably helped him to perform at his best. When the patient understands himself better at the end of the examination than he did at the beginning, the examiner knows he conducted the examination in a spirit of mutual cooperation and treated the patient as a reasoning, responsible individual. It is a truism that good psychological treatment requires continuing assessment. By the same token, good assessment will also contribute to the patient's psychological well-being.

6

The Neuropsychological
Examination: Interpretation

The Nature of Psychological Examination Data

The basic data of psychological examinations, like any other psychological data, are
behavioral observations. In order to have a broad and meaningful sample of the
patient's behavior from which to draw diagnostic inferences or conclusions relevant
to patient care and planning, the psychological examiner needs to have made or
obtained reports of many different kinds of observations, including historical and
demographic information (see pp. 92, 94–96).

The Different Kinds of Examination Data

Background Data

Background data are essential for providing the context in which current observations
can be best understood. In most instances, accurate interpretation of the patient's
examination behavior and test responses requires at least some knowledge of the
patient's developmental and medical history, family background, educational and
occupational accomplishments (or failures), and his current living situation and level
of social functioning (see pp. 102–105). The examiner must take into account sensory
and motor defects when evaluating test performances (G. Goldstein, 1974). An appreciation of the patient's current medical and neurological status can guide the examiner's search for a pattern of neuropsychological deficits.

The importance of background information in interpreting examination observations is obvious when evaluating a test score on school-related skills such as arithmetic
and spelling, or in the light of a vocational history that implies a particular performance level (e.g., a journeyman millwright must be of at least *average* ability but is
more likely to achieve *high average* or even better scores on many tests; to succeed
as an executive chef requires at least *high average* ability but, again, many would
perform at a *superior* level on cognitive tests). However, the importance of such back-

ground variables as age or education has not always been appreciated in the interpretation of many different kinds of tests, including those purporting to measure neuropsychological integrity.

A 54-year-old housewife with a history of very heavy alcoholic intake pled not guilty by reason of mental defect to a charge of murdering her husband with a shotgun. Her attorney bolstered this claim with a psychologist's report that stated that her scores of 58 on the Halstead Category Test (see p. 480f.), 22.5′ Total Time on the Tactual Performance Test (pp. 459–462), 41 for each hand on the Finger Tapping Test (p. 529), and 51″ and 98″ for forms A and B, respectively, of the Trail Making Test (556-559) were all within the "Brain-damaged Range." The psychologist had used Halstead's (1947) norms, based on a young (mean age = 28.3) sample in evaluating her performances on the first three tests (see p. 142), and army norms, also based on a relatively young sample, for drawing conclusions about her Trail Making Test performance. He did note that her scores on cognitive ability tests, which take age into account, and on the Wechsler Memory Scale (pp. 463–466) were all *average* or better. On the basis of her scores on the tests in the neuropsychological battery, the psychologist concluded that the patient suffered "chronic, alcohol induced brain pathology . . . akin to . . . *senility*." However, when the scores from the neuropsychological test battery were reevaluated on the basis of age norms (Davies, 1968; Lewinsohn, 1973), all of the scores given above were within normal limits excepting Trail Making A, which was between the 20th and 25th percentile, just below the *average* score range. Using this reinterpretation of the test data, the court rejected her not guilty plea and convicted her of manslaughter.

BEHAVIORAL OBSERVATIONS

Naturalistic observations can provide extremely useful information about how the patient functions outside the formalized, usually highly structured, and possibly intimidating examination setting. Psychological examiners rarely study patients in their everyday setting, but reports from nursing personnel or family members may help set the stage for evaluating examination data, or at least raise questions about what the examiner observes or should look for.

The value of naturalistic observations may be most evident when formal examination findings alone would lead to conclusions that the patient is more or less capable than he actually is. Such an error is most likely to occur when the examiner confounds observed *performance* with *ability*, what Tryon (1979) calls the "test-trait fallacy." For example, most people who survive even quite severe head trauma in motor vehicle accidents, by the second year after the accident achieve scores that are within or close to the *average* ability range on most tests of cognitive functions (Levin, Grossman et al., 1979; Naquet et al., 1970; K. O'Brien and Lezak, 1981). Yet, by some counts, as few as 30% of them hold jobs in the competitive market as so many are troubled by problems of attention, temperament, and self-control (Lezak, 1982a; Najenson, 1980). The behavioral characteristics that compromise their adequate and sometimes even excellent cognitive skills are not elicited in the usual neuropsychiatric or neuropsychological examination. However, they become painfully apparent to anyone who is with the patient as he goes about his usual activities—or, in many cases, inactivities. In contrast, there is the shy, anxious, or suspicious patient who responds only minimally to a white-coated examiner but whose everyday behavior is far superior to anything the examiner sees.

How the patient conducts himself in the course of the examination is another source of useful information. It needs to be documented and evaluated as his attitudes toward the examination, his conversation or silence, the appropriateness of his demeanor and social responses, can tell a lot about his neuropsychological status as well as enrich the context in which his responses to the examination proper will be evaluated.

TEST DATA

Testing differs from these other forms of psychological data gathering in that it elicits behavior samples in a standardized, replicable, and more or less artifical and restrictive situation. Its strengths lie in the approximate sameness of the test situation for each subject, for it is the sameness that enables the examiner to compare behavior samples between individuals, over time, or with expected performance levels. Its weaknesses too lie in this sameness, in that psychological test observations are limited to the behaviors occasioned by the test situation. They rarely include observations of patients in more familiar settings engaging in their usual activities.

To apply examination findings to the problems that have brought the patient to him, the psychological examiner extrapolates from a limited set of observations to the patient's behavior in real life situations. Extrapolation from the data is a common feature of other kinds of psychological data handling as well, since it is rarely possible to observe a human subject in every problem area. Extrapolations are likely to be as accurate as the observations on which they are based are pertinent and precise, as the situations are similar, and as the generalizations are apt.

> A 48-year-old advertising manager with originally *superior* intellectual abilities sustained a right hemisphere stroke with minimal sensory or motor deficits. He was examined at the request of his company when he wanted to return to work. His verbal skills in general were *high average* to *superior,* but he was unable to construct two-dimensional geometric designs with colored blocks, put together cut-up picture puzzles, or draw a house or person with proper proportions. The neuropsychologist did not observe the patient on the job but, generalizing from these samples, she concluded that the visual-perceptual distortions and misjudgments demonstrated on the test would be of a similar kind and occur to a similar extent with layout and design material. The patient was advised against retaining responsibility for the work of the display section of his department. Later conferences with the patient's employers confirmed that he was no longer able to evaluate or supervise the display operations.

130

Quantitative and Qualitative Data

Every psychological observation can be expressed either numerically as quantitative data or descriptively as qualitative data. Each of these classes of data can constitute a self-sufficient data base as demonstrated by two different approaches to neuropsychological assessment. An actuarial approach developed by Ralph Reitan (undated; Reitan and Davison, 1974) and elaborated by others (e.g., K. M. Adams et al., 1975; E. W. Russell et al., 1970; Swiercinsky, 1978) exemplifies the quantitative method. It relies on scores, derived indices, and score relationships for diagnostic predictions. Practitioners using this approach may have a technician examine the patient so that, except for an introductory or closing interview, their data base is exclusively in numerical, often computer-processed, form. At the other extreme is a clinical approach built upon richly detailed observations without objective standardization (Christensen, 1979; Luria, 1966, 1973). The clinician documents his observations in careful detail, much as a neurologist or psychiatrist describes what he observes. Both approaches have contributed significantly to the development of contemporary neuropsychology. However, to do justice to the complexity, variability, and subtleties of patient behavior, the neuropsychological examiner needs to consider quantitative and qualitative data together.

QUANTITATIVE DATA

Scores are summary statements about the observed behavior. Scores may be obtained for any set of behavior samples that can be categorized according to some principle. For example, Golden (1981) put into a highly structured format the examination material developed by Christensen to facilitate mastery of Luria's very sensitive qualitative approach. By categorizing responses and assigning numerical scaled values to the categories, he made a score-based actuarial system using material designed for a hypothesis-testing clinical approach. Ideally, the scorer evaluates each behavior sample to see how well it fits a predetermined category and then gives it a place on a numerical scale (Cronbach, 1970).

The most commonly used scale for individual test items has two points, one for "good" or "pass" and the other for "poor" or "fail." Three-point scales, which add a middle grade of "fair" or "barely pass," are often used for grading intellectual test items. Few scales contain more than five to seven scoring levels because the gradations become so fine as to be confusing to the scorer and meaningless for interpretation.

Scored tests with more than one item produce a summary score that is usually the simple sum of the scores for all the individual items. Occasionally, test-makers incorporate a correction for guessing into their scoring systems so that the final score is not just a simple summation.

Thus, a final test score contains at least two sources of inaccuracy. It represents only one narrowly defined aspect of a set of behavior samples, and it is two or more steps removed from the original behavior. "Global," "aggregate," or "full scale" scores calculated by summing or averaging a set of subtest scores are three to four steps removed from the behavior they represent. Index scores based on subtest scores that have had their normal range restricted to just two points representing either pass or fail, or "within normal limits" or "brain damaged," are also many steps removed from the original observations.

The inclusion of test scores in the psychological data base satisfies the need for objective, readily replicable data cast in a form that permits reliable interpretation and meaningful comparisons. By using standard scoring systems, the examiner can reduce a vast array of different behaviors to a single numerical system. This enables him to compare the score of any one test performance of a patient with all other scores of that patient or of any other person.

Completely different behaviors, such as writing skills and visual reaction time, can be compared on a single numerical scale: one person might receive a high score for elegant penmanship but a low one on speed of response to a visual signal; another might be high on both kinds of tasks or low on both. Considering one behavior at a time, a scoring system permits direct comparisons between the handwriting of a 60-year-old stroke patient and that of school children at various grade levels, or between the patient's visual reaction time and that of other stroke patients of the same age.

PROBLEMS IN THE EVALUATION OF QUANTITATIVE DATA

"To reason—or do research—only in terms of scores and score-patterns is to do violence to the nature of the raw material." Roy Schafer (1948)

When interpreting test scores, it is important to keep in mind their artificial and abstract nature. Some examiners come to equate a score with the behavior it is supposed to represent. Others prize standardized, replicable test scores as "harder," more "scientific" data at the expense of unquantified observations. Reification of test scores can lead the examiner to overlook or discount direct observations. A test-score approach to psychological assessment that minimizes the importance of qualitative data can result in serious distortions in the interpretations, conclusions, and recommendations drawn from such a one-sided data base.

To be neuropsychologically meaningful, a test score should represent as few kinds of behavior or dimensions of intellectual functions as possible. The simpler the test task, the clearer the meaning of scored evaluations of the behavior elicited by that task. Correspondingly, it is difficult to know just what functions contribute to a score obtained on a complex, multidimensional test task. If the test score is overinclusive, as in the case of summed or averaged test battery scores, it becomes virtually impossible to know just what behavioral or intellectual characteristics it stands for. Its usefulness for highlighting differences in ability and skill levels is nullified, for the patient's behavior is hidden behind a hodgepodge of intellectual functions and statistical operations (Butler et al., 1963; A. Smith, 1966b).

Further, the range of observations an examiner can make is restricted by the test.

This is particularly the case with paper and pencil tests and those that restrict the patient's responses to button pushing or other mechanized activity that limits the patient's opportunities for self-expression. Typically, a busy examiner does not stay to observe the cooperative, comprehending, or docile patient manipulating buttons or levers or taking a paper and pencil test. Multiple-choice and automated tests offer no behavior alternatives beyond the prescribed set of responses. Qualitative differences in these test performances are recorded only when there are frank aberrations in test-taking behavior, such as qualifying statements written on an MMPI answer sheet, or more than one alternative marked on a single-answer multiple-choice test. For most paper and pencil or automated tests, *how* the patient solves the problem or goes about answering the question remains unknown or is, at best, a matter of conjecture based on such relatively insubstantial information as heaviness or neatness of pencil marks, test-taking errors, patterns of nonresponse, erasures, and the occasional pencil-sketched spelling tryouts, mathematical equations, or arithmetic computations in the margin.

In addition, the fine-grained scaling provided by the most sophisticated instruments for measuring cognitive competence is not suited to the assessment of many of the behavioral symptoms of cerebral neuropathology. Defects in behaviors that have what I call "species-wide" norms (see pp. 88–89), i.e., that occur at a developmentally early stage and are performed effectively by all but the most severely impaired school-age children, such as speech and dressing, are usually readily apparent. Quantitative norms generally do not enhance the observer's sensitivity to these problems. Using a finely scaled vocabulary test to examine an aphasic patient, for example, is like trying to discover the shape of a flower with a microscope: the examiner will simply miss the point. Moreover, in many of these cases the behavioral aberration is so highly individualized and specific to the associated lesion that its distribution in the population at large, or even in the brain damaged population, does not lend itself to actuarial prediction techniques.

The evaluation of test scores in the context of direct observations is essential when doing neuropsychological assessment. For many brain damaged patients, test scores alone give relatively little information about the patient's functioning. The meat of the matter is often *how* a patient solves a problem or approaches a task rather than what his score is. "There are many reasons for failing and there are many ways you can go about it. And if you don't know in fact which way the patient was going about it, failure doesn't tell you very much" (K. W. Walsh, 1978a). There can also be more than one way to pass a test.

A 54-year-old sales manager sustained a right frontal lobe injury when he fell as a result of a heart attack with several moments of cardiac arrest. On the Hooper Visual Organization Test (see pp. 357–358), he achieved a score of 26 out of a possible 30, well within the "normal" range. However, not only did his errors reflect perceptual fragmentation (e.g., he called a cut-up broom a "long candle in holder") but his correct responses were also fragmented (e.g., "Wrist and hand and fingers" instead of the usual response, "hand"; "Ball stitched and cut" instead of "baseball").

133

Furthermore, two patients who achieve the same score on the Arithmetic subtest of the WAIS may have very different problems and abilities with respect to arithmetic. One patient performs the easy, single operation problems quickly and correctly, but fails the more difficult items requiring two operations or more for solution because of an inability to retain and juggle so much at once in his immediate memory. The other patient has no difficulty remembering item content. He answers many of the simpler items correctly but very slowly, counting aloud on his fingers. He is unable to conceptualize or perform the operations on the more difficult items. The numerical score masks the disparate performances of these patients.

QUALITATIVE DATA

Qualitative data are direct observations. In the formal neuropsychological examination these include observations of the patient's *test-taking* behavior as well as test behavior per se. Observations of the patient's appearance, his verbalizations, gestures, tone of voice, mood and affect, personal concerns, habits, and idiosyncrasies can provide a great deal of information about his life situation and overall adjustment, as well as his attitude toward the examination and his condition (see pp. 105–107). More specific to the test situation are observations of the patient's reactions to the examination itself, his approach to different kinds of test problems, and his expressions of feelings and opinions about his performance. Observations of the manner in which the patient handles test material, the wording of his test responses, the nature and consistency of his errors and his successes, fluctuations in attention and perseverance, his emotional state, and the quality of his performance from moment to moment as he interacts with the examiner and with the different kinds of test material are the qualitative data of the test performance itself.

LIMITATIONS OF QUALITATIVE DATA

Distortion or misinterpretation of information obtained by direct observation results from different kinds of methodological and examination problems. All of the standardization, reliability, and validity problems inherent in the collection and evaluation of data by a single observer are ever-present threats to objectivity (Bolgar, 1965; Sundberg, 1977). In neuropsychological assessment, the vagaries of neurological impairment compound these problems. When the patient's communication skills are questionable, the examiner can never be certain that he understood his transactions with the patient. Worse yet, the communication disability may be so subtle and well masked by the patient that the examiner is not aware of communication slips. There is a more than ordinary likelihood that the patient's actions will be idiosyncratic and therefore unfamiliar and subject to misunderstanding. Also, the patient may be entirely or variably uncooperative, sometimes quite unintentionally.

Moreover, when the neurological insult does not produce specific defects but rather reduces efficiency in the performance of behaviors that tend to be normally distributed among adults, such as response slowing, recall of words or designs, ability to abstract and generalize, most examiners, especially the young and inexperienced, benefit from scaled tests with standardized norms. The early behavioral evidence of a deteriorating disease and much of the behavioral expression of traumatic brain injury or little strokes can occur as a quantifiable diminution in the efficiency of the affected system(s) rather than as a qualitative distortion of the normal response. This can be the case with conditions of rapid onset, such as trauma, stroke, or certain infections, particularly after the acute stages have passed and the first vivid and highly specific symptoms have dissipated. In many such cases I have found it difficult or impossible to appreciate the nature or extent of cognitive impairment without recourse to quantifiable examination techniques that permit a relatively objective comparison between different functions.

It is true that as clinicians gain experience with many patients from different backgrounds, representing a wide range of abilities, and suffering from a variety of cerebral insults, they are increasingly able to estimate or at least anticipate the subtle deficits that show up as lowered scores on tests. This sharpening of observational talents may be attributed to the development of internal norms based on clinical experience accumulated over the years (K. M. Adams and Rennick, 1978).

INTEGRATED DATA

The integrated use of qualitative and quantitative examination data treats these two different kinds of information as different parts of the whole data base. Test scores that have been interpreted without reference to the context of the examination in which they were obtained may be objective but meaningless in their individual applications. Clinical observations unsupported by standardized and quantifiable testing, although full of import for the individual, lack the comparability necessary for many diagnostic and planning decisions. Descriptive observations flesh out the skeletal structure of numerical test scores. Each is incomplete without the other.

Evaluation of Neuropsychological Examination Data

Qualitative Aspects of Examination Behavior

Two kinds of behavior are of special interest to the neuropsychological examiner when evaluating the qualitative aspects of a patient's behavior during the examination. One, of course, is behavior that differs from normal expectations or customary activity for the circumstances. Responding to Block Design instructions (see pp. 277f.) by matter of factly setting the blocks on the stimulus cards is obviously an aberrant response that deserves more attention than a score of zero alone would indicate. Satisfaction with a blatantly distorted response, or tears and agitation when finding some test items difficult also should elicit the examiner's interest, as should statements of displeasure with a mistake unaccompanied by any attempt to correct it. Each of these behavioral aberrations may arise for any number of reasons. However, each is most likely to occur in association with certain neurological conditions and thus can also alert the knowledgeable examiner to look for other evidence of the suspected condition.

Setting blocks on the stimulus cards usually indicates relatively severe frontal lobe pathology, such as that which can occur with very severe trauma or advanced pre-senile dementia of the Alzheimer's type (PSDA). The inappropriately pleased patient may have suffered prefrontal damage, most likely involving the right frontal lobe, or he could have fairly extensive right posterior damage from a stroke or tumor. Tears and agitation in the face of a difficult task suggest a catastrophic reaction, which is most likely to accompany left hemisphere disease (see p. 61). Patients who may correctly evaluate their performance errors but do nothing to rectify them are usually displaying the behavioral discontinuities characteristic of prefrontal damage.

Regardless of their possible diagnostic usefulness, each of these aberrant responses also affords the examiner a sample of behavior which, if characteristic, tells a lot about how the patient thinks and how he perceives himself, the world, and its expectations of him. The patient who sets blocks on the card not only has not comprehended the instructions, but also is not aware of this failure as he proceeds—unself-consciously?—with this display of very concrete, structure-dependent behavior. The patient who expresses pleasure over an incorrect response is also unaware of his failure but, along with a distorted perception of the task, his product, or both, he demonstrates self-awareness and some sense of a scheme of things or set of self-expectations that his performance satisfied. And so on.

The second kind of qualitatively interesting behaviors deserves special attention whether or not they are aberrant. Gratuitous responses are the comments patients make about their test performance or while they are taking the test, or the elaborations beyond the necessary requirements of a task that may enrich or distort their drawings, stories, or problem solutions, and usually individualize them. The value of gratuitous responses is well recognized in the interpretation of projective test material, for it is the gratuitously added adjectives, adverbs, or action verbs, flights of fancy whether verbal or graphic, spontaneously introduced characters, objects, or situations, that reflect the patient's mood and betray his preoccupations. Gratuitous responses are of similar value in neuropsychological assessment. The unnecessarily detailed spokes and gears of a bike with no pedals (see Fig. 6-1) tell of the patient's involvement with details at the expense of practical considerations. Expressions of self-doubt or self-criticism repeatedly voiced during a mental examination may reflect perplexity or depression and raise the possibility that the patient is not performing as well as he might (Lezak, 1978b).

In addition, patient responses gained by testing the limits or using the standard test material in an innovative manner to explore one or another working hypothesis have to be evaluated qualitatively. For example, should the examiner ask the patient to recall a set of designs ordinarily presented as a copy task (e.g., Wepman's variations of the Bender-Gestalt Test, see p. 388), he will look for systematically occurring distortions—in size, angulation, simplifications, perseverations—which, if they did not

136

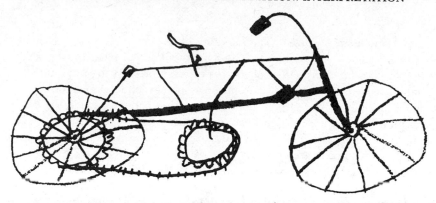

Fig. 6-1. This bicycle was drawn by a 61-year-old retired millwright with a high school education. Two years prior to the neuropsychological examination he had suffered a stroke involving the right parietal lobe. He displayed no obvious sensory or motor deficits, and was articulate, alert, and cheerful but so garrulous that his talking could be interrupted only with difficulty. His highest WAIS scores, Picture Completion and Picture Arrangement, were in the *high average* ability range.

occur on the copy trial, may shed some light on the patient's visual memory problems. As the examiner looks for systematic deviations in these and other drawing characteristics that may reflect dysfunction of one or more behavioral systems (see Hutt, 1977, and pp. 389–391), he also analyzes the patient's stories and comments for such qualities as disjunctive thinking, appropriateness of vocabulary, simplicity or complexity of grammatical constructions, richness or paucity of descriptions, etc. (For an example of a carefully thought-out, comprehensive, and practical system that was developed for evaluating narrative responses to pictures but can be applied to many other aspects of verbal performance as well, see W. E. Henry's 1947 monograph on the Thematic Apperception Technique.)

Test Scores

Test scores can be expressed in a variety of forms. Rarely does a test-maker use a *raw score*—the simple sum of correct answers or correct answers minus a portion of the incorrect ones—for in itself a raw score communicates nothing about its relative value. Instead, test-makers generally report scores as values of a scale based on the raw scores made by a *standardization population* (the group of individuals tested for the purpose of obtaining normative data on the test). Each score then becomes a statement of its value relative to all other scores on that scale. Different kinds of scales provide more or less readily comprehended and statistically well-defined standards for comparing any one score with the scores of the standardization population. The most widely used scale is based on the *standard score*.

STANDARD SCORES

The need for standard scores.   The handling of test scores in neuropsychological assessment is often a more complex task than in other kinds of intellectual evaluations because there can be many different sources of test scores. In the usual intellectual examination, generally conducted for purposes of academic evaluation or career counseling, the bulk of the testing is done with one test battery, such as the WAIS or the California Test of Mental Maturity. Within such a battery, the scores for each of the subtests are on the same scale and standardized on the same population so that subtest scores can be compared directly.

On the other hand, there is no single test battery that provides all the information needed to adequately assess most patients presenting neuropsychological questions. Techniques employed in the assessment of different aspects of intellectual functioning have been developed at different times, in different places, on different populations, for different ability and maturity levels, with different scoring and classification systems, and for different purposes. Taken together, they are an unsystematized aggregate of more or less standardized tests, experimental techniques, and observational aids that have proven useful in demonstrating the loss or disturbance of some intellectual function or activity. Their scores are not directly comparable with one another.

To make the comparisons necessary for evaluating impairment, the many disparate test scores must be convertible into one scale with identical units. Such a scale can serve as a kind of test users' *lingua franca*, permitting direct comparisons between many different kinds of measurements. The scale that is most meaningful statistically and that probably serves the intermediary function between different tests best is one derived from the normal probability curve and based on the standard deviation unit (Anastasi, 1982; Lyman, 1963) (see Fig. 6-2).

The value of basing a common scale on the standard deviation unit lies primarily in the statistical nature of the standard deviation (s) as a measure of the spread or dispersion of a set of scores (X_1, X_2, X_3, etc.) around their mean ($\overline{X}$). Standard deviations units describe known proportions of the normal probability curve (see Fig. 6-2, "Percent of cases under portions of the normal curve"). This has very practical applications for comparing and evaluating psychological data in that the position of any test score on a standard deviation unit scale, in itself, defines the proportion of people taking the test who will obtain scores above and below the given score. Virtually all scaled psychological test data can be converted to standard deviation units for inter-test comparisons. Furthermore, a score based on the standard deviation, a *standard score*, can generally be estimated from a percentile, which is the most commonly used nonstandard score in adult testing.

The likelihood that two numerically different scores are significantly different can also be estimated from their relative positions on a standard deviation unit scale. This use of the standard deviation unit scale is of particular importance in neuropsychological testing, for evaluation of test scores depends upon the significance of their distance from one another or from the comparison standard. Since direct statistical

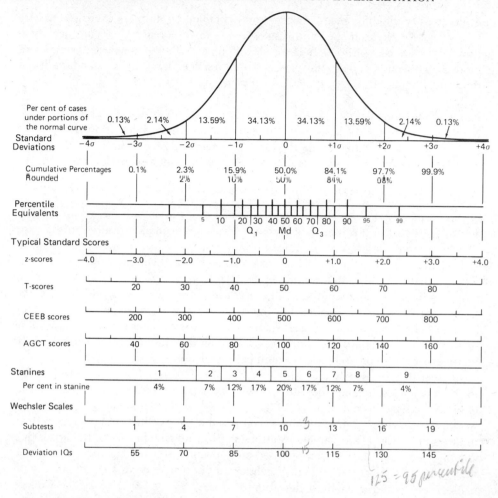

NOTE: This chart cannot be used to equate scores on one test to scores on another test. For example, both 600 on the CEEB and 120 on the AGCT are one standard deviation above their respective means, but they do not represent "equal" standings because the scores were obtained from different groups.

Fig. 6-2. The relationship of the most commonly used test scores to the normal curve and to one another. (Reprinted from the *Test Service Bulletin* of The Psychological Corporation, No. 48, 1955.)

evaluations of the difference between scores obtained on different kinds of tests are rarely possible, the examiner must use estimates of the ranges of significance levels based on score comparisons. In general, differences of two standard deviations or more may be considered significant, whereas differences of one to two standard deviations suggest a trend (Field, 1960; R. W. Payne and Jones, 1957).

Kinds of standard scores. There are a variety of standard scores that are all translations of the same scale, based on the mean and the standard deviation. The *z-score* is the basic, unelaborated standard score from which all others can be derived. The z-score represents, in standard deviation units, the amount a score deviates from the mean of the population from which the score is drawn $\left(z = \dfrac{X - \overline{X}}{s} \right)$. The mean of the normal curve is set at zero and the standard deviation unit has a value of one. Scores are stated in terms of their distance from the mean as measured in standard deviation units. Scores above the mean have a positive value; those below the mean are negative. Neuropsychological test data can be handled very appropriately in a z-score format (e.g., Birri and Perret, 1980).

Elaborations of the z-score are called *derived scores*. Derived scores provide the same information as do z-scores, but the score value is expressed in scale units that are more familiar to some test users than z-scores. A test-maker can assign any value he wishes to the standard deviation and mean of his distribution of test scores. Usually he follows convention and chooses commonly used values.

Among the most widely used derived scores are *T-scores*, which are very popular in educational testing and paper and pencil personality tests. The *T-score* has a mean of 50 and a standard deviation of 10 (i.e., $T = 50 + 10z$). Some neuropsychologists working with scores from test batteries composed of many different tests report their findings in *T*-scores (Kiernan and Matthews, 1976; Lewinsohn, 1973; Reitan, 1964). Another popular standard score is based on a mean of 100 and a standard deviation unit of 15 (i.e., $SS = 100 + 15z$). Wechsler subtest scaled scores are computed with a mean of 10 and a standard deviation of 3 (i.e., $SS_w = 10 + 3z$). The College Entrance Examination Board uses a mean of 500 and 100 as the standard deviation size for their Scholastic Aptitude Tests (i.e., $CEEB = 500 + 100z$). Still other test means and standard deviations are set at other values. When their standardization populations are similar, all of these different scores are directly comparable with one another, the standard deviation and its relationship to the normal curve serving as the key to translation (see Table 6-1).

Estimating standard scores from nonstandard scores. Since most published standardized tests today use a standard score format for handling the numerical test data, their scores present little or no problem to the examiner wishing to make intertest comparisons. However, there are still a few test-makers who report their standardization data in percentile or IQ score equivalents. In these cases, standard score approximations can be estimated.

Unless there is reason to believe that the standardization population is not normally

140

Table 6-1   Comparisons of Common Scoring Systems in Terms of Given z-score Values

When the z-score $\left(\dfrac{X - \overline{X}}{s}\right)$ =	−0.60	+0.80	+2.10
the T-score (50 + 10z) =	44	58	71
SS (100 + 15z) =	91.0	112.0	131.5
SS_w (10 + 3z =	8.0	12.4	16.3
CEEB (500 + 100 z) =	440	580	710
and the percentile =	27.4	78.8	98.2

distributed, a standard score equivalent for a percentile score can be estimated from a table of normal curve functions. Table 6-2 gives z-score approximations, taken from a normal curve table, for 21 percentiles ranging from 1 to 99 in five-point steps. The z-score that best approximates a given percentile is that one that corresponds to the percentile closest to the percentile in question. The mean percentile score of 50 is equivalent to a z-score of zero. All z-scores for percentiles above 50 are positive; those for percentiles below 50 are negative.

IQ scores can also be converted to standard score approximations without much difficulty. This is done by using the standard deviation of the distribution of test scores to measure the distance of any score from the test mean. The size of the discrepancy between a score in IQ score units and the mean, when measured in standard deviation units, is the approximate z-score for that IQ score. Thus, if the IQ score is 123 and the standard deviation of the distribution is 16, the z-score estimate is 23/16 standard deviation units above the mean, or approximately +1.44. This kind of conversion is rarely necessary since most tests that give IQ score equivalents for their raw scores also provide tables of percentile and standard score equivalents.

EXCEPTIONS TO THE USE OF STANDARD SCORES

Standardization population differences.   In evaluating a patient's performance on a variety of tests, the examiner can only compare scores from different tests when the standardization populations of each of the tests are identical or at least reasonably

Table 6-2.   Standard Score Equivalents for 21 Percentile Scores Ranging from 1 to 99

Percentile Score	z-score	Percentile Score	z-score	Percentile Score	z-score
99	+2.33	65	+0.39	30	−0.52
95	+1.65	60	+0.25	25	−0.68
90	+1.28	55	+0.13	20	−0.84
85	+1.04	50	0	15	−1.04
80	+0.84	45	−0.13	10	−1.28
75	+0.68	40	−0.25	5	−1.65
70	+0.52	35	−0.39	1	−2.33

similar. Otherwise, even though their scales and units are statistically identical, the operational meanings of the different values are as different as the populations from which they are drawn. This restriction becomes obvious should an examiner attempt to compare a vocabulary score obtained on the Wechsler intelligence tests, which were standardized on cross sections of the general adult population, with a score on the Graduate Record Examination (GRE), standardized on college graduates. A person who receives a mean score on the GRE would probably achieve a score of one to two standard deviations above the mean on the WAIS, since the average college graduate typically scores around two standard deviations above the general population mean on tests of this type (Anastasi, 1982). Although each of these mean scores has the same z-score value, the performance levels they represent are very different.

Test-makers usually describe their standardization populations in terms of sex, race, age, or education. Intraindividual comparability of scores may differ between the sexes in that women tend to do less well on advanced arithmetic problems (Nash, 1979; Petersen and Wittig, 1979; Sherman, 1978, 1982) and visuospatial items (Dodrill, 1979; L. J. Harris, 1978; Vandenburg and Kuse, 1979). By and large, men display a verbal skill disadvantage (D. Cohen and Wilkie, 1979; McGlone, 1976; Verhoff et al., 1979). Education, too, affects level of performance on different kinds of tests differentially, making its greatest contribution to tasks involving verbal skills, stored information, and other school-related activities (see pp. 259–271 *passim*, for details regarding the relationship of education and social class to performance on subtests of the Wechsler Scales). Differential education effects have shown up only inconsistently in studies of tests designed to measure neuropsychological status (Finlayson et al., 1977; Prigatano and Parsons, 1976). No significant differences between major racial groups have been demonstrated in the score patterns of tests of various cognitive abilities or in neuropsychological functioning. Vocational and regional differences between standardization populations may also contribute to differences between test norms. However, vocational differences generally correlate highly with educational differences, and regional differences tend to be relatively insignificant compared to age and variables that are highly correlated with income level, such as education or vocation (Anastasi, 1982).

Age can be a very significant variable when evaluating test scores of older patients. Functions such as immediate memory and learning, which decline sharply with advanced age, are also extremely susceptible to the effects of organic impairment (see Chapter 8, the section on aging). In patients over 50, the normal changes with age may obscure subtle intellectual changes that could herald early, correctable stages of a tumor or vascular disease. The use of age-graded scores puts the aging patient's scoring pattern into sharper focus. Age-graded scores are important aids to differential diagnosis in patients over 50 and are essential to the evaluation of test performances of patients over 65. Although not all tests an examiner may wish to use have age-graded norms or age corrections, enough are available to determine the extent to which a patient might be exceeding the performance decrements expected at his age.

Most tests of a single intellectual function, ability, or skill do not have separate norms for age, sex, education, etc. A few widely used tests of general intellectual abilities take into account the geographic distribution of their standardization population; the rest are usually standardized on local people. Tests developed in Minnesota will have Minnesota norms; New York test-makers use a big city population; and British tests are standardized on British populations. Although this situation results in less than perfect comparability between the different tests, in most cases the examiner has no choice but to use norms of tests standardized on an undefined mixed or nonrandom adult sample. Experience quickly demonstrates that this is usually not a serious hardship, for these "mixed-bag" norms generally serve their purpose adequately. Perhaps the chief normative fault of many single-purpose tests is that they lack discriminating norms for the top 5 or 10% of the population.

Children's tests. Some children's tests are well-suited for the examination of patients with severe intellectual impairment or profound disability. There are also many good tests of academic abilities such as arithmetic, reading, and spelling that have been standardized for child or adolescent populations. The best of these invariably have standard score norms that, by and large, cannot be applied to an adult population because of the significant effect of age and education on performance differences between adults and children.

Senior high school norms are the one exception to this rule. On tests of intellectual ability that provide adult norms extending into the late teens, the population of 18 year-olds does not perform much differently than the adult population at large (Wechsler, 1955, 1981), and four years of high school is a reasonable approximation of the adult educational level. This exception makes a great number of very well-standardized and easily administered paper and pencil academic skill tests available for the examination of adults, and no scoring changes are necessary.

All other children's tests are best scored and reported in terms of mental age (MA), which is psychologically the most meaningful score derived from these tests. Most children's tests provide mental age norms or grade level norms (which readily convert into mental age). With mental age scores, the examiner can readily estimate the extent of impairment, or he can compare performances on different tests or between two or more tests administered over time, just as he does with test performances in terms of standard scores. Mental age scores are also useful for planning educational or living activity retraining programs.

A rough approximation to standard scores can be obtained for mental age scores of 5-3 (five years three months) and above by using the age 18 norms in the Conversion Tables (for converting mental age scores into standard scores) of the third revision of the Stanford-Binet Intelligence Scale (Terman and Merrill, 1973, pp. 257–335). In this test the standard score is entitled the "deviation IQ" (DIQ) and is based on a mean of 100 and a standard deviation of 16, i.e., DIQ $= 100 + 16\ z$).

As with any other score, the examiner must make appropriate allowances for normal testing error so that he does not draw unwarranted conclusions about nonsignificant differences between mental age scores. When one or more of the scores to be compared are mental age scores, he can convert the MA to a standard score by using the DIQ conversion tables as long as the mental age is 5-3 or above. Care in evaluating the discrepancy between scores is particularly important when mental age scores are used, since differences that are quite significant for children may be well within the limits of chance variation for adults. At age four years three months, for example, an MA of 5-6 converts to a DIQ of 128, and an MA of 7-0 is equivalent to a DIQ of 164. Thus, at age four years three months, this one and one-half year mental age difference can be considered significant because the discrepancy is 2.25 standard deviations. At age 18, on the other hand, an MA of 5-6 converts to a DIQ of 23, and an MA of 7-0 converts to a DIQ of 42, a difference of only 10 DIQ points or ¹⁰⁄₁₆ths of a standard deviation. Such small differences between scores are most likely due to chance.

Standard scores for mental age scores below 5-3 are not available for the 18-year-old norms. At this level, for age 18, the DIQ is 30, 4.38 standard deviations below the mean. Any adult mental age score below 5-3 can be considered significantly below any comparison standard for all but the frankly retarded.

Sometimes test norms for children's tests are given in standard scores or percentiles for each age or set of ages. The examiner can convert the score to a mental age score by finding the age at which the obtained score is closest to a score at the 50th percentile or the standard score mean (see Tables 6-3 and 6-4).

Small standardization populations. A number of interesting and potentially useful tests of specific skills and abilities have been devised for studies of particular neuropsychological problems in which the standardization groups are relatively small (often under 20) (e.g., Talland, 1965a; Tow, 1955). Standard score conversions are inappropriate if not impossible in such cases. When there is a clear relationship between the condition under study and a particular kind of performance on a given test, there is frequently a fairly clear-cut dichotomy between patient and control group scores. Any given patient's score can be evaluated in terms of how closely it compares with the score ranges of either the patient or the control group reported in the study.

On paragraph recall (Talland and Ekdahl, 1959; see p. 439, below), 22 patients with a severe memory disability (Korsakoff's psychosis) recalled an average of 3.97

Table 6-3. Sample Table of Raw Scores for Converting Raw Scores into Percentiles for an Age-related Skill Test

Ages	Percentiles				
	10	25	50	75	90
3	3	5	7	9	12
4	5	7	10	12	14
5	8	11	13	15	18
6	10	14	16	19	22

If the patient receives a score of 10, his mental age is estimated to be 4, for 10 is the middle or most typical score for that age. A patient who gets a score of 14 on the same test is in the 5- to 6-year mental age range—approximately 5-4, by interpolation.

144

Table 6-4. Sample Table of Standard Scores for Converting Raw Scores into Standard Scores for an Age-related Skill Test[a]

Raw Scores	Mental Age Scores (years)			
	3	4	5	6
8	98	83	88	82
9	101	96	91	85
10	104	100	94	89
11	106	102	97	93
12	109	105	100	96

A raw score of 10 converts to a mental age score of 4 years, for 10 is the mean score for age 4. Similarly, a patient with a raw score of 11 would receive a mental age score between 4-0 and 5–0, or approximately 4-5 by interpolation.
[a]Mean = 100; Standard Deviation = 10.

out of a possible total of 27 units, compared with 22 control subjects' average recall of 8.32 units. The difference between the means of the groups was evaluated by a t-test and found to be significant at the .01 level. Thus, should a patient's score on this test be markedly below the control group's average, a memory disability may be suspected.

Reporting Scores

The practice of reporting test performances in terms of scores can be confusing and misleading, particularly since most recipients of test reports are teachers, guidance counselors, physicians, and lawyers who lack training in the niceties of psychometrics. One important source of faulty communication is the variability in the size of assigned standard deviations. This can be seen most clearly when one compares derived scores based on a mean of 100 but with standard deviations ranging from 10 to 20 (see Table 6-5). With four different common magnitudes of the standard deviation, a score of 110 can range as widely as from the 69th to the 84th percentile. Unless the person

Table 6-5. z-score and Percentile Values of a Score of 110 on Four Tests with Means of 100 and Different Standard Deviations

	$s = 10$[a]	$s = 15$[b]	$s = 16$[c]	$s = 20$[d]
z	+1.00	+0.67	+0.62	+0.50
Percentile	84	75	73	69

Among the tests with these four standard deviations are (a) the Wide Range Achievement Test; (b) the Wechsler Intelligence Scales; (c) the Stanford-Binet (Form L-M); and (d) the General Aptitude Test Battery.

who receives the test report is statistically sophisticated and knowledgeable about the scaling idiosyncrasies of test-makers, it is unlikely that he will notice or appreciate these kinds of discrepancies.

Another difficulty in reporting scores lies in the statistically naive person's natural assumption that if one measurement is larger than another, there is a difference in the quantity of whatever is being measured. Unfortunately, few persons unschooled in statistics understand measurement error; they do not realize that two different numbers need not necessarily stand for different quantities but may be chance variations in the measurement of the same quantity. When a layman sees a report listing a WAIS Similarities score of 9 and an Arithmetic score of 11, he is likely to draw the possibly erroneous conclusion that the subject does better in mathematics than in verbal reasoning. Since most score differences of this magnitude are chance variations, it is more likely that the subject is equally capable in both areas.

Ignorance about the meaning of test scores has its gravest consequences in school testing programs in which children's test scores are reported as numerical "IQs" (B. F. Green, 1978). Teachers and school administrators who really think that a child with an "IQ" score of 108 is not as bright as one with a score of 112 treat each child accordingly. Similar ignorance can compromise a nonpsychologist's understanding of a psychological report (Wright, 1970), particularly a neuropsychological report in which conclusions often rest on proper interpretation of test score discrepancies.

Further, there has been a tendency, both within school systems and in the culture at large, to reify test scores (Tryon, 1979). In many schools, this has too often resulted in the arbitrary and rigid sorting of children into different parts of a classroom, into different ability level classes, and onto different vocational tracks. In its extreme form, reification of test scores has provided a predominant frame of reference for evaluating people generally. It is usually heard in remarks that take some real or supposed IQ score to indicate an individual's personal or social worth. "Sam couldn't have more than an 'IQ' of 80," means that the speaker thinks Sam is socially incompetent. "My Harold's IQ is 160!" is a statement of pride.

Although these numerical metaphors presumably are very meaningful for the people who use them, the meanings are not standardized or objective, nor do they bear any necessary relationship to the meaning a test-maker defines for the scores in his scoring system. Thus, the communication of numerical test scores, particularly if the test-maker has labeled them "IQ" scores, becomes a very uncertain business since the examiner has no way of knowing what kind of meaning his reader has already attached to mental test scores.

One way to avoid the many difficulties inherent in test score reporting is to write about test performances in terms of the commonly accepted classification of ability levels (Terman and Merrill, 1973; Wechsler, 1955, 1981). In the standard classification system, each ability level represents a statistically defined range of scores. Both percentile scores and standard scores can be classified in terms of ability level (see Table 6-6).

Test performances communicated in terms of ability levels have generally accepted and relatively clear meanings. Should the examiner doubt whether such classifications

THE NEUROPSYCHOLOGICAL EXAMINATION: INTERPRETATION

Table 6-6. Classification of Ability Levels

Classification	z-score	Percent Included	Lower Limit of Percentile Range
Very superior	+2.0 and above	2.2	98
Superior	+1.3 to 2.0	6.7	91
High average	+0.6 to 1.3	16.1	75
Average	±0.6	50.0	25
Low average *91-80*	−0.6 to −1.3	16.1	9
Borderline *80-70*	−1.3 to −2.0	6.7	2
Retarded *<70*	−2.0 and below	2.2	—

as *average, high average,* and so on, make sense to his reader, he can qualify them with a statement about the percentile range they represent, for the public generally understands the meaning of percentiles. For example, in reporting Wechsler intelligence test scores of 12 and 13, the examiner can say, "The patient's performance on [the particular subtests] was within the *high average* ability level, which is between the upper 75th and 85th percentiles, approximately."

This method also enables the examiner to report clusters of scores that may be one or two—or in the case of tests with fine-grained scales, several—score points apart but that probably represent a normal variation of scores around a single ability level. Thus, in dealing with the performance of a patient who receives scores of 8, 9, or 10 on each Wechsler Scale subtest involving verbal skills, the examiner reports that, "The patient's verbal skill level is *average.*" Significant performance discrepancies can also be readily noted. Should a patient achieve *average scores* on verbal tests, but *low average* to *borderline defective* scores on constructional tasks, the examiner can note both the levels of the different clusters of test scores and the fact that discrepancies between these levels approach or reach significance.

Interpreting the Examination Data

Examination data can be used for diagnostic decision-making, treatment, and planning purposes in several ways. *Screening techniques* are used to determine whether an organic defect is likely to be present. A *pattern approach* to test score analysis can provide diagnostically useful information as well as greater efficacy than simple screening techniques in identifying organically impaired persons. *Integrated interpretation* takes into account test signs of brain damage and test score patterns in conjunction with the qualitative aspects of the examination. Each of these approaches will be discussed below.

Screening Techniques

Different screening techniques make use of different kinds of behavioral manifestations of brain damage. Some patients suffer only a single highly specific defect or a

147

cluster of related disabilities while the greater part of their intellect remains intact. Others sustain widespread impairment involving changes in cognitive, self-regulating, and executive functions, attention, and personality. Still others display aberrations characteristic of brain damage (*signs*) with more or less subtle evidence of intellectual or emotional deficits. Thus, brain damaged patients can be identified on screening tests in terms of a particular defect or set of associated defects, or general impairment, or characteristic signs of organicity.

The accuracy of screening tests varies in a somewhat direct relationship to the narrowness of range or specificity of the behaviors assessed by them. As a rule, the specific cognitive defects associated with neurological disorders affect a relatively small proportion of the brain damaged population as a whole, and virtually no one whose higher brain functions are intact. For instance, *perseveration* (the continuation of a response after it is no longer appropriate, as in writing three or four "e's" in a word such as "deep" or "seen," or copying a 12-dot line without regard for the number, stopping only when the edge of the page is reached) is so strongly associated with brain damage that the examiner should suspect brain damage on the basis of this defect alone. However, since most brain damaged patients do not give perseverative responses, it is not a useful criterion for screening purposes. Use of a highly specific symptom such as perseveration as a screening criterion for brain damage results in few persons without brain damage misidentified as brain damaged (*false positive* errors), but such a narrow test of brain damage will let many persons who are brain damaged slip through the screen (*false negative* errors) (Ehrfurth and Lezak, 1982).

On the other hand, those defects that affect intellectual functioning generally, such as distractibility, impaired immediate memory, and concrete thinking, are not only very common symptoms of brain damage but tend to accompany a number of emotional disorders as well. As a result, a screening test that uses a defect impairing intellectual functioning generally will identify many brain damaged patients correctly with few false negative errors, but a large number of psychiatric patients will also be included as a result of false positive errors of identification.

Limitations in predictive accuracy do not invalidate either tests for specific signs or tests that are sensitive to conditions of general dysfunction. Each kind of test can be used effectively as a screening device as long as its limitations are known and the information it elicits is interpreted accordingly. When testing is primarily for screening purposes, a combination of tests including some that are sensitive to specific impairment, some to general impairment, and others that tend to draw out diagnostic signs will make the best diagnostic discriminations.

Signs

The sign approach is based on the assumption that there are some distinctive behavioral manifestations of brain damage. In part this assumption reflects early concepts of brain damage as a unitary kind of dysfunction (Hebb, 1942; Shure and Halstead, 1958), and in part it results from observations of behavioral characteristics that do distinguish the test performances of many patients with organic damage.

Most "organic signs" refer to specific aberrant test responses or modes of response. Some signs are isolated response deviations that, in themselves, may indicate the presence of an organic defect. Rotation in copying a block design (Satz, 1966b) or a geometric figure (Fuller and Laird, 1963) has been considered a sign of brain damage. Specific test failures or test score discrepancies have also been treated as signs of organicity, as for instance, marked difficulty on a serial subtraction task (Ruesch and Moore, 1943) or a wide spread between the number of digits recalled in the order given and the number recalled in reversed order (Wechsler, 1958). The manner in which the patient responds to the task may also be considered an organic sign. M. Williams (1965) associated three response characteristics with brain damage: "stereotyping and perseveration"; "concreteness of behavior" defined by her as "response to all stimuli as if they existed only in the setting in which they are presented"; and "catastrophic reactions" of perplexity, acute anxiety, and despair when the patient is unable to perform the presented task.

Another common sign approach relies on not one but on the sum of different signs, i.e., the total number of different kinds of specific test response aberrations or differentiating test item selections made by the patient. This method has been widely used with the Rorschach test with some success (Harrower, 1965; Piotrowski, 1937) (see pp. 603–604) and has been attempted with the Minnesota Multiphasic Personality Inventory (Hovey, 1964; Zimmerman, 1965) (see pp. 610–611).

CUTTING SCORES

The score that separates the "normal" or "not diagnostic" from the "abnormal" or "organic" ends of a continuum of test scores is called a *cutting score*. The use of cutting scores is akin to the sign approach, for their purpose is to separate patients in terms of the presence or absence of the condition under study. A statistically derived cutting score for organicity is that score that differentiates organic patients from others with the fewest instances of error on either side. A cutting score may also be derived by simple inspection, in which case it is usually the score just below the poorest score attained by any member of the "normal" comparison group.

Cutting scores are a prominent feature of most screening tests. However, many of the cutting scores used for neuropsychological diagnosis may be less efficient than the claims made for them (Meehl and Rosen, 1967). This is most likely to be the case when the establishment of a cutting score does not take into account the base rate at which the predicted condition occurs in the sample from which the cutting score was developed (Cronbach, 1970; Satz et al., 1970). The criterion groups are often not large enough for optimal cutting scores to be determined. Further, cutting scores developed on one kind of population may not apply to another. R. L. Adams and his co-workers (1982) point out the importance of adjusting cutting scores for "age, education, premorbid intelligence, and race-ethnicity," by demonstrating that the likelihood of false positive predictions of brain damage tends to increase directly with age and for non-whites, and inversely with education and intelligence test scores.

When the recommended cutting scores are used, these tests generally do identify

Table 6-7. Sample Table of Scores on a Timed Test for a Brain Damaged Group and a Normal Control Group

Performance Time (seconds)	Percent Achieving a Given Raw Score	
	Control Group	Brain Damaged Group
20	6	
25	12	1
30	23	0
35	29	2
40	20	6
45	8	15
50	2	24
55		28
60		16
65		5
70+		2

A cutting score set at 41 seconds misidentifies 10% of the control group and 9% of the brain-damaged group for the lowest number of total errors. If the cutting score is set at 51 to exclude all false positives, i.e., all normal controls, then 48% of the brain damaged patients will be excluded as well. A cutting score set to exclude all false negatives would exclude all but 6% of the normal control group.

the organically impaired patients better than by chance. They all also misdiagnose both organically intact persons (false positive cases) and persons with known organic defects (false negative cases) to varying degrees. The nature of the errors of diagnosis depends on where the cutting score is set: if it is set to minimize misidentification of organically sound persons, then a greater number of organically impaired patients will be called "normal" by the screening. Conversely, if the test-maker's goal is to identify as many patients with brain damage as possible, he will then include more organically sound persons in his brain damaged group (see Table 6-7). As a general rule, even when these tests screen brain damaged patients from a normal control group, they do not discriminate well between them and psychiatric patients (Lilliston, 1973). Only rarely does the cutting score provide a distinct separation between the two populations, and then only for tests that are so simple no nonretarded intact adult could fail. For example, there are few false positive cases screened in by the Token Test, which consists of verbal instructions involving basic concepts of size, color, and location (Boller and Vignolo, 1966; see pp. 321–326).

Single Tests for Organicity

Interest in using behavioral techniques to identify the presence of brain damage has given rise to numerous "tests of organicity." These tests typically comprise a single task or small set of tasks, usually of a similar character. Some of them, like the Bender-Gestalt test, were originally developed for some other purpose (L. Bender, 1938) but entered the neuropsychological test repertory to become, for some examiners, a kind of psychological litmus paper for the detection of brain damage (e.g., Brilliant and Gynther, 1963; Hain, 1964) (see pp. 385–393). Other tests were developed especially for the detection of brain damage, without regard to anatomical or functional differences between organically impaired patients. For example, Elithorn's Mazes and Hooper's Visual Organization Test examine visuoconceptual functions (see pp. 368–369 and 357–358). Others are based on one relatively complex task, such as the Graham-Kendall Memory for Designs Test, which involves visuoconstructional *and* memory functions (see pp. 451–453).

The use of single tests for identifying brain damaged patients is also based on the assumption that brain damage, like measles perhaps, can be treated as a single entity. Considering the heterogeneity of organic brain disorders, it is not very surprising to find that single tests have high misclassification rates (G. Goldstein and Shelly, 1973; Spreen and Benton, 1965). Most single tests, including many that are not well standardized, can be rich sources of information about the functions, attitudes, and habits they elicit. But to look to any single test for decisive information about overall intellectual behavior is not merely foolish, it can be dangerous as well, since the absence of positive findings does not rule out the presence of a pathological condition (Ehrfurth and Lezak, 1982). Teuber (1962) pointed out, for example, that, "certain standard tests of so-called general intelligence . . . (that) depend maximally on overlearned information and skills" may be insensitive to some large brain lesions but sensitive to others, depending on which parts of the brain have been damaged. The same can be said of almost every other single test that has been used in examining for brain damage except those that are so complex and involve so many different functions that they register almost every brain disorder—and many psychiatric, personality, situational, and medical conditions as well.

Usefulness of Screening Techniques

In the 1940s and 1950s, when brain damage was still thought by many to have some general manifestation that could be demonstrated by tests, screening techniques were popular, particularly for identifying the organically impaired patients in a psychiatric population (Klebanoff, 1945; Yates, 1954). As a result of our better understanding of the multifaceted nature of brain pathology and of the accelerating development and refinement of other kinds of neurodiagnostic techniques, neuropsychological screening has only limited usefulness at present. Screening is unnecessary or inappropriate in most cases referred for neuropsychological evaluation: either the presence of neuropathology is obvious or otherwise documented, or diagnosis requires more than a simple screening for organicity. Furthermore, the extent to which screening techniques produce false positives and false negatives compromises their reliability for making decisions about individual patients.

However, screening may still be useful with populations in which neurological disorders are more frequent than in the general population but occur at unknown base rates or at base rates so low that thorough examination of each person in that population is impracticable. The most obvious clinical situations in which neuropsychological screening may be called for are the examinations of patients entering a psychiatric inpatient service or at-risk groups such as the elderly or alcoholics when they seek medical care. Moreover, when screening tests are used along with tests that allow for many gradations of behavior, organic signs and positive cutting scores do lend support to findings suggestive of brain damage, although their absence does not weaken an interpretation of brain damage based on data from graded tests. Dichotomizing screening techniques are also useful in research for evaluating tests or treatments, or for comparing populations with respect to the presence or absence of organic defects.

Once a patient has been identified by screening techniques as possibly having an organic disorder, the problem arises of what to do about him, for simple screening at best operates only as an early warning system. These patients still need careful neurological and neuropsychological study to evaluate the possibility of organicity and to diagnose organic conditions so that treatment and planning can be undertaken.

EVALUATING SCREENING TECHNIQUES

"Hit Rates." It has become the custom of some investigators in clinical neuropsychology to judge the "goodness" of a test or measure in terms of its "hit rate," i.e., the percent of cases it correctly identifies as belonging to either one of two predetermined clinical populations (of which one may be a control group). This practice is predicated on questionable assumptions, one of which is that *the accuracy with which a test makes diagnostic classifications is a major consideration in evaluating its clinical worth.* Yet the criterion of diagnostic accuracy is only important when evaluating some tests (e.g., an aphasia screening test). Most tests (e.g., the Wechsler intelligence tests) are not used for this purpose most of the time.

The "hit rate" concept also implies an assumption that the "hit rate" is a measure of test efficiency and, as such, is an inherent characteristic of the test. However, the percent of cases classified accurately by any given test will depend on the base rate of condition(s) to which the test is sensitive in the population(s) used to evaluate its goodness. With judicious selection of populations, an investigator can virtually predetermine the outcome. If high hit rates are desired, then the brain damaged population (e.g., patients with left hemisphere lesions) should consist of subjects who are known to suffer the condition(s) (e.g., communication disorders) measured by the test(s) under consideration (e.g., an aphasia screening test); the comparison population (e.g., normal control subjects, neurotic patients) should be chosen on the basis that they are unlikely to have the condition(s) measured by the test. Using a population in which the frequency of the condition measured by the test(s) under consideration is much lower (e.g., patients who have had only one stroke, regardless of site) will necessarily lower the hit rate. However, this lower hit rate does not reflect upon the value of the test. The extent to which hit rates vary as populations differ is shown by the large differences reported in studies using the same test(s) on different kinds of clinical (and control) populations (e.g., Heaton et al., 1978; Spreen and Benton, 1965).

A number of authors (e.g., Ehrfurth and Lezak, 1982; Walsh, 1978b; Yates, 1966) have called attention to a fallacy that underlies the development and cross-validation of screening tests and even entire batteries in terms of how well their hit rates differentiate between an unequivocally brain damaged population and normal controls or neurotic subjects. When history, simple observation, or well-established laboratory techniques clearly demonstrate a neurological disorder, neuropsychological tests are not needed to document the presence of brain damage.

> For example, Duffala (1978) used the battery developed by Golden (see pp. 569–572) to compare 20 "head trauma patients . . . who had injuries resulting from airplane, car, or motor cycle accident, gunshot wound, or severe blow to the head in falling . . . [when] the patients reached an appropriate level of awareness" with "volunteers from a university community or . . . hospital staff." Not surprisingly, she found that this battery "does discriminate between groups of people having brain injury and those without." However, the ability to use a can opener would probably have discriminated as well between these two groups.

Although a "hit rate" standard is virtually meaningless as a measure of a test's capacity to identify "organic" or "not organic" subjects, it can be applicable when examining a particular test's sensitivity to a specific disorder (Ehrfurth and Lezak, 1982). To be useful diagnostically, neuropsychological techniques must be able to make diagnostic discriminations among patients whose presenting symptoms or complaints are hard to diagnose by traditional approaches.

Limitations of screening techniques. In neuropsychology as in medicine, limitations in predictive accuracy do not invalidate either tests for specific signs or disabilities or tests that are sensitive to conditions of general dysfunction. Each kind of test can be used effectively as a screening device as long as its limitations are known and the information it elicits is interpreted accordingly. When testing is primarily for screening purposes, a combination of tests including some that are sensitive to specific impairment, some to general impairment, and others that tend to draw out diagnostic signs will make the best diagnostic discriminations.

When evaluating tests for screening purposes, it is important to realize that although neuropsychological tests have proven effective in identifying the presence of cerebral dysfunction, they cannot guarantee its absence, i.e., "rule out" organicity (Talland, 1963). Not only may cerebral disease occur without behavioral manifestations, but the examiner may also neglect to look for those neuropsychological abnormalities that are present. Inability to prove the negative case in neuropsychological assessment is shared with every other diagnostic tool in medicine and the behavioral sciences. Thus, when a neuropsychological examination produces no positive findings, the only tenable conclusion is that the person in question performed within normal limits on the tests that he took at that time. The neuropsychologist cannot give a "clean bill of health."

Pattern Analysis

The many differences in cognitive performance between diagnostic groups and between individuals within these groups can only be appreciated and put to clinical use when the evaluation is based on subtest score patterns and item analyses that are taken from tests of many different functions. Neither a narrow range of tests nor an interpretation approach that disregards subtest and item discrepancies can make available the amount of information generally required for adequate description and analysis of the patient's deficits (Bigler, 1982).

The basic element of test score analysis is a significant discrepancy between any two or more scores. Implicitly or explicitly, all score-based approaches to neuropsychological assessment rest on the assumption that one intellectual performance level best represents each person's general intellectual abilities (see pp. 22–23, 94–95). Marked quantitative discrepancies in a person's performance suggest that some abnormal condition is interfering with that person's overall ability to perform at his characteristic level of intellectual functioning. It then becomes the examiner's responsibility to determine the nature of that limitation.

History and observations will help the examiner evaluate the possible contributions that cultural differences or disadvantages, emotional disturbances, developmental anomalies, and so on, may make to performance discrepancies. Test score discrepancies may provide the critical information for determining whether the patient is brain damaged or, when diagnosis is not a question, how his brain damage affects his behavior. Any single discrepant score or response error can usually be disregarded as a chance deviation. A number of errors or test score deviations, however, may form a pattern that can then be analyzed in terms of whether or not it makes neurological sense, i.e., whether the score discrepancies fit neuroanatomically probable behavior patterns. The possibility that a given pattern of scores reflects an organic brain disorder is supported to the extent that the scores conform to a neuropsychologically reasonable discrepancy pattern.

The question of neuroanatomical or neurophysiological likelihood underlies all analyses of test patterns undertaken for differential diagnosis. As in every other diagnostic effort, the most likely explanation for a behavioral disorder is the one that requires the least number of unlikely events to account for it. Organicity is suspected when a neurological condition best accounts for the patient's behavioral abnormalities.

INTRAINDIVIDUAL VARIABILITY

Discrepancies, or variability, in the pattern of successes and failures in a test performance is called *scatter*. Variability within a test is *intratest scatter;* variability between the scores of a set of tests is *intertest scatter* (D. Wechsler, 1958).

Intratest scatter. Scatter within a test is said to be present when there are marked deviations from the normal pass-fail pattern of a test. On tests in which the items are presented in order of difficulty, it is usual for the subject to pass almost all items up to the most difficult passed item, with perhaps one or two failures on items close to the last passed item. Rarely do nondefective persons fail very simple items, or fail many items of middling difficulty and pass several difficult ones. On tests in which all items are of a similar difficulty level, most subjects tend to do all of them correctly, with perhaps one or two errors of carelessness, or they tend to flounder hopelessly with maybe one or two lucky "hits." Variations from these two common patterns deserve the examiner's attention.

Efforts to relate intratest scatter to either organicity or emotional disturbance have not produced much evidence that intratest scatter patterns alone differentiate reliably between diagnostic groups (Guertin et al., 1966; Rabin, 1965). However, certain kinds of organic problems as well as some functional disturbances may manifest themselves in intratest scatter patterns. Hovey and Kooi (1955) demonstrated that when taking mental tests, those epileptic patients who suffered paroxysmal brain wave patterns (sudden bursts of activity) were significantly more likely to be randomly nonresponsive or forgetful than were psychiatric, brain damaged, or other epileptic patients. Some patients who have sustained severe head injuries respond to questions that draw on prior knowledge as if they had randomly lost chunks of stored information. For example, a high school graduate may recall the main theme of the Book of Genesis and the boiling point of water, but have no memory for the author of Hamlet or the capital of Italy, even though he is sure he once knew them. Psychiatric patients who tend to block or distort responses to verbalizations they perceive as emotionally threatening may also give highly scattered intratest performances (Rapaport et al., 1968). A review of the failed items will often give clues to the nature of the failure: if the only items failed were those with potentially anxiety-arousing content, then the examiner can reasonably suspect a functional basis for the scatter. On the other hand, if premature failures occur in an apparently meaningless fashion, then organicity may account for them.

The presence of *intratest* scatter may aid psychodiagnosis, but its absence has no bearing on anything whatsoever. Since intratest scatter tends to be the exception rather than the rule, it is not relevant to the majority of test evaluations.

Intertest scatter. Probably the most common approach to the psychological evaluation of organic brain disorders is through comparison of the test score levels obtained by the subject, in other words, analysis of the intertest score scatter (McFie, 1975; Reitan and Davison, 1974; E. W. Russell, 1979). By this means, the examiner attempts to relate variations between test scores to probable neuropsychological events. This technique can often provide clarification of a seeming confusion of signs and symptoms of behavioral disorder by giving the examiner a frame of reference for organizing and evaluating his data.

Consistency in the expression of intellectual functions is the key concept of pattern analysis. Damage to cortical tissue in an area serving a specific function changes or abolishes the expression of that function. Once a function is changed or lost, the character of all activities that originally involved that function will change to a greater or lesser degeee, depending upon how much the function itself has changed and the extent to which it entered into the activity.

In analyzing test score patterns, the examiner looks for both commonality of dysfunction and evidence of impairment on tests involving neuroanatomically related functions or skills (G. Goldstein, 1974; K. W. Walsh, 1978b). He first estimates the patient's original intellectual endowment from his history, qualitative aspects of his performance, and his test scores, using the examination or historical indicators that reasonably allow the highest estimate (see p. 97). This enables the examiner to identify the impaired test performances. He then notes which functions contribute to the impaired test performances. Out of these he identifies which if any functions or functional systems are *consistently* associated with lowered test scores, for these are the possible behavioral correlates of an organic brain condition. When the pattern of lowered test scores does not appear to be consistently associated with a single pattern of intellectual dysfunction, then the discrepant scores can be attributed to psychogenic, developmental, or chance deviations.

Reliable neuropsychological assessment based on impairment patterns requires a fairly broad review of functions. A minor or well-circumscribed intellectual deficit may show up on only one or a very few depressed test scores, or may not become evident at all if the test battery samples a narrow range of behaviors. Moreover, most of the behaviors that a psychologist examines are complex. When attempting to analyze behavior in order to identify the deficit(s) contributing to the observed impairments, the psychologist cannot examine a specific function in a vacuum but must look at it in combination with many different functions.

By and large, the use of pattern analysis has been confined to Wechsler subtests because of their obvious statistical comparability. However, by converting different kinds of test scores into comparable score units, the examiner can compare data from many different kinds of tests in a sysematic manner, permitting the analysis of patterns formed by the scores of tests from many sources. Many neuropsychologists using the Halstead-Reitan test battery (see pp. 562–566) augment the Wechsler subtest score pattern with scores of the other tests in the Halstead-Reitan battery by converting the scores to the T-score scale (Harley et al., 1980; Lewinsohn, 1973; Reed and Reitan, 1963). Lewinsohn also converts the scores of a number of memory, learning, and visual pattern recognition tests he devised into T-scores.

The Intellectual Performance Chart

Charting the test performance graphically may enable the examiner to perceive performance patterns and trends more readily. With A. E. Popov, I have developed a chart on which test performance levels can be laid out graphically. It is particularly useful when there are more than a handful of test scores and they do not all lie within a relatively narrow ability range. This technique for organizing the neuropsychological examination data also lends itself well to communicating the information to clinicians who are not familiar with psychological tests (see Figs. 6-3a and 6-3b).

Most test performances can be charted easily. When dealing with a test that has a wide enough range of difficulty and a sufficiently graduated scale as to generate normally distributed scores, i.e., most standardized tests of cognitive abilities and academic skills (see Chapter 10), the examiner simply converts the score to its appropriate ability level and charts it in the row of white spaces corresponding to that level.

Some functions and activities, tests, and examination techniques do not generate a normally distributed range of scores. This is particularly the case with tests devised for screening purposes as they typically have a very low ceiling of difficulty (such as the Token Test or the Hooper Visual Organization Test). Tests of skills and abilities possessed by all intact adults (e.g., aphasia tests, body and spatial orientation tests), tests and examination techniques that do not yield graded scores (e.g., many concept formation tests), and tests of function that have a very narrow range in the normal population (e.g., immediate memory span) also do not generate scores that can be adapted to the standard classification system for normally distributed intellectual abilities. Scores obtained on such tests generally fit better into a three-category scale of "within normal limits," "borderline to normal limits," and "defective." Performances that are "within normal limits" or "borderline to normal limits" on these tests should be entered in the appropriate one of the two hatched rows of our chart; those that are "defective"should be noted in the bottom row shared by both classification systems. The hatched rows were placed within the seven-level classification scheme so that both kinds of performances, those that are normally distributed and those that are not, could be charted closely enough together to make an integrated performance picture for ease of inspection.

The three-category scale may also be used for test performances that are usually not scored but evaluated qualitatively, such as the human figure drawing test. Experience with these tests and familiarity with the literature usually enable the examiner to distinguish between performances in terms of this three-category classification system.

Using the Intellectual Performance Chart. The chart is divided into two one-page sections to allow room to document the many kinds of observations that may be made in a neuropsychological examination. The first page (Fig. 6-3a) contains spaces for recording the test performances which, by and large, have a significant verbal component. Records of test performances that have a major nonverbal component—again, by and large—go into the second section (Fig. 6-3b).

In actuality, the complexity of human cognitive activity does not allow for many clear-cut distinctions between verbal and nonverbal tests. Tests that have pictorial stimuli requiring verbal responses, such as Goodglass and Kaplan's "Cookie Theft Description" test of verbal expression (see p. 328), the Wechsler tests' Picture Completion subtest (see pp. 274–275) or the Hooper Visual Organization Test (see pp. 357–358) can theoretically be assigned to either page. Usually, I chart such tests according to whichever is the modality of prime interest, whether by the test-maker's design or common practice. Thus, since the "Cookie Theft" picture was designed to stimulate oral expression, I record the performance in the "Reasoning and Judgment" column under the "Verbal/Symbolic" section of page 1. However, Picture Comple-

I. Intellectual Performance Chart M.D. LEZAK AND A.E. POPOV

Name _____
Date _____ Place _____

Level of Performance \ Stimulus Function	VERBAL / SYMBOLIC							
	Old Learning and Verbal Skills	Reasoning and Judgment	MEMORY			Arithmetic	Concept Formation & Abstraction	Attention Concentration Tracking
			Immediate Span	Short-Term	Learning			
Very Superior								
Superior								
High Average	Reading Vocab Spelling[2] Functional Vocab (writing & speech)	C[4] (except proverbs)						
Within Normal Limits			DF[7] AVLT I+B[8]		AVLT Ⅴ		WCS[11]	DB[12]
Average	I(WAIS + SAB)[3]	S[5] Reading Compr.[6]				A-WAIS[9] A-SAB[10]		
Low Average								
Borderline to Normal Limits					AVLT Ⅺ AVLT Ⅴ-Ⅵ			
Borderline Defective								
Defective Below Normal Limits		Proverbs (WAIS+SAB)						SDMT[13] WCS A(WAIS)
Comment								

Fig. 6-3a. Charted performance of a 27-year-old high-school graduate, recently demoted from a skilled to a semiskilled position following onset of seizures and subsequent apathy, irritability, and complaints of memory problems. As can be seen from the chart, the most impaired functions were concentration and tracking, visual and spatial organization, and visual memory with some reduction of verbal learning capacity as well. On visual reasoning and visuoconstruction tests, his performance tended to vary directly with the degree to which the test is structured and therefore his performance level ranged from *average* on well-structured tasks to *defective* on those requiring very much organizing activity for success. On the Wisconsin Card Sorting Test (WCS), he demonstrated both good capacity for concept formation and the ability to shift concepts appropriately, but after the third shift he lost track of the current concept, performing poorly because of defective concentration and tracking. This pattern suggests right hemisphere involvement, probably in the parietotemporal region. Neuroradiological tests indicated a right anterior parietal lesion which, on surgery, proved to be a slow-growing tumor.

KEY: 1. Gates-MacGinite Reading Test, Survey F. 2. Self-administered Battery (SAB) and Personal History Inventory (PHI). 3. Information subtest of the Wechsler Adult Intelligence Scale (WAIS) and of the SAB. 4. Comprehension (WAIS). 5. Similarities (WAIS). 6. Gates-MacGinitie Reading Test. 7. Digits Forward (WAIS). 8. Rey's Auditory-Verbal Learning Test; Roman numerals and B on this and other AVLT notations refer to different trials of the test. 9. Arithmetic (WAIS). 10. Arithmetic story problems (SAB). 11. Wisconsin Card Sorting Test. 12. Digits Backward (WAIS). 13. Symbol Digit Modalities Test.

2. Intellectual Performance Chart M.D. LEZAK AND A.E. POPOV

Name _____

Date _____ Place _____

Level of Performance \ Stimulus Function	NONVERBAL					Self Regulation	Motor Functions: Praxis	Miscellaneous
	Perception and Reasoning	Construction	MEMORY					
			Immediate Span	Short-Term	Learning			
Very Superior								
Superior								
High Average								
Within Normal Limits		B-GT(form)[20]				WCS(shift)		
Average	PC[14] PA[15] Mooney[16] Rorschach	BD[21] Lady[22]						
Low Average	RPM[17]							
Borderline to Normal Limits		Bicycle[23] DAP[24]						
Borderline Defective		Mazes[25]						
Defective Below Normal Limits	HVOT[18] Rorschach[19] 3 rejects	OA[26] B-GT(space)		BVRT-A[27] nC+nE			PPT→Ⓡ[28]	
Comment								

Fig. 6-3b. 14. Picture Completion (WAIS). 15. Picture Arrangement (WAIS). 16. Mooney Closure Faces Test. 17. Raven's Progressive Matrices. 18. Hooper Visual Organization Test. 19. No response to three of ten Rorschach cards. 20. Bender-Gestalt Test. 21. Block Design (WAIS). 22. Lady Walking in the Rain. 23. Bicycle drawing test. 24. Draw a Person. 25. Maze Test of the Wechsler Intelligence Scale for Children. 26. Object Assembly (WAIS). 27. Benton Visual Retention Test performance was defective according to both "number correct" and "error" scores. 28. Purdue Pegboard Test performance discrepancy implicated right hemisphere dysfunction.

tion and the Hooper Visual Organization Test are used primarily to examine reasoning and perceptual organization in the visual modality, so I document these performances under "Perception and Reasoning" in the "Nonverbal" section of page 2.

Concept formation and abstraction probably are most often examined by verbal similarities and differences tests (see pp. 265–266 and 478–480) and explanations of proverbs (pp. 476–477) or fables, yet other sensitive techniques for measuring these functions have minimal dependence on verbal mediation (e.g., Object Sorting Test, pp. 486–487; Wisconsin Card Sorting Test, pp. 487–491). The decision to place "Concept Formation and Abstraction" and "Attention, Concentration, Tracking" on page

1 and "Self-Regulation" and "Motor Functions," which may have significant verbal or other symbolic components, on page 2 was based on my subjective impression of relatedness.

One other kind of scoring problem involves tests in which two classes of functions play significant roles, one of which may be intact and the other impaired. In this case, I chart the test twice, at the appropriate level for each of the functions (see "A[WAIS]" and "WCS," Fig. 6-3a). When all the functions involved in a test performance are intact, the patient's responses tend to be consistent and the test is usually charted only once under the most predominant of the functions in question.

The second step in charting test performances is to determine the predominant function(s) examined by the test. This too is a relatively simple task for most tests. Tests involving verbal skills, such as vocabulary, reading, or sentence construction tests or tests of information or reasoning in the verbal modality, can usually be subsumed under one of the two classes of "Verbal" functions. Construction tasks belong under "Construction," and when verbal memory and learning are emphasized, the predominant functional category is one of the classes of "Memory" on page 1. Tests that do not lend themselves readily to a single classification can be charted twice. For example, a drawing task involving short-term memory may be represented under the "Construction" category and under "Memory/Short-Term" on page 2. If the patient is also dyspractic, this would be additionally noted in the "Motor Functions" column of page 2.

Arithmetic tests present a special problem because several functional classes may vie for the predominant role depending on both the format of the test and the nature of the patient's disability (see pp. 134, 262–265). However, when a disability, such as defective concentration and mental tracking, interferes with the ability to perform oral arithmetic, or a visuospatial defect prevents a mathematically knowledgeable patient from doing paper and pencil calculations correctly, I chart the test performance under both "Arithmetic" and the other significant category (see "A[WAIS]" under "Arithmetic" and "Attention, Concentration, and Tracking," Fig. 6-3a).

When used to organize graphically a large set of data about a person, this charting technique can make very evident the presence—or the absence—of clear-cut performance patterns. However, the examiner must remember that ability level categories represent only rough approximations to performance levels, that one's own arbitrary and subjective judgments enter into classification decisions, and that, except as noted, qualitative aspects of the test performance are represented on the chart only indirectly if at all. The relative simplicity of the chart should keep the test-wise examiner from falling into the dangerous and all too common error of confusing graphic representations of psychological test scores with reality.

The charted test score pattern can make neuropsychological sense only to the extent to which the examiner knows what patterns are likely, given the patient's age, background, and concomitant physical status and medical data. However, the neuropsychologically naive examiner who is well grounded in clinical psychology can interpret the charted scores in terms of the patient's cognitive strengths and weaknesses, and thus provide a description that may be useful for many purposes, such as rehabilitation or vocational planning.

For example, an interpretation of the pattern of scores charted in Figures 6-3a and 6-3b and described on page 157 would point out that the patient has retained a number of verbal skills at the *high average* level, suggesting that his original intellectual endowment was in this ability range. Moreover, both well-learned verbal skills, such as vocabulary, and his ability to apply these skills in reading comprehension and in verbal reasoning tasks are in the same *average* to *high average* range with the single exception of proverbs interpretations. The statistically significant discrepancy between the higher level of other verbal skills and a relatively poorer performance on a task requiring both conceptual reorganization of the material and abstraction suggests that he will be able to make the best use of his good verbal abilities within familiar, well-structured settings. Given his very inadequate interpretations of proverbs, a Similarities score in the *average* range probably reflects a good vocabulary with well-learned associations rather than an *average* ability to form abstract verbal concepts. However, he did demonstrate an ability to form low-level abstract concepts and flexibility in shifting them suggesting that his problem is not concept formation in itself, but rather the level of concept formation.

His *average* Arithmetic performance probably gives a low estimate of his mathematical background since he lost some points because he could not do the oral problems in his head, and lost other points, on written Arithmetic, because of small errors that could reflect either carelessness or calculation and number manipulation slips. Although, under ideal conditions, he can probably solve more difficult problems correctly, the usefulness of his arithmetic skills is probably lower than his scores predict because of inadequate self-monitoring of errors.

The patient's perceptual accuracy and ability to reason in the visual modality are *average* so long as he deals with familiar and fairly well-structured material. When the burden for making structure—i.e., organizing percepts from fragmented or vague stimuli—is on the subject, his performance deteriorates to the *defective* level. He displays a similar pattern on construction tasks, best illustrated on the Bender-Gestalt Test by defective placement on the paper—e.g., overlapping figures and figures abutting one another, disorganized order on the page—of accurate copies of the designs. He displays some diminution of motor speed and dexterity in his left hand.

His immediate verbal memory span and verbal learning curve are well within normal limits. However, his retention is relatively impaired so that, in order to retain new verbal information he will require more exposure or rehearsal than normal at his age and verbal skill level. In contrast, his ability to hold on to new visual information, even for a minute, is practically nonexistent. He was not tested for learning in the visual modality.

The patient displayed normal conceptual tracking when handling a limited amount of verbal material within a 5–10-second range. In contrast, he repeatedly demonstrated an inability to keep mental track of larger amounts of data over longer periods of time, regardless of the modality.

The practical conclusions that can be drawn from such a purely psychological

161

interpretation of his test performances are that this patient can perform many tasks at an *average* level so long as he has careful supervision, a well-structured and familiar situation, and is not expected to exercise judgment. Moreover, he has lost some dexterity as well as the capacity to concentrate well and track mentally, and will be slow to learn anything new, particularly if it is not put into words.

Taking the next step of relating the psychological data to neurological conditions requires more acquaintance with clinical neuropathology than the scope of this or any other book allows if the reader has not also had clinical experience. In describing typical patterns of neuropsychological functioning and some other salient aspects of the major categories of neuropathological disorders, Chapter Seven offers an introduction to neuropathology from a neuropsychologist's perspective.

Integrated Interpretation

Pattern analysis is insufficient to deal with the numerous exceptions to characteristic patterns, with the many rare or idiosyncratically manifested neurological conditions, and with the effects on test performance of the complex interaction between the patient's intellectual status, his emotional and social adjustment, and his appreciation of his brain damage. For the examination to supply answers to many of the diagnostic questions and most of the treatment and planning questions requires integration of all the data—from tests, observations made in the course of the examination, and the history of the problem.

Many conditions do not lend themselves to pattern analysis beyond the use of large and consistent test score discrepancies to implicate brain damage. This is particularly the case with head injuries in which neither the location nor the extent of the damage can be definitely determined before autopsy, and with malignant tumors, which are unlikely to follow a regular pattern of growth and spread. In order to determine which functions are involved and the extent of their involvement, it is usually necessary to evaluate the qualitative aspects of the patient's performance very carefully for evidence of complex or subtle aberrations that betray damage in some hitherto unsuspected area of the brain. Such painstaking scrutiny is often not as necessary when dealing with a fairly typical stroke patient, for instance, or a patient whose disease generally follows a well-known and regular course.

Test scores alone do not provide much information about the emotional impact of the patient's disease on his intellectual functioning. However, his behavior during the test is likely to reveal a great deal about how he is reacting to his disabilities and how these reactions in turn affect the efficiency of his performance. The common emotional reactions of brain damaged patients tend to affect their intellectual functioning adversely. The most prevalent and most profoundly handicapping of these are anxiety and depression. Euphoria and carelessness, while much less distressing to the patient, can also seriously interfere with full expression of a patient's abilities.

Brain damaged patients have other characteristic problems that generally do not depress test scores but which must be taken into account in rehabilitation planning.

These are motivational and control problems that show up in an inability to organize, to react spontaneously, to initiate goal-directed behavior, or to carry out a course of action independently. They are rarely reflected in test scores since almost all tests are well structured and administered by an examiner who plans, initiates, and conducts the examination. Yet, no matter how well the patient does on tests, if he cannot develop or carry out his own course of action, he is incompetent for all practical purposes. Such problems become apparent during careful examination, but they usually must be reported descriptively unless the examiner sets up a test situation that can provide a systematic and scorable means of assessing the patient's capacity for self-direction and planning (see pp. 507–527).

7
Neuropathology for Neuropsychologists

The practitioner can make diagnostic sense out of the behavioral patterns that emerge in neuropsychological assessment only to the extent that he is knowledgeable about the neuropsychological presentation of many kinds of neurological disorders and with their underlying pathology. This knowledge gives the examiner a diagnostic frame of reference that will help him identify, sort out, appraise, and put into a diagnostically meaningful context the many bits and pieces of observations, scores, family reports, and medical history that typically make up the material of a case. Furthermore, such a frame of reference should help the examiner know what additional questions need be asked or what further observations or behavioral measurements need be made in order to arrive at a diagnostic formulation of the patient's problems.

This chapter aims to provide such a frame of reference. The major disorders of the nervous system having neuropsychological consequences will be reviewed according to their customary classification by known or suspected etiology or by the system of primary involvement. While this review cannot be comprehensive, it covers the most common neuropathological conditions seen in the usual hospital or clinic practice in this country. The reader may wish to consult Strub and Black's *Organic Brain Syndromes* (1981) or Lishman's *Organic Psychiatry* (1978) for a more detailed presentation of the medical aspects of these and other less common conditions which have behavioral ramifications.

As in every other aspect of neuropsychology, or any other personalized clinical assessment procedure, the kind of information the examiner needs to know will vary from patient to patient. For example, hereditary predisposition is not an issue with traumatic injuries or a *hypoxic* (condition of insufficient oxygenation) episode during surgery, but it becomes a very important consideration when a previously unexceptional person begins to exhibit uncontrollable movements and poor judgment coupled with impulsivity. Thus, it is not necessary to ask every candidate for neuropsychological assessment for family history going back a generation or two, although family history is important when the diagnostic possibilities include a hereditary disorder such as Huntington's disease (see pp. 187–189). In certain populations, the incidence of alcohol or drug abuse is so high that every person with complaints suggestive of a cerebral disorder should be carefully questioned about his or her drinking or drug habits; yet for many persons, such questioning becomes clearly unnecessary early in a clinical examination and may be offensive as well. Moreover, a number of different kinds of disorders produce similar constellations of symptoms. For example, apathy, affective dulling, and memory impairment occur in Korsakoff's psychosis, with heavy exposure to certain organic solvents, as an aftermath of severe head trauma or herpes encephalitis, and with conditions in which the supply of oxygen to the brain has been compromised. Many conditions with similar neuropsychological features can be distinguished by differences in other neuropsychological dimensions. Other conditions are best identified in terms of the patient's history, associated neurological symptoms, and the nature of the onset and course of the disorder.

No single rule of thumb will tell the examiner just what information about any particular patient is needed to make the most effective use of the examination data. Whether the purpose of the examination is diagnosis or delineation of the behavioral expression of a known condition, knowledge about the known or suspected condition(s) provides a frame of reference for the rational conduct of the examination.

The Major Classes of Brain Disorders

Head Trauma

Traumatic head injuries are among the most common forms of brain damage, leading all others in childhood and the younger (to age 42) adult years (Gurdjian and Gurdjian, 1978; Kraus, 1978; Selecki et al., 1982). Modern medical techniques for the management of acute brain conditions are saving many accident victims today who ten— or even five—years ago would have succumbed to the metabolic, hemodynamic, and other complications that follow severe brain trauma. (For a detailed description of the series of physiological events that head injury is likely to trigger, see Jennett and Teasdale, 1981; Plum and Posner, 1980.) As a result, an ever-increasing number of survivors of severe head injury, mostly children and young adults at the time of injury, are rapidly familiarizing us with this relatively new and usually tragic phenomenon of physically fit young people whose brains have been significantly damaged.

The behavioral effects of all brain lesions hinge upon a variety of factors, such as severity, age, site of lesions, and premorbid personality (see Chapter 8). The psychological consequences of head trauma also vary according to how the injury happened, e.g., whether it occurred in a moving vehicle, as a result of a blow to the head, or from a missile furrowing through it. With knowledge of the kind of head injury, its severity, and the site of focal damage, an experienced examiner can generally predict the broad outlines of a patient's major behavioral and neuropsychological disabilities and his psychosocial prognosis. Of course, only careful examination can demonstrate the individual features of the patient's disabilities, such as whether verbal or visual functions are more depressed, and the extent to which retrieval problems, frontal inertia, or impaired learning ability each contribute to the patient's poor performance on memory tests. Yet, the similarities in the behavioral patterns of many patients, especially those with severe closed head injuries, tend to outweigh the individual differences.

OPEN HEAD INJURIES

Traumatic brain injuries in which the skull is penetrated, as in gunshot or missile wounds, are called open head injuries. They differ from closed head injuries (see pp. 167–169) in ways that have important behavioral implications.

Open head injuries are likely to be "clean" wounds in the sense that significant tissue damage tends to be concentrated in the path of the intruding object (Newcombe, 1969). Since surgical cleansing of the wound (debridement) typically removes damaged tissue along with debris, most of the brain usually remains intact. Conditions such as these, which result in a circumscribed focal lesion, typically produce relatively circumscribed and predictable intellectual losses. (Their predictability is subject, of course, to normal interindividual variability in brain organization.) Neuropsychologists who have taken advantage of this "clean" characteristic of penetrating head wounds that received prompt surgical attention have been able to make major contributions to the understanding of functional brain organization (e.g., Luria, 1970a; Newcombe, 1969, 1974; Semmes et al., 1960, 1963; Teuber, 1962, 1964).

However, the penetrating object may also cause damage throughout the brain as a result of shock waves and pressure effects (Grubb and Coxe, 1978, Gurdjian and Gurdjian, 1978). The extent and severity of diffuse damage to brain tissue, which depends on such physical qualities as speed and malleability of the penetrating object, usually remain unknown (K. W. Walsh, 1978b). Moreover, transient physiological conditions (of swelling, bleeding) during the acute stages may leave permanent tissue damage. Thus, in addition to the behavioral changes and specific intellectual deficits that can usually be traced to the site of the lesion, patients with open head injuries may also show some of the impairments of memory functions, attention and concentration, and mental slowing that tend to be associated with diffuse brain damage (see pp. 171–174). Teuber, for example, noted "subtle but pervasive changes in our patients' capacity to deal with everyday intellectual demands," which he considered to be among the "general effects" of penetrating head wounds.

These patients tend to make relatively rapid gains in the first year or two following injury (A. E. Walker and Jablon, 1961), with further improvement coming very slowly and more likely as a result of learned accommodations and compensations than return or renewal of function. Certain specific impairments and general deficits tend to improve, while others remain essentially unchanged over the years. Of the specific defects, language and constructional disorders are among those that may show significant improvement. Yet other localized defects, such as visual blind spots and reduced tactile sensitivity persist unchanged indefinitely (Teuber, 1975a). Many of the general effects of brain damage, such as distractibility or slowing, tend to improve but may never return to the premorbid level of efficiency. However, 15 years after the Russian invasion of Finland, 89% of the surviving Finnish head trauma patients were working (Hillbom, 1960), and Newcombe (1969) and Teuber (1975a) each reported that approximately 85% of their war wound victims were gainfully employed 20 or more years after injury. These data suggest that penetrating head wounds tend to be somewhat but not severely handicapping. Dresser and his co-workers (1973) found that frontotemporal injuries and pretraumatic low performance each significantly reduced the employability of war-injured patients.

Closed Head Injuries

Neuropathology. The mechanics of closed head injuries explain many of their common symptom patterns (Grubb and Coxe, 1978; Walton, 1977). Several kinds of damaging mechanical forces have been identified (Gurdjian and Gurdjian, 1978). The most obvious of these is the force of impact, the predominant cause of brain damage in *static injuries*, in which a relatively still victim receives a blow to the head. Damage appears to result from a rapid sequence of events beginning with the inward molding of the skull at point of impact and compensatory adjacent outbending followed by rebound effects. With sufficient stress, the skull may be fractured, complicating the picture with the possibility of infection and additional tissue damage.

The blow at point of impact is called *coup*. *Contrecoup* lesions, in which the brain sustains a bruise *(contusion)* in an area opposite the blow, occur in most cases of occipital injury (Grubb and Coxe, 1978). E. Smith (1974) estimates that approximately half of all focal injuries involving direct impact to the side of the head are due to contrecoup, although Roberts' (1976) data suggest that 80% of his less seriously injured subjects sustained contrecoup damage as judged by the motorically disabled side. Contrecoup damage results from translation of the force and direction of impact to the brain sitting on its flexible stem in a liquid medium (Gurdjian, 1975). The force of the blow may literally bounce the brain off the opposite side of its bony container, bruising brain tissue where it strikes the skull. Coup and contrecoup lesions account for the specific and localizable behavioral changes that accompany closed head injuries.

Another neuropsychologically important kind of brain damage that occurs in closed head injury results from the combination of translatory force and rotational acceleration of the brain within the bony structure of the skull (Jurko, 1979). The movement of the brain within the skull puts strains on delicate nerve fibers and blood vessels that can stretch them to the point of shearing (Strich, 1961). Shearing effects, in the form of microscopic lesions, which occur throughout the brain (Oppenheimer, 1968; Walton, 1977), tend to be concentrated in the frontal and temporal lobes (Grubb and Coxe, 1978).

Rotational velocity appears to play a significant role in producing loss of consciousness, the *concussion* (Harper, 1982; Ommaya and Gennarelli, 1974). Involvement of brain stem reticular formation structures in the injury may be a requirement for concussion, although postmortem microscopic examination of concussion victims typically shows that damage to the brain has been widespread through white matter and cortex as well. Moreover, significant physiological changes in blood pressure, heart rate, breathing patterns, etc., begin to take place immediately upon impact and tend to heighten the disruptive effects of the injury on cerebral functions.

The bruises, shearing, and strains caused by the traumatic impact and consequent movements of the brain within the skull may be thought of as direct effects of the injury. Indirect effects, resulting from the ensuing physiological processes, may be as destructive of brain tissue as the immediate effects of the impact, if not more destructive (Grubb and Coxe, 1978; Jennett and Teasdale, 1981; Plum and Posner, 1980).

Damage caused by hemorrhage may be considered an indirect effect of trauma. When blood flows in between the coverings of the brain, it acts as a more or less rapidly growing mass, the *hematoma* (Grubb and Coxe, 1978). As a hematoma grows, it exerts increasing pressure on surrounding structures. Since the bony cranium does not give way, the air- and liquid-filled spaces surrounding and within the brain are first compressed. The swelling mass then pushes against the softer mass of the brain, deforming and damaging brain tissue pressed against the skull and ultimately squeezing brain tissue through the base of the cranium.

As with bruises and tissue damage to other parts of the body, damage to brain tissue, whether by impact or from increased intracranial pressure, produces swelling as a result of *edema*, the collection of fluid in and around damaged tissue. Whereas swelling on the surface of the body—such as the "goose egg" that temporarily bulges out in response to a superficial blow to the head—can expand without putting pressure on body tissue, swelling within the cranium only compounds whatever damage has taken place, whether direct or indirect. Moreover, since edema is one of the normal physiological responses to tissue damage, the additional damage it causes serves to perpetuate and accelerate the edematous process. Like pressure from hematoma, swelling due to edema can produce further direct damage to brain tissue.

Loss of consciousness may occur at the time of injury when the head accelerates freely and rapidly (Gronwall and Sampson, 1974; Ommaya and Gennarelli, 1974), probably as a result of extraordinary stress on the reticular formation with consequent shearing effects (Grubb and Coxe, 1978). In the past, unconsciousness due to concussion when there were no other apparent injuries to the brain was thought to be a fully reversible phenomenon. Recent studies, however, have demonstrated that some destruction of brain stem cells and fibers accompanies concussion (Ommaya et al., 1973; Walton, 1977). Loss of consciousness that is prolonged beyond a day or that sets in following an initial period of lucidity signals the effects of elevated intracranial pressure on the reticular formation. When this happens, other brain structures generally sustain damage due to pressure as well (Plum and Posner, 1980). The duration of loss of consciousness—or length of coma—can serve as a measure of the severity of damage as it correlates directly with mortality (Heiskanen and Sipponen, 1970), psychosocial dependency (Gilchrist and Wilkinson, 1979; Najenson et al., 1974), and intellectual impairment (Kløve and Cleeland, 1972; Levin, Benton and Grossman, 1982; Levin, Grossman et al., 1979).

The most dangerous effects of swelling are on the lower brain stem structures concerned with vital functions, for when compression seriously compromises their activity the patient dies. The brain stem is also a common site of severe damage in surviving patients (Broe, 1982). Thus, control of intracranial pressure is the most important medical consideration in the acute care of head trauma. Heightened intracranial pressure is the usual cause of death in closed head injuries (Seitelberger and Jellinger, 1971). The increasing survival rate of patients with such injuries attests to the success of modern medical and surgical techniques for controlling intracranial pressure.

Many other physiological changes take place in the brain, and in other organ systems as well, in response to brain injury (Lishman, 1978). Some are ameliorative; others compound destructive processes. Full discussions of the body's physiological response to acute brain damage are given by Plum and Posner (1980) and Jennett and Teasdale (1981).

The victim's situation when he sustains head trauma while moving rapidly, as in a motor vehicle, is greatly aggravated by the additional impact of the brain bouncing around inside the skull upon sudden deceleration. The undersides of the frontal and temporal lobes tend to take the brunt of the impact (Ommaya et al., 1971; K. W. Walsh, 1978b). Additionally, the high velocity of impact in a moving vehicle intensifies shearing, stress, and shock wave effects on brain tissue, thus multiplying the number and severity of small lesions involving nerve fibers and blood vessels throughout the brain. Ventricular enlargement, as demonstrated by CT scan, has been found in 72 percent of a series of patients with severe closed head injuries (Levin, Meyers, Grossman, and Sarwar, 1981). Enlarged ventricles were most likely to occur in patients with prolonged coma following moving vehicle accidents and were associated with poorer outcomes. For these reasons, head injuries incurred in moving vehicle accidents are often treated separately from other head injuries in clinical or research discussions of the problems of these patients.

Behavioral manifestations. Two kinds of specific behavioral impairments occur with closed head injuries. Coup and contrecoup lesions result in discrete impairment of those functions mediated by the cortex at the site of the lesion. Such specific impairment patterns are most likely to appear as the sole or predominate neuropsychological disturbance when the victim has been struck by an object or has struck his head against an object through a sudden move or short fall in which he did not gain much momentum.

I examined a 28-year-old right-handed man about one year after he fell from a work station eight feet above ground, striking the left side of his head. He displayed no language or neurological deficits and all aspects of response speed, motor control, and attention, concentration, and mental tracking were well above average. However, he could no longer perform complex mechanical construction work efficiently or safely, nor could he draw a house in perspective. He failed miserably on an employee aptitude test of visuographic functions and had difficulty with block and puzzle construction tasks. His thinking displayed the fragmented quality characteristic of patients with right hemisphere damage, and his wife complained that he had become insensitive to her emotional states as well as socially gauche.

There was no question that this man had localized brain damage. Without further tests, one could not disprove the possibility that he was one of the one-in-a-hundred right-handed persons whose lateral cortical organization was the reverse of normal (see pp. 221–222). However, a more likely explanation was that he was one of the 50 per cent who sustain a localized contrecoup lesion when the traumatic impact is to the side of the head.

Clearly distinguishable focal deficits are much less likely to be seen when there was a great deal of momentum on impact, as occurs in moving vehicle accidents. In such cases damage tends to be widespread so that some deficits associated with damage at the site of impact may be observed as well as deficits that can only be attributed to focal lesions elsewhere in the brain. As a result, victims of trauma occurring with momentum generally give a pattern of multifocal or bilateral damage without clear-cut evidence of lateralization regardless of the site of impact (Bigler, 1981; Brooks and Aughton, 1979b; Levin et al., 1982).

The second pattern of specific impairments that can be associated with localized brain lesions involves the frontal and temporal lobes, those areas most susceptible to the damaging effects of head injury (Ommaya and Gennarelli, 1974; K. W. Walsh, 1978b). Thus, problems in the regulation and control of activity, in conceptual and problem-solving behavior (see pp. 79–83), and in various aspects of memory and learning are common among closed head injury victims (Hécaen and Albert, 1975; Lezak, 1979b; Luria, 1966; Schachter and Crovitz, 1977). The more severe the injury, the more likely it is that the patient will display deficits characteristic of frontal and temporal lobe injuries and the more prominent these deficits will be (Brooks, 1972; Levin et al., 1976b; Lezak, 1979b).

Damage involving the frontal and temporal lobes tends to have significant effects on the patient's personality and social adjustment as well (Blumer and Benson, 1975; Lezak et al., 1980). These personality changes, even when subtle, are more likely to impede the patient's return to psychosocial independence than cognitive impairment or physical crippling (Bond, 1975; Jennett, 1975; Oddy et al., 1978a, b). Severely injured patients may display a pattern of acute confusional behavior shortly after return to consciousness that may last for days but rarely for more than several weeks. The confusional state is typically characterized by motor restlessness, agitation, incomprehension and incoherence, and uncooperativeness, including resistive and even assaultive behavior. Relatively few victims of traffic accidents who have sustained severe head injuries ever resume their studies or return to gainful employment (Bond, 1975; Eson and Bourke, 1980b; Najenson, 1980), or if they do reenter the work force, it is likely to be at a lower level than before (Lezak et al., 1980; Vigoroux et al., 1971; Weddell et al., 1980). Despite residual abilities that often are considerable, one combination or another of impaired initiative and apathy, lack of critical capacity, defective social judgment, childishness and egocentricity, inability to plan or sustain activity, impulsivity, irritability, and low frustration tolerance is likely to render these patients unemployable or only marginally employable. These same qualities also make a person who has sustained moderate to severe head injuries at best a nuisance at home, at worst a terror (Brooks et al., 1979; McKinlay et al., 1981; Panting and

Merry, 1972). By virtue of these qualities, and again despite their residual capacities, these patients are rarely able to form or maintain close relationships (Weddell et al., 1980), so that those who have not been rendered silly and euphoric or apathetic by their injuries, are often lonely and depressed as well (Lezak et al., 1980; Oddy and Humphrey, 1980).

The diffuse damage that accompanies much traumatic brain injury consists of minute lesions and lacerations scattered throughout the brain substance that eventually become the sites of degenerative changes and scar tissue or simply little cavities (Seitelberger and Jellinger, 1971; Strich, 1961). This kind of damage tends to compromise mental speed, attentional functions, cognitive efficiency, and when severe, high-level concept formation and complex reasoning abilities (Deelman, 1977; Gronwall, 1980; Gronwall and Sampson, 1974; Van Zomeren and Deelman, 1978). These problems are typically reflected in patients' complaints of inability to concentrate or to perform complex mental operations, confusion and perplexity in thinking, irritability, fatigue, and inability to do things as well as before the accident. This latter complaint is particularly poignant in bright, mildly damaged subjects who may still perform well on standard ability tests but who are aware of a loss of mental power and acuity that will keep them from realizing premorbid goals or repeating premorbid accomplishments. In contrast to these bright patients are those whose severe injuries include considerable frontal lobe damage that has limited their capacity for self-awareness and self-evaluation. The performance of these latter patients may be significantly compromised yet they can appear quite untroubled by this and may even continue to announce intentions to return to work, fly airplanes, or enter a profession despite the most obvious cognitive or motor deficits.

Problems associated with diffuse damage readily become apparent in an appropriate examination. Slowed thinking and reaction times may result in significantly lowered scores on timed tests despite the capacity to perform the required task accurately. Tracking tasks tend to be particularly sensitive to diffuse effects (Eson and Bourke, 1980a; Gronwall, 1980). In general, patients with diffuse damage perform relatively poorly on tasks requiring concentration and mental tracking such as oral arithmetic or sequential arithmetic and reasoning problems that must be performed mentally (Gronwall and Wrightson, 1981). Eson and Bourke (1980b) suggest that this common problem represents a deficit in processing information that "has gone before or . . . that require(s) the carrying forward of a rule for making decisions sequentially." Other difficulties experienced by patients with diffuse damage include confusion of items or elements of orally presented questions, feelings of uncertainty about the correctness of their answers, distractibility, and fatigue (Lezak, 1978b).

Occasionally, a head trauma patient with a strong mathematics background will perform surprisingly well on arithmetic problems, even those involving oral arithmetic with its mental tracking requirements, although most head trauma patients run into difficulty with problems that require them to juggle several elements mentally. Observations of arithmetically exceptional patients who perform poorly on other tests of mental tracking give the impression that their arithmetic thinking habits are so ingrained that the solutions come to them automatically, before they have time to lose

171

or get confused about the problems' elements. Similar manifestations of other kinds of overlearned behaviors can also crop up unexpectedly, usually to the examiner's amazement.

Many of the problems associated with diffuse traumatic brain damage commonly occur in the acute stages of brain disease, regardless of etiology (see pp. 206, 210). When traumatic damage is predominantly localized, much of the impairment associated with diffuse damage may diminish in a year or, at the most, two. If the injury was mild, diffuse symptoms may seem to dissipate within the first three to six months after trauma (Gronwall and Sampson, 1974). However, many patients experience problems during the early postraumatic period. For example, of 424 mildly injured patients (i.e., unconscious less than 20 minutes, a Glasgow Coma Scale score of 13 to 15 [see p. 592]), 79% reported persistent headaches, 59% complained of memory problems, and 34% of those who had been employed at the time of injury had not yet returned to work three months later (Rimel et al., 1981). On neuropsychological examination, as a group, these patients displayed a variety of mild deficits, particularly on tasks involving "higher level cognitive functioning, new problem-solving skills, and attention and concentration." Memory functions were not examined. Yet only 2% of this group showed positive neurological signs on the three-month examination.

Moreover, some patients continue to complain of headaches, dizziness, and symptoms commonly associated with mental or emotional stress, such as anxiety, insomnia, irritability, fatigue, and dulled intellect long after they were injured (Lewin, 1968; Lishman, 1978). A recent New Zealand study suggests that persistent complaints of memory and concentration problems made by many victims of mild head injury may be less of a neurotic phenomenon than previously suspected. Testing bright young adults under the stress of mild hypoxia in a simulated altitude of 3,800 meters, Ewing and his colleagues (1980) demonstrated that those subjects who had sustained mild head injury within the previous one to three years performed a little less well on immediate memory and vigilance tasks than did their peers who had not had concussions. Obvious problems associated with diffuse damage are most likely to persist indefinitely when moderate and severe head injuries have been incurred in motor vehicle accidents or other situations involving high-velocity impact.

Few persons with traumatic brain damage exhibit only one pattern of impairment, with the exception of patients with mild injuries. The most severely injured suffer all three. Even many who are moderately damaged will usually have symptoms of focal damage *and* some temporal and frontal lobe deficits *and* diffuse impairment as well.

Judging from their complaints, "memory problems" seem to trouble most traumatically brain injured patients at some time (Brooks and Aughton, 1979b; Oddy et al., 1978b). Often the patient feels that his memory difficulties are predominant even though they may not actually handicap him as much as impaired motivational and self-regulating capacities do. Moreover, "memory problems" may mean any number of specific disabilities involving registration, attention, and tracking; immediate memory span, learning, or retrieval in one or more modalities (Gronwall and Wrightson, 1981); or a condition in which the patient has stored and can retrieve required memories but seems unable to do so without response-directed questioning or cuing (Schachter and Crovitz, 1977). In short, what patients and their families call "memory problems" may result from diffuse damage and reticular formation dysfunction, damage to the memory system per se, or frontal lesions, and, of course, any combination of these. Thus, memory impairments present very differently from one patient to the next.

One distinguishing feature of the postconcussional aspects of closed head injury is *posttraumatic amnesia* (PTA), the period following injury during which the patient is unable to store or retrieve new information. Patients with penetrating head wounds are likely to exhibit this problem when their injury involves concussive effects as well. Posttraumatic amnesia correlates significantly with both coma (C. D. Evans, 1975) and the severity of the injury and therefore has often been used as a measure of severity (Ruesch and Moore, 1943; W. R. Russell and Nathan, 1946; A. Smith, 1961). Brooks and his colleagues (1980), for example, found that duration of posttraumatic amnesia was more closely associated with cognitive status two years after head injury than was length of coma. However, difficulties in defining and therefore determining the duration of posttraumatic amnesia have made its usefulness as a measure of severity questionable (Gronwall, 1980; Jennett, 1972; Schachter and Crovitz, 1977). For example, while it is generally agreed that posttraumatic amnesia does not end when the patient first begins to register experience again, but only when registration is continuous, deciding when continuous registration returns may be difficult with confused or aphasic patients (Gronwall and Wrightson, 1980). Techniques for standardizing assessments of posttraumatic amnesia have been developed for use with hospitalized patients (see p. 593). For those patients who have returned home while still suffering memory gaps, it may be impossible to find out exactly when registration did return to normal. For the patient, posttraumatic amnesia can be a psychologically painful issue. When confusion has settled down and continuous registration has returned, patients are likely to become aware that they have no memory or perhaps very spotty memory for days—sometimes weeks or months—following their injury. Many are quite uncomfortable about this, sometimes troubled indefinitely by uneasiness about their period of posttraumatic amnesia despite being told what happened to them and being reassured as to the propriety of their behavior during this time.

Retrograde amnesia, usually involving the minutes, sometimes hours, and more rarely days immediately preceding the accident, commonly accompanies posttraumatic amnesia (Lishman, 1978; Schachter and Crovitz, 1977). Its duration too tends to correlate with severity of injury. In my experience, patients are less disturbed by their experience of retrograde amnesia than by anterograde amnesia, while their lawyers tend to find retrograde amnesia difficult to accept.

Since the variety of functions that tend to be lumped together as memory are mediated by different structures and disrupted in different ways, it is not surprising that their posttraumatic courses differ. Thus, those activities that have a large attentional component, such as immediate span, tend to improve quickly and reach a plateau within the first six months to a year after injury (Gronwall and Sampson, 1974; Lezak, 1978b; Vigouroux et al., 1971). Activities such as new learning that involve the memory system tend to improve over a longer period of time (K. O'Brien and Lezak, 1981; Vigoroux et al., 1971). Those deficits having to do with retrieval rather than registration and learning are either apt to improve as specific verbal or visuospatial functions return, making stored information and response patterns available again, or, in the case of sluggishness in engaging in retrieval activity, should the deficits result from extensive frontal or subcortical damage, they may show only minimal improvement and that fairly soon after return of consciousness.

During the early stages following head injury, many patients exhibit moderate to severe communication or perceptual disturbances that ultimately clear up or remain as subtle defects that are not always apparent to casual observers (Broe, 1982; Lezak et al., 1980; M. T. Sarno, 1980). However, after the acute symptoms have subsided, most head trauma patients, even some who have sustained severe injuries, tend to show remarkably little deficit on verbal tests that measure overlearned material or behaviors such as culturally common information and reading, writing, and speech (when the damage does not directly involve the language centers). Yet, residual problems of word retrieval (dysnomia) may continue to plague head trauma victims even when other verbal functions have improved to normal or near normal levels (Levin, Grossman, Sarwar, and Meyers, 1981). The extensiveness and severity of residual language difficulties tends to be associated with the severity of the injury as well as with the extent of left hemisphere damage. Head injured patients may also do well on tests that elicit responses primarily mediated by the posterior areas of the cortex, which are less likely to be damaged except when under the point of impact. The latter include tests of constructional abilities and perceptual accuracy that are uncomplicated by memory, organization, or speed requirements.

Yet these are the kinds of tasks that, in large part, make up the tests and test batteries used for both general intellectual assessment and examination of brain dysfunction. Unless examination techniques are geared to eliciting impairments that are common to head trauma victims, these often seriously handicapping deficits may not become evident (Eson and Bourke, 1980a; Gronwall and Sampson, 1974; K. W. Walsh, 1978b). Many patients can perform adequately on a conventional psychological examination or one of the prepackaged neuropsychological test batteries. For example, long after the acute stages have passed, traumatically brain injured adults achieve score patterns on the Wechler Adult Intelligence Scale "that tended to approximate the average" (McFie, 1976). Yet many of these patients continue to suffer frontal apathy, memory deficits, severely slowed thinking processes, or a mental tracking disability that makes them unable to resume working or, in some instances, to assume any social responsibility at all. Insufficient or inappropriate behavioral examinations of head trauma can lead to unjust social and legal decisions concerning employability and competency, can invalidate rehabilitation planning efforts, and can confuse patient and family, not infrequently adding financial distress to their already considerable stress and despair. In this vein, it should be noted that Brooks (unpublished) has observed that patients seeking compensation for their injuries do not present more symptoms or deficits than similar patients who do not have compensation claims, but the claimants tend to complain more than other patients. Rimel and her

174

coworkers (1981) also found that the pending litigation had a negligible effect if any on the level of adjustment achieved by head injury patients.

Although most cases of head trauma involve blows to the head or penetration of the skull by missiles or other objects, other sources of traumatic brain injuries include lightning, electrical accidents, and blast injuries. These latter may also have neuropsychological effects as a result of temporary paralysis of brain centers with consequent cardiac or respiratory malfunction creating a transient hypoxic condition. Some of these accident victims sustain head injuries through falling or being knocked over. A variety of other kinds of injuries to brain and associated tissue can also occur in lightning, electrical, blast, or radiation injuries. For a detailed discussion of these less common forms of head trauma, see Gurdjian (1975) Gurdjian and Gurdjian (1978), and Panse (1970).

Vascular Disorders

Vascular diseases of the brain cause more deaths and debilitation than any other diseases except heart conditions and cancer (Kuller, 1978; WHO, 1980). A knowledge of the structure and dynamics of the cerebrovascular circulation and its relationship to the rest of the circulatory system and its diseases is necessary for understanding the events that characterize the course of cerebrovascular diseases. However, a technical description of the cerebral circulation and its vicissitudes is beyond the scope of this book. Readers wishing such a description at a relatively nontechnical level should consult Kevin Walsh's *Neuropsychology* (1978b) or M. T. O'Brien and Pallett's *Total care of the stroke patient* (1978). More detailed discussions of the cerebral circulatory system and how it relates to the common cerebrovascular disorders are given in Bannister (1978), Barr (1979), Eliasson et al. (1978), Walton (1977), and in other basic neurology and neuroanatomy texts.

The considerable variety of disorders affecting cerebral circulation and their many subtypes precludes a comprehensive treatment of the neuropsychological implications of cerebral vascular disease. Instead, this section deals with those conditions that a neuropsychologist is most likely to encounter. The focus is on the broad outlines of their structural and pathophysiological antecedents and on their neuropsychological ramifications.

STROKE AND RELATED DISORDERS

The most frequently encountered of the cerebrovascular diseases is the *cerebrovascular accident* (CVA) (J. S. Meyer and Shaw, 1982). It was once called *apoplexy* or an *apoplectic attack* and is now commonly referred to as *stroke*. Medically speaking, a stroke is a "focal neurological disorder of abrupt development due to a pathological process in blood vessels" (Walton, 1977).

The cardinal pathogenic feature of CVAs is the disruption of the supply of nutrients—primarily oxygen and glucose—to the brain as a result of disrupted blood flow. The inability of the nervous tissue of the brain to survive more than several minutes of oxygen deprivation accounts for the rapidity with which irreversible brain damage takes place. The disruption of normal blood flow, *infarction*, creates an area of damaged or dead tissue, an *infarct*. Most strokes are caused by ischemic infarctions, i.e., infarctions due to tissue starvation resulting from insufficient or absent blood flow rather than from insufficient or absent nutrients in the blood.

Two prominent mechanisms that can account for the tissue starvation of CVAs are obstructions of blood vessels and hemorrhage. Because the symptoms and course of these two major stroke-producing disorders differ, they are considered separately below. This separation, however, is an oversimplification as some kinds of obstructions are hemorrhagic in nature and some hemorrhages give rise to spasmodic constriction of the blood vessels (vasospasms) that so severely impedes blood flow as to create focal sites of obstruction.

Obstructive strokes.   The buildup of fat deposits within the artery walls *(arteriosclerotic plaques)* involves fibrous tissue and is susceptible to hemorrhage and ulceration. These deposits are the most common source of obstruction of blood flow to the brain. In *thrombotic* strokes, the infarction results from occlusion of blood vessel by the clump of blood particles and tissue overgrowth, a *thrombus*, that accumulates in arteriosclerotic plaques that most usually form where blood vessels branch or, less frequently, on traumatic or other lesion sites on the vessel wall. Growth of the thrombus narrows the opening in the blood vessel, thus reducing blood flow, or closes off the vessel altogether. Thrombotic strokes may occur suddenly with no further increase in symptoms. Often, however, they take as long as half an hour to develop fully. In some cases, thrombotic strokes evolve for hours or even days. Most usually (approximately 80% of the cases) they are preceded by one or more "little strokes," i.e., *transient ischemic attacks* (TIA's) with symptoms that dissipate within a day or, more likely, within hours (see pp. 177–178).

Obstruction in *embolic* strokes is caused by an *embolus*, a plug of thrombic material or fatty deposit broken away from blood vessel walls, or of foreign matter such as clumps of bacteria or even obstructive gas bubbles. Most emboli are fragments of thrombotic lesions that developed outside the intracranial circulatory system, many in the heart and its blood vessels. Relatively few thrombotic emboli arise from lesions within the major arterial pathways to the brain. The onset of embolic strokes is generally sudden and becomes complete within minutes. Unlike thrombotic strokes, there are no warning signs.

The effects of ischemic infarctions vary from person to person, or from time to time when a person suffers repeated strokes. These variations are due to a host of factors such as individual differences in the anatomical organization of the cerebral circulation, in the capacity to develop and utilize collateral brain circulation, and in cerebral blood pressure and blood flow. Variations in the extent, sites, and severity of arteriosclerotic disease, in the large extracranial arteries that feed the cerebral circulation, in the smaller intracranial and intracerebral vessels, and within the circulatory system of the heart contribute to individual differences in the manifestations of stroke, as do such health variables as heart disease, diabetes, or blood conditions that affect

176

its viscosity or clotting capacity. Even age and sex may play a role in determining the presentation of a stroke (Brown and Jaffe, 1975; Eslinger and Damasio, 1981; Seron, 1979). For example, embolic strokes, usually associated with heart disease, tend to occur at an earlier age than thrombotic strokes and are more likely to involve anterior areas of the brain. Patients with Broca's (expressive) aphasia tend to be younger than those with Wernicke's (receptive) aphasia or global aphasia (Harasymiw and Halper, 1981). A tendency toward bilateralization of function in the female may account for less severe behavioral manifestations of strokes in women (Castro-Caldas et al., 1979). Thus, each stroke is an individual event.

Yet with all these variations, certain overall patterns in onset and manifestations tend to stand out. Stroke tends to have one-sided effects. While there is an enormous range of differences between stroke patients with respect to the depth, extent, and site (e.g., from front to back and crown to base of the brain) of damaged tissue, most strokes lateralize either to the right or to the left. For this reason, many stroke patients make good subjects for neuropsychological research into the lateral organization of the brain and the development of tests of specific cognitive functions.

During the acute stages, secondary diffuse effects typically add symptoms of widespread brain pathology as edema and other physiological reactions take place. Sometimes the symptoms improve relatively early in the course of the illness. Such a change for the better is thought to reflect the dislodgement of an embolus and return of more normal blood flow to the ischemic area (Bannister, 1978). Swelling and other secondary effects of the stroke can cause more serious bilateral or diffuse damage than the stroke itself and may—as may secondary physiological reactions to trauma—result in death. Thus, stroke patients frequently display signs of bilateral or diffuse damage during the early stages of their illness. As swelling diminishes and other physiological disturbances return to a more normal state, signs of bilateral or diffuse dysfunction gradually diminish and may dissipate altogether, while the severity of the lateralized impairments usually decreases too.

Most patients whose strokes were ischemic in nature are left with some more or less obvious lateralized deficits and relatively minimal evidence of diffuse damage. Moreover, their focal deficits typically fit into a pattern of dysfunction associated with areas of the brain that share a common artery or network of smaller arterial vessels. Thus, it is unlikely that decreased verbal fluency, suggestive of frontal damage, will occur with alexia without agraphia, a condition that typically implicates an occipital lesion, unless the patient has had two or more successive strokes. On the other hand, the four symptoms that make up Gerstmann's syndrome (see p. 71) occur together because the cortical areas in which each of the four is mediated are close together within a common arterial flow pattern (Geschwind and Strub, 1975; Hécaen and Albert, 1978).

Transient ischemic attacks (TIAs)   These episodes of temporary obstruction of a blood vessel last less than 24 hours by definition, and many last for only moments (Bannister, 1978; Lishman, 1978). They are characterized by mild strokelike symptoms that follow the same patterns of presentation—lateralization and clustering of symptoms within defined arterial territories—as do full-blown strokes. Furthermore, like strokes, most transient ischemic attacks are associated with arteriosclerotic disease. They typically represent little infarctions resulting from thrombotic microemboli that pass on before they can do much damage. Patients may experience few or many such attacks, relatively frequently or spaced out over months or years (Lishman, 1978). Half or more of patients who have had transient ischemic attacks ultimately sustain a major stroke (Brust, 1977; Toole et al., 1978; Ziegler and Hassanein, 1973).

In stating that transient ischemic attacks are "followed by complete recovery" and that "these attacks are not accompanied by irreversible infarction of the affected brain substance," Walton (1977) has reported the common wisdom. However, a closer look at these patients, through the eyes of relatives or a careful clinician (Lishman, 1978) or by means of neuropsychological tests (Delaney et al., 1980; Kelly et al., 1980), indicates that in fact patients who have had TIAs do suffer mild cognitive impairment. The tests used by Delaney and his co-workers elicited both problems with slowing and tracking suggestive of bilateral or diffuse brain damage and focal deficits indicating that lateralized damage had occurred in those areas in which blood flow is most commonly disrupted by stroke. F. B. Wood and his colleagues (1981) also report that a substantial number of patients who have had TIA's show some neuropsychological deficits, most often on delayed recall tasks.

Hemorrhagic strokes. Strokes in which hemorrhage is the primary and most significant agent of damage may result from the rupture of an *aneurysm* (weak vessel wall that can balloon out and ultimately burst under pressure). Although aneurysms are present at the rate of two percent of the population at large (Raichle et al., 1978), ruptured aneurysms attract attention because their manifestations can be quite dramatic. Warning symptoms rarely precede these hemorrhagic strokes. Typically, the patient suffers extremely painful headaches that are often accompanied by nausea and vomiting and followed within hours by evidence of neurological dysfunction such as stiff neck and focal neurological signs. The patient may or may not lose consciousness, depending on the severity of the bleed. The condition can be fatal when massive bleeding occurs. Yet, if the bleeding is arrested soon enough, the patient may sustain relatively little brain damage. The in-between cases, in which damage is extensive but not fatal, tend to display behavioral impairments attributable to focal damage. For example, patients who have had ruptured aneurysms of the anterior communicating artery are likely to display the kinds of behavioral disturbances—such as lack of spontaneity, childishness, indifference, and the Korsakoff memory disorder—associated with frontal lobe lesions (Okawa et al., 1980). However, neuropsychological deficits resulting from ruptured aneurysms differ from the impairments of ischemic cerebrovascular accidents in that the damage is likely to be more widespread and does not necessarily follow anatomically well-defined or neuropsychologically common patterns.

Hemorrhages of the small blood vessels lying within the cerebral hemispheres have been associated with *hypertension* (high blood pressure). The blood vessels at the base of the cerebral hemispheres are most vulnerable to this kind of hemorrhage so that the usual area of involvement is subcortical. Thus, these strokes mostly affect the thalamus, basal ganglia, and brain stem. These hypertensive cerebral hemorrhages or intracerebral hemorrhages, as they are variously called, have a mortality rate of 50% (Raichle et al., 1978). The condition of surviving patients can be anything from near-vegetative to relatively good return to independence. However, even the patients who show greatest improvement continue to suffer some attention and memory problems and irritability (Walton, 1977), and they also show the more subtle changes in psychosocial and self-regulatory behavior typically associated with frontal lobe lesions.

Even without documented cerebral changes, hypertension has been associated with mild cognitive impairments that worsen with the duration and severity of the hypertensive condition (Eisdorfer, 1977; Wilkie et al., 1976). Deficits have been reported in visual memory (Visual Reproduction subtest of the Wechsler Memory Scale, see p. 444) and on a complex concept formation task (the Category Test, see pp. 480-481) (H. Goldman et al., 1974; 1975). Reduction of blood pressure was related to fewer errors on the Category Test. Eisdorfer (1977) notes, however, that while elderly patients with significant hypertension suffered gradual intellectual deterioration over a ten-year period, those with mild hypertension actually showed some improvement. Cognitive functioning of normotensive subjects did not change appreciably over the years.

Degenerative Disorders

Many disease processes involve progressive deterioration of brain tissue and of behavior. Some of these conditions are commonplace, and others are rare. Together they may affect as many as 16% of the over-65 population, or some 4,000,000 Americans in 1978 (Tower, 1978).

Neuropsychological differences between the degenerative disorders show up in the early stages before the disease process has become so widespread as to obliterate them (Fuld, 1978; Gainotti et al., 1980). By the time these various diseases have run much of their course, their victims tend to share many behavioral features. Prominent among these are psychosocial regression; disorders of attention such as inattentiveness, inability to concentrate or track mentally, and distractibility; apathy with impaired capacity to initiate, plan, or execute complex activities; and the full spectrum of memory disorders. In the long run, most degenerative conditions become neuropsychologically indistinguishable.

Therefore, the following descriptions of degenerative disorders pertain to the patient's presentation early enough in the course of his illness that distinguishing characteristics are still present. How many months or years it takes from the first appearance of subtle behavioral harbingers of the disorder to full-blown deterioration varies with the conditions and probably with individual differences as well (Kaszniak et al., 1979). The end point for most persons suffering these conditions is total dependency, loss of general awareness including loss of sense of self, and inability to make self-serving or goal-directed responses. Death typically results from pneumonia or other diseases associated with inactivity and debilitation.

DEMENTIA

All of the degenerative disorders and many other chronic brain conditions such as stroke qualify as *dementias* under broad interpretations of this variously defined nosological construct. C. E. Wells (1977), for example, considers dementia to be "the spectrum of mental states resulting from diseases of man's cerebral hemispheres in adult life." Other investigators reserve this term for progressive "global deterioration of mental functions due to organic diseases of the cerebral hemispheres . . . which have a chronic and irreversible course" (Golper and Binder, 1981; see also Lipowski, 1975). Imprecision in using the term "dementia" can confuse discussions of patients and conceptualizations of their disorders. For the sake of clear communication, I will use the term "dementia" only in the narrow sense quoted except when it is qualified, as in "subcortical dementia." When working with patients with dementing disorders, it is also important to keep in mind that these are not mutually exclusive conditions. Symptoms and neuropathological changes associated with two or even more of them may occur together (Boller et al., 1980; Roth, 1978).

Alzheimer's disease (AD)/senile dementia of the Alzheimer's type (SDAT). Alzheimer's disease, characterized by inexorably progressive degenerative nerve cell changes within the cerebral hemispheres with concomitant progressive global deterioration of intellect and personality has been considered the paradigm of the dementias (Roth, 1980). With one-half of all cases of dementia attributed to this condition and affecting an estimated five to six percent of persons aged 65 and over, it is the most widespread of the dementing diseases (Plum, 1979; Schneck et al., 1982; C. E. Wells, 1982). The usual presentation of senile dementia is indistinguishable from Alzheimer's disease, both behaviorally and at the cellular level (Gruenberg, 1978; Terry, 1980). Local or personal convention seems to dictate whether a dementing condition of the Alzheimer's type is considered a presenile dementia (called Alzheimer's disease) or a senile dementia (called senile dementia of the Alzheimer's type). Some authorities use age 59 (e.g., Gruenberg, 1978; Seltzer and Sherwin, 1978) and others age 64 (e.g., Berry, 1975; Roth, 1978) as the upper limit for diagnosing a presenile dementia. Thus, the diagnosis of many patients with this condition may depend both on their age and on their physician's opinion of when old age (the *senium*) begins.[1] This discussion will follow C. E. Wells's (1978a) resolution of the terminological differences among authorities and will refer to this condition as Alzheimer's disease regardless of the patient's age when the condition was first suspected. In current psychiatric usage, Alzheimer's disease is called "primary degenerative dementia (PDD)" (American Psychiatric Association, 1980; Reisberg and Ferris, 1982).

The neuropathological hallmark of Alzheimer's disease is the presence of *neurofi-*

---

[1] In clinical practice, this is a diagnosis by exclusion; i.e., when all other diagnostic possibilities have been eliminated and the patient displays the behavioral alterations characteristic of Alzheimer's disease, this becomes the suspected diagnosis. The diagnosis can only be confirmed in autopsy when pathognomonic changes in brain tissue are demonstrated.

brillary tangles and *senile plaques*. The former are tangled bundles of fine fibers within the cell bodies of neurons that occur throughout the brain, but particularly in hippocampal and amygdaloid areas (Berry, 1975; Lishman, 1978; Terry, 1980). The latter are products and by-products of neuronal degeneration that can be found in all areas of the cerebral cortex, particularly the parietal lobe (Roth, 1978), but they too are likely to appear in great profusion in hippocampal and amygdaloid areas. These alterations in the fine structure of the brain tend to be consistently associated with mental deterioration, regardless of the patient's age (Blessed et al., 1968; Roth, 1980). On CT scans, more than half of all patients suffering Alzheimer's disease show evidence of cerebral atrophy in the form of thinning of the cortical mantle, usually with enlargement of the lateral ventricles and a flattening of the surface of the cortex (Berry, 1975; deLeon et al., 1980; Pear, 1977). CT scan measurements of patients in the 62 to 81 year age range, diagnosed as having senile dementia, have indicated lower tissue densities in areas confined to the frontal and temporal lobes and to the anterior portion of the *caudate nucleus* within the corpus striatum (see p. 48) (Bondareff et al., 1981). A biochemical abnormality involving an important neurotransmitter (choline acetyltransferase: CAT) has been repeatedly found in post-mortem examination of the brain tissue of patients with Alzheimer's disease, giving new hope for its treatment (D. M. Bowen, 1980; Corkin, 1981; C. M. Smith and Swash, 1980; E. V. Sullivan et al., 1981). C. E. Wells (1982) reports recent findings of dysfunction in the noradrenergic system of some of these patients. Abnormally high levels of aluminum in brain structures of some Alzheimer patients have been reported (Crapper et al., 1973; Schneck et al., 1982). In any event, its etiology remains a mystery (Crapper-McLachlan and DeBoni, 1980; Sherwin and Seltzer, 1976).

Disagreement regarding the extent to which this condition is genetically transmissible is reflected in conflicting reports. Whalley et al., 1982 and Tower (1978) find that only in a small proportion of cases does Alzheimer's disease run in families. Heston and his colleagues (1981), however, found probable cases of Alzheimer's disease among close family members of 40% of their patients. A greater incidence of this disease has been reported for women, with relatively greater frequencies of occurrence in the range of two to one and three to one (Lishman, 1978). These findings are coming under question as they have been based on hospitalization rates, which tend to run higher for women than for men (Schneck et al., 1982).

The earliest signs that herald Alzheimer's disease are usually a failing recent memory, depression, and irritability, although occasionally a seizure will give the first indication of neurological disease. The condition typically begins so insidiously that often the family is unaware that anything is wrong until a sudden disruption in routine leaves the patient disoriented, confused, and unable to deal with the unfamiliar situation. Because the early behavioral decline is so gradual and unsuspected and because most simple functions—as measured by elementary tests of language and of sensory and motor functions—remain intact in the early stages of the disease (M. P. Kelly et al., 1980), it is difficult to date the onset of the condition with any sureness. Moreover, early symptoms of inattentiveness, mild cognitive dulling, social withdrawal, and emotional blunting or agitation are often confused with depression so that it is not extraordinary to find an Alzheimer's patient who has recently been treated quite vigorously for depression (Liston, 1978; Roth, 1978). In these cases, families attempting to identify a date or period of significant behavior change that would signal the onset of the disease run into difficulty. Even with all the hindsight that one can muster, it is still usually impossible to distinguish the patient's premorbid personality and emotional disturbances from his earliest symptoms and reactions to the evolving experience of personal disintegration. Thus, the published range of duration of the disease from 1½ to 15 years (Walton, 1977) probably represents a range of starting points, from very early in the course of the disease to much further along for socially isolated patients or those whose families are not very observant. Nevertheless, a tendency for early onset (under age 55) to be associated with a more severe and rapid course than later onset has been documented (Heston et al., 1981).

By the time a neurological disorder is suspected, many patients have developed the characteristic behavioral disorders of Alzheimer's disease. When the deterioration has progressed to the point that the disoriented patient has lost the capacity for purposeful action beyond satisfaction of immediate need states or fragments of reruns of old habit patterns, the problem of differential diagnosis has usually been resolved. The deteriorating patient may still want to drive or continually pester others to take him out, but with no goal beyond the desired activity. Periods of restless apathy may alternate with aggressive demands for attention and petulant irritability. In the early stages of the disease, and even when the erosion of cognitive functions has become apparent, orientation may still be intact (Eisdorfer and Cohen, 1980). By the time most cognitive functions have deteriorated significantly, the patient's sense of person, capacity for judgment, or ability to care for himself will be lost although well-ingrained social habits may still be retained.

Severely handicapping apraxias, disruption of effective speech production, disturbances of posture and gait, and incontinence eventually render the mindless patient helpless and totally dependent. Ultimately, the patient ends his days in bedridden oblivion.

Neuropsychological assessment can be an important diagnostic aid for differentiating Alzheimer's disease from depression or other psychiatric conditions, or from treatable neurological disorders such as normal pressure hydrocephalus (see pp. 189–190). Using standard measurement instruments, Coolidge and his co-workers (undated), Fuld (1978, 1982) and Horenstein (1977) have delineated the broad outlines of the pattern of cognitive dysfunction in early Alzheimer's disease. On the Wechsler Intelligence Scales (see Chapter 9), the highest scores are obtained on tests of overlearned behaviors presented in a familiar format and of immediate memory recall. Thus, Information, Vocabulary, many Comprehension and Similarities items, and Digits Forward (digit span) will be performed relatively well, even long after the patient is not capable of caring for himself. The more the task is unfamiliar, abstract, speed-dependent, and taxes the patient's dwindled capacity for attention and learning, the more likely it is that he do poorly: Block Design, Digit Symbol, and Digits Backward typically vie for the bottom rank among test scores. Object Assembly tends to be low, too, but generally runs a little higher than Block Design and Digit Symbol. Based on their study of seven WAIS subtests (excluding Information, Comprehension, Picture Arrangement, and Object Assembly), the Coolidge group (undated) suggest that a Vocabulary subtest score that is at least twice as large as the Block Design subtest score is a highly likely indicator of dementia and rarely if ever occurs among depressed patients. This pattern generalizes to other tests, so that these patients fail other reasoning, unfamiliar, or timed tests such as Raven's Matrices (pp.502–505), verbal fluency tests (pp. 330–333), and both storage and retrieval components of memory learning tests (Fuld, 1978, and see pp. 574–575; Gainotti et al., 1980).

Immediate span and short-term memory tend to be relatively spared (Tweedy et al., 1982). Kaszniak and his co-workers (1979b; R. S. Wilson, Kaszniak, and Fox, 1981a) have demonstrated marked deficits in the learning ability and remote recall of dementia patients with cerebral atrophy. Learning impairments appear to stem from an inability to process new material for "deep" (i.e., semantic) encoding (R. S. Wilson, Kaszniak, and Fox, 1980). These patients tend to have a normal Digits Forward span with little or no capacity to recite Digits Backward. Defective memory for faces is also common among these patients, but does not appear to be functionally linked with their verbal memory impairments (R. S. Wilson, Kaszniak, and Bacon, in press).

The disturbances in verbal thought and language production that occur in Alzheimer's disease reflect the nature of the cognitive deterioration generally. Language defects may appear quite early in the course of the disease, but so rarely and in such mild form as to be easily overlooked. Yet the occurrence of several instances of characteristic speech or language anomalies, such as perseverations or paralogisms with syntax preserved (Golper and Binder, 1981; Marin and Gordon, 1979) may be strong evidence of a dementing process, particularly if other early symptoms of the disease are present as well. Alzheimer patients experience increasing difficulty with word finding *(dysnomia)* that blocks the flow of speech (R. S. Wilson, Kaszniak, Fox, et al., 1981b). Fuld and her co-workers (1982) have documented a relationship between the presence and frequency of *intrusive* errors in speech (i.e., *intrusions:* the "inappropriate recurrence of a response [or type of response] from a preceding test item, test, or procedure") and cholinergic deficiency as inferred from administration of anticholinergic drugs to young volunteers, and from diminished levels of choline acetyltransferase in the brain tissue of Alzheimer's patients (see also p. 181).

One dimension of verbal impairment that appears early in the course of the disease is loss of spontaneity so that conversation always has to be initiated by someone else or something else (Irigaray, 1973). In extreme cases, a verbally capable patient may become mute.

A 49-year-old married salesman, father of three, had been variously diagnosed as depressed and paranoid schizophrenic during a six-month period in which he withdrew socially, communicating at one point only to the living room radiator. On his third psychiatric hospitalization, he was diagnosed as catatonic, as he remained immobile most of the time, and mute. Neuropsychological consultation was requested as one staff member suspected aphasia since it is not usual for catatonic schizophrenia to make its first appearance in midlife. I visited the patient in his room to see whether he would be amenable to formal examination. While I began talking to him, he fixated on the bright yellow button pinned to the lapel of my white lab coat and slowly began speaking for the first time in weeks, reading the red printed words over and over; "Thank you for not smoking. Thank you for not smoking," etc. Once he had started talking, it became possible to engage his attention enough for him to answer questions. He was promptly referred for a neurological workup, which resulted in a probable diagnosis of Alzheimer's disease.

The loss of verbal spontaneity characteristic of patients with Alzheimer's disease is typically reflected in *dysfluency*, i.e., difficulty in generating words. Thus verbal fluency tests are sensitive to this problem (see pp. 330–333).

The example of the "catatonic" patient also illustrates the perseverative aspect of verbal dysfunction in these patients. Like nonresponsiveness, perseveration is not limited to speech. It shows up early in written spellings, such as "streeet," CCCcarl," or "Reagagen," in the meaningless appearance in writing or speech of words or expressions just recently used, in drawings that resemble the last or next-to-the-last thing drawn, or movements or gestures left over from a preceding response (Golper and Binder, 1981). Fuld (1980; 1982) notes the usefulness of this latter kind of perseverative response (intrusions) in differentiating Alzheimer's disease from other dementing processes.

Paraphasias and articulatory errors that may be a form of oral apraxia appear as the disease progresses (Golper and Binder, 1981; Obler and Albert, 1980). Dysarthria and jumbling of sounds and words tend to parallel the performance apraxias that eventually interfere with the patient's accomplishment of almost any intentional act, including intentional speech.

A breakdown in the ability to maintain consistent and accurate use of verbal concepts, either in speaking or making responses to verbal stimuli (M. F. Schwartz et al., 1979; Irigaray, 1973), tends to parallel the patient's increasing inability to respond to or use appropriately nonverbal material such as everyday objects or their own body parts. Disabilities in almost all aspects of writing have been observed, particularly in association with deterioration in language functions generally (R. S. Wilson, Kaszniak, Fox, et al., 1981b). In these patients, verbal retrieval capacity appears to deteriorate while the basic organizing principles of language, the syntax, remain relatively intact. Ultimately, these patients all become wordless and verbally uncomprehending.

Pick's disease. This relatively rare condition has also been called "circumscribed cortical atrophy" (Walton, 1977). Pick's disease is so similiar to Alzheimer's disease— even to affecting at least twice as many women as men—that diagnosis usually has to wait until autopsy (Lishman, 1978; Sjögren et al., 1952). Its pathological presentation shares many of the features of Alzheimer's disease, but enough differences can be detectable microscopically. Cellular degeneration and atrophy are typically confined to frontal and temporal cortex, which accounts for "frontal lobish" kinds of personality changes, such as silliness, social disinhibition, and impulsivity with apathy or impaired capacity for sustained motivation (Roth, 1978; Walton, 1977). Whereas memory impairments are usually an early feature of Alzheimer's disease with significant personality deterioration coming somewhat later, in Pick's disease personality disturbances precede memory loss (Berry, 1975). The course may run a little longer than in Alzheimer's disease, but it also terminates in a bedridden, mindless state (Lishman, 1978).

Multi-infarct dementia (arteriosclerotic dementia; arteriosclerotic psychosis). This vascular disease of the brain is usually considered among the degenerative disorders. Typically, it has a progressive stepwise course and its manifestations are sufficiently like those of Alzheimer's disease that it can be mistaken for it (Scheinberg, 1978; Walton, 1977). Although *arteriosclerosis* (hardening of the arteries due to loss of elasticity with thickening of arterial walls) contributes to the occurrence of this condition, the immediate pathological process is multiple strokes (often small strokes) that eventually lead to diffuse softening and degeneration of cerebral tissue (Torack, 1978; Walton, 1977).

The behavioral counterpart of this process to some extent reflects focal lesions as they occur (Roth, 1978). As more and more infarcted areas involve increasing amounts of cerebral tissue, a picture of diffuse cognitive and personality deterioration emerges. Although the behavioral presentation of multi-infarct dementia can be indistinguishable from that of Alzheimer's disease (Torack, 1978), multi-infarct dementia tends to have a number of distinguishing features (Hachinski et al., 1975; Roth, 1978; Walton, 1977. See also pp. 585–586). Its course often has an acute onset and progresses in a "stuttering" or stepwise manner. The severity of symptoms may fluctuate from hour to hour, or day to night with nocturnal confusion. Early in its course, cognitive deficits are likely to predominate while personality deterioration lags behind, although eventually both aspects of behavior may become profoundly disordered. Perhaps most distinctive of this condition are the motor abnormalities, such as gait disturbances and rigidity, which reflect lesions involving subcortical structures (Scheinberg, 1978). More men than women have multi-infarct dementia and hypertension is prevalent (Ladurner et al., 1982).

SUBCORTICAL DEMENTIAS

This relatively new concept refers to the behavioral symptoms of degenerative disorders involving primarily subcortical structures (M. L. Albert, 1978; Joynt and Shoulson, 1979). Rather than the widespread cognitive and personality disorganization that characterizes diffuse dementing processes, patients with subcortical dementias are more likely to experience decreased initiation, slowing in their rate of response, and specific defects in memory functions. Differences in the behavioral presentation of the various subcortical disease processes have been related to the structures each involves and to associated variations in the production of neurotransmitters (Lishman, 1978; Walton, 1977).

Parkinson's disease. This is primarily a condition of neuronal degeneration of basal ganglion structures, particularly the *substantia nigra*, bilateral, small, darkly pigmented areas that are part of the motor system of the basal ganglia. Diffuse cortical degeneration may be present as well (Boller, 1980; Lishman, 1978). It is usually progressive. Parkinsonism's outstanding feature is a motor disorder with a number of component symptoms (Walton, 1977). These include "resting tremor," a relatively rapid rhythmical shaking, usually of the hands, ankles, or head, that diminishes or disappears with voluntary movement; muscular rigidity; difficulties initiating movements *(akinesia)* and *bradykinesia* (motor slowing) resulting in the characteristic *masked fascies* (an expressionless, unblinking stare), dysarthric speech, and general loss of grace, agility, and fine coordination. These patients are further hampered by a slowed, shuffling gait with little steps *(marche à petits pas)*, difficulty in starting to walk and, once started, difficulty in stopping. Few patients display all of these symptoms, particularly early in the course of the disease. Parkinsonism is a syndrome rather than a disease; there appear to be a number of causative agents, some known or suspected and some unknown (Kessler, 1978). Among known etiologies are encephalitis and multi-infarct dementia; toxic reactions are suspected in some instances, familial tendencies in a few others. However, most cases remain unexplained (i.e., *idiopathic*) (Lishman, 1978; Pincus and Tucker, 1978).

Examinations of samples of parkinsonism patients have generally indicated that between 40 and 50% suffer mental deterioration (Boller, 1980; Boller et al., 1980; Hakim and Mathieson, 1979; Loranger et al., 1972). Some studies suggest that mental changes occur in only about one-third of all patients with Parkinson's disease and may represent a subtype of the disorder in which both cortical and subcortical structures are affected (C. E. Wells, 1982). In many of these patients, Boller and his colleagues found the tangles and plaques of Alzheimer's disease on autopsy, suggesting a related degenerative process. However, fewer than half of those with mild mental deterioration showed the Alzheimer's signs. Boller (1980) points out that dementia in these patients is not associated with aging. He also notes that some investigators have suggested an association between dementia and dopaminergic drugs used to control motor symptoms of the disease (see also pp. 226–227).

Specific impairments of cognitive functioning in parkinsonism patients suggest how the basal ganglia contribute to cognitive activity. These impairments include slowed scanning on a visual recognition task (Wilson et al., 1980), diminished conceptual flexibility (M. L. Albert, 1978; F. P. Bowen, 1976), and slowing on motor response tasks that may reflect both bradykinesia and a central defect of motor programming (Bowen, 1976; Matthews and Haaland, 1979; Talland and Schwab, 1964). The writing and drawing of many patients with Parkinson's disease tend to be more than ordinarily small and cramped appearing. M. L. Albert's additional finding of decreased output on verbal fluency tasks, without dysarthria or aphasia, suggests a central problem of impaired initiative or spontaneity.

Certain cognitive and motor impairments tend to occur together, implicating the same subcortical lesion site (Mortimer et al., 1982; Pirozzolo et al., 1982). While Mortimer, Pirozzolo, and their co-workers observed no relationship in the occurrence of the three cardinal symptoms of parkinsonism (i.e., tremor, rigidity, and bradykinesia), they found that bradykinesia correlated significantly with poorer performances on tests involving psychomotor speed, visuospatial performances (both timed and untimed), and memory for spatial orientation. In contrast, severity of tremor was related to *better* scores on the test of memory for spatial orientation. These studies also reported a general decrease in verbal memory that was unrelated to specific motor deficits. Only on tests of apraxia, object naming, and vocabulary did the parkinsonism patients do as well as matched controls. Moreover, 56 of the 60 patients with idiopathic Parkinson's disease showed some evidence of intellectual dysfunction.

In general, parkinsonism patients tend to perform at a significantly lower level on the timed "performance" tests of the Wechsler scales than on the mostly untimed Verbal Scale subtests. Specific impairments tend to worsen with increased severity of the motor symptoms and with duration of the disease (Riklan and Diller, 1961).

Of all groups of patients with dementing conditions, parkinsonism patients are most likely to enjoy a normal level of cognitive functioning in many areas. When time is not a consideration, their performance on block design constructions (F. P. Bowen, 1976) and on visual organization (e.g., Raven's Matrices, pp. 502–505) and drawing tests (Gainotti et al., 1980) may be relatively unimpaired. Attention, concentration, and immediate memory are also likely to remain intact (J. A. Walker et al., 1982), particularly if the movement disorder has not become seriously disabling (Talland, 1962).

There are some contradictory data. Both F. P. Bowen (1976) and Pirozzolo and his co-workers (1982) describe short-term verbal memory deficits (on Wechsler Memory Scale subtests, pp. 429, 436–437) while the small (15) group of parkinsonism patients studied by Gainotti and his colleagues performed slightly above *average* on their measures of short-term verbal memory and retention (Rey's Auditory-Verbal Learning Test, pp. 422–429). Another contradiction, between M. L. Albert's (1978) findings of depressed verbal fluency and the Gainotti group's report that their parkinsonism patients had *average* verbal fluency, suggests that the patients studied by the Gainotti group were singularly well preserved.

Irritability, suspiciousness, and egocentricity appear with sufficient frequency to suggest they may be characteristic of parkinsonism (Lishman, 1978). Depression, too, is a common concomitant of the condition, as it is with any disabling disease in which self-awareness and social orientation are preserved (Cohn and Neumann, 1978; C. E. Wells, 1982). The deleterious effects of depression on such aspects of cognitive functioning as attention, memory, and calculations should be taken into account when evaluating the performance of Parkinson patients on neuropsychological tests (Mayeux et al., 1981).

Huntington's disease. This hereditary condition also involves basal ganglion structures, principally the caudate nucleus and the putamen. However, there is usually significant atrophy of the frontal cortex and the corpus callosum as well (Berry, 1975; Lishman, 1978). The involved brain structures show a progressive loss of neurons with proliferation of connective tissue cells. The onset of this disease may be as early as 20 years, but more often it first becomes unequivocally evident in the fourth or fifth decade (Burch, 1979), thus giving the carrier—who will inevitably succumb to it—

ample opportunity to have children of whom one-half also will be carrier-victims, regardless of their sex.

This disease was originally called Huntington's *chorea* (from the Greek word *choreia*, dance) because of the prominence in its symptom picture of the involuntary, spasmodic, often tortuous movements that ultimately become profoundly disabling. The disease is also manifested both cognitively and in personality disturbances. With the possible exception of those whose symptoms do not appear until relatively late in life and, as a group, may not exhibit cognitive deterioration or emotional disorders as do the others (Bird, 1978; Burch, 1979), most patients suffer cognitive, personality, and motor impairments although each aspect of the disease may differ in time of onset and in severity (Caine et al., 1978; Dewhurst, et al., 1969; Paulson, 1979). Since most people at risk for this disease are known and are aware of their possible fate, early diagnosis is more common than in Alzheimer's disease and other dementias associated with aging. Thus, estimates of ten to 15 years as the usual duration of the disease are trustworthy. Walton (1977) notes that some patients may live with it as long as 30 years.

Irritability, anxiety, emotional lability, impaired social judgment, and impulsivity involving aggressive or sexual behavior are common traits of Huntington's patients while they are still sufficiently mobile and independent to be dangerous to themselves and others (Bear, 1977; Caine et al., 1978). Many receive psychiatric diagnoses of schizophrenia, paranoia, or affective disorder before their condition has evolved sufficiently to be recognized by most medical examiners (Dewhurst et al., 1969; James et al., 1969; McHugh and Folstein, 1975), though they may have previously lived relatively stable lives. What appears to be apathy in many of these patients seems to come from an increasing inability to plan, initiate, or carry out complex activities (Caine et al., 1978), a problem shared by many patients with frontal lobe damage. Eventually, the movement disorder gets in the way of sustained performance of any kind of behavior, even maintenance of posture, and the patient becomes bedridden and increasingly debilitated.

There is a fairly consistent pattern of cognitive deterioration in Huntington's disease in which overlearned skills, such as reading and writing, word usage, and simple visual recognition, tend to be relatively well preserved. Drawing, too, particularly when structure is provided, tends to hold up (Gainotti et al., 1980). The more a task requires speed or mental tracking, lacks familiarity and structure, involves overstimulation or much perceptual or response complexity, the poorer will be the patient's performance (Aminoff et al., 1975; Fedio et al., 1979; Norton, 1975). This pattern shows up nicely on the Wechsler Intelligence Scales (Chapter 9) in highest scores on Information, Comprehension, Similarities, and Vocabulary; middling scores on Arithmetic (which, presented orally, requires mental tracking) and Picture Completion (dependent on well-ingrained verbal skills and visual recognition, but requiring an "abstract attitude" in making judgments of relevancy); and significantly depressed scores on the other very time-dependent and relatively unfamiliar "Performance" tasks and on other tests that combine these difficulty variables such as the Trail Making Test (Boll et al., 1974; Josiassen et al., 1982). Huntington's patients also show early difficulties performing verbal abstraction tasks (Lyle and Gottesman, 1977) and diminished verbal fluency (Butters et al., 1978; Gainotti et al., 1980).

Memory deficits in Huntington's disease have been subjected to careful scrutiny. Immediate span is the least impaired of the memory functions in the early stages and tends to hold up best over time as well, although on the more demanding task requiring recitation of a digit string in reverse order, these patients do poorly (Caine et al., 1977). Despite preservation of many cognitive capacities, these patients' ability to retain new information, even over a short period of time is relatively impaired, regardless of modality (Aminoff et al., 1975; Butters and Cermak, 1976; Fedio et al., 1979) and severely disrupted by distraction (Butters, 1977a; Meudell et al., 1978). These learning failures are associated with defective encoding (Weingartner et al 1979). Remote memory, too, deteriorates as the disease progresses (M. S. Albert et al., 1981a, b), with the amount of loss being essentially the same across decades. Early in the course of the disease, remote recall benefits greatly from cuing, indicating a retrieval rather than storage problem. Cuing adds much less to the remote recall performance of patients with advanced Huntington's disease.

Normal Pressure Hydrocephalus (NPH)

This reversible condition involving mental deterioration is not a primary degenerative disorder, such as the dementias. Rather, it results from obstruction of the flow of cerebral spinal fluid (CSF), usually by scarring from old trauma or infection, or from hemorrhage or tumor (Pincus and Tucker, 1978; C. E. Wells, 1978a). Sometimes the source of the obstruction cannot be identified. With obstruction, pressure builds up within the lateral ventricles, gradually enlarging them (R. D. Adams, 1980). The main area of damage is in the midbrain reticular formation (Torack, 1978). As the ventricles enlarge to accommodate the steady, usually slow fluid increase within them, CSF pressure returns to normal. Thus, the onset of this condition can be very slow and insidious. If left to run its course, it produces a symptom pattern of confusion, disorientation, incontinence, and increasing mental debilitation. A gait disturbance eventually interferes with ambulation. A casual or naive observer can easily misdiagnose the steadily deteriorating mental and physical condition of these patients whose enlarged ventricles readily show up on pneumoencephalographic or CT scan studies, for in the later stages it resembles primary dementias such as Alzheimer's disease (Pincus and Tucker, 1978; Pear, 1977). Because the deteriorating process may be reversed by a relatively simple surgical procedure, correct diagnosis is of the utmost importance.

Although gait disturbances, incontinence, and memory impairment are features of Alzheimer's disease, as well as of normal pressure hydrocephalus, the usual order of their appearance in the course of each disease can help the examiner distinguish between these two conditions (R. D. Adams, 1980; Torack, 1978). Incontinence and a clumsy, wide-based gait are commonly but not necessarily among the earliest symptoms of normal pressure hydrocephalus (Benson, 1975). Mental changes involve disorientation, confusion, decreased attention span, and both mental and motor slowing, with good preservation of cognitive functions, judgment, and self-awareness.

In the early stages, lowered scores on the Wechsler Intelligence Scales will be on Arithmetic, Digit Span, and the timed tests, reflecting slowing and impaired attention and mental tracking. When surgery is successful, scores on these subtests typically rise, indicating that component functions were relatively intact. Eventually, all scores become proportionately depressed if the condition is not relieved by surgery. In contrast to normal subjects who usually get higher scores using both hands than with one hand on tasks such as block construction and pegboard tests, these patients tend to do no better on the two-handed condition than when using their best hand alone (Botez et al., 1975). The appearance of this phenomenon may precede more obvious evidence of mental deterioration. Poor performance on tests of immediate recall, short-term memory, and learning in the early stages probably reflects confusion and impaired attention rather than a primary registration or learning disability. As the condition evolves, however, the destructive process does involve the memory system (M. M. Wood and Jeffries, 1979). This sequence of events runs counter to Alzheimer's course in which memory defects are among the earliest symptoms and incontinence and loss of ability to walk herald the terminal stage. Since patients with normal pressure hydrocephalus retain self-awareness and are appreciative of their socially handicapping impairments until they become severely confused, they are also usually quite appropriately depressed (H. Rosen and Swigar, 1976). When surgery can return these patients to social independence, even though some clumsiness and loss of mental acuity usually remain, the depression will typically be relieved as well.

MULTIPLE SCLEROSIS (MS)

This degenerative nervous system disease involves patchy deterioration of the fatty insulation around nerve fibers, the *myelin sheath*, disrupting the normal transmission of nerve impulses. Proliferating connective tissue cells at the demyelinated sites contribute to the formation of the grayish-colored sclerotic plaques. It is now thought that the degenerative process represents a breakdown in the patient's autoimmune system (B. Matthews, 1978). A predisposing viral infection may be a contributing etiological agent (Walton, 1977). Nerve cells are affected only secondarily to the degenerative changes in the myelin sheath.

Multiple sclerosis tends to be a progressive disease affecting young adults; the age of onset is usually between 20 and 40 (Lishman, 1978). Its course is typically bumpy, with stable periods of more or less long duration punctuated by acute flare-ups. Each acute attack may involve a quite different area of the brain's white matter than the last, and thus each attack may produce very different symptoms that often resolve for the most part but still leave the patient a little worse off each time. Prominent symptoms are weakness or loss of control of a limb; dysarthria with a characteristic spasmodically paced speech ("scanning speech"); eye muscle imbalance causing double vision; blindness, usually transient, in one eye; loss of sphincter control; and patchy painless sensory changes such as numbness (Walton, 1977). This disease progresses at different rates in different people. In some cases it continues in a very mild form for decades, and in others it reduces the patient to helpless dependency in five to ten years.

In this disease, perhaps more than any other degenerative condition, the enormous differences in rate and extent of mental and physical decline make the concepts of "early" and "late" stages dependent on the severity of the disease, not its duration. It is probably for this reason that so many equivocal findings are reported in the literature.

Although there is no question that most MS patients who are severely disabled physically also suffer significant global mental deterioration, few early stage mental changes have been documented with any regularity. Impairment of conceptual reasoning (Beatty and Gange, 1977; Lishman, 1978; Staples and Lincoln, 1979), of the specific memory functions involved in short-term recall and new learning have been consistently reported (Beatty and Gange, 1977; Rao et al., 1982; Vowels, 1979). Monti (1981) found that 51% of MS patients with cognitive disorders showed deficits suggestive of localized damage. However, in a group of 108 patients, none older than 40, of whom 85% had been diagnosed as having MS for at least five years and some for as many as 25 years, almost two-thirds gave evidence of intellectual impairment on mental status examination (Surridge, 1969). In the early stages, MS patients may not exhibit deficits in attention, immediate memory span, or information retrieval, although these functions may be profoundly affected when the disease is severe. Interestingly, the Wechsler Intelligence Scales and the Halstead Battery show depressed scores primarily on timed motor subtests, tests of cognitive function that have important motor components, and sensory discrimination tests (G. Goldstein and Shelly, 1974; Ivnik, 1978; R. Kaplan and Tsaros, 1979).

These studies demonstrate that examination of MS patients for cognitive changes in the early stages of multiple sclerosis requires a variety of tests. Monti (1981) points out that the heterogeneous character of cognitive deficits in multiple sclerosis cannot be adequately assessed by formalized batteries but rather requires an individualized "experimental investigation of the single case." However, as many as 40% of patients with only mild neurological signs of multiple sclerosis may show no cognitive impairment at all (Vowels, 1979).

While depression is common among MS patients (Whitlock and Siskind, 1980), perhaps an equal number of them display the frankly euphoric mood that once was thought to be the hallmark of the personality of these patients (Lishman, 1978; B. Matthews, 1978). The euphoria may mask or fluctuate with an underlying depression (Surridge, 1969). Depression and preoccupation with their physical disabilities tend to characterize MS patients with moderate physical impairment whose cognitive functioning is intact (Peyser et al., 1980). Cognitively intact patients whose physical impairments are relatively mild are likely to deny that they have worries or problems. Especially when cognitive capacities are severely compromised, the patient may display unbounded optimism with a thoroughly unrealistic assessment of his disability, his situation, and the future. Emotional lability, irritability, and distractibility are common symptoms, particularly as the disease progresses. Fatigue is generally a problem from the outset.

Toxic Conditions

The list of substances that can be deleterious to brain tissue is virtually endless (e.g., Walton, 1977; Lishman, 1978). It includes substances that are poisonous in any form or amount as well as the substances of abuse and drugs that may promote central nervous system efficiency at one dose level but interfere with it at another. There is not space in this chapter to review the many kinds of neurotoxic substances, the variety of pathological processes they can produce, or their multitudinous effects.

The examiner must keep in mind the possibility of a toxic reaction with every patient. With the exception of patients with an alcohol-related condition, relatively few people who are seen for neuropsychological assessment have disorders that are primarily due to toxicity. Not infrequently, however, the effects of proprietary or street drugs, of industrial and other chemicals, or of alcoholism will complicate the presentation of another kind of neurological disorder. The examiner needs to remain alert to this possibility, particularly with patients inclined toward the use of street drugs and alcohol, and those who are prone to self-medication or apt to be careless about a medical regimen. For example, in their comprehensive review of the literature on neuropsychological consequences of drug abuse, Parsons and Farr (1981) report few findings of cognitive deficits among street drug users. They note, however, the relative youthfulness of the population under consideration. A closer look at some of these data suggests a pattern of relationships between performance decrements and duration of drug use.

Problems of medicinal drug toxicity are addressed in the section on drug effects in Chapter 8 (see pp. 226–227). Here the salient neuropsychological features of the major source of toxic brain damage—alcohol abuse—of marihuana intoxication, and of poisoning with an industrial solvent are reviewed.

ALCOHOL-RELATED DISORDERS

Different kinds of brain changes have been associated with the alcohol-related behavioral disturbances (Bolter and Hannon, 1980; Lishman, 1981). Alcohol *(ethanol)* acts as a central nervous system depressant and has effects like those of some tranquilizing and hypnotic drugs. The metabolism of alcohol and its metabolites initiates chains of biochemical and physiological events involving many other organ systems of the body. Thus, "the characteristic action of alcohol . . . may reflect not only the intrinsic properties of the drug, but also the whole constellation of secondary events that are determined by the amounts, routes and frequencies with which [it is] customarily used" (Kalant, 1975).

A relatively high incidence of brain atrophy that shows up on CT scan or pneumoencephalographic study in widened and flattened sulci and enlarged ventricles occurs among chronic alcoholics (Lishman, 1978, 1981; Lishman et al., 1980; Wilkinson, 1982). Some of the data on brain atrophy suggest a selective shrinking of frontal and perhaps parietal lobe structures (Berglund and Risberg, 1980; Bergman et al., 1980). Other investigators, however, have not found localized areas of atrophy (Lishman, 1981; C. E. Wells, 1982). Most studies do agree, though, in finding ventricular enlargement, particularly involving the third ventricle. Widespread cortical atrophy tends to be more prominent than ventricular enlargement, although both are likely to occur together (Jernigan et al., 1982; C. E. Wells, 1982). Atrophy appears to be associated with the duration of problem drinking and the extent of cognitive deficit (Kroll et al., 1980; Lusins et al., 1980;), increases with age (Carlen et al., 1981), and is thought to be due to the effects of alcohol itself (Walton, 1977).

Lesions in the mamillary bodies and in specific thalamic nuclei, usually with lesions in other structures of the limbic system (see pp. 46–47, 75–77), have been implicated in the condition of severe mental deterioration, *Korsakoff's psychosis* (Lhermitte and Signoret, 1976; Brion and Mikol, 1978; Victor et al., 1971) (see pp. 196–197). Korsakoff's psychosis appears to be due to a nutritional deficiency of vitamin B_1 (thiamine) (Lishman, 1981; Walton, 1977). The diet of chronic alcoholics, particularly during periods of binge drinking, is often insufficient to meet the body's thiamine needs. When treated promptly in the acute stage with thiamine, this condition may be ameliorated (Victor et al., 1971). Freund (1982) links it with alcohol toxicity per se (see also Butters, 1981). M. L. Albert (1978) classifies Korsakoff's psychosis among the subcortical dementias. Deficiency of another vitamin—nicotinic acid—has been associated with a confusional disorder that occurs among alcoholic patients (Lishman, 1981).

Delirium tremens is an acute disorder in which the most prominent symptoms are tremulousness, visual and other sensory hallucinations, and profound confusion and agitation that can lead to death from exhaustion. It is often associated with abrupt cessation of long-term drinking, but its exact etiology remains unknown (Lishman, 1978). Alcohol-precipitated seizures are not uncommon among seizure-prone persons such as those who have had a traumatic brain injury or who have focal lesions from some other cause. Seizures and transient amnesic episodes ("blackouts") also occur in chronic alcoholics of long standing, usually during a heavy bout of drinking or soon after (Walton, 1977).

The performance of chronic alcoholics and patients with Korsakoff's psychosis falls on a continuum of severity of impairments on certain visuoperceptive (Butters et al., 1977; Kapur and Butters, 1977), dichotic information processing (Butters et al., 1975), and memory tasks (Ryan and Butters, 1980a), which might suggest that Korsakoff's psychosis represents an end stage in a continuum of alcoholic deterioration. However, certain distinctive features of Korsakoff's patients such as their tendency to confabulate (Howieson, 1980a), their gross memory defects (Butters and Cermak, 1974; Talland, 1968), and their usual state of affective blandness and passivity clearly differentiate them from other alcohol abusers. A condition of significant mental deterioration secondary to long-term alcohol abuse, *alcoholic dementia,* in which loss of the abstract attitude and impaired visuomotor performance are cardinal features, has been distinguished from Korsakoff's psychosis (Horvath, 1975; Lishman, 1978,

1981). Alcoholic dementia may represent the end stage of a dementing process associated with alcohol-induced cerebral atrophy. That some patients diagnosed as having alcoholic dementia display some of the symptoms typical of Korsakoff's psychosis (Horvath, 1975; Lishman, 1981), and vice versa, suggests that these patients have sustained more than one kind of alcohol-related brain damage.

Social drinking. There is some evidence that the moderate amounts of alcohol intake associated with social drinking result in mild cognitive impairments. In one study specific deficits on tests of abstract reasoning and mental flexibility were positively associated with the subjects' normal amount of alcohol intake (Parker and Noble, 1977). B. M. Jones and M. K. Jones (1977) found a positive relationship between blood alcohol levels and lowered performance on a word learning task in which the specific impairment appeared to be a learning rather than a retrieval deficit. They also noted a greater succeptibility to this problem among women, particularly during premenstrual and menstrual phases of their cycles.

Chronic alcoholism. Chronic alcohol abuse affects certain aspects of intellectual functioning while leaving many intellectual activities relatively unimpaired (Parsons, 1977; Parsons and Farr, 1981; Tarter, 1975, 1976). The severity of the specific intellectual deficits associated with chronic alcoholism tends to be directly related to the duration of the drinking problem (Tarter, 1973; Tarter and Jones, 1971a) and to age (Carlen et al., 1981; Ryan and Butters, 1982). Binge drinkers appear to be less prone to alcohol-related cognitive deficits than those with a heavy daily alcohol intake (Sanchez-Craig, 1980). A high incidence of malnutrition has been observed among chronic alcoholics (A. Guthrie and Elliott, 1980). The most seriously malnourished tend to display more cognitive deficits than well-nourished subjects.

Intellectual deficits consistently appear on tasks involving functions associated with frontal lobe activity (Bolter and Hannon, 1980b; Parsons, 1977b; Talland, 1965; Tarter, 1975, Tarter and Jones, 1971b). Thus, difficulties in maintaining a cognitive set, impersistence, decreased flexibility in thinking, defective visual searching behavior, deficient motor inhibition, perseveration, loss of spatial and temporal orientation, and impaired ability to organize perceptuomotor responses and synthesize spatial elements characterize the test behavior of chronic alcoholics. There is not much evidence to suggest that alcoholics suffer a defect in their ability to make abstractions or to generalize from particulars. Rather, their failures on tests involving abstractions tend to result from the performance defects listed here (Ryan and Butters, 1982). This pattern of deficits may also accompany diffuse brain damage and resembles aging (Blusewicz, 1977a, b; G. Goldstein and Shelly, 1980; Hochla and Parsons, 1982).

Chronic alcoholics characteristically perform relatively poorly on speed-dependent visual scanning tasks such as the Digit Symbol subtest of the Wechsler Intelligence Scales or the Trail Making Test (pp. 556–559), on tests of motor speed, and on tests of visuospatial organization of which the Wechsler Block Design subtest and the Tactual Performance Test (pp. 459–462) are representative examples (Parsons and Farr,

1981; Kapur and Butters, 1977; Tarter, 1975). The verbal and arithmetic skills examined by Wechsler Verbal Scale subtests generally remain relatively unimpaired. These perceptuomotor problems associated with chronic alcoholism may appear at first to implicate functions associated with the right hemisphere. However, analysis of the perceptuomotor failures of chronic alcoholics suggests that they involve impaired motor control and integration. Furthermore, alcoholics show no consistent performance decrement on perceptuomotor tasks or motor coordination tasks that require little or no synthesizing, organizing, or orienting activity (Hirschenfang et al., 1968; Tarter, 1975; Vivian et al., 1973). As yet, no neuropathological data support a hypothesis of right hemisphere susceptibility to the depredations of alcohol (Ryan and Butters, 1982). In fact, G. Goldstein and Shelly (1980) found that tendencies to lateralized performance patterns on neuropsychological tests were about equally divided among 77 alcoholics in one study. Inadequate evaluation of test performances may best account for the probably unfounded conclusions of right hemisphere deficits in chronic alcoholism (Bolter and Hannon, 1980).

Chronic alcoholics tend to sustain subtle but consistent short-term memory and learning deficits that become more evident as task difficulty increases (for example, by increasing the number of items to be learned or inserting distractor tasks between learning and recall trials) (Ryan and Butters, 1980b; 1982; Ryan, DiDario et al., 1980). These deficits appear to be the product of a breakdown in encoding strategies similar to the encoding defects associated with Korsakoff's psychosis (Ryan, Butters et al., 1980) (see p. 196 below). However, serious memory and learning defects are not a regular feature of chronic alcoholism. When they do occur, they may be symptomatic of other specific neurological conditions that are present in addition to the neuropathology of chronic alcoholism (Butters et al., 1977). Remote memory is particularly resistant to deterioration in alcoholics (M. S. Albert et al., 1980).

There has been much interest in the extent to which intellectual deficits associated with alcohol consumption are ameliorated by abstinence. During the detoxification period, usually the first two weeks after cessation of drinking, most alcoholics will exhibit a variety of neuropsychological deficits involving just about every cognitive functions that has been subject to testing, including the usually stable verbal skills (M. S. Goldman, 1982; D. W. Goodwin and Hill, 1975). Thus, most newly abstinent alcoholics show remarkable "improvements" when test scores obtained weeks or months later are compared with performance levels obtained during the acute withdrawal stage. Valid measurements of improvement of function can only be made when scores for a comparison baseline have been obtained after the acute condition has dissipated. Ryan and Butters (1982) point out that the greatest amount of return of function takes place in the first week of abstinence. The rate of return slows down rapidly thereafter, leveling off at three to six weeks. Reports of continuing improvement are inconsistent (Tarter, 1976).

Memory, for example, tends to improve significantly but less than completely in the first several weeks of abstinence (Ellenberg et al., 1980; Jonsson et al., 1962; Parsons and Farr, 1981). I. Grant and his colleagues (1979) reported that both recently detoxified and abstinent (for 18 months or longer) alcoholics in their late 30s performed within normal limits on a variety of neuropsychological tests. However, the group that had been detoxified for only three weeks when first tested did not exhibit the practice effects displayed by the other group on retest one year later (K. M. Adams et al., 1980). This learning failure suggests the presence of subtle deficits at three weeks of abstinence that the usual test procedures do not pick up. Improvements in short-term memory approaching normal levels have been observed in alcoholics abstinent for five or more years (Ryan and Butters, 1982). There is little data, however, to indicate continuing improvement on complex memory tasks. For example, five or more years of abstinence resulted in no improvements for 30 previously alcoholic men on a paired-associated learning test used to measure long-term memory (Brandt et al., 1983). Although some studies report complete return of impaired perceptuomotor skills following prolonged sobriety (Farmer, 1973; Tarter and Jones, 1971), others indicate that even when improvement occurs during prolonged abstinence, performance on tests involving visuomotor functions remains depressed (Parsons, 1977). Activities involving response speed and attention, such as those measured in symbol substitution tasks, for example (see pp. 272–274, 554–555), may also show a tendency to improvement over a year or more of abstinence (Ryan and Butters, 1982). Age may be a significant variable in determining the reversibility of alcohol-related deficits. M. S. Goldman (1982) compared under- and over-35-year-old alcoholics and, in separate studies, those under 40 with those over 40, on a variety of speed-dependent perceptual and motor tasks. He found that the younger subjects generally returned to normal performance levels within three months after they stopped drinking while the older ones improved but remained relatively impaired. Recent reports that the CT scans of some chronic alcoholics with cerebral atrophy show improvement following abstinence suggest a parallel between the structural status of the brain and cognitive functioning of these patients (Carlen et al., 1978; Lishman, 1981).

Korsakoff's psychosis.   The most striking neuropsychological deficit associated with alcoholism is the gross memory impairment of Korsakoff's psychosis. The condition typically affects alcoholics with a long drinking history. It may be brought on by a particularly heavy bout with alcohol (usually two weeks or more) during which the patient eats little if any food. Clinically similar memory deficits can result from a variety of other cerebral diseases (Lishman, 1978; Walton, 1977).

The memory problem of Korsakoff's psychosis appears as a defective ability to consolidate, retrieve, and utilize newly registered data (M. S. Albert et al., 1979; Buschke and Fuld, 1974; Butters and Cermak, 1975, 1976, 1980; Talland, 1968). In an ingenious series of studies of Korsakoff's psychosis, Butters and his co-workers (e.g., Biber et al., 1981; Butters, 1977b; Butters and Cermak, 1974, 1980; Butters et al., 1975, 1977) have implicated defective encoding of new information as the common component of the Korsakoff memory disorder. Defective encoding results in the patient's retaining access to much of the immediate experience of the past two or three minutes, with little or no ability to utilize whatever might have been stored in recent memory (i.e., since the onset of the condition), and a tendency toward inconsistent

196

and poorly organized retrieval of remote memory with retrograde amnesia on a steep temporal gradient. Many Korsakoff patients can perform Digit Span, Subtracting Serial Sevens, and other tasks involving immediate memory and attention quite well, although they are not likely to resume interrupted activities and show little if any learning curve on repetitive tasks (Talland, 1965a). Even recall for immediate memory may be impaired in severely affected patients (Butters, 1971). One interesting aspect of their memory disorder that is not usually mentioned is a breakdown in the capacity to appreciate or use time relationships to guide or evaluate their responses. Korsakoff patients tend to be oblivious to chronology in their recall of remote events so that they report impossible sequences unquestioningly and without guile, such as going into service before going to high school, or watching television before World War II. When they attempt to answer questions about events, it is as though they respond with the first association that comes to mind no matter how loosely or inappropriately it might be linked to the questions (Lezak et al, 1983; Lhermitte et Signoret, 1972).

Oscar-Berman (1980) describes other aspects of cognitive and motivational impairment, such as slowed perceptual processing, premature responding, diminished ability to profit from mistakes (i.e., change unrewarding response patterns), and diminished ability to perceive and use cues. She suggests that, "The multiplicity of deficits observed in alcoholic Korsakoff patients can be linked to [a] multiplicity of . . . sites of brain damage."

The performance of Korsakoff patients on the usual tests of cognitive functions, such as the Wechsler Intelligence Scales, is virtually identical with that of chronic alcoholics (Kapur and Butters, 1977; Malerstein and Belden, 1968). Thus, their performance on well-structured, untimed tests of familiar, usually overlearned, material such as vocabulary and arithmetic holds up while their scores on the other tests decline to the extent that speed, visuoperceptual, and spatial organization components are involved.

Behavioral defects specifically and consistently associated with the Korsakoff syndrome are disorientation for time and place; apathy characterized by a virtually total loss of initiative, disinterest, and a striking lack of curiosity about past, present, or future; and emotional blandness with a capacity for momentary irritability, anger, or pleasure that quickly dissipates when the stimulating condition is removed or the discussion topic is changed. In the early stages, many patients tend to produce unconsidered, frequently inconsistent, foolish, and sometimes quite exotic confabulations in response to questions for which they feel they ought to know the answer, such as "What were you doing last night?" or "How did you get to this place?" Although the patient may have retained many specific abilities and skills, unlike the chronic alcoholic whose memory functions remain relatively intact, the memory defects of the Korsakoff's syndrome render the severely impaired patient utterly dependent and call attention to the central organizing function of retention and recall for emotional and intellectual behavior alike.

Some patients with Korsakoff's psychosis show improvement in memory, orientation, and general responsiveness when given large doses of thiamine early in the course of this disease (Berglund et al., 1979). This improvement tends to be steady, although it can be quite slow. Many patients reach a plateau without regaining enough capacity to maintain social independence, but some others do return to independent living.

Marihuana

The most apt generalization that can be made about studies of the neurological and neuropsychological effects of marihuana use is that their findings are equivocal (Parsons and Farr, 1981). A comparison of test scores of college student marihuana users and nonusers on the Wechsler Intelligence Scale and the Halstead Battery taken a year apart showed no difference on any measure (Culver and King, 1974). This finding was supported by a Danish study of several groups of polydrug users, all of whom used marihuana, in which the the same set of tests plus learning and reaction time tests showed no differences between the users and control groups (P. Bruhn and Maage, 1975). Similar studies have come up with similar negative results (D. W. Goodwin and Hill, 1975; Satz et al., 1976; Schaeffer et al., 1981). I. Grant and his coworkers (1978a, b) concluded, on the basis of a large-scale collaborative study of polydrug abuse, that marihuana "is not neurotoxic, at least in the short run (i.e., approximately 10 years of regular use)." However, they qualify this conclusion by noting that their subjects "were not, in general, heavy hallucinogen consumers."

A number of studies (M. Evans, 1975; Kolansky and Moore, 1972; Lishman, 1978) point to personality changes in heavy users of marihuana or hashish. The most commonly described characteristics are affective blunting, mental and physical sluggishness, apathy, restlessness, some mental confusion, and defective recent memory. M. Evans (1975) reported enlarged ventricles in youthful marihuana smokers, but these findings have been subject to debate (Lishman, 1978).

Laboratory studies of behavior during marihuana use also tend to be equivocal. In a very detailed review, L. L. Miller (1976) found that for each study that demonstrated a marihuana-related change on one or another test of cognitive functions, there was at least one and usually more that did not show change. Yet, a pattern of deficits is suggested by Miller's data. While studies using Digit Span were too equivocal to allow any conclusions to be drawn, scores on digit symbol substitution tests showed a possible dose-related tendency toward response slowing on this task. On simple tracking tasks, no deficits were found, but a study using a complex tracking task did elicit evidence of impairment following marihuana inhalation. Memory test data are the most conclusive, generally showing reduced memory efficiency during marihuana usage. This deficiency appears to be associated with storage but not retrieval (C. F. Darley and Tinklenberg, 1974) and may be due more to impaired attention, loss of ability to discriminate between old and new learning, or insufficient rehearsal, than to a storage defect per se. Slowed visual processing during marihuana use has also been demonstrated (Braff et al., 1981). Time perception, which under normal conditions tends to be underestimated, the subject thinking less time has passed than actually has, is underestimated even more when marihuana is used. However, these effects, observed in the laboratory within 30 minutes of administration of the drug, tend to dissipate within the subsequent 40 minutes (Dornbush and Kokkevi, 1976).

INDUSTRIAL TOXINS

The neuropsychological effects of exposure to industrial toxins such as the organic solvents that are common components of house paint give one example of the neuropsychological disorders that can affect persons in particular occupations. The literature indicates that a large proportion of workers exposed to house paint (Hane et al., 1977; Lindström, 1980) or other organic solvents (Axelson et al., 1976; Olsen and Sabroe, 1980), to styrene used in plastics manufacturing (Härkönen et al., 1978), or to petroleum-distilled fuels (Knave et al., 1978), for example, are subject to a variety of mental and physical symptoms. The most frequent of these are memory problems, fatigue, poor concentration, irritability, and headaches. On neuropsychological examination, workmen who have had long-term exposure to these substances tend to display significant deficits, primarily involving memory, learning, and attention (Arlien-Søborg et al., 1979; Grandjean et al., 1955; Seppäläinen et al., 1980). Some impaired ability to form abstractions, reaction time slowing, and reduced manual dexterity have also been noted (Hane et al., 1977; Knave et al., 1978; Lindström, 1981; Lindström et al., 1976). Both abnormal electroencephalograms (Härkönen et al., 1978) and CT scan findings suggestive of cerebral atrophy (Arlien-Søberg et al., 1979) have also been reported to occur more frequently among these workers, particularly those with long exposure histories, than others not exposed to organic solvents. "Paint sniffers," who use paint fumes to induce intoxication, display a similar pattern of psychological deficits that becomes more pronounced with longer usage (Tsushima and Towne, 1977).

The similarity of these complaints to those of neurotic or depressed patients, coupled with the absence of distinctive neurological symptoms, can mislead an examiner into discounting the patient's complaints if supporting neuropsychological findings are not available. Mikkelsen (1980) and his colleagues (Mikkelsen et al., 1978; Gregersen et al., 1978) found that painters and other industrial workers exposed to organic solvents suffer conditions of debilitating dementia at a higher than normal rate in their middle years. They raise the question of whether such exposure "is one probable cause of development of . . . incapacitating presenile dementia" (Gregersen et al., 1978). In a two-year follow-up study of house painters with cerebral atrophy, little change was observed (P. Bruhn et al., 1981).

Infectious Processes

Many of the infectious diseases that have long-lasting mental effects, such as measles encephalitis or tuberculous meningitis, can be severely crippling, if not fatal. Others, such as *general paresis (neurosyphilis)* or certain fungal infections, may have a fairly long course that leaves the patient's mental capacities progressively impaired with very specific deficits that are peculiar to the disease or relate to a focal lesion. Some idea of how many infectious diseases can have direct effects on brain functioning is given by Lishman (1978), who lists 23 varieties of encephalitis and notes several other conditions suspected of having a viral etiology.

One infectious condition of special neuropsychological interest is *herpes simplex encephalitis*. Relatively few people contract the disease and of these, relatively few survive the acute stage (Lishman, 1978; Walton, 1977). However, those who survive have lost much medial temporal and orbital brain tissue, usually including the hippocampal memory registration substrate, the amygdala with its centers for control of primitive drives, and that area of the frontal lobes involved in the kind of response inhibition necessary for goal-directed activity and appropriate social behavior. These patients typically display an exceedingly dense memory defect with profound anterograde amnesia, usually considerable retrograde amnesia as well, and severe social dilapidation (Hierons et al., 1978). The memory defect makes them interesting subjects for the study of memory functions (Butters and Cermak, 1976; Lhermitte et Signoret, 1972; Wallack, 1976) since their hippocampal lesions compromise new learning in contrast to the Korsakoff patients with thalamic and mamillary body lesions who demonstrate some new learning but have difficulty with retrieval.

Localized infections such as encysted abscesses may also be of neuropsychological interest in producing focal damage in areas that normally are not subject to isolated lesions. If they are sufficiently slowly developing as to have minimal pressure effects and produce little edematous reactions, so that diffuse repercussions are slight, highly specific neuropsychological deficits can result. The neuropsychological effects of such cysts often cannot be differentiated from those of a slow-growing tumor.

Neoplasms

Of the many kinds of tumors that may invade or impinge upon brain tissue, several occur most often in adults (Walton, 1977). Tumors that arise from the glial cells that form the connective tissue of the brain, *gliomas*, are the most common and include both highly malignant and some relatively benign types. *Glioblastoma multiforme*, which is also called an *astrocytoma*, grade 3 or 4 (grades indicate the degree of malignancy from 1—least, to 4—most malignant), are rapidly growing malignancies that infiltrate the brain's tissue so that clean surgical removal is impossible. Patients with these tumors, who are usually middle-aged, typically die within months of diagnosis. Grade 1 astrocytomas also infiltrate brain tissue but grow so slowly that survival of five years or more is commonplace. The tumors that are the second most common type in the brain are metastatic neoplasms that have their origin in some other part of the body, most often the lungs. Since metastatic tumors, or secondary carcinomas, tend to be fast-growing, the effects of the tumor of second growth may exceed those of the tumor of origin. Unlike the infiltrating gliomas, *meningiomas*, tumors evolving out of tissue covering the brain, grow between the brain and skull but may penetrate the skull itself, producing characteristic changes in its bony structure. Meningiomas tend to grow relatively slowly. Because they are typically self-contained and do not invade the brain itself, many may be completely removed by surgery. These three major types constitute about three-quarters of all brain tumors in adults.

Brain tumors compromise brain functioning in one or more of four different ways (Coxe, 1978): (1) by increasing intracranial pressure (see pp. 168–169); (2) by inducing seizures; (3) by destroying brain tissue through invasion or replacement; and (4) by secreting hormones or altering endocrine patterns that affect a variety of body functions. To a large extent, tumors act as localized lesions affecting behavior in much the same way that other kinds of discrete brain lesions do (Lishman, 1978). However, neuropsychological effects of tumors depend not only on their size and location but also on their rate of growth (Finger, 1978). Fast-growing tumors tend to put pressure on surrounding structures, disrupting their function, while the gradual displacement of brain tissue by slow-growing tumors may allow for shifts in position and reorganization of structures with minimal behavioral repercussion occurring until the tumor has become quite large. By increasing pressure and contributing to the displacement of brain structures, edema also tends to exacerbate the tumor's symptoms and add diffuse effects to the focal symptom picture (Coxe, 1978). The degree to which edema may contribute to the severity of symptoms is probably best appreciated when one sees the often dramatic effects of steroid therapy, which can rapidly shrink edema-swollen tissues. Severely confused patients with serious impairments in all dimensions of brain function may return in relatively short order to an alert and responsive state with control over many of the functions that seemed lost even hours before.

Anoxia

Patients suffering the effects of insufficient blood oxygen *(hypoxia)* or lack of blood oxygen *(anoxia)* who are seen in a general clinical neuropsychological practice, will most likely have sustained this condition in the course of surgery under general anesthesia, in an acute cardiac crisis (Bengtsson et al., 1969; Falicki and Sep-Kowalik, 1969; Lishman, 1978), as an aftermath of open-heart surgery (Walton, 1977), or from carbon monoxide poisoning (in which saturation of red blood cells with carbon monoxide interferes with their normal oxygen transport) (K. M. Adams et al., 1980; Lishman, 1978). Pulmonary disease, too, can reduce the supply of oxygen to the brain (K. M. Adams et al., 1980; Prigatano et al., 1983). Whatever the etiology of the condition, these patients may exhibit one or more aspects of a constellation of symptoms. New learning ability tends to be more or less impaired. The degree of this impairment relates in a general way to the severity and duration of oxygen insufficiency and tends to be concomitant with hippocampal damage (Muramoto et al., 1979). The learning disability can be so profound as to render the patient fully dependent, or so slight as to be a nuisance for which the patient can contrive some compensatory techniques. A general dampening of mental acuity with impaired attention, concentration, and tracking, and tendencies to concrete thinking may also be present, suggesting (usually) mild diffuse damage (I. Grant et al., 1982). Some patients exhibit affective dulling and disinhibition (McFarland, 1952; D. Wechsler, 1963). McSweeny and his colleagues (1982) report a positive relationship between overall impairment on

201

neuropsychological measures and depression among patients with chronic obstructive pulmonary disease (COPD).

A third important aspect of this symptom complex is a reduced capacity for planning, initiating, and carrying out activities. In its most extreme forms, the patient is apathetic and dependent upon external stimulation to spur him into activity. In milder cases, the patient can carry out routine activities without prompting, particularly if they are well structured and familiar, but is hard put to come up with new solutions to unfamiliar problems or even to identify new problems, to define new goals, or to restructure his activities. This latter set of problems can be most puzzling to the patient, his family, or employer since the bulk of his mental capacities and most aspects of his personality remain the same and yet he has become more or less nonfunctional for no reason apparent to the naive or casual observer.

Visual defects, possibly associated with cortical lesions (Jefferson, 1976), may accompany the neuropsychological impairments. One patient with whom I have worked sustained pronounced bilateral blind spots along with the memory, attentional, and motivational problems he incurred during general anesthesia for minor surgery. Pillon and his colleagues (1977) described a case of carbon monoxide poisoning in which pronounced visuospatial drawing distortions seemed to implicate a lateralized focal (right posterior) lesion along with the characteristic memory deficits. After the acute stage, these impairments tend to be relatively stable (Muramoto et al., 1979).

Metabolic and Endocrine Disorders

Metabolic disorders of the brain are secondary to pathological changes that occur elsewhere in the body. Many of the cerebral concomitants show up as transient confusion, delirium, or disordered consciousness during acute conditions of metabolic dysfunction (Bleuler, 1975; Dodson, 1978). Mental disturbances are usually global in nature with particular involvement of attentional and memory functions and often reasoning and judgment (e.g., Whelan et al., 1980).

The neuropsychological effects of uremic poisoning, which occurs with kidney failure, are in many ways typical of the mental changes associated with metabolic disorders. A progressive development of lethargy, apathy, and cognitive dysfunction with accompanying loss of sense of well-being takes place as the uremic condition develops (Lishman, 1978; Yager, 1973). While Yager describes marked relief from these symptoms when patients are dialyzed, Beniak (1977) demonstrated a pattern of deficits that did not improve with dialysis. These included attentional deficits that interfered with performance on memory tasks and impaired performance on several different visual perceptual tasks. Beniak attributed this pattern to an impairment of the arousal system. In addition, he noted visuomotor coordination difficulties. In a review of the literature, Chui and Damasio (1980) reported a more global form of mental deterioration in uremic patients who had been dialyzed for more than six months, most more than two years. Approximately two-thirds of these patients exhibited symptoms of disorientation and (unspecified) memory impairment.

202

Psychiatric disturbances are a more common feature of endocrine disorders than are neuropsychological impairments (Lishman, 1978). However, cognitive deterioration is a fairly consistent feature of pronounced thyroid insufficiency, or hypothyroidism *(myxedema)*. Like the dementia of Alzheimer's disease, the onset and development of the cognitive impairments in this condition are usually subtle and insidious. The patient becomes sluggish, lethargic, and suffers concentration and memory disturbances. Unlike Alzheimer's disease, of course, this condition is reversible with thyroid replacement therapy.

Nutritional Deficiency

The best known of the disorders of nutritional deficiency is Korsakoff's psychosis and the related vitamin B_1 deficiency disease, beriberi (Walton, 1977). Other conditions of mental deterioration have been attributed to dietary deficiency. Folic acid, or folate, deficiency, for example, is suspected in the etiology of a progressive condition of mental deterioration with concomitant cerebral atrophy (M. I. Botez, T. Botez, et al., 1979; M. I. Botez, Peyronnard, et al., 1979; Manzoor and Runcie, 1976). This condition gives rise to a variety of neurological and neuropsychological symptoms including sensory and reflex abnormalities, depressed mood, and impairments on memory, abstract reasoning, and visuoconstructional tests specifically, and general depression of cognitive functions is also reported. Significant improvements on neuropsychological testing have been observed with folate replacement therapy. This condition, like many other diseases of nutritional deficiency, needs further study. If, as suspected, folate deficiency is the etiological factor, education alone should go a long way toward eliminating a crippling disorder that is counteracted by a moderate intake of lettuce.

8

Diagnostic Issues

Variables Affecting the Expression of Brain Damage

Like all other psychological phenomena, behavioral changes that follow brain injury are determined by multiple factors. The size, location, and kind of lesion certainly contribute significantly to the altered behavior pattern. Another important predisposing variable is the duration of the condition. The patient's age at the onset of the organic disorder, the pattern of cerebral dominance, background, life situation, and psychological makeup also affect how the patient responds to the physical insult and to its social and psychological repercussions. Moreover, these changes are dynamic, reflecting the continually evolving interactions between behavioral deficits and residual competencies, the patient's appreciation of his strengths and weaknesses, and family, social, and economic support or pressure.

Lesion Characteristics

SITE OF LESION

Diffuse and focal effects. The concepts of "diffuse" and "focal" brain injury are more clear-cut than their manifestations. Diffuse brain diseases do not affect all brain structures equally, and it is rare to find a focal injury in which some diffuse repercussions do not take place either temporarily or ultimately (Goodglass, 1973; A. Smith, 1975; Teuber, 1969. Also see Chapter 7).

Diffuse brain injury typically results from a widespread condition such as infection, anoxia, hypertension, intoxication (including alcohol intoxication, drug overdose, and drug reactions), and certain degenerative, metabolic, and nutritional diseases. Behavioral aftereffects reflecting diffuse brain dysfunction are common to most closed-head injuries, particularly those sustained under conditions of fast acceleration or deceleration as in motor vehicle accidents or falls (e.g., see pp. 167–169). These usually

204

include memory, attention, and concentration disabilities; impaired higher level and complex reasoning resulting in conceptual concretism and inflexibility; and general response slowing. Emotional flattening or lability may also be present. These symptoms tend to be most severe immediately after an injury or the sudden onset of a disease, or they may first appear as subtle and transient problems that increase in duration and severity as a progressive condition worsens.

Trauma, space-displacing lesions (e.g., tumors, blood vessel malformations), localized infections, and cerebrovascular accidents cause most focal brain injuries. Some systemic conditions, too, such as a severe thiamine deficiency, may devastate discrete brain structures and result in a predominantly focal symptom picture (p. 193). Occasionally, focal signs of brain damage accompany an acute exacerbation of a systemic disorder, such as diabetes mellitus, confusing the diagnostic picture until the underlying disorder is brought under control and the organic symptoms subside. Symptoms of diffuse damage almost always accompany focal lesions of sudden onset. Initially, cloudy consciousness, confusion, and generally slowed and inconsistent responsiveness may obscure focal residual effects so that clear-cut evidence of the focal lesion may not appear until later. On the other hand, the first sign of a progressive localized lesion such as a growing tumor may be some slight, specific behavioral impairment that becomes more pronounced and inclusive. Ultimately, diffuse behavioral effects resulting from increased intracranial pressure and circulatory changes may obliterate the specific defects due to local tissue damage.

Focal lesions can often be distinguished by lateralizing signs since most discrete lesions involve only one hemisphere. Even when the lesion extends to both hemispheres, the damage is apt to be asymmetrical, resulting in a predominance of one lateralized symptom pattern. In general, when one function or several related specific functions are significantly impaired while other functions remain intact and alertness, response rate, either verbal or nonverbal learning ability, and orientation are relatively unaffected, the examiner can safely conclude that the cerebral insult is focal.

Site of focal lesion. From a neuropathological perspective, the site of the lesion should determine many characteristics of the attendant behavioral alterations. Yet the expression of these changes—their severity, intransigence, burdensomeness—depends upon so many other variables that predicting much more than the broad outlines of the behavioral symptoms from knowledge of the lesion's location is virtually impossible (A. Smith, 1975, 1979). In ordinary clinical practice there are relatively few patients with primary focal lesions whose damage is confined to the identified area. Stroke patients may have had other small or transient and therefore unrecognized cerebral vascular accidents and, at least in the first few weeks after the stroke, physiological and metabolic changes and depression of neural functioning (*diaschisis*, see p. 206) take place in some areas of the brain other than the site of tissue damage. With the exception of some missile or puncture wounds, traumatic brain injuries are rarely "clean," for damage is generally widespread. Tumors do not respect the brain's midline or any other of the landmarks or boundaries we use to organize our knowledge about the brain. Thus, in most cases, information about where in the brain a discrete lesion is located must be viewed as only a partial description that identifies the primary site of damage. The patient's pattern of behavior or his neuropsychological test performance often may not meet textbook expectations for a lesion in the designated area (Geschwind, 1974b; A. Smith, 1980).

Depth of lesion.   Subcortical damage associated with a cortical lesion also contributes to the amount and kind of impairment the patient suffers. It compounds the symptom picture with the added effects of disrupted pathways or damaged lower integration centers. The depth and extent to which a cortical lesion involves subcortical tissue will alter the behavioral correlates of similar cortical lesions. Depth of lesion has been clearly related to the severity of impairment of verbal skills (Newcombe, 1969). The varieties of *anosognosia* (impaired awareness of one's own disability or disabled body parts, associated with right parietal lobe damage) illustrate the differences in the behavioral correlates of similarly situated cortical lesions with different amounts of subcortical involvement. Gerstmann (1942) reported three forms of this problem and their subcortical correlates: (1) Anosognosia with neglect of the paralyzed side, in which the patient essentially ignores the fact of his paralysis although he may have some vague awareness that he is disabled, is associated with lesions of the right optic region of the thalamus. (2) Anosognosia with amnesia for or lack of recognition of the affected limbs or side occurs with lesions penetrating only to the transmission fibers from the thalamus to the parietal cortex (3) Anosognosia with such "positive" psychological symptoms as confabulation or delusions (in contrast to the unelaborated denial of illness or nonrecognition of body parts of the other two forms of this condition) is more likely to occur with lesions limited to the parietal cortex.

Distance effects. 1. Diaschisis.   Diaschisis refers to depression of activity that takes place in areas of the brain outside the immediate site of damage, usually in association with acute focal brain lesions (Kempinsky, 1958). Von Monakow ([1914], 1969) originally conceived of diaschisis as a form of shock to the nervous system due to disruptions in the neural network connecting the area damaged by the lesion with functionally related areas that may be situated at some distance from the lesion itself, even in the opposite hemisphere. Some investigators have extended the concept of diaschisis to include acute depression of neuronal activity in areas outside the immediate site of damage resulting from "vegetative" changes such as edema (Kertesz, 1979; E. W. Russell, 1981a). However, the concept of diaschisis applies more appropriately to the depression of relatively discrete or circumscribed clusters of related functions (Seron, 1979; A. Smith, 1979) than to the global dampening of cerebral activity associated with the often radical physiological alterations that take place following an acute injury to the brain (Plum and Posner, 1980). Diaschisis has been viewed as a transient phenomenon that, as it dissipates, allows the depressed functions to improve spontaneously (Gazzaniga, 1974; Laurence and Stein, 1978). Yet it may also account for the appearance of permanent changes in functions that are not directly associated with the lesion site (A. Smith, 1980).

206

2. Disconnection syndromes. The chronic condition of diaschisis is similar to disconnection syndromes in that both involve depression or loss of a function primarily served by an area of the brain that is intact and can be some distance from the lesion. Both phenomena thus involve disrupted neural transmission through subcortical white matter. However, the similarity ends here. Cortical lesions that may or may not involve white matter give rise to diaschisis while disconnection syndromes result from damage to white matter that cuts cortical pathways, disconnecting one or another cortical area from the communication network of the brain (Geschwind, 1965; K.W. Walsh, 1978b). These disconnection problems can simulate the effects of a cortical lesion or produce an atypical symptom pattern. Even a small subcortical lesion can result in significant behavioral changes if it interrupts a critical pathway running to or from the cortex or between two cortical areas. Cortical involvement is not necessary for a cortical area to be rendered nonfunctional. Geschwind (1972) analyzed a case in which a patient with normal visual acuity suddenly could no longer read, although he was able to copy written words. Postmortem examination revealed that an occluded artery prevented blood flow to the left visual cortex and the interhemispheric visual pathways, injuring both structures and rendering the patient blind in his right visual field. His left visual field and right visual cortex continued to register words that he could copy. However, the right visual cortex was disconnected from the left hemisphere so that this verbal information was no longer transmitted to the left hemisphere for the symbol processing necessary for verbal comprehension and therefore he could not read.

The most dramatic disconnection syndromes are those that occur when interhemispheric connections are severed, whether by surgery or as a result of disease or developmental anomaly (Bogen, 1979; Hécaen and Albert, 1978; Sperry, 1974). For example, under laboratory conditions that restrict stimulation to one hemisphere, information received by the right hemisphere, for instance, does not transfer across the usual white matter pathway to the left hemisphere that controls the activity of the right hand. Thus, the right hand does not react to the stimulus or it may react to other stimuli directed to the left hemisphere while the left hand responds appropriately (see also pp. 54–55).

NATURE OF LESION

Type of Damage. Differences in the nature of the lesion also affect the symptom picture. Where there has been a clean loss of cortical tissue, as a result of surgery or missile wounds, those functions specifically mediated by the lost tissue can no longer be performed. When white matter has also been removed, some disconnection effects may also occur. In short, when the lesion involves tissue removal with little or no diseased tissue remaining, repercussions on other, anatomically unrelated functions tend to be minimal and the potential for rehabilitation runs high (Newcombe, 1969; Teuber, 1969) (see also pp. 283–284).

Dead or diseased brain tissue, which alters the neurochemical and electrical status of the brain, produces more extensive and severe behavioral changes than a clean surgical or missile wound that removes tissue (J. A. Deutsch, 1960; Diller, 1962; Weiskrantz, 1968). Thus, the functional impairments associated with diseased or damaged tissue, as in strokes or closed-head injuries, tend to result in behavioral distortions involving other functions, to have high level cognitive repercussions, and to affect personality. Dailey's (1956) finding that patients who received surgical treatment for their posttraumatic epilepsy tended to outperform a similar, medically treated group with posttraumatic epilepsy on a number of mental ability tests, also illustrates this principle. Hécaen (1964) found that fully two-thirds of his frontal lobe tumor patients presented with confused states and dementia, whereas patients who had had even extensive loss of prefrontal tissue were apt to be properly oriented and to suffer little or no impairment of reasoning, memory, or learned skills. Even so, Klebanoff (1945) noted, on the basis of an extensive review of case reports of patients with frontal lobe disease, that, "several of the [behavioral] alterations . . . do not appear as consistently in cases of tumor as they do in [closed head] traumatic lesions.

The presence of diseased or dead brain tissue can also affect the circulation and metabolism of surrounding tissue both immediately and long after the cerebral insult has occurred, with continuing psychological dysfunction of the surrounding areas (Hillbom, 1960; A. Smith, 1960; Woltman, 1942). This may include such secondary effects of tissue damage as buildup of scar tissue, microscopic blood vessel changes, or cell changes due to lack of oxygen following interference with the blood supply, which often complicate the symptom picture.

Severity.   There is little question that the severity of damage plays an important role in determining the behavioral correlates of a brain lesion. Yet no single measure of severity applies to all the kinds of damage that can interfere with normal brain functioning. Even the CT scan, which in most instances can provide reliable information about the extent of a lesion, does not reliably detect some kinds of damage such as the degenerative changes of a dementing process, many recent as well as old traumatic lesions, and cerebral vascular accidents within the first day or two after they occur (deLeon et al., 1980; L. Jacobs et al., 1976; Tunks, 1976; Weisberg, 1979). Duration of coma is a good index of the severity of a stroke or traumatic injury (see p. 168) but much less useful for assessing the severity of a toxic or hypoxic episode in which loss of consciousness does not occur with predictable regularity (Plum and Posner, 1980). Extent of motor or sensory involvement certainly reflects the dimensions of some lesions, so that when large portions of the body are paralyzed or sensory deficits are multiple or widespread, an extensive lesion with many behavioral ramifications should be suspected. However, injury or disease can involve large areas of frontal or posterior association cortex or limbic structures and yet have only minimal or subtle motor or sensory effects. Furthermore, some degenerative conditions, such as Alzheimer's disease, display only behavioral symptoms until very late in their course. Thus, in many cases, to evaluate the severity of a brain disorder one should rely on a number of different kinds of measures, including the behavioral measures obtained in neuropsychological assessment. The latter are often quite sensitive to subtle alterations in the brain's activity or to changes in areas of the brain that do not involve consciousness, or motor or sensory behavior directly.

Momentum. Dynamic aspects of the lesion contribute to behavioral changes too (Fitzhugh et al., 1961; Reitan, 1966). As a general rule, regardless of the cause of damage, the more rapid the onset of the condition, the more severe and widespread will its effects be (Ajuriaguerra et Hécaen, 1960; Finger, 1978; A. Smith, 1980). This phenomenon has been observed in comparisons of the behavioral effects of damage from rapidly evolving cerebrovascular accidents with the behavioral effects of tumors in comparable areas, for stroke patients usually have many more and more pronounced symptoms than tumor patients with similar kinds of cerebral involvement. Joynt (1970) points out that rapid-onset conditions such as stroke tend to set into motion such alterations in brain function as reduced cerebral circulation, depressed metabolism, and diaschisis. The effect of the rapidity with which the lesion evolves can also be seen in comparing tumors developing at different rates. Self-contained, slow-growing tumors that only gradually alter the spatial relationships between the brain's structural elements but do not affect its physiological activity or anatomical connections tend to remain "silent," i.e., do not give rise to symptoms, until they become large enough to exert pressure on or otherwise damage surrounding structures. A fast-growing tumor is more likely to be accompanied by swelling of the surrounding tissues resulting in a greater amount of behavioral dysfunction with more diffuse effects than a slow-growing tumor.

Time

Brain damage is a dynamic phenomenon, even when the lesions are nonprogressive (Newcombe et al., 1975; Scherer et. al., 1955; A. Smith, 1980). There appear to be regular trends in patterns of improvement and deterioration, depending on the nature of the cerebral insult, the age of the patient, and the function under study. The length of time following the onset of the condition must be taken into account in any evaluation of neuropsychological examination data. Ideally, every patient would be examined more than once, for changes in intellectual status can be expected throughout the brain damaged person's lifetime.

NONPROGRESSIVE BRAIN DISORDERS

In this category can be found all brain disorders that have an end to their direct action on the brain. Head trauma, aneurysms, *anoxia* due to heart stoppage or the effect of anesthesia during surgery, infectious processes that are ultimately halted, temporary toxic conditions, and nutritional deficiencies are the usual sources of "nonprogressive" brain damage. Strokes may come under this heading, for the typical stroke results from a single cerebrovascular event that has a fairly predictable course similar in many respects to the course of other nonprogressive brain diseases. Strokes do not necessarily reoccur or, if there is another one, it may take place in a different part of the brain. However, once a patient has suffered a stroke, the likelihood of reoccurrence is sufficiently great that in some patients stroke can be considered a progressive brain condition in which the ongoing deterioration is irregularly slowed by periods of partial improvement (Hutchinson and Acheson, 1975; Torack, 1978).

Psychological characteristics of acute brain conditions.   With nonprogressive or single-event brain disorders, the recency of the insult may be the most critical factor determining the patient's psychological status (Gronwall and Wrightson, 1974; Kertesz and McCabe, 1977; Lezak et al., 1980; M. T. Sarno, 1976). This is particularly evident in those stroke or trauma patients who are comatose for days or weeks as an immediate aftermath of cerebral damage. When they return to consciousness, and usually for several weeks to several months, severely damaged patients are confused, unable to track the sequence of time or events, emotionally unstable, unpredictably variable in their alertness and responsiveness, behaviorally regressed, and most often they display profound cognitive deficits (Lishman, 1978; Vigouroux et. al., 1971). In many such patients, these symptoms of acute disorganization recede so rapidly that noticeable improvement takes place from day to day during the first few weeks or months until the rate of improvement begins to level off. Even patients with less severe damage are likely to experience confusion to some degree for days, weeks, and sometimes months following a head injury or stroke (Gronwall and Sampson, 1974; Ruesch and Moore, 1944). This confusion is often accompanied by disorientation, difficulty in concentration, poor memory and recall for recent experiences, fatigability, irritability, and labile affect. However, these patients too tend to make the most rapid gains in the first weeks and months following onset.

   Apart from specific functional defects that vary from patient to patient with the site and extent of the lesion, the most common behavioral characteristics of an acute brain condition in conscious patients are impaired retention, concentration, and attention, emotional lability, and fatigability. The disruption of memory functions may be so severe that months later the patient can recall little or nothing of the acute stage of his condition although he appeared to be fully conscious at the time (posttraumatic amnesia, see p. 173). So much of a patient's behavioral reintegration usually takes place the first month or two following a brain injury that psychological test data obtained during this time may be obsolete within weeks or even days. The rapidity with which change typically occurs and the patient's great vulnerability to fatigue and emotional upset make premature testing inadvisable. As a general rule, formal psychological testing should not be initiated before six, or even better, eight weeks after the patient regains consciousness. The greatest cognitive gains will be achieved within the first six months after onset (Bond, 1979; Kertesz and McCabe, 1977).

Psychological characteristics of chronic brain conditions.   Even after the acute stage has passed, the patient's condition rarely remains static. Intellectual functions, particularly those involving immediate memory, attention and concentration, and specific disabilities associated with the site of the lesion generally continue to improve markedly during the first six months or year, and improvement at an increasingly slower rate may go on for a decade and more following a stroke or other single-event injury to the brain (Blakemore and Falconer, 1967; Eson et al., 1978; Newcombe and Artiola i Fortuny, 1979; Seron, 1979). However, improvement probably never amounts to full recovery[1], even when the insult may appear to be slight (Brodal, 1973; Milner, 1969; Schachter and Crovitz, 1977; S. Weinstein and Teuber, 1957).

Although the rate of improvement following onset of nonprogressive brain damage may vary with the patient's age, and the nature, site, and severity of the lesion, and probably other factors as well, improvement almost always takes place very rapidly at first, then gradually slows until it reaches the plateau that marks the level of ultimate gain (Newcombe et al., 1975; K. O'Brien and Lezak, 1981; Seron, 1979). The regularity with which test performances change in the early months and years following nonprogressive brain damage necessitates repeated neuropsychological examination, continuing until the examiner is satisfied that, at least for most functions, the patient has reached a plateau. Without repeated examinations, a plateau cannot be established, and without knowledge of the patient's ultimate performance levels, planning and guidance cannot be intelligently undertaken.

Some functions that appear to be intact in acute and early stages may deteriorate over the succeeding months and years (Dikmen and Reitan, 1976; A. Smith, 1964). Findings from studies of traumatically injured patients (Anttinen, 1960; Daghighian, 1973; Hillbom, 1960) and of patients who underwent brain surgery for psychiatric disorders (North and Zubin, 1956; A. Smith and Kinder, 1959) suggest that for both these conditions, following an initial improvement and a plateau period of several years or more, some mental deterioration may take place. Behavioral deterioration generally involves the highest levels of intellectual activity having to do with mental flexibility, efficiency of learning and recall, and reasoning and judgment about abstract issues or complex social problems. It may be compounded by diminished self-control with consequent dilapidation of personal habits and performance standards (McReynolds and Weide, 1960). As for the neuropathology, decades after psychosurgery the brains of lobotomized patients tend to be noticeably smaller than normal for their age (Johnstone et al., 1976). Geschwind (1974b) suggests that "extensive trans-synaptic and transneuronal degeneration" may account for this shrinkage.

Patients with organic disorders who have been invalids and patients institutionalized over long periods of time tend to perform with a sameness characterized chiefly by poor memory and attention span, apathy, concrete thinking, and generally regressive behavior. Such general behavioral deterioration can obscure the pronounced test performance discrepancies between differentially affected functions that are characteristic of acute and progressive brain conditions.

---

[1] I no longer use the term "recovery" when discussing brain damage. Brain damage that is severe enough to alter the level of consciousness even momentarily, or to result in even transient impairment of sensory, motor, or cognitive functions, is likely to leave some residual deficits. In cases where the damage is more than mild, the use of the word "recovery," which implies restoration or return to premorbid status, when discussing the patient's prognosis can give the patient and family false hopes, delay practical planning, and may cause unnecessary anxiety and disappointment.

Few symptoms distinguish the behavior of persons suffering chronic brain damage of adult onset with sufficient regularity to be considered characteristic. The most common complaints are of temper outbursts, fatigue, and poor memory (Brodal, 1973; Brooks, 1979; Lezak, 1978a, b; Oddy et al., 1978b). Rest and a paced activity schedule are the patient's best antidotes to debilitating fatigue. Patients who read and write and are capable of self-discipline can aid their failing memory with notebooks. Some patients benefit from mnemonic training techniques using visual imagery (Binder and Schreiber, 1980) and repetition (Schachter, 1980).

However, the reality of memory complaints is not always apparent, even on careful examination. When this occurs, these complaints may reflect the patient's feelings of impairment more than an objective deficit. Care must be taken to distinguish true memory defects from attention or concentration problems, for patients may easily interpret the effects of distractibility as a memory problem (Milner, 1969). A common chronic problem is an abiding sense of unsureness about mental experiences (*perplexity*) (Lezak, 1978b). Patients express this problem indirectly with hesitancies and statements of self-doubt or bewilderment; they rarely understand that it is as much a natural consequence of brain injury as their fatigue. Reassurance that guesses and solutions that come to mind first are generally correct, and advice to treat the sense of unsureness as an annoying symptom rather than a signal that he must heed, often relieve the patient's distress.

Depression troubles most adults who were not rendered grossly defective by their injuries (Brooks and Aughton, 1979b; Lezak, 1978b, Lezak et al., 1980; Lishman, 1978). It is usually first experienced within the year following the onset of brain damage. The severity and duration of the depressive reaction vary greatly among patients, depending on a host of factors both intrinsic and extrinsic to their brain condition (Merskey and Woodforde, 1972; E. D. Ross and Rush, 1981). Patients whose permanent disabilities are considerable and who have experienced no depression have either lost some capacity for self-appreciation and reality testing, or are denying their problems. In both cases, rehabilitation prospects are significantly reduced, for the patient must have a fairly realistic understanding of his strengths and limitations to cooperate with and benefit from any rehabilitation program. For most patients, the depression resolves or becomes muted with time (e.g., Dikmen and Reitan, 1977a). Some patients remain chronically depressed and, when their emotional distress is severe, may become suicidal (M. W. Buck, 1968).

Heightened irritability is another common complaint of both patients and their families (Bond 1979; Lezak et al., 1980). A greatly—and permanently—decreased tolerance for alcohol should also be anticipated following brain injury of any consequence.

Predicting outcome.   Outcome can be evaluated on a number of dimensions. Self-report and the presence and severity of sensory and motor symptoms are most often used in clinical practice. This custom can create serious problems for the many brain damaged patients whose motor or sensory status and ability to respond appropriately to such simple questions as, "How are you feeling today?" far exceed their judgment, reasoning abilities, self-understanding, and capacity to care for themselves or others (Broe, 1982; Lezak, 1982b). Neuropsychological assessment data and evaluations of the status of particular impaired functions, such as speech, also serve as outcome measures. Social outcome criteria tend to vary with the age of the population. The usual criterion of good outcome for younger adults, and therefore for most head trauma patients, is return to gainful employment. For older people, usually stroke patients, the social outcome is more likely to be judged in terms of degree of independence, self-care, and whether the patient could return home rather than to a care facility.

Regardless of the nature of the lesion, its severity is by far the most important variable in determining the patient's ultimate level of improvement (Dresser et al., 1973; Gilchrist and Wilkinson, 1979; Kertesz and McCabe, 1977; Lezak et al., 1980). For example, Levin and his co-workers (1979) have demonstrated that patients whose posttraumatic amnesia (PTA) lasts less than two weeks are likely to have good outcomes. Longer periods of PTA are associated with greater dependency as measured on the Glasgow Outcome Scale (see p. 593f). Unexplained exceptions to this general rule, however, do occur (e.g., Geschwind, 1974b). The nature of the lesion, too, may play some role since traumatically injured patients tend to enjoy more return of impaired functions such as arm or leg movements or speech than do stroke patients (Geschwind, 1974b). Of course, trauma patients are younger than stroke patients by and large, and the likelihood that they had preexisting brain disease or conditions that may work against the healing process is less. Among stroke patients, those whose strokes are due to infarction, whether thrombotic or embolic, have longer survival times than patients with hemorrhagic strokes (Abu-Zeid et al., 1978).

Age may affect outcome at the age extremes but appears to have little influence within the young to middle-aged adult range (see pp. 215–216). Premorbid intelligence, too, may contribute to outcome (see p. 225). General physical status is related to outcome for stroke patients (J.F. Lehmann et al., 1975). Family support has been found to contribute to good outcomes of both trauma and stroke patients (Gilchrist and Wilkinson, 1979; Greif and R. Matarazzo, 1982; J. F. Lehmann et al., 1975). For example, married stroke patients tend to outlive single ones (Abu-Zeid et al., 1978). Yet the extent to which the family continues its involvement with the patient may, in turn, be related to the severity of the patient's behavior and self-care problems. Thus, at least in some instances, the presence of family support may depend on how well the patient is doing rather than serve as an independent predictor of outcome success.

A most interesting finding is that stroke patients with left hemiplegia (right hemisphere damage) tend to have poorer outcomes than those with left-sided brain damage (Knapp, 1959; J. F. Lehmann et al., 1975; A. Smith, 1971). Denes and colleagues (1982) suggest that this difference is due to unilateral spatial agnosia, not indifference reaction. Moreover, among patients with right hemisphere damage, those who show the inattention phenomenon tend to be more impaired and improve less than the ones who are not troubled by inattention (Campbell and Oxbury, 1976).

Testing done during the third to sixth months after severe brain injury may give some indication of what the patient's ultimate mental condition will be. However,

213

many patients continue to improve significantly through much of the first year and into the second and third (K. O'Brien and Lezak, 1981). Repeated testing during the first year following injury may provide a better basis for estimating how much improvement can be expected. The rule of thumb for predicting extent of improvement is that the more rapid the rate of improvement, the more further improvement can be expected.

Both the rate and nature of the improvement are almost always uneven. Improvement does not follow a smooth course but tends to proceed by inclines and plateaus, and different functions improve at different rates (Kertesz, 1979; K. O'Brien and Lezak, 1981). Old memories and well-learned skills generally return most quickly; recent memory, ability for abstract thinking, mental flexibility, and adaptability are more likely to return at a slower rate. Of course, these general tendencies vary greatly depending upon the site and extent of the lesion and the patient's premorbid abilities.

Brain injured patients' test scores are likely to fluctuate considerably, over time and between functions, particularly during the first few years after injury. Therefore, predicting a patient's ultimate ability to perform specific functions or activities can be a very chancy business for at least a year or two after the event. Unless the patient's handicaps are so severe as to be permanently and totally disabling, it is unwise for binding decisions or judgments to be made concerning his legal, financial, or vocational status until several years have passed. Even then, arrangements made for legal settlements, compensation benefits, or working agreements should provide for the possibility that the patient's mental status may yet change.

Progressive Brain Diseases

In progressive brain disease, behavioral deterioration tends to follow an often bumpy but fairly predictable downhill course for particular sets of functions that may deteriorate at varying rates, depending on the disease (Chapter 7. See also Klebanoff et al., 1954; Lishman, 1978; Strub and Black, 1981). When the diagnosis is known, the question is not so much *what* will happen, but *when* it will happen. Past observations provide some rules of thumb to guide clinicians in their predictions. The clinical rule of thumb for predicting the rate of mental decline holds that conditions that are progressing rapidly are likely to continue to worsen at a rapid rate whereas slow progressions tend to remain slow.

For instance, most patients with multiple sclerosis can expect that, ultimately, higher level mental activities, vision, and motor functions will deteriorate. The rate at which the disease progresses in the early stages of the illness gives some indication as to whether these disabilities will occur in a few years or a few decades, for the rapid appearance of serious symptoms generally presages a rapid decline, and a slower course with long periods of remission is a favorable sign that deterioration will be slow and perhaps less profound (B. Matthews, 1978; McAlpine et al., 1972). Similar progression patterns obtain in other degenerative disorders such as Huntington's chorea or Alzheimer's disease (Lishman, 1978).

Patients with newly diagnosed progressive brain disease may benefit from an early "baseline" assessment of their psychological status with one or two reexaminations at two- to four- or six-month intervals. Such a longitudinal study can provide a rough basis for forecasting the rate at which mental deterioration is likely to take place, to aid the patient and his family in their planning for his care.

Predicting the course of the behavioral effects of a brain tumor differs from making predictions about other progressively deteriorating diseases. Biopsy, performed in the course of surgery, takes some of the guesswork out of estimating the rate of progression, for different kinds of brain tumors grow at fairly predictable rates. The severity of the behavioral disorder, too, bears some relationship to the type of tumor. Extensive edema and elevated intracranial pressure for instance, are more likely to accompany fast-growing astrocytomas and glioblastomas than other tumorous growths and thus involve more of the surrounding and distant tissue (Lishman, 1978; A. Smith, 1966b). On the other hand, the *direction* of growth is not predictable so that the neurologist cannot forewarn the patient or his family about *what* behavioral changes they can expect as the disease runs its course, short of terminal apathy, stupor, and coma.

Predicting mortality. Large-scale studies of aging populations consistently show that performance on measures of cognitive functioning correlates negatively with biological factors associated with decreased longevity, such as cigarette smoking, cardiovascular disease, and hypertension (Jarvik, 1975; Torack, 1978). A sudden drop in an elderly person's mental competency can be an early indicator of biological changes that will lead to death (Botwinick, 1977; Eisdorfer and Wilkie, 1973). Severe cognitive impairment is also associated with approaching death in patients with presenile or senile dementia of the Alzheimer's type. Kaszniak and his co-workers (1978) found that a measure of verbal fluency (a sentence production test) was the single best predictor of death within one year. Disorientation and poor performance on memory and vocabulary tests were also correlated with death within the year, while cerebral atrophy (as measured by CT scan) and EEG abnormalities did not differentiate survivors and nonsurvivors. Defective learning ability, as measured by verbal learning tests, was predictive of mortality for a group of elderly psychiatric patients (Sanderson and Inglis, 1961). Nine of the 15 patients with a documented learning disorder had died within 16 months of testing, while all 15 of the slightly older (on the average) patients whose learning ability had been relatively intact were still alive. However, H. S. Wang (1977) warns against making predictions in the individual case, pointing out that such variables as quality of care, age of the patient, and intercurrent illnesses will also contribute to the length of time that a demented person will survive.

Patient Variables

AGE

By and large, the adverse effects of brain damage on behavior tend to increase with advancing age. Yet this is not a simple linear relationship. In any given study of behavioral changes associated with brain damage, the question of whether age will

215

show up as a significant variable turns upon such dimensions as the coarseness of age intervals, narrowness of overall age range under study, and the nature and severity of the lesion.

Age at onset. Studies of patients who have suffered head trauma (Brooks, 1972, 1974; Jennett et al., 1975) or stroke (J. W. Brown and Jaffe, 1975; A. Smith, 1971, 1972b) consistently demonstrate how age and severity interact, with advancing age significantly enhancing the impact of severity of damage. This effect is probably less evident in younger (below 30) than older persons. However, youthfulness (under 25) has also been associated with greater cognitive impairment (Jurko, 1979) due to head injury. When severity is not taken into account, age alone does not appear to make much difference in outcome for traumatically impaired patients within the young to middle-age adult range (Gilchrist and Wilkinson, 1979; Lezak, 1979b). In age groups at least above 45, negative effects of age have been reported for stroke patients (Ben-Yishay et al., 1970; Sands et al., 1969), tumor patients (Benton, 1977b; Hamsher and Benton, 1978), and psychosurgery patients (A. Smith, 1960). In progressive deteriorating conditions, the normal mental changes of advancing years, such as reduced learning efficiency, tend to compound mental impairments due to the disease process (Kaszniak et al., 1979a). Thus functions normally not affected by age deteriorate at the same rate in elderly as in younger patients while rapidity of deterioration increases with age for those functions vulnerable to both normal age changes and the disease process.

Normal cognitive changes in the elderly. The aging brain normally undergoes structural changes of which decreasing size, flattening of the surface, and increasing amounts of intracranial space are most obvious on inspection (Jernigan et al., 1980). Concomitant microscopic, biochemical, and electrophysiological changes take place as well (Berry, 1975; Brizzee et al., 1980; Hansch et al., 1980; Zatz et al., 1982a and b).

The pattern of normal intellectual decline bears an overall similarity to the pattern of deficits that has emerged from studies of heterogeneous populations of organically impaired persons (Kramer and Jarvik, 1979). Thus, verbal skills, particularly the well-learned skills of reading, writing, vocabulary, and word usage, tend to hold up (Botwinick, 1977). Moreover, the general intellectual status of healthy older people, as measured by neuropsychological tests, tends to remain within normal limits through the eighth decade (Benton et al., 1981). Even among subjects in their early eighties when an increasing number showed deficits on one or more tests, most subjects gave performances within normal limits on most of the tests.

Along with verbal skills, arithmetic ability is generally stable among elderly groups (Kramer and Jarvik, 1979; Wechsler, 1958; M. Williams, 1970b). Older persons retain and retrieve once-learned information as well as do younger ones (Botwinick and Storandt, 1980). Contrary to conventional belief, normal aging processes do not affect the immediate memory span (G. Goldstein and Shelly, 1973a; M. Williams, 1970b). Lowered Wechsler Digit Span subtest scores at older age levels result mainly in a greatly shortened span of recall for Digits Backward, reflecting impaired concentration and mental tracking. However, a normal tendency for digit and letter span to be a little longer in the auditory than visual modality appears to increase with age (Craik, 1977a; Kramer and Jarvik, 1979).

Those cognitive abilities that tend to decrease with age typically involve speed, unfamiliar material, complexity of task, and active problem solving (in comparison to activation of well-learned response patterns by vocabulary or standard arithmetic test items) (Botwinick, 1977; Botwinick and Storandt, 1974; Kramer and Jarvik, 1979). For example, each of the WAIS subtests most vulnerable to advancing age—Digit Symbol, Block Design, and Object Assembly—involves these characteristics to some degree.

Reports that some verbal skills, such as vocabulary, continue to improve into the seventh and eighth decade (G. Goldstein and Shelly, 1973a; Traxler, 1972) have been questioned on methodological grounds. Different studies show great differences in what happens to verbal skills in the later years depending upon whether comparisons between age groups are done on a cross-sectional or a longitudinal basis (Botwinick, 1981; Torack, 1978). Cross-sectional studies suggest that between middle and old age a sharp drop occurs in verbal skills as measured by the WAIS verbal subtests, Information, Comprehension, and Similarities, for instance (Kramer and Jarvik, 1979). In contrast, longitudinal studies tend to show modest gains over the years with increasingly smaller increments ultimately reaching a plateau and then declining in the eighth to ninth decades (Horn and Donaldson, 1976). The sharp losses observed in the cross-sectional studies of different age groups must be interpreted in the light of differences in education, medical status, motivation, and test-wiseness that characterize the different generations included in such studies (Horn and Donaldson, 1976). The continuing gains noted in longitudinal studies, on the other hand, may be largely accounted for by the greater longevity of those persons who have been more amply endowed with health, financial security, social status, cognitive abilities, and willingness to exercise common sense, all variables that correlate with one another and with longevity (Lehr and Schmitz-Scherzer, 1976; Torack, 1978). Botwinick (1977) refers to this increasingly higher representation of the more fortunate members of society in aging populations as "selective availability." These contradictory findings and different methodological approaches highlight some of the central issues in the evaluation of cognitive function in the elderly. Moreover, all authors who have addressed the issue of individual differences emphasize the importance of recognizing when exceptions to overall tendencies arise.

The normal intellectual decline associated with old age shows up most strikingly in four areas of intellectual activity:

1. The primary, or working, memory capacity of intact elderly persons differs little from that of younger adults (Erickson, 1978) except when the amount of material to be remembered exceeds the normal primary storage capacity of six or seven items, as in tests of supraspan (see pp. 418–419) (Craik, 1977a). Craik points out that in memorization of lists that are longer than immediate storage capacity, for example, whatever is retained after the eighth or ninth item must have been stored (i.e.,

learned) in the secondary memory system. The relative impairment of elderly persons on supraspan memory tests suggests a storage or retrieval failure in secondary memory. Both storage and retrieval problems tend to occur with advanced age (Botwinick, 1981). The elderly use less effective learning procedures (e.g., less elaborate encoding) than younger persons and tend to show a greater differential between recall and recognition of learned material, particularly when the recognition tasks are easy (Botwinick and Storandt, 1974). Noting parallels in the patterns of impaired learning of elderly subjects and of younger persons under conditions of intoxication, fatigue, and divided attention, Craik and Byrd (1981) have suggested that all of these conditions reduce the amount of "mental energy" available for learning with consequent reduction in the deliberate, effortful activity required for effective encoding of new material. D. M. Burke and Light (1981) attribute the normal memory problems of the elderly to poor utilization of contextual information in the retrieval process and to changes that take place in the organization of semantic memory over the years, contributing to the reduced efficiency of retrieval. Interference does not appear to impede learning in the elderly but may reduce effective retrieval through confusion due to information overload (what Craik calls "cue overload"). A speed factor may contribute to learning disability in the aged since slowed presentation of material to be learned gives elderly subjects greater benefits than younger ones although the level of learning of the elderly never reaches that of younger subjects under the same conditions (Craik, 1977a; Hulicka and Wheeler, 1975).

Contrary to studies that indicate a progressive loss in recall of public events (Craik, 1977a; Squire, 1974), Botwinick and Storandt (1980) reported that memory for remote events does not appear to change with the passage of time. However, younger persons displayed a better memory than the older subjects for the more recent events. A finding that runs contrary to conventional belief is that memory for old personal events does not hold up as well over time as memory for more recent ones (Craik, 1977a). Craik pointed out that the few favorite anecdotes often retold by some elderly persons are not a representative sample of old memories. Some may not even be old memories as they changed in the process of retelling over the years. Moreover, in contradiction to the greater number of memory complaints voiced by older persons, by and large they have the same expectations of learning well as do younger persons, even when their ability to recall newly learned material has diminished (Bruce et al., 1980; Perlmutter, 1978).

An age decrement that varies with the modality has also been shown for learning nonverbal material (Riege and Williams, 1980). Visual nonverbal memory declines more rapidly than other forms of nonverbal memory in the 60 to 80 decades, auditory or tactile memory shows greater decline than visual in the decades between 40 and 60.

2. Diminished ability for abstract and complex conceptualization typifies the intellectual functioning of elderly persons (Botwinick, 1977; Denney, 1974; Reitan, 1967). The more meaningful and concrete the presentation of a reasoning problem, the greater is the likelihood that older people will succeed at it (Botwinick, 1978).

3. Mental inflexibility, appearing as difficulty in adapting to new situations, solving

novel problems, or changing mental set, characterizes intellectual performance failures of old age (Botwinick, 1977, 1978; Kramer and Jarvik, 1979; M. Williams, 1970b; Schaie, 1958).

4. General behavioral slowing is a predominant characteristic of aging that affects perceptual (Hines and Posner, n.d.; Kramer and Jarvik, 1979), cognitive (Botwinick, 1977; J. C. Thomas et al., 1977), and memory functions as well as all psychomotor activity (Benton, 1977b; Hicks and Birren, 1970; Welford, 1977). Slowing contributes to the lower scores typically achieved by elderly persons on timed tests of cognitive functions such as the Block Design, Object Assembly, and Digit Symbol subtests of the WAIS (Kramer and Jarvik, 1979). However, even when the speed factor is removed, elderly subjects' scores improve relative to those of younger persons, but still do not reach their higher level (Botwinick, 1977). Accurate evaluation of an elderly patient's poor performance on any timed test must depend on careful observation and analysis of the effect of time limits on the scores, for the score alone will tell little about the effects of slowing per se (Lorge, 1936).

Organic brain disease and old age.   The known incidence of organic deteriorating diseases of the brain increases sharply with advancing age (Eisdorfer and Cohen, 1978; Roth, 1980), creating an ever-growing social burden. Moreover, the awesome dimensions of this problem are only now beginning to be appreciated as diagnostic sensitivity to these problems improves (H. S. Wang, 1977). Furthermore, as the number of elderly persons in the population increases, proportionally fewer of them live in family units that can tolerate or care for them if they become mentally disabled. The social burden of the problem is further compounded in that, with advancing age, patients presenting with dementia symptoms are more apt to be suffering from an irreversible disease than such treatable conditions as normal pressure hydrocephalus or arteriosclerosis (C. E. Wells, 1978b). With advancing age, elderly people generally have fewer social resources, such as family availability and income (H. E. Lehmann et al., 1977; Lehr and Schmitz-Scherzer, 1976) so that when they require care, it is increasingly likely to be given in a nursing home or institution where unfamiliar surroundings and lack of stimulation and personalized care contribute to the severity of their symptoms.

Determining whether the mental slowing and dulling experienced by an elderly person represent the effects of the "normal" aging process or of an abnormal brain condition often amounts to determining the extent to which the older person's mental disabilities either exceed those expected for his years or differ from the normal aging pattern (Bolton et al., 1966). The most common problem complicating differential diagnosis of behavioral disturbances in older persons is depression, which can mimic or exacerbate symptoms of progressive dementing conditions such as Alzheimer's disease (see pp. 180–184). Since the depressive features of the patient's disturbance may respond to psychiatric treatment, it is important to ascertain whether depression is contributing to the patient's symptoms. Most often, the disturbed behavior of an elderly psychiatric patient has a mixed etiology in which his emotional reaction to significant losses—of loved ones, of ego-satisfying activities, and of physical and intel-

lectual competence—interacts with the behavioral effects of physiological and anatomical brain changes to produce a complex picture of behavioral dilapidation (Post,
1975). There are also many physical disorders to which elderly persons are prone that
may create disturbances in mental functioning that mimic the symptoms of degenerative brain disease (Libow, 1977). Since many of these conditions are reversible,
with proper treatment, the differential diagnosis can be extremely important (E.D.
Ross and Rush, 1981).

SEX

In large-scale studies comparing the performances of males and females on tests of
cognitive functions, a pattern of differences has emerged (Bock, 1973; Bock and Kolakowski, 1973; Buffery and Gray, 1972; L. J. Harris, 1978; A. C. Petersen and Wittig,
1979) that crosses ethnic and socioeconomic lines (Backman, 1972). Females consistently do better on verbal tasks, including verbal fluency (Benton et al., 1983; A. C.
Petersen, 1976), symbol substitution (A. Smith, 1968), and verbal learning (Ivison,
1977) and relatively less well on tests involving visuospatial processing (Coltheart et
al., 1975; Levy, 1972; McGee, 1979). For males, this pattern is reversed. These differences, which tend to be fully developed by adolescence, continue into old age (D.
Cohen and Wilkie, 1979). Examinations of normal subjects using neuropsychological
techniques for demonstrating cerebral lateralization, such as dichotic listening (Bryden, 1979a; Buffery and Gray, 1972; L. J. Harris, 1978), measurement of visual field
superiority for verbal or visual material (Bryden, 1979a; Hannay, 1976), or recognition of shapes by touch (Witelson, 1976) show sex differences in patterns of cerebral
organization. Lateralization of verbal and visuospatial functions to the left and right
hemispheres, respectively, tends to be greater for males than for females.

Differences in cerebral organization between the sexes may account for many of
the observed performance differences. For example, men who have had unilateral
brain damage tend to show more profound deficits in functions associated with the
side of lesion than do women with similar lesions (L. J. Harris, 1978; McGlone, 1976).
With unilateral damage, women's deficits may be less profound and more diffuse.
However, variations in degree of cerebral lateralization are also associated with handedness (Piazza, 1980; see pp. 221–222); socialization patterns may alter the development and expression of particular skills (Sherman, 1978); and age at maturation has
been implicated in the development of spatial ability (Herbst and A. Peterson, 1980).
Whether the usual finding of male superiority in mathematics reflects differences
between the sexes in cerebral organization or in socialization is as yet an unresolved
question (see F. C. Richardson and Woolfolk, 1980, for a recent review of this
problem).

When taking sex into account in evaluating neuropsychological text performances,
it is perhaps most important to keep in mind that group differences rarely amount to
as much as one-half of a standard deviation (e.g., Ivison, 1977; D. Wechsler, 1958) so
that the overlap in the distribution of male and female scores is much greater than
the distance between them. Interpretation of any individual's test performance in the

light of general knowledge about cognitive differences between the sexes must be done with caution.

LATERAL ASYMMETRY

Cerebral organization and hand preference.   Based on clinical and laboratory studies of cerebral lateralization, Levy (1974) estimated that 99.67% of right-handed people have left hemisphere language representation. The remaining right-handers have right hemisphere language representation. Clinical data support her estimate in that 98% or more of aphasic disturbances in right-handed persons are associated with left-sided lesions (Hicks and Kinsbourne, 1978; Searleman, 1977). These proportions have also been observed in the production of aphasic speech phenomena when right-handed patients are treated with special procedures such as injection of sodium amytal directly into the common or internal carotid artery to inactivate one hemisphere (see p. 60), direct cortical stimulation before brain surgery, and electroconvulsive therapy. Visuospatial and other functions having a significant configurational component are predominantly mediated by the right hemisphere in right-handers.

Three different patterns of cerebral dominance for speech have been identified among left-handed and ambidextrous persons (Hicks and Kinsbourne, 1978; Milner, 1974, 1975; Satz, 1980; Searleman, 1977). Approximately two-thirds of them show the pattern of lateral asymmetry that is characteristic for right-handers. In approximately one-third of non-right-handers, aphasic disorders are associated with right-sided lesions, and about one-half of these (reports from different studies range in the neighborhood of 13 to 16%) appear to have bilateral speech representation. Aphasia occurs with greater frequency in left-handed and ambidextrous patients than in right-handers because both right and left hemisphere lesions may result in an aphasic condition (Humphrey and Zangwill, 1952; Satz, 1980). It is also much more likely to be mild or transient (Gloning and Quatember, 1966), suggesting bilateral localization of speech functions. The extent to which cerebral organization is lateralized may be reflected in the strength of hand preference (D. G. Thomas and Campos, 1978; see pp. 222–223).

For the most part, left-handers with left cerebral dominance for verbal functions are those with a strong left-hand bias who do not have a familial history of left-handedness (Corballis and Beale, 1976; Hardyck and Petrinovich, 1977; Hécaen and Albert, 1978). Familial left-handers, who usually have only a moderate degree of left-hand preference (i.e., show some ambidexterity), are more likely to have right or mixed hemisphere dominance for speech. Ability patterns of familial left-handers also differ according to sex as the performance of these females on visuospatial tasks is higher, and that of males is lower, than either their right-handed or their nonfamilial left-handed counterparts (Healey et al., 1982). However, those relatively uncommon familial left-handers with a very strong left-hand bias are apt to resemble nonfamilial strongly left-handed people more than other familial left-handers in having predominantly left hemisphere representation of speech. Moreover, right-handers with left-handers in the family tend to show more and faster improvement from aphasia due to left hemisphere lesions than do other right-handers, suggesting that they too may have some bilateral cerebral representation for language functions (Carter-Saltzman, 1979).

Determining handedness.   Because of the relationship of handedness to cerebral organization, it is often important to know the patient's handedness status. For clinical purposes, the determination of handedness is usually made by such self-report methods as questioning the subject about his writing habits. For most right-handed people this is a quite satisfactory procedure since right-handers typically show strong right-sided preferences, using the right hand, arm, leg, eye, or ear when they can choose between sides (Annett, 1967; Levy and Gur, 1980). However, this simple approach to the question of handedness does not identify persons with a left-sided or mixed (ambi-lateral) preference who, by training or as a result of illness or injury, learned to write with the right hand. In this vein, Searleman (1980) has observed that the side and strength of foot preference ("footedness") may be an even more reliable predictor of the direction and extent of lateral asymmetry in cortical organization, probably because it is less subject to cultural pressure.

Eye or ear preference does not help to clarify lateral preference in left-handed persons as many have a right eye or right ear preference regardless of their strength of handedness (Klisz, 1978). Nor does ear advantage, as determined by dichotic listening tests, indicate lateralization of verbal functions in left-handers with any greater accuracy than does the determination of hand preference (Warrington and Pratt, 1981). Moreover, Teng (1979, 1981) notes that unreliability and large error variance in ear difference scores make dichotic ear difference "a poor index" of functional asymmetry between the cerebral hemispheres.

A number of behavioral techniques have been devised to help ascertain both lateral preference and its strength (as measured by the consistency of side of choice). Many clinicians use an informal set of tasks or questions having to do with a variety of one-sided activities. For example, Kimura and Vanderwolf (1970) asked their subjects to show how they "write, brush teeth, comb hair, hammer a nail, cut bread, use a key, strike a match, and hold a tennis or badminton racquet." Subjects were classified as right- or left-handed if they met at least six of these criteria on one hand.

Formal questionnaires typically ask about choice of side in performing a variety of one-hand activities and other acts, including choice of foot for kicking or dressing first (Humphrey, 1951; Raczkowski et al., 1974). Milner's (1975) 18-item questionnaire also inquires into hand preference for such two-handed activities as hammering a nail. A. J. Harris's *Test of Lateral Dominance* (1958) involves both questions and activities, including a test of eye preference in which the subject is asked to look through a rolled-up piece of paper or into a kaleidoscope.

A revision of Annett's (1967) hand preference questionnaire takes into account the fact that for many left-handed and ambidextrous persons, lateral preference is not easily dichotomized (G. G. Briggs and Nebes, 1975) (see Fig. 8-1). The five-point scale measuring strength of laterality for each item was added to make this inventory more sensitive to ambidexterity than Annett's questionnaire. A handedness score can be

Name_____ Sex_____ Age_____

Indicate hand preference	Always left	Usually left	No pre-ference	Usually right	Always right
1. To write a letter legibly					
2. To throw a ball to hit a target					
3. To play a game requiring the use of a racquet					
4. At the top of a broom to sweep dust from the floor					
5. At the top of a shovel to move sand					
6. To hold a match when striking it					
7. To hold scissors to cut paper					
8. To hold thread to guide through the eye of a needle					
9. To deal playing cards					
10 To hammer a nail into wood					
11. To hold a toothbrush while clean-ing teeth					
12. To unscrew the lid of a jar					

Are either of your parents left-handed? If yes, which? _____
How many siblings of each sex do you have? Male _____ Female _____
How many of each sex are left-handed? Male _____ Female _____
Which eye do you use when using only one (e.g., telescope, keyhole)? _____
Have you ever suffered any severe head trauma? _____

Fig. 8-1. *The handedness inventory.* (Modified from Annett, 1967. Source: Briggs and Nebes, 1975).

obtained by assigning two points to "always" responses, one point to "usually," and none to "no preference". Scoring left preferences as negative and right preferences as positive gives a range of scores from −24 for the most left-handed to +24 for the most right-handed. The authors arbitrarily called persons receiving scores of +9 and above right-handed, those with scores between −9 and +8 were called mixed-handed, and scores from −9 to −24 indicated left-handedness. Using this method, 14% of a large (n = 1599) group of students were designated non-right-handers, a figure in accord with the literature. Factor analysis of the items in this inventory identified three distinct factors (power, skills, and rhythm), as well as distinctive factor structures for two different student populations (Loo and Schneider, 1979).

For most practical purposes, informal questioning is sufficient, since most patients will be right-handed and will answer the questions consistently. When the patient's responses differ from the expected pattern of consistent right bias, then the examiner may want to explore the laterality issue further by having the patient pantomime or demonstrate one-sided activities and answer questions involving the leg, ear, and eye, as well as the hand. Freides (1978) recommends that when investigating "footedness," the examiner inquire into the subject's preference for hopping or standing on one foot rather than kicking since children with lateralized dysfunction often learn to stand on the stronger leg and kick with the weaker one. Thus, foot preference for kicking may reflect compensatory behavior, not dominance.

Determination of the side and strength of hand preference only tells the examiner the odds that the subject's cerebral lateralization follows one or another pattern (Warrington and Pratt, 1981). Most examiners do not have access to laboratory techniques for ascertaining cerebral lateralization and thus have to use clinical observations if they wish to refine their conjectures. When the side of the lesion is known, the pattern of test performance will often answer this question.

Jerre Levy (Levy, 1972; Levy and Reid, 1976) has hypothesized that hand position in writing may reflect cerebral lateralization. She observed that both right- and left-handers using a normal hand position tended to have language representation on the hemisphere side opposite the writing hand while subjects holding their writing instrument in an inverted position (i.e., "hooked") were more likely to have language represented in the hemisphere on the same side as the writing hand. Some contradictory findings have been reported as well as supporting data regarding language and even music functions (J. Levy, personal communication; McKeever and VanDeventer, 1980; Searleman, 1980; Volpe et al., 1981). McKeever (1979) concluded that left-handedness in the family predicts lateralization of language functions better than hand position. L. C. Smith and Moskovitch (1979), however, suggested that hand position may reflect cerebral organization of visual and visuomotor but not auditory functions. The findings of the many studies generated by Levy's interesting hypothesis suggest that the extent to which hand posture may be predictive of cerebral organization appears to be limited by a number of variables, some known, some only guessed at (Weber and Bradshaw, 1981; Levy, 1982).

A tendency for right-handers to perform better than left-handers on visuospatial tasks has been consistently observed (Buffery, 1974; Levy, 1972). These group differences in visuospatial abilities may be due to the greater likelihood that left-handers, like women, have visuospatial functions mediated in a more diffuse manner by both hemispheres than localized on the right, as is most typical for male right-handers. Levy wisely cautions that these data only represent overall group tendencies and cannot be indiscriminately applied to individuals.

Although the incidence of right hemisphere or mixed dominance is low in right-handed people, test behavior must be evaluated with these possibilities in mind. The first hint that there has been an unexpected switch is often the examiner's bewilderment when a hemiplegic patient displays the "wrong" set of behavioral symptoms. Since left-handed patients generally are less likely to conform to the common dominance pattern, their behavior should be routinely scrutinized for evidence of an irregular dominance pattern. When deviations from the normal left-right organization of the brain appear, a very thorough study of all functional systems is necessary to delineate the nature of the patient's intellectual disabilities fully, for in these exceptional cases no systematic relationships between functions can be taken for granted.

PREMORBID PSYCHOLOGICAL STATUS

"It is not only the kind of injury that matters, but the kind of head" Symonds, (1937).

Prior intellectual endowment tends to be directly related to intellectual achievement following brain damage (Chapman et al., 1958; Dresser et al., 1973; Hillbom, 1960). Education is positively associated with performance on neuropsychological tests including those, such as immediate memory and scanning tasks, that appear to be independent of academic achievement (Finlayson et al., 1977; Hilbert et al., 1976; Kaszniak et al., 1979a). Education has also been associated with level of outcome (J. F. Lehmann et al., 1975; A. Smith, 1971).

The premorbid personal and social adjustment of brain damaged patients also appears to have some effect, not only on the quality of their ultimate adjustment but also on the amount of gain they make (Gloning et al., 1968; Symonds and Russell, 1943; A. E. Walker and Jablon, 1959). Premorbid personality contributes both directly and indirectly to the kind of adjustment a patient makes following brain injury (A. L. Anderson, 1950; Lishman, 1973).

Direct effects are fairly obvious since premorbid personality characteristics are generally not so much changed as exaggerated by brain injury. Tendencies to dependent behavior, hypochondriasis, passivity, perfectionism, irresponsibility, etc., can be major obstacles to the patient whose rehabilitation depends on active relearning of old skills and reintegration of old habit patterns while he copes with a host of unrelenting and often humiliating frustrations.

The indirect effects of premorbid adjustment may not become apparent until the handicapped patient needs emotional support and acceptance in a protective but not institutional living situation. Patients who have conducted their lives in an emotionally stable and mature manner are also those most likely to be supported through their critical personal and social transitions by steadfast, emotionally stable and mature family and friends. On the other hand, patients with marked premorbid personality disorders or asocial tendencies are more apt to lack a social support system when they need it most. Many of this latter group have been social isolates, and others are quickly rejected by immature or recently acquired spouses, alienated children, and opportunistic or irresponsible friends who want nothing of the dependent patient who can no longer cater to their needs. The importance of a stable home environment to rehabilitation often becomes inescapable when determining whether a patient can return to the community or must be placed in a nursing home or institution in lieu of any alternative living situation.

SOCIAL AND CULTURAL VARIABLES

The evaluation of neuropsychological data must take into account the contribution of educational, social, and cultural experiences to the patient's test performance and to his attitudes and understanding of his condition. (Anastasi, 1982; Loehlin et al., 1975; Vernon, 1979). Persons growing up under conditions of deprivation, without adequate medical care, nutrition, environmental stimulation, or other benefits of modern society are more prone to developmental and other childhood disorders that can affect brain function (Amante et al., 1977; Winick, 1976). These conditions may make them less resilient to brain damage incurred in adulthood (Jennett et al., 1975). When characteristics of cultural background or socioeconomic status are overlooked, interpretations of test scores are subject both to errors of overinclusion (false positives) and errors of overexclusion (false negatives) (R. L. Adams et al., 1982; see also p. 142). Poorly learned or insufficiently practiced skills can produce a test profile with a lot of scatter that may be misinterpreted as evidence of organic disease. Members of some subcultures that stress intellectual development at the expense of manual activities may be so clumsy and perplexed when doing tasks involving hand skills as to exhibit a large discrepancy between verbal and visuoconstructional test scores (Backman, 1972). A bright but shy farmhand may fail dismally on any task that requires speaking or writing. On the other hand, the test performance of a patient whose intellectual development was lopsided and who sustained brain injury involving his strongest abilities may show so little intertest variability as to appear, on casual observation, to be intellectually intact.

MEDICATION

Many patients referred for neuropsychological assessment are on a drug regimen, whether for a behavioral or mood disturbance, tension, anxiety, sleep disturbance, or a neurological or medical disorder. Others may be treating themselves with nonprescription cold or headache remedies, or an over-the-counter analgesic. Judging from the relatively few studies on this large subject, the effects of most drugs in common use on neuropsychological test performance tend to be negligible (Heaton and Crowley, 1981; R. R. Baker, 1968; L. L. Judd et al., 1977; Telford and Worrall, 1978) or are as yet only demonstrated on relatively discrete functions in special populations (Dodrill, 1975; Gillis, 1977; Legg and Stiff, 1976).

However, some drugs alone or in interaction with other medications may have pronounced behavioral effects that can alter a subject's performance on particular tests. For example, Donnelly and his co-workers (1972, 1978) studied the effects on "judgment" as measured by the Comprehension subtest of the WAIS (see pp. 259–262) of dopamine activity in the brain. They found that increasing dopamine activity by administering L-Dopa resulted in lower scores only on this WAIS subtest, while administration of alpha-methyl-*para*-tyrosine (AMPT), a drug that decreases dopamine synthesis, was associated with score elevations on Comprehension. Sweet and his colleagues (1976) noted an increase in the incidence of dementia among Parkinson patients taking L-Dopa. Their interpretation of these findings was that the medication prolonged their patients' lives, thus allowing the dementing aspects of the disease to appear. Psychiatric disorders, such as hallucinations and formal thought disorders, have been observed in L-Dopa treated parkinsonism patients who had no prior psychiatric history. Moreover, the drug appears to exacerbate pre-existing schizophrenia (Klawans and Weiner, 1981). High serum levels of phenytoin (dilantin) in epileptic patients have been associated with deficits on tests of motor performance, while epileptic patients taking carbamazepine (tegretol) showed improvements in attentional functions and problem solving efficiency with decreased feelings of tension and anxiety (Dodrill, 1980) (see also p. 229). L. L. Judd and Grant's (1975) study of polydrug users suggested that longstanding heavy barbiturate intake may produce a pattern of mental dysfunction similar to that seen in chronic alcoholics in which concept formation, learning ability, visuomotor coordination, perceptual accuracy, and response speed are all impaired.

Examiners should also be aware that some patients take several weeks to adjust to a new drug and experience changes in mental efficiency in the interim. Geriatric patients are particularly susceptible to drug reactions that can affect—usually impair—some aspect of their cognitive functioning, or their alertness, or general activity level (Eisdorfer and Cohen, 1978; Salzman and Shader, 1977).

This topic is too broad and too complex to be satisfactorily dealt with here. The examiner needs to find out (1) what medications the patient is taking, (2) the patient's reports on their subjective effects, and (3) the usual effects of these drugs on behavior. For a general review of this issue the reader may wish to consult Barchas et al. (1977), Goodman and Gilman (1980), Heaton and Crowley (1981), or Khantzian and McKenna (1979).

EPILEPSY

Seizure disorders can arise from any condition that heightens the excitability of brain tissue (Pincus and Tucker, 1978; D. F. Scott, 1976). The diagnosis of epilepsy relates to the observed seizure behavior and, in many but not all cases, to certain characteristic EEG patterns that reflect disturbances in the electrical rhythms of the brain. Epilepsy does not refer to a single disease entity or brain condition but to a large class of symptoms that have in common some form of episodic disturbance of behavior or perception arising from hyperexcitability and hypersynchronous discharge of nerve cells in the brain. The underlying causes relate to scarring or brain damage from birth trauma or head injury, the presence of a tumor, an infection, a metabolic disorder, a cerebrovascular accident, a deteriorating brain disease or a host of other conditions (Glaser, 1973). In many cases, no physiological or anatomical abnormality appears to account for either the seizures or epileptiform brain wave patterns, but there may be a history of epilepsy in the family. Epilepsy of unknown etiology is commonly called *idiopathic* to distinguish it from *symptomatic* epilepsy, for which the etiology is known.

The class of adult seizure patients includes persons whose seizures began in infancy and those whose seizures began yesterday, older persons who spent a considerable amount of time in an institution because modern medical techniques for controlling seizures were not available in their youth, and equally old persons who have enjoyed a lifetime of independent and productive activity in spite of a seizure disorder of long standing or before developing epileptic symptoms. Thus, it is not surprising to find that the seizure condition itself has no characteristic patterning effect on intellectual functioning (P. C. Fowler et al., 1980; Klebanoff et al., 1954; Kløve and Matthews, 1974). Taken as a whole, however, epileptic patients are more than ordinarily prone to personality disturbances (Dodrill, 1981; Lishman, 1978; D. F. Scott, 1978).

Despite the plethora of conditions underlying the variety of epileptic phenomena that afflict the different kinds of persons who are seizure-prone, some kinds of seizure disorders tend to be associated with certain patterns of intellectual dysfunction. Not surprisingly, intelligence test scores tend to decline with increased brain wave abnormalities, reflecting the degree of underlying brain damage (Dodrill and Wilkus, 1976a,b; Tarter, 1972; Wilkus and Dodrill, 1976). Patients with generalized seizure activity tend to show greater and more generalized cognitive deficits than those with focal seizures, and cognitive functioning with both kinds of seizure patterns worsens as the rate of seizures increases (Dodrill, 1980). The most defective performances on cognitive tests generally are given by patients with generalized seizure activity occurring at a discharge rate of less than one per minute. When the seizure activity arises from a localized cortical lesion, the seizure-prone patient is likely to display a pattern of test performance like that of patients with similar lesions who are not troubled by seizures (Milner, 1975). Thus, left hemisphere epileptic foci, whether due to chronic, acute, or progressive conditions, tend to be associated with impaired verbal function (Kløve, 1959; Kløve and Fitzhugh, 1962; V. Meyer and Jones, 1957). Patients with acute or progressive right hemisphere lesions and those whose right hemisphere lesion involves the parietal lobe are likely to display the visuoconstructional disabilities that tend to be associated with right hemisphere lesions (Kløve, 1959; V. Meyer and Jones, 1957). The test performance patterns of chronic seizure patients with right temporal lobe lesions show little if any difference from those of normal control subjects (Kløve and Fitzhugh, 1962; Dennerll, 1964), except that seizure patients with temporal lobe lesions may experience impaired recall of narrative material regardless of the side of the lesion (Glowinski, 1973). Bilateral temporal lobe foci are associated with more general impairment of memory functions (Mirsky et al., 1960; Rausch et al., 1978).

Disrupted attention is a common but not universal problem of epileptic patients (J. Allison et al., 1968; Lansdell and Mirsky, 1964; Mirsky et al, 1960). It has been studied by EEG monitoring of patients taking standard psychological tests (Hovey and Kooi, 1955; Kooi and Hovey, 1957). Patients with petit mal epilepsy demonstrated a marked tendency to fail to respond at the moments when the EEG was recording the characteristic slow wave of the petit mal attack. They also tended to give "don't know" responses, to ask that questions be repeated, and to answer incorrectly at such moments; only rarely (14% of the time) did they give a correct answer during a brief seizure discharge. When the performance of a memory task was punctuated by paroxysmal activity, the item was usually failed regardless of its level of difficulty.

These EEG abnormalities were also significantly related to response slowing in this group of patients. Attention problems underlie the distractibility factor extracted in a factor analytic study of the WAIS performance of brain damaged patients with an epileptogenic focus in the temporal lobe (Dennerll, 1964). This factor, which is not ordinarily found in similar studies of Wechsler test results of normal populations, is weighted on Digit Span, Arithmetic, and Digit Symbol and appears to be related to the size of the associated brain lesion. P. C. Fowler and his co-workers (1980) also found this factor had a small Block Design weighting. Attention problems are probably related to a tendency for some epileptic patients to have lower scores on Digit Span, Arithmetic, and Digit Symbol, than on Comprehension, Block Design, and Object Assembly subtests of the Wechsler Scales (Tarter, 1972). Seizure patients also tend to do poorly on those General Aptitude Test Battery motor tasks that are scored for speed and require sustained activity, but their performance did not differ significantly from the norms on tests involving the more intellectual functions (Tellegen, 1965).

Because of the narrow margins between a prophylactic and a toxic dose of many anticonvulsant drugs (Lishman, 1978; Vajda, 1979), it is important to keep a record of the kinds and amounts of medication a patient is taking and to note whether the patient's drug regimen is routinely monitored. Toxic blood levels of these drugs tend to depress performance on a number of cognitive and response variables and may impair perceptual functions and motor coordination as well (Dodrill, 1981; Dodrill and Troupin, 1975; C. G. Matthews and Harley, 1975; Reynolds, 1977). On the basis of his findings that anticonvulsant drugs tend to lower response speed and reduce attention span, Hartlage (1981) asks, "How many of our closed head injury patients who show improvement over time are actually showing the effects of reduced anticonvulsant medication?" since the standard practice has been to give anticonvulsant drugs for the first year after injury and then discontinue if the patient has been seizure free. Hartlage reported that of the four drugs he studied, phenobarbital, primidone (mysolene), carbamazepine (tegretol), and phenytoin (dilantin), phenobarbital had the greatest negative effects on test performance and phenytoin the least.

Problems of Differential Diagnosis

Many of the questions asked of the neuropsychologist concern problems of differential diagnosis. The most common ones, the ones in which differential diagnosis is the central issue, have to do with the possibility that brain disease may underlie an emotional or personality disturbance, or contribute to a premature senility.

Most often, these questions of differential diagnosis are asked as "either-or" problems even when lip service is given to the likelihood of interaction between the effects of a brain lesion and the patient's emotional predisposition or advanced years. In perplexing cases of differential diagnosis, a precise determination may not be possible unless an ongoing disease process eventually submerges the functional aspects of the patient's confusing behavior or "hard" neurological signs show up. The frequency

229

h neurological and neuropsychological diagnostic techniques mistakenly
ith organic and functional behavioral disturbances demonstrates how diffi-
ential diagnosis can be in some cases, particularly since the populations used
of diagnostic accuracy have already been identified by other means (Spreen
ton, 1965; Filskov and Goldstein, 1974; Woody, 1968). Large test batteries
that serve as multiple successive sieves tend to reduce but still do not eliminate neuropsychodiagnostic errors (K. M. Adams et al., 1975; Benton and Van Allen, 1972a;
G. Goldstein and Shelly, 1973).

Problems of differential diagnosis involving the question of organic versus functional disorder tend to arise from two different referral sources. Neurologists and other
medical specialists seek neuropsychological assistance when they suspect the patient's
complaints have a significant functional—usually neurotic or personality—component. Clinicians working with emotionally or behaviorally disturbed patients refer
them when there appears to be a likelihood that the patient's psychiatric disturbance
has an organic basis.

Pankratz and Glaudin (1980) have categorized two kinds of diagnostic errors that
may be made with many of these patients. Type I errors involve the diagnosis of a
physical disease when the patient's condition represents a functional solution to psychosocial stress. Type II errors are diagnoses of functional disorders when patients'
complaints have an organic basis. The subtle behavioral expression of many brain
diseases, particularly in their early stages, and the not uncommon sameness or overlap
of symptoms of organic brain diseases and functional disturbances make such errors
common. When the findings of a neuropsychological examination leave the examiner
in doubt about a differential diagnosis, the best bet for ultimate resolution of the question is reexamination three to six months hence, and three to six months after that if
need be (A. Smith, 1980).

Neurotic and Personality Disorders

Patients who complain of headaches, dizziness, "blackout" spells, memory loss, mental
slowing, peculiar sensations, or weakness and clumsiness usually find their way to a
neurologist. These complaints can be very difficult to diagnose and treat: symptoms
are often subjective and wax or wane with stress or attention; with regular events such
as going to work, arriving home, or family visits; or unpredictably. The patient's complaints may follow a head injury or a bout with an illness as mild as a cold or as severe
as a heart attack, or they may simply occur spontaneously. When there are objective
neurological findings, they may be unrelated to the patient's complaints or, if related,
insufficient to account for his distress or incapacitation. Sometimes treatment—medication, psychotherapy, physical therapy, rest, activity, or a change in the patient's
routine or living situation—will relieve the problem permanently. Sometimes relief
lasts only temporarily, and the patient returns to his doctor again and again, each
time getting a new drug or a different regimen that may give him respite from his
complaints for a while. The temptation is great to write off patients who present these

230

kinds of diagnostic problems or who do not respond to treatment as neurotic, inadequate, or dependent personalities (J. M. Goodwin et al., 1979), or—if there is a pending law suit or disability claim—as compensation seekers.

However, many very serious and sometimes treatable neurological diseases first present with vague, often transient symptoms that can worsen with stress and temporarily diminish or even disappear altogether with symptomatic or psychological treatment. The first symptoms of multiple sclerosis and early cerebrovascular arteriosclerosis, for instance, are often transient, lasting hours or days, and may appear as reports of dizziness, weakness, ill-defined peculiar sensations, and fatigue. Diagnostically confusing complaints can herald a tumor and persist for months or even years before clear diagnostic signs emerge. Vague complaints are also common to postconcussion patients who may suffer headaches as well (Merskey and Woodforde, 1972; Rimel et al., 1981). Persons who have sustained head trauma tend to show significantly elevated profiles on the popular Minnesota Multiphasic Personality Inventory (MMPI) (pp. 609–610, 612) suggestive of neurotic emotional disturbances involving "depression, agitation, confusion, oversensitivity, problems with concentration, and a loss of efficiency in carrying out everyday tasks" (Casey and Fennell, 1981).

Early diagnosis of neurological disease can be complicated by the fact that these are the same complaints expressed by many persons for whom functional disorders serve as a life-style or a neurotic reaction to stress. Particularly when the patient's complaints and his reactions to them appear to be typically neurotic or suggestive of a character disorder may his neurological complaints have been discounted.

A 34-year-old high school teacher originally sought neurological help for seizures that began without apparent reason. Each of several neurologists, upon finding no evidence of organic disease, referred him to a psychiatrist for evaluation and treatment. Since his wife, a somewhat older woman, continued to press for a neurological answer to his seizures, by the end of the first year following the onset of this problem, he had been seen by several neurologists, several psychiatrists, and at least one other psychologist besides myself.

The patient's passive-dependent relationship with his wife, his tendency to have seizures in the classroom, which ultimately gained him a medical retirement and relief from the admitted tension of classroom teaching, and his history as an only child raised by a mother and grandmother who were teachers led to agreement among the psychiatrists that he was suffering from an hysterical seizure disorder. Both personality and cognitive test data supported this diagnosis. When his seizures dissipated during a course of electroconvulsive thereapy (ECT), all of the clinicians involved in the case were relieved to learn that their diagnostic impressions were validated in such a striking manner. During a routine interview after several symptom-free months, however, his psychiatrist observed a slight facial asymmetry suggesting weakness or loss of innervation of the muscles around the left side of his mouth and nose. He immediately referred the patient for neurological study again. An abnormal EEG was followed by radiographic studies in which a small right frontotemporal lesion showed up that, on surgery, proved to be an inoperable tumor. The patient died about a year and a half later.

231

Neuropsychological opinions about the etiology of these symptom pictures rely on criteria for both functional and organic disorders. An inappropriate—usually bland or indifferent—reaction to the complaints, symbolic meaningfulness of the symptoms, secondary gains, perpetuation of a dependent or irresponsible life-style, a close association between stress and the appearance of the patient's problem, and an unlikely or inconsistently manifested pattern of psychological impairment suggest psychogenic contributions to the patient's problems, regardless of his neurological status. Occasionally, a happily unconcerned patient will maintain frankly bizarre and medically unlikely symptoms with such good will that their hysterical origin is indisputable. With more commonplace aches, weaknesses, and sensory disabilities, the patient's attitude of *la belle indifférence* may be the first clue to a conversion hysteria. Pincus and Tucker (1978) urge caution in making a diagnosis of hysteria in an adult who does not have a history of psychosomatic disorders.

Medical folklore has held that only women can suffer a conversion hysteria (*hysteria* means uterus in Greek, and was originally thought to result from a displacement of that organ). Occasionally this traditional thinking still leads to a misdiagnosis in a male patient with an hysterical reaction. Cheerfully unrealistic attitudes about visual or motor defects or debilitating mental changes may also mislead the examiner when they mask an appropriate underlying depressive reaction from the patient himself as well as others and result in an erroneous functional diagnosis.

Complaints of headache, dizziness, fatigue, and weakness can be accurate reports of physiological states or the patient's interpretation of anxiety or an underlying depression (Pincus and Tucker, 1978). The presence of anxiety symptoms or depression in the absence of "hard" findings is not in itself evidence that the patient's condition is functional, for the depressive reaction may have resulted from the patient's awareness or experience of as yet subtle mental or physical symptoms of early neurological disease (Lipowski, 1978; Lishman, 1978; Post, 1975). Memory complaints, too, are common symptoms of depression and may be particularly prominent among the complaints of elderly depressed patients. However, Z. Goldberg, Syndulko, Montan, and their colleagues (1981) have found that some older persons complaining of poor memory who give no evidence of depression or dementia appear to be experiencing an abnormal degree of mental slowing and attention and tracking problems.

Identification of organicity in the differential diagnostic process is no different than when the diagnostic questions call for a simple yes or no. An organic behavior aberration may appear on neuropsychological examination as a single sign, such as rotation on a visuoconstructional task or perseverative writing, an otherwise inexplicable low test score or a few low scores on tests involving the same function, or a pattern of intellectual impairment that makes neuroanatomical or neuropsychological sense. Evidence of lateralized impairment lends strong support to the possibility of organic involvement. Should any of the behavioral aberrations associated with organicity be consistently evident, the examiner can suspect an organic brain disorder *regardless* of how much of the patient's problem is clearly functional in nature.

It is rare to find a case in which the behavioral manifestations of brain disease are uncomplicated by the patient's emotional reactions to the mental changes and the

232

consequent personal and social disruptions he is experiencing. As a rule, only ⎸ simplistic or severely impaired persons will present clear-cut symptoms of bra⎸ age without some functional contribution to the symptom picture.

Psychotic Disturbances

An organic brain disorder can also complicate or imitate severe functional behavioral disturbances (Lishman, 1978; Merskey and Buhrich, 1975; Wahl et al., 1967). The primary symptoms may involve marked mood or character change, intellectual confusion or disorientation, disordered thinking, delusions, hallucinations, bizarre ideation, ideas of reference or persecution, or any other of the thought and behavior disturbances typically associated with schizophrenia or the affective psychoses. The neuropsychological identification of an organic component in a severe behavior disturbance relies on the same criteria used to determine whether neurotic complaints have an organic etiology. Here, too, a pattern of intellectual dysfunction selectively involving predominantly lateralized abilities and skills makes a strong case for organicity, as does an organic pattern of memory impairment in which recent memory is more severely affected than remote memory, or a pattern of lowered scores on tests involving attention functions and new learning relative to scores on tests of knowledge and skill. The inconsistent or erratic expression of cognitive defects suggests a psychiatric disturbance. Organic behavioral disturbances are not likely to have symbolic meaning (Malamud, 1975).

Identifying those psychotic conditions that have an organic component is often more difficult than distinguishing neurotic conditions or character disorders from symptoms of brain damage, because some psychiatric disorders are as likely to disrupt attention, mental tracking, and memory as are some organic conditions (Cutting, 1979). Psychiatric disorders may also disrupt perceptual, thinking, and response patterns as severely as organic conditions. Therefore, a single test sign or markedly lower score does not identify the organic patient in a psychotic population with the same degree of reliability as a similar sign or lowered score among neurotic patients (R. W. Payne, 1970). Moreover, studies comparing different diagnostic groups of patients in psychiatric hospitals have shown that groups of patients with mixed organic diagnoses have test profile patterns that are similar to but lower than those of groups of functionally psychotic patients, and also similar to but even lower than the profile patterns of patients hospitalized for other functional conditions (e.g., neurotic or personality disorders) or for alcoholism (Chelune et al., 1979; Holmes, 1968; Overall et al., 1978). Thus, in attempting to determine whether a psychotically disturbed patient is brain damaged, the examiner will require a clear-cut pattern of lateralized dysfunction or organic memory impairment, a number of signs, or a pattern of lowered test scores before concluding that brain damage is probably present.

Neuropsychological differentiation of organic and functional disorders tends to be easier when the condition is acute and to become increasingly difficult with chronicity, for institutionalization tends to have a behaviorally leveling effect on organic and functional patients alike. The identification by neuropsychological techniques alone of long-term institutionalized patients with organic disorders in a chronic mental hospital population is often little more than a chance operation (DeWolfe et al., 1971; Heaton et al., 1978). In some cases, the history is useful in differentiating the organic from the purely functionally disturbed patients. Organic conditions are more apt to appear during or following physical stress such as an illness, intoxication, head trauma, or some forms of severe malnutrition. Emotional or situational stress more often precedes functionally disturbed behavior disorders. Unfortunately for diagnosticians, stress does not always come neatly packaged, for an illness that is sufficiently severe to precipitate an organic psychosis, or a head injury incurred in a family feud or a traffic accident, is also emotionally upsetting. Among diagnosed schizophrenic patients, those who tend to display symptoms of anxiety and emotionality are less likely to appear organic on neuropsychological testing than are the more apathetic patients and those with perceptual disorders (Lilliston, 1973).

The behavioral symptoms of some organic conditions are easily misinterpreted. Unlike many postcentral lesions that announce themselves with distinctive lateralized behavioral changes or highly specific and identifiable intellectual defects, the behavioral effects of frontal lobe tumors may be practically indistinguishable from progressive character or behavioral disturbances. Hécaen (1964) found that 67% of patients with frontal lobe tumors exhibit confused states and dementia, and almost 40% have mood and character disturbances. The confusion tends to be relatively mild and is often limited to time disorientation; the dementia, too, is not severe and may appear as general slowing and apathy, which can be easily confused with chronic depression. Euphoria, irritability, and indifference resulting in unrealistically optimistic or socially crude behavior may give the appearance of a psychiatric disturbance, particularly when compounded by mild confusion or dullness. Tests of tracking behavior, motor and conceptual flexibility, verbal fluency and productivity, and executive functions, including planning and regulation of behavior, may help identify those psychiatric patients who have frontal lobe involvement.

Another difficult to diagnose group are psychiatric patients with suspected temporal lobe lesions. These patients tend to be erratically and irrationally disruptive or to exhibit marked personality changes or wide mood swings (Blumer, 1975; Meier, 1980; Pincus and Tucker, 1978; D. F. Scott, 1978). Severe temper or destructive outbursts, or hallucinations and bizarre ideation may punctuate periods of rational and adequately controlled behavior, sometimes unpredictably and sometimes in response to stress. Positive neuropsychological test results may provide clues to the nature of the disturbance when EEG or neurological studies do not (Tunks, 1976). Memory for auditory and visual, symbolic and nonsymbolic material should be reviewed as well as complex visual pattern perception and logical—propositional—reasoning.

Differentiating Dementia and Depression

Probably the knottiest problem of differential diagnosis is that of separating depressed dementia patients who, early in the course of the disease, do not yet show the characteristic symptoms of dementia, from psychiatrically depressed patients in the depths of their depression when they may display a pattern of dysfunctional behavior that appears so much like dementia that it has been labeled "pseudodementia" (Salzman and Shader, 1979; C. E. Wells, 1979). Depressive reactions are often the first overt sign of something wrong in a person who is experiencing the very earliest subjective symptoms of a dementing process (Liston, 1977, 1978; Roth, 1980). Those aspects of the clinical presentation of both an early dementing process and depression that are most likely to contribute to misdiagnosis are depressed mood or agitation; a history of psychiatric disturbance; psychomotor retardation; impaired immediate memory and learning abilities; defective attention, concentration, and tracking; impaired orientation; an overall shoddy quality to cognitive products; and listlessness with loss of interest in one's surroundings and, often, in self-care (Lishman, 1978; Cainotti et al., 1980; C. E. Wells, 1979).

Nonetheless, functionally depressed patients and those with organic disease are likely to differ in a number of ways. Dementia patients are much less likely to suffer vegetative symptoms of depression such as loss of appetite, disturbed sleep, and constipation (Kaszniak et al., 1981). The structure and content of speech remain essentially intact in depression but deteriorate in dementia of the Alzheimer's type (see pp. 183–184). Depressed pseudodemented patients can learn, showing this on delayed recall and recognition memory tasks even when their immediate recall performance may have been significantly impaired (Caine, 1981). The presence of aphasias, apraxias, or agnosias clearly distinguishes an organic dementia from the pseudodementia of depression (Golper and Binder, 1981; R. S. Wilson et al., 1981). Quite early in the course of their illness, dementia patients show relatively severe impairment on drawing and constructional tasks, making virtually no appropriate response or a fragment of a response that may be distorted by perseverations despite their obvious efforts to do as asked. In contrast, the performance of depressed patients on drawing and construction tasks may be careless, shabby, or incomplete due to apathy, low energy level, and poor motivation but, if given enough time and encouragement, they may make a recognizable and often fully adequate response. J. P. Schaie (1976) identifies "an attentional-motivational deficit" as the most significant variable contributing to poor performance by depressed patients. It also can account for the inconsistency that tends to distinguish the orientation disorder of depressives from the more predictable disorientation of dementia patients. Moreover, depressed patients are more likely to be keenly aware of their impaired cognition, making much of it; in fact, their complaints of poor memory in particular may far exceed measured impairment (Kahn et al., 1975; C. E. Wells, 1979). Dementia patients, in contrast, are not likely to be aware of the extent of their cognitive deficits and may even report improvement as they lose the capacity for critical self-awareness.

Other aspects of their conditions may also help to differentiate dementia patients who are depressed from depressed patients who appear to be demented (Hutton, 1980). The cognitive deterioration of a dementing process typically has a slow and insidious onset while cognitive impairments accompanying depressive reactions are more likely to evolve over several weeks' time (Folstein and McHugh, 1978). The context in which the dysfunctional symptoms appear can be extremely important in the differential diagnosis, as depressive reactions are more likely to be associated with an identifiable precipitating event or, as so often happens to the elderly, a series of precipitating events, usually losses. However, precipitating events, such as divorce or loss of a job or a business, may also figure in depressive reactions of dementia patients early in their course. In the latter cases, hindsight usually shows that what looked like a precipitating event was actually a harbinger of the disease, occurring as a result of early symptoms of ineptitude and social dilapidation.

It can also be important to identify treatable depression in other brain damaged patients whose poor insight or impaired capacity to communicate may prevent them from seeking help on their own. E. D. Ross and Rush (1982) suggest a number of clues to the presence of depression in these patients. Among these are an unexpectedly low rate of improvement from the neurological insult or unexpected deterioration in a condition that had been stable or improving; uncooperativeness in rehabilitation and other "management" problems; or "*pathological* laughing and crying in patients who do not have pseudobulbar palsy." Ross and Rush recommend that the family be interviewed as well as the patient regarding the presence of vegetative indicators of depression. They also note that the monotonic voice and reduced emotional responsiveness of patients with right hemisphere lesions may deceive the observer who, in these cases, must listen to *what* the patients say rather than *how* they say it.

Although enumerating these distinguishing characteristics may make the task of diagnosing such patients seem reasonably simple, in practice, it is sometimes impossible to formulate a diagnosis when the patient first comes to professional attention. In such cases, only time and repeated examinations will ultimately clarify the picture.

Malingering

Malingering is a special problem in neuropsychological assessment because so many neurological conditions present few "hard" findings and so often defy documentation by clinical laboratory techniques, particularly in their early stages. The problem is complicated by the compensation and retirement policies of companies and agencies which can make poor health well worth some effort.

Inconsistency in performance levels or between a patient's reports of disability and his performance levels, unrelated to any fluctuating physiological condition, is the hallmark of malingering. Generally, but not always, a thorough neuropsychological examination performed in conjunction with careful neurological studies will bring out performance discrepancies that are inconsistent with normal neuropsychological expectations. If inpatient facilities are available, close observation by trained staff for several days will often answer questions about malingering. There are a number of special techniques for testing the performance inconsistencies characteristic of malingerers (see pp. 618–622). When malingering is suspected, the imaginative examiner may also be able to improvise tests and situations that will reveal deliberate efforts to withhold or mar a potentially good performance.

II

A Compendium of Tests
and Assessment Techniques

In the last 12 chapters of this book, most tests of intellectual function and personality in common use, and many relatively uncommon tests, are reviewed. These are tests and assessment techniques that are particularly well suited for *clinical* neuropsychological examination. Clinical examiners can employ the assessment techniques presented in these chapters for most neuropsychological assessment purposes in most kinds of work settings.

An effort has been made to classify the tests according to the major functional activities they elicit, and for many of them this was possible. Many others, though, call upon several functions so that their assignment to a particular chapter was somewhat arbitrary. For example, the Complex Figure Test, which is a test of both visuographic copying and visuographic memory, and the Rorschach, which also involves many functions, are discussed in two different chapters. Raven's Progressive Matrices, a test of both visuoperception and abstract reasoning, was assigned to Chapter 15, Conceptual Functions. The Tactual Performance Test, which assesses tactile form perception, form and spatial learning, and recall, is reported in Chapter 14, which deals with memory functions. Still other tests are useful even though the functions they examine are ill-defined or so complex that it is hard to separate individual functions and therefore hard to assign the test to one or another classification. A number of the individual tests discussed in Chapter 10 under the heading "Intellectual Ability Tests" are in this category.

Not all of these tests are well standardized. Those which have been insufficiently or questionably standardized were included because their clinical value seems to outweigh their statistical weaknesses. Rather than waiting for formal standardization of experimental neuropsychological examination techniques, I recommend that clinicians try out those that appear to meet their clinical needs. In most busy clinical settings, a clinical examiner—or better yet, a group of examiners—can try out a new technique on a number of patients whose conditions have been well documented along with those who present diagnostic puzzles or treatment challenges. When proceeding in this manner, it does not take long for an experienced clinician to ascertain whether a technique elicits or measures the target behavior as anticipated. For those interested in test development, this pilot approach can give a good idea of which tests are most worthy of the time and effort a thoroughgoing job of standardization requires.

Space, time, and energy set a limit to the number of tests reviewed here. Selection favored tests that are in relatively common use, represent a subclass of similar tests, illustrate a particularly interesting assessment method, or uniquely demonstrate some significant aspect of behavior. The selection criteria of availability and ease of administration eliminated those tests that require bulky, complicated, expensive equipment or material that cannot be easily obtained or reproduced by the individual clinician. These criteria cut out all tests that have to have a fixed laboratory installation, as well as all those demanding special technical knowledge of the examiner. The tests described in these chapters are portable for use at bedside, in jails, or anywhere the examiner might need to conduct a thorough examination. They are almost all relatively inexpensive to obtain and to administer. Most of the testing materials can be ordered from test publishers or they are easily assembled by the examiner; only a few must be ordered from the author or an unusual source. Some instruments, such as the Trail Making Test, are in the public domain. Such tests are identified wherever possible so that the user can decide whether to copy test forms or to buy the material from a test purveyor. Examiners wishing to use tests requiring material that is not being marketed—and is usually experimental—should contact individual authors for information about how to obtain these instruments.

Psychophysiological tests of specific sensory or motor deficits, such as tests of visual and auditory acuity, of one- and two-point tactile discrimination, of perceptual inattention, or of motor response speed and strength are all also part of the standard neurological examination. Because they are well described elsewhere, this book will not deal with them systematically. With few exceptions, the tests considered here are essentially psychological.

9

Intellectual Ability Tests 1
The Wechsler Intelligence Scales

Although early psychological theorists treated intelligence as a unitary capacity, test makers have always acknowledged the multidimensionality of intellect by producing many-faceted measuring instruments. With few exceptions, the most widely used mental ability tests have been *composite tests* made up of a variety of tasks testing different skills and capacities.

Composite tests come in one of two formats. In *omnibus* composite tests, the order of task presentation varies so that each test item or subtest differs from its neighbors. For instance, an arithmetic problem may follow a verbal or pictorial reasoning item and be followed in turn by an immediate memory or a drawing task. Generally, different kinds of tasks reappear at different difficulty levels. Omnibus tests provide frequent activity changes to hold the interest of youngsters and mentally impaired persons of all ages. They also expose the subject to many different kinds of tasks in a practicable amount of administration time. However, their quick change format keeps the examiner so busy manipulating material and giving new instructions that he may find it difficult to observe the patient and keep track of the test performance. The patient who thinks, learns, and shifts slowly may be unable to acquire sufficient task familiarity to perform at his best. Furthermore, when a test contains a very wide variety of tasks, there is usually not enough time for each kind of task to be given at every ability level.

The other kind of composite test is actually a test *battery* comprising a number of distinct subtests. The battery format solves the administration problems of the omnibus approach. Fewer shifts from task to task reduce the amount of instructing and material handling to more manageable proportions and give the slow patient time to become oriented to the new task. Subtests with many similar items at different levels of difficulty permit relatively fine gradations in item scaling and development of highly standardized subtest norms for comparing performances on the various subtest tasks. These features have led to the now almost universal use of battery-type ability tests (Lubin et al., 1971). Tests of the omnibus type still make up part of the usual test repertory, but they are apt to serve as a source of additional specific tasks that the standardized battery does not contain, or as a substitute for a battery-type test when inattentiveness or restlessness become serious administration problems.

Both battery and omnibus-type tests are available in individually administered and paper and pencil forms. For clinical decision-making, individually administered tests are essential. Paper and pencil tests can provide valuable supplementary information (see pp. 299–307).

The Wechsler Intelligence Scales are individually administered composite tests in battery format (Matarazzo, 1972; Wechsler, 1955, 1958, 1981; Zimmerman and Woo-Sam, 1973). The earliest of these scales were the Wechsler-Bellevue Intelligence Scales, Forms I and II (WB-I, -II, Wechsler, 1944). The Wechsler Adult Intelligence Scale (WAIS) was first published in 1955, and its revision, the WAIS-R, in 1981. When discussing these latter two tests together, I will use the expression, "WAIS battery." When dealing with one or the other, I will continue to call the 1955 version the WAIS and will refer to the new edition as the WAIS-R.

For all but the most severely impaired adults, a WAIS battery constitutes a substantial portion of the test framework of the neuropsychological examination. When paper and pencil tests of the basic communication, arithmetic, and drawing skills, and additional individually administered tests involving mental tracking, recent memory, and learning are administered along with a WAIS battery, the examiner will have obtained some information about the most important aspects of the patient's intellectual functioning. He will also have a great deal of information about how the patient behaves (J. Allison et al., 1968; Rapaport et al., 1968). A basic review of intellectual functions, in which a WAIS battery serves as the core instrument, is usually sufficient to demonstrate an absence of significant intellectual disability or to provide clues to altered functions.

Eleven different subtests make up the WAIS battery. Wechsler classified six of them as "Verbal" tests: Information (I), Comprehension (C), Arithmetic (A), Similarities (S), Digit Span (DSp), and Vocabulary (V). The other five he termed "Performance" tests. They include Digit Symbol (DSy), Picture Completion (PC), Block Design (BD), Picture Arrangement (PA), and Object Assembly (OA). (See pp. 256–286 for a detailed description of the WAIS battery subtests).

Two functionally distinct subtest groups have consistently emerged on factor analysis of the WAIS. The first group shares a common *verbal* factor, weighting on the Information, Comprehension, Similarities, and Vocabulary subtests. The subtests in the second group, always including Block Design and Object Assembly and sometimes including Picture Completion or Picture Arrangement, share a common factor variously termed *perceptual organization* (J. Cohen, 1957b), *nonverbal organization* (Wechsler, 1958), *space performance* (Maxwell, 1960), *spatial* (McFie, 1961), and *performance* (E. W. Russell, 1972a). This will be called the *visuospatial* factor here. A general intellectual factor, akin to Spearman's g (see pp. 22–23), has been extracted as a discrete factor (J. Cohen, 1957a; E. W. Russell, 1972b) and also as part of the first, "verbal-intellectual" factor (Maxwell, 1960). A *memory* factor, weighting primarily on Digit Span and infrequently on Arithmetic, has been identified with some regularity (J. Cohen, 1957b; McFie, 1961). J. Cohen reports two other, "minor specific" factors, one weighting primarily but inconsistently on Picture Completion and the other weighting primarily on Digit Symbol and occasionally on Digit Span and Picture Arrangement. Because of their tenuous intersubtest relationships, Cohen does not relate these two test-specific factors to intellectual functions. Wechsler suggests that the first of these minor factors may relate to relevance, or "the appropriateness of response," and the second may be a "measure of the individual's capacity to resist distraction" (1958, p. 126).

Since the pattern and strengths of the subtest intercorrelations of the WAIS-R differ somewhat from those of the WAIS, it is possible that the factor structure and other characteristics of the WAIS-R will also differ in some respects. Thus, knowledge about the composition and interrelationships of the WAIS subtests cannot be unquestioningly applied to the WAIS-R.

Although a WAIS battery's capacity to test different kinds of intellectual functions contributes much to its important role in neuropsychological assessment, the WAIS battery subtests assess neither pure nor readily defined functions, nor do they facilitate the systematic examination of the different functions (e.g., Lansdell and Donnelly, 1977; E. W. Russell, 1979). Still, there are many reasons why the WAIS battery is the most commonly used psychological test. Clinicians who become familiar with the virtues and limitations of each of the various subtests often are very sensitive to behavioral nuances and score relationships elicited by these subtests, both individually and in their many combinations. Furthermore, an enormous body of knowledge has grown up around the Wechsler tests. The WAIS batteries and their predecessors, the Wechsler-Bellevue Scales, Forms I and II, have served as the primary test standards in all intellectual test development since shortly after the introduction of the Wechsler-Bellevue Scale in 1939. The Wechsler scales have also been the most commonly used tests of intellectual ability for research purposes. They have been the intellectual ability tests of choice for many neuropsychologists, who have incorporated them into both clinical and research batteries (e.g., Reitan and Davison, 1974; E. W. Russell et al., 1970; A. Smith, 1975). Finally, Wechsler tests, with their variants in other English-speaking countries and their many translations, have the advantage of being used throughout the world.

The new revision of the Wechsler scales has been in preparation for several years. It was needed because some of the WAIS items are outdated (e.g., Washington's birthday is no longer generally celebrated on February 22, but has been incorporated into a Monday holiday, President's Day, that does not have an exact date. Persons reaching adulthood within the last ten years do not share an historical association for February 22 with their elders). Another defect of the WAIS is that some of the age-graded norms for older subjects, particularly on the Similarities and Picture Arrangement subtests, are spuriously low, giving standard scores in the *low average* to *average* ranges for performances that are clearly impaired (see pp. 265 and 282).

It is still too soon to know how well the WAIS-R measures the cognitive functions of interest to neurpsychologists, as independent studies have not yet been published. However, since the format of each subtest is essentially unchanged, it is not likely that WAIS-R factor analyses and performance patterns of discrete groups of brain impaired patients will differ much from those of the WAIS. The similarity of the WAIS-R to its predecessors will probably make the transition to the WAIS-R easier for practitioners who have become accustomed to the WAIS. Nevertheless, it is unfortunate that the WAIS-R has preserved the IQ concept and the subtest alignment into Verbal and Performance Scales in the face of the body of literature that contradicts the assumptions underlying conglomerate scores and Wechsler's pre-1939 classification of the subtests.

It is certainly possible that another test maker will devise a set of tests for appraising adult intellectual functions that is more scientifically founded and systematic than the Wechsler scales. The question remains as to whether test efficiency would then supplant the hard-won achievements of familiarity and experience.

Scoring Issues

There are a number of issues involved in interpreting the WAIS battery scores, such as item scaling, interexaminer reliability, and the influence of testing conditions (Matarazzo, 1972; Wechsler, 1981; Zimmerman and Woo-Sam, 1973). Those most relevant to neuropsychological assessment concern IQ scores, the effects of age, sex differences, and the evaluation of the significance of score discrepancies.

IQ Scores

Educators have found that the Full Scale IQ score of the WAIS battery, which is calculated from the sum of all the subtest scaled scores (or their prorated values if fewer than 11 subtests are given), is an excellent predictor of academic achievement. However, neither the IQ scores calculated for the Verbal or the Performance tests, nor the Full Scale IQ score, are useful in neuropsychological testing (see pp. 22–23).

Much neuropsychological research has focused on comparisons between Wechsler Verbal and Performance Scale IQ scores, under the assumption that differences between these scores would reflect impairment of one or the other major functional system and thus significantly aid in the diagnosis. Both Verbal and Performance Scale IQ scores, however, are based on averages of some quite dissimilar functions that have relatively low intercorrelations and bear no regular neuroanatomical or neuropsychological relationship to one another (Parsons et al., 1969; J. Cohen, 1957a). There is also considerable functional overlap between these two scales (Maxwell, 1960). These findings are not surprising since "common sense" reasoning rather than factor analytic or neuropsychological studies dictated the assignment of the individual subtests to either the Verbal or the Performance Scale.

The inadvisability of drawing inferences about neuropsychological status from Verbal Scale and Performance Scale IQ score comparisons has been demonstrated in a number of ways (Anastasi, 1982; A. Smith, 1975). Although there is some general tendency for Verbal Scale IQ scores to be reduced relative to Performance Scale IQ scores when the lesion is predominantly or only in the left hemisphere, this decline does not occur regularly enough for clinical reliability (Lewinsohn, 1973; A. Smith, 1966a; Vega and Parsons, 1969). A lowered Performance Scale IQ score is even less useful as an indicator of right hemisphere damage since the time-dependent Performance Scale subtests are sensitive to any cerebral disorder that impairs the brain's efficiency, they call upon more unfamiliar activities than do the Verbal Scale subtests, and the constructional disorders experienced by many patients with left-sided lesions result in relatively low scores on Performance as well as Verbal Scale subtests (Lebrun and Hoops, 1974; Tissot et al., 1963). Thus, although the relative lowering of Performance Scale IQ scores is most pronounced for patients with extensive right hemisphere damage, left hemisphere lesions and certain degenerative disorders, for example, can produce relative lowering of the Performance Scale IQ score or depress both the Verbal and the Performance Scale IQ scores about equally. In addition, the Verbal Scale IQ score relative to the Performance Scale IQ score varies systematically as the Full Scale IQ score varies, with a strong tendency for Verbal Scale IQ scores to be relatively high at the higher Full Scale IQ score levels and for the tendency to be reversed in favor of higher Performance Scale IQ scores when the Full Scale IQ score is very much below 100 (A. Smith, 1966a). Cultural patterns can also contribute to wide disparities between Verbal and Performance Scale IQ scores (Dershowitz and Frankel, 1975; Tsushima and Bratton, 1977).

Moreover, the subtests in each scale differ in their sensitivity to both general effects, such as slowing or concrete thinking, that may accompany many kinds of brain damage, and to specific effects associated with lesions in areas of the brain subserving particular verbal, mathematical, visuospatial, memory, or other functions. When brain damage impairs performance on only one or two subtests in a scale, it is not uncommon for the lower score(s) to be obscured when averaged in with the other subtests measuring capacities that were spared by the damage. Botez and his colleagues (1977) demonstrated this problem when they found a number of patients with normal pressure hydrocephalus who achieved Performance Scale IQ scores within the *average* ability range. These patients did poorest on the Block Design subtest and also on Kohs Block Design Test, which is essentially identical to the Block Design subtest of the Wechsler batteries but contains many more items (see p. 407). In this case, the patients' impaired ability to do block designs was immediately obvious when communicated in the form of a score on Kohs' test, but was lost to sight in the aggregate Performance Scale IQ score.

In short, averaged scores on a WAIS battery provide just about as much information as do averaged scores on a school report card. There is no question about the performance of a student with a four-point average: he can only have had an A in each subject. Nor is there any question about individual grades obtained by the student with a zero grade point average. Excluding the extremes, however, it is impossible to predict a student's performance in any one subject from his grade point average alone. In the same way, it is impossible to predict specific disabilities and areas of intellectual competency or dysfunction from the averaged ability test scores. For these reasons, IQ scores have not been reported for test data presented in this book.

Age-Graded Scores

The WAIS batteries take account of age differentials in the computation of the IQ scores but not in the standard subtest scaled score equivalents. These latter scores were ascertained for a randomized sample of 500 persons from ages 20 to 34, and therefore are not suitable for neuropsychological purposes. Instead, the examiner should use the Tables of Scaled Score Equivalents for Raw Scores by Age Group when converting subtest raw scores into standard scores. (See the Appendix of the WAIS Manual, pp. 99–110, or the WAIS-R Manual, pp. 139–150, for these tables and instructions on how to use them.) The number of years in each age group's range is not equal owing to the relatively rapid intellectual changes of the early and later adult years. McFie (1975, p. 31) gives age corrections for each five-year span from 30–34 to 65–69 that can be added to Wechsler-Bellevue subtest scores.

The standard scaled score values for the 11 WAIS battery subtests are practically identical to the age-graded score values for the young adult ranges of most of the subtests. A scaled score of 11 on a subtest that is relatively impervious to the effects of age, such as Information, requires much the same number of correct items for the seven age groups from 18–19 to 65–69. However, even on one of the least age-sensitive tests as Information, fewer correct responses are needed to achieve a scaled score of 11 at age groups 16–17, 70–74, and 75 and over. The range of applicability of the standard scaled score values is much narrower for the five timed subtests of the Performance Scale, than for the more age-resistant Verbal Scale subtests, particularly Information, Vocabulary, Comprehension, and Arithmetic (Botwinick, 1977). The Digit Symbol subtest provides the most extreme example of how norms on which the standard scaled score values are based change with age. From ages 16 to 34, 52 to 57 correct responses are needed for a standard scaled score of 10 on this subtest. At age 35 a raw score of 55 correct responses will earn a scaled score of 12. At age 65, the same number of correct responses earns a scaled score of 18.

Below age 20 and above age 35, age-graded subtest scaled scores are necessary when making subtest comparisons. In these age ranges, for which the normal pattern of test behavior differs from the pattern of the large, mixed-age standardization group, it becomes difficult to interpret many of the subtest scores and virtually impossible to compare them or to attempt pattern analysis unless the patient's performance has been graded according to the norms of his own age group (Simpson and Vega, 1971) (see Table 9-1). Caution is still needed when interpreting even the age-graded WAIS scores of subjects aged 65 and over as the normative samples' performances— particularly for the Performance Scale subtests—have tended to run higher than performances of other presumably representative groups of older persons (Price et al., 1980). Like the WAIS norms, the WAIS-R norms for the 55-and-over age groups were based on smaller samples than for any other of the age groups that have a five or ten year range. However, unlike the WAIS, the groups comprising the older samples of the WAIS-R were formed on the same stratified sampling basis as the younger groups.

Practical considerations may require the neuropsychological examiner to obtain both the age-graded and the standard scaled score equivalents. Although the standard

Table 9-1 Standard Scaled Score Equivalents for the Average Score Obtained by Three Age Groups on the WAIS

	16–17		45–54		70–74	
	Raw Score	Scaled Score	Raw Score	Scaled Score	Raw Score	Scaled Score
Information	18	9	15	10	12	8
Comprehension	16	10	17	10	14	8
Arithmetic	10	9	11	10	8	7
Similarities	13	10	13	10	9	8
Digit Span	10	9.5	10	9	9.5	8
Vocabulary	29	8	39	9	33	9
Digit Symbol	51	9	40	7	19	4
Picture Completion	13	9	11	8	7	6
Block Design	30	9	27	8	23	7
Picture Arrangement	22	9	17	7	12	6
Object Assembly	30	9	27	8	24	7

When the raw score is converted to standard scaled score equivalents, what appears to be a slight edge of Verbal Scale over Performance Scale scores at ages 45–54 becomes a large differential at ages 70–74 with the numerical discrepancy between one pair of scores (V-DSy) approximating statistical significance, in the overall trend toward higher verbal subtests. In a much younger person, this score pattern would be sufficiently suggestive of organicity to warrant further study. For people in their early 70s, the pattern of raw scores given above is most typical.

scaled score equivalents distort the test data for neuropsychological purposes, they represent the patient's performance relative to the younger segment of the working population and thus can guide the psychologist in vocational and educational planning for his patient. For example, a 55-year-old former cabinetmaker who achieves a raw score of 24 on Block Design may be performing well in the *average* range for his age group; but compared to the younger working population, his score, in the *low average* range, is only at the 25th percentile. On the basis of his age-graded scaled score alone, he seems capable of working at his former occupation; but when compared to people entering the job market, his relative disability on the Block Design task (which tests visuospatial functions and response speed) puts him at a decided disadvantage.

Sex Differences

Although men and women perform differently on some subtests of the WAIS batteries, the overlap between their scores is too great to allow these differences to enter into interpretations of the scores of the individual case. With few exceptions, studies of the original Wechsler tests found that men regularly obtained slightly higher full scale scores than women. This tendency has persisted in the WAIS (D. A. Payne and

Lehmann, 1966; Wechsler, 1958) and probably continues in the WAIS-R. However, the WAIS-R Manual does not give separate scores for men and for women. The men of the standardization sample for the 1955 WAIS revision of the Wechsler-Bellevue Scales achieved higher scores on Information, Comprehension, Arithmetic, Picture Completion, and Block Design, whereas the women had a small advantage on Similarities, Vocabulary, and Digit Symbol. Yet the combined age group differences were greater than one scaled score point only for Arithmetic and Digit Symbol; one combined age group difference was approximately two-thirds of a scaled score point and all others were approximately one-third of a scaled score point or less.

The years since the WAIS was standardized have seen critical changes in the nature and extent of women's education and vocational pursuits. These changes have not been limited to younger women alone, for the proportion of working middle-aged women continues to grow, as does the number of older women returning to school. Thus, without more current data, it is not possible to estimate the presence or the pattern of sex differences more than two decades later. It is certainly likely that significant differences remain between the sexes in WAIS response patterns (see pp. 220–221. What these differences are and how they vary from age group to age group remains to be answered.

Evaluating Significance

It is generally agreed that the psychodiagnostic meaningfulness of test score deviations depends on the extent to which they exceed expected chance variations in the subject's test performance. However, there is a lack of agreement about the standard against which deviations shall be measured.

Commonly employed comparison standards for the Wechsler tests are the subtest mean scaled score, which is 10 for all subtests; the patient's own mean subtest score, which can be broken down into Verbal Scale and Performance Scale subtest mean scores (Rabin, 1965; D. Wechsler, 1958); the Vocabulary test scaled score (Gonen and Brown, 1968); and the average of the Vocabulary and Picture Completion subtest age-graded scaled scores (McFie, 1975). Jastak developed an "intellectual altitude" measure by averaging the scores of the three highest subtests (Thorp and Mahrer, 1959). Wechsler uses deviations from the patient's subtest mean to obtain a pattern of scores that deviates in both positive and negative directions.

Neuropsychologically, the most meaningful comparison standard is the one that gives the highest estimate of the original ability level based on the patient's test scores (see Chapter 4). This is usually the highest WAIS battery subtest score, which then becomes the best estimate of the original general ability level. When the highest WAIS battery subtest score is used as the estimated comparison standard, lower scores are subtracted from it and all scaled score discrepancies will have a negative arithmetic value.

There are two exceptions to the use of the highest WAIS battery subtest score as the comparison standard. First, evidence that the patient once enjoyed a level of intellectual competency higher than that indicated by the Wechsler subtest scores, such as life history information, non-Wechsler test data, or isolated Wechsler item responses, takes precedence over Wechsler subtest scores in the determination of the comparison standard.

> A 52-year-old general contractor and real estate developer with severe progressive arteriosclerosis had successfully completed two years of the Business Administration program at an outstanding private midwestern university just after World War II when this school had a highly selective admissions policy. On the verbal subtests, his highest age-graded scaled score was 9, suggesting no better than an *average* original ability level. Knowledge of his previous academic experience led the examiner to estimate his original ability level as having been at least in the *superior* range, at the 90th percentile or above. The WAIS subtest scaled score at this level is 14, which became the comparison standard against which the obtained subtest scores were measured for significance. It is interesting to note that this same patient, who obtained an age-graded scaled score of 9 on the Arithmetic subtest, produced a highly variable arithmetic performance in which he betrayed his original *superior* ability level by answering one difficult problem correctly while failing many easier items.

The second exception is that high scores on the test of span of attention and immediate (working) memory (Digit Span) and on a set of picture puzzle constructions (Object Assembly) are less likely to reflect the original general ability level than any other subtests. Correlational studies show that the highest correlation of the score for the combined subsections of Digit Span with any other subtest of the WAIS is .60 (with Vocabulary) and that six of the remaining ten subtest correlations range below .50. On the WAIS-R, Digit Span's highest correlation is with Arithmetic (.56) and all but one other subtest correlation (Vocabulary) are .45 or below. Although the highest intersubtest correlation of Object Assembly is .69 (with Block Design), six of its other ten subtest intercorrelations also are .50 or lower on the WAIS. Eight of the ten subtest intercorrelations with Object Assembly are lower than .50 on the WAIS-R, and four of these are .40 or lower. In comparison, the highest correlation of Information is .81 (with Vocabulary) and none of the other subtest intercorrelations is lower than .54 on the WAIS. Three of the WAIS-R subtests—Digit Span, Object Assembly, and Digit Symbol—have correlations below .50 with Information. Knowledge of the astonishing feats of memory of idiots savants should also make the examiner wary of using attention span and immediate memory scores as a basis for estimating original ability level (Anastasi, 1965). In clinical practice, the tendency for both Object Assembly and Digit Span to vary independently of other subtest scores becomes readily apparent as some rather dull people turn in excellent performances on these subtests and some bright subjects do no better than *average* on them. The symbol-number substitution task (Digit Symbol) also correlates as poorly with the other subtests as does Digit Span, but Digit Symbol is so rarely a subject's best subtest that the question of its score serving as a comparison standard is practically irrelevant.

Wechsler originally recommended that a subtest score deviation measured from the subject's mean should be of the magnitude of two subtest scaled score units to be considered a possibly meaningful deviation, and that a deviation of three be considered significant. The applicability of this rule of thumb depends to some extent upon the stability of the subtest scores. For most of the subtests, it is likely that the obtained score is within two to three scaled score points of the true score 95% of the time. Digit Span (WAIS) and Object Assembly are the only subtests that consistently vary so greatly that the 95% range of variability of individual scores exceeds three scaled score points. Picture Arrangement exceeds this range for some age groups but not for others. Vocabulary and Information scores display the least variability (Wechsler, 1955, 1981).

A discrepancy of three points between any two Wechsler subtest scores may occur as often as 15% of the time (Wechsler, 1958, 1981) and therefore does not satisfy the 5% significance level that psychologists typically use as the upper limit when assessing the probability that an event has not occurred by chance. Field (1960) computed estimates of the magnitude of difference between any two WAIS scaled scores required for that difference to reach the 1 and 5% significance levels and found that the minimum differences between pairs of scaled scores that could be interpreted as nonchance discrepancies were in the 3.5–4.3 range at the 5% level, in the 4.6–5.5 range at the 1% level (see Table 9-2). Thus, for most practical purposes, the examiner can consider discrepancies of four scaled score points as approaching significance and discrepancies of five or more scaled score points to be significant, i.e., nonchance. This rough rule for estimating significance permits the examiner to evaluate the Wechsler test score discrepancies at a glance without having to resort to extra computations or formulae. Table 9-3 (p. 252) provides several examples of subtest score patterns. McFie's (1975) suggestion that patterns of discrepancies should be considered by the clinician even when the score differences are not large enough to reach the 5% level given in Field's table reflects common practice among experienced clinicians.

Identifying the Presence of Brain Damage

Indices, Ratios, and Quotients

Most early studies of the neuropsychological sensitivity of the Wechsler tests were of mixed organic populations, with little or no attention paid to the nature, location, or extent of the brain lesion (Heaton et al., 1978; Wechsler, 1944). A consistent pattern of subtest scores emerged from these studies in which subtests requiring immediate memory, concentration, response speed, and abstract concept formation were most likely to show the effects of brain damage. The performance of these same patients on tests of previously learned information and verbal associations tended to be least affected. While recognizing the inconstancy of relationships between Wechsler subtest patterns and various kinds of brain lesions, Wechsler and others noted the similarities between these apparently organicity-sensitive subtests and the subtests most prone to age-related changes. Efforts to apply this apparent relationship to questions of differential diagnosis resulted in a number of formulae for ratios on which to base cutting scores.

Table 9-2 Reliability of Differences between Any Two Subtest Scores for Different Values of the Range (WAIS)[a]

Range	2		3		4		5		6		7		8		9		10	
Significance Level (percent)	5	1	5	1	5	1	5	1	5	1	5	1	5	1	5	1	5	1
Age (years)																		
18–19	3.5	4.7	3.7	4.9	3.9	5.0	4.0	5.1	4.0	5.2	4.1	5.2	4.1	5.3	4.2	5.3	4.2	5.4
25–34	3.6	4.8	3.8	5.0	4.0	5.1	4.0	5.2	4.1	5.3	4.2	5.4	4.2	5.4	4.3	5.5	4.3	5.5
45–54	3.5	4.6	3.7	4.8	3.8	4.9	3.9	5.0	4.0	5.1	4.0	5.2	4.1	5.2	4.1	5.2	4.1	5.3

To use this table, a subject's scaled scores must first be arranged in order of magnitude. The two scores to be compared are located and their range is found by adding the number of intervening scores to the number of scores being compared, which is 2. The difference between the scores must be equal to or greater than one of the two values in the table, under the appropriate Range and Age, to reach the level of significance shown in the second row of the table (Field, 1960, p. 5).

[a]Adapted from Field (1960), p. 4. By permission.

249

Wechsler devised a *deterioration quotient* (DQ), also called a *deterioration index* (DI), which enables the examiner to compare scores on those tests that tend to withstand the onslaughts of old age (*"Hold"* tests) with those that are most likely to decrease over the years (*"Don't Hold"* tests). His assumption was that deterioration indices that exceed normal limits reflect early senility or an abnormal organic process, or both. For the WAIS, calculation of the deterioration index uses age-graded scores in a comparison of "Hold" tests (Vocabulary, Information, Object Assembly, and Picture Completion) with "Don't Hold" tests (Digit Span, Similarities, Digit Symbol, and Block Design). The formula for the deterioration quotient is $\dfrac{Hold - Don't\ Hold}{Hold}$. The cutting score for "possible deterioration" is .10, and .20 is the suggested indicator of "definite deterioration" (Wechsler, 1958, p. 211). Unfortunately, neither the earlier *mental deterioration index* (MDI) calculated on Wechsler-Bellevue subtest scores (using Information, Comprehension, Object Assembly, and Picture Completion as "Hold" tests and Digit Span, Arithmetic, Digit Symbol, and Block Design as "Don't Hold" tests) (Wechsler, 1944) nor the WAIS DQ proved effective in identifying patients with organic damage (V. Meyer, 1961; Rabin, 1965; C. G. Watson et al., 1968). Wechsler's 1944 formula classified anywhere from 43 to 75% of patients correctly (Yates, 1954). and the WAIS deterioration quotient has not produced better results (Bersoff, 1970; E. W. Russell, 1972b; Savage, 1970).

Dissatisfaction with the equivocal results of Wechsler's deterioration indices led to more elaborate efforts to develop a numerical touchstone for organicity. Other proposed formulae for ascertaining the presence of organic deterioration followed Wechsler's "Hold" versus "Don't Hold" subtest format. For the most part, these formulae involved rather slight variations on Wechsler's basic theme. W. L. Hunt (1949) and more recently Gonen (1970) recommended a deterioration quotient derived by using Information and Comprehension as the "Hold" and Digit Symbol and Block Design as the "Don't Hold" subtests, which Gonen describes as particularly sensitive to the effects of diffuse, nonlateralized cerebral atrophy. R. D. Norman (1966) attributed some of the failures of Wechsler's deterioration index to differences between the sexes with respect to the "Hold" or "Don't Hold" qualities of subtests and offered a new formula for women based on Vocabulary, Information, Object Assembly, and Block Design as the "Hold" tests and Similarities, Digit Span, Digit Symbol, and Picture Arrangement as the "Don't Hold" tests, although he recommended retaining Wechsler's 1955 formula for men and the same cutting scores for both sexes.

Recognizing the heterogeneity of the brain damaged population, Hewson developed not one but a set of ratios in hopes of using Wechsler subtest scores to identify organic patients (1949). This ratio method shuffles subtest scores into seven different formulae, each of which discriminates with more or less accuracy between normal control subjects, neurotic, and postconcussion patients. If none of the computed ratios results in a significant value, the subject is considered to be probably organically intact and without a marked neurosis. A. Smith (1962b) claimed relatively good success in identifying brain tumor patients by means of Hewson's ratios, classifying 81.3% of 128 of them correctly. However, he obtained much lower accuracy rates with other categories of patients. In another study, age-graded subtest scaled scores tuted for the standard scaled scores, and this increased the accuracy of by means of the Hewson ratios from 67% to 71%; but the ratios still miscl of the patients with known cerebral pathology (Woolf, 1960). Compar indices and ratios based on Wechsler subtest scores, the Hewson ratios organicity relatively well, but they misclassify too many cases for clinical application and also have the disadvantage of being rather complicated and time consuming to calculate.

A comprehensive review of the literature concerning the diagnostic efficiency of various neuropsychological tests with psychiatric populations, including the WAIS, was published by Heaton and his colleagues (1978). They pointed out that, by and large, the performance level of psychiatric patients, other than chronic or process schizophrenics, is sufficiently similar to that of normal control subjects that patients with functional psychiatric disorders can be identified by test scores alone as "not organic" at the same level of accuracy as normal or medical control subjects are identified. The highest accuracy levels reported (in the 85–88% range) were from studies using the WAIS to identify nonpsychotic psychiatric patients as not organic, supporting the use of WAIS scores in making such discriminations for research purposes. However, actuarial techniques alone do not give a clue as to which one of every seven to ten of these patients has been misclassified by the test.

Pattern Analysis

David Wechsler and others have looked to the pattern of Wechsler subtest score deviations for clues to the presence of brain damage and, more recently, for evidence of specific kinds of brain damage (C. G. Matthews et al., 1962; McFie, 1975; Reitan, 1955b; E. W. Russell, 1979b; Simpson and Vega, 1971). The most common Wechsler organicity patterns reflect the most commonly seen neuropathological conditions. A pattern of clear-cut differences between subtests involving primarily verbal functions on the one hand and those involving primarily visuospatial functions on the other is likely, but not necessarily, a product of lateralized brain injury (Lansdell and Smith, 1972; E. W. Russell, 1979b) (see Table 9-3). Not infrequently, one or more subtests in the vulnerable group will not be significantly depressed. Occasionally a verbal subtest score will even be among the highest a patient with left hemisphere disease achieves. It is much less likely for a visuospatial subtest to be highest, regardless of the side of the lesion, because of the effect of motor slowing on these timed tests. Picture Completion, which has both verbal and visual components and does not require motor response, may vary a little with either the verbal or the visuospatial tests, or take some middling position, but will rarely be among the lowest subtests (McFie, 1975).

Other Wechsler subtest patterns may be superimposed on relatively clear-cut differences between verbal and visuospatial subtests. Immediate memory, attention, and concentration problems show up in depressed performances on Digit Span and Arithmetic, whereas problems involving attention and response speed primarily affect

Table 9-3 Sample Age-Graded Subtest Score Patterns

Subtest	A	B	C
Information	8	8	16
Comprehension	7	8	15
Arithmetic	6	10	13
Similarities	7	9	12
Digit Span	5/4	6/5	8/6
Digit Symbol	6	10	9
Picture Completion	8	8	11
Block Design	6	11	6
Picture Arrangement	6	10	13
Object Assembly	8	13	10

A glance at pattern A shows that the greatest discrepancy between subtests is of a magnitude of two points and therefore probably due to chance. This could be a typical profile of an intact person who generally functions at a *low average* level (at approximately the 16th percentile). On pattern B, except for a *high average* score on Object Assembly, there are only chance variations between subtest scores. Since the single high score is Object Assembly, it too will be considered a chance deviation unless some other information suggestive of a better than *average* ability level becomes available (see pp. 247, 284). Sample pattern C, on the other hand, contains nine discrepancies of six or seven points. Two Block Design items were correctly completed after the time limit. Even if they had been counted as "passed" (see pp. 122 and 272 regarding double-scoring WAIS battery subtests), raising the Block Design age-graded scaled score to 8, there still would remain five discrepancies of six points or more and three of five points. Pattern C was produced by a patient of originally *very superior* general ability who suffered impairment of visuospatial functions with some slowing.

Digit Symbol scores (E. W. Russell, 1972b). These depressed scores are not necessarily associated with lateralized defect but also tend to characterize the Wechsler performance of many organically impaired persons with diffuse brain disease.

An additional feature that may appear with any kind of brain damage is concrete thinking. Concrete thinking—or absence of the abstract attitude—may be reflected in lowered scores on Similarities and Picture Completion, and in failures or one-point answers on the three proverb items of Comprehension when responses to the other Comprehension items are of good quality. Concrete behavior can show up on Block Design, too, as inability to conceptualize the squared format or appreciate the size relationships of the blocks relative to the pictured designs. Concrete thinking is also characteristic of persons whose general intellectual functioning tends to be low in the *average* range or below *average* and of certain kinds of psychiatric patients (R. W. Payne, 1970).

Concrete thinking associated with brain damage may be distinguished from the normal thinking of persons of lower intellectual ability when the examiner finds one or more scores or responses reflecting a higher level of intellectual capability than the patient's present inability to abstract would warrant. Further, in the brain damaged patient, concrete thinking is usually accompanied by lowered scores on subtests sensitive to memory defect, distractibility, and motor slowing, whereas these problems are not characteristic of people who are simply dull and not organically impaired. The concrete thinking of brain damage is distinguishable from that of psychiatric conditions in that the former tends to occur consistently, or at least regardless of the emotional meaningfulness of the stimulus, whereas the latter is more apt to vary with the emotional impact of the stimulus on the patient or with any number of factors external to the examination. Concrete thinking alone is not indicative of brain damage in patients of normally low intellectual endowment or in long-term chronic psychiatric patients. A concrete approach to problem solving, which shows up in a relatively depressed Similarities score, with perhaps some lowering of Comprehension, Block Design, or Picture Completion scores, may be the most pronounced residual intellectual defect of a bright person who has had a mild brain injury. However, patients with lesions primarily involving prefrontal structures may be quite impaired in their capacity to handle abstractions or to take the abstract attitude and yet not show pronounced deficits on the close-ended, well-structured Wechsler test questions (see pp. 78–79, 82).

Other than a few fairly distinctive but not mutually exclusive patterns of lateralized and diffuse damage, the Wechsler-based evaluation of whether brain damage is present depends on whether the subtest score pattern makes neuropsychological sense. For instance, the widespread tissue swelling that often accompanies a fresh head injury or rapidly expanding tumor results in confusion, general dulling, and significant impairment of memory and concentration functions that appear on the WAIS batteries as significantly lowered scores on almost all subtests, except perhaps time-independent verbal tests of old, well-established speech and thought patterns (Gonen and Brown, 1968). Bilateral lesions generally produce changes in both verbal and visuospatial functions and involve aspects of memory and attention as well.

Evaluation of organicity by pattern analysis requires knowledge of what is neuropsychologically possible and an understanding of the patient's behavioral capabilities as demonstrated on a WAIS battery and other measures of mental functions that have been examined within the context of the patient's life experiences, current psychosocial situation, and the medical history. Pattern analysis applies best to patients with recent or ongoing brain changes and is less effective in identifying organic disorders in psychiatrically disturbed patients. The Wechsler subtest score patterns of patients with old, static brain injuries, particularly those who have been institutionalized for a long time, tend to be indistinguishable from those of chronic institutionalized psychiatric patients and is less effective in identifying organic disorders in psychiatrically disturbed patients (see pp. 233–234).

The Wechsler Intelligence Scales Subtests

The standard examination procedure calls for the administration of the 11 subtests of the Wechsler scales in the order of their presentation below. When all 11 tests are given, testing time generally runs from one and one quarter to two hours. The WAIS and WAIS-R Manuals give the standard administration instructions in detail (D. Wechsler, 1955, 1981).

In the interests of maintaining a standardized administration, the examiner should not attempt to memorize the questions but rather should read them from the manual. When questions have been memorized, the examiner is liable to insert a word here or change one there from time to time without being aware of these little changes. Ultimately they add up so that the examiner may be asking questions that differ not only in a word or two but in their meaning as well. I have found that the only way to guard against this very natural tendency is to use the manual for every administration.

Administration of the 11 subtests need not follow the standard order of presentation (see p. 114). Rather, the examiner may wish to vary the subtest order to meet the patient's needs and limitations. Patients who fatigue easily can be given more taxing subtests, such as Arithmetic or Digit Span, early in the testing session. If the patient is very anxious about the tests, the examiner will want him first to take tests on which he is most likely to succeed before he tackles more difficult material.

Edith Kaplan recommends alternating Verbal and Performance Scale subtests of the WAIS so that patients who may have predominantly verbal or predominantly visuospatial deficits are not faced with a series of failures but rather can enjoy some successes throughout the examination. I have found this presentation pattern very helpful in preventing buildup of tension or discouragement in these patients. Alternating between the school-like question-and-answer items of the Verbal Scale subtests and the puzzle-and-games Performance Scale items also affords a change in pace that keeps the interest of patients whose insight, motivation, or capacity to cooperate is impaired better than does presentation in the originally prescribed order. The WAIS-R incorporates these advantages in a recommended order of administration that alternates Verbal Scale and Performance Scale subtests.

The examiner also need not complete all subtests in one sitting but can stop whenever he or his patient becomes restless or fatigued. In most instances, the examiner calls the recess at the end of a subtest and resumes testing at some later time. Occasionally, a patient's energy or interest will give out in the middle of a subtest. For most subtests, this creates no problem; the test can be resumed where it had been stopped. However, the easy items on Similarities, Block Design, and Picture Arrangement provide some people the practice they need to succeed at more difficult items. If the examination must be stopped in the middle of any of these three tests, the first few items should be repeated at the next session so the patient can reestablish the set necessary to pass the harder items.

Savage and his colleagues (1973) found that people over the age of 70 tended to be uncomfortably sensitive to failures. Negative reactions were likely to show up when the examiner was following the requirement that subtests be continued for a given number of failures. Since many older people enjoyed doing "puzzles," they tolerated failure better on Performance Scale than on Verbal Scale subtests. When faced with the choice of giving the required number of items or discontinuing early to reduce the elderly patient's discomfort, I usually discontinue. In most cases, even if the patient succeeded on one or two of the more difficult items, continuation would not make a significant difference in the score. When the patient appears to be capable of performing at a higher level than he seems willing to attempt and it is important to document this information, the omitted items can be given at a later time, after the patient has had some obvious successes or when he seems more relaxed.

A verbatim record of the patient's answers and comments makes this important dimension of his test behavior available for leisurely review. The examiner who has learned shorthand has a great advantage in this respect. Slow writers in particular might benefit from an acquaintance with brief-hand or speedwriting.

Many examiners routinely use only nine or ten of the eleven WAIS battery subtests (McFie, 1975; A. Smith, 1966b). Most of my examinations do not include Vocabulary because the information it adds is redundant when the other verbal subtests have been given. It also takes the longest of any of the verbal subtests to administer and score. In my examinations a vocabulary test is usually included in the paper and pencil battery or a picture vocabulary test is substituted for patients unable to read or write. Sometimes I exclude Digit Symbol and give the Symbol Digit Modalities Test instead (when I want to compare auditory and graphic response speed on the symbol substitution task and also look for tendencies toward spatial rotation or disorientation, I may give them both). When a symbol substitution test is given to patients with pronounced motor disability or motor slowing who will obviously perform poorly on this highly time-dependent test, their low scores add no new information, making this test redundant, too.

When there are time pressures, the examiner may wish to use a "short form" of the WAIS battery, that is, a set of only three, four, or five subtests selected to give a reasonably representative picture of the patient's functioning (Duke, 1967). Short forms were originally developed to produce a quick estimate of the Full Scale IQ score. Since estimation of an aggregate IQ score is not the goal of the neuropsychological examination, selection of subtests for brief neuropsychological screening need not be made on the basis of how well the combined score from the small set of tests approximates the Full Scale score. So long as the subtests are handled as discrete tests in their own right, the examiner can include or exclude them to suit his patient's needs and abilities and the requirements of the examination.

"Split-half" administrations, in which only every other item is given, also save time but may lose accuracy. One study (Zytowski and Hudson 1965) found that with the exception of Vocabulary, the validity coefficients of split-half scores correlated with whole subtest scores range below .90; and of the Performance Scale subtests, only Block Design is above 80. Satz and Mogel (1962) devised an abbreviated set of scales that includes all the WAIS scales. It uses mostly split-half (odd items only) administrations excepting on Information, Vocabulary, and Picture Completion in which every third item is given. Digit Span and Digit Symbol administrations remain unchanged. The authors report that only Information ($r = .89$), Comprehension ($r = .85$), Block Design ($r = .84$), and Object Assembly ($r = .79$) have correlations below .90 with the whole subtests. G. G. Marsh (1973) obtained fairly comparable correlations on a cross-validation study of the Satz-Mogel format and concluded that

255

this format "is an adequate substitute for the long-form WAIS when it is used as a test of general intelligence with neurology or psychiatry patients." She found, however, that with the abbreviated forms of Information, Comprehension, Picture Completion, and Picture Arrangement, 15–20% of the scores of the group of neurology patients and 18–30% of the scores of the psychiatry patients showed a deviation of three or more scaled scores from their whole subtest performances. Marsh cautioned against using this format when doing pattern analysis. Goebel and Satz (1975) examined the relationship between subtest scaled score profiles obtained on the Satz-Mogel abbreviation of the WAIS and profiles derived in the standard administration, using multivariate procedures. Their data suggest that the abbreviated format does generate subtest profiles that can be used with relative confidence when comparing an individual profile with a set of statistically derived clinical profile types. These findings, though, apply only to the classification of overall profiles, and do not answer the questions raised by Marsh's study regarding the clinical use of abbreviated scale scores when doing inductive pattern analysis.

Neuropsychologically useful information can be gained by incorporating the face-sheet identification and personal information questions into the examination proper. These questions give the examiner the opportunity of evaluating the patient's orientation in a very naturalistic—and thus quite inoffensive—manner and also of ensuring that the important employment and education data have been obtained. ("Race" or "color" is usually obvious.) Only the examiner who routinely asks patients about the date, their age and date of birth, and similar kinds of information usually taken for granted, can appreciate how often neurologically impaired patients fail to answer these questions reliably and how important it is to know this when evaluating and planning for a patient. I also always make a point of filling in my name along with the rest of the information requested at the top of the page and repeating it while I write as many patients, particularly in a large medical center where they may be examined by many people, may not remember the examiner's name and may be too embarrassed to ask.

Many of the subtests present administration or scoring problems peculiar to that subtest. These will be noted in the discussion of each subtest below.

Verbal Scale Subtests

INFORMATION

The Information items test general knowledge normally available to persons growing up in the United States. WAIS battery forms for other countries contain suitable substitutions for items asking for peculiarly American information. The items are arranged in order of difficulty from the four simplest, which all but severely retarded or organically impaired persons answer correctly, to the most difficult, which only few adults pass. The relative difficulty level of some of the WAIS items has probably changed over the years, particularly for the younger age groups. The recent ramblings of the date for celebrating Washington's birthday from year to year (see p.

241), the almost universal (in the United States) inclusion of the *Odyssey* or the *Iliad* in the high school curriculum, and the increased popular interest in Islamic culture will necessarily be reflected in differences in the proportion of persons within and between the different age groups who can answer these questions correctly. In addition, increases in the level of education in the United States, particularly in the older age groups, may have raised the population mean score on the Information subtest. Certainly my clinical experience suggests that this is the case.

I make some additions to Wechsler's instructions. When a patient taking the WAIS gives a very low or very high estimate of the height of the average American woman, I usually ask, as if it were the next question in the test, "What does *average* mean?" to determine whether the response represents an estimation error (see pp. 501–502) or ignorance of the concept of average. I spell "Koran" after saying it since it is a word people are more likely to have read than heard, and if heard, may have been pronounced differently. When patients who have not gone to college answer any of the items from 21 to 25 correctly so that they will be given one or more of the last four items, I usually make some comment such as, "You have done so well that I have to give you some questions that only a very few, usually college-educated, people can answer," thus protecting them as much as possible from unwarranted feelings of failure or stupidity if they are unfamiliar with the items' topics. When a patient gives more than one answer to a question and one of them is correct, the examiner must insist on the patient telling which answer he prefers to be scored as it is not possible to score a response containing both right and wrong answers. I usually ask patients to "vote for one or another of the answers."

Although the standard instructions call for discontinuation of the test after five failures, the examiner may use discretion in following this rule, particularly with brain injured patients. On the one hand, some neurologically impaired patients with prior *average* or higher intellectual achievements are unable to recall once-learned information on demand and therefore fail several simple items in succession. When such patients give no indication of being able to do better on the increasingly difficult items and are also distressed by their failures, the examiner loses little by discontinuing this task early. If he has any doubts about the patient's inability to answer the remaining questions, he can give the next one or two questions later in the session after the patient has had some success on other subtests. On the other hand, bright but poorly educated subjects will often be ignorant of general knowledge but have acquired expertise in their own field which will not become evident if the test is discontinued according to rule. Some mechanics, for example, or nursing personnel, may be ignorant about literature, geography, and religion, but know the boiling point of water. When testing an alert person with specialized work experience and a limited educational background who fails five sequential items not bearing on his personal experience, I usually give all higher level items that might be work-related.

When giving the Information subtest to a patient with known or suspected organic impairment, it is very important to differentiate between failures due to ignorance, loss of once-stored information, and inability to retrieve old learning or say it on command. (See *Testing the Limits*, pp. 114–115.) Patients who cannot answer questions at levels higher than warranted by their educational background, social and work experiences, and vocabulary and current interests have probably never known the answer. Pressing them to respond may at best waste time, at worst make them feel stupid or antagonize them. However, when patients with a high school education cannot name the capital of Italy or give the direction from Chicago to Panama, I generally ask them if they once knew the answer. Many patients who have lost information that had been in long-term storage or have lost the ability to retrieve it, usually can be fairly certain about what they once knew but have forgotten or can no longer recall readily. When this is the case, the kind of information they report having lost is usually in line with their social history. The examiner will find this useful both in evaluating the extent and nature of the patient's impairments and in appreciating his emotional reactions to his condition.

Should a patient acknowledge that he could have answered the item at one time, appear to have a retrieval problem or difficulty verbalizing the answer, or have a social history that would make it likely he once knew the answer (e.g., a Catholic who cannot identify the Vatican), then information storage can be tested by giving the patient several possible answers to see whether he can recognize the correct one. I always write out the multiple-choice answers so the patient can see all of them simultaneously and need not rely on a possibly failing auditory memory. For example, when patients who have completed high school are unable to recall *Hamlet's* author, I write out, "Longfellow (or Kipling on the WAIS-R), Tennyson, Shakespeare, Wordsworth." Occasionally a patient taking the WAIS points to "Longfellow." If there are other indications of perseverative behavior, then this response probably gives one more instance of it; certainly it raises the suspicion of perseveration since the patient had just recently heard that name. More often, the patient identifies Shakespeare correctly, thus providing information both about his fund of knowledge (which he has just demonstrated is bigger than his Information subtest score will indicate) and his retrieval problem. Nonaphasic patients who can read but still cannot identify the correct answer on a multiple-choice presentation probably do not know, cannot retrieve, or have truly forgotten the answer.

The additional information that the multiple-choice technique may communicate about the patient's fund of knowledge raises scoring problems. Since the test norms were not standardized on this kind of administration, additional score points for correct answers to the multiple-choice presentation cannot be evaluated within the same standardization framework as scores obtained according to the standardization rules. On the other hand, this valuable information should not be lost or misplaced. To solve this problem, I use *double scoring;* that is, I post both the age-graded standard score the patient achieves according to the standardization rules and, usually following it in parentheses, another age-graded standard score based on the "official" raw score plus raw score points for the items on which the patient demonstrated knowledge but could not give a spontaneous answer. This method allows the examiner to make an estimate of the patient's fund of background information based on a more representative sample of behavior, given the patient's impairments. The disparity between the

two scores can be used in making an estimate of the amount of deficit the pat
sustained, while the lower score alone indicates the patient's present level c
tioning when he must retrieve verbal information without assistance.

On this and other subtests, test administration adapted to the patient's defic.. ....
double-scoring to document performance under both standard and adapted conditions enables the examiner to discover the full extent of the neurologically impaired
patient's capacity to perform the task under consideration. Effective use of this
method involves both testing the limits of the patient's capacity and, of equal importance, standardized testing to ascertain a baseline against which performance under
adapted conditions can be compared. In every instance, the examiner should test the
limits only after giving the test item in the standard manner with sufficient encouragement and a long enough wait to satisfy any doubts about whether the patient can
perform correctly under the standard instructions.

Information and Vocabulary are the best WAIS battery measures of general ability,
that ubiquitous test factor that appears to be the statistical counterpart of learning
capacity plus mental alertness, speed, and efficiency. Information also tests verbal
skills, breadth of knowledge, and—particularly in older populations—remote memory. Information tends to reflect formal education and motivation for academic
achievement (Saunders, 1960a). It is one of the few subtests in the WAIS batteries
that can give spuriously high ability estimates for overachievers, or fall below the
subject's general ability level because of early lack of academic opportunity or interest. Information (WAIS) contains ten items that are not equally difficult for men and
women, the difference favoring men to a significant degree.

In brain injured populations, Information tends to appear among the least affected
WAIS battery subtests (K. O'Brien and Lezak, 1981; Sklar, 1963). Although a slight
depression of the Information score can be expected with brain injury of any kind,
because performance on this subtest shows such resiliency it often can serve as the
best estimate of original ability. In individual cases, a markedly low Information score
suggests left hemisphere involvement, particularly if verbal tests generally tend to be
relatively depressed and the patient's history provides no other kind of explanation
for the low score. Thus, the Information performance can be a fairly good predictor
of the hemispheric side of a suspected brain lesion (Reitan, 1955b; A. Smith, 1966b;
Spreen and Benton, 1965).

COMPREHENSION

This subtest includes two kinds of open-ended questions: 11 (13 in the WAIS-R) test
common-sense judgment and practical reasoning, and the other three ask for the
meaning of proverbs. Comprehension items range in difficulty from a common-sense
question passed by all nondefective adults to a proverb that is fully understood by
fewer than 22% of adults (Matarazzo, 1972).

Since some of the items are lengthy, the examiner must make sure that patients
whose immediate verbal memory span is reduced have registered all of the elements

of an item. The instructions call for this subtest to be discontinued after four failures, but the examiner needs to use discretion in deciding whether to terminate early or continue beyond four "near misses."

Except for the first two items of the WAIS, which are scored on a pass-fail basis, the subject can earn one or two points for each question, depending on the extent to which the answer is either particular and concrete or general and abstract. Scoring of Comprehension creates a judgment problem for the examiner since so many answers are not clearly of one- or two-point quality but somewhere in between (R. E. Walker et al., 1965). There are even answers that leave the examiner in doubt as to whether to score two points or zero! I have found that scoring of the same set of answers by several psychologists or psychology trainees usually varies from two to four points in raw score totals. When converted to scaled scores, the difference is not often more than one point, which is of little consequence so long as the examiner treats individual subtest scores as likely representatives of a *range* of scores.

Comprehension is only a fair test of general ability, but the verbal factor is influential. Like Information, it appears to measure remote memory in older persons. Six of the fourteen WAIS items have a sex bias with an overall tendency (at the 5% level of significance) for men to make slightly higher scores. Comprehension subtest scores also reflect the patient's social knowledgeability and judgment. It is important, however, to distinguish between the capacity to give reasonable-sounding responses to these structured questions dealing with single, delimited issues and the judgment needed to handle complex, multidimensional real-life situations (Lezak, 1979a). In real life, the exercise of judgment typically involves defining, conceptualizing, structuring, and delimiting the issue that requires judgment as well as rendering an action-oriented decision about it. Thus, as demonstrated most vividly by many patients with right hemisphere lesions, high scores on Comprehension are no guarantee of practical common sense or reasonable behavior.

A 62-year-old retired supervisor of technical assembly work achieved a Comprehension age-graded scaled score of 15 two years after sustaining a right hemisphere CVA that paralyzed his left arm and weakened his left leg. He was repeatedly evicted for not paying his rent from the boarding homes his social worker found for him because he always spent his pension on cab fares within the first week of receiving it. On inquiry into this problem, he reported that he likes to be driven around town. During one hospitalization, when asked about future plans, he announced that upon discharge he would buy a pickup truck, drive to the beach, and go fishing.

Another 62-year-old patient obtained a Comprehension age-graded scaled score of 13 a year after having an episode of left-sided weakness that dissipated within days, leaving minimal sensory and motor residual effects and an identifiable right frontotemporal lesion on CT scan. This man with two graduate degrees had enjoyed a distinguished career in an applied science until, beginning several months after the stroke, he made a series (over 70) of decisions in blatant violation of the regulations he was responsible for carrying out. When confronted with possible criminal action against him, he defended himself quite guilelessly by explaining that he had

260

been conducting his own independent experiments to test the appropriateness of the regulations.

Of all the WAIS battery subtests, Comprehension best lends itself to interpretation of content because the questions ask for the patient's judgment or opinion about a variety of socially relevant topics, such as marriage or taxes, which may have strong emotional meanings for the patient. Tendencies to impulsivity or dependency sometimes appear in responses to questions about dealing with a found letter or finding one's way out of a forest. The most dramatic evidence of poor judgment and impulsivity often comes on the question asking for an appropriate response to the discovery of a theatre fire. In a random count of 60 patients with a variety of brain disorders, 17 (28%) said they would "yell," "holler," or otherwise inform the audience themselves, or leave precipitously. (For example, a 58-year-old lawyer, mentally deteriorated as a result of long-standing, severe alcoholism, achieved a Comprehension age-graded scaled score of 15. His answer was, "Generally one would call out 'fire'". A 63-year-old man with suspected Alzheimer's disease, who received a Comprehension age-graded scaled score of 8, responded, "head for exit.") Of these patients, nine had Comprehension age-graded scaled scores of 10 or higher.

Comprehension test scores hold up well as a record of the premorbid intellectual achievement of brain damaged patients generally, except that they are even more sensitive than other predominantly verbal subtests to left hemisphere damage. Thus, when damage is diffuse, bilateral, or localized within the right hemisphere, the Comprehension subtest score is likely to be among the best test indicators of premorbid ability, whereas its vulnerability to verbal defects makes it a useful indicator of left hemisphere involvement. Impulsive answers to emotionally arousing questions may contrast vividly with well thought out judgments about land values or child labor laws, reflecting impaired self-control in once intellectually competent and socially sophisticated persons whose impulsivity is associated with brain injury.

Occasionally a patient, usually elderly, whose reasoning ability seems quite defective for any practical purposes will give two-point answers to many of the questions related to practical aspects of everyday living or to business issues, such as the need for taxes or the market value of property. In such instances, a little questioning typically reveals a background in business or community affairs and suggests that their good responses represent recall of previously learned information rather than on-the-spot reasoning. For those patients, Comprehension has become a test of old learning. The same holds true for good interpretation of one or more proverbs by a mentally dilapidated elderly patient. Two and more generations ago, proverbs were common conversational coin so that many elderly patients can express suitable meanings for familiar ones while being unable to think abstractly. On the other hand, proverbs really test abstract verbal reasoning in young people, particularly those with little interest in or exposure to the ways of older generations (also see pp. 476–477).

Because the three proverbs appear to test somewhat different abilities—and experiences—than do the other items of this subtest, when evaluating a performance, it

261

can be useful to look at the subject's responses to the practical reasoning questions separately from his responses to the proverbs. Most usually, when there is a disparity between these two different kinds of items, the quality of performance on proverbs (i.e., abstract reasoning) will be akin to that on the Similarities subtest (see pp. 265–266).

ARITHMETIC

This subtest consists of 14 items, but testing routinely begins with the third item since the first two are ordinarily given only to persons who fail both items 3 and 4. The simplest item, which calls for block counting, should also be given to patients with known or suspected right hemisphere lesions since they may be unable to count more than a few visually presented items correctly while they are still capable of performing fairly difficult arithmetic problems conceptually. All nonretarded, organically intact adults can answer the first of the routinely administered items correctly. On the WAIS, a few brain damaged patients who can perform the simple addition respond incorrectly on this item because they interpret the question concretely (pp. 120–121). Approximately 20% of the adult population can do the last item (Matarazzo, 1972), which is like, "Four men can finish a job in eight hours. How many men will be needed to finish it in a half hour?"). When the patient is distressed by his failures or very unlikely to improve his performance, I may discontinue this test after a second or third consecutive failure, rather than continue for the four consecutive failures called for in the instructions. Arithmetic items have time limits ranging from 15 seconds on the first four to 120 seconds on the fourteenth. A subject can earn raw score bonus points for particularly rapid responses on the last four items. As a result, all scores above a scaled score of 13 for ages 18–70 differ only in terms of time bonus increments.

When recording test data using the WAIS test form, the examiner will obtain more information by noting the patient's exact responses on the Record Form, rather than writing in "R" or "W" as the WAIS printed material suggests. Every answer should be written in, the correct ones as well as the incorrect, so that the subject gets no hint of failure from the pace or amount of the examiner's writing. Although all Arithmetic failures receive the same zero score, some approach correctness more closely than others, and a simple "W" tells nothing about this. On the question above that is similar to the last one on the WAIS and WAIS-R, for example, an incorrect response of "32" indicates that the patient has sorted out the elements of the problem and used the appropriate operation, but has failed to carry it through to the proper conclusion. An answer of "48" suggests that he performed the correct operations but miscalculated one step, whereas an answer of "1½" or "16" reveals ignorance or confusion. Thus, although "32", "48" "1½" and "16" are equally incorrect as far as scoring is concerned, only a person with a reasonably good grasp of arithmetic fundamentals and ability to reason about a complex arithmetic idea could get "32" as an answer; a person who says "48" can handle mathematical concepts well but is either careless or has forgotten his multiplication tables.

The total Arithmetic score of a bright intact person will usually be compounded both of number correct and time credit points. In the case of a slow responder who takes longer than the time limit to formulate the correct answer, the total Arithmetic score may not reflect his arithmetic ability so much as his response rate. Each of these persons may get the same number of responses correct, say 11; but the intact subject could earn a raw score of 12 and a scaled score of 11, whereas a neurologically impaired patient whose arithmetic skills are comparable might receive a raw score of only 8 or 9 and a scaled score of 7 or 8. To do justice to the slow responder and gain a full measure of data about him, the examiner should obtain two Arithmetic scores: one based on the sum of correct responses given within time limits plus time bonuses, and the other on the sum of correct responses regardless of time limits. The first score can be interpreted in terms of the test norms and the second gives a better indication of the patient's arithmetic skills in themselves. When testing for maximum productivity, the examiner will not interrupt the patient to give another item until he has indicated he cannot do it or he becomes too restless or upset to continue working on the unanswered item.

Difficulties in immediate memory, concentration, or conceptual manipulation and tracking can prevent even very mathematically skilled patients from doing well on this orally administered test. These patients typically can perform the first several questions quickly and correctly, since they involve only one operation, few elements, and simple, familiar number relationships. When there is more than one operation, several elements, or less common number relationships requiring "carrying," these patients lose or confuse the elements or goal of the problems. They may succeed with repeated prompting but only after the time limit has expired, or they may be unable to do the problem "in their head" at all, regardless of how often the question is repeated. The standard WAIS battery Arithmetic procedure does not begin to test the arithmetic skills of these patients. After discovering how poorly the patient performs when he has to rely on his immediate memory, the examiner can find out how well he can do on these problems by giving him paper and pencil and letting him work out the problems. I use one sheet of unlined paper for this purpose, handing it to the patient after each failure, *if the failure appears to be due to an immediate memory, concentration, or conceptual clarity defect*. Use of unlined paper has two advantages: spatial orientation problems are more apt to show up if there are no guide lines, and there is no visual interference to distract vulnerable patients. By providing only one sheet of paper, the examiner forces the patient to organize the two or three and sometimes more problems on the one page, a maneuver that may reveal defects in spatial organization, ordering, and planning. An alternative method, recommended by Edith Kaplan and suitable for patients who also have difficulty writing, is to give the patient the problem printed out on a card that he can study as long as he wants. In either case, the examiner should obtain two scores. One based on the patient's performance under standard conditions will give a good measure of the extent to which his memory and mental efficiency problems are interfering with his ability to handle problems mentally. The other, compounded of all of his correct answers regardless of timing or administration format, will give a better estimate of his arithmetic skills per se.

Arithmetic scores, like Comprehension scores, are of only mediocre value as measures of general ability in the population at large, but they do reflect concentration and "ideational discipline" (Saunders, 1960a). In early adulthood, the memory component plays a relatively small role in Arithmetic, but it becomes more important with age. Arithmetic performance, like Information, may suffer from poor early school attitudes or experiences. In the case of women generally. Arithmetic's vulnerability to culturally ingrained attitudes may well be reflected in their significantly lower scores.

For normal subjects this subtest is not a good measure of verbal ability. The subtests that are heavily weighted with the verbal factor (Information, Comprehension, Similarities, and Vocabulary) correlate less with Arithmetic (.49–.66) than their comparable correlations with the Performance Scale subtest, Picture Completion (.56–.67) (Wechsler, 1958). Thus, under ordinary circumstances, it should not be considered a verbal subtest. However, McFie (1975) noted that subjects who have some kind of difficulty with verbal comprehension may be confused by the wording of some of the problems and fail for this reason. He recommends that when the examiner suspects this to be the case, the question should be restated. As one example, McFie rewords item 8 (7 on the WAIS-R) to say, "If you walk at three miles an hour, how long would it take you to walk 24 miles?"

When obtained from brain damaged patients following standard procedure, the Arithmetic subtest score of the WAIS battery may be more confusing than revealing. The problem lies in the oral administration format, which emphasizes the considerable memory and concentration components of oral arithmetic. This results in a tendency for Arithmetic scores to drop in the presence of brain damage generally (Morrow and Mark, 1955; Newcombe, 1969). In addition, using the oral format, the examiner may overlook the often profound effects of the spatial type of dyscalculia that become apparent only when the patient must organize arithmetic concepts on paper (i.e., spatially) In other cases, the examiner may remain ignorant of a figure or number alexia that would show up if the patient had to look at arithmetic symbols on paper (Hécaen, 1962). Further, a distinct verbal component emerges from the Arithmetic performance of organic populations that may account for the slight but regular tendency for left hemisphere patients to do a little worse on this subtest than those whose lesions are located within the right hemisphere (Spreen and Benton, 1965; Warrington and Rabin, 1970). McFie found that patients with left parietal lesions tended to have significantly lowered Arithmetic scores (1975) and Long and Brown (1979) reported similar findings for a group with left temporal lobe lesions. I have seen a number of patients with right hemisphere damage who also do poorly on this subtest, particularly relative to their scores on the verbal subtests. In some of these cases, the difficulty appears related to an impaired ability to organize the elements of the problems; in others, it tends to be due to memory or attention deficits. A lowered Arithmetic subtest score should lead the examiner to suspect an immediate memory or concentration problem and to raise questions about verbal functions, but it does not necessarily reflect the patient's arithmetic skills, particularly if there are other indications of impaired memory, concentration, or verbal functions. To evaluate the patient's ability to do arithmetic, the examiner must turn to the untimed WAIS battery Arithmetic score, the paper and pencil score, qualitative aspects of the patient's performance, and other arithmetic tests.

SIMILARITIES

This is a test of verbal concept formation. The subject must explain what each of a pair of words has in common. The word pairs range in difficulty from the simplest ("orange-banana"), which only retarded or impaired adults fail, to the most difficult ("fly-tree" on the WAIS, "praise-punishment" on the WAIS-R). The test begins with the first item for all subjects and is discontinued after four failures. Here, too, common sense should dictate whether to present the last one or two items to a patient who has ceased to comprehend the nature of the problem and is fatigued or upset. Items are passed at the two-point level if the patient gives an abstract generalization and at the one-point level if he responds with a specific concrete likeness.

There are fewer scoring problems on Similarities than on Comprehension, but some variation between scorers does occur. Deteriorated patients, as well as persons whose general functioning is *borderline defective* or lower, sometimes respond with likenesses to the first few items but name a difference, which is generally easier to formulate, when the questions become difficult for them. In such cases, I record the incorrect response, scoring the item zero, but repeat the request for a similarity the first time this happens. Sometimes this extra questioning will help the patient attend to the demand for a likeness on the next and subsequent questions.

It is my impression that for older patients (age ranges of 55–64 and above), the age-graded WAIS Similarities scaled scores are skewed in the direction of leniency in the lower score ranges. As a result, older patients with raw scores of 5 or 6, gained from perhaps one good abstraction and three or four concrete answers, obtain age-graded scaled scores within the *average* range, scores that seem to belie their limited capacities to make verbal abstractions and generalizations. When giving the WAIS to older people, the examiner should use discretion in drawing conclusions from the Similarities age-graded scaled scores. This appears to be less of a problem on the WAIS-R, since 10 raw score points are needed for a scaled score of 8 at ages 65 to 69. However, a scaled score of 8 is relatively easy to earn at ages 70 to 74, since only 8 raw score points are required.

Similarities is an excellent test of general intellectual ability, but through middle age it reflects the verbal factor only to a moderate degree. Since Similarities is virtually independent of any memory component, for older people whose memory assumes much more importance on other verbal tests, it becomes the best test of verbal ability per se. Of all the verbal subtests, Similarities is least affected by the subject's background and experiences. Unlike Information and Arithmetic, it does not depend on academic skills, so that a bright person with inadequate schooling may do significantly better on this than on the other, more school-dependent verbal subtests. Unlike Comprehension, Similarities is relatively independent of social or educational background and unaffected by the impulsivity and social misjudgments that accompany some kinds of brain injuries. Compared to schizophrenic patients and normal subjects, brain damaged patients tend to give many more "Don't know" responses to Similarities questions, and proportionately fewer brain damaged patients attempt conceptual responses (Spence, 1963).

Similarities tends to be more sensitive to the effects of brain injury regardless of localization than the other verbal subtests (Hirschenfang, 1960b). Its vulnerability to brain conditions that affect verbal functions compounds its vulnerability to impaired concept formation, so that a relatively depressed Similarities score tends to be associated with left temporal and frontal involvement (McFie, 1975; Newcombe, 1969) and is one of the best predictors of left hemisphere disease in the WAIS battery. Rzechorzek (1979) found that patients with left frontal lobe lesions had significantly lower Similarities scores than did those with anterior lesions on the right, whose Similarities scores tend to be unaffected (Bogen et al., 1972; McFie, 1975). Lower Similarities scores are also associated with bilateral frontal lesions (Sheer, 1956).

An occasional concrete-minded patient—usually one suffering from a diffuse dementing process—will do surprisingly well on this subtest, despite its usual independence from memory functions. Since these are almost always persons who had once enjoyed excellent verbal skills, it appears that in these cases the patient is calling upon old, well-formed verbal associations so that the test is actually eliciting old verbal memories.

DIGIT SPAN

The Digit Span subtest used in the Wechsler tests (the intelligence scales and the Wechsler Memory Scale, pp. 463, 465–466) comprises two different tests, Digits Forward and Digits Backward, which involve different mental activities and are affected differently by brain damage. Both tests consist of seven pairs of random number sequences that the examiner reads aloud at the rate of one per second, and both thus involve auditory attention. Here much of the similarity between the two tests ends.

In combining the two digit span tasks to obtain one score, which is the score that enters into most statistical analyses of the Wechsler tests, these two tests are treated as if they measured the same behavior or very highly correlated behaviors. The latter assumption holds for most normal control subjects through middle age. With advancing age, the Digits Forward span tends to be stable while the Digits Backward span typically shrinks (Botwinick and Storandt, 1974; Hayslip and Kennelly, 1980). Differences between these two tests become most evident in studies of brain damaged patients in which straightforward digit span and reversed digit span are dissociated in some patient groups (Costa, 1975; Lezak, 1979b; Weinberg et al., 1972) but not in others (Black and Strub, 1978).

The risk of losing information by dealing with these two tests as if they were one and combining their scores becomes obvious when one considers what the WAIS scaled score, based on the combined raw scores, might mean. To obtain a scaled score of 10, the *average* scaled score, a young adult needs to achieve a raw score of 11 which, in the majority of cases, will be based on a Digits Forward score of 6 and a Digits Backward score of 5. However, he can get this *average* rating based on a Digits

Forward score of 7 and a Digits Backward score of 4 with a three-point difference between the scores, a difference that occurs more often in brain damaged than in intact populations. The same scaled score of 10 may also be based on a Digits Forward score of 8 and a Digits Backward score of 3. A disparity between scores of this magnitude is almost never seen in normal, intact subjects. Moreover, a Digits Backward score of 3 in a young adult, in itself is indicative of brain dysfunction.

The problem of obscuring meaningful data is further compounded in the WAIS-R. In order "to increase the variability of scores," two trials are given of each item (i.e., at each span length) and the subject receives one raw score point for each correct trial. Thus, information about the length of span is confounded with information about the reliability of span performance. A person in the 18- to 34-year-old range who passes only one of the two trials on each pair of Digits Forward items containing four to six digits and Digits Backward items of three to five digits in length would receive a total raw score of 10, which would be classified at the level of a scaled score of 6, just above the *borderline* level. Yet, for neuropsychological purposes, this subject has demonstrated an *average* span for both digit span forward and the reversed digit span. That this subject is more prone to error than most people whose span for digits is the same length is interesting information. However, neither the subject's *average* capacity nor his proneness to error are evident in the final score. Rather, the final score can easily be misinterpreted by anyone who does not know that the subject's *span* of recall was within normal limits.

For neuropsychological purposes, neither the WAIS nor the WAIS-R scoring systems are useful. Digit span forward and digit span backward are meaningful pieces of information that require no further elaboration for interpretation (see pp. 550–551). The examiner who is interested in assessing the reliability of a patient's attention span may give three or more trials at each span length, but should not confound data about the consistency of response with data concerning its length.

Digits Forward. This is the first of the two to be administered. The subject's task is to repeat each sequence exactly as it is given. When a WAIS sequence is repeated correctly, the examiner reads the next longer number sequence, continuing until the patient fails a pair of sequences or repeats a nine-digit sequence correctly. On the WAIS-R, both trials are given at each span length until both trials are failed. To find out whether the patient can perform this task at all, I will occasionally administer a third sequence of the same length after two failures. This is not routine, but done only in one of two circumstances: (1) When the patient's failure on at least one of the two trials of a sequence appears to be due to distraction, noncooperation, inattentiveness, etc., I give the third digit series, usually taking the requisite number of digits out of one of the nine forward or eight backward sequences that are unlikely to be used. (2) When the patient recalls more digits reversed than forward, the examiner can assume that the patient is capable of doing at least as well on the much less difficult Digits Forward as on Digits Backward and that this rarely seen disparity probably reflects the patient's lack of effort on a simple task. Almost invariably, such a patient will pass a third trial and occasionally will pass one or two of the longer sequences.

The WAIS and the Wechsler-Bellevue Manuals provide a method to convert raw scores into standard scores that can be juggled into separate standard score estimates for each of the two Digit Span tests. However, because Digit Span has a relatively restricted range and does not correlate very highly with other measures of cognitive prowess, it makes more sense to deal with the data in raw score form than to convert them. Taking into account that the normal range for Digits Forward is 6 ± 1 (Spitz, 1972), and that education appears to have a decided effect on this task (Weinberg et al., 1972), it is easy to remember that spans of 6 or better are well *within normal limits*, a span of 5 may be marginal to *normal limits*, a span of 4 is definitely *borderline*, and 3 is *defective*.

What Digits Forward measures is more closely related to the efficiency of attention than to what is commonly thought of as memory (Spitz, 1972). It has perhaps been most aptly described as a test of the "passive span of apprehension" (Hayslip and Kennelly, 1980). Anxiety tends to reduce the number of digits recalled (Mueller, 1979; Pyke and Agnew, 1963), but it may be difficult to identify this effect in the individual case. For example, one study of 144 students (half tested as high, half as low anxiety) reported a Digits Forward mean score of 7.15 for the high-, 7.54 for the low-anxiety students, a difference indicating a large overlap between the two groups (Mueller and Overcast, 1976). Stress-induced lowering of the Digit Forward score has been shown to dissipate with practice (Pyke and Agnew, 1963). When the examiner suspects that a stress reaction is interfering with a subject's Digit Span performance, he can repeat the test later in the examination. If the scores remain low even when the task is familiar and the patient is presumably more at ease, then the patient's poor performance is probably due to something other than stress.

Digit Span tends to be more vulnerable to left hemisphere involvement than to either right hemisphere or diffuse damage (Newcombe, 1969; Weinberg et al.,1972). It is a relatively stable capacity that is likely to be resistant to the effects of many dementing diseases. It does decline with age, a little in the late sixties to early seventies, more sharply after that (Hulicka, 1966; Kramer and Jarvik, 1979). (See Chapter 7, pp. 217–218.) Since it appears to be primarily a measure of attention, it is not surprising to find that, in the first months following head trauma or psychosurgery, the Digits Forward span of some patients is likely to fall below normal limits, but it is also likely to show returns to normal levels during the subsequent years (Lezak, 1979b; Scherer et al., 1957).

Digits Backward. The Digits Backward number sequences are two to eight digits long and, on hearing them read, the subject's task is to say them in an exactly reversed order. Again, the test continues until the subject fails a pair of sequences or recalls eight reversed correctly.

Although Wechsler's instructions suffice for most subjects, when dealing with patients who are known or suspected to have brain damage, some variants may help to elicit maximum performance on this test without violating the standardization. Many patients whose thinking is concrete or who become easily confused comprehend the standard instructions for Digits Backward with difficulty if at all. Typically, these patients do not appreciate the transposition pattern of "backwards" but only understand that the last number need be repeated first. To reduce the likelihood of this misconception, I introduce the Digits Backward task using the wording in the Wechsler Manual (1955, 1981), but give as the first example the two-digit number sequence, which even very impaired patients can do with relative ease. Everyone who recalls two digits reversed on either the first or second trial then receives the following instructions: "Good! [or some other expression of approval]. Now I am going to say some more numbers, and once again, when I stop I want you to say them *backwards*. For example, if I say *1–2–3*, what would you say?" Most patients can reverse this three-number sequence because of its inherent familiar pattern. If the subject fails this example, it is given again verbally with the admonition, "Remember, when I stop, I want you to say the numbers *backwards*—the last number first and the first one last, just as if you were reading them backwards." The examiner may point in the air from the patient's left to his right as he says each number, and then point in the reverse direction as the patient repeats the reversed numbers so as to add a visual and directional reinforcement to the concept "backwards." If the patient still is unable to grasp the idea, the examiner can write each number down as he repeats *1–2–3* the third time. The examiner needs to write the numbers in a large hand on a separate sheet of paper or at the top of the Record Form so that they face the subject and run from the subject's left to right, i.e., ε-ζ-I. Then when the examiner asks the patient to repeat the numbers backwards, he points to each number as the patient says or reads it. No further effort is made to explain the test. As soon as the subject reverses the *1–2–3* set correctly or has received all of the above explanations, the examiner continues the rest of Digits Backward according to Wechsler's procedure.

The normal raw score difference between Digits Forward and Digits Backward tends to range around 1.0 (Costa, 1975) with a spread of reported differences running as low as .59 (Mueller and Overcast, 1976) and as high as 2.00 (Black and Strub, 1978). The examiner who chooses to evaluate the Digits Backward performance on the basis of the raw score should consider raw scores of 4 to 5 as *within normal limits*, 3 as *borderline defective* or *defective*, depending on the patient's educational background (Botwinick and Storandt, 1974; Weinberg et al., 1972), and 2 to be *defective* for persons up to the age of 60. The Digits Backward span typically decreases about one point during the seventh decade. However, as age groups 60 and over are increasingly likely to be better educated than the groups examined in the reported studies, these classifications may be increasingly appropriate to age 70.

The Digits Backward requirement of storing a few data bits briefly while juggling them around mentally is an effortful activity that calls upon the working memory, as distinct from the more passive span of apprehension measured by Digits Forward (Hayslip and Kennelly, 1980; Vernon, 1979). It is therefore more of a memory test than Digits Forward. The task involves mental *double-tracking* in that both the memory and the reversing operations must proceed simultaneously. M. B. Bender (1979) suggests that the ability to reverse digits, or to spell a word or recite a letter sequence backwards, is "probably characteristic of normal cognitive function and language processes" related to the brain's normal function of temporal ordering. Based on data showing that right hemisphere damaged patients with visual field defects did less well on this test than right hemisphere damaged patients without such defects, Weinberg and his group (1972) have hypothesized that the reversing operation depends upon internal visual scanning. Most intact adults, when asked to spell a word backwards, for example, will report when questioned afterwards that their eyes moved in response to a mental visual scanning approach to the task, so that an hypothesis linking the capacity to reverse digits to visual scanning efficiency appears to be potentially fruitful. Costa (1975), however, has suggested that both lowered Digits Backward scores and visual field defects may each simply reflect greater impairment.

Like other tests of working memory, Digits Backward is generally sensitive to brain damage. By and large, patients with left hemisphere damage (Newcombe, 1969; Weinberg et al., 1972), and patients with visual field defects have shorter Backward spans than those without such defects. Older patients get lower scores than younger ones, and, in general, the more severe the lesion the lower the Digits Backward score. This test is very vulnerable to the kind of diffuse damage that occurs with many dementing processes but may not be affected in Korsakoff's psychosis (see Chapter 7, pp. 193, 196–197). Unlike Digits Forward, Digits Backward shows little improvement over time following trauma (Lezak, 1979b) or psychosurgery (Scherer et al., 1957).

VOCABULARY

This subtest consists of 40 words in the WAIS, 35 in the WAIS–R, arranged in order of difficulty. The examiner reads the question, "What does＿＿＿＿ mean?" The easiest word on the list is "bed," but the administration usually begins with the fourth word, "winter," which practically all adults can define. It continues until the subject fails five words consecutively or until the list is exhausted. The most difficult words on the WAIS are "impale" and "travesty,"; on the WAIS–R they are "audacious" and "tirade," items 34 and 36 of the WAIS. Except for the first three words on the WAIS list, which are scored two or zero, the subject can obtain one or two points for each acceptable definition, depending on its accuracy, precision, and aptness. Thus, the subject's score reflects both the extent of his recall vocabulary and the effectiveness of his speaking vocabulary.

Vocabulary normally takes 15 to 20 minutes to administer, and at least 5 minutes to score, which makes it the most time-consuming subtest by far. In clinical practice, particularly with easily fatigued brain damaged patients, the high time cost of administering Vocabulary rarely compensates for the information gain it affords.

One kind of patient for whom the information gain may be uniquely relevant is the puzzling psychiatric patient who generally responds well to standard personality tests but exercises poor judgment and appears increasingly inefficient in his activities. The differential diagnosis is between a functional thought disorder and brain disease. With no other clear-cut findings, Vocabulary is the most likely of the WAIS battery subtests to aid in discriminating between the two diagnostic categories, because patients with thought disorders occasionally let down their guard on this innocuous-appearing verbal skill test to reveal a thinking problem in "clangy" expressions, idiosyncratic associations, or personalized or confabulatory responses. For any other purpose, another kind of vocabulary test will not only provide an estimate of the patient's vocabulary but will do so in terms of dimensions not tested by the WAIS batteries, such as reading and writing, or visual recognition and discrimination (see pp. 306–308, 335).

Attention has been called to the nature of the Vocabulary response in other contexts as well. Storck and Looft (1973) note that synonyms are the most common form of response among normal adults, but their frequency tends to decrease a little in the sixth or seventh decade. Definitions in terms of descriptions, use, or demonstrations are relatively uncommon, except among children, and explanations—although also not commonly given—tend to increase in frequency gradually throughout the adult years. These findings assume particular interest in the light of a study of patients who had undergone psychosurgery (Schalling, 1957). All groups, regardless of lesion site, gave fewer synonyms and more "inferior" definitions (such as illustrations, poor explanations, repetitions with slight modifications, demonstrations, and loose associations). Lobotomized patients showed the greatest reduction in response quality while the patients whose lesions were more "selective" (e.g., inferior lobotomy, convexity, or orbital undercutting) displayed less qualitative change. Schalling warned that some of these differences would not show up in a simple "pass-fail" scoring system.

In the interests of standardizing scoring, accurate scaling, reducing redundancy, and increasing the discrimination power of each item, Jastak and Jastak (1964) devised a scale using just 20 words of the WAIS Vocabulary list. The great care they exercised in selecting the items and providing a detailed set of examples to aid in scoring each item appears to have paid off in split-half reliability coefficients of .972 and .963 for groups of 300 men and 200 women, respectively. Examiners looking for a less time-consuming way of giving Vocabulary may wish to try this short form.

Vocabulary has been identified as the single best measure of both verbal and general mental ability, although Information serves equally well as a measure of general ability and Comprehension does about as well as a measure of verbal functions. Early socialization experiences tend to influence vocabulary development even more than schooling, so that the Vocabulary score is more likely to reflect the patient's socioeconomic and cultural origins and less likely to have been affected by academic motivation or achievement than Information or Arithmetic.

When brain injury is diffuse or bilateral, Vocabulary tends to be among the least affected of the WAIS battery subtests (Gonen and Brown, 1968). Like all other highly verbal tests, it is relatively sensitive to lesions in the left hemisphere (Parsons et al., 1969). Among the WAIS battery verbal subtests, however, Vocabulary is generally not one of those most depressed by left hemisphere damage.

Performance Scale Subtests

Four of the next five tests require motor response, writing on Digit Symbol and manipulating material on the other three. The question arises as to the validity of scores obtained on these tests when the patient is hemiplegic and can use only one hand, which often will be the nonpreferred hand. Normal control subjects obtained

271

no significant score difference on the three manipulation tasks when only one hand was used, whether or not it was the preferred hand, although both Picture Arrangement and Object Assembly showed a small scaled score point loss for either hand alone (P. F. Briggs, 1960). When the subject used only the nonpreferred hand, Digit Symbol suffered slightly but with enough consistency to produce a significant lowering of the score.

All Performance Scale subtests except Digit Symbol lend themselves to double-scoring, since many subjects, particularly brain injured and elderly persons, may complete one or more items on these subtests satisfactorily after the time limit has expired. For those who are slow, the score for all satisfactory answers, regardless of time to completion, provides a better estimate of how well they can perform the task than does the score obtained by standard, time-limited scoring rules. The latter score, however, is more useful for diagnostic interpretations.

DIGIT SYMBOL

This symbol substitution task is printed in the test booklet. It consists of four rows containing, in all, 100 small blank squares, each paired with a randomly assigned number from one to nine (see Fig. 9-1). Above these rows is a printed key that pairs each number with a different nonsense symbol. Following a practice trial on the first ten squares (seven on the WAIS–R), the subject's task is to fill in the blank spaces with the symbol that is paired to the number above the blank space as quickly as he can. After 90 seconds he is stopped. His score is the number of squares filled in correctly. Of all the WAIS battery tests, this is the only one that I time openly, for in this case the importance of speed must be stressed.

Persons unused to handling pencils and doing fine handwork under time pressure are at a disadvantage on this test. The great importance that motor speed plays in the scoring, particularly at ages below 35, renders Digit Symbol of doubtful validity for

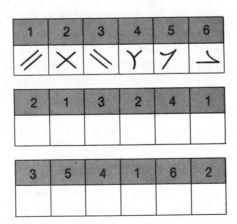

Fig. 9-1. The symbol-substitution format of the Digit Symbol subtest of the WAIS battery.

many low-skilled manual workers and for anyone whose motor responses tend to be slow. It is particularly difficult for elderly subjects whose vision or visuomotor coordination is impaired or who have difficulty comprehending the instructions (Savage et al., 1973). This test should not be given to patients with pronounced motor slowing or to unskilled manual laborers who have not completed high school or who graduated more than 15 years before the examination, for these persons invariably do poorly regardless of their neuropsychological status. An exception to this rule is made for those few patients suspected of having visual perception or orientation problems whose defects might show up as rotations, simplification, or other distortions under the stress of this task. Thus, I usually give this test to patients with known or suspected right hemisphere damage, particularly if it is right frontal, since these patients are most likely to make orientation errors, usually reversals.

Edith Kaplan gets extra mileage out of this test by using it to measure incidental learning in addition to obtaining a score on a standardized performance. She notes which square the patient filled in at 90 seconds, but allows the patient to continue until the end of the next-to-the-last row. She then folds the test under so that only the unmarked last row shows and requests the patient to fill in from memory as many of the symbols as he can recall. She reports that a recall of seven out of the nine symbols is at the low end of *average* for normal persons. When a patient cannot place seven or more correctly, he is encouraged to write as many of the symbols as he can recall in the margin below. Kaplan also recommends that the examiner make a note of the patient's progress on the test at each 30-second interval in order to evaluate the rate at which he proceeds.

For most adults, Digit Symbol is a test of psychomotor performance that is relatively unaffected by intellectual prowess, memory, or learning (Erber et al., 1981; Glosser et al., 1977; Murstein and Leipold, 1961). Motor persistence, sustained attention, response speed, and visuomotor coordination play important roles in a normal person's performance. Estes (1974) points out that skill in encoding the symbols verbally also appears to contribute to success on this test, and may account for a consistently observed feminine superiority on symbol substitution tasks (e.g., A. Smith, 1967; Wechsler, 1958). Some weak perceptual organization components do show up in the performance of older persons, but the natural response slowing that comes with age seems to be the most important variable contributing to the age differential on this test.

This test is consistently more sensitive to brain damage than other WAIS battery subtests in that its score is most likely to be depressed even when damage is minimal, and to be the most depressed when other subtests are affected as well (Hirschenfang, 1960b). Because Digit Symbol tends to be affected regardless of the locus of the lesion, it is of little use for predicting the laterality of a lesion.

Digit Symbol's nonspecific sensitivity to brain dysfunction should not be surprising since it can be affected by so many different components of a performance. In an interesting series of studies, Butters and Cermak (1976) and Glosser with Butters and E. Kaplan (1977) have demonstrated that failures on this test may be the result of different factors or their interplay. For example, diminished speed alone contributes to but does not account for the much lower scores, obtained by patients with right hemisphere lesions or Korsakoff's psychosis than by chronic alcoholics (whose performance also suffers from psychomotor slowing). By manipulating the symbol substitution task using both familiar and unfamiliar symbols and the standard and reversed (see p. 555) administrations, they were able to identify a visuoperceptual component that contributed significantly to both the Korsakoff and the right hemisphere damaged patients' performances. On the other hand, Tissot and his colleagues (1963) report that the greatly lowered scores that aphasics typically earn on this test result from virtually error-free but exceedingly slow performances.

PICTURE COMPLETION

To give this test, the examiner shows the subject 21 (WAIS) or 20 (WAIS–R) incomplete pictures of human features, familiar objects, or scenes, arranged in order of difficulty with instructions to tell what *important part* is missing (see Fig. 9-2). The tests always begins with the first picture (a knobless door), to which most mentally retarded persons respond correctly, and continues through the last picture (a profile lacking an eyebrow on the WAIS, snow missing from a woodpile on the WAIS–R). This test does not discriminate well between *superior* and *very superior* ability levels.

Twenty seconds are allowed for each response. When testing a slow responder, the examiner should note the time of completion and whether the response was correct so that he can obtain a timed and untimed score. The patient's verbatim responses on failed items may yield useful clues to the nature of the underlying difficulty. For example, the response "flagpole" to the WAIS picture of an American flag with 35 stars is a common error of persons with little initiative who respond to the obvious or

Fig. 9-2. WAIS-type Picture Completion subtest item.

who tend to think in simple, concrete terms; but the response "red in the stripes" to the eleventh of a black and white series is rare and obviously represents very concrete and uncritical thinking. Here too, I record the patient's words rather than merely noting whether or not the answer was correct. Patients who have difficulty verbalizing a response may indicate the answer by pointing (e.g., to the rim of the rowboat where an oarlock would normally be found). I credit such responses. Doubts about the subject's intentions in pointing can usually be clarified by multiple-choice questioning (e.g., for the missing oarlock, the examiner can ask if the subject is pointing to a missing "oar, paddle, oarlock, anchor holder").

Of all the Performance Scale subtests, Picture Completion has the highest weighting of the general ability factor with modest weightings on both verbal and visuospatial factors (Lansdell and Donnelly, 1977; Maxwell, 1960; E. W. Russell, 1972a and b). At the most basic level it tests visual recognition. The kind of visual organization and reasoning abilities needed to perform Picture Completion differs from that required by other Performance Scale subtests as the subject must supply the missing part from long-term memory but does not have to manipulate the parts. On the WAIS, Picture Completion correlates higher (.67) with the Information subtest than any other except Comprehension, thus reflecting the extent to which it also tests remote memory and general information. Its highest correlation on the WAIS–R, .55, is with Vocabulary. There are also reasoning components to this test involving judgments about both practical and conceptual relevancies (Saunders, 1960b). J. Cohen considers this test to be a nonverbal analogue of Comprehension (1957b). Picture Completion is biased to a slight but statistically significant degree in favor of men.

Picture Completion consistently demonstrates resilience to the effects of brain damage. Lateral damage does not have any significant differentiating effect. When brain impairment is lateralized, the Picture Completion score is usually higher than the scores on the tests most likely to be vulnerable to that kind of damage. For example, a patient with left-sided damage is likely to do better on this subtest than on the four highly verbal ones; with right-sided involvement, the Picture Completion score tends to exceed that of the other subtests in the Performance Scale. Picture Completion can serve as the best test indicator of previous ability, particularly when left hemisphere damage has significantly affected the ability to formulate the kinds of complex spoken responses needed for the Verbal subtests.

> One example of the sturdiness of Picture Completion is given by the WAIS age-graded subtest score pattern of a 50-year-old retired mechanic. This high school graduate had a right superficial temporal and middle cerebral artery anastomosis two months after a right CVA and three years before the neuropsychological examination. A little more than one year after he had undergone the neurosurgical procedure he reported seizures involving the right arm and accompanied by headache and right-sided numbness. An EEG showed diffuse slowing, which agreed with a history that implicated bilateral brain damage. Bilateral damage was also suggested by WAIS age-graded subtest scores of 7 on Information, Similarities, and Object Assembly, and of 5 on Block Design and Picture Arrangement. His highest score—10—was Picture Completion.

BLOCK DESIGN

This is a construction test in which the subject is presented with red and white blocks, four or nine, depending on the item. The task is to use the blocks to construct replicas of two block constructions made by the examiner and eight (on the WAIS) or seven (WAIS–R) designs printed in smaller scale (see Fig. 9-3). The order of presentation differs from the order of difficulty. Diller and his co-workers (1974) found that, for elderly subjects, the second design had a difficulty level intermediate between WAIS designs 5 and 6. Generally speaking, at each level of complexity, the WAIS even-numbered items are likely to be more difficult than the odd-numbered items. Designs

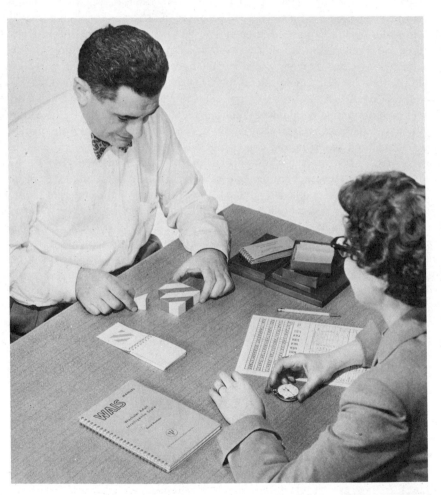

Fig. 9-3. Block Design subtest. (Reproduced by permission of The Psychological Corporation.)

1, 3, 5, and 7 (1, 4, and 6 of the WAIS–R) are made up of distinguishable block faces, mostly plain squares; diagonals occur discretely so that when patients with visuospatial disorders or dull or careless persons fail one of these items, it is more likely to be due to incorrect orientation of the diagonal of a red-and-white block than to errors in laying out the overall pattern. In contrast, the diagonal patterns of the even-numbered designs reach across two- and three-block spans. Concrete-minded persons and patients (particularly those with right hemisphere damage) with visuospatial deficits have particular difficulty constructing these diagonal patterns. The four-block designs have one-minute time limits and the nine-block designs two-minute limits. The subject can earn one or two bonus points for speed on the last four designs of the WAIS, and speed credits are given on items 3 to 9 of the WAIS–R.

Unlike the example pictured in Figure 9-3, the designs to be copied should be placed directly in front of the patient, just back far enough to allow the patient room to work. (Also unlike the example depicted in Figure 9-3, the patient's working area should be free of distractions such as other test material, the examiner's booklet, etc.) All subjects begin with the first item, which is presented and demonstrated as a block-copying rather than a design-copying test. The first and second items can be repeated should the subject fail to produce a correct design within the time limits, and the manual allows some leeway for demonstration and explanation of these items (Wechsler, 1955, 1981). Only severely retarded or impaired adults are unable to succeed on either trial of the first two items. The third item of the WAIS is much easier than the second one and is given to all subjects, regardless of their performance on items 1 or 2. No demonstrations are allowed after the first two items. The test is normally discontinued after three failures.

The examiner may wish to vary the standard procedures to give the patient an opportunity to solve problems failed under standard conditions or to bring out different aspects of the patient's approach to the Block Design problems. As on the other timed tests, it is useful to obtain two scores if the patient fails an item because he exceeded the time limit. When the examiner times discreetly, the patient remains unaware that he has overrun his time so that if he completes the design correctly, he will have the full satisfaction of his success. Usually, permitting the patient to complete the design correctly means waiting an extra minute or half minute beyond the allotted time. With a very slow patient, the examiner has to decide whether waiting the five or seven minutes the patient takes to work at a problem is time well spent observing him or providing an opportunity for success; whether the patient's struggle to do a difficult or perhaps impossible task distresses him excessively; or whether the patient needs the extra time if he is to succeed at this kind of task at all. It is usually worthwhile to wait out a very slow patient on at least one design to see him work through a difficult problem from start to finish and to gauge his persistence. However, if the patient is obviously in over his depth and either does not appreciate this or refuses to admit defeat, the examiner needs to intervene tactfully before the task so upsets or fatigues him that he becomes reluctant to continue taking any kind of test.

Brain damaged patients sometimes do not comprehend the Block Design task when given the standard instructions alone. An accompanying verbal explanation like the following may help clarify the demonstration: "This lower left-hand [patient's left] corner is all red, so I put an all red block here. The lower right-hand corner is also all red, so I put another all red block there. Above it in the upper right corner goes what I call a 'half-and-half' block [red and white halves divided along the diagonal]; the red runs along the top and inside so I'll put it above the right-hand red block this way (emphasizing the angulation of the diagonal)", etc. Following completion of the test the examiner can bring out any design that puzzled the patient or elicited an atypical solution and ask him to try again. The examiner can then test for the nature of the patient's difficulty by having him verbalize as he works, by breaking up the design and constructing and reconstructing it in small sections to see if simplification and practice help, or by giving the patient blocks to copy instead of the smaller sized and unlined printed design. The examiner can test the patient's perceptual accuracy alone by asking him to identify correct and incorrect block reproductions of the designs (Bortner and Birch, 1962).

Block Design lends itself well to qualitative evaluation. The manner in which the patient works at Block Design can reveal a great deal about his thinking processes, work habits, temperament, and attitudes toward himself. The ease and rapidity with which the patient relates the individual block sides to the design pattern give some indication of his level of visuospatial conceptualization. At the highest level is the patient who comprehends the design problem at a glance (forms a *gestalt* or unified concept) and scarcely looks at it again while putting the blocks together rapidly and correctly. Patients taking a little longer to study the design, who perhaps try out a block or two before proceeding without further hesitancy, or who refer back to the design continually as they work, function at a next lower level of conceptualization. Trial and error approaches contrast with the gestalt performance. In these the subject works from block to block, trying out and comparing his positioning of each block with the design before proceeding to the next one. This kind of performance is typical of persons in the *average* ability range. These people may never perceive the design as a total configuration, nor even appreciate the squared format, but by virtue of accurate perception and orderly work habits, many can solve even the most difficult of the design problems. Most people of *average* or better ability do form immediate gestalts of at least five of the easiest designs and then automatically shift to a trial and error approach at the point that the complexity of the design surpasses their conceptual level. Thus, another indicator of ability level on this perceptual organization task is the level of the most difficult design that the subject comprehends immediately.

The patient's problem-solving techniques reflect his work habits. Orderliness and planning are among the characteristics of working behavior that the block-manipulating format makes manifest. Some patients always work in the same direction, from left to right and up to down, for example, whereas others tackle whatever part of the design meets their eye and continue in helter-skelter fashion. Most subjects quickly appreciate that each block is identical, but some turn around each new block they pick up, looking for the desired side, and if it does not turn up at first they will set that block aside for another one. Some work so hastily that they misposition blocks and overlook errors through carelessness, whereas others may be slow but so methodical that they never waste a movement. Ability to perceive errors and willingness to correct them are also important aspects of the patient's work habits that can be readily seen on Block Design.

Temperamental characteristics, such as cautiousness, carefulness, impulsivity, impatience, apathy, etc., appear in the manner in which the patient responds to the problems. Self-deprecatory or self-congratulatory statements, requests for help, rejection of the task and the like betray the patient's feelings about himself.

The examiner should record significant remarks as well as the kinds of errors and manner of solution. For quick, successful solutions, he usually needs to note only whether the approach was conceptual or trial and error, and if trial and error, whether it was methodical or random. To some extent, time taken to solve a design will also indicate the patient's conceptual level and working efficiency since gestalt solutions generally take less time than those solved by methodical trial and error, which, in turn, generally are quicker than random trial and error solutions. It thus makes sense that high scores on this test depend to some extent on speed, particularly for younger subjects. For example, persons under the age of 35 cannot get scores above the 75th percentile (i.e., above the *average* range) without earning time credits. The examiner can document the patient's difficulties, his false starts, and incorrect solutions by sketching them on the margin of the Record Form, on a piece of paper kept handy for this purpose, or on a supplemental form that provides spaces for recording the designs. Of particular value in understanding and describing the patient's performance are sequential sketches of the evolution of a correct solution out of initial errors or of the compounding of errors and snowballing confusion of an ultimately failed design (e.g., Fig. 3-4a, p. 57).

Block Design is generally recognized as the best measure of visuospatial organization in the Wechsler scales. It reflects general ability to a moderate extent so that intellectually capable but academically or culturally limited persons frequently obtain their highest score on this test.

Block Design scores tend to be lower in the presence of any kind of brain injury. They are likely to be least affected when the lesion is confined to the left hemisphere, except when the left parietal lobe is involved (McFie, 1975). They tend to be moderately depressed by diffuse or bilateral brain lesions such as those resulting from traumatic injuries or diffuse degenerative processes that do not primarily involve cortical tissue.

Patients with diffuse loss of cortical neurons like that which characterizes Alzheimer's disease, severe damage to prefrontal cortex, or extensive right hemisphere damage that includes the parietal lobe are all likely to perform very poorly on this test, but in different ways (e.g., Luria, 1973). In the very early stages of the disease, Alzheimer's patients will understand the task and may be able to copy one or two designs. However, these patients soon get so confused between one block and another or between their constructions and the examiner's model that they may even be unable to imitate the placement of just one or two blocks. The quality of "stickiness," often used to describe the performance of organically impaired patients but hard to define, here takes on concrete meaning when patients place their blocks on the design cards or adjacent to the examiner's model and appear unable to respond in any other way.

Patients with severe damage to the frontal lobes may display a similar stickiness despite assertions that they understand the task. With less severe damage, frontal lobe patients may fail items because of impulsivity and carelessness, a concrete perspective that prevents logical analysis of the designs with resulting random approaches to solving the problem or not seeing or correcting errors. Concrete thinking tends to show up in the first item, for such patients will try to make the sides as well as the top of their construction match that of the model; some even go so far as to lift the model to make sure they have matched the underside as well. These patients may be able to copy many of the designs quickly and accurately, but tend to fail item 8 (7 of the WAIS–R), for instance, by laying out red and white stripes with whole blocks rather than abstracting the 3×3 format and shifting their conceptualization of the design (from the mostly squared format of the first 3×3 design) to a solution based on diagonals.

The Alzheimer's patients and those frontal lobe patients who cannot make the blocks do what they want them to do can be properly described as having *constructional apraxia*. The discontinuity between intent, typically based on accurate perceptions, and action reflects the breakdown in the program of an activity that is central to the concept of apraxia.

Slowness in learning new response sets may develop with a number of conditions such as aging, a dementing process, frontal lobe disease, or head injury. The Block Design format is sufficiently unfamiliar that patients capable of performing well may do poorly at first if they have this problem. Since the first five items (four on the WAIS–R) are quite easy for persons with *average* or better constructional ability, they give the patient who is slow to learn a new set the opportunity to gain needed familiarity. These patients tend to display an interesting response pattern in which the first two items are failed or, at best, passed only on the second trial while the succeeding two or three or more items are passed, each more rapidly than the last. Those patients who are slow in learning a response set but whose ability to make constructions is good may succeed on most or even all the difficult items despite their early failure.

Block Design deficits associated with lateralized lesions are usually most common and most pronounced when the lesions involve posterior, particularly parietal, areas and are on the right side (Black and Strub, 1976; Newcombe, 1969; A. Smith, 1966b). Defective block design constructions made by patients with lesions in either hemisphere or when—under experimental conditions—a "split-brain" patient can use only one hemisphere, demonstrate that each hemisphere contributes to the realization of the design: "neither hemisphere alone is competent in this task" (Geschwind, 1979). However, the nature of the impairment tends to differ according to the side of the lesion (Consoli, 1979) (See pp. 285–286 for a discussion of these differences as they show up in relationships of scores on Block Design and Object Assembly to one another and to performances on purely visuoperceptual tests.)

Patients with left, particularly parietal, lesions tend to show confusion, simplification, and concrete handling of the design. However, their approach is likely to be orderly, they typically work from left to right as do intact subjects, and their construction usually preserves the square shape of the design. Their greatest difficulty is likely to be in placing the last block (which will typically be on their right) (McFie, 1975).

Patients with right-sided lesions may begin at the right of the design and work left. Their visuospatial deficits show up in disorientation, design distortions, and misperceptions. Some patients with severe visuospatial deficits lose sight of the squared or self-contained format of the design altogether (see Fig. 3-4a, p. 57). Left visuospatial inattention may compound these design-copying problems, resulting in two- or three-block solutions to the four-block designs, in which the whole left half or one left quadrant of the design has been omitted.

Both right and left hemisphere damaged patients make many more errors on the side of the design contralateral to the side of the lesion. Edith Kaplan has called attention to the importance of noting whether errors tend to occur more at the top or at the bottom of the constructions, as the upper visual fields have temporal lobe components while the lower fields have parietal components. Thus, a pattern of errors clustering at the top or at the bottom can also give some indication of the site and extent of the lesion.

PICTURE ARRANGEMENT

This test consists of eight sets (WAIS) or ten sets (WAIS–R) of cartoon pictures that make up stories. Each set is presented to the subject in scrambled order with instructions to rearrange the pictures to make the most sensible story (see Fig. 9-4). There are from three to six pictures in each set. Presentation is in order of increasing difficulty. Unless the subject fails both the first and second sets, all eight WAIS sets are administered. On the WAIS–R testing is discontinued after four consecutive failures. All but seriously retarded adults can do the first set (Matarazzo, 1972). Time limits range from one minute on the easiest items to two minutes on the two most difficult items. On five of the sets in each test there are two levels of accuracy. The subject can also earn time bonuses on the last two sets of the WAIS. Below age 55, the subject

Fig. 9-4. WAIS-type Picture Arrangement subtest item.

taking the WAIS must get time bonuses to obtain age-graded scaled scores in the *superior* to *very superior* classifications. As on other timed tests, the examiner should note correct solutions completed outside the time limits.

The age-graded scaled scores for Picture Arrangement, like those for Similarities, appear to be overly lenient at older age levels. From age 55 on, a person can fail all but the three easiest items and still obtain a score within the *average* range (e.g., at 55 a raw score of 12 on the WAIS, 5 on the WAIS–R, becomes a scaled score of 8; at 70 they each become a scaled score of 10! Yet at age 20, the same raw scores convert to a scaled score of 5, within the *borderline defective* range, which classification gives a more accurate estimate of the level of such a performance. This skew also gives what strikes me as spuriously high age-graded scaled scores to performances that at younger ages, receive scaled scores in the *average* to *high average* ranges. Therefore, discretion is recommended in interpreting the WAIS Picture Arrangement age-graded scaled scores for older persons.

Like most of the other subtests, there are common failures made by patients whose functioning on this test is not organically impaired, and there are atypical failures that most likely result from conceptual confusion, perceptual distortion, or judgmental and reasoning problems. For example, many persons, particularly young men who have been arrested and detained for a minor offense, quite reasonably arrange item 3 on the WAIS incorrectly, for they were jailed briefly before appearing in court to be acquitted or placed on probation. Although this common, incorrect arrangement receives zero credit, the examiner should take this "correct" solution into account when evaluating subtest scores. Another common failure involves displacement of the last card to the beginning of the sequence on item 4. This arrangement reflects orderly sequential thinking in a person who misses the point of the joke. It needs to be interpreted differently than some other erroneous sequence on this set. A few sharp-eyed persons have difficulty solving the WAIS version of item 4 because they spot the printing error which left one boy's pants white on card 6 although they are black on the other cards (Cooley and Miller, 1979).

It is good practice to have the subject "tell the story" of his arrangement of the cartoons. This enables the examiner to sample the subject's ability for verbal organization of complex sequentially ordered visual data. In order to prevent the subject from noticing an error while telling the story, the examiner can remove the cards first. Since this makes the story-telling requirement a test of immediate memory as well, stories given by those few patients whose memory defects involve confabulation are likely to deviate from their arrangements considerably, but they are also likely to be identifiable by extraneous intrusions that, in themselves, will be of interest. Absence of the pictures does not seem to affect the stories given by most subjects. To save time, I usually request stories for only two or three items and, on less than perfect performances, I always include at least one passed and one failed item. On those not infrequent occasions when I discover that a patient made the correct arrangement by chance or for the wrong reasons, I have them tell stories for all subsequent items.

I usually include item 5, whether passed or failed, among the requests for stories because it can be misinterpreted in ways that may show patients' preoccupations along with their difficulties comprehending visual information or integrating sequential material. The most common erroneous solution to this item (OPESN) was explained by a 31-year-old construction worker with a high school education who had incurred a head injury in an accident ten months earlier:

> It looks like the man is trying a door. He walks up to the door and tries to open it. He just tries to open it and he walks away and another man follows just behind him and just opens the door and doesn't have any trouble opening it.

This patient's age-graded scaled score for Picture Arrangement was 12. A 49-year-old investment counselor, who had done graduate work in Business Administration, was examined approximately one year after he had a cardiac arrest and fell to the ground, receiving a right frontal injury. He obtained a WAIS scaled score of 5 on this test as he only did the first two items correctly. His arrangement on this item was correct, but not his explanation:

> Looks like it was locked there. But there must be room for more than one. There's three darned people involved. One guy with the black hat went into wherever it was and then he came out and then the other gentleman entered.

Not surprisingly, this once highly organized patient was having a great deal of difficulty appreciating his changed situation and dealing with it reasonably. Another patient, an architectural draftsman aged 35, had sustained a severe left frontal head injury with coma and transient right-sided weakness ten years before being seen for neuropsychological assessment. He too made a correct arrangement for this item, which he interpreted as, "A guy tried to break into the house and the owner was coming home. Then he walked away."

Other than a modest correlation with the general ability factor, Picture Arrangement has little in common with other subtests or with the prominent WAIS battery factors. It tends to reflect social sophistication so that, in unimpaired subjects, it serves as a nonverbal counterpart of that aspect of Comprehension. Its humorous content not only enhances its sensitivity to socially appropriate thinking, but also provides an opportunity for a particular kind of social response and interplay within the test setting. Sequential thinking—including the ability to see relationships between events, establish priorities, and order activities chronologically—also plays a significant role in this subtest.

Picture Arrangement tends to be vulnerable to brain injury in general. Right hemisphere lesions have a more depressing effect on these scores than left hemisphere lesions (McFie, 1975). A low Picture Arrangement score in itself is likely to be associated with right temporal lobe damage (Dodrill and Wilkus, 1976b; Long and Brown, 1979; Piercy, 1964). Meier and French (1966) reported that right temporal lobectomy for control of seizures had a significantly depressing effect on their patients' Picture Arrangement scores relative to the other subtest scores when measured one and three years after surgery. Patients whom I have seen with focal right temporal damage consistently do poorly on this subtest but, contrary to Meier and French's findings, patients who have undergone a lobectomy on the right have typically obtained Picture Arrangement scores that were not lower than their other scores. Milner (1954) concluded from similar observations that, "greater deterioration may result from the presence of abnormally functioning tissue than from mere absence of tissue" (see also pp. 207–208).

McFie (1975) and K. Walsh (1978b) call attention to tendencies displayed by some patients with frontal damage to shift the cards only a little if at all and to present this response (or nonresponse) as a solution. Walsh suggests that this behavior is akin to the tendency, described by Luria (1973a), of patients with frontal lobe lesions to make hypotheses impulsively and uncritically based on first impressions or on whatever detail first catches the eye, without analyzing the entire situation.

OBJECT ASSEMBLY

This test contains four cut-up cardboard figures of familiar objects given in order of increasing difficulty (see Fig. 9-5). In order of presentation, the objects are a manikin, a profile, a hand, and an elephant. All responses are scored for both time and accuracy. Although each item has a time limit (2 minutes for the two easiest puzzles, three minutes for the others), unlike Block Design and Picture Arrangement, partially complete responses receive credit too. All the items are administered to every subject.

Object Assembly has the lowest association with general intellectual ability of all the Performance Scale subtests and is second only to Digit Span in weakness on this factor. In normal individuals, the Object Assembly performance level tends to vary relatively independently of other subtest performances. Like Block Design, it is a relatively pure measure of the visuospatial organization ability. It requires little abstract thinking. Ability to form visual concepts is needed for an adequate performance on this test; ability to form visual concepts *quickly* and translate them into rapid hand responses is essential for an *average* or better score. Thus, Object Assembly

Fig. 9-5. WAIS-type Object Assembly subtest item.

is as much a test of speed of visual organization and motor response as it is of the capacity for visual organization itself.

The puzzles are relatively simple. Even moderately retarded adults can put the manikin together, and more than half of all adults can complete all four puzzles successfully (Matarazzo, 1972). Since 15 of the 44 possible WAIS points and 12 of the WAIS–R's 41 Object Assembly score points are awarded for performance speed, up to age 35 differentiation of performance levels above the *average* range depends solely on time bonuses. Beyond that age, the importance of time diminishes, but even at age 70, all differentiations among the 25% of the population scoring above the 75th percentile occur on the basis of time alone.

The speed component of Object Assembly renders it relatively vulnerable to brain damage generally. Since it tests constructional ability, Object Assembly tends to be sensitive to posterior lesions, more so to those on the right than the left (Black and Strub, 1976; Long and Brown, 1979). Object Assembly and Block Design correlate more highly with one another than with any other WAIS subtests, reflecting their similarity in requiring the subject to synthesize a construction from discrete parts, and probably reflecting the speed component as well. Thus, many patients, particularly those with right posterior lesions, who do poorly on one of these two tests are also likely to do poorly on the other.

The patterns of variations of Block Design and Object Assembly scores relative to one another and to other tests allow the examiner to infer the different functions that contribute to success on these tasks.

1. *Impaired ability for visuospatial manipulation.* The constructional rather than the perceptual component of these constructional tasks is implicated when the patient performs better on such tests of visuoperceptual conceptualization and organization as the Hooper Visual Organization Test (see pp. 357–358) than on those requiring a constructed solution. This problem was described well by a 64-year-old logger who had had a right, predominantly temporoparietal stroke with transient mild left hemiparesis two years before taking the WAIS. When confronted with the Elephant puzzle he said, "I know what it's supposed to be but I can't do anything."

2. *Impaired ability for visuospatial conceptualization.* Patients who appear unable to visualize or conceptualize what the Object Assembly constructions should be can put them together in piecemeal fashion by matching lines and edges in a methodical manner although, typically, they do not recognize what they are making until the puzzle is almost completely assembled. They are as capable of accepting grossly inaccurate constructions as correct solutions. They also tend to fail Block Design items that do not lend themselves to a verbalized solution. Like the next group, they have difficulty with purely perceptual tasks such as the Hooper. Unlike the next group, their ability to conceptualize what they are doing does not seem to benefit from visuomotor stimulation, although their visuomotor coordination and control may be excellent. Their damage almost invariably involves the right posterior cortex.

3. *Ability for visuospatial conceptualization dependent on visuomotor activity.* Another group of patients, who typically have at least some right parietal damage, perform both Block Design and Object Assembly by using trial and error to manipulate their way to acceptable solutions without having to rely solely on discrete features or verbal guidance. They do much worse on purely perceptual tasks such as the Hooper. These patients seem unable to form visuospatial concepts before seeing the actual objects, but their perceptions are sufficiently accurate and their self-correcting abilities sufficiently intact that as they manipulate the pieces they can identify correct relationships and thus use their evolving visual concepts to guide them.

4. *Impaired ability to appreciate details.* Patients with left hemisphere damage who do poorly on this test usually get low scores on Block Design as well. These patients tend to rely on the overall contours of the puzzle pieces but disregard such details as internal features or relative sizes of the pieces (e.g., of the fingers on Hand).

5. *Structure dependency.* Patients who can only perform satisfactorily when a framework or pattern is given that they can follow may be able to put together the block designs and perform Raven's Matrices (see pp. 502–504) at an acceptable level since they can follow or pick out a ready-made pattern, but they tend to have much more trouble with Object Assembly or the Hooper since these latter tests require them to conceptualize, or at least identify, the finished product in order to assemble it mentally or actually. These patients usually have at least some frontal lobe pathology.

6. *Concrete-mindedness.* Still other patients may do all right with the first two block models but have difficulty comprehending the abstract designs on the reduced-scale pictures and thus perform poorly on Block Design. Yet they perform relatively well on Object Assembly since it involves concrete, meaningful objects. Again, some frontal pathology is usually implicated in these cases.

7. *Slowing.* The speed component probably contributes to the association of lowered Object Assembly scores with frontal lobe lesions (A. Smith, 1966b; Sheer, 1956).

10
Intellectual Ability Tests 2
Special Purpose Tests

While not designed for neuropsychological purposes, the tests described in this chapter may be useful in neuropsychological assessment in one of two ways. Some, such as many of the Stanford-Binet subtests, may contribute information about specific cognitive disabilities. Others that are not used as neuropsychological techniques can serve to make estimates of premorbid ability or to evaluate a patient's potential for schooling or employment. For tests that can help answer specific educational or vocational questions, the reader is referred to *The Eighth Mental Measurements Yearbook* (Buros, 1978).

Composite Tests

Problems of learning and adjustment in school instigated the development of most tests of intellectual ability. These tests tend to reflect their educational origins in the age ranges to which they apply and in the type of questions they contain. Moreover, although the intellectual ability tests for adults usually have been developed to aid in job assignment or vocational counseling, the influence of school testing programs can be seen in formats that tend to emphasize academically acquired skills. Thus, intellectual ability tests are more likely to provide data about verbal than other kinds of functions, and those ability tests that purport to measure nonverbal functions have verbal instructions or have been validated on verbal criteria.

Wide Range Tests

"Wide range" refers to the age span covered by a test. In contrast to the WAIS battery, children's tests, and most paper and pencil ability tests, these tests provide items and norms for age levels ranging from early childhood into the adult years. Composite wide range tests meet the need for measures of different functions at many levels of difficulty.

287

THE STANFORD-BINET INTELLIGENCE SCALE (Terman and Merrill, 1937, 1973)

The Stanford-Binet differs greatly from the WAIS. It is an omnibus test of intellectual abilities containing a very wide variety of short, one- to six-item subtests (Sattler, 1965). Its norms span the age range from two to the young adult.

Subtests are arranged in order of difficulty starting with year II at which the subject is asked to build a four-block tower, to identify pictures of three common objects by name (e.g., tree, plane, cup), to place three simple geometric wooden forms into a formboard, and to point out four body parts on a large cardboard doll (e.g., hair, mouth, feet). There are six subtests and an alternate at each level. The subtests are grouped into half-yearly age level intervals from years II to V. From V to XIV, subtest grouping continues by yearly intervals. The average child of a given age can pass most of the subtests at his own age level and few at higher levels so that the activities required at any given age level are typical for children of that age.

After year XIV, there are four more subtest groups, for Average Adult (AA) and Superior Adult (SA) I, II, and III levels. Sample SA III subtests are vocabulary test words "limpet," "flaunt," and "philanthropy"; interpretation of two proverbs such as "Let sleeping dogs lie"; and a mathematical reasoning test involving an arithmetic progression. Subtests at the AA level are equivalent in difficulty to WAIS items passed by adults of *average* intellectual ability. SA I level corresponds to the *high average* WAIS range, SA II to the *superior* WAIS range, and SA III to the *very superior* range.

Each subtest has its own administration and scoring instructions. At each level, the "pass" criterion for any given subtest is the subtest score achieved by a majority of persons at that age level. Some subtests are repeated at several age levels with a different "pass" criterion for each. For instance, Ingenuity I, which consists of three arithmetic reasoning problems (see p. 500) is one of the tests at levels XIV, AA, and SA II. At XIV, the "pass" criterion is one correct solution; at AA the criterion is two, and three correct solutions are required for credit at SA II.

The Binet also differs from the WAIS in that only 7 of its almost 120 subtests have time limits and no bonuses are awarded for fast responses. Unlike the Wechsler tests, the Binet's emphasis on purely verbal functions varies at different ages. Below age VI, roughly two out of five subtests draw on visuospatial functions, but from age VI on, less than one subtest in seven has much of a visuospatial component. Thus, adults with verbal impairments are at a decided disadvantage on the Binet, although the range and variety of verbal tasks permit testing of many more aspects of verbal functioning than does the WAIS. By the same token, although adult subjects whose disabilities are limited mainly to visuomotor, attention and tracking, or visuospatial functions will fare relatively well on the Binet, it gives the psychologist little opportunity to examine their problem areas.

In selecting subtests for their 1960 revision of the Binet, Terman and Merrill favored those correlating highly with the general ability factor, which may account for the heavy bias toward verbal tests. A content analysis of this revision divided the subtests into seven categories: language, memory, conceptual thinking, reasoning, numerical reasoning, visual-motor, and social intelligence (Sattler, 1965). Table 10-1 lists the tests by category in the order of their appearance on the test.

The Binet contributes to the neuropsychologist's test repertory in two ways. First, it provides a wide enough range of item difficulty for testing those patients who are so seriously impaired that they are unable to pass enough WAIS items to earn subtest scores much above zero. Second, many of the individual items are excellent tests of one or another of the functions and skills that come under investigation in neuropsychological studies. In reviewing Binet data from a series of patients who had had neurosurgery, Hebb (1942, p. 281) noted the sensitivity of such subtests as "Maze tracing, sentence completion, differentiation of abstract words, giving of opposites, analogies, speeded block-manipulation tasks, and picture absurdities" to the presence of brain injury. Some of these Binet subtests have similar counterparts in WAIS items. However, many of them measure very different aspects of common mental activities. They may provide data to confirm or reject the presence of a specific kind of intellectual dysfunction or to clarify its nature or its functional relationships. Although few of the Binet items reoccur at enough levels of the test to allow discriminating scoring at every level, the item by item age or ability level grading enables the examiner to evaluate each Binet subtest performance separately and also to compare it with performance on other tests.

To use the Binet Scale for a severely retarded adult, the examiner can simply follow the administration instructions in the manual. Neuropsychological evaluation does not require computation of the MA score or IQ score. The Binet examination can provide a richly descriptive evaluation in which the age-grades of the subtests serve as points of reference. The summed MA or IQ scores, like WAIS scores, obscure the strengths and weaknesses of the patient's performance. The examiner may prefer to use a battery-type children's test for a wider range of difficulty and finer scaling of individual subtests and for their ease of administration and interpretation (see pp. 295–299 for a discussion of children's tests).

Individual Binet subtests can be given as single tests. Since there are few guidelines for selecting a test of some particular function or set of functions (see for example, Table 10-1), the examiner must select most Binet subtests on the basis of their face validity and can only draw a conclusion about the patient's performance relative to the average person at the age or ability level at which the subtest appears on the scale. With the exception of those subtests that have counterparts at other levels of the scale, if the patient passes a subtest, the examiner does not know how much better he could do, and if he fails, the examiner does not know at what lower level he could pass it.

The neuropsychologist who wants an extensive repertory of easily administered and scored assessment techniques should familiarize himself with both the 1937 and 1960 revisions of the Binet Scale. A few subtests were omitted, mostly from Form M, when the two alternate forms of the 1937 revision were merged into the current Form L-M. Some of the omitted subtests are like Form L-M subtests, but their content puts them at different levels of difficulty. By making use of these Form M subtests, the examiner can evaluate similar test behavior at different levels of difficulty.

Table 10-1 Analysis of Functions Tested in the 1960 Stanford-Binet Intelligence Scale[a]

Language (L)

(1)II,3:	Identifying parts of the body; (5) II–6, 2
(2) II, 5:	Picture vocabulary: (7) II–6, 4; (8) III, 2; (9) IV, 1
(3) II, 6:	Word combinations
II, A:	Identifying objects by name
(4) II–6, 1:	Identifying objects by use
(6) II–6, 3:	Naming objects
(10) IV, 4:	Pictorial identification; IV–6, A
(11) V, 3:	Definitions
(12) VI, 1:	Vocabulary; (13) VIII, 1; (15) X, 1; (19) XII, 1; (24) XIV, 1; (25) AA, 1; (28) SAI, 1; (31) SAII, 1; (32) SAIII, 1
(14) IX, 4:	Rhymes: New form
IX, A;	Rhymes: Old form
(16) X, 3:	Abstract words I; (20) XII, 5
(17) X, 5:	Word naming
(18) XI, 3:	Abstract words II; (22) XIII, 2
(21) XII, 6:	Minkus completion I
(23) XIII, 5:	Dissected sentences
(26) AA, 3:	Differences between abstract words
(27) AA, 8:	Abstract words III
(29) SAI, 3:	Minkus completion II
(30) SAI, 5:	Sentence building

Memory (M)

Meaningful Memory (mM)

(3) IV, 2:	Naming objects from memory
IV, A:	Memory for sentences I
(4) IV–6, 5:	Three commissions
(6) VIII, 2:	Memory for stories: The Wet Fall
(11) XI, 4:	Memory for sentences II
(13) XIII, 3:	Memory for sentences III
(16) SAII, 6:	Repeating thought of passage I: Value of Life
(17) SAIII, 6:	Repeating thought of passage II: Tests

Nonmeaningful Memory (nmM)

(1) II–6, 5:	Repeating 2 digits
III, A:	Repeating 3 digits
(5) VII, 6:	Repeating 5 digits
VII, A:	Repeating 3 digits reversed
(8) IX, 6:	Repeating 4 digits reversed
(9) X, 6:	Repeating 6 digits
(12) XII, 4:	Repeating 5 digits reversed
(15) SAI, 4:	Repeating 6 digits reversed

Visual Memory (vM)

(2) III, 4:	Picture memories
(7) IX, 3:	Memory for designs I; (10) XI, 1
XII, A:	Memory for designs II
(14) XIII, 6:	Copying a bead chain from memory

Conceptual Thinking (CT)

(1) IV, 3:	Opposite analogies I; (2) IV–6, 2
(3) VI, 2:	Differences
(4) VI, 5:	Opposite analogies II
(5) VII, 2:	Similarities: Two things
(6) VII, 5:	Opposite analogies III
(7) VIII, 4:	Similarities and differences
(8) XI, 6:	Similarities: Three things
(9) XIV, 6:	Reconciliation of opposites; SAI, A
(10) AA, 5:	Proverbs I
(11) AA, 7:	Essential differences; (14) SAII, 5
(12) SAI, 6:	Essential similarities
(13) SAII, 3:	Proverbs II
(15) SAIII, 2:	Proverbs III
(16) SAIII, 3:	Opposite analogies IV
SAIII, A:	Opposite analogies V

Reasoning (R)

Nonverbal Reasoning (nvR)

(1) II, 2:	Delayed response
(2) III–6, 1:	Comparison of balls
(3) III–6, 2:	Patience: Pictures
(4) III–6, 3:	Discrimination of animal pictures

290

(5) III–6, 5:	Sorting buttons		*Visual-Motor* (VM)	
III–6, A:	Comparison of sticks	(1) II, 1:	Three-hole form board	
(6) IV, 5:	Discrimination of forms	(2) II, 4:	Block building; Tower	
(7) IV–6, 3:	Pictorial similarities and differences I	II–6, A:	Three-hole form board: Rotated	
(8) V, 5:	Pictorial similarities and differences II	(3) III, 1:	Stringing beads	
		(4) III, 3:	Block building: Bridge	
(9) V, 6:	Patience: Rectangles	(5) III, 5:	Copying a circle	
(10) VI, 3:	Mutilated pictures	(6) III, 6:	Drawing a vertical line	
(15) XIII, 1:	Plan of search	(7) V, 1:	Picture completion: Man	
(18) XIV, 5:	Orientation: Direction I	(8) V, 2:	Paper folding: Triangle	
(19) AA, 6:	Orientation: Direction II	(9) V, 4:	Copying a square	
(21) SAIII, 1:	Orientation: Direction III	V, A:	Knot	

Verbal Reasoning (vR)

(11) VIII, 3:	Verbal absurdities I
(12) IX, 2:	Verbal absurdities II; (14) XII, 2
X, A:	Verbal absurdities III
(13) XI, 2:	Verbal absurdities IV
(16) XIII, 4:	Problems of fact
(17) XIV, 3:	Reasoning I
(20) SAII, 2:	Finding reasons III
SAII, A:	Codes
(22) SAIII, 5:	Reasoning II

(10) VI, 6:	Maze tracing
(11) VII, 3:	Copying a diamond
(12) IX, 1:	Paper cutting; XIII, A
AA, A:	Binet paper cutting

Social Intelligence (SI)

(1) II–6, 6:	Obeying simple commands
(2) III–6, 4:	Response to pictures; VI, A
(3) III–6, 6:	Comprehension I
(4) IV–6:	Comprehension II
(5) IV–6, 1:	Aesthetic comparison
(6) IV–6, 4:	Materials
(7) IV–6, 6:	Comprehension III
(8) VII, 1:	Picture absurdities I
(9) VII, 4:	Comprehension IV; (10) VIII, 5
(11) VIII, 6:	Naming the days of the week
VIII, A:	Problem situations I
(12) X, 4:	Finding reasons I
(13) XI, 5:	Problem situation II
XI, A:	Finding reasons II
(14) XII, 3:	Picture absurdities II: The Shadow

Numerical Reasoning (NR)

(1) VI, 4:	Number concepts
(2) IX, 5:	Making change
(3) X, 2:	Block counting
(4) XIV, 2:	Induction
(5) XIV, 4:	Ingenuity I; (6) AA, 2; (9) SAII, 4
XIV, A:	Ingenuity II
(7) AA, 4:	Arithmetical reasoning
(8) SAI, 2:	Enclosed box problem

Note: Alternate items not designated by number.
[a]Form L-M (Sattler, 1965).

Individual Binet subtests fit well into larger test batteries constructed for specific research purposes. For example, Eson and his co-workers (1978) include 20 Binet subtests from age levels IV through IX in a battery designed for serial neuropsychological assessment of adult head injury patients from the time they emerge from coma until maximum return of function.

For clinical purposes, Binet material can be used with patients who are too impaired to make meaningful responses to the relatively complex Wechsler items.

A right-handed, 68-year-old retired logger was referred for neuropsychological assessment with a three-year history of increasing confusion. He was described as withdrawn, apathetic, and forgetful, and his speech had become "vague." Most recently he was unable to recognize his children and his grandchildren. CT scan showed general cortical atrophy, consistent with Alzheimer's disease, and an old left hemisphere infarct.

On examination it quickly became evident that this patient was unable to respond to the WAIS subtests calling for verbal response, although he did copy the third block design correctly (after first placing the blocks *on* the design booklet). The examiner therefore turned to the Binet for easier items to evaluate functions that could not be examined effectively with the WAIS. On the Binet, the patient gave evidence of low-level and variable verbal comprehension (Identifying Objects, year II [1 of 1]; Obeying Simple Commands, year III–6 [1 of 3]; Identifying Objects by Use, year II–6 [3 of 3]); a ten-second simple immediate memory span (a variant of Naming Objects from Memory, year IV, using pointing rather than naming [1 of 1]); and basic counting ability (Number Concepts, year VI [3 of 3]), but he could not verbalize at will (Identifying Objects by Name, year II [0/5]). The findings of this examination were used to help his wife accept and plan for nursing home placement.

Application of particular Binet subtests to specific problems in neuropsychological assessment will be discussed in Chapters 11 through 16 under the appropriate topic heading.

THE PEABODY INDIVIDUAL ACHIEVEMENT TEST (PIAT) (Dunn and Markwardt, 1970)

This test battery measures academic achievement for school grades from kindergarten to grade 12. Its wide coverage of achievement levels makes it a valuable instrument for measuring residual intellectual competency of brain injured adults. By virtue of its focus on academic skills, the PIAT primarily tests verbal conceptual functions. However, the stimulus material is mostly visual—both verbal and pictorial in content—so that a variety of visuoperceptual functions enter into the PIAT performance too. No complex motor responses are required of the subject, making this an excellent instrument for use with physically handicapped patients. It was standardized on a carefully randomized national population. The PIAT is an untimed test designed to take from 30 to 40 minutes to administer (Fig. 10-1).

There are five subtests in the battery. (1) Mathematics is a multiple-choice test on which patients with impaired speech need only point to an answer. It begins with simple number and symbol recognition and ends with algebra and geometry problems. (2) On Reading Recognition, the subject answers the first nine items by pointing, but the remaining items require his verbal response. Items 10 to 17 present single letters, and the remaining items call for correct pronunciation of increasingly difficult words. At the lowest reading level are the words "run," "play," and "jump"; the most difficult word is "apophthegm." (3) The Reading Comprehension subtest requires the subject to select which of four line drawings is described in a printed sentence. Items range in difficulty from a simple, straightforward sentence containing six one-syllable

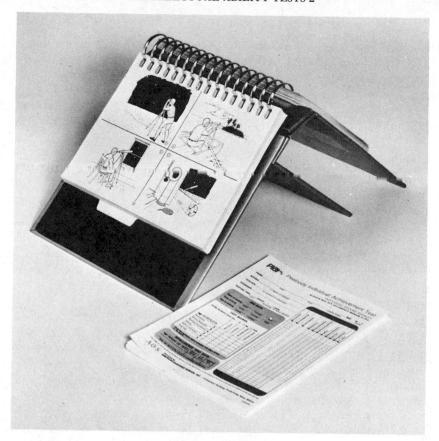

Fig. 10-1. The Peabody Individual Achievement Test.

words to a complex sentence with several modifying clauses and 31 words of which 12 are at high school and college reading levels. (4) The Spelling subtest is also multiple choice and covers the full range of difficulty levels. The first 14 items test letter and word recognition; the remainder present the correct spelling and three incorrect alternatives for words in a sentence read aloud by the examiner. (5) The General Information subtest is a question and answer test of common information.

All subtests have 84 items except Reading Comprehension, which has 66. Each subtest has its own norms for converting raw scores into grade equivalents and age equivalents, as well as percentile ranks for each grade level, Kindergarten through 12, and percentile ranks for each age level "5–3 to 5–5" through "18–0 to 18–3." Thus, each subtest can be used apart from the battery as a whole. Further, the PIAT's variety of norms gives the examiner the option of using different norms to facilitate comparisons of PIAT performance with that of almost any other test.

The Wide Range Achievement Test (WRAT) (Jastak and Jastak, 1965)

This battery format instrument earns its "wide range" title by its applicability from early childhood through the middle adult years. It tests three academic skills—spelling, reading, and arithmetic—each at two age ranges or "Levels." The Level I age range is from five through 11; Level II covers ages 12 to "45–0 and over."

The Level I Spelling test comes in three parts: copying a short set of nonsense figures and writing one's name are tasks only at Level I; a dictation task differs from the Level II Spelling test in word difficulty. Both Arithmetic levels have two parts, an orally administered section for the lowest achievement levels, and a written arithmetic test. Ten minutes are allowed for written arithmetic at both levels. Reading begins with letter reading and recognition at Level I and continues with a 75-word reading and pronunciation list. At Level II, Reading involves only the word list.

This test is carefully standardized with a full set of norms for each subtest. Level I has age norms for each half-yearly interval between ages 5 and 12. Level II age norms continue at half-yearly intervals from 12 to 16; from 16 to 20, they span two-year intervals, and from 20 to 45 they cover five-year intervals. All raw scores can be converted to school grades, standard scores, or percentiles. Thus, this is a flexible test, adaptable for inclusion in any set of tests.

The standard deviation of the WRAT is only 10 (see p. 145). With a mean set at 100, an examiner familiar with the scoring systems of the Wechsler or Stanford-Binet scales may misinterpret the WRAT scores if the smaller standard deviation is not taken into account.

All three WRAT subtests are heavily weighted with the general ability factor, and the verbal factor contributes a large component to Reading and Spelling. Arithmetic has little of the verbal factor, but a "motivation" factor is involved.

The WRAT Arithmetic subtest tests the ability to perform written arithmetic. A feature of the WRAT Arithmetic test that is valuable for neuropsychological assessment is the variety of mathematical problems it poses. These include application of the four basic arithmetic operations to two- and three-digit numbers, to decimals, percentages, fractions, and to algebraic problems, as well as the translation of Roman numerals, weights, and measures. Problems concerning squares, roots, and some geometric constructs are also presented. Thus, when a patient's mathematical performance is defective, the examiner can determine by inspection of his worksheet whether his difficulties are due to a dyscalculia of the spatial type, a symbol or number alexia, or an anarithmetria in which number concepts or basic operations have been lost. The lower level arithmetic problems can be given when the patient is unable to do enough at the adult level for a fair sampling of his arithmetic skills.

The Arithmetic subtest does have some drawbacks when used for neuropsychological purposes. Many brain damaged patients are unable to answer more than a few items within the allotted ten minutes. To evaluate a performance on the basis of the test norms, which take time into account, the examiner need only note how much of the test the patient completed at ten minutes, without disturbing the patient. Stopping the patient before he has finished may greatly restrict the amount of information that can be obtained about his ability to do arithmetic and the nature of any disability he may have in this area. The small print and scant space surrounding each problem can create some difficulty, particularly for older patients and patients with visual acuity problems. A larger scale version of this test, allowing for more computation space around each problem, would solve this difficulty and make it easier for the examiner to follow the patient's computational efforts. The standard score and percentile norms reflect a performance decline from ages 25 to 50, but they do not take into account differences at older age levels.

Children's Tests

Patients with severe intellectual handicaps may give so few scorable responses to some or all of the WAIS subtests that the examiner has little opportunity to assess their capabilities or the relative strengths and weaknesses of different functions. Children's or infant's tests may enable them to display a broader range of their behavior than and preschool levels but lacks the advantages of battery tests. Four of the best known children's tests—the Wechsler Intelligence Scale for Children, The Wechsler Preschool and Primary Test of Intelligence, the Pictorial Test of Intelligence, and the Illinois Test of Psycholinguistic Abilities—are in battery form. A fifth, the Leiter, is a nonverbal counterpart of the Binet intended for use with patients who have speech and hearing handicaps.

The Wechsler Intelligence Scale For Children (WISC and WISC-R)
(Wechsler, 1949, 1974)

The WISC covers the age range from 5 to 15 years 11 months, and the age range of its revision, the WISC-R, is 6 years to 16 years 11 months. They contain the same subtests as the WAIS in an almost identical format, but all of the subtests except Digit Span begin with considerably simpler items. Although most WISC and WISC-R items are the same, outmoded WISC items have been dropped from the WISC-R, and some of the new WISC-R picture items have black or female subjects. The WISC-R blocks conform to the two-color (red and white) WAIS blocks, replacing the four-color WISC blocks. The number sequences of the WISC and WISC-R Digit Span subtest are the same length and difficulty as those of the WAIS. There is an alternate form of Digit Symbol (called Coding on the WISC) for children under nine on the WISC, under eight on the WISC-R, and suspected mental defectives. Coding uses five geometric symbols (star, circle, etc.) instead of numbers, and the symbols to be written in are simpler than those of the more difficult WISC version of the WAIS. Administration instructions are similar, and for many subtests, identical, to those of the WAIS.

Standard score equivalents of WISC and WISC-R subtest raw scores are given for each four-month interval covered by the scale. However, in interpreting WISC and WISC-R scores for adult patients, the examiner should use the Table of Test Age Equivalents (p. 113 of the WISC Manual, p. 189 of the WISC-R Manual), which will give the age equivalents of the patient's score on any of the WISC subtests.

The WISC contains a maze test that has no WAIS counterpart. It consists of printed mazes (eight on the WISC, nine on the WISC-R) of varying sizes and complexity, which are given in order of difficulty. Scoring is based on the number of errors; there are no time bonuses. Although the range of difficulty is neither as high nor as low as the Porteus Mazes, I find the all-on-one-page format of the WISC mazes easier to administer. Mazes have been used to measure general ability as well as specific non-verbal reasoning and visuopractic functions. For further discussion of maze tests, see pp. 511–512.

There is no overlap between the WAIS and the WISC age norms. The WISC-R overlaps the WAIS at age 16, but 16 year olds tend to obtain slightly higher scores on the WAIS than the WISC-R. However, there is a great deal of overlap in item difficulty. Thus, severely impaired patients cannot succeed on many more WISC or WISC-R than WAIS items, although several of the WISC-R subtests provide a fuller coverage than their WISC counterparts at the youngest age levels. Even the WISC's simpler items may be too difficult for the profoundly impaired patient.

Wechsler Preschool and Primary Scale of Intelligence (WPPSI)
(Wechsler, 1967)

This scale was developed to provide better Wechsler test norms at the lowest WISC levels where the original WISC standardization tends to be unsatisfactory for children of average or lower ability and to extend Wechsler test coverage downward another year below the WISC. Its age range is four to six and one-half years.

Eight of the eleven subtests of the WPPSI have WISC counterparts, and of these eight, one-third to two-thirds of the test questions are similar or identical to WISC items. All the Verbal Scale subtests of the WISC and WAIS are represented on the WPPSI except Digit Span. Apart from the first four Arithmetic items, which use pictures to test quantity concepts, the formats of the verbal subtests are identical with those of their WISC and WAIS counterparts, differing only in range and difficulty level. The Sentences test substitutes for Digit Span as the test of immediate memory span.

Of the five Performance Scale subtests, Picture Completion, Mazes, and Block Design have WISC counterparts. Instead of cubes, Block Design uses two-sided flat blocks, some painted solid red or white, some half red and half white. Of the ten designs, only the last three are copied from pictures; the rest are copied from models the examiner builds. The flat blocks change the nature of the task radically so that, although the last three designs are from the WISC, this subtest is actually not an extension of the WAIS Block Design. The first six mazes are line mazes; the rest of the test consists of all but the most difficult of the WISC mazes. Animal House is new to the Wechsler tests. It presents a substitution format similar to Digit Symbol or Coding, but instead of being a paper and pencil test, it uses animal pictures and colored pegs. The child's task is to put the colored pegs into holes under the animal pictures following the pairing of animals and colored pegs displayed in a model at the top of the pegboard. Any slight motor clumsiness that slows performance penalizes the subject since the scoring is heavily dependent on time: a six year old who takes 4 minutes and 59 seconds to complete the test correctly receives a scaled score of 4; if he takes 1 minute and 59 seconds his scaled score is 9, and a 59-second performance earns him a scaled score of 14. Geometric Design is a copying task using ten simple geometric figures as models.

The WPPSI is not a test for the severely impaired patient, although a few items on each scale will be suitable for some patients who cannot handle the WISC. The added range afforded by this test is so small that few patients who are unable to perform WISC items could perform on the WPPSI instead.

THE PICTORIAL TEST OF INTELLIGENCE (PTI) (French, 1964)

This children's test in battery format was standardized on a well-randomized sample of American children from ages three to eight. It contains six subtests: (1) Picture Vocabulary tests comprehension of spoken words and picture recognition, (2) Form Discrimination is a design-matching test. (3) Information and Comprehension measures the subject's understanding of the nature and use of common objects. (4) Similarities tests the ability to abstract and generalize. (5) Size and Number involves both quantity and number concepts. (6) Immediate Recall is a recognition test based on a 5-second exposure to a picture or design.

The PTI requires no verbal or fine motor response from the subject. He need only point to or otherwise indicate one of four designs, pictures, symbols, etc., printed on a large (27 cm × 27 cm) response card. All the printed materials are uncomplicated black and white line drawings. This untimed test typically takes about half an hour to complete. Each subtest has a short form covering a restricted range of the questions for three and four-year-old children. These short forms are not appropriate for many profoundly impaired adults who may still possess some unexpected residual abilities enabling them to pass test items at higher levels than those represented on the short forms. Any given subtest can be discontinued after six consecutive failures.

The examiner may wish to change some of the wording to suit adult patients. For example, the recommended introduction to the test, "I believe that you will have a lot of fun looking at the pictures which I have in this box," might sound better to an adult as "I have a lot of pictures in this box for you to look at." Some of the Size and Number subtest questions, in particular, would benefit from rewording. For example, item 7 shows a picture of children in party dress and the examiner's introduction is, "Let's pretend that we are going to a party," which is more appropriately read to an adult as, "These pictures show a children's party."

THE LEITER INTERNATIONAL PERFORMANCE SCALE (Leiter, 1969a,b)

This instrument was devised especially for testing verbally handicapped and foreign language-speaking children. The instructions can be either spoken or pantomimed. This is not a test that is used frequently with adult populations, but it should be available as part of a standard neuropsychological battery. The Leiter was originally developed for ages 2 to 12, and it is well standardized for this group. The test also includes a set of upper level (ages 14 to Adult) subtests that are not as well standardized for validity or reliability. Test presentation follows the omnibus format.

The test material consists of a long wooden form with a slot on the top side for holding cardboard strips of varying length. Cutout squares form pockets along the length of the wooden form into which wooden block cubes can be fitted. Problems are printed on the cardboard strips. Each problem has its own set of blocks that carry the printed or painted "answers" on one side. The subject's task is to figure out the principle of the problem posed by the printed strip and insert the blocks correctly into the square pockets (see Fig. 10-2). Items include a wide variety of tasks involving pictures, colors, numbers, and geometric designs. Although this is a portable test, its bulk and weight make transportation difficult.

Like the Binet, Leiter subtests are arranged and presented in age groups, ranging from year II to year XVIII, with four subtests in each group. After year X, only even-numbered years are represented, making 13 age levels and 52 subtests in all. As with the Binet, the examiner can estimate the patient's performance level from the age grade of passed subtests. Since a number of similar tests appear at different ages and levels of difficulty, this test does provide some differentiation of performance levels for some functions such as serial reasoning and two-dimensional construction. The instructions recommend that the test begin at a level two years below the child's age to acquaint him with this unfamiliar activity on relatively easy tasks. When using the Leiter with adults, the examiner should follow the principle of beginning the test at an easily comprehended level. The examination stops when the subject has failed all the subtests of two consecutive age groups. The test is untimed except for four difficulty levels of Block Design, which allow from two and one-half to five minutes for the most difficult and easiest problems, respectively.

Fig. 10-2. The Leiter International Performance Scale test materials.

Many of the Leiter subtests are nonverbal analogues of tests that appear elsewhere, such as color, form, or picture matching; Block Design; Block Counting; and Similarities. Others are unique to the Leiter. These include tests of perceptual recognition, size and number estimation, and comprehension of sequences and progressions. For these latter subtests, the examiner must rely on his own content analysis when interpreting a patient's performance.

The Illinois Test of Psycholinguistic Abilities (ITPA) (Kirk, McCarthy, and Kirk, 1968)

This test was devised in response to the need to delineate areas of deficit in communication-related functions in young children (ages 2–7 to 10–1). It consists of 12 subtests that have been carefully standardized so that derived scores are statistically comparable. Its intended use—to provide a test profile to aid in developing an individualized remediation program—has little place in the neuropsychological assessment of adults. Nevertheless, individual subtests, such as Visual Closure (see p. 365), Visual Sequential Memory, Visual Reception, or Auditory Reception (see p. 374), are suited to the examination of some disabilities of adult patients. Of course, the lack of adult norms is a drawback. Interpretation of an adult's performance must rely on rather loose extrapolation from the highest (10+ years) norms, which does not allow for evaluation of fine gradations of performance. However, the assumption that the average adult would obtain a score at least commensurate with the highest age norm allows the examiner to judge whether an adult's performance is defective. The format of the individual tests is such that the perceptive examiner can analyze the patient's approach to a problem set and his errors so that useful inferences can be drawn from qualitative aspects of the patient's performance.

Paper and Pencil Tests

The large-scale needs of academic and vocational selection, placement, and counseling programs occasioned the development of numerous paper and pencil tests designed to measure a variety of intellectual abilities. Although some of the earlier tests of intellectual ability followed the omnibus format, most group ability tests now are batteries with two, three, or more subtests of different skills and abilities.

Paper and pencil test batteries will rarely be used in neuropsychological examinations. However, many persons seen for neuropsychological assessment will have taken one or more of them at some time in the past or recently in the course of a vocational or educational evaluation. The test results may help in estimating the level of premorbid functioning and may augment the examiner's knowledge about the patient's current abilities. The content of many of them parallels or complements individually administered batteries for testing visuospatial functions as well as verbal ones, thus permitting the testing of similar functions with different input and output modalities. Further, their large-scale, elaborate standardization procedures generally ensure statistically well-defined norms and high reliability.

Even though many of these batteries serve their purpose well, they do not substitute for individually administered tests. Many handicapped patients cannot take paper and pencil tests. Furthermore, the qualitative aspects of behavior rarely show up on multiple-choice answer sheets.

ARMED SERVICES TESTS

Army General Classification Test (AGCT) (Science Research Associates, 1948).   This is like a battery test in that it contains three different kinds of test items, (Vocabulary, Arithmetic Story Problems, and Block Counting), but it presents them in an omnibus format. The three kinds of multiple-choice items are sequentially rotated in sets of five or ten items, beginning with the ten easiest of each and continuing in order of difficulty, for a total of 150 items. The results are summed in one score.

The single score is based on a mean of 100 and a standard deviation of 20. Percentiles are also given for raw score conversions. Scores cover the entire range of nondefective adults from three standard deviations below the mean (AGCT Standard Score = 41) to three standard deviations above the mean (AGCT SS = 161). The examiner must inspect the answer sheet to find out whether there are marked performance differences between the subtests.

This test was designed to provide quick screening and classification of the intellectual ability of newly enlisted armed services personnel. Millions of young people took this test during the years 1940 to 1945. Scores from AGCT tests taken at induction were utilized in several brain function studies. The military stopped using this test in 1945, replacing it with an updated version, the *Armed Forces Qualification Test (AFQT)* (Montague et al., 1957). The AGCT then entered the civilian domain, like the Army Alpha a generation before (Army General Classification Test, 1948).

The single summed test score reduces reliable interpretation of AGCT data to the single dimension of general ability which restricts its sensitivity to brain damage. Brain injured patients generally tend to have lower postmorbid than premorbid AGCT scores (H. L. Williams, 1962). Significantly greater score depressions following frontal lobe and left hemisphere—particularly parietal and temporal lobe—injuries reflect the large role that language and speed play in this test (S. Weinstein, 1964). In reporting that patients whose lesions were situated in other areas of the brain showed no losses on this test, Teuber (1962) notes "the notorious lack of sensitivity of such routine psychometric tests in revealing residuals of brain injury."

Army Classification Battery (ACB) (Montague et al., 1957).   The ACB is not available for civilian examinations. However, all army recruits take it routinely and their scores are filed in their permanent service record. Data from this battery can provide direct measures of premorbid intellectual functioning for evaluating the extent of impairment in patients who have served in the army.

The ACB contains ten separately scored subtests. The first subtest, Reading and Vocabulary (RV), is a verbal skill test that correlates .76 with the Wechsler-Bellevue

Information and Vocabulary subtests. Arithmetic Reasoning (AR) involves story problems and thus tests both verbal and arithmetic skills, as it correlates .71 with the Wechsler Information subtest and .70 with Arithmetic and Vocabulary. The Pattern Analysis test (PA) purports to measure spatial ability but it is actually a nonverbal test of general ability, correlating most highly with the Wechsler Full Scale score (.81) and more highly with Information (.63) than with Block Design (.58). The Army Clerical Speed test (ACS-1 and ACS-2), which includes a symbol substitution task like the WAIS Digit Symbol subtest, involves visual accuracy and graphomotor speed. The Army Radio Code Aptitude test (ARC-1) is an auditory learning test. The remaining five subtests measure different areas of technical information.

VOCATIONAL GUIDANCE BATTERIES

The batteries that are most highly recommended for vocational counseling contain many subtests covering a variety of skills and abilities. They are designed as multiple-choice tests with both machine- and hand-scoring keys to facilitate group administration. This limits their applicability to patients whose verbal skills and ability to follow directions and work independently are relatively intact. With such patients, they do enable the examiner to obtain a considerable amount of information with very little effort on his part. These advantages make them attractive research tools for the study of many kinds of brain damage. Examiners may also find them clinically useful, both for the broad range of data the complete battery can provide and for testing a specific function or ability by means of one or more of the individual subtests.

Differential Aptitude Tests (DAT) (Bennett et al., 1972). This test, now in its fifth edition, consists of eight separately scored subtests, each with its own norms. Because it was designed for guidance in high schools, norms are given for each sex separately and for grades 8 through 12. Twelfth grade norms apply to young adults as well. There is a Spanish language form of the DAT.

Of the eight subtests, (1) is Verbal Reasoning (VR), a verbal analogies test. (2) Numerical Ability (NA) involves arithmetic calculation. (3) Abstract Reasoning (AR) concerns nonverbal conceptual sequences. (4) Clerical Speed and Accuracy (CSA) measures perceptual response speed. (5) Mechanical Reasoning (MR) tests the practical understanding of basic physical principles. (6) Space Relations (SR) requires translation of two-dimensional designs to three-dimensional figures. (7) Spelling (LU-1) requires identification of spelling errors. (8) Language Usage (LU-2) tests grammar. These are timed tests, the five longest taking 35–40 minutes each to explain and administer. Total testing time is five to five-and-one-half hours. Raw score conversion is to percentiles.

Studies of brain injured patients suggest that all DAT subtest scores are affected by the extent of the lesion (Lansdell, 1971). The scores of the verbal subtests (VR and LU-1 and 2) and the visuospatial tests show the greatest shift downward. The Abstract Reasoning Test may be particularly sensitive to temporal lobe damage.

Employee Aptitude Survey (EAS) (F. L. Ruch and W. W. Ruch, 1963). Ten short (testing time of 5 minutes or less) multiple-choice subtests make up a battery designed to give a profile of vocationally relevant abilities. Scoring can be done by stencils or machines. Each subtest is printed on a separate sheet and has two forms (Word Fluency has three) to allow for retesting and to reduce opportunities for "motivated applicants" to become familiar with the questions. The authors recognize the need for face validity in a battery of this type.

Each of the ten subtests is similar in format to other tests in use. (1) Verbal Comprehension is a synonym test of vocabulary. (2) Numerical Ability includes three separately timed subtests that together cover the basic arithmetic operations for integers, decimals, and fractions. (3) Visual Pursuit is similar to the Pursuit subtest of the MacQuarrie Tests (see p. 370). (4) Visual Speed and Accuracy involves checking the identity of pairs of number series. (5) Space Visualization is a block-counting task similar to MacQuarrie's Block Counting subtest (see p. 304). (6) Numerical Reasoning is a symbol pattern test that uses numbers (see p. 482). (7) Verbal Reasoning tests the ability to relate facts to conclusions. (8) Word Fluency requires the subject to write words to a given letter (see pp. 333–334). (9) Manual Speed and Accuracy is a lengthened version of MacQuarrie's Dotting subtest (see p. 303). (10) Symbolic Reasoning measures ability to evaluate symbolic relations.

Besides norms for a category called "General Productive Male Population," based on subjects aged 16 to 55 in an age distribution proportional to that of the 1950 census, norms for 40 other categories of males are given, such as Design Engineer, Inside Salesman, Junior Executive, or Electronic Technician Students. The eleven female norms include only one requiring more than a high school education (Female College Student). The ten other norms for women are for traditional office-work positions such as Typist, Figure Clerk, or Telephone Operator.

The format of these tests, their ease of presentation, and the wide choice of norms (at least for men) make these suitable for clinical and particularly research use for certain kinds of neurologically impaired patients. Binder and Schreiber (1980), for example, used the Verbal Comprehension and Space Visualization subtests to examine cognitive functions of recovering alcoholic patients and control subjects.

General Aptitude Test Battery (GATB) (United States Department of Labor, 1965). The main purpose of this battery is to provide information for job counseling and only secondarily for educational guidance. Like the armed services tests, the GATB is not available commercially. However, many patients have taken it when seeking vocational help from state employment and rehabilitation agencies either prior or subsequent to incurring their brain injury. Neuropsychologists can usually obtain a patient's scores from the appropriate agency.

There are 12 subtests in this battery, of which seven are multiple-choice paper and pencil tests. The five other subtests involve aspects of motor speed and coordination. The seven paper and pencil subtests are: (1) Name Comparisons, involving the comparison of similar and different names on two lists, is associated with a factor called Clerical Perception (Q). (2) Computation consists of nonverbal arithmetic problems testing Numerical Aptitude (N). (3) Three-Dimensional Space requires the patient to relate two- and three-dimensional aspects of the same figure, like Space Relations on the DAT, and is associated with Spatial Aptitude (S). (4) Vocabulary tests identification of similar and different words and measures Verbal Aptitude (V). (5) Tool Matching involves perceptual accuracy and a Form Perception (P) factor. (6) Arithmetic Reasoning consists of story problems and is also a measure of Numerical Aptitude (N). (7) Form Matching is another test of perceptual accuracy associated with the Form Perception (P) factor. A general ability (G) factor score is compounded from the scores on the Three-Dimensional Space, Vocabulary, and Arithmetic Reasoning subtests. The eighth test, Mark Making, is a motor speed and accuracy test associated with a Motor Coordination (K) factor. Tests 9 through 12 require apparatus, a Pegboard for the (9) Place and (10) Turn subtests measuring Manual Dexterity (M); and a Finger Dexterity Board with rivets and washers for subtests (11) Assemble and (12) Disassemble, which are both tests of Finger Dexterity (F). Total testing time runs from two to two-and-a-half hours.

The five GATB motor tests involving motor speed tend to be particularly vulnerable to chronic seizure conditions (Tellegen, 1965) and chronic alcoholism (Kish, 1970). Alcoholics displayed little deficit on the Vocabulary subtest, and the seizure patients' performance on the nonmotor parts of the test was unremarkable. The thorough factorial analysis of these tests recommends their further application to both neuropsychological research and clinical problems.

The MacQuarrie Test for Mechanical Ability (MacQuarrie, 1925, 1953). This little battery-type test was developed to aid in employee selection and job placement. Although it is a paper and pencil test designed for group administration, it examines a variety of functions that are of neuropsychological interest, such as simple visuomotor speed and accuracy, visuospatial estimation, and visual tracking. Moreover, individual subtest items enable the examiner to make informative intersubtest comparisons. For these reasons this test has a great deal to offer as a neuropsychological instrument.

This paper and pencil test differs from most in that the responses to six of the seven subtests require visuomotor activity from the subject; only the block-counting subtest calls for a graphic response in which hand–eye interactions are not a component. Each subtest is preceded by a practice test which enables the subject to establish a set and the examiner to make sure the subject understands the task.

The first three subtests measure manual speed and more or less fine motor control. In Tracing, the subject must draw a continuous line through 80 irregularly placed 1½ mm gaps in as many small (28 mm) vertical lines. The score is the number of gaps the pencil line penetrates in 50 seconds without touching the lines. Tapping presents the subject with 70 circles 9 mm in diameter with instructions to make three pencil dots in each circle with a 30 second time limit. The emphasis in this subtest is on speed rather than accuracy, so that the score is all the circles in which a response was attempted, including circles with dots outside the perimeter. In contrast, accuracy is emphasized in Dotting. In this subtest the subject must place one dot in each of 100

303

little (4 mm diameter) circles placed irregularly along a pathway that runs from left to right and back again in ten horizontal lines down a page. Score is the number of circles containing dots placed fully within them in the 30 seconds allowed.

The next three subtests involve visuospatial functions. The Copying task presents the subject with 20 figures to copy onto a grid of dots (see Fig. 10-3). The score is the sum of correct lines drawn in two-and-one-half minutes. Location consists of a large square containing a 6 $\times$ 6 array of letters arranged so that no two of the twelve duplicated letters are in the same quadrant. Along the sides of the large square are eight smaller squares, each containing five dots scattered in the same relative positions as five corresponding letters in the large square. The subject is given two minutes to write in the letter corresponding to each dot. The number of dots correctly lettered in that time makes up the score. Blocks is a block-counting test consisting of line representations of six three-dimensional constructions made up of one size of block. The task is to figure out the number of blocks touched by the five designated blocks (marked with an x) in each construction. Time allowed on this subtest is two-and-one-half minutes. The last test, Pursuit, measures speed and accuracy of visual tracking by presenting a line-tracing format requiring the subject to follow lines visually through a tangle of other lines. Each of the four patterns are more complicated versions of the Line Tracing Task (see Fig. 12-15, p. 370), having ten starting points instead of seven and lines ending at ten different end points rather than five. The time limit is two-and-one-half minutes and the score is the number of lines correctedly tracked.

The test manual provides separate percentile norms for each subtest for men and women "aged sixteen up," based on test performances of 1000 adults of each sex. It also gives some data showing how well these tests correlate with performance on a variety of industrial jobs. Sterne (1969) found small negative correlations between age and the Tapping and Dotting tests which are reflected in the data he collected on three age groups (unpublished document) (see Table 10-2).

Patterns of differences in subtest performance levels tend to show up clinically. Patients whose visuospatial abilities are intact but who have poor regulation or coordination of fine motor activity will perform less well on the first three subtests than on Tracing or Location. When visuospatial functions are impaired but motor activity remains intact and under good control, large differences in performance levels will appear in low Tracing and Location scores and high scores on the motor speed and

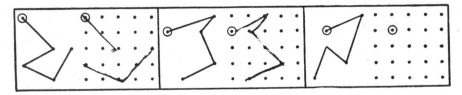

Fig. 10-3. Practice items of the MacQuarrie Tracing subtest. The subject who made the responses shown here performed as poorly on the test items as well (see text).

Table 10-2 Means and Standard Deviations for the Tapping and Dotting Subtests of the MacQuarrie Test for Mechanical Ability for Three Age Groups

	Age Groups		
	24–35 (n = 17)	36–45 (n = 33)	46–55 (n = 24)
Tapping	34.4 ± 8.5	36.9 ± 7.7	32.3 ± 7.9
Dotting	17.1 ± 3.2	16.9 ± 3.3	14.7 ± 3.3

(Adapted from D. M. Sterne, unpublished document)

accuracy tasks. The sample Tracing task items, for example (see Fig. 10-3) show the failed responses of a 30-year-old surveyor two years after he fell eight feet onto the side of his head sustaining right temporoparietal injuries. He performed in the first to fifth percentiles on this subtest and on Location as well, but scores on Tracing, Tapping, and Dotting were all above the 90th percentile.

EDUCATIONAL GUIDANCE TESTS

Several tests of academic ability are organized into a battery format with separate subtests scores. Because these are academically oriented tests, they provide data on a much narrower range of abilities than do the more vocationally oriented batteries.

Some of the academic ability tests, like the Cooperative School and College Ability Tests (SCAT) (1966) and the Scholastic Aptitude Test (SAT) of the College Entrance Examination Board, consist of just two subtests, one testing verbal and the other mathematical abilities. The College Qualification Test (CQT) (Bennett et al., 1961) has three subtests, V-verbal, N-numerical, and I-information. The California Short-Form Test of Mental Maturity, 1963 Revision (CTMM–SF) (E. T. Sullivan et al., 1963), gives norms for four factors: Logical Reasoning, Numerical Reasoning, Verbal Concepts, and Memory. In their present form, the Primary Mental Ability Tests (PMA) (Thurstone and Thurstone, 1962) provide subtests of three factors, Verbal Meaning, Number Facility, and Spatial Relations, at all levels from Kindergarten through 12th grade plus subtests of Perceptual Speed for grades K–6, and of Reasoning for grades 4–12. All of these tests except the SAT can be purchased by qualified individual examiners. The SAT tests are highly restricted and cannot be given in a clinical setting. However, for patients who took the test before the onset of an organic brain condition, they provide a very reliable measure of premorbid verbal and mathematical skills.

The applicability of the College Qualification Tests is limited to persons who have completed high school and have not experienced a general retardation. The College Qualification Tests are best suited for estimating the premorbid general ability level of patients who have fairly specific nonverbal deficits. Since the SCAT norms begin at grade 4 and the CTMM and PMA test norms begin at the kindergarten level, these tests can assess residual verbal skills in moderately deteriorated patients. Individual

Primary Mental Abilities subtests, such as Reasoning (see p. 482), may be sensitive to specific neuropsychological deficits. Earlier editions of the PMA included subtests no longer in general use but still employed by neuropsychologists, such as Word Fluency (see pp. 333–334) and the Line Tracing Task or its variants (see pp. 302, 370–371).

There are also multiple-scale paper and pencil educational tests that purport to measure visual and spatial factors as well as verbal and quantitative ones. Unfortunately, claims for their performance have not been substantiated to an extent that warrants their regular use in neuropsychological studies (Buros, 1978).

Single Tests of General Ability

Single tests for estimating the general intellectual ability level of intact persons typically measure some aspect of intellectual functioning associated with such evidence of mental prowess as school grades, academic attainment, or occupational status. Their usefulness in providing an estimate of the general ability of brain injured patients varies with the nature of the cerebral insult. When functions involved in one of these tests remain relatively unaffected, that test will serve its intended purpose well. When a function critical to the performance of one of these tests is impaired, the test can provide much information about the nature and extent of the intellectual disability when it is given as one of a set of different kinds of tests.

Vocabulary Tests

Vocabulary level has long been recognized as an excellent guide to the general intellectual performance of intact, well-socialized persons. Vocabulary tests have proven equally valuable in demonstrating the effects of dominant hemisphere disease. This dual function has placed vocabulary tests among the most widely used of all mental ability tests, whether alone or as part of test batteries.

PAPER AND PENCIL VOCABULARY TESTS

Single paper and pencil vocabulary tests are rarely used. Most of the time, the assessment of vocabulary takes place as part of an academic aptitude test battery, a reading test battery, or one of the multiple test guidance batteries. When neuropsychological studies have included a single vocabulary test in their paper and pencil battery, it has usually been the 100-word Atwell and Wells' Wide Range Vocabulary Test (Atwell and Wells, 1937) or the 80-word Mill Hill Vocabulary Scale (Raven, 1958). These multiple-choice tests take relatively little time to administer and are easily scored. The Atwell and Wells test gives grade level equivalents for raw scores with a range from grade three to college. Mill Hill raw scores convert to percentiles and a standard score (expressed as a "deviation IQ" score [Peck, 1970]) for age levels from 20 to 65 (see Table 15-5, p. 504). Both of these well-standardized tests have proven to be sensitive to left hemisphere disease (Costa and Vaughan, 1962; Lansdell, 1968). Performance on the Mill Hill was only slightly (5 IQ score points) but significantly diminished in a group of head injured patients mostly tested within six months of injury (Brooks and Aughten, 1979a,b). No Mill Hill score differences were found between groups of elderly patients with and without diffuse brain disease (Irving, 1971). Particularly when compared with lower performances on other kinds of tests, these data reflect the relative sturdiness of vocabulary tests.

NONVERBAL RESPONSE VOCABULARY TESTS

Vocabulary tests in which the patient signals that he recognizes a spoken or printed word by pointing to one of a set of pictures permit evaluation of the recognition vocabulary of many verbally handicapped patients. These tests are generally simple to administer. They are most often used for quick screening and for estimating the general ability level of intact persons when time or circumstances do not allow a more complete examination. Slight differences in the design and standardization populations of the picture vocabulary tests in most common use affect their appropriateness for different patients to some extent.

Peabody Picture Vocabulary Test (PPVT) (Dunn, 1965).   This easily administered vocabulary test was standardized for ages two and one-half to 18. It consists of 150 picture plates, each with four pictures (see Fig. 10-4). There is one plate for each of the 150 words of the two equivalent word lists, arranged in order of difficulty. The subject points to or gives the number of the picture most like the stimulus word, which is spoken by the examiner or shown on a printed card. The simplest words are given only to young children and obviously retarded or impaired adults. The PPVT items span both very low age ranges and levels of intellectual functioning and levels considerably above average adult ability. Care should be taken to enter the word list at the level most suitable for the subject so that both basal (the highest six consecutive passes) and ceiling (six failures out of eight) scores can be obtained with minimum effort. Points for passed items are simply counted and entered into tables giving derived mental age scores, percentiles, and deviation IQ scores.

This test was standardized on a suitable number of white children, all from Nashville, Tennessee. The validity of its IQ scores has been questioned because of relatively low correlations (.47, .66) with verbal IQ scores obtained from Wechsler tests (Frankenburg and Camp, 1975). The median correlation between the two forms had been reported as .77 (Bochner, 1978); the median test-retest correlation is .73 (range .28–.97) (Weiner, 1979). The MA score level may be somewhat more suitable for use in estimating premorbid ability. The examiner obviously must exercise very cautious judgment when making generalizations about premorbid verbal ability from a patient's PPVT performance.

However, this test will give some idea of the range of vocabulary still available to the patient and of the range of knowledge once possessed by him. For severely impaired patients, particularly when their ability to communicate has been compromised, this test may give the examiner the best access to the patient's residual vocab-

307

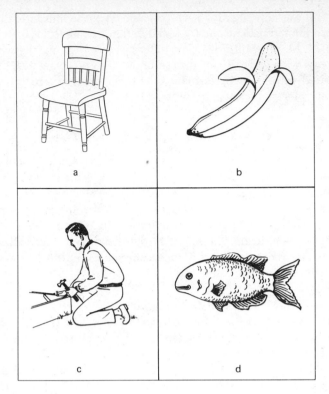

Fig. 10-4. Sample item from the Peabody Picture Vocabulary Test. The word to be matched is "Banana."

ulary and fund of information. In addition, the simplicity of the pictures makes it eminently suitable for those brain damaged patients who have so much difficulty sorting out the elements in a complex stimulus that they are unable to respond to the intended problem.

Nonverbal Tests of General Intellectual Ability

There have been many attempts to devise a simple, easy to administer test that would predict academic success or vocational achievement as well as the Wechsler tests and the Binet do. There are also many tests that claim to measure the general intellectual level of verbally handicapped persons. A few tests aim to accomplish both these goals. These various tests measure different sets of functions but have in common a nonverbal format.

RAVEN'S PROGRESSIVE MATRICES (RPM) (Raven, 1960)

This multiple-choice paper and pencil test was developed in England as a "culture fair" test of general ability. Although widely used as a test of general ability, its sensitivity to particular reasoning and visuoperceptual disorders makes it a valuable instrument for neuropsychological assessment. A full discussion of this test is given in Chapter 15, pp. 502–505.

HUMAN FIGURE DRAWING TESTS

The quality and complexity of children's drawings increase with age at a sufficiently regular pace to warrant the inclusion of drawing tests in the standard repertory of tests of intellectual development. In the United States, the Goodenough "Draw a Man" test and its revision utilizing drawings of a man and a woman have provided the most popular systems for estimating developmental level from human figure drawings (D. B. Harris, 1963). A similar test, developed in Europe, uses a system for scoring drawings of "A lady walking in the rain *(Une dame qui se promène et il pleut)*" from which the child's developmental level can be estimated (E. M. Taylor, 1959). These tests have been particularly prized for measuring the intellectual potential of handicapped or neurologically impaired children. They have also been used as brief intellectual screening procedures with young children.

The upper age norms of both these tests end at 15, reflecting the normal leveling off of scores on drawing tests in the early teens. However, because drawing tests are relatively independent of language skills they can be used to obtain rough estimates of the general ability of adults with verbal impairments.

Each test is administered with verbal instructions to produce the desired drawing, a man and a woman, or a lady walking in the rain. Neither test is timed. The subject can achieve a maximum of 73 and 71 points for figures of a man and woman, respectively, whereas André Rey's standardization of "Lady" allows for a maximum 49 score points to provide a somewhat coarser-grained scale than the Harris-Goodenough test (see Table 10-3).

The Harris scoring system converts the raw score points to standard scores based on a mean of 100 and a standard deviation of 15, for each year from 3 to 15. However, test score increments beyond the age of 12 do not reflect age increments, thus fixing the test age ceiling at 12 years (L. H. Scott, 1981). The Rey scoring system for "Lady" converts the raw score to percentiles at five percentile levels for each age from 4 to 15+ (see Table 10-4). The age 15 norms of both tests should be used for adult patients.

Human figure drawings provide the neuropsychologist with a sample of behavior that is not only relatively culture free and language independent but also sufficiently complex and closely related to normal human development to afford some measure of the intellectual endowment of patients whose ability to draw has remained essentially intact. This method of assessing premorbid intellectual ability is not applicable

Table 10-3 Rey's Scoring System for *Une dame qui se promène et il pleut*

Item	Points
1. Human form (head with legs)	1
2. Body distinct from arms and legs	1
3. Some clothing (buttons, scribbles on body)	1
4. A female figure	1
5. Profile: head and at least one other part of body in profile (body, feet, arms)	1
6. Motion indicated (gait, posture)	1
7. Rain roughly indicated	1
8. Rain properly indicated (touching ground, regularly distributed, raindrops on umbrella and lower parts of picture)	1
For drawing featuring umbrella	
9. Umbrella roughly indicated	1
10. Umbrella in two lines (round, oblong, top, handle)	1
11. Umbrella clearly shown (ribs, points, scallops)	1
12. Umbrella dimensions ⅛ to ⅜ of body length	1
13. Umbrella positioned to cover at least half of body	1
14. Umbrella attached to hand at end of arm	1
15. Position of arm adequate	1
For drawing featuring raincoat, raincape, hood, without umbrella	
16. Hood indicated (if there is a hood and an umbrella count only point 42—clothing)	1
17. Head well covered by hool	1
18. Raincoat or raincape	1
19. Shoulders, arms covered by coat or cape, only hands showing	1
20. Arms fully covered by cape, with shoulders clearly indicated	1
21. Shoulders not shown, but asked, "where are the arms?" child answers, "under coat."	1
22. Eyes shown (one line, dot)	1
23. Eyes in double lines, several parts	1
24. Nose shown	1
25. Mouth shown (one line)	1
26. Mouth shown in double lines, lips front or profile	1
27. Ears shown	1
28. Chin shown (front or profile)	1
29. Hair or headgear (except hood)	1
30. Neck or collar shown clearly	1
If the lady's face is covered by umbrella or if her back is turned, give credit for nose, mouth, eyes, etc. Credit 2 points if the quality of the picture suggests the more mature form of these details.	
31. Hands (credit one point if hands are in pocket)	1
32. Arms shown (one line)	1
33. Arms in double lines	1
34. Arms attached to body at shoulder level	1
35. Arms in proportion to body or slightly longer	1
36. Legs shown (one line)	1
37. Legs in double lines	1
38. Legs properly attached	1
39. Legs in proportion to body	1
40. Feet shown	1
41. Shoes shown clearly	1
42. Clothing: 2 articles (skirt and blouse, jacket and skirt; if the hood goes with an open umbrella, it is considered clothing)	1

Item	Points
43. No transparency, if such could be possible	1
For a picture that shows a definite artistic trend or technique (silhouette, etching, skilled schematization), credit total number of points possible up to here: 37 points.	
For landscape	
44. A baseline, a road, a path, in one line or dots	1
45. Figure clearly positioned on baseline or road	1
46. Road or path shown	1
47. Pavement or gravel shown	1
48. Flower border, tree, doorway, house shown	1
49. Special details showing imagination	1
	Maximum 43 points

(From E. M. Taylor, *Psychological appraisal of children with cerebral defects*, 1959, by courtesy of Harvard University Press and the Commonwealth Fund. Adapted from André Rey, *Monographies de psychologie appliquées, No. 1, 1947*)

to the many brain damaged patients with perceptual and constructional disabilities or to those whose predominant mental symptoms include mental deterioration. The Harris and Rey scoring systems can greatly aid the assessment of impairment of those functions contributing to the free drawing performance. Use of these techniques in evaluating the nature and extent of an organic impairment is discussed on pp. 404–405.

Table 10-4 Rey's Norms for Ages 15 and Older for *Une dame qui se promène et il pleut*

Percentiles	0	25	50	75	100
Scores	17	30	33	37	43

(From E. M. Taylor, 1959)

11
Verbal Functions

The most prominent disorders of verbal functions are the aphasias and associated difficulties in verbal production such as *dysarthria* (defective articulation) and apraxias of speech. Other aspects of verbal functions that are usually affected when there is an aphasic disorder, such as fluency and reading and writing abilities, may be impaired without aphasia being present. Assessment of the latter functions will therefore be discussed separately from aphasia testing.

Testing for Aphasia

Aphasic disorders can be mistakenly diagnosed when the problem actually results from a global confusional state, a dysarthric condition, or pathological inertia (e.g., see pp. 183–184). The reverse can also occur when mild deficits in language comprehension and production are attributed to generalized intellectual impairment or to a memory or attentional disorder. Defective auditory comprehension, in particular, whether due to a hearing disorder or to impaired language comprehension, can result in unresponsive or socially inappropriate behavior that is mistaken for negativism, dementia, or a psychiatric condition (Brookshire and Manthie, 1980). In fact, aphasia occurs as part of the behavioral picture in many brain disorders (Golper and Binder, 1981) so that often the question is not whether the patient has aphasia, but rather how (much) the aphasia contributes to the patient's behavioral deficits. Questions concerning the presence of aphasia can usually be answered by careful observation in the course of an informal but systematic review of the patient's capacity to perceive, comprehend, remember, and respond with both spoken and written material, or by using an aphasia screening test (see pp. 320ff). A review of language and speech functions that will indicate whether communication problems are present will include examination of the following aspects of verbal behavior:

1. *Spontaneous speech.*
2. *Repetition* of words, phrases, sentences. "Methodist Episcopal" and similar

tongue-twisters elicit disorders of articulation and sound sequencing. "No ifs, ands, or buts" tests for the integrity of connections between the center for expressive speech (Broca's area) and the receptive speech center (Wernicke's area) (see pp. 32–34).

3. *Speech comprehension.* a. Give the subject simple commands (e.g., "Show me your chin." "Put your left hand on your right ear"). b. Ask "yes-no" questions (e.g., "Is a ball square?"). c. Ask the subject to point to specific objects.

4. *Naming.* The examiner points to various objects and their parts asking, "What is this?" (e.g., glasses, frame, nose piece, lens). Ease and accuracy of naming in other categories, such as colors, letters, numbers, and actions should also be examined (Goodglass, 1980).

5. *Reading.* To examine for accuracy, have the subject read aloud. For comprehension, have the subject follow written directions (e.g., "Tap three times on the table"), explain a passage he has read.

6. *Writing.* Have the subject copy, write to dictation, and compose a sentence or two (see pp. 339–341).

Formal aphasia testing should be undertaken when aphasia is known or strongly suspected to be present. It may be done for any of the following purposes: "(1) diagnosis of presence and type of aphasic syndrome, leading to inferences concerning cerebral localization; (2) measurement of the level of performance over a wide range, for both initial determination and detection of change over time; (3) comprehensive assessment of the assets and liabilities of the patient in all language areas as a guide to therapy" (Goodglass and Kaplan, 1972).

Aphasia tests differ from other verbal tests in that they focus on disorders of symbol formulation and associated apraxias and agnosias (Benton, 1967b). They are usually designed to elicit samples of behavior in each communication modality—listening, speaking, reading, writing, and gesturing. The examination of the central "linguistic processing of verbal symbols" is their common denominator (F. L. Darley, 1972; Wepman and Jones, 1967).

Aphasia Test and Batteries

The most widely used aphasia tests are actually test *batteries* comprising numerous subtests of many discrete verbal functions. Their product may be a score or index for diagnostic purposes or an orderly description of the patient's communication disabilities. Most aphasia tests involve lengthy, precise, and well-controlled procedures. They are best administered by persons, such as speech pathologists, who have more than a passing acquaintance with aphasiology and are trained in the specialized techniques of aphasia examinations.

Aphasia test batteries always include a wide range of tasks so that the nature and severity of the language problem and associated deficits may be determined. Because aphasia tests concern disordered language functions in themselves, and not their intellectual ramifications, test items typically present very simple and concrete tasks most children in the lower grades can pass. Common aphasia test questions ask the patient (1) to name simple objects ("What is this?" asks the examiner pointing to a cup or a pen or the picture of a boy or a clock); (2) to recognize simple spoken words ("Point to your ear," or "Put the spoon in the cup"); (3) to act on serial commands; (4) to repeat words and phrases; (5) to recognize simple printed letters, numbers, words, primary level arithmetic problems, and common symbols; (6) to give verbal and gestural answers to simple printed questions; and (7) to print or write letters, words, numbers, etc. In addition, some aphasia tests ask the patient to tell a story or draw. Some examine articulatory disorders and apraxias as well.

Aphasia test batteries differ primarily in their terminology, internal organization, the number of modality combinations they test, and the levels of difficulty and complexity to which the examination is carried. The tests discussed here are both representative of the different kinds of aphasia tests and among the best known. Some clinicians devise their own batteries, taking parts from other tests and adding their own, so that apart from the published batteries, there are also a number of unpublished sets of tests (Eisenson, 1973; Osgood and Miron, 1963). A detailed review of most batteries and tests for aphasia can be found in F. L. Darley's *Evaluation of appraisal techniques in speech and language pathology* (1979).

THE APHASIA LANGUAGE PERFORMANCE SCALES (ALPS) (Keenan and Brassell, 1975)

The format of this test evolved from the author's experiences in examining aphasic patients to determine whether and how these patients might benefit from speech therapy. It therefore has a practical orientation. The authors stress the need for informality in the patient-examiner interaction to maintain a level of rapport and patient comfort that will permit the patient to perform at his best. The ALPS examines four aspects of language ability—listening, talking, reading, and writing—each in a ten-item scale that is graded in difficulty. Normal and self-corrected responses earn one point; when prompted (usually repetition of the question) a response earns half a point. The test generally takes no more than 30 minutes since the examiner begins each scale at a level deemed appropriate on the basis of pretest conversation or attempts to converse. In addition to the score sheet, a cumulative record sheet is provided for reporting patients' progress over time. Equipment was deliberately kept light (a set of reading cards and some coins, keys, and a watch) to ensure portability so the test could be administered at bedside or elsewhere, as in a patient's home. Standardization groups were small. The four ALPS scales tend to correlate highly with PICA (see pp. 318–319) subtest scores that presumably measure the same functions.

The authors make no attempt to relate performance on this test to aphasia subtypes or to neuroanatomic sites. Rather, they emphasize the importance of the patient's history in making prognostic statements and illustrate how the four scores together with demographic and historical data can be used in planning a treatment program. Ritter (1979) recommends this instrument for screening purposes but questions its usefulness in planning treatment. The ALPS is far from comprehensive in its review of communication and communication-related functions. Its pragmatic rather than

314

statistically based scaling reduces comparability between scales and the instrument's usefulness for research.

The Boston Diagnostic Aphasia Examination (BDAE) (Goodglass and Kaplan, 1972)

This test battery was devised to provide information about the "components of language" that would aid in diagnosis and treatment and in the advancement of knowledge about the neuroanatomic correlates of aphasia. It provides for a systematic examination of communication and communication-related functions in 12 areas defined by factor analysis, with a total of 34 subtests, not including two for "music" and seven for the "parietal lobe battery." Time is the price paid for such thorough coverage, for a complete examination takes from one to four hours. As a result many examiners use portions of this test selectively, often in combination with other tests (e.g., see p. 328). A number of "supplementary language tests" are also given that can be used to make discriminations of such aspects of psycholinguistic behavior as grammar and syntax, and to examine for disconnection syndromes. Subtests are scored for number correct; subtest scores can then be coverted to z-scores derived from a normative study of aphasic patients mostly presenting with relatively selective deficits and representing all but the most severely impaired (global) aphasics. In addition, this battery will yield a "Rating Scale Profile" for qualitative speech characteristics that, the authors point out, "are not satisfactorily measured by objective scores" but can be judged on seven seven-point scales, each referring to a particular feature of speech production. The subtest and rating scale profiles can aid in differential diagnosis but do not automatically classify patients into the diagnostic subtypes of aphasia.

The range and sensitivity of the "Boston" battery makes it an excellent tool for the description of aphasic disorders and for treatment planning. However, an examiner must be experienced to use it diagnostically. The original standardization procedures and population leave the comparability of the subscale z-scores in question and thus limit the battery's research application. Recent norms (means, standard deviations, ranges, and suggested cut-off scores) have been published by Borod and the battery's authors (1980). These should further enhance its general clinical usefulness.

Communication Abilities in Daily Living (CADL) (Holland, 1980)

The disparity between scores that patients obtain on the usual formal tests of language competency and their communicative competency in real life led to the development of an instrument that might reduce this disparity by presenting the patient with language tasks in familiar, practical contexts. The CADL examines how the patient might handle daily life activities by engaging him in role-playing in a series of simulated situations such as "the doctor's office" or "the grocery store." In keeping with the goal of making the examination as naturalistic as possible, the examiner is encouraged to carry out a dual role as examiner/play-acting participant with informality, "a flourish," and such props as a toy stethoscope or boxes of packaged soup. Responses are scored on a three-point scale according to their communicative effectiveness, regardless of the modality used (i.e., spoken, written, or gestural responses are all acceptable). With the high score of 2 indicating satisfactory communication, the middle score of the scale is used for responses that bear a relationship to the topic although they fail to convey the requisite meaning. The 68 CADL items sample ten categories of behavior, such as "speech acts," "utilizing context," "social convention," and capacity to participate in role-playing. Most items (46) involve more than one of these categories. A series of evaluations of CADL performances of 130 aphasic patients demonstrated that this test was sensitive to aphasia, age, and institutionalization (unspecified), but not sex or social background. The CADL also differentiated patients with the major types of aphasia on the single dimension of severity of communicative disability based on the summation score. The ten category scores also differentiated aphasia subtypes. The manual provides category patterns for differentiating aphasia types and cut-off scores for identifying aphasics within predominantly nonaphasic populations. Self-training procedures for examiners that mainly focus on scoring standardization are also provided, with a training tape to supplement written patient response samples.

Because responses need not be vocalized to earn credits, this test tends to be more sensitive to the communication strengths of many speech-impaired (e.g., Broca's aphasia) patients than are traditional testing instruments. This instrument is as yet too new to have been thoroughly tested in the marketplace. However, it is used in the Veterans Administration's cooperative treatment study, "A comparison of hospital and home treatment-programs for aphasic patients," and therefore its worthiness should soon become known.

EXAMINING FOR APHASIA (Eisenson, 1954)

Although this test uses diagnostic categories that have generally been superseded by current formulations of the nature of aphasia, it offers a thorough approach to the examination of communication dysfunction. Almost two decades after it first appeared, its author described it as "a clinical instrument intended to provide a protocol of type and degree of severity of language and related deficits" (Eisenson, 1973). It contains 37 discrete subtests, each differing from the others in modalities tested, content, or level of difficulty. Eisenson suggests the test can be used for aphasia screening by giving only the first item in each subtest, although administration of the full test permits the examiner to determine gradations of dysfunction. The test may take anywhere from half an hour to two hours to complete. Eisenson offers no normative data or objective criteria for evaluating responses since he considers a formal scoring system inapplicable to a condition for which inconsistency of response is a hallmark. Performances on each subtest can be summarized on a five-point scale rating the extent of impairment from "Complete" to "None." "Despite its total lack of psychometric merit" (G. J. Canter, 1979), this test offers the examiner a range of well-constructed stimulus material with guidelines that can be profitably used by clinicians who prefer a flexible approach to the highly structured procedures that characterize many of the more recently published tests.

The Functional Communication Profile (M. T. Sarno, 1969)

This is a 45-item inventory that takes 20 to 40 minutes to administer. It permits serial scaled ratings of a patient's practical language behavior elicited "in an informal setting," as distinguished from language on more formal testing instruments since "improvement as meaured by higher (formal) test scores does not always reflect useful improvement" in the patient's day-to-day activities (J. E. Sarno et al., 1971). Like battery type aphasia tests, the *Functional Communication Profile* also requires an experienced clinician to apply it reliably and sensitively. Evaluation proceeds in five different performance areas: "Movement," "Speaking," "Understanding," "Reading," and "Other," not exclusively verbal, adaptive behaviors. Scoring is on a nine-point scale, and ratings are assigned on the basis of the examiner's estimate of the patient's premorbid ability in that area. Scores are recorded on a histogram. Sarno recommends color coding to differentiate the initial evaluation from subsequent reevaluations for easy visual review (M. L. Taylor, 1965). She also offers a rather loose method of converting the item grades into percentages that may be too subjective for research purposes or for comparisons with clinical evaluations made by different examiners. However, this test is of practical value in predicting functional communication (Swisher, 1979).

The Minnesota Test for Differential Diagnosis of Aphasia; rev. ed. (Schuell, 1972)

This lengthy test involves 57 different subtests that thoroughly cover the breadth and depth of communication disturbances. It focuses on many different aspects of each of five areas, defined by factor analysis, in which aphasic patients commonly have problems: "auditory disturbances," "visual and reading disturbances," "speech and language disturbances," "visuomotor and writing disturbances," and "disturbances of numerical relationships and arithmetic processes." The battery usually takes from one to three hours to administer, although profoundly impaired patients will finish much sooner because they are unable to respond to more than a few of the items. Each subtest is scored for errors, but Schuell also stresses that the kind of errors a patient makes tells more about his condition than does their number. Test performances are summarized in a diagnostic scale organized into functional performance categories. The examination booklet also contains a six-point scale for rating extratest observations of comprehension of spoken speech, reading, writing, and dysarthria (impaired articulation). Data from this test provide a systematic description of the patient's language disability that can serve as a basis for planning therapy (Osgood and Miron, 1963; Zubrick and A. Smith, 1979). Its research applications are limited as it is not standardized.

Multilingual Aphasia Examination (MAE) (Benton and Hamsher, 1978)

This eight-part battery was developed to provide for a systematic, graded examination of receptive, expressive, and immediate memory components of speech and language functions. Some of its subtests, such as "Token Test," "Digit Repetition," and "Controlled Oral Word Association," are variations of tests in general use; others, for instance the three forms of the Spelling subtest (Oral, Written, and Block—using large metal or plastic letters), were developed for this battery. Most of the subtests have two or three forms, thus reducing practice effects on repeated administrations. For each subtest, age and education effects are dealt with by means of a Correction Score, which, when added to the raw score, gives an Adjusted Score. Percentile conversions for each adjusted score and their corresponding classification (for example, see Tables 11-4 and 11-5, p. 331) have been worked out so that scores on each subtest are psychometrically comparable. This means of scoring and evaluating subtest performances has the additional virtue of allowing each subtest to be used separately as, for instance, when an examiner may wish to study verbal fluency or verbal memory in a patient who is not aphasic and for whom administration of many of the other subtests would be a waste of time.

Neurosensory Center Comprehensive Examination for Aphasia (NCCEA)
(Spreen and Benton, 1969)

This battery consists of 24 short subtests, 20 involving different aspects of language performance, and four "control" tests of visual and tactile functions. Most of the subtests normally take less than five minutes to administer. The control tests are given only when the patient performs poorly on a test involving visual or tactile stimuli. A variety of materials are used in the tests, including common objects, sound tapes, printed cards, a screened box for tactile recognition, and the Token Test "tokens" (see pp. 321–326). An interesting innovation enables patients whose writing hand is paralyzed to demonstrate "graphic" behavior by giving them "Scrabble" letters for forming words. All of the materials can be easily purchased, or they can be constructed by following instructions in the manual. Scores for each subtest are entered on two profile sheets, one providing norms for the performance of normal adults that take age and performance into account, the other with norms based on the performance of aphasic patients. This double scoring enables the examiner to identify patients whose performance differs significantly from normal adults, while providing for score discriminations within the aphasic score range so that small amounts of change can be registered. This test has proven sensitivity, particularly for moderately and severely aphasic patients (Greenberg, 1979), but suffers from insufficient standardization data and a low ceiling that diminishes its usefulness for examining patients with mild impairments.

The Porch Index of Communicative Ability (PICA) (Porch, 1967)

The *PICA* was developed as a highly standardized, statistically reliable instrument for measuring a limited sample of language functions. This battery contains 18 ten-item subtests, four of them verbal, eight gestural, and six graphic. The same ten common items (cigarette, comb, fork, key, knife, matches, pencil, pen, quarter, toothbrush) are used for each subtest with the exception of the simplest graphic subtest in which the patient is asked to copy geometric forms. The examiner scores each of the patient's responses according to a 16-point multidimensional scoring system (Porch, 1971). Each point in the system describes performance. For example, a score of 1 indicates no response; a score of 15 indicates a response that was judged to be accurate, responsive, prompt, complete, and efficient. Qualified and trained PICA testers undergo a 40-hour training period after which they administer ten practice tests. This training leads to high interscorer reliability correlation coefficients.

By virtue of its tight format and reliable scoring system, the PICA provides a sensitive measure of small changes in patient performance. This sensitivity can aid the speech pathologist in treatment planning so long as the patient's deficits are not so mild that they escape notice because of the test's low ceiling. Its statistically sophisticated construction and reliability make it a useful research instrument as well (F. L. Darley, 1972; McNeil, 1979). Martin (1077) called into question a number of aspects of the PICA that can lead a score-minded examiner to misinterpret the examination, particularly with respect to the patient's capacity for functional communication. McNeil (1979) recommends that Martin's criticisms be treated as "cautions" that can reduce interpretation error in the course of using this versatile instrument.

THE WESTERN APHASIA BATTERY (Kertesz, 1979)

This battery grew out of efforts to develop an instrument from the Boston Diagnostic Aphasia Examination that would generate diagnostic classifications and be suitable for both treatment and research purposes (Kertesz and Poole, 1974). Thus, many of the items were taken from the Boston examination. The Western Aphasia Battery consists of four oral language subtests that yield five scores based on either a rating scale (for Fluency and Information content of speech) or conversion of summed item-correct scores to a scale of 10. Each score thus can be charted on a ten-point scale; together, the five scores, when scaled, give a "profile of performance." An "Aphasia Quotient" (AQ) can be calculated by multiplying each of the five scaled scores by 2 and summing them. Normal (i.e., perfect) performance is set at 100. The AQ gives a measure of discrepancy from normal language performance, but like any summed score in neuropsychology, it tells nothing of the nature of the problem. The profile of performance and the AQ can be used together to determine the patient's diagnostic subtype according to pattern descriptions for eight aphasia subtypes. In addition, tests of reading, writing, arithmetic, gestural *praxis* (i.e., examining for apraxia of gesture, see pp. 31–32, 528) construction, and Raven's Progressive Matrices (see pp. 502–505) are included to provide a comprehensive survey of communication abilities and related functions. Scores on the latter tests can be combined into a "Performance Quotient" (PQ); the AQ and PQ together give a summary "Cortical Quotient" (CQ) score for diagnostic and research purposes. The language portions of the test may take as long as an hour, and less time with the more impaired patients.

Only the two scores obtained by ratings should present standardization problems. However, the other items leave little room for taking the qualitative aspects of performance into account and thus may provide a restricted picture of the patient's functioning. Another drawback is that the classification system does not take account of the many patients whose symptoms are of a "mixed" nature (i.e., have components of more than one of the eight types delineated in this classification system). How well this test realizes its diagnostic promise remains to be seen.

Aphasia Screening Tests

Aphasia screening tests do not replace the careful examination of language functions afforded by the test batteries. Rather, they are best used as supplements to a neuropsychological test battery. They signal the presence of an aphasic disorder and may even call attention to its specific characteristics, but they do not provide the fine discriminations of the complete aphasia test batteries (Eisenson, 1973). Since these tests do not require technical knowledge of speech pathology for satisfactory administration or interpretation, they can be given and interpreted reliably by clinicians familiar with aphasia syndromes.

THE APHASIA SCREENING TEST (Halstead and Wepman, 1959)

This is the most widely used of all aphasia tests since it or its variants have been incorporated into many formally organized neuropsychological test batteries. As originally devised, the Aphasia Screening Test has 51 items that cover all the elements of aphasic disabilities as well as the most commonly associated communication problems. It is a fairly brief test, rarely taking longer than 30 minutes to complete. There are no rigid scoring standards, but rather the emphasis is on determining the nature of the linguistic problem, once its presence has been established. Erroneous responses are coded into a diagnostic profile intended to provide a description of the pattern of the patient's language disabilities. Obviously, the more areas of involvement and the more a single area is involved, the more severe the disability. However, no provisions are made to grade test performance on the basis of severity, nor information provided for classifying patients. Tikofsky (1979) recommends that this test not be used by inexperienced examiners because it offers no guidelines for clinical application.

Reitan included the Aphasia Screening Test with a number of other different tests in the Halstead-Reitan Neuropsychological Test Battery (see pp. 562–563). He pared down the original test to 32 items but still handled the data descriptively, in much the same manner as originally intended (Boll, 1981; Reitan, undated). A second revision of the Aphasia Screening Test appeared in E. W. Russell, Neuringer, and G. Goldstein's amplification of the Reitan battery (1970). This version is called the "aphasia examination" and contains 37 items. It is essentially the same as Reitan's revision except that four easy arithmetic problems and the task of naming a key were added. E. W. Russell and his colleagues established a simple error-counting scoring system for use with their computerized diagnostic classification system, which converts to a six-point rating scale. This scale indicates the severity of an aphasic disorder, but not its nature.

A very shortened version of the Halstead and Wepman Aphasia Screening Test consists of four tasks (Heimburger and Reitan, 1961):

1. Copy a square, Greek cross, and triangle *without lifting the pencil from the paper.*
2. Name each copied figure.
3. Spell each name.
4. Repeat: "He shouted the warning"; then explain and write it.

This little test may aid in discriminating between patients with left and right hemisphere lesions, for many of the former can copy the designs but cannot write, while the latter have little trouble writing but many cannot reproduce the designs.

THE TOKEN TEST (Boller and Vignolo, 1966; De Renzi and Vignolo, 1962)

The Token Test is extremely simple to administer, to score and, for almost every nonaphasic person who has completed the fourth grade, to perform with few if any errors. Yet it is remarkably sensitive to the disrupted linguistic processes that are central to the aphasic disability, even when much of the patient's communication behavior has remained intact. Scores on the Token Test correlate highly with scores on tests of auditory comprehension (Morley et al., 1979). The Token Test performance also involves immediate memory span for verbal sequences and capacity to use syntax (Lesser, 1976). It can identify those brain damaged patients whose other disabilities may be masking a concomitant aphasic disorder, or whose symbolic processing problems are relatively subtle and not readily recognizable. However, it contributes little to the elucidation of severe aphasic conditions because its difficulty level is too high (Wertz, 1979).

Twenty "tokens" cut from heavy construction paper or thin sheets of plastic or wood make up the test material. They come in two shapes—circles and squares[1]; two sizes—big and little; and five colors. The tokens are laid out horizontally in four parallel rows of large circles, large squares, small circles, and small squares with colors in random order (e.g., see De Renzi and Faglioni, 1978). The only requirement this test makes of the patient is that he comprehend the token names and the verbs and prepositions in the instructions. The diagnosis of those few patients whose language disabilities are so severe as to prevent them from cooperating on this task is not likely to depend on formal testing; almost all other brain injured patients can respond to the simplest level of instructions. The test consists of a series of oral commands, 62 altogether, given in five sections of increasing complexity (Table 11-1).

Although this test seems easy to administer, the examiner must guard against unwittingly slowing his rate of delivery in response to the quality of the patient's

---

[1]When originally published, the instruction called for rectangles. Squares have been universally substituted to reduce the number of syllables the patient must process.

Table 11-1   The Token Test

PART 1

(Large squares and large circles only are on the table)

(1) Touch the red circle
(2) Touch the green square
(3) Touch the red square
(4) Touch the yellow circle
(5) Touch the blue circle (2)[1]
(6) Touch the green circle (3)
(7) Touch the yellow square (1)
(8) Touch the white circle
(9) Touch the blue square
(10) Touch the white square (4)

PART 2

(Large and small squares and circles are on the table)

(1) Touch the small yellow circle (1)
(2) Touch the large green circle
(3) Touch the large yellow circle
(4) Touch the large blue square (3)
(5) Touch the small green circle (4)
(6) Touch the large red circle
(7) Touch the large white square (2)
(8) Touch the small blue circle
(9) Touch the small green square
(10) Touch the large blue circle.

PART 3

(Large squares and large circles only)

(1) Touch the yellow circle and the red square
(2) Touch the green square and the blue circle (3)
(3) Touch the blue square and the yellow square
(4) Touch the white square and the red square
(5) Touch the white circle and the blue circle (4)
(6) Touch the blue square and the white square (2)
(7) Touch the blue square and the white circle
(8) Touch the green square and the blue circle
(9) Touch the red circle and the yellow square (1)
(10) Touch the red square and the white circle.

PART 4

(Large and small squares and circles)

(1) Touch the small yellow circle and the large green square ((2)
(2) Touch the small blue square and the small green circle

[1]A second number at the end of an item indicates that the item is identical or structurally similar to the item of that number in De Renzi and Faglioni's "short version" (see p. 326). With the exceptions that "blue" and "black" are transposed, "touch" is substituted for "pick" and "take," and there are a few changes in the wording of Part 6 (from the original Part 5), the second numbered items provide the essential content of Parts 2 through 6 of the "short version." To preserve the complexity of the items in Part 5 of the short version, item 3 of the original Part 4 should read, "Touch the large white square and the *small* red circle."

322

(3) Touch the large white square and the large red circle (1)
(4) Touch the large blue square and the large red square (3)
(5) Touch the small blue square and the small yellow circle
(6) Touch the small blue circle and the small red circle
(7) Touch the large blue square and the large green square
(8) Touch the large blue circle and the large green circle
(9) Touch the small red square and the small yellow circle
(10) Touch the small white square and the large red square (4).

PART 5

(Large squares and large circles only)

(1) Put the red circle on the green square (1)
(2) Put the white square behind the yellow circle
(3) Touch the blue circle with the red square (2)
(4) Touch—with the blue circle—the red square
(5) Touch the blue circle and the red square (3)
(6) Pick up the blue circle or the red square (4)
(7) Put the green square away from the yellow square (5)
(8) Put the white circle before the blue square
(9) If there is a black circle, pick up the red square (6)
   N.B. *There is no black circle.*
(10) Pick up the squares, except the yellow one
(11) Touch the white circle without using your right hand
(12) When I touch the green circle, you take the white square.
   N.B. *Wait a few seconds before touching the green circle.*
(13) Put the green square beside the red circle (7)
(14) Touch the squares, slowly, and the circles, quickly (8)
(15) Put the red circle between the yellow square and the green square (9)
(16) Except for the green one, touch the circles (10)
(17) Pick up the red circle—no!—the white square (11)
(18) Instead of the white square, take the yellow circle (12)
(19) Together with the yellow circle, take the blue circle (13)
(20) After picking up the green square, touch the white circle
(21) Put the blue circle under the white square
(22) Before touching the yellow circle, pick up the red square

(From Boller and Vignolo, 1966.)

performance (Salvatore et al., 1975). Slowed presentation of instructions ("stretched speech" produced by slowing an instruction tape) significantly reduced the number of errors made by aphasic patients while not affecting the performance of patients with right hemisphere lesions (Poeck and Pietron, 1981). However, even with slowed instructions, aphasic patients still make many more errors than do patients with right-sided lesions.

Items failed on a first command should be repeated and, if performed successfully the second time, scored separately from the first response. When the second but not the first administration of an item is passed, only the second performance is counted under the assumption that many initial errors will result from such nonspecific vari-

323

ables as inattention and lack of interest. Each correct response earns one point, so that the highest attainable total score is 62. When scoring, the examiner should note whether the patient makes the behavioral distinction between "touch" and "pick up" as directed in Part 5.

Boller and Vignolo have developed a slightly modified version of De Renzi and Vignolo's original Token Test format. They give the full record of scores achieved by their standardization groups. Their cut-off scores correctly classified 100% of the control patients, 90% of nonaphasic patients with right hemisphere lesions, 65% of nonaphasic patients, for an overall 88% correctly classified. Table 11-2 summarizes these data.

It should be noted that Part V, which consists of items involving relational concepts, by itself identified only one less patient as a "latent aphasic" than did the whole 62-item test of Boller and Vignolo. This finding suggests that Part V could be used without the other 40 questions to identify those left hemisphere damaged patients misclassified as nonaphasic because their difficulties in symbol formulation are too subtle to impair their communication for most ordinary purposes.

Age and education effects have been inconsistently reported (De Renzi and Faglioni, 1978; Wertz, 1979a). Wertz and his colleagues (1971, reported in Brookshire and Manthie, 1980) observed a gradual increase in errors with advancing age. Normal subjects aged 35 to 39 made a median error score of 0 on Part V. At ages 65–69, the median error score on this section was 3.2; it increased to 3.4 for the 70- to 74-year-olds, and to 4.4 for those in the 75 to 79 age range. There is also disagreement on whether general intellectual ability (as measured by Raven's Matrices) affects the Token Test performance (Coupar, 1976). Coupar's reported correlation of .35 for the Matrices test with the Token Test suggests that if intelligence plays any role at all, it is practically negligible.

Despite the simplicity of the called-for response—or perhaps because of its simplicity—this direction-following task can give the observant examiner insight into the nature of the patient's comprehension or performance deficits. Patients whose failures on this test are mostly due to defective auditory comprehension tend to confuse colors or shapes, and to carry out fewer than the required instructions. They may begin to perseverate as the instructions become more complex. A few nonaphasic patients may also perseverate on this task because of conceptual inflexibility or an impaired capacity to execute a series of commands (Lezak, 1982b). For example, although he could repeat the instructions correctly, a 68-year-old retired laborer suffering multi-infarct dementia was unable to perform the two-command items because he persisted in placing his fingers on the designated tokens simultaneously despite numerous attempts to lead him into making a serial response.

When a patient has difficulty on this task, his problem is usually so obvious that, for clinical purposes, the examiner may not find it necessary to begin at the beginning of the test and administer every item. I usually start at the highest level at which success seems likely and move to the next higher level if the patient easily succeeds on three or four items. When a score is needed, as for research purposes or when preparing a report that may enter into litigation proceedings, the examiner may wish to use one of the several short forms.

Table 11-2 A Summary of Scores Obtained by the Four Experimental Groups on the Token Test

| | | Brain Damaged Patients: | | |
| | | Right | Left | |
Partial scores	Control Patients (n = 31)	(n = 30)	Nonaphasic (n = 26)	Aphasic (n = 34)
Part I				
10	31	30	26	30
9 & lower				4
Part II				
10	31	30	25	23
9 & lower		1	1	11
Part III				
10	29	28	25	13·
9	2	2	1	10
8 & lower				11
Part IV				
10	29	25	21	5
9	2	3	3	4
8 & lower		2	2	25
Part V				
20 & above	28	22	14	3
18 & 19	3	7	5	2
17 & lower		1	7	29
Total score				
60 & above	26	21	14	2
58–59	5	6	4	1
57 & lower		3	8	31

(Adapted from Boller and Vignolo, 1966.)

Spreen and Benton (1969) developed a 39-item modification of De Renzi and Vignolo's long form, which is incorporated in the Neurosensory Center Comprehensive Examination for Aphasia. From this, Spellacy and Spreen (1969) constructed a 16-item short form that uses the same 20 tokens as both the original and the modified long forms and includes many of the relational items of Part V.

A 22-item Token Test is part of Benton and Hamsher's Multilingual Aphasia Examination battery (1976, 1978) (see pp. 317–318). The first ten items contain representative samples from sections I to IV of the original test, the last 11 items involve the more complex relational concepts found in the original section V. The 16-item short form identified 85% of the aphasic and 76% of the nonaphasic brain damaged patients, screening as well as Part V of the 62-item long form, but not quite as well as the entire long form. These data suggest that for screening, either Part V or a short form of the Token Test will usually be adequate. Patients who achieve a borderline score on one of these shorter forms of the test should be given the entire test to clarify the equivocal findings.

A *"Short Version" of the Token Test* (De Renzi and Faglioni, 1978).   This 36-item "short version" takes half the time of the original test and is therefore less likely to be fatiguing. This version differs from others in the inclusion of a sixth section, Part 1, to lower the test's range of difficulty. The new Part 1 contains seven items requiring comprehension of only one element (aside from the command, "touch"); e.g., "1. Touch a circle"; "3. Touch a yellow token"; "7. Touch a white one." To keep the total number of items down, De Renzi and Faglioni use only 13 items in Part 6 (taken from the original Part 5), and each of the other parts, from 2 through 5, contains four items (see the double-numbered items of Table 11-1 and its footnote). On the first five parts, should the patient fail or not respond for five seconds, the examiner returns misplaced tokens to their original position and repeats the command. Success on the second try earns half a credit. The authors recommend that the earned score be adjusted for education (see Table 11-3). The adjusted score that best differentiated their control subjects from aphasic patients was 29, with only 5% of the control subjects scoring lower and 7% of the patients scoring higher. A scheme for grading auditory comprehension based on the adjusted scores (see Table 11-3) is offered for making practical clinical discriminations. De Renzi and Faglioni reported that scores below 17 did distinguish patients with global aphasia from the higher-scoring ones with Broca's aphasia.

Revised Token Test (RTT) (McNeil and Prescott, 1978).   This expanded version of the original Token Test contains ten ten-item subtests. The materials and layout are essentially the same as for other forms of the test. Its length is a result of the authors'

Table 11-3   Adjusted Scores and Grading Scheme for the "Short Version" of the Token Test

Conversion of Raw Scores to Adjusted Scores		Severity Grades for Adjusted Scores	
For years of education	Change raw scores by	Score	Grade
3–6	+1	25–28	Mild
10–12	−1	17–24	Moderate
13–16	−2	9–16	Severe
17+	−3	8 or less	Very severe

(Adapted from De Renzi and Faglioni, 1978)

efforts to set the Token Test in a framework that satisfies accepted psychometric criteria for test construction. Each of the first four subtests contains items that are structurally identical to its counterpart in the first four parts of the original Token Test. Subtests V, VI, IX, and X contain variations on the syntactically complex items of the original Part 5. Subtests VII and VIII test right-left orientation. Four to eight "linguistic elements" of each of the responses are scored on a 1- to 15-point scale that parallels the 15-point scale devised for the PICA (see pp. 318–319). The authors state that "detailed analysis of the RTT score sheet and profiles" should disclose the specific deficits contributing to auditory processing impairments, and they provide six tables (12 full pages) of normative data (from 90 control subjects, 30 left brain and 30 right brain damaged patients) to facilitate this analysis. Whether this format adds enough clinically useful information to what can be gained from a shorter form of the Token Test to warrant its considerable redundancy and the additional examination and scoring time is a question that will probably be answered by practical considerations, at least until the RTT is subjected to disinterested cross-validation.

Verbal Skills

Word Usage

Individually administered tests of word knowledge typically give the examiner more information about the patient's verbal abilities than just an estimate of vocabulary level. Responses to open-ended vocabulary questions, for example, can be evaluated for conceptual level and complexity of verbalization (see p. 271). Descriptions of activities and story telling can demonstrate how expressive deficits interfere with effective communication and may bring out subtle deficits that have not shown up on less demanding tasks.

PICTURE-NAMING TESTS

Another form of vocabulary test, naming pictures, can also provide useful information about the patient's ability to use words. Snodgrass and Vanderwart (1980) have developed a set of 260 pictures with norms for "name agreement, image agreement, familiarity, and visual complexity" that should enable the examiner to make up naming tasks suitable for particular patients or research questions. The two tests described below each deal with picture naming differently. Although their pictures are not available for commercial distribution, they deserve mention because together they can give the reader a working perspective on the kinds of clinically applicable information a naming test can yield.

Object-Naming Test (Newcombe et al., 1971). A set of 36 line drawings put together by Oldfield and Wingfield (1965) was used to examine the naming errors (i.e., "misnaming," which includes descriptions by use or correct associations, "misidentification," and "not known") and response latencies of patients with focal missile wounds. The drawings represent nouns selected from Thorndike and Lorge's word list (1944) for their different frequencies of usage (from more than 100 occurrences in a million words of text to one per three million). With a cut-off score of 20 correct responses, derived from the performances of two control groups comparable in age to the patients, only 4% of the control subjects and 3% of right brain damaged patients scored below 20 correct, but 16% of those with left brain damage and 15% with bilateral damage scored that low. Differences between the groups also appeared in the nature of their errors; the left brain damaged patients made a preponderance of misnaming errors and those with bilateral lesions made somewhat more misidentification errors than the others. Response latency was measured only for those persons who named a set, including at least 20 pictures, correctly. This procedure excluded 51% of the left brain damaged patients but only 25% of the controls. Even with such select patient groups, the control subjects had shorter latencies than the other groups at all word frequency levels. When pictures of low-frequency words were shown, bilaterally damaged patients' response latencies were very long (means in the range of 1.5–3.0 seconds) relative to the other patients as well as the control subjects.

The Boston Naming Test (Kaplan et al., 1978.)[1] This test consists of 85 large pen and ink drawings of items ranging in familiarity from such common ones as tree and pencil at the beginning of the test to sphinx and trellis at its end. When a patient is unable to name a drawing, the examiner gives a stimulus cue; if he is still unable to give a correct name, a phonetic cue is provided (e.g., for pelican, "it's a bird," "pe"). The examiner notes how often cues are needed and which ones are successful. Borod and her co-workers (1980) give age-graded norms for the number of items identified, including means, ranges, and cut-off scores based on a normal control population ranging in age from 25 to 85. Although this test was designed for the evaluation of naming deficits, Kaplan recommends using it with patients with right hemisphere damage, too. She notes that, particularly for patients with right frontal damage, some of the drawings elicit responses reflecting perceptual fragmentation (e.g., the mouthpiece of a harmonica may be reinterpreted as the line of windows on a bus!).

EXPRESSIVE DEFICITS

Story telling. Pictures are good standard stimuli for eliciting free speech. The Cookie Jar Theft picture from the Boston Aphasia Examination (Goodglass and Kaplan, 1972) is an excellent one for sampling propositional speech since the simple line drawing depicts familiar characters (e.g., mother, mischievous boy) engaged in familiar activities (washing dishes) in a familiar setting (a kitchen). To make sense out of F. L. Wells and Ruesch's (1969) Smashed Window picture, the subject must

---

[1]This test material can be ordered from Dr. Edith F. Kaplan, Psychology Service (116B), Veterans Administration Medical Center, 150 S. Huntington Ave., Boston, MA 02130.

appreciate social cues and integrate a number of discrete elements. The Birthday Party picture from the Stanford-Binet Scales (Terman and Merrill, 1973), although a less complex stimulus, can also be used for this purpose. Responses to such picture tests provide information about how effectively the subject perceives and integrates the elements of the picture (Lezak, 1982b) and about such aspects of verbal ability as word choice, vocabulary level, grammar and syntax, and richness and complexity of statements.

Describing activities.   Open-ended questions about a patient's activities or skills also elicit samples of speech that can show how well the patient expresses himself verbally. I have asked patients to describe their work (e.g., "Tell me how you operate a drill press?"), a behavior day ("Beginning with when you get up, tell me what you do all day."), or their plans. While these questions may enable the examiner to learn about the patient's abilities to plan and carry out activities, they do not allow for much comparison between patients (e.g., How do you compare a farmer's description of his work with that of a sawmill worker who pulls logs off of a conveyor belt all day?). Moreover, the patient's work may be so routine or his plans so ill-formulated that the question does not elicit many words. De Renzi and Ferrari (1978) have solved this problem for their Italian population by asking men to describe how they shave and women how to cook spaghetti. "Tell me how to make scrambled eggs" is a counterpart of the spaghetti question that most Americans can answer. D. Cohen and Eisdorfer (in press) ask their patients to give the steps in changing a tire or baking a cake.

Verbal Fluency

Following brain injury, many patients experience changes in the speed and ease of verbal production. Greatly reduced verbal productivity accompanies most aphasic disabilities, but it does not necessarily signify the presence of aphasia. Impaired verbal fluency is also associated with frontal lobe damage, particularly the left frontal lobe anterior to Broca's area (Milner, 1975; Ramier and Hécaen, 1970; Tow, 1955). A fluency problem can show up in speech, reading, and writing; generally it will affect all three activities (Perret, 1974; L. B. Taylor, 1979).

FLUENCY OF SPEECH

Fluency of speech is typically measured by the quantity of words produced, usually within a restricted category or to a stimulus, and usually within a time limit. Almost any test format that provides the opportunity for unrestricted speech will test its fluency. For example, Dailey (1956) found that trauma patients whose damage predominantly involved the frontal lobes produced many fewer responses to the Rorschach test than patients with posterior lesions. Usually, verbal fluency is measured by word-naming tests. Estes (1974) pointed out that successful performance on these tests depends in part on the subject's ability to "organize his output in terms of clusters of meaningfully related words." He also noted that word-naming tests indirectly involve short-term memory in keeping track of what words have already been said. Age, sex, and education have been found to influence performance on these tests (Benton et al., 1983; Verhoff et al., 1979; Wertz, 1979b), with women's performances holding up increasingly better than men's after age 55.

As Estes suggested, word fluency tests provide an excellent means of finding out whether and how well the subject organizes his thinking. Fluency tests requiring the subject to generate words according to an initial letter give the greatest scope to the subject seeking a strategy for guiding his search for words and are most difficult for subjects who cannot develop strategies of their own. Examples of effective strategies are use of the same initial consonant (e.g., content, contain, contend, etc.), variations on a word (shoe, shoelace, shoemaker), or variations on a theme (sew, stitch, seam). Fluency tests calling for items in a category (e.g., animals, what you find in a grocery store) provide the structure lacking in those asking for words by initial letter. However, even within categories, subjects to whom strategy-making comes naturally will often develop subcategories for organizing their recall. For example, the category "animals" can be addressed in terms of domestic animals, farm animals, wild animals, or birds, fish, mammals, etc.

Word Naming (Stanford-Binet). One of the earliest fluency tests, Word Naming, simply requires the subject to say as many words as possible in one minute, without saying sentences or number series. In Terman and Merrill's 1960 standardization of the Stanford-Binet, 59% of the ten-year-olds tested gave a minimum of 28 words, which is the Binet Form L-M norm for that age.

Controlled Oral Word Association Test (Benton and Hamsher, 1976; Benton et al., 1983). Benton and his group have systematically studied the oral production of spoken words beginning with a designated letter. The associative value of each letter of the alphabet except X and Z was determined in a normative study using normal control subjects (Borkowski et al., 1967). Control subjects of low ability tended to perform a little less well than brighter brain damaged patients. This result highlights the necessity of taking the patient's premorbid verbal skill level into account when evaluating verbal fluency.

The Controlled Oral Word Association Test (first called the Verbal Associative Fluency Test and then the Controlled Word Association Test) consists of three word-naming trials. The set of letters that were first employed, FAS, has been used so extensively that this test is sometimes called "FAS." The 1976 version was developed as part of Benton and Hamsher's Multilingual Aphasia Examination (see pp. 317–318). It provides norms for two sets of letters, CFL and PRW. These letters were selected on the basis of the frequency of English words beginning with these letters. In each set, words beginning with the first letter of these two sets have a relatively high frequency, the second letter has a somewhat lower frequency, and the third letter has a still lower frequency. In keeping with the goal of developing a multilingual battery for the examination of aphasia, Benton and Hamsher also give the frequency rank for letters in French, German, Italian, and Spanish.

330

Table 11-4 Controlled Oral Word Association Test: Adjustment Formula for Males (M) and Females (F)

Add points to raw scores of 10 and above as indicated:

Education (years completed)	Age					
	25–54		55–59		60–64	
	M	F	M	F	M	F
Less than 9	9	8	11	10	14	12
9–11	6	5	7	7	9	9
12–15	4	3	5	4	7	6
16 or more	—	—	1	1	3	3

(Adapted from Benton and Hamsher, 1976)

To give the test, the examiner asks the subject to say as many words as he can think of that begin with the given letter of the alphabet, excluding proper nouns, numbers, and the same word with a different suffix. The multilingual battery version also provides for a warm-up trial using the very high frequency letter "S." The practice trial terminates when the subject has volunteered two appropriate "S" words. This method allows the examiner to determine whether the subject comprehends the task before attempting a scored trial. The score, which is the sum of all acceptable words produced in the three one-minute trials, is adjusted for age, sex, and education (see Table 11-4). The adjusted scores can then be converted to percentiles (see Table 11-5). Benton (personal communication) advises that these are tentative norms and that new normative data are being collected. Moreover, since variability at lower educational levels tends to be wide, the performances of persons with less than a high school education must be interpreted with caution.

Word fluency as measured by FAS and similar techniques calling for generation of word lists has proven to be a sensitive indicator of brain dysfunction. Frontal lesions,

Table 11-5 Controlled Oral Word Association Test: Summary Table

Adjusted Scores	Percentile Range	Classification
53+	96+	Superior
45–52	77–89	High normal
31–44	25–75	Normal
25–30	11–22	Low normal
23–24	5–8	Borderline
17–22	1–3	Defective
10–16	<1	Severe defect
0–9	<1	Nil—Trace

(Adapted from Benton and Hamsher, 1976)

regardless of side, tend to depress fluency scores, with left frontal lesions resulting in lower word production than right frontal ones (Miceli et al., 1981; Perret, 1974; Ramier et Hécaen, 1970). Benton (1968a) found that not only did patients with left frontal lesions produce on the average almost one-third fewer FAS words than patients with right frontal lesions, but bilateral lesions tended to lower verbal productivity even more. Reduced capacity to generate words has also been associated with Alzheimer's-type dementia (E. Miller and Hague, 1975). In contrast, verbal fluency holds up when symptoms of depression mimic organic deterioration (Kronfol et al., 1978).

Other verbal fluency tests. Studying the effect of set on the verbal productions of patients with severe memory disorder (Korsakoff's psychosis, see pp. 196–197), Talland (1965a) asked his subjects to "name as many different things as you can that one is likely to see in the street" in 60 seconds, and to "name as many different animals as you can" in 30 seconds. A control group of 17 normal persons with a mean Wechsler Vocabulary scaled score of 10 gave an average of 15.7 street sights and 12.5 animals, whereas patients named an average of 8.8 street sights and 9.1 animals.

The *Set Test* is another test of the effect of set on verbal fluency (Isaacs and Kennie, 1973). The subject is asked to name as many items as he can from four successive categories: colors, animals, fruits, and towns. He names items in the first category until he recalls ten items or can remember no more, at which point the next category is announced, and so on. His score is the total number of items recalled, 40 being the highest possible score. This test has been given to a random sample of 189 persons aged 65 and older. Healthy old people averaged 31.2 names. Of the old people in this sample, 95% achieved scores of 15 or over; scores below 15 are considered abnormal for this age group. All of the 22 persons in the sample group who named fewer than 15 words had other symptoms of brain disease. Six persons diagnosed as demented achieved scores between 15 and 24, as did three depressed persons and 12 who were healthy and in good spirits. In contrast, only one of the 146 patients with scores of 25 or better was described as confused, and 11 were considered "anxious or depressed."

Newcombe (1969) used another variant of these tests, asking her patients first to name objects, then animals, and then to alternate in naming birds and colors, each for 60 seconds. The first two tasks were scored for number of correct words emitted, the last for each correct alternation (e.g., B-C-B = 2, BB-C-B-CC = 3). She found that patients with left hemisphere lesions performed more poorly than those with right hemisphere lesions, but no regular performance differential related to the injured lobe (see Table 11-6). The fluency test discriminated between right and left hemisphere lesions better than most of the tests in Newcombe's considerable battery, but the overlap between groups is too large for these data to indicate much more than a tendency to impaired fluency in the left hemisphere group.

W. G. Rosen (1980) used the CFL form of the Controlled Word Association Test along with an animal-naming task to study the verbal fluency of patients with Alzheimer's-type dementia. She found that both elderly control subjects and mildly

Table 11-6 Performance Averages of Patients with Left and Right Hemisphere Damage and of Controls on Three Verbal Fluency Tests

Group	Object Naming	Animal Naming	Alternations
Left hemisphere	24.25 (n = 50)	14.43 (n = 35)	12.00 (n = 50)
Right hemisphere	29.02 (n = 42)	18.00 (n = 31)	14.24 (n = 42)
Controls (n = 20)	30.20	16.95	16.95

(Adapted from Newcombe, 1969)

demented patients named more animals than CFL words. This difference was most pronounced among the elderly subjects who averaged more than seven animal names within the first quarter of the minute-long trial in contrast to the mildly demented group's average of little more than four. Both normal subjects and mildly demented patients gave more than twice as many animal names within the first quarter of the trial than in subsequent quarters. Patients in moderate to severe stages of deterioration did equally poorly on both fluency tests, averaging fewer than two words per minute. Rosen suggests that differences in the hierarchical organization of the two categories (letters and animal names) may account for the performance differences as retrieval by letter requires exploration of more category subsets than does retrieval by animal name.

In a variation of the animal naming task, R. S. Wilson, Kaszniak, Fox et al. (1981b) scored the most productive 60 seconds of a 90-second trial. A control group composed of 32 subjects (mean age = 67.7, mean education = 13.1) averaged 18.8 animal names, more than twice as many as an age-matched sample of dementia patients. Fuld (1980) explores verbal fluency in elderly and demented persons by asking her subjects to name fruits, vegetables, and happy and sad events (see p. 575).

WRITING FLUENCY

Word fluency. A written test for word fluency first appeared in the Thurstones' Primary Mental Abilities tests (1938; 1962). The subject must write as many words beginning with the letter S as he can in five minutes, and then write as many four-letter words beginning with C as he can in four minutes. The average 18-year-old can produce 65 words within the nine-minute total writing time. Milner and her colleagues at the Montreal Neurological Institute use a cutting score of 45 to identify fluency problems. Milner (1964, 1975) found that the performance of patients with left frontal lobectomies was significantly impaired on this test relative to that of other patients with left hemisphere lobectomies whose frontal lobes remained intact, and to that of patients whose surgery was confined to the right hemisphere. She observed that this task is more discriminating than object-naming fluency tests because the writing task, particularly for C words, is harder.

Quantity of writing. Clinical observations that many patients with right hemisphere damage tend to be verbose led to speculation that these patients may use more words when writing than do other persons (Lezak and Newman, 1979). The number of words used to answer personal and WAIS-type questions, complete the stems of a sentence completion test, and write interpretations to proverbs and a story to TAT card 13MF was counted for 29 patients who had predominantly right hemisphere damage, 15 whose damage was predominantly in the left hemisphere, 25 with bilateral or diffuse damage, and also for 41 control subjects hospitalized for medical or surgical care. On a number of these items, proportionately more patients with predominately right hemisphere damage gave very wordy responses than other brain damaged patients or the control patients. This phenomenon appeared most clearly on the open-ended questions of the sentence completion test and a personal history question, neither of which required much conceptual prowess or writing skill. On proverb interpretations and the TAT story, education level played the greatest role in determining response length except for the tendency of the left brain damaged group to give the shortest responses to proverbs.

Speed of writing. Talland (1965a) measured writing speed in two ways: speed of copying a 12-word sentence printed in one-inch type and speed of writing dictated sentences. On the copying task, his 16 control subjects averaged 33.9 seconds for completion, taking significantly less time ($p < .05$) than patients with Korsakoff's psychosis. No significant score differences distinguished the control subjects from the patients in their speed of writing a single 12-word sentence. However, when writing down a 97-word story, read to them at the rate of one to two seconds per word, the control subjects averaged 71.1 words within the three-minute time limit, whereas the patient group's average was 53.1 ($t = 2.69$, $p < .02$). It would appear that when writing speed has been slowed by brain damage, the slowing may become more evident as the length of the task increases.

Moreover, the amount of time it took to write the word "television" with the non-preferred hand differentiated neurologically normal and abnormal schizophrenic patients better than 30 other measures, mostly taken from the standard Halstead-Reitan battery (see pp. 562–566) (G. Goldstein and Halperin, 1977). The investigators acknowledged being at a loss to explain this finding and wondered whether this sensitivity might be a function of the task's midrange level of complexity. Times in the range of 6.6 and 5.7 seconds have been reported for the organically intact schizophrenic patients studied by Goldstein and Halperin and for medicated epileptics (R. Lewis and Kupke, 1977), respectively. Nondominant hand times tend to run just

334

about twice as long as times for the dominant hand suggesting that pronounced deviations from this pattern may reflect unilateral brain damage.

READING FLUENCY

The Stroop Test has been used to measure reading fluency, but because of its sensitivity to impairments in executive functions—particularly those relating to mental control and response flexibility—it is more widely used as a measure of frontal lobe dysfunction than a reading test. For this reason, the detailed discussion of the Stroop Test will be given in Chapter 16, pp. 523–525, in the section on Executive Functions.

Academic Skills

With the exception of aphasia tests, surprisingly few neuropsychological batteries contain tests of learned verbal skills such as reading, writing, spelling, and arithmetic. Yet, impairment in these commonplace activities can have profound repercussions on a patient's vocational competence and ultimate adjustment. It can also provide clues to the nature of the underlying organic condition. Some standard tests measure a single skill and other tests measure more than one (see pp. 299–307, and Buros, 1978).

Reading

THE GATES-MACGINITIE READING TESTS (Gates and MacGinitie, 1965, 1969)

These are good examples of academic skill tests that lend themselves to neuropsychological assessment. These paper and pencil multiple-choice tests come in four primary levels and three grade and high school levels. The highest level, Survey F, contains norms for grades 10, 11, and 12. Grade level 12-8 (last quarter of the 12th year) norms are suitable for most adults, although the ceiling is apt to be too low for college graduates. Patients for whom Survey F is too difficult can take the test at a lower level. Survey D, for instance, extends down to grade 4. Patients who are unable to handle it should be given the individualized PIAT or an aphasia test for an evaluation of their reading skills.

The Gates-MacGinitie tests measure different aspects of reading separately. The first subtest, Speed and Accuracy, has a four-minute limit and determines how rapidly the subject reads with understanding. The second subtest, Vocabulary, involves simple word recognition. The last subtest, Comprehension, measures ability to understand written passages. Both Vocabulary and Comprehension scores tend to be lower when verbal functioning is impaired. When verbal functions remain essentially intact, but higher level conceptual and organizing activities are impaired, a marked differential favoring Vocabulary over Comprehension may appear between the scores of these two subtests. The norms of Speed and Accuracy are so time-dependent as to tell little about brain damaged patients except that they tend to be slow. The other two tests also have time limits, but they are more generous. They can be administered as untimed tests without much loss of information since most very slow patients fail a large number of the more difficult items they complete outside the standard time limits.

THE DIAGNOSTIC SCREENING PROCEDURE (Boder, 1973)

This simple test, designed for diagnosing developmental dyslexia, can be useful in analyzing reading disorders associated with adult onset brain damage as well. All the materials necessary for administering it are given in Boder's article. The first section contains eight 20-word lists graded in order of difficulty from pre-primer (e.g., "and," "go") to sixth grade (e.g., "earthquake," "foreign") reading levels. Responses are scored according to speed. Responses made within one second of exposure get credit for "flash" recognition and the subject is shown the next word. Words read correctly within ten seconds are given "untimed" credit. "Flash" recognition words are considered to be part of the subject's "sight vocabulary." The highest grade level at which 50 or more of the words are read by sight is the subject's reading level. To determine the extent to which the subject reads by sight or phonetically, the examiner need only compare the number of "flash" and "untimed" words that the subject reads correctly.

The second section of this test, the spelling test, also comes in two parts, "known words" from the sight vocabulary, and "unknown words," i.e., words not in the sight vocabulary. The examiner first dictates ten words from the three highest grades of the sight vocabulary for spelling. Next he dictates ten "unknown" words at the subject's grade level or higher. Analysis of spelling focuses on the relative number of phonetic and nonphonetic "known" words correctly spelled and on the effectiveness of phonetic spelling of "unknown" words.

Boder defines three classifications of childhood dyslexia. Reversals and letter-order errors characterize the reading and writing of all three groups. 1. *Dysphonetic Dyslexia:* These children have the capacity for immediate recognition and fluent reading of a limited number of words, i.e., their sight vocabulary, which they read "*globally* as instantaneous visual gestalts." They cannot read phonetically or spell phonetically, but can spell known words that they are able to revisualize. Both their reading and their spelling are characterized by conceptually related word substitutes. 2. *Dyseidetic Dyslexia:* Boder describes these children as "letter blind," in that they have difficulty learning to distinguish the letters because of a disability in forming visual gestalts. Once they have learned to associate sounds with letter forms, they read by phonetic analysis and develop little if any sight vocabulary. They then have their greatest difficulty with nonphonetic words. Their misspellings are phonetic but not bizarre. These children usually misspell nonphonetic words that they know by sight but spell unknown phonetic words correctly. 3. *Mixed Dysphonetic-dyseidetic Dyslexia (Alexia):* As one might expect, children who can use neither sight nor sound readily have difficulty with all aspects of reading and spelling.

MINKUS COMPLETION (subtest of the Stanford-Binet scales, years XII and SA I)
(Terman and Merrill, 1973)

This fill-in sentence-completion test requires an appreciation of syntactical construction at average and above-average difficulty levels. It examines word usage as well as reading comprehension. I have combined the four items from each age level into a single eight-item test given routinely as part of a paper and pencil test packet for neuropsychological assessment (see pp. 108–109). I use Terman and Merrill's scoring standards to document the level of a patient's performance when evaluating it in reference to a comparison standard or for formal reporting. Thus, a patient who has completed high school satisfactorily but fails three items at the SA I level may be doing as well as can be expected, but the same performance by a college graduate would put his reading comprehension or word usage into question. This test is sensitive to the higher level deficits in verbal comprehension and conceptual integration that may be associated with right hemisphere damage (Eisenson, 1962).

NEW ADULT READING TEST (NART) (Nelson, no date; Nelson and O'Connell, 1978)

Since vocabulary correlates best with overall ability level and tends to resist the dementing process better than any other intellectual attainment, the residual vocabulary of patients with dementing conditions may be the best indicator of premorbid intellectual ability. Although dementing patients may not be able to give definitions, their correct pronunciation of words when reading has been used as evidence of premorbid familiarity with a word (Nelson and O'Connell, 1978). However, demented patients can sound out unfamiliar but phonetically regular words (see Table 11-7) as well as can normal control subjects, giving the impression of having known words that had actually been in their vocabularies. To better estimate the actual premorbid vocabulary of patients with dementing conditions, Nelson and O'Connell recommend using pronunciation of phonetically irregular words that can only be read correctly by someone who has had prior familiarity with them.

The NART list comprises 50 phonetically irregular words (see Table 11-8). Patients with cortical atrophy made many more errors reading the NART list of phonetically irregular words than a list of regularly formed words, also given in the authors' 1978 article. A control group made as many errors as did the patients on the irregular list but fewer errors on the list of phonetically regular words. NART's increased sensitivity to premorbid vocabulary level appears to permit more accurate prediction of premorbid ability for patients who had been of *high average* or better intelligence than do other reading vocabulary tests.

READING/EVERYDAY ACTIVITIES IN LIFE (REAL) (Lichtman, 1972)

This is a test of practical reading ability. It contains a representative sampling of every-day reading situations, such as a movie ad, a recipe, and a job application.

Table 11-7 Phonetically Regular Words

Adventurously	Indiscoverable	Chitterling	Tipularian
Individual	Manufactured	Herpetology	Gressorial
Uninterested	Organizations	Fleeringly	Paraboloid
Experimenter	Particularly	Huckaback	Hectographic
Apprehensive	Trajectory	Intertergal	Shibboleth

(Adapted from Nelson and O'Connell, 1978)

Table 11-8 The New Adult Reading Test

Ache	Subtle	Superfluous	Gouge	Beatify
Debt	Nausea	Radix	Placebo	Banal
Psalm	Equivocal	Assignate	Facade	Sidereal
Depot	Naive	Gist	Aver	Puerperal
Chord	Thyme	Hiatus	Leviathan	Topiary
Bouquet	Courteous	Simile	Chagrin	Demesne
Deny	Gaoled	Aeon	Detente	Labile
Capon	Procreate	Cellist	Gauche	Phlegm
Heir	Quadruped	Zealot	Drachm	Syncope
Aisle	Catacomb	Abstemious	Idyll	Prelate

(Adapted from Nelson and O'Connell, 1978)

Questions are on tape, but the subject can write his answers at his own pace. Available norms only make discriminations between functionally literate, marginally literate, and illiterate, so that this test is more useful for limited practical purposes than for clinical ones.

READING COMPREHENSION—SIMPLE COMMANDS (A. Smith, no date)

The five-sentence reading subtest of The *Michigan Neuropsychological Battery* (see p. 572) consists of cards, each with a simple command written on it, such as, "Put the lock in the cup"; "Close your eyes and touch your nose." Reading comprehension is reflected in the patient's motor responses. Gross screening tests such as this need no norms. Should a patient fail to perform the commands satisfactorily, the examiner must then analyze the reading disability in terms of its basic elements (e.g., form recognition, visual scanning, verbal comprehension, etc.) to determine the nature of the disability.

Writing and Spelling

Qualitative aspects of writing may distinguish the script of patients whose brain damage is lateralized (Brodal, 1973; Hécaen and Marcie, 1974). Patients with right hemisphere lesions tend to repeat elements of letters and words and to leave a wider than normal margin on the left-hand side of the paper. Left visuospatial inattention may be elicited by copying tasks (see Fig. 11-1). Edith Kaplan has called attention to "little perseverative errors" in the writing of patients with right brain lesions, such as extra bumps on n's and m's. Patients with left hemisphere lesions are more likely to have a wide right-sided margin and tend to leave separations between letters or syllables that disrupt the continuity of the writing line. Kaplan has also noted that aphasic patients tend to print when asked to write.

In studying the writing disturbances of acutely confused patients, Chédru and Geschwind (1972) devised a three-part writing test: (1) writing to *command,* in which patients were told to write a sentence about the weather and a sentence about their jobs; (2) writing to *dictation* of words (business, president, finishing, experience, physician, fight) and sentences ("The boy is stealing cookies." "If he is not careful the stool will fall."); and (3) *Copying* a printed sentence in script writing ("The quick brown fox jumped over the lazy dog."). They found that the writing of these patients

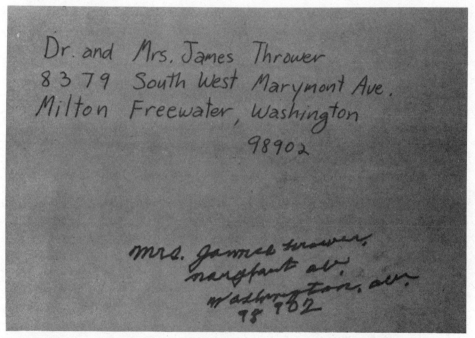

Fig. 11-1 This attempt to copy an address was made by a 66-year-old retired papermill worker two years after he had suffered a right frontal CVA. His writing not only illustrates left visuospatial inattention, but the tendency to add "bumps" (e.g., the m in "James") and impaired visual tracking (e.g., "Ave" is repeated on the line below the street address line)—all problems that can interfere with the reading and writing of patients with right hemisphere lesions.

339

SELF-ADMINISTERED BATTERY

General Information Questionnaire

Name ____________________

Address ____________________

City ____________________ State ____________________

Phone ____________________ Age ____________________

Soc. Sec. # ____________________ Date ____________________

Circle by number the highest year you completed in school:

1 2 3 4 5 6 7 8	1 2 3 4	1 2 3 4 5 6	______
Elementary School	High School	College	Graduate Degree

Please Circle:

Single Married Separated Divorced

Number of children ____________ Number of dependents ____________

What date were you admitted to the hospital? ____________ What Ward ____________

What is (or was) your occupation ____________________

When did you last work steadily prior to coming to the hospital ____________________

What problems brought you to the hospital ____________________

____

Fig. 11-2 Face sheet of the Self-Administered Battery.

was characterized by dysgraphia in the form of motor impairment (e.g., scribbling), spatial disorders (e.g., of alignment, overlapping, cramping), agrammatisms, and spelling and other linguistic errors. Moreover, dysgraphia tended to be the most prominent and consistent behavioral symptom displayed by them. The authors suggest that the fragility of writing stems from its dependence on so many different components of behavior and their integration. They also note that for most people, writing, unlike speaking, is far from an overlearned or well-practiced skill.

SENTENCE BUILDING (subtest of the Stanford-Binet scales, year SA I) (Terman and Merrill, 1973)

This task requires the patient to compose a sentence around three given words. It is sensitive to slight impairments of verbal functions that may show up in occasional speech hesitancies or neologisms but are not reflected in significantly depressed WAIS verbal subtest scores. Sentence Building can be given as a written test, either as part of a paper and pencil test battery in which the instructions and words are printed on an answer sheet, or it can be orally administered with the request to "write" the sentence. Besides testing verbal and sequential organizing abilities and use of syntax, the written format elicits spelling, punctuation, and graphomotor behavior. A written form of this subtest is included in my paper and pencil test packet for neuropsychological assessment (see pp. 108–109). The 1937 revision, Form M version of the Sentence Building subtest at age level VII broadens the applicability of this test to adults with limited verbal skills.

A five-item version of this task using two or three words is included in the Neuropsychological Test Battery developed by Miceli and his colleagues (Miceli et al., 1977, 1981). A scoring system takes into account both production of meaningful sentences that are grammatically correct (3 points each) and response time (1 point for sentences composed within 20 seconds, 2 points if response time is ten seconds or less). Performances of nonaphasic patients with left hemisphere lesions and of patients with right hemisphere lesions did not differ on the basis of their scores.

Writing and spelling can be readily assessed by questions requiring written responses such as those of the paper and pencil test battery that I use (see Fig. 11-2 and pp. 108–109). A self-report questionnaire, the *Personal History Inventory* (PHI) (Lezak, 1968), also provides incidental information about the patient's reading and writing skills.

341

12

Perceptual Functions

The tests considered in this chapter are essentially perceptual, requiring no physical manipulation of the test material; verbal or gestural responses suffice. Most of them test other functions as well, such as attention, spatial orientation, or memory, for the complexities of brain function make such overlap both inevitable and desirable. Only by testing each function in different modalities, in combination with different functions, and under different conditions can the examiner gain an understanding of which functions are impaired and how that impairment is manifested.

Visual Functions

Many aspects of visual perception may be impaired by brain disease. Typically an organic condition involving one visual function will affect a cluster of functions. Some other stimulus dimensions that may highlight different aspects of visual perception are the degree to which the stimulus is structured, the amount of old or new memory involved in the task, the spatial element, and the presence of interference.

Visual functions are broadly divided along the lines of verbal/symbolic and configural stimuli. When using visually presented material in the examination of lateralized disorders, however, the examiner cannot categorically assume that the right brain is doing most of the processing when the stimuli are pictures, or that the right brain is not engaged in distinguishing the shapes of words or numbers. Visual symbolic stimuli have spatial dimensions and other visual characteristics that lend themselves to processing as configurations, and most of what we see, including pictorial or design material, can be labeled. Materials for testing visuoperceptual functions do not conform to a strict verbal/configurational dichotomy any more than the visual stimuli of the real world do.

Visual Inattention

The visual inattention phenomenon (sometimes called visual neglect or visual extinction) usually involves absence of awareness of visual stimuli in the left field of vision, reflecting its common association with right hemisphere lesions (see pp. 72–73). Visual inattention is more likely to occur with posterior (usually parietal lobe) than anterior lesions (Frederiks, 1969a) but may result from frontal lobe lesions as well (Heilman and Valenstein, 1972). The presence of homonymous hemianopsia increases the likelihood of visual inattention, but these conditions are not necessarily linked (De Renzi, 1978; Diller and Weinberg, 1977). Visual inattention is more apt to be apparent during the acute stages of a sudden-onset condition such as stroke or trauma, when a patient may be inattentive to people on his neglected side, even when they speak to him, or eat only food on the side of the plate ipsilateral to the lesion—and complain that he is being served inadequate portions. Long after the acute stages of the condition and blatant signs of inattention have passed, when the patient's range of visual awareness seems intact on casual observation, careful testing may elicit evidence that some subtle neglect of visual stimuli remains.

In showing visual material to brain damaged patients, the examiner must always be alert to the possibility that the patient suffers visuospatial inattention and may not be aware of stimuli that appear on one side (usually the left) of the examination material (e.g., see D.C. Campbell and Oxbury, 1976; Colombo et al, 1976; Costa et al., 1969). For tests in which response choices are laid out in a horizontal format (e.g., 3×2 or 4×2 as in Raven's Matrices, Southern California Figure-Ground Visual Recognition Test, Test of Facial Recognition), the examiner may wish to realign the material so that all response choices are set in a column that can be presented to the patient's midline (or right side, if left-sided inattention is pronounced). Alternatively, when visuospatial inattention is obvious or suspected, tests with horizontal formats must be shown to the patient's right side.

LINE-MARKING TASKS FOR TESTING VISUAL INATTENTION

Although these tasks require a motor response, that response is typically so minimal that it hardly qualifies them as tests of visuomotor functions. Rather, their usefulness is in their sensitivity to disorders of visual inattention.

Crossing-out tests.　M. L. Albert (1973) standardized an informal technique for eliciting visual inattention, the *Test of visual neglect*. Patients were asked to cross out lines drawn randomly on a sheet of paper. Albert's version consists of a sheet of paper (20 × 26 cm) with 40 lines, each 2.5 cm long, drawn out at various angles and arranged so that 18 lines are widely dispersed on each side of a central column of four lines. Three weeks or more after unilateral surgery, 30 patients with right-sided lesions and 36 with lesions in the left hemisphere did not differ significantly in the percentage displaying inattention on this task (37% and 30% respectively). They did differ greatly, however, in the severity of the inattention phenomenon, patients with right-sided lesions left approximately seven times as many lines uncrossed as did the left-lesioned patients.

Line bisection tests.　The technique of examining for unilateral inattention by asking a patient to bisect a line has been used for years (Diller et al., 1974; Kinsbourne,

343

1974a). The examiner can draw the line for the patient or ask the patient to copy an already drawn horizontal line. (Diller and his group use a 10-mm line.) He then instructs the patient to divide the line by placing an "X" at the center point. The score is the length by which the patient's estimated center deviates from the actual center. When Diller's technique is used, a second score can be obtained for the deviation in length of the patient's line from that of the copied line. Numerical norms are not available for this technique. Noticeable errors are most often made by patients with visual field defects who tend to underestimate the side of the line opposite to the defective field, although the reverse error appears occasionally (Benton, 1969b). However, many patients with visuospatial inattention problems do not make these errors consistently. Thus, a single trial is often insufficient to demonstrate the defect.

With the *Line Bisection test* (*LB*), Schenkenberg and his colleagues (1980) have made a multiple-trial version of this technique.[1] In this test, the subject is asked to mark the middle of each of a set of 20 lines of different sizes arranged so that six are centered to the left of the midline of a typewriter-paper size page (21.5 × 28 cm), six to the right of midline, six in the center. A top and bottom line, to be used for instructions, is also centered on the page (see Fig. 12-1). Since only the middle 18 lines are scored, 180° rotation of the page produces an alternate form of the test. Instructions ask the patient to "Cut each line in half by placing a small pencil mark through each line as close to its center as possible," to take care to keep the nondrawing hand off the table, and to make only one mark on a line without skipping any. All capable patients take one trial with each hand, with randomized orientation of the page on first presentation and 180° rotation of the page on the second trial.

Two scores are obtained. One gives the number and position of unmarked lines (e.g., 4R, 1C, 2L). The other is a Percent Deviation score for left-, right-, and center-centered lines derived by means of the formula:

$$\text{Percent Deviation} = \frac{\text{measured left half} - \text{true half}}{\text{true half}} \times 100$$

Percent Deviation scores are positive for marks placed right of center and negative for left-of-center marks. Average Percent Deviation scores can be computed for each of the three sets of differently centered lines or for all lines.

Schenkenberg and his colleagues found that 15 out of 20 patients with right hemisphere damage totally neglected an average of 6.6 lines, while only ten of the 60 patients in the left-damaged, diffusely damaged, and control groups neglected any lines, and these ten omitted an average of only 1.4 lines each. Patients with right hemisphere lesions tended to miss lines, mostly those on the left and center of the page, regardless of hand used. Only one control subject neglected to mark one line. When patients with right hemisphere damage used their right hands, their cutting marks tended to deviate to the right on both left- and center-centered lines, but not

---

[1]A copy of this test can be obtained by writing to Dr. Thomas Schenkenberg, Psychology Service (116B), Veterans Administration Medical Center, Salt Lake City, Utah 84148.

Fig. 12-1 The Line Bisection test (Schenkenberg et al., 1980).

on right-centered lines. The other groups displayed no consistent deviation tendencies when using the right hand. A tendency to deviate to the left was generally manifested on left-hand trials, regardless of the site or presence of a brain lesion.

Although the task of bisecting a line has proven useful in eliciting the inattention phenomenon that is prominent among the visuoperceptual disorders of many patients with right brain lesions, inattention does not necessarily appear the first or even the second time these patients use their right hand to bisect a left-centered line. The Line Bisection test format is a sensitive one because it provides many trials, thus increasing the likelihood of demonstrating the presence of inattention, particularly when a patient's tendency to neglect the left half of space is only mild.

Use of Spatial Preference to Test for Visual Inattention

A series of techniques that elicit the visuospatial inattention phenomenon require the subject to indicate preferred positions on several kinds of patterns (Vernea, 1978). The patient is given a 9 × 9 grid of squares and asked to put an "X" in any three squares he chooses. When presented with a horizontal row of nine circles, he is asked to draw lines through any three. Two horizontal rows of nine dots are presented in parallel and the subject's task is to draw a vertical line between any three pairs of corresponding dots. Patients with left visuospatial inattention will show a predominant right-sided preference. Vernea has not found a similar preference bias among patients with left hemisphere lesions.

PICTURE DESCRIPTION TASKS FOR TESTING VISUAL INATTENTION

Symmetrically organized pictures can elicit "one-sided" response biases that reflect unilateral visual inattention. I use two pictures taken from travel advertisements: One has a columned gazebo in its center with seven lawn bowlers pictured along the horizontal expanse of the foreground; the other is a square composed of four distinctly different scenes, one in each quadrant. I ask patients to count the people and the columns in the first card and to tell me everything they see in the second one. Each of these pictures has successfully brought out the inattention phenomenon when it was not apparent to casual observation.

Meaningful Pictures (Battersby et al., 1956).   This test has a systematized format in which the patient is shown colored magazine illustrations or photographs that are essentially symmetrical on either side of the median plane. Each picture is presented first as a verbal recall task in which, after a ten-second exposure, the subject is asked to name and indicate the relative position of the details he recalls. On completion of the recall task, the subject sees each picture again with instructions to describe all the details while looking at the card. Card sides are compared for the number of responses they elicit; a preponderance on one side or the other suggests a lateralized visual inattention to the opposite side.

Picture Matrix Memory Task (G. Deutsch et al., 1980).   This technique was developed to verify suspected left unilateral visual inattention so that its potential for eliciting subtle defects of unilateral inattention has not been examined. However, its format is not unlike that of the 3 × 2 or 4 × 2 horizontal layout of Raven's Progressive Matrices (see p. 502) on which patients demonstrate inattention. Thus, it could be a promising clinical as well as research tool. It consists of a 4 × 2 horizontally extended array of eight line drawings of familiar subjects such as a baby, a flying kite, and a package of crayons. The patient sees this array for 10 seconds and then must recall as many objects as he can after the picture card has been removed. This simple format can lend itself to a number of variations—in number of pictures, length of exposure time, recall delay, and interference trials—to make it more or less difficult, more or less sensitive to inattention.

READING TASKS FOR TESTING VISUAL INATTENTION

Two kinds of word recognition problems can trouble nonaphasic patients. Both aphasic and nonaphasic patients with visual field defects, regardless of which hemisphere is damaged, tend to ignore the part of a printed line or even a long printed word that falls outside the range of their vision when the eye is fixated for reading.

346

This can occur in spite of the senselessness of the partial sentences they read. Patients with left hemisphere lesions may ignore the right side of the line or page, and those with right hemisphere lesions will not see what is on the left. This condition shows up readily on oral reading tasks in which sentences are several inches long. Newsprint is unsatisfactory for demonstrating this problem because the column is too narrow. To test for this phenomenon, Battersby and his colleagues (1956) developed a set of ten cards on which were printed ten familiar four-word phrases (e.g., GOOD HUMOR ICE CREAM, NEWS PAPER HEAD LINE) in letters 1 inch high and ⅙ inch in line thickness. Omission or distortion of words on only one side was considered evidence of a unilateral visual defect.

Left unilateral visual inattention for words, a defect that interferes with the reading accuracy and pleasure of many patients with right brain damage, may be clearly shown by having the patient copy sentences or phrases. Names and addresses make good copying material for this purpose since missing words or numbers are less apparent than a word or two omitted from the left-hand side of a meaningful line of print. When set up in a standard address format, patients' efforts to copy model addresses readily reveal inattention defects (see Fig. 11-1).

INATTENTION IN SPATIAL REPRESENTATION

Unilateral visuospatial inattention is a spatial as well as a visual phenomenon. This can be demonstrated in tests of spatial representation in which the visual component has been eliminated.

A scene-recall task for testing spatial inattention. Left-sided spatial neglect has been elicited by requesting the subject to describe a familiar locale (Bisiach and Luzzatti, 1978). Patients were asked to name the prominent features of a scene from two specific viewing points directly opposite one another. Their left-sided neglect was reflected in either absence or scant mention of features on the left, in marked contrast to detailed descriptions of structures to the right of each given perspective.

Dotting a target circle. A dotting task requires the subject to put five dots in a circle, approximately 1 cm in diameter, that has been drawn in the middle of a large sheet of paper (Vernea, 1978). After placing each dot, the subject must move his hand away from the drawing position to a center position below the paper or on his lap. Following this, the task is to continue placing dots within the circle with eyes closed and, again, moving the hand away between trials. When their eyes are closed, patients with left-sided inattention tend to place the dots to the right of the circle, straying increasingly further away as they continue dotting.

Color Perception

Tests of color perception serve a dual purpose in neuropsychological assessment. They can identify persons with congenitally defective color vision, or "color blindness," whose performance on tasks requiring accurate color recognition might otherwise be misinterpreted. Knowledge that the patient's color vision is defective will affect the examiner's evaluation of responses to colored material, such as the color cards of the *Rorschach* technique (see pp. 361, 602–604), and should militate against use of color-dependent tests such as the *Color Sorting Test* (see below and p. 483). They can also be used to test for color agnosia and related defects. Evaluation of color recognition (usually measured by color association tasks such as *Coloring of Pictures* or *Wrongly Colored Pictures*, discussed below) is important in examining aphasic patients since many of them have pronounced color recognition deficits (Benton, 1979). A small proportion of patients with lesions on the right and of nonaphasic patients with left-sided lesions also have color recognition problems.

TESTING FOR ACCURACY OF COLOR PERCEPTION

In neuropsychological assessment, the *Ishihara* (1964) and the *Dvorine* (1958) screening tests for the two most common types of color blindness are satisfactory. The *H-R-R Pseudoisochromatic Plates* (Hardy et al., 1955) screen for two rare forms of color blindness, which would not be correctly identified by the Ishihara or Dvorine tests, as well as for the two common types (Hsia and C. H. Graham, 1965). The stimulus materials of all three of these tests are cards printed with different colored dots, which form recognizable figures against a ground of contrasting colored dots. The Farnsworth-Munsell *100-hue and Dichotomous Test for Color Vision* (Farnsworth, 1943), which requires the subject to arrange colored paper chips according to hue, can be used to identify color agnosias and also to screen for the purely sensory disorder. The Color Sorting Test presents the patient with four different color identifying and sorting tasks with skeins of wool of different color and brightness (K. Goldstein and Scheerer, 1953a,b).

A COLOR PERCEPTION BATTERY (De Renzi and Spinnler, 1967)

This is a six-test battery for examining impaired response to color in patients with known lateralized lesions, including a color matching test, the Ishihara plates, color naming, point to color, verbal memory for color, and color drawing. The authors found that patients with visual field defects associated with right hemisphere lesions were most likely to have difficulty with the two purely perceptual tasks, color matching and the Ishihara plates, and to do poorly on the other tests as well. As expected, aphasic patients had more difficulty than any other group on tasks involving language.

DISCRIMINATING BETWEEN COLOR AGNOSIA AND COLOR ANOMIA

The problem of distinguishing color agnosia from an anomic disorder involving use of color words was ingeniously addressed in two tasks devised by Damasio and his colleagues (1979). *Coloring of Pictures* requires the subject to choose a crayon from a multicolored set and fill in simple line drawings of familiar objects that have strong color associations (e.g., banana—yellow; frog—green). In *Wrongly Colored Pictures*, the examiner shows the subject a line drawing that has been inappropriately colored (e.g., a green dog, a purple elephant), and asks what the picture represents.

In a refinement of these techniques which investigates the correctness of color associations, Varney (1982) developed a set of 24 line drawings of familiar objects (e.g., banana, ear of corn). Each drawing is accompanied by samples of four different colors of which only one is appropriate for the item. This format requires only a pointing response. Just four of 100 normal control subjects failed to identify at least 20 colors correctly. In contrast, 30% of the 50 aphasic patients failed this standard. It is interesting to note that all of the aphasic patients who failed the color association test also failed a reading comprehension task while none who succeeded on the reading task failed the color association test.

Visual Recognition

Interest in visual recognition has grown with the rapid expansion of knowledge of the different roles played by the hemispheres and with more precise understanding of the different functional systems. When the presence of brain damage is suspected or has been identified grossly, the examination of different aspects of visual recognition may lead to a clearer definition of the patient's condition.

ANGULATION

The perception of angular relationships tends to be a predominantly right hemisphere function except when the angles readily lend themselves to verbal description (e.g., horizontal, vertical, diagonal) and therefore can be mediated at least as easily by the left hemisphere as by the right (Berlucchi, 1974; Kimura and Durnfurd, 1974). Thus, it is not surprising that inaccurate perception of angulation may accompany right hemisphere damage (Benton et al., 1975).

Judgment of Line Orientation (Benton et al., 1975, 1978, 1983).[1] This test examines the ability to estimate angular relationships between line segments by visually matching angled line pairs to 11 numbered radii forming a semicircle (see Fig. 12-2). The test consists of 30 items, each showing a different pair of angled lines to be matched to the display cards. Its two forms, H and V, present the same items but in different order. A five-item practice set precedes the test proper. Normative data show that only 5% of the 144 normal control subjects obtained scores lower than 19 while only 3% of them made scores below 17 (Benton et al., 1978). Scores between 15 and 18 are interpreted as representing mild to moderate defects in the ability to judge line orientation; scores below 15 (made by one of 144 control subjects) indicate severe defect in this ability. As might be predicted from other studies of the ability to judge angular relationships, most (45 of 48) of the patients with left hemisphere

---

[1]The test material may be ordered from the Medical Sales Department, Oxford University Press, 200 Madison Ave., New York, N.Y. 10016.

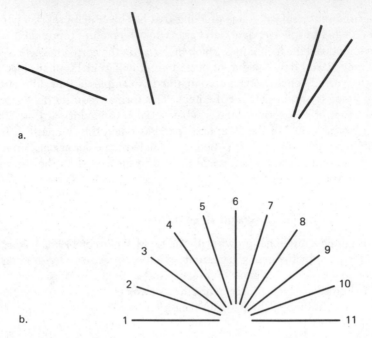

Fig. 12-2 Examples of double-line stimuli (a) to be matched to the multiple-choice card below (b).

damage performed in the normal range, and none obtained a score below 17. Again as might be predicted, many more (17 of 43) of the right hemisphere damaged patients had scores below 19 and, of these, 13 were in the severely defective range. However, only right hemisphere damaged patients with posterior lesions performed defectively.

RECOGNITION OF PICTURED OBJECTS

Warrington and Taylor (1973) examined the relative accuracy with which patients with right or left hemisphere lesions could identify familiar objects under distorting conditions. The first condition involved 20 enlarged drawings of small objects, such as a safety pin. Comparisons of patients' responses with those of control subjects to the enlarged pictures and to realistic-size drawings showed that neither patients nor control subjects had difficulty recognizing objects when drawn in their realistic size. Although the patient groups made significantly more errors than the control group in recognizing the enlarged objects, the difference in error score between the right and left brain damaged groups was negligible. In the second condition, photographs showed 20 familar objects from a conventional and an unconventional view. For example, a bucket was shown in a side view (the conventional view) and straight down from above (the unconventional view). This condition resulted in a clear-cut separation of patients with right brain damage who did poorly on this task from the left damaged group or the control subjects. In addition, patients with right posterior lesions made significantly more errors than any other of the brain damaged groups, whether right or left lesioned.

FACE RECOGNITION

Warrington and James's (1967b) demonstration that there is no regular relationship between inability to recognize familiar faces *(prosopagnosia)* and impaired recognition of unfamiliar faces has led to a separation of facial recognition tests into those involving a memory component and those that do not. Two kinds of facial recognition tests involve memory. All tests of familiar faces call on stored information. Typically, these tests require the subject to name or otherwise identify pictures of well-known persons (Milner, 1968; Warrington and James, 1967b). Two kinds of errors have been noted: Left hemisphere damaged patients identified but had difficulty naming the persons whereas defective recognition characterized the right hemisphere damaged patients' errors.

Recognition tests of unfamiliar faces involving memory have appeared in several formats. Photos can be presented for matching either one at a time or in sets of two or more. When the initial presentation consists of more than one picture, this adds a memory span component, which further complicates the faces recognition problem. The second set of photos to be recognized can be presented one at a time or grouped, and presentation may be immediate or delayed. By having to match unfamiliar faces following a delay, patients with brain damage involving the right temporal lobe demonstrated significant performance decrements, again linking memory for configural material with the right temporal lobe (Warrington and James, 1967b).

Test of Facial Recognition (Benton and Van Allen, 1968; Benton et al., 1983).[1]   This test was developed to examine the ability to recognize faces without involving a memory component. The patient matches identical front views, front with side views, and front views taken under different lighting conditions (see Fig. 12-3). The original test has 22 stimulus cards and calls for 54 separate matches. Six items involve only single responses (i.e., only one of six pictures on the stimulus card is of the same person as the sample), and 16 items call for three matches to the sample photograph. It may take from 10 to 20 minutes to administer, depending on the patient's response rate and cautiousness in making choices.

In order to reduce administration time, a short form of this test was developed that is half as long as the original (Levin et al., 1975). The 16-item version calls for only 27 matches based on six one-response and seven three-response items. Correlations between scores obtained on the long and short forms range from .884 to .940, reflect-

---

[1]The test material may be ordered from the Medical Sales Department, Oxford University Press, 200 Madison Ave.,New York, N.Y. 10016.

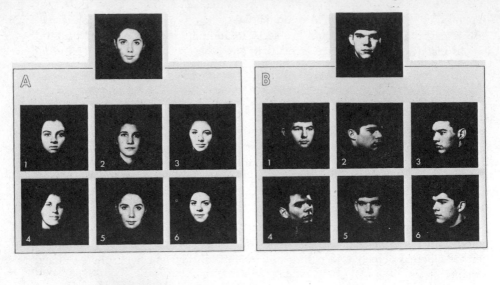

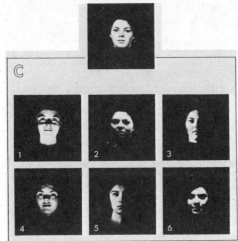

Fig. 12-3 Test of Facial Recognition (Benton and Van Allen, 1968; Benton et al., 1983). These photographs illustrate the three parts of the test: A. Matching of identical front-views. B. Matching of front-view with three-quarter views. C. Matching of front-view under different lighting conditions.

ing a practical equivalence between the two forms. Instructions and norms for both forms are included in the test packet.

Patients with right parietal lesions perform more poorly than those with right temporal lesions on the facial recognition task, which suggests that this task has a substantial visuospatial processing component (Dricker et al., 1978; Warrington and James, 1967b). That the task has a linguistic component is suggested by findings that aphasic patients with defective language comprehension fail on this test at rates similar to those of patients with right hemisphere damage (Hamsher et al., 1979). For both these groups, many more patients with posterior lesions had defective performances than did patients with anterior lesions. The performances of patients with left hemisphere lesions who were not aphasic or who were aphasic but did not have comprehension defects were indistinguishable from normal controls. Visual field defects do not necessarily affect facial recognition scores, but facial recognition deficits tend to occur with spatial agnosias and dyslexias, and with dysgraphias that involve spatial disturbance (Tzavaras et al., 1970). Normal subjects who are weakly left-handed may do less well on facial recognition tests than right-handed or strongly left-handed normal control subjects (Gilbert, 1973). This tendency has been related to the relatively decreased lateralization of functions hypothesized as characterizing the brain organization of weakly left-handed persons (see p. 221).

Recognition of the facial expression of emotion. Observations suggesting that patients with right-sided lesions appear to be somewhat insensitive emotionally have led investigators to examine whether the perception of facial emotion is differentially impaired by right hemisphere disease. DeKosky and his colleagues (1980) used photographs of four actors, each depicting four emotional states: happiness, sorrow, anger, and indifference. Overall, right hemisphere damaged subjects matched faces and made emotional discriminations less well than either control subjects or those with left-lateralized lesions. Patients with left hemisphere damage tended to perform less well than the control subjects on two of the four tasks involving discrimination of facial emotion, but significantly better than right hemisphere damaged patients and not very different from the control subjects on the other two tasks. In using a more complex experimental design that required recall as well as identification of emotional expression, Prigatano and Pribram (1982) found that patients with right posterior lesions were relatively more impaired than those with anterior lesions or than left hemisphere damaged patients. These findings were also supported by a study in which the right hemisphere damaged group displayed a similar difficulty in appreciating the emotional import of descriptive phrases (e.g., "A man sinking in quicksand") as well as of emotional facial expressions (Cicone et al., 1980). In this study, frontal leucotomy patients exhibited overall an even greater degree of emotional incomprehension than the right hemisphere damaged group. Patients with left hemisphere lesions had less difficulty than the other patient groups in appreciating facial expressions but were on a par with the right hemisphere group when the stimulus was verbal.

FIGURE AND DESIGN RECOGNITION

Simple recognition. Perceptual recognition of meaningless designs is usually tested by having the patient draw them from models or memory (see pp. 384ff, 443ff). When a subject's design reproductions contain the essential elements of the original from which they are copied and preserve their interrelationships with reasonable accuracy, his perceptual accuracy with this kind of material has been adequately demonstrated. A few correct responses to the WAIS Picture Completion subtest or a similar task show that the subject can recognize meaningful pictures. At lower levels of functioning, picture vocabulary tests, such as the Peabody Picture Vocabulary Test (pp. 307–308) or the *Picture Vocabulary* subtest of the Stanford-Binet Scales (pp. 288–289) may be used to assess recognition of meaningful pictures. Patients with verbal comprehension problems can be examined by the picture-matching tests of the Leiter (pp. 297–299) or the ITPA (p. 299). When the patient's graphic reproductions are inaccurate, markedly distorted, or simplified, or have glaring omissions or additions, or when he is unable to respond correctly to drawings or pictures, there is further need to study his perceptual accuracy.

There are many techniques for examining simple perceptual recognition. A low-level visual recognition task is *Discrimination of Forms* at age level IV of the Stanford-Binet. The patient is shown ten line drawings of common geometric figures such as a square, a circle, an oval, one at a time and asked to point out one like it on a card on which all ten geometric figures are displayed. Of the four-year-old normative group, 79% made correct responses on this test. The first 12 items of both forms of Raven's Progressive Matrices also test simple recognition of designs (Knehr, 1965; see pp. 502–506). The GATB (pp. 302–303) examines visuoperceptual accuracy on two visual matching subtests, 5-Tool Matching and 7-Form Matching. The most recent revision of the Beta Examination, originally developed by the U.S. Army to test the intellectual ability of World War I recruits who were illiterate or could not read English, contains a two-part perceptual acuity subtest (The Revised Beta Examination, Kellogg and Morton, 1935). The first part involves identifying like pairs of a variety of pictured items such as tools, birds, and geometric figures. The second part consists of paired numbers to match for identity.

Visual Organization

Tests requiring the subject to make sense out of ambiguous, incomplete, fragmented, or otherwise distorted visual stimuli call for perceptual organizing activity beyond that of simple perceptual recognition. Although the perceptual system tends to hold up well in the presence of organic brain changes for most ordinary purposes, any additional challenge may be beyond its organizing capacity. For this reason, tests of perceptual organization were among the earliest psychological instruments to be used for evaluating neuropsychological status. Roughly speaking, there are three broad categories of visual organization tests: test requiring the subject to fill in missing elements; tests presenting problems in reorganizing jumbled elements of a percept; and those stimuli lacking inherent organization onto which the subject must impose structure of his own making.

TESTS INVOLVING INCOMPLETE VISUAL STIMULI

Of all tests of visual organization, those in which the subject fills in a missing part, such as Picture Completion, are least vulnerable to the effects of brain damage, probably because their content is usually so well structured and readily identifiable. Thus, although technically they qualify as tests of perceptual organization, they are not especially sensitive to problems of perceptual organization except when the perceptual disorder is relatively severe.

Recognition of missing parts.   For most patients, the WAIS Picture Completion subtest is a good measure of the ability to fill in incomplete parts. An examiner who wants
to assess the capacity for visual organization of a severely impaired patient can use
Mutilated Pictures at age level VI of the Stanford-Binet. This test consists of one card
with five simple line drawings of incomplete objects, such as a glove without a finger
and a teapot without a handle. Three-quarters of all six-year-olds can identify the
missing part correctly.

Recognition of incomplete stimuli.   Several sets of incomplete pictures have been
used to examine the perceptual closure capacity. Although poor performance on
gestalt completion tests has generally been associated with right brain damage
(DeRenzi and Spinnler, 1966; Lansdell, 1970; Newcombe and Russell, 1969), Wasserstein (1980) and her colleagues (1980) found a low correlation between four such tests
when given to college students, the *Street Completion Test* (Street, 1931), unpublished Street items (Street, 1944), Mooney's *Closure Test* (see p. 356), and the Educational Testing Service's *Gestalt Completion Test* (Ekstrom et al., 1976). However,
analysis of the performance of unilaterally brain damaged patients indicated a relationship between performance on the gestalt completion tests and the perception of
subjective contour illusions (i.e., visual illusions in which brightness or color gradients
are seen when not present; for example, most people will see Fig. 12-4 as a solid white
triangle overlaying an inverted triangular frame and three black circles although no
solid triangle is physically present). Relationships between performances on the gestalt
completion tests and on a subjective contours task indicated that, unlike patients with
right hemisphere damage, the patients with left-sided lesions used a common solution
mechanism for solving both gestalt completion and subjective contour problems.
None of the four gestalt completion tests discriminated between the two patient
groups although the patients with left brain damage consistently had higher scores.

Eight items from the gestalt completion tests shared 75% or more of their variance
with performance on the subjective contours task for patients with left-sided lesions:
items 4, 8, and 18 of the Street Completion Test, and items 37, 39, 41, 51, and 53 of
the ETS test (Fig. 12-5). These items were extracted to make a new "subjective con-

Fig. 12-4 Example of subjective contour effect (E.L. Brown and Deffenbacher, 1979).

Fig. 12-5 Figure 8 of the Street Completion Test.

tour closure" test. When examined for its ability to discriminate patients on the basis of side of lesion, this new test demonstrated greater sensitivity to hemisphere side of lesion (p. <02) than any of the original gestalt completion tests. Moreover, left hemisphere damaged patients did better on this test than control subjects. Patients over 50, however, generally performed poorly on all of these tests, a finding in accord with other studies of closure functions in older people (Fozard et al. 1977). These authors note that performance on closure tests appears to be independent of performance on facial recognition tests, suggesting that two different perceptual processes having different anatomical correlates underlie the two different tests.

Closure Faces Test (CFT) (Mooney and Ferguson, 1951; Mooney, 1957) has enjoyed extensive use as a research instrument (e.g., Lansdell, 1968a, 1970; Newcombe, 1969, 1974). Each item depicts a face so extensively shaded that it has become a perceptual puzzle of the gestalt completion type. This test requires the subject to sort these pictures into one of six piles: B (boy), G (girl), M (grown man), W (grown woman), O (old man), or X (old woman). It has a demonstrated sensitivity to right hemisphere lesions, particularly those involving right temporoparietal areas, and could have clinical applications as well. Unfortunately, it has not been made available for clinical use and is therefore not generally accessible.

Gollin figures (Gollin, 1960) also made use of incomplete drawings to assess perceptual functions. The original test consists of 20 picture series of five line drawings of familiar objects (e.g., duck, tricycle, umbrella) ranging in completeness from a barely suggestive sketch (Set I) to a complete drawing of the figure (Set V). The score is the sum of all the set numbers at which each picture is correctly identified. Warrington (Warrington and James, 1967a; and Rabin, 1970) used Gollin's original procedure, but Warrington and Taylor (1973) used only three rather than five of the pictures in each of the 20 picture series. The Gollin figures did not discriminate between right and left hemisphere damaged groups in the Warrington and Rabin study, patients with right parietal lesions showing only a trend toward poor performance. However, this test was more sensitive to right brain lesions than other perceptual tests used by Warrington and James or Warrington and Taylor in their studies, successfully discriminating between patients with right and left hemisphere damage and implicating the right posterior (particularly parietal) lobe in the perception of incomplete contours.

TESTS INVOLVING FRAGMENTED VISUAL STIMULI

Perceptual puzzles requiring conceptual reorganization of disarranged pieces test the same perceptual functions as does Object Assembly. This kind of test material can have either meaningful or meaningless visual content.

The Hooper Visual Organization Test (HVOT) (Hooper, 1958).   The HVOT was developed to identify those patients in mental hospitals with organic brain conditions. Thirty pictures of more or less readily recognizable cut-up objects make up the test. The subject's task is to name each object verbally if the test is individually administered or by writing the object's name in spaces provided in the test booklet (see Fig. 12-6). This test does not correlate significantly with sex, education, age, or intelligence except at borderline defective and lower intellectual ability levels and at ages above 70. On three administrations repeated after six and then after 12 months, mean HVOT scores did not shift to any appreciable degree and a coefficient of concordance (W) of .86 indicated that test-retest reliability is high (Lezak, 1982d).

Intellectually intact persons generally fail no more than five HVOT items. Persons

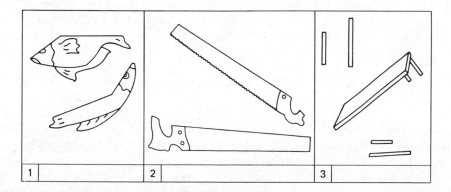

Fig. 12-6   Easy items of the Hooper Visual Organization Test. (By H. Elston Hooper, Ph.D. © 1958 by Western Psychological Services. Reprinted by permission.)

who make six to ten failures comprise a "borderline" group that includes emotionally disturbed or psychotic patients as well as those with mild to moderate brain disorders. More than ten failures usually indicate organic brain pathology. When this many errors result from a psychotic rather than a neuropathological condition, qualitative aspects of the responses will generally betray their functional etiology. Many brain injured persons perform well on the HVOT. However, a low score on this test usually indicates the presence of brain damage as false positive performances are rare.

The frequency of low scores (below 22; Mack and Levine, no date) on this test does not differ on the basis of side of lesion. Yet when Mack and Levine's patients with right-sided lesions scored below the cutting score, they tended to make significantly more errors than those whose brain damage was confined to the left hemisphere. However, J. L. Boyd (1981) reported no mean differences between groups with left, right, or diffuse/medial damage. Brain tumors and stroke tend to be associated with much lower scores than does head trauma (J. L. Boyd, 1981). The HVOT can be useful in investigations of the nature of a patient's disability since it may provide a means for separating the perceptual component from a patient's performance on Object Assembly and other visuoconstructional tests.

Several of the HVOT items are particularly effective in eliciting the kind of perceptual fragmentation that is most likely to be associated with lesions of the right frontal lobe, although all patients with right frontal lesions do not make this kind of error. Patients who exhibit this phenomenon will often be able to identify most of the items correctly, thus demonstrating that they understand the organizing demand of the instructions. Some may even obtain a score in the low 20s, reflecting accurate perceptual recognition. Yet, on one or more of the three items that contain one piece most clearly resembling an object in itself, patients who have a tendency to view their world in a fragmented manner will interpret that one piece without attending to any of the others in the item. For example, the top piece of item 1 may be called a "duck" or a "flying goose" (see Fig. 12-6. Also see pp. 285–286 for a discussion of the relationship of the HVOT and constructional tasks.) Item 21 becomes "a desert island" when only the center piece is taken into account, and the tail of the "mouse" of item 22 turns into "a pipe." When fragmentation is more severe, the mesh of item 12 may be called "a tennis net," item 14 becomes "a pencil," and item 30 "a plumber's helper" or "plunger."

The Minnesota Paper Form Board Test (Likert and Quasha, 1970).   This test uses nonobjective material—fragmented circles, triangles, and other geometric figures— to elicit perceptual organizing behavior (see Fig. 12-7). It calls on perceptual scanning and recognition and the ability to perceive fragmented percepts as wholes. In its standard form, it is a 64-item multiple-choice paper and pencil test with norms based on a 20-minute time limit. The manual gives norms for a variety of populations including high school students, men from various occupations and job applicant groups, and women factory work applicants. By and large, eleventh- and twelfth-grade student groups averaged 39 to 40 correct responses, as did groups of adult males. Female groups had average scores of 34 or 35. Correlations with paper and pencil intellectual

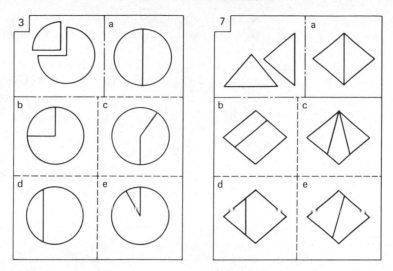

Fig. 12-7 Sample items from the Revised Minnesota Paper Form Board Test, Series BB. (Reproduced by permission. © 1941, renewed 1969, by The Psychological Corporation, New York, N.Y. All rights reserved.)

ability tests tend to be low, positive, and insignificant. In finding that this task could be readily solved by analytic processing, Guay and his co-workers (1978) questioned its usefulness as a spatial task.

Dee (1970) views this test as measuring "a higher level of perceptual ability" than does a simple matching task. He simplified the original formboard test by enlarging the 2″ × 3″ items to 6″ × 9″ and presenting only the first 40 of them individually rather than side by side in a test booklet. Dee used a 25-minute time limit, thereby allowing approximately twice as much time for each item. With this format, patients who performed constructional tasks satisfactorily averaged 32 correct responses, and mean scores for patients with visuoconstructive deficits were approximately 19, regardless of side of lesion. Statistical analysis of the data indicated a strong association between poor performance on this task and on construction tasks (e.g., assembling, drawing).

Gazzaniga and LeDoux (1978) showed how the procedures used in examining performance on this kind of perceptual puzzle problem can alter the findings. Their reported observations were limited to one split-brain patient who, without seeing the puzzle pieces, formed simple designs significantly better with his left than his right hand. However, when the whole form was presented to each visual field with instructions to select the correct set of fragmented pieces, the subject performed very well under both conditions. Rather than offering an explanation of these observations that draws upon hemisphere differences in perceptual processing, Gazzaniga and LeDoux concluded that a "manipulospatial dimension . . . accounts for these qualitative differences" between the functions of the two hemispheres. However, their presentation of the completed figure with one correct and several incorrect sets of design fragments is the reverse of the Paper Form Board and Hooper procedures. Since the procedure used by Gazzaniga and LeDoux does not require the subject to conceptualize a gestalt but only to check the size and shape of the fragments with an already formed gestalt, it may be a task that can be performed by either left or right hemisphere strategies and thus one that is inappropriate for studying lateralization of perceptual organization functions.

Tests Involving Ambiguous Visual Stimuli

Most tests that use ambiguous stimuli were developed as personality tests and not as tests of intellectual functioning. They were applied to neuropsychological problems as examiners became familiar with the kinds of responses made by different patient groups.

The *Rorschach* technique exemplifies how ambiguous stimuli, originally used for personality assessment, can provide information about a patient's perceptual abilities. When handling Rorschach responses as data about personality (e.g., behavioral predispositions), the examiner looks at many different aspects of the patient's test performance, such as his productivity, response style, and the affective quality of his associations. In neuropsychological assessment, Rorschach protocols can be evaluated for a variety of qualitative and quantitative response characteristics that tend to be associated with brain disease. Chapter 18 contains a discussion of the Rorschach as a projective technique and as a tool for making neuropsychodiagnostic discriminations. Although perceptual accuracy enters into both personality evaluations and diagnostic discriminations, it can also be treated in its own right, apart from these broader applications of the test.

Evaluation of the perceptual component of a Rorschach response can focus on four aspects of perceptual activity. The first of these is the accuracy of the percept. Since the Rorschach inkblots are ambiguous and composed by chance, no a priori "meaning" inheres in the stimulus material. Nevertheless, certain areas of the blots tend to form natural gestalts and to elicit similar associations from normal, intact adults. The test for perceptual accuracy, or "good form," is whether a given response conforms in content and in the patient's delineation of a blot area to common ways of looking at and interpreting the blot. Some Rorschach specialists leave the determination of good form to the examiner's judgment (Klopfer and Davidson, 1962; Rapaport et al., 1968). A more reliable method of determining whether a given response reflects a normal organization of the stimulus uses a frequency count, differentiating "good form" (F+) from "poor form" (F−) responses on a strictly statistical basis (S. J. Beck et al., 1961; Beizmann, 1970; Exner, 1974). Beck lists usual and rare responses to all the commonly used parts of the Rorschach ink blots so that the examiner need only compare the patient's responses with the listed responses to determine which are good and which are poor form. Of the hundreds of good form responses, 21 are given with such frequency that they are called "popular" (P) responses. They are thought to reflect the ability not merely to organize percepts appropriately but also to do so in a socially customary manner. The percentage of good form responses (F+%) and the incidence of popular responses thus can be used as measures of perceptual accuracy.

That these response variables do reflect the intactness of the perceptual system can be inferred from the consistent tendency for brain damaged patients to produce lower F+% and P scores than normal control or neurotic subjects (Aita, Reitan, and Ruth, 1947; Brussel et al., 1942; Goldfried et al., 1971; Piotrowski, 1937). In normal Rorschach protocols, 75–85% of unelaborated form responses are of good quality. Brain damaged patients tend to produce fewer good form responses, generally from 40 to 70%. Their poor form responses reflect the kind of perceptual problems that are apt to accompany brain injury, such as difficulties in synthesizing discrete elements into a coherent whole, breaking down a perceptual whole into its component parts, clarifying figure-ground relationships, and identifying relevant and irrelevant details (G. Baker, 1956). Patients' verbatim associations will often shed light on the nature of their perceptual disabilities. Their behavior too may betray the perceptual problems, for only brain damaged patients attempt to clarify visual confusion by covering parts of the blot with the hand.

A second aspect of perceptual organization that may be reflected in Rorschach responses is the ability to process and integrate multiple stimuli. Some organic brain conditions reduce the capacity for handling a large perceptual input at once, resulting in a narrowed perceptual field and simplified percepts. This shows up in relatively barren, unelaborated responses in which one characteristic of the blot alone dictates the content of the response, for the patient ignores or does not attempt to incorporate other elements of the blot into his percept. The reduced capacity for handling multiple stimuli also appears as difficulty in integrating discrete parts of the blot into a larger, organized percept, or in separating associations to discrete blot elements that happen to be contiguous. Thus, the patient may correctly interpret several isolated elements of card X as varieties of sea animals without ever forming the organizing concept, "underwater scene." Or, on card III, the side figures may be appropriately identified as "men in tuxedos" and the central red figure as a "bow tie," but the inability to separate these physically contiguous and conceptually akin percepts may produce a response combining the men and the bow tie into a single forced percept such as, "they're wearing tuxedos and that is the bow tie." Sometimes mere contiguity will result in the same kind of overinclusive response so that the blue "crab" on card X may be appropriately identified, but the contiguous "shellfish" becomes the crab's "shellfish claw." These latter two responses are examples of confabulation on the Rorschach.

In terms of specific Rorschach variables, the number of form responses that also take into account color (FC) is likely to be one per record for brain damaged patients, whereas normal subjects typically produce more than one FC response (Lynn et al., 1945). Some patients simply name colors (C_n), whereas normal subjects do not give this kind of response. There may be relatively few responses involving shading (FT, FY), and those introducing movement into the percept (M or FM) are apt to be minimal (Dörken and Kral, 1952; Hughes, 1948; Piotrowski, 1937).

A third aspect of perception is its reliability. Many brain damaged patients feel that they cannot trust their perceptions. Lack of certainty—the Rorschach term for expressions of doubt and confusion is *perplexity*—about one's interpretations of the ink blots is relatively common among brain damaged patients but rare for other patient groups or normal subjects (G. Baker, 1956, Piotrowski, 1937).

Lastly, brain damaged patients tend to have slower reaction times on the Rorschach than do normal persons (Goldfried et al., 1971). Average reaction times of 1 minute or longer suggest impaired perceptual organization on an organic basis.

Visual Interference

Tasks involving visual interference are essentially visual recognition tasks complicated by distracting embellishments. The stimulus material contains the complete percept but extraneous lines or designs encompass or mask it so that the percept is less readily recognizable. Visual interference tasks differ from tests of visual organization in that the latter call on synthesizing activities whereas visual interference tests require the subject to analyze the figure-ground relationship in order to distinguish the figure from the interfering elements.

FIGURE-GROUND TESTS

Hidden Figures (L. L. Thurstone, 1944). This 34-item version of Gottschaldt's (1928) *Hidden Figures Test* has been used in many studies of abilities of patients with brain damage (see Fig. 12-8). *Closure Flexibility (Concealed Figures)* is a 49-item multiple-choice version of this task (Thurstone and Jeffrey, 1982). The hidden figures task requires the subject to identify the hidden figure by marking the outline of the simple figure embedded in the more complex one. At the most difficult levels, the subject has to determine which of two intricate designs contains the simpler figure. In Thurstone's study of normal perception, successful performance on this task was strongly associated with "the ability to form a perceptual closure against some distraction . . . [and] the ability to hold a closure against distraction" (L. L. Thurstone, 1944, p. 101).

Teuber and his colleagues (Teuber et al., 1960; S. Weinstein, 1964) found that all groups with brain injuries due to missile wounds performed more poorly on the Hidden Figures Test than did normal controls. Not all missile wound victims have difficulty on this test, however. Corkin (1979) found that the degree of impairment of test performance was related to the size of the lesion regardless of side. Patients who had had surgery involving the frontal cortex (Teuber et al., 1951) and aphasic patients made significantly lower scores than other brain injured patients. Patients whose aphasia resulted from other kinds of brain lesions, mostly vascular, also did poorest among patients studied for the effects of lateralized lesions (Russo and Vignolo, 1967). Interestingly, left hemisphere damaged patients who did not have aphasia performed within the range of the control group. The performance level of patients with right hemisphere damage was midway between the two groups with left hemisphere dam-

362

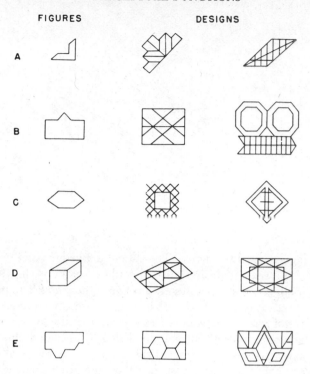

Fig. 12-8 Sample items from the Hidden Figures Test. (Talland, 1965a. © Academic Press, Reprinted by permission.)

age. The presence of visual field defects did not affect performances of these patients. This test proved sensitive to the sometimes subtle alterations in brain functioning occasioned by uremic disease (Beniak, 1977). Talland (1965a) reported that patients with Korsakoff's psychosis performed very poorly on this test. He attributed their almost total failure to problems in perceptual shifting and focusing, for in order to perform successfully, the subject must shift his attention from the discrete figure to the inclusive design, necessitating a change of perceptual set in the process. Perceptual flexibility also appeared to contribute significantly to the successful performance of normal teenage youngsters on this test (Beard, 1965).

Overlapping Figures Test. This little test was originally devised by Poppelreuter (1917) to study the psychological effects of head injuries incurred in Word War I (see Fig. 12-9). Ghent (1956) employed similar overlapping figures to examine the development of perceptual functions in children. Luria (1966) used several versions of the overlapping or "superimposed" figures test to examine the phenomenon of simultaneous agnosia (see p. 66). In her systematization of Luria's examination methods, Christensen (1979) includes three Poppelreuter-type figures in the section on "the

Fig. 12-9 Example of a Poppelreuter-type overlapping figure.

investigation of higher visual functions." The patient is asked to name as many of the objects as he can. Both Luria and Christensen describe several ways in which a patient can fail this test. Both point out the difference between the *inability* to perceive more than one object at a time or to shift gaze that may accompany a posterior lesion and passivity or inertia of gaze, perseverated responses, or confused responses that are more likely to be associated with an anterior lesion. Christensen also reminds her readers that a perceptual bias to the right of these figures may reflect left visuospatial inattention. Tests in abbreviated forms, such as those used by Luria and Christensen, do not lend themselves to graded answers or standardized norms. Rather, erroneous responses must be evaluated on the kind of qualitative basis exemplified by Luria's and Christensen's discussions of patients' response styles in order to make fruitful use of this method.

Using the nine stimulus figures, each with four overlapping objects, which Ghent developed, De Renzi and Spinnler (1966) found that right-lesioned patients performed significantly more poorly than control subjects and patients with left-sided damage (who also did less well than the controls). An expanded version of this test included ten stimulus figures with a total of 40 objects presented in such categories as "clothing" or "animals." It was used by Masure and Tzavaras (1976) under the name of Ghent's test (i.e., *le test de Ghent*). Although Masure and Tzavaras did not set a limit, total time to completion was recorded and subjects indicated their responses on a multiple-choice form. With this approach, patients with posterior lesions performed less well as a whole than the anterior group. No differences occurred between right and left hemisphere damaged groups in number of correct responses, but patients with left posterior lesions were by far the slowest.

Southern California Figure-Ground Visual Perception Test. (Ayres, 1966). Although this test was developed for use with children, it is appropriate for adult populations as the most difficult items are challenging at all ages. The eight easiest items consist of overlapping figures (e.g., stool, spoon, shoe). The last ten items are complex geometric designs. Six possible responses are pictured for each item, of which three, the correct responses, are represented in the test figure. The subject can respond by pointing, reading the response number, or naming the responses (in the first eight items). Data concerning use of this test with adults are not now available. However, its similarity to other figure-ground tests that have proven useful in identifying perceptual disorders in brain damaged adults warrants its use with adults. Its value lies in its simplicity of administration and the inclusion of both types of figure-ground problems in one test.

Visual Closure   (subtest of the Illinois Test of Psycholinguistic Abilities, see p. 299). This task, which involves visual search and recognition of parts of objects or of objects at unusual angles, appears to have much in common with children's play-book games requiring the players to count faces or animals hidden all over the page, in unlikely places as well as likely ones. This subtest consists of five horizontal picture strips that are 9 cm wide and approximately 43 cm long. Each strip shows a line drawing of a scene that contains 14 or 15 items in whole or part view (e.g., fish under water; soda pop bottles at a birthday party; hammers and saws at a construction site). A time limit of 30 seconds is allowed for each trial. The first trial is given for practice. The score is the sum of the other four trials. Since age norms for this test do not go beyond 10 years 10 months, it is not possible to evaluate adult performances that may be depressed but still earn higher scores than the 10 year 10 month mean (of 34 raw score points out of a possible 58). Scores that run much lower than the 10 year 10 month mean (e.g., performances in which half or less of the items are spotted), however, would certainly suggest a visual scanning or recognition problem. Again, analysis of qualitative aspects of the performance, including the nature of the errors, is the best source for clues as to the nature of the perceptual problem. The Luria and Christensen guide to analyzing visuoperceptual defects that show up on the Poppelreuter figures (see the previous section) is also applicable in analyzing performance deficits on this test.

Optical illusions.   Some optical illusions are variants of the embedded figure problem. L. Cohen (1959) used the number of figure-ground or alternate figure reversals, i.e., the "rate of apparent change (RAC)" to measure perceptual fluctuation in normal control subjects and a brain injured population. Brain injured subjects reported fewer reversals of the *Rubin Vase* and *Double Necker Cube* illusions (see Fig. 12-10) than did the control group. Of the brain injured population, those with lesions on the right reported fewer reversals than did those with left hemisphere damage. Frontal lobe patients differed from this pattern in that no right-left differential occurred, and except for those patients with bilateral frontal lesions, who saw the most reversals of all, the reversal rate of patients with frontal lobe lesions was the slowest (Teuber, 1964; Yacorzynski, 1965). Of an older (65–90) institutionalized group, the few (6 of 31) subjects who could perform the task also reported a smaller number of reversals than younger control subjects (Heath and Ohrbach, 1963).

Illusions involving line size and angle distortions have been used to examine the

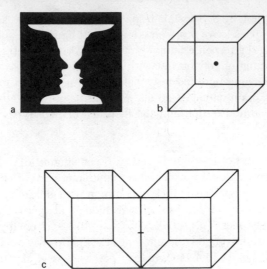

Fig. 12-10 Classical optical illusions: a. Rubin Vase, b. Necker Cube, and c. Double Necker Cube.

differential effects of lateralized brain damage on visual perception. The most extensive work has been done with the familiar Müller-Lyer illusion (see Fig. 12-11a). Two studies have shown that left-sided lesions tend to be associated with an accentuation of the illusion (Houlard et al., 1976; Barton, 1969). These findings are in accord with a demonstrated tendency for the Müller-Lyer illusion to be greater when normal sub-

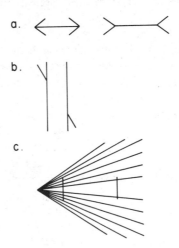

Fig. 12-11 Line illusions: (a) Müller-Lyer, (b) Poggendorff, (c) Ponzo.

366

jects view it in the left rather than the right field (Mizusawa, 1978). One study (Greene and Tager, 1979), which did not find an enhanced magnitude of illusion among patients with left hemisphere damage, required the subjects to draw their size estimates rather than communicate their judgments by gestural or sorting techniques. In another study (Basso et al., 1974) in which subjects selected the size match from an ascending and descending series of lines of graded length, the illusion was strongest for patients with right hemisphere damage who had field defects, and weakest for those with left hemisphere damage and field defects. Only the latter group differed significantly from the control group. Houlard and his colleagues also found no appreciable difference between control subjects and patients with right hemisphere damage in the magnitude of the Müller-Lyer illusion. Unlike other familiar line illusions, the Müller-Lyer illusion tends to become stronger with advancing age (Fozard et al., 1977).

Other line illusions have also elicited differential response patterns between right and left hemisphere damaged patients. Patients with right-sided lesions can see the Ponzo illusion (see Fig. 12-11c) weakly if at all, though it tends to be magnified by patients whose lesions are on the left (Houlard et al., 1976). Still other illusions have been presented in such different formats that it becomes difficult to determine whether they produce lateralized distortion patterns consistently. For example, A. E. Edwards (1972) displayed the Poggendorf illusion (see Fig. 12-11b) on a vertical axis and found that patients with left hemisphere lesions saw less of an illusion than other brain damaged patients. Greene and Tager (1979), however, presented it horizontally and varied the direction of the intersecting line, and found that differences in illusion size between patients with right and left hemisphere damage depended upon the direction of the intersect. Until standard formats for the administration and presentation of illusions have been established, their clinical value remains questionable.

Visual Masking Problems

Cross-hatching or shading over simple drawings, letters, or words may destroy the underlying percept for some patients (see Fig. 12-12). Luria (1965a, 1966) found this disability among patients whose lesions involved the occipital lobe; left hemisphere patients experienced difficulty with letters and right hemisphere patients were unable to identify such simple drawings as a clock face or a table when they were shaded.

Visual Scanning

The visual scanning defects that often accompany brain lesions can seriously compromise such important activities as reading, writing, performing paper and pencil calculations, and telling time (Diller et al., 1974), and are associated with accident-prone behavior (Diller and Weinberg, 1970). They are most common and most severe in patients with right hemisphere lesions (Weinberg et al., 1976). Their relatively high incidence in brain damaged populations means that tests of visual scanning can be used to screen for brain damage. Tests for inattention (pp. 343–347) and cancellation

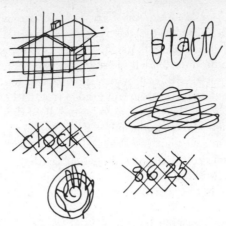

Fig. 12-12 Visual masked words and pictures.

tasks (see pp. 548–550) will often disclose scanning problems. These deficits also show up on the purely perceptual tests involving scanning behavior.

VISUAL SEARCH TESTS

Perceptual Maze Test (Elithorn et al., 1964).   Elithorn's Mazes are based on his view that "perceptual skills are phylogenetically fundamental components of intelligent behavior." Elithorn originally intended the Perceptual Maze Test to be a culture-free, nonverbal "intelligence test" (see Fig. 12-13). One version of the test consists of 18 lattice-type mazes that require the subject to trace a line as quickly as he can from the top to the bottom of the lattice through as many of the randomly placed choice points as possible. Thus, besides perceptual activities, the patient must comprehend a

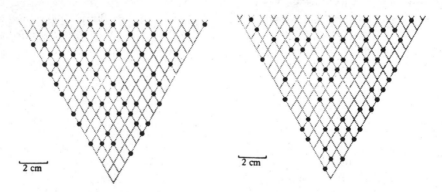

Fig. 12-13   Two patterns from Elithorn's Perceptual Maze Test. (Elithorn et al., 1964; reproduced by permission of the Cambridge University Press.)

somewhat complex task, count, keep track of several numbers and the paths they represent, and choose between alternate routes. The tests are scored on the basis of a one-minute time limit without informing the patient. Each maze has its own norms that give the percentage of control subjects who passed it.

In one large study, which included relatively few aphasic patients, this test discriminated well between brain damaged and control patients with more failures among right than left hemisphere patients (Benton et al., 1963). Aphasic patients consistently do poorly on the standard timed administration (Archibald et al., 1967; Colonna and Faglioni, 1966). However, Archibald (1978) has shown that low scores obtained by patients with left hemisphere lesions result from their slowed performances rather than poor solutions. On untimed administrations of this task, the performances of aphasic and nonaphasic left-lesioned patients were indistinguishable from normal control subjects on the untimed condition, and they did not differ from one another on either condition. Patients with right hemisphere damage were consistently inferior to both the controls and those patients whose lesions were lateralized on the left. Patients with diffuse brain dysfunction associated with uremia do very poorly on this test (Beniak, 1977). The Colonna and Faglioni study also demonstrated a low but significant relationship between the Perceptual Maze Test and education ($r = +.377$) and a higher significant correlation with Raven's Matrices ($r = +.668$).

The intricacy of the Mazes' patterning and the complexity of the task limit the number of patients who can follow the instructions and handle the task. Kevin Walsh (1978b) points out, for example, that patients with frontal lobe damage tend to disregard the rules (i.e., "the pathway must be completely on the lattice lines" and "must not double back" [Elithorn et al., 1964]).

Visual Search (G. Goldstein et al., 1973). This test is part of both the computer-assisted and the manual forms of the Repeatable-Cognitive-Perceptual-Motor Battery (RCPM) (see p. 566). The test booklet of the manual form contains four versions of the 9×9 checkerboard pattern stimulus figures (see Fig. 12-14). The subject's task is to indicate in which of the outlying grids is the position of the two little black squares like that of eight center test grids. The test is scored for time and errors. In its original format, using 16 stimulus figures projected on a screen, brain damaged patients performed the Visual Search task at a much slower rate than normal control subjects, and considerably more slowly than neurologically intact psychiatric patients (G. Goldstein et al., 1973). Error scores did not discriminate between these groups. Time scores have also proven useful in evaluating the effects of medication changes on the mental functioning of epileptics (R. Lewis and Kupke, 1977).

Counting dots. This very simple device for testing visual scanning behavior can be constructed to meet the occasion (McFie et al., 1950). The subject is asked to count a number of dots, 20 or more, widely scattered over a piece of paper with an equal number in each quadrant. Errors may be due to visual inattention to one side, to difficulty in maintaining an orderly approach to the task, or to problems in tracking numbers and dots consecutively.

Fig. 12-14   One of the Visual Search stimulus figures.

VISUAL TRACKING TESTS

Two tests for visual tracking do not differ greatly in their format. Talland's *Line Tracing* task (1965a) consists of four separate tangled line patterns numbered only on the left (see Fig. 12-15). The subject's task is to write the number of each line beginning on the left in the empty space to the right of the line he thinks is the line's right end. The test patterns differ in the number of lines originating on the left, ending on the right, or both. These line problems are derived from those used by L. L. Thurstone

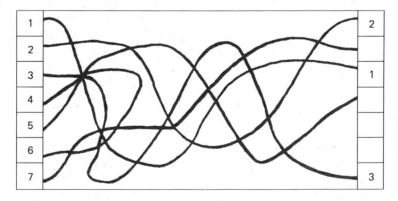

Fig. 12-15   One of four patterns of the Line Tracing task. (Talland, 1965a, © Academic Press, Reprinted by permission.)

in *A Factorial Study of Perception* (1944). Time is recorded. Talland's 16 control subjects made no errors on the two easiest patterns, less than one error on the next most difficult pattern, and less than two errors on the most difficult pattern. Average time taken per line on the simpler patterns ranged from 3.4 to 6.3 seconds, but it more than tripled on the most difficult pattern. Pursuit, a similar but more complex line-tracing task, is a subtest of the MacQuarrie Test for Mechanical Ability (see p. 304).

Auditory Functions

As is the case with vision, the verbal and nonverbal components of auditory perception appear to be functionally distinct (Kimura, 1967; Milner, 1962). Also as with vision, there are many psychological techniques for examining the verbal auditory functions. Unlike visual perception, however, psychologists have paid relatively little systematic attention to nonverbal auditory functions. Thus, although verbal tests involving audition are abundant, the psychological examination of nonverbal aspects of auditory perception is limited to a few techniques.

Sources of Defective Auditory Comprehension

The most common sources of defective auditory comprehension are deficiencies in auditory acuity resulting from conduction and/or sensorineural hearing losses, and deficits in auditory processing associated with aphasia.

DECREASED AUDITORY ACUITY

Most patients whose hearing is impaired are aware of their problem. Unfortunately, some individuals with mild to moderate deficits are embarrassed and do not report them to the examiner, or they may try to hide their disability even at the cost of a poor performance on the tests. Occasionally a patient incurs a reduction in hearing sensitivity as a result of his brain injury, in which case hearing on the ear opposite the side of the lesion is likely to be the more impaired. When such a hearing loss is slight, and particularly when it is recent or when aphasic defects also contribute to his speech comprehension problems, the patient may be unaware of it.

Usually, if the patient does not report that he is hard of hearing, his behavior will betray his problem. Persons whose hearing is better on one side tend to favor that side by turning the head toward the examiner and placing themselves so the better ear is closer to him. The mild to moderately hard of hearing person may display erratic speech comprehension as the examiner's voice becomes louder or softer, or not hear well if the examiner turns away when speaking to the patient. The examiner who suspects that the patient has a hearing loss can test for it crudely by changing his voice level and noting whether the patient's level of comprehension varies. When the patient appears to have a hearing loss, the examiner should insist that the patient see an audiologist for a thorough audiological examination. An audiological assessment is of particular importance when a tumor is suspected, for an early sign of some forms of brain tumor is decreased auditory acuity. It is also important for the brain damaged patient with other sensory or cognitive defects to be aware of his hearing problems so that he can learn to compensate for them and, when indicated, get the benefits of a hearing aid.

Auditory Discrimination Problems

Some patients have difficulty discriminating sounds even when thresholds for sound perception remain within the normal hearing range and no aphasic disability is present. Auditory discrimination can be tested by having the patient repeat words and phrases spoken by the examiner, or by asking the patient to tell whether two spoken words are the same or different, using pairs of different words, such as "cap" and "cat," or "vie" and "thy," interspersed with identical word pairs. Auditory discrimination is evaluated routinely in audiometric examinations. When the problem is suspected, referral to an audiologist is indicated.

Speech Sounds Perception Test (Reitan and Davison, 1974; E. W. Russell et al., 1970). This is one of the tests in the Halstead-Reitan battery (see pp. 562–563). Sixty sets of four nonsense syllables beginning and ending with different consonants but based on the vowel sound "ee" comprise the items, which are administered by tape recording. The patient notes what he thinks he heard on a multiple-choice form. This test is sensitive to brain damage generally, and to left hemisphere damage in particular. Secondarily, it may test the subject's capacity to attend to a mechanically administered, boring task. Although Halstead (1947) defined the normal error range as 0–7, many intact older subjects make eight or more errors on this test (Lewinsohn, 1973; Pauker, 1977).

Aphasia

When the patient's comprehension problem clearly does not relate to deficits in auditory acuity, aphasia must be suspected. The neuropsychologist always looks for evidence of aphasia when the patient displays a right-sided weakness or complains of sensory changes on the right half of his body. Aphasia must also be considered whenever the patient's difficulty in comprehending speech appears to be clearly unrelated to hearing loss, attention or concentration defects, a foreign language background, or a functional thought disorder. The patient's performance on an aphasia screening test (see pp. 320ff.) should help the examiner determine whether a more thorough study of the patient's language functions is indicated.

Auditory Inattention

Some patients with lateralized lesions involving the temporal lobe or central auditory pathways tend to ignore auditory signals entering the ear opposite the side of the lesions, much as other brain damaged patients exhibit unilateral visual neglect or *extinction* (unawareness of one of a pair of similar stimuli simultaneously presented to different parts of the body, different areas of the fields of vision, etc.) on the side contralateral to the lesion (Oxbury and Oxbury, 1969).

A simple method for testing auditory inattention can be performed without special equipment by an examiner standing behind the patient so that he can deliver stimulation to each ear simultaneously. He then makes soft sounds at each ear separately and simultaneously, randomly varying single and simultaneous presentations of the stimuli. Production of a soft rustling sound by rubbing the thumb and first two fingers together is probably the method of choice (e.g., G. Goldstein, 1974), as Strub and Black (1977) point out that few examiners can snap their fingers with equal intensity.

DICHOTIC LISTENING

Dichotic testing, in which the auditory recognition capacity of each ear is tested separately but simultaneously, uses stimulus sets, such as digits, delivered through headphones by a dual-track sound system (Kimura, 1967). By this means, the patient receives the stimulus pairs, one to each ear, at precisely the same time. Normally, when different digits or words are received by each ear, both of them are heard. When only one word set is heard clearly and the other is only poorly understood or not recognized at all, a lesion involving the auditory system on the contralateral side can be suspected (K. W. Walsh, 1978b).

Auditory-Verbal Perception

Every thorough neuropsychological examination provides some opportunity to evaluate the auditory perception of verbal material. When the examiner orally presents problems of judgment and reasoning, learning, and memory, he also has an opportunity to make an informal estimate of the patient's auditory acuity, comprehension, and processing capacity. Significant defects in the perception and comprehension of speech are readily apparent during the course of administering most psychological tests. For example, a patient must have a fairly intact capacity for auditory-verbal perception in order to give even a minimal performance on the WAIS.

If a few tasks with simple instructions requiring only motor responses or one- or two-word answers are given, however, subtle problems of auditory processing may be missed. These include difficulty in processing or retaining lengthy messages although responses to single words or short phrases may be accurate, inability to handle spoken numbers without a concomitant impairment in handling other forms of speech, or inability to process messages at high levels in the auditory system when the ability to repeat them accurately is intact. In the absence of a hearing defect, any impairment in the recognition or processing of speech usually indicates a lesion involving the left or speech dominant hemisphere (Milner, 1962).

When impairment in auditory processing is suspected, the examiner can couple an auditorally presented test with a similar task presented visually. This kind of paired testing enables the examiner to compare the functioning of the two perceptual systems under similar conditions. A consistent tendency for the patient to perform better under one of the two stimulus conditions should alert the examiner to the possibility of neurological impairment of the less efficient perceptual system. Test pairs can be readily found or developed for most verbal tests at most levels of difficulty. For example, I include both paper and pencil and orally administered personal history, information, arithmetic reasoning, and proverbs questions in my basic battery. Comprehension, sentence building, vocabulary items, and many memory and orientation tasks also lend themselves well to this kind of dual treatment.

AUDITORY RECEPTION (subtest of the Illinois Test of Psycholinguistic Abilities, see p. 299)

A simple test of how well speech is received and comprehended is to ask a subject nonsense as well as sensible questions. This test contains 50 subject-verb sentence questions of which half are sensible (e.g., "Do caterpillars crawl?") and half are nonsensical ("Do dishes yodel?"). Word difficulty of the items increases so that performance on this test may also provide an estimate of vocabulary up to 10 years-2 months of age. Since this test can be answered verbally or by gestures, most patients can respond. The average adult should make no errors on this task. A few errors suggest inattentiveness or carelessness. More than a few errors indicate a need for more thorough examination of auditory verbal receptive and processing functions.

Nonverbal Auditory Perception

So much of a person's behavior is organized around verbal signals that nonverbal auditory functions are often overlooked. However, the recognition, discrimination, and comprehension of nonsymbolic sound patterns, such as music, tapping patterns, and the meaningful noises of sirens, dog barks, and thunderclaps are subject to impairment much as is the perception of language sounds (Frederiks, 1969a). Defects of nonverbal auditory perception tend to be associated with lesions of the right temporal lobe (Gordon, 1974; Milner, 1962, 1971).

Most tests for nonverbal auditory perception use sound recordings. The *Seashore Rhythm Test* is probably the one used most widely since Halstead (1947) incorporated it into his test battery and Reitan (undated) subsequently included it in his neuropsychological assessment program. This test, which is a subtest of the *Seashore Test of Musical Talent* (Seashore et al., 1960), requires the subject to discriminate between like and unlike pairs of musical beats. Aging appears to have no appreciable effect on the capacity measured by this test (Lewinsohn, 1973; Reed and Reitan, 1963). Milner (1971) has recorded a set of familiar sounds (train whistle, squealing brakes) for an auditory recognition test. Patients with right temporal brain damage tend to do poorly on both of these tests, whereas patients with brain lesions localized elsewhere are much less likely to experience difficulty with them.

When the perceptual task is as simple as asking for a discrimination between three evenly spaced taps and three taps spaced so that the first two are close together with a lag between the second and third taps, more than one failure suggests defective nonverbal perception. The patient who fails two or three of as many as five trials on this kind of discrimination task should be given another five to ten trials with similar material. This may help clarify whether he misunderstood the instructions, was having difficulty concentrating on the task, or whether in fact he has a perceptual disability since rhythm pattern recognition may be depressed by diffuse cerebral dysfunction, too (e.g., Beniak, 1977). Pairing similar tasks involving verbal and nonverbal material can help clarify the interpretation of a patient's failures. For example, the examiner can ask the patient to repeat four- and five-syllable sentences and to mimic four- and five-beat tapping patterns. Patients who display confusion on both tasks may have an attention defect or may not have understood the instructions. Those who fail to repeat only sentences or only tapping patterns correctly probably have a specific defect of auditory perception. Adding a memory component to these tasks is likely to increase their sensitivity in demonstrating a perceptual defect. However, memory techniques can be included in perception tests only when the patient has demonstrated adequate memory in other perceptual modalities. The examiner should also note whether the patient seems to comprehend such extraneous noises as a door slamming, a plane flying overhead, or the ring of a phone.

TESTING FOR AMUSIA

Defective perception of music or of its components (e.g., rhythm, pitch, timbre, melody, harmonics) is usually associated with temporal lobe disease, and is more likely to occur with right- than with left-sided involvement (see pp. 55,74). Tests for this aspect of auditory perception can be easily improvised. The examiner can whistle or hum several simple and generally familiar melodies such as "America" ("God Save the Queen"), "Silent Night," or "Frère Jacques." He can test pitch discrimination with a pitch pipe, asking the patient to report which of two sounds is higher or whether two sounds are the same or different. Recognition for rhythm patterns can be evaluated by requiring the patient either to discriminate similar and different sets of rhythmic taps or to mimic patterns tapped out by the examiner with a pencil on the table top.

Formalized batteries may be used for systematic examination of musical functions. Benton (1977a) outlines a seven-part battery developed by Dorgeuille that contains four sections for assessing receptive functions: II Rhythmic expression (reproduction of tapped rhythm patterns); IV Discrimination of sounds (comparing two tones for highest pitch); V Identification of familiar melodies; and VI Identification of types of music (e.g., whether dance, military, or church). Botez and Wertheim (1959; Wertheim and Botez, 1961) developed a comprehensive examination for studying amusic phenomena in musically trained patients with cerebral disorders that, in its review of perceptual aspects of musicianship, tests for: A. Tonal, Melodic, and Harmony Elements; B. Rhythmic Element; C. Agogial (tempo-related) and Dynamic Elements; and D. Lexic Element (testing for ability to read musical notation). Each of these sections contains a number of subsections for examining very discrete aspects of musical dysfunction. This latter battery provides a comprehensive format for reviewing residual musical capacities in a musician who has sustained brain damage, but it is much too technical for general use.

RECOGNITION OF EMOTIONAL TONE IN SPEECH

That nonverbal aspects of speech may be as important to communication as its verbal content becomes evident when listening to the often flat or misplaced intonations of patients with right hemisphere damage. Using four sentences with emotionally neutral content (e.g., "He tossed bread to the pigeons."), Daniel M. Tucker and his co-workers (1976, 1977) examined whether the capacity to identify or discriminate the emotional toning of speech was also subject to impairment resulting from lateralized cerebral damage. Tape recordings were made of each sentence read with a happy, sad, angry, or indifferent intonation, making a total of 16 sentences that were presented in random order on the recognition task. These sentences were paired for the discrimination task in which the subject was asked to indicate which of the pair expressed a specified one of the four moods. Although their patient sample was small (11 with right-sided, 7 with left-sided dysfunction), patients whose damage involved right-sided brain structures (i.e., had left visuospatial neglect) were much less able to appreciate the emotional qualities of the sentences than the conduction aphasics who comprised the left-lesioned group.

This technique very clearly differentiated between the two patient groups with no overlap on scores on either task, which suggests that it may be a useful diagnostic adjunct. Moreover, the technique may bring to light another dimension of the deficits that are likely to accompany left visuospatial neglect, that may debase the quality of these patients' social adjustment, and that can lead to an underestimation of their affective capacity when their problem is one of perceptual discrimination rather than emotional dulling.

Tactile Functions

Investigations into defects of touch perception have employed many different kinds of techniques to elicit or measure the different ways in which tactile perception can be disturbed. Most of the techniques present simple recognition or discrimination problems. A few involve more complex behavior.

Tactile Sensation

Before examining complex or conceptually meaningful tactile-perceptual functions, the integrity of the somatosensory system in the area of neuropsychological interest—usually the hands—should be evaluated. Some commonly used procedures involve asking the patient to indicate whether he feels the sharp or the dull end of a pin, whether he feels pressure from one or two points (applied simultaneously and close together), or whether he can feel a pressure from a graded set of plastic hairs, the Von Frey hairs, which have enjoyed wide use in the examination of sensitivity to touch (Christensen, 1979; Luria, 1966; E. W. Russell, 1980b). The patient's eyes should be closed or his hand out of sight when sensory functions are tested.

Tactile Inattention

The tactile inattention phenomenon, sometimes called "tactile extinction" or "tactile suppression," most often occurs with right hemisphere—particularly right parietal—damage (see pp. 72–73). Although it frequently accompanies visual or auditory inattention, it can occur by itself. Testing for tactile inattention typically involves a procedure used in neurological examinations in which points on some part of the body (usually face or hands) on each side are touched first singly and then simultaneously (double simultaneous stimulation). This is the method, in standardized format, that is used with the Halstead-Reitan battery (e.g., E. W. Russell et al., 1970; Reitan and Davison, 1974). If the patient is experiencing left hemi-inattention, he will report a right-sided touch on simultaneous stimulation although when only one side is touched, he may have no difficulty reporting it correctly.

FACE-HAND TEST (Bender et al., 1951; Fink et al., 1952)

An examination for tactile inattention that involves two stimulation points on each trial—the method of double simultaneous stimulation—has been formalized as a brief, ten-trial test administered first with eyes closed. Upon each stimulation trial, the subject must indicate where he felt he was touched (see Table 12-1). Should the subject make errors with his eyes closed, the test is readministered with his eyes open. Interestingly, under the eyes-open condition, only 10–20% of patients who had made errors with their eyes closed improved on their original performances (Kahn et al., 1960–61). This technique has proven useful for demonstrating the presence of tactile inattention. Not all errors, though, are errors of extinction. Errors on trials 2 and 6

Table 12-1 The Face-Hand Test

Trial		
1. Right cheek	and	left cheek
2. Left cheek	and	left hand
3. Right cheek	and	right hand
4. Left cheek	and	right hand
5. Right hand	and	left hand
6. Right cheek	and	right hand
7. Right hand	and	left hand
8. Left cheek	and	right hand
9. Right cheek	and	left hand

(Adapted from Kahn and Miller, 1978)

suggest that the patient has either a sensory impairment or difficulty following instructions. Displacement errors, in which the patient reports that the stimulus was felt on another part of the body, tend to occur with diffuse deteriorative conditions (Fink et al., 1952). Beyond middle age, errors on this test tend to increase with advancing years (Kahn and Miller, 1978).

Aaron Smith includes a 20-item *Face-Hand Sensory Test* in the Michigan Neuropsychological Test Battery (p. 572). It differs from the Face-Hand Test in that eight single stimulation items are interspersed between 12 double simultaneous stimulation items calling for touch to hand or cheek on one or both sides. Smith recommends that the tactile stimulation be applied as "a brisk stroke." The patient responds by pointing to where he felt the stroke, giving a verbal response only if unable to point. Smith and his colleagues (Berker et al., 1982) demonstrated an association between sensory deficits identified by this test and cognitive impairments.

Quality Extinction Test (QET) (A. S. Schwartz et al., 1977)

Dissatisfaction with the number of patients with parietal lobe damage who did not display the tactile extinction phenomenon on the usual testing procedures led to the development of a test that requires more complex discriminations. In this test, after becoming familiarized by sight and touch with an assortment of different surface textures (e.g., wire mesh, sandpaper, velvet), the subject is required to identify these materials when they are brushed against his hand while he is blindfolded. On some trials, each hand receives the same material; on other trials, different material is brushed against each hand. This method proved to be more sensitive to extinction than classical testing methods, eliciting the phenomenon when it did not show up with usual testing procedures.

Tactile Recognition and Discrimination Tests

Finger Agnosia

Gainotti and his colleages (1972) modified Benton's (1959, 1979; Benton et al., 1983) technique of examining for finger agnosia by substituting pointing for a verbal response. In this essentially nonverbal task, patients must indicate which finger is touched by pointing to a life-size paper model of the back of the hand on which each finger is numbered 1 through 5, starting with the thumb. For each of three stimulation procedures, ten trials are given for each hand. In procedure A the subject's task is to indicate which finger the examiner touches while the hand is in plain view. Procedure B is identical except that the hand is shielded from view. The hand is also shielded for procedure C in which the examiner touches two fingers at a time on each trial. The fingers are touched in a set random order that is different for each hand and each procedure. When examined by this method, only two of 40 normal control subjects made as much as one error, in each case on the left hand. Thus, the presence of any error may be taken as evidence of finger agnosia when using this technique.

A variety of techniques designed to elicit finger agnosia demonstrate that it can

378

occur with lesions on either side of the brain (Benton, 1979; Boll, 1974; Kinsbourne and Warrington, 1962). However, in order to avoid biasing the examination of even mildly aphasic patients, the nonverbal response used by Gainotti and his colleagues (1972) is the method of choice.

Tactile Finger Recognition (Reitan and Davison, 1974; called *Tactile Finger Localization* by Boll, 1974). In this test the examiner assigns a number to each finger. When the subject's eyes are closed and his hands extended, the examiner touches the fingers of each hand in a predetermined order and the subject reports the number of the finger he thinks was touched.

Stereognosis (Recognition of Objects by Touch)

Object recognition (testing for astereognosis) is commonly performed in neurological examinations. The patient closes his eyes and is asked to recognize by touch such common objects as a coin, a paper clip, a pencil, or key. Each hand is examined separately. Size discrimination is easily tested with coins. The examiner can use bits of cloth, wire screening, sandpaper, etc., for texture discrimination. Organically intact adults are able to perform tactile recognition and discrimination tests with complete accuracy: a single erroneous response or even evidence of hesitancy suggests that this function is impaired. Somesthetic defects are generally associated with lesions of the contralateral hemisphere (S. Weinstein, 1964).

Luria (1966) used four procedures to satisfy reasonable doubts about whether a patient's inability to identify an object placed in his palm results from astereognosis or some other problem. If the patient does not identify the object on passive contact with the hand, then he is encouraged to feel the object and move it around in his hand. Should he not be able to name the object, he is given an opportunity to pick out one like it from other objects set before him. Should he still not recognize it, Luria put the object in the other hand, noting that, "if the patient now recognizes the object without difficulty, when he could not do so before, it may be concluded that astereognosis is present." Of course, as soon as the patient accurately identifies the object, the remaining procedural steps become unnecessary.

Some workers (e.g., Boll, 1974; Reitan and Davison, 1974; S. Weinstein, 1964, 1978) have standardized their procedures for examining stereognosis and developed scoring systems as well. Although such refinements are necessary for many research purposes, the extra testing they entail adds little to a clinical examination that gives the patient three or four trials with different objects (or textures) for each hand with sensation sufficiently intact to warrant doing this test.

Skin Writing

The technique of tracing letters or numbers on the palms of the subject's hands is also used in neurological examinations. Rey (1964) formalized the skin-writing procedure into a series of five subtests in which the examiner writes (1) the figures 5 1 8 2 4 3 on the dominant palm (see Fig. 12-16a); (2) V E S H R O on the dominant palm; (3)

Fig. 12-16 Rey's skin-writing procedures. (Courtesy of Presses Universitaires de France.)

3 4 2 8 1 5 on the nondominant palm (Fig. 12-16b); (4) 1 3 5 8 4 2 in large figures extending to both sides of the two palms held 1 cm apart (Fig. 12-17c–h); and (5) 2 5 4 1 3 8 on the fleshy part of the inside dominant forearm. Each subtest score represents the number of errors. Rey provides data on four different adult groups: manual and unskilled workers (M), skilled technicians and clerks (T), people with the baccalaureate degree (B), and persons between the ages of 68 and 83 (A) (see Table 12-2). In the absence of a sensory deficit or an aphasic condition, when the patient displays an error differential between the two hands, a contralateral cortical lesion is suspected; defective performance regardless of side implicates a tactile perceptual disability.

Fingertip Number-Writing Perception (G. Goldstein, 1974; Reitan and Davison, 1974; also called *Fingertip Writing*, e.g., E. W. Russell et al., 1970). As part of his

Table 12-2 Skin-Writing Test Errors Made by Four Adult Groups

Group		Right Hand Numbers	Right Hand Letters	Left Hand Numbers	Both Hands Numbers	Forearm Numbers
M	Mdn	0	1	0	2	1
$n = 51$	CS[a]	2	3	2	5	3
T	Mdn	0	1	0	1	0
$n = 25$	CS	2	3	1	3	3
B	Mdn	0	1	0	0	0
$n = 55$	CS	1	2	1	2	2
A	Mdn	1	2	1	2	2
$n = 14$	CS	3	4	3	6	3

(Adapted from Rey, 1964)
[a]CS = Cutting score.

modification of Halstead's original test battery (see pp. 562–563), Reitan formalized neurological procedures by devising a test in which the examiner writes with a pencil each of the numbers 3, 4, 5, and 6 in a prescribed order on each of the fingertips of each hand, making a total of 20 trials for each hand. Skin-writing tests are useful for lateralizing the site of damage when there are no obvious signs such as hemiparesis or aphasia. The two tests presented here can also provide some indication of the severity of a tactile-perceptual defect.

13

Constructional Functions

Constructional performance combines perceptual activity with motor response and always has a spatial component. In order to distinguish it from the neuropsychologically meaningful concept of *praxis*, which "in the strict (neurological) sense, refers to the motor integration employed in the execution of complex learned movements" (Strub and Black, 1977), I will follow Strub and Black's lead by maintaining a terminological distinction between these functional classes. Thus, I will use the term "constructional impairment" rather than "constructional apraxia," and reserve the term "apraxia" for the special class of dysfunctions characterized by a breakdown in the direction or execution of complex motor acts.

The integral role of the visuoperceptual functions in constructional activity becomes evident when persons with more than very mild perceptual disabilities experience some difficulty on constructional tasks. However, constructional disturbances can occur without any concomitant impairment of visuoperceptual functions. Because of the complexity of functions entering into constructional performances, numerical scores convey only a limited amount of information about the test performance. Careful observation is needed to distinguish between perceptual failures, apraxias, spatial confusion, or attentional or motivational problems.

The concept of constructional functions embraces two large classes of activities, drawing and building or assembling. The tendency for drawing and assembling disabilities to occur together, although significant, is so variable that these two classes of activity need to be evaluated separately.

Awareness that the two cerebral hemispheres differ in their information-processing capacities has brought increasing attention to the differences in how patients with ulilateral lesions perform constructional tasks. A number of characteristic tendencies in the constructions of these patients have been described (Hécaen and Albert, 1978; Mack and Levine, 1981, no date; K. W. Walsh, 1978b). Patients with right hemisphere damage tend to take a piecemeal, fragmented approach, losing the overall gestalt of the construction task. They may neglect the left side of the construction or—occasionally—pile up items (lines in a drawing, blocks or puzzle pieces) on the left. Although some patients with right hemisphere damage produce very sparse, sketchy drawings, others create highly elaborated pictures that do not "hang together," i.e., frequently lack important components or contain serious distortions in perspective or proportions, and yet have a repetitive overdetailing that gives the drawing a not unpleasant, rhythmical quality (see Fig. 6-1). Unlike patients with left hemisphere damage, those with lesions on the right do not benefit from having a model (Hécaen and Assal, 1970). Patients with left-sided lesions may get the overall proportions and the overall idea of the construction correct, but they tend to lose details and generally turn out a shabby production. The frequency of errors does not seem to differentiate patients with left and right hemisphere lesions so much as their nature (Archibald, no date; Gainotti and Tiacci, 1970; Hécaen and Assal, 1970). However, in a very simple copying task (drawing one or two crosses on a blank card in the position corresponding to that in which they appear on the stimulus card), both right and left hemisphere damaged patients made the same number of errors on the side of the response card contralateral to the lesion, but only the patients with right-sided lesions made an abnormal number of errors on the side of the card ipsilateral to the lesion (Tartaglione et al., 1981). Patients whose damage was on the left made no more errors than normal control subjects when copying crosses on the left side of space thus, in this case, making fewer overall errors than right lesioned patients.

Warrington and her colleagues (1966) examined copies of simple geometric figures made by patients with lateralized lesions and they reported the following differences between the right- and left-lesioned groups: (1) Left hemisphere patients tend to improve with practice; right hemisphere patients do not. (2) Right hemisphere patients are significantly poorer than left hemisphere patients at estimating diagonal distances between dots, but both groups position horizontally placed dots equally well. (3) Left hemisphere patients tend to produce more—and right hemisphere patients tend to produce fewer—right angles than there are in the cube. (4) Right hemisphere patients consistently underestimate, and left hemisphere patients consistently overestimate, the angles of the star. (5) Right hemisphere patients produce more errors of symmetry than do left hemisphere patients. (6) Left hemisphere patients copied as much of the structure of the structured drawings as the right hemisphere patients but significantly failed to use it to build their drawings. (7) Visual inattention to the side opposite the lesion predominated among right hemisphere patients at a rate of six to one. Edith Kaplan notes that patients with right hemisphere damage may proceed from right to left in their drawings although the common approach is to draw from left to right.

These tendencies represent the predominant research findings. They may not be applicable in the individual case since the site of the lesion along the anterior-posterior axis also affects the expression of constructional impairment (A. Smith, 1979; K. W. Walsh, 1978b). Thus, while patients with right posterior lesions will, in general, be most likely to have impaired constructional functions, right hemisphere damaged patients whose lesions are anterior are least likely to experience constructional deficits.

Drawing

The major subdivisions within this class are copying and free drawing. The overlap between them is considerable and yet many persons whose drawing skills are impaired can copy with reasonable accuracy. Instances of the reverse case are relatively rare (Messerli et al., 1979).

Drawing tasks have achieved a central position in neuropsychological testing by virtue of their sensitivity to many different kinds of organic disabilities. Andrews and his colleagues (1980), for example, found that the presence of abnormalities in drawings (both free and copied) was a powerful predictor of poor outcome following stroke. This sensitivity may be the reason that the discriminating power of drawing tasks at times has assumed mythic proportions. Unfortunately, it has not been uncommon for some psychologists to think that a complete neuropsychological examination consists of the WAIS and one or two drawing tests, usually the Bender-Gestalt and a Draw-a-Person test. (There are even a few intrepid purists who prefer to form their diagnostic opinions on the basis of a single drawing test.) However, although they are rich sources of data, drawing tests too have limits to the amount of information they can provide. The examiner who uses them needs to remember that every kind of drawing task has been performed successfully by brain injured patients including some with lesions that should have prevented them from doing the tasks. Furthermore, no matter how sensitive these tests might be to perceptual, practic, and certain cognitive and motor organization disabilities, they still leave many intellectual functions untouched.

In drawings, the phenomenon of unilateral inattention tends to be reflected in the omission of details on the side of the drawing opposite the lesion (see Figs. 3-7 and 3-8a, pp. 67, 69; Colombo et al., 1976). Burton (1978) and Gur and her colleagues (1977) also observed a tendency for patients with unilateral damage to position their drawings on the same side of the page as the lesion, thus underutilizing the side of space that is most susceptible to inattention. This tendency was much more prominent among patients with left than with right hemisphere lesions studied by Gasparinni and his co-workers (1980), perhaps because those with left hemisphere damage were more likely to use a smaller part (typically the upper left quadrant and immediately adjacent areas) of the page while the right-lesioned group's overall shift to the right of the midline was less apparent because their drawings covered most of the page. The drawings (both free and copy) of patients with right hemisphere damage also tend to be larger than those done by patients with left-sided lesions (Larrabee and Kane, 1983). Frederiks (1963) reports that free drawings (i.e., drawing to command) tend to elicit evidence of inattention more readily than does copying from a model. (It is of interest to note that, in 1963, Frederiks's definition of "constructional apraxia" was essentially identical with what we now call "visuospatial inattention or neglect" in drawings.)

When using drawings as a means of testing for inattention, as when examining inattention by perceptual or spatial preference techniques (see pp. 343–346), a complete copy of a single drawing is not an adequate demonstration that the patient does not suffer unilateral neglect as this phenomenon, particularly in its milder forms and with relatively simple drawings, may not show up readily (Colombo et al., 1976). When neglect is suspected, it should be looked for by a variety of means (see pp. 346–347).

The skillfulness of the hand used in drawing may also be relevant to the quality of the performance. Semenza and his colleagues (1978) found no differences between preferred and nonpreferred hands in the way in which normal subjects approached the task of copying a relatively simple figure. However, Archibald's (no date) right-handed patients with left hemisphere damage who had to draw with their left hands showed a marked tendency to simplify their copies of a complex figure (see pp. 383, 403).

Copying Tests

The Bender-Gestalt Test (L. Bender, 1938; Hutt, 1977)

Of all drawing tests, the *Bender-Gestalt* has been the subject of the most study, theory, and research. Conceptual approaches to the interpretation of nonobjective drawings that have evolved out of this work can be applied to the evaluation of drawing performances generally, This test's quick and easy administration probably contributes to its first-place position among the most frequently used psychological tests in the United States (Lubin et al., 1971). The fact that it serves as a projective technique for studying personality as well as a visuoconstructional task for neuropsychological assessment also accounts for its popularity.

The Bender material is a set of nine designs[1] originally used to demonstrate the tendency of the perceptual system to organize visual stimuli into *Gestalten* (configurational wholes) (see Fig. 13-1). The designs were assembled and numbered (A and 1 through 8) by Lauretta Bender for the study of mental development in children. She called this method a "Visual Motor Gestalt Test." Time and custom have grafted Dr. Bender's name onto the formal title of her test. Most clinicians simply refer to it as the "Bender."

Exact reproductions of the designs are necessary for reliable evaluation of drawing distortions. If the circles of design 2, for example, are depicted as ovals, or the line quality of the model designs is uneven, then the examiner is hard put to decide whether similar distortions in a patient's copy represent distortion or finicking accuracy. Also, if the curves of design 7 do not cross in such a way that the figure can be seen as either two contiguous or two overlapping sinusoidal curves, then the examiner can not find out whether the patient would perceive them in a simplified (uncrossed) or complex (crossed) manner.

---

[1]The set of Bender cards with the most evenly and clearly reproduced design elements is Hutt's adaptation of the Bender test figures (Hutt, 1977). These are exact reproductions of the original stimulus designs as depicted in Figure 13-2.

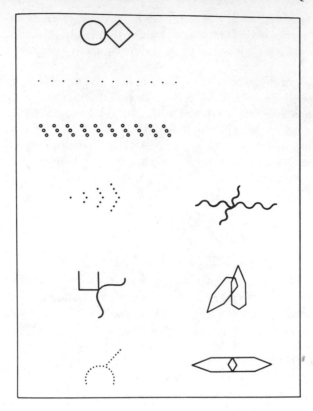

Fig. 13-1   The Hutt Adaptation of the Bender-Gestalt figures. (Hutt, 1977. Reproduced by permission.)

Almost every clinician who has written about the Bender at any length has prescribed at least one set of instructions. My administration of this test begins with laying three sharpened number one or two pencils and a small stack of unlined white typewriter paper in front of the patient so that the short side is horizontal to him. Three pencils with good erasers ensure against having to interrupt the test when a heavy-handed, intense, or clumsy patient breaks one or more pencil points. Pencils any harder than number two tend to resist pressure so that drawing becomes more effortful and the pencil marks are less apt to reflect individual pressure differences in their shading or thickness. The main purpose of putting out more than one piece of paper is to create a softer drawing surface that will increase ease of drawing and pick up pressure marks on the second sheet. Sometimes patients set aside the top sheet of paper on completion of the first drawing, or after three or four drawings. When they do so, I ask them to draw all the designs on the first sheet unless there is no usable space left, in which case I ask them to complete the test on the second sheet. Forcing the patient to confine his drawings to one or, at the most, two sheets provides one way to see how—or whether—the patient organizes the designs within limited space.

386

The instructions are: "I've got nine of these altogether (hold up the pack of cards with the back facing the patient). I'm going to show them to you one at a time and your job is (or "you are") to copy them as exactly as you can. Here you go." The first card is then placed in front of the patient with its length running horizontally to him and its edges squared with the edges of the work surface. When the patient finishes the first drawing, the second card is placed on top of the first and so on to completion. When all the designs have been copied, I ask the subject to write his name and the date on the paper with no instructions about where these should be placed, and I offer no suggestions if asked.

These instructions afford the patient the barest minimum of structure and virtually no information on how to proceed. This method not only enhances the test's projective possibilities, but makes it a test of the patient's ability to organize his activities as well. By letting the subject know there are nine cards, the examiner gives him the opportunity to plan ahead for his space needs. By omitting any reference to the nature of the cards, i.e., by not calling them "designs," the examiner avoids influencing the subject's perceptual organization of the stimuli. By lining the cards up with the edges of the work surface, the examiner provides an external anchoring point for the angulation of the stimulus so that, should the subject rotate his copy of the design, the examiner knows exactly how much the drawing is angled relative to the original stimulus.

Many subjects need no more instruction than this to complete the tests comfortably. Others ask questions about how to draw the figures, whether they can be larger or smaller, have more or less dots, need to be numbered, lined up along the edge, or spread over the page, etc. To each of these questions, the answer is, "Just copy the card as exactly as you can." Should the subject persist in his questioning, the examiner may tell him that, "I can only give you these instructions; the rest is up to you." The subject who asks to erase is given permission without special encouragement. If the subject attempts to turn either the stimulus card or his sheet of paper, he should be stopped before he begins copying the card at an incorrect or uncommon angle, as the disorientation of the drawing might no longer be apparent when the paper is righted again. I do not let the patient turn the page more than is needed for a comfortable writing angle. The total time usually runs from five to ten minutes.

Besides different versions of the standard adminstration, there are a number of other ways to give the test, most of which were developed for personality assessment (Hutt, 1977). Those that enable the examiner to see how well the subject can function under pressure provide interesting neuropsychological data as well. For instance, in the "stress Bender," the patient is given the whole test a second time with instructions to "copy the designs as fast as you can. You drew them in _____ seconds (any reasonable time approximation will do) the first time; I want to see how much faster you can do them this time." The examiner then begins timing as noisily and ostentatiously as possible. Some patients who can compensate well for mild constructional disabilities when under no pressure will first betray evidence of their problem as they speed up their performance. Interestingly, many organically intact subjects actually improve their Bender performance under the stress condition. (Regardless of how much time the patient takes the second time, I always congratulate him on his speed and, if need be, shade a few seconds off his performance time in telling him about it.) Hutt (1977) suggests that tachistoscopic exposure of the designs may be a more sensitive technique than the standard copy administration for purposes of differential diagnosis, but in the absence of definitive research he wisely urges more investigation of this procedure.

Wepman (personal communication, 1974) incorporated two recall procedures into his three-stage standard administration of the Bender. Each card is shown for five seconds, then removed, and the subject is instructed to draw it from memory. After this, the cards are shown again, one at a time, with instructions to copy them exactly. This second stage is the same as the standard copy administration. Finally, the cards are removed, the subject is handed one more blank sheet of paper, and asked to draw as many of the figures as he can remember. Wepman views difficulty with items 1, 2, 4, and 5 as particularly suggestive of a constructional disorder. He found that normal subjects typically recall five designs or more, and he considers recall scores under five to be suggestive of brain injury. This impression is supported by Tolor's findings (1956, 1958) that functionally disturbed psychiatric patients recall six designs on the average, whereas organic patients average three and a half recalled designs. Lyle and Gottesman (1977) obtained similar results when they compared normal persons at risk for Huntington's disease with afflicted patients and found that the patients recalled only 3.7 designs on the average while those still free of the disease recalled an average of 5.6 designs. Recall scores obtained by these subjects were as effective in making diagnostic discriminations between them as was clinical judgment. Approximately two-thirds of each diagnostic group was correctly identified by each method, not enough to serve as the sole basis for prediction of neuropsychological status (Lyle and Quast, 1976).

Research reported in the considerable literature on Bender recall (see Hutt, 1977) is consistently in accord with these data. Undoubtedly, recall of these designs can be a useful technique for examining visuospatial memory. However, administration and scoring procedures of the many reported studies have not been standardized, leaving many important questions unanswered, such as how many designs would normally be recalled after interference or a delay, and how strict the criteria for correct recall should be.

Lauretta Bender conceived of her test as a clinical exercise in which "(d)eviate behavior . . . should be observed and noted. It never represents a test failure" (1946). She did not use a scoring system. The Bender variables that can be scored are numerous and equivocal, and their dimensions are often difficult to define. The profusion of scoring possibilities has resulted in many attempts to develop a workable system to obtain scores for diagnostic purposes.

Probably the best known scoring system is the one devised by Pascal and Suttell (1951), who viewed deviations in the execution of Bender drawings as reflecting "disturbances in cortical function," whether on a functional or an organic basis. By assigning each deviant response a numerical value, they enabled the examiner to compute a score indicating the extent to which the drawings deviate from normal productions. As a general rule, the scores of neurotic patients are almost indistinguishable from those of normal subjects, the highest scores tend to be obtained by brain damaged patients, and the considerable overlap between groups of brain damaged and psychiatric patients makes differentiation between them on the basis of a Bender score alone a very questionable matter.

The Pascal-Suttell system identifies 106 different scorable characteristics of the drawings, from 10 to 13 for each figure (excluding A) plus seven layout variables applied to the performance as a whole. Significant distortions of these characteristics earn score points. For example, there are 12 scorable characteristics for design 6 that yield scores for specific deviations: (1) Asymmetry (score 3); (2) Angles in the Curve (score 2); (3) Point of Crossing (score 2); (4) Curve Extra (score 8); (5) Double Line (score 1 for each); (6) Touch-up (score 8); (7) Tremor (score 4); (8) Distortion (score 8); (9) Guide Lines (score 2); (10) Workover (score 2), (11) Second Attempt (score 3 for each); and (12) Rotation (score 8). An examiner who knows this system can score most records in two to three minutes. The average mean raw score for seven age groups of men and women with high school education is 18.0 ± 9.4; for the same number of age groups of both sexes with college educations, the average mean score is 12.7 ± 8.8.

Approaching the test performance as a whole rather than card by card, Hain (1964) developed a 15-category scoring system from inspection of the Bender protocols of brain damaged patients (see Table 13-1). Any single instance of a category characteristic earns the score points for that category. The total possible range of scores is from 0 for a perfect performance to 34 for a protocol in which every category of deviant response occurs at least once. Hain compared small groups of brain damaged, psychiatric, and "non-brain damaged" patients to obtain cut-off scores for discriminating between the brain damaged group and the others (see Table 13-2). He set the optimal cut-off point between scores 8 and 9, which identifies approximately 80% of all subjects correctly, but misidentifies 41% of the brain damaged patients and only 8% of the combined groups without brain damage.

Hutt designed a 17-factor Psychopathology Scale to measure the severity of psychopathology (1977). Although the scale was evaluated with groups of normal subjects

Table 13-1 Hain's 15-Category Scoring System for the Bender-Gestalt Test

The Scoring Categories Classified by Their Score Weights			
4 points	3 points	2 points	1 point
Perseveration	Added Angles	Embellishments	Omission
Rotation or Reversal	Separation of Lines	Partial Rotation	Abbreviation of Designs 1 or 2
Concretism	Overlap		Separation
	Distortion		Absence of Erasure
			Closure
			Point of Contact on
			Figure A

(Adapted from Hain, 1963)

Table 13-2 Distribution of Hain Bender-Gestalt Scores for Brain Damaged and Non-brain Damaged Groups

Classification	Score	Brain Damaged (%) ($n = 21$)	Non-brain Damaged (%) ($n = 84$)[a]
Normal area	0–5	20	80
Borderline	6–12	41	18
Critical area	13–24	39	2

(Adapted from Hain, 1963)
[a]Includes 21 psychiatric patients.

and neurotic and schizophrenic patients, Hutt anticipated that scores of schizophrenic and brain damaged patients would overlap, with the highest scores going to the latter. Like Hain's scoring approach, this scoring system differs from the Pascal-Suttell system in treating the test performance as a whole. Thus, for a factor such as "curvature difficulty," Hutt has a four-point scale ranging from Severe (scale value = 10.0), scored when curves in all three figures containing curves are distorted, to Absent (scale value = 1.0), when all the curves are drawn well. In contrast, Pascal and Suttell's system scores for six different kinds of curve distortion on design 4, one kind of curve distortion on design 5, and two on design 6.

The first five of Hutt's factors relate to the organization of the drawings on the page and to one another: (1) Sequence, (2) Position, 1st Drawing, (3) Use of Space, I, (4) Collision, and (5) Shift of Paper. The next factors concern changed gestalts: (6) Closure Difficulty, (7) Crossing Difficulty, (8) Curvature Difficulty, and (9) Change in Angulation. Factors related to distorted gestalts are associated with severe psychopathology: (10) Perceptual Rotation, (11) Retrogression, (12) Simplification, (13) Fragmentation, (14) Overlapping Difficulty, (15) Elaboration, (16) Perseveration, and (17) Redrawing, Total Figure. Scale values of each factor range from 10 to 1 with the exception of the second factor, which has only two scale values, 3.25 for Abnormal and 1.0 for Normal. Score range is from 17 for a perfect performance (or at least a performance without scorable imperfections) to 163.5 for a performance in which maximum difficulty is encountered in handling each factor characteristic.

Criteria for scoring each factor are presented in detail and are sufficiently clear to result in reliable judgments. Hutt reports that interjudge reliability correlations for the 17 factors for two judges scoring 100 schizophrenic records ranged from 1.00 to .76, with five factor correlations running above .90 and nine above .80. An interjudge reliability correlation of .96 was obtained for the total scale. Hutt reports that by means of this system the examiner can discriminate reliably between normal and neurotic, schizophrenic and organic groups, with all differences between groups significant beyond the .001 level except that between "chronic schizophrenics" and "organics," which was significant at the .05 level. His standardization group of 140 normals (which included 60 "unselected" college students) obtained a mean score of

32.8 ± 4.9. The mean score for "outpatient neurotics" was 53.5 ± 9.6, for "chronic schizophrenics" it was 97.1 ± 12.1, and the patients with "chronic disease processes or traumatic brain injury" who comprised the "organic brain damage" group obtained a mean score of 100.3 ± 14.3.

Hutt also describes a number of other characteristic distortions, such as size changes and line quality, that are not included in the scale but which may be associated with organic conditions and have all been included in one or more other scales. He identifies 11 kinds of deviations that are particularly associated with brain damage: (1) Collision (and Collision Tendency), i.e., the running together or overlapping of two discrete designs; (2) Angulation Difficulty (marked); (3) Perceptual Rotation (severe, which increases in seriousness when the subject does not perceive or cannot correct it); (4) Simplification; (5) Fragmentation (severe); (6) Overlapping Difficulty (moderate to severe); (7) Perseveration (of elements in a design and of elements of one design in another, especially if severe); (8) Elaboration (moderate); (9) Redrawing of a Total Figure; (10) Line Incoordination (both fine and coarse); and (11) Concreteness. He also regards sketching that is so loose or crude as to diminish the quality of the drawing or distort the gestalt, and expressions of feelings of impotence, as indicators of organicity. Hutt suggests that four or more of these deviant response characteristics in a record is strongly indicative of neuropathology. A careful reading of Hutt's description and interpretation of these deviant characteristics will enhance the examiner's perceptiveness in dealing with Bender data (see Hutt and Gibby, 1970, for examples).

Hutt's interest in the projective potentials of the Bender led him to develop a second scale, the Adience-Abience Scale, to measure "perceptual approach-avoidance behavior." The scale appears to add little to the study of visuographic functions although it may ultimately contribute information about the social and emotional adjustment of brain damaged patients.

Although some scoring system is necessary when doing research with the Bender, for clinical purposes formal scoring is usually unnecessary. Familiarity with one or more of the scoring systems will make the examiner aware of the common Bender distortions. Familiarity with the kinds of aberrations that tend to be associated with visuospatial disabilities and organic response styles will improve the examiner's accuracy in making discriminations on the basis of inspection rather than scores of the Bender drawings. This was demonstrated in L. R. Goldberg's study (1959) comparing a group of psychology trainees, another group consisting of psychologists' secretaries, scores obtained by the Pascal-Suttell system, and Professor Max Hutt for accuracy in sorting the Bender protocols of subjects with and without brain damage. Trainees, secretaries, and the scoring system all did equally well; Professor Hutt made the most correct sorts.

E. W. Russell (1976) demonstrated how misleading a score can be in clinical practice when he used Hutt's system to test an aphasic patient with pronounced right hemiplegia who had sustained a severe depressed skull fracture some 17 years earlier, and the patient obtained a score within normal limits (less than 2 SD above the "Normals" mean). His performance included an insufficient number of dots on four designs, perseveration of dots from design 1 to design 2, a 45° rotation of the curve on design 4, poor planning in his placement of the design, and several instances in which the designs were crowded together (Hutt calls this, "Collision Tendency"). He also left a few little "tag ends" on angles. These kinds of errors in such quantity far exceed the errors of haste or carelessness that might detract from the drawings of a neurologically intact subject. However, the patient did preserve all the gestalts and, while his drawing line was a little shaky at times, his reproductions were for the most part "clean" in appearance, providing a good example of how relatively well this test can be handled by some brain damaged patients.

Pascal and Suttell's mean score differences between high-school and college-educated populations suggested that the Bender-Gestalt performance correlates with general intellectual ability. In a psychiatric population, this was borne out by consistently significant correlations (around .50) between Pascal and Suttell and WAIS subtest scores, with only Digit Span and Object Assembly correlations running below .40 (Aylaian and Meltzer, 1962). On the other hand, a study of college students found "little if any" relation between an academic achievement test and Pascal and Suttell Bender scores, whereas Bender score differences in this relatively homogeneous, intellectually superior population were associated with GPA differences (Peoples and Moll, 1962). Since most nine-year-olds can copy the Bender designs with a fair degree of accuracy (Koppitz, 1964), Bender performance differences between competent intact adults apparently result from the same kind of temperamental or character traits that influence behavior in school or at work. Only when an organically intact group contains both dull and bright persons can intellectual differences be expected to show up in Bender score differences.

Neuropsychological research with the Bender has demonstrated its relative efficiency in making the frequently difficult discrimination between brain damaged and psychiatric patients (Yates, 1966). Brilliant and Gynther (1963) and Lacks and her colleagues (1970), each using Hutt's scoring system, found that the Bender identified members of each diagnostic group as well or better than any other instrument. In Brilliant and Gynther's study, the Bender-Gestalt showed a diagnostic accuracy of 82%, performing better than either of two visuographic memory tests. In the Lacks study, the Bender-Gestalt score identified organic patients as well or better (74%) than four of eight scores on the Halstead Battery and far and away better (91%) than any of the Halstead Battery tests in identifying "nonorganic" patients. In another study using the Pascal-Suttell scoring system, 74% accuracy in discriminating brain damaged from mixed psychiatric patients was reported (Korman and Blumberg, 1963). A summary of studies concerned with making neuropsychological discriminations between psychiatric and neurological disorders that were published from 1960 through 1975 is given by Heaton, Baade, and Johnson (1978). In this review of the literature, a median score for percent of correct classifications of 76% was computed for the Bender. In a comparison with four other neuropsychological techniques that have been used for diagnostic screening purposes (Background Interference Procedure, p. 393; Benton Visual Retention Test, pp. 447–451); Memory for Designs, pp.

451–453; and Trail-Making Test, pp. 556–559), the Bender's discrimination accuracy was exceeded only by that of the Background Interference Procedure.

Bender scores have also proven sensitive in documenting changes in neuropsychological status. Farmer (1975) followed 100 alcoholics through their first two-and-a-half months of abstinence and found that their mean Bender scores (using the Pascal-Suttell system) dropped an average of 17.2 points, showing significant decreases at one-and-a-half as well as two-and-a-half months. Differences in response to chemosurgery of 54 patients with Parkinson's disease were documented by using Pascal and Suttell's scoring system in comparisons between those patients who had chemosurgery of left-sided and those whose chemosurgery was of right-sided basal ganglia structures (Riklan and Diller, 1961). Another treatment response, of patients with chronic obstructive pulmonary disease treated with continuous oxygen therapy, was also reflected in an improvement in Bender scores that did not occur in an untreated patient group (Krop et al., 1972).

Like other visuographic disabilities, difficulties with the Bender are more likely to appear with parietal lobe lesions (Garron and Cheifetz, 1965), and of these, lesions of the right parietal lobe are associated with the poorest performances (Diller et al., 1974; Hirschenfang, 1960a). Patients with right hemisphere damage are much more susceptible to errors of rotation (Billingslea, 1963) and fragmentation than those with left-sided lesions (Belleza et al., 1979). Diller and Weinberg (1965) reported that both their right and left hemisphere damaged patients tended to make additions but only those with lesions on the right made omissions. In my experience, however, patients with either right- or left-sided lesions—certainly those with bilateral damage—make errors of omission (see also E. W. Russell's case reported on pp. 391–392).

The unlikelihood of finding manifest impairment in the Bender drawings of patients with left frontal lesions should serve to remind the examiner that "an adequate [Bender] copy does not necessarily rule out organic brain pathology" (Garron and Cheifetz, 1965). However, a normal-appearing Bender does reduce the likelihood of parietal involvement. The sensitivity of this test to diffuse cortical disease or subcortical lesions (Lyle and Gottesman, 1977; and Lyle and Quast, 1976; Riklan and Diller, 1961) suggests that copying tasks require a high level of integrative behavior that is not necessarily specific to visuographic functions but tends to break down with many kinds of cerebral damage.

BACKGROUND INTERFERENCE PROCEDURE-BENDER (BIP) (A. Canter, 1966, 1968)

In an effort to enhance the usefulness of the Bender-Gestalt Test for neuropsychological screening, Canter devised the Background Interference Procedure. It uses an 8½ × 11 inch (21.6 × 28.1 cm) sheet of white paper covered with heavy black curved lines that crisscross over the entire sheet. The Bender is first administered in standard form and then given again with instructions to copy it on the BIP sheet. Canter also does not allow his subjects to turn either the paper or the card. By attaching a carbon paper with a plain white sheet under the BIP sheet, Canter found that he could get a clear copy of the BIP performance that made comparisons with the standard performance easier. Scoring of the BIP rests on comparisons between the raw Pascal-Suttell score for each administration with some elaborations (Canter, 1968). An attempt to adapt the less cumbersome Hain scoring system to this procedure was unsuccessful (Pardue, 1975).

A review of the efficacy of neuropsychological screening tests in discriminating between organic and psychiatric patients suggests that Canter realized his goal (Heaton, Baade, and Johnson, 1978). Of the many tests and batteries examined in the 94 studies reviewed by Heaton and his co-workers, the BIP was by far the most effective with a median 84% of correct classifications. Its effectiveness as a screening device for brain impairment was also demonstrated in an elderly population in which 5 of the 17 healthy elderly persons obtained Bender error scores within Pascal and Suttell's range for mild to moderate deficit, but only one of the 17 received a BIP score suggestive of neuropsychological abnormality (A. Canter and Straumanis, 1969). In the same study, senile patients were readily identified by both testing techniques. The BIP was also sensitive to improvement in the neuropsychological status of patients with chronic obstructive pulmonary disease who had oxygen inhalation therapy (Krop et al., 1972). As with the Bender, there are laterality effects with this techique in that the BIP is more likely to disrupt the performance of patients with right hemisphere damage than of those whose damage is on the left (Nemec, 1978).

MINNESOTA PERCEPTO-DIAGNOSTIC TEST (MPD) (Fuller, 1969; Fuller and Laird, 1963)

This copying task is designed to test for the presence of a tendency toward rotation in drawings. It uses two of the designs included in the Bender-Gestalt test, A and 4, presenting each in three different combinations of design and card orientation. Scoring is based on the amount of rotation of the drawings, which is measured with a protractor. The manual gives norms for diagnostic groups of both children and adults. Much of the literature on this test pertains to studies of children with school or personal/social adjustment problems.

This test may be useful in discriminating between brain damaged and other patients and nonpatient groups (Uyeno, 1963). Score differences on the MPD correctly identified 89% of the "Normal" subjects, 80% of a "Personality Disturbance" group (consisting of persons diagnosed as "neurotic," "sociopathic," and "psychotic" in unreported numbers), and 78% of the "Chronic Brain Syndrome" (CBS) group (described as "diagnosed CBS by the medical staff") of the standardization population, the latter group obtaining higher (error) scores (Fuller and Laird, 1963). However, the ages of these groups leave serious question as to their comparability for standardization purposes since the mean age of the Normal group was 29.11 ± 10.94, of the Personality Disturbance group 43.21 ± 14.20, and of the Chronic Brain Syndrome group 51.21 ± 11.50, which brings the last-named group to the borderland of old age and all the normal functional changes of senility. In a study of its efficacy in differentiating organic from psychiatric patients in which age and education variables

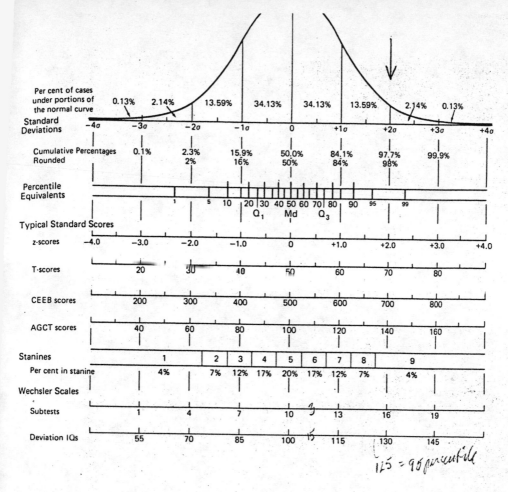

Per cent of cases under portions of the normal curve	0.13%	2.14%	13.59%	34.13%	34.13%	13.59%	2.14%	0.13%

Standard Deviations	-4σ	-3σ	-2σ	-1σ	0	+1σ	+2σ	+3σ	+4σ

Cumulative Percentages Rounded	0.1%	2.3% 2%	15.9% 16%	50.0% 50%	84.1% 84%	97.7% 98%	99.9%	

Percentile Equivalents

1   5   10   20 30 40 50 60 70 80   90   95   99
                 Q₁   Md   Q₃

Typical Standard Scores								
z-scores	-4.0	-3.0	-2.0	-1.0	0	+1.0	+2.0	+3.0	+4.0
T-scores		20	30	40	50	60	70	80	
CEEB scores		200	300	400	500	600	700	800	
AGCT scores		40	60	80	100	120	140	160	

Stanines		1	2	3	4	5	6	7	8	9	
Per cent in stanine		4%	7%	12%	17%	20%	17%	12%	7%	4%	

Wechsler Scales

Subtests		1	4	7	10	13	16	19	
Deviation IQs		55	70	85	100	115	130	145	

125 = 95 percentile

NOTE: This chart cannot be used to equate scores on one test to scores on another test. For example, both 600 on the CEEB and 120 on the AGCT are one standard deviation above their respective means, but they do not represent "equal" standings because the scores were obtained from different groups.

Fig. 6-2. The relationship of the most commonly used test scores to the normal curve and to one another. (Reprinted from the *Test Service Bulletin* of The Psychological Corporation, No. 48, 1955.)

from: M. LEZAK Neuropsychological Assessment.

were controlled, this test proved worthless (Helmes et al., 1980). Cultural background may also influence performance on this test (D. M. Harrison and Chagnon, 1966).

THE COMPLEX FIGURE TEST (CFT): COPY ADMINISTRATION *also see p 444* ♯

A "complex figure" was devised by Rey (1941) to investigate both perceptual organization and visual memory in brain damaged subjects. (See pp. 444–447 for a discussion of the complex figure in memory testing.) Osterrieth (1944) standardized Rey's procedure, obtaining normative data from the performance of 230 normal children of ages ranging from four to 15 and 60 adults in the 16–60 age range. In addition to two groups of children with learning and adjustment problems, he studied a small number of behaviorally disturbed adults, 43 who had sustained traumatic brain injury, and a few patients with endogenous brain disease. More recently, L. B. Taylor made up an alternate complex figure for use in retesting (Milner, 1975; L. B. Taylor, 1969, 1979). Although normative data have not been obtained for the Taylor figure, its comparability to the Rey figure in design elements and complexity is reflected in the similarity of scores obtained on retest by patients with left temporal lobectomies whose drawing abilities, ordinarily, are unaffected by left temporal epileptic foci or surgery for this condition.

The test material consists of Rey's complex figure (see Fig. 13-2) or Taylor's complex figure (see Fig. 13-3), blank typewriter-size paper, and five or six colored pens or pencils. The subject is first instructed to copy the figure, which has been so set out that its length runs along the subject's horizontal plane. The examiner watches the subject's performance closely. Each time the subject completes a section of the drawing, the examiner hands him a different colored pencil and notes the order of the colors. Instead of using color for tracking the subject's performance, some examiners keep a detailed record of the subject's copying sequence by reproducing the performance, numbering each unit in the order that it is drawn (Binder, 1982; Edith Kaplan, personal communication). Visser (1973) uses a "registration sheet" containing the printed Rey figure, which the examiner numbers in the order in which the subject makes his copy. This latter method is a satisfactory and effort-saving procedure except when the subject produces a drawing that deviates significantly from the original. When this happens, Visser's instructions to ignore extra lines and to deal with "wrongly placed [lines] . . . as if they were placed correctly" can result in a confusing and misleading record. For most clinical purposes, switching colors generally affords an adequate representation of the subject's overall approach. When using the CFT for research, the technique of drawing exactly what the subject draws and numbering each segment (I use directional arrows as well) will best preserve the drawing sequence accurately. Time to completion is recorded and both the test figure and the subject's drawings are removed. This is usually followed by one or more recall trials. Some subjects who are dissatisfied with a poorly executed copy show improvement on a second copy trial.

Osterrieth analyzed the drawings in terms of the patient's method of drawing as well as specific copying errors. He identified seven different procedural types: (I) Sub-

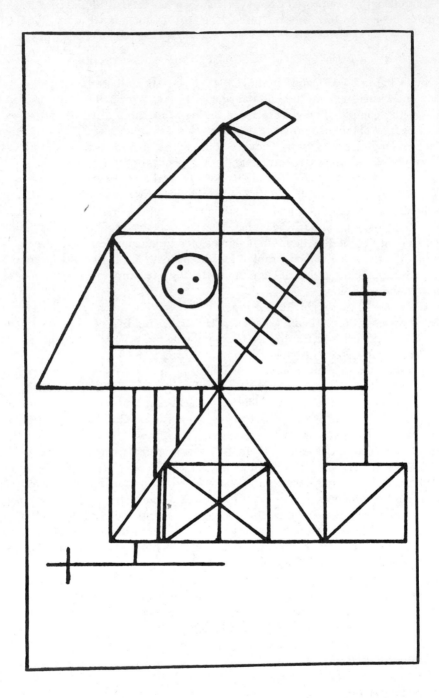

Fig. 13-2   Rey Complex Figure (Osterrieth, 1944).

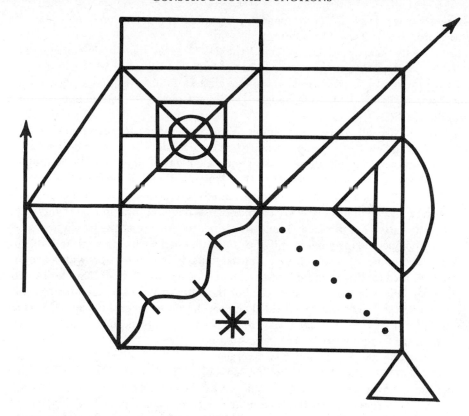

Fig. 13-3. Taylor Complex Figure (actual size).

ject begins by drawing the large central rectangle and details are added in relation to it. (II) Subject begins with a detail attached to the central rectangle, or with a subsection of the central rectangle, completes the rectangle and adds remaining details in relation to the rectangle. (III) Subject begins by drawing the overall contour of the figure without explicit differentiation of the central rectangle and then adds the internal details. (IV) Subject juxtaposes details one by one without an organizing structure. (V) Subject copies discrete parts of the drawing without any semblance of organization. (VI) Subject substitutes the drawing of a similar object, such as a boat or house. (VII) The drawing is an unrecognizable scrawl.

In Osterrieth's sample, 83% of the adult control subjects followed procedure Types I and II, 15% used Type IV, and there was one Type III Subject. Past the age of seven, no child proceeded on a Type V, VI, or VII basis, and from age 13 onward, more than half the children followed Types I and II. No one, child or adult, produced a scrawl. More than half (63%) of the traumatically brain injured group also followed Type I and II procedures, although there were a few more Type III and IV subjects in this group and one of Type V. Three of four aphasic patients and one with senile dementia gave Type IV performances; one aphasic and one presenile dementia patient followed a Type V procedure.

In line with Osterreith's observations, Visser (1973) noted that "brain-damaged subjects deviate from the normals mainly in the fact that the large rectangle does not exist for them . . . [Thus] since the main line clusters do not exist, (parts of) the main lines and details are drawn intermingled, working from top to bottom and from left to right" (p. 23).

Although, like all overgeneralizations, Visser's statement has exceptions, Binder (1982) showed how stroke patients tend to lose the overall configuration of the design. By analyzing how subjects draw the structural elements of the Rey-Osterrieth figure (the vertices of the pentagon drawn together, horizontal midline, vertical midline, and two diagonals) (Fig. 13-4). Binder obtained three scores: Configural Units is the number of these five elements that were each drawn as one unit; Fragmented Units is the number that were not drawn as a unit (this is not the inverse of the Configural score as it does not include incomplete units, i.e., those that had a part missing); and Missing Units is the number of incomplete or omitted units. Fourteen patients with left brain damage tended to display more fragmentation (mean score of 1.64) than the 14 with right-sided lesions (mean score of 0.71), but the latter group's average Missing Units score of 1.71 (primarily due to left-sided neglect) far outweighed a negligible Missing Units score of 0.07 for the left CVA group. In contrast, 14 normal control subjects averaged 0.21 Fragmented Units and omitted none. These copying approaches were reflected in the low Configural Unit average of 2.57 for patients with right-sided CVAs, a higher average Configural Unit score of 3.29 for those with left CVAs, and a near-perfect average score of 4.79 achieved by the control subjects.

Visser (1973) suggests that the fragmented or piecemeal approach to copying the complex figure that is so characteristic of brain damaged persons reflects their inabil-

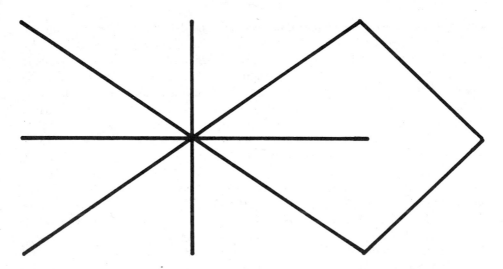

Fig. 13-4. Structural elements of the Rey Complex Figure (Binder, 1982).

ity to process as much information at a time as do normals. Thus, brain damaged persons tend to deal with smaller visual units, building the figure by accretion. Many ultimately produce a reasonably accurate reproduction in this manner, although the piecemeal approach increases the likelihood of size and relationship errors (Messerli et al., 1979).

Messerli and his colleagues (1979) looked at copies of the Rey figure drawn by 32 patients whose lesions were entirely or predominantly localized within the frontal lobes. They found that, judged overall, 75% differed significantly from the model. The most frequent error (in 75% of the defective copies) was the repetition of an element that had already been copied, an error resulting from the patient's losing track of what he had drawn where because of a disorganized approach. In one-third of the defective copies, a design element was transformed into a familiar representation (e.g., the circle with three dots was rendered as a face). Perseveration occurred less often, usually showing up as additional cross-hatches (scoring unit 12) or parallel lines (scoring unit 8). Omissions were also noted.

Laterality differences in approach to these drawings emerge in several ways. Binder's study (1982) showed that patients with left hemisphere damage tend to break up the design into units that are smaller than normally perceived while right hemisphere damage makes it more likely that elements will be omitted altogether. However, on recall of the complex figure, patients with left hemisphere damage who may have copied the figure in a piecemeal manner tend to reproduce the basic rectangular outline and the structural elements as a configural whole, suggesting that their processing of all these data is slow but, given time, they ultimately reconstitute the data as a gestalt. This reconstitution is less likely to occur with right hemisphere damaged patients who, on recall, continue to construct poorly integrated figures (also see Chapter 14, pp. 445–446). Archibald (no date) found that, overall, patients with left-sided lesions tend to make more simplifications in their copies than do patients with right-sided lesions. These two groups differ in that the simplifications of patients with right brain damage involve partial omissions (e.g., fewer dots or lines than called for) while left brain damaged patients tend to simplify by rounding angles (e.g., giving curved sides to the diamond of the Rey figure), drawing dashes instead of dots, which are more difficult to execute, or leaving the cross of the Rey figure in an incomplete, T-shaped form. Of the 32 simplifications made by patients with left hemisphere damage, however, only five were made with the right hand, and three of these errors were made by patients who had residual right upper limb weakness. All others were made by the nonpreferred (left) hand of hemiparetic patients. These data suggest that, for the most part, simplification errors of patients with left hemisphere damage are the product of the left hand's deficient control over fine movements; i.e., simplification in patients with left-sided lesions is a defect of execution, not one of perception or cognition. Binder's right and left hemisphere damaged patients also differed significantly in the accuracy of their reproductions. Patients with right hemisphere damage produced much less accurate copies than patients with left CVAs who, although on the whole less accurate than the normal control group, still showed some overlap in accuracy scores with the control group.

Differences between patients with parietal-occipital lesions and patients with fron-

tal lobe damage were demonstrated in their failures to copy the complex figure correctly (Pillon, 1981b). Errors made by the frontal patients reflected disturbances in
their ability to program the approach to copying the figure. Patients with parietal-
occipital lesions, on the other hand, had difficulty with the spatial organization of the
figure. When given a plan to guide their approach to the copy task, the patients with
frontal damage improved markedly. The patients with posterior lesions also improved
their copies when provided spatially reference points. However, use of spatial reference points did not improve the copies made by the patients with frontal damage,
nor did those with parietal-occipital lesions benefit from a program plan.

Overall evaluations of the success of a drawing of the complex figure can be
obtained by using an accuracy score based on a unit scoring system (see Tables 13-3
and 13-4). The scoring units refer to specific areas or details of the figures that have
been numbered for scoring convenience. Since the reproduction of each unit can earn
as many as two score points, the highest possible number of points is 36. From age

Table 13-3   Scoring System for the Rey Complex Figure

Units
1. Cross upper left corner, outside of rectangle
2. Large rectangle
3. Diagonal cross
4. Horizontal midline of 2
5. Vertical midline
6. Small rectangle, within 2 to the left
7. Small segment above 6
8. Four parallel lines within 2, upper left
9. Triangle above 2 upper right
10. Small vertical line within 2, below 9
11. Circle with three dots within 2
12. Five parallel lines within 2 crossing 3, lower right
13. Sides of triangle attached to 2 on right
14. Diamond attached to 13
15. Vertical line within triangle 13 parallel to right vertical of 2
16. Horizontal line within 13, continuing 4 to right
17. Cross attached to 5 below 2
18. Square attached to 2, lower left

Scoring
Consider each of the 18 units separately. Appraise accuracy of each unit and relative position within
the whole of the design. For each unit count as follows:

Correct	placed properly	2 points
	placed poorly	1 point
Distorted or incomplete	placed properly	1 point
but recognizable	placed poorly	½ point
Absent or not recognizable		0 points
Maximum		36 points

(From E. M. Taylor, 1959, adapted from Osterrieth, 1944)

Table 13-4   Scoring System for the Taylor Complex Figure

Units

1. Arrow at left of figure.
2. Triangle to left of large square.
3. Square, which is the base of figure.
4. Horizontal midline of large square, which extends to 1.
5. Vertical midline of large square.
6. Horizontal line in top half of large square.
7. Diagonals in top left quadrant of large square.
8. Small square in top left quadrant.
9. Circle in top left quadrant.
10. Rectangle above top left quadrant.
11. Arrow through and extending out of top right quadrant.
12. Semicircle to right of large square.
13. Triangle with enclosed line in right half of large square.
14. Row of 7 dots in lower right quadrant.
15. Horizontal line between 6th and 7th dots.
16. Triangle at bottom right corner of lower right quadrant.
17. Curved line with 3 cross-bars in lower left quadrant.
18. Star in lower left quadrant.

Scoring

Follow instructions given in Table 13-3 for scoring the Rey figure.

eight onward, the average score is 30 or above; the average adult's score is 32 (see Table 13-5). The accuracy score provides a good measure of how well the subject reproduces the design, regardless of the approach he uses. Since the memory trial of the CFT is scored in the same manner, the accuracy score permits a comparison between the different trials of the test (see Chapter 14, pp. 445, 447). For example, although almost half of the 43 traumatically brain injured adult patients in Osterrieth's sample achieved "copy" scores of 32 or better, one-third of this group's scores were significantly low. On the memory trial, fewer than one-third of the traumatically brain injured group were able to achieve the normal group's mean score of 22. In general, there was a wider disparity between the copy and memory scores of the brain injured group than in Osterrieth's normal group of 60 persons ages 16 to 60. Four patients performed relatively better on the memory than the copy task, suggesting delayed perceptual organization or slowed ability to adapt to new tasks. Seven patients diagnosed as having severe psychiatric disorders were the only adults to add

Table 13-5   Percentile Norms for Accuracy Scores Obtained by Adults on the Copy Trial of the Complex Figure Test

Percentile	10	20	30	40	50	60	70	80	90	100
Score	29	30	31	32	32	33	34	34	35	36

(Adapted from Osterrieth, 1944)

bizarre embellishments to their drawings, interpret details concretely, or fill in parts of the design with solid color. No behavior of this kind appeared among the brain damaged patients.

THE BENTON VISUAL RETENTION TEST (BVRT): COPY ADMINISTRATION
(Benton, 1974)

The three alternate forms of this test permit the use of one of them for a copy trial. (See pp. 447–448 for a description and picture of the test.) The copy trial usually precedes the memory trials, which allows the subject to familiarize himself with the test and the test materials before undertaking the more difficult memory tests. Benton's normative population of 200 adults provides the criteria for evaluating the scores. Each patient's drawings must be evaluated in terms of his estimated original level of functioning. Persons of *average* or better intelligence are expected to make no more than two errors. Subjects making three or four errors who typically perform at *low average* to *borderline* levels on most other intellectual tasks have probably done as well as could be expected on this test; for them, the presence of a more than ordinary number of errors does not signify a visuographic disability. On the other hand, the visuographic functioning of subjects who achieve a cluster of test scores on other kinds of tasks in the ranges above *average* and who make four or five errors on this task is suspect.

The performance of patients with frontal lobe lesions differs with the side of injury: those with bilateral damage average 4.6 errors; with right-sided damage, 3.5 errors; and with left-sided damage the average 1.0 error is comparable to that of the normative group (Benton, 1968). Other studies tend to support a right-left differential in defective copying of these designs, with right hemisphere patients two or three times more likely to have difficulties (Benton, 1969a). However, in one study that included aphasic patients in the comparisons between groups with lateralized lesions, no differences were found in the frequency with which constructional impairment was present in the drawings of right and left hemisphere damaged patients (Arena and Gainotti, 1978).

MISCELLANEOUS COPYING TASKS

Since any copying task can produce meaningful results, the examiner should feel free to improvise tasks as he sees fit. He can learn to reproduce a number of useful figures and then draw them at bedside examinations or in interviews when his test material is not available. Hécaen and co-workers (1951) and Warrington (1970) give some excellent examples of how easily drawn material for copying, such as a cube, a Greek cross, and a house can contribute to the evaluation of visuographic disabilities (see Fig. 13-5). Bilaterally symmetrical models for copying such as the cross and the star in Figure 13-5, or the top left and bottom designs from the Stanford-Binet Scale (Fig. 14-2, p. 444) are particularly suited to the study of unilateral inattention.

Another simple copying technique that is sensitive to visual inattention as well as

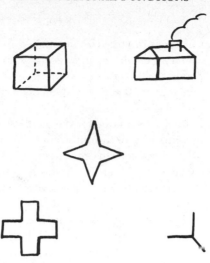

Fig. 13-5. Sample freehand drawings for copying.

preservation of relationships in space is *Copying Crosses*. Different investigators have used different numbers of crosses, two to six small ones arranged horizontally on a large (27 cm × 22 cm) sheet of paper (De Renzi and Faglioni, 1967) or ten small crosses, also arranged horizontally but in groups of five on either side of the paper's midpoint (Gainotti and Tiacci, 1970). Gianotti and Tiacci differentiate between "unilateral spatial inattention," which they define in terms of one or two absent crosses, and "unilateral spatial neglect," defined as the absence of five or more crosses. They also note whether the crosses are constructed in an organized or a piecemeal, fragmented fashion.

Free Drawing Tests

The absence of a model changes the perceptual component of free drawing from the immediate act of perception involved in copying tasks to arousal of a perceptual construct, a picture in the mind. This difference may account for the failure of Warrington et al. (1966), to find a systematic way to sort freehand drawings on the basis of the side of the lesion despite the many clear-cut differences between the drawings of right and left hemisphere damaged patients. Yet some differences do persist, such as a greater likelihood of left-sided visual inattention, an increased tendency to sketch over drawings, and more details—both relevant and inconsequential—among patients with right hemisphere lesions; drawings of left hemisphere patients have fewer details, giving them an "empty" or poorly defined appearance. The presence of these lateralizing characteristics will enable the examiner to identify some brain damaged patients on the basis of their free drawings.

Human Figure Drawings

Combining the number of times the test was mentioned for the *Draw-a-Person* test with those for the *House-Tree-Person* test in a recent study of the frequency of test use (Lubin et al., 1971) brings the total mention of tests involving human figure drawing far ahead of the front-runner, the Bender-Gestalt. This is not surprising, since human figure drawing has long been a staple in personality and neuropsychological test batteries as well as a popular technique for the intellectual assessment of children. Among its virtues are its simplicity of administration, for it requires nothing more than pencils, paper, and the instructions to draw a person; its relative speed of administration, for few patients take more than 5 minutes to complete a drawing; and its applicability to all but those patients with such severe handicaps that they cannot draw.

Different kinds of scoring systems have been devised for evaluating human figure drawings. The Goodenough-Harris scoring system (D. B. Harris, 1963) and Rey's system for scoring A *lady walking in the rain (Une dame qui se promène et il pleut)* (E. M. Taylor, 1959) measure intellectual maturation in the child and the level of intellectual organization of the visuographic response when used in the neuropsychological assessment of adults (see pp. 309–311). Machover (1948) and J. N. Buck (1948) developed the best-known systems for appraising personality on the basis of human figure drawings. Both of these systems attend to dimensions and characteristics of the drawings that are, for the most part, irrelevant to neuropsychological questions. Reznikoff and Tomblen (1956) proposed a simple plus and minus scoring system they hoped would provide an indication of brain damage. Although their system did differentiate between brain damaged and other patient groups, the large overlaps preclude its use as a single screening technique for individual cases. Nevertheless, this study does identify six characteristics of human figure drawings that are strongly associated with organicity: (1) lack of details, (2) parts loosely joined, (3) parts noticeably shifted, (4) shortened and thin arms and legs, (5) inappropriate size and shape of other body parts (except the head), and (6) petal-like or scribbled fingers.

Descriptions of human figure drawings by brain damaged patients with either specific visuographic disturbances or conditions of more generalized intellectual debilitation usually include such words as childlike, simplistic, not closed, incomplete, crude, unintegrated (e.g., Hécaen et al., 1951). Asymmetry may appear either as a difference in the size of limbs and features of one side of the body relative to those on the other side, or in a tendency of the figure to lean to one side or the other. The absence of a portion of the figure is also more common in the drawings of brain damaged patients than in those of any other group but it does not necessarily imply visual inattention, for patients with somatosensory defects of a limb or side of the body may "forget" to draw the affected part although they perform well on visual field and visual attention tests (Cohn, 1953; Schulman et al., 1965). Riklan and his colleagues (1962) observed a tendency for parkinsonism patients to make their drawings abnormally small, the size of the drawings decreasing as severity of rigidity increased. This tendency is exhibited by other brain damaged patients as well (e.g., see drawings by a traumatically injured patient, p. 452). Perseverative loops also characterize the drawings of severely impaired patients (M. Williams, 1965). Patients with severe drawing disability may display acute emotional distress that subsides soon after the task is removed *(catastrophic reaction)*. In evaluating human figures drawn by brain damaged patients, the impact of their emotional status should not be overlooked. This is particularly true for mildly impaired patients whose sensitivity to their loss has occasioned a highly anxious or depressed mental state that may lower the quality of their drawings or exaggerate the extent of their drawing disability.

BICYCLE DRAWING TEST

Most of the noncontent characteristics of the human figure drawings of brain damaged patients apply to other free drawings, too. Bicycle drawings can serve as a test of mechanical reasoning as well as visuographic functioning (E. M. Taylor, 1959). The instructions are simply, "Draw a bicycle." The material consists of typewriter paper and pencils. When the drawing is completed, the examiner who is interested in whether the patient can think through the sequential operation of a bicycle can ask, "How does it work?" Mildly confused, distractible, and structure-dependent patients who consider their drawing complete when it still lacks a necessary element such as pedals or drive chain or a seat will usually note and repair the omission on questioning. Patients with problems of visual neglect, visual scanning, or more than mild confusion may refer to the missing component but remain satisfied with the incomplete drawing, or may overlook the missing part but add an inconsequential detail or superficial embellishments (see Figs. 3-8a,b and 6-1). To maintain the original, incomplete drawing while giving the patient an opportunity to improve his performance, Diane Howieson recommends handing the patient a colored pen or pencil should he attempt to make additions or corrections after first indicating that he had finished.

In order to quantify the bicycle-drawing task, I devised a 20-point scoring system (see Table 13-6). Lebrun and Hoops (1974) report a 29-point scoring system devised by Van Dongen to investigate drawing behavior of aphasic patients. This latter system includes scoring for many details (such as the tires, the taillight, or crossbars on a parcel carrier) that are infrequently drawn by normal subjects and rarely, if ever, drawn by brain damaged patients.

The bicycle-drawing task tends to bring out the drawing distortions characteristic of lateral damage. Right hemisphere patients tend to reproduce many of the component parts of the machine, sometimes with much elaboration and care, but misplace them in relation to one another; left hemisphere patients are more likely to preserve the overall proportions but simplify (Lebrun and Hoops, 1974; McFie and Zangwill, 1960). Severely impaired patients, regardless of the site of the lesion, perform this task with great difficulty, producing incomplete and simplistic drawings.

MISCELLANEOUS DRAWING TASKS

Specific aspects of the visuographic disability may be studied by means of other drawing tasks. *House* may elicit difficulties in handling perspective that are common among intellectually deteriorated patients; the alert, bright patient who struggles with

Table 13-6   Scoring System for Bicycle Drawings

Score one point for each of the following:
1. Two wheels
2. Spokes on wheels
3. Wheels approximately same size (smaller wheel must be at least three-fifths the size of the larger one)
4. Wheel size in proportion to bike
5. Front wheel shaft connected to handle bars
6. Rear wheel shaft connected to seat or seat shaft
7. Handlebars
8. Seat
9. Pedals connected to frame at rear
10. Pedals connected to frame at front
11. Seat in workable relation to pedals (not too far ahead or behind)
12. Two pedals (one-half point for one pedal)
13. Pedals properly placed relative to turning mechanism or gears
14. Gears indicated (i.e., chain wheel and sprocket; one-half point if only one present)
15. Top supporting bar properly placed
16. Drive chain
17. Drive chain properly attached
18. Two fenders (one-half point for one fender; when handlebars point down, always give credit for two fenders)
19. Lines properly connected
20. No transparencies

a roof line or flattens the corner between the front and side of the house is more likely to have right than left hemisphere involvement. Patients who complain of difficulty in finding their way, getting lost even in familiar places, can be asked to reproduce a ground plan of their home or their ward. Drawings of such symmetrical objects as a *clock face* or a *daisy* may expose a unilateral visual inattention problem (Battersby et al., 1956). Even when they include all the numbers or petals in their drawings, right hemisphere patients may have a great deal of difficulty rounding out the left side of the clock, or spacing the numbers or petals properly, particularly on the left side of their drawing. Copying a clock picture and drawing it freehand is part of the Parietal Lobe Battery (Borod et al., 1980; Goodglass and Kaplan, 1972). On the free drawing, the patient is instructed to "set the time for 10 after 11," which gives additional information about the patient's time orientation and capacity to process numbers and number/time relationships.

Building and Assembling

More than any other kind of test, building and assembling tasks involve the spatial component in perception, at the conceptual level, and in motor execution. Inclusion of both construction and drawing tests in the test battery will help the examiner discriminate between the spatial and the visual aspects of a constructional disability and estimate the relative contributions of each.

With Block Design and Object Assembly, the Wechsler tests contribute two of the basic kinds of construction tasks to the neuropsychological examination, both involving two-dimensional space. Three-dimensional construction tasks call upon a somewhat different set of functions, as demonstrated by patients who can put together either the two- or the three-dimensional constructions but not both (Benton and Fogel, 1962). Other construction tasks test the ability to execute reversals in space and to copy and reason about different kinds of visuospatial maneuvers.

Two-Dimensional Construction

KOHS BLOCKS

This is the original block design test, differing from the WAIS Block Design subtest in that each block is four colored—red, white, blue, and yellow (Arthur Point Scale of Performance, Arthur, 1947). The 17 designs are different, too. Many of them are more complex than the Wechsler designs, but the administration and interpretation of the test results are the same. This test has proven unsuccessful as a screening instrument, particularly in attempts to differentiate psychiatric from brain injured patients (Yates, 1954). However, its sensitivity to postcentral lesions (Benton, 1969a; Luria, 1973b) and to degenerative disorders (e.g., Botez and Barbeau, 1975; Botez, Botez, and Lévielle et al., 1979) is well established.

The almost universal use of the Wechsler scales has made the administration of the *Kohs Blocks* redundant in most cases. However, because it has some more difficult designs, this test may be useful in bringing out mild visuoconstructive deficits in very bright patients.

STICK CONSTRUCTION

Stick construction is a two-dimensional task in which the subject puts sticks together in patterns. In its usual format as a copying task, the subject is required to reproduce stick patterns arranged by the examiner (Fogel, 1962; K. H. Goldstein and Scheerer, 1953a,b). The subject can also be asked to construct his own designs with them, to copy a drawing, or to compose simple geometric figures or letters (Hécaen et al., 1951; Hécaen and Assal, 1970). Twice as many right as left hemisphere patients show a severe deficit on stick construction tasks (14% to 7%). Approximately 20% of patients with lateralized lesions have some difficulty on this task regardless of the side of lesion (Benton, 1967). The six patients with severe visuoconstructive difficulties studied by Hécaen and his co-workers (1951) made both copy and spontaneous stick arrangements that were close to being correct, but they tended to take a long time. A later study brought out a difference between right and left hemisphere patients attempting to construct a cube pattern with the sticks: patients with left hemisphere lesions copied stick models best, whereas right hemisphere patients copied drawings best (Hécaen and Assal, 1970).

407

Stick test (Benson and Barton, 1970; Butters and Barton, 1970). One version of the stick construction task includes a rotation condition as well as a standard copy condition. This ten-item test is first administered as a copying task. The examiner remains seated *beside* the patient throughout the first "match condition" part of the test. He gives the patient four wooden sticks (approximately 5 inches long and ¼ inch wide with a ½-inch blackened tip) and then makes a practice pattern with two other sticks, instructing the patient to copy his pattern exactly. The examiner does not proceed until he is satisfied that the patient understands and can perform this two-stick problem. The examiner then gives the test by constructing each design in numbered order (see Fig. 13-6) and requesting that the patient make his copy directly under that of the examiner. On completing the ten copy items, the examiner moves to the other side of the examining table so that he is seated opposite the patient. He constructs the same two-stick practice pattern he made originally, but this time asks the patient to "make your pattern look to you like mine looks to me." If the patient does not understand, the examiner demonstrates the right-left and up-down reversals with the practice pattern. Once again, when the examiner is confident that the patient knows what is expected of him, he gives the items of the test again in the same order as the first time. There is no time limit, but rather patients are encouraged to take as much time as they feel they need to be accurate. Each condition is scored for the number of failed items. On the reversal condition, the test is discontinued after five consecutive failures.

Again, the findings on the copy task implicate postcentral lesions, particularly those localized in the right hemisphere. However, on the rotation condition, there was a significant ($p < .05$) tendency for patients with left postcentral lesions to make more

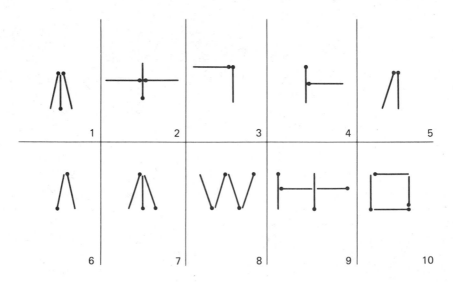

Fig. 13-6. The ten stick designs employed in the match and rotation conditions (Butters and Barton, 1970). (©, Pergamon Press. Reprinted with permission.)

errors (mean = 2.74) than any other group. Those with right anterior lesions made the second greatest number of errors (mean = 2.13), and the left anterior group made almost as few (mean = 1.69) as did the 16 control subjects (mean = 1.59) (Benson and Barton, 1970). The need for verbal mediation to handle the rotation task successfully was suggested as one possible reason for the relatively poor performance of the left posterior patients. Regardless of hemispheric localization, when the constructional disability is pronounced on other constructional tasks, it is likely to be present on the match condition and to be very pronounced on the rotation condition of this test (Butters et al., 1970).

Three-Dimensional Construction

CUBE CONSTRUCTION

The simple block construction tasks described here will elicit three-dimensional visuoconstructive defects. The level at which age-graded tasks are failed provides a useful indicator of the severity of the disability.

The 1960 revision of the Stanford-Binet battery contains two simple block construc-

Fig. 13-7. Block model used by Hécaen et al. (1951) to examine three-dimensional constructional ability.

Fig. 13-8. Test of Three-Dimensional Constructional Praxis, Form A (A. L. Benton). The three block models successively presented to the subject.

tion tasks: *Tower* at age level II is simply a four-block-high structure; *Bridge* at age level III consists of three blocks, two forming a base with the third straddling them. At age 3, most children can copy a four-block train (three blocks in a row with the fourth placed on one of the end blocks); most four-year-olds can build a six-block pyramid and a five-block gate composed of two two-block "towers", less than one inch apart, with each top block set a little back from the bottom block's edge, making

410

room for a middle block to rest at a 45° angle. Most five-year-old children can copy six-block steps but ten-block steps are too difficult for most six-year-olds (E. M. Taylor, 1959). Hécaen and his colleagues (1951) used seven blocks in their cube construction task (four blocks, not touching, form the corners of a square; two blocks bridge a parallel pair of the bottom blocks, and the seventh block tops the middle two), which none of their six patients with severe visuoconstructive disabilities associated with right parietal lesions was able to perform correctly (see Fig. 13-7).

TEST OF THREE-DIMENSIONAL BLOCK CONSTRUCTION (Benton, 1967, 1968b, 1973;
Benton et al., 1983)

Six block constructions are included in this test (originally called the *Test of Three-Dimensional Constructional Praxis*), three on each of two equivalent forms (see Fig. 13-8). The number of (1) omissions, (2) additions, (3) substitutions, and (4) displacements (angular deviations greater than 45°, separations, misplacements) in the test constructions is subtracted from the total of 29 possible correct placements. There is no score for rotation of the entire model although Benton notes when this occurs. The scoring standard requires that the score represent the fewest corrections needed to reproduce an accurate copy of the original construction. When the construction is so defective that it is impossible to count errors, then the score is the number of correctly placed blocks. When the total time taken to complete all three constructions is greater than 380 seconds, two time-correction points are subtracted from the total score. Both control and brain damaged groups performed better with a block model presentation of the constructions than with photographic presentation (see Table 13-7).

Some of the construction problems exhibited by patients with impaired ability to build structures in three-dimensions parallel those made on two-dimensional construction and drawing tasks. Thus, simplification (see Fig. 13-9) and neglect of half the model are not uncommon. Failure on this task, defined as a performance level exceeded by 95% of the control group, occurs twice as frequently among patients with right hemisphere lesions (54%) than among those whose lesions are on the left (23%) (Benton, 1967a). A higher rate of defective performance on this task also distinguished right from left frontal lobe patients (Benton, 1968a). An interesting finding was that, unlike other visuoconstructive tasks (e.g., block designs and stick construction), this

Table 13-7 Scores on Block Model and Photographic Presentations of the Three-Dimensional Construction Tasks

| Score | Block Model | | Photographic Presentation | |
	Control Group ($n = 120$)	Organic Group ($n = 40$)	Control Group ($n = 100$)	Organic Group ($n = 40$)
25 & above	120	30	92	10
17 to 24	0	3	8	17
16 & below	0	7	0	13

(Adapted from Benton, 1973a)

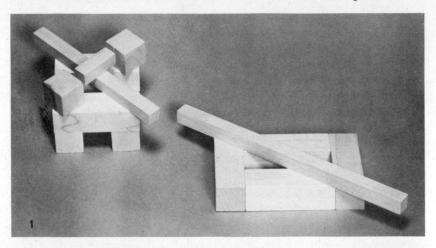

Fig. 13-9. Illustrations of defective performances: (1) Simplified construction with inaccurate choice of blocks. (2) "Closing-in phenomenon" in which the patient utilizes part of the model in his own construction.

test discriminates between groups of right and left hemisphere patients who are moderately impaired as well as between those who are severely impaired (Benton, 1967a). One plausible interpretation of this finding is that visuoconstructive deficits may show up on this complex task when they are too mild to interfere with performance on a less challenging one.

412

Miscellaneous Construction Tasks

In *Paper Folding: Triangle* at age level V of the 1960 revision of the Stanford-Binet, the subject is requested to copy a three-dimensional maneuver in which the examiner folds a square of paper along the diagonal into a triangle and folds that triangle in half. In Beard's factorial analysis of test performances of high school age children (1965), a set of three more complex paper folding tasks involved a number of different factors including a high weighting (.592) of a spatial factor involving "imagination of movement in space and awareness of orientation," and low weightings of a "speed of closure" factor (.290) and a verbal reasoning factor (.263).

A different kind of spatial maneuver is required by Poppelreuter's test, in which the subject must cut out a four-pointed star following a demonstration by the examiner (Paterson and Zangwill, 1944). Patients with right parieto-occipital lesions were unable to perform this task. Paterson and Zangwill also used simple Meccano models to test visual space perception. The possibility of using erector sets or Lego type plastic blocks, which fit together, for testing visuospatial functions should not be overlooked even though they have not been reported as standard assessment procedures.

14

Memory Functions

Memory is the means by which an organism registers some previous exposure to an event or experience. However, the mental activities that people generally call "memory" include a variety of functions (see pp. 25–30) that, in organically intact people, operate at less than perfectly correlated levels of efficiency. Certain emotional disturbances, pathological brain impairment, and the normal pattern of loss of mental efficiency that accompanies the aging process tend to magnify the ordinary disparities in performance levels between these various functions. The differences in the degrees to which "memory functions" become impaired and the differences in their patterns of impairment attest to their anatomical and functional distinctions.

The use of the same word to identify some very different mental activities can create confusion. Many patients whose learning ability is impaired claim a good "memory" because early recollections seem so vivid and easy to retrieve. Other patients who complain of memory problems actually have disorders of attention or mental tracking that interfere with learning and recall but are distinguishable from these memory functions. Thus questions concerning memory disorders have to be put in terms of the specific functions under study. Maintaining terminological distinctions between these functions will help the clinician to keep their differences in mind when evaluating patients and conceptualizing findings and theory.

A General Review of Memory Functions

At a minimum, the memory examination should cover *span of immediate retention; learning* in terms of extent of recent memory, learning capacity, and how well newly learned material is retained; and efficiency of *retrieval* of both recently learned and long-stored information (i.e., remote memory). Ideally, these different memory functions would be systematically reviewed through the major receptive and expressive modalities using both recall and recognition techniques. When memory problems do not appear to be central or unusual, thoroughness can be sacrificed for practical considerations of time, patient cooperation, and fatigue.

414

For most adults, a WAIS battery is a good starting place for testing memory functions. It directly tests (1) *span* of immediate verbal retention and (2) *extent* of remote memory (Information) stored in verbal form. The longer Arithmetic and Comprehension questions also offer the observant examiner incidental information on (3) the duration and stability of the immediate verbal span for meaningful material. This aspect of the examination can also be conducted with a sentence recall task (see pp. 433–434). The mental status examination (see pp. 576–578) augments the WAIS data with (4) items involving remote personal (i.e., episodic) memory; (5) a verbal retention task requiring the subject to recall three or four spoken items, such as battleship, sidewalk, and tangerine or New York, Denver, Boston, and Miami, after five minutes of interpolated interview, and with (6) personal orientation questions to assess the retention of ongoing experience at the minimal level necessary for independent living. The addition of (7) a test of configural recall and retention such as the Complex Figure Test (see pp. 444–447) or Wepman's administration of the Bender-Gestalt test (see p. 388), (8) a paragraph for recall to examine learning and retention of meaningful verbal material (see pp. 434–439), and (9) a test of learning ability that gives a learning curve, such as Rey's Auditory-Verbal Learning Test (see pp. 422–429), completes a review of the major dimensions and modalities of memory.

The examiner can usually integrate the memory tests into the rest of the examination so as to create a varied testing format, to avoid stressing those memory-impaired patients who may be concerned about their deficits, and to use nonmemory tests as interference activities when testing delayed recall. Thus, much mental status information can be obtained quite naturalistically during the introductory interview and in the course of filling out the patient information section at the top of the WAIS answer sheet. For example, rather than simply noting the patient's report of his years of schooling and letting it go at that, the examiner can ask for dates of school attendance and associated information such as dates of first employment or entry into service and how long after finishing school these events took place, and then inquire into the patient's living situation while attending school, including where, with whom, and when. Although the examiner will frequently be unable to verify this information, internal inconsistencies or vagueness are usually evidence of confusion about remote personal memory or difficulty retrieving it. When using a single paragraph for both immediate and delayed recall (see pp. 437, 466), the examiner may give it initially just before the WAIS Comprehension subtest and ask for recall on completion of Comprehension, which provides five to ten minutes of verbal interference. Other tests with delayed recall trials, such as the Complex Figure Test, can also be first given in the course of the WAIS administration for recall later in the session.

When the patient's performance on these tasks is not significantly depressed relative to his best performance on other kinds of tests, and particularly when his performance on tests of remote memory is not significantly better than his handling of the learning tasks, the examiner can assume that memory and learning functions are fairly intact. Pronounced deficits on the general review of memory call for a detailed study involving systematic comparisons between functions, modalities, and the length, type, and complexity of the content.

A relatively poor performance only on tests of immediate memory and retention should alert the examiner to the possibility that the patient may be severely depressed (G. M. Henry et al., 1973; M. Williams, 1978; D. E. Sternberg and Jarvik, 1976). In depression, however, complaints and concerns about failing memory may exceed performance deficits. Furthermore, the preoccupying worries or obsessional thinking often associated with depression tend to disrupt performance on any tasks calling for attention and concentration. Therefore, when I suspect that depression may account for much of a patient's memory dysfunction, I inquire into his preoccupations and, following each demonstrated lapse in attention or memory, I ask him what he had been thinking just then, where his mind had wandered. Impaired immediate memory and retention are also common early symptoms of many neurological conditions that ultimately result in general intellectual deterioration. As the still-alert neurological patient experiences his failing competence, he may also be quite appropriately depressed, thus compounding the problem of differential diagnosis (see pp. 234–236).

Verbal Memory Functions

The almost unlimited possibilities for combining different kinds of verbal stimuli with input and output modalities and presentation formats have resulted in a proliferation of verbal memory tests. Many of them were developed in response to specific clinical problems or research questions. Only a few have received enough use or careful standardization to have reliable norms. Because of the lack of systematic comparisons between the different verbal memory tests, their relative usefulness and potential interchangeability remain unknown.

Therefore, the examiner's choice of memory tests must depend more on clinical judgment than on scientific demonstration that this or that test is most suitable for answering the question under study. Even with many tests available, the examiner may occasionally find that none quite suits the needs of a particular patient or research question, and will devise a new one.

Verbal memory tests are presented here by content. Under each content heading the reader will find a number of tests that differ in format, in emphasis on immediate span, retention, or the learning process, and in the nature of the response. Not every kind of test is represented under every content heading, but taken altogether, the major techniques for examining verbal memory functions are reviewed.

Immediate recall involving the amount or *span* of material that can be grasped for entry into short-term storage or encoded for learning has most often been examined by means of unrelated data bits such as numbers, nonsense syllables, or words. These or any other immediate memory tasks can be converted into a test of retention by providing an interference task or trial. For studying short-term retention, the most popular method has been to use the distractor technique developed by L. R. Peterson and Peterson (1959; L. R. Peterson, 1966) in the United States and J. Brown in England (see Baddeley, 1976) that has come to be called the "Brown-Peterson technique." The purpose of the distractor task is to prevent rehearsal of material being held for short-term retention testing. The Petersons' technique requires the subject, upon hearing (or seeing) the stimulus material, to count backward from a given number until signaled to stop counting, and then to report or identify the stimulus item. The examiner tells the subject the number from which he is to begin counting—typically a three-digit number—immediately after giving the test item. For example, if the test item is the three letters of a nonsense syllable, the examiner says, "V O R 386" and the subject begins counting—"385, 384," etc.—until stopped at the end of the predesignated time interval to recall the item. One version of the Brown-Peterson technique, used by Butters and his co-workers (1973), requires the subject to count backward from 100 by twos. This group has also used word naming (e.g., colors) as a distractor. However, the Brown-Peterson distractor technique is not appropriate for testing retention over long periods of time. Thus, retention may also be tested after an interference trial or the interposition of one or more other, different, tasks.

Almost any verbal stimulus can be used to measure the variety of memory functions. Variations in the length of the stimulus, stimulus repetition, timing, and use of interference techniques will determine which functions come under scrutiny.

Verbal Automatisms

Patterned material learned by rote in early childhood and frequently used throughout life is normally recalled so unthinkingly, effortlessly, and accurately that the response is known as an *automatism*. Examples of automatisms are the alphabet, number series from 1 to 20 or 100 by 10s, days of the week and months of the year, and the Pledge of Allegience or a long-practiced prayer. Automatisms are among the least perishable of the learned verbal habits. Loss or deterioration of these well-ingrained responses in nonasphasic patients may reflect the attentional disturbances or fluctuations of consciousness in acute conditions. It occurs in nonacute conditions only when there is severe, usually diffuse, cerebral damage. To test for automatisms, the examiner simply asks the subject to repeat the alphabet, the days of the week, etc. More than one error usually indicates brain dysfunction. Inability to begin, or if the subject does recall the first few items, inability to complete the response sequence, signifies that the dysfunction is severe.

Digits

Digit Span

The WAIS (or Wechsler Memory Scale) Digit Span subtest is the test format in most common use for measuring span of immediate verbal recall (see pp. 266–270). On the Binet, *Repeating of Digits* and *Repeating of Digits Reversed* appear at a number of difficulty levels from II-6 (two digits forward) to SA I (six digits reversed). The Binet format differs from The WAIS and Wechsler Memory Scale Digit Span items only in allowing three rather than two trials for each span length (Terman and Merrill, 1973). The rate of presentation for all digit span tests is one per second unless otherwise stated.

417

POINT DIGIT SPAN (A. Smith, 1975)

Along with the standard administration of Digit Span, Aaron Smith (1975) also has his subjects point out the digit series on a numbered card. The "point" administration parallels Digit Span in all respects except that the response modality does not require speech, so that the verbal span of patients who cannot speak can be tested. When given with Digit Span to the speaking patient, marked performance differences favoring the "point" administration suggest a problem in speech production. A "point" performance much below the performance on the standard presentation suggests problems in integrating visual and verbal processes (A. Smith, personal communication, 1975).

Point Digit Span requires a large (approximately 30 cm × 30 cm) white cardboard card on which the numbers 1 through 9 appear sequentially in a 3 × 3 arrangement in big (approximately 6 cm high) black print. The subject is instructed to *point out* the number sequence read by the examiner or the reverse sequence for Digits Backward. The procedure is identical with that of Digit Span; i.e., presentation begins with three digits (two for Digits Backward), and increases one digit following each success. The test is usually discontinued after two failures at the same level.

INCREASING THE TESTED SPAN

Many elderly subjects and patients with brain damage have an immediate memory span as long as that of younger, intact adults. Thus, digit span, as traditionally administered, frequently does not distinguish brain damaged or aged persons from normal subjects (Botwinick and Storandt, 1974; Hamsher et al., 1980; Lezak, 1979b), nor does it elicit the immediate recall problems characteristic of many persons in these clinical groups. Because of these limitations, longer and more complex testing formats have been devised for measuring digit span that have greater sensitivity to memory deficits.

Number Span (Barbizet and Cany, 1968).   This technique tests the span of new verbal learning. The patient is given increasingly longer number sequences, each succeeding sequence differing from the one before it in its last number only, e.g., 8-3, 8-3-6, 8-3-6-1, 8-3-6-1-4, etc. Barbizet and Cany reported that 88 medical students retained an average of 9.06 numbers whereas the average retention of 51 persons over the age of 65 was 5.87.

Hebb's Recurring Digits (Milner, 1970, 1971).   This is a disguised learning test. The subject is asked to recall orally presented digit lists, each of them one digit longer than his immediate memory span. He is not informed that every third list is identical whereas none of the intervening lists are alike. Normal subjects tend to learn the repeated lists but patients with verbal learning disabilities do not. This test was failed by patients who had had left temporal lobectomies but not by those with right temporal lobectomies, the extent of the defect varying with the amount of hippocampal

418

involvement. The technique has also been used to test learning in older, intact subjects (Talland, 1968).

Supraspan. A variety of techniques for examining recall of strings of eight or more random numbers have demonstrated the sensitivity of the supraspan task to age, educational level, brain impairment, and anticholinergic medication (e.g., Crook et al., 1980; Drachman and Leavitt, 1974). Problems in identifying and scoring the supraspan (e.g., it may begin at 7, 8, 9, or 10 in the normal population; should partial spans be counted?) resulted in some complex scoring systems that are unsuited to clinical use. Drachman and Arbit (1966) gradually increased the length of digit strings by one each time the subject learned a list correctly in 25 or fewer repetition trials. By means of this technique for extending the digit span, a small group of patients with profound learning defects (i.e., "amnesics;" the famous patient, H. M., who was extensively studied by Brenda Milner and her co-workers, was in this group) could store as many as 12 digits, although normal control subjects stored a minimum of 20.

In the *Digit Sequence Learning* (or *Serial Digit Learning*) test (Benton et al., 1983; Hamsher et al., 1980), subjects with less than a twelfth grade education are given eight digits to learn (form D8), subjects with 12 or more years of schooling learn a nine digit span (form K9). The task continues until the subject has repeated the digit string correctly for two consecutive trials or after the twelfth trial. Based on a scoring system in which each correct trial earns two points and two points are added for each trial to 12 that did not have to be given, the maximum score is 24. For form K9, defective performance is defined by a score of 7 or less; failure on form D8 is defined by 6 points or less. This technique proved to be more sensitive to the mental changes that accompany the normal aging of persons aged 65 years and older (Benton et al., 1981) and to the presence of brain damage than a digit span score based on the longest span correctly recalled. It also identified a higher proportion of patients with bilateral than unilateral damage.

Letters

LETTER SPAN

Normal letter span (6.7 in the 20s, 6.5 in the 50s) is virtually identical with digit span except beyond age 60 when some relative loss has been documented (5.5 in the 60s, 5.4 in the 70s) (Botwinick and Storandt, 1974). Every brain injured patient group in Newcombe's study (1969) had lower average scores on a simple letter span task, analogous to Digits Forward, than on the digit version of the task. On *Letter Span*, with the single exception of the left frontal group, the left hemisphere damaged groups also obtained lower average scores than the right hemisphere groups. The mean score range for the left hemisphere groups was from 5.00 (temporal or temporoparietal, and mixed) to 5.75 (frontal); for the right hemisphere patients, group mean scores ranged from 5.50 (frontal and mixed) to 6.00 (temporal or temporoparietal). The

419

overlap of scores of the different patient groups was too great to permit inferences about localization of the lesion in any individual case.

Consonant Trigrams

The verbal learning defect associated with left temporal lobectomy shows up on this learning task which requires recall of a spoken set of three consonants following the interpolated task of counting backward from a given three-digit number by threes or fours (Milner, 1970, 1972). As in Hebb's Recurring Digits, the degree of the learning defect was related to the extent of removal of the left hippocampus. Patients with right temporal lobectomies suffered no pre- to postoperative loss on this test. The average recall accuracy of college students was 72% of 48 consonant sets when recall came 3 seconds after the subject began counting backward, and 38% when counting backward continued for nine seconds (Peterson and Peterson, 1959).

Syllables

Nonsense syllables have been a popular medium for studying memory since Ebbinghaus first reported in 1885 on their use to explore retention and forgetting. They may be the stimulus of choice when the examiner wants to study verbal functions while minimizing or controlling the confounding effects of meaning. Noble's tables (1961) contain 2100 nonsense syllables of the consonant-vowel-consonant (CVC) type along with their measured association and meaningfulness values for use in test syllable sets.

Memory for nonsense syllables has been studied in some neuropsychological research projects but typically has not been included in batteries devised for clinical use. Newcombe (1969) demonstrated that patients with left hemisphere damage did less well than those with lesions in the right hemisphere on both immediate and delayed recall trials using nonsense syllables. Normal control subjects examined by Talland (1965a) recited as many CVC nonsense syllables as three-letter words on immediate recall. On succeeding repetitions minutes apart, they recalled fewer words although their recall of nonsense syllables remained the same. Memory-impaired (due to Korsakoff's psychosis) patients retained words better than syllables although their scores for both were much lower than the control subjects' scores on all trials.

Words

The use of words, whether singly in word lists or combined into phrases, sentences, or lengthier passages, introduces a number of dimensions into the memory task that can affect test performances differentially, depending upon the patient's age, nature of impairment, intellectual capacity, etc. These dimensions include familiar-unfamiliar, concrete-abstract, low-high imagery, low-high association level, ease of categorization, low-high emotional charge, and structural dimensions such as rhyming or other phonetically similar qualities (e.g., see Baddeley, 1976; Mandler, 1967; Poon et al., 1980, *passim*). The amount of organization inherent in the material also affects ease of retention (Schonen, 1968). This is obvious to anyone who has found it easier to learn words than nonsense syllables, sentences than word strings. When using words for testing memory—and particularly when making up alternate word lists, sentences, etc.—the examiner must be alert to the potential effects that these dimensions have on the comparability of items, for instance, or when interpreting differences between groups on the same task. (For example, see Butters and Cermak, 1975; Butters et al., 1977, for differences in performances on the same verbal tasks by control subjects, chronic alcoholics, and patients with diseases involving different memory subsystems.) When developing one's own material for testing memory and learning functions, the examiner may find Toglia and Battig's *Handbook of semantic word norms* (1978) a useful reference. These authors give ratings for 2854 English words (and some "non-words") along the seven dimensions of *concreteness, imagery, categorizability, meaningfulness, familiarity, number of attributes or features,* and *pleasantness,* thus enabling the examiner to develop equatable or deliberately biased word lists on a rational, tested basis. A "meaningfulness" list of 319 five-letter (alternating consonant with vowel, e.g., "vapor," "money," "sinew") words and wordlike constructs (i.e., paralogs) was developed by Locascio and Ley (1972). Palermo and Jenkins's *Word association norms* (1964) provides a great deal of data on word frequencies and their relatedness. Paivio and his colleagues (1968) graded 925 nouns for concreteness, imagery, and meaningfulness.

Brief Word Learning Tests

Probably the most widely familiar word learning test comes from the mental status examination used by medical practitioners, particularly psychiatrists and neurologists, to evaluate their patients' mental conditions (see pp. 576–577). In the course of the evaluation interview, the patient is given three or four unrelated, familiar words (e.g., p. 582) (some examiners use a name or date, an address, and a flower name or florist's order, such as "one dozen red roses") to repeat with instructions to remember these items for recall later. The patient must demonstrate accurate immediate repetition of all the words or phrases so that there is no question about their having been registered in the first place. For some patients, this may require several repetitions. Once assured that the patient has registered the words, the examiner continues to question the patient about other issues—work history, family background—or may give brief items of the examination for 5 minutes. The patient is then asked to recall the words. Most persons have no difficulty recalling all three or four words or phrases after five minutes. Thus, correct recall of two out of three or three out of four raises the question of a retention deficit. Recall of only one of three or two of four words usually indicates that verbal learning is impaired.

There are a number of variants to the basic three- or four-word learning test. In one of these the examiner identifies their categories when naming the words (e.g., "Detroit, a city; yellow, a color; petunia, a flower; apple, a fruit."). On the first recall trial, the examiner asks for the words. If the patient omits any, the examiner can then see whether cuing by category will help the patient recall the word. When cuing improves recall, then a retrieval rather than a storage problem is implicated. Strub and Black (1977) recommend both a ten-minute and a 30-minute delay, using four words that can be cued in different ways. Should any be missed on spontaneous recall, the examiner then provides different cues, such as the initial phoneme of the abstract word, the category of the color, a familiar characteristic of the flower, etc. Should cuing fail, they recommend using a recognition technique (e.g., "Was the flower a rose, tulip, daisy, or petunia?") to help determine whether the patient has a storage or a retrieval problem. Upon satisfying himself that the patient could recall several words after a short time span, Luria (1973) used two three-word lists, giving the patient "Series 2" after the patient had learned the three common words in "Series 1." When the second series had been learned, Luria then asked for recall of series 1 as a test of the patient's capacity to maintain the organization and time relationships of subsets of learned material. Ryan and Butters (1980a, b) used four words in a short-term retention test design. Following the one-per-second reading of four unrelated words (e.g., anchor, cherry, jacket, and pond), patients were given a three-digit number with instructions to count backward from that number by threes for 15 or 30 seconds, at which time they were instructed to recall the words. This technique was quite sensitive in eliciting an age gradient for normal subjects that was paralleled, at significantly lower levels, for alcoholics at the three tested age levels.

Word Span

The number of words normal subjects recall remains relatively stable through the early and middle adult years. Five age groups (20s, 30s, 40s, 50s, and 60s) comprising a total of 200 men, were tested with familiar one-syllable words in lists ranging in length from four to 13 words (Talland, 1965b, 1968). Beyond five-word lists, average recall scores hovered around 5.0. The five age groups did not differ on recall of lists of four to seven words. There was a very slight but statistically significant tendency for the two oldest groups to do a little less well than the youngest groups on the nine- and 11-word lists, and the three-oldest groups did less well on the 13-word list. The greatest difference between the oldest and youngest groups was on the nine-word list on which the 20–29 age group averaged 5.6 words and the 60–69 age group averaged 5.0 words. When tested in the same manner as Digit Span—i.e., beginning with a two-word list and adding a word with each successful repetition maintaining the original word order—the word span of a group of control subjects again averaged 5.0 (E. Miller, 1973). Control subjects learned word lists of one, two, and three words longer than their word span in two, four, and more than ten trials, respectively.

Auditory-Verbal Learning Test (AVLT) (Rey, 1964; E. M. Taylor, 1959)

This easily administered test measures immediate memory span, provides a learning curve, reveals learning strategies—or their absence, elicits retroactive and proactive interference tendencies and tendencies to confusion or confabulation on memory tasks, and also measures retention following an interpolated activity. It consists of five presentations with recall of a 15-word list, one presentation of a second 15-word list, and a sixth recall trial, which altogether take ten to 15 minutes. Retention may be examined after 30 minutes or hours or days later.

It begins as a test of immediate word span. For trial I, the examiner reads a list (A) of 15 words (see Table 14-1) at the rate of one per second after giving the following instructions:

> I am going to read a list of words. Listen carefully, for when I stop you are to say back as many words as you can remember. It doesn't matter in what order you repeat them. Just try to remember as many as you can.

The examiner writes down the words the patient recalls *in the order recalled.* In this way, he can keep track of the patient's pattern of recall, noting whether the patient has associated two or three words, whether he proceeds in an orderly manner, or whether recall is hit or miss. If the patient asks whether he has already said a word, the examiner should tell him, but the examiner should not volunteer that a word has been repeated because this tends to distract some patients and interfere with their performance.

When the patient indicates he can recall no more words, the examiner rereads the list following a second set of instructions:

> Now I'm going to read the same list again, and once again when I stop I want you to tell me as many words as you can remember, *including words you said the first time.* It doesn't matter in what order you say them. Just say as many words as you can remember whether or not you said them before.

Table 14-1 Rey Auditory-Verbal Learning Test Word Lists

List A	List B	List C
Drum	Desk	Book
Curtain	Ranger	Flower
Bell	Bird	Train
Coffee	Shoe	Rug
School	Stove	Meadow
Parent	Mountain	Harp
Moon	Glasses	Salt
Garden	Towel	Finger
Hat	Cloud	Apple
Farmer	Boat	Chimney
Nose	Lamb	Button
Turkey	Gun	Log
Color	Pencil	Key
House	Church	Rattle
River	Fish	Gold

(Taken in part from E. M. Taylor, *Psychological appraisal of children with cerebral defects.* © 1959 by Harvard University Press)

This set of instructions must emphasize inclusion of previously said words for otherwise some patients will assume it is an elimination test.

The list is reread for trials III, IV, and V using trial II instructions each time. The examiner may praise the patient as he recalls more words. He may tell the patient the number of words he has recalled, particularly if the patient is able to use the information for reassurance or as a challenge. On completion of each ten-word trial of a similar word-learning test, Luria (1966) asked his patients to estimate how many words they would recall on the next trial. In this way, along with measuring verbal learning, one can also obtain information about the accuracy of patients' self-perceptions, appropriateness of their goal setting, and their ability to apply data about themselves. This added procedure requires very little time or effort for the amount of information it can provide, and it does not seem to interfere with the learning or recall process.

On completion of trial V, the examiner tells the patient:

> Now I'm going to read a second list of words. This time, again, you are to say back as many words of this second list as you can remember. Again, the order in which you say the words does not matter. Just try to remember as many as you can.

The examiner then reads the second word list (B), again writing down the words *in the order in which the patient says them.* Following the B-list trial, the examiner asks the patient to recall as many words from the first list as he can (trial VI). The third word list (C) is available should either the A- or B-list presentations be spoiled by interruptions, improper administration, or confusion or premature response on the patient's part. A 30-minute delayed recall trial will give additional information on how well the patient can recall what was once learned. Although there are no norms for recall after such a lengthy delay, clinical experience suggests that few if any words recalled on trial VI are normally lost after half an hour.

The score for each trial is the number of words correctly recalled. A total score, the sum of trials I through V, can also be calculated. Words that are repeated can be marked R; RC if the patient corrects himself; or RQ if the patient questions whether he has repeated the word but remains unsure. Subjects who want to make sure they did not omit saying a word they remembered may repeat a few words after recalling a suitable number for that trial. However, lengthy repetitions, particularly when the subject can recall relatively few words, most likely reflect a problem in self-monitoring and tracking associated with a learning defect.

Words that are not on the list are errors and are marked E. Frequently an error made early in the test will reappear on subsequent trials, often in the same position relative to one or several other words. Diane Howieson (personal communication) recommends distinguishing between frank confabulations and phonemic or semantic associations by marking the former EC and the latter EA. Intrusions from list A into the recall of list B, or from B into recall trial VI are errors that can be marked A or B. (See Table 14-2 for an example of scored errors. The 28-year-old ranch hand and packer who gave this set of responses had sustained a right frontotemporal contusion

424

Table 14-2 Sample AVLT Record Illustrating Error Scoring

I	II	III	Trial IV	V	B	VI
Hat 1	Drum 1	River 1	Drum 1	River 1	Desk 1	Drum 1
Garden 2	Curtain 2	House 2	Curtain 2	House 2	Ranger 2	Curtain 2
Moon 3	Bell 3	Turkey 3	Hat 3	School 3	Glasses 3	Bell 3
Turkey 4	House 4	Farmer 4	School 4	Bell 4	Bell A	Parent 4
Hose EA	River 5	Water EC	Parent 5	Farmer 5	Pet EC	School 5
	Hose EA	Color 5	Farmer 6	Drum 6	Fish 4	Moon 6
	Drum R	Drum 6	Color 7	Curtain 7	Glasses R	Teacher EA
	Bell R	Curtain 7	Nose 8	Bell R	Mountain 5	Turkey 7
	Curtain R	Garden 8	Turkey 9	School R	Cloud 6	Coffee 8
	Drum R	Hat 9	Color R	Parent 8	Bell AR	Color 9
		Hose EA	School R	Coffee 9		
		Garden R	Nose R	School R		
		Turkey R	Drum R	Parent R		
		Farmer R	Turkey R	Color 10		
		School 10	Farmer R	Moon 11		
		Parent 11				

requiring surgical reduction of swelling just two years before the examination. Since the accident he had been unable to work because of poor judgment, disorientation, and personality deterioration.) This method of marking errors enables the examiner to evaluate the quality of the performance at a glance. Patients who make these kinds of errors tend to have difficulty in maintaining the distinction between information coming from the outside and their own associations, or in distinguishing between data obtained at different times. Some, such as the patient whose performance is given in Table 14-2, have difficulty maintaining both kinds of distinctions, which suggests a serious breakdown in self-monitoring functions.

Rey gives norms for trials I through V and includes data on the performance of children and adolescents, ages five to 15 years. His adult norms differ according to social class and age groups (see Table 14-3).

I gathered data on recall following the interpolated word list from 70 mixed brain damaged patients and 21 graduate and postgraduate students. On trial VI the patient group recalled 6.88 words, an average of 1.97 fewer words than on trial V; the average difference between the number of words recalled on trials V and VI for the graduate students was 1.52. The difference between these average differences was not significant ($t = 1.16$). However, for a significantly larger proportion of the patient group

Table 14-3 Average Recall on Each Learning Trial of the Rey Auditory-Verbal Learning Test for Five Groups of Adults

Subject Groups		I	II	Trial III	IV	V
Manual laborers	Mean	7.0	10.5	12.9	13.4	13.9
(n = 25)	SD	2.1	1.9	1.6	2.0	1.2
Professionals	Mean	8.6	11.8	13.4	13.8	14.0
(n = 30)	SD	1.5	2.0	1.4	1.1	1.0
Students	Mean	8.9	12.7	12.8	13.5	14.5
(n = 47)	SD	1.9	1.8	1.5	1.3	0.7
Elderly laborers	Mean	3.7	6.6	8.4	8.7	9.5
(70–90 years)	SD	1.4	1.4	2.4	2.3	2.2
(n = 15)						
Elderly professionals	Mean	4.0	7.2	8.5	10.0	10.9
(70–88 yrs)	SD	2.9	2.9	2.5	3.3	2.9
(n = 15)						

(Adapted from Rey, 1964)

(one-third) than the student group (one-tenth), recall dropped by more than three words from trial V to trial VI (χ^2 = 5.66, $p < .02$). These results suggest that a decrease of more than three words recalled from trials V to VI is an abnormal amount of shrinkage and probably reflects a retention or retrieval problem. They are supported by findings in a more recent study (O'Brien and Lezak, 1981) involving 26 control subjects and 17 recently (within six months of testing) traumatically brain injured patients in the 18–49 age group and of comparable education levels in which auditory and pictorial (see pp. 428–429) presentations of this test were compared (Table 14-4). In this study, the control subjects demonstrated significantly greater retention from trial V to VI than the patients, with an average loss that was virtually identical to that of the graduate students.

Ordinarily, the immediate memory span for digits and the number of words recalled on trial I will be within one or two points of each other, providing supporting

Table 14-4 Average AVLT and PVLT[a] Performances on Trials V and VI

Trials	AVLT V	VI	V–VI	PVLT V	VI	V–VI
Patients	7.12	4.06	3.06	8.88	7.53	1.88
Controls	13.15	11.62	1.53	14.38	14.27	0.11

[a]*Pictorial Verbal Learning Test* (see pp. 428–429).

evidence regarding the length of span. Larger differences usually favor the digit span and seem to occur in patients with intact immediate memory and concentration who become confused by too much stimulation. These patients tend to have difficulty with complex material or situations of any kind, doing better with simplified, highly structured tasks. When the difference favors the more difficult word list retention task, the lower digit span score is usually due to inattention, lack of motivation, or anxiety at the time Digit Span was given.

Slowness in shifting from one response to another can show up in a low score on trial I. When this occurs in a person whose immediate verbal memory span is within normal limits, recall B will be at least two or three words longer than that of trial I, usually within normal limits. Trial II recall, in these cases, will show a much greater rate of acquisition than what ordinarily characterizes the performance of persons whose initial recall is abnormally low; occasionally a large jump in score will not take place until trial III. When this phenomenon is suspected, the examiner should review the pattern of the patient's performance on other tests in which slowness in establishing a response set might show up, such as Block Design (e.g., a patient who gets two points at most on each of the first two designs, and does designs 4, 5, and 6 accurately and, often, faster than the first two; or a verbal fluency performance in which the patient's productivity increases with each trial, even though the difficulty of the naming task may also have increased). In those cases in which recall of list B is much (two or three words) lower than immediate recall on trial I, what was just learned has probably interfered with the acquisition of new material; i.e., there is a *proactive inhibition* effect. When proactive inhibition is very pronounced, intrusion words from list A may show up in the list B recall, too.

Most brain damaged patients show a learning curve over the five trials. The appearance of a curve, even at a low level—i.e., from three or four words on trial I to eight or nine on V—demonstrates some ability to learn if some of the gain is maintained on the delayed recall trial, VI. Such a patient may be capable of benefiting from psychotherapy or personal counseling and may profit from rehabilitation training and even formal schooling since he can learn, although at a slower rate than normal. Occasionally a once-bright but now severely memory impaired patient will have a large immediate memory span, recalling eight or nine words on trial I, but no more than nine or ten on V and very few on VI. Such a performance demonstrates the necessity of evaluating the scores for each trial in the context of the other trials.

Craik (1977a) suggests that on supraspan learning tasks such as this, both short-term retention and learning capacities (i.e., primary and secondary memory in Craik's terminology) of intact subjects are engaged. Thus, many brain damaged patients do as well as normal subjects on the initial trial, but have less learned carry-over on subsequent trials (e.g., Lezak, 1979b). Short-term retention in patients whose learning ability is defective also shows up in a far better recall of the words at the end of the list than of those at the beginning (the *recency effect*), as the presentation of new words in excess of the patient's immediate memory span interferes with retention of the words first heard. Normal subjects, on the other hand, tend to show a *primacy* as well as a recency effect, consistently having better recall for the words at the beginning of the list than most of the other words. Moreover, subjects whose memory system is intact are much more likely to develop an orderly recall pattern that does not vary much from trial to trial except as new words are added. By trial V, many subjects with good memory capacity repeat the list in almost the same order as it is given.

When given three times at six and 12 month intervals to 20 control subjects, practice effects showed up on the second administration of trials V and VI which were maintained on the third administration of trial VI but not trial V (Lezak, 1982d). This finding suggests that alternative word lists should be given on repeated administrations of the AVLT.

A recognition trial can be used when a patient's performance of the recall trial, VI, runs three or more words below the last learning trial, V. The recognition procedure will clarify the nature of the patient's recall problem, for if he has retained the data but cannot retrieve it easily, he will probably perform well on the recognition task. However, if his problem is simply that he has difficulty retaining new information, he will perform as poorly on the recognition task as on trial VI. In testing recognition, the examiner asks the patient to identify as many words as he can from the first list when shown (or read from) a list of 50 words containing all the items from both the A and B lists as well as words that are semantically associated (S) or phonemically similar (P) to words on lists A or B (see Table 14-5). This can show not only how much the patient has stored, but also his capacity to discriminate when or with what other information a datum was learned. This technique can be used to look for evidence of disordered recall like that which troubles patients with impaired frontal lobe functions who can learn readily enough but cannot keep track or make order out of what they have learned.

The five-trial learning format lends itself to use with pictures—the *Pictorial Verbal Learning Test (PVLT)*—or printed words (see also p. 442). I use 15 items of the Binet *Picture Vocabulary*, turning the picture cards at a rate of one per second, thereby exposing each picture for about a half second. The data reported in Table 14-4 were obtained using paragraph recall (the Logical Memory subtest of the Wechsler Memory Scale) as the interference trial. Picture sets can also be made out of the flash card

Table 14-5   Word List for Testing AVLT Recognition

Bell (A)°	Home (SA)	Towel (B)	Boat (B)	Glasses (B)
Window (SA)	Fish (B)	Curtain (A)	Hot (PA)	Stocking (SB)
Hat (A)	Moon (A)	Flower (SA)	Parent (A)	Shoe (B)
Barn (SA)	Tree (PA)	Color (A)	Water (SA)	Teacher (SA)
Ranger (B)	Balloon (PA)	Desk (B)	Farmer (A)	Stove (B)
Nose (A)	Bird (B)	Gun (B)	Rose (SPA)	Nest (SPB)
Weather (SB)	Mountain (B)	Crayon (SA)	Cloud (B)	Children (SA)
School (A)	Coffee (A)	Church (B)	House (A)	Drum (A)
Hand (PA)	Mouse (PA)	Turkey (A)	Stranger (PB)	Toffee (PA)
Pencil (B)	River (A)	Fountain (PB)	Garden (A)	Lamb (B)

°(A) Words from list A; (B) words from list B; (S) word with a semantic association to a word on list A or B as indicated; (P) word phonemically similar to a word on list A or B.

or word-learning material used by speech pathologists and others doing language therapy. Most persons recall two or three more pictures than words on the first trial and reach their ceiling—often 14 or 15—by the fourth trial. As a group, the traumatically brain injured patients whose performance is reported in Table 14-4 both learned more words on the pictorial than the auditory presentation of this task and retained more (O'Brien and Lezak, 1981). When categorized according to predominant side of injury (as determined by the presence of hemiplegia or aphasia, and by neurological and laboratory studies), in the second posttrauma year both predominantly right- and predominantly left-brain damaged patients learned approximately the same number of words on auditory and pictorial presentation (trial V), but differed in retention (trials V–VI). Patients with left-sided damage tended to retain pictorial information better whereas auditory presentation benefited patients with right-sided damage. Older patients with left CVA's but not those with right-sided lesions also benefited from pictorial presentation of this test, as did matched controls (M.E. Davis et al., 1983).

Miceli and his colleagues (1981), using a modification of this test in their Neuropsychological Test Battery (see p. 573), also found that patients with right hemisphere lesions did significantly better than patients with lesions involving the left hemisphere, even though these latter patients were not aphasic. In their presentation, recall takes place after a 15 minute period during which the patient performs visuospatial tasks. They derive two scores: 15W-ST is the sum of all words recalled following each learning trial; 15W-LT is the number of words given on the delayed recall trial.

ASSOCIATE LEARNING SUBTEST OF THE WECHSLER MEMORY SCALE (see pp. 463ff)

This is perhaps the most familiar of the paired word-learning tests. It consists of ten word pairs, six forming "easy" associations (e.g., baby—cries) and the other four "hard" word pairs that are not readily associated (e.g., cabbage—pen) (Wechsler, 1945). The list is read three times, with a memory trial following each reading. Total score is one-half the sum of all correct associations to the easy pairs plus the sum of all correct associations to the hard pairs, made within five seconds after the stimulus word is read. Thus, the highest possible score is 21.

Several standardization efforts together provide a somewhat rough set of norms for this test, with no data for ages 50 to 59 (see Table 14-13). Women tend to average about one point higher than the men at each age level until the 60s when they have an approximately two-point lead (Ivison, 1977; Verhoff et al., 1979). This test is sensitive to learning (i.e., secondary memory) deficits involving complex or novel information (Kaszniak et al., 1979b; Kear-Colwell, 1973; Wilson et al., 1982). However, Verhoff and her colleagues (1979) point out that the score reflects not simply what is learned but errors of commission resulting from pathological response tendencies such as perseveration and confabulation. The juxtaposition of "hard" and "easy" pairs in one test has the practical result of testing two different activities (i.e., recall of well-learned verbal associations and retention of new, unfamiliar verbal material) and obscuring the status of each in the combined score.

A fourth-trial variation on the standard administration of the Associate Learning task has been introduced by Edith Kaplan, who tells the patient, "I'm going to give you the second word and you give me the first." In this way, the examiner can determine whether the associations of the new words were truly learned, or whether the patient's correct responses represent strings of passively learned phonetic associations.

WORD LEARNING TESTS

Two tests require the patient to learn definitions of unfamiliar words, thus sampling a common learning activity. The *New Word Learning and Retention Test (NWLT)* (V. Meyer and Yates, 1955; V. Meyer and Falconer, 1960) and the *Modified Word Learning Test (MWLT)* (Savage, 1970; D. Walton and Black, 1957; D. Walton and Mather, 1961; D. Walton et al., 1959) differ only in the length of the list of words to be learned.

Each of these tests uses a standard word list, either the Binet or Wechsler Vocabulary list (NWLT), or just the Binet Vocabulary (MWLT). Exceptionally bright subjects who have fewer than ten consecutive failures on these standard vocabulary subtests are given the most difficult words from the Mill Hill Vocabulary Scale, Form 1, Senior (Raven, 1958) (though American examiners might have more ready access to Atwell and Wells's Wide Range Vocabulary Test). The material of the NWLT consists of the first five consecutively failed words on the Vocabulary subtest list; the MWLT uses the first ten consecutively failed words. The examiner teaches the meaning of the failed words to the subject and asks him to define the words immediately afterward. The criterion for success on the five-word test is three correct—not necessarily consecutive—definitions; on the ten-word list the criterion is doubled to six. If the subject is unable to meet the criterion, the meanings for all the words are given to him again and the testing repeated until he has given the required three or six definitions.

The MWLT has a scoring system that rewards speed of learning by giving the highest score (10) to subjects who learn six words on the first presentation of the ten-word list. One point is subtracted from the score for each additional presentation of the list until the subject succeeds at the task. Thus, if six words are learned on the second presentation, the subject earns a score of nine; if six words are not learned until the fifth presentation, the subject's score will be six.

Normal individuals generally learn three of the five words of the NWLT after hearing all of them defined just once. Without exception, 57 normal control subjects learned six of the ten-word series within three full repetitions, whereas only one of a 46-member organic group succeeded in fewer than five repetitions of the list (Walton and Black, 1957). A cutting score of five (success on the sixth repetition) identified 93.5% of the organic group and 97% of the normal control subjects and the 155 psychiatric patients with functional disorders (neuroses and psychoses). A cutting score of six (fifth repetition) produced no false positives among the normal control subjects and classified 71% of the organic patients correctly (Bolton et al., 1967). Because performance on this test does correlate significantly with level of intellectual ability, the scores of persons of *low average* or lower ability should be interpreted with caution.

Data concerning use of the MWLT with elderly psychiatric patients are equivocal. Poor performance on the MWLT was strongly predictive of mortality in one group of patients (Sanderson and Inglis, 1961), misclassified schizophrenics in another elderly psychiatric group (Orme et al., 1964), and did not discriminate between patients with and without diagnosed organic disease in a third study (Newcombe and Steinberg, 1964). Newcombe and Steinberg concluded that the MWLT "criterion (six words learned out of 10) was too tiring and difficult for some elderly patients." Riddell (1962b) found that this test discriminated between functional and organic elderly psychiatric patients when given with the Stanford-Binet but not with the WAIS vocabulary list.

One variation of the MWLT uses neologisms to reduce the advantage of educated subjects who are more sophisticated about words and to provide items with concrete definitions that are easier for dull subjects to learn (Hetherington, 1967). This method uses the six out of ten criterion for success, discontinuing after ten repetitions. The use of neologisms produced a very large separation between control and organic group scores.

WICKEN'S RELEASE FROM PI TEST (Craik and Birdwistle, 1971; Wickens, 1970)

This procedure uses the phenomenon of proactive inhibition (PI) to determine the level at which material to be learned is encoded. It is presented as a test of short-term retention. In the basic five-trial format, the stimulus words are different for each trial. However, the words given in the first four trials come from one category, and the words of the fifth trial are from a different category. Thus, Butters and Cermak (1974, 1975) used stimulus material from one category (e.g., animals, consonant trigrams) with a distractor task (e.g., naming colors or counting backward) between presentation and recall for the first four trials. These were followed by a fifth trial in which the stimulus material came from a different category (e.g., vegetables, a three-digit number), also administered with an intervening distractor task. Moscovitch (1976) presented this technique as a word-learning task, using five 12-word lists read at a rate of one word per two seconds. The words on the first four lists came from the world of sports and the fifth list consisted of words relating to professions.

Normal persons who encode in terms of semantic categories show a release from PI in that recall of the new category of material returns to the level of recall on the first list, although level of recall had gradually lowered on the subsequent trials using lists of items in the same category as the first list. No increase in the number of items recalled when the category shifts signifies an abnormal response to this test. Butters and Cermak (1974, 1975) and Cermak (1979, 1982) compared alcoholic patients, who served as control subjects, and showed a normal release from PI, with patients with Korsakoff's psychosis, demonstrating that the latter also showed a normal release from PI when the two kinds of material to be encoded are as different as letters and numbers. However, when the shift was from one semantic category to another, the Korsakoff patients did not experience the release phenomenon, indicating that they were not encoding in semantic categories. Moscovitch (1976) demonstrated a dissociation between level of short-term retention and the presence or absence of the release phenomenon. His study showed that patients with anterior left hemisphere damage had normal recall with no release from PI, and those with left temporal lobe lesions did poorly on the recall task but showed release from PI. Patients with right hemisphere damage also showed release from PI regardless of the site of lesion along the longitudinal axis.

SERIAL WORD LEARNING

The ability to maintain the order of learned material has been studied by a variety of techniques. Luria's (1966) interest in the order in which patients reproduced a ten-word list was formalized in a *Serial Word-Learning Test* (Vowels, 1979). The subject is instructed to recall ten relatively high frequency, unrelated words in the order in which they were read. Middle-aged normal control subjects learned the list in three to four trials.

Serial word learning has been used to study whether the relationships (imagery or associative) of stimulus words affect the learning of patients with Huntington's disease (Caine et al., 1977) or alcoholics (Weingartner et al., 1971). The paradigm for these studies is the use of pairs of word lists eight to ten words long, each constructed according to a different principle (e.g., high and low imagery, associatively related, random). Each list is presented until it is learned or a given number of trials (e.g., 6 or 10) is reached. Scoring may be on the basis of trials to learning or number of words repeated in serial order on each trial or on a given trial.

Serial word learning is also well suited for studying the ability to use sequential organization as an aid to learning (Weingartner 1968). In contrast to normal control subjects whose ability to learn benefits from sequentially organized word lists, patients who had undergone unilateral temporal lobectomies (right or left) for control of seizures did no better on highly organized word lists than on unorganized lists or lists of random words. The highly organized lists were those in which adjacent words had strong associational links, e.g., *moth, butterfly, insect, bug, bird, wing, bees, fly, sunshine, summer, garden, spring*. In an alternate, less highly organized list, the words with the strongest associations were separated, e.g., *bird, moth, summer, fly, garden, insect, wing, sunshine, butterfly, bees, spring, bug*. Learning was measured in terms of accuracy of anticipation of the next word on the list.

Sentences

The technique of evaluating memory by means of tests of sentence recall merits more attention than it has received. Unlike many memory tests, memory for sentences has a naturalistic quality that can be directly related to the patient's everyday functioning. Further, developmental norms provide ready-made criteria for evaluating a patient's performance when it is impaired. The average adult can correctly recall sentences of 24 or 25 syllables in length (M. Williams, 1965).

Comparing sentence span with word or digit span, the examiner can determine the extent to which meaning contributes to the patient's span of immediate memory. As on other verbal memory tasks, failure on memory for sentences is associated with lesions of the left hemisphere. McFie (1960) reported that left frontal, temporal, and parietal lobe lesions tend to result in impaired performance on this task with no similar deficits noted for patients with right hemisphere lesions. Moreover, since sentences are composed of both function and content words, sentence recall may be used to examine aphasic disorders in which function words are more apt to be misused or omitted than content words (Caramazza et al., 1978).

Memory for Sentences

The Stanford-Binet scales include a sentence memory test at three age levels, beginning with 12-syllable sentences at age level IV. Each item in Memory for Sentences II at age level XI contains 20 syllables. At age level XIII the two Memory for Sentences III items contain 19 and 16 syllables, respectively, but the syntax and vocabulary are more complex than at age level XI.

Sentence Repetition (Benton and Hamsher, 1976, 1978)

This subtest of the Multilingual Aphasia Examination (MAE) (see p. 317f.) can do double duty. The fourteen sentences in Form I graduate in length from three to 24 syllables (see Table 14-6). They thus provide a measure of span for meaningful verbal material ranging from abnormally short to the expected normal adult length of 24 syllables. In addition, seven different linguistic constructions are represented among each of the two sets of sentences, Forms I and II (e.g., positive declaration, negative interrogation, etc.). This allows the examiner to test for the patient's sensitivity to syntactical variations in what he hears. This feature appears useful for registering mild or subtle linguistic deficits of patients whose communication abilities may seem

Table 14-6 Sentence Repetition: Form I

1. Take this home.
2. Where is the child?
3. The car will not run.
4. Why are they not living here?
5. The band played and the crowd cheered.
6. Where are you going to work next summer?
7. He sold his house and they moved to the farm.
8. Work in the garden until you have picked all the beans.
9. The artist painted many of the beautiful scenes in this valley.
10. This doctor does not travel to all the towns in the country.
11. He should be able to tell us exactly when she will be performing here.
12. Why do the members of that group never write to their representatives for aid?
13. Many men and women were not able to get to work because of the severe snow storm.
14. The members of the committee have agreed to hold their meeting on the first Tuesday of each month.

intact when taking the usual neuropsychological tests. A scoring system is available that gives one point for each sentence repeated correctly and provides an adjustment formula for additional points to be added to the raw score of persons in the age groups 25 to 29 and 60 to 64 who have had 15 years or less of schooling. However, when this test is administered apart from the MAE battery, the presence or absence of deviations from the expected 24-syllable span or a pattern of errors that suggests selective mishearing of the sentences will provide the needed clinical information.

Although the two forms of this test were found to be equivalent in difficulty for two matched groups of 85 patients each (average adjusted scores were 10.67 and 10.96 for Forms I and II, respectively), they differ in that the two longest sentences of Form II consist of only 18 and 19 syllables (16 and 15 words, respectively). Thus, while Form II sentences test for syntactical integrity, they are less suitable for examining span for sentences in the strict sense.

SILLY SENTENCES (Botwinick and Storandt, 1974)

The contribution of meaning to retention was examined by means of a set of long silly sentences developed as a parallel task to paragraph recall:

1. The Declaration of Independence/ sang/ overnight/ while/ the cereal/ jumped/ by the river./
2. Two dates/ ate/ the bed/ under the car/ seeing/ pink flowers/ forever./
3. They slept/ in the fire/ to avoid the draft./ It was cold there/ and their sweaters kept them/ cool./
4. I eat pink mice./ They are delicious/ but their green fur/ gives me heartburn./

Each of these silly sentences is read to the subject and is immediately followed by a recall trial. Correct recall of each unit—marked by slashes—merits one point so that the total possible score is 24. The average recall of subjects by decades was 21.9 for the 20s, 20.7 for the 30s, 20.6 for the 40s, 20.0 for the 50s, 19.0 for the 60s, and 15.6 for the 70s. A comparison of these data with scores obtained for paragraph recall indicated that meaningfulness of material played an increasingly greater role in recall in the later decades.

Paragraphs

The quantity of words and ideas in paragraph tests takes them out of the class of tests that measure simple immediate memory span. Rather, they provide a measure of the amount of information that is retained when more is presented than most people can remember on one hearing. In this sense, memory for paragraphs is analogous to a "supraspan" test, for there, too, more data are presented than can be fully grasped. The comparison of a patient's memory span on a paragraph test with that on sentences shows the extent to which an overload of data compromises functioning. Thus, if a patient has an average recall for digits forward and can remember a 26- or 28-

word sentence, but is unable to repeat as many as six words on the first presentation of the AVLT word list and recalls only five or six ideas of a paragraph containing 22 or 24 memory units, then the examiner can better define the conditions under which the patient's capacity for immediate recall becomes ineffective. Like sentences, paragraphs afford a more naturalistic medium for testing memory than do smaller speech units.

F.B. Wood and his co-workers (1982) suggest that the difference between immediate and delayed recall of a paragraph is an indirect measure of episodic memory. They point out that this measure of paragraph recall is more sensitive to the memory defects of amnesia patients than are either immediate recall scores or tests of old learning or digit learning. They consider that, unlike paragraph recall, these latter forms of verbal memory tests measure semantic memory which correlates most highly with measures of verbal skill.

Scoring paragraph recall presents a number of problems, since few people repeat the test material exactly. This leaves the examiner with the problem of deciding how pronounced alterations must be to require loss of score points. Common alterations include a variety of *substitutions* (of synonyms, of similar concepts, of less-precise language, of different numbers or proper names); *omissions* (large and small; irrelevant to the story, relevant, or crucial); *additions* and *elaborations* (ranging from inconsequential ones to those that distort or alter the story or are frankly bizarre); and *shifts in the story's sequence* (that may or may not alter its meaning). Rapaport and his colleagues (1968) attempted to deal with questions of how to judge these alterations by scoring as correct all segments of the story in which "the change does not alter the general meaning of the story or its details." Without a more elaborate scoring scheme, this rule is probably the most reasonable one that can be followed in a clinical setting. In addition, the Rapaport group developed a four-point "Distortion Score" that reflects the extent to which alterations change the gist of the story. Thus, they give credit to all minor (one-point) alterations as accurate "meaningful memories."

Talland and Ekdahl (1959) made a welcome distinction between verbatim and content (semantic) recall of paragraphs. They divided meaningful verbal material into separate scoring units for verbatim recall and for content *ideas*, which are credited as correctly recalled if the subject substitutes synonyms or suitable phrases for the exact wording (see p. 439). In a study comparing semantic and verbatim scoring methods, Mills and Burkhart (1980) found that semantic scoring results in higher scores than does verbatim scoring. While intercorrelations were so high ($r = .94$) as to suggest that the two methods measured identical functions, only verbatim scoring differentiated hemisphere side of lesion in immediate recall trials. Moreover the verbatim method was more sensitive to lesion lateralization on delayed recall trials than was semantic scoring which also differentiated lesion side on delayed recall trials. A high degree of interscorer agreement ($r \geq .97$) was found for each method.

One method of scoring alterations was devised for the Logical Memory subtest of the Wechsler Memory Scale (pp. 436–437), but may be generally applicable to tests of paragraph recall (Power et al., 1979). This method takes minor alterations into account by (1) giving one-half credit for synonym substitutes that do not alter the basic idea; (2) giving one-half credit when omission of an adjective, adverb, or article changes the basic idea only a little. The authors report high ($r \geq .95$) interscorer agreement for immediate recall trials of both forms of this test.

Unless scoring rules for alterations are specified, as by Rapaport and his colleagues, or a method for scoring slight alterations is used, the examiner will inevitably have to make scoring decisions without clear-cut, objective standards. In most cases, the likelihood that a score for a paragraph memory test may vary a few points (depending on who does the scoring and how the scorer feels that day) is not of great consequence. The sophisticated psychological examiner knows that there is a margin of error for any given score. However, alterations in some patients' responses may make large segments unscorable as verbatim recall although the patient demonstrated a quite richly detailed recall of the story. Other patients may reproduce much material verbatim, but in such a disconnected manner, or so linked or elaborated with bizarre, confabulated, or perseverated introjections that a fairly high verbatim recall score belies their inability to reproduce newly learned verbal material accurately.

MEMORY FOR STORY AND PARAGRAPH RECALL (STANFORD- BINET)

The Binet scales again provide several memory items in this category. For *The Wet Fall* at age level VII, the subject looks at a card with the story printed on it while the examiner reads the story aloud. Immediately after the reading, the examiner takes the card from the subject and asks a set of close-ended questions about the story, such as, "What is the name of this story?" Both the 1937 and 1960 Binet scales also contain two paragraphs in *Repeating Thought of Passage*, which deal with abstract topics, *Value of Life* and *Tests* at SA II and SA III levels, respectively. These items differ from the easier paragraph memory task in that the subject does not see the passage and can give a free recall.

LOGICAL MEMORY SUBTEST OF THE WECHSLER MEMORY SCALE (Wechsler, 1945) (see pp. 463–466)

Free recall immediately following auditory presentation characterizes most story memory tests. The Logical Memory test of the Wechsler Memory Scale, probably the most widely used story memory test, employs this format. The examiner reads two paragraphs, stopping after each reading for the patient to give his immediate free recall. Paragraph A contains 24 memory units or "ideas" and paragraph B contains 22. The subject gains one point of credit for each "idea" he recalls. The total score is the average number of ideas recalled for each paragraph. The highest possible score is 23, i.e., $\dfrac{A + B}{2}$. A fairly steady decline in scores with age characterizes the Logical Memory performance (see Table 14-13, p. 464).

Although Logical Memory involves verbal learning, women are not only not superior to men on this test (Ivison, 1977) but, in at least one study, men outscored women (Verhoff et al., 1979). In a factor analysis of the Wechsler Memory Scale, this subtest correlated most highly with Associate Learning (see p. 429) and the test of immediate recall of designs (Visual Reproduction, see p. 444) (Kear-Colwell, 1973). This correlation pattern may be interpreted as indicating that Logical Memory involves learning and immediate recall of complex, unfamiliar information.

Many examiners give delayed recall trials 20 minutes (Edith Kaplan), 30 minutes (E. W. Russell, 1975a; see pp. 466–467), or 45 minutes (Mills and Burkhart, 1980) to an hour (Foliart and Mack, 1979) later, following administration of other tests. In general, delayed recall scores of control subjects run one to two points below their immediate recall scores. Verhoff and her colleagues (1979) found that sex differences were somewhat magnified on delayed recall. In a study of patients who had undergone surgical resection of a temporal lobe, this test did not discriminate between the right and left hemisphere groups on immediate recall (Delaney et al., 1980). On a recall trial after 30 minutes, however, patients with left-sided lesions recalled significantly fewer story elements.

THE BABCOCK STORY RECALL TEST (Babcock, 1930; Babcock and Levy, 1940; Rapaport et al., 1968)

In this paragraph recall test, a 21-unit story is used to measure both immediate and delayed recall:

> December 6./ Last week/ a river/ overflowed/ in a small town/ ten miles/ from Albany./ Water covered the streets/ and entered the houses./ Fourteen persons/ were drowned/ and 600 persons/ caught cold/ because of the dampness/ and cold weather./ In saving/ a boy/ who was caught/ under a bridge,/ a man/ cut his hands.

The test begins with the instructions, "I am going to read a short story to you now. Listen carefully because when I finish I'm going to ask you to tell me as much of the story as you can remember." Upon reading the paragraph, the examiner instructs the patient, "Now tell me everything you can remember of the story." When a patient reports only a few items, the examiner should encourage him to try to recall more. If the patient still does not produce much, the examiner can provide some structure for recall with questions such as, "What happened?"; "Where did it happen?"; "Who was involved?" The examiner should note where questioning began to keep track of spontaneous versus directed recall. The patient should not be questioned to the point of discomfort. As testing proceeds, the examiner can usually make some estimate about the extent to which a low response level reflects pathological inertia, a communication disorder, or a specific memory deficit, and will thus have some sense of when to push a patient and when to let well enough alone.

Immediately following the first recall trial, the examiner says, "In a little while I'm going to ask you to tell me how much of the story you can still remember. I'm going to read the story to you again now so that you'll have it fresh in your memory for the next time." Recall following the second reading comes after approximately 20 minutes of testing involving verbal material. Once again the examiner asks the subject to

"Tell everything you can remember," and presses for more responses as appears appropriate.

Four points are added to the immediate recall score to equate for the second reading of the paragraph before the delayed recall trial. Expected scores at the median and two quartiles for three ability levels show a recall increment from the immediate to the delayed trial when the four-point adjustment of the immediate recall score has been made (see Table 14-7).

Diane Howieson and I have developed a second paragraph (the *Portland Paragraph*) of similar length and conceptual and syntactical complexity, and divided into the same number of scoring units for retest purposes:

> Two/ semi-trailer trucks/ lay on their sides/ after a tornado/ blew/ a dozen trucks/ off the highway/ in West Springfield./ One person/ was killed/ and 418 others/ were injured/ in the Wednesday storm/ which hit an airport/ and a nearby residential area./ The governor/ will ask/ the President/ to declare/ the town/ a major disaster area.

These two paragraphs can be used in tandem to look for the effects of interference of newly learned material on ongoing learning. The format for administering these paragraphs consists of giving the Babcock paragraph twice following the standard instructions. The Portland paragraph is then given immediately on completion of the second Babcock recall following the Babcock format of reading the paragraph, immediate recall, rereading, 20-minute interference period, and then delayed recall. No norms are available for evaluating performance on the Portland paragraph, but the Babcock norms can provide a rough standard. Of special interest are intrusions of content or ideas from the first to the second paragraph and wide disparities in amount of recall.

The decision about which paragraph recall format to use, Wechsler's or Babcock's, depends on whether the examiner is more interested in testing for proactive inhibition or learning. The paragraphs in each of these tests can be adapted to either format. The addition of the delayed recall trial to the Wechsler paragraphs (E. W. Russell, 1975a; see pp. 466–467) allows the examiner to see what happens to delayed recall

Table 14-7 Expected Scores for Immediate and Delayed Recall Trials of the Babcock Story Recall Test

Intellectual level[a]	Sample n	Immediate Recall			Delayed Recall		
		Q_1	Median	Q_3	Q_1	Median	Q_3
Average	27	12	13	14	13	15	16
High average	41	12	14.5	17	16	17	19
Superior	45	13	15	18	15	17	19

(Adapted from Rapaport et al., 1968)
[a]For statistical definitions of these levels, see Chap. 9.

when the stage is set for proactive inhibition (i.e., when two stories are read, one after the other, for immediate recall). With no further reading of the paragraphs, the Wechsler format provides less of a learning test than does the Babcock. The greater content similarity of the Babcock and the Portland stories makes this pair more suitable for the examination of proactive inhibition, or simply confusion of story lines, than the Wechsler pair.

One paragraph recall format that clearly differentiated organic from functionally disturbed elderly psychiatric patients involved a first reading of a short story followed at once by immediate recall, a second reading and second immediate recall trial. There were five subsequent recall trials, at one day, three days, one week, two weeks, and one month, each followed by another reading and immediate recall trial (Newcombe and Steinberg, 1964). The organic group's low first trial recall indicated impaired immediate registration. They then showed marked gains in each subsequent recall trial immediately following each reading, but forgot most of what they had learned in each trial that followed a delay of 24 hours or more. The functionally disturbed group, rather than forgetting much of what they learned, continued to make and maintain gains throughout the 28-day testing period.

The Cowboy Story

Because it has been included in many mental status examinations since it first appeared in 1919, this is the paragraph best known to medical practitioners. Talland (1965a; with Ekdahl, 1959) used it to make a welcome distinction between verbatim and content recall of paragraph. He divided it into 27 memory units for quantitative verbatim recall and identified 24 content *ideas* (italicized words or phrases), which are credited as correctly recalled if the subject substitutes synonyms or suitable phrases for the exact wording.

> A *cowboy*/ from *Arizona*/ went to *San Francisco*/ with his *dog*,/ which he *left*/ at a *friend*'s/ while he *purchased*/ a *new* suit of *clothes*./ Dressed finely,/ he *went* back/ to the *dog*,/ *whistled* to him,/ *called him* by name/ and *patted* him./ But the dog would *have nothing to do* with him,/ in his new *hat*/ and *coat*,/ but gave a *mournful*/ *howl*./ *Coaxing* was of no effect/; so the cowboy *went away*/ and donned his *old garments*,/ whereupon the *dog*/ *immediately*/ showed his wild *joy*/ on *seeing his master*/ as he thought he *ought* to be./ (Talland, 1965).

On immediate recall testing, a 22-subject control group gave an average of 8.32 of the 27 verbatim memory units; their average content recall score was 9.56.

Pattern, Design, and Other Configural Tests of Visual Memory Functions

Tests of visual memory using configural stimulus material often call for a visuomotor response, usually drawing. This, of course, complicates the interpretation of defective performances, for the patient's failure may arise from a constructional disability or impaired visual or spatial memory, or it may represent an interaction between these disabilities and include others as well. Even on recognition tasks, which do not call for a visuomotor response, such perceptual defects as visuospatial inattention may compound memory problems. Therefore, the examiner must pay close attention to the quality of the patient's responses in order to estimate the relative contributions of memory, perceptual, and constructional or visuomotor components to the final product.

To reduce the possibility of verbal mediation, most visual recall test stimuli consist of designs or nonsense figures. However, unless they are quite complex or unfamiliar, geometric designs do not fully escape verbal labeling. Moreover, it is virtually impossible to design a large series of nonsense figures that do not elicit verbal associations. One series of 180 random shapes includes values for frequency and heterogeneity of verbal associations that allow the examiner to take into account the stimulus potential for verbal mediation (Vanderplas and Garvin, 1959).

Visual Memory: Tests of Recognition and Verbal Recall

RECURRING FIGURES TEST (Kimura, 1963[1])

In this test, the stimulus material consists of 20 cards on which are drawn geometric or irregular nonsense figures. After looking at each of these cards in succession, the patient is shown a pack of 140 cards one by one for three seconds each. This pack contains seven sets of eight of the original 20 designs interspersed throughout 84 one-of-a-kind-design cards. The patient must indicate which of the cards he has seen previously. A perfect performance would yield a score of 56. False positive responses are subtracted from right responses to correct for guessing. The 11 control subjects in Kimura's study, with an average age in the 20s, obtained a mean net (correct minus false positive responses) score of 38.9. There was essentially no difference in the gross average scores of right and left temporal lobectomized patients (43.4 and 44.4, respectively), although the right temporal lobe patients had more than twice as many false positive responses as the left temporal lobe group, resulting in a net score difference that significantly favored the left hemisphere patients. The members of both groups remembered geometric figures much better than nonsense figures, and the left hemisphere patients remembered a much larger proportion of the nonsense figures than did the right hemisphere patients, although the two groups did not differ greatly in their recognition of geometric figures.

An older group of 28 control subjects, most of them in their forties, averaged 28.5 ± 6.92 on this task (Newcombe, 1969). The tendency for patients with left hemisphere lesions was to fare better on this test than patients with right hemisphere lesions

---

[1]The test material may be ordered from D. K. Consultants, Department of Psychology, University of Western Ontario, London, Ontario, Canada, N6A 3K7.

and control subjects, too. Net means for three left-lesioned groups exceeded the control subjects' mean while none of the groups with right hemisphere damage had a mean as high as the control subjects. However, none of the group score differences in Newcombe's study reached significance. Net correct scores on this test did differentiate traumatically brain injured patients from a group of matched control subjects, although these groups were indistinguishable in terms of number of false positive errors (Brooks, 1974b). In Brooks's study, each performance was broken into a series of seven trials of 20 items each so that the data could be examined for evidence of learning curves. Learning curves did show up in net score increases over the seven trials for both control and head injured groups, and in decreases in false positive errors for both groups; but neither group showed any regular pattern of reduction of false negative errors.

VISUAL RETENTION TEST (METRIC FIGURES) (Warrington and James, 1967a)

With the goal of minimizing verbal mediation, Warrington and James developed a multiple-choice recognition task. Twenty 5 × 5 inch white squares, each containing four blackened squares variously positioned so that no two stimulus figures are alike, comprise the test material (see Fig. 14-1). Following a two-second exposure of each stimulus figure, the patient must choose the identical figure from a set of four similar figures. A second administration follows the first, differing in duration of exposure (10 seconds) and in a 180° rotation of the stimulus figures. Three error scores result, one for each administration and one for their sum. Ten control subjects made an average of 3.3 errors on the first and 2.2 errors on the second administration for an average total of 5.5 errors out of a maximum possible error score of 40.

Although the 37 left hemisphere patients' average total error score (8.6) differed very little from that of the 40 right hemisphere patients (10.2), ten right parietal damaged patients made significantly more errors on the two-second administration than

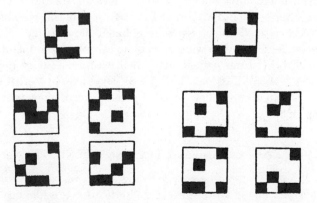

Fig. 14-1. Visual Retention Test (Metric Figures) (Warrington and James, 1967). (©, 1967, Pergamon Press. Reprinted with permission)

441

eight left parietal lobe patients. A significant association between performance on Block Design and this test attests to its usefulness for evaluating visuospatial perceptual processing. The nature of the right hemisphere damaged patients' errors on this test suggests that unilateral spatial neglect may contribute significantly to the higher error score of the right parietal lobe patients, since patients who demonstrated unilateral neglect on a drawing task tended to select their answers from the two choices on the right side of the multiple choice set (Oxbury et al., 1974; Campbell and Oxbury, 1976).

OBJECT AND PICTURE MEMORY SPAN

Pictures or real objects may be used to test span of visual retention. Tests can differ in the number of stimuli, in length of exposure, in the presence and length of a delay interval, and in the kind of response requested. The verbalizability of these measures of visual memory span may make them as much tests of verbal as of visual memory. Therefore, generalizations about visual memory cannot be freely drawn from performances on these tests.

A recognition format was used by Squire (1974) in his study of the remote memory of older people grouped in the four decades from the 50s to the 80s. He used 15 stimulus pictures of objects presented one at a time for three seconds while the subject named each object aloud. Following a 30-minute delay, the patient was shown a 30-picture array with the 15 original stimulus pictures and 15 new ones mixed together. One point was scored for each correct 'yes' or 'no' regarding previous exposure, which gave a maximum of 30 points. A slight age effect was found ($p < .05$) although the highest score was 29.2 for the 60–69-year-old group and the 70–79-year-old group had the lowest, 26.3. A *Memory Span for Objects* test is described in F. L. Wells and Ruesch's *Mental Examiner's Handbook* (1969). The patient is shown ten or 20 object pictures, which he names and then recalls, much like a word-span test. When shown 20 pictures, the average adult should be able to recall 11 of them. For ten objects, Wells and Ruesch report a normal span of 7 $\pm$ 1.4. Despite considerable overlap, the number of objects recalled out of ten differentiated those patients with diagnosed presenile or senile dementia who were alive one year after examination (their mean score was 5.89 $\pm$ 3.54) from patients who died within a year of the examination (mean score, 2.94 $\pm$ 4.85) (Kaszniak et al., 1978). The Pictorial-Verbal Learning Test (PVLT) measures span of immediate recall of printed words along with learning and retention (see p. 428).

NON-LANGUAGE PAIRED ASSOCIATE LEARNING TEST (R. S. Fowler, 1969)

This test was devised to assess the new learning ability of patients whose language deficits preclude their taking a word-learning test. Its format is identical to that of the Associate Learning test of the Wechsler Memory Scale after which it was patterned (see pp. 429, 464). Instead of words, however, the stimulus material consists of objects taken from the Object Sorting Test kit (see pp. 486–487), which were arranged into six sets of easily associated pairs (e.g., real fork—real knife, pipe—matches) and four hard-to-associate pairs (e.g., real pliers—sugar cube, real cigar—red rubber ball). After being shown each series of ten pairs, the subject's task is to pick out from a set of 22 items those that had been shown with a paired item when the first item of the pair is presented to the subject. Like the Associate Learning test, the order in which each item is presented varies from trial to trial.

In comparisons made of the performance of control subjects on Easy Words with Easy Objects, and Hard Words with Hard Objects, there was very little difference between the two administrations involving the well-known—i.e., "easy"—associations at any of the four age levels (30s, 40s, 50s, and 60+). However, scores for all age groups were consistently lower for "hard" words than for "hard" object pairs, although the differences between the two administrations became practically negligible by the third trial. A slight but significant decrease in learning efficiency with age showed up on both "easy" and "hard" object items, which was more pronounced for the "hard" pairs. No sex differences were observed, however.

This test was standardized with approximately the same number of subjects in each age group (40) as was Wechsler's test, so that its norms are certainly as sturdy as Wechsler's. It is unfortunate that norms for delayed recall trials were not also obtained to round out the memory examination made possible by this useful and handy non-speech alternative for testing old associations and new learning.

Visual Memory: Recall Tests

DESIGN REPRODUCTION

There are any number of abbreviated tests of memory for designs that call for a five- or ten-second exposure followed immediately, or after a brief delay, by a drawing trial in which the subject attempts to depict what he remembers. Probably the most popular designs are the two of the Binet *Memory for Designs I* task at age levels IX and XI (see Fig. 14-2). They are among the four designs of the Visual Reproduction subtest of the Wechsler Memory Scale and appear in other test sets as well (e.g., Gainotti and Tiacci, 1970; L. Wood and Shulman, 1940). Both the Binet and the Wechsler Memory Scale administrations call for a ten-second exposure followed by an immediate response. A third Binet design, composed of embedded diamonds, appears at age level XII (see Fig. 14-2). The Binet item scaling permits some discrimination between performance levels but far less than the detailed scoring breakdown for the four Wechsler Memory Scale designs (see below). However, the larger and more carefully selected Binet standardization population probably makes the Binet norms more reliable. Memory for design tests requiring reproduction of the design are particularly sensitive to right hemisphere damage. McFie (1960) found a significant number of impaired Binet design reproductions associated with right hemisphere lesions regardless of their specific site, although this disability was not associated with left hemisphere patients.

443

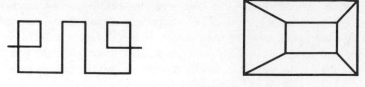

IX- and XI-year level

XII-year level

Fig. 14-2. Memory for Designs models (Terman and Merrill, 1973). (Courtesy of Houghton Mifflin Co.)

Visual Reproduction subtest of the Wechsler Memory Scale (see pp. 464–466). This is an immediate recall test but some examiners also recommend a delayed trial (e.g., E. W. Russell, 1975a; see pp. 466–467). Each of three cards with printed designs is shown for five seconds (the third card of each form of the test has a double design; Form I contains the IX- and XI-year level designs of the Binet pictures shown in Figure 14-2, for example. The other two Form I designs are from the Babcock-Levy test battery [1940]). Following each exposure, the subject draws what he remembers of the design. This subtest has the steepest age gradient of all the Wechsler Memory Scale subtests (see Table 14-12). No sex differences were found among the older (55+) persons examined in the Framingham study (Verhoff et al., 1979), but in the large-scale Australian standardization, the women obtained an average score that was almost one point lower than the men's average score (Ivison, 1977). On immediate recall this test does not discriminate between patients with right- and left-sided lesions (Delaney et al., 1980). The relative simplicity of the designs encourages verbal encoding and may account for their insensitivity to lateralization effects. Lateralized differences do show up on recall after a 30-minute delay as patients with right temporal lesions then obtain significantly lower scores than those with left temporal lesions or normal control subjects.

Complex Figure Test (CFT): Recall Administrations. Most examiners give both immediate and delayed recall trials of the CFT; however, the amount of delay varies among examiners. Edith Kaplan recommends a 20-minute delay, Brooks (1972) uses

444

a 30-minute delay, Snow's (1979) delay is 40 minutes, and the Montreal Neurological Institute group gives the delay trial after 45 minutes of intervening tasks (L. B. Taylor, 1979). Within the limits of an hour or so, the length of delay is apparently of little consequence, as Ebert found no differences in either patient or control subjects' performances using the Taylor figure following delays of 30 minutes or one hour (cited in Wood et al., 1982). As in the copy trial, the examiner should see that the order of approach is recorded, whether by giving the subject different colors to mark his progress, by drawing a numbered copy of what the subject draws, or—ideally—both.

Osterreith's (1944) norms are useful for comparing copy and recall trials (see Tables 13-5, p. 401, and 14-8). Since Ebert (in F.B. Wood et al., 1982) found that few patients' performances showed more than a one- or two-point difference between immediate and delayed recall trials, and mean differences between the two recall administrations were negligible, the examiner can use Table 14-8 to evaluate both immediate and delayed recall trials so long as the delay does not go much beyond one hour.

Performance on the two recall trials helps the examiner sort out different aspects of the constructional and memory disabilities that might contribute to defective recall of the complex figure (Snow, 1979; Wood et al., 1982). Those patients (more likely with left-sided lesions) whose defective copy is based more on slow organization of complex data than on disordered visuospatial abilities may improve their performances on the immediate recall trial (Osterreith, 1944). Patients whose lesions are on the left tend to show preserved recall of the overall structure of the figure with simplification and loss of details. Patients with right-sided lesions who have difficulty copying the figures display even greater problems with recall (Milner, 1975; L. B. Taylor, 1969). Patients with right hemisphere damage tend to lose many of the elements of the design, making increasingly impoverished reproductions of the original figure as they go from the immediate to the delayed recall trial. Those right hemisphere damaged patients who have visuospatial problems or who are subject to perceptual fragmentation will also increasingly distort and confuse the configurational elements of the design. This shows up in the three trials—copy (a), immediate recall (b), and (approximately) 40-minute delayed recall (c)—drawn by a 50-year-old graduate civil engineer 12 years after suffering a ruptured aneurysm of the right anterior communicating artery, which resulted in left hemiparesis, significant behavioral deterioration, and pronounced impairment of arithmetic and complex reasoning abilities along with other intellectual deficits (see Fig. 14-3).

Traumatically brain injured patients also tend to have difficulty on recall trials of the CFT. Patients in one study, most of whom had sustained their injuries in motor vehicle accidents and thus had at least some frontal lobe involvement, showed much

Table 14-8 Percentile Norms for Accuracy Scores Obtained by Adults on Memory Trials of the Complex Figure Test

Percentile	10	20	30	40	50	60	70	80	90	100
Score	15	17	19	21	22	24	26	27	28	31

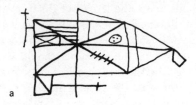

a

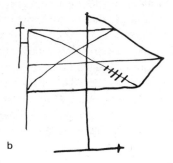

b

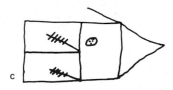

c

Fig. 14-3. Complex Figure Test performance of a 50-year-old hemiparetic engineer with severe right frontal damage of 12 years duration (see text). (a) Copy trial. (b) Three-minute recall with no intervening activities. (c) Recall after approximately 40 minutes of intervening activities including other drawing tasks. This series illustrates the degradation of the percept over time when there is a pronounced visual memory disorder.

446

greater impairment (and a much wider score range) than did normal control subjects on (probably the three-minute) recall (Benayoun et al., 1969). However, Brooks's (1972) patients with traumatic brain damage did as well as the controls on immediate recall but gave impaired performances after a 30-minute delay. Tendencies of patients with frontal lobe damage to perseverate, confabulate, personalize, or otherwise distort the design that first appears on the initial copy or the immediate recall trial tend to be exaggerated with repeated recall.

In addition to Osterreith's (1944) norms (see Table 14-8), two scores have been devised for making more precise distinctions between performances obtained under the three different administration conditions. Snow (1979) uses a "% recall" score $\left(\dfrac{CFT \cdot R}{CFT \cdot C} \times 100 \right)$ "to remove the effects of the level of performance on the . . . Copy administration $(CFT \cdot C)$ from the memory performance" $(CFT \cdot R)$. Brooks's (1972) "% Forgetting" score $\left(\dfrac{CFT \cdot RI - CFT \cdot RD}{CFT \cdot RI} \times 100 \right)$ gives the amount of data lost from the immediate $(CFT \cdot RI)$ to the delayed $(CFT \cdot RD)$ trial. These scores probably have their greatest usefulness in research, but may also be helpful when an examiner needs to document a patient's deficits concretely and with precision.

The Benton Visual Retention Test (BVRT) (Benton, 1974).   This widely used visual recall test is most often called by its originator's name alone. The *BVRT* owes its popularity to a number of virtues. It has three forms which are roughly equivalent; some studies demonstrate no differences in their difficulty level and other studies indicate that Form D may be a little more difficult than Forms C or E (Benton, 1974; Riddell, 1962a). Its norms include both age and estimated original intellectual capacity. The three-figure design format is sensitive to unilateral spatial neglect (see Fig. 14-4). The complex but easily learned scoring system helps the examiner identify error patterns. Benton furnishes adult norms for three administration procedures: Administration A allows a ten-second exposure to each card with immediate recall by drawing (and has norms for children ages 8 through 14). Administration B, like A, is also a simple recall test but follows a five-second exposure. Administration C is a copying test in which the subject is encouraged to draw the designs as accurately as possible (and C also includes children's norms). No norms are given for Administration D, which requires the subject to delay his response for 15 seconds after a ten-second exposure.

All but two of each ten-card series have more than one figure in the horizontal plane; most have three figures, two large and one small, with the small figure always at one side or the other. Besides its sensitivity to visual inattention problems, the three-figure format provides a limited measure of the immediate span of recall since some patients cannot retain the third or both of the other figures while drawing the first or second one, even though they may be able to do a simple one-figure memory task easily. Further, spatial organization problems may show up in the handling of size and placement relationships of the three figures.

447

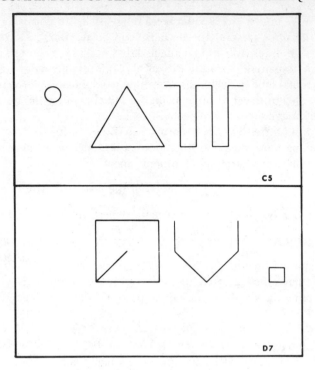

Fig. 14-4. Two representative items of the Benton Visual Retention Test. © A. L. Benton. Courtesy of the author.

The examiner should give the patient a fresh sheet of paper, approximately the size of the card, for each design. To avoid the problem of a patient "jumping the gun" on the memory administrations—and particularly on Administration D—I remove the pad of paper after completion of each drawing and do not give it back until it is time for the patient to draw the next design. The drawings should be numbered in some standard manner to indicate the orientation of the drawing on the paper. Although usually there is no question as to the orientation of the paper relative to the subject when there are numerous errors of omission, perseveration, and particularly rotation, it can be difficult to tell from the drawing alone not only which side was up, but even which design was copied.

When the copy administration is given first, the examiner is able to determine the quality of the patient's drawings per se and also familiarize the subject with the three-figure format. Well-oriented, alert patients generally do not require the practice provided by administration C, so that it need not be given if there is another copying task in the battery. Patients who have difficulty following instructions and lack "test-wiseness" should be given at least the first three or four designs of a series for copy practice.

Each administration is scored for both the number of correct designs and the number of errors. Six types of error are recognized: omissions, distortions, perseverations, rotations, misplacements (in the position of one figure relative to the others), and errors in size. Thus, there can be, and not infrequently are, more than one error to a card. Both the Number Correct Score and the Error Score norms for administration A take into account intelligence level and age (see Table 14-9). Klonoff and Kennedy (1965, 1966) found that extrapolations of correction scores to evaluate the Administration A performances of very elderly persons gave estimates that were too high. The 115 subjects they studied, aged 80–92, who were living in the community and were—for the most part—active, achieved an average 3.94 Number Correct Score and an average Error Score of 11.90 (see p. 400 also).

Interpretation of performance is straightforward. Taking the subject's age and intellectual endowment into account, the examiner can enter the normative tables for Administration A and quickly determine whether the Number Correct or the Error Score falls into the impairment categories. On Administration B, the normal tendency for persons in the age range 16–60 is to reproduce correctly one design less than under the 10-second exposure condition of Administration A. The examiner who wishes to evaluate Administration B performances need only add one point and use the A

Table 14-9 BVRT Norms for Administration A: Adults Expected Number Correct Scores, by Estimated Premorbid IQ and Age

Estimated Premorbid IQ	Expected Number Correct Score, by Age		
	15–44	45–54	55–64
110 and above (Superior)	9	8	7
95–109 (Average)	8	7	6
80–94 (Low Average)	7	6	5
70–79 (Borderline)	6	5	4
60–69 (Defective)	5	4	3
59 and below (Very Defective)	4	3	2

BVRT Norms for Administration A: Adults
Expected Error Scores, by Estimated Premorbid IQ and Age

Estimated Premorbid IQ	Expected Error Score, by Age			
	15–39	40–54	55–59	60–64
110 and above (Superior)	1	2	3	4
105–109 (High Average)	2	3	4	5
95–104 (Average)	3	4	5	6
90–94 (Low Average)	4	5	6	7
80–89 (Dull Average)	5	6	7	8
70–79 (Borderline)	6	7	8	9
60–69 (Defective)	7	8	9	10
59 and below (Very Defective)	8	9	10	11

norms. Only Error Score norms with no age or intelligence corrections are available for Administration C (see p. 402). The Number Correct Scores of Administration D for normal control subjects are, on the average, 0.4 point below their Administration A score.

Tabulation of errors by type allows the examiner to determine the nature of the patient's problems on this test. Impaired immediate recall or an attention defect appears mostly as simplification, simple substitution, or omission of the last one or two design elements of a card. Normal subjects exhibit these tendencies too; the difference is in the frequency with which they occur. The first two designs of each series consist of only one figure so simple and easily named that it is rare for even patients with a significantly impaired immediate memory capacity to forget them. Unilateral spatial neglect shows up as consistent omission of the figure on the same side as the lesion. Visuospatial and constructional disabilities appear as defects in the execution or organization of the drawings. Rotations and consistent design distortions generally indicate a perceptual problem. Perseverations on this test should alert the examiner to look for perseveration on other kinds of tasks. Widespread perseveration suggests a monitoring or activity control problem; perseveration limited to this test is more likely evidence of a specific visuoperceptual or immediate memory impairment. Simplification of designs, including disregard of size and placement, may be associated with overall behavioral regression in patients with bilateral or diffuse damage.

When given with Administration A, Administration D (10-second exposure, 15-second delay) sometimes provides interesting information about the patient's memory processes that is not obtainable elsewhere. The average loss from D to A by brain damaged patients seen in a general clinical practice has been reported as 0.7 (Benton, 1974). Occasionally, the 15-second delay elicits a gross memory impairment when memory defects were not pronounced on Administration A. A few brain injured patients do better on Administration D than on A, apparently profiting from the 15-second delay to consolidate memory traces that would dissipate if they began drawing immediately. For example, fewer errors on the delay administration (D) compared with the immediate recall administration (A) were made by each patient in a study of five stroke patients and five other elderly men hospitalized for nonneurological conditions (Crow and Lewinsohn, 1969). Patients who improve their performance when they have the quiet delay period may be suffering attention and concentration problems rather than memory problems per se, or they may need more than an ordinary amount of time to consolidate new information.

The BVRT is very stable and has a high reliability on repeated administrations (Lezak, 1982d). Three administrations, given to normal control subjects six and 12 months apart, produced no significant differences between either number correct or error score means. Coefficients of concordance (W) between scores obtained for each administration were .74 for number correct and .77 for errors.

When deciding whether to give the BVRT or some other visually presented memory test, it is important to recognize that many of the designs can be conceptualized verbally (e.g., for C5 in Fig. 14-4, "small circle up, triangle, and a squared-off 'W'"). Thus, this test is sensitive to left brain damage as well as right. For example, Zubrick and Smith (1978) reported that aphasia patients' scores on the BVRT tended to improve as their language functions improved. Zubrick and Smith also found that patients with focal right posterior lesions who, as a group, do least well on the Block Design and Object Assembly subtests of the WAIS battery, also do less well on this test than patients with left hemisphere damage or right anterior lesions. Taken with reports that the BVRT has higher correlations with tests of design copying ability than with memory tests (e.g., A. B. Silverstein, 1962; Snow, 1979), these data suggest that the constructional component far outweighs the memory component measured by this test.

The BVRT can serve several purposes. When perseveration or visuospatial inattention is suspected or when there is a need to record these problems in the patient's own hand, the BVRT may be the instrument of choice. It can be particularly useful for documenting these problems in patients who monitor their performances and are thus apt to catch inattention or perseveration errors when they see them. The 15-minute delay administration can be given following Administration A to patients who either seem overwhelmed by too much stimuli or are slow to process information, to see whether they can use the brief interlude to sort out and consolidate the material. This test may also be used to measure the immediate retention span of language-impaired patients.

Since this test involves so many different capacities—visuomotor response, visuospatial perception, visual and verbal conceptualization, immediate memory span—it is not surprising that it is quite sensitive to the presence of brain damage. The preponderance of research on the BVRT shows that it is better than many other tests for brain damage in distinguishing patients with cerebral brain damage from those with psychiatric disorders (Benton, 1974; Heaton et al., 1978; G.G. Marsh and Hirsch, 1982). It also appears to be sensitive to the cognitive alterations that accompany normal aging, as approximately 40% of a group of 162 healthy persons in the 75 to 84-year-old age range gave defective performances. However, like other single tests, it cannot be used alone as it does not identify organic patients with enough reliability to make individual diagnostic decisions.

The Memory for Designs Test (MFD) (F. K. Graham and Kendall, 1960). This test consists of 15 geometric designs that vary in complexity (see Fig. 14-5). They are shown to the subject one at a time for five seconds. Immediately after each exposure, the subject draws what he remembers of the design.

The reproductions are scored for errors, based on a point system that awards one point for two or more errors when the essential design is preserved, two points when the configuration of the design has been lost or a major element is missing or greatly distorted, and three points for rotations and reversals. Surprisingly, no points are given for designs that have been completely forgotten. Thus, the error score of patients with extremely defective immediate recall who forget some or all of the designs may not be significantly elevated. On the other hand, the three-point penalties placed on rotations and reversals expand some patients' scores disproportionately (Grundvig et al., 1970). This heavy a penalty seems particularly unwarranted in view of Kendall's

451

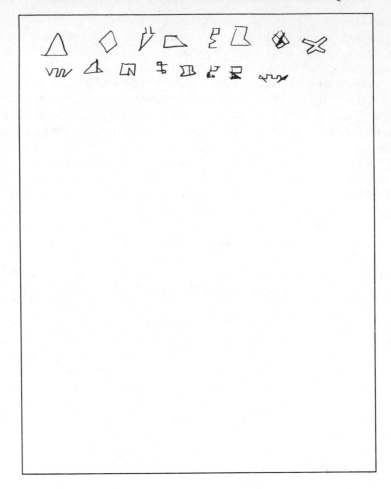

Fig. 14-5. Memory for Designs performance by a 39-year-old minister one year after a car accident in which he sustained a cerebral concussion and was unconscious for 16 days. The MFD scoring system gives this performance a "perfect" score of zero, although reproduction errors of three of the designs (3, 14, and 15), the line quality, handling of erasures, and the size and placement of the designs on the paper are distortions common to design reproductions of brain damaged persons.

(1966) report that normal control subjects made almost one-third as many rotational errors as did brain damaged patients. A correction for age and general ability level (based on the Wechsler-Bellevue or Binet Vocabulary subtest score) is recommended when evaluating the performance of children or mentally dull or aged adults. For all other adults, raw scores may be interpreted directly. Test norms were developed from 535 normal control subjects and a very mixed sample of 243 "brain-disordered" patients.

452

Studies of the efficiency of the MFD test as a predictor of brain damage in psychiatric populations have most often compared it with the Bender-Gestalt and BVRT and found that, by and large, the MFD has the lowest accuracy rate (Heaton et al., 1978). G.G. Marsh and Hirsch (1982) report misclassification rates of 64% (errors) and 61% (difference score). A correlation of .851 between the MFD and the Bender (scored by the Hain method) suggests that, although the MFD involves immediate recall, by and large these two tests measure the same functions (Quattlebaum, 1968).

Moreover, the MFD scoring system tends to be too stringent and of questionable reliability (McFie, 1975). Not infrequently, patients will produce a set of MFD reproductions that appear frankly defective on inspection but that earn scores within the "Normal" (0–4) or "Borderline" range (5–11) (see Fig. 14-5). Because the scoring system is so strict, this test yields very few false positives: short of deliberate faking, it would be difficult for an organically intact subject to earn a score in the "Brain Damage" range (12 error points or more).

RECALL OF SEQUENCES

Block-tapping. Milner (1971) described a Block-tapping task devised by P. Corsi for testing memory impairment of patients who had undergone temporal lobe resection. It consists of nine black 1½-inch cubes fastened in a random order to a black board (see Fig. 14-6). Each time the examiner taps the blocks in a prearranged sequence, the patient must attempt to copy his tapping pattern. By adding one tap to each succeeding successful sequence, the examiner ascertains the patient's span for immediate recall. Then the 24 test trials of tapping sequences one tap greater than the patient's immediate span are conducted. As in Hebb's Recurring Digits task (see pp. 418–419), the same sequence is repeated every third trial.

Normal subjects gradually learn the recurring pattern during the 24 test trials, as

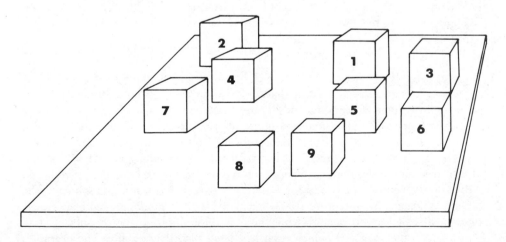

Fig. 14-6. Corsi's Block-tapping board. (After Milner, 1971)

do patients with both large and small left temporal resections, but patients whose right temporal resections included significant amounts of the hippocampus show no learning on this task. De Renzi and his co-workers (1977) tested stroke patients and found that those who had a visual field defect had a shorter immediate recall span on Corsi's test than patients without such a defect, regardless of hemisphere side of lesion. When a superspan criterion of span + 2 was used, again, patients with a visual field defect were more likely to fail (in 50 trials!) than the others. However, patients with visual field defects whose lesions were on the right failed at a ratio of 2:1 (13 failures, 7 successes), while those whose lesions were on the left failed at the lower ratio of less than 1:2 (6 failures, 14 successes).

Knox Cube Imitation Test. Corsi's Block-tapping test is a variant of the Knox Cube Imitation Test, one of the tests in the *Arthur Point Scale of Performance* battery (Arthur, 1947). The four blocks of the Knox Cube Test are affixed in a row on a strip of wood. Again, the examiner taps the cubes in prearranged sequences of increasing length and complexity, and the subject must try to imitate the tapping pattern exactly. Administration time runs from two to five minutes. Mean scores of a large general hospital population of middle-aged and elderly men tested twice on four different administrations of this test correlated significantly ($p < .01$) with the WAIS Digit Span, Arithmetic, Block Design, and Picture Arrangement tests, but less highly with Vocabulary (Sterne, 1966). The ease of administration and simplicity of the required response recommend this task for memory testing of patients with speech and motor disabilities and low stamina, and elderly or psychiatric patients (Inglis, 1957). Edith Kaplan has pointed out that the straight alignment of four blocks allows the patient to use a numerical system to aid recall so that there may be both verbal and nonverbal contributions to any given patient's responses on this test. Having demonstrated improved performance on the Knox Cube Test immediately following electroconvulsive shock therapy to the right hemisphere, Horan and his colleagues (1980) concluded that this test examines the sequential, time-dependent functions of the left hemisphere.

Learning logical and sequential order (Lhermitte and Signoret, 1972, 1976). A series of tasks was devised to aid in analyzing and differentiating conditions in which memory impairment is a prominent feature. In *Learning a place in space*, a square frame partitioned into nine smaller squares (or a card divided by lines into a 3 × 3 set of squares) is placed in front of the subject. Each of nine pictures of different objects (e.g., key, pear, rug, motorcycle) is placed in one of the squares for 5 seconds with instructions to "remember where each picture was placed," and then removed and the next picture—placed in some different part of the frame—is shown to the patient. When all nine pictures have been exposed in their predesignated places once, they are all shown again, one at a time, but in a different order, and the subject's task is to identify the square in which each had been placed originally. The examiner informs the subject when he is correct and corrects each error as soon as it is made. This procedure continues until the subject demonstrates learning for the spatial place-

454

ments by succeeding for three consecutive trials of nine pictures. If the subject continues to fail on the tenth trial, the examiner leaves each correct card in place, thus increasingly reducing likelihood of error on all subsequent items of that trial and providing a greater amount of information on each learning trial. This modified administration continues until three consecutive successes or the tenth of this second set of trials, at which point the test is discontinued. Three minutes after the first trial, and then at one hour, 24 hours, and four days later, three types of recall tests are given: (1) recall of which pictures went where by pointing and naming, using the empty frame without any pictures present; (2) recall by placing the pictures as they are given to the patient in the order of original presentation; and (3) recall by placing the pictures when all are handed together to the patient.

A control group of 20 subjects, ages 20 to 72, learned the place in space in one to four trials and made from six or seven to nine correct identifications of place with picture on the three kinds of recall tests at each of the time periods. Eleven patients with Korsakoff's psychosis learned this task relatively slowly and demonstrated learning on recall tests 2 and 3 at all four time periods. However most of the Korsakoff patients made no more than two correct associations between picture and place on the immediate recall trial of the uncued recall test (1), one of these patients made one correct uncued match after 24 hours, and all failed at four days without cuing. Three patients with bilateral hippocampal damage due to herpes encephalitis showed virtually no learning on this task by any means.

A second spatial learning test, *Learning a logical order*, used the same 3 × 3 square frame but presented stimuli in a logical arrangement such that each figure in the top horizontal row consisted of two triangles, three circles appeared in each figure in the middle horizontal row, and each square of the bottom row contained a square figure. The figures in each vertical row were of the same color and differed in color from the other two rows. Thus, the subjects had to learn only one color sequence that went from side to side and one shape sequence from top to bottom. Many subjects could identify the organization principle by the sixth item of the first trial. Only ten trials are given for this task if the subject has not already satisfied the criterion of three correct consecutive trials. The control subjects learned this pattern in one to six trials. Nine of 11 Korsakoff patients were unable to learn this task at all, yet two encephalitis patients learned it as rapidly as did the control subjects, and one took eight trials.

Learning a code also requires the subject to learn a principle, in this case the principle that governs the sequential arrangement of bead colors. The examiner begins by hiding a bead of specified color in his hand, asking the subject to guess which is the first color in the bead sequence, and then showing the palmed bead. At the beginning, therefore, the subject must make random guesses. Each learning series continues until the subject reaches the criterion of three consecutive correct sets of responses. Code patterns come in four lengths: (1) G (green) Y (yellow); (2) B (blue) R (red) R; (3) B Y R Y; and (4) G Y Y R G. Control subjects and all three encephalitis patients learned all code lengths in six or fewer repetitions, except for an unreported number of control subjects who took 12 repetitions to learn the longest code. Eight of the Korsakoff patients, in contrast, were unable to learn a code of any length.

MISCELLANEOUS RECALL TESTS OF VISUAL MEMORY

Memory subtests of the Stanford-Binet Scales.   The Binet scales contain two simple visual recall tasks suitable for very regressed patients, *Delayed Response* at age level II and *Naming Objects from Memory* at age level IV. The former involves a little cat figurine and three small boxes. On each of the three trials the examiner hides the cat under a different one of the three boxes, screens the boxes for a count of ten, and then invites the patient to point to the box hiding the cat. The latter test uses a box and nine different small objects, such as the cat, a thimble, and a spoon. On each of three trials, three of the objects are set out and named by (or named for) the patient, who then keeps his eyes closed while the examiner covers one of the three objects with the box. The patient's task is to recall which object is hidden. Two correct responses satisfy the passing standard for each of these tests.

At the XII year level of the Stanford-Binet, the patient must copy a nine-bead pattern made by stringing differently shaped wooden beads onto a shoestring. After the subject observes the examiner make the chain, it is exposed for five seconds more and then removed. The subject must replicate it in two minutes. This task proved relatively easy for the 13-year-old standardization group, since 70% of them passed it.

Cross or circle on a line (Posner task) (Milner, 1972, 1974).   Another nonverbal task failed by patients with significant loss of right or bilaterial hippocampal tissue but performed successfully by patients with similar left-sided lesions involves recall of a model drawing a cross on a line. In this test, the patient notes the position of a small circle on an eight-inch line or observes the examiner mark a cross on a line. The stimulus is removed, and the patient counts backward from ten or is engaged in some other distractor task (Squire and Slater, 1978). After a designated number of seconds the patient attempts to draw a circle or cross in the same relative position on the line as the model. Squire and Slater found this technique to be sensitive to the adverse effects of electroconvulsive therapy on retention.

7/24 (Barbizet and Cany, 1968).   This completely nonverbal memory task has the virtue of testing visuospatial recall without requiring either keen eyesight or good motor control. In the original version of this test, seven poker chips are randomly placed on a 6 × 4 checkerboard. Presentation is in 10-second units. After each 10-second exposure, the subject attempts to reproduce the original seven chip pattern with nine chips and an empty board. Learning trials are repeated until the subject masters the task or has exhausted 15 trials. After each trial, the examiner notes the number of correctly placed chips. On the first trial this number represents the immediate visual recall span. The total number of trials and the time taken to learn the task is also recorded. Retesting is conducted after five minutes, 30 minutes, and 24 hours. Patients who cannot learn 7/24 in 15 trials are tested a week later with five chips. If they fail this simpler task after 15 trials, the following week the test is repeated with three chips. Normal control subjects between the ages of 41 and 79 (average age of 58) recalled four chips correctly on the first trial. At five and 30 minutes, and at 24 hours, these subjects averaged a little over six correctly placed chips on the first trial.

In a rational modification of this test using the materials described above, five learning trials are given of an array of seven poker chips (Design A, see Fig. 14-7), each with a 10-second exposure (Rao et al., 1982). These are followed by a single learning trial, based on a different seven chip array (Design B). This sixth learning trial measures proactive interference and serves as a distractor for the first free recall of Design A, which is the next trial in the series. After 30 minutes of intervening tasks, a second—delayed—recall trial of Design A is given. The score is the number of correctly placed chips. In comparisons of a group of 35 relatively disabled MS patients with 18 control subjects of comparable age and education (see Table 14-10 for control group data), this technique differentiated the two groups on four of the five learning trials (trials 1, 2, 3, and 5) and on the first (immediate) recall trial. Fewer learning deficits were found for the MS group on a verbal learning test that seemed comparable in difficulty.

Chess figures (king, queen, five pawns) replaced poker chips in a study comparing learning and recall of patients with multiple sclerosis, and control subjects (Vowels, 1979). Control subjects took three to four trials to learn the positions compared to an average of six trials for the MS patients. The control subjects recalled the positions of six to seven of the figures at one and 24 hours, showing a small improving trend in

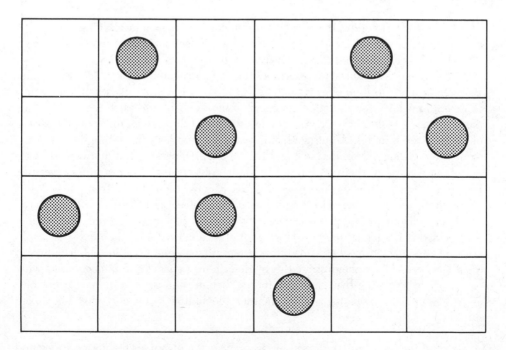

Fig. 14-7.   7/24, Design A. (After Rao et al., 1982)

457

Table 14-10 7/24: Control Group Data

Subjects	n		Age			Education
	18 (9M, 9F)		44.4 ± 10.7			13.9 ± 2.6

Learning Trials			Design A			Design B
	1	2	3	4	5	
	5.1	5.9	6.6	6.6	6.8	4.4

Recall Trials	Immediate	30-Minute Delay
	6.1	5.6

(Adapted from Rao et al., 1982)

their average recall from the first to the second recall trial. The MS patients, in contrast, recalled fewer figure positions than the control subjects at both one and 24 hours, thus losing a little ground at 24 hours rather than gaining. All comparisons between patients and controls were significant. This task may have a lower level of difficulty for experienced chess players who are accustomed to visualizing spatial relationships on the board.

Hidden objects.   Testing the patient's immediate memory and learning for spatial orientation and span of immediate memory by asking for recall of where and what objects have been hidden is an examination technique that has been used in the Binet (see p. 456) and in mental status examinations (e.g., Strub and Black, 1977). Strub and Black hide four common objects, such as a pen, keys, watch, or glasses, in the examining room while the patient observes, naming each object as it is hidden. The patient's task is to find or point out each hiding place following an interpolated period of at least ten minutes. Adults with unimpaired visual learning remember all four objects and hiding places. Barbizet and Duizabo (1980) also use familiar objects (e.g., pen, button, cork) in their version of the hidden objects test: The examiner gives the patient five objects to name and place in a box which is then hidden from view. After 15 minutes, the examiner asks the patient if these objects had been hidden, where, and to describe them. Recall is tested again at one and 24 hours. Barbizet and Duizabo point out that the technique of asking for immediate recall and then delayed recall at two subsequent times helps to differentiate among conditions in which memory disorders occur. They demonstrate this by describing a jovial *"grand alcoolique"* who found a bottle of wine that had been hidden behind him three minutes earlier, but after ten minutes more he recalled neither the hiding place nor what had been hidden.

A pictorial memory test (Butters et al., in press).   An ingenious technique for examining visual memory involves material from the *Make-A-Picture-Story* test (MAPS), a projective test developed for the assessment of children's personality disorders (Shneidman, 1952). Butters and his co-workers presented to their subjects a series of six pictures of different scenes (e.g., a living room) on which three cardboard cutout test figures (e.g., happy boy, angry man, dog), changed for each scene, were placed. This technique enables the examiner to compare performances for both recall (by asking subjects to select from 18 target and 15 distractor figures each set of three that had been shown with each of the six scenes) and recognition (by forced-choice, asking the subject to indicate which one of each of 15 pairs of figures had been presented with the pictures). This format also enables the examiner to study the subject's use of verbal mediators by comparing the strictly visual presentation with a visual presentation accompanied by a reading of a story about the scene. Using this technique, Butters and his group were able to demonstrate significant differences between recall and recognition for four patient groups (Alzheimer's disease, Huntington's disease, Korsakoff's disease, right hemisphere damaged) as all patient groups performed better than chance on the recognition test while recalling a significantly smaller number of figures than did normal control subjects. Moreover, the four patient groups displayed distinctive differences in both the number of figures recalled and the extent to which hearing a story improved their performance: the patients with right hemisphere damage and Huntington's disease both recalled relatively more figures than the Korsakoff and Alzheimer patients and benefited more from the accompanying verbal material than did the latter two patient groups.

Tests of Tactile Memory

TACTUAL PERFORMANCE TEST

Like the Knox Cubes, the material for this test, the *Seguin Formboard* came from the Arthur (1947) battery of tests (see Fig. 14-8). Although originally administered as a visuospatial performance task, Halstead (1947) converted it into a tactile memory test by blindfolding subjects and adding a drawing recall trial. Reitan incorporated Halstead's version of this test into the battery he recommends for neuropsychological testing (Reitan and Davison, 1974) (see pp. 562–563). Three trials are given in Halstead's administration, the first two with the preferred and nonpreferred hands, respectively, and the third with both hands. The score for each trial is the time to completion, which Halstead recorded to the nearest tenth of a minute. Their sum is the "Total Time" score.

On completion of the formboard trials, and only after the formboard has been concealed, the examiner removes the blindfold and instructs the subject to draw the board from memory, indicating the shapes and their placement relative to one another. The drawing trial gives two scores: The Memory score is the number of shapes reproduced with reasonable accuracy; the Location score is the total number of blocks placed in proper relationship to the other blocks and the board.

The cutting scores developed by Halstead have been retained by Reitan for predicting the likelihood of organic impairment (see Table 14-11). These cutting scores become questionable when applied to persons over the age of 40 (see p. 564) (Bak

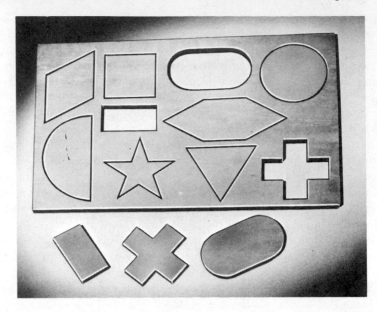

Fig. 14-8. One of the several available versions of the Seguin-Goddard Formboard used in the Tactual Performance Test. (Courtesy of the Stoelting Co.)

and Greene, 1980; Blusewicz et al., 1977; Cauthen, 1978). In a study of healthy retired teachers whose average age was 71.9, for example, Price and his co-workers (1979) found that the cutting scores for the Total Time score would place 88.9% of this group in the "impaired" category. Prigatano and Parson's (1976) study also found some significant age effects on Tactual Performance Test scores and, in one group of control subjects but not in a second group, a small correlation between the Total Time score and education.

Teuber and Weinstein (1954) administered this test somewhat differently than Halstead and Reitan. They gave only two trials to blindfolded subjects, one with the board in the usual position and one with the board rotated 180°. Like Halstead and Reitan, they followed the formboard task with a drawing recall, but scored only for memory,

Table 14-11 Tactual Performance Test Norms

	Total Time (minutes)	Memory	Localization
Average performance of normal subjects	10.56	8.17	5.92
Cutting Score	15.6	6	5

(From Halstead, 1947)

not for location. Performances of their frontal lobe injured patients were consistently superior to those of patients whose injuries involved other cortical areas (Teuber, 1964). The frontal lobe patients also recalled more forms on the drawing trial than any other group and the occipital lobe patients recalled the fewest.

Although there appears to be little doubt that markedly slowed or defective performances on the formboard test or the recall trial are generally associated with brain damage, the nature of the organic defect remains in dispute. Some investigators have found a right-left hemisphere differential favoring performance by patients with left hemisphere lesions (Reitan, 1964; Teuber and Weinstein, 1954). However, opposite results on the recall task, in which the left hemisphere damaged group tended to do a little worse than the right hemisphere group have also been reported (De Renzi, 1968). De Renzi attributed the better recall scores of right hemisphere patients to their access to verbal mediators. Halstead (1947), Reitan (1964), and Scherer and his colleagues (1957) consider this test to be particularly sensitive to frontal lobe lesions; yet Teuber and Weinstein's posterior brain injured patients performed least well and their anterior brain injured patients made the best scores of their three brain injured subgroups (1954; Teuber, 1964). Teuber notes that their findings are "not unreasonable, in view of the known symptomatology of parietal and temporal lesions. What is difficult to understand is that this formboard task should have been considered a test of frontal pathology at all" (1964, p. 421). That Reitan's significant anterior-posterior differences occurred between *right* frontal and *left* nonfrontal, and between *left* frontal and *right* nonfrontal groups—and not between groups of patients whose anterior and posterior lesions were on the same side—may account for the magnitude of his findings, but it still does not explain the contradiction between the relatively poor performance of his right frontal group and the relatively good performance of Teuber and Weinstein's patients whose lesions were similarly located.

The difference between the time taken on the preferred hand and that on the non-preferred hand trials may provide a clue as to the side of the lesion. Normally, if learning takes place, trial II takes a little less time than trial I even though it is performed with the nonpreferred hand, and trial III takes the least amount of time.

A fairly consistent pattern of dysfunction on this test has emerged in studies of chronic alcoholics (Fabian et al., 1981; Parsons and Farr, 1981). When administered in the Halstead-Reitan format, right-handed alcoholics tend to show the most slowing on the nonpreferred hand trial, significant slowing on the preferred hand trial, and an abnormally low Location score with a normal or near normal Memory score. This pattern was essentially the same for both men and women alcoholics, although women (both alcoholics and controls) tended to exceed men on the Memory score but do relatively poorer than their male counterparts on the Location task (Fabian et al., 1981).

Probably because of its inclusion in the popular Halstead-Reitan battery—and perhaps because this battery is so often administered by a technician rather than by the clinician responsible for deciding which tests to give—this test continues to enjoy wide usage despite several drawbacks. I consider one of these drawbacks so serious that I now use this test only under special circumstances such as a need to assess tactile

461

learning in a blind person. The chief clinical drawback is the enormous discomfort experienced by many patients when blindfolded, which, when added to their frustration in performing a trial that may take as many as ten or even more minutes for some to complete, creates a degree of psychological distress that does not warrant use of an instrument that may give very little new information in return. The other major drawbacks are the amount of time consumed in giving this test to older and brain injured patients, and the equivocal and often redundant nature of the data obtained. My experience has been that what one gets from this test is simply not worth the time and trouble.

De Renzi (1968, 1978) has always used a six-figure rather than the ten-figure formboard in his studies. It is possible that the smaller board reduces time sufficiently to make this test feasible for ordinary clinical use. Certainly the reduction in number of forms does not seem to have reduced the discriminating power of this technique for De Renzi.

OTHER TACTILE MEMORY TESTS

Four pieces of wire, each twisted into a distinctly different nonsense shape (see Fig. 14-9), comprise the material for a tactile test of immediate memory (Milner, 1971). The patients never see the wire figures. After several training trials on matching the figures with no time delay, matching follows an increasing delay length up to two minutes. During 30-second delay trials, a distractor task of copying match stick patterns was introduced (Milner and Taylor, 1972). Six out of seven commissurotomized patients performed better with their left than with their right hand, indicating that complex perceptual learning can take place without words and that it is mediated by the right hemisphere. Milner and Taylor (1972) found little difference between patients with unilaterial lesions and intact interhemispheric connections, and control subjects on this task. Both groups performed rapidly and virtually without errors except for a single error made by each of two left temporal lobectomy patients using their right hands. These findings suggest that even after delay with an intervening distractor task, this test may be too easy for patients whose lesions are as localized and circumscribed as temporal lobectomy patients.

Shaped wire has also been used in a paired recognition task in which pairs of wire

Fig. 14-9. Tactile nonsense figures (Milner, 1971). (©, 1971, Pergamon Press. Reprinted with permission)

patterns, placed in the palm of the blindfolded subject, are first learned, following which recognition for the learned pair is tested as a paired-associates task (V. Meyer and Falconer, 1960). Using simple geometric designs projecting above a block to test tactile discrimination learning of 36 patients with unilateral brain injuries, Ghent and her co-workers (1955) found that learning took place when the patient used the hand on the same side as the injury, but no learning occurred with the contralateral hand. A comparison of errors made on verbal (alphabet letters) and configural (four-line meaningless figures) forms of a tactile retention test using raised figures tacked to a board indicated that recognition of verbal figures (by matching for identity) following delay with a distractor task was much easier for all subjects than was the configural version of this test (Butters et al., 1973). Moreover, this technique demonstrated that Korsakoff patients had more difficulty learning in the tactile modality than did alcoholic patients or control subjects.

Memory Batteries

To provide a thorough coverage of the varieties of memory disabilities, batteries of memory tests have been developed or are in the making. By and large, the older batteries have only haphazard norms, and each has limitations in its scope and emphases such that none provides a suitably well-rounded and generally applicable means of examining the memory functions (see Erickson and Scott, 1977). A well-standardized battery that could provide an overall review of memory functions taking into account modality differences and all major aspects of the memory system without requiring much more than an hour would be most welcome. The memory review that I use (see pp. 414–415) in lieu of a formal battery lacks the standardization that assures reliability and that generates a scoring system with intertest equivalency. The ideal memory battery would be more extensive than intensive. When a review of memory systems indicates likely areas of impairment, the examiner can then undertake a more detailed assessment of deficits. Many times even a general review is not needed, for the problem areas requiring careful study are clearly apparent from observation or history.

Wechsler Memory Scale (WMS) (Stone et al., 1946; Wechsler, 1945)

The two forms of this test each contain seven subtests. The first two consist of questions common to most mental status examinations: *I Personal and Current Information* asks for age, date of birth, and identification of current and recent public officials (Who is president of the United States? Who was president before him?); and *II Orientation* has questions about time and place. *III Mental Control* tests automatisms (alphabet) and simple conceptual tracking (count by fours from 1 to 53). *IV Logical Memory* tests immediate recall of verbal ideas with two paragraphs (see pp. 436–437). *V Digit Span* differs from the WAIS Digit Span subtest by omitting the three-digit trial of Digits Forward and the two-digit trial of Digits Backward, and not giving score credits for performances of nine forward or eight backward. *VI Visual Reproduction* is an immediate visual memory drawing task (see p. 444). *VII Associate Learning* tests verbal retention (see p. 429).

All major studies of the Wechsler Memory Scale have dealt with form I. There are no useful norms or standardization data available for form II. One small study found that the Visual Reproduction subtest of form I was significantly more difficult than its form II counterpart, and that the Associative Learning subtest of form I was significantly easier than that of form II (Bloom, 1953). It would therefore appear likely that the two forms of the test can not be used interchangeably.

The Wechsler Memory Scale's normative population is relatively small (approximately 200) and is composed of an undisclosed number of age groups between the ages 20 and 50. Wechsler gives no information about the intellectual ability of the normative subjects. Its very restricted age range stops at the point where the greatest normal changes in memory function begin to take place and where the incidence of central nervous system abnormalities increases. This serious deficiency in normative data has been somewhat remedied by Hulicka (1966), who reported the average scores made by five groups of normal subjects at five different age levels (15–17, 30–39, 60–69, 70–79, and 80–89) for all of the subtests except II. Composite age norms for the three subtests of the WMS that measure immediate recall and learning—Associate Learning, Logical Memory, and Visual Reproduction—give an overview of how performance on these tests changes with age (see Table 14-12).

Besides its unsatisfactory age norms, this collection of subtests has other serious failings. Perhaps the greatest of these is its use of the Memory Quotient (MQ), a score based on the sum of the subtests which purportedly is a representative measure of

Table 14-12 Composite Norms for the Immediate Memory and Learning Subtests of the Wechsler Memory Scale

Age Range	20–29	30–39	40–49	60–69	70–79	80–92	20–69
Investigator	W[a]	H[b]	W	H	H	K[c]	I[d]
n	50	53	46	70	46	115	500
Associate Learning							
Mean	15.72	15.48	13.91	11.94	10.98	10.15	12.89
SD	2.81	3.48	3.12	4.53	4.78	3.80	3.93
Logical Memory							
Mean	9.28	7.99	8.09	7.34	7.35	5.72	7.77
SD	3.10	2.95	2.52	2.90	3.83	2.91	3.70
Visual Reproduction							
Mean	11.00	10.09	8.35	6.03	4.95	3.76	8.46
SD	2.73	3.01	3.17	3.72	3.42	2.70	3.25

[a]D. Wechsler, 1945.   [c]Klonoff and Kennedy, 1966.
[b]Hulicka, 1966.   [d]Ivison, 1977.

memory abilities. This procedure can be faulted on a number of counts, such as (1) the assumption that memory is a unidimensional function; (2) an overly inclusive concept of memory that incorporates personal orientation, verbal information, immediate verbal span, drawing competency, and mental tracking in a formula that is supposed to provide information about the status of the patient's memory functions; and (3) insensitivity to the patterns of deficit of the various memory functions associated with neurological and psychiatric conditions. This latter failing means that the MQ is useless for purposes of differential diagnosis (Bornstein, 1982). The battery is also of very questionable value as a screening technique (Erickson and Scott, 1977; Prigatano, 1977, 1978).

Other objections to this battery concern its limitations with respect to the kinds of memory functions it tests (e.g., see Erickson and Scott, 1977; E. W. Russell, 1975a, 1980a). Six of its seven subtests are verbal, and some aspects of the designs of the Visual Reproduction subtest are verbalizable so that it slights nonverbal memory functions and unduly penalizes persons with verbal impairments. In addition, the reliability of the Wechsler Memory Scale has been questioned on a number of counts, including the low internal consistency of subtests and the disparate difficulty levels between the subtests. Subtest intercorrelations are so low as to nullify the assumption that intact subjects will perform the various subtests at a sufficiently similar level that subtest deviations may predict brain pathology (J. C. Hall, 1957b). Furthermore, positive correlations between many of the subtests and tests of intellectual ability raise questions as to just what these subtests measure (Clément, 1966; Hulicka, 1966; Kear-Colwell, 1973).

Defects of Form II of this scale are even more serious. No data on its standardization are offered beyond the total score means and the mean differences between total scores on two administrations of the test given two weeks apart to three young adult student groups. Total score means for one of the three groups differed significantly, raising doubts about the reliability of Form II.

Despite its considerable psychometric defects, scores on the Wechsler Memory Scale subtests do tend to fall with advancing age and with memory disorders associated with bilateral, diffuse, and particularly with left hemisphere lesions (although it is relatively insensitive to memory disorders that occur with lesions localized on the right) (see Prigatano, 1978). Moreover, a consistent factor structure exists, comprised of three component factors: (I) immediate learning and recall; (II) attention and concentration; and (III) orientation and long-term information recall (Kear-Colwell, 1973; Skilbeck and Woods, 1980). Skilbeck and Woods report a fourth factor, "visual short-term memory," that appeared in the analysis of Wechsler Memory Scale performances by a group of elderly (54–88 years old) psychiatric patients in which both organic and functional diagnoses were represented. When subject to factor analysis in conjunction with WAIS subtest scores (Larrabee, Kane, and Schuck, 1983), the expected Learning/Memory factor (I) and an Attention/Concentration factor (II, which also comprised a WAIS A/C factor) emerged. However, rather than loading on factor I, the Visual Reproduction subtest showed a strong relationship with the Visual Organization (visuospatial) factor of the WAIS such that the Learning/Memory factor accounted for only 5% of the variance of Visual Reproduction while the Visual Organization factor accounted for 83%. This finding calls into question the usual interpretations of this subtest as a memory test.

Kear-Colwell (1973) recommends that interpretations of the Wechsler Memory Scale utilize factor scores as "more rational scales of measurement" than the subtest scores. Based on a stepwise multiple regression analysis, he developed the following formulae for converting subtest scores to factor scores:

> I = −0.27 + (0.25 × Logical Memory) + (0.19 × Visual Reproduction) + (0.21 × Associate Learning).
> II = −1.80 + (0.28 × Information) + (−.34 × Orientation) + (0.43 × Mental Control) + (0.45 × Digit Span).
> III = −9.68 + (0.78 × Information) + (2.34 × Orientation).

Although the Wechsler Memory Scale does not stand up well as a memory battery; the Associate Learning, Logical Memory, and Visual Reproduction subtests have proven to be useful in research as well as clinically (see, for example, pp. 179, 183, 471). When using them, however, the presently available norms given in Table 14-12 can only be regarded as advisory.

REVISED WECHSLER MEMORY SCALE (E. W. Russell, 1975a)

Dissatisfaction with the many weaknesses of the Wechsler Memory Scale prompted Russell to develop a new memory test using Logical Memory and Visual Reproduction, the two subtests that he identifies as measures of immediate recall which together provide a balanced assessment of verbal (Russell calls it "semantic") and configural (i.e., "figural") memory. Administration of each subtest follows the same procedures. Each test is first given as originally directed by Wechsler and then by a second recall trial following a half an hour later during which the subject takes "quite different" tests. This method produces two sets of three scores: one is the short-term memory score used in the original WMS; a second, calculated by the same criteria as the first, is the long-term score for the delayed recall trial; and the third score is a computation of "percent retained" (i.e., $\frac{Delayed\ Recall}{Immediate\ Recall} \times 100$). On the delay trials, the examiner is instructed to prompt the subject who denies any recall for either the stories or the designs. For stories, Russell suggests questions such as, "Do you remember a story about a washerwoman?" He also suggests verbal cuing for the "figural" subtest, e.g., "Do you remember a design that looks like flags?"

Reliability (measured by correlating the scores for the two stories and by correlating scores on two pairs of the four designs of the Visual Reproduction subtest) was .83 or higher for all scores except "figural percent retained." Adding a half-credit category to the scoring system for Logical Memory increased the interscorer reliability coefficient for both immediate and delayed trials from .83 and .88, respectively, to .97 and .96 (Power et al., 1979. See also p. 435f.). All six scores discriminated well between normal control subjects and a group of organic patients with a variety of diagnoses. Russell also found high correlations between these six scores and the Average Impairment score derived from the version of the Halstead-Reitan battery that he uses (E. W. Russell et al., 1970). A set of "scale scores", which range from 0 for best performance to 5 for most defective, was developed so that scores from the verbal and configural subtests could be compared. This comparison did distinguish between left and right lateralized lesions. The scale scores were then used to develop a "lateralization memory index" on which numbers above 5 indicate right impairment greater than left; below 5 the opposite holds. This index, too, discriminated between patients with right- and left-sided lesions when it was greater than 6 or less than 5. This scale also proved effective in discriminating between a group of dementia patients and and normal aging (55- to 85-year-old) control subjects matched for age, sex, and education (Logue and Wyrick, 1979). Significant differences between groups were present for all six scores. Both groups did less well on the Figural than on the Semantic tests, and both groups displayed a high degree of intragroup variability.

LEARNING TEST BATTERY (V. Meyer and Falconer, 1960)

Unlike the Wechsler Memory Scale, this one tests neither remote nor immediate recall, but focuses on retention of newly learned material. The subtests systematically differ in their input and output modalities to provide thorough coverage of modality-specific learning defects. There are seven tests in this battery: (1) the New Word Learning Test (see pp. 430–431), and six other learning tests in the paired associates format: (2) Auditory-Verbal Recall; (3) Auditory-Verbal Recognition; (4) Visual-Verbal Recognition; (5) Visual-Design Recognition; (6) Visual-Design Recall (a drawing test in which pictures of objects and designs are paired); and (7) Tactile Design Recognition (see pp. 462–463).

MEMORY TEST BATTERY (Cronholm and Molander, 1957; Cronholm and Ottoson, 1963)

A set of tests and testing patterns that provide a comparison between immediate recall and retention (with and without rehearsal) was developed to study the memory impairment and effects of psychiatric treatment of depressed patients. The battery has proven useful in demonstrating how levels of immediate and delayed recall may vary as a consequence of different disorders of the central nervous system (Erickson and Scott, 1977) and of depression, and how the immediate memory impairments often associated with depression may be relieved by medication (Sternberg and Jarvik, 1976). The battery consists of three sets of material—each with two equivalent forms, A and B—that the subject learns: (1) 15 word pairs with a low (under 1%) association value (the *15 word-pair test*); (2) 15 drawings of familiar objects (the *15 figure test*); and (3) three fictitious facts associated with each of three photographs of persons (the *9 personal data test*). Both the 15 word-pair test and the 9 personal data test require a recall response; on the 15 figure test, the patient must recognize the learned material when it appears in a larger picture with drawings of 15 other objects.

467

Testing with each set of material involves six steps: (1) The patient learns Form A. (2) The patient is immediately tested on Form A. (3) The patient then learns Form B. (4) He waits three hours. (5) The patient is tested on Form B. (6) The patient is tested on Form A. Obviously, this testing pattern can be applied to other learning tasks. The addition of a second learning trial, using the *savings* method (see below) adds a more sensitive test of retention for evaluating the patient's retrieval ability.

MEMORY TEST (Randt et al., 1980, no date)

This set of tests was "specifically designed for longitudinal studies" of patients with mild to moderate impairment of storage and retrieval functions. Randt and his co-workers anticipate that this instrument may be useful in investigating drug effects, particularly memory-enhancing drugs. Although this easy to administer test contains seven subtests (referred to as "modules"), it is brief, taking approximately 20 minutes. It has a set order of presentation in which acquisition and retrieval from storage are differentiated by separating immediate recall and recall following fixed tasks (a subsequent subtest serves as the distractor task for each one of the four subtests that have delayed recall trials). An interesting feature is the use of telephone interviews to obtain 24-hour recall data.

The Memory Test has five different forms for repeated examinations. The first and last modules (General Information and Incidental Learning) are identical in all forms. For patients with at least some ability to recall new experiences, Incidental Learning, which asks for recall of the names of the subtests, cannot remain a test of "incidental learning" for more than one or two repeated administrations of the test. Each form of the other five modules has been equated on the basis of such relevant characteristics as word length, frequency, and imagery levels. Thus, each form appears to be quite similar though no reliability studies are available yet. The middle five modules test recall of five words, of digits forward and backward, of word pairs, and of a paragraph, and also include a module testing recognition of line drawings of common objects. Scores between subtests are not comparable.

Excepting General Information, at least one trial of each subtest module has demonstrated sensitivity to the effects of aging or to the memory impairments of a group of patients with memory complaints of one or more years' duration. However, this highly verbal test cannot qualify for general use in neuropsychological assessment since it necessarily penalizes patients with language disorders and would probably be relatively insensitive to memory impairments involving nonverbal (e.g., configural, spatial) material. Thus its usefulness in evaluating memory dysfunction appears to be limited to conditions associated with aging and diffuse brain diseases.

Special Memory Problems

In trying to define the nature of a memory defect, the examiner may wish to explore several aspects of learning and memory that are not covered in the usual neuropsy-

468

chological examination. These include very long term (i.e., remote) memory, the rate of forgetting, differentiation of storage and retrieval problems, and input and output modality differences studied by parallel techniques. Most tests that explore these problems have been developed through use with hospitalized patients. Many of them are not adaptable to general clinical use because they either take an impracticable amount of time to administer or require many hourly or daily repetitions on a schedule that is virtually impossible for the clinical practitioner to maintain, particularly when working with outpatients. However, innovative practitioners will be able to modify these tests to conform with the demands of an active practice and the needs of the patients.

Remote Memory

The need to assess very long term memory generally arises only when retrograde amnesia is present and the examiner wants to know how far back it extends. Thus, testing for the integrity of remote memory usually concerns persons of advanced age, those with brain conditions that result in retrograde amnesia, such as Korsakoff's disease, and those with memory problems incurred in special circumstances, such as treatment with electroconvulsive therapy (ECT). Several approaches to the problem of measuring retrograde amnesia involve recall or recognition of information that is commonly held. Unfortunately, in using test items that range from recent to remote topics, an instrument developed to assess gradients of long-term memory must be constantly updated or it will soon become obsolete. This precludes the development of a really well-standardized test of remote memory because of the impossibility of going through elaborate standardization procedures every few years. Bahrick and Karis (1982) describe methods for assessing remote memory (what they call "long-term ecological memory") and discuss some of the attendant methodological problems.

TESTS OF RECALL OF PUBLIC EVENTS

Recall and recognition of public events were investigated in Great Britain by Warrington and Silberstein (1970) who examined the usefulness of both a recall and a multiple-choice questionnaire for assessing memory of events that had occurred in the previous year. Subjects took this test three times at six-month intervals. This technique showed that both age and the passage of a year's time affected recall and recognition of once-known information, and that recall was much more sensitive to age and time effects than was recognition. This method was then extended over longer periods of time with the development of a multiple-choice questionnaire covering events for the four preceding decades selected to give even coverage over the 40-year span (Warrington and Sanders, 1971). A companion test of "well-known" faces covering the previous (approximately) 25 years was also developed in both free recall and multiple-choice versions. With long periods of time, both recognition and recall techniques registered significant decrements for age and the passage of time.

A public events questionnaire covering a slightly larger time span (1930–1972) was developed in the United States, also to assess the effects of aging on remote memory (Squire, 1974). Using a multiple-choice instrument, Squire found that the amount retained decreased with age for all time periods but there was no time gradient.

Sanders (1972) and later, Squire (1974), questioned the interpretation of the data from remote memory studies since some of the material may have been relearned years after the event (when presented in an article, a book, or a television program, for example). Sanders also wondered how even-handed this examination technique was since the amount of interest in events such as the death of a prime minister of another country or in personalities such as politicians or movie stars, varies so greatly from person to person. Scores on a test of familiarity with television program titles, for example, were positively related to the amount of time the subjects watched television (Harvey and Crovitz, 1979). Squire also speculated about the role played by intellectual capacity and questioned whether these tests may simply be measuring learning ability.

FAMOUS PEOPLE TESTS

M. S. Albert and her colleagues (1979a, b; 1981a, b; Butters and Albert, 1982), as part of their studies of memory disorder in Korsakoff's disease, have developed tests invoking recall or recognition of famous people. *Facial Recognition Test* consists of approximately 25 photographs of persons who achieved fame in each of six decades (1920s to 1970s), making a total of 180 pictures presented as a recognition test. Twenty-nine photographs from the Facial Recognition Test, taken when the subjects were young, were paired with photographs of these same people who were still famous when they were old (e.g., Charlie Chaplin) and presented in randomized order to make up the *Old-Young Test*. In addition, two questionnaires about famous people from these decades were constructed, one testing recall, the other recognition. The patients with Korsakoff's disease averaged almost 60 years of age and 12 years of education. Control subjects were matched on these variables. This latter group did not show a gradient of loss of information with the passage of time. On most analyses of the data from these tests, the patients showed a marked gradient, from low scores for recent material to scores approaching normal for material from early decades. When this set of tests was given to patients with Huntington's disease and to senile dementia patients, most of whom had been diagnosed within two years of testing, no temporal gradient was found for either of the patient groups, as both sets of patients performed poorly on material from all decades. However, both patients with Alzheimer's disease and controls recognized photographs of familiar faces taken when the person was old more readily than those taken earlier (Wilson, Kaszniak, and Fox, 1981).

TESTS OF TELEVISION TITLES

A multiple-choice test format consisting of 32 questions about titles of television shows that appeared for one season of an eight-year period was used by Levin and his co-workers (1977) to examine memory deficits in a group of mixed brain damaged patients. The patients consistently displayed poorer recognition than control subjects, but no regular gradient appeared with the passage of time for either group. Squire and Slater (1975) used an 80-item multiple-choice questionnaire about one-season TV shows that appeared during a 15-year period. Over the longer time period covered by this questionnaire, a time gradient was found for a group of 17 adults ranging in age from 26 to 71. When used to study the effects of ECT on remote memory, this technique demonstrated a prominent retrograde amnesia that extended back for two to three years but no further, and generally cleared up within six months after treatment.

Forgetting

Forgetting curves require repetition over time. Most techniques for measuring retention can be used to examine forgetting by adding recall or recognition trials spaced over time. Talland (1965) used the delayed recall format, for example, with recall trials of hours, days, and up to a week to establish forgetting curves for many different kinds of material.

The *savings* method provides an indirect means of measuring the amount of material retained after it has been learned. This method involves teaching the patient the same material on two or more occasions, which are usually separated by days or weeks but the second learning trial may come as soon as 30 minutes after the first. The number of trials the patient takes to reach criterion is counted each time. Reductions in the number of trials needed for criterion learning (the "savings") at a later session is interpreted as indicating retention from the previous set of learning trials. Ingham (1952) devised a formula for expressing savings based on the proportion of relearning to learning trials: $10 \left(\dfrac{N_1 - N_2}{N_1} \right) + 5$, where $N_1 =$ the number of repetitions needed to learn the material completely, and $N_2 =$ the number of repetitions required to relearn it completely at a later time. Ingham added the constant to make all scores positive in case N_2 is greater than N_1.

Warrington and Weiskrantz (1968) demonstrated some retention in severely amnesic patients over one- and four-week intervals by using the savings method with both verbal and nonverbal material. No other method they used gave evidence that these patients had retained any material from the initial exposure to the tests. Lewinsohn and his co-workers (1977), using the savings method, looked at both the number of trials to correct recall up to ten trials and the number correct on the first recall trial to examine the effects of imagery training after 30 minutes and again after one week. With this method they could show that the effects of imagery training lasted 30 minutes but not a week among both brain injured patients and control subjects.

The scores devised by Brooks (1972) and by Snow (1979) to document the relative amount of information lost between the various trials of the Complex Figure Test can be applied to other tests as well (see p. 447). Brooks demonstrated this by using his "% Forgetting" score to compare performances on immediate and and delayed trials of the Logical Memory and Associate Learning subtests of the Wechsler Memory Scale.

471

INVENTORY OF MEMORY EXPERIENCES (IME) (Herrmann and Neisser, 1978)

Recall of both remote and recent personal experiences are examined by this inventory. Forty-eight questions (Part F) have to do with how often one forgets personal day-to-day events and details. Examples of items in this section are, "How often are you unable to find something that you put down only a few minutes before?" or "When you want to remember an experience, a joke, or a story, how often do you find that you can't do so?" Part R consists of 24 questions of remote memory such as, "Do you remember any toys you had as a young child?" and "Do you remember the first time you earned any money yourself?" Each of these questions are accompanied by a follow-up question that asks, "How well do you remember . . .?" All 72 questions are answered on a 7-point scale that ranges from "not at all" to "perfectly."

Data on this inventory come from a study using college students. Eight factors emerged when the scores for Part F were factor analyzed: (1) rote memory (e.g., telephone numbers); (2) absent-mindedness; (3) names; (4) people; (5) conversations (e.g., forgetting jokes, conversations); (6) errands (e.g., forgetting lists of chores); (7) retrieval (i.e., inability to account for a sense that something is familiar); and (8) places (i.e., forgetting the location of something). The college students' greatest problems were with rote memory and names, while they remembered people and conversations best. On Part R, women recalled memories having to do with early childhood a little better than men. Response patterns having to do with other aspects of long-term memories were not well differentiated. Whether different patterns of forgetting will be found in older groups or for patients with brain damage remains to be seen. However, the possibility of discovering such differences and the advantages of being able to use the same format for making comparisons between recall of recent and of remote memories should make this an attractive instrument for neuropsychological investigators. Herrman (1982) reviews similar questionnaires.

Differentiation of Storage and Retrieval

The amount of material a person recalls depends upon both the amount of information he has stored and the efficiency of his retrieval processes. Direct evaluation of the relative contributions of storage and retrieval to what is recalled is not possible. However, there are ways to differentiate between these two functions.

One method of evaluating the relative efficiency of a patient's storage and retrieval capacities compares performance on a test requiring the patient to *recall* the answers with performance on a multiple-choice test, comparable to the first in difficulty level and content, in which the patient need only *recognize* the correct answer. This comparison has been made systematically in several studies of remote memory (see pp. 469–470 and Botwinick, 1978). Vocabulary tests are useful for making this comparison; for example, the patient's performance on the WAIS or Stanford-Binet Vocabulary subtest (both recall tests) can be compared with his performance on the Vocabulary subtest of the Gates-MacGinitie Reading Test or the SCAT (both multiple-choice recognition tests). A score on the paper and pencil test that is very much higher

472

than the score on the orally administered test suggests a retrieval problem. When the score of the orally administered test is notably higher than that on the paper and pencil test, the patient's capacity for self-direction or independence may be compromised.

Another method for differentiating storage and retrieval is to compare recall with savings, inasmuch as the method of savings measures storage indirectly. If the memory impairment is due to retention problems, then recall will be down and there will be little savings on later learning trials. If the problem is one of retrieval, recall will be down, but relearning at a later time will occur rapidly, indicating that the material had been stored.

A number of techniques using cues to facilitate recall have been developed that also allow the examiner to evaluate the efficiency of free recall. Butters and his colleagues (1976) compared patients with Huntington's disease and patients with Korsakoff's disease on serial word list learning. Category cues (e.g., vegetables, tools) aided neither of these patients groups. However, cuing by category improves word recall of normal subjects (Baddeley, 1976; Tulving and Pearlstone, 1966). In M. William's *delayed recall test* (1978, 1979), the subject is shown a card with line drawings of nine familiar objects to name and instructions to remember them for later recall. Free recall is obtained after 8–10 minutes of vocabulary or other verbal testing. Items not recalled are each prompted by a cue that may refer to the object's category, its use, its usual location, etc. Using a scoring system that gives a penalty when cues are needed and a greater penalty when even cuing does not aid recall, Williams showed a significantly greater dependence on cues by psychiatric and neurological patients than by control subjects.

When evaluating performance on tests of retention, the examiner also needs to take special care to differentiate poor performance due to structural damage or dysfunction involving one or another of the memory subsystems from defective performance on recall tasks by patients with frontal lobe or certain kinds of subcortical damage. The latter may be patients who register the stimulus material but lack the spontaneity or drive to reproduce more than a bit of what they remember, if that. When absence of initiating activity, lack of spontaneity, or apathy suggests that the patient may be suffering from defective drive or motivational capacity, the examiner should press for additional responses. With story material, for example, I may ask such questions as, "How did it begin?" "What was the story about?" "Who were the characters in the story?" or, if the patient repeats only an item or two, "What happened next?" When the task involves reproduction of configural material, the patient can be encouraged with, "That's fine; keep going," or by being asked, "What more do you remember?"

THE METHODS OF SELECTIVE REMINDING AND RESTRICTED REMINDING (Buschke and Fuld, 1974; Fuld, 1975)

The differentiation of retention, storage, and retrieval can be facilitated by the methods of selective reminding and restricted reminding. In selective reminding, the subject recalls as many words as he can in any order from a list just read to him. After each trial, the examiner repeats all the words the patient omitted in that trial. The reminding and the recall trials continue until the patient recites the whole list. This technique tends to facilitate learning by focusing attention on unlearned items only. Normal subjects typically recall ten of ten-word lists of animals or articles of clothing by the third trial, all ten without any immediately prior prompting on the fourth trial (Buschke and Fuld, 1974).

Using this technique, Levin, Grossman, and their colleagues (1979) were able to differentiate the efficiency with which patients who had sustained head trauma of varying degrees of severity learned a list of 12 high frequency words. They used four measures: "long-term storage" (the number of words recalled in each of 12 trials); "total long-term storage" (the sum of words in storage across trials); "consistent long-term retrieval (from storage)" (the number of words recalled in any given trial that were recalled on all subsequent trials without reminding); and "total consistent long-term retrieval" (of course, the sum of the latter scores). It is interesting to note that on long-term storage, only the seriously damaged group did not continue to show improvement across all 12 trials, but leveled off (with an average recall of approximately six words) at the sixth trial. The mildly impaired group achieved near-perfect scores on the last two trials and the moderately impaired group maintained about a one-word-per-trial lag behind them throughout. However, the moderately impaired group showed a much less consistent retrieval pattern than the mildly impaired group.

In restricted reminding, following the first reading of the word list, the examiner again repeats those words the subject did not recall and tells him to recall as many words as he can. All subsequent reminding is limited to words not recalled on any trial. Recall trials and reminding continue until he has named each word at least once. Thus, the first recall tests immediate retention span. Spontaneous recall is demonstrated each time he recalls a word he had previously named. Retrieval problems become evident when a once-named word is recalled only sporadically thereafter. Once all words have been named, the stability of storage can be tested by the method of *extended recall* in which the patient is given 12 more recall trials without any further reminding. The patient's response can be evaluated for the number of items recalled and the consistency with which items are recalled. With a 20-word list of animal names, normal control subjects named an average of 16 items on extended recall and tended to recall items consistently once they were named during the extended recall trials (Fuld, 1975).

Buschke and Fuld have done most of their work with lists of words taken from a single category such as animals or clothing. Erickson and Scott's (1977) questioning of this procedure as inviting guessing has been borne out in my experience using categorically restricted lists. Moreover, when using such a list, it is often difficult to know when a subject is guessing, unlike the situation when one is using a categorically open list and guesses stand out like crows in snow.

15
Conceptual Functions

Unlike receptive or expressive defects, conceptual dysfunctions are not necessarily associated with injury to a particular cortical area but tend to be sensitive to the effects of brain injury regardless of site (Luria, 1966; Yacorzynski, 1965). This is not surprising since conceptual activities always involve at least (1) an intact system for organizing perceptions even though specific perceptual modalities may be impaired; (2) a well-stocked and readily available store of remembered learned material; (3) the integrity of the cortical and subcortical interconnections and interaction patterns that underlie "thought"; and (4) the capacity to process two or more mental events at a time. In addition, the translation of cognitive activity into overt behavior requires (5) a response modality sufficiently integrated with central cortical activity to transform conceptual experience into manifest behavior; and (6) a well-functioning response feedback system for continuous monitoring and modulation of output.

Concrete thinking is the most common sign of impaired conceptual functions. It usually appears as an inability to think abstractly. The patient may have difficulty forming concepts, using categories, generalizing from a single instance, or applying procedural rules and general principles, be they rules of grammar or conduct, mathematical operations, or good housekeeping practices. Loss of the abstract attitude often results in a preference for obvious, superficial solutions. The patient may be unaware of subtle underlying or intrinsic aspects of a problem and thereby be unable to distinguish what is relevant from what is irrelevant, essential from unessential, and appropriate from outlandish. To the extent that the patient cannot conceptualize abstractly, each event is dealt with as if it were novel, an isolated experience with a unique set of rules.

Conceptual concreteness and mental inflexibility are sometimes treated as different aspects of the same disability. When they occur together, they tend to be mutually reinforcing in their effects. However, they can be separated. Although both are associated with extensive or diffuse damage, significant conceptual inflexibility can be present without much impairment of the ability to form and apply abstract concepts, particularly when there is frontal lobe involvement (Zangwill, 1966). Furthermore,

475

conceptual concreteness does not imply impairment of specific reasoning abilities. Thinking may be concrete even when the patient can perform many specific reasoning tasks well, such as solving arithmetic problems or making practical judgments. On the other hand, thinking is likely to be concrete when the patient has specific reasoning disabilities.

Most tests of conceptual functions are designed to probe for concrete thinking in one form or another, usually testing concept formation by itself or in conjunction with mental flexibility. Tests of other cognitive functions, such as planning and organizing, or problem solving and reasoning, do not treat concrete thinking as the primary examination object, but they often supply information about it. Tests that deal with mental flexibility per se are discussed later (see pp. 518–523).

Tests of Concept Formation

Tests of concept formation differ from most other mental tests in that they focus on the *quality* or *process* of thinking more than the content of the response. Many of these tests have no "right" or "wrong" answers. Their scores stand for qualitative judgments of the extent to which the response was abstract or concrete, complex or simple, apt or irrelevant. Tests with right and wrong answers belong in the category of tests of abstract conceptualization to the extent that they provide information about *how* the patient thinks.

Patients with moderate to severe brain damage or with a diffuse injury tend to do poorly on all tests of abstract thinking, regardless of their mode of presentation or channel of response. However, patients with mild, modality specific, or subtle organic defects may not engage in concrete thinking generally, but only on those tasks that directly involve an impaired modality, are highly complex, or touch upon emotionally arousing matters. Furthermore, concretism takes different forms with different patients, and varies in its effect on mental efficiency with the type of task. The examiner who is interested in finding out how his patient thinks will use more than one kind of concept formation test involving more than one sensory or response modality.

Proverbs

Tests of interpretation of proverbs are among the most widely used techniques for evaluating the quality of thinking. The Wechsler tests, the Stanford-Binet scales, and the mental status examination include proverb interpretation items. Their popularity rests on their usefulness in indicating where the patient's thinking lies on an abstract-concrete dimension. Further, all but mentally defective patients and those with serious communication disabilities can make some response without a great deal of effort or loss of dignity.

Although it is assumed that the abstract-concrete dimension is a continuum, interpretations of proverbs are usually evaluated dichotomously, as either abstract or concrete. The commonly used three-point scoring system preserves this dichotomy (e.g.,

Bromley, 1957; Gorham, 1956; Wechsler, 1955, 1981). It is also implicit in informal evaluations of patients' responses in mental status examinations. In this system, appropriate abstract interpretations earn two points (e.g., *A rolling stone gathers no moss:* "You will have nothing if you keep on moving"); concrete interpretations earn one point (e.g., "Most turning objects never gather anything" or "Because of moss will fall off"), or no points if the response misses the gist of the proverb or misinterprets it (e.g., "If you keep busy you will feel better"). Usually this scoring system creates no problems, but occasionally patients' interpretations will be borderline or difficult to classify.

THE PROVERBS TEST (Gorham, 1956)

This test formalizes the task of proverb interpretation, presenting it as an important source of information about the quality of thinking in its own right rather than as a part of another examination. Its standardization reduces variations in administration and scoring biases and provides norms that take into account the difficulty level of individual proverbs. The Proverbs Test has three forms, each containing 12 proverbs of equivalent difficulty. It is administered as a written test in which the subject is instructed to "tell what the proverb *means* rather than just tell more about it." The three-point scoring system is used. Mean scores for each form of the test do not differ significantly. A multiple-choice version of the Proverbs Test (the Best Answer Form) contains 40 items, each with four choices of possible answers. Only one of the choices is appropriate and abstract; the other three are either concrete interpretations or common misinterpretations.

Proverbs Test scores vary with education level (and probably social class) (Gorham, 1956). Using the multiple-choice version in a study of frontal lobe functions, Benton (1968a) reported very poor performance by seven patients with bilateral frontal lobe disease (mean = 11.4 ± 6.1), a somewhat better performance by eight patients with right frontal lobe disease (mean = 20.1 ± 6.8), and unexpectedly adequate scores achieved by ten patients with left frontal lobe disease (mean = 26.4 ± 9.4). On the multiple-choice form of the Proverbs Test, the scores of groups of schizophrenic and organic patients are significantly lower than those of normal control subjects, but they do not differ significantly among one another (Fogel, 1965).

Bromley (1957) used both a multiple choice and a "creative response" form of the proverb interpretation technique to compare quantitative aspects of the thinking of healthy persons in different age groups ranging from the 20s to the 70s. A pronounced tendency for the relative number of concrete responses to increase with age was demonstrated on both test formats.

Word Usage Tests

Tests calling for abstract comparisons between two or more words provide a sensitive measure of concrete thinking. However, word usage is also very dependent upon both the integrity of the patient's communication system and the level of his verbal skills.

Thus, patients who have even a mild aphasic disorder and those who have always been intellectually dull or educationally underprivileged will do poorly on these tests, regardless of the extent to which their cognitive functions have been preserved.

When ability to form verbal concepts is evaluated, the patient's verbal skill level must always be taken into account. Easy items (such as those through age level XII on the Binet) can be used with most adults who have completed the sixth grade. Difficult items may elicit evidence of cognitive dysfunction in bright, well-educated adults when their performance on easier words would seem to indicate that their ability to make verbal abstractions is intact.

THE ABSTRACT WORDS TEST (Tow, 1955)

As in the Similarities subtest of the WAIS, this test calls for comparisons between two words. However, instead of giving likenesses, the subject must tell how two words differ from one another, which is usually a simpler task (see Table 15-1). This test is part of a battery given pre- and postoperatively to evaluate the effects of psychosurgery (frontal leucotomy) on intellectual functioning. The patients scored significantly lower on this test after surgery.

LURIA'S METHODS FOR EXAMINING CONCEPT FORMATION (Luria, 1966; Christensen, 1979)

Luria used a number of tasks involving words to examine conceptual thinking. In addition to questions about similarities and differences between verbal concepts, he gave subjects tasks of identifying "logical relationships." These relationships include general categories for specific ideas (e.g., "tool" for "chisel"), specific ideas for general categories (e.g., "rose" for "flower"), parts of a whole (e.g., "leg" of a "table"), and the whole from a part (e.g., "house" from "wall"). Luria also asked subjects to give opposites (e.g., "healthy—*sick*"), to find analogies (e.g., "table : leg :: bicycle :

Table 15-1 Abstract Word Test: Word List

Instructions: What is the difference between _____ and _____ ?

1.	MISTAKE	and	LIE
2.	THRIFT	and	AVARICE
3.	MURDER	and	MANSLAUGHTER
4.	LAZINESS	and	IDLENESS
5.	COURAGE	and	BOLDNESS
6.	POVERTY	and	MISERY
7.	ABUNDANCE	and	EXCESS
8.	TREACHERY	and	DECEIT
9.	CHARACTER	and	REPUTATION
10.	EVOLUTION	and	REVOLUTION

(From Tow, 1955)

wheel"), and to identify "the superfluous fourth" word of a series in which three words are similar and one is different (e.g., "spade, saw, ax, *log*"). Luria did not give many examples of each category of concept formation problems, nor does Christensen. However, it would not be difficult for the examiner interested in using this approach to make up a series of items for these tasks. More extensive samples of similar items are represented in the Stanford-Binet scales (see next section) where they also have the advantage of age norms.

STANFORD-BINET SUBTESTS (Terman and Merrill, 1973)

The Stanford-Binet scales test verbal abstraction in a number of ways. All of the Binet items are scored on a pass-fail basis. Unlike Wechsler's and Gorham's three-point scoring system, both concrete interpretations and misinterpretations of words and proverbs receive no credit.

There are three *Similarities* subtests: *Two Things* at age level VII contains such questions as, "In what way are *wood* and *coal* alike?" *Three Things* at age level XI is identical with the lower level similarities test except that likenesses have to be found for three words, i.e., "In what way are *book, teacher,* and *newspaper* alike?" *Essential Similarities* at the SA I level is a two-word similarities test requiring a high level of abstraction for credit.

There are also three *Differences* subtests in the Binet. At age VI, *Differences* consists of three items asking for the differences between two words with fairly concrete referents, i.e., "What is the difference between a *bird* and a *dog*?" *Differences between Abstract Words* at the AA level and *Essential Differences* at levels AA and SA II both ask for the differences between two abstract words. The only difference between these two subtests, besides the content of the word pairs, is the insertion of the word "principal" in the question, "What is the (principal) difference between . . .?" on the Essential Differences subtest.

There are three *Similarities and Differences* subtests on the Binet. The simplest, *Pictorial Similarities and Differences I* at age level IV-6 presents six pictures, each with four figures, of which three are alike and one different (e.g., three crosses and a dash); the subject's task is to point to the one unlike figure. At year V, *Pictorial Similarities and Differences II* consists of 12 cards, each containing two figures that are either the same (e.g., two trees) or different (e.g., a circle and a square); the subject must tell whether the figures are the same or different. At year VIII, *Similarities and Differences* is completely verbal; the subject has to tell how two familiar objects, such as a *baseball* and an *orange*, are alike and how they differ.

In addition to the word comparison subtests, the Binet scales contain three subtests asking for definitions of *Abstract Words*, with scoring standards for years X and XII *(Abstract Words I)*, XI and XIII *(Abstract Words II)*, and the AA level *(Abstract Words III)*. Word difficulty ranges from words of emotion such as "pity" at the X and XII year levels to words like "generosity" and "authority." The definitions too are scored on a two-point pass-fail basis.

Opposite Analogies is another form of word abstraction test. The Binet scales carry it in five versions spread over six age and ability levels from age level IV ("Brother is a boy; sister is a _____") to SA III ("Ability is native; education is _____").

THE CATEGORY TEST (Halstead, 1947; E. W. Russell et al., 1970; Swiercinsky, 1978)

In this test of abstracting ability, the stimulus figures making up the 208 items are projected on a screen (see Fig. 15-1). Six sets of items, each organized on the basis of different principles, are followed by a seventh set made up of previously shown items. For example, the first set shows roman numerals from I to IV, guiding the subject to the use of the four answer keys. In the third set, one of the four figures of each item differs from the others (e.g., three squares and a circle). The fifth set shows geometric figures made up of solid and dotted lines for which the proportion in solid lines is the correct answer (e.g., *one*-fourth, *two*-fourths, etc.). The seventh set tests the subject's recall. The subject's task is to figure out the principle presented in each set and signal the answer by pressing the appropriate key on a simple keyboard. A pleasant chime rewards correct answers; errors receive a buzz. The score is the number of errors.

When using the cutoff score (50–51) recommended by Reitan (undated) and derived from Halstead's small and relatively young normative sample (see p. 564), this test discriminates well between brain damaged and neurologically intact groups

Fig. 15-1. The Category Test in use.

of younger patients (De Wolfe et al., 1971; Shaw, 1966; Spreen and Benton, 1965). However, its sensitivity to aging shows up in higher error scores beginning in the 40s (Lewinsohn, 1973; Pauker, 1977) and increasing with each succeeding decade (Harley et al., 1980). Significant education effects have also been reported (Pauker, 1977; Prigatano and Parsons, 1976).

Along with measuring abstract concept formation (Pendleton and Heaton, 1982) and ability to maintain attention to a lengthy task, this test has a visuospatial component, correlating most highly with the Block Design and Picture Arrangement subtests of the WAIS (Lansdell and Donnelly, 1977). Boll (1981) notes that the test is also "a learning experiment" that requires learning skills for effective performance.

Variations of the Category Test. In its standard form, the Category Test has a number of practical drawbacks. It is very time-consuming, taking many normal control subjects the better part of an hour. Brain damaged patients may require as much as two hours to complete it. The equipment is too bulky to be portable and is costly. A number of workers have attempted to remedy these defects.

A 108-item short form of the Category Test uses just the first four sets of the test (Calsyn et al., 1980). Correlations of error scores of the Category Test and this abbreviated version were .89 and .88 respectively, suggesting that subtests V and VI add little to the value of this test. In a cross-validation study, correlations between the total score estimate based on the score of the first four subtests and the total score of the standard test ranged from .83 to .88, further supporting use of this abbreviated format (Golden, Kuperman et al., 1981). In order to evaluate performance on the abbreviated Category Test according to the accustomed norms, the error score can be converted by multiplying it by 1.4 and adding 15.

Dropping the last items from subtests II to V and all of subtests VI and VII resulted in a 120-item short form (Gregory et al., 1979). A single study reported a correlation between the long and short forms of .95. The short form's cutoff score of 35 errors classified three of 80 subjects differently than did the long form and its cutoff score of 51 errors. However, in two of these cases, the short form made the correct classification.

Two paper and pencil forms of the Category Test have recently been developed. R. L. Adams and Trenton (1981) have reproduced the stimulus figures on 3 × 5-in. cards presented in seven booklets, one for each set. The answer sheet is chemically treated so that when a chemically treated pen is used, marks that are made on the correct answer place turn red, incorrect responses turn green, providing a colorful substitute for the chimes and buzzes of the original format. Split-half correlations between the two forms of the test produced correlations in a similar range to reliability coefficients for the test in its original form. DeFilippis and his colleagues (1979) also present the test material in booklet form, preserving the appearance of the slides as much as possible. The stimulus material is presented in two letter-size notebooks. At the bottom of each, the numbers 1 through 4 are mounted so that the subject can point to each answer. The test is individually administered by an examiner who records the answer and informs the subject whether the response was "correct" or "incorrect." Performances of both normal and control subjects and alcoholics on the mechanically administered and paper and pencil forms of this test correlated highly (.913 for controls, .804 for alcoholics). Both of these groups, tended to make fewer errors on the booklet version, but this difference was not significant. Moreover, the booklet version discriminated effectively between the control subjects and the alcoholic group.

S. D. Kimura (1981) has redrawn the Category Test stimulus figures onto 10 × 15 cm cards. The examiner exposes and turns the cards while keeping a record of the patient's verbalized responses. Correlations between this and the traditional slide-projector format run in the same range as test-retest correlations for the traditional presentation.

Symbol Pattern Tests

Deductive reasoning combines with ability for conceptual sequencing in symbol pattern tests, exemplified by the Thurstones' *Reasoning Tests* in the *Primary Mental Abilities* (PMA) battery (1962) or their *American Council on Education Psychological Examination* (ACE) (1953, 1954). These tests are composed of such number or letter patterns as 1-2-4-2-4-8-3- — or A-B-D-C-E-F-H- —. The subject must indicate, usually by selecting one of several choices, what symbol should follow in the sequence. Both the ACE and the PMA have norms for different age and education levels. The Numerical Reasoning subtest of the Employee Aptitude Survey (p. 302) gives norms for different occupational groups. This kind of reasoning problem seems to require an appreciation of temporal or consequential relationships for success.

Sorting Tests

Sorting tests are the most common form of tests of abstraction and concept formation. In sorting tasks, the subject must sort collections of objects, blocks, tokens, or other kinds of items into subgroups following instrucitons such as "sort out the ones that go together" or "put together the ones that have the same thing in common." Most sorting tests assess the patient's ability to *shift* concepts as well as his ability to use them. The manner in which the subject proceeds will give some indication of his ability to form and handle abstract concepts.

Few sorting tests produce numerical scores, for it is more the patient's procedures than his solutions that interest the examiner. Attention is paid to whether the patient sorts according to a principle, whether he can formulate the principle verbally, whether it is a reasonable principle, and whether the patient follows it consistently.

Although sorting tests demonstrate how the patient thinks and handles certain kinds of abstraction problems, they have not proven successful in differentiating brain damaged from functionally psychotic patients (K. Goldstein and Scheerer, 1941, 1953; Yates, 1954), particularly when the psychiatric disorder has been chronic (Tutko and Spence, 1962). On scored sorting tests, few significant differences show up between the mean scores obtained by groups of brain injured patients and normal control subjects (De Renzi et al., 1966; McFie and Piercy, 1952; Newcombe, 1969). This does not invalidate sorting tests except for screening purposes. It does suggest, however, that deficits registered by these tests occur only mildly or infrequently in many brain injured populations. When marked impairment of performance does appear, an organic brain disorder is likely to be present.

SIMPLE SORTING TESTS

There are two well-known nonverbal tests of concept formation that are simply sorting tests. Both highlight the processes used by the patient to solve concept formation problems. Neither is scored.

The Color Sorting Test (K. Goldstein and Scheerer, 1941, 1953; Weigl, 1941). With the Color-Form Sorting Test (see p. 485) and the Object Sorting Test (see pp. 486–487), this is one of a set of tests designed to measure "abstract and concrete thought." It is also known as the *Gelb-Goldstein Wool Sorting Test*. It consists of 61 little skeins of wool, each of a different combination of hue, shade, and brightness. There are about ten skeins in each of the major colors—green, red, blue, and yellow, plus shades of brown, gray, purple, and other combined hues. The test requires the patient (1) to sort to sample; (2) to match two of three different skeins, two of which are similar in hue and two in brightness; (3) to explain the sameness principle underlying groupings of six skeins of the same hue but different shades and six skeins of different hue but the same brightness; and (4) to select all skeins of the same hue such as "red" or "green," giving his reasoning for the selection. The examiner judges the patient's level and his ease of abstract thinking from his own observations and from the patient's accompanying explanations.

The Kasanin-Hanfmann Concept Formation Test (Hanfmann, 1953). This test is sometimes called the *Vigotsky Test*. Its purpose is to "evaluate an individual's ability to solve problems by the use of abstract concepts and provide information both on the subject's level of abstract thinking and on his preferred type of approach to problems." It consists of 22 different blocks varying in color, size, shape, and height. On the underside of each is printed one of four nonsense words (or a number, in a variant of the test) designating the group to which the block belongs when the blocks are sorted by both shape and height (see Fig. 15-2). The subject continues to group and regroup the blocks, with a correcting clue given following each incorrect attempt, until he combines both the principles of shape and height to achieve the correct sorting solution. This may take anywhere from five minutes to one hour. He is encouraged to "think aloud" as he works, and the examiner is encouraged to keep a detailed record of both performance and verbalizations.

Card sorting (Caine et al., 1977). This word sorting task uses two sets of 32 3 × 5 cards with a word printed on each card. Four cards from each of eight categories (e.g., clothes, animals, etc.) make up one set; the second set consists of random words. The subject is simply asked to group the cards. Performance is evaluated on the basis of the number and appropriateness of the sorts. This technique was used to investigate

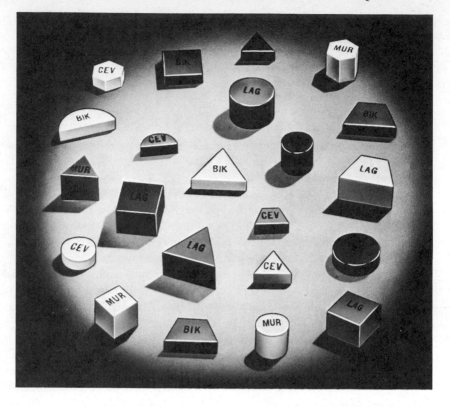

Fig. 15-2. The Kasanin-Hanfmann Concept Formation Test. (Courtesy of The Stoelting Co.)

the "clustering" phenomenon in the organization of semantic memory (Mandler, 1976).

The ability to think in categories can also be examined with sets of pictures of many different kinds of plants, animals, or other classes of entities that have hierarchically organized subclasses. For example, the animal set may contain pictures of different kinds of mammals, such as felines, canines, primates, hooved animals, etc. Different kinds of birds (fowl, shorebirds, birds of prey), different kinds of insects (butterflies, beetles), and so on. The patients' task is simply to sort the set of randomized pictures as they deem appropriate. Upon completing the task, patients who can talk should be asked for an explanation of their sorting array.

SORT AND SHIFT TESTS

Sorting tests, which include a requirement to shift concepts, spread a wider screening net than the simple sorting tests. Observation will clarify whether the patient's primary difficulty is in sorting or in shifting. For those sort and shift tests that produce a numerical score, the need to augment numerical data with behavioral description is obvious.

The Color Form Sorting Test (K. Goldstein and Scheerer, 1941, 1953; Weigl, 1941). This test may also be called *Weigl's Test* or the *Weigl-Goldstein-Scheerer Color Form Sorting Test*. It consists of 12 tokens or blocks, colored red, blue, yellow, or green on top and all white underneath, which come in one of three shapes—square, circle, or triangle. The patient is first asked to sort the test material. On completion of his first sort, he is told to "group them again, but in a different way." On completion of each sort, the examiner asks, "Why have you grouped them this way?" or "Why do these figures go together?" If the patient has difficulty in his second attempt at sorting, the examiner can give clues such as turning up the white sides for the patient who spontaneously sorted by color, or showing the patient who sorted by form a single grouping by color and asking if he can see why the three blocks belong together.

Inability to sort is rarely seen in persons whose premorbid functioning was much above *borderline defective*. K. W. Walsh (1978b), for example, reported that this part of the Color Form Sorting Test task was failed by only three of 13 patients who had had *orbitomedial leucotomy* (psychosurgery involving the severing of thalamofrontal connections near the tip of the frontal horn of the lateral ventricle). *Inability to shift* from one sorting principle to another is seen more often, particularly among patients with frontal lobe damage (e.g., five of Walsh's patients needed help to make the shift). Inability to shift is evidence of impaired mental functioning in persons who were operating at a better than *dull normal* level to begin with. Frontal lobe lesions are often implicated in failures on the Color Form Sorting Test, but aging also takes its toll (Kramer and Jarvik, 1979). McFie and Piercy (1952) found that many more patients with left hemisphere lesions (8 out of 17) fail on this test than those with right hemisphere lesions (2 of 32) although the presence or absence of aphasia did not appear to affect the ratio of poor performances among patients with left hemisphere brain disease. In a study of patients with unilateral frontal disease, those with left hemisphere lesions "had great difficulty" on this test, particularly when compared to the relatively satisfactory performances of patients whose damage was confined to the right frontal lobe (Rzechorzek, 1979).

The Object Classification Test (R. W. Payne and Hewlett, 1960). This modification of the Color Form Sorting Test increases the number of possible sorts. It also uses 12 tokens. Besides differing in shape and color, they are of different weights, thicknesses, sizes, materials, hues, and brightness. This permits up to ten different sorts (including a sort by surface area and one by presence or absence of curved corners). The instructions are identical to those of the Color Form Sorting Test; following each correct sort the patient is asked to sort the tokens another way. The patient's score is the number of abstract (A) sorts he makes. A standardization group of 20 normal control subjects made an average of 4.20 ± 1.61 different sorts on this test, the average score of a group of schizophrenics was 2.80 ± 2.62, and the average scores of three groups of patients with neurotic or affective disorders fell inbetween. The number of acceptable sorts made by Newcombe's brain injured population (1969) did not differ greatly from the mean of the normal control subjects. In fact, four patients with mixed right hemisphere lesions made an average of 4.25 sorts, and five patients with posterior right hemisphere lesions averaged 4.00 sorts. The lowest average scores attained by her patient groups were 2.70 and 2.80 for the left parietal and right frontal groups, respectively.

Weigl's Test, modified version (De Renzi, et al., 1966).   This is another modification of the Color Form Sorting Test. It increases the number of possible sorts to five, using thickness, size, and "suit" (a club, heart, or diamond printed at the block's center) in addition to the four standard colors and three common shapes. The first part of the test proceeds much as the original and the Payne modifications, except for a three-minute time limit. When the patient is unable to make an acceptable sort within three minutes, the examiner makes each of the sorts not used by the patient and allows the patient one minute to identify the principle. Spontaneous patient sorts earn three score points each; correct classification of the examiner's sort earns one point. Scores can range from 0 to 15. Forty control subjects achieved a mean score of 9.49. The presence of aphasia tended to result in markedly depressed scores, but other kinds of brain dysfunction had little effect on performance of this test. This finding receives support from the other sorting test studies that associate left hemisphere lesions with relatively lower scores.

The Object Sorting Test (K. Goldstein and Scheerer, 1941, 1953; Weigl, 1941)   This test is based on the same principles and generally follows the same administration procedures of the block and token sorting tests, except that the materials consist of 30 familiar objects (see Fig. 15-3). The objects can be grouped according to such principles as *use, situation* in which they are normally found, *color, pairedness, material,* etc. Variations on the basic sorting task require the patient to find objects compatible with the one preselected by the examiner, to sort objects according to a category named by the examiner, to figure out a principle underlying a set of objects grouped by the examiner, or to pick out one object of an examiner-selected set of objects that does not belong to the set. Most variations also ask for a verbal explanation. By providing a wider range of responses than most sorting tests, the Object Sorting Test allows the examiner more flexibility in the conduct of the examination and more opportunities to observe the patient's conceptual approach. The use of common objects also eliminates any need to familiarize the patient with the test material, or devise names for unfamiliar objects.

Weigl and K. Goldstein and Scheerer focused on the qualitative aspects of the patient's performance, but Tow (1955) emphasized the number of different solutions. Preoperatively, his frontal leucotomy patients averaged 2.5 spontaneous solutions for a total of 3.2 solutions including both spontaneous ones and those achieved with cues. Postoperatively, these same patients' average number of spontaneous solutions was 1.8, and the average number of combined solutions was 2.1. Tow concluded that frontal leucotomy interfered with concept formation.

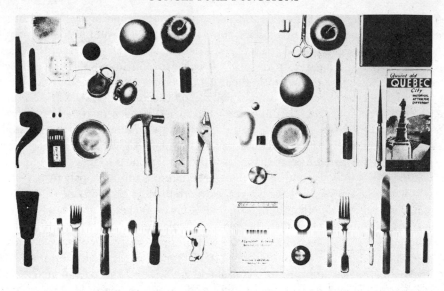

Fig. 15-3. The Object Sorting Test. (K. Goldstein and Scheerer, in *Contributions toward Medical Psychology,* edited by A. Weider. © Ronald Press, New York.) This version consists of a set of objects for men (left half) and a second set for women (on the right).

Free and serial classification (Krauss, 1978). Playing cards have been used to examine different aspects of cognitive competency in elderly persons. The rationale has been to give older people testing material that is already familiar and easy for them to see and handle, so that they can feel comfortable in taking the tests. The cards used in the sorting test devised by Krauss come in four shapes (standard, round, oversized, and zigzag) and consist of all four suits and two numerical values. The first—"free"—classification requires the subject to make as many groups as desired. Following this, and each subsequent—"serial classification"—sort, the subject is asked to resort the cards in some other way, continuing until he can think of no more bases for sorting. The number of groups sorted in the free trial does not vary with age, nor does the number of attributes on which the sorting for this and later trials are based. However, with increasing age, the number of subsequent sortings does decrease. Education tends to increase the number of rationales offered for classification but does not increase the number of different sorts.

The Wisconsin Card Sorting Test (WCST) (Berg, 1948; D. A. Grant and Berg, 1948).[1] This widely used test was devised to study "abstract behavior" and "shift of set". The subject is given a pack of 64 cards on which are printed one to four symbols, triangle, star, cross, or circle, in red, green, yellow, or blue. No two cards are identical

---

[1]The cards may be ordered from Wells Printing Co., Inc., P.O. Box 1744, Madison, Wisconsin 53701.

(see Fig. 15-4). The patient's task is to place them one by one under four stimulus cards—one red triangle, two green stars, three yellow crosses, and four blue circles—according to a principle that the patient must deduce from the pattern of the examiner's responses to the patient's placement of the cards. For instance, if the principle is color, the correct placement of a red card is under *one red triangle*, regardless of the symbol or number, and the examiner will respond accordingly. The subject simply begins placing cards and the examiner tells him whether each placement is correct. After a run of ten correct placements in a row, the examiner shifts the principle, indicating the shift only in the changed pattern of his "right" and "wrong" statements. The test begins with color as the basis for sorting, shifts to form, then to number, returns again to color, and so on. The test continues until the patient has made six runs of ten correct placements, has placed more than 64 cards in one category, or spontaneously reports the underlying principle (e.g., "you keep changing what is correct—from the number of spots to their shape or color and back again"). If the pack is exhausted before six successful runs, the card order is rearranged and the pack is used again. I usually discontinue the test after 30 or 40 cards have been misplaced and the patient seems unlikely to comprehend the task. If the patient makes four correct runs of ten consecutively (not counting the one or two trials between runs for determining the new principle), I ask the patient to state the general principle and discontinue if he is correct. Milner (1963) used a 128-card pack and discontinued after six runs or when all 128 cards were placed. She counted both the number of categories achieved and the number of erroneous responses for scores.

In using the Wisconsin Card Sorting Test with brain injured war veterans, Teuber and his colleagues (1951) shifted the response principle every ten trials regardless of the correctness of the subject's performance. Although this practice gives many patients more exposure to the *shifting* aspect of the task, E. Miller (1972) wisely observed that it does not allow frontal patients a long enough exposure to each sorting principle "to develop a strong response set to any dimension."

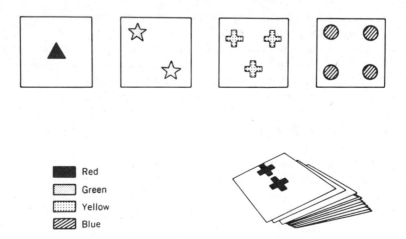

Fig. 15-4. The Wisconsin Card Sorting Test (Milner, 1964).

Wisconsin Card Sorting Test performances can be scored in a number of ways. The most widely used scores are for Categories Achieved and Perseverative Errors. Following Milner's (1963) criteria, Categories Achieved refers to the number of correct runs of ten sorts, ranging from 0 for the patient who never gets the idea at all to 6, at which point the test is normally discontinued. Using a double pack of 128 cards, which allows for an optimal number of 11 runs of ten correct sorts each, Malmo (1974) and Moscovitch (1976) identified a Category Achieved score of 4 or 6 as representing a successful performance.

Perseverative Errors occur either when the subject continues to sort according to a previously successful principle or, in the first series, when the subject persists in sorting on the basis of an initial erroneous guess. The Perseverative Error score is useful for documenting problems in forming concepts, profiting from correction, and conceptual flexibility. Control subjects studied by A. L. Robinson and her co-workers (1980) averaged only 12.06 errors in the course of completing six runs while patients with right frontal lesions made an average of almost 60 such errors. When Total Errors are also tabulated, then the Other Errors score is the difference between Total Errors and Perseverative Errors (e.g., see Table 15-2). Other errors may represent guessing, losing track of the current sorting principle, or occasionally, an effort to devise a complex scheme, which usually indicates that a verbally clever person has failed to keep track of the pattern of the examiner's responses or to accept the simplicity of that pattern. Tarter and Parsons (1971) tabulated two other interesting aspects of the performance: the percentage of errors that occurred after a sequence of correct responses and the percentage of errors occurring after a sequence of errors of a given length. The former figure indicates how well the subject can maintain a set. The latter indicates the extent to which the patient profits from correction or perpetuates an error pattern. Data using these two percentages discriminated well between long-term alcoholics who have difficulty maintaining a set or sustaining an orderly pattern of search (see Fig. 15-5 and p. 194) and short-term alcoholics and normal control subjects who do not exhibit these problems.

Recording a performance, particularly if the patient works rapidly, can be difficult. The system I use allows me to keep an accurate record without undue effort, to evaluate the performance at a glance, and to make score counts as needed. This simplified system involves identifying the category to be achieved at the left of a line of note paper and marking a slash for each correct sort, the category initial of each incorrect sort (C, F, N; CF, CN, etc., when an erroneous sort satisfies two categories), and an X when none of the categories match the sort (e.g., when three blue circles are placed under the card with two green stars). When the category has been achieved (i.e., when there are ten slash marks), I move to the left of the next line, mark the new category, and continue recording as before (see Fig. 15-5).

A poor performance on this test can result from different kinds of intellectual deficits. The patient may have difficulty sorting according to category, which suggests an impaired ability to form concepts. This problem occurs most often in patients with frontal lobe—particularly left frontal lobe—damage involving the medial area (Drewe, 1974). A series of schizophrenic patients who had undergone frontal leucotomy approximately 25 years prior to examination with the WCST achieved as many

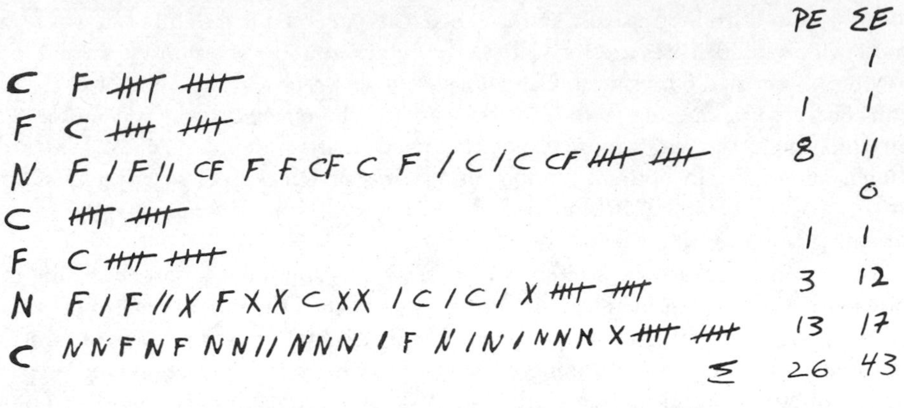

PE ΣE

C F ̶H̶H̶T ̶H̶H̶T   1

F C ̶H̶H̶T ̶H̶H̶T   1   1

N F / F // CF F F CF C F / C / C CF ̶H̶H̶T ̶H̶H̶T   8   11

C ̶H̶H̶T ̶H̶H̶T   0

F C ̶H̶H̶T ̶H̶H̶T   1   1

N F / F // X F X X C X X / C / C / X ̶H̶H̶T ̶H̶H̶T   3   12

C N N F N F N N // N N N / F N / N / N N N X ̶H̶H̶T ̶H̶H̶T   13   17

≤   26   43

Fig. 15-5. A method for recording the Wisconsin Card Sorting Test performances.

categories on the first 64 cards as did normal control subjects (Benson et al., 1981). All subjects were then told about the three possible sorting categories. With this information, the control subjects' performances improved significantly while the patients' performance deteriorated "as though hampered by the additional information."

Difficulty in shifting when the category changes, i.e., perseveration, was also a common error made by Drewe's brain injured patients regardless of the side or site of lesion. Milner (1963, 1964) reported that both before and after surgical removal of brain tumors, the performance of patients with dorsolateral frontal lobe lesions was significantly poorer than that of patients with lesions localized elsewhere. The frontal lobe patients achieved fewer sorting categories and made more perseverative errors than the other brain tumor patients (see Table 15-2). A. L. Robinson and her coworkers (1980) found that both frontal lobe patients and those with diffuse damage were highly susceptible to making perseverative errors.

L. B. Taylor (1979) associated perseverative errors with dorsolateral lesions of the frontal lobes, but reported that more patients with left-sided lesions displayed per-

Table 15-2 Mean Categories Achieved and Card Sorting Errors Made by Two Groups of Patients with Surgical Brain Lesions

		Errors	
Locus of Lesion	Categories Achieved	Perseverative	Other
Dorsolateral frontal ($n = 18$)	1.4	51.5	21.7
Posterior cortex ($n = 46$)	4.6	18.1	18.0

(Adapted from Milner, 1964)

manent impairments on this task after lobectomy (usually for epilepsy control or excision of a tumor) than did those whose damage was on the right. Robinson's group reported just the opposite, using as supporting evidence Drewe's study, which suggested a tendency for patients with right frontal damage to make slightly more perseverative errors than those with left-sided lesions. The question of whether this difference arises from differences in the nature of the lesions or other patient variables needs exploration.[1] There is no question, however, that patients with frontal lesions are prone to perseverate on the WCST.

Perseveration also characterizes the performance of long-term alcoholics (Parsons, 1975; Tarter and Parsons, 1971). Parsons called attention to a third common error (after difficulty in forming concepts and difficulty shifting) that he referred to as "difficulty in maintaining . . . [the] set," in which the patient is able to form categories easily and shift readily, but after several shifts he loses track of the present category and may end up hopelessly confused. (Figure 15-5 is an example of this phenomenon in a 55-year-old inventory control clerk who had completed 13 years of schooling and had a 20-year history of alcohol abuse. This erratic error pattern illustrates the interruptions and impersistence described by Parsons that characterize the performance of chronic alcoholics.)

The Modified Card Sorting Test (MCST) (Nelson, 1976).   This modification of the WCST eliminates all cards from the pack that share more than one attribute with a stimulus card. For example, all red triangle cards would be removed leaving only yellow, blue, and green triangles, and of these the two green, three yellow, and four blue triangle cards would also be removed. Only 24 of the original 64-card deck satisfy the requirement of being correct for only one attribute at a time. This method removes ambiguity in the examiner's responses, thereby simplifying the task for the patient and clarifying the nature of errors for the examiner.

Nelson uses a 48-card pack with the four stimulus cards set up as in the WCST. Whatever category the patient chooses first is designated "correct" by the examiner who then proceeds to inform the patient whether each choice is correct or not until the patient has achieved a run of six correct responses. At this point, the patient is told that the rule has changed and is instructed to "find another rule." This procedure is continued until six categories are achieved or the pack of 48 cards is used up. Nelson notes that her pilot studies indicated that explicitly announcing each shift did not seem to affect the tendency to perseverate. However, letting the patient know that the rule had changed made it easier for patients to deal with being told their answers were wrong.

Besides a score for the number of categories obtained, Nelson derived a score for

[1]Taylor's subjects have all had surgical excision of frontal tissue. Not only is the number of patients whose damaged tissue had been surgically removed unspecified in the Robinson study, but Robinson and her co-workers include in the "focal" groups several closed head injury patients who may also have sustained diffuse damage (see pp. 167–169). It is interesting to note that Drewe, whose findings on this issue come between the opposite poles represented by the two other studies, included in her sample both postlobectomy patients and patients with diseased frontal tissue.

the total number of errors (TE) and scored as perseverative errors (PN) only those of the same category as the immediately preceding response (in contrast to Milner's criteria given on p. 489). A third score $\left(\dfrac{PN}{TE} \times 100\% \right)$ gives the percentage of errors that are perseverative.

Comparison of the 53 patients with unilateral lesions and 47 control subjects in the pilot study sample on number of categories achieved readily separated the patients from the controls. The pilot study demonstrated a tendency for patients with posterior lesions to perform better than patients whose lesions involved the frontal lobes, with considerable overlap between these two groups and no difference with respect to side of lesion. However, although frontal patients made many more perseverative errors than the 15 control subjects whose performances were noticeably less than perfect, the control subgroup and the patients with posterior lesions made a similar, relatively small number of perseverative errors. Again, no lateralized differences were observed. Analyses using the number or the proportion of perseverative errors resulted in the same pattern of significance. Nelson's data also suggest that this method is sensitive to aging effects.

The advantages and disadvantages of this method probably carry different weight according to population and purpose. The clarification that unambiguous card patterns bring to the evaluation of a performance is offset by the fact that hemisphere differences no longer show up, a finding that Nelson attributes at least in part to a decreased need for verbal mediation in sorting the unambiguous cards. The advantage that a shorter run requirement has in reducing fatigue and keeping the patient attentive may be more than counterbalanced in some populations—such as chronic alcoholics—by interruptions that can come after six or more correct sorts (see Parsons, 1975). Moreover, the shorter run, like Teuber's procedure of changing categories every ten trials, may not give frontal patients an adequate opportunity to develop a strong response set. Having dealt with the distress that some patients experience when a category shifts with no more warning than an unexpected "wrong" called out by the examiner, I can empathize with Nelson's desire to alleviate unnecessary pain. However, alerting patients to a shift in sorting principle changes the task radically as the need to appreciate the fact of change is no longer present.

Innovative examiners who tend to be flexible in their approach will probably find one or more of Nelson's procedural changes useful for some purposes and some patients. Although there are no scoring norms for selective use of her techniques, in clinical practice norms are rarely needed for determining whether or how a performance is unsatisfactory.

Sequential Concept Formation Tests

Talland (1965a) used two decks of playing cards without aces in his most complex test of *Sequential concept formation.* He considered this task to be conceptually similar to maze learning. The black and red cards are arranged in 16 runs of B-B-R-B-R-R. The subject must discover the pattern in order to predict the color of the next card as he turns the cards up one by one. The subject proceeds at his own pace until he correctly predicts three sequences (18 cards) in a row. To add a dimension of immediate memory to this task, the examiner interjects a moment or two of verbal praise after the subject has completed a three-run sequence correctly and then permits him to resume the task. A final task requires the subject to reconstruct the pattern from a pack of disarranged cards. If a patient fails to see the pattern before going through both decks (16 six-card sequences), the examiner shows it to him, gives several demonstrations, and then if the patient still is unable to perform the task independently, the examiner has him copy the sequence from a model placed in front of him. In one study of patients with severe memory disorders, all 20 control subjects succeeded by the third trial and ten were not set back by the interruption. However, only two of the 20 patients with severe memory disorder solved the problem, one after two trials and one after five.

When this sequential concept formation task was given to 76 men and women ranging in age from the fifth to the ninth decade and without history or evidence of neurological or psychiatric disorder, Talland (1961) found that the proportion of subjects who could solve the task (i.e., predict a run of 18 cards correctly) varied inversely with age (see Table 15-3). Noting no appreciable age differences until the ninth decade on a sorting type of concept formation task, Talland attributed the decline on the sequential concept formation task to its short-term storage component, suggesting that the length of the pattern to be learned increasingly taxed the aging short-term memory span capacity.

An easier sequential concept formation test uses five geometric figures drawn in black ink on white cards, a 1-inch circle, two small circles, a triangle, a square, and a 2-inch circle. The goal is to predict when the large circle will appear. Talland devised three different patterns: (A) With a varying number of intervening cards, the combination 1-inch circle, double circle, 1-inch circle heralded the 2-inch circle. (B) With a varying number of intervening blank cards, the combination 1-inch circle and two blank cards preceded the large circle. (C) Again a varying number of blank cards appeared, among which one square and one triangle were placed a different number of cards apart each time they appeared; the 2-inch circle immediately followed the appearance of the second of these two figures. All of the 21 control subjects solved patterns A and B but four of them had to be told the rule for pattern C before they could apply it. Eighteen of the memory impaired patients solved pattern A, ten solved

Table 15-3   Effects of Age on the Sequential Concept Formation Test

Decade	Fifth	Sixth	Seventh	Eighth	Ninth
n	14	13	19	20	10
% successful	57	64	42	25	0

(Adapted from Talland, 1961)

pattern B, but only seven solved C. Several of the patients verbalized C correctly but failed to apply the rule.

The easiest of these tests also uses playing cards, sorted into suit sequences, i.e., D-S-C-H. The subject has to anticipate the next suit that will be turned up. The 20 control subjects deduced the principle within the first three four-card sequences. The 17 (of 20) memory impaired patients who solved this problem took an average of 8.41 four-card sequences to do so.

Reasoning Tests

Reasoning tests call for different kinds of logical thinking, comprehension of relationships, and practical judgments. The WAIS furnishes examples of different kinds of reasoning tests in Comprehension, Arithmetic, Picture Completion, and Picture Arrangement. Tests of other functions may also provide information about the patient's reasoning ability, such as the Reading Comprehension subtest of the Gates-MacGinitie Reading Test, and the Bicycle drawing test. The Stanford-Binet scales contain a variety of reasoning tests, some of which have counterparts in other tests. All the Stanford-Binet subtest references in this section are to the 1973 revision except as otherwise noted.

Verbal Reasoning Problems

STANFORD-BINET SUBTESTS

Although these reasoning tests have not had enough neuropsychological use to result in published studies, they are effective in drawing out defects in reasoning. The verbal reasoning tests of the Binet cover a sufficiently broad range of difficulty to provide suitable problems for patients at all but the highest and lowest levels of intellectual ability. For example, *Problem Situations I* and II at ages VIII and XI and *Problems of Fact* at age XIII involve little stories for which the patient has to supply an explanation, such as "My neighbor has been having queer visitors. First a doctor came to his house, then a lawyer, then a minister (preacher, priest, or rabbi). What do you think happened there?"

The *Verbal Absurdities* (VA) subtest items call for the subject to point out the logical impossibilities in several little stories. At the IX year old level, for example, one item is, "Bill Jones's feet are so big that he has to pull his trousers on over his head." There are four forms of Verbal Absurdities with scoring standards for five age levels, VIII (VA I), IX (VA II), X (VA III), XI (VA IV), and XII (VA II). Verbal Absurdities can sometimes elicit impairments in the ability to evaluate and integrate all elements of a problem that may not become evident in responses to the usual straightforward questions testing practical reasoning and common sense judgment, particularly when the mature patient with a late-onset condition has a rich background of experience to draw upon.

Three-and-a-half months after surgical removal of a left temporal hematoma incurred in a fall from a bar stool, a 48-year-old manufacturers' representative who had completed one year of college achieved age-graded scaled scores ranging from *average* to *superior* ability levels on the WAIS. However, he was unable to explain "what's funny" in a statement about an old gentleman who complained he could no longer walk around a park since he now went only halfway and back (at age level VIII). The patient's first response was, "Getting senile." [Examiner: "Can you explain . . ."] "Because he is still walking around the park; whether he is still walking around the park or not is immaterial." Another instance of impaired reasoning appeared in his explanation of "what's funny" about cooing icebergs that had been melted in the Gulf Stream (at age level IX), when he answered, "Icebergs shouldn't be in the Gulf Stream."

POISONED FOOD PROBLEMS (Arenberg, 1968)

This test was developed to examine changes in reasoning ability that might occur with aging. The subject's task is to deduce the unique event from a set of statements about a number of events. Arenberg chose the "poisoned foods" format when he found that abstract concepts (e.g., color, form, number) made a similar task so abstract that his elderly (60 to 77 years of age) subjects had difficulty comprehending it.

For each of the ten problems and a practice problem, the subject receives a sheet of paper printed with a list of the nine foods contained in the sets of meals and a grid on which the subject can keep track of the meals and their consequences (i.e., whether the consumer lived or died) (see Fig. 15-6). After instructing the subject in how to keep a record of the foods as they are read, by crossing out each food that could not be the poisoned food, the examiner reads the contents of each meal in the set (see Table 15-4).

Five kinds of problems (differing in terms of presence and number of positive, negative, and redundant items) are each represented once in the first five and the second five problems. Arenberg tabulated the number correct for subject and the number correct and number of errors for each kind of problem.

Arenberg's findings of a significant difference ($p < .001$) between the elderly subjects and a group of 17- to 22-year-olds were supported by Hayslip and Sterns (1979), who report increasingly higher error scores on this test with advancing age. Arenberg's 21 young subjects got an average of 7.6 $\pm$ 2.4 problems correct while the 21 older subjects succeeded on an average of only 4.5 $\pm$ 2.5 of the problems.

Arenberg (personal communication, 1979) noted that matching age groups on a culture-fair test reduced much of the age-related variance found with unmatched subjects. An analysis of performances by types of problems showed that old and young groups did not differ in susceptibility to error on positive and negative items, but the

Look at each of the nine foods listed across the page.

Figure out whether it could be the poisoned food or could not be the poisoned food.

If a food *cannot be the poisoned food*, it should be *crossed out*.

Do not cross out any foods which could be the poisoned food.

After you decide which foods should be crossed out, tell me all the foods which could be the poisoned food. The foods you tell me are all the foods which are not crossed out.

MEAL	coffee	milk	tea	beef	lamb	veal	rice	corn	peas	LIVED or DIED

Fig. 15-6. Worksheet for the Poisoned Food Problem.

Table 15-4 Poisoned Food Test Problems

Practice Problem Meals and Consequences
Coffee Lamb Peas—Died
Coffee Veal Peas—Died
Coffee Lamb Corn—Lived

Possibly Poisoned Foods
Coffee Lamb Peas
Coffee Peas
Peas

On the practice problem: Correct all errors of recording and indicate all discrepancies. If the subject has not solved the problem after the last meal, discontinue, saying, "Sometimes I will interrupt a problem and go on to the next." Ask for clarification questions now, explaining that once the test proper is begun you can give no further help. *Starting a new problem;* Say, "The first person's meal in *this* problem is _____ ."

Test Problems

I Milk Beef Corn—Died
   Tea Beef Corn—Died
   Milk Beef Peas—Died

II Coffee Veal Corn—Died
    Coffee Veal Rice—Lived

III Tea Beef Rice—Lived
     Milk Veal Rice—Lived
     Tea Veal Peas—Lived
     Tea Lamb Rice—Lived
     Milk Beef Corn—Lived

IV Milk Lamb Rice—Died
    Tea Lamb Rice—Died
    Coffee Lamb Rice—Died
    Milk Veal Rice—Died

V Tea Lamb Corn—Died
   Coffee Lamb Rice—Lived
   Milk Beef Rice—Lived
   Tea Beef Corn—Died
   Coffee Veal Corn—Lived

VI Tea Veal Corn—Died
    Tea Veal Rice—Died
    Tea Veal Peas—Died
    Milk Veal Corn—Died

VII Tea Beef Peas—Died
     Coffee Beef Corn—Lived
     Coffee Beef Rice—Lived
     Tea Lamb Peas—Died
     Tea Veal Rice—Lived

VIII Coffee Lamb Corn—Lived
      Coffee Beef Peas—Lived
      Coffee Veal Peas—Lived
      Milk Veal Peas—Lived
      Tea Veal Corn—Lived

IX Coffee Lamb Peas—Died
    Coffee Beef Peas—Lived

X Milk Lamb Corn—Died
   Milk Lamb Peas—Died
   Milk Veal Corn—Died

After the fifth problem: Give the subject a minute or two of rest.

older subjects made many more errors than younger ones when dealing with redundant data (Arenberg, 1968, 1970).

Picture Problems

On the Binet, the visual analogue of Verbal Absurdities is *Picture Absurdities* I and II at years VII and XIII (see Fig. 15-7). These subtests depict a logically or practically impossible situation the patient must identify. The *McGill Picture Anomalies Test*

Fig. 15-7. Picture Absurdities I, Card B (Terman and Merrill, 1973). (Courtesy of Houghton Mifflin Co.)

(Hebb and Morton, 1943) also depicts practically or logically impossible situations. It consists of two equivalent series of 30 pictures, with instructions to "Show me what is funny or out of place." Patients with surgical lesions of the right temporal lobe tended to make more errors on this test than did other patient groups and also were slower and more hesitant in their responses, whereas patients with parietal lobe lesions performed well (Milner, 1958). However, these findings were not reflected in another study of patients with temporal lobe epilepsy in which no pre- or postsurgical differences were found (Shalman, 1961). The McGill pictures are dated, and this may well make them unreliable for present-day use, whereas the six Binet pictures seem ageless.

Focusing on functions involved in the appreciation of humor, Wapner and her colleagues (1981) reported patient responses to a three-frame funny cartoon. In contrast to control subjects and aphasic patients who "invariably" saw the humor, those whose lesions were in the right hemisphere did not even realize that a joke was intended. Their responses are described as "serious and critical," suggesting difficulty in spontaneous integration of all the elements of the story so that particular elements are taken out of the overall context and thus interpreted as inappropriate in some way.

Arithmetic Problems

CALCULATIONS

An assessment of cognitive functions that does not include an examination of calculation skills is incomplete. An adequate review for neuropsychological purposes should give the patient an opportunity to demonstrate that he recognizes the basic arithmetic symbols (plus, minus, times, division, and equals) and can use them to calculate problems mentally and on paper. Story problems, like those given in the Wechsler tests, while assessing knowledge of and ability to apply arithmetic operations, do not test symbol recognition or spatial dyscalculia (see pp. 72, 264f.). Nor do the Wechsler Arithmetic subtest problems test whether more advanced mathematical concepts (e.g., fractions, decimals, squares, algebraic formulations) that are mastered by most adults who complete high school have survived a cerebral insult.

Many examiners who have the Wide Range Achievement Test (WRAT) available use its Arithmetic subtest for this purpose (see pp. 293–295). A test with a larger proportion of problems at lower (grade school) difficulty levels, which makes it more suitable than the WRAT for neuropsychological evaluations, is the Calculations subtest of Woodcock's *Psycho-Educational Battery* (1977). Moreover, Woodcock's Calculations subtest also includes problems dealing with concepts and operations usually studied in advanced high school or college mathematics courses involving, for example, logarithms, exponents, and other mathematical functions. Thus, the average score for senior high school students, reported with its standard deviation, can be meaningfully applied to adults taking the test. Unfortunately, like the WRAT, the layout of Woodcock's test does not allow much space for calculations, although the typeface is bigger and thus easier to read. The Calculations subtest also does not provide for a large enough sampling of performances on arithmetic problems involving two- and three-place numbers in the four basic operations, to meet the needs of neuropsychological assessment, particularly when spatial dyscalculia, carelessness in handling details, or impaired ability to perceive or correct errors is suspected. In the latter circumstances, the examiner may wish to make up a set of ten or 12 arithmetic problems. Most of them should require carrying, some of the multiplication and division problems should involve decimals, and at least a few of them should have zeros in the multiplier and in the dividend. In addition to giving the patient a sheet with the problems already laid out, the examiner can also dictate some problems representing each of the four kinds of operations to see how well the patient can set them up.

Luria described a series of questions designed to test various aspects of arithmetic ability in an orderly manner (1966; see also Christensen, 1979). He began with addition and subtraction of one-digit numbers and gradually increased the size and complexity of the problems. At the simplest levels, many of the problems, such as multiplication of numbers memorized in times tables, have a virtually automatic character for most adults. Inability to respond accurately at these low levels signals an impairment in symbol formulation characteristic of aphasic disturbances, or a severe breakdown in conceptual functions. More complex problems involving arithmetic operations with two- and three-place numbers test the immediate auditory memory span, attention, and mental tracking functions as well as the integrity of arithmetic skills. The examiner must take care to identify the nature of the failure on these problems by comparing the ability to perform problems with paper and pencil that are similar to those the patient may have failed to do mentally. A similar sequence of arithmetic problems, ranging from "Verbal Rote Examples" such as $2 + 5$, 4×4, $8 - 2$, and

42 ÷ 7, to "Verbal Complex Examples," e.g., 15 + 18, 18 × 4, 52 − 27, and also 126 ÷ 9, is part of the mental status examination recommended by Strub and Black (1977; see also pp. 576–577). These authors also include two-, three-,and four-place number problems in their "Written Complex Examples."

ARITHMETIC REASONING PROBLEMS

Luria (1973) used arithmetic problems of increasing difficulty to examine reasoning abilities. These problems do not involve much mathematical skill. They implicitly require the subject to make comparisons between elements of the problem, and they contain intermediate operations that are not specified. An easy example would be, "The green basket contains three apples; the blue basket has twice as many. How many apples are there altogether?" A more difficult problem of the type suggested by Luria is "Two baskets together contain 24 apples. The blue basket has twice as many apples as the green basket. How many apples in each basket?" The most difficult problem format of this series requires the "inhibition of the impulsive direct method" for solution: "There are 12 apples in the green basket; the blue basket contains 36 apples more than the green basket. How many times more apples are in the blue than the green basket?" Luria pointed out that the tendency to set the problem up as a "direct operation" (i.e., 36 ÷ 12) must be inhibited in favor of the more complex set of operations required for solution (i.e., [12 + 36] ÷ 12). Arithmetic problems were also used by Luria to examine conceptual flexibility (1966; Christensen, 1979). He set familiar problems up in unfamiliar ways—for example, placing the smaller number above rather than below the larger one in a written subtraction problem.

Besides the usual Arithmetic Story problems, the Binet scales contain some interestingly complex reasoning problems involving arithmetic operations and concepts. These problems may expose subtle difficulties in formulating problems or in conceptual tracking that are not readily apparent in patients whose well-ingrained thinking patterns suffice for handling most test reasoning tasks. *Ingenuity* I and II are arithmetic "brain teasers" such as "(A boy) has to bring back exactly 13 pints of water. He has a 9-pint can and a 5-pint can. Show me how he can measure out exactly 13 pints of water using nothing but these 2 cans and not guessing at the amount." This type of question calls for a "process" rather than content answer, eliciting information about how the patient reasons. The *Enclosed Box Problem* at the SA I level is also a mathematical brain teaser. It is a serial reasoning task that begins with "Let's suppose that this box has 2 smaller boxes inside it, and each one of the smaller boxes contains a little tiny box. How many boxes are there altogether, counting the big one?" The next three items elaborate on the first, compounding the number of boxes at each step. *Induction* at year XIV involves a serial paper folding and cutting problem in which the number of holes cut increases at an algebraic ratio to the number of folds. After observing the folding and cutting procedure, the patient is asked to state the rule that will enable him to predict the number of holes from the number of folds. *Reasoning* I and II are brain teasers, too, requiring the patient to organize a set of numerical facts and deduce their relationship in order to solve the problem.

500

Block counting. The Block Counting task at age level X, sometimes called *Cube Analysis* (Newcombe, 1969) or *Cube Counting* (McFie and Zangwill, 1960) is another Binet test that lends itself well to the study of reasoning processes. The material consists of two-dimensional drawings of three-dimensional block piles (see Fig. 15-8). The subject must count the total number of blocks in each pile by taking into account the ones hidden from view. Several studies comparing right and left hemisphere patients on this task have found mildly to significantly impaired performances by right hemisphere patients relative to those with left hemisphere lesions (Newcombe, 1969; McFie and Zangwill, 1960; Warrington and Rabin, 1970). Moreover, among patients with right hemisphere lesions, those who exhibited left visuospatial inattention made many more errors on a 25-item modification of the Binet drawings than patients with right-sided damage who did not display the inattention phenomenon (D. C. Campbell and Oxbury, 1976). Although Newcombe's right and left hemisphere patients' scores did not differ significantly, right hemisphere patients were slower.

Luria described a similar block counting task that he ascribed to Yerkes. He gives four examples of "Yerkes' test" that, in turn, are available in Christensen's (1979) test card material (see pp. 567–568). Although use of these block pictures should give some idea of whether the patient can perform this kind of spatial reasoning operation and how he goes about it, lack of norms and of a large enough series of graded problems limit the usefulness of this material. A set of block counting problems calling upon similar abilities to reason about spatial projections is one of the subtests of the MacQuarrie Test for Mechanical Ability (see p. 304). Although not presented in a graded manner, individual items are of different difficulty levels and subtest norms are provided.

Estimations. Estimations of sizes, quantities, etc., also test a patient's ability to apply what he knows, to compare, to make mental projections, and to evaluate conclusions. Some questions calling for estimations are in the Wechsler tests' Information subtest, such as those that ask the height of the average American (or other nationality, depending upon the country in which the test is given) man or woman, the distance from New York to Paris, or the population of the United States. The examiner can make up others as appropriate, using familiar subjects such as the height of telephone poles or the number of potatoes in a ten-pound sack.

Shallice and Evans (1978) constructed a set of *Cognitive Estimate Questions* for examining practical judgment. They found that patients with anterior lesions tended to give more bizarre responses than those with posterior lesions, supporting observa-

Fig. 15-8. Sample items from the Block Counting task (Terman and Merrill, 1973). (Courtesy of Houghton Mifflin Co.)

tions that patients with frontal lobe damage often use poor judgment, particularly in novel situations. Of the 15 questions, the four which elicited more bizarre responses from frontal lobe patients were, "How fast do race horses gallop?" ($p < .10$); "What is the largest object normally found in a house?" ($p < .10$); "What is the best paid occupation in Britain today?" ($p < .05$); and "How tall is the average English woman?" ($p < .01$). Unfortunately, the last question has been dropped from the WAIS-R. However, the examiner can easily include it with the other Information questions, giving it in approximately the same position (after "Brazil" and before "Italy") as it appeared in the WAIS. However, on one of the questions, "What is the length of a pound note?" the percentage of patients with posterior lesions who gave bizarre answers exceeded that of the anterior group.

Miscellaneous Reasoning Problems

RAVEN'S PROGRESSIVE MATRICES (RPM) (Raven, 1960)

This multiple-choice paper and pencil test was developed in England and has received widespread attention in this country and abroad. It was intended to be a "culture fair" test of general ability, but even though it requires neither language nor academic skills for success, educational level influences the RPM performance (Bolin, 1955; Colonna and Faglioni, 1966). The test consists of a series of visual pattern matching and analogy problems pictured in nonrepresentational designs. It requires the subject to conceptualize spatial, design, and numerical relationships ranging from the very obvious and concrete to the very complex and abstract (see Fig. 15-9). The Coloured Progressive Matrices provides a simpler alternate three-series form of this test for use with children and defective adults. Some workers (e.g., Costa, 1976; A. Smith, 1972a) use this form of the test for neuropsychological assessment (see p. 572).

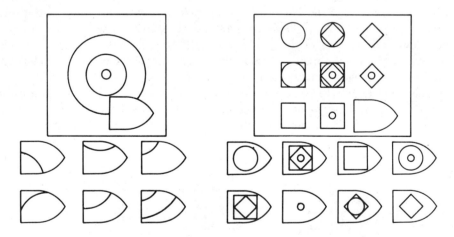

Fig. 15-9. Examples at two levels of difficulty of Progressive Matrices type items.

Raven's Matrices is easy to administer. A secretary or clerk can give or demonstrate the instructions. It has no time limit; most people take from 40 minutes to an hour. It consists of 60 items grouped into five sets. Each item contains a pattern problem with one part removed and from six to eight pictured inserts of which one contains the correct pattern. The subject points to the pattern piece he selects as correct or writes its number on an answer sheet.

Norms are available for ages 8 to 65. Score conversion is to percentiles. Seven percentile levels are given for age groups ranging from 20 to 65. For finer scaled scoring, the examiner can use Peck's table for converting raw scores into percentiles (see Table 15-5). The age group changes reported by Raven and Peck were found in other studies of the vicissitudes of conceptual thinking through the adult years (Botwinick, 1973). Retest reliability correlations run in the range of .7 to .9 (Eichorn, 1975), even when retesting involves three administrations six and 12 months apart (Lezak, 1982d). The lowest reliability coefficient was .67 obtained in an odd even correlation (Dulke, 1976). Moreover, the RPM has proven very stable, with no significant shift in mean scores between three administrations (Lezak, 1982d).

The first (A) set of 12 items consists of incomplete figures; the missing part is depicted in one of the six response alternatives given below the figure. All of the items call for pattern matching (e.g., the left-hand item in Fig. 15-8) and test the kind of visuoperceptual skills associated with normal right hemisphere functioning (Denes et al., 1978). In the other sets of RPM items, the task shifts from one of pattern completion to reasoning by analogy at levels ranging from quite simple (in Set B) to increasingly difficult (in the subsequent sets) and ultimately to very complex. These analogical reasoning problems appear to call upon left hemisphere functions predominantly (Denes et al., 1978). The example on the right in Figure 15-8 is similar to some of the problems in Set D. Many of the more difficult analogy problems involve mathematical concepts. Most of the analogy problems in Set B and the three more difficult sets (C, D, E) have nameable features so that it is not surprising that factor analytic studies have demonstrated a significant verbal component in this test (Bock, 1973; Burke and Bingham, 1969). However, the Progressive Matrices correlates most highly with "nonverbal" tests and most poorly with tests that predict academic achievement (J. C. Hall, 1957a; Talland, 1965a; Urmer et al., 1960). Although it fails to achieve its purpose as a test of general intellectual ability, it does assess reasoning in the visuospatial modality (Archibald et al., 1967; Colonna and Faglioni, 1966).

The effectiveness of the Progressive Matrices in identifying organically impaired patients appears to be related to the extent of the damage (Zimet and Fishman, 1970). This was demonstrated nicely in Brooks and Aughton's study (1979b) of traumatically injured patients whose RPM scores decreased quite regularly with increases in the duration of posttraumatic amnesia. However, the test's usefulness in screening for brain damage is limited (Heaton et al., 1978; Newcombe, 1969). Newcombe and Artiola i Fortuny (1979) attribute some of its insensitivity to a tendency for the old (from the 1950s) norms to overestimate performance slightly, citing one case in which a socially incompetent trauma patient achieved a score above the 95th percentile.

The standard form of this test does not discriminate well between undifferentiated

Table 15-5. Table for Converting Progressive Matrices Raw Scores into Percentiles

Raw Score	Age Group								
	25	30	35	40	45	50	55	60	65
13								2	5
14								5	7
15					2.5	3.0	5	8	10
16					3.0	3.5	7	10	13
17				2.0	4	5	8	13	17
18				3.0	5	6.5	10	15	20
19			2.0	4	7	7.5	12	18	25
20	2.0	2.0	2.5	5	8	10	15	22	30
21	2.5	3	3.5	7	10	12	20	25	34
22	3.0	4	5	8	12	15	24	28	38
23	3.5	5	7	10	15	19	28	32	42
24	4.0	7	9	12	17	21	32	36	46
25	5	8	11	15	20	25	36	40	50
26	8	10	14	17	23	28	40	45	55
27	9	12	16	20	25	32	44	50	60
28	10	14	19	23	28	36	48	54	64
29	11	16	21	26	31	40	50	59	68
30	12	18	25	28	35	46	54	63	72
31	14	20	28	31	39	50	58	66	75
32	15	22	30	34	43	54	62	70	78
33	17	25	34	37	47	58	64	73	81
34	19	28	38	40	50	61	68	75	83
35	21	30	40	43	54	64	71	78	85
36	24	32	42	46	57	67	73	80	87
37	26	34	45	50	60	70	76	82	88
38	28	38	48	53	63	72	78	84	89
39	32	40	50	57	66	74	80	85	90
40	35	42	53	60	69	76	83	87	91
41	38	45	56	64	72	78	86	89	93
42	42	48	60	68	75	80	88	90	94
43	45	50	62	71	78	83	90	92	95
44	48	54	66	75	81	85	92	93	96
45	52	58	70	79	85	87	93	95	97
46	56	62	74	82	87	90	94	96	98
47	61	66	77	85	90	92	95	97	>98
48	66	70	80	88	92	93	96	98	
49	70	74	84	90	94	95	97	>98	
50	74	78	86	92	95	96	98		
51	78	82	89	94	96	97	>98		
52	82	85	91	95	98	98			
53	85	90	93	96	>98	>98			
54	88	95	95	97					
55	94	98	>98	98					
>56	>98	>98							

(From Peck, 1970)

groups of patients with right and left hemisphere damage (Arrigoni and De Renzi, 1964; Costa and Vaughan 1962). Finding that commissurotomized patients used different strategies for the right and left hands when solving a tactile RPM task, Sperry (1974) concluded that, "the scores for the Progressive Matrices Test do not in themselves eminently distinguish left and right hemisphere capabilities." With visual presentations restricted to each visual half-field and responses made by the contralateral hand, two commissurotomized and two hemispherectomized patients also failed to produce significant differences between performances of the two hemispheres (E. Zaidel et al., 1981). A positive association has been reported between poor performances on the Matrices and on drawing and constructional tasks (Piercy and Smyth, 1962).

Positional preferences in selecting a response can affect performance on this test. Using a sample of mostly middle-aged to elderly psychiatric patients that included some with diagnosed organic disease and others with functional disturbances, Bromley (1953) found that "certain answer positions are preferred more than others." However, he also reported position preferences of a group of school girls that differed somewhat from those of the psychiatric patients. Overall, top line alternatives tended to be chosen by both groups more than those on the bottom line and the first and last positions were also favored, but no consistent pattern of right-left preferences emerged. However, patients with lateralized lesions—particularly those who have demonstrated unilateral visuospatial inattention—show a consistent tendency to prefer alternatives on the side of the page ipsilateral to the lesion, neglecting answers on the side opposite the lesion (D. C. Campbell and Oxbury, 1976; Colombo et al., 1976; Costa et al., 1969). This phenomenon occurs with both right- and left-sided lesions, but much more so with lesions on the right, and particularly when the patient with right hemisphere damage also has a visual field defect (De Renzi and Faglioni, 1965).

Thus, the presence of unilateral neglect may be elicited by this test (see p. 000). Other kinds of error patterns can also provide insight into the patient's mishandling of conceptual problems. Error tendencies may be determined in an item-by-item inspection of errors in which the examiner looks for such error patterns as choosing a whole for a part response (on set A), choosing a response that repeats a part of the matrix, performing a simplified abstraction (e.g., by attending to only one dimension of patterns involving both vertical and horizontal progressions), and perseverating (the direction of pattern progression, a solution mode, a position.) Some patients' errors will make no sense at all. Questioning them about their choices may reveal tendencies to personalized, symbolic, or concrete thinking, incomprehension, or confusion (see Bromley, 1953).

RAVEN'S COLOURED PROGRESSIVE MATRICES (RCPM) (Raven, 1965)

The RCPM provides a simplifed 36-item format with norms for children in the five to 11-year-old range, and for adults 65 years and older. It consists of sets A and B of the RPM and an intermediate set Ab that, like set B, contains both gestalt completion items and some simple analogies. Each item is printed with a bright background color that may make the test more appealing to children and does not seem to detract from its clarity. Miceli and his colleagues (1977, 1981) have included the Coloured Matrices in their Neuropsychological Test Battery (see p. 573), using a modified format in which the response choices are presented in a vertical array to minimize the effects of visuospatial inattention (see also p. 343).

In contrast to performances on the RPM, the consistent tendency for patients with right-sided lesions to fare less well than those whose cerebral damage is on the left appears in research on the RCPM (Costa et al., 1969; A. Smith, 1972a, personal communication, 1976). This is not surprising since only one-fifth of the RPM items test visuoperceptual skills almost exclusively, while more than one-third of the RCPM is composed of predominantly visuospatial items. Costa and his colleagues noted that patients with receptive or mixed aphasia do poorly on this test as well (of course, these are the aphasic patients most likely to exhibit constructional disabilities), an observation that is in accord with Costa's later (1976) finding that posterior lesions tend to compromise ability to solve the Matrices problems more than anterior lesions. These research data suggest that the two forms of the test are not interchangeable (see also Zaidel et al., 1981).

MISCELLANEOUS REASONING PROBLEMS OF THE BINET

Codes at AA (Form M, 1937 Revision) and SA II is another kind of reasoning task. Each difficulty level of Codes contains one message, "COME TO LONDON," printed alongside two coded forms of the message. The patient must find the rule for each code. This task requires the subject to deduce a verbal pattern and then translate it. Codes can be sensitive to mild verbal dysfunctions that do not appear on tests involving well-practiced verbal behavior but may show up when the task is complex and unfamiliar.

In Binet *Paper Cutting* subtests at IX, XIII, and AA levels, the examiner cuts holes in folded paper so that the subject can see what he is doing but not how the unfolded paper looks. The subject's task is to draw a picture of how he thinks the paper will look when unfolded. This test was included in a battery for studying the visual space perception of patients with lateralized lesions (McFie and Zangwill, 1960; Paterson and Zangwill, 1944). It discriminated left and right hemisphere damaged patients well: four out of four left hemisphere lesion patients could pass it at the IX year level, whereas only one out of ten right hemisphere damaged patients succeeded.

16
Executive Functions and Motor Performance

The Executive Functions

The executive functions can be conceptualized as having four components: (1) goal formulation; (2) planning; (3) carrying out goal-directed plans; and (4) effective performance. Each involves a distinctive set of activity-related behaviors. All are necessary for appropriate, socially responsible, and effectively self-serving adult conduct. Moreover, it is rare to find a patient with impaired capacity for self-direction or self-regulation who has defects in just one of these aspects of executive functioning. Rather, defective executive behavior typically involves a cluster of deficiencies of which one or two may be especially prominent.

A medically retired financial manager whose cardiac arrest was complicated by a hard fall onto his right temple is very responsive to his own needs and energetic in attempts to carry out plans. Unfortunately, he can no longer formulate plans well because of an inability to take all aspects of a situation into account and integrate them. This disability is further aggravated by his lack of awareness of his mistakes. Problems occasioned by this man's emotional lability and proneness to irritability are overshadowed by the crises resulting from his efforts to carry out inappropriate and sometimes financially hazardous plans.

The young woman mentioned in Chapter 2 (p. 38) who sustained serious brain injuries in a head-on collision is emotionally unresponsive and seems to have lost the capacity for pleasure along with the capacity to be motivated. Unless someone else defines her activities and gets her started, she remains inert except when roused by toileting needs or sleepiness. Yet she is meticulously careful and accurate in everything she does do.

In these cases and in much of the literature concerning the executive functions, frontal lobe damage is implicated (e.g., Damasio, 1979; Hécaen and Albert, 1978; Luria, 1966, 1973; Seron, 1978). This is not surprising since most patients who have

507

had significant injury or disease of the prefrontal regions, particularly when orbital or medial structures are involved, experience behavioral and personality changes stemming from defective executive functions (see pp. 79–82). However, the executive functions are also sensitive to damage in other parts of the brain. Impairment of executive functions may be associated with subcortical damage. Some disturbances in executive functions result from anoxic conditions that involve limbic structures (Falicki and Sep-Kowalik, 1969; Jefferson, 1976; Muramoto et al., 1979) and can be among the sequelae of inhalation of organic solvents (Arlien-Søborg et al., 1979; Gregersen et al., 1978; Tsushima and Towne, 1977). Korsakoff patients, whose lesions primarily involve thalamic nuclei and other subcortical components of the limbic system, typically exhibit profound distrubances in executive behavior. Many of them are virtually immobilized by apathy and inertia. Some Parkinson patients display diminished conceptual flexibility and impaired initiative and spontaneity (Bowen, 1976; M. L. Albert, 1978). Moreover, patients with right hemisphere damage who can "talk a good game" and are neither inert nor apathetic are often ineffective because their difficulties in organizing all facets of an activity conceptually and integrating it with their behavior may keep them from carrying out their many intentions (Lezak, 1979a).

The system of executive functions can break down at any stage in the behavioral sequence that makes up planned or intentional activity. Systematic examination of the capacities that enter into the four aspects of executive activity will help to identify the stage or stages at which a breakdown in executive behavior takes place. Such a review of a patient's executive functions may also bring to light impairments in self-direction or self-regulation that would not become evident in the course of the usual examination or observation procedures.

One obstacle to examining the executive functions is the paradox of having to structure a situation in which the patient can show whether and how well he can make structure for himself. Typically, in formal examinations, the examiner determines what activity the subject is to do with what materials, when, and how. Most cognitive tests, for example, allow the subject little room for discretionary behavior. The problem for clinicians who want to examine the executive functions becomes how to transfer goal setting, structuring, and decision making from the clinician to the subject within the structured examination. Only a limited number of established examination techniques give the subject sufficient leeway to think of and choose alternatives as needed to demonstrate the main components of executive behavior.

The following review covers techniques that may be useful in exploring and elucidating this most subtle and central realm of human activity. Other instruments presented in this chapter test more peripheral but equally important executive capacities, such as those that enter into self-regulation and self-correction.

Goal Formulation

Goal formulation refers to the complex process of determining what one needs or wants and conceptualizing some kind of future realization of that need or want. The

508

capacity to formulate a goal or, at a less well-conceptualized level, form an intention is bound up both with motivation and with awareness of oneself psychologically, physically, and in relation to one's surroundings. Persons who lack the capacity to formulate goals simply do not think of anything to do. In extreme cases they may be apathetic, unappreciative of themselves as distinctive persons (much as an infant or young child), or both, as is often the case. They may be unable to initiate activities except in response to internal stimuli such as bladder pressure or external stimuli, for example, an annoying mosquito. Such persons may be fully capable of performing complex activities and yet not carry them out unless instructed to do so. For instance, although able to use eating utensils properly, some will not eat what is set before them without continuing explicit instructions. Less impaired persons may eat or drink what is set before them, but will not seek nourishment spontaneously, even when hungry. Patients whose capacity for goal formulation is only mildly impaired can do their usual chores and engage in familiar games and hobbies without prompting. However, they are typically unable to assume responsibilities requiring appreciation of long-term or abstract goals and do not enter into new activities independently. Without outside guidance, many wander aimlessly or sit in front of the television or at the same neighborhood bar or coffee shop when they have finished their routine activities.

Observations of the patient in the normal course of day-to-day living and reports by caretakers, family, and others who see him regularly are the best sources of information about his capacity for formulating goals and forming intentions. The examination of the patient's emotional capacity should include questioning both the patient and the people who know him best about his likes and dislikes, what he does for fun, and what makes him angry. Oftentimes a patient reports what sound like normal activity programs when asked how he spends his leisure time or how he performs his chores. It is always important for the examiner to find out when the patient last dated or went on a camping trip, for example, or who plans the meals he cooks. It is not unusual to find that a patient who reports that he likes to take his girl to the movies has not had "a girl" since before his accident three years ago and has not gone to a theater since then either; nor that one who tells how competent he is in the kitchen actually prepares the same few dishes over and over again exactly as he had been taught.

Assessment of the patient's self awareness and awareness of his surroundings will also depend greatly upon observations and interviews. Lack of normal adult self-consciousness may show up in reports or observations of poor grooming and childish or crude behavior that contrast sharply with a premorbid history of social competence. The extent to which the patient is aware of and responsive to what goes on around him is likely to be reflected in his use of environmental cues. This can be examined with questions about the time of day, the season of the year, or other temporal events or situational circumstances (e.g., Christmas time, the dining hall, office, or waiting room, etc.) that can be easily deduced or verified by an alert patient who is attentive to his surroundings.

Story and picture material from standard tests can also be used to examine the patient's ability to pay attention to situational cues. The "Problems of Fact" items of

509

the Stanford-Binet scales (see p. 494) require the patient to use cues to interpret a situation. The Cookie Theft picture from the Boston Diagnostic Aphasia Examination (Goodglass and Kaplan, 1972) is excellent for testing the patient's ability to infer a story from a picture (see p. 328). The patient can make up a single integrated story involving the important elements of the picture; he can give a bit-by-bit description of the picture that raises questions about whether he can integrate what he sees; or he may disregard all but one or two items because of an impaired capacity to attend systematically to what he sees.

Planning

The determination and organization of the steps and elements (e.g., skills, material, other persons) needed to carry out an intention or achieve a goal constitute planning and involve a number of capacities. In order to plan, a person must be able to conceptualize change from present circumstances, deal objectively with himself in relation to the environment, and view the environment objectively, i.e., take the abstract attitude (see p. 81f.). The planner must also be able to conceive of alternatives, weigh and make choices, and evolve a conceptual framework or structure that will give direction to the carrying out of a plan. Moreover, all of this conceptual activity requires a capacity for sustained attention.

USE OF STANDARD EXAMINATION PROCEDURES

There are few formal tests of these abilities. However, the patient's handling of many of the standard psychological tests will provide insight into how he performs these important conceptual activities. For example, the layout of Bender designs on the page indicates the patient's awareness of space use and spatial relations. Responses to story telling tasks, such as the Thematic Apperception Test (see pp. 606–607), reflect the patient's handling of sequential verbal ideas. For example, stories may be complex and highly organized, have simple and straight story lines, be organized by accretion, or be loose or disjointed associations or descriptions (W. E. Henry, 1947). Even the patient's approach to such highly structured tests as Block Design will provide information about whether he orders and plans ahead naturally and effectively, laboriously, inconsistently, or not at all (see pp. 278–280). Sentence Building at SA I of the 1960 Revision of the Stanford-Binet, and age level VII on the 1937 Form M of the Binet scales affords the patient a good opportunity to demonstrate how he organizes his thoughts into a sensible and linguistically acceptable construct (p. 341). The Complex Figure Test (Messerli et al., 1979; Rey, 1941) also elicits planning behavior. Osterrieth's (1944) analysis of approaches to copying the complex figure provides standards for evaluating how systematic is the patient's response to this task. A haphazard, fragmented mode of response suggests poor planning (see pp. 395, 397).

Questioning can bring out defective planning. How a patient who is living alone or keeping house describes food purchasing and preparation may reveal how well he or she can organize and plan. Other issues that may bring out organizing and planning abilities concern personal care, how the patient's illness affects his activities and his family, what accommodations he has to make to his disabilities, to his altered financial and vocational status, etc. Some patients, particularly those whose brain lesions are in the right hemisphere, may give lucid and appropriate answers to questions involving organization and planning of impersonal situations or events but show poor judgment in unrealistic, confused, often illogical or nonexistent plans for themselves, or lack the judgment to recognize that they need to make plans if they are to remain independent (Lezak, 1979a).

PORTEUS MAZE TEST (Porteus, 1959, 1965)

The maze tracing task was designed to yield data about the highest levels of mental functioning involving planning and foresight, i.e., "the process of choosing, trying, and rejecting or adopting alternative courses of conduct or thought. At a simple level, this is similar to solving a very complex maze" (Porteus, 1959, p. 7).

There are three sets of the *Porteus Maze Test* currently in use: the Vineland Revision, which contains 12 mazes for years III through XII, year XIV, and Adult; the eight-maze Porteus Maze Extension covering years VII through XII, year XIV, and Adult; and the Porteus Maze Supplement, which also has eight mazes for years VII through XII, XIV, and Adult (Porteus, 1965) (see Fig. 16-1). The latter two series were developed to compensate for practice effects in retesting, so that the maze at each year of the Porteus Maze Extension is a little more difficult than its counterpart in the

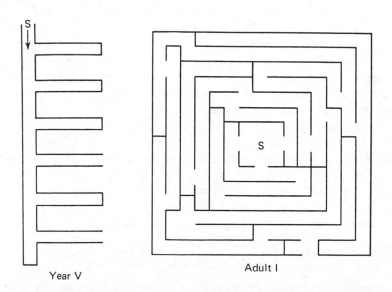

Year V

Adult I

Fig. 16-1. Two of the Porteus mazes. (Reproduced by permission.) (Copyright 1933, 1946, 1950 by S. D. Porteus, Published by the Psychological Corporation, New York. All rights reserved.)

Vineland Revision, and each year of the Porteus Maze Supplement is more difficult than its corresponding test in the Extension series.

To achieve a successful trial, the subject must trace the maze without entering any blind alleys. The test is not timed and may take some patients an hour or more to complete all the mazes given to them. Scores are reported in terms of test age (TA), which is the age level of the most difficult maze the patient completes successfuly. The upper score is 17 for success on the Adult level maze. The test can be done with either hand without lowering the score although the nonpreferred hand makes about twice as many qualitative errors—such as crossing a line or lifting the pencil—as the preferred hand (P. F. Briggs, 1963).

The Porteus Maze Test is quite sensitive to the effects of brain damage (Klebanoff et al., 1954). Perhaps the most notable research was undertaken by A. Smith and Kinder (1959) and A. Smith (1960), who did an eight-year follow-up study of psychosurgical patients, comparing younger and older groups who had undergone superior or orbital topectomy with younger and older patient controls. Following a score rise in a second preoperative testing, scores on tests taken within three months after surgery were lower than the second preoperative scores in all cases. The superior topectomy group's scores dropped still lower during the eight-year interval to a score significantly ($p < .05$) lower than the original. The control group mean scores climbed slightly following the first and second retest (10.87, 11.89, and 12.59), but the eight-year and the original maze test scores were essentially the same. Maze test scores have also successfully predicted the severity of brain damage (Meier, 1974; Meier et al., 1982). Those patients who achieved test age (TA) scores of VIII or above during the first week after a stroke made significant spontaneous gains in lost motor functions, whereas those whose scores fell below this standard showed relatively little spontaneous improvement. Tow (1955) found that frontal leucotomy patients tested pre- and postoperatively were significantly slowed ($p < .02$) in their maze test performance by the psychosurgery and averaged more errors; their preoperative mean time for mazes VI to XII plus XIV of the Vineland Revision was 313 seconds whereas postoperatively their mean time lengthened to 546 seconds.

The Wechsler Intelligence Scale for Children contains a shorter maze test with time limits and an error scoring system (see pp. 295–296). Although the most difficult item is a little less complex than the most difficult items in the Porteus series, the highest (15 years 10 months) norms allow the examiner to make a rough estimate of the adequacy of the adult patient's performance. Moreover, the one-page format and the time limits make the WISC mazes easy to give. I find that for most clinical purposes, they are a satisfactory substitute for the lengthier Porteus test.

Carrying Out Activities

The translation of an intention or plan into productive, self-serving activity requires the actor to initiate, maintain, switch, and stop sequences of complex behavior in an orderly and integrated manner. Disturbances in the programming of activity can thwart the carrying out of reasonable plans regardless of motivation, knowledge, or capacity to perform the activity. However, such disturbances are less likely to impede impulsive actions.

Patients who have trouble programming activity may display a marked dissociation between their verbalized intentions and plans and their actions.

> Korsakoff and head injury patients who do not always know where they are may still talk repeatedly about wanting to leave (to get some money, return to a wife, visit parents, etc.). When informed that they were free to go whenever they wished and even given an explanation of how they might do so, they either quickly forgot what they were told, changed the subject, or ignored the message. One young head injury victim repeatedly announced his very reasonable intention to get a much-needed haircut. Although he knew the way to the barbershop and was physically capable of going there, he never did get his hair cut on his own.

Programming difficulties may affect large-scale purposive activities or the regulation and fine-tuning of discrete intentional acts or complex movements. Patients who have trouble performing discrete actions also tend to have difficulty carrying out broader purposive activities. For example, youthful offenders who displayed an inability to switch ongoing activity by making errors on an untimed trial of the Trail Making Test, part B (see pp. 556–559) also tended to be those whose self-report of their criminal activities contained evidence of an inability to make appropriate shifts in the "principle of action (POA)" during the commission of the crime (Pontius and Yudowitz, 1980).

Purposive Behavior

The Tinkertoy® Test (TTT) (Lezak, 1981, 1982). This constructional test was devised to give patients an opportunity within the necessarily highly structured formal examination to demonstrate executive capacities. The Tinkertoy Test allows them to undertake initiation, planning, and structuring of a potentially complex activity, and to carry it out independently. In the normal course of most neurological or neuropsychological examinations such functions are carried out by the examiner, or they are made unnecessary (or even unwelcome) by the structured nature of the test material and the restricted number of acceptable responses in most tests of cognitive functions. Thus, these functions typically remain unexamined although they are absolutely essential to the maintenance of social independence in a complex society (see pp. 38–40, 507ff.).

The Tinkertoy Test also gives the patient an opportunity to perform a "free" construction without the constraints of a model to copy or a predetermined solution. The interplay between executive and constructional functions will more or less limit the extent to which this examination technique tests the constructional capacity of any individual patient. Its usefulness as a constructional test will vary, largely, with the patient's productivity. For example, Figure 16-2 was put together by a youthful head injury patient whose constructional abilities had remained relatively intact (WAIS

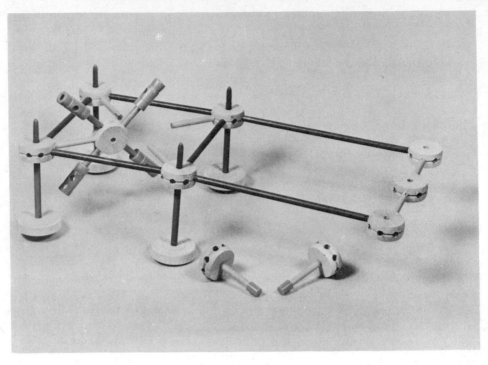

Fig. 16-2. A 23-year-old craftsman with a high school education made this Tinkertoy "space platform" after he had first tried to construct "a design," and then "a new ride at the fair" (see text).

scaled scores for Block Design = 10, Object Assembly = 14) but whose capacity for integrating complex stimuli was impaired (Picture Arrangement = 6). The ambitiousness, complexity, and relative symmetry of this "space platform" reflect his good constructional skills, although its instability, lack of integration (he could not figure out how to put the two little extra constructions onto the main construction), growth by accretion rather than plan, and the inappropriateness of the name given to it are concrete evidence of defective executive functioning.

Administration of this test is simple. Fifty pieces of a standard Tinkertoy set (see Table 16-1) are placed on a clean surface in front of the subject, who is told, "Make whatever you want with these. You will have at least five minutes and as much more time as you wish to make something." The necessity for a five-minute minimum time limit became evident when, without such a limit, bright, competitive-minded control subjects did a slapdash job thinking this was a speed test and poorly motivated or self-deprecating patients gave up easily. Deteriorated patients may stop handling the items after two or three minutes, but should be allowed to sit for several minutes more before being asked whether they have finished with the material. Except for the five-

Table 16-1 Items Used in the Tinkertoy Test

Wooden Dowels			Wooden Rounds		Plastic Pieces	
Green	(18.9 cm)	4	Knobs	10	Connectors	4
Red	(12.6 cm)	4	Wheels	4	Caps	4
Blue	(8.3 cm)	4			Points	4
Yellow	(5.3 cm)	6				
Orange	(3.2 cm)	6				

minute minimum, the test is not timed since a pilot study involving both patients and control subject showed that the amount of time taken did not vary either with neuropsychological status or with the quality of the performance. Encouragement is given as needed.

Most patients find this test interesting or amusing. Of the 35 subjects with diagnosed neurological disorders who participated in the pilot study, many seemed to enjoy the constructional activity and none raised any objections. Even the one patient who made no construction played with a few pieces, fitting them together and taking them apart, before his attention drifted away. Only those patients who cannot manipulate small objects with both hands are unable to take this test.

On completion, the examiner asks what the construction represents (e.g., "What is it?"). If it does represent something (usually a named object), the construction is evaluated for its appropriateness to the indicated name (or concept). The following scores are then obtained: (1) whether the patient made any construction(s) *(mc)*; (2) total number of pieces used *(np)*; (3) whether the construction was given a name appropriate to its appearance *(name)*; (4a) mobility (wheels that work) and (4b) moving parts *(mov)*; (5) symmetry *(sym)*; (6) whether it has three dimensions *(3d)*; (7) whether the construction is freestanding *(stand)*; and (8) whether there is a performance *error* such as *misfit* in which parts of pieces are forced together that were not made to be combined, *incomplete fit* in which connections are not properly made, or *dropping* pieces on the floor without attempting to recover them (see Fig. 16-3). The complexity score *(comp)* is based on all of these performance variables (see Table 16-2). A modified complexity score *(mComp)* does not include the number of pieces used.

An initial evaluation of the effectiveness of the Tinkertoy Test in measuring executive capacity was made using the *np* and *comp* scores of 35 unselected patients with cerebral pathology and of ten normal control subjects. On the basis of history, records, or family interviews, 18 patients who required total support and supervision were classified as Dependent (D), and 17 were classified as Not Dependent (ND) as they all managed daily routines on their own and could drive or use public transportation, and five of them were capable of working independently. The two patient groups did not differ in age, education, or scores on the Information subtest of the WAIS. On the average, the control subjects were younger and better educated than the patients.

Both *np* and *comp* scores differentiated the constructions of the three groups (see Table 16-3). All but one of the Dependent patients used fewer than 23 pieces, those

Fig. 16-3. This patient said he was trying to make "a car" (see text pp. 517–518). He has been totally dependent since the initial illness. Speech is dysfluent, he feeds and toilets himself, and walks with a parkinsonism-like gait.

Table 16-2 Tinkertoy Test: Scoring for Complexity

Variable	Scoring Criteria	Total Possible
1. *mc*	Any combination of pieces	1
2. *np*	n ≲ 20 = 1, 30 = 2, ≲ 40 = 3, ≲ 50 = 4	4
3. *name*	+ = 1	1
4. *mov*	Mobility = 1, moving parts = 1	2
5. *sym*	× 2 = 1, × 4 = 2	2
6. *3d*	3-Dimensional = 1	1
7. *stand*	Free-standing = 1	1
8. *error*	One or more errors (misfit, incomplete fit, drop and not pick up)	−1

Highest score possible	12
Lowest score possible	−1

Table 16-3 Comparisons Between Groups on *np* and Complexity Scores

| Group | Patient | | Control | |
	Dependent	Nondependent		
Measure				*F*
np				
Mean ± SD	13.5 ± 9.46	30.24 ± 11.32	42.2 ± 10.03	26.91[a]
Range	0–42	9–50	23–50	
Complexity				
Mean ± SD	2.22 ± 2.10	5.47 ± 1.77	7.8 ± 1.99	28.27[a]
Range	−1–8	2–9	5–12	

[a]One-way ANOVA, $p < .001$

who were Not Dependent used 23 or more, and half of the control group used all 50 pieces. The *np* and *comp* scores of the control subjects and the 19 patients who had age-graded scaled scores of 10 or higher on the WAIS Information or Block Design subtests were significantly different. The lower Tinkertoy Test scores of the patients whose cognitive performances were relatively intact suggest that this test measures more than cognitive abilities. As measured by correlations with the Block Design scaled scores, constructional ability contributes to the complexity of the construction $(r_{comp \times BD} = .574, p < .01)$ but has a much lower association with the number of pieces used $(r_{np \times BD} = .379, p < .05)$.

A number of executive functions appear to contribute to high scoring constructions, including the abilities to formulate a goal and to plan, initiate, and carry out a complex activity to achieve the goal (e.g., Figure 16-4, "space vehicle," depicts the product of a distinguished neuropsychologist, well known for innovative research, that reflects her technical competence and well-organized and systematic approach).

Initial observations suggest that patients who have difficulty initiating or carrying out purposive activities tend to use relatively few pieces although some make recognizable and appropriately named constructions (e.g., see Figure 16-5, the construction of a 60-year-old left-handed but right-eyed medically retired plumbing contractor who had had a cerebrovascular accident involving a small area of the left parietal lobe that resulted in transient aphasic symptoms). Those who have an impaired capacity for formulating goals or planning but can initiate activity and are well motivated may use relatively more pieces, but their constructions are more likely to be unnamed or inappropriate for their names and poorly organized (e.g., Fig. 16-2). Patients with extensive impairment involving all aspects of the executive functions may pile pieces together or sort them into groups without attempting any constructions or they use few pieces to make unnamed and unplanned constructions. For example, Figure 16-3 was the product of a 40-year-old appliance salesman who suffered a bout of meningitis following a left endarterectomy and thrombectomy undertaken several days after an initial right-sided cerebrovascular accident had resulted in a mild left hemiparesis and slurred speech. Four months after the meningitis had subsided his WAIS

Fig. 16-4. "Space vehicle" was constructed by a neuropsychologist unfamiliar with Tinkertoys. Although she used only 34 pieces, her complexity score is 11, well above the control mean.

Information, Comprehension, and Block Design scaled scores were 10, 9, and 6, respectively. Pathologically inert patients who can usually be coaxed into giving some response to standard test items are likely to do nothing with as open-ended a task as this.

The appropriateness of the scoring system for evaluating constructional aspects of the Tinkertoy Test has not been systematically examined. It is certainly possible that sensitive measurement of the constructional component will require a different set of scoring dimensions, or perhaps different weights for the individual variable scores. However, examiners using this test will find that qualitative characteristics of the constructions are often a rich source of data about the patient's capacity to handle a three-dimensional construction problem.

SELF-REGULATION

Flexibility and the capacity to shift.   The ability to regulate one's own behavior can be demonstrated on tests of flexibility that require the subject to shift a course of thought or action according to the demands of the situation. The capacity for flexibility in behavior extends through perceptual, cognitive, and response dimensions.

Fig. 16-5. The creator of this "cannon" achieved WAIS age-graded scaled scores of 16 and 17 on Comprehension and Block Design, respectively (see p. 517).

Defects in mental flexibility show up perceptually in defective scanning and inability to change perceptual set easily. Conceptual inflexibility appears in concrete or rigid approaches to understanding and problem solving, and also as *stimulus-bound* behavior in which the patient cannot dissociate his responses or pull his attention away from whatever is in his perceptual field. It may appear as inability to shift perceptual organization, train of thought, or ongoing behavior to meet the varying needs of the moment.

Inflexibility of response results in perseverative, stereotyped, nonadaptive behavior and difficulties in regulating and modulating motor acts. In each of these problems there is an inability to shift behavior readily, to conform behavior to rapidly changing demands on the person. This disturbance in the programming of behavior appears in many different contexts and forms and is associated with lesions of the frontal lobes (Luria, 1966; Luria and Homskaya, 1964). Its particular manifestation depends at least in part on the site of the lesion.

By and large, techniques that tend to bring out defects in self-regulation do not have scoring systems or even standardized formats. Neither is necessary or especially desirable. Once perseveration or inability to shift smoothly through a movement, drawing, or speaking sequence shows up, that is evidence enough that the patient is having difficulty in self-regulation. The examiner may then wish to explore the dimensions of the problem: how frequently it occurs, how long it lasts, whether the patient can self-recover (for instance, when perseverating on a word or movement, or when an alternating sequence breaks down), and what conditions are most likely to bring out the dysfunctional response (kind of task, lateral differences, stress, fatigue, etc.). An efficient examination should be different for each patient as the examiner follows up on the unique set of dysfunctional responses displayed by the patient at each step in the course of the examination. When a subtle defect is suspected, for example, the examiner may give a series of tasks of increasing length or complexity. When a broad, very general defect is suspected, it may be unnecessary to give very long or complex tasks, but rather for planning and rehabilitation purposes it may be more useful to expose the patient to a wide range of tasks.

At the conceptual level, mental inflexibility can be difficult to identify, shading into personality rigidity on the one hand and stupidity on the other. Tests of abstraction that emphasize shifts in concept formation (see pp. 484–492) touch upon mental flexibility.

Another kind of test that assesses inflexibility in thinking is the *Uses of Objects* test (Getzels and Jackson, 1962,) which has also served to identify creativity in bright children. The printed instructions ask the subject to write as many uses as he can for five common objects: brick, pencil, paper clip, toothpick, sheet of paper. Two examples are given for each object, such as "Brick—build houses, doorstop," or "Pencil—write, bookmark," with space on the answer sheet for a dozen or more uses to be written in for each object. The tendency to give obvious, conventional responses such as Brick: "to build a wall," or "line a garden path," reflects a search for the "right" or logical solution, which is called *convergent* thinking. In *divergent* thinking, on the other hand, the subject generates many different and often unique and daring ideas without evident concern for satisfying preconceived notions of what is correct or logical. The divergent thinker, for example, might recommend using a brick for a bedwarmer or as a weapon. In recommending this test for use in evaluating mental inflexibility, Zangwill (1966) notes that "frontal lobe patients tend to embroider on the main or conventional use of an object, often failing to think up other, less probable uses. This is somewhat reminiscent of the inability to switch from one principle of classification to another" (p. 397).

A *Design Fluency Test* (Jones-Gotman and Milner, 1977) that was developed as a nonverbal counterpart of Thurstone's Word Fluency Test (pp. 333–334) also can be used to examine conceptual productivity. In the first—*free condition*—trial, the subject is asked to "invent drawings" that represent neither actual objects nor nameable abstract forms (e.g., geometric shapes) and that are not merely scribbles. After being shown examples of acceptable and unacceptable drawings, subjects are given five-minutes in which to make up as many different kinds of drawings as they can, "many" and "different" being emphasized in the instructions. The first of each type of unacceptable drawing or too similar a drawing is pointed out as is a drawing so elaborate as to decrease quantity production. The second, four-minute trial is the *fixed (four-line) condition* in which acceptable drawings are limited to four lines, straight or curved. Again the subject is shown acceptable and unacceptable examples and the instructions place emphasis on the subject's making as *many different* drawings as possible. The control subjects' average output on the free five-minute condition was 16.2 designs, on the fixed (four-minute) condition it was 19.7. Approximately 10% of their responses were judged perseverative. Frontal lobe patients tended to have reduced output on both free and fixed conditions relative to normal subjects and patients with posterior lesions. Patients with right-sided lesions generally tended to have lower productivity (except right posterior patients on the free condition), and those with right frontal lesions were least productive. Patients with frontal—particularly right frontal—and right central lesions showed the greatest tendency to perseveration relative to the control group on both free and fixed conditions.

Perseverative behavior is one of the hallmarks of response inflexibility. When perseveration or difficulty in shifting is suspected, the patient can be asked to copy and maintain alternating letters (e.g., *mnmnmn* in script) or repetitive sequential patterns of hand movements (see also pp. 522–523) with separate trials for each hand to determine whether there are laterality differences in hand control (e.g., see Christensen, 1979; Luria, 1966; pp. 567–568). Luria (1966) gave patients a sheet of paper with several word series typed in rows such as "circle, circle, circle, cross, circle" or "square, cross, circle, cross, cross," with instructions to draw the indicated figure below each word as fast as possible. Similar chains of verbal commands also elicit perseverative tendencies. A variety of figures can be named, including the simple geometric forms, letters, and numbers. Of the common geometric figures, circles are least likely, squares more likely, and triangles most likely to be perseverated (E. Goldberg, 1975). E. Goldberg and David Tucker (1979) have identified four types of perseveration that can occur in simple drawing responses to these kinds of chained verbal commands: (1) "Hyperkinetic-like motor perseveration" refers to inability to terminate an elementary movement that, on a drawing, shows up in multiple overdrawings of single elements of the task or continuation of an element until stopped by the edge of the page. (2) In "perseveration of elements," the patient can reproduce discrete elements but introduces elements of previously drawn figures into subsequent ones. (3) "Perseveration of features" involves the perpetuation of some characteristic of a previously drawn figure, such as "openness," which produces, for example, a cross drawn in outline following an outlined ("open") figure such as a circle or a crescent rather than the more usual form of intersecting lines. (4) In "perseveration of activities," different categories of stimuli, for example, words and numbers, mathematical and geometrical symbols, become confounded. These authors point out that only type 1 is a true motor perseveration. The other types result from breakdown of cognitive processing at different levels, from unification of the elements in different graphic sequences (2), to confusion of spatial characteristics (3), to confusion of semantic categories (4) at the highest level of this hierarchy of complexity in processing.

The Bender-Gestalt test (see pp. 385–393), particularly cards 1, 2, and 6, and the Benton Visual Retention test (see pp. 447–451) tend to bring out perseverative tendencies, as do tasks involving writing to command or copying letters, numbers, or words. Perseverative patients often have difficulty in just writing the alphabet, a number series, or their address. Perseveration is least likely to show up in signatures as they are so overpracticed as to be automatic for almost all but the most impaired patients.

· Difficulties in regulating motor responses can be brought out by tests in which the patient must make converse responses to the examiner's alternating signals (Luria, 1966; Luria and Homskaya, 1964; see also p. 527). For example, if the examiner taps once, the patient must tap twice and vice versa; or if the examiner presses a buzzer to give a long signal, the patient must press for a short signal. Patients with self-regulation problems may irresistibly follow the examiner's response pattern.

Self-regulation problems also appear as difficulty in reversing a motor set. Talland (1965a) had both his memory defective patients and his control subjects write S's for 30 seconds, then write reverse S's for 60 seconds and again write standard S's for 60 seconds. On the two 60-second trials, the control subjects wrote an average of 78.2 standard S's and 65.8 reversed S's. The patients produced an average of 78.0 standard S's, but their average of reversed S's was only 35.3.

When giving tasks designed to examine the capacity for motor regulation, the examiner must continue them long enough for defective responses to show up. Frequently, patients can maintain the correct response set for the first few sequences and only become confused or slip into a perseverative pattern after that. If the patient's response deteriorates, the examiner should ask the patient to recall the instructions as patients with frontal lobe damage may be able to repeat the instructions accurately while continuing to respond incorrectly, thus demonstrating a dissociation between comprehension and action.

I have devised a *Line Tracing Task (LTT)* to examine fine motor regulation (see Fig. 16-6). The subject is given a brightly colored felt-tipped pen and a sheet of paper

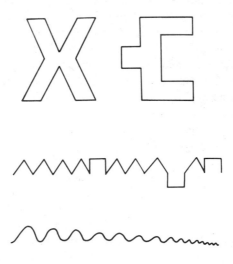

Fig. 16-6. Line Tracing Task (reduced in size).

printed with these figures and told to draw over the lines of each figure as rapidly as possible. Since the focus is on how well the subject can follow the twists and turns in the figures rather than on response speed, timing is not necessary. Motor regulation problems tend to show up in difficulties with angles, overshooting lines at corners, perseveration of an ongoing response, and inability to follow the graduated size reduction of the curves in the bottom figure. The task is well within the ability of any normal ten-year-old so that noticeable deviations are suggestive of problems in motor regulation.

The *MacQuarrie Test for Mechanical Ability* (MacQuarrie, 1925, 1953) contains several subtests—Tracing, Tapping, and Dotting—that appear to be sensitive to impairments in fine motor regulation (for a description of the MacQuarrie subtests, see pp. 303–304). Since these are timed tests, the scores may reflect the effects of motor slowing *per se* as well as the response slowing that results from motor performance defects. Only an analysis of the quality of the performance and an evaluation of the scores within the context of the pattern of test scores overall can identify the source of the slowing when scores on these subtests are unexpectedly low.

Scanning tests (see pp. 367–371) are sensitive to a diminished capacity for mental flexibility. Decreased perceptual shifting also shows up on optical illusions and attention tests involving visual scanning (see pp. 365–367, 548–550, 554–559). Analysis of the performance on these and other perceptual tests will enable the examiner to determine whether the disability results from a perceptual defect or from an inability to accommodate to variety and change.

The Stroop Test (Stroop, 1935).   This test measures the ease with which the patient can shift his perceptual set to conform to changing demands. Talland (1965a) used the Stroop Test to examine the effects of perceptual interference and incidentally found that it provided data on reading fluency. Dodrill (1978c) includes it in his Neuropsychological Battery for Epilepsy (p. 566) as a test of concentration which, if impaired, may contribute to problems in shifting responsively.

The material for this test in its original form consists of three white cards, each containing ten rows of five items. Randomized color names—blue, green, red, and yellow—are in black print on card A. Card B is identical, except each color name is printed in some color other than the color it names. Card C displays colored dots in the same array of four colors. There are four trials, each consisting of a different task. On trial I, the subject reads card A; on II he reads card B and ignores the color of the print; for III he names the colors on card C; and on IV he names the colors of the print on card B. The subject is instructed to read or call out the color "as fast as you can" (see Table 16-4). The *Press Test* (Baehr and Corsini, 1980) is a paper and pencil form of the Stroop Test that was modified for group administration but is suitable for clinical use as well.

Nehemkis and Lewinsohn (1972) administered the same tasks in the same order but, unlike Stroop's cards, the test cards they used contained 100 rather than 50 items. Their left hemisphere patients took approximately twice as long as their control subjects to perform each trial, but the interference effect of the second and fourth trials

Table 16-4 Control Subject Performances (in Seconds) on Four Conditions of the Stroop Test

		Read black print	Read color print	Name color dots	Name color print
50-item[a]	Mean	24.7	32.9	40.9	71.8
cards	SD	8.7	12.6	8.1	19.4
100-item[b]	Mean	45.6	47.2	68.3	147.4
cards	SD	9.1	10.3	14.5	73.3

[a]Talland, 1965a.
[b]Nehemkis and Lewinsohn, 1972.

was no greater for left than for right hemisphere patients. A longitudinal survey of performance on a three-color, 100-word variation of the Stroop Test covered each year between ages seven and 12, and age groups 17–19, 25–34, 35–44, and 65–80 (Comalli et al., 1962). Time taken on the word-reading task decreased from an average 89.8 seconds at age seven to a low point for young adults (39.4 seconds) but did not increase greatly for the elderly subjects (45.1 seconds). Time taken on the color-naming task was highest for the young children (264.7 seconds), lowest by a few points for the late teens (103.0 seconds), not much greater through the middle adult years (109.9 seconds), but increased for the 65–80-year-olds (165.1 seconds).

Dodrill (1978c) has developed a modification of the Stroop Test that uses only one sheet containing 178 (11 across, 22 lines down) color word names (red, orange, green, blue) randomly printed in these colors. In Part I of this test, the subject reads the printed word name. Part II requires the subject to report the color in which each word is printed. The times taken to complete the readings are recorded halfway through and at the end on a sheet the examiner uses for recording the subject's responses. The Part I side of the examiner's record sheet shows the correct word names, the other side has printed in correct order the color names for Part II. This device greatly facilitates the recording of this task since many patients move along quite rapidly, particularly on Part I. Dodrill evaluates the performance on the basis of the total time for Part I and the difference between the total time for Parts I and II (Part II minus Part I) (see Table 16-5). The time at which the patient is halfway

Table 16-5 Performance of Control and Epileptic Groups and Cutoff Scores on Dodrill's Modification of the Stroop Test

		Control Group ($n = 50$)	Epileptic Group ($n = 50$)	Cutoff Scores
Part I	Mean	84.76	115.12	93/94 seconds
	SD	20.60	43.91	
Part II − Part I	Mean	123.04	194.68	150/151seconds
	SD	35.77	86.44	

(From Dodrill, 1978c)

through each part, when compared with the total time, indicates whether task familiarity and practice, or difficulty in maintaining a set or attention changes the performance rate.

Perseverance. Problems in perseverance may also compromise any kind of mental or motor activity. Inability to persevere can result from distractibility, or it may reflect impaired self-control usually associated with frontal lobe damage. In the former case, ongoing behavior is interrupted by some external disturbance; in the latter, dissolution of ongoing activity seems to come from within the patient as he loses interest, slows down, or gives up. *Motor impersistence*, the inability to sustain certain discrete voluntary motor acts on command, tends to occur in those patients with right hemisphere or bilateral cortical damage who display fairly severe mental impairment (Joynt et al., 1962; Joynt and M. N. Goldstein, 1975).

Tow (1955) examined perseverance following frontal lobe surgery by having the seated patient hold a leg a little above a chair in front of him as long as possible and by requiring the patient to write as many three-letter words as he can make up from the letters in the words "constable," "speculate," and "overstate." These three words were chosen because many small words can be formed from each. The words were given one after the other as three separate trials. After surgery, patients tended to let their leg down sooner than before surgery. There was also a decided tendency for their productivity to fall off on the second and third trials of the word task. Tow concluded that "Tests of perseveration measure the tendency of mental processes to lag. Perseveration is involuntary; perseverance implies a voluntary control of the act" (pp. 130–131).

Tests of motor impersistence (Joynt et al., 1962; Benton et al., 1983). The eight little subtests combined to examine this phenomenon reflect their origins in the neurological examination. They are (1) keeping eyes closed; (2) protruding tongue, blindfolded; (3) protruding tongue, eyes open; (4) fixating gaze in lateral visual fields; (5) keeping mouth open; (6) fixating on examiner's nose (during confrontation testing of visual fields); (7) sustaining "ah" sound; and (8) maintaining grip. Motor impersistence may also show up when a patient is asked to hold his breath or maintain a lateral gaze. Ben-Yishay and his colleagues (1968) found that only three patients in their group of 24 left hemiplegics failed tongue protrusion while 20 could not maintain a fixated gaze. The proportion of patients failing these tasks increased in the same order as task difficulty determined by Joynt and his co-workers (1962). Such an orderly progression suggests a common underlying deficit that occurs with varying degrees of severity. Scaling (by number of tests failed) also reflected severity of impairment as documented by measurements of cognitive abilities, visuomotor efficiency, and functional competence (Ben-Yishay et al., 1968).

Effective Performance

A performance is as effective as the performer's ability to monitor, self-correct, and regulate the intensity, tempo, and other qualitative aspects of delivery. Brain damaged patients often perform erratically and unsuccessfully since abilities for self-correction and self-monitoring are vulnerable to many different kinds of brain damage. Some patients cannot correct their mistakes because they do not perceive them. Patients with pathological inertia may perceive their errors, even identify them, and yet do nothing to correct them. Defective self-monitoring can spoil any kind of performance, showing up in such diverse ways as unmowed patches in an otherwise manicured lawn, one or two missed numbers in an account book, or shoelaces that snapped and buttons that popped from too much pressure. In a neuropsychological examination, self-monitoring defects may appear in cramped writing that leaves little or no space between words or veers off the horizontal; in missed or slipped (e.g., answer to item 9 on line 10) responses on paper and pencil tests; in speech that comes in quick little bursts or a monotonic, unpunctuated delivery; and in incomplete sentences and thoughts that trail off or are disconnected or easily disrupted by internal or external distractions.

While few examination techniques have been developed for the express purpose of studying self-monitoring or self-correcting behavior, all test performances can provide information about how the subject performs. The nature of the patient's errors, attitudes (including awareness and judgment of them), idiosyncratic distortions, and compensatory efforts will often give more practical information about the patient than test scores that can mask either defects or compensatory strengths.

Maze Learning

Milner (1965, 1969) was the first to show how maze-learning tests may elicit defects in the ability of patients with frontal lobe damage (lobectomized patients in Milner's studies) to carry out instructions despite apparent verbal comprehension of them. In studies comparing these patients with others who had undergone surgery of other parts of the brain, only those with frontal lesions exhibited "rule-breaking" behavior, i.e., an inability to follow the instructions ("return to last point on maze after making an error"; "do not retrace the correct path"; "do not make diagonal moves") despite correct recall of them. As might be expected, Milner also observed that patients with bilateral hippocampal lesions were defective in learning the pathway.

The Austin Maze (Walsh, 1978a).   This electrically activated "stepping stone" maze was developed to study self-correcting behavior as well as the ability to follow instructions. It requires the subject to learn a long pathway through a 10×10 grid of button switches that momentarily light up—green for correct steps and red for incorrect steps along the pathway. Initially the maze must be traversed by trial and error. With each subsequent trial, the number of errors normally diminishes until the subject has learned the maze perfectly. Scores are obtained for both the number of errors per trial and the number of trials to a perfect performance. Normal subjects also tend to adhere to the rules (e.g., no retracing, only right-angled turns). Patients whose executive abilities are impaired may have difficulty learning from their mistakes, switching to alternative response patterns, or attending to the rules. Observation and com-

526

parisons with the patient's performance on learning tests enable the examiner to determine whether a poor performance is due to learning or to executive disabilities. A similar technique for studying the ability to profit from correction can be devised by printing a 10 × 10 grid of dots on paper. The patient can trace a path by touching dots on paper with the eraser end of a pencil (so that no visual track remains), receiving verbal cuing ("right" or "wrong") from the examiner.

Motor Performance

Distinctions between disturbances of motor behavior resulting from a supramodal executive dysfunction and specific disorders of motor functions are clearer in the telling than in fact. A defective sequence of alternating hand movements, for example, may occur—with a cortical lesion—as a specific disability of motor coordination or it may reflect perseveration or inability to sustain a motor pattern; however, it may be a symptom of subcortical rather than cortical pathology (Heilman, 1979). Some diagnostic discriminations can be made from observations of the defective movement. But the classification of a particular disability may also depend on whether the pattern of associated symptoms implicates a cerebellar or a frontal lesion, whether the disorder appears bilaterally or involves one side only, or whether it may reflect a sensory deficit or motor weakness rather than a disorder of movement per se. E. Goldberg and David Tucker (1979) note that the typology of graphic perseverations does not carry with it any focal anatomic associations, at least as yet. Many of the other motor disorders that may accompany cerebral brain damage also cannot, by themselves, necessarily be linked with particular anatomic areas.

The motor dysfunctions within the purview of neuropsychology are those that can occur despite intact capacity for normal movement. They also have an intentional component that makes them psychological data unlike reflex jerks, for example, or the random flailing of a delirious patient.

Motor Functions

A neuropsychological review of motor functions will cover the gamut of motor behavior from the response to a command or imitation of the simplest hand, finger, mouth, or foot and leg movements; to coordination of movements of one or two limbs or fingers, or hand and head; to maintaining movements or changing their rates and direction; to complex motor sequences involving the hands and mouth in particular; to integration of motor behavior with speech and verbal thought. Christensen (1979) provides an orderly review of the techniques Luria used for the neuropsychological examination of these basic motor functions (see pp. 567–568). Other descriptions of these techniques can be found in Luria's writings (1966, 1973). The techniques have not been graded or equated for difficulty or level of complexity, nor are they suited to such statistical manipulations. Rather, Christensen's list can serve as an orderly framework for eliciting motor behavior and articulating clinical observations.

Examining for Apraxia

The examination for apraxia reviews a variety of learned movements of the face, the limbs, and—less often—the body (Hécaen, 1981; Heilman, 1979; Kimura and Archibald, 1974; Strub and Black, 1977). The integrity of learned movements of the face and limbs, particularly the hands, is typically examined under two conditions: *imitation* of the examiner (a) making symbolic or communicative movements, such as familiar gestures, (b) using actual objects, or (c) pantomiming their use without objects; and *to command* for each of these three kinds of activities.

Table 16-6 lists activities that have been used in examinations for apraxia. The examiner may demonstrate each activity for imitation or direct its performance, asking the subject to "do what you see me doing" or "show me how you. . . ." Some of these activities should involve the use of objects either with the object or in pantomine. The examiner should be alert to those patients who are not apraxic but, when pantomiming to command, use their hand as if it were the tool (e.g., hammering with their fists, cutting with fingers opening and closing like scissors blades). The concreteness of their response reflects their concreteness of thought.

As with so many aspects of executive dysfunctions, the presence of apraxia is signalled by any single instance of inability to perform the required movements that is not a result of sensory deficit or motor weakness, or subcortical disease involving components of the motor system (e.g., parkinsonism, cerebellar disorders). The range of activities tested enables the examiner to assess the extent and severity of the disorder. Among patients with unilateral lesions, most apraxias of use and gesture affect both sides of the body but typically occur with lesions in the left cerebral cortex (Kimura, 1979). Dee and his colleagues (1970) observed that symbolic and use apraxias tend to be closely associated with receptive language disorders (Dee et al., 1970) and with gesture recognition (Ferro et al., 1980). However, a high proportion of brain damaged patients had difficulty *imitating* symbolic gestures, regardless of the side of lesion.

Table 16-6 Activities for Examining Practic Functions

	Use of Objects	Symbolic Gestures	Other
Face (Buccofacial)	Blow out match	Stick out tongue	Whistle
	Suck on straw	Blow a kiss	Show teeth
Upper Limb	Use toothbrush	Salute	Snap fingers
	Hammer nail	Hitchhike	Touch ear with index finger
	Cut paper	"OK" sign	Hold up thumb and little finger
	Flip coin	"Stop" sign	Make a fist
Lower Limb	Kick ball		
	Put out cigarette		
Whole Body	Swing baseball bat	Bow	Stand (or sit)
	Sweep with broom	Stand like boxer	Turn around

Heilman (1979) reports that patterns of hand apraxia differing with respect to side of involvement and task condition may relate to different lesion sites.

Manual Dexterity

Many neuropsychologists include tests of manipulative agility in their examination batteries. These are all timed speed tests that either have an apparatus with a counting device or elicit a countable performance. These tests may aid in the detection of a lateralized disability.

THE FINGER TAPPING TEST (FTT) (Reitan and Davison, 1974; E. W. Russell et al., 1970)

Probably the most widely used test of manual dexterity, this was originally called the *Finger Oscillation Test* (Halstead, 1947). It is one of the tests in the Halstead-Reitan battery (see pp. 562–566). It consists of a tapping key with a device for recording the number of taps. Each hand makes five 10-second trials with brief rest periods between trials. The score for each hand is the average for each five trials. The 29 subjects who comprised Halstead's control group (see p. 564) averaged 50 taps per 10-second period for their right hand, 45 taps for their left. Two larger samples of men and women (47 each) using their preferred hands achieved mean scores of 55.87 ± 4.91 and 51.08 ± 4.87, respectively (Dodrill, 1979). The almost five-point difference between the groups is significant at the .001 level. The mean Finger Tapping score of 54.12 ± 4.35 reported by Matarazzo and his co-workers (1974) for 29 young men supports Dodrill's data, as do findings of a 4.4-point difference ($p < .01$) in favor of males using Finger Tapping scores averaged "across hands" (G. D. King et al., 1978). G. D. King and his group also observed that anxiety tended to depress Finger Tapping scores of the women in his study, but not the men. As one might expect, slowing occurs with age, tending to show up in the fifth to sixth decades and increasing significantly thereafter (Bak and Greene, 1980; Harley et al., 1980; Pauker, 1977).

Brain damage generally, but not always, tends to have a slowing effect on finger tapping rate (Dodrill, 1978a; Haaland et al., 1977; Lansdell and Donnelly, 1977). Lateralized lesions usually result in slowing of the tapping rate of the contralateral hand (Finlayson and Reitan, 1980; Haaland and Delaney, 1981). However, these effects do not appear with sufficient distinctiveness or consistency to warrant the use of this test for screening purposes (Heaton et al., 1978; Lewinsohn, 1973). The test is sensitive to diphenylhydantoin (Dilantin) levels (Dodrill, 1975).

THE PURDUE PEGBOARD TEST (Purdue Research Foundation, 1948)

This neuropsychologically sensitive test was developed to test manual dexterity for employment selection. It has been applied to questions of lateralization of lesions (Costa et al., 1963; Vaughan and Costa, 1962) and motor dexterity (Diller et al., 1974) among brain damaged patients. Following the standard instructions, the patient places the pegs with the left hand, right hand, and then both hands simultaneously (see Fig. 16-7). Each condition lasts for 30 seconds so that the total actual testing time is 90 seconds. Although the standard instructions call for only one trial for each condition, when examining patients with known or suspected brain damage, a practice trial is recommended for each condition to allow the patient to learn the test set. The score is the number of pegs placed correctly. Average scores of normative groups, consisting of production workers and applicants for production work jobs, range from 15 to 19 for the right hand, from 14.5 to 18 for the left hand, from 12 to 15.5 for both hands, and from 43 to 50 for the sum of the first three scores (Tiffin, 1968). Averages for groups of women tend to run two or more points above the averages for men's groups.

Although brain damaged patients as a group tend to perform below the control

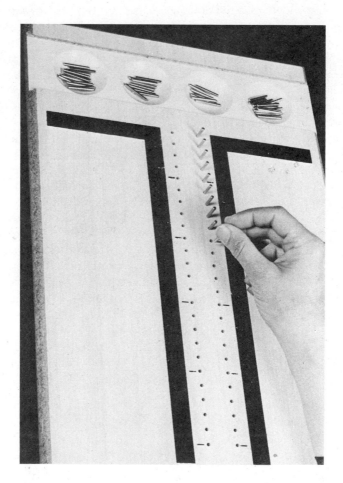

Fig. 16-7.   The Purdue Pegboard Test. (Courtesy of the Lafayette Instrument Co.)

Table 16-7   Purdue Pegboard Test Mean Scores

	Control Subjects	Left Damaged Patients	Right Damaged Patients
Right hand	14	9	10
Left hand	13	10	0

(Adapted from Vaughan and Costa, 1962)

group, patients with right hemisphere damage may be virtually nonfunctional when using their left hand (see Table 16-7). However, Diller found that group mean scores—averaged for the three 30-second trials—did not differ significantly for right and left hemiplegic stroke patients. Their mean scores ranged between 10.40 and 11.83 with standard deviations no smaller than 2.41.

In a study of the efficiency of the Purdue Pegboard Test in making diagnostic discriminations, cutoff scores were developed that proved 70% accurate in predicting a lateralized lesion in the validation sample, 60% accurate in predicting lateralization in the cross-validation sample, and 89% accurate in predicting brain damage in general for both samples (Costa et al., 1963). Since the base rate of brain damaged patients in this population was 73%, the Pegboard accuracy score represented a significant ($p < .05$) prediction gain over the base rate. Two separate sets of cutting scores were developed for older and younger age groups (see Table 16-8). Further, for patients of all ages, a brain lesion is likely to be present whenever the left hand score exceeds that of the right (preferred) hand, or the right (preferred) hand score exceeds that of the left by three points or more. One-sided slowing suggests a lesion on the contralateral hemisphere; bilateral slowing occurs with diffuse or bilateral brain damage.

T. E. Goldberg and A. Smith (1976) have also developed cutoff scores for two age groups, using an expanded administration that includes two 30 second trials and a 60 second trial for each condition (preferred, nonpreferred, and both hands). Their cutting scores differ from those developed by Vaughn and Costa (see Table 16-8) in only two respects: their Both Hands cutting score for their younger (13 to 40) group is 9; their Preferred Hand cutting score for their older (41 to 70) group is 12. Although the age ranges of the younger and older groups in these two studies were not the same, the other cutting scores for the younger and older groups in these studies were

Table 16-8   Purdue Pegboard Test Cutting Scores for Brain Damage for Two Age Groups

	Under Age 60	60 and Older
Right (preferred) hand	<13	<10
Left (nonpreferred) hand	<11	<10
Simultaneous (both hands)	<10	<8

(Adapted from Vaughan and Costa, 1962)

identical. Goldberg and Smith's criteria for each 60 second condition is simply two times the 30 second criterion for that condition. Performances are considered indicative of brain damage when one or more score below criterion occurs on both the first and the second trial for one or more 30 second conditions, or occurs on the 60 second trial for one condition. A 60 second score achieved by the nonpreferred hand that exceeds the preferred hand's score by three or more points indicates a lesion contralateral to the preferred hand. A 30 second score for the preferred hand that exceeds the 30 second score of the nonpreferred hand by five or more points suggests that the lesion is ipsilateral to the preferred hand.

Like many other useful neuropsychological instruments, the Purdue Pegboard Test varies greatly in the efficiency with which it identifies brain impairment. T. E. Goldberg and A. Smith (1976) report that, using their norms based on two trials for each condition, this test identified 80% (10% false positive, 10% false negative) of a large group of normal subjects and neurological patients correctly. Also using these norms, Berker and his colleagues (1982) found that in a group of 228 diagnostically mixed brain damaged persons, a larger number had motor than sensory deficits (using the Face-Hand Sensory Test, see p. 378), although both kinds of deficits are usually present with lateralized lesions. However, Heaton and his co-workers (1978) report that the proportion of correct differentiations between organic and various groups of psychiatric patients made by this test alone ranges from 76% to 46%. These are not very good odds on which to attempt a screening program.

GROOVED PEGBOARD (Kløve, 1963; Matthews and Kløve, 1964)

This test adds a dimension of complex coordination to the pegboard task. It consists of a small board containing a 5×5 set of slotted holes angled in different directions. Each peg has a ridge along one side requiring it to be rotated into position for correct insertion. It is part of the Wisconsin Neuropsychological Test Battery (Harley et al., 1980; Matthews and Kløve, 1964) and the Lafayette Clinic Repeatable Neuropsychological Test Battery (R. Lewis and Kupke, 1977) (see p. 566). Its complexity makes it a highly sensitive instrument for studying improvement in motor functions following stroke (Meier, 1974) and hemispheric components of motor performance (Haaland et al., 1977; Haaland and Delaney, 1981).

Time to completion is scored. Data have been handled in a variety of ways. Matthews and Haaland (1979) give the mean time averaged for both hands in a small (n = 16) group of mostly middle-aged (55 ± 5) control subjects as 85 seconds. One group of 14-year-old boys and girls performed the task in 66.5 ± 13.3 seconds using their preferred hands and 70.1 ± 7.5 seconds with the nonpreferred hand (Knights and Moule, 1968). Another group of 14 year olds, all male, took longer and showed much greater variability, performing the task in 78 ± 40.5 seconds with the preferred hand and in 81 ± 23.8 seconds with the nonpreferred hand (Trites, no date). R. Lewis and Kupke (1977) report that average scores for the preferred hand only were in the range of 71–79.5 seconds for epileptic patients under different drug conditions.

17

Orientation and Attention

Orientation

Orientation, the awareness of self in relation to one's surroundings, requires consistent and reliable integration of attention, perception, and memory. Impairment of particular perceptual or memory functions can lead to specific defects of orientation; more than mild or transient problems of attention or retention are likely to result in global impairment of orientation. Its dependence on the intactness and integration of so many different mental activities makes orientation exceedingly vulnerable to the effects of brain dysfunction (Schulman et al., 1965).

Orientation defects are among the most frequent symptoms of brain disease, and of these, impaired awareness for time and place is the most common, accompanying every brain disorder in which attention or retention is significantly affected (Gooddy, 1969; McGhie, 1969). It is not difficult to understand the fragility of orientation for time and place, since each depends on both continuity of awareness and the translation of immediate experience into memories of sufficient duration to allow the person to keep in touch with his ongoing history. Thus, impaired orientation for time and place typically occurs with widespread cortical involvement (e.g., in senile dementia, acute brain syndromes, or bilateral cerebral lesions), lesions in the limbic system (e.g., Korsakoff's psychosis), or damage to the reticular activating system of the brain stem (e.g., disturbances of consciousness). However, when cognitive impairments or deficits in attention are relatively mild, orientation can still be intact (Eisdorfer and Cohen, 1980). Thus, while impaired orientation, in itself, is strongly suggestive of cerebral dysfunction, good orientation is not evidence of cognitive or attentional competence.

Assessment of orientation for time, place, and person is generally covered in the mental status examination (see Chap. 19, pp. 576–578). Tests of specific facets of orientation are not ordinarily included in the formal neuropsychological examination. However, their use is indicated when a patient's lapses on an informal mental status examination call for a more thorough evaluation of his orientation or when scores are needed for documenting the course of a condition or for research. For these purposes, a number of little tests and examination techniques are available.

Tests for Orientation

PLACE

Assessment of orientation for place generally begins with questions about the name or location of the place in which the patient is being examined. The examiner needs to find out if the patient knows the *kind* of place he is in, e.g., hospital, clinic, office; the name, if it has one, e.g., Veteran's Hospital, Marion County Mental Health Clinic; and where it is located, e.g., city, state. Orientation for place also includes an appreciation of direction and distance. To test for this, the examiner might ask where the patient's home is in relation to the hospital, clinic, etc., in what direction the patient must travel to get home, and how long it takes to get there. The examiner can also check the patient's practical knowledge of the geography of the locale or state and his awareness of the distance and direction of the state capital, another big city, or an adjacent state relative to his present location.

TIME

To test for time orientation, the examiner asks for the date (day, month, year, and day of the week) and the time of day. The patient's sense of temporal continuity should also be assessed, since he may be able to remember the number and name of the present day and yet not have a functional sense of time, particularly if he is in a rehabilitation unit or in the care of a conscientious family whose members make every effort to keep him oriented. On the other hand, some patients will have a generally accurate awareness of the passage of time but be unable to remember the specifics of the date. Questions concerning *duration* will assess the patient's appreciation of temporal continuity. The examiner may ask such questions as "How long have you been in this place?"[1] "How long is it since you last worked?" "How long since you last saw me?" "What was your last meal (i.e., breakfast, lunch, or dinner)?[2] How long ago did you have it?"

TEMPORAL ORIENTATION TEST (Benton et al., 1964; Benton et al., 1983)

This is a scoring technique in which negative numerical values are assigned to errors in any one of the five basic time orientation elements: day, month, year, day of week, and present clock time. It has a system of differentially weighted scores for each of the five elements. Errors in naming or numbering days and errors in clock time are

[1] It is important not to give away answers before the questions are asked. The examiner who is testing for time orientation before place must be careful not to ask, "How long have you been in the *hospital?*" or "When did you arrive in *Portland?*"

[2] Some mental status examinations for recent memory include questions about the foods served at a recent meal. Unless the examiner checks with the family or the dietician, he has no way of knowing whether the paitent had chicken for dinner or is drawing on old memory of what people usually eat in the evening. The menu problem is most apparent with breakfast, for the usual variety of breakfasts is so limited it is impossible to tell whether the patient is calling on old memory or new when he reports that he had "toast, cereal, eggs, and coffee."

given one point for each day difference between the correct and the erroneously stated day and for each 30 minutes between clock time and stated time. Errors in naming months are given 5 points for each month of difference between the present and the named month. Errors in numbering years receive 10 points for each year of difference between the present and the named year. The total error score is subtracted from 100 to obtain the test score. Scores of 60 patients with brain disease were compared with 110 control patients (see Table 17-1).

Both control (patients without cerebral disease) and brain damaged patients most commonly erred by missing the number of the day of the month by one or two. For both groups, the second most common error was misestimating clock time by more than 30 minutes. The brain damaged group miscalled the day of the week with much greater frequency than the control patients. Patients with undifferentiated bilateral cerebral disease performed most poorly of all. Applying this test to frontal lobe patients, Benton (1968a) found that it discriminated between bilaterally and unilaterally brain injured patients, for none of the frontal lobe patients with unilateral lesions and 57% of those with bilateral lesions had defective performances. In a group of long-term hospitalized patients, a larger proportion of those who were organically impaired (39%) received scores in the defective range (94 or less) on this test than did schizophrenic patients (9%) (Joslyn and Hutzell, 1979). However, two-thirds of this organic patient group and 44% of the schizophrenic group were unable to respond well enough to obtain any score at all. The disparity between organic and schizophrenic patients was even greater for newly admitted patients as 57% of the organic patients scored 94 or lower in contrast to only 9% of the newly admitted schizophrenic patients. Interestingly, all recently admitted patients gave scorable performances.

Using a set of ten differentially weighted temporal orientation questions (*Temporal Disorientation Questionnaire*), P. L. Wang and Uzzell (1978) reported findings similar to Benton's. Their brain damaged patients also had a high rate of failure in naming the day of the week (96%). Patients with bilateral lesions were the most severely disoriented. Performance on this test did not discriminate between patients with right- or left-sided lesions. As a group, patients with unilateral lesions made more errors than control subjects or patients with brain stem lesions, but many fewer errors than the bilateral group. A preponderance of the brain damaged patients also could not give their date of admission (77%) or the current date (73%).

Table 17-1 Temporal Orientation Test Scores for Control and Brain Damaged Patients

	Score			
Subjects	100	99	98–95	94 & below
Control (*n* = 110)	67 (61%)	33 (30%)	10 (9%)	0
Brain damaged (*n* = 60)	27 (45%)	6 (10%)	19 (32%)	8 (13%)

(Adapted from Benton et al., 1964)

TIME ESTIMATION

Benton and his colleagues (1964) also asked their subjects to estimate the passage of a minute. They report that error scores of 21–22 seconds are in the "average range," an error score of 33 seconds is "moderately inaccurate," and scores over 38 seconds are "extremely inaccurate." For neither the control nor the brain injured patient group was there a relationship between poor scores on the Temporal Orientation Test and size of time estimation error, leading the authors to conclude that "temporal orientation and the ability to estimate brief temporal durations reflect essentially independent behavior processes" (p. 119). Another simple time estimation task requires the patient to guess the length of time taken by a just-completed test session (McFie, 1960). Estimations under one-half the actual time are considered failures. Only one of 15 patients whose lesions were localized on the left temporal lobe failed this task although one-third or more of each of the other groups of patients with localized lesions and one-half of those suffering presenile dementia failed.

Talland (1965a) used buzzers in testing time estimation of patients with severe memory impairments. The test involves matching durations of and intervals between buzzer signals. These patients made larger errors of both underestimation and overestimation than the control subjects, but the difference between the two groups was not significant. On another series of time estimation tasks, each given on a different day, both control and memory impaired groups underestimated the time lapse while engaged on a task but the memory impaired patients made larger errors, particularly on the longer (3 minutes) rather than the shorter (30 seconds) time interval. Judgments by control subjects of the amount of lapsed time were much less variable than those of the patients.

Recognition of recency.   The *Discrimination of Recency* task (Milner, 1971) was developed to test the hypothesis that memories normally carry "time tags" that facilitate their retrieval (Yntema and Trask, 1963). The verbal form consists of 184 cards on which are printed two spondaic words such as "pitchfork" and "smokestack." Each card has a different word pair, but the same word may occur on a number of cards. At intervals in the deck are cards with a question mark between two words. The subject reads the word pairs aloud, and when he comes to the card with the question mark, his task is to indicate which of the two words he saw more recently. Usually both words have come up previously; occasionally only one had already been seen. The nonverbal form of this task presents paired pictures of abstract art.

On the verbal form of this task, normal control subjects recognized an average of 94% of previously seen words when they were paired with new words and correctly guessed relative recency an average of 71% of the time. Both left frontotemporal and left temporal groups were significantly impaired on one or both of these tasks relative to the control subjects and right brain injured patients. However, the patients with right-sided lesions were defective relative to controls and left brain injured patient groups on the nonverbal version of this task. Patients with frontal lobe involvement had difficulty with the recency aspect of the task; those with temporal lobe involvement had difficulty with recognition.

Huppert and Piercy (1976) used a picture recognition technique to examine the ability to make recency estimations. Korsakoff patients and chronic alcoholics (used as control subjects) had to identify which pictures they had seen (1) three times the day before the recognition test (40 familiar filler pictures), (2) both three times the day before and once ten minutes before the recognition test (40 familiar stimulus pictures), (3) once ten minutes before the recognition test (40 unfamiliar stimulus pictures), and (4) for the first time on the recognition test (40 unfamiliar fillers). Half of the pictures were presented in pairs of which only one was the stimulus picture shown just prior to testing. On this, the two-choice form, the patient's task was to identify the stimulus picture. The other 80 pictures were presented one by one with the question, "Did you see this picture *today?*" When the answer was negative, the subject was asked if he had seen it before.

The control subjects made more correct identifications than the Korsakoff patients on both forms of the test. However, the interpretation of results with the two-choice form is difficult because a correct answer may reflect correct identification of either one of the pictures or could result from a comparative judgment. Results with the yes-no form of the test are less ambiguous as the responses to the different kinds of items can be analyzed separately and unequivocally. Thus, an analysis of errors on the yes-no form clearly differentiated response patterns of the Korsakoff patients and the control subjects; the Korsakoff patients gave 50.6% false positive responses to the familiar filler pictures in contrast to the control subjects' false positive rate of 3.1, and they made 400% more false positive responses to the familiar than the unfamiliar filler pictures.

Space

"Spatial disorientation" refers to different kinds of defects that in some way interfere with the ability to relate to the position, direction, or movement of objects or points in space. In identifying different kinds of spatial disorientation, Benton (1969b) pointed out that they do not arise from a single defect but are associated with damage to different areas of the brain and involve different functions. With the exception of right-left, topographic, and body schema disorientation, however, most disturbances of spatial orientation occur with lesions of the posterior right hemisphere (S. Weinstein, 1964). As in every other kind of defective performance, an understanding of the disoriented behavior requires careful analysis of its components to determine the extent to which the problem is one of verbal labeling, specific amnesia, visual scanning, visual agnosia, or a true spatial disorientation. Thus, comprehensive testing for spatial disorientation requires a variety of different tests.

Spatial orientation is one of the components of visual perception. For this reason, some tests of visuospatial orientation are presented in Chapter 12, Perceptual Functions, such as Judgment of Line Orientation (pp. 349–350), which measures the accuracy of angular orientation, and the line bisection tests (pp. 343–345), which involve distance estimation.

BODY ORIENTATION

Disorientation of personal space *(autotopagnosia)* tends not to be associated with problems of localization in space. It is most apt to occur with left frontal lesions (Teuber, 1964) and is also a common concomitant of aphasia (Diller et al., 1974; S. Weinstein, 1964). The examination of body orientation has complications. Tests for disorientation of personal space typically require the patient to make right-left discriminations that may be disrupted by left posterior lesions. Moreover, communication disabilities resulting from the aphasic disorders likely to accompany left hemisphere lesions can override subtle disorders of body or directional orientation.

Informal tests for body orientation are part of the neurological examination (Fredericks, 1969d; Strub and Black, 1977). Finger orientation is examined in tests for finger agnosia (see pp. 378–379). Orientation to body parts can be reviewed through different operations: pointing on command, naming body parts indicated by the examiner, and imitating body part placements or movements of the examiner. A thorough examination will require the patient to identify parts of his body and of the examiner's body and will include crosswise imitation (e.g., right-side response to right-side stimulus) (Fredericks, 1969d).

Personal Orientation Test (Semmes et al., 1963; S. Weinstein, 1964). This test calls for the patient (1) to touch the parts of his body named by the examiner, (2) to name parts of his body touched by the examiner, (3) to touch those parts of the examiner's body the examiner names, (4) to touch his body in imitation of the examiner, and (5) to touch his body according to numbered schematic diagrams of the body (see Fig. 17-1). A sixth task tests for astereognosis by asking for the names of seen and felt objects.

A comparison of left and right hemisphere damaged patients' performances on this task indicates that the left hemisphere patients have greatest difficulty following verbal directions, whereas patients with right hemisphere lesions are more likely to ignore the left side of their body or objects presented to their left (Raghaven, 1961). Much of the impaired body orientation associated with left posterior lesions appears to be an aspect of a more global asphasic disorder; or it may follow from incomprehension of how single parts relate to a whole structure (De Renzi and Scotti, 1970). Disturbances of body schema occurring with frontal lesions seem to result from disturbances in scanning, perceptual shifting, and postural mechanisms (Teuber, 1964). Using part 5 of this test, which is mostly nonverbal, F. P. Bowen (1976) showed that Parkinson patients, whose lesions primarily involve subcortical areas, suffered some defects in body orientation. Those whose symptoms were predominantly left-sided or bilateral made many more errors than patients with predominantly right-sided symptoms.

538

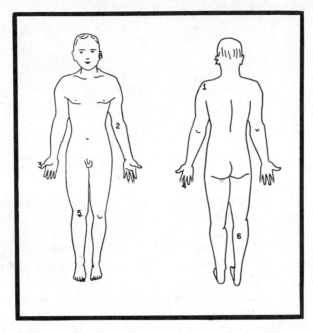

Fig. 17-1. One of the five diagrams of the Personal Orientation Test (Semmes etal. 1963).

Body Center Test (Diller et al., 1974).   This test was devised to study body disorientation in relation to scanning problems. While the examiner taps along the patient's back from shoulder to shoulder, the patient must indicate when he thinks the examiner has reached the center of his back. This procedure is repeated six times, three from each shoulder. Deviations of the guessed center from the actual center are measured in fractions of inches from zero. As on other scanning tests, the performance of patients with severe aphasic disorders was much worse than that of patients with mild aphasia. From the data, it is not possible to determine whether this finding is a function of the severity of the cerebral insult per se or is associated with a sensory disturbance.

DIRECTIONAL (RIGHT-LEFT) ORIENTATION

As the examination of body orientation almost necessarily involves right-left directions, so the examination of right-left orientation usually refers to body parts (e.g., Strub and Black, 1977; K. W. Walsh, 1978b). When verbal communication is sufficiently intact, gross testing of direction sense can be accomplished with a few commands, such as "Place your right hand on your left knee," "Touch your left cheek with your left thumb," or "Touch my left hand with your right hand."

Table 17-2. Right-Left Body Parts Identification: Show Me

"Show Me Your:"	"Show Me My:"
(a) Left Hand	(b) Right Ear
(c) Right Hand	(d) Left Eye
(e) Left Ear	(f) Right Hand
(g) Right Eye	(h) Left Ear
(i) Right Ear	(j) Right Eye

(From A. Smith, undated)

Right-Left Body Parts Identification: "Show Me" (A. Smith, undated). This little test is part of the Michigan Neuropsychological Test Battery (p. 572) (see Table 17-2). Because the hand the patient should use to indicate the named body part is not specified, patients with lateralized motor disabilities are not put at a disadvantage.

The Standardized Road-Map Test of Direction Sense (Money, 1976). This easily administered test provides developmental norms for a quick paper and pencil assessment of right-left orientation (Fig. 17-2). As the examiner traces a dotted pathway with his pencil, he asks the subject to tell the direction he takes at each turn, right or left. The test is preceded by a demonstration trial on an abbreviated pathway in a corner of the map. Although norms for ages above 18 are not available, a cutoff point

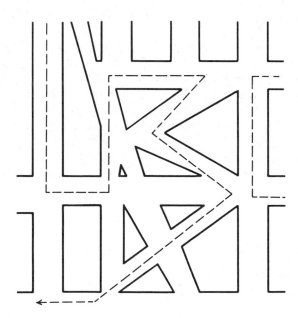

Fig. 17-2. A section of *The Standardized Road-Map Test of Direction Sense* (© J. Money. Courtesy of the author).

of ten errors (out of the 32 choice points) is recommended for evaluating performance, regardless of age. Since it is unlikely that persons who make fewer than ten errors are guessing, their sense of direction is probably reasonably well-developed and intact.

Almost all brain injured patients who are capable of following simple instructions pass this test so that failure is a clear sign of impaired right-left orientation. It may also result from inability to shift right-left orientation, which will show up particularly at those choice points involving a conceptual reorientation of 90° to 180°.

Butters and his colleagues (1972) examined the performances of four groups of patients with localized lesions (right parietal and temporal, left frontal and temporal). The left frontal group averaged 11.9 errors, more than twice as many as the right parietal patients who were next highest with a mean error score of 5.5. The authors suggest that the failures of the left frontal patients reflect the test's conceptual demands for making mental spatial rotations. However, the absence of left parietal and right frontal groups leaves unanswered the question of whether the right-left confusion that some patients with left hemisphere damage experience may have contributed as much or more than conceptual disabilities to the left frontal patients' poor performances.

DISTANCE ESTIMATIONS

Both spatial disorientation (Benton, 1969b) and visual scanning defects (Diller et al., 1974) may be involved in impaired judgment of distances. Benton divides problems of distance estimation into those involving local space, i.e., "within 'grasping distance,'" and those involving points in the space "beyond arm's reach." He notes a tendency for patients with disordered spatial orientation to confuse retinal size with actual size, ignoring the effects of distance.

In examining distance estimation, Hécaen and Angelergues (1963) presented their patients with a number of informal tasks. They asked for both relative (nearer, farther) and absolute (in numerical scale) estimations of distances between people in a room, between the patient and objects located in different parts of the room, and for rough comparisons between the relative estimates. The patient also had to indicate when two moving objects were equidistant from him. These distance estimation tasks were among other tests for visuospatial deficits. Although some visuospatial deficits accompanied lesions in the left posterior cortex, more than five times as many such deficits occured in association with right posterior—particularly occipital—lesions.

MENTAL TRANSFORMATIONS IN SPACE

Defective abilities to conceptualize such spatial transformations as rotations, inversions, and three-dimensional forms of two-dimensional stimuli have received considerable neuropsychological attention (e.g., Boller et al., 1981; Butters et al., 1970; Levy, 1974; Luria, 1966). Most of these examination methods are paper and pencil tests that require the subject to indicate which of several rotated figures matches the stimulus

541

figure, to discriminate right from left hands, or to mark a test figure so that it will be identical with the stimulus figure. Luria (1966, p. 371) shows samples of the last two kinds of items in the "parallelogram test" and the "hands test." These items and most others have been taken from paper and pencil intelligence and aptitude tests (e.g., the Differential Aptitude Test, the California Tests of Mental Ability, the Primary Mental Ability Tests, among others). A list of those subtests that appear to weigh substantially on Spatial Visualization and Spatial Orientation factors is provided by McGee (1979).

Mental Re-orientation (Ratcliff, 1979) is an example of a spatial orientation test devised for neuropsychological studies (see Fig. 17-3). The "Little Men" figures can be presented by slide projection or on cards. Each of the four positions is shown eight times; in half the cases the black disc is on the figure's right, in half on the left. The subject's task is to state whether the black disc is on the figure's right or left side. Before and after the test, the subjects were given 12 trials of a simple right-left discrimination task (indicating whether a black circle was right or left of a white one) that did not involve reorientation in order to evaluate accuracy of simple right–left discrimination. Comparing small subgroup samples (e.g., only 11 in the "nonposterior" group), Ratcliff found that patients with right posterior lesions made more errors ($p < .05$) than any other group. Although patients with bilateral posterior damage made the second highest number of errors, differences between this patient group and the groups with the lowest error scores (control, nonposterior, left posterior) did not reach statistical significance.

Using a variation of the Mental Re-orientation task, Boller and his colleagues (1981) looked for differences in the abilities of four groups of patients (with left- or right-sided lesions each divided into a posterior and an anterior group) to make spatial

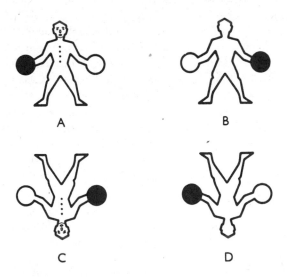

A B

C D

Fig. 17-3. "Little Men" figures of the Mental Re-orientation test.

reorientations on visuoperceptual and visuomotor tasks. On the visuoperceptual form of the test, Little Men figures were presented in pairs, each oriented differently; the subject's task was to say whether the black discs were on the same or different sides. The visuomotor form of the task also presented pairs of variously oriented Little Men, only one with a black disc; the task here was to blacken the disc on the same side of the other figure as the sample figure's black disc. With these modifications, also using small groups of patients, no statistically significant right-left group differences appeared on either task, although patients with left anterior lesions made the most errors. Performances on the two tasks were highly correlated in both groups with right hemisphere lesions ($r = .68$), but not in the group with left hemisphere damage or the control subjects. This finding suggests that visuoperceptual defects played a large role in the visuospatial disorder of the patients with right hemisphere damage, but contributed minimally to the visuospatial impairments of those with left hemisphere lesions.

Performance deficits on tests involving mental rotations have been associated with parietal lobe lesions (Butters and Barton, 1970). Studies involving conceptual transformations from two to three dimensions have consistently demonstrated the importance of the right hemisphere to these operations (Nebes, 1978). In the absence of fully consistent findings, standardized methods, and large patient samples, however, the examiner should not rely on these tests for making diagnostic discriminations. They are of value in gaining information about visuospatial orientation for planning, treatment, and research purposes.

SPATIAL ORIENTATION MEMORY TEST (Wepman and Turaids, 1975)[1]

This test of immediate recall of the orientation of geometric and design figures is predominantly a measure of visual discrimination and spatial orientation and also has an immediate memory component (Pirozzolo et al., 1982). It is based on observations of rotational and reversal tendencies in the perceptual orientation of young children which dissipate for the most part by age seven but are often still present in older children with reading problems. Like a number of special function tests designed for children, this test has a sufficiently high ceiling for adult use.

Each of the 20 items of this test consists of a stimulus card containing a single target figure that is reproduced in the identical orientation and in four different orientations on the multiple-choice response card. Target figures include, for example, an isosceles triangle, a dotted circle transected by a broken dotted line, and a three-quarter moon. The items increase in difficulty, as the range of angulation of the alternative figures goes from 90° and 180° differences from the target on the two sample and first six items to angulation ranges differing from the target by less than 90°. The stimulus card is displayed for just five seconds and immediately thereafter the subject is shown the response card and asked to indicate the one figure that is turned in the same

[1]This test is available through Language Research Associates, P.O. Box 2085, Palm Springs, Ca., 92262.

direction as the target. From ages five to ten, the mean scores steadily increase from just under 7.00 to approximately 13.00, with the largest increment occurring between ages six and seven. Sixty normal control subjects with a mean age in the early 60s did a little better than the 12 and 13 year olds in the normative groups ($\overline{X} = 14.82 \pm 2.79$). However, a group of 60 patients with Parkinson's disease in the same age range achieved a significantly lower mean score (10.80 ± 3.81) (Pirozzolo et al., 1982), reflecting a tendency to spatial disorientation compounded by impairments in immediate memory that were also documented by other tests taken by these patients.

SPATIAL DYSCALCULIAS

Difficulty in calculating arithmetic problems in which the relative position of the numbers is a critical element of the problem, as in carrying numbers or long division, tends to occur with posterior right hemisphere lesions (see p. 72). This shows up in distinctive errors of misplacement of numbers relative to one another, confusion of columns or rows of numbers, and neglect of one or more numbers, although the patient understands the operations and appreciates the meaning and value of the mathematical symbols.

Tests for spatial dyscalculia are easily improvised. When making up arithmetic problems to bring out a spatial dyscalculia, the examiner should include several relatively simple addition, subtraction, multiplication, and long division problems using two- to four-digit numbers that require carrying for their solution. Problems set up by the examiner should be written in fairly large numbers. The examiner can also dictate a variety of computation problems to see how the patient sets them up. I use unlined letter-size sheets of paper for this task so that the patient does not have ready-made lines for visual guidance. Large paper gives the patient a greater opportunity to demonstrate spatial organization and planning than do smaller pieces of paper on which abnormally small writing or unusual use of space (e.g., crowding along one edge) is less apparent.

TOPOGRAPHICAL ORIENTATION

Defective memory for familiar routes or for the location of objects and places in space involves an impaired ability for "revisualization," the retrieval of established visuospatial knowledge (Benton, 1969b). Testing for this defect can be difficult, for it typically involves disorientation around home or neighborhood, sometimes in spite of the patient's ability to verbalize the street directions or descriptions of the floor plan of his home. When an alert patient or his family complains that he gets lost easily, or seems bewildered in familiar surroundings, his topographical memory can be tested by asking him first to describe the floor plan of his house or his ward and the route to the nearest grocery store or gas station from his home, and then having him draw the floor plan or a map, showing how to get from home to store or station, or a map of the downtown or other familiar section of his city (Paterson and Zangwill, 1944).

A reasonably accurate performance of these kinds of tasks is well within the capacity of most of the adult population. Thus, a single blatant error, such as an east-west reversal or a gross distortion or logically impossible element on a diagram or map, should raise the suspicion of impairment. More than one error probably results from defective visuospatial orientation. Failure on any of these tasks does not necessarily indicate impaired topographical memory. Visuographic disabilities, unilateral spatial inattention, a global memory disorder or a confusional state may also interfere with performance on tests of visuospatial orientation. Evaluation of the source of failure should take into account the nature of the patient's errors on this task and the presence of visuographic, perceptual, or memory problems on other tasks.

Topographical Localization (Lezak, no date). Topographical memory can be further tested by requesting the patient to locate prominent cities on a map of the country. An outline map of the United States of convenient size can be easily made by tracing the Area Code map in the telephone directory onto letter-size paper. When using this technique, I first ask the patient to write in the compass directions on this piece of paper. I then ask the patient to show on the map where a number of places are located by writing in a number assigned to each of them. For example, "Write 1 to show where the Atlantic Ocean is; 2 for Florida; 3 for Portland; 4 for Los Angeles; 5 for Texas; 6 for Chicago; 7 for Mexico; 8 for New York; 9 for the Pacific Ocean; 10 for the Rocky Mountains; and 11 for your birthplace" (see Fig. 17-4). The places named will be different in different locales and for different patients as they should be likely to be familiar given the place of the examination and the patient's background. To insure this test's sensitivity to visuospatial inattention, at least as many of the places named should be in the west as in the east.

For clinical purposes, scoring is not necessary as disorientation is usually readily apparent. It is important, however, to distinquish between disorientation and ignorance when a patient misses more than one or two items. Committing a few errors, particularly if they are not all eastward displacements of western locales, usually reflects ignorance. Making many errors usually reflects disorientation. Most patients mark the points of the compass correctly. However, a scoring system that gives one point for each correct compass direction and one point for each of the 11 named locales (including the patient's place of birth) has proven sensitive in discriminating better than chance ($p < .05$) between best performances made by 45 head injury patients in the second year post trauma or later ($\overline{X} = 12.40 \pm 3.07$) and 27 normal control subjects ($\overline{X} = 14.26 \pm 1.26$). (The control subjects and 41 of the patients had been given neuropsychological examinations as part of a Veterans Administration funded research project on the long-term cognitive consequences of nonprogressive brain damage. All of the control subjects were in the 19 to 49 age range; the patients were in that age range when injured. Two were in their 50s when tested.) In contrast, none of an older (age range 42 to 76) group of six patients with right CVAs achieved scores above 11 ($\overline{X} = 7.83 \pm 2.79$).

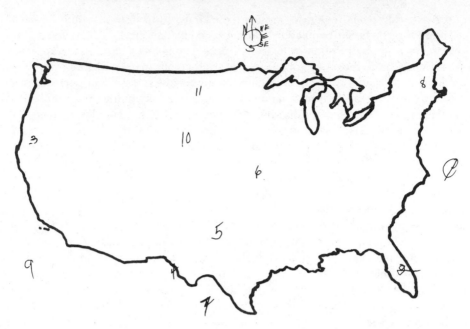

Fig. 17-4. Topographical Localization responses by a 50-year-old engineer who had been hemiparetic for 14 years since suffering a ruptured aneurysm of the right anterior communicating artery. Although only two of his responses are notably displaced (4 and 6), he betrayed left visuospatial inattention in an overelaborated set of compass points in which West was omitted.

Geographic orientation tests (Benton et al., 1974). Tests of three different aspects of geographical knowledge were given to patients with unilateral brain disease and to medically hospitalized control subjects. In the *verbal association* test, the subject's task is to tell in which state 15 cities (e.g., Birmingham, Butte, Providence) are located. The relative unfamiliarity of some of these cities was reflected in scores that varied according to educational level but did not differentiate between groups. *Verbal directions* requires the subject to indicate the direction of travel between two places, either cities or states. On this test, amount of education made no difference in scores but the brain damaged groups did less well then the control subjects. However, this task did not discriminate between side of lesion. *Map localization* utilizes a printed 22 × 35 cm of the United States map on which the states are outlined and the locations of Canada, Mexico, and Chicago are noted in print. The subject's task is to make an "x" to indicate the location of six cities and four states. This procedure yields two scores: "map deviation" gives the number of states the check mark was placed away from the correct state (e.g., if the patient placed the state of Washington in Nebraska, the deviation score would be 3 [for Wyoming, Idaho, Washington]; "map vector" accounts for east-west (i.e., right-left) deviations, with eastward deviations scored plus, westward deviations scored minus. The two scores reflected both the level of schooling and the presence of brain damage. With relatively small subgroups and significant education effects (few subjects with 12 or more years of schooling made errors on any of the tests), a tendency for more patients with right-sided lesions to make errors did not reach significance. Vector scores suggested that patients with unilateral lesions (right more than left) were somewhat prone to pile up responses on the same side of the paper as the lesion with fewer responses on the contralateral side.

Route finding.   The inability of brain damaged patients to find their way around familiar places or to learn new routes is not uncommon. The problem can be so severe that it may take days before an alert and ambulatory patient can make his way to the bathroom on his ward. It often dissipates as the acute stage of the illness passes, but some confusion about locations and slowness in learning new routes may remain. A test for this disability, the *Extrapersonal Orientation Test,* uses visual and tactile route maps laid out on a nine-point square (S. Weinstein et al., 1956). The patient's task is to translate the drawn lines of the visual map or the string lines of the tactile map into locomotion by walking the designated pattern on a nine-dot square laid out on the floor. Regardless of the sensory mode of presentation or the side of the lesion, frontal lobe patients showed the least impairment, and parietal lobe patients showed the most impairment on this task (Semmes et al., 1963; Teuber, 1964). S. Weinstein (1964) noted that head wound patients with aphasia were relatively more disabled on this task than those without aphasia. Parkinson patients tend to score lower than control subjects. (F. P. Bowen, 1976). Those with predominantly left-sided symptoms did least well in Bowen's study while the performances of those whose symptoms mostly involved their right side were statistically indistinguishable from the control group.

Sense of direction.   The status of the sense of direction has been examined by having the patient draw a series of arrows (Gooddy and Reinhold, 1963). As a first step, the patient is asked to draw an arrow. If unable to do so, he is shown a simple three-line model consisting of the shaft and the point, which he is asked to reproduce from memory. If the patient does not have immediate recall of the model, he is asked to copy it. Following this, the patient is instructed to draw arrows in specified directions, such as "up" or "down," "the other way," and "toward a corner." The examiner can also request that a number of arrows (such as four) be drawn in "different directions." The more complex requirements may bring out defects that do not appear on simpler forms of the task. Patients with right posterior lesions tend to have the greatest difficulty with this test, although impaired performances are not confined to this group.

Attention, Concentration, and Tracking

Although attention, concentration, and tracking can be differentiated theoretically, in practice they are difficult to separate. Purely attentional defects appear as distractibility or impaired ability for focused behavior of any kind, regardless of the patient's

547

intention. Intact attention is a necessary precondition of both concentration and mental tracking activities. Concentration problems may be due to a simple attentional disturbance, or to inability to maintain a purposeful attentional focus or, as is often the case, to both problems. At the next level of complexity, conceptual tracking can be prevented or interrupted by attention or concentration problems and also by diminished ability to maintain focused attention on one's mental contents while solving problems or following a sequence of ideas.

Clarifying the nature of an attention problem depends on observations of the patient's general behavior as well as his performance on tests involving concentration and tracking, for only by comparing these various observations can the examiner begin to distinguish the simpler global defects of attention from the more discrete, task-specific problems of concentration and tracking. Further, there is evidence that even impaired attention is not always a global disability but may be specific to the visual or verbal modality and associated with a lesion on the corresponding side of the brain (Diller and Weinberg, 1972)

Vigilance

Successful performance of any test of attention, concentration, or tracking requires sustained attention. However, vigilance tests examine the ability to sustain attention in itself. These tests typically involve the sequential presentation of stimuli (such as strings of letters or numbers) over an extended period of time with instructions for the patient to indicate in some way (tap, raise hand) when a given number or letter (the target stimulus) is perceived. Thus, lists of 60 or more items are usually read, played on a tape, or presented in a visual display at a rate of one per second (Strub and Black, 1977). Franz (1970) used 150 items presented at the rate of one each half-second. The simplest form of the task uses only one target item. Two or more target items can be used. More complex variations of the vigilance task require the subject to respond only when the target item is preceded by a specified item (e.g., to tap B only when if follows D). Strub and Black's list of letters, for which A is the target letter, contains one run of three and two runs of two A's, which additionally sample the patient's ability to stop an ongoing activity. These vigilance tasks are performed easily by persons whose capacity for sustained attention is intact. Thus, even one or two lapses on these tests may reflect an attention problem.

CANCELLATION TESTS

These paper and pencil tests require visual selectivity at fast speed on a repetitive motor response task. They assess many functions, not least of which is the capacity for sustained attention. Visual scanning and activation and inhibition of rapid responses are also necessary to the successful performance of cancellation tasks. Lowered scores on these tasks can reflect the general response slowing and inattentiveness of diffuse damage or acute brain conditions or more specific defects of response shifting and motor smoothness or of unilateral spatial neglect.

The basic format for these tests follows the vigilance test pattern. It consists of rows of letters or numbers randomly interspersed with a designated target letter or number. The patient is instructed to cross out all target letters or numbers. The performance is scored for errors and for time to completion; or if there is a time limit, scoring is for errors and number of targets crossed out within the allotted time. The possibilities for variations on the basic format are virtually limitless. Several similar tasks can be presented on one page (Weinberg and Diller, 1968). The task can be made more difficult by decreasing the space between target characters or by the number of non-target characters between the targets (Diller et al., 1974). The task can be made more complex by using gaps in the line as spatial cues (e.g., "cross out every . . . letter that is preceded by a gap" [Talland, 1965]), or by having two target characters instead of one.

Diller and his colleagues (1974) constructed nine different cancellation tasks: two using digits, two using letters, two using easy three-letter words, two using geometric figures (taken from the WISC Coding task), and one using simple pictures. Their basic version of the task consists of six 52-character rows in which the target character is randomly interspersed approximately 18 times in each row (see Fig. 17-5). Thirteen control patients had a median error score of 1 on the basic version of the letter and digit cancellation tasks with median performance times of 100 seconds on Letters and 90 seconds on Digits. Stroke patients with right hemisphere lesions were not much slower than the control subjects but had many more errors (median Letters errors = 34, median Digits errors = 24), always of omission and usually on the left side of the page (Diller and Weinberg, 1977). Patients with left hemisphere lesions made few errors but took up to twice as long (median Letters time = 200 seconds; median Digits time = 160 seconds). Failure on the cancellation tasks appeared to be associated with "spatial neglect" problems of the patients with right hemisphere lesions and with difficulties in the temporal processing of information of left hemisphere patients.

Letter Cancellation Test (Talland and Schwab, 1964; Talland, 1965). Variations of the cancellation test have also been used to examine the capacity of Korsakoff patients (Talland, 1965a) and of patients with Parkinsons disease (Horne, 1973; Talland and Schwab, 1964) to deal with alternative response possibilities. Each sheet for this task contains 16 rows of 26 lower case letters interspersed with ten capitals. Four double

Fig. 17-5. Letter Cancellation task: "Cancel C's and E's" (reduced size) (Diller et al., 1974).

spaces occur in random positions on each sheet where all other letters are separated by a single space. Three forms of the test, of presumably increasing difficulty, were devised. In Test A the patient must cross out capitals. Test B calls for crossing out capitals and letters immediately following the four double spaces. Test C instructions add to those of Test B in the requirement of crossing out all letters preceding the double spaces. Scoring can be for speed (correct cancellations per 60 seconds), errors, and omissions. Both alcoholic and Parkinson patients were slower than control subjects and made more errors, except Talland and Schwab's group of Parkinson patients who performed as well as the control subjects on Test A, the simplest of the three. Talland and Schwab interpreted their finding as reflecting impairment in central programming. Horne suggested that the poor Test A scores of his patients may have been due to their being more impaired than the patients studied by Talland and Schwab.

Digit Vigilance Test (R. Lewis and Kupke, 1977). This cancellation task is included in the manual form of the Lafayette Clinic Repeatable Neuropsychological Test Battery (see p. 566). It is two pages long, containing 59 rows of 35 digits. On alternate forms, the target number is 6 or 9 as these yielded equal time scores. This test is scored for total time and errors of omission only.

Perceptual Speed (PS) (Moran and Mefferd, 1959). This cancellation task differs from others in that the target shifts with each line. Thus it measures both speed of visual tracking and ability to shift attention. Each form of the Perceptual Speed test consists of two pages of 25 rows of 30 randomized digits. The first digit at the left of each line is circled, indicating that it is the target digit for that line. Practice on a small sample precedes the test proper. The score is the number of digits correctly cancelled in two-and-one-half minutes. The only available data come from a small number of subjects, all employed, with a wide range of education. Their mean score (based on scores for each of the 20 forms of the test) was 87 ± 5.6. As it was designed to be part of a battery of repeatable tests, the original series has 30 alternate forms. Obviously, a format such as this lends itself to many variations.

Mental Tracking

The simplest test of mental tracking is digit recall, or Digit Span, as it is usually called (see pp. 266–270), which merely tests how many bits of information a person can attend to at once and repeat in order. Most tests of attention and concentration involves some perceptual tracking or more complex mental operations as well, and many of them also involve some form of scanning. The importance of visual scanning in visual perception is well known (Hebb, 1949; Luria, 1965; Weinberg and Diller, 1968; Weinberg et al., 1976). The role of visual scanning in conceptual tracking has only recently become apparent in studies demonstrating the scanning eye movements that accompany the performance of such conceptual tracking tasks as Digits Backward or spelling a long word or name in reverse (Weinberg et al., 1972). Tracking tasks can be complicated by requiring the subject to track two or more stimuli or associated ideas simultaneously, alternatively, or sequentially in what I call *double* or *multiple* tracking behavior. The capacity for double or multiple tracking is one of the first most likely to break down with brain damage. Occasionally, loss of this capacity may be the only documentable mental change following head injury or brain disease. The disturbance appears as difficulty in keeping two or more lines of thought going, as in a cocktail party conversation, in solving two- or three-number addition or multiplication problems mentally, or in remembering one thing while doing another.

Reversing Serial Order

The sensitivity of Digits Backward to brain dysfunction also is seen in other tasks requiring reversals in the serial order of letters or numbers (M. B. Bender, 1979). Bender used a variety of reversal tasks to assess normal children, adults, and several groups of older persons (over 60); adult patients with a dementing disease or diffuse encephalopathy (*organic mental syndrome*, or OMS), or with aphasia; and dyslexic children. In addition to counting forward and backward (mostly to establish a set for reversing serial order on subsequent tasks), subjects were given the following reversing tasks. *Spelling* two- (I-T), three- (C-A-T), four- (H-A-N-D), and five- (W-O-R-L-D) letter words backward was the first. Any word of the designated length in which each letter appears only once can be substituted as needed, (e.g., H-O-U-S-E, Q-U-I-C-K.) Bender also compared letter reversing with serial word reversing; for example, the days of the week, months of the year. *Reading* words forward and backward, and vertically printed words from top to bottom and bottom to top was examined next.

Normal children made the least spelling errors (5%). Approximately one in ten normal adults and older subjects over 60 made reversed spelling errors. The older the subject group, the greater the incidence of errors, up to an error rate of 38% for a group of normal adults aged 75 to 88. The percentage of patients with diffuse encephalopathy making reverse spelling errors was less (78%) than the percentage of aphasic patients failing this task (90%). The aphasic patients also had more difficulty than any others reading in reverse or from bottom to top, although many who failed these tasks could read satisfactorily in the left-right or top to bottom directions. Bender described four stages of severity of the reversing disability that distinguish progressive levels of impairment for the patients with diffuse brain conditions (Organic Mental Syndrome—OMS) and the aphasic patients (see Table 17-3). He suggested that the ability to reverse letter, number, and word strings is characteristic of normal thinking and language processes. It is vulnerable to many different kinds of cerebral disorders because defects in reversal ability can result from (a) reading disability; (b) memory disorder; (c) aphasia; (d) the mental rigidity that may accompany aging; (e) perseverative tendencies; (f) a specific disability for learning to reverse symbolic material; or (g) "latent" alexia that shows up on the unfamiliar reversing task.

Table 17-3 Progressive Stages of Impairment in Mental and Speech Functions

Stage	OMS due to diffuse encephalopathy	Aphasia due to localized lesion
I	Defects in memory and calculation. Defect in reversal of five-letter words.	Normal speech except for dysnomia or word groping. Slight memory defect. Occasional defect in reversal of five-letter words.
II	As Stage I and defects in orientation, impairment in reversals of serial order of four-letter words.	Plentiful speech but gross errors in language and communication with impairment in reversal of serial order of four-letter words.
III	As Stage II plus impaired alertness, defects in perception. Dysnomia. Defects in reversals of three-letter words.	Speech almost unintelligible. Severe impairment of communication but can count from 1 to 10. Inability to reverse three- or two-letter words.
IV	As in Stage II, Illusions, hallucinations, delusions, and abnormalities in social behavior (Dementia). Defects in reversals of two-letter words.	No speech or any form of communication. (Global aphasia) Reversals can not be tested.

(Reprinted with permission from [*Neuropsychologia, 17,* M.B. Bender, Defects in reversal of serial order of symbols], Copyright [1979], Pergamon Press, Ltd.)

SUBTRACTING SERIAL SEVENS

There is little statistical data on this test for it is not generally used by psychologists. It is part of the mental status examination given by psychiatrists, neurologists, and other medical examiners. The subject is first instructed to "Take seven from 100." When he has done this, he is told, "Now take seven from 93 and continue subtracting sevens until you can't go any further." Patients who are unable to perform Serial Sevens can sometimes handle serial threes ("Take three from 50 . . ."). Patients who cannot perform the simpler serial subtraction task can be asked to count from 20 backward or say the months of the year backward, both very simple mental tracking tasks. Occasionally a patient will have been given this task so many times that much, if not all, of the number sequence will have been committed to memory. When a well-oriented patient has been given many mental status examinations, particularly during the previous weeks or months, the examiner should start the test at 101 or 102 instead of 100.

A. Smith (1967b) gave Serial Sevens to 132 employed adults, most of them with college or professional educations, and found that only 99 performed the task with two errors or less. He thus proved that this test's usefulness in discriminating between normal and brain injured populations does not rest simply on the presence or absence of errors. He also demonstrated that grossly impaired performances are rarely seen in the normal population—only three (2%) of Smith's subjects were unable to complete the task and only six made more than five errors. The women in Smith's study were more error-prone than the men, particularly women over 45 who had not attended or completed college. Very defective recitations of Serial Sevens are fairly common among brain injured patients (Luria, 1966; Ruesch and Moore, 1943). Serial Sevens can be scored for time taken as well as number of errors by counting pauses that last for five seconds or more. Pauses of more than five seconds between responses also tend to be characteristic of brain injured patients.

PACED AUDITORY SERIAL ADDITION TEST (PASAT) (Gronwall and Sampson, 1974; Gronwall and Wrightson, 1974)

This sensitive test simply requires that the patient add 60 pairs of randomized digits so that each is added to the digit immediately preceding it. For example, if the examiner reads the numbers "2-8-6-1-9," the subject's correct responses, beginning as soon as the examiner says "8," are "10-14-7-10." The digits are presented at four rates of speed, each differing by 0.4 seconds and ranging from one every 1.2 seconds to one every 2.4 seconds. Precise control over the rate at which digits are read requires a taped presentation. Gronwall begins the tape with a brief repetition task that is followed by a ten-digit practice series presented at the 2.4-second rate. Sixty-one digits are given at each rate. The performance can be evaluated in terms of the percentage of correct responses or the mean score (see Table 17-4; the data are rounded to the nearest whole number).

Postconcussion patients consistently perform well below control group averages immediately after injury or return to consciousness. The overwhelming tendency is for their scores to return to normal within 30 to 60 days. Based on an evaluation of how the PASAT performance was associated with performances on memory and attention tasks, Gronwall and Wrightson (1981) concluded that the PASAT is very sensitive to deficits in information processing ability. By using the PASAT performance as an indicator of the efficiency of information processing following concussion, the examiner can determine when a patient is able to return to a normal level of social and vocational activity without experiencing undue stress, or when a modified activity schedule would be best (Gronwall, 1977).

Although this technique was developed for taped presentation in order to control the presentation rate, with practice the examiner should be able to deliver the numbers at a reasonably steady one or two second rate. The task can also be presented at

Table 17-4 Average PASAT Percent Correct and Mean Scores Made by Control Group at Four Presentation Rates

Presentation rate (seconds)	1.2	1.6	2.0	2.4
Average percent correct	51	66	73	82
Mean score ($\pm$ SD)	22 $\pm$ 5	32 $\pm$ 8	40 $\pm$ 7	46 $\pm$ 6

(Adapted from Gronwall and Wrightson, 1974; Gronwall, 1977)

the subject's response rate (i.e., unpaced), in which case the examiner should record pauses of five seconds and longer. Although the paced delivery format identifies patients whose responses are slowed as well as those who have a tracking disability, the unpaced delivery is more likely to identify those patients whose defective performance is due to a tracking defect.

Complex Tests of Attention Functions

All visual perception tests require visual attention and concentration for successful performance. Visual search and visual scanning tests involve sustained, focused concentration and directed visual shifting. Visual attention functions also enter into the complex scanning and tracking tasks that have proven sensitive to the intellectual impairments resulting from brain injury (see pp. 367–371).

SYMBOL DIGIT MODALITIES TEST (SDMT) (A. Smith, 1968, 1973)

This test preserves the substitution format of Wechsler's Digit Symbol subtest but reverses the presentation of the material so that the symbols are printed and the numbers are written in (see Fig. 17-6). This not only enables the patient to respond with the more familiar act of number writing, but also allows a spoken response trial. Both written and oral administrations of the SDMT should be given whenever possible to permit comparisons between the two response modalities. When, in accordance with the instructions the written administration is given first, the examiner can use the same sheet to record the patient's answers on the oral administration by writing them in under the answer spaces. Neither order of presentation nor recency of the first administration appears to affect performance (A. Smith, personal communication). As with Wechsler's Digit Symbol subtest, 90 seconds are allowed for each trial; but unlike the Wechsler Intelligence Scales, there are 110 rather than 90 items. The written form of this substitution test also lends itself to group administration for rapid screening of many of the verbal and visual functions necessary for reading (A. Smith, 1975).

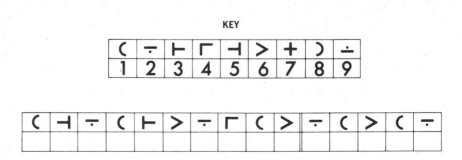

Fig. 17-6. The Symbol Digit Modalities Test (SDMT). (By Aaron Smith, Ph.D. © 1973 by Western Psychological Services. Reprinted by permission.)

Table 17-5 Symbol Digit Modalities Test Norms for Ages 18 to 74

Age Group	Mean Education	Mean Written Administration	Mean Oral Administration
18–24 (*n* = 69)	12.7	55.2 (± 7.5)	62.7 (± 9.1)
25–34 (*n* = 72)	13.5	53.6 (± 6.6)	61.2 (± 7.8)
35–44 (*n* = 76)	12.1	51.1 (± 8.1)	59.7 (± 9.7)
45–54 (*n* = 75)	11.7	46.8 (± 8.4)	54.5 (± 9.1)
55–64 (*n* = 67)	11.3	41.5 (± 8.6)	48.4 (± 9.1)
65–74 (*n* = 61)	10.7	37.4 (± 11.4)	46.2 (± 12.8)

(Based on studies by Carmen C. Centofanti)

The adult normative population was composed of 420 persons ranging in age from 18 to 74 (see Table 17-5). When applied to 100 patients with "confirmed and chronic" brain lesions, these norms correctly identified 86% of the patient group and 92% of the normal population, using a cutoff point of −1.5 standard deviations below the age norm (A. Smith, personal communication). Smith considers scores below the 1.5 SD cutoff to be "indicative" and those between 1.0 and 1.5 SDs below the age norm to be "suggestive" of cerebral dysfunction. A −1.0 SD cutoff gives a somewhat high (9 to 15%) rate of false positive cases (Rees, 1979). It should be noted that education is positively correlated with the scores of both the written and oral administrations of this test and therefore needs to be taken into account when interpreting the SDMT performance.

A significant performance decrement in one response modality relative to the other naturally points to a dysfunction of that modality. Significant impairment on both administrations reflects visual perceptual, visual scanning (shifting), or oculomotor defects, or general mental or motor slowing (Kaufman, 1968). Glosser and her co-workers (1977) and Butters and Cermak (1976) compared symbol substitution test formats that differed in familiarity of the symbols and whether a digit or symbol response was required. All subjects, normal controls as well as brain damaged patients, performed both the familiar and unfamiliar digit response tests more slowly than those calling for symbol responses (of which the Wechsler's Digit Symbol subtest is an example). This phenomenon was attributed, at least in part, to absence of an orderly sequence in the stimulus array. As with the Digit Symbol subtest, the SDMT is sensitive to the normal effects of aging as well as to brain dysfunction. A complete set of children's norms appears in the test manual (A. Smith, 1973).

SEQUENTIAL MATCHING MEMORY TASK (SMMT) (Collier and N. Levy, undated)

This task requires "*intense* attention over a considerable period of time" for success-ful performance (Collier and Levy, undated). It also involves perceptual and response flexibility, since the reference point continually shifts. The test material consists of decks of 3×5-inch cards that each have one of two distinctive symbols, such as a plus or a minus. Other than the restriction that four cards with the same symbol not occur in a sequence, the cards are randomly arranged to be exposed to the subject one by one. In a practice trial using 20 cards, the subject must recall the symbol of the card before the previous card (i.e., the card once removed). On test trials, the card to be recalled can be two or more times removed, depending on how difficult the examiner wants the task to be. In the standard administration there are three 35-card trials requiring the subject to remember the card twice removed. In a preliminary study comparing hospitalized epileptic patients and hospitalized postlobotomy patients with a control group of hospitalized psychiatric patients, mostly diagnosed as paranoid schizophrenic, this test differentiated between each patient group and the control group significantly ($p < .01$). The control patients averaged 9+ errors, the epileptic group 13+, and the lobotomized patients 16+ errors per 35-card trial.

TRAIL MAKING TEST

This test, originally part of the Army Individual Test Battery (1944), has enjoyed wide use as an easily administered test of visual conceptual and visuomotor tracking. Like most other tests involving motor speed and attention functions, the Trail Making Test is highly vulnerable to the effects of brain injury (Armitage, 1946; Reitan, 1958; Spreen and Benton, 1965). It is given in two parts, A and B (see Fig. 17-7). The patient must first draw lines to connect consecutively numbered circles on one work sheet (Part A) and then connect the same number of consecutively numbered and lettered circles on another work sheet by alternating between the two sequences (Part B). The subject is urged to connect the circles "as fast as you can" without lifting the pencil from the paper.

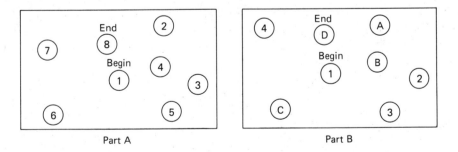

Part A   Part B

Fig. 17-7. Practice samples of the Trail Making Test.

Some administration and scoring procedures have changed over the years. Originally, the examiner removed the work sheet after three uncorrected errors. Each trial received a score on a ten-point scale depending on the amount of time taken to complete it. Armitage changed this procedure, allowing the patient to finish regardless of the number of errors but accounting for the errors by giving a score of zero to performances in which errors were left uncorrected. Reitan (undated) made further changes, requiring the examiner to point out errors as they occur so that the patient could always complete the test without errors and scoring is based on time alone.

This latter method is the one in most common use today. However, the price for a simplified scoring system may have been paid in diminished reliability, for the measured amount of time includes the examiner's reaction time (in noticing errors), his speed in pointing them out, and the speed with which the patient comprehends and makes the correction. This method penalizes for errors indirectly but does not control for differences in response times and correction styles that can conceivably result in significant biases in the time scores obtained with different examiners. While the reliability of Part A, as measured by the coefficient of concordance remained high throughout three administrations to 19 normal control subjects at six and 12 month intervals ($W = .78$), it was somewhat lower ($W = .67$) on form B (Lezak, 1982d). However, in this same study a cumulative practice effect on Part A reached significance on the third administration ($p < .001$) although average time scores on Part B did not drop significantly.

When interpreting the performance of any test in which response speed contributes significantly to the score, allowances need to be made for the normal slowing of age. The Trail Making Test is no exception, since performance time increases with each succeeding decade (Davies, 1968; Harley et al., 1980; Lindsey and Coppinger, 1969) (see Table 17-6). In the single reported study not showing this trend, the average educational level of control subjects in the 45 and older age group was almost 15 years (Boll and Reitan, 1973). Davies (1968) found that when Trail Making Test performances of 80 normal control subjects in their 70s were evaluated by the cutting scores recommended by Reitan (undated), 92% of the 40 men and 90% of the 40 women were misclassified as brain damaged. Davies' norms, although somewhat coarse-grained, provide standards for evaluating Trail Making Test performances throughout the adult years. The extensive T-score norms developed by Harley and his co-workers (1980) offer a more sensitive set of norms for older men (55–79).

Intellectual ability as measured by Wechsler-Bellevue scores (Reitan, 1959) and by scores on both "verbal" and "nonverbal" tests of intellectual ability (Fleming, 1975) does seem to contribute to speedy Trail Making Test performances. Based on a review of studies concerned with the role that intellectual ability plays on this test, Kramer and Jarvik (1979) recommend ability-based norms as well as age norms. Unfortunately, ability-based norms are not available.

When the number of seconds taken to complete Part A is relatively much less than that taken to complete Part B, the patient probably has difficulties in complex—double or multiple—conceptual tracking. Slow performances at any age on one or both

Table 17-6 Distribution of Trail Making Test Scores (in Seconds) for Normal Control Subjects for the Six Decades Beginning with Age 20

Age	20 to 39 (n = 180)		40 to 49 (n = 90)		50 to 59 (n = 90)		60 to 69 (n = 90)		70 to 79 (n = 90)	
Part	A	B	A	B	A	B	A	B	A	B
Percentile										
90	21	45	22	49	25	55	29	64	38	79
75	26	55	28	57	29	75	35	89	54	132
50	32	69	34	78	38	98	48	119	80	196
25	42	94	45	100	49	135	67	172	105	292
10	50	129	59	151	67	177	104	282	168	450

(Adapted from Davies, 1968)

Parts A and B point to the likelihood of brain damage, but in themselves do not indicate whether the problem is one of motor slowing, incoordination, visual scanning difficulties, poor motivation, or conceptual confusion.

Reitan and Tarshes (1959) suggested that patients who perform very much better on Part A than B are likely to have left-sided lesions. However, data concerning this formulation are equivocal. Some studies have supported it (Lewinsohn, 1973; Wheeler and Reitan 1963). Korman and Blumberg (1963) found that their patients with left hemisphere damage did less well on Part B than A, but so did their patients with bilateral lesions. On the other hand, 25% of the 44 left hemisphere patients and 28% of the right hemisphere patients making up the population studied by Reitan and Tarshes performed contrary to Reitan and Tarshes's formula. All of a group of seven patients, each diagnosed as having a right hemisphere lesion, were significantly slower on Part B than Part A; Reitan's rules would have called each a left hemisphere patient (Lezak, unpublished study). A recent analysis of over 300 cases, including many different kinds and sites of brain impairment, "failed to support . . . the idea that the ratio of Trails A to Trails B is a useful indicant of lesion laterality" (Wedding, 1979). The lack of agreement between these studies makes use of this test to lateralize a lesion highly questionable.

Yet this test is among those that are most sensitive to the presence of brain damage (Lewinsohn, 1973). Like many other tests, high diagnostic prediction rates are found only when the discrimination has been between brain injured patients and normal control subjects. Its diagnostic effectiveness in differentiating brain injured from psychiatric patients has not been consistent (Heaton et al., 1978; Spreen and Benton, 1965; Zimet and Fishman 1970).

However, the Trail Making Test's clinical value goes far beyond whatever it may contribute to diagnostic decisions. Lewinsohn (1973) found that performance on Trails A was predictive of vocational rehabilitation following brain injury. Visual scanning and tracking problems that show up on this test can give the examiner a good idea of how effectively the patient responds to a visual array of any complexity, how well he performs when following a sequence mentally or dealing with more than one stimulus or thought at a time (Eson et al., 1978), or how flexible he is in shifting the course of an ongoing activity (Pontius and Yudowitz, 1980; see pp. 518ff.). When a patient has difficulty performing this task, careful observation of how he gets off the track and the kinds of mistakes he makes can provide insight into the nature of his neuropsychological disabilities.

18

Batteries and Composite
Tests for Brain Damage

Batteries

Two purposes guide the development of most neuropsychological test batteries. One is, "Accuracy in prediction" which Filskov and S. Goldstein (1974) state "is the hall-mark of a good diagnostic instrument." Tests are chosen—or test data are handled—on the basis of predictive efficiency alone.

A second purpose is the understanding of the nature of organic disabilities. Batteries developed for this purpose provide a standard data collection procedure to include tests that yield a broad behavior sample. Tests in such batteries measure the major intellectual functions across at least auditory and visual, verbal and nonsymbolic modalities, and provide for comparisons between the modalities for each of the major functions (A. Smith, 1975). Test selection may be based as much if not more on use-fulness in eliciting different kinds of behavior as on predictive efficiency.

These purposes may appear to be mutually exclusive. In fact, it is possible to con-struct a test battery that identifies organicity better than chance but still does not cover the major intellectual functions in all significant modalities. However, it is dif-ficult to conceive of a set of tests that could satisfy the requirements of the second purpose but not make good diagnostic discriminations.

The strengths and limitations of set batteries for neuropsychological assessment were aptly stated by Davison (1974, p. 354):

> Utilization of a standardized battery, particularly when it is administered by someone other than the neuropsychologist who will interpret it, presents great advantages for research in that the objective data can be evaluated without contam-inating influences, and all subjects secure scores on the same variables. However, the method also presents great liabilities for *some* clinical diagnostic problems, among them adequate specification of an individual's characteristics for the purpose of predicting behavior in his ambient existence. For this purpose the data collector must have a clear idea of the practical problem to which he is predicting and the

freedom, knowledge, and ingenuity to add tests to the battery for individual cases and to *improvise* individualized assessment when necessary . . . The clinician must recognize his responsibility not simply for addressing the referral problem, but toward the patient as a whole.

There are few formalized batteries for general clinical use although several have been constructed to meet specific clinical or research needs. Among formalized batteries, the best known is the set of tests assembled by Reitan (undated; Reitan and Davison, 1974). Among batteries constructed for specific purposes are Halstead's battery for testing "biological intelligence" in frontal lobe patients (1947); the Columbia-Greystone battery for studying the intellectual consequences of psychosurgery (Landis, 1952); Benton's six-test frontal lobe battery (1968a) and seven-test battery for assessing elderly persons (Benton et al., 1981); and Newcombe's 23-test battery for evaluating the intellectual effects of missile wounds (1969).

Many experienced neuropsychologists assemble their own test batteries for the psychological assessment of brain disorders. A. Smith's (1975) selection of tests for clinical assessment and the set of tests that make up my basic battery (see p. 572 and 107–109) are examples of informal batteries that are subject to change and can be applied flexibly with additions or subtractions to suit the needs of each patient. The clinical and theoretical benefits that can come from using a flexible approach to neuropsychological assessment were amply demonstrated by Luria, who "was always experimenting, changing the situations and trying new methods in a highly precise scientific way" (Christensen, 1979).

In deciding whether to use a ready-made battery, to organize one's own battery, or to reorganize someone else's, the clinician needs to evaluate the battery for suitability, practicability, and usefulness. A battery that is deficient in one of these areas, no matter what its other virtues, will be inadequate for general clinical purposes even though it may satisfy the requirements for some individual cases or research designs.

A *suitable* battery provides an examination that is appropriate to the patient's needs, whether they call for a baseline study, differential diagnosis, rehabilitation planning, or any other type of assessment. Thus, the examination of a patient who seeks help for a memory complaint should contain visual and verbal learning tests and tests of retention and retrieval. Suitability also extends to the specific needs of patients with sensory or motor defects. A suitable battery contains test variations or possibilities for such variations sufficient to provide data on all the major intellectual functions through the handicapped patient's remaining sensory and response modalities.

A *practicable* battery is relatively easy to administer and has inexpensive equipment. It is adaptable to the limitations of the wheelchair or bedridden patient, can be moved by one person, and is transportable by car. Further, a practicable battery does not take so much time as to be prohibitive in cost, exhaust the patient, or greatly limit the number of patients that can be tested by one examiner.

A *useful* battery provides the information the examiner wants. If the examiner decides to rely primarily on one battery of tests for unselected clinical patients, then it must be a multipurpose battery that will aid in diagnosis, give baselines, and supply data for planning and treatment.

There are now no batteries that satisfy all these criteria, i.e., provide the minimum, maximum, and only set of tests needed in every examination. It is as doubtful whether such a battery can be constructed as whether physicians can devise a single set of examination procedures and laboratory tests that can be efficiently or practicably applied to all patients. Further, although standardized procedures are the heart of reliable assessment, at the present stage of neuropsychological understanding not enough is known to enshrine any set of procedures with a full-scale standardization. Present-day batteries, both the informal collections and those for which there are elaborate statistical evaluation procedures, can be no more than early and tentative efforts to deal with the subtle and complex problems of neuropsychological assessment.

Representative Batteries

THE HALSTEAD-REITAN BATTERY

This set of tests has grown by accretion and revision and continues to be modified by many of its users. It began as a battery of seven tests selected for their power to discriminate between patients with frontal lobe lesions and those with other lesions or normal subjects (Halstead, 1947; Reitan and Davison, 1974). Most current modifications of the Halstead-Reitan battery use five of the original seven, dropping the *Critical Flicker Fusion Test* and the *Time Sense Test* because they do not identify brain damaged patients with sufficient accuracy to be diagnostically useful (Boll, 1981; E. W. Russell et al., 1970). The tests listed here typically constitute the core Halstead-Reitan battery. Many clinicians also add tests of verbal and visuospatial memory (e.g., Dodrill, 1978c, 1979; Matarazzo et al., 1974; E. W. Russell, 1980c), perceptual integrity (e.g., Reitan, 1966b; E. W. Russell et al., 1970) and motor performance (e.g., Matthews and Haaland, 1979; Harley et al., 1980) to the common core of the Halstead-Reitan battery (see pp. 566–567).

The Halstead part of the battery consists of the following tests:

1. The *Category Test* is reviewed on pp. 480–481.
2. The *Tactual Performance Test* is reviewed on pp. 459–462.
3. The *Rhythm Test* originally appeared in the *Seashore Measures of Musical Talent* (see p. 374).
4. *Speech Sounds Perception Test* is described on p. 372.
5. The *Finger Oscillation Test,* or *Finger Tapping Test,* has also been reviewed (p. 529).

These five tests together yield seven scores: three (total time, memory, location) come from the Tactual Performance Test; each of the four other tests contributes a single score. An *Impairment Index*, which Halstead devised for making gross diagnostic discriminations, is the proportion of scores that exceed the cutting scores established by Halstead in his study of frontal lobe patients. It runs from 0, obtained when no subtest performance is in the impaired range, to 10, which indicates that they all were in that range. Halstead's original set of tests produced ten scores, making calculation of the Impairment Index a simple matter of adding up the number of scores on the impaired side of the designated cutting scores. With only seven scores, the Impairment Index becomes the proportion of scores out of the seven that are in the impaired range (Boll, 1981). However, the interpretation remains the same as when Halstead used ten scores and set the cutting score for the Impairment Index at 5 with scores of 4 and lower characterizing the control subjects.

Other tests in this battery are the *Trail Making Test* (see pp. 556–559); various modifications of the *Aphasia Screening Test* by Halstead and Wepman (see pp. 320–321); a sensory examination that tests for finger agnosia, skin writing recognition, and sensory extinction in the tactile, auditory, and visual modalities; one of the Wechsler intelligence tests (see Chapter 9); a measure of grip strength using a hand dynamometer, and the *Minnesota Multiphasic Personality Inventory* (see pp. 607–613). Administration time for the complete Halstead-Reitan Battery runs from six to eight hours.

A distinctive feature of Reitan's handling of the examination data of the Halstead-Reitan Battery has been reliance on test scores for predicting the nature and the site of the lesion as well as its presence (Wheeler et al., 1963; Wheeler and Reitan, 1963). Predictions about the site of the lesion and its nature (diffuse or focal, static or changing) are based on statistically identified relationships between test scores. This actuarial approach has encouraged development of computerized interpretations of Halstead-Reitan test protocols (K.M. Adams et al., 1975; E. W. Russell et al., 1970; Swiercinsky, 1978; Swiercinsky and Warnock, 1977).

The relative value of interpretations based on statistical analyses compared with clinical interpretations of the test data has been a subject of interest. G. Goldstein (1974) concluded that, "Clinical interpretation still has the advantage of being able to make more precise statements about individual cases than can the quantitative, objective methods" (p. 304). He also pointed out that by using linear discriminant function analysis, high degrees of accuracy have been obtained in identifying side of lesion.

Heaton and his colleagues (1981) compared interpretations by two relatively experienced clinicians with those generated by the Key Approach to semiautomated interpretation of the Halstead-Reitan battery (E. W. Russell et al., 1970) for accuracy of classification along the dimensions of presence, chronicity, and laterality of brain damage. All three ratings of severity were highly correlated ($r = .95$). The clinicians, however, made significantly more accurate classifications of both presence and laterality of brain damage. Only on the chronicity dimension did the semiautomated Key Approach have a higher accuracy rate, but it was not significantly higher than the clinicians' accuracy rate, nor did either the Key Approach or the clinicians predict chronicity any better than the base rate. An analysis of lateralization errors suggested that the Halstead-Reitan battery did not provide sufficient information for making judgments regarding lateralization for approximately 25% of the 250 cases reviewed in this study. These authors concluded that, "The current advantage of the clinicians is probably due to their ability to analyze and weight flexibly the significance of the complex, highly variable combinations of HRB data, and also to the relatively crude nature of the actuarial competition." They wondered whether future refinements in actuarial approaches might not significantly increase their accuracy.

In another study investigating the diagnostic effectiveness of automated interpretation systems, Anthony and his coworkers (1980) compared two different programs, the Key Approach (E. W. Russell et al., 1970) and a Fortran IV program called BRAIN 1 devised to simulate clinical inference. Although both programs classified subjects as brain damaged or normal at a better than chance rate, neither performed as well as its authors had reported. Moreover, predictions of site of lesion or recency of damage were unacceptably low for clinical purposes.

In other studies, diagnostic conclusions regarding simply presence or absence of brain damage based on the Impairment Index were found to be much less accurate than those obtained by clinical judgment based on tests, interviews, and medical history (Tsushima and Wedding, 1979). However, Wedding (1979) found that discriminant function analysis was superior to other statistical techniques for obtaining diagnostic classifications from selected Halstead-Reitan scores and was also superior to clinical judgment. It is not surprising that there are different opinions on this subject and that the findings of different studies are not in agreement since all the Halstead-Reitan variables and their interrelationships have not yet been adequately validated or standardized (Davison, 1974; E. W. Russell, 1980c).

The original norms of the Halstead tests (see Boll, 1981) are not well founded. Halstead's "normal" population consisted of 29 subjects (eight women) and 30 sets of scores. Ten of these subjects were servicemen who became available for this study because they were under care for "minor" psychiatric disturbances. One was awaiting sentencing for a capital crime (in Illinois at that time it could have been either life imprisonment or execution; Halstead observed that the subject appeared "anxious"). Four were awaiting lobotomies because of behavior threatening their own life and/ or those of others. Two sets of scores made by one of these, a young man, were entered twice since he was still waiting after two months and so took the tests again. This is the group whose test performances defined the unimpaired range for the cutting scores in general use with these tests.

A serious problem with Halstead's cutting scores is that they are based on the performance of a young sample. The group representing a "normal" population ranged from 14 to 50 years of age, with an average age of 28.3. Yet performance on most of the subtests in the Halstead-Reitan battery falls off with age (Bak and Greene, 1980; Lewinsohn, 1973; Prigatano and Parsons, 1976). This can result in spuriously elevated Impairment Indices and erroneous diagnostic conclusions (e.g., see Ehrfurth and Lezak, 1982; Price et al., 1979). However, age-graded norms are now available. Pauker (1977) provides means and standard deviations at five age levels from 19 to 76 according to three levels of WAIS Full Scale IQ scores (84–109, 110–119, 120–133), for the seven commonly used Halstead-Reitan scores plus the Impairment Index. Harley and his colleagues (1980) give T-score conversions for all the scores in the full

Halstead-Reitan battery and also for a number of measures of motor proficiency at five age ranges from 55 to 79 based on performances by a veteran population.

Level of education may also contribute to performances on Halstead-Reitan measures (Finlayson, Johnson, and Reitan, 1977). Scores of neurologically sound subjects with little education can dip into the impaired range while well-educated brain damaged patients may achieve spuriously high scores. The Seashore Rhythm Test and the Speech-Sounds Perception Test are most susceptible to this effect (see also Vega and Parsons, 1967)., although it showed up on all the Halstead-Reitan subtests in the Finlayson, Johnson, and Reitan study.

Evaluations of the Halstead-Reitan battery that have focused on its effectiveness in correctly identifying organic patients, distinguishing them from neurologically intact control subjects, report high rates of correct predictions (Boll, 1981; Reitan, 1955b). However, as with all other psychological tests, prediction rates are less likely to be high when the discriminations to be made are between organic and psychiatric patients (Heaton et al., 1978). Several studies have questioned whether the Halstead-Reitan battery discriminates between these two kinds of patients better than just one or a few tests. In one, the Bender-Gestalt alone had a higher prediction rate than any of the Halstead tests (Lacks et al., 1970). In another study, only two of 36 discriminations between organic and psychiatric patients made by Halstead test scores proved to be significant, whereas six of 44 WAIS score discriminations were significant (DeWolfe et al., 1971). In a third study, the rate of correct predictions made on the basis of WAIS scores alone was a little better than those made with the full Halstead-Reitan battery (C. G. Watson et al., 1968).

Efforts to use the Halstead-Reitan battery for localizing lesions have had equivocal results. This battery does elicit differential performance patterns between patients with left and right hemisphere lesions (Kløve, 1974, Reitan, 1955a). However, without the sensory examination added to the battery by Reitan (1966b), right-left hemisphere differences are not identified with sufficient consistency to warrant basing clinical decisions regarding lesion localization on the Halstead-Reitan test scores alone (e.g., Schreiber et al., 1976; Wheeler and Reitan, 1963). With the sensory examinations, diagnosis and lesion localization by means of multivariate statistical analyses of Halstead-Reitan scores have been relatively successful (K. M. Adams et al., 1975; Wedding, 1979). This is not surprising since G. Goldstein and Shelly (1973b) found that "suppression" (i.e., unilateral inattention, extinction) "was the single variable [among all the Halstead-Reitan variables] that produced the greatest separation between the left and right hemisphere damaged] groups. Lateralized motor and tactile recognition dysfunctions also appear to be good lateralization indicators." Thus, it is interesting to note that this battery's greatest diagnostic strengths come from several brief examination techniques on which neurologists have relied for decades to make the same diagnostic distinctions.

Data from two reliability studies (three different populations: young normal control subjects, older patients with diffuse cerebrovascular disease, and chronic epileptics) suggest that neither the Impairment Index nor many of the subtests are highly stable measures in some populations (Dodrill and Troupin, 1975; Matarazzo et al., 1974).

Both the chronic epileptic group and the normal young subjects made ten-point drops on their Category Test scores on a second testing. By the fourth testing, the mean Category Test score of the epileptic patients had dropped another ten points. The young controls and the epileptic patients also made gains on the Location score of the Tactual Performance Test. Overall score improvements made by the chronic epileptics lowered the average Impairment Index from .6 to .45 by the fourth round of testing, which placed more patients in the unimpaired range than had been so classified initially. In contrast, the older patients with diffuse disease did not register much change on any of the subtests or the Impairment Index.

Although the Halstead-Reitan battery has practical limitations in that it is unwieldy, takes a relatively long time to administer, and is not suitable for the thorough examination of patients with sensory or motor handicaps, it does afford one of the more reliable psychological means of identifying patients with brain damage. However, its greatest contribution may not be to diagnostic efficiency, but rather to the practice of neuropsychological assessment, for Reitan has been singularly instrumental in making psychologists aware of the need to test many different kinds of behavior when addressing neuropsychological questions.

VARIATIONS OF THE HALSTEAD-REITAN BATTERY

Variations on this battery tend to reflect the interests of their creators. The *Wisconsin Neuropsychological Test Battery* (Harley et al., 1980) has been used in studies of parkinsonism (Matthews and Haaland, 1979) and to help elucidate motor disturbances associated with other brain disorders (e.g., Haaland et al., 1977; Matthews and Harley, 1975). In addition to the tests from the Halstead-Reitan battery, the Wisconsin battery includes the *Wisconsin Motor Battery* which contains five measures of motor proficiency and also Finger Tapping. Dodrill (1978b; 1980) developed a *Neuropsychological Battery for Epilepsy,* which includes tests of memory, motor control, concentration, and mental flexibility. These additions provide greater sensitivity to the test performances of epileptic patients than do most of the tests in the basic Halstead-Reitan battery (Dodrill, 1978a). Swiercinsky (1978) has been interested in computer applications of neuropsychological tests. His test program, *SAINT* (System for Analysis and Interpretation of Neuropsychological Tests), was developed on the Halstead-Reitan battery. However it does not require any specific tests as it was constructed to provide "a comprehensive, flexible, and empirical approach to the automated interpretation of neuropsychological tests" (Swiercinsky, 1978). Thus, the test core of this approach is a modified Halstead-Reitan battery, but other tests and nontest data can be entered into the program. The *Lafayette Clinic Repeatable Neuropsychological Test Battery* (R. Lewis and Kupke, 1977) includes a number of the tests in the Halstead-Reitan battery (Trail Making Test, Finger Tapping, grip strength, and the Digit Symbol and Digit Span subtests of the WAIS), the Critical Flicker Fusion test from the original Halstead Battery, and a variety of other, all time-dependent, tests measuring such neuropsychologically relevant behavior as verbal fluency, visual scanning, and fine hand coordination. Because those of its subtests that are susceptible to practice effects come in different versions, it is well suited to studies using repeated measurements. It has been used with a modified Halstead-Reitan battery (K. M. Adams and Schoof 1975), but it is presented as a complete battery in itself.

Luria's Neuropsychological Investigation (Christensen, 1979)

Luria's neuropsychological examination techniques have been brought together in a single set of materials comprising a text, manual of instructions, and test cards. Included are the testing instructions and test material for examining the whole range of functions—both neurosensory and intellectual—that he has studied. The techniques and test materials presented in this battery are identical with techniques and materials that Luria describes in his work (e.g., *Higher cortical functions in man,* 1966; *The working brain,* 1973b). Christensen has made this material readily accessible to those who wish to use the methods that were so fruitful in Luria's hands. She did this in two ways: by replicating Luria's techniques in card form, using his instructions (e.g., see Luria, 1966, 1973b) with detailed directions for administration; and, perhaps more importantly, by organizing the items into a framework that follows Luria's conceptualization of the roles and relationships of the brain's cortical functions and guides the course of the examination.

Christensen's collection of Luria's material is organized into ten sections according to particular functions (motor functions, acoustico-motor organization, higher cutaneous and kinesthetic functions, higher visual functions, impressive [i.e., receptive] speech, expressive speech, writing and reading, arithmetical skill, mnestic processes, and investigation of intellectual processes). The examination techniques and test fragments included in this battery reflect the range of methods Luria incorporated into his neuropsychological investigations. For example, he used familiar psychological tests such as Kohs blocks (see p. 407), Raven's Matrices (see pp. 502–505), and Gottschaldt's Hidden Figures (see p. 302f.). A few items from these tests are included in this battery. In addition, many tasks asked of the patient have the same format as items in popular tests of mental abilities or speech disorders (e.g., building a sentence using three given words, following instructions that involve prepositional relationships such as "draw a cross beneath a circle," or arranging a set of pictures to make a story). A number of items in this battery come from the mental status examination (e.g., recitation of months forward and backward, serial sevens, telling how two verbal concepts such as boat and train are similar or different, retention of three or four words following an interference activity). Some tasks are procedures included in other parts of the neurological examination (e.g., rapid alternating hand movements, discrimination of sharp or dull pressure on the skin, testing limb position sense). Some of the most interesting items or item sequences are those developed by Luria. These include a series of tasks involving "speech regulation of the motor act": "conflict" commands requiring the patient to make a hand response that is the alternate of the examiner's hand movement (e.g., "tap once when the examiner taps twice and vice versa"; "show a fist when the examiner points a finger and vice versa"); "go-no-go" instructions which test the patient's capacity to respond to one cue and withhold response to another (e.g., squeeze the examiner's hand at the word "red"; do nothing at the word "green"); alternating commands, which examine the patient's ability to establish a stereotyped motor pattern (e.g., "raise the right hand in response to one signal, the left to two signals") or to break out of it (e.g., continue the alternating pattern of cue presentation until the stereotyped response pattern is established, and then change the pattern, repeating one or the other signal at random). Another interesting set of items tests arithmetic skills by systematically varying the task in terms of stimulus (written, oral), response (written in Roman or Arabic numbers, oral), operation (addition, subtraction, etc.), difficulty level (one-, two-place numbers), and complexity (serial sequences using different operations). Many of the unique features of this battery may be found in Luria's variations on conventional examination practices, such as testing short-term retention of rhythmic taps or hand position, writing (in addition to repeating) dictated phonemes, indicating differences between phoneme pairs by gesture), and solving arithmetic story problems that require several steps (see p. 500 for examples).

In keeping with the spirit of what Luria referred to as an "experimental" approach to the clinical examination, Christensen points out the value of adapting the many brief examination procedures that comprise this battery to each patient's capacity. While acknowledging the benefits that standardized procedures afford, she also stresses the need for the examiner to modify these procedures in whatever manner will most likely challenge the patient without defeating him.

This battery can not satisfy all neuropsychological examination requirements. For one thing, it was not meant to be comprehensive. Among its more obvious omissions are tests of attention, concentration, and mental tracking. Few techniques are offered for assessing nonverbal memory or nonverbal concept formation. Fund of information also is not assessed. Another problem is that many of the subtests examine functions such as speech or simple finger and hand coordination that all intact adults can perform. Deficits elicited by these subtests may reflect either very circumscribed or relatively severe conditions. However, these same subtests are often not useful in detecting most mild or diffuse impairments, such as the residuals of a mild concussion or stroke or early changes in a dementing disorder. For example, although some aspects of verbal memory and learning are reviewed by the tests in this battery, these tests are not of sufficient difficulty to pick up subtle learning deficits, particularly in bright persons. Moreover, absence of normative data makes performance on the learning tests and a number of other items in this battery difficult to evaluate.

Many examiners use some of the subtests in this battery selectively. I find, for example, that a number of the routines for investigating motor functions (section D, pp. 38–45) test aspects of the integration and effectiveness of motor performance and motor control that are not addressed in most neurological or neuropsychological examination procedures and often provide valuable information. Because of its incompleteness, when this battery comprises the core of the neuropsychological examination, supplemental testing will be needed for most patients. Christensen typically includes a (Danish version) WAIS and also uses standardized memory tests in her clinical examinations (personal communication).

THE LURIA-NEBRASKA NEUROPSYCHOLOGICAL BATTERY[1] (Golden, 1981; Golden et al., 1980)

The title of this battery is somewhat of a misnomer. To the extent that the examination techniques used by A. R. Luria, which were collected and organized by Christensen (see above), have been converted into test items in this battery, it traces its lineage to that preeminent Russian neuropsychologist. However, as Spiers (1981) so aptly stated, "It is not these items, per se, but the manner in which Luria made use of them as a means of testing hypotheses concerning various abilities, deficits or functions which is his method and his unique contribution to neuropsychological assessment. Consequently, the incorporation of items drawn from Luria's work into a standardized test should not be interpreted to mean that the test is an operationalization or standardization of Luria's method."

With the stated goal of developing an "ideal test battery" that would "consist of Luria's test procedures administered and evaluated in a standardized manner," Golden (1981) and his colleagues selected items from Christensen's manual on the basis of whether they descriminated between normal subjects and an unspecified group of neurologically impaired patients. Items were assigned to 11 scales according to their placement among the test procedures presented by Christensen, differing from Christensen's categorization only in that "Reading" and "Writing" are separate scales in Golden's battery. Performance on each item is evaluated on a three-point scale, from 0 for no impairment to 2 for severely impaired. Score values were also determined on the basis of how well scores separated control and neurologically impaired groups and therefore bear little relationship to the ways in which neuropsychological disorders are manifested. For example, scores for a story recall task are given in items 166 and 167 (on the Receptive Speech scale), which grossly measure response time and number of correct words repeated by the patient. With a slowed response counted in the same category as verbal memory impairment, a six second response delay receives the same score (2) as inability to recite even one word correctly, regardless of how accurately or completely the slow responder recalled the story. (This verbal recall item, which requires a spoken response and yet is scored on the "Receptive Speech" scale, is an excellent example of the confounded items, items that overlap scales, and misplaced items that create insoluble psychometric and interpretation problems.) The summed scores for each of these scales produce 11 scoring indices. Three additional scales are made up of items from the other scales: the Pathognomonic, Right Hemisphere, and Left Hemisphere scales. The latter two scales are composed of all the tactile and motor function items for each side of the body. An average of the 14 scale sums "represents the subject's average performance," although the relative contributions of each item to this score will necessarily vary with the number of failures on the tactile and motor scales and on the items included in

---

[1]In the earliest publications about this battery, while C.G. Golden was still associated with the University of South Dakota, it was called the "Luria-South Dakota Neuropsychological Battery," undergoing a name change when Golden moved to Nebraska.

the Pathognomonic scale since scores on these items are counted twice. Age and education corrections are provided.

Because it was taken directly from Christensen's work, this battery has the same content limitations. It has also acquired a serious one of its own. By limiting scorable response times to ten seconds for the questions in 57 items (of 248; another 26 "items" are simply reaction time scores) and to longer times (15 to 90 seconds) on 32 other items, this test penalizes slow responders without providing the means for evaluating the quality of their performance or distinguishing between failures due to generalized slowing or to impairment of specific functions associated with an item. The timing issue is actually greater than suggested by the numbers here since many of the items in which response times are limited to ten or 15 seconds are made up of three or four subitems.

A considerable gap separates the evaluations of this battery made by Golden and his colleagues from those by neuropsychologists who are not affiliated with them. Golden and his group, without exception, offer data supporting their claims that this battery is a diagnostically efficient instrument (e.g., Golden, 1980, 1981; Golden et al., 1978; Hammeke et al., 1978; Purisch et al., 1978). Other neuropsychologists have concluded that this battery is diagnostically unreliable (K. M. Adams and Brown, 1980; Crosson and Warren, 1982; Delis and Kaplan, 1982). In evaluating the literature on this instrument, it is important to know the nature of the data on which such differing conclusions have been based.

Golden and his colleagues have evaluated this battery in terms of how well it discriminates between diagnostically different groups, mostly between normal control subjects and neurologically impaired patients, but also between psychiatric and neurological patients, and between patients with localized or diffuse lesions (G. P. Lewis et al., 1979). The standard of comparison they use is the "hit rate," which, as shown on pp. 152–153, is a function of the number of diagnostic characteristics identified by the instrument and the base rates of these diagnostic characteristics in the particular population under study. It also varies with the relative proportions of the groups under examination. Thus, an investigator can manipulate the hit rate by including more or less severely damaged patients, more or fewer control subjects (see K. M. Adams, 1980a, b; Ehrfurth and Lezak, 1982). The reliance on hit rates to demonstrate the worthiness of this instrument implies that the purpose of neuropsychological assessment is to make the crude diagnostic discriminations these investigators report. However, the neuropsychological disorders sustained by the group of 50 patients used in three of the validation studies cited by Golden (1981; an additional two studies referred to in Golden, 1980, also used this same patient group; see K. M. Adams, 1980a) are such that most would be identified as impaired within the first few minutes of observation and questioning (10 were trauma victims, 6 had neoplasms, 3 had had infectious diseases, 14 had cerebrovascular disorders, 6 suffered from degenerative diseases, 4 had epilepsy, 3 presented with metabolic and toxic disorders, and 4 had congenital disorders). When patient's impairments are obvious on observation, the ability of an assessment instrument to make the same discriminations does not make it a valuable diagnostic tool.

Clinical evaluations by other neuropsychologists have focused on how well this battery provides diagnostically accurate information in the individual case. K. M. Adams and Brown (1980) examined scores from this battery obtained by six patients with cerebral vascular disease. They found that these "tests either overestimate the degree of pathology in certain areas, or fail to detect critical focal deficit." Moreover, they noted that the Intellectual Processes scale (which Golden [1980] says "represents an evaluation of a subject's intellectual level") is "highly unstable" and produces ability estimates that are widely at variance with WAIS scores.

Delis and Kaplan (1982) compared the diagnostic profile and conclusions obtained on the Boston Diagnostic Aphasia Examination with the diagnostic profile and conclusions of Golden's battery for a patient with a left posterior temporal lesion (documented by CT scan). The patient received an evaluation of "mild residual deficits indicative of . . . a posterior fluent aphasia" on the basis of the Boston battery, administered by a speech pathologist. However, he received a critically high T-score on the Expressive Speech scale of Golden's battery, with a much lower Receptive Speech scale T-score that placed the patient within the unimpaired range on this scale. On this basis, "the standardized scores would indicate that (the patient) is suffering from expressive speech deficits, with receptive speech functions intact. The lesion would therefore be interpreted as being most likely anterior to the Rolandic fissure." The patient, who failed several drawing and motor response items because he could not readily comprehend the verbal instructions, also received a higher score on the Right Hemisphere scale than the Left Hemisphere scale. If this had been "evaluated in a standardized manner," as recommended by Golden (1981), the lesion would have been placed on the right side of this right-handed patient's brain. An analysis of the speech scales that produced these erroneous results demonstrated two contributing problems: First, "The assessment of certain cognitive functions is confounded by requiring that other cognitive functions, associated with anatomically disparate structure, be intact." (E.g., more than three-fourths of the "Expressive Speech" items involve activities, such as verbal repetition or reading, which are vulnerable to posterior lesions. Thus, a patient with a receptive disability may have quite adequate spontaneous speech and yet fail these Expressive Speech items if receptive speech functions are impaired.) The second problem lies in an insufficient number of speech items that do not require other functions for a successful response.

Crosson and Warren (1982) also found that this battery misidentified the side of lesion of an aphasic patient with a posterior lesion while another patient with two right-sided CVAs had significant scale elevations indicating left hemisphere damage as well as right. They identified several items that are sensitive to left visuospatial inattention, but none of these are on the Visual scale. Failure due to left visuospatial inattention will show up on other scales (e.g., Receptive Speech, Memory) so that "a relatively low score on the Visual scale does not guarantee that visual problems do not exist." Crosson and Warren also point out that many items that are purportedly nonverbal involve verbal skills.

It is not surprising that this battery is of questionable value in making individual diagnostic predictions since its theoretical and psychometric bases are unsound. E. W.

Russell (1980c) has observed that with only a three-point scale for each item, and scales composed of many heterogeneous items, it is impossible to examine gradations in impairment of a function or functional system. Delis and Kaplan (in press) show that the heterogeneity of the scales makes it impossible to interpret the score of any given scale. Russell demonstrated this by listing the variety and uneven representation of specific aspects of memory that are included in the Memory scale, noting that, "One item is not even a memory item" (item 224: accuracy with which the subject predicts the number of items recalled). The confounding of functions within scales, discussed by a number of authors, was carefully detailed by Spiers (1982), who also noted "its overlapping item content on different scales and its failure to determine the actual source of error relative to such items."

Of course this battery discriminates between brain damaged patients and normal control subjects at a better than chance rate. Any collection of tests of sensory, motor, and assorted cognitive functions would do the same. Moreover, when given with the Halstead-Reitan battery, each of these batteries identifies some subjects with organic brain damage who were not accurately diagnosed by the other, although both batteries made the same discriminations most of the time (Kane et al., 1981). Still, given its many psychometric defects, the examiner must be extremely cautious about drawing conclusions based on the scores and indices of this battery as presently constituted.

Golden and his colleagues (1982) also advise against indiscriminate use of this battery, noting that simplistic interpretations of this or "any test . . . are limited, at best." They cite the importance of behavioral observations in interpreting scores obtained on this battery, of testing hypotheses by looking for internal consistency in the response pattern, and of making evaluations within the context of the patient's background and history. In pointing out that effectiveness of this battery depends on knowledge about neuropsychology and neurology as well as an understanding of Luria's theory, they remind potential users that this instrument is not suitable for use by any examiner who does not have a good grounding in neuropsychology and its related disciplines.

MICHIGAN NEUROPSYCHOLOGICAL TEST BATTERY (A. Smith, 1981)

The tests that constitute Smith's basic neuropsychological examination were chosen to provide a well-balanced review of intellectual functions. He includes six standard tests with the WAIS (or WISC for younger subjects): the Visual Organization Test (see pp. 357–358); Raven's Coloured Matrices (see pp. 505–506); Administrations A and C of the Benton Visual Retention Test (see pp. 402, 447ff.); the Purdue Pegboard Test (see pp. 529–532); the Symbol Digit Modalities Test (see pp. 554–555); and the Peabody Picture Vocabulary Test (see pp. 307–308). In addition, he uses a number of unpublished tests of reading, writing, color naming, identifying body parts (see p. 540), tactile inattention, and sentence memory to round out the battery. The complete battery takes approximately three hours to give. There are no norms for the battery as a whole, but each test in it has demonstrated sensitivity to a well-defined modality or function impairment or is presently undergoing evaluation.

NEUROPSYCHOLOGICAL TEST BATTERY (Miceli et al., 1977; 1981)

The six tests in this battery were selected as representative measures of "intelligence, memory, and visuoconstructive functions." The three "Verbal Tasks" are (1) *Word Fluency* (described by Benton, 1968; see pp. 330–332); (2) *Phrase Construction*, requiring the subject to compose a sentence from two or three words (see p. 341); and (3) *Rey's 15 Word Memory Test*, using a slightly modified presentation and scoring system (see pp. 422–429). The "Visual-Spatial Tasks" consist of (1) *Raven's Coloured Progressive Matrices*, modified so that response items are presented vertically (see pp. 505–506); (2) *Immediate Visual Memory* which uses some of the Coloured Matrices designs in a recognition format involving the presentation of the stimulus for three seconds immediately followed by a display of the stimulus among four alternative response choices; and (3) *Copying Drawings*, in which the subject first copies a star, a cube and a house on blank paper and then copies them on paper containing "landmarks" for guidance. Raw scores are converted to T-scores ($\overline{X} = 50$, SD $= 10$) for ease of comparison of subtest performances.

Specific performance deficits, whether they appear on individual tests or in the test battery profile, show regular associations with neuroanatomically defined lesions of the cerebral hemispheres (Miceli et al., 1981). The expected dissociation between performance deficits on the verbal and the visual tasks by patients with right and left hemisphere lesions was observed. Even though the patients with left-sided lesions were not aphasic, they showed this effect more prominently than those whose lesions involved the right hemisphere, particularly when the right-sided lesion was confined to one lobe. Word Fluency and Copying Drawings demonstrated particular sensitivity to anterior and posterior lesions respectively.

Composite Tests for Brain Damage

As more becomes known about neuropsychological assessment and is reported in journals of general interest to psychiatrists, neurologists, and clinical psychologists, there seems to be less interest in and acceptance of screening tests that were simply devised to identify "organicity." Thus, some once-popular tests that have been around for decades, such as the *Hunt-Minnesota Test for Organic Brain Damage* (H. F. Hunt, 1943) have faded into obsolescence. Only the "Shipley" has survived into the 1980s.

THE SHIPLEY INSTITUTE OF LIVING SCALE (Shipley, 1940, 1946)

This test, which consists of only two subtests, is fully reproduced with the scoring key and all the normative tables in Pollack (1942). It was originally developed to screen mentally deteriorated psychiatric patients from other patient groups, but its use has been extended to screening for organicity as well. An easily administered paper and pencil test, it is based on the observation that performance on vocabulary tests is often least affected by brain injury. Vocabulary performance is compared with performance on a verbal abstraction test under the assumption that, with mental deterioration, the ability to form abstractions will erode sooner than the basic verbal skills reflected in vocabulary test scores. The test is not standardized for age, sex, or performance on intellectual ability tests, and in fact, the frequency of "organic" scores increases with age (Yates, 1954).

The vocabulary score is the number correct of 40 multiple-choice items. The comparison between the vocabulary and abstraction test scores yields a Conceptual Quotient (CQ) that is the "index of impairment." Shipley (1940) warns, however, that, "quotients obtained from vocabulary scores below 23 are of doubtful validity." Yet in one sample of 38 relatively young male psychiatric outpatients, eight (21%) received scores below 23. That so many of these clinic patients did not achieve vocabulary scores within the acceptable range is not surprising. Many of the words (e.g., 26—rue, 32—lissom, 40—pristine) rarely appear in print and are heard even less frequently.

Although this test is still in clinical use (Lubin, 1971), most research studies report that it fails to discriminate between organic patients and normal control subjects as well as between different categories of neuropsychiatric patients (Aita, Armitage et al., 1947; J. W. Parker, 1957; Savage, 1970). In one study the Shipley Scale was described as "the most useful single instrument" for separating neurotic from brain concussion patients, but schizophrenic and depressive patients had been eliminated from the patient pool (Abbott et al., 1943). Another study in which the Shipley Scale did identify patients with intellectual impairment indicates that it may be useful for coarse screening of thought disorders without distinguishing between organic and functional problems (Prado and Taub, 1966).

FULD OBJECT-MEMORY EVALUATION (Fuld, 1977, 1980)

This set of procedures was designed to assess several aspects of learning and retrieval in elderly persons and also provides information about tactile recognition, right-left discrimination, and verbal fluency. The test material consists of a bag containing ten small common objects that can be identified by touch (ball, bottle, button, card, cup, key, matches, nail, ring, and scissors). The procedures must be given in the prescribed order.

In the first task in the procedural sequence, the patient is asked to name or describe each of the ten objects while feeling it in the bag, using the right or left hand alternatively as requested by the examiner. With each response, the indicated object is pulled out of the bag so the subject can see it and check guesses. When needed, a suitable name or mutually satisfactory gesture or description is established for each one of the objects at this time. The next task is a verbal fluency test (called here, "rapid semantic retrieval"), which serves as a distractor and requires the patient to say as many given names (same sex as the patient) as he can think of in one minute. Then comes a one-minute recall trial followed by four learning and recall trials using the method of selective reminding (see p. 473f.). For these trials, the examiner reminds the patient of omitted items at the slow rate of one item every five seconds. One of four 30-second "rapid semantic retrieval" trials comes after each learning trial as a

Table 18-1 Fuld Object-Memory Evaluation Scores Made By Elderly Subjects Residing in the Community

Age Groups		Total Recall	Storage	Repeated Retrieval	Ineffective Reminders
70–79	Mean	38.73	10.00	25.87	2.13
(n = 15)	SD	4.53	0.00	4.96	1.81
80–89	Mean	33.59	9.47	21.00	6.29
(n = 15)	SD	6.61	1.12	5.69	5.28

distractor for the next recall trial. The word categories for these distractor trials are, respectively, foods, "things that make people happy," vegetables, and "things that make people sad." A one-minute recall trial follows this series of learning, recall, and distractor trials. Next comes 15 minutes during which the patient does other tests. If the patient can name all ten items after this delay, the test is terminated. If not, recognition of each item not named within the one minute allowed for recall is tested in a three-choice recognition format: e.g., "In the bag is there a stone, a block, or a *ball?*"

Several memory scores can be derived from each completed performance of this test. (See Table 18-1). *Total Recall* is the sum of items correctly named in all five trials. *Storage* refers to the total number of items (of ten) that have been recalled at least once during the first five recall trials. *Repeated Retrieval,* which is the sum of items named without reminding, is offered as a measure of retrieval efficiency. *Ineffective Reminders* is the sum of instances in which reminding was not followed by recall on the next trial. It is the measure of the extent to which the patient does not use feedback and is dependent, in part, on the amount of reminding required.

Fuld (1980) reported that of 15 persons residing in the community who were in their eighth decade, 14 recalled seven of the ten words on the delay trial, 13 of 15 in their ninth decade recalled six. When used to compare moderately impaired with unimpaired elderly nursing home residents, these procedures elicited higher storage and recall scores for the latter group. Intact residents also showed a tendency to improve their recall scores on each trial while the impaired subjects' span of recall leveled off at the second trial.

The verbal fluency test included in this set of procedures may contribute to the discrimination of "pseudodementia" from a genuine dementing process, particularly when the patient is depressed since decreased verbal productivity is a common finding in Alzheimer's disease (see pp. 183–184). Moreover, the use of "happy" and "sad" categories may aid in identifying psychotically depressed patients as Fuld (1980) observed that unlike most people, depressed patients tend to make more sad than happy associations. Normative data for the neutral "rapid semantic retrieval" task categories were developed on 32 unimpaired persons in the 70 to 93 age range residing in the community. The women performed significantly better than the men, giving an average of 21.91 ± 4.17 items in the food and vegetable categories combined, and 16.35 ± 2.96 names. The men in this group gave an average of only 15.64 ± 6.13 food and vegetable responses and 13.21 ± 6.12 names.

19

Observational Methods, Rating Scales, and Inventories

The techniques presented in this chapter tend to be relatively brief, based on observations, and not rigorously standardized. Many are essentially schedules for directing and organizing behavioral observations and diagnostic interviews. Some have evolved out of clinical experience, and others were developed for specific assessment purposes. They all provide behavioral descriptions that can amplify or humanize test data and may be useful in following a patient's course or forming gross diagnostic impressions.

The Mental Status Examination

The mental status examination, a structured interview, usually takes place during the examiner's initial session with the patient. It is the only formal procedure for assessing intellectual functions in psychiatric or neurological examinations. Psychologists often dispense with it since most of the data obtained in the mental status examination are acquired in the course of a thorough neuropsychological evaluation. However, by beginning the examination with the brief review of intellectual and social behavior afforded by the mental status examination, the psychologist may be alerted to problem areas that will need intensive study. The mental status examination will usually indicate whether the patient's general level of functioning is too low for standard adult assessment techniques. It is also likely to draw out personal idiosyncracies or emotional problems that may interfere with the examination or require special attention or procedural changes.

Mental status information comes from both direct questioning and careful observation of the patient during the course of the interview. Almost every clinical textbook or manual in psychiatry and neurology contains a guide to the mental status examination. Examples of a variety of questions that touch upon many different areas of intellectual and social/emotional functioning and guidelines for reviewing the areas covered by the mental status examination are given in Strub and Black (1977, 1981), Volle (1975), and F. L. Wells and Ruesch (1972). Different authors organize the components of the mental status examination in different ways and different examiners ask some of the questions differently, but it always covers the following aspects of the patient's behavior:

1. *Appearance.* The examiner notes the patient's dress, grooming, carriage, facial expressions and eye contact, mannerisms, and any unusual movements.

2. *Orientation.* This concerns the patient's appreciation of time, place, person, and of his present situation (see pp. 553ff.). Some examiners also inquire about the patient's awareness of the examiners' role.

3. *Speech.* Observations are made of both delivery and content of speech. The examiner looks for deviations from normal rate, tone quality, articulation, phrasing, and smoothness and ease of delivery as well as for misuse or confusion of words, grammatical and syntactical errors, perseverations, dysnomia, and other defects in word production and organization.

4. *Thinking.* In patients with aphasic disorders or verbal dyspraxias, and in some with severe functional disturbances such as profound depression with motor slowing, it can be difficult to distinguish speech and thought disorders. In most patients, speech can be evaluated separately from such characteristics of thinking as mental confusion, quality and appropriateness of associations, logic, clarity, coherence, rate of thought production, and such specific thinking problems as blocking, confabulation, circumstantiality, or rationalization.

5. *Attention, concentration, and memory.* In this review of span of attention, immediate, recent, and remote memory, the examiner inquires about the patient's early and recent history, asking for names, dates, places, and events (p. 103f.). He gives digit span (see pp. 266–270) and asks for recall of three or four words immediately and again after an intervening task or five more minutes of interview (see pp. 421–422). Serial Sevens (see pp. 552–553) and digits reversed are the standard mental status concentration tasks.

6. *Intellectual functioning.* Estimation of the level of general intellectual functioning is based on quality of vocabulary, reasoning, judgment, and organization of thought as well as answers to questions about topics of general information, fairly simple arithmetic problems, and abstract reasoning tasks. Usually the patient is asked to explain one or two proverbs (see pp. 476–477) and to give "similarities" and "differences" (see pp. 478–479). When examining patients with known or suspected neurological impairment, the examiner should include simple drawing and copying tasks (e.g., draw a clock and a house, copy a cube or geometric design drawn by the examiner) and a brief assessment of reading and writing.

7. *Emotional state.* Both *mood* (the patient's prevailing emotional tone) and *affect* (the range and appropriateness of his emotional responses) need to be distinguished and reported. Mood constitutes the ground, affect the figure of the patient's emotional behavior.

8. *Special preoccupations and experiences.* The examiner looks for reports or expressions of bodily concerns, distortions of self-concept, obsessional tendencies, phobias, paranoidal ideation, remose or suicidal thoughts, delusions, hallucinations, and strange experiences such as dissociations, fugue states, feelings of impersonalization or unreality.

9. *Insight.* This is evaluated on the basis of the patient's self-understanding, his appreciation of his condition, and his expectations and plans.

The mental status examination of a reasonably cooperative, verbally intact patient takes 20 to 30 minutes. The examiner's experience and training provide the standards for evaluating much of the patient's responses and behavior, for outside of questions drawn from such standardized tests as the Wechsler or Stanford-Binet scales, there are no quantitative norms. Thus, the data obtained in the mental status examination are impressionistic and tend to be coarse-grained, compared with the fine scaling of psychometric tests. It does not substitute for formal testing; rather, it adds another dimension. However, for many seriously impaired patients, particularly those who are bedridden, have significant sensory or motor deficits, or whose level of consciousness is depressed or fluctuating, the mental status examination may not only be the examination of choice, but may also be the only examination that can be made of the patient's neuropsychological condition. For example, for severely injured head trauma victims, the mental status examination is often the best tool for following the patient's course during the first six to eight weeks after return of consciousness.

Many of the mental status items can be integrated into an introductory interview to provide data on most of the behavior covered by a mental status examination in the course of taking the patient's history and discussing his present situation and future plans. For example, the patient's knowledge about his present income, where it comes from, how much he gets from what sources, and his most recent living arrangements reflects the integrity of his recent memory. He will also be performing calculations and indirectly demonstrating the quality of his concentration ability if asked to tell the amount of his total income when it comes from several sources, his annual rent or house payments based on the monthly cost, or the amount of monthly income left after he has paid for housing. Some patients who are concerned about being "crazy" or "dumb" are very touchy about responding to the formal arithmetic questions or memory tests of the mental status examination. These same patients often remain cooperative if they do not perceive the questions as challenging their mental competence.

Rating Scales and Inventories

The content of most scales, inventories, and other patient rating schemes falls into one of three categories: (1) more or less complete mental status examinations that have been given scoring systems; (2) observer's descriptions of some specified class of behavior (e.g., activities, psychiatric symptoms); and (3) reactions or perceptions of nonprofessional persons familiar with the patient, usually family members. Most of these instruments have been devised with a particular population or diagnostic question in mind and therefore have become associated with that population or question. Moreover, the problems that some of these scales measure are peculiar to the population for which they were developed. Therefore, scales and inventories are grouped for review here according to the purpose for which they were originally devised.

Rating scales and inventories typically include scoring schemes that, as likely as not, were devised without benefit of psychometric scaling techniques or substantial reliability or cross-validational studies. Most of the behavioral characteristics that are scored in these instruments tend to separate members of the target population from the population at large at sufficiently respectable rates to warrant their use for gross clinical screening or documentation in research. For clinical purposes, the value of a scale or inventory is more likely to be in the framework it gives to the conduct and evaluation of a brief examination than in its scores.

Dementia Evaluation

The often very difficult problem of differentiating patients with behavioral disturbances due to organic deterioration from those with psychiatric disorders has inspired many clinicians to systematize the observational schemes that seemed to work for them. The depressive reactions and other behavioral disorders common among elderly persons can be virtually indistinguishable from the behavioral changes accompanying many of the organic diseases that are also common among the aged. Most of these instruments were developed to aid in making these difficult discriminations. Thus, some contain questions that are best suited for middle-aged and older people or include simplified forms of tasks used in examinations for the general population. Most of them, however, have general applicability. Diagnostic accuracy may be enhanced by combining data from several of these instruments (Eisdorfer and Cohen, 1980).

MENTAL STATUS TYPE SCALES

Thirteen scales for the evaluation of "organic mental status" are very briefly described by Kochansky (1979). Most scales based on the mental status examination come in one of three levels of complexity.

(1) Lengthy scales composed of many different kinds of items contain most of the elements of the mental status examination plus a scoring system. The most extensive of these is probably the *Mattis Organic Mental Syndrome Screening Examination* (MOMSSE) (Mattis, 1976). This scale covers ten areas. The first four, (I) State of consciousness, (II) Insight into illness, (III) Affect, and (IV) Estimate of premorbid intellectual abilities, serve as guides to a structured interview and observation. The last six sections each contain a number of scorable items: (V) General information, (VI) Verbal abstraction, (VII) Attention (digits forward to 7, digits backward to 6), (VIII) Memory (orientation for time and place, immediate and delayed sentence recall with a sentence-building task serving as interference, and recall of design D-V of Benton's Visual Retention Test [see pp. 447–451]), (IX) Language (nine different verbal tasks), and (X) Construction (drawing and copying, WAIS Block Designs 2, 4, and 6). Responses to sections V, VI, and VII are scored and classified on a four-point scale ranging from *Above Average* through *Average* and *Below Average* to *Defective*. These sections provide a small sample of the WAIS performance. For example, instead of the 29 graded items of the WAIS Information subtest, section V is composed of only six of the WAIS Information items, mostly from the lower end and the

middle of the subtest (numbers 6, 8, 10, 12, 15, and 21). Mattis reports that the MOMSSE takes 15 to 20 minutes. He suggests that a review of cognitive functions as extensive as this is unlikely to make false negative discriminations.

Mattis (1976) also developed a shorter, less taxing set of mental status examination items, the *Dementia Rating Scale*. This scale examines five areas that are particularly sensitive to the behavioral changes that characterize senile dementia of the Alzheimer's type (SDAT) (see pp. 180–184). Five areas are covered: (I) Attention (digits forward and backward up to four; follow two successive commands, e.g., "Open your mouth and close your eyes"; (II) Initiation and perseveration (e.g., name articles in supermarket, repeat series of one-syllable rhymes; perform double alternating hand movements, copy a row of alternating O's and X's); (III) Construction (e.g., copy a diamond in a square, copy a set of parallel lines, write name); (IV) Conceptual (e.g., four WAIS-type Similarities items, identify which of three items is different); and (V) Memory (e.g., delayed recall of a five-word sentence, personal orientation, design recall). A scoring system permits test-retest comparison. "Split-half" scoring of responses given by a group of elderly deteriorated patients indicates that this scale has high internal reliability (r ; .90) (R. Gardner, Oliver-Muñoz, et al., 1981).

An interesting feature of both the Mattis scales is that, instead of giving items in the usual ascending order of difficulty, the most difficult item is given first (except the digits series and the Block Design subtest items of the MOMSSE). Since the most difficult items on the Dementia Rating Scale and the second or third (of six) most difficult items in each section of the MOMSSE are within the capacity of most intact older persons, this feature can be a time-saver. An intact subject would only have to give three abstract answers on the first subtest (Similarities) of the Conceptualization section of the Dementia Rating Scale, for example; the other 26 items in this section would be skipped. On the other hand, Mattis reports that the examination of demented patients can take 30–45 minutes. The two kinds of items on which practice and set are most likely to make a difference, digit span and block constructions, are given in the traditional order.

(2) In abbreviated mental status examinations, each section is represented by only one or a few items. Those most suitable for use in diagnostic screening, to evaluate a treatment regimen, or to follow the course of a condition contain questions testing personal orientation, attention and mental tracking, verbal abstraction, language usage, and recent and remote memory, and include a drawing or writing task and sometimes both. The *Mental Status Check List* (Lifshitz, 1960), for example, covers just these specific areas. The *Geriatric Interpersonal Rating Scale* (Plutchik et al., 1971) contains all of these kinds of items and also includes digits forward and reversed, a series of simple multiplication problems, two items testing humor, and some card sorting and matching tasks using playing cards.

The *Confabulation* questionnaire (Mercer et al., 1977) was constructed to elicit confabulation in amnesic patients (primarily those with Korsakoff's psychosis). It consists of four kinds of questions. (I) Twelve of the 41 questions draw upon remote memory (e.g., "Where were you living when you began school?"). (II) Among the 29 items testing recent memory are orientation questions and questions about recent events (e.g., "Who won the world series?" "Who is president?"). (III) Six items can be answered by using available cues (e.g., the examiner's name tag, a calendar and an envelope imprinted with the name and address of the hospital). (IV) Questions to which neurologically intact patients frequently responded, "I don't know" (the patient's area code, the winner of the world series and of the "Superbowl"). Among the items in group II are four that tend to be "leading," i.e., likely to elicit a confabulated response: "Do you remember what we did the last time we met?" "Something important is going to happen soon. Can you tell me what it is?" "What were you doing yesterday?" and "Have you done any traveling recently?" Using this instrument, its authors were able to distinguish mild from severe confabulators and characterize each group in terms of memory deficits (greater among severe confabulators), response latencies (briefer among severe confabulators), self-corrections (virtually nonexistent among severe confabulators, but mild confabulators displayed some tendency to self-correction), and use of cues (much less by severe confabulators). In general, items where an answer was expected (e.g., date, birthdate, place) were most likely to elicit a confabulated response.

The *Mini-Mental State* (Folstein et al., 1975) was designed to test cognitive functions simply and quickly. It has no abstraction items, but includes a diagnostically valuable verbal retention test. Administration takes from five to ten minutes. Both administration and scoring are easily learned and are standardized (see Fig. 19-1). Sixty-three elderly (mean age = 73.9) normal control subjects comprised the standardization population. With a maximum obtainable score of 30, the elderly control subjects and younger patients with functional psychiatric disorders achieved scores in the 24.6 to 27.6 range. Scores of several groups of senile patients ranged from 9.6 to 12.2. There was no overlap between the aged control subjects and the senile patients. This test has proven useful in registering changes in the intellectual functioning of psychiatric patients as they respond to treatment.

(3) The shortest instruments are composed of a small number of items that test one to three areas reviewed in the usual mental status examination. Orientation questions figure most prominently in these little tests.

The *Memory Loss Scale* (Markson and Levitz, 1973) consists of just five orientation questions (age, address, birthdate, today's date and day, and request for directions to a "common reference point known to respondent"). Impaired orientation, as measured by this little scale, was significantly predictive of mortality in an elderly population: 23% of low scorers but only 3% of high scorers had died within a year after taking the test.

Ten questions make up the *Mental Status Questionnaire* (R. L. Kahn and Miller, 1978). Five are listed as "Orientation Questions." Three of the five "General Information Questions" concern personal orientation (age, month and year of birth); the other two ask for the names of the current and immediate past presidents. The authors note that errors on questions of place involving misnaming or confusion of the place where hospitalized with another institution is more apt to characterize responses of patients with acute brain syndromes than those with chronic brain syndromes. They also observed that patients with chronic brain syndromes are more amenable to cor-

581

Patient _____

Examiner _____

Date _____

MINI MENTAL STATE

Score   Orientation

(   )   What is the (year) (season) (month) (date) (day)? (5 points)

(   )   Where are we? (state) (county) (town) (hospital) (floor) (5 points)

Registration

(   )   Name 3 objects: 1 second to say each. Then ask the patient to repeat all three after you have said them. 1 point for each correct. Then repeat them until he learns them. Count trials and record _____. (3 points)

Attention and Calculation

(   )   Serial 7's. 1 point for each correct. Stop at 5 answers. Or spell "world" backwards. (Number correct equals letters before first mistake - i.e., d l o r w = 2 correct). (5 points)

Recall

(   )   Ask for the objects above. 1 point for each correct. (3 points)

_____

Language Tests

(   )   name - pencil, watch (2 points)

(   )   repeat - no ifs, ands or buts (1 point)

(   )   follow a 3 stage command: "Take the paper in your right hand, fold it in half, and put it on the floor." (3 points)

```
Mini Mental State
Page 2


Score

            Read and obey the following:

( . )       CLOSE YOUR EYES.  (1 point)

(   )       Write a sentence spontaneously below.  (1 point)



(   )       Copy design below.  (1 point)
```

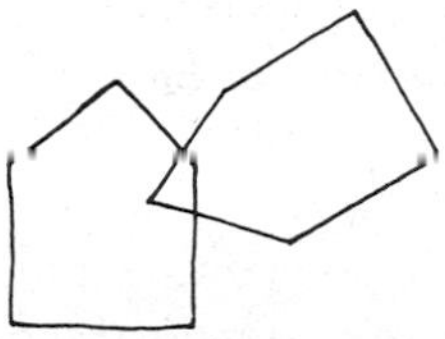

```
 (   )       TOTAL 30 POINTS
```

```
The above test does not include abstraction.  You may want to test this
for your own information:

            Proverbs
            Similarities
```

Fig. 19-1. Mini-Mental State (Folstein et al., 1975).

rection on this point than are patients whose disorientation has resulted from an acute condition.

The *Short Portable Mental Status Questionnaire* (SPMSQ) (Pfeiffer, 1975) also consists of ten questions, of which seven involve orientation (e.g., date, place, mother's maiden name), two ask for current and previous presidents, and the last tests concentration and mental tracking with serial threes. Using a ten-point error score and impairment ratings that take into account level of education, this test consistently identified organically impaired patients ($p < .001$), with very few false positive errors (4 of 133 intact subjects were misclassified); however, of 80 patients with diagnoses of Organic Brain Syndrome (OBS), 37 were misclassified with false negative ratings.

SCALES for RATING OBSERVATIONS

These scales can focus on many different aspects of behavior. The two described below illustrate this. One important difference between these two scales is in the amount of discretion given to the rater, a difference that is reflected in different levels of interrater agreement.

The 31-item *Geriatric Rating Scale* (GRS) (Plutchik et al., 1970) is based on the *Stockton Geriatric Rating Scale* (Meer and Baker, 1966). It was developed for use by "nonprofessional ward staff" to rate patients' behavior in such areas as eating, toileting, self-direction, and sociability. Each item is scored from 0 to 2 according to the severity of the problem as briefly described in the item (e.g., "The patient talks with other people on the ward: Often—0; Sometimes—1; Almost never—2"). The authors report high reliability ($r = .86, .87$) and indicate that high scores (in the direction of severity) are associated with severity of impairment of geriatric patients. However, Plutchik (1979) states that this scale is not applicable to outpatients who can still care for themselves as the items are too "easy" for this population. He criticizes the single global score yielded by this scale because it provides no information regarding the nature of the patient's dysfunctions. In one study reported by Plutchik, three factors were identified: Withdrawal/Apathy; Antisocial Disruptive Behavior; and Deficits in Activities of Daily Living. Plutchik recommends the use of subscales based on these factors to enhance the instrument's sensitivity.

Of the 19 items in the *Sandoz Clincal Assessment—Geriatric* (SCAG) (Shader et al., 1974), some are activity-focused such as "Self-Care," "Appetite," and "Unsociability." However, most have to do with behaviors and response characteristics that are usually symptomatic of psychopathology, such as "Mood Depression," "Irritability," "Emotional Lability," and "Anxiety." The items are couched in general terms (e.g., "UNSOCIABILITY: Poor relationships with others, unfriendly, negative reaction to social and communal recreational activities, aloof. Rate on observed behavior and not on patient's own impression."). Each item is scored on a seven-point scale that ranges from 1 = Not Present to 7 = Severe. Thus, a lot of item interpretation is left to the rater. Kochansky (1979) notes that the rater should be a "skilled clinician." In the research that Shader and his co-workers reported on this scale, the rating was done by psychiatrists or psychiatric residents. Interrater reliability was determined for 18 items ("Dizziness" occurred too rarely for statistical evaluation of this item) and ranged from .93 to .24. Of the 18 reliability correlation coefficients, 11 fell below .80; five were below .60. However, this instrument did discriminate between groups of intact volunteers and elderly patients with mild and severe dementia, or depression. Kochansky (1979) reports that one factor analytic study identified a "mood," a "bewilderment," and an amotivational ("aboulia") factor.

RATING RELATIVE REPORTS

Noting that dementing processes have a significant effect on the patient's "ability to cope with the task of daily living," Hachinski and his colleagues (1975) developed a

Dementia Score scale, which measures how well the patient gets along in his usual environment (see Table 19-1). Demented patients suffering from "primary degenerative" dementia. (i.e., Alzheimer's and related diseases) or multi-infarct dementia received scores ranging from 4 to 25 on this scale with group averages of 11.6 (SD = 5.4) and 12.0 (SD = 5.1), respectively. However, these two patient groups are clearly differentiated by an *Ischemic Score* (Hachinski et al., 1975; M. J. G. Harrison et al., 1979) (see Table 19-2) based partly on patient and family information, and partly on clinical data. The higher the score the more likely it is that the patient is suffering from multi-infarct dementia.

Table 19-1 Dementia Score

Feature	Score
Changes in Performance of Everyday Activities	
1. Inability to perform household tasks	1
2. Inability to cope with small sums of money	1
3. Inability to remember short list of items, e.g., in shopping	1
4. Inability to find way about indoors	1
5. Inability to find way about familiar streets	1
6. Inability to interpret surroundings	1
7. Inability to recall recent events	1
8. Tendency to dwell in the past	1
Changes in Habits	
9. Eating	
Messily with spoon only	1
Simple solids, e.g., biscuits	2
Has to be fed	3
10. Dressing	
Occasionally misplaced buttons, etc.	1
Wrong sequence, commonly forgetting items	2
Unable to dress	3
11. Sphincter control	
Occasional wet beds	1
Frequent wet beds	2
Doubly incontinent	3
12. Increased rigidity	1
13. Increased egocentricity	1
14. Impairment of regard for feelings of others	1
15. Coarsening of affect	1
16. Impairment of emotional control	1
17. Hilarity in inappropriate situations	1
18. Diminished emotional responsiveness	1
19. Sexual misdemeanor (appearing de novo in old age)	1
20. Hobbies relinquished	1
21. Diminished initiative or growing apathy	1
22. Purposeless hyperactivity	1

(From Hachinski et al., 1975, *Archives of Neurology 32*, p. 633. © 1975, American Medical Association.)

Table 19-2 Ischemic Score

Feature	Score
Abrupt onset	2
Stepwise deterioration	1
Fluctuating course	2
Nocturnal confusion	1
Relative preservation of personality	1
Depression	1
Somatic complaints	1
Emotional incontinence	1
History of hypertension	1
History of strokes	2
Evidence of associated atherosclerosis	1
Focal neurological symptoms	2
Focal neurological signs	2

(From Hachinski et al., 1975, *Archives of Neurology 32*, p. 634. © 1975, American Medical Association.)

Developmental Scales

If a severely impaired patient is unable to respond consistently to examination questions or tasks, it is possible to obtain a standardized evaluation of his behavioral status by using one of the infant and child developmental scales. These are inventories of behavior expected at specified ages based on large-scale normative observations. The examiner obtains much of the information about the child (patient) from interviews with a parent (nurse, family member). Some information is obtained through observation, and some from tests for specific responses or skills. Eson and his colleagues (1978, 1979) for example, in devising a series of measures for the longitudinal evaluation of head trauma victims, have brought together 97 items taken from a number of infant scales (e.g., the *Boyd Developmental Progress Scale*, see below; the *Vineland Social Maturity Scale*, p. 587). These are used to document the return of adaptive behaviors in the earliest stages following severe head injury.

CHILD DEVELOPMENT SCALES

Boyd Developmental Progress Scale (R. D. Boyd, 1974). This easily administered scale tests behavior in the three areas of motor, communication, and self-sufficiency skills from birth through the seventh year (see Fig. 19-2). The scale focuses on the *adaptive* aspects of behavior in each of the three test areas so that its data can be immediately useful in rehabilitation planning and training. Some of the items are inappropriate for adult patients (e.g., "Rides Tricycle" at 2–3 years) but most are very relevant (e.g., "Cuts with Scissors," or "Feeds—Uses Fork to Spear" at the 2- to 3-year level). The arrangement of test items on the record sheet facilitates both the conduct of the examination and interpretation of the data for it allows comparison of performance by age and by behavioral area. The communication age scale correlates .95 with the mental age score of the Stanford-Binet (1972 norms) (Boyd, personal communication).

The Gesell Developmental Schedules (Gesell, 1940; Gesell et al., 1949). These are probably the most famous of the developmental scales. They cover the age range from four weeks to six years. No score or overall value is computed. Rather, the child's (patient's) developmental level can be compared with normative data for the many age levels reported in each of four major areas of behavior: motor, language, adaptive, and personal-social.

The Vineland Social Maturity Scale (Doll, 1953, 1965). The range of this scale is from birth to age 25 and over. It is used for assessing the social-adaptive behavior of normal adults, children, and infants. This scale has a checklist format in which the individual items are arranged in order of difficulty by age levels. The eight categories in which the Vineland Scale measures social competence are (1) General Self-Help, (2) Self-Help in Eating, (3) Self-Help in Dressing, (4) Self-Direction, (5) Occupation, (6) Communication, (7) Locomotion, and (8) Socialization. The test yields a Social Age score from which a Social Quotient can be derived. The focus of the test is on personal responsibility and independence; the evaluation of motor and communication skills is incidental. Item answers are obtained by interviewing informants or the subject himself rather than from direct observation. To facilitate scoring and interpretation of this scale, some investigators have developed scoring profiles in which the items are reorganized into content categories having to do with functional areas such as eating, communication, and self-help (Holroyd, 1966; Iscoe, 1960).

Developmental Scales for the Mentally Retarded

Scales for evaluating the level of development of mentally retarded persons are also applicable to the adaptive and cognitive deficits exhibited by some severely damaged or deteriorated patients. The 66-item *AAMD Adaptive Behavior Scale* (Nihira et al., 1975) is available through the American Association on Mental Deficiency. It was developed to evaluate all levels of retardation and thus includes many items relating to independent living. The first part of this scale provides graded evaluations for adaptive behavior in ten "Domains," for example, (I) Independent Functioning (which includes among its eight areas of behavior, Eating, Appearance, Travel); (III) Economic Activity (which has two subdomains, Money Handling and Budgeting, and Shopping Skills); and (VII) Self-Direction (comprised of items pertaining to Initiative, Perseverance, and Leisure Time). The second part contains 14 Domains concerned with such maladaptive behaviors as: (I) Violent and Destructive Behavior; (V) Withdrawal; (VIII) Unacceptable Vocal Habits; and (XI) Hyperactive Tendencies. Factor analysis of the ratings of 734 adult (19 to 67) mentally retarded persons on the scales in part I yielded eight factors in three major divisions (Nihira, 1978): Personal Self-

BOYD DEVELOPMENTAL PROGRESS SCALE

Robert D. Boyd, Ph.D.

DATE   Year   Month   Date

BIRTH ___ ___ ___

AGE ___ ___ ___

NAME _____

UNIT NO. _____

	B	6 mos.	1	18 mos.	2	3	4	5	6	7	8
MOTOR SKILLS	Follows object	Takes two cubes	Builds tower of 2 blocks	Builds tower of 4 blocks	Builds bridge of 3 blocks	10 pellets in bottle 30 sec.	Catches ball, bounced 2/3	10 pellets in bottle 20 sec.	Rides bicycle	Arranges material neatly	
	Rolls over	Sits without support	Walks alone	Walks upstairs	Cuts with scissors	Alternates downstairs	Cuts–follows simple outline	[1]Prints first name	[1]Prints full name	Cuts round outline well	
	Grasps object	Walks holding on	Walks backwards	Jumps	Balances on 1 foot 1 sec.	Balances on 1 foot 5 sec.	Balances on 1 foot 10 sec.	Builds steps of 6 blocks	[1]Prints 1-20 few reversals	[1]Prints 1-20 no revs. 1/2 inch	
	Bears weight	Stands alone	Stoops and recovers	Throws overhand	Rides tricycle	Hops on 1 foot	[2]Draws Man 4 parts	[2]Draws Man 6 parts	[2]Draws Man 9 parts	Writes full name (cursive)	
	Transfers objects	Pincer grasp	Scribbles	[1]Imitates line	Copies circle	Copies cross	Copies square	Copies triangle	Copies vertical diamond	Constructs objects/cooks	

[1]On back of drawing sheet

[2]On back of this sheet

COMMUNICATION SKILLS

B	6 mos.	1	18 mos.	2	3	4	5	6	7	8
Responds to bell	Says—mama, dada	Plays ball	Show-mouth, eyes, hair, nose 1/4	Show-mouth eyes, hair nose 4/4	2What do we— 6/7	Made of-car window dress 2/3	Made of-fork floor, shoe 3/3	2Names animals 1 min. 9	Names days of week	
Babbles	Imitates Sounds	Uses 3 to 5 words	Block-on table to me; on floor 2/3	Block-on, under, front back 2/4	Block-on, under, front, back 3/4	2Completes analogies 2/3	2Definitions 6/9	Alike—boat/airplane; hat/shoe 1/2	Tells own address	
Follows person visually	Responds to no-no, bye-bye	Indicates specific wants	Combines words	Uses plurals	Do—tired, cold, hungry 2/3	Do—cross street	2Reads .5 grade level	3Reads 1.5 grade level	3Reads 2.5 grade level	
Smiles	Hesitates with strangers	Mimics chores	Brings objects on request	Gives full name	Show—"longer" 3/3 or 5/6	Show— "smoother" 3/3 or 5/6	Show—R-ear -eye, R-leg -arm 4/4	When—breakfast, bed, afternoon 3/3	Show—upper R, lower L; middle 3/3	
Turns to whisper	1 Word—not mama, dada	Solitary play	Parallel play	Cooperative play	Separates—without fuss	Tells age	Plays competitive games	Answers phone-takes message	Plays organized group games	

2On back of this sheet
3Use WRAT

SELF SUFFICIENCY SKILLS

B	6 mos.	1	18 mos.	2	3	4	5	6	7	8
Head upright and steady	Drinks from cup with help	Feeds—scoops with spoon (or fork)	Discriminates edible substances	Feeds—uses fork to spear	Feeds—cuts with fork	Brushes own teeth	Games—penny, dime, nickel 2/3	Spreads own bread	Cuts own meat (knife)	
Recovers toy from chest	Uncovers face	Chews food	Unwraps candy or gum	Blocks—give "just one"	Counts-2 blocks/pellets 2/2	Counts—4 and 3 blocks 2/2	Counts—10 and blocks 2/2	Solves—2+1, 3+2, 5-1 2/3	Solves—8+6, 9-5, 7+4 2/3	
Reaches for objects	Works for toy	Drinks without help	Solves pellet bottle	Washes, dries own hands	Ident.—blue, yellow, red, green 3/4	Washes own face	Blows own nose	Bathes self, complete	Buys with money	
Occupies self, unattended	Pulls self upright	Opens closed doors	Goes about house	Avoids danger —street	Cares for self at toilet	Goes about within block	Goes about, crosses streets	Goes to bed unassisted	Tells time, quarter hour	
Feeds self cracker	Gets to sitting position	Removes clothing	Puts on some clothing	Gets own drink	Dresses without help	Buttons-correct, complete	Errands outside home	Ties own shoes	Grooms self	

Fig. 19-2. The Boyd Developmental Progress Scale.

sufficiency, Community Self-sufficiency, and Personal-Social Responsibility. An evaluation of the validity of the ratings on these scales when compared with structured criterion tests found that about half of the ratings differed from criterion test performances, mostly by one level (Millham et al., 1976). This study suggests that these scales are best used for documenting changes or for planning rather than for classification of patients.

In contrast, the *Balthazar Scales of Adaptive Behavior* (Balthazar, 1971) are intended for use with "the profoundly and severely mentally retarded." The finely scaled items were developed to provide highly specific data upon which to base training programs. For example, the Eating Scales contain five subclasses: (I) Dependent Feeding; (II) Finger Foods; (III) Spoon Usage; (IV) Fork Usage; and (V) Drinking. Among the nine Finger Foods items are (2) Holds finger foods; (4) Reaches for finger foods; and (8) Bites off appropriate-size pieces of finger foods. Accompanying these scales and instructions for their use are scoring forms and *The Workshop and Training Manual* for use in developing specific training programs from the ratings.

Epileptic Patient Evaluations

Scales and inventories for documenting the behavior of epileptic patients have been used for two quite different purposes. One has been to document the behavioral and psychosocial consequences of surgery, typically temporal lobectomy for control of psychomotor (complex partial) seizures. Serafetinides (1975) reported a study of patients with temporal lobectomies in which psychiatric rating scales were used to document postsurgical changes in the level of psychopathology (*Brief Psychiatric Rating Scale, BPRS*, Overall and Gorham, 1962; see p. 591) and early postoperative reduction in depression (*Self-Rating Depression Scale, SDS*, Zung, 1965; see p. 614). In another investigation that focused on the psychosocial ramifications of temporal lobectomies, Horowitz and her colleagues constructed the *Psychosocial Rating Scale (PRS)* (1970). Each of the seven subscales is scored on a six-point continuum from the most socially desirable status to the least desirable. Thus, the range of (I) Personal satisfaction scale, is from 1 (Satisfied and self-fulfilled) to 6 (Despair, depression, or suicide). The other scales are (II) Pervasive negative affects (e.g., depression, anger, fear, shame, disgust, or guilt); (III) Adaptation to illness; (IV) Psychopathology; (V) Degree of dependency; (VI) Communication of thought; and (VII) Paranoia. The authors point out that, "The psychosocial scales are only a shorthand method of reporting our clinical judgments." They used the rating scores both to describe the pattern of responses of individual patients and to draw conclusions about the patient groups (seizure condition improved, not improved, etc.).

Dodrill and his colleagues developed the *Washington Psychosocial Seizure Inventory (WPSI)* (Dodrill, 1978a; Dodrill et al., no date) to document the extent and improve the understanding of the social maladaptations that tend to be associated with chronic epilepsy. The 132 Yes-No items take about 15 to 20 minutes to answer. This inventory includes three validity scales (A—number of items left blank; B—a "Lie" scale with items such as, "Is your life free from problems?" which, when answered Yes would be scored on this scale; and C—Rare Items, i.e., items endorsed by 15% or fewer of the standardization population). The seven pyschosocial scales relate closely to important aspects of the patient's life: Background factors (primarily pertaining to family and predisposing influences); Emotional concerns; Interpersonal problems; Vocational difficulties; Financial concerns; Acceptance of Seizures; and Medicine and Medical Management.

Psychiatric Symptoms

Brief Psychiatric Rating Scale (BPRS) (Overall and Gorham, 1962). This 16-item instrument has enjoyed wide use with organically impaired subjects (e.g., Kochansky, 1979; Levin and Grossman, 1978; Seratetinides, 1975). Each item represents a "relatively discrete symptom area"; most of the items were derived from psychiatric rating data. Ratings are made on a seven-point scale from Not Present to Extremely Severe. The scale is intended for use by psychiatrists and psychologists. Although many of the items are more appropriate for a psychiatric population than for brain damaged patients (e.g., Guilt feelings, Grandiosity), there are also items involving symptoms that are prominent features of some organic conditions (e.g., Motor retardation, Conceptual disorganization, Blunted affect). Others, although usually considered psychiatric symptoms, also appear in many patients with organic brain damage (e.g., Uncooperativeness, Depressive mood, Suspiciousness).

Traumatic Brain Injury

Many of the established behavioral rating scales and inventories can be adapted for use with traumatically brain injured patients. However, the special problems of many head trauma victims have led to the development of specialized assessment instruments. Perhaps the most important of these problems is predicting outcome. Since many aspects of outcome have been found to be closely associated with the severity of damage (see pp. 212–213), particular attention has been given to assessing severity on the basis of clinical observations. A second problem has been the assessment of a condition in which rapid change is the rule, as is the case particularly in the first few months after return to consciousness. Not infrequently I have begun a examination of such a patient on a Thursday or Friday and had to discontinue a test before completing it only to find, on the following Monday or Tuesday, that the patient's new performance level has rendered the original data obsolete. However, in the early stages, the rate of change becomes an important feature in itself. Still another problem concerns the enormous intraindividual variability in performance levels that characterizes so many head injury patients. A thorough neuropsychological examination of some patients may require use of many different measures ranging in complexity and sophistication from infant scales to college aptitude tests. Social adjustment is another area that has increasingly gained notice as, more and more, traumatically brain dam-

591

aged people are surviving who regain most of their premorbid physical competencies and many of their original cognitive abilities while their judgment, self-control, and social skills and sensitivity remain impaired. The disparities between what these patients are capable of doing and what they are competent to do result in patterns of social maladaptation peculiar to them that the usual inventories of behavioral or social problems do not handle well.

EVALUATING SEVERITY

Glasgow Coma Scale (Teasdale and Jennett, 1974). Although it has "coma" in its title, this brief assessment technique can be used to describe all posttraumatic states of altered consciousness from the mildest confusional state to deep coma (see Table 19-3). A coma score, the sum of the highest score in each dimension, can be calculated. With a possible score range of 3 to 13, scores of 8 or higher in the first few days after injury are considered to be predictive of good outcome. Its simplicity allows it to be used by nursing personnel as well as doctors. The inclusion of three response dimensions make it possible to evaluate level of consciousness when vision or speech, for example, is compromised by factors other than impaired consciousness. Moreover, it can be used repeatedly to provide longitudinal data on the course of improvement during the earliest posttrauma period. Its greatest virtue is that is has proven to be a good predictor of outcome (e.g., Jennett et al., 1975; Levin, Grossman et al., 1979. Plum and Caronna, 1975, used it to predict outcome of coma resulting from medical conditions). The Glasgow Coma Scale has been generally accepted as the standard measure for determining severity of injury in patients whose consciousness is compromised.

Table 19-3 Glasgow Coma Scale

Dimension		Score
Eyes open	Spontaneously	4
	To speech	3
	To pain	2
	Not at all	1
Best verbal response	Oriented	5
	Confused	4
	Inappropriate	3
	Incomprehensible	2
	None	1
Best motor response	Obeys commands	4
	Localizes pain	3
	Flexion to pain	2
	None	1

Galveston Orientation and Amnesia Test (GOAT) (Levin, O'Donnell, and Grossman, 1979). This is a short mental status examination devised to assess the extent and duration of confusion and amnesia following traumatic brain injury (see Fig. 19-3). Like the Glasgow Coma Scale, it was designed for repeated measurements and can be used many times a day and repeated over days or weeks as necessary. Eight of the ten questions involve orientation for time, place, and person. The two questions asking for the first event the patient can remember "*after* injury" and the last event "*before* the accident" relate specifically to amnesia. The error scoring system results in a score from 0 to 100. This test can serve two purposes. In light of the relationship between early return of orientation and good outcome, and its converse, it can serve as an outcome predictor. It also provides a fairly sensitive indicator of level of responsivity in recently brain injured patients. For example, Levin recommends that formal testing begin only after the patient achieves a GOAT score of 75 or better (within the "normal" range), i.e., when orientation is relatively intact. He notes that problems with amnesia are apt to persist after orientation has returned to normal.

Questionnaire for evaluating posttraumatic amnesia (Artioli i Fortuny et al., 1980). Success on a picture and person recognition test was as effective in determining the status of posttraumatic amnesia as were the usual questions about personal history, orientation, and events surrounding the accident. Each day the patient is shown a different set of three colored pictures and asked to recall them or recognize them among a set containing five distractor items. The patient is also tested each day for recall or recognition of the examiner's first name and for recognition of the examiner's face ("Have you seen me before?"), using a photograph of the previous day's examiner when there was a change. A perfect score for three consecutive days signals that posttraumatic amnesia had ended on the first of the three days. The authors note that this daily examination technique also can identify mental status changes indicative of a deterioration in the patient's condition.

Outcome Evaluation

Glasgow Outcome Scale (Jennett and Bond, 1975; Bond, 1979). This scale complements the Glasgow Coma Scale by providing criteria for evaluating the "goodness" of outcome. It has five levels: (1) *Death* (due to brain damage. This typically occurs within the first 48 hours after injury. It is rare that death after 48 hours, of persons who improved to an outcome level of 4 or 5, will be attributable to primary brain damage); (2) *Persistent vegetative state* (absence of cortical function); (3) *Severe disability (conscious but disabled)* (These patients are "dependent for daily support."); (4) *Moderate disability (disabled but independent)*; (5) *Good recovery* (resumption of "normal life" is the criterion rather than return to work which, the authors note, can be misleading when economic factors prevent an able person from finding employment or particularly favorable circumstances allow a relatively disabled person to earn money). Although this scale is attractive in its simplicity, this same quality

Name _____   Date of Test └─┴─┴─┘
                                                         mo day yr
Age _____ Sex   M   F   Day of the week   s m t w th f s
Date of Birth └─┴─┴─┘   Time   AM   PM
              mo day yr
Diagnosis _____   Date of injury └─┴─┴─┘
                                                            mo day, yr

GALVESTON ORIENTATION & AMNESIA TEST (GOAT)   Error Points

1. What is your name? (2) _____   When were you born? (4) _____   └─┴─┘
    Where do you live?   (4) _____
2. Where are you now? (5) city_____   (5) hospital _____   └─┴─┘
    (unnecessary to state name of hospital)
3. On what date were you admitted to this hospital? (5) _____   └─┴─┘
    How did you get here? (5) _____
4. What is the first event you can remember <u>after</u> the injury? (5)_____   └─┴─┘
    Can you describe in detail (e.g., date, time, companions) the first event you can recall after injury? (5) _____
    _____
5. Can you describe the last event you recall <u>before</u> the accident? (5) _____   └─┴─┘
    _____ Can you describe in detail (e.g., date, time, companions)
    the first event you can recall <u>before</u> the injury? (5) _____
6. What time is it now? _____(−1 for each ½ hour removed from correct time to maximum of −5)   └─┴─┴─┘
7. What day of the week is it?_____(−1 for each day removed from correct one)   └─┴─┘
8. What day of the month is it?_____(−1 for each day removed from correct date to maximum of −5)   └─┴─┘
9. What is the month?_____(−5 for each month removed from correct one to maximum of −15)   └─┴─┘
10. What is the year? _____(−10 for each year removed from correct one to maximum of −30)   └─┴─┘

Total Error Points   └─┴─┴─┘

Total Goat Score (100-total error points)   └─┴─┴─┘

76-100 = NORMAL
66-75 = BORDERLINE
≤65 = IMPAIRED

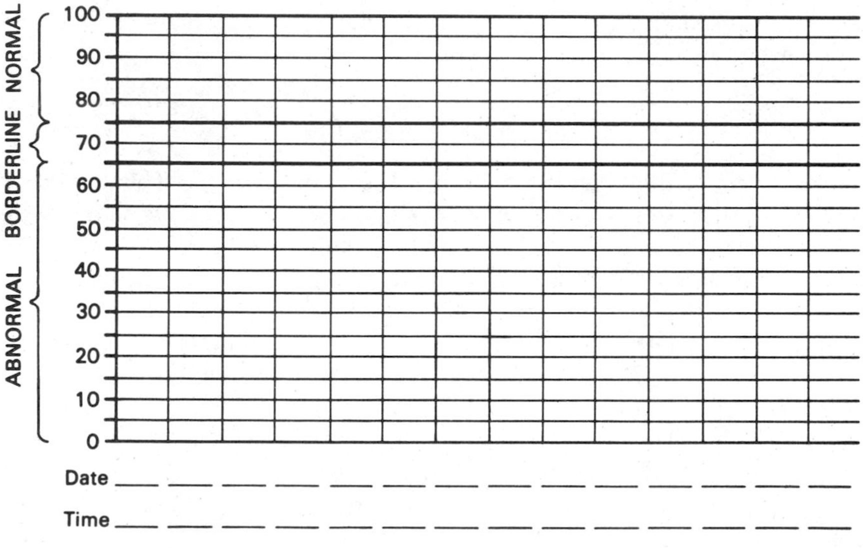

Figure 19-3

makes it difficult to categorize many patients who are semidependent or independent. The authors advise that, "aspects of social outcome should be included . . . such as leisure activity and family relationships" in making outcome determinations. However, they do not offer a solution to the complex classification problem presented by so many patients whose level of social or emotional functioning is very different from the level of their cognitive skills, sensory-motor competence, or daily activities.

Evaluating the Psychosocial Consequences of Head Injury

An appreciation of the effects of traumatic brain injury on personal and social adjustment and of their impact on family, friends, and the community has led a number of workers to develop schedules and scales for standardizing the examination and documentation of these problems. Brooks and his co-workers (Brooks and Aughton, 1979b; Brooks et al., 1979; McKinlay et al., 1981) have devised techniques to assess the subjective and objective "burdens" that traumatic brain damage imposes on the patient's family. A 90-item structured interview schedule, for use with family members, inquires about the patient's physical and mental conditions, his behavior, and his self-care. Problems documented on this schedule constitute the "objective burdens." The "subjective burden" is measured by a seven-point scale on which the family members give a rating of the degree of strain or distress experienced "because of changes in patient since the accident."

Rosenbaum and Najenson (1976) were also interested in the repercussions of brain damage on patients' spouses. They constructed a four-point interview questionnaire for wives of men who had incurred head injury during the "Yom Kippur War" in Israel. Each wife was asked first to compare her current situation with her situation prior to her husband's injury in 23 areas of family life (e.g., sex, leisure, children, social activities) on a five-point scale ranging from 1 (much less) to 5 (much more often). A second set of questions inquired into the interpersonal behavior of the injured spouse with wife, children, in-laws, etc.,—also measured on a five-point scale ranging from 1 (very disturbing) to 5 (a great improvement). The third part of the questionnaire was an inventory of marital roles. The fourth part was a 22-symptom checklist assessing mood disturbances. Like the schedule used by Brooks and his co-workers, this composite questionnaire documents both the changes associated with the brain injury and the effects of these changes on the spouse and other family members.

Katz Adjustment Scale: Relative's Form (KAS-R) (Katz and Lyerly, 1963). This scale was developed to assess the personal, interpersonal, and social adjustment of psychiatric patients in the community, but much of it is appropriate for neuropsychologically impaired patients as well (e.g., McSweeny et al., 1982). The issues dealt with in this scale are particularly relevant to head trauma victims living with their families or in noninstitutionalized settings. The authors' rationale for assessing the patient's adjustment from a relative's perspective is that "the patient's overall functioning is . . . intimately linked with the working out of mutually satisfactory relationships within the family." Additionally, the informant can provide a close view of the patient's day to day activities. Moreover, as is the case with psychiatric patients, some brain damaged patients cannot respond reliably to a self-rating inventory or may be unable to cooperate with this kind of assessment at all so that the only way to get dependable information about these patients is through an informant. The questionable objectivity of a close relative led to the development of items concerning specific behaviors.

The scale consists of five inventories, or subscales, each designed to assess a different aspect of the patient's life or the relatives' perception of it. Form R1 asks for "Relatives Ratings of Patient Symptoms and Social Behavior." It includes 127 questions about such indicators of patient adjustment as sleep, fears, quality of speech, and preoccupations, for rating on a scale ranging from "1-almost never" to "4-almost always."

Forms R2 and R3, "Level of Performance of Socially-expected Activities" and "Level of Expectations for Performance of Social Activities," use the same 16 items dealing with such ordinary activities as helping with household chores, going to parties, and working. Form R2 requires the informant to indicate the patient's level of activity for each item on a 3-point scale on which a rating of 1 is given for "not doing," 2 for "doing some," and 3 for "doing regularly." A 3-point scale is used for Form R3 too, but the rating criteria are reworded to include the informant's expectations of the patient; i.e., 1—"did not expect him to be doing," etc. McSweeny and his colleagues (1982) have added a fourth response alternative, "does not apply," to both of the original 3-point scales.

The 22 items of Forms R4 and R5 have to do with how the patient spends his or her free time. Like Forms R2 and R3, these two inventories share the same items which list specific leisure activities such as watching television, shopping, or playing cards, plus a 23rd item asking for activities to be listed that were not included in the previous items. These too are on 3-point scales. Form R4 asks for the frequency of activity (1—"Frequently" to 3—"Probably Never"). R5 inquires about the relative's level of satisfaction with the patient's activities (1—"Satisfied with what he does here" to 3—"Would like to see him do less"). Again McSweeny and his colleagues have added a "Does not apply" response alternative to each of these scales.

Portland Adaptability Inventory (Lezak et al., 1980).   This set of three scales was constructed to provide a systematic record of the personal and social maladaptations that tended to prevent many head trauma patients from resuming normal family relationships and social activities. Each scale covers a different area of behavior. *Temperament and Emotionality* contains seven items: (1) Irritability to Aggression, (2) Anxiety to Agitation, (3) Indifference, (4) Depression, (5) Delusions and Hallucinations, (6) Paranoia, and (7) Initiation. *Activities and Social Behavior* are examined by 11 items: (1) Significant Relationships (status of), (2) Residence (i.e., where residing), (3) Social Contact, (4) Self-Care, (5) Work/School, (6) Leisure Activities, (7) Driving, (8) Law Violations, (9) Alcohol, (10) Drugs, (11) Appropriate Social Interaction. The *Physical Capabilities* scale was included so that the relationship between physical impairment and personal/social adjustment could be examined. Physical disabilities were included that would seem to have an obvious bearing on personal or social adjustment. This scale covers (1) Ambulation, (2) Use of hands, (3) Sensory status: Audition, (4) Sensory status: Vision, (5) Dysarthria, and (6) Aphasia. All items are rated from 0 for no problem or the normal situation (e.g., living in a single or family residence) to 3 for severe problems or a most abnormal situation (e.g., institutionalization), except Alcohol and Drugs, which are on three-point scales. The ratings should be made by trained persons who are familiar with the problems of traumatically brain injured patients and are experienced interviewers and observers. Ratings can be given on the basis of patient or family reports, clinical observations, medical records, and social history. In many cases, the conscientious rater will base ratings on most or all these sources.

In a longitudinal study of 42 traumatically brain damaged men, ratings were made at yearly intervals, for over five years (Lezak et al., 1990). Anger (Irritability to Aggression), Social Contact, Work/School, and Leisure were the issues among the initial high-frequency problems occurring among 70% or more of the patients' problems that continued to be high-frequency problems through the fifth year after injury. Other problems which had initially occurred at high frequencies in the first year or two tended to ameliorate somewhat in time (e.g., Depression, Initiation, Significant Relationships). Increasing independence was reflected in large drops in the number of high scorers on Residence, Self-Care, and Driving, even while these patients remained socially dislocated. Except for Aphasia, physical handicaps did not relate in any regular manner to emotional well-being or social adjustment generally. Scores on items that related to social dependency (i.e., Residence, Self-Care, and Driving), however, did vary directly with improvements in Ambulation.

20

Tests of Personal Adjustment
and Functional Disorders

Personality Tests

The assessment of personality and personal adjustment contributes to the neuropsychological examination in several important ways. In order to evaluate the patient's performance on the cognitive tests, the examiner needs a basis for estimating the extent to which emotional state, motivation, and characterological predisposition affect the patient's efficiency. In some cases, documentation of emotional and social behavior patterns that are symptomatic of particular brain disorders may play as much or more of a role in the formulation of a diagnosis as do test score patterns of intellectual impairment. Furthermore, subtle aspects of cognitive dysfunction sometimes show up in the patient's responses to relatively unstructured tests of personal adjustment when they are masked by the more familiar and well-structured formats of the cognitive tests.

Efforts to diagnose brain disease from personality test responses have proceeded in two different directions. Some investigators have sought to identify "organic personalities" from qualitative characteristics or patterns of test responses. Others have looked for traces of brain disease in tell-tale "organic signs." Both avenues of investigation have been fruitful. Some tests, such as the MMPI or Draw-a-Person, lend themselves more readily to one kind of data handling than the other. Projective tests such as the Rorschach yield both kinds of data. In some instances projective assessment techniques can serve as particularly rich sources of information about the interaction between cognitive deficits, personality characteristics, and personal adjustment.

The convenient classification of personality tests into "objective" or "projective" is used here. The distinction between projective and objective personality tests follows the common practice of calling "projective" those tests with relatively less structured stimulus material that allow the patient open-ended responses. Questionnaire-type tests that restrict the range of response are called "objective" without regard to the extent to which questionnaire test responses also register projection (Carson, 1969b; Cronbach, 1970).

598

Projective Personality Tests

Clinical psychology's credibility as a science rests on the assumption that a person's behavior is the product of the totality of his experiences, his attitudes, his capacities, and his uniquely organized perceptual, cognitive, and response characteristics. From this cornerstone derive many of the principles that guide the clinical psychologist's thinking and activities. One of these is the *projective hypothesis,* which holds that when confronted with an ambiguous or unstructured stimulus situation, people tend to *project* onto it their own needs, experiences, and idiosyncratic ways of looking at the world. In other words, each person perceives external stimuli through a reflection of his or her attitudes, understandings, and perceptual and response tendencies, and interprets the compounded percept as external reality (C. H. Graham, 1965).

Projective testing utilizes this principle to elicit the patient's characteristic response tendencies. A projective test may be comprised of cloud or inkblot pictures, or pictures of persons in vague or ill-defined scenes, or it may consist of a set of instructions to draw a person or to complete sentence stems. The common denominator for all projective tests is that they are techniques that tend "to induce the individual to reveal his way of organizing experience by giving him a field . . . with relatively little structure and cultural patterning so that the personality can project upon that plastic field his way of seeing life, his meanings, significances, patterns, and especially his feelings. Thus we elicit a projection of the individual's private world because he has to organize the field, interpret the material, and react affectively to it" (Frank, 1939, p. 391).

Projective responses tend to differ between persons, between diagnostic groups, and between age groups, sexes, and cultures. These differences show up in both the *content* of the responses and in the *formal*—structural and organizational— qualities of the content: in the *how* as well as the *what* of a response. Analysis of these complementary aspects of projective productions can often give the examiner a look at the inner workings of the subject's mind that would be difficult to obtain as quickly or in as clear-cut a fashion by any other method.

Projective techniques can be compared to the EEG or any other diagnostic technique that may contribute to the evaluation of a highly complex system in which there are multiple interacting variables. No single instrument can provide definitive answers to all questions about such a system. By themselves EEG findings are of only limited usefulness, but in the context of a complete neurological study they can be invaluable. The same holds true for the data of a projective study. Projective test data alone tell only part of the story. When taken out of context of interviews, history, and medical findings, projective test data become insubstantial and unreliable. When used appropriately, projective material complements other kinds of examination data.

Certain projective techniques have contributed significantly to the evaluation and understanding of brain injury. The effects of brain injury may influence the patient's perceptions of the world. It may compromise the ease and flexibility with which he sorts, selects, organizes, or critically evaluates his own mental contents. Close and extensive observation of the patient as he goes about his daily affairs is the best method of finding out when and how mental impairments affect his behavior. Short of such exacting procedures, projective testing may be the most effective means of answering these questions.

A number of projective response tendencies characterize the behavior of brain damaged persons. Regardless of the technique employed, these response tendencies show up in the *protocols* (the record of test responses) of some brain injured patients and occur much less frequently in the responses of neurologically intact subjects.

1. *Constriction.* Responses become reduced in size. If they are verbal, the patient employs few words, a limited vocabulary, a decreased range of content. If the responses are graphic, drawings are small, unelaborated, and important details may be left out. There will be little if any evidence of creativity, spontaniety, or playfulness in the responses.

2. *Stimulus-boundedness.* Responses tend to stick closely to the bare facts of the stimulus (i.e., to a story-telling task with a picture stimulus, "This is a man, this is a woman and a young woman, and there is a horse. It's a farm"; or to an inkblot, "This is an ink splotch; that's all I see. Just an ink splotch"). There may be a "sticky" quality to the patient's handling of the test material in that once he attends to one part of the stimulus, or gives one association, he seems helpless to do much more than reiterate or elaborate on his initial response.

3. *Structure-seeking.* The patient has difficulty in spontaneously making order or sense out of his experiences. He will search for guidance anywhere he can and depend on it uncritically. Structure-seeking is reflected in tendencies to adhere to the edge of the page or to previously drawn figures when drawing (see Fig. 14-5 for a classic example of this tendency), or to seek an inordinate amount of help from the examiner.

4. *Response rigidity.* Difficulty in shifting, in being flexible, in adapting to changing instructions, stimuli, and situations shows up in projective tests as response perseverations (e.g., mostly "bat" or "butterfly" responses to the inkblot cards; an unusual number of identical phrases given to sentence completion stems such as "Most bosses *good*," "Thinking of my mother *good*," "A wife *good*," "When I was a child *good*."). Response rigidity may also show up in failure to produce any reponse at all in a changing situation, or in poorer quality of response under changing conditions than when repetitively dealing with a similar kind of task or working in the same setting.

5. *Fragmentation.* Fragmented responses are related to the "organic" tendency to *concreteness* and difficulty in organization. Many brain injured patients are unable to take in the whole of a complex situation and to make unified sense out of it, and therefore can only respond in a piecemeal, pedantically matter-of-fact manner. This can be seen in responses that comprehend only part of a total stimulus situation normally grasped in a single gestalt (i.e., human figure drawing constructed by accretion of the parts; an inkblot response, "leg," to what is commonly perceived not as an isolated leg but as the leg of a whole human).

6. *Simplification.* Simplified responses are poorly differentiated or detailed whole percepts and responses (such as "bat" without details, or "leaf" or "tree stump" to inkblot stimuli; or crudely outlined human figure drawings with minimal elaborations; or six- or eight-word descriptions instead of a creative response on a story telling task).

600

7. *Conceptual confusion* and *spatial disorientation*. Both organic and functionally disturbed patients may give responses reflecting logical or spatial confusion. Differential diagnosis depends on such other response characteristics as symbolic content, expansiveness, variability of quality, and emotional tone.

8. *Confabulated responses*. Illogical or inappropriate compounding of otherwise discrete percepts or ideas is a response characteristic common to both organic and functional thought disorders.[1] Organic patients are most likely to produce confabulated responses in which naturally unrelated percepts or ideas become irrationally linked because of spatial or temporal contiguity, giving them a stimulus-bound or "sticky" quality. Confabulations in which the linkage is based on a conceptual association are more typical of functionally disordered thinking.

9. *Hesitancy and doubt*. Regardless of performance quality or the amount and appropriateness of reassurance, many brain damaged patients exhibit continuing uncertainty and dissatisfaction about their perceptions and productions (Lezak, 1978b).

It is rare to find the protocol of a brain damaged patient in which all of these characteristics occur, although many brain injured persons display at least a few of them. When one type occurs two or three times in a single test or crops up on several different tests, or when two or three different "organic" characteristics appear in a single test protocol, brain damage should be suspected.

THE RORSCHACH TECHNIQUE

The Rorschach test is probably the best known of the projective techniques. It was developed in the early 1920s by Hermann Rorschach, a Swiss psychiatrist, who was interested in how his patients' mental disorders affected their perceptual efficiency. He selected the present set of ten inkblots out of approximately 1,000 he made by dropping ink on paper, folding it, and opening it again to get a generally symmetrical design. His criterion for selection was how well the design elicited imaginal responses (Rorschach, 1942).

The subject is shown the blots one card at a time and invited to "tell what the blot looks like, reminds you of, what it might be; tell about everything you see in the blot." The examiner keeps a record of what the patient says. Most examiners note response time for the first response to each card, and many record the total testing time, but there is no time limit. If the patient gives no response or only one response to the first or second blot, the examiner can encourage him to produce more once or twice. I tell patients who offer only one response to the first card that, "Sometimes people can

---

[1]The category of "confabulated responses" to projective test stimuli needs to be distinguished from the term "confabulation" as it is applied to the often quite elaborated fabrications that some patients with memory disorders offer as responses to questions, particularly to questions of personal fact that they can no longer answer reliably (R. J. Campbell, 1981; see also pp. 580–581). S. J. Beck and his co-workers (1961) define the confabulated response as one in which the subject "seldom engages in any directed organizing activity. The details happen to be seen in relation and eventually all are included. The (response) is accidental, not intellectual work" (p. 22).

make out more than one thing in a blot." If they still produce only one response to the second blot, I repeat the same statement and then let the matter drop. Other than occasional encouragement as needed, the examiner says nothing during this first, *free association*, phase of the test administration.

Some examiners still follow Rorschach's instructions calling for the examiner to be seated behind and facing the subject's back (Exner, 1974). While this seating arrangement might seem to help create as unstructured and emotionally neutral a setting as possible, the advantages of having an unobtrusive examiner are countered by loss of the rich observational data of facial expression, coloring, and nonverbal communication. Rapaport and his colleagues (1968) note that when the examiner faces the patient, "difficulties in the course of the test, particularly the appearance of negativism, may be more easily coped with" (p. 278). Structure-dependent patients and those who tend to be suspicious can also be expected to respond better when they can see the examiner.

After going through all the cards, the examiner conducts the *inquiry* phase in which he questions the patient about what part of the blot was used for each response and what qualities in the blot contributed to each percept. During the inquiry, the examiner also attempts to clarify confusing or vague responses and elicit associations to the responses.

The last part of the Rorschach examination, *testing the limits*, is not always conducted. In this phase, the subject is asked about response categories or card qualities he failed to handle spontaneously, to see if he is capable of making that kind of response at all.

There are a number of scoring systems in general use, all of them variants of Rorschach's original system, and all of them equally effective in the hands of a skilled examiner (S. J. Beck, 1961; Exner, 1974; Klopfer et al., 1954; Rapaport et al., 1968). The scoring systems are used for categorizing and quantifying the responses in terms of mode of approach and subject matter. Every scoring system includes scoring for the following major response variables:

1. Number of responses.
2. The portion of the inkblot involved in the response: whole, obvious part, or obscure part.
3. Color and shading.
4. Movement (e.g., "*dancing* bears," "*bowing* waiters").
5. Percentage of percepts that are "good," i.e., commonly perceived.
6. Figure-ground reversals.

Responses are also scored for

7. Content, such as human, animal, anatomy, or landscape.
8. Very great popularity or rarity of the response.

The scoring pattern and the verbatim content of the responses are then interpreted in terms of actuarial frequencies and the overall configuration of category scores and content. A number of rules of thumb and statistical expectancies have evolved over 50 years of Rorschach experience that suggest relationships between category scores or score proportions and behavioral or emotional characteristics. These rules and expectancies are only suggestive. Any attempt to relate *this* Rorschach response or category score or proportion between scores to *that* specific behavior or mental or emotional characteristic, out of context of the panoply of responses and the total examination situation, is a misuse of this technique. No single Rorschach response or set of responses, taken alone, has any more or less meaning or diagnostic value than any other single statement or gesture taken by itself.

Variables that contribute to the *formal* aspect of the Rorschach performance include the number and appropriateness (form quality) of the responses; use of shape, color, shading, and movement (the *determinants*) in the formulation of a response; and the location, relative size, and frequency of use of identifiable parts of the blots. In analyzing the *content* of the responses, the examiner notes their appropriateness and usualness as well as any repetition or variation of topics, the presence and nature of elaborations on a response, emotional tone, and evidence of thought disorder or special preoccupations. Gratuitous (i.e., unnecessary for clear communication) or extraneous elaborations of a percept may reflect the patient's special preoccupations and concerns. Unusual or idiosyncratic elaborations, particularly of the most common and easily formed percepts (i.e., the whole blot animal—bat or crab—of card I, the "dancing" figures of card III, the "flying" creature of card V, the pink animals at the sides of card VIII, and the tentacled blue creatures of card X) sometimes convey the patient's self-image. Thus, it is not uncommon for a brain injured patient to perceive the "bat" or "butterfly" of card V or the blue "crab" of card X as dead or injured, or to volunteer descriptions of these creatures as "crazy" or "dumb", e.g., a "crazy bat," a "dumb bunny."

The appeal of a sign system for simple and reliable identification of patients with brain disease has attracted the attention of many Rorschach clinicians and researchers. Most Rorschach sign systems are similar as they are constructed of quantifiable aberrant responses or response tendencies which have appeared with sufficient frequency in protocols of brain injured patients and sufficient rarity in the protocols of other kinds of patients to warrant the conclusion that they are associated with brain damage to a significant degree (Goldfried et al., 1971; Hughes, 1948; Piotrowski, 1937; W. D. Ross and Ross, 1942).

The most widely used sign system consists of ten signs (Piotrowski, 1937):

1. *R.* Less than 15 responses in all.
2. *T.* Average *time* per response is greater than 1 minute.
3. *M.* There is but one *movement* response if any.
4. *Cn.* The subject *names colors* (e.g., "a pinkish splotch") instead of forming an association (e.g., "pinkish clouds").
5. *F%*. Percentage of *good form* responses is below 70 (see pp. 360–361 for a discussion of Rorschach form quality).
6. *P%*. Percentage of *popular* responses is below 25 (see pp. 360–361).
7. *Rpt. Repetition* refers to perseveration of an idea in response to several inkblots.

8. *Imp. Impotency* is scored when the patient recognizes his response is unsatisfactory but neither withdraws nor improves it.

9. *Plx. Perplexity* refers to the hesitancy and doubt displayed by many organic patients about their perceptions.

10. *AP.* The examiner must determine when a pet expression is repeated so often and indiscriminately as to qualify as an *automatic phrase*.

In introducing these signs, Piotrowski notes that, "no single sign alone points to abnormality in the psychiatric sense, to say nothing of organic involvement of the brain. It is the accumulation of abnormal signs in the record that points to abnormality" (p. 529). He also recommends that the examiner use caution by not scoring doubtful signs. He considers five to be the minimum number of his signs needed to support an inference of cortical brain disease. The likelihood that five or more of these signs will appear in the records of patients with organic brain disease increases with age (Piotrowski, 1940).

Piotrowski's signs have consistently demonstrated their usefulness in distinguishing brain damaged patients from control subjects, including neurotic personality disorders (Piotrowski, 1940). However, like so many other "organic" signs, they do not differentiate chronic schizophrenics from organic patients (Goldfried et al., 1971; Suinn, 1969). Thus, psychotic populations will produce a good many false positive protocols. On the other hand, Piotrowski's signs also produce false negatives, for absence of the requisite five signs is no guarantee that the patient is free of brain damage (Sklar, 1963). Yet, with all these problems, the fact that the Piotrowski signs identify the diagnostic category of no fewer than 51% and as many as 97% of the patients (organic and mixed psychiatric) and control subjects in 11 reported studies testifies to its usefulness, particularly with populations in which the frequency of chronic schizophrenia tends to be low. Of the ten Piotrowski signs, all but three—M, P%, and Cn— effectively separate brain injured from nonpsychiatric groups (Goldfried et al., 1971). Four of these—Plx, Imp, Rpt, and AP—have been reported as particularly sensitive to mild and moderate organic conditions (Baker, 1956a).

Other investigators have developed lists of response and behavioral aberrations that can be treated as "organic" signs without offering cutting scores or frequency norms. G. Baker (1956a) reported 23 different signs and response characteristics of organicity, including four of Piotrowski's signs. Four of her indicators are also among the nine listed by Aita, Reitan, and Ruth (1947) in addition to Piotrowski's ten. Neither Baker nor Aita and his colleagues provided scoring standards for the additional signs. Instead, their signs describe behavior that frequently accompanies brain injury, none of them being diagnostic in itself. The signs common to both lists are (1) *inflexibility*, difficulty in producing alternative interpretations of the same blot, identified as an organic tendency by Lynn et al. (1945), too; (2) *concrete response*, difficulty in organizing whole responses, lack of characterizing or attributing elaboration; (3) *catastrophic reaction*, emotional reaction to testing so disruptive as to render the patient unable to respond; and (4) *covers part of card*, an uncommon but reliable sign (see p. 361).

Identification of brain injured patients on the basis of clinical interpretations of the Rorschach protocol rests in part on recognition of aberrant responses and in part on the reconstruction of relevant dimensions of personality from the content and pattern of responses as well as the patient's nonverbal behavior and extraneous verbalizations (G. Baker, 1956b; Brussel et al., 1942). M. M. Hall and G. C. Hall (1968) took this approach to evaluate the Rorschach response characteristics of right and left hemisphere damaged patients by statistical analysis (discriminant functions). They used such data as perplexity, fabulizing, (making story elaboration), the total number of responses, and the sum of movement responses to describe the personality characteristics that differentiate patients with right from those with left hemisphere lesions. Their patients with right hemisphere lesions tended to be uncritically free in the use of determinants and overexpansive, creating imaginative responses by readily combining parts into wholes, thus generating many bizarre or preposterous responses. In contrast, patients with left-sided lesions expressed a great deal of perplexity, frequently rejected cards, and tended to give "correct" and unelaborated form-dependent responses. Harrower-Erickson (1940) studied the personality of brain tumor patients by means of the Rorschach, evaluating their performance by the Piotrowski sign method. She also interpreted the behavior and personality implications of such aberrant features as the low number of responses, relative absence of color or movement responses, and lack of shading responses as indicating emotional constriction and diminished capacity for introspection.

Studies of Rorschach performances of head trauma victims show some consistent response characteristics. Prominent among these are a reduction in number of responses, stereotypy (repetition, perseveration), and concreteness (Dailey, 1956; Klebanoff et al., 1954; Vigouroux et al., 1971). Vigouroux and his colleagues also note that, "Twelve to 18 months after the injury . . . the profound disturbances of personality which appeared in the first months remained with little change."

With advancing age, the Rorschach responses of normal subjects also tend toward reduction in number, in range of content with increased stereotypy, and in use of color and shading (Ames, 1960; Kahana, 1978). However, even with these changes, the Rorschach test protocols of intact elderly persons are readily distinguishable from those of demented patients who give very few responses ($\overline{X} = 16$), use color and shading infrequently, and have a narrow range of content (Ames et al., 1954). These authors noted that pronounced differences between demented patients and elderly intact subjects showed up in qualitative aspects of the performance. The most frequently observed and distinguishing features of the demented patient's response patterns were: "Express insecurity as to ability to give a good answer" (62%); "General vagueness of expression" (61%); "Perseveration of remarks" (61%); "Argue and discuss with selves the accuracy of responses" (59%); and "Make excuses for not giving better responses: brain not good" (44%).

The Rorschach can be useful in the differential diagnosis of psychiatric patients suspected of having an organic brain disorder. These patients usually carry a diagnosis of schizophrenia because of withdrawn, disruptive, or erratic behavior and complaints of intrusive ideas, mental confusion, or difficulty in thinking. Many have histories of head injury. The behavioral changes of others just seemed to happen, sometimes following a period of stress, sometimes without apparent reason. The discrimination between an organic and functional diagnosis is based on the much greater frequency with which schizophrenic patients produce bizarre, symbolic, personalized, or "crazy" associations to the inkblots. The absence of frankly psychotic associations does not rule out the possibility of a functional disorder. Many chronic schizophrenics, particularly if they have been institutionalized or have settled into a fairly simple living routine for a long time, tend to produce few, barren, and vague Rorschach responses without frankly psychotic ideation. By the same token, the presence of psychotic thinking does not preclude the possibility of brain damage. However, absence of psychotic thinking tendencies on the Rorschach increases the likelihood that the patient's behavioral disturbances arise at least in part from brain injury.

It is difficult to cast much of the data on which clinical inferences are based, or the inferences themselves, into a form suitable for statistical analysis (Potkay, 1971). However, for clinical purposes, the integration of inferences drawn from both the sign and the clinical interpretation approaches is apt to yield the most information, with each approach serving as a check on the appropriateness of conclusions drawn from the other. By this means, symptomatic cognitive and behavioral defects can be viewed in interaction with personality predispositions so that the broader social and personal implications of the patient's brain injury may be illuminated.

STORY TELLING TECHNIQUES

Story telling is a particularly rich test medium, since it elicits the flow of verbal behavior, brings out the quality of the patient's abilities to organize and maintain ideas, and may reveal characteristic attitudes and behavioral propensities. Stories told to pictures or themes can also be analyzed for both their formal and content characteristics (W. E. Henry, 1947; Stein, 1955). Of the several story telling projective tests for adults, the *Thematic Appreception Test (TAT)* (Murray, 1938) is the most widely used (Lubin et al., 1971). Although the familiar test pictures of the TAT have the advantage of known expectations for the kinds and characteristics of stories each elicits (Murstein, 1963), the examiner without TAT or other story test material can easily improvise with illustrations from magazine stories or with photographs.

Stories composed by brain injured patients possess the same response qualities that characterize Rorschach protocols. Thus, the brain injured patient is likely to use fewer words and ideas in telling his stories (R).[1] Response times are apt to be longer with many punctuating pauses (T). Brain injured patients are more likely to describe the picture than make up a story; or if they make up a story, its content is apt to be trite with few characters and little action (M). The organic patient may be satisfied with simple descriptions of discrete elements of the picture and unable to go beyond this level of response when encouraged to do so (Cn). A more than ordinary number of

[1]The symbols in parentheses refer to the corresponding Piotrowski organic sign for Rorschach responses (see pp. 603–604).

misinterpretations of either elements of the picture or the theme may occur due to tendencies toward confusion, simplification, or vagueness ($F\%$). The organic patient may give relatively few of the most common themes ($P\%$). Perseveration of theme (Rpt) and automatic repetition of certain phrases or words (AP) rarely appear in stories of subjects without brain damage. Inability to change an unsatisfactory response (Imp) and expressions of self-doubt (Plx) may be present. Inflexibility, concrete responses, catastrophic reactions, and difficulties in dealing with the picture as a whole are also likely to be of organic etiology (Fogel, 1967). Kahana (1978) reports that the TAT productivity of elderly persons also tends to be relatively lowered and may be limited to descriptions.

DRAWING TASKS

It is much more difficult to handle the drawings of organic patients as projective material than their verbal products. When perceptual, motor, or constructional defects interfere with the ability to execute a drawing, the resultant distortions make doubtful any interpretations based on the projective hypothesis. Even when distortions are slight, the examiner cannot tell whether paucity of details, for instance, reflects a barren inner life, or is due to low energy or feelings of uncertainty and self-consciousness; or whether reduced drawing size is a product of lifelong habits of constriction or of efforts to compensate for tendencies to spatial disorientation or motor unsteadiness or some interaction between them.

As a rule, formal characteristics of the drawings of brain injured persons, such as size, proportion, angulation, perspective, and line quality, should not be subject to projective interpretations, nor should underdetailing, simplification, or incompleteness. Gratuitous elaborations, on the other hand, may usually be treated as projective material, in which case inferences may be drawn following the principles and practices of projective interpretation (J. N. Buck, 1948; Machover, 1948).

Objective Personality Tests

Objective personality tests are self-report instruments: the patient describes himself by checking those items he wishes to claim to be true about himself. On these tests, the effects of impairment may be manifested through the patient's responses to items concerning intellectual disabilities or personality changes related to his impairment. The test used most frequently in medical settings, the Minnesota Multiphasic Personality Inventory, has only questionable usefulness in the evaluation of personality components of a neuropsychological complaint or disability.

THE MINNESOTA MULTIPHASIC PERSONALITY INVENTORY (MMPI) (Hathaway and McKinley, 1951; Welsh and Dahlstrom, 1956; Dahlstrom et al., 1975)

This 566-item true-false questionnaire was developed in a medical setting—the University of Minnesota Medical School Hospital and Clinics. Computerized scoring forms, scoring services, and interpretation systems are available (Butcher, 1978; J. R. Graham, 1977). The MMPI has been translated into other languages, tape-recorded forms have been devised for semiliterates and the visually handicapped, and there is a form for patients who cannot write but may have enough motor coordination to sort item cards. It is an untimed test, suitable for older adolescents and adults. Neither age nor education is taken into consideration in the scoring, but there are separate male and female norms. Verbal comprehension must be at the *low average* or better level (minimum reading skills at the sixth grade level) for useful results (Dahlstrom and Welsh, 1960). Very impaired patients who have difficulty following or remembering instructions, who cannot make response shifts readily, or whose verbal comprehension is seriously compromised cannot take this test.

The MMPI was constructed on principles of actuarial prediction. Rigorous statistical discrimination techniques were used to select the items and construct the scales. The criterion for item selection and scale construction was the efficiency with which items discriminated between normal control subjects and persons with diagnosed psychiatric disorders.

The inventory is ordinarily scored for 14 scales. Four *validity scales* provide information about the subject's competency to take the test, the likelihood that he is malingering or denying real problems, and such test-taking attitudes as defensiveness or help-seeking. On the ten *clinical scales* the patient's response pattern is compared with those of the normal control subjects and the different diagnostic groups of psychiatric patients. Interpretation is on the basis of the overall scale *patterns*, not on any one response or the score for any one scale. Dozens of scales other than the 14 in most common use have been developed, but many have not been adequately standardized and most are primarily of research interest (Dahlstrom et al., 1975).

Spurred by the discriminating power of actuarial predictions (Meehl, 1954; Sines, 1966), numerous investigators have been developing and refining "cookbook" programs for computerized scoring and interpretation of the MMPI (Butcher, 1978; R. D. Fowler, 1969). The predictive prowess of these programs when applied to large populations has been demonstrated repeatedly. Their application to the individual case, however, is questionable since the programs in general use interpret the patient's highest but not lowest scores and not all of them account for age or physical condition (J. R. Graham, 1977). Butcher (1978) has pointed out that, "Most MMPI computer services are not pure actuarial systems but operate from programmed clinical decision rules with, in many cases, clinical lore as the basic data. . . . At this stage, *computerized narratives using psychological test based information is little more than an art (or craft) disguised as a science*" (p. 942). Moreover, every program produces a statistically ascertainable number of false positive and false negative predictions. Use of computerized or "cookbook" interpretations of the MMPI requires sophisticated clinical judgment. The "highly mechanized and 'objective' appearance of the MMPI profile often tempts people to abandon their usual approach in evaluating clinical data and to adopt a kind of rigidly psychometric—sign—actuarial method of interpretation. . . . However, most clinicians who regularly use the MMPI in clinical practice see this as being at best, a relatively barren procedure. At its worst, from the point of view of the individual case, it is productive of sometimes serious diagnostic errors" (Carson, 1969a).

The problem of purely actuarial handling of MMPI responses is demonstrated in the computer interpretation of the MMPI profile of the victim of a car accident, a 23-year-old male high school graduate.

> He suffered left-sided weakness with some left-sided tremor and spasticity, dysarthria, and a tendency to convulsions, which was adequately controlled by medication. Intellectual impairment was minimal, showing up mostly in mild concentration and attention problems, weakened retention of newly learned material, and some visuoconstructional distortions.
>
> The program developed by Dr. Harold Gilberstadt for the Veterans Adminstration (1970) produced the following interpretation of his MMPI profile (see Fig. 20-1)ı
>
> "The patient's current state appears to be characterized by hypomania. Test taking attitude seems to reveal naïveté. Professes rigid adherence to social mores. Sees self as conforming, self-controlled. Normal defensiveness and/or ego strength.
>
> "Single and pair-wise scale analysis suggests the possibility of the following traits and characteristics: histrionic, emotionally labile, may develop atypical symptoms which may yield to superficial treatment, may have episodic attacks of acute distress, may develop symptoms impossible to reconcile with organic etiology. Behavior controls may be tenuous. Veneer of gaiety and friendliness but may be irascible, restless and impulsive, hostile, hyperactive, grandiose, talkative.
>
> "The following should be looked for among trait and diagnostic alternatives: hostile, emotionally labile personality."
>
> This print-out gives a very good description of the young man except that his significant coordination and motor disabilities and his mild intellectual impairment are not included, nor is his history of chronic conflict with his father, which tends to generalize into conflict with other persons in positions of authority.

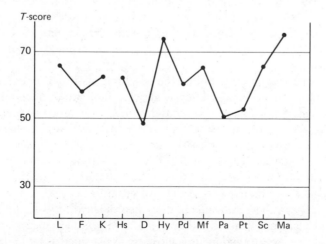

Fig. 20-1. MMPI profile of trauma victim described above.

This example illustrates both the strengths and weaknesses of the computerized MMPI. The patient tends to deny disability and social difficulties and therefore did not repond as a disabled person. The computerized interpretation accords well with the patient's perception of himself as whole and on top of things. It correctly identifies him as angry and having some behavioral control problems. However, it does not register the very significant discrepancy between the patient's self-concept and reality, except to indicate the possibility of grandiosity and, by implication ("histrionic," "veneer of gaiety"), the patient's tendency to deny unpleasantness at the expense of reality. Furthermore, not only does it not identify the central problem of organicity, but it also suggests that the possibility of organic etiology of his complaints should be viewed rather skeptically.

Following the actuarial principles underlying this test, there have been a number of efforts to develop MMPI scales that would effectively predict the likelihood of brain damage (Mack, 1979). Hovey's five-item scale (1964) has met with very limited success. This scale consists of four items marked *false* (10, 51, 192, and 274) and one (159) marked *true*. Four is the cutting score for organicity. Hovey recommends that this scale be used only when the K-scale score is 8 or above to minimize the likelihood of false positive errors. This scale was ineffective in discriminating between patients with organic impairment and groups of organically intact patients with functional disorders (Maier and Abidin, 1967), schizophrenic patients (C. G. Watson, 1971), and normal control subjects (Weingold et al., 1965). In one study, the Hovey scale identified only 28% of a small ($n = 25$) mixed "brain damaged" group, but 64% of a similar-sized group of patients diagnosed as having multiple sclerosis (Jortner, 1965). Jortner questioned the discriminating power of item 274, "My eyesight is as good as it has been for years," for persons over age 40. Classification of chronic alcoholic patients by the Hovey scale was not found to bear any systematic relationship to cognitive indices of organic impairment (Chaney et al., 1977). One exception to this catalogue of failures is a study by Zimmerman (1965) who found that Hovey's scale identified 62% of severely damaged patients seven years after injury, but only 29% and 25% respectively, of moderately and mildly injured patients. He concluded that "Hovey's five MMPI items identify the permanent or residual impairment due to severe brain damage."

Two other scales that purport to differentiate brain damaged from other patients illustrate the problem of using clinical scales for individual diagnosis. A 17-item *Pseudo-Neurologic Scale* (Shaw and Matthews, 1965), designed to identify patients whose neurological complaints are not supported by positive neurological findings, contains five items marked *true* (38, 47, 108, 238, 253) and 12 *false* (3, 8, 68, 171, 173, 175, 188, 190, 230, 237, 238, and 243) with a cutting score of 7 in the scored direction. In the original study, this scale differentiated 81% of the patients with symptoms suggestive of brain damage who had negative neurological work-ups while misclassifying 25% of those with unequivocal neurological disease. But cross-validation results, although statistically significant ($p < .01$), were less successful, since there were 33% false negatives (pseudoneurologic patients classified as brain damaged) and 22% false positives. An 80-item *Sc-0* scale (with a 30-item short form) discriminated between groups of hospitalized schizophrenic and brain damaged patients to a significant degree, but prediction rates, which ranged from 72 to 75% for the male patients, make their application to the individual case a questionable procedure (C. G. Watson, 1971). In addition, C. G. Watson and Plemel (1978) constructed the 56-item *P-0* scale for separating organic patients from "all types of functional disorders." Their group of 60 functionally disordered patients contained mostly alcoholics (35). The *P-0* scale correlates positively with age ($r = .30$). Like the *Sc-0* scale, it differentiated between the two patient groups successfully, However, when the *Sc-0* scores are used in combination with Benton Visual Retention Test error scores to maximize discriminative efficiency, the best pair of cutting scores misdiagnosed 31% of the organic patients and 25% of the psychiatric group. This scale identified 90% of the normal subjects in another study, but only 57% of a mixed group of brain damaged patients and 77% of diagnosed schizophrenics (Golden et al., 1979). This large a margin of error makes the scale unsuitable for clinical use.

An alternative method of using the MMPI to aid in differential diagnosis of organic from schizophrenic disorders has been proposed by E. W. Russell (1975b). Essentially, this "key" approach is a set of successive sieves for identifying schizophrenic patients within a group of psychiatric inpatients. With this key approach, Russell made correct classifications of 80% of the schizophrenics and 72% of the brain damaged patients. He later found that simply by using a cut off *T*-score of 80 on the Sc scale, he successfully identified organic and schizophrenic patients from one another in 78% of the cases (E. W. Russell, 1977). However, when schizophrenics comprised only half of the group of patients with functional disorders, an Sc cut-off score of 80 made only 67% correct classifications.

Efforts to use the MMPI for differential diagnosis of organic defects have produced a variety of scales. Several epilepsy scales have been developed, but none has held up well under cross-validation studies (Dahlstrom and Welsh, 1960; Rosenman and Lucik, 1970). S. H. Friedman constructed a 32-item *Parietal-frontal* (*Pf*) scale (1950) and H. L. Williams a *Caudality* (*Ca*) scale (1952). Both claim to provide some discrimination between brain injured patients with anterior lesions and those with posterior lesions (Dahlstrom and Welsh, 1960; Meier, 1969). However, Reitan (1976) reports that recent research has not supported the earlier findings.

A sign approach to the identification of epileptic patients on the basis of the standard 14 MMPI scales has not met with more success than has scale development (Hovey et al., 1959; Jordan, 1963; Weingold et al., 1965). Other studies seeking to use MMPI scoring systems for identifying the presence of epilepsy have also had disappointing results (Lachar et al., 1979; Mack, 1979).

The sheer variety of brain injuries and of problems attendant upon organicity probably helps explain the unsatisfactory results of MMPI scale and sign approaches. Moreover, the MMPI was not constructed for neuropsychological assessment and may be inherently inappropriate for this purpose. This becomes most evident in evaluations of the effectiveness of the MMPI in making diagnostic determinations about organic brain disorders (Dikmen and Reitan, 1977b). Results of studies seeking MMPI correlates of localized cerebral lesions have been negative (Dikmen and Reitan,

1974b; Vogel, 1962) or questionable (Mack, 1979). The findings of investigations into the effects of lesion lateralization on MMPI performance have been variable. Studies that have found lateralization differences consistently report that patients with left hemisphere damage tend to have elevated scores on scale 2 (Depression). Scales 8 (Schizophrenia), 1 (Hypochrondriasis), and 7 (Psychasthenia) may also be higher with left-sided lesions (Black, 1975; Gasparini et al., 1978). High scale 8 scores also distinguished a group of predominantly left hemisphere damaged patients, all of whom had aphasic symptoms, from a predominantly right hemisphere damaged group without aphasic symptoms (Dikmen and Reitan, 1974a). Black interpreted the high (T-score ≥ 70) 8–2–1 scale pattern as reflecting a tendency to catastrophic reaction in young (mean age = 21.7 ± 2.1) missile wound patients whose injuries were predominantly on the left. Gasparini and his colleagues pointed out that the 2-8-7 pattern of high mean scores made by their relatively young (mean age = 36.5) patients with left-sided lesions of mixed etiology was characteristic of a major affective disorder. The right hemisphere damaged patients in these latter two studies were comparable to the left hemisphere groups in age and etiology but, in both cases, produced essentially normal profiles. In three other studies, two involving organic populations with mixed diagnoses (Dikmen and Reitan, 1974b; Flick et al., 1970), and one of patients with temporal lobe epilepsy (Meier and French, 1965), no lateralization differences were found.

Thus, the MMPI appears to be an inefficient instrument for identifying or localizing cerebral lesions, particularly when so many other more effective methods have been specifically developed to perform these diagnostic tasks.

Nevertheless, there are very general *pattern* tendencies that characterize the responses of many patients with neurological disorders. To some extent, the pattern of MMPI profiles of brain damaged patients is an artifact of the test items and scale composition. Among the 51 items of the 357 scored items on a short form of the MMPI (omitting scale *Si* and all items normally not scored) referrable to symptoms of physical disease, 26 relate to central nervous system diseases and 8 describe problems associated with being ill (Lezak and Glaudin, 1969). Most of the "neurological symptom" items appear on the *Sc* scale, and many have double and triple scale loadings, particularly on scales *Hs*, *D*, and *Hy*. As a result, nonpsychiatric patients with central nervous system disease tend to have an elevated "neurotic triad" (*Hs*, *D*, and *Hy*) (Dikmen and Reitan, 1974a) and higher than average *Sc* scores (see Fig. 20-2). *Pt* is also among the scales most likely to be elevated in an organic population (Mack, 1979). The 2-9 and 1-3-9 scale elevations once thought to represent organic patterns have not been validated (E. W. Russell, 1977). However, Casey and Fennell (1981) reported elevations on scales 2, 8, and 1 (in that order) that characterized the MMPI profiles of traumatically injured patients; Heaton, Smith, and their colleagues (1978) also observed that head injured patients tended to have elevated scores on scales 2 and 8. In general, elevated MMPI profiles tend to be common among brain damaged populations, reflecting the relatively frequent incidence of emotional disturbance in these patients (Filskov and Leli, 1981).

The tendency for *Sc* to be the highest or one of the highest scales has been noted

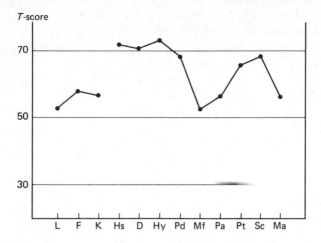

Fig. 20-2. Mean MMPI profile for patients with diagnosed brain disease (Lezak and Glaudin, 1969).

for epileptic patients (Kløve and Doehring, 1962; Meier, 1969). High scores on the neurotic triad have characterized the MMPI profiles of patients with multiple sclerosis (Dahlstrom and Welsh, 1960). Huntington's disease patients, too, have abnormally high score profiles, but they are indistinguishable from the profile pattern of heterogeneous groups of brain damaged patients (Boll et al., 1974; Norton, 1975).

Thus, for brain damaged patients, acknowledgment of specific symptoms accounts for some of the elevation of specific scales. Premorbid personality tendencies and the patient's reactions to his disabilities also contribute to the MMPI profile. The combination of symptom description, the anxiety and distress occasioned by central nervous system defects, and the need for heroic psychological adaptive measures probably account for the frequency with which brain damaged patients produce neurotic profiles.

SELF-RATING SCALES

Like the MMPI, the applicability of self-rating scales to brain damaged patients is limited by the patients' often restricted capacity to take paper and pencil tests. Still, a number of self-rating scales have been widely used both clinically and in research, mostly to evaluate depressive reactions and to aid in the differential diagnosis of patients presenting symptoms of dementia. Psychiatric and social adjustment scales may also be useful in gaining a better understanding of the patient's view of his circumstances.

Self-rating of depression. Any one of the three self-rating instruments described here can be used as an aid in determining the presence and extent of depression. The *Beck Depression Inventory* (A. T. Beck et al., 1961) consists of 21 items, each concerned with a particular aspect of the experience and symptomatology of depression (e.g., Mood, Sense of Failure, Indecisiveness, Work Inhibition, and Appetite). Each item contains four statements of graded severity expressing how a person might feel or think about the aspect of depression under consideration. The statements carry scores ranging from 3 for most severe to 0 for absence of problem in that area. For example, the range of statements under Self-Hate is "3-I hate myself," "2-I am disgusted with myself," "1-I am disappointed in myself," "0-I don't feel disappointed in myself." The higher the overall score, the more depressed is the patient. This format gives a symptom profile at a glance. However, this advantage can be of little value when used with a depressed patient who denies or is unaware of his distress. Its obviousness also makes it readily susceptible to manipulation.

These problems have been addressed in the *Self-rating Depression Scale (SDS)* (Zung, 1965, 1967; sometimes referred to as "the Zung"). This 20-item scale also uses a four-point grading system on a scale ranging from "None OR a Little of the Time" to "Most OR All of the Time." However, since half of the items are worded in the negative, severity is represented by "None OR a Little" in one-half of the cases and by "Most OR All" in the other half. For example, the severity scoring for item 1 ("I feel downhearted, blue and sad") runs counter to the severity scoring for item 18 ("My life is pretty full"). Besides items obviously relating to depression, a number of items concerning physiological and psychological disturbances are not so obvious. Scores can be evaluated in terms of symptom groups (affect—two items; physiological disturbances—eight items; psychomotor disturbance—two items; and psychological disturbances—eight items) or in an overall "SDS Index." This index is obtained by converting scores from the raw score scale of 20 to 80 to a 25–100 SDS scale on which 100 represents maximum severity. Fabry (1980) notes that this scale is best used with persons between the ages of 19 and 65 as older and younger subjects tend to get excessively elevated scores.

On the *Depression Adjective Check List* (Lubin, 1965), the patient discribes himself by selectively checking a list of 32 adjectives relating to mood and state. Ten of the adjectives relate to positive feelings (e.g., Safe, Strong, Sunny). The 22 others that describe different aspects of depression (e.g., Wilted, Gloomy, Tortured, Weary) are the scored items. Four forms of the checklist with no overlapping items have been developed and show high intercorrelations (.85 to .92).

Scales for rating social adjustment. In her evaluation of 15 scales for examining the social functioning of psychiatric patients, Weissman (1975) describes two based on the patient's self-report and several others devised to elicit information about the patient from family members. Although these scales were intended for the examination of psychiatric patients, much of the information requested is relevant to brain damaged patients.

A *Life Satisfaction Index* (Neugarten et al., 1961), developed for use with elderly persons, consists of a self-report subscale (Index A) and a set of open-ended questions with scoring standards to be applied by an interviewer. The 20 items of Index A mainly cover three areas associated with life satisfaction: Mood Tone (e.g., "I am just as happy as when I was younger."), Zest for Life (e.g., "I have made plans for things I'll be doing a month or a year from now."), and Congruence (e.g., "I've gotten pretty much what I expected out of life.") (D. L. Adams, 1969). One point is scored for each item on which the response is in the positive direction. Thus, low scores on this scale will tend to reflect depression. Because its wording is suitable for elderly persons, when used "in reverse," it can be a useful measure of depression in older patients. However, the absence of scoring ranges on individual items makes it a less sensitive instrument than the depression scales reported above.

The *Patient's Assessment of Own Functioning Inventory* (Heaton, Chelune, & Lehman, 1981) assesses how well the patient appreciates his condition by asking the patient to grade his capacities in eight categories of functioning: "memory," "language and communication," "use of hands," "sensory-perceptual," "higher level cognitive and intellectual functions," "work," "recreation," and "general." As few as two and as many as ten items cover different aspects of each category. Almost all questions ask the subject to estimate the identified function, activity, or problem on a six-point scale ranging from "almost always" to "almost never." Some items ask the subject to list activities. The last category contains only two questions, "What are the activities that you need help with at this time?" and "What do you think are your major areas of difficulty at this time?" If assistance was required in order to fill out the inventory, there is a place to note this. A companion inventory, *Relative's Assessment of Patient Functioning Inventory*, is provided for close relatives to document their observations of the patient. The eight categories in this inventory differ from the patient's inventory only in adding a 22-item section on "personality" and omitting the "sensory-perceptual" category. These items, too, are mostly presented in a six-point scale format. These inventories were developed to bring to light discrepancies between the patient's condition and his self-perceptions (Heaton & Pendleton, 1981).

Tests for Functional Complaints

The direct financial benefits of illnesses and injuries related to job, service, or accident, and the indirect emotional and social rewards of invalidism make malingering and functional disabilities an attractive solution to all kinds of social, economic, and personal problems for some people. Functional disorders frequently take the form of neurological symptoms and complaints since many neurological conditions are easily confused with the psychogenic complaints accompanying common emotional disturbances, such as headaches, "blackouts," and memory or sensory problems. The differential diagnosis is further complicated by the fact that early neurological disease often does not show up on physical examination or in laboratory studies.

Another problem complicating diagnosis is that the distinction between unconscious symptom production and the conscious decision to feign illness for personal gain is often blurred, for both conscious and unconscious motivations may contribute to the pseudosymptoms of physical disease. Moreover, even the issue of whether a complaint is psychogenic is not simple for often the patient presents a mixture of functional and organic symptoms or of organic disabilities with a functional reaction to his handicaps that increases their severity or interferes with treatment or rehabilitation of the organic problem. Therefore, motivation will not be dealt with here; we will examine only the question of determining whether the patient's complaints are likely to be psychogenic.

In clinical practice, the determination of whether there is a functional component to the patient's symptoms usually rests (1) on evidence of inconsistency in the history or examination; (2) on the likelihood that the set of symptoms and complaints the patient brings makes medical sense, i.e., fits a reasonable disease pattern; (3) on an understanding of the patient's present situation, personal/social history, and emotional predispositions, i.e., his personality "dynamics"; and (4) on his emotional reactions to his complaints, particularly if he presents the classic *la belle indifference* (the beautiful unconcern) characteristic of patients whose symptoms, due to conversion hysteria, are at least in part unconsciously motivated and usually bring significant secondary gains. In addition, there are some administration techniques and guidelines for evaluating performance on a number of standard assessment instruments as well as a few tests of dissimulation that can be given to patients when their motivations or complaints are suspect.

Examining for Functional Complaints: (1) Standard Examination Techniques

Some of the recommendations for testing or evaluating test performances for functional complaints or symptoms are based on studies, and others come from clinical experience. In general, functional distortions of test performances show up in inconsistencies, bizarre or unusual responses, and in performance levels *below* the usual range for persons who have the complained-of symptoms or disorder on an organic basis.

BENDER-GESTALT

Hutt (1977) recommends that when malingering or poor motivation is suspected the standard copy administration of the test be given after all the rest of the testing is completed, and if possible, after a delay of several days. The longer the delay between the initial testing and the retest, the more likely it is that the subject who has deliberately altered his reproductions will have forgotten what alterations he had made. Hutt also points out that on retesting several days later, circumstances may have changed so that the once poorly motivated subject may be more willing to cooperate. If a question remains about the patient's willingness to perform well after a delayed retest, Hutt suggests that the cards be readministered for copying in the inverse position as few persons would be able to maintain the same deliberate distortions with the changed gestalt.

In a study investigating whether college students could successfully produce "organic" Bender reponses, A. R. Bruhn and Reed (1975) found that they could not. An experienced clinician was able to identify all of the student records using guidelines developed from four general criteria: (1) Organics tend to simplify, not complicate their drawings. (2) When an organic patient markedly distorts an element in one design, similar elements in other designs will show the same kind of distortion. (3) Organics are unlikely to make both good and poor copies of designs at the same difficulty level. (4) There are some kinds of distortions made only by brain damaged patients such as rotations and difficulty with the intersection of card 6.

Benton Visual Retention Test (BVRT)

Benton and Spreen (1961) investigated the effects of deliberate faking on the ten-second recall administration (A) of this test by comparing the performances of brain damaged patients with those of college students directed to perform like brain damaged patients. The simulators made many more errors of distortion than the patients, but not as many errors of omission. The patients were more likely to forget the small peripheral figure and also to perseverate than were the simulators. In a similar study, Spreen and Benton (1963) asked college students to simulate feeble-mindedness when taking the BVRT. The overall frequency profile of errors was similar between the two groups. However, like the students faking head injury, these simulators, too, exaggerated the imagined impairment by making both significantly more errors and fewer correct responses than mentally retarded subjects.

Halstead-Reitan Battery (including the WAIS)

Heaton, Smith, and their colleagues (1978) also used college students to examine how malingering might affect performance on the tests in this battery. With instructions to respond as if they had sustained head injury, college students performed at significantly lower levels than head injury victims on the Speech Sounds Perception Test, the Finger Oscillation (Finger Tapping) Test, the tests for Finger Agnosia and Sensory Suppression, and on the Hand Dynamometer. The simulators also did significantly more poorly on Digit Span. The head injured patients did much worse on the Category Test and on all three scored components of the Tactual Performance Test, and made many more errors on part B of the Trail Making Test. Using these data, Heaton's group derived a discriminant function formula for this set of data and for the MMPI (see below), which they have applied to protocols of claimants in litigation actions.

Minnesota Multiphasic Personality Inventory (MMPI)

The Heaton group (1978) examined differences in MMPI performances between the same head injured patients and college student simulators as above. The college students produced much more disturbed-appearing profiles, exceeding the head injured patients on scales F, 1, 3, 6, 7, 8, and 10. The head injured patients had T-scores above 70 on scales 2 and 8. The college students, in their efforts to appear head injured, achieved T-scores above 70 on F, 1, 2, 3, 6, 7, 8 (93.9 $\pm$ 21.2!), and 10. Casey and

Fennell (1981), however, found similar patterns and no differences in scale elevations in the profiles of MMPI scores of head injured patients involved in litigation of compensation claims and those not involved in litigation.

PORCH INDEX OF COMMUNICATIVE ABILITY (PICA)

To test whether aphasic disorder can be simulated on the PICA, Porch et al. (1977) compared the performances of 25 normal subjects (including both naive and well-informed persons) with a composite aphasia PICA pattern. Porch had hypothesized that normal persons simulating aphasia would have higher scores than aphasics on the difficult end of the profile curve and lower scores on the easier end because of inability to judge difficulty levels on tasks that were all easy to perform. In fact, this is essentially what the simulators did. A discriminant analysis of the data permitted the development of cutoff criteria for each score and a "discriminant score" useful for identifying nonaphasic patients.

RORSCHACH

As a psychologist in the armed forces, Benton (1945) had to make diagnostic decisions about servicemen presenting pseudoneurologic symptoms. He reported that the Rorschach was particularly useful for this problem because the "unfamiliar, seemingly irrational task" typically aroused the malingering patient's suspicions and defenses. As a result, their Rorschach productions tended to be very sparse, constricted, and given with characteristically slow reaction times. When this response pattern was in marked contrast to the patient's performance on the "rational and understandable" intelligence tests, Benton considered that it strongly supported a supposition of malingering.

Examining for Functional Complaints: (2) Special Techniques

Since questions concerning the extent to which a patient's symptoms or complaints have an organic basis are so common, it is not surprising that a number of techniques for testing dissimulation have been developed by both neurologists (e.g., S. Walker III, 1967) and psychologists. The first four tests below were devised by André Rey. With the exception of the 15-item "memory" test, they are reported in *L'examen psychologique dans les cas d'encéphalopathie traumatique* (1941).

MEMORIZATION OF 15 ITEMS

This technique can be used to test the validity of a memory complaint (1964). The principle underlying it is that the patient who consciously or unconsciously wishes to appear impaired will fail at a task that all but the most severely brain damaged or retarded patients perform easily.

The task is presented as a test requiring the memorization of 15 *different* items. In the instructions, the number "15" is stressed to make the test appear to be difficult. In reality, the patient need remember only three or four ideas to recall most of the items. The examiner marks on a piece of paper the following, in five rows of three character to a line:

A	B	C
1	2	3
a	b	c
O	□	△

The patient sees this display for 10 seconds whereupon the examiner withdraws it and asks the patient to copy what he remembers. A 10- or 15-second quiet delay period can be interpolated. Anyone who is not significantly deteriorated can recall at least three of the five character sets.

DOT COUNTING: UNGROUPED DOTS

This test can be used with patients complaining of general intellectual impairment or specific visuoperceptual defects. It is based on the technique of randomizing stimulus intensity or difficulty levels to determine whether the patient's failures are regularly associated with the altered intensity (as in audiometric examination) or level of difficulty of a task.

The test material consists of six serially numbered 3 × 5-inch cards on which are printed (1) 7, (2) 11, (3) 15, (4) 19, (5) 23, and (6) 27 dots, respectively. The cards are shown to the patient, one at a time, in the order: 2, 4, 3, 5, 6, 1. The patient is told to count and tell the number of the dots as quickly as he can, and his response times are noted. His response times can then be compared with those made by normal adult subjects (percentiles 25 to 100, Table 20-1) and brain injured patients (percentile 0, Table 20-1). The cooperative patient's time will increase gradually with the increased number of dots. More than one pronounced deviation from this pattern raises the likelihood that the patient is not acting in good faith.

Table 20-1 Percentile Norms for Time (in Seconds) Taken to Count Ungrouped Dots

		Percentile				
Card	Dots	100	75	50	25	0
1	7	1	2	4	5	11
2	11	2	3	4	5	17
3	15	3	4	6	7	17
4	19	4	6	7	9	19
5	23	5	8	10	12	30
6	27	6	9	11	16	30

(Adapted from Rey, 1941)

Dot Counting: grouped and ungrouped dots

This test adds six more numbered cards to the Dot Counting task. These cards contain (1) 8, (2) 12, (3) 16, (4) 20, (5) 24, and (6) 28 dots, respectively, arranged as follows: (1) two four-dot squares; (2) two five-dot squares and two separate dots; (3) four four-dot diamonds; (4) four five-dot squares; (5) four six-dot rectangles; and (6) four five-dot squares and two four-dot squares. Again the cards are presented in the order, 2, 4, 3, 5, 6, 1. For this set of cards, however, because the dots are grouped, the time taken to count the dots is much less than for the ungrouped dots (see Table 20-2).

The patient's performance is evaluated in terms of the difference between the total time for the two performances. When there is little difference or the time taken to count the grouped dots exceeds that for the ungrouped dots, the subject's cooperation becomes suspect.

Dorothy Gronwall (personal communication) employs the same principle in using the Associate Learning subtest of the Wechsler Memory Scale to evaluate malingering. Since more easy word pairs will be recalled than hard word pairs, a change from the expected pattern of recall may reflect poor cooperation.

Word Recognition

This is a memory test based on the principle that recognition is easier than recall. It involves a 15-word stimulus list and a 30-word list that contains the 15 words of the stimulus list mixed in with 15 other words. First the word recognition test is given by reading the stimulus words at a one per second rate in the following order:

> half, camel, mistake, toy, morning, hair, wax, grain, cookie, fly, place, cherry, door, knee, state

After 5 seconds, the examiner hands the patient a sheet of paper on which appear the 30 words with the instructions to underline with a pencil all the words he remembers being used.

Table 20-2 Percentile Norms for Time (in Seconds) Taken to Count Grouped Dots

Card	Dots	Percentile				
		100	75	50	25	0
1	8	0.5	1	1	2	3
2	12	1	2	2	2	3
3	16	1	2	2	4	5
4	20	1	1	2	4	5
5	24	2	2	2	5	6
6	28	2	2	3	5	7

(Adapted from Rey, 1941)

hello	today	door	thread	light
gift	grain	concert	wall	knee
camel	power	grass	hair	fly
morning	toy	bottle	cheese	mistake
half	style	cookie	horse	cherry
airplane	wax	place	smile	state

Some time later (at least 10 minutes), the examiner gives Rey's Auditory-Verbal Learning Test.

The number of words recalled on the first trial of the AVLT is then compared with the number of words recognized on the word recognition task. A performance in which the number of words recalled equals or exceeds the number of words recognized raises the possibility that the patient is feigning a memory defect or is not cooperating fully or consistently.

THE SYMPTOM VALIDITY TEST

This simple procedure may be used to evaluate the validity of symptoms and complaints involving perception and short-term memory (Pankratz, 1979; Pankratz et al., 1975). It is presented as a test of whatever disability the patient claims to have. It requires the patient to make 100 forced-choice decisions of a simple, two-alternative problem involving his symptom or complaint. By chance alone, approximately 50% of the patient's choices will be correct. This is the expected result when the patient's complaints are valid, e.g., when he is deaf or has an impaired short-term memory or no position sense in his toes. Since so many trials are conducted, even quite small deviations from the expected value become significant. When the patient's percent correct score runs much below 40, the examiner can suspect a functional etiology; if he is in doubt, a second set of 100 trials should clarify the question, for the likelihood that the percent correct score would be significantly lower than chance on two sets of 100 trials is so slight as to be highly improbable. Percent correct scores that run significantly above the chance expectation obviously indicate that the patient is able to perform the task.

The adaptability of this task to perceptual and memory complaints is probably limited only by the examiner's imagination. The task is always presented to the patient as a straightforward but very difficult test of the claimed disability. Loss of feeling on the hand, for example, can be tested by having the patient tell whether he was touched on the palm or the back, or on his thumb or his middle finger. A patient with a visual complaint, such as eyesight too blurry for reading, can be shown two cards, each containing a different simple word or phrase. For testing "blurred" vision, we use cards with the statements "This card is number one" and "Number two is this card" printed in small type. The patient's task is to identify the card he is shown as "one" or "two." Short-term memory can be tested by presenting the patient with one of two similar visual or auditory stimuli, such as colored lights or four- or five-digit numbers, and then having him perform an intervening task, such as a repetitive task or counting backwards for ten or 15 seconds, before reporting which stimulus he remembered. Even if the patient insists he cannot perform the task at all, he can be required to make the 100 choices.

The Symptom Validity Test confronts malingering patients quite directly for it is difficult to maintain a properly randomized response pattern that will result in a score within the range of chance for 100 trials. Since the examiner reports to the patient whether his choice was correct after each trial, patients may get the impression that they are doing better than they thought they could when half the time they hear that they are correct. The impression of doing well can have an unsettling effect on malingerers. Patients who attempt to avoid the confrontation by giving most or all of one kind of answer are obviously uncooperative. Those who naively give a wrong answer more often than chance betray their competency. To avoid the dilemma presented by this technique, patients may attempt to subvert the procedure by circumventing it or withdrawing altogether. Pankratz (1979) recommends providing the patient with a "neurological" rationale for regaining the function in question by means of this technique. For example, in treating patients with "paralyzed" limbs, he explains the procedure as an attempt to determine whether any "nerve pathways" are "still available."

Skillful use of this technique can encourage some functionally disabled patients to experience "recovery" without loss of dignity. The task may be presented as being difficult. For example, the examiner can introduce it by saying, "A lot of people have trouble getting many correct answers." Or the examiner can emphasize that the task is difficult for persons with the patient's disability. The examiner can applaud a naive patient who has demonstrated the functional nature of his complaint by making only 20 or 30% correct responses and reassure him that his performance demonstrated that he can recover the "lost" or weakened function. On subsequent trials, the examiner can encourage him to increase his percent correct score gradually. Higher percent correct scores then become evidence of "improvement," increasing the patient's expectation of "recovery." When this procedure is followed for a series of trials, conducted in a supportive setting, the suggestible patient may be able to relinquish his symptoms within a few days with little threat to his self-esteem.

References

Abbott, W. D., Due, F. O., & Nosik, W. A. Subdural hematoma and effusion as a result of blast injuries. *Journal of American Medical Association*, 1943, *121*, 739–741.

Abu-Zeid, H. A. H., Choi, N. W., Hsu, P. H., & Maini, K. K. Prognostic factors in the survival of 1,484 stroke cases observed for 30 to 48 months.*Archives of Neurology*, 1978, *35*, 121–125.

Adams, D. L. Analysis of a life satisfaction index. *Journal of Gerontology*, 1969, *24*, 470–474.

Adams, K. M. An end of innocence for behavioral neurology? Adams replies. *Journal of Consulting and Clinical Psychology*, 1980a, *48*, 522–524.

Adams, K. M. In search of Luria's battery: a false start. *Journal of Consulting and Clinical Psychology*, 1980b, *48*, 511–516.

Adams, K. M. & Brown S. J. *Standardized behavioral neurology: useful concept, mixed metaphor, or commercial enterprise?* Paper presented at the American Psychological Association Convention, Montreal, Quebec, Canada, September, 1980.

Adams, K. M., Grant, I., & Reed, R. Neuropsychology in alcoholic men in their late thirties: one-year follow-up. *American Journal of Psychiatry*, 1980, *137*, 928–931.

Adams, K. M. & Rennick, P. M. *Early development of clinical neuropsychology: data file of Ward Halstead*. Paper presented at the American Psychological Association Convention, Toronto, Canada, 1978.

Adams, K. M., Rennick, P., & Rosenbaum, G. *Automated clinical interpretation of the neuropsychological battery: an ability-based approach*. Paper presented at the third annual meeting of the International Neuropsychological Society, Tampa, Florida, February, 1975.

Adams, K. M., Sawyer, J. D., & Kvale, P. A. Cerebral oxygenation and neuropsychological adaptation. *Journal of Clinical Neuropsychology*, 1980, *2*, 189–208.

Adams, K. M. & Schooff, K. G. *Are neuropsychological assessments satisfactory measures of drug-induced CNS deficits?* Paper presented at the American Psychological Association Convention, Chicago, Illinois, 1975.

Adams, R. D. Altered cerebrospinal fluid dynamics in relation to dementia and aging. In L. Amaducci, A. N. Davison, & P. Antuono (eds.), *Aging of the brain and dementia*. New York: Raven Press, 1980.

Adams, R. D., Collins, G. H., & Victor, M. Trouble de la mémoire et de l'apprentissage chez l'homme. Leurs relations avec des lésions des lobes temporaux et du diencéphale. In *Phy-*

siologie de l'hippocampe (Colloques Internationaux du Centre National de la Recherche Scientifique, No. 107). Paris: C. N. R. S., 1961.

Adams, R. L., Boake, C., & Crain, C. Bias in a neuropsychological test classification related to education, age, and ethnicity. *Journal of Consulting and Clinical Psychology*, 1982, *50*, 143–145.

Adams, R. L. & Trenton, S. L. Development of a paper-and-pen form of the Halstead Category test. *Journal of Consulting and Clinical Psychology*, 1981, *49*, 298–299.

Aita, J. A., Armitage, S. G., Reitan, R. M. & Rabinowitz, A. The use of certain psychological tests in the evaluation of brain injury. *Journal of General Psychology*, 1947, *37*, 25–44.

Aita, J. A., Reitan, R. M., & Ruth, J. M. Rorschach's test as a diagnostic aid in brain injury. *American Journal of Psychiatry*, 1947, *103*, 770–779.

Ajuriaguerra, J. de & Hécaen, H. *Le Cortex Cérébral* (2nd ed.). Paris: Masson, 1960.

Alajouanine, T. Aphasia and artistic realization. *Brain*, 1948, *71*, 229–241.

Albert, M. L. A simple test of visual neglect. *Neurology*, 1973, *23*, 658–664.

Albert, M. L. Subcortical dementia. In R. Katzman, R. D. Terry, & K. L. Bick (Eds.), *Alzheimer's disease: senile dementia and related disorders*. New York: Raven Press, 1978.

Albert, M. L. Alexia. In K. M. Heilman & E. Valenstein (Eds.), *Clinical neuropsychology*. New York: Oxford University Press, 1979.

Albert, M. L., Silverberg, R., Reches, A., & Berman, M. Cerebral dominance for consciousness. *Archives of Neurology*, 1976, *33*, 453–454.

Albert, M. S. Geriatric neuropsychology. *Journal of Consulting and Clinical Psychology*, 1981, *49*, 835–850.

Albert, M. S., Butters, N., & Levin J. Memory for remote events in chronic alcoholics and alcoholic Korsakoff patients. In H. Begleiter & M. Kissen (Eds.), *Alcohol intoxication and withdrawal*. New York: Plenum Press, 1972a.

Albert, M. S., Butters, N., & Levin, J. Temporal gradients in the retrograde amnesia of patients with alcoholic Korsakoff's disease. *Archives of Neurology*, 1979b, *36*, 211–216.

Albert, M. S., Butters, N., & Brandt, J. Memory for remote events in alcoholics. *Journal of Studies on Alcohol*, 1980, *41*, 1071–1081.

Albert, M. S., Butters, N., & Brandt, J. Development of remote memory loss in patients with Huntington's disease. *Journal of Clinical Neuropsychology*, 1981a, *3*, 1–12.

Albert, M. S., Butters, N., & Brandt, J. Patterns of remote memory in amnesic and demented patients. *Archives of Neurology*, 1981b, *38*, 495–500.

Allison, J., Blatt, S. J., & Zimet, C. N. *The interpretation of psychological tests*. New York: Harper & Row, 1968.

Amante, D., VanHouten, V. S., Grieve, J. H. et al. Neuropsychological deficit, ethnicity, and socioeconomic status. *Journal of Consulting and Clinical Psychology*, 1977, *45*, 524–535.

American Psychiatric Association, *Diagnostic and statistical manual of mental disorders* (3rd ed.). Washington, D.C.: American Psychiatric Association, 1980.

Ames, L. B. Age changes in the Rorschach responses of a group of elderly individuals. *Journal of Genetic Psychology*, 1960, *97*, 257–285.

Ames, L. B., Learned, I., Metraux, R. W., & Walker, R. N. *Rorschach responses in old age*. New York: Hoeber-Harper, 1954.

Aminoff, M. J., Marshall, J., Smith, E. M., & Wyke, M. A. Pattern of intellectual impairment in Huntington's chorea. *Psychological Medicine*, 1975, *5*, 169–172.

Anastasi, A. *Differential psychology* (3rd ed.). New York: Wiley, 1965.

Anastasi, A. *Psychological testing* (5th ed.). New York: Macmillan, 1982.

Andersen, R. Cognitive changes after amygdalotomy. *Neuropsychologia*, 1978, *16*, 439–51.

REFERENCES

Anderson, A. L. The effect of laterality localization of brain damage on Wechsler-Bellevue indices of deterioration. *Journal of Clinical Psychology*, 1950, *6*, 191–194.

Andrews, K., Brocklehurst, J. C., Richards, B., & Laycock, P. J. The prognostic value of picture drawings by stroke patients. *Rheumatology and Rehabilitation*, 1980, *19*, 180–188.

Annett, M. The binomial distribution of right, mixed, and left handedness. *Quarterly Journal of Experimental Psychology*, 1967, *19*, 327–333.

Anthony, W. Z., Heaton, R. K., & Lehman, R. A. W. An attempt to cross-validate two actuarial systems for neuropsychological test interpretation. *Journal of Consulting and Clinical Psychology*, 1980, *48*, 317–326.

Anttinen, E. E. On the apoplectic conditions occurring among brain injured veterans. *Acta Psychiatrica et Neurologica Scandinavica*, 1960, *35*, Suppl. 143.

Archibald, Y. M. Time as a variable in the performance of hemisphere-damaged patients on the Elithorn Perceptual Maze Test. *Cortex*, 1978, *14*, 22–31.

Archibald, Y. M. Simplification in the drawings of left hemisphere patients—a function of motor control? Unpublished manuscript, no date.

Archibald, Y. M., Wepman, J. M., & Jones, L. V. Performance on nonverbal cognitive tests following unilateral cortical injury to the right and left hemispheres. *Journal of Nervous and Mental Disease*, 1967, *145*, 25–36.

Arena, R. & Gainotti, G. Constructional apraxia and visuopractic disabilities in relation to laterality of cerebral lesions. *Cortex*, 1978, *14*, 463–473.

Arenberg, D. Concept problem solving in young and old adults. *Journal of Gerontology*, 1968, *23*, 279–282.

Arenberg, D. Equivalence of information in concept identification. *Psychological Bulletin*, 1970, *74*, 355–361.

Arlien-Søborg, P., Bruhn, P., Gyldenstead, C., & Melgaard, B. Chronic painters' syndrome. *Acta Neurologica Scandinavica*, 1979, *60*, 149–156.

Armitage, S. G. An analysis of certain psychological tests used for the evaluation of brain injury. *Psychological Monographs*, 1946, *60*, (Whole No. 277).

Army General Classification Test. Chicago: Science Research Associates, 1948.

Army Individual Test Battery. Manual of directions and scoring. Washington, D.C.: War Department, Adjutant General's Office, 1944.

Arnold, M. B. *Mind, memory, and the brain*. Presidential address presented at the meeting of Division 24, American Psychological Association, New Orleans, September, 1974.

Arndt. S. & Berger, D. E. Cognitive mode and asymmetry in cerebral functioning. *Cortex*, 1978, *14*, 78–86.

Arrigoni, G. & De Renzi, E. Constructional apraxia and hemispheric locus of lesion. *Cortex*, 1964, *1*, 170–197.

Arthur, G. *A Point Scale of Performance Tests*. Revised Form II. New York: Psychological Corporation, 1947. Chicago: Stoelting, no date.

Artiola i Fortuny, L., Briggs, M., Newcombe, F., Ratcliff, G., & Thomas, C. Measuring the duration of post traumatic amnesia. *Journal of Neurology, Neurosurgery, and Psychiatry*, 1980, *43*, 377–379.

Astrom, K. E. & Vander Eecken, H. Traumatic diseases of the brain. In G. W. Thorn, R. D. Adams, E. Braunwald, et al. (Eds.), *Harrison's Principles of internal medicine* (8th Ed.). New York: McGraw-Hill, 1977.

Atwell, C. R. & Wells, F. L. *Wide Range Vocabulary Test*. New York: Psychological Corporation, undated.

Atwell, C. R. & Wells, F. L. Wide range multiple-choice vocabulary tests. *Journal of Applied Psychology,* 1937, *21,* 550–555.

Axelson, O., Hane, M., & Hogstedt, C. A case-referent study on neuropsychiatric disorders among workers exposed to solvents. *Scandinavian Journal of Work Environment and Health,* 1976, 2, 14–20.

Aylaian, A. & Meltzer, M. L. The Bender Gestalt Test and intelligence. *Journal of Consulting Psychology,* 1962, *26,* 483.

Ayres, A. J. *Southern California Figure-Ground Visual Perception Test. Manual.* Los Angeles: Western Psychological Services, 1966.

Babcock, H. An experiment in the measurement of mental deterioration. *Archives of Psychology,* 1930, *117,* 105.

Babcock, H. & Levy, L. *The measurement of efficiency of mental functioning (revised examination). Test and manual of directions.* Chicago: C. H. Stoelting, 1940.

Babinsky, J. & Joltrain, E. Un nouveau cas d'anosognosie. *Revue Neurologique,* 1924, *31,* 638–640.

Backman, M. E. Patterns of mental abilities: ethnic, socioeconomic, and sex differences. *American Educational Research Journal,* 1972, *9,* 1–12.

Baddeley, A. D. *The psychology of memory.* New York: Basic Books, 1976.

Baddeley, A. D. The trouble with levels: a reexamination of Craik and Lockhart's framework for memory research. *Psychological Review,* 1978, *85,* 139–152.

Baddeley, A. D. & Hitch, G. Working memory. *Psychology of Learning and Motivation,* 1974, *8,* 47–89.

Baehr, M. E. & Corsini, R. J. *The Press Test.* Chicago: Human Resources Center, University of Chicago, 1980; Park Ridge, Ill.: London House Press, 1982.

Bahrick, H. P. & Karis, D. Long-term ecological memory. In C. R. Puff (Ed.), *Handbook of methodology for memory and cognition.* New York: Academic Press, 1982.

Bak, J. S. & Greene, R. L. Changes in neuropsychological functioning in an aging population. *Journal of Consulting and Clinical Neuropsychology,* 1980, *48,* 395–399.

Baker, G. Diagnosis of organic brain damage in the adult. In B. Klopfer (Ed.), *Developments in the Rorschach technique.* New York: World Book, 1956.

Baker, R. R. The effects of psychotropic drugs on psychological testing. *Psychological Bulletin,* 1968, *69,* 377–387.

Balthazar, E. E. *Balthazar Scales of Adaptive Behavior for the profoundly and severely mentally retarded.* Champaign, Ill.: Research Press, 1971.

Bannister, R. *Brain's clinical neurology* (5th ed.). London: Oxford University Press, 1977.

Barbizet, J. Defect of memorizing of hippocampal-mammillary origin: a review. *Journal of Neurology, Neurosurgery, and Psychiatry,* 1963, *26,* 127–135.

Barbizet, J. *Human memory and its pathology.* San Francisco: W. H. Freeman, 1970.

Barbizet, J. Le monde de l'hémiplégique gauche:essai de théorization. In J. Barbizet, M. Ben Hamida, & Ph. Duizabo (Eds.), *Le monde de l'hémiplégique gauche.* Paris: Masson & Cie., 1974a.

Barbizet, J. Rôle de l'hémisphère droit dans les perceptions auditives. In J. Barbizet, M. Ben Hamida, & Ph. Duizabo (Eds.), *Le monde de l'hémiplégique gauche.* Paris: Masson & Cie., 1974b.

Barbizet, J. & Cany, E. Clinical and psychometrical study of a patient with memory disturbances. *International Journal of Neurology,* 1968, *7,* 44–54.

Barbizet, J. & Duizabo, Ph. *Neuropsychologie* (2nd ed.). Paris: Masson, 1980.

Barchas, J. D., Berger, P. A., Ciaranello, R. D., & Elliott, G. R. (Eds.). *Psychopharmacology: from theory to practice.* New York: Oxford University Press, 1977.

Bardach, J. L. Group sessions with wives of aphasic patients. *International Journal of Group Psychotherapy*, 1969, *19*, 361–365.

Barondes, S. H. Protein-synthesis dependent and protein-synthesis independent memory storage processes. In D. Deutsch & J. A. Deutsch, *Short-term memory*. New York: Academic Press, 1975.

Barr, M. L. *The human nervous system. An anatomic viewpoint* (3rd ed.). Hagerstown, Md.: Harper & Row Medical Department, 1979.

Barton, M. Perception of the Mueller-Lyer illusion in normal and aphasic adults. *Perceptual and Motor Skills*, 1969, *28*, 403–406.

Basso, A., Bisiach, E., & Faglioni, P. The Mueller-Lyer illusion in patients with unilateral brain damage. *Cortex*, 1974, *10*, 26–34.

Battersby, W. S., Bender, M. B., Pollack, M., & Kahn, R. L. Unilateral "spatial agnosia" ("inattention") in patients with cortical lesions. *Brain*, 1956, *79*, 68–93.

Bear, D. M. *Position paper on emotional and behavioral changes in Huntington's disease.* (Commission for the control of Huntington's disease and its consequences. Vol. 3, Part 1). Washington, D.C.: U.S. Department of Health, Education, and Welfare, 1977.

Bear, D. M. & Fedio, F. Quantitative analysis of interictal behavior in temporal lobe epilepsy. *Archives of Neurology*, 1977, *34*, 454–467.

Bear D. M., Levin, K., Blumer, D. et al. Interictal behavior in hospitalised temporal lobe epileptics: relationship to idiopathic psychiatric syndromes. *Journal of Neurology, Neurosurgery & Psychiatry*, 1982, *45*, 481–488.

Beard, R. M. The structure of perception: a factorial study. *British Journal of Educational Psychology*, 1965, 210–221.

Beatty, P. A. & Gange, J. J. Neuropsychological aspects of multiple sclerosis. *Journal of Nervous and Mental Disease*, 1977, *164*, 42–50.

Bechtereva, N. P. *The neurophysiological aspects of human mental activity* (2nd ed.). New York: Oxford University Press, 1978.

Beck, A. T., Ward, C. H., Mendelson, M., Mock, J., & Erbaugh, J. K. An inventory for measuring depression. *Archives of General Psychiatry*, 1961, *4*, 561–571.

Beck, S. J., Beck, A. G., Levitt, E. E., & Molish, H. B. *Rorschach's test: basic processes* (3rd ed.). New York: Grune & Stratton, 1961.

Beizmann, C. *Handbook for scorings of Rorschach responses* (S. J. Beck, trans.). New York: Grune & Stratton, 1970.

Belleza, T., Rappaport, M., Hopkins, H. K., & Hall, K. Visual scanning and matching dysfunction in brain-damaged patients with drawing impairment. *Cortex*, 1979, *15*, 19–36.

Benayoun, R., Guey, J., & Baurand, C. Étude corrélative des données cliniques électroencéphalographiques et psychologiques chez des traumatisés cranio–cérébraux. *Journal de Psychologie Normale et Pathologique*, 1969, *66*, 167–193.

Bender, L. A visual motor gestalt test and its clinical use. *American Orthopsychiatric Association Research Monographs*, 1938, No. 3.

Bender, L. *Instructions for the use of Visual Motor Gestalt Test.* New York: American Orthopsychiatric Assoc., 1946.

Bender, M. B. Defects in reversal of serial order of symbols. *Neuropsychologia*, 1979, *17*, 125–138.

Bender, M. B., Fink, M., & Green, M. Patterns in perception on simultaneous tests of face and hand. A.M.A. Archives of Neurology and Psychiatry, 1951, *66*, 355–362.

Bengtsson, M., Holmberg, S., & Jansson, B. A psychiatric-psychological investigation of patients who had survived circulatory arrest. *Acta Psychiatrica Scandinavica*, 1969, *45*, 327–346.

627

Beniak, T. E. The assessment of cognitive deficits in uremia. Paper presented at European meeting of the International Neuropsychological Society, Oxford, England, 1977.

Bennett, G. K., Bennett, M.G., Wallace, M., & Wesman, A. G. *College Qualification Tests.* New York: Psychological Corporation, 1961.

Bennett, G. K., Seashore, H. G., & Wesman, A. G. *Differential Aptitude Tests. Manual* (5th ed.). New York: Psychological Corporation, 1972.

Benson, D. F. Psychiatric aspects of aphasia. *British Journal of Psychiatry,* 1973, *123,* 555–566.

Benson, D. F. The hydrocephalic dementias. In D. F. Benson & D. Blumer (Eds.), *Psychiatric aspects of neurologic disease.* New York: Grune & Stratton, 1975.

Benson, D. F. The third alexia. *Archives of Neurology,* 1977, *34,* 327–331.

Benson, D. F. *Aphasia, alexia, and agraphia.* New York: Churchill Livingstone, 1979.

Benson, D. F. & Barton, M. I. Disturbances in constructional ability. *Cortex,* 1970, *6,* 19–46.

Benson, D. F., Stuss, D. T., Naeser, M. A., Weir, W. S., Kaplan, E. F., & Levine, H. L. The long-term effects of prefrontal leukotomy. *Archives of Neurology,* 1981, *38,* 165–169.

Benton, A. L. Rorschach performance of suspected malingerers. *Journal of Abnormal and Social Psychology,* 1945, *40,* 94–96.

Benton, A. L. *Right-left discrimination and finger localization: development and pathology.* New York: Hoeber-Harper, 1959.

Benton, A. L. The fiction of the Gerstmann syndrome. *Journal of Neurology, Neurosurgery, and Psychiatry,* 1961, *24,* 176–181.

Benton, A. L. Constructional apraxia and the minor hemisphere. *Confinia Neurologica,* 1967a, *29,* 1–16.

Benton, A. L. Problems in test construction in the field of aphasia. *Cortex,* 1967b, *3,* 32–58.

Benton, A. L. Differential behavioral effects in frontal lobe disease. *Neuropsychologia,* 1968a, *6,* 53–60.

Benton, A. L. La praxie constructive tri-dimensionelle. *Revue de psychologie appliquée,* 1968b, *18,* 63–80.

Benton, A. L. Constructional apraxia: some unanswered questions. In A. L. Benton, *Contributions to clinical neuropsychology.* New York: Aldine, 1969a.

Benton, A. L. Disorders of spatial orientation. In P. J. Vinken & G. W. Bruyn (Eds.), Handbook of clinical neurology (Vol. 3, *Disorders of higher nervous activity*). New York: Wiley, 1969b.

Benton, A. L. Test de praxie constructive tridimensionnelle: forme alternative pour la clinique et la recherche. *Revue de psychologie appliquée,* 1973, *23,* 1–5.

Benton, A. L. *The Revised Visual Retention Test* (4th ed.). New York: Psychological Corporation, 1974.

Benton, A. L. The amusias. In M. Critchley & R. A. Henson (Eds.), *Music and the brain.* London: William Heinemann, 1977a.

Benton. A. L. Interactive effects of age and brain disease on reaction time. *Archives of Neurology,* 1977b, *34,* 369–370.

Benton, A. L. Visuoperceptive, visuospatial, and visuoconstructive disorders. In K. M. Heilman & E. Valenstein (Eds.), *Clinical neuropsychology.* New York: Oxford University Press, 1979.

Benton, A. L. The neuropsychology of facial recognition. *American Psychologist,* 1980, *35,* 176–186.

Benton, A. L., Elithorn, A., Fogel, M. L., & Kerr, M. A perceptual maze test sensitive to brain damage. *Journal of Neurology, Neurosurgery and Psychiatry,* 1963, *26,* 540–544.

REFERENCES

Benton, A. L., Eslinger, P. J., & Damasio, A. R. Normative observations on neuropsychological test performances in old age. *Journal of Clinical Neuropsychology*, 1981, *3*, 33–42.

Benton, A. L. & Fogel, M. L. The assumption that a common disability underlies failure in copying drawings and in copying two- and three-dimensional block patterns is not justified. *Archives of Neurology*, 1962, *7*, 347.

Benton, A. L. & Hamsher, K. deS. *Multilingual Aphasia Examination*. Iowa City: University of Iowa, 1976. (*Manual*, revised, 1978).

Benton, A. L., Hamsher, K. deS., Varney, N. R., & Spreen, O. *Contributions to neuropsychological assessment*. New York: Oxford University Press, 1983.

Benton, A. L., Hannay, H. J., & Varney, N. R. Visual perception of line direction in patients with unilateral brain disease. *Neurology*, 1975, *25*, 907–910.

Benton, A. L., Levin, H. S., & Van Allen, M. W. Geographic orientation in patients with unilateral cerebral disease. *Neuropsychologia*, 1974, *12*, 183–191.

Benton, A. L. & Pearl, D. (Eds.). *Dyslexia*. New York: Oxford University Press, 1978.

Benton, A. L. & Spreen, O. Visual memory test: the simulation of mental incompetence *Archives of General Psychiatry*, 1961, *4*, 79–83.

Benton, A. L. & Van Allen, M. W. Impairment in facial recognition in patients with cerebral disease. *Cortex*, 1968, *4*, 344–358.

Benton, A. L. & Van Allen, M. W. Aspects of neuropsychological asssessment in patients with cerebral disease. In C. M. Gaitz (Ed.), *Aging and the brain*. New York:Plenum Press, 1972.

Benton, A. L., Varney, N. R., & Hamsher, K deS. Visuospatial judgment. A clinical test, *Archives of Neurology*, 1978, *35*, 364–367.

Benton, A. L., Van Allen, M. W., & Fogel, M. L. Temporal orientation in cerebral disease. *Journal of Nervous and Mental Disease*, 1964, *139*, 110–119.

Ben-Yishay, Y., Diller, L., Gerstman, L. & Haas, A. The relationship between impersistence, intellectual function and outcome of rehabilitation in patients with left hemiplegia. *Neurology*, 1968, *18*, 852–861.

Ben-Yishay, Y., Diller, L., & Mandelberg, I. Ability to profit from cues as a function of initial competence in normal and brain-injured adults: a replication of previous findings. *Journal of Abnormal Psychology*, 1970, *76*, 378–379.

Berg, E. A. A simple objective test for measuring flexibility in thinking. *Journal of General Psychology*, 1948, *39*, 15–22.

Berglund, M., Gustafson, L., & Hagberg, B. Amnestic-confabulatory syndrome in hydrocephalic dementia and Korsakoff's psychosis in alcoholism. *Acta Psychiatrica Scandinavica*, 1979, *60*, 323–333.

Berglund, M. & Risberg, J. Reversibility in alcohol dementia. In H. Begleiter (Ed.), *Biological effects of alcohol*. New York: Plenum Press, 1980.

Bergman, H., Borg, S., Hindmarsh, T., et al. Computed-Tomography of the brain and neuropsychological assessment of alcoholic patients. In H. Begleiter (Ed.), *Biological effects of alcohol*. New York: Plenum Press, 1980.

Berker, E., Whelan, T., & Smith, A. *The significance of manual motor and somatosensory tests in neuropsychological assessments*. Paper presented at the tenth annual meeting of the International Neuropsychological Society, Pittsburgh, February, 1982.

Berlucchi, G. Cerebral dominance and interhemispheric communication in normal men. In F. O. Schmitt & F. G. Worden (Eds.), *The Neurosciences. Third Study Program*. Cambridge, Mass.: Massachusetts Institute of Technology Press, 1974.

Berlucchi, G. Interhemispheric integration of simple visuomotor responses. In P. A. Buser & A. Rougeul-Buser (Eds.), *Cerebral correlates of conscious expreience*. INSERM Symposium No. 6. Amsterdam: Elsevier/North Holland Biomedical Press, 1978.

629

Berry, R. G. Pathology of dementia. In J. G. Howells (Eds.), *Modern perspectives in the psychiatry of old age*. Edinburgh/London: Churchill Livingstone, 1975.

Bersoff, D. N. The revised deterioration formula for the WAIS. *Journal of Clinical Psychology*, 1970, *26*, 71–73.

Bever, T. G. & Chiarello, R. J. Cerebral dominance in musicians and nonmusicians. *Science*, 1974, *185*, 537–539.

Biber, C., Butters, N., Rosen, J., et al. Encoding strategies and recognition of faces by alcoholic Korsakoff and other brain-damaged patients. *Journal of Clinical Neuropsychology*, 1981, *3*, 315–330.

Bigler, E. D. Clinical assessment of cognitive deficit in traumatic and degenerative disorders: brain scan and neuropsychologic findings. In R. N. Malathesa (Ed.), *Neuropsychology and cognition*. Netherlands: Martinus Nijhoff, 1982.

Bigler, E. D. & Ehrfurth, J. W. The inappropriate continued use of the Bender Visual Motor Gestalt Test. *Professional Psychology*, 1981, *12*, 562–569.

Bigler, E. & Steinman, D. R. Neuropsychology and computerized axial tomography: further comments. *Professional Psychology*, 1981, *12*, 195–197.

Billingslea, F. Y. The Bender-Gestalt. A review and a perspective. *Psychological Bulletin*, 1963, *60*, 233–251.

Binder. L. M. Constructional strategies on complex figure drawings after unilateral brain damage. *Journal of Clinical Neuropsychology*, 1982, *4*, 51–58.

Binder, L. M., & Schreiber, V. Visual imagery and verbal mediation as memory aids in recovering alcoholics. *Journal of Clinical Neuropsychology*, 1980, *2*, 71–73.

Binet, A. & Simon Th. Le développement de intelligence chez les enfants. *L'Année Psychologique*, 1908, *14*, 1–94.

Bird, E. D. The brain in Huntington's chorea. *Psychological Medicine*, 1978, *8*, 357–360.

Birnbaum, I. M. & Parker, E. S. Acute effects of alcohol on storage and retrieval. In I. M. Birnbaum & E. S. Parker (Eds.), *Alcohol and human memory*. Hillsdale, N.J.: Lawrence Erlbaum Associates, 1977.

Birren, J. E. & Schaie, K. W. (Eds.). *Handbook of the psychology of aging*. New York: Van Nostrand, 1977.

Birri, R. & Perret, E. *Differential age effects on left-right and anterior-posterior brain functions*. Paper presented at the third European conference of the International Neuropsychological Society, Chianciano-Terme, Italy, June, 1980.

Bisiach, E. & Luzzatti, C. Unilateral neglect of representational space. *Cortex*, 1978, *14*, 129–133.

Black, D. W. Pathological laughter. *Journal of Nervous and Mental Disease*, 1982, *170*, 67–71.

Black, F. W. Unilateral brain lesions and MMPI performance: a preliminary study. *Perceptual and Motor Skills*, 1975, *40*, 87–93.

Black, F. W. & Strub, R. L. Constructional apraxia in patients with discrete missile wounds of the brain. *Cortex*, 1976, *12*, 212–220.

Black, F. W. & Strub, R. L. Digit repetition performance in patients with focal brain damage. *Cortex*, 1978, *14*, 12–21.

Blakemore, C. & Falconer, M. A. Long term effects of anterior temporal lobectomy on certain cognitive functions. *Journal of Neurology, Neurosurgery, and Psychiatry*, 1967, *30*, 364–367.

Blakemore, C., Iversen, S. D., & Zangwill, O. L. Brain functions. *Annual Review of Psychology*, 1972, *23*, 413–456.

Blessed, G., Tomlinson, B. E., & Roth, M. The association between quantitative measures of dementia and of senile changes in the cerebral grey matter of elderly subjects. *British Journal of Psychiatry,* 1968, *114,* 797–811.

Bleuler, M. Acute concomitants of physical disease. In D. F. Benson & D. Blumer (Eds.), *Psychiatric aspects of neurologic disease.* New York: Grune & Stratton, 1975.

Blinkov, S. M., & Glezer, I. I. *The human brain in figures and tables.* New York: Plenum Press, 1968.

Bloom B. L. Comparison of the alternate Wechsler Memory Scale forms. *Journal of Clinical Psychology,* 1959, *15,* 72–74.

Blumer, D. Temporal lobe epilepsy and its psychiatric significance. In D. F. Benson & D. Blumer (Eds.), *Psychiatric aspects of neurologic disease.* New York: Grune & Stratton, 1975.

Blumer, D., & Benson, D. F. Personality changes with frontal and temporal lobe lesions. In D. F. Benson & D. Blumer (Eds.), *Psychiatric aspects of neurologic disease.* New York: Grune & Stratton, 1975.

Blumstein. S. Neurolinguistic disorders: Language-brain relationships. In S. B. Filskov & T. J. Boll (Eds.), *Handbook of clinical neuropsychology.* New York: Wiley-Interscience, 1981.

Blumstein, S. & Cooper, W. E. Hemispheric processing of intonation contours. *Cortex,* 1974, *10,* 146–158.

Blusewicz, M. J., Dustman, R. E., Schenkenberg, T., & Beck, E. C. Neuropsychological correlates of chronic alcoholism and aging. *Journal of Nervous and Mental Disease,* 1977a, *165,* 348–355.

Blusewicz, M. J., Schenkenberg, T., Dustman, R. E., & Beck E. C. WAIS performance in young normal, young alcoholic, and elderly normal groups: An evaluation of organicity and mental aging indices. *Journal of Clinical Psychology,* 1977b, *33,* 1149–1153.

Bochner, S. Reliability of the Peabody Picture Vocabulary Test: A review of 32 selected research studies between 1965 and 1974. *Psychology in the Schools,* 1978, *15,* 320–327.

Bock, R. D. Word and image: sources of the verbal and spatial factors in mental test scores. *Psychometrika,* 1973, *38,* 437–457.

Bock, R. D. & Kolakowski, D. Further evidence of sex-linked major-gene influence on human spatial visualizing ability. *American Journal of Human Genetics,* 1973, *25,* 1–14.

Boder, E. Developmental dyslexia: a diagnostic approach based on three atypical reading-spelling patterns. *Developmental Medicine and Child Neurology,* 1973, *15,* 663–687.

Bogen, J. E. The other side of the brain I: dysgraphia and dyscopia following cerebral commissurotomy. *Bulletin of the Los Angeles Neurological Societies,* 1969a, *34,* 73–105.

Bogen, J. E. The other side of the brain II: an appositional mind. *Bulletin of the Los Angeles Neurological Societies,* 1969b, *34,* 135–162.

Bogen, J. E. The callosal syndrome. In K. E. Heilman & E. Valenstein (Eds.), *Clinical neuropsychology.* New York: Oxford University Press, 1979.

Bogen, J. E., DeZure, R., Tenhouten, W. D., & March, J. F. The other side of the brain IV: the A/P ratio. *Bulletin of the Los Angeles Neurological Societies,* 1972, 37, 49–61.

Bolgar, H. The case study method. In B. B. Wolman (Ed.), *Handbook of clinical psychology.* New York: McGraw-Hill, 1965.

Bolin, B. J. A comparison of Raven's Progressive Matrices (1938) with the A.C.E. Psychological Examination and the Otis Gamma Mental Ability Test. *Journal of Consulting Psychology,* 1955, *19,* 400.

Boll, T. J. Right and left cerebral hemisphere damage and tactile perception: performance of the ipsilateral and contralateral sides of the body. *Neuropsychologia,* 1974, *12,* 235–238.

Boll, T. J. The Halstead-Reitan Neuropsychology Battery. In S. B. Filskov & T. J. Boll (Eds.), *Handbook of clinical neuropsychology.* New York: Wiley-Intersciences, 1981.

REFERENCES

Boll, T. J., Heaton, R., & Reitan, R. M. Neuropsychological and emotional correlates of Huntington's chorea. *Journal of Nervous and Mental Disease*, 1974, *158*, 61–69.

Boll, T. J. & Reitan, R. M. Effect of age on performance of the Trail Making Test. *Perceptual and Motor Skills*, 1973, *36*, 691–694.

Boller, F. Mental status of patients with Parkinson Disease. *Journal of Clinical Neuropsychology*, 1980, *2*, 157–172.

Boller, F. & Frank, E. *Sexual functions in neurological disorders*. New York: Raven Press, 1981.

Boller, F., Kim, Y., Morrow, L., et al. *Rotation of visual designs and locus of hemispheric lesions*. Paper presented at the ninth annual meeting of the International Neuropsychological Society, Atlanta, February, 1981.

Boller, F., Mizutani, T., Roessmann, U., & Gambetti, P. Parkinson disease, dementia, and Alzheimer disease: clinicopathological correlations. *Annals of Neurology* 1980, 7, 329–335.

Boller, F. & Vignolo, L. A. Latent sensory aphasia in hemisphere-damaged patients: an experimental study with the Token Test. *Brain*, 1966, *89*, 815–831.

Bolter, J. F. & Hannon, R. Cerebral damage associated with alcoholism: a reexamination. *The Psychological Record*, 1980, *30*, 165–179.

Bolton, N., Britton, P. G., & Savage, R. D. Some normative data on the W.A.I.S. and its indices in an aged population. *Journal of Clinical Psychology*, 1966, *22*, 184–188.

Bolton, N., Savage, R. D., & Roth, M. The Modified Word Learning Test and the aged psychiatric patient. *British Journal of Psychiatry*, 1967, *113*, 1139–1140.

Bond, M. R. Assessment of the psychosocial outcome after severe head injury. In Ciba Foundation Symposium, no. 34 (New Series). *Symposium on the outcome of severe damage to the central nervous system*. Amsterdam: Elsevier. Excerpta Medica, 1975.

Bond, M. R. The stages of recovery from severe head injury with special reference to late outcome. *International Rehabilitation Medicine*, 1979, *1*, 155–159.

Bondareff, W., Baldy, R., & Levy, R. Quantitative computed tomography in senile dementia. *Archives of General Psychiatry*, 1981, *38*, 1365–1368.

Bonin, G. von. Anatomical asymmetries of the cerebral hemispheres. In V. B. Mountcastle (Ed.), *Interhemispheric relations and cerebral dominance*. Baltimore: Johns Hopkins University Press, 1962a.

Bonin, G. von. Brain and mind. In S. Koch (Ed.), *Psychology: a study of a science* (Vol. 4, *Biologically oriented fields*). New York: McGraw-Hill, 1962b.

Bonner, F., Cobb, S., Sweet, W. H., & White, J. C. Frontal lobe surgery. *Psychiatric Treatment. Proceedings of the Association for Research in Nervous and Mental Disease*, 1953, *31*, 392–421.

Borkowski, J. G., Benton, A. L., & Spreen, O. Word fluency and brain damage. *Neuropsychologia*, 1967, *5*, 135–140.

Bornstein, R. A. Effects of unilateral lesions on the Wechsler Memory Scale. *Journal of Clinical Psychology*, 1982, *38*, 389–392.

Borod, J. C., Goodglass, H., & Kaplan, E. Normative data on the Boston Diagnostic Aphasia Examination, Parietal Lobe Battery, and the Boston Naming Test. *Journal of Clinical Neuropsychology*, 1980, *2*, 209–216.

Bortner, M. & Birch, H. G. Perceptual and perceptual-motor dissociation in brain-damaged patients. *Journal of Nervous and Mental Disease*, 1962, *134*, 103–108.

Botez, M. I. Frontal lobe tumors. In P. J. Vinken & G. W. Bruyn (Eds.), *Handbook of clinical neurology*, Vol 17, Pt. II, New York, American Elsevier, 1974.

Botez, M. I. & Barbeau, A. Role of subcortical structures, and particularly of the thalamus, in the mechanism of speech and language. *International Journal of Neurology*, 1971, *8*, 300–320.

Botez, M. I. & Barbeau, A. Neuropsychological findings in Parkinson's disease: a comparison between various tests during long-term Levodopa therapy. *International Journal of Neurology*, 1975, *10*, 222–232.

Botez, M. I., Botez, T., & Aubé, M. *Amusia: clinical and computerized tomographic scanning (CT) correlations.* Iberoamerican Society of Neurological Sciences, International Symposium Phronesis II, Barcelona, October, 1979.

Botez, M. I., Botez, T., Léveillé, J., Bielmann, P., & Caddotte, M. Neuropsychological correlates of folic acid deficiency: facts and hypotheses. In M. I. Botez & E. H. Reynolds (Eds.), *Folic acid in neurology, psychiatry, and internal medicine.* New York: Raven Press, 1979.

Botez, M. I., Ethier, R., Léveillé, J., & Botez-Marquard, T. A syndrome of early recognition of occult hydrocephalus and cerebral atrophy. *Quarterly Journal of Medicine, New Series*, 1977, *46*, (183), 365–380.

Botez, M. I., Léveillé, J., Bérubé, L. & Botez-Marquard, T. Occult disorders of the cerebrospinal fluid dynamics. *European Neurology*, 1975, *13*, 203–223.

Botez, M. I., Peyronnard, J-M., Bérubé, L., & Labrecque, R. Relapsing neuropathy, cerebral atrophy and folate deficiency. *Applied Neurophysiology*, 1979, *42*, 171–183.

Botez, M. I. & Wertheim, N. Expressive aphasia and amusia following right frontal lesion in a right-handed man. *Brain*, 1959, *82*, 186–202.

Botwinick, J. Intellectual abilities. In J. E. Birren & K. W. Schaie (Eds.), *Handbook of the psychology of aging.* New York: Van Nostrand, 1977.

Botwinick, J. *Aging and behavior* (2nd ed.). New York: Springer, 1978.

Botwinick, J. Neuropsychology of aging. In S. B. Filskov & T. J. Boll (Eds.), *Handbook of clinical neuropsychology.* New York: Wiley-Interscience, 1981.

Botwinick, J. & Storandt, M. *Memory, related functions, and age.* Springfield, Ill.: C. C. Thomas, 1974.

Botwinick, J. & Storandt, M. Recall and recognition of old information in relation to age and sex. *Journal of Gerontology*, 1980, *35*, 70–76.

Bowen, D. M. Biochemical evidence for nerve cell changes in senile dementia. In L. Amaducci, A. N. Davison, & P. Antuono (Eds.), *Aging of the brain and dementia.* New York: Raven Press, 1980.

Bowen, F. P. Behavioral alterations in patients with basal ganglia lesions. In M. D. Yahr (Ed.), *The basal ganglia.* New York: Raven Press, 1976.

Boyd, J. L. A validity study of the Hooper Visual Organization Test. *Journal of Consulting and Clinical Psychology*, 1981, *49*, 15–19.

Boyd, R. D. *The Boyd Developmental Progress Scale.* San Bernardino, Calif.: Inland Counties Regional Center, 1974.

Braff, D. L., Silverton, L., Saccuzzo, D. P., & Janowsky, D. S. Impaired speed of visual information processing in marijuana intoxication. *American Journal of Psychiatry*, 1981, *138*, 613–617.

Brain, W. R. Disorders of memory. In W. R. Brain & M. Wilkinson, (Eds.), *Recent advances in neurology and neuropsychiatry.* Boston: Little, Brown, 1969.

Brandt, J., Butters, N., Ryan, C., & Bayog, R. Differential recovery of memory functions in abstinent alcoholics. *Archives of General Psychiatry*, 1983, *40*, 435–442.

Bray, G. P., De Frank, R. S., & Wolfe, T. L. Sexual functioning in stroke survivors. *Archives of Physical Medicine and Rehabilitation*, 1981, *62*, 286–288.

REFERENCES

Brierly, J. B. The neuropathology of amnesic states. In C. W. M. Whitty & O. L. Zangwill (Eds.), *Amnesia*. London: Butterworth, 1966.

Briggs, G. G. & Nebes, R. D. Patterns of hand preference in a student population. *Cortex*, 1975, *11*, 230–238.

Briggs, P. F. The validity of WAIS performance subtests completed with one hand. *Journal of Clinical Psychology*, 1960, *16*, 318–319.

Briggs, P. F. The validity of the Porteus Maze Test completed with the nondominant hand. *Journal of Clinical Psychology*, 1963, *19*, 169–171.

Brilliant, P. J. & Gynther, M. D. Relationships between performance on three tests for organicity and selected patient variables. *Journal of Consulting Psychology*, 1963, *27*, 474–479.

Brion, S. & Mikol, J. Atteinte du noyau lateral dorsal du thalamus et syndrome de Korsakoff alcoolique. *Journal of Neurological Sciences*, 1978, *38*, 249–251, 258–261.

Brizzee, K. R., Ordy, J. M., Knox, C., & Jirge, S. K. Morphology and aging in the brain. In G. J. Maletta & F. J. Pirozzolo (Eds.), *The aging nervous system*. New York: Praeger, 1980.

Broadbent, D. E. Recent analyses of short-term memory. In K. H. Pribram & D. E. Broadbent (Eds.), *Biology of memory*. New York: Academic Press, 1970.

Broadbent, D. E. Division of function and integration of behavior. In F. O. Schmitt & F. G. Worden (Eds.), *The neurosciences. Third study program*. Cambridge, Mass.: Massachusetts Institute of Technology Press, 1974.

Brodal, A. Self-observations and neuro-anatomical considerations after a stroke. *Brain*, 1973, *96*, 675–694.

Brodal, A. *Neurological anatomy* (3rd ed.). New York: Oxford University Press, 1981.

Brody, E. B. & Brody, N. *Intelligence. Nature, determinants, and consequences*. New York: Academic Press, 1976.

Broe, G. A. The concept of head injury rehabilitation. In G. A. Broe & R. L. Tate (Eds.), *Brain impairment. Proceedings of the Fifth Annual Brain Impairment Conference*. Sydney: Postgraduate Committee in Medicine of the University of Sydney, 1982.

Bromley, D. B. Primitive forms of response to the Matrices Test. *Journal of Mental Science*, 1953, *99*, 374–393.

Bromley, D. B. Some effects of age on the quality of intellectual output. *Journal of Gerontology*, 1957, *12*, 318–323.

Brooks, D. N. Memory and head injury. *Journal of Nervous and Mental Disease*, 1972, *155*, 350–355.

Brooks, D. N. Recognition memory, and head injury. *Journal of Neurology*, Neurosurgery, and Psychiatry, 1974, 37, 794–801.

Brooks, D. N. Psychological deficits after severe blunt head injury: their significance and rehabilitation. In D. J. Oborne, M. M. Gruneberg, & J. R. Eiser (Eds.), *Research in psychology and medicine* (Vol. 2). London: Academic Press, 1979.

Brooks, D. N. & Aughton, M. E. Cognitive recovery during the first year after severe blunt head injury. *International Rehabilitation Medicine*, 1979a, *1*, 166–172.

Brooks, D. N. & Aughton, M. E. Psychological consequences of blunt head injury. *International Rehabilitation Medicine*, 1979b, *1*, 160–165.

Brooks, D. N., Aughton, M. E., Bond, M. R., Jones, P., & Rizvi, S. Cognitive sequelae in relationship to early indices of severity of brain damage after severe blunt head injury. *Journal of Neurology, Neurosurgery, and Psychiatry*, 1980, 43, 529–534.

Brooks, D. N., McKinlay, W., & Bond, M. R. *The burden on the relatives of head injured adults*. Paper presented to the second European Conference of the International Neuropsychological Society, Noordvijkerhout, The Netherlands, June, 1979.

REFERENCES

Brookshire, R. H. *An introduction to aphasia* (2nd ed.). Minneapolis, Minn.: BRK Publishers, 1978.

Brookshire, R. H. & Manthie, M. A. Speech and language disturbances in the elderly. In G. F. Maletta & F. J. Pirozzolo (Eds.), *The aging nervous system*. New York: Praeger, 1980.

Brown, E. L. & Deffenbacher, K. Perception and the senses. New York: Oxford University Press, 1979.

Brown, J. W. Language, cognition and the thalamus. *Confinia Neurologica,* 1974, *36,* 33–60.

Brown, J. W. On the neural organization of language: thalamic and cortical relationships. *Brain and Language,* 1975, *2,* 18–30.

Brown, J. W. & Jaffe, J. Hypothesis on cerebral dominance. *Neuropsychologia,* 1975, *13,* 107–110.

Bruce, P. R., Coyne, A. C., & Botwinick, J. *Adult age differences in metamemory.* Paper presented at the American Psychological Association Convention, Montreal, 1980.

Bruhn, A. R. & Reed, M. R. Simulation of brain damage on the Bender-Gestalt test by college subjects. *Journal of Personality Assessment,* 1975, *39,* 244–255.

Bruhn, P., Arlien-Søborg, P., Gyldensted, C., & Christensen, E. L. Prognosis in chronic toxic encephalopathy. *Acta Neurologica Scandinavica,* 1981, *64,* 259–272.

Bruhn, P. & Maage, N. Intellectual and neuropsychological functions in young men with heavy and long-term patterns of drug abuse. *American Journal of Psychiatry,* 1975, *132,* 397–401.

Brussel, I. A., Grassi, J. R., & Melniker, A. A. The Rorschach method and post-concussion syndrome. *Psychiatric Quarterly,* 1942, *16,* 706–743.

Brust, J. C. M. Transient ischemic attacks: Natural history and anticoagulation. *Neurology,* 1977, *27,* 701–707.

Bryden, M. P. Evidence for sex-related differences in cerebral organization. In M. A. Wittig & A. C. Petersen (Eds.), *Sex-related differences in cognitive functioning.* New York: Academic Press, 1979a.

Bryden, M. P. Strategy effects in the assessment of hemispheric asymmetry. In G. Underwood (Ed.), *Strategies of information proprocessing.* New York: Academic Press, 1979b.

Buck, J. N. The H-T-P test. *Journal of Clinical Psychology,* 1948, *4,* 151–159.

Buck, M. W. *Dysphasia.* Englewood Cliffs, N.J.: Prentice-Hall, 1968.

Buffery, A. W. H. Asymmetrical lateralisation of cerebral functions and the effects of unilateral brain surgery in epileptic patients. In S. J. Dimond & J. G. Beaumont (Eds.), *Hemisphere function in the human brain.* New York: Halsted Press, 1974.

Buffery, A. W. H. & Gray, J. A. Sex differences in the development of spatial and linguistic skills. In C. Ounsted & D. C. Taylor (Eds.), *Gender differences: their ontogeny and significance.* Edinburgh/London: Churchill Livingstone, 1972.

Burch, P. R. J. Huntington's disease: Types, frequency, and progression. In T. N. Chase, N. S. Wexler, & A. Barbeau (Eds.), *Advances in neurology* (Vol. 23). New York: Raven Press, 1979.

Burke, H. R. & Bingham, W. C. Raven's Progressive Matrices: More on construct validity. *Journal of Psychology,* 1969, *72,* 247–251.

Burke, D. M. & Light, L. L. Memory and aging: The role of retrieval processes. *Psychological Bulletin,* 1981, *90,* 74–88.

Buros, O. K. The eighth mental measurements yearbook. Highland Park, N.J.: The Gryphon Press, 1978.

Burton, C. Unilateral spatial neglect after cerebrovascular accident. In G. V. Stanley & K. W.

REFERENCES

Walsh (Eds.), *Brain impairment. Proceedings of the 1977 Brain Impairment Workshop.* Parkville, Victoria, Australia: Neuropsychology Group, Dept. of Psychology, University of Melbourne, 1978.

Buschke, H. & Fuld, P. A. Evaluating storage, retention, and retrieval in disordered memory and learning. *Neurology*, 1974, *11*, 1019–1025.

Butcher, J. N. Minnesota Multiphasic Personality Inventory. In O. K. Buros (Ed.), *The eighth mental measurements yearbook*. Highland Park, N.J.: The Gryphon Press, 1978.

Butler, J. M., Rice, L. N., & Wagstaff, A. K. *Quantitative naturalistic research*. Englewood Cliffs, N.J.: Prentice-Hall, 1963.

Butters, N. *An analysis of the Korsakoff patient's memory disorder*. Paper presented at the American Psychological Association Convention, Washington, D. C., 1971.

Butters, N. *Position paper on neuropsychology and Huntington's disease; a current assessment*. (Commission for the control of Huntington's disease and its consequences. Vol. 3, Part 1.) Washington, D.C.: U.S. Department of Health, Education, and Welfare, 1977a.

Butters, N. Effect of predistractor delays on the short-term memory performance of patients with Korsakoff's and Huntington's disease. *Neuropsychologia*, 1977b, *15*, 701–706.

Butters, N. Amnesic disorders. In K. M. Heilman & E. Valenstein (Eds.), *Clinical neuropsychology*. New York: Oxford University Press, 1979.

Butters, N. The Wernicke-Korsakoff syndrome: A review of neuropsychological, neuropathological and etiological factors. In M. Galanter (Ed.), *Currents in alcoholism* (Vol. 8). New York: Grune & Stratton, 1981.

Butters, N. & Albert, M. S. Processes underlying failures to recall remote events. In L. S. Cermak (Ed.), *Human memory and amnesia*. Hillsdale, N.J.: Lawrence Erlbaum Associates, 1982.

Butters, N. & Barton, M. Effect of parietal lobe damage on the performance of reversible operations in space. *Neuropsychologia*, 1970, *8*, 205–214.

Butters, N., Barton, M. & Brody, B. A. Role of the right parietal lobe in the mediation of cross-modal associations and reversible operations in space. *Cortex*, 1970, *6*, 174–190.

Butters, N. & Cermak, L. S. The role of cognitive factors in the memory disorders of alcoholic patients with the Korsakoff syndrome. *Annals of the New York Academy of Sciences*, 1974, *233*, 61–75.

Butters, N. & Cermak, L. Some analyses of amnesic syndromes in brain-damaged patients. In R. L. Isaacson & K. H. Pribram, *The Hippocampus*, Vol. 2. New York: Plenum Press, 1975.

Butters, N. & Cermak, L. S. Neuropsychological studies of alcoholic Korsakoff patients. In G. Goldstein & C. Neuringer (Eds.), *Empirical studies of alcoholism*. Cambridge, Mass.: Ballinger, 1976.

Butters, N. & Cermak, L. S. *Alcoholic Korsakoff's syndrome*. New York: Academic Press, 1980.

Butters, N., Cermak, L. S., Jones, B., & Glosser, G. Some analyses of the information processing and sensory capacities of alcoholic Korsakoff patients. *Advances in Experimental Medical Biology*, 1975, *59*, 595–604.

Butters, N., Cermak, L. S., Montgomery, K., & Adinolfi, A. Some comparisons of the memory and visuoperceptive deficits of chronic alcoholics and patients with Korsakoff's disease. *Alcoholism: Clinical and Experimental Research*, 1977, *1*, 73–80.

Butters, N., Lewis, R., Cermak, L. S., & Goodglass, H. Material-specific memory deficits in alcoholic Korsakoff patients. *Neuropsychologia*, 1973, *11*, 291–299.

Butters, N., Miliotis, P., Albert, M. S., & Sax, D. S. Memory assessment: evidence of the heterogeneity of amnesic symptoms. In G. Goldstein (Ed.), *Advances in clinical neuropsychology*. New York: Plenum Press, in press.

Butters, N., Samuels, I., Goodglass, H., & Brody, B. Short-term visual and auditory memory disorders after parietal and frontal lobe damage. *Cortex*, 1970, *6*, 440–459.

Butters, N., Sax, D., Montgomery, K., & Tarlow, S. Comparison of the neuropsychological deficits associated with early and advanced Huntington's disease. *Archives of Neurology*, 1978, *35*, 585–589.

Butters, N., Soeldner, C., & Fedio, P. Comparison of parietal and frontal lobe spatial deficits in man: extrapersonal vs. personal (egocentric) space. *Perceptual and Motor Skills*, 1972, *34*, 27–34.

Butters, N., Tarlow, S., Cermak, L. S., & Sax, D. A comparison of the information processing deficits of patients with Huntington's chorea and Korsakoff's syndrome. *Cortex*, 1976, *12*, 134–144.

Caine, E. D. Pseudodementia. *Archives of General Psychiatry*, 1981, *38*, 1359–1364.

Caine, E. D., Ebert, M. H., & Weingartner, H. An outline for the analysis of dementia. *Neurology*, 1977, *23*, 1087–1092.

Caine, E. D., Hunt, R. D., Weingartner, H., & Ebert, M. H. Huntington's dementia. *Archives of General Psychiatry*, 1978, *35*, 377–384.

Calsyn, D. A., O'Leary, M. R., & Chaney, E. F. Shortening the Category Test. *Journal of Consulting and Clinical Psychology*, 1980, *48*, 788–789.

Campbell, D. C. & Oxbury, J. M. Recovery from unilateral visuo-spatial neglect. *Cortex*, 1976, *12*, 303–312.

Campbell, R. J. *Psychiatric dictionary* (5th ed.). New York: Oxford University Press, 1981.

Canter, A. A background interference procedure to increase sensitivity of the Bender-Gestalt test to organic brain disorder. *Journal of Consulting Psychology*, 1966, *30*, 91–97.

Canter, A. BIP Bender test for the detection of organic brain disorder: modified scoring method and replication. *Journal of Consulting and Clinical Psychology*, 1968, *32*, 522–526.

Canter, A. & Straumanis, J. J. Performance of senile and healthy aged persons on the BIP Bender test. *Perceptual and Motor Skills*, 1969, *28*, 695–698.

Canter, A. H. Direct and indirect measurement of psychological deficit in multiple sclerosis: Parts I and II. *Journal of General Psychology*, 1951, *44*, 3–25, 27–50.

Canter, G. J. Examining for aphasia (review). In F. L. Darley (Ed.), *Evaluation of appraisal techniques in speech and language pathology*. Reading, Mass.: Addison-Wesley, 1979.

Capitani, E., Scotti, G., & Spinnler, H. Colour imperception in patients with focal excisions of the cerebral hemispheres. *Neuropsychologia*, 1978, *16*, 491–496.

Caramazza, A. & Berndt, R. S. Semantic and syntactic processes in aphasia: A review of the literature. *Psychological Bulletin*, 1978, *85*, 898–918.

Caramazza, A., Zurif, E. B., & Gardner, H. Sentence memory in aphasia. *Neuropsychologia*, 1978, *16*, 661–669.

Carlen, P. L., Wilkinson, D. A., Wortzman, G., et al. Cerebral atrophy and functional deficits in alcoholics without clinically apparent liver disease. *Neurology*, 1981, *31*, 377–385.

Carlen, P. L., Wortzman, G., Holgate, R. C., Wilkinson, D. A., & Rankin, J. G. Reversible cerebral atrophy in recently abstinent chronic alcoholics measured by computed tomography scans. *Science*, 1978, *200*, 1076–1078.

Carmon, A. Spatial and temporal factors in visual perception of patients with unilateral cerebral lesions. In M. Kinsbourne (Ed.), *Asymmetrical function of the brain*. Cambridge: Cambridge University Press, 1978.

Carmon, A. & Nachshon, I. Effect of unilateral brain damage on perception of temporal order. *Cortex*, 1971, *7*, 410–418.

Carson, R. C. Interpretative manual to the MMPI. In J. N. Butcher (Ed.), *MMPI: Research developments and clinical applications*. New York: McGraw-Hill, 1969a.

Carson, R. C. Issues in the teaching of clinical MMPI interpretation. In J. N. Butcher (Ed.), *MMPI: Research developments and clinical applications*. New York: McGraw-Hill, 1969b.

Carter, J. W., Jr. & Bowles, J. W. A manual on qualitative aspects of psychological examining. *Clinical Psychology Monographs* (No. 2). *Journal of Clinical Psychology*, 1948, *4*, 110–150.

Carter-Saltzman, L. Patterns of cognitive functioning in relation to handedness and sex-related differences. In M. A. Wittig & A. C. Petersen (Eds.), *Sex-related differences in cognitive functioning*. New York: Academic Press, 1979.

Casey, V. A. & Fennell, E. B. *Emotional consequences of brain injury: effect of litigation, sex, and laterality of lesion*. Paper presented at the ninth annual meeting of the International Neuropsychological Society, Atlanta, February, 1981.

Cassel, R. H. The order of the tests in the battery. *Journal of Clinical Psychology*, 1962, *18*, 464–465.

Casson, I. R., Sham, R., Campbell, E. A., et al. Neurological and CT evaluation of knocked-out boxers. *Journal of Neurology, Neurosurgery, and Psychiatry*, 1982, *45*, 170–174.

Castro-Caldas, A., Ferro, J. M., & Grosso, J. T. *Age, sex, and type of aphasia in stroke patients*. Paper presented at the second European meeting of the International Neuropsychological Society, Noordwijkerhout, Holland, June, 1979.

Cauthen, N. Normative data for the Tactual Performance Test. *Journal of Clinical Psychology*, 1978, *34*, 456–460.

Cavalli, M., De Renzi, E., Faglioni, P., & Vitale, A. Impairment of right brain-damaged patients on a linguistic cognitive task. *Cortex*, 1981, *17*, 545–556.

Cermak, L. S. Amnesic patients' level of processing. In L. S. Cermak & F. I. M. Craik (Eds.), *Levels of processing in human memory*. Hillside, N.J.: Lawrence Erlbaum Associates, 1979.

Cermak, L. S. The long and short of it in amnesia. In L. S. Cermak (Ed.), *Human memory and amnesia*. Hillsdale, N.J.: Lawrence Erlbaum Associates, 1982.

Chaney, E. F., Erickson, R. C., & O'Leary, M. R. Brain damage and five MMPI items with alcoholic patients. *Journal of Clinical Psychology*, 1977, *33*, 307–308.

Chapman, L. F., Thetford, W. N., Berlin, L., Guthrie, T. C., & Wolff, H. G. Highest integrative functions in man during stress. In H. C. Solomon, S. Cobb, & W. Penfield (Eds.), *The brain and human behavior. Research Publication of the Association for Nervous and Mental Disease*, 1958, *36*, 491–534.

Chapman, L. F. & Wolff, H. G. The cerebral hemispheres and the highest integrative functions of man. *A.M.A. Archives of Neurology*, 1959, *1*, 357–424.

Chédru, F. & Geschwind, N. Writing disturbances in acute confusional states. *Neuropsychologia*, 1972, *10*, 343–353.

Chelune, G. J., Heaton, R. K., Lehman, R. A. W., & Robinson, A. Level versus pattern of neuropsychological performance among schizophrenic and diffusely brain-damaged patients. *Journal of Consulting and Clinical Psychology*, 1979, *47*, 155–163.

Chi, J. G., Dooling, E. C., & Gilles, F. H. Left-right asymmetries of the temporal speech areas of the human fetus. *Archives of Neurology*, 1977, *34*, 346–348.

Chiarello, C., Dronkers, N. F., & Hardyck, C. *Choosing sides: Some questions concerning the apparent instability of language lateralization in normal as compared to aphasic pop-*

ulations. Paper presented at the fifth European conference of the International Neuropsychological Society, Deauville, France, June, 1982.

Christensen, A.-L. *Luria's neuropsychological investigation. Text* (2nd ed.). Copenhagen: Munksgaard, 1979.

Chui, H. C. & Damasio, A. R. Progressive dialysis encephalopathy ("Dialysis dementia"). *Journal of Neurology*, 1980, *222*, 145–157.

Chusid, J. G. *Correlative neuroanatomy and functional neurology* (17th ed.). Los Altos, Calif: Lange Medical Publication, 1979.

Cicone, M., Wapner, W., & Gardner, H. Sensitivity to emotional expressions and situations in organic patients. *Cortex*, 1980, *16*, 145–158.

Clark, R. G. *Manter & Gatz's essentials of clinical neuroanatomy and neurophysiology* (5th ed.). Philadelphia: F. A. Davis, 1975.

Cleeland, C. S. Inferences in clinical psychology and clinical neuropsychology: similarities and differences. *Clinical Psychologist*, 1976, *29* (2), 8–10.

Clément, F. Analyse de l'Échelle de Mémoire de Wechsler. Facteurs qui influent sur ses résultats. *Revue de Psychologie Appliqué*, 1966, *16*, 197–244.

Cohen, D. & Eisdorfer, C. *The cognitive evaluation battery*. New York: Springer, in press.

Cohen, D. & Wilkie, F. Sex-related differences in cognition among the elderly. In M. A. Wittig & A. C. Petersen (Eds.), *Sex-related differences in cognitive functioning*. New York: Academic Press, 1979.

Cohen, J. Factor-analytically based rationale for Wechsler Adult Intelligence Scales. *Journal of Consulting Psychology*, 1957a, *21*, 451–457.

Cohen, J. The factorial structure of the WAIS between early adulthood and old age. *Journal of Consulting Psychology*, 1957b, *21*, 283–290.

Cohen, L. Perception of reversible figures after brain injury. A.M.A. *Archives of Neurology and Psychiatry*, 1959, *81*, 765–775.

Cohn, R. Role of "body image concept" in pattern of ipsilateral clinical extinction. A.M.A. *Archives of Neurology and Psychiatry*, 1953, *70*, 503–509.

Cohn, R. & Neumann, M. A. Discussion of subcortical dementias. In R. Katzman, R. D. Terry, & K. L. Bick (Eds.), *Alzheimer's disease: senile dementia and related disorders* (*Aging*, Vol. 7). New York: Raven Press, 1978.

Collier, H. L. & Levy, N. *A preliminary study employing the Sequential Matching Memory task in an attempt to differentially diagnose brain damage*. Unpublished manuscript, undated.

Colombo, A., De Renzi, E., & Faglioni, P. The occurrence of visual neglect in patients with unilateral cerebral disease. *Cortex*, 1976, *12*, 221–231.

Colonna, A. & Faglioni, P. The performance of hemisphere-damaged patients on spatial intelligence tests. *Cortex*, 1966, *2*, 293–307.

Coltheart, M., Hull, E., & Slater, D. Sex differences in imagery and reading. *Science*, 1975, *253*, 438–440.

Comalli, P. E., Jr., Wapner, S., & Werner, H. Interference effects of Stroop color-word test in childhood, adulthood, and aging. *Journal of Genetic Psychology*, 1962, *100*, 47–53.

Consoli, S. Étude des strategies constructives secondaires aux lésions hémisphèriques. *Neuropsychologia*, 1979, *17*, 303–313.

Cooley, F. B., & Miller, T. W. Can you think of a *good* reason to reject a WAIS Picture Arrangement card? *Journal of Consulting and Clinical Psychology*, 1979, *47*, 317–318.

Coolidge, F. L., Brown, R. E., & Harsch, T. L. *Differential diagnosis of dementia or depression with the WAIS*. Unpublished manuscript. Colorado Springs: University of Colorado.

Cooperative School and College Ability Tests (SCAT). Princeton, N.J.: Educational Testing Service, 1966.

Corballis, M. C. & Beale, I. L. *The psychology of left and right*. Hillsdale, N. J.: Lawrence Erlbaum Associates, 1976,

Corkin, S. Acquisition of motor skill after bilateral medial temporal lobe excision. *Neuropsychologia*, 1968, *6*, 255–266.

Corkin, S. Hidden-Figures-Test performance: lasting effects of unilateral penetrating head injury and transient effects of bilateral cingulotomy. *Neuropsychologia*, 1979, *17*, 585–605.

Corkin, S. Brain acetylcholine, aging, and Alzheimer's disease: implications for treatment. *Trends in Neurosciences*, 1981, *4*, 287–290.

Corkin, S., Growdon, J. H., Sullivan, E. V., & Shedlack, K. Lecithin and cognitive function in aging and dementia. *Excerpta Medica*, 1981.

Costa, L. D. The relation of visuospatial dysfunction to digit span performance in patients with cerebral lesions. *Cortex*, 1975, *11*, 31–36.

Costa, L. D. Interest variability on the Raven Coloured Progressive Matrices as an indicator of specific ability deficit in brain-lesioned patients. *Cortex*, 1976, *12*, 31–40.

Costa, L. D. & Vaughan, H. G., Jr. Performance of patients with lateralized cerebral lesions. I. Verbal and perceptual tests. *Journal of Nervous and Mental Disease*, 1962, *134*, 162–168.

Costa, L. D., Vaughan, H. G., Jr., Howitz, M., & Ritter, W. Patterns of behavioral deficits associated with visual spatial neglect. *Cortex*, 1969, *5*, 242–263.

Costa, L. D., Vaughan, H. G., Levita, E., & Farber, N. Purdue Pegboard as a predictor of the presence and laterality of cerebral lesions. *Journal of Consulting Psychology*, 1963, *27*, 133–137.

Coupar, A. M. Detection of mild aphasia: a study using the Token Test. *British Journal of Medical Psychology*, 1976, *49*, 141–144.

Coxe, W. S. Intracranial tumors. In S. G. Eliasson, A. L. Prensky, & W. B. Hardin, Jr. (Eds.), *Neurological pathophysiology* (2nd ed.). New York: Oxford University Press, 1978.

Craik, F. I. M. *Short-term storage in a "levels of processing" framework*. Paper presented at the meeting of the Midwestern Psychology Association, Chicago, 1973.

Craik, F. I. M. Age differences in human memory. In J. E. Birren & K. W. Schaie (Eds.), *Handbook of the psychology of aging*. New York: Van Nostrand, 1977a.

Craik, F. I. M. Similarities between the effects of aging and alcoholic intoxication on memory performance, construed with a "levels of processing" framework. In I. M. Birnbaum & E. S. Parker (Eds.), *Alcohol and human memory*. Hillsdale, N.J.: Lawrence Erlbaum Associates, 1977b.

Craik, F. I. M. Human memory. *Annual Review of Psychology*, 1979, *30*, 63–102.

Craik, F. I. M. & Birtwistle, J. Proactive inhibition in free recall. *Journal of Experimental Psychology*, 1971, *91*, 120–123.

Craik, F. I. M. & Byrd, M. Aging and cognitive deficits: the role of attentional resources. In F. I. M. Craik & S. E. Trehub (Eds.), *Aging and cognitive processes*. New York: Plenum Press, 1981.

Craik, F. I. M. & Lockhart, R. S. Levels of processing: a framework for memory research. *Journal of Verbal Learning and Verbal Behavior*, 1972, *11*, 671–684.

Crapper, D. R., Krishnan, S. S., & Dalton, A. J. Brain aluminum distribution in Alzheimer's disease and experimental neurofibrillary degeneration. *Science*, 1973, *180*, 511–513.

Crapper-McLachlan, D. R. & De Boni, U. Etiologic factors in senile dementia of the Alzheimer type. In L. Amaducci, A. N. Davison, & P. Antuono (Eds.), *Aging of the brain and dementia*. New York: Raven Press, 1980.

Critchley, M. *The parietal lobes*. Baltimore: Williams & Wilkins, 1953.

Critchley, M. Disorders of highest nervous activity: introductory remarks. Chap. 1, Vol. 3, *Disorders of higher nervous activity*. In P. J. Vinken & G. W. Bruyn (Eds.), *Handbook of clinical neurology*. New York: Wiley, 1969.

Critchley, M. Inter-hemispheric partnership and inter-hemispheric rivalry. In M. Critchley & J. L. O'Leary (Eds.), *Scientific foundation of neurology*. Philadelphia: F. A. Davis, 1972.

Cronbach, L. J. *Essentials of psychological testing*. N.Y.: Harper & Row, 1970.

Cronholm, B. & Molander, L. Memory disturbances after electroconvulsive therapy. *Acta Psychiatrica et Neurologica Scandinavica*, 1957, *32*, 280–306.

Cronholm, B. & Ottosson, J.-O. Reliability and validity of a memory test battery. *Acta Psychiatrica Scandinavica*, 1963, *39*, 218–234.

Crook, T., Ferris, S., McCarthy, M., & Rae, D. Utility of digit recall tasks for assessing memory in the aged. *Journal of Consulting and Clinical Psychology*, 1980, *48*, 228–233.

Crosson, B. & Warren, R. L. Use of the Luria-Nebraska Neurophysical Battery in aphasia: a conceptual critique. *Journal of Consulting and Clinical Psychology*, 1982, *50*, 22–31.

Crow, C. M. & Lewinsohn, P. M. Performance of left hemiplegic stroke patients on the Benton Visual Retention Test. Doctoral dissertation, University of Oregon, 1969.

Culver, C. M. & King, F. W. Neuropsychological assessment of undergraduate marijuana and LSD users. *Archives of General Psychiatry*, 1974, *31*, 707–711.

Cutter, F. Intelligence: a heuristic frame of reference. *American Psychologist*, 1957, *12*, 650–651.

Cutting, J. Study of anosognosia. *Journal of Neurology, Neurosurgery, and Psychiatry*, 1978, *41*, 548–555.

Cutting, J. Memory in functional psychosis. *Journal of Neurology, Neurosurgery, and Psychiatry*, 1979, *42*, 1031–1037.

Daghighian, I. Le vieillissement des anciens traumatisés du crâne. *Archives Suisses de Neurologie, Neurochirurgie et de Psychiatrie*, 1973, *112*, 399–447.

Dahlstrom, W. G. & Welsh, G. S. *An MMPI handbook*. Minneapolis: University of Minnesota Press, 1960.

Dahlstrom, W. G., Welsh, G. S., & Dahlstrom, L. E. *An MMPI handbook* (Vol. 1. *Clinical interpretation*, Rev ed.). Minneapolis: University of Minnesota Press, 1975.

Dailey, C. A. Psychological findings five years after head injury. *Journal of Clinical Psychology*, 1956, *12*, 440–443.

Damasio, A. R. Varieties and significance of the alexias. *Archives of Neurology*, 1977, *34*, 325–326.

Damasio, A. R. The frontal lobes. In K. M. Heilman & E. Valenstein (Eds.), *Clinical neuropsychology*. New York: Oxford University Press, 1979.

Damasio, A. R., Damasio, H., & Chui, H. C. Neglect following damage to frontal lobe or basal ganglia. *Neuropsychologia*, 1980, *18*, 123–132.

Damasio, A. R., Damasio, H., & Van Hoesen, G. W. Prosopagnosia: anatomic basis and behavioral mechanisms. *Neurology*, 1982, *32*, 331–341.

Damasio, A. R., McKee, J., & Damasio, H. Determinants of performance in color anomia. *Brain and Language*, 1979, *7*, 74–85.

Darley, C. F. & Tinklenberg, J. R. Marijuana and memory. In L. L. Miller (Ed.), *Marijuana. Effects on human behavior*. New York: Academic Press, 1974.

Darley, C. F., Tinklenberg, J. R., Roth, W. T., et al. Influence of marihuana on storage and retrieval processes in memory. *Memory and Cognition*, 1973, *1*, 196–200.

REFERENCES

Darley, F. L. *Apraxia of speech: 107 years of terminological confusion*. Paper presented at the American Speech and Hearing Association Convention, Chicago, 1967.

Darley, F. L. The efficacy of language rehabilitation. *Journal of Speech and Hearing Disorders*, 1972, 37, 3–21.

Darley, F. L. *Evaluation of appraisal techniques in speech and language pathology*. Reading, Mass: Addison-Wesley, 1979.

Davies, A. The influence of age on Trail Making test performance. *Journal of Clinical Psychology*, 1968, 24, 96–98.

Davis, A. E. & Wada, J. A. Lateralization of speech dominance by spectral analysis of evoked potentials. *Journal of Neurology, Neurosurgery, and Psychiatry*, 1977, 40, 1–4.

Davis, M. E., Binder, L. M., & Lezak, M. D. *Hemisphere side of damage and encoding capacity*. Paper presented at the eleventh annual meeting of the International Neuropsychological Society, Mexico City, February, 1983.

Davison, L. A. Current status of clinical neuropsychology. In R. M. Reitan & L. A. Davison (Eds.) *Clinical Neuropsychology: current status and applications*. New York: Hemisphere, 1974.

DeArmond, S. J., Fusco, M. M., & Dewey, M. M. *Structure of the human brain* (2nd ed.). New York: Oxford University Press, 1976.

Dee, H. L. Visuconstructive and visuoperceptive deficit in patients with unilateral cerebral lesions. *Neuropsychologia*, 1970, 8, 305–314.

Dee, H. L., Benton, A. L., & Van Allen, M. W. Apraxia in relation to hemisphere locus of lesion and aphasia. *Transactions of the American Neurological Association*, 1970, 95, 147–148.

Dee, H. L. & Fontenot, D. J. Use of the non-preferred hand in graphomotor performance: a methodological study. *Confinia Neurologica*, 1969, 31, 273–280.

Deelman, B. *Memory deficits after closed head injury*. Paper presented at the first European conference of the International Neuropsychological Society, Oxford, England, 1977.

DeFillippis, N. A., McCampbell, E., & Rogers, P. Development of a booklet form of the Category Test: normative and validity data. *Journal of Clinical Neuropsychology*, 1979, 1, 339–342.

DeKosky, S. T., Heilman, K. M., Bowers, D., & Valenstein, E. Recognition and discrimination of emotional faces and pictures. *Brain and Language*, 1980, 9, 206–214.

Delaney, R. C., Rosen, A. J., Mattson, R. H., & Novelly, R. A. Memory function in focal epilepsy: a comparison of non-surgical, unilateral temporal lobe and frontal lobe samples. *Cortex*, 1980, 16, 103–117.

Delaney, R. C., Wallace, J. D., & Egelko, S. Transient cerebral ischemic attacks and neuropsychological deficit. *Journal of Clinical Neuropsychology*, 1980, 2, 107–114.

deLeon, M. J., Ferris, S. H., George, A. E. et al. Computed tomography evaluations of brain-behavior relationships in senile dementia of the Alzheimer's type. *Neurobiology of Aging*, 1980, 1, 69–79.

Delis, D. & Kaplan, E. F. The assessment of aphasia with the Luria-Nebraska Neuropsychological Battery: a case critique. *Journal of Consulting and Clinical Psychology*, 1982, 50, 32–39.

Delis, D. C. & Kaplan, E. F. Hazards of a standardized neuropsychological test with low content validity: common on the Luria-Nebraska Battery. *Journal of Consulting and Clinical Psychology*, in press.

DeLong, M. R. & Georgopoulos, A. P. Physiology of the basal ganglia—a brief overview. In T. N. Chase et al. (Eds.), *Advances in Neurology*, Vol. 23. New York: Raven Press, 1979.

Denes, F., Semenza, C., & Stoppa, E. Selective improvement by unilateral brain-damaged patients on Raven Coloured Progressive Matrices. *Neuropsychologia*, 1978, *16*, 749–752.

Denes, G., Semenza, C., Stoppa, E., & Lis, A. Unilateral spatial neglect and recovery from hemiplegia: a follow-up study. *Brain*, 1982, *105*, 543–52.

Dennerll, R. D. Cognitive deficits and lateral brain dysfunction in temporal lobe epilepsy. *Epilepsia*, 1964, *5*, 177–190.

Denney, N. W. Evidence for developmental changes in categorization criteria for children and adults. *Human Development*, 1974, *17*, 41–53.

Denny-Brown, D. Clinical symptomatology in right and left hemisphere lesions. Discussion. In V. B. Mountcastle (Ed.), *Interhemispheric relations and cerebral dominance*. Baltimore: John Hopkins Press, 1962.

Denny-Brown, D., Meyer, J. S., & Horenstein, S. The significance of perceptual rivalry resulting from parietal lesion. *Brain*, 1952, *75*, 433–471.

De Renzi, E. Nonverbal memory and hemispheric side of lesion. *Neuropsychologia*, 1968, *6*, 181–189.

De Renzi, E. Hemispheric asymmetry as evidenced by spatial disorders. In M. Kinsbourne (Ed.), *Asymmetrical function of the brain*. Cambridge, England: Cambridge University Press, 1978.

De Renzi, E. & Faglioni, P. The comparative efficiency of intelligence and vigilance tests in detecting hemispheric cerebral damage. *Cortex*, 1965, *1*, 410–433.

De Renzi, E. & Faglioni, P. The relationship between visuo-spatial impairment and constructional apraxia. *Cortex*, 1967, *3*, 327–342.

De Renzi, E. & Faglioni, P. Normative data and screening power of a shortened version of the Token Test. *Cortex*, 1978, *14*, 41–49.

De Renzi, E., Faglioni, P., & Previdi, P. Spatial memory and hemispheric locus of lesion. *Cortex*, 1977, *13*, 424–433.

De Renzi, E., Faglioni, P., Savoiardo, M., & Vignolo, L. A. The influence of aphasia and of the hemisphere side of the cerebral lesion on abstract thinking. *Cortex*, 1966, *2*, 399–420.

De Renzi, E., Faglioni, P., & Scotti, G. Hemispheric contribution to exploration of space through the visual and tactile modality. *Cortex*, 1970, *6*, 191–203.

De Renzi, E., Faglioni, P., & Sorgato, P. Modality-specific and supramodal mechanisms of apraxia. *Brain*, 1982, *105*, 301–312.

De Renzi, E. & Ferrari, C. The Reporter's Test. *Cortex*, 1978, *14*, 279–293.

De Renzi, E., Motti, F., & Nichelli, P. Imitating gestures, *Archives of Neurology*, 1980, 37, 6–10.

De Renzi, E. & Scotti, C. Autotopagnosia. fiction or reality? *A.M.A. Archives of Neurology*, 1970. *23*, 221–227.

De Renzi, E. & Spinnler, H. Visual recognition in patients with unilateral cerebral disease. *Journal of Nervous and Mental Disease*, 1966, *142*, 515–525.

De Renzi, E. & Spinnler, H. Impaired performance on color tasks in patients with hemispheric damage. *Cortex*, 1967, *3*, 194–217.

De Renzi, E. & Vignolo, L. A. The Token Test: a sensitive test to detect disturbances in aphasics. *Brain*, 1962, *85*, 665–678.

Dershowitz, A. & Frankel, Y. Jewish culture and the WISC and WAIS test patterns. *Journal of Consulting and Clinical Psychology*, 1975, *43*, 126–134.

Deutsch, G. Tweedy, J. R., & Lorinstein, I. B. *Some temporal and spatial factors affecting visual neglect*. Paper presented at the eighth annual meeting of the International Neuropsychological Society, San Francisco, February, 1980.

Deutsch, J. A. *The structural basis of behavior*. Chicago: University of Chicago Press, 1960.

REFERENCES

Dewhurst, K., Oliver, J., Trick, K. L. K., & McKnight, A. L. Neuro-psychiatric aspects of Huntington's disease. *Confinia Neurologia*, 1969, *31*, 258–268.

DeWolfe, A. S., Barrell, R. P., Becker, B. C., & Spaner, F. E. Intellectual deficit in chronic schizophrenia and brain damage. *Journal of Consulting and Clinical Psychology*, 1971, *36*, 197–204.

Dikmen, S. & Reitan, R. M. Minnesota Multiphasic Personality Inventory correlates of dysphasic language disturbance. *Journal of Abnormal Psychology*, 1974a, *83*, 675–679.

Dikmen, S. & Reitan, R. M. MMPI correlates of localized cerebral lesions. *Perceptual and Motor Skills*, 1974b, *39*, 831–840.

Dikmen, S. & Reitan, R. M. Psychological deficits and recovery of functions after head injury. *Transactions of the American Neurological Association*, 1976, 72–77.

Dikmen, S. & Reitan, R. M. Emotional sequelae of head injury. *Annuals of Neurology*, 1977a, 492–494.

Dikmen, S. & Reitan, R. M. MMPI correlates of adaptive ability deficits in patients with brain lesions. *Journal of Nervous and Mental Disease*, 1977b, *165*, 247–254.

Diller, L. Hemiplegia. In J. F. Garrett & E. S. Levine (Eds.), *Psychological practices with the physically disabled*. New York. Columbia University Press, 1962.

Diller, L. Brain damage, spatial orientation, and rehabilitation. In S. J. Freedman (Ed.), *The neuropsychology of spatially oriented behavior*. Homewood, Ill.: Dorsey, 1968.

Diller, L., Ben-Yishay, Y., Gerstman, L. J., Goodkin R., Gordon, W., & Weinberg, J. *Studies in cognition and rehabilitation in hemiplegia* (Rehabilitation Monograph No. 50). New York: New York University Medical Center Institute of Rehabilitation Medicine, 1974.

Diller, L. & Weinberg, J. Bender Gestalt Test distortions in hemiplegia. *Perceptual and Motor Skills*, 1965, *20*, 1313–1323.

Diller, L. & Weinberg, J. Evidence for accident-prone behavior in hemiplegic patients. *Archives of Physical Medicine and Rehabilitation*, 1970, *51*, 358–363.

Diller, L. & Weinberg, J. Differential aspects of attention in brain-damaged persons. *Perceptual and Motor Skills*, 1972, *35*, 71–81.

Diller, L. & Weinberg, J. Hemi-inattention in rehabilitation: the evolution of a rational remediation program. In E. A. Weinstein & R. P. Friedland (Eds.), *Advances in neurology* (Vol. 18). New York: Raven Press, 1977.

Dimond, S. J. & Beaumont, J. G. Experimental studies of hemispheric function in the human brain. In S. J. Dimond & J. G. Beaumont (Eds.), *Hemispheric function in the human brain*. New York: Halsted, 1974.

Divac, I. Does the neostriatum operate as a functional entity? In A. R. Cools, A. H. M. Lohman, & I. H. L. Van den Bereken (Eds.), *Psychobiology of the striatum*. Amsterdam: Elsevier/North-Holland Biomedical Press, 1977.

Dodrill, C. B. Diphenylhydantoin serum levels, toxicity, and neuropsychological performance in patients with epilepsy. *Epilepsia*, 1975, *16*, 593–600.

Dodrill, C. B. The hand dynamometer as a neuropsychological measure. *Journal of Consulting and Clinical Psychology*, 1978a, *46*, 1432–1435.

Dodrill, C. B. *Neuropsychological assessment in epilepsy rehabilitation*. Paper presented at the 86th annual convention of the American Psychological Association, Toronto, 1978b.

Dodrill, C. B. A neuropsychological battery for epilepsy. *Epilepsia*, 1978c, *19*, 611–623.

Dodrill, C. B. Sex differences on the Halstead-Reitan Neuropsychological Battery and on other neuropsychological measures. *Journal of Clinical Psychology*, 1979, *35*, 236–241.

Dodrill, C. B. Neuropsychological evaluation in epilepsy. In J. S. Lockard & A. A. Ward, Jr. (Eds.), *Epilepsy: a window to brain mechanisms*. New York: Raven Press, 1980.

REFERENCES

Dodrill, C. B. Neuropsychology of epilepsy. In S. B. Filskov & T. J. Boll (Eds.), *Handbook of clinical neuropsychology*. New York: Wiley-Interscience, 1981.

Dodrill, C. B., Batzel, L. W., Queisser, H. R., & Temkin, N. R. *An objective method for the assessment of psychological and social problems among epileptics*. Unpublished manuscript, no date.

Dodrill, C. B. & Troupin, A. S. Effects of repeated administrations of a comprehensive neuropsychological battery among chronic epileptics. *Journal of Nervous and Mental Disease*, 1975, *161*, 185–190.

Dodrill, C. B. & Wilkus, R. J. Neuropsycholological correlates of the electroencephalogram in epileptics: III Generalized non-epileptiform abnormalities. *Epilepsia*, 1976a, *17*, 101–109.

Dodrill, C. B. & Wilkus, R. J. Relationships between intelligence and electroencephalographic epileptiform activity in adult epileptics. *Neurology*, 1976b, 525–531.

Dodson, E. W. Metabolic encephalopathies. In S. G. Eliasson, A. L. Prensky, & W. B. Hardin, Jr. (eds.), *Neurological pathophysiology* (2nd ed.). New York: Oxford University Press, 1978.

Dolke, A. M. Investigation into certain psychometric properties of Raven's Standard Progressive Matrices Test. *Indian Journal of Psychology*, 1976, *51*, 225–236.

Doll, E. A. *Measurement of social competence*. Minneapolis: Educational Publishers, 1953.

Doll, E. A. *Vineland Social Maturity Scale: Manual of directions* (Revised ed.). Minneapolis: American Guidance Service, 1965.

Donnelly, E. F., Dent, J. D., Murphy, D. L., & Mignone, R. J. Comparison of temporal lobe epileptics and affective disorders on the Halstead-Reitan Battery. *Journal of Clinical Psychology*, 1972, *28*, 61–62.

Donnelly, E. F., Nasrallah, H. A., Wyatt, R. J., et al. Effects of dopamine synthesis inhibition on WAIS Comprehension. *Journal of Consulting and Clinical Psychology*, 1978, *46*, 385–388.

Dordain, M., Degos, J. D., & Dordain, G. Troubles de la voix dans les hémiplégies gauches. *Revue d'Otolaryngologie, Otologie, et Rhinologie*, 1971, *92*, 178–188.

Dörken, H., Jr. & Kral, V. A. The psychological differentiation of organic brain lesions and their localization by means of the Rorschach test. *American Journal of Psychiatry*, 1952, *108*, 764–770.

Dornbush, R. L. & Kokkevi, A. Acute effects of Cannabis on cognitive, perceptual, and motor performance in chronic hashish users. *Annals of the New York Academy of Science*, 1976, *282*, 313–322.

Doty, R. W. Neurons and memory: some clues. In M. A. B. Brazier (Ed.), *Brain mechanisms in memory and learning: from neurons to man*. New York: Raven Press, 1979.

Doyle, J. C., Ornstein, R., & Galin, D. Lateral specialization of cognitive mode: II. EEG frequency analysis. *Psychophysiology*, 1974, *11*, 567–577.

Drachman, D. A. & Arbit, J. Memory and the hippocampal complex. II. Is memory a multiple process? *Archives of Neurology*, 1966, *15*, 52–61.

Drachman, D. A. & Leavitt, J. Human memory and the cholinergic system. *Archives of Neurology*, 1974, *30*, 113–121.

Dresser, A. C., Meirowsky, A. M., Weiss, G. H., McNeel, M. L., et al. Gainful employment following head injury. *Archives of Neurology*, 1973, *29*, 111–116.

Drewe, E. A. The effect of type and area of brain lesion on Wisconsin Card Sorting Test performance. *Cortex*, 1974, *10*, 159–170.

Dricker, J., Butters, N., Berman, G., Samuels, I., & Carey, S. The recognition and encoding of faces by alcoholic Korsakoff and right hemisphere patients. *Neuropsychologia*, 1978, *16*, 683–695.

Duffala, D. *Validity of the Luria-South Dakota Neuropsychological Battery for brain injured persons*. Doctoral dissertation. Berkeley, Calif.: California School of Professional Psychology, 1978.

Duke, R. B. Intellectual evaluation of brain-damaged patients with a WAIS short form. *Psychological Reports*, 1967, *20*, 858.

Dunn, L. M. *Expanded manual for the Peabody Picture Vocabulary Test*. Minneapolis: American Guidance Service, 1965.

Dunn, L. M. & Markwardt, F. C., Jr. *Manual. Peabody Individual Achievement Test*. Circle Pines, Minn.: American Guidance Service, 1970.

Dvorine, I. *Dvorine Pseudo-Isochromatic Plates* (2nd ed.). Baltimore: Waverly Press, 1953.

Edguer, B., Graves, R., & Strauss, E. *Hemispheric differences in processing pictorial material*. Paper presented at the tenth annual meeting of the International Neuropsychological Society, Pittsburgh, February, 1982.

Edwards, A. E. Dissolution of illusion: a sign of a lesioned brain. *Proceedings of the 80th Annual Convention of the American Psychological Association*, 1972, *7*, 419–420. (summary).

Ehrfurth, J. W. & Lezak, M. *The battering of neuropsychology by the "hit rate": an appeal for peace and reason*. Paper presented at the tenth annual meeting of the International Neuropyschological Society, Pittsburgh, February, 1982.

Ehrlichman, H. & Wiener, M. W. Consistency of task-related asymmetries. *Psychophysiology*, 1979, *16*, 247–252.

Eichorn, D. H. *The Raven Progressive Matrices* (Review). In W. K. Frankenburg & B. W. Camp. *Pediatric screening tests*. Springfield, Ill.: C. C. Thomas, 1975.

Eisdorfer, C. Stress, disease and cognitive change in the aged. In C. Eisdorfer & R. O. Friedel (Eds.), *Cognitive and emotional disturbance in the elderly*. Chicago: Year Book Medical Publishers, 1977.

Eisdorfer, C. & Cohen, D. The cognitively impaired elderly: differential diagnosis. In M. Storandt, I. Seigler, & M. Ellis (Eds.), *The clinical psychology of aging*. New York: Plenum Press, 1978.

Eisdorfer, C. & Cohen, D. Diagnostic criteria for primary neuronal degeneration of the Alzheimer's type. *Journal of Family Practice*, 1980, *11*, 553–557.

Eisdorfer, C. & Wilkie, F. Intellectual changes with advancing age. In L. F. Jarvik, C. Eisdorfer, & J. E. Blum (Eds.), *Intellectual functioning in adults*. New York: Springer, 1973.

Eisenson, J. *Examining for aphasia. A manual for the examination of aphasia and related disturbances*. New York: Psychological Corporation, 1954.

Eisenson, J. Language and intellectual findings associated with right cerebral damage. *Language and Speech*, 1962, *5*, 49–53.

Eisenson, J. *Adult aphasia*. New York: Appleton-Century-Crofts, 1973.

Ekstrom, R. B., French, J. W., Harman, H. H., & Dermen, D. *Manual for Kit of Factor-Referenced Cognitive Tests*. Princeton, N.J.: Educational Testing Service, 1976.

Eliasson, S. G., Prensky, A. L., & Hardin, W. B. Jr. (Eds.), *Neurological pathophysiology* (2nd ed.). New York: Oxford University Press, 1978.

Elithorn, A., Jones, D., Kerr, M., & Lee, D. The effects of the variation of two physical parameters on empirical difficulty in a perceptual maze test. *British Journal of Psychology*, 1964, *55*, 31–37.

Ellenberg, L., Rosenbaum, G., Goldman, M. S., & Whitman, R. D. Recoverability of psychological functioning following alcohol abuse: Lateralization effects. *Journal of Consulting and Clinical Psychology*, 1980, *48*, 503–510.

Ellenberg, L. & Sperry, R. W. Lateralized division of attention in the commissurotomized and intact brain. *Neuropsychologia*, 1980, *18*, 411–418.

Ellenberger, C., Jr. The visual system. In S. G. Eliasson, A. L. Prensky, & W. B. Hardin, Jr. (Eds.), *Neurological pathophysiology* (2nd ed.). New York: Oxford University Press, 1978.

Erber, J. T., Botwinick, J., & Storandt, M. The impact of memory on age differences in Digit Symbol performance. *Journal of Gerontology*, 1981, *36*, 586–590.

Erickson, R. C. Problems in the clinical assessment of memory. *Experimental Aging Research*, 1978, *4*, 255–272.

Erickson, R. C. & Scott, M. L. Clinical memory testing: a review. *Psychological Bulletin*, 1977, *84*, 1130–1149.

Eolinger, P J & Damasio, A. R. Age and type of aphasia in patients with stroke. *Journal of Neurology, Neurosurgery, and Psychiatry*, 1981, *44*, 377–381.

Eson, M. E. & Bourke, R. S. *Assessment of information processing deficits after serious head injury*. Paper presented at the eighth annual meeting of the International Neuropsychological Society, San Francisco, February, 1980a.

Eson, M. E. & Bourke, R. S. *Assessment of long-term information processing deficits after serious head injury*. Paper presented at the NATO Advanced Study Institute of Neuropsychology and Cognition, Augusta, Georgia, September, 1980b.

Eson, M. E., Yen, J. K., & Bourke, R. S. Assessment of recovery from serious head injury. *Journal of Neurology, Neurosurgery, and Psychiatry*, 1978, *41*, 1036–1042.

Estes, W. K. Learning theory and intelligence. *American Psychologist*, 1974, *29*, 740–749.

Evans, C. D. Discussion of the clinical problem. In Ciba Foundation Symposium, No. 34 (New Series). *Symposium on the outcome of severe damage to the CNS*. Amsterdam: Elsevier-Excerpta Medica, 1975.

Evans, M. Cerebral disorders due to drugs of dependence and hallucinogens. In J. G. Rankin (Ed.), *Alcohol, drugs and brain damage*. Proceedings of Symposium. Toronto: Addiction Research Foundation, 1975.

Ewing, R., McCarthy, D., Gronwall, D., & Wrightson, P. Persisting effects of minor head injury observable during hypoxic stress. *Journal of Clinical Neuropsychology*, 1980, *2*, 147–155.

Exner, J. E. *The Rorschach*. New York: Wiley-Interscience, 1974.

Fabian, M. S., Jenkins, R. L., & Parsons, O. A. Gender, alcoholism, and neuropsychological functioning. *Journal of Consulting and Clinical Psychology*, 1981, *49*, 138–140.

Fabry, J. J. Depression. In R. H. Woody (Ed.), *Encyclopedia of Clinical Assessment* (Vol. 2). San Francisco: Jossey-Bass, 1980.

Falicki, Z. & Sep-Kowalik, B. Psychic disturbances as a result of cardiac arrest. *Polish Medical Journal*, 1969, *8*, 200–206.

Farmer, R. H. Functional changes during early weeks of abstinence, measured by the Bender-Gestalt. *Quarterly Journal of Studies on Alcohol*, 1973, *34*, 786–796.

Farnsworth, D. Farnsworth-Munsel 100-hue and dichotomous test for color vision. *Journal of the Optical Society of America*, 1943, *33*, 568–578.

Fedio, P. *The cortical and thalamic mechanisms of memory*. Paper presented at the fourth annual meeting of the International Neuropsychological Society, Toronto, Canada, 1976.

Fedio, P., Cox, C. S., Neophytides, A. et al. Neuropsychological profile of Huntington's disease: patients and those at risk. In T. N. Chase, N. S. Wexler, & A. Barbeau (Eds.), *Advances in Neurology* (Vol. 23). New York: Raven Press, 1979.

647

REFERENCES

Fedio, P. & Van Buren, J. *Electrical stimulation of thalamic mechanisms for immediate memory in man.* Paper presented at the American Psychological Association Convention, Honolulu, Hawaii, 1972.

Fedio, P. & Van Buren, J. M. Memory deficits during electrical stimulation of the speech center in consicous man. *Brain and Language,* 1974, *1,* 29–42.

Fedio, P. & Van Buren, J. M. Memory and perceptual deficits during electrical stimulation in the left and right thalamus and parietal subcortex. *Brain and Language,* 1975, *2,* 78–100.

Ferro, J. M., Santos, M. E., Castro-Caldas, A., & Mariano, G. Gesture recognition in aphasia. *Journal of Clinical Neuropsychology,* 1980, *2,* 277–292.

Field, J. G. Two types of tables for use with Wechsler's Intelligence Scales. *Journal of Clinical Psychology,* 1960, *16,* 3–7.

Filskov, S. B. & Boll, T. J. *Handbook of clinical neuropsychology.* New York: Wiley Interscience, 1981.

Filskov, S. B. & Goldstein, S. G. Diagnostic validity of the Halstead-Reitan neuropsychological battery. *Journal of Consulting and Clinical Psychology,* 1974, *42,* 382–388.

Filskov, S. B., & Leli, D. A. Assessment of the individual in neuropsychological practice. In S. B. Filskov & T. J. Boll (Eds.), *Handbook of clinical neuropsychology.* New York: Wiley-Interscience, 1981.

Finger, S. Lesion momentum and behavior. In S. Finger (Ed.), *Recovery from brain damage.* New York: Plenum Press, 1978.

Fink, M., Green, M., & Bender, M. B. The Face-Hand Test as a diagnostic sign of organic mental syndrome. *Neurology,* 1952, *2,* 46–58.

Finlayson, M. A. J., Johnson, K. A., & Reitan, R. M. Relationship of level of education to neuropsychological measures in brain-damaged and non-brain-damaged adults. *Journal of Consulting and Clinical Psychology,* 1977, *45,* 536–542.

Finlayson, M. A. J. & Reitan, R. M. Effect of lateralized lesions on ipsilateral and contralateral motor functioning. *Journal of Clinical Neuropsychology,* 1980, *2,* 237–243.

Fisher, C. M. Disorientation for place. *Archives of Neurology,* 1982, *39,* 33–36.

Fitzhugh, K. B., Fitzhugh, L. C., & Reitan, R. M. Psychological deficits in relation to acuteness of brain dysfunction. *Journal of Consulting Psychology,* 1961, *25,* 61–66.

Fleming, M. *The Trail Making Test with industrially injured workers.* Unpublished manuscript, September, 1975.

Fletcher, J. M., Rice, W. J., & Ray, R. M. Linear discriminant function analysis in neuropsychological research: some uses and abuses. *Cortex,* 1978, *14,* 564–577.

Flick, G. L., Edwards, K. R., Rinards, K., & Freund, J. *MMPI performance of patients with organic brain dysfunction.* Paper presented at the meeting of the Southwestern Psychological Association, St. Louis, 1970.

Fogel, M. L. The Gerstmann syndrome and the parietal symptom complex. *Psychological Record,* 1962, *12,* 85–99.

Fogel, M. L. The Proverbs Test in the appraisal of cerebral disease. *Journal of General Psychology,* 1965, *72,* 269–275.

Fogel, M. L. Picture description and interpretation in brain-damaged patients. *Cortex,* 1967, *3,* 433–448.

Foliart, R. H. & Mack, J. L. *The form of recall of prose material in normal and brain damaged subjects.* Paper presented at the seventh annual meeting of the International Neuropsychological Society, New York, February, 1979.

Folstein, M. F., Folstein, S. E., & McHugh, P. R. "Mini-Mental State." *Journal of Psychiatric Research,* 1975, *12,* 189–198.

REFERENCES

Folstein, M. F., Maiberger, R., & McHugh, P. R. Mood disorder as a specific complication of stroke. *Journal of Neurology, Neurosurgery, and Psychiatry*, 1977, *40*, 1018–1020.

Folstein, M. F. & McHugh, P. R. Dementia syndrome of depression. In R. Katzman, R. D. Terry, & K. L. Bick (Eds.), *Alzheimer's disease: senile dementia and related disorders* (*Aging*, Vol. 7). New York: Raven Press, 1978.

Fowler, P. C., Richards, H. C., & Boll, T. J. WAIS factor patterns of epileptic and normal adults. *Journal of Clinical Neuropsychology*, 1980, *2*, 115–123.

Fowler, R. D., Automated interpretation of personality test data. In J. N. Butcher (Ed.), *MMPI: research developments and clinical applications*. New York: McGraw-Hill, 1969.

Fowler, R. S., Jr. A simple non-language test of new learning. *Perceptual and Motor Skills*, 1969, *29*, 895–901.

Fowler, R. S., Jr. & Fordyce, W. E. *Stroke: Why do they behave that way?* Seattle, Washington: Washington State Heart Association, 1974.

Fox, J. H., Kaszniak, A. W., & Huckman, M. Computerized tomographic scanning not very helpful in dementia—nor in cranio-pharyngioma (letter). *New England Journal of Medicine*, 1979, *300*, 437.

Fozard, J. L., Wolf, E., Bell, B., et al. Visual perception and communication. In J. E. Birren & K. W. Schaie (Eds.), *Handbook of the psychology of aging*. New York: Van Nostrand, 1977.

Frank, L. K. Projective methods for the study of personality. *Journal of Psychology*, 1939, *8*, 389–413.

Frankenburg, W. K. & Camp, B. W. (Eds.), *Pediatric screening tests*. Springfield, Ill.: C. C. Thomas, 1975.

Franz, S. I. *Handbook of mental examination methods*. New York: Journal of Nervous and Mental Disease, 1912; Reprint, N.Y.: Johnson Reprint Co., 1970.

Frederiks, J. A. M. Constructional apraxia and cerebral dominance. *Psychiatria, Neurologia, Neurochirurgia*, 1963, *66*, 522–530.

Frederiks, J. A. M. The agnosias. In P. J. Vinken & G. W. Bruyn (Eds.), *Handbook of clinical neurology* (Vol. 4). Amsterdam: North-Holland, 1969a.

Frederiks, J. A. M. Consciousness. In P. J. Vinken & G. W. Bruyn (Eds.), *Handbook of clinical neurology* (Vol. 3). Amsterdam: North-Holland, 1969b.

Frederiks, J. A. M. Disorders of attention in neurological syndrome In P. J. Vinken & G. W. Bruyn (Eds.), *Handbook of clinical neurology* (Vol. 3). Amsterdam: North-Holland, 1969c.

Frederiks, J. A. M. Disorders of body schema. In P. J. Vinken & G. W. Bruyn (Eds.), *Handbook of clinical neurology* (Vol. 4). Amsterdam: North-Holland, 1969d.

Freides, D. On determining footedness. *Cortex*, 1978, *14*, 134–135.

French, J. L. *Manual. Pictorial Test of Intelligence*. New York: Houghton-Mifflin, 1964.

Freund, G. The interaction of chronic alcohol consumption on brain structure and function. *Alcoholism. Clinical and Experimental Research*, 1982, *6*, 13–21.

Fried, I., Mateer, C., Ojemann, G., et al. Organization of visuospatial functions in human cortex. *Brain*, 1982, *105*, 349–371.

Friedman, S. H. *Psychometric effects of frontal and parietal lobe brain damage*. Unpublished doctoral dissertation. Minneapolis: University of Minnesota, 1950.

Fritsch, G. & Hitzig, E. On the electrical excitability of the cerebrum. In K. H. Pribram (Ed.), *Brain and behavior 2. Perception and action*. Baltimore, Penguin Books, 1969.

Fuld, P. A. *Storage, retention, and retrieval in Korsakoff's syndrome*. Paper presented at the third annual meeting of the International Neuropsychological Society, Tampa, Fla., February, 1975.

REFERENCES

Fuld, P. A. *Fuld Object-Memory Evaluation*. New York: Saul R. Korey Department of Neurology, Albert Einstein College of Medicine, 1977; Chicago: Stoelting, no date.

Fuld, P. A. Psychological testing in the differential diagnosis of the dementias. In R. Katzman, R. D. Terry, & K. L. Bick (Eds.), *Alzheimer's disease: senile dementia and related disorders (Aging,* Vol. 7). New York: Raven Press, 1978.

Fuld, P. A. Guaranteed stimulus-processing in the evaluation of memory and learning. *Cortex,* 1980, *16,* 255–272.

Fuld, P. A. Behavioral signs of cholinergic deficiency in Alzheimer dementia. In S. Corkin (Ed.), *Memory and aging.* New York: Raven Press, 1982.

Fuld, P. A. Cognitive changes associated with Alzheimer's dementia. In R. N. Malathesa (Ed.), *Neuropsychology and cognition,* Netherlands: Martinus Nijhoff, 1982.

Fuld, P. A., Katzman, R., Davies, P., & Terry, R. D. Intrusions as a sign of Alzheimer dementia: chemical and pathological verification. *Annals of Neurology,* 1982, *11,* 155–159.

Fuller, G. B. *Minnesota Percepto-Diagnostic Test.* (Rev. Ed.). Brandon, Vt.: Clinical Psychology Publishing Co., 1969.

Fuller, G. B., & Laird, J. T. The Minnesota Percepto-Diagnostic Test. *Journal of Clinical Psychology, Monograph Supplement,* 1963, No. 16.

Fuster, J. M., *The prefrontal cortex.* New York: Raven, 1980.

Gainotti, G. Emotional behavior and hemispheric side of the lesion. *Cortex,* 1972, *8,* 41–55.

Gainotti, G., Caltagirone, C., Masullo, C., & Miceli, G. Patterns of neuropsychologic impairment in various diagnostic groups of dementia. In L. Amaducci, A. N. Davison, & P. Antuono (Eds.), *Aging of the brain and dementia.* New York: Raven Press, 1980.

Gainotti, G., Cianchetti, C., & Tiacci, C. The influence of the hemispheric side of lesion on nonverbal tasks of finger localization. *Cortex,* 1972, *8,* 364–381.

Gainotti, G. & Tiacci, C. Patterns of drawing disability in right and left hemisphere patients. *Neuropsychologia,* 1970, *8,* 379–384.

Galaburda, A. M., LeMay, M., Kemper, T. L., & Geschwind, N. Right-left asymmetries in the brain. *Science,* 1978, *199,* 852–856.

Galin, D. Implications for psychiatry of left and right cerebral specialization. *Archives of General Psychiatry,* 1974, *31,* 572–583.

Gardner, R., Jr., Oliver-Muñoz, S., Fisher, L., & Empting, L. Mattis Dementia Rating Scale: internal reliability study using a diffusely impaired population. *Journal of Clinical Neuropsychology,* 1981, *3,* 271–275.

Gardner, R. W., Jackson, D. N., & Messick, S. J. Personality organization in cognitive controls and intellectual abilities. *Psychological Issues,* 1960, *2,* Monograph 8.

Garron, D. C. & Cheifetz, D. I. Comment on "Bender Gestalt discernment of organic pathology." *Psychological Bulletin,* 1965, 63, 197–200.

Gasparrini, W. G., Satz, P., Heilman, K. M., & Coolidge, F. L. Hemispheric asymmetries of affective processing as determined by the Minnesota Multiphasic Personality Inventory. *Journal of Neurology, Neurosurgery, and Psychiatry,* 1978, *41,* 470–473.

Gasparrini, B., Shealy, C. & Walters, D. Differences in size and spatial placement of drawings of left versus right hemisphere brain-damaged patients. *Journal of Consulting and Clinical Psychology,* 1980, *48,* 670–672.

Gates, A. I. & MacGinitie, W. H. *Gates-MacGinitie Reading Tests.* New York: Teachers College Press, Teachers College, Columbia University, 1965, 1969.

Gazzaniga, M. S. *The bisected brain.* New York: Appleton, 1970.

Gazzaniga, M. S. Determinants of cerebral recovery. In D. G. Stein, J. J. Rosen, & N. Butters (Eds.), *Plasticity of function in the central nervous system.* New York: Academic Press, 1974.

REFERENCES

Gazzaniga, M. S. (Ed.), Handbook of behavioral neurobiology (Vol. 2) *Neuropsychology*. New York: Plenum Press, 1979.

Gazzaniga, M. S. & LeDoux, J. E. *The integrated mind*. New York and London: Plenum Press, 1978.

General Aptitude Test Battery. Washington, D.C.: U.S. Department of Labor, 1965.

Gerstmann, J. Syndrome of finger agnosia, disorientation for right and left, agraphia, and acalculia. *Archives of Neurology and Psychiatry*, 1940, *44*, 398–408.

Gerstmann, J. Problems of imperception of disease and of impaired body territories with organic lesions. *Archives of Neurology and Psychiatry*, 1942, *48*, 890–913.

Gerstmann, J. Some notes on the Gerstmann syndrome. *Neurology*, 1957, 7, 866–869.

Geschwind, N. Disconnexion syndromes in animals and man. *Brain*, 1965, *88*, 237–294.

Geschwind, N. The organization of language and the brain. *Science*, 1970, *170*, 940–944.

Geschwind, N. Language and the brain. *Scientific American*, 1972, *226*, 76–83.

Geschwind, N. The anatomical basis of hemispheric differentiation. In S. J. Dimond & J. G. Beaumont (Eds.), *Hemisphere function in the human brain*. New York: Halsted Press, 1074a.

Geschwind, N. Late change in the nervous system: an overview. In D. G. Stein, J. J. Rosen, & N. Butters (Eds.), *Plasticity and recovery of function in the central nervous system*. New York: Academic Press, 1974b.

Geschwind, N. The apraxias: neural mechanisms of disorders of learned movement. *American Scientist*, 1975, *63*, 188–195.

Geschwind, N. Specializations of the human brain. *Scientific American*, 1979, *241*, 180–199.

Geschwind, N. & Levitsky, W. Human brain: left–right asymmetries in temporal speech region. *Science*, 1968, *161*, 186–187.

Geschwind, N. & Strub, R. Gerstmann syndrome with aphasia: a reply to Poeck and Orgass. *Cortex*, 1975, *11*, 296–298.

Gesell, A. *The first five years of life*. New York: Harper and Row, 1940.

Gesell, A. & Associates. *Gesell Developmental Schedules*. New York: Psychological Corporation, 1949.

Getzels, J. W. & Jackson, P. W. *Creativity and intelligence*. New York: Wiley, 1962.

Ghent, L. Perception of overlapping and embedded figures by children of different ages. *American Journal of Psychology*, 1956, *69*, 575–587.

Ghent, L., Weinstein, S., Semmes, J., & Teuber, H. L. Effect of unilateral brain injury in man on learning of tactual discrimination. *Journal of Comparative and Physiological Psychology*, 1955, *48*, 478–481.

Gilberstadt, G. *Comprehensive MMPI Code Book for males*. Minneapolis, Minn.: MMPI Research Lab., Veterans Administration Hospital, 1970.

Gilbert, J. G. Thirty-five-year follow-up study of intellectual functioning. *Journal of Gerontology*, 1973, *28*, 68–72.

Gilchrist, E. & Wilkinson, M. Some factors determining prognosis in young people with severe head injuries. *Archives of Neurology*, 1979, *36*, 355–359.

Gillis, J. S. The effects of selected antipsychotic drugs on human judgment. *Current Therapeutic Research*, 1977, *21*, 224–232.

Gilmann, S. & Winans, S. (Eds.). *Manter and Gatz's Essentials of clinical neuroanatomy and neurophysiology* (6th ed.). Philadelphia: F. A. Davis, 1982.

Glaser, G. H. Convulsive disorders (epilepsy). In H. H. Merritt, *A textbook of neurology* (5th ed.). Philadelphia: Lea & Fibiger, 1973.

Gloning, I., Gloning, K., & Hoff, H. *Neuropsychological symptoms and syndromes in lesions of the occipital lobe and adjacent areas*. Paris: Gauthier-Villars, 1968.

REFERENCES

Gloning, K. & Hoff, H. Cerebral localization of disorders of higher nervous activity. In P. J. Vinken & G. W. Bruyn (Eds.), *Handbook of clinical neurology* (Vol. 3, *Disorders of higher nervous activity*). New York: Wiley, 1969.

Gloning K. & Quatember, R. Statistical evidence of neuropsychological syndrome in left-handed and ambidextrous patients. *Cortex*, 1966, *2*, 484–488.

Glosser, G., Butters, N., & Kaplan, E. Visuoperceptual processes in brain damaged patients on the digit symbol substitution test. *International Journal of Neuroscience*, 1977, *7*, 59–66.

Glowinski, H. Cognitive deficits in temporal lobe epilepsy. *Journal of Nervous and Mental Disorders*, 1973, *157*, 129–137.

Goebel, R. A. & Satz, P. Profile analysis and the abbreviated Wechsler Adult Intelligence Scale: a multivariate approach. *Journal of Consulting and Clinical Psychology*, 1975, *43*, 780–785.

Goldberg, E. *Motor perserverations and languages of coding visual information.* Paper presented at the third annual meeting of the International Neuropsychological Society, Tampa, Fla., 1975.

Goldberg, E. & Costa, L. D. Hemisphere differences in the acquisition and use of descriptive systems. *Brain and Language*, 1981, *14*, 144–173.

Goldberg, E. & Tucker, D. Motor perseveration and long-term memory for visual forms. *Journal of Clinical Neuropsychology*, 1979, *1*, 273–288.

Goldberg, L. R. The effectiveness of clinicians' judgments: the diagnosis of organic brain disease from the Bender-Gestalt test. *Journal of Consulting Psychologyy*, 1959, *23*, 25–33

Goldberg, T. E. & Smith, A. *Revised criteria for Purdue Pegboard neuropsychodiagnostic applications.* Unpublished manuscript, Neuropsychological Laboratory, University of Michigan Medical School, 1976.

Goldberg, Z., Syndulko, K., Montan, B., et al. *Older adults with subjective memory problems: results of personality and neuropsychological tests.* Paper presented at the meeting of the Western Psychological Association, Los Angeles, April, 1981.

Golden, C. J. Validity of the Halstead-Reitan neuropsychological battery in a mixed psychiatric and brain-injured population. *Journal of Consulting and Clinical Psychology*, 1977, *45*, 1043–1051.

Golden, C. J. In reply to Adams' "In search of Luria's battery: a false start." *Journal of Consulting and Clinical Psychology*, 1980, *48*, 517–521.

Golden, C. J. A standardized version of Luria's neuropsychological tests. In S. Filskov & T. J. Boll (Eds.), *Handbook of clinical neuropsychology*. New York: Wiley-Interscience, 1981.

Golden, C. J., Ariel, R. N., Moses, J. A., Jr., Wilkening, G. N., McKay, S. E., & MacInnes, W. D. Analytic techniques in the interpretation of the Luria-Nebraska Neuropsychological Battery. *Journal of Consulting and Clinical Psychology*, 1982, *50*, 40–48.

Golden, C. J., Hammeke, T. A., & Purisch, A. D. Diagnostic validity of a standardized neuropsychological battery derived from Luria's neuropsychological tests. *Journal of Consulting and Clinical Psychology*, 1978, *46*, 1258–1265.

Golden, C. J., Hammeke, T. A., & Purisch, A. D. *Manual for the Luria-Nebraska Neuropsychological Battery.* Los Angeles: Western Psychological Services, 1980.

Golden, C. J., Kuperman, S. K., MacInnes, W. D. & Moses, J. A. Cross-validation of an abbreviated form of the Halstead Category Test. *Journal of Consulting and Clinical Psychology*, 1981, *49*, 606–607.

Golden, C. J., Sweet, J. J., & Osmon, D. C. The diagnosis of brain-damage by the MMPI: a comprehensive evaluation. *Journal of Personality Assessment*, 1979, *43*, 138–142.

652

Goldfried, M. R., Stricker, G., & Weiner, I. B. *Rorschach handbook of clinical and research applications*. Englewood Cliffs, N.J.: Prentice-Hall, 1971.

Goldman, H., Kleinman, K. M., Snow, M. Y., et al. Correlation of diastolic blood pressure and signs of cognitive dysfunction in essential hypertension. *Diseases of the Nervous System*, 1974, *35*, 571–572.

Goldman, H., Kleinman, K. M., Snow, M. Y., et al. Relationship between essential hypertension and cognitive functioning: Effects of biofeedback. *Psychophysiology*, 1975, *12*, 569–573.

Goldman, M. S. Reversibility of psychological deficits in alcoholics: The interaction of aging with alcohol. In A. Wilkinson (Ed.), *Symposium on cerebral deficits in alcoholism*. Toronto: Addiction Research Foundation, 1982.

Goldstein, G. The use of clinical neuropsychological methods in the lateralization of brain lesions. In S. J. Dimond & J. G. Beaumont (Eds.), *Hemisphere function in the human brain*. New York: Halsted Press, 1974.

Goldstein, G. & Halperin, K. M. Neuropsychological differences among subtypes of schizophrenia. *Journal of Abnormal Psychology*, 1977, *86*, 34–40.

Goldstein, G. & Shelly, C. H. *Age, mental deterioration, and brain damage*. Paper presented at the American Psychological Association Convention, Montreal, Canada, 1973a.

Goldstein, G. & Shelly, C. H. Univariate vs. multivariate analysis in neuropsychological test assessment of lateralized brain damage. *Cortex*, 1973b, *9*, 204–216.

Goldstein, G. & Shelly, C. H. Neuropsychological diagnosis of multiple sclerosis in a neuropsychiatric setting. *Journal of Nervous and Mental Disease*, 1974, *158*, 280–290.

Goldstein, G. & Shelly, C. Neuropsychological investigation of brain lesion in localization in alcoholism. In H. Begleiter (Ed.), *Biological effects of alcohol*. New York: Plenum Press, 1980.

Goldstein, G., Welch, R. B., Rennick, P. M., & Shelly, C. H. The validity of a visual searching task as an indication of general brain disease. *Journal of Consulting and Clinical Psychology*, 1973, *41*, 434–437.

Goldstein, K. H., *The organism*. New York: American Book Co., 1939.

Goldstein, K. H., The mental changes due to frontal lobe damage. *Journal of Psychology*, 1944, *17*, 187–208.

Goldstein, K. H. *Language and language disturbances*. New York: Grune & Stratton, 1948.

Goldstein, K. H. & Scheerer, M. Abstract and concrete behavior; an experimental study with special tests. *Psychological Monographs*, 1941, *53*, No. 2 (Whole No. 239).

Goldstein, K. H. & Scheerer, M. Tests of abstract and concrete behavior. In A. Weider, *Contributions to medical psychology* (Vol. 2). New York: Ronald Press, 1953.

Gollin, E. S. Developmental studies of visual recognition of incomplete objects. *Perceptual and Motor Skills*, 1960, *11*, 289–298.

Golper, L. C. & Binder, L. M. Communicative behaviors in aging and dementia. In J. Darby (Ed.), *Speech evaluation in medicine and psychiatry* (Vol. 2). New York: Grune & Stratton, 1981.

Gonen, J. Y. The use of Wechsler's deterioration quotient in cases of diffuse and symmetrical cerebral atrophy. *Journal of Clinical Psychology*, 1970, *26*, 174–177.

Gonen, J. Y. & Brown, L. Role of vocabulary in deterioration and restitution of mental functioning. *Proceedings of the 76th Annual Convention of the American Psychological Association*, 1968, *3*, 469–470. (Summary)

Gooddy, W. Disorders of the time sense. In P. J. Vinken & G. W. Bruyn (Eds.), *Handbook of clinical neurology* (Vol. 3, *Disorders of higher nervous activity*). New York: Wiley, 1969.

Gooddy, W. & Reinhold, M. The sense of direction and the arrow-form. In E. Halpern (Ed.), *Problems of dynamic neurology*. Jerusalem, Israel: Hebrew University Hadassah Medical School, 1963.

Goodglass, H. *Psychological effects of diffuse vs. focal lesions*. Paper presented at the American Psychological Association Convention, Montreal, August, 1973.

Goodglass, H. Disorders of naming following brain injury. *American Scientist*, 1980, *68*, 647–655.

Goodglass, H. & Kaplan, E. *Assessment of aphasia and related disorders*. Philadelphia: Lea and Febiger, 1972.

Goodglass, H. & Kaplan, E. Assessment of cognitive deficit in the brain-injured patient. In M. S. Gazzaniga (Ed.), *Handbook of behavioral neurobiology* (Vol. 2, *Neuropsychology*). New York: Plenum Press, 1979.

Goodman, L. S. & Gilman, A. *The pharmacological basis of therapeutics* (6th ed.). New York. Macmillan, 1980.

Goodwin, D. W. & Hill, S. Y. Chronic effects of alcohol and other psychoactive drugs on intellect, learning and memory. In J. G. Rankin (Ed.), *Alcohol, drugs and brain damage*. Proceedings of Symposium. Toronto: Addiction Research Foundation, 1975.

Goodwin, J. M., Goodwin, J. S., & Kellner, R. Psychiatric symptoms in disliked medical patients. *Journal of American Medical Association*, 1979, *241*, 1117–1120.

Gordon, H. W. Auditory specialization of the right and left hemispheres. In M. Kinsbourne & W. L. Smith (Eds.), *Hemispheric disconnection and cerebral function*. Springfield, Ill.: C. C. Thomas, 1974.

Gorham, D. R. A Proverbs Test for clinical and experimental use. *Psychological Reports*, 1956, *1*, 1–12.

Gottschaldt, K. Über den Einfluss der Erfahrung auf die Wahrnehmung von Figuren. *Psychologische Forschung*, 1928, *8*, 18–317.

Graham, C. H. Visual form perception. In C. H. Graham (Ed.), *Vision and visual perception*. New York: Wiley, 1965.

Graham, F. K. & Kendall, B. S. Memory-for Designs-Test: revised general manual. *Perceptual and Motor Skills, Monograph Supplement* No, 2--VIII, 1960, *11*, 147–188.

Graham, J. R. *The MMPI: a practical guide*. New York: Oxford University Press, 1977.

Grandjean, E., Munchinger, R., Turrian, V., et al. Investigations into the effects of exposure to trichlorethylene in mechanical engineering. *British Journal of Industrial Medicine*, 1955, *12*, 131–142.

Grant, D. A. & Berg, E. A. A behavioral analysis of degree of reinforcement and ease of shifting to new responses in a Weigl-type card-sorting problem. *Journal of Experimental Psychology*, 1948, *38*, 404–411.

Grant, I., Adams, K. M., Carlin, A. S., et al. Neuropsychological effects of polydrug abuse. In D. R. Wesson, A. S. Carlin, K. M., Adams, & G. Beschner (Eds.), *Polydrug abuse*. New York: Academic Press, 1978a.

Grant, I., Adams, K. M., Carlin, A. E., et al. Organic impairment of poly drug users: risk factors. *American Journal of Psychiatry*, 1978b, *135*, 178–184.

Grant, I., Adams, K. M., & Reed, R. Normal neuropsychological abilities in late thirties alcoholics. *American Journal of Psychiatry*, 1979, *136*, 1263–1269.

Grant, I., Heaton, R. K., McSweeny, A. J., et al. *Neuropsychological findings in hypoxemic chronic obstructive pulmonary disease*. Paper presented at the tenth annual meeting of the International Neuropsychological Society, Pittsburgh, February, 1982.

Green, B. F., Jr. In defense of measurement. *American Psychologist*, 1978, *33*, 664–670.

Green, E. & Boller, F. Features of auditory comprehension in severely impaired aphasics. *Cortex*, 1974, *10*, 133–145.

Green, J. D. The hippocampus. *Physiology Review*, 1964, *44*, 562–608.

Greenberg, F. R. Neurosensory Center Comprehensive Examination for Aphasia (NCCEA) (Review). In F. L. Darley (Ed.), *Evaluation of appraisal techniques in speech and language pathology.* Reading, Mass.: Addison-Wesley, 1979.

Greene, E. & Tager, R. M. The influence of stroke on visual illusion magnitude. *Neurological Research*, 1979, *1*, 169–177.

Gregersen, P., Middelsen, S., Klausen, H., et al. (A chronic cerebral syndrome in painters. Dementia due to inhalation or of cryptogenic origin?) *Ugeskrift for Läeger*, 1978, *140*, 1638–1644.

Gregory, R. J., Paul, J. J., & Morrison, M. W. A short form of the Category Test for adults. *Journal of Clinical Psychology*, 1979, *35*, 795–798.

Greif, E. & Matarazzo, R. *Behavioral approaches to rehabilitation.* New York: Springer, 1982.

Grewel, F. Acalculia. *Brain*, 1952, *75*, 397–407.

Gronwall, D. M. A. Paced auditory serial-addition task: a measure of recovery from concussion. *Perceptual and Motor Skills*, 1977, *44*, 367–373.

Gronwall, D. M. A. *Information processing capacity and memory after closed head injury.* Paper presented at the ninth annual meeting of the International Neuropsychological Society, San Francisco, 1980.

Gronwall, D. M. A. & Sampson, H. *The psychological effects of concussion.* Auckland, N. Z.: Auckland University Press/Oxford University Press, 1974.

Gronwall, D. M. A. & Wrightson, P. Delayed recovery of intellectual function after minor head injury. *Lancet*, 1974, *ii* (7874), 1452.

Gronwall, D. M. A. & Wrightson, P. Duration of post-traumatic amnesia after mild head injury. *Journal of Clinical Neuropsychology*, 1980, *2*, 51–60.

Gronwall, D. & Wrightson, P. Duration of post-traumatic amnesia after mild head injury. *Journal of Clinical Neuropsychology*, 1980, *2*, 51–60.

Gronwall, D. & Wrightson, P. Memory and information processing capacity after closed head injury. *Journal of Neurology, Neurosurgery, and Psychiatry*, 1981, *44*, 889–895.

Grubb, R. L. & Coxe, W. S. Trauma to the central nervous system. In S. G. Eliasson, A. L. Prensky, & W. B. Hardin, Jr. (Eds.), *Neurological pathophysiology.* New York: Oxford University Press, 1978.

Gruenberg, E. M. Epidemiology of senile dementia. In B. S. Schoenberg (Ed.), *Advances in neurology* (Vol. 19). New York: Raven Press, 1978.

Grundvig, J. L., Needham, W. E., & Ajax, E. T. Comparisons of different scoring and administration procedures for the Memory-for-Designs Test. *Journal of Clinical Psychology*, 1970, *26*, 353–357.

Guay, R., McDaniel, E., & Angelo, S. *Analytic factor confounding spatial ability measurement.* Paper presented at the American Psychological Association Convention, Toronto, August, 1978.

Guertin, W. H., Ladd, C. E., Frank, G. H., Rabin, A. I., & Hiester, D. S. Research with the Wechsler Intelligence Scales for Adults: 1960–1965. *Psychological Bulletin*, 1966, *66*, 385–409.

Gur, R. E. Conjugate lateral eye movements as an index of hemispheric deterioration. *Journal of Personal and Social Psychology*, 1975, *31*, 751–757.

Gur, R. E., Levy, J., & Gur, R. C. Clinical studies of brain organization and behavior. In A.

Frazer & A. Winokur (Eds.), *Biological bases of psychiatric disorders*. New York: Spectrum Publications, 1977.

Gurdjian, E. S. Recent developments in biomechanics, management, and mitigation of head injuries. In D. B. Tower (Ed.), *The nervous system. Vol. 2: The clinical neurosciences.* New York: Raven Press, 1975.

Gurdjian, E. S. & Gurdjian, E. S. Acute head injuries. *Surgery, Gynecology, and Obstetrics*, 1978, *146*, 805–820.

Guthrie, A. & Elliot, W. A. The nature and reversibility of cerebral impairment in alcoholism. *Journal of Studies on Alcohol*, 1980, *41*, 147–155.

Haaland, K. Y., Cleeland, C. S., & Carr, D. Motor performance after unilateral hemisphere damage in patients with tumor. *Archives of Neurology*, 1977, *34*, 556–559.

Haaland, K. Y. & Delaney, H. D. Motor deficits after left or right hemisphere damage due to stroke or tumor. *Neurospsychologia*, 1981, *19*, 17–27.

Hachinski, V. C., Iliff, L. D., Zilhka, E., et al. Cerebral blood flow in dementia. *Archives of Neurology*, 1975, *32*, 632–637.

Hain, J. D. *Scoring system for the Bender Gestalt test: preliminary manual.* Unpublished manuscript, 1963.

Hain, J. D. The Bender Gestalt test: a scoring method for identifying brain damage. *Journal of Consulting Psychology*, 1964, *28*, 34–40.

Hakim, A. M. & Mathieson, G. Dementia in Parkinson disease: a neuropathologic study. *Neurology*, 1979, *29*, 1209–1214.

Hall, J. C. Correlation of modified form of Raven's Progressive Matrices (1938) with the Wechsler Adult Intelligence Scale. *Journal of Consulting Psychology*, 1957a, *21*, 23–26.

Hall, J. C. Reliability (internal consistency) of the Wechsler Memory Scale and correlation with the Wechsler-Bellevue Intelligence Scale. *Journal of Consulting Psychology*, 1957b, *21*, 131–135.

Hall, M. M. & Hall, G. C. Antithetical ideational modes of left versus right unilateral hemisphere lesions as demonstrated on the Rorschach. *Proceedings of the 76th Annual Convention of the American Psychological Association*, 1968, *3*, 657–658.

Halstead, W. C. *Brain and intelligence.* Chicago: University of Chicago Press, 1947.

Halstead, W. C. & Wepman, J. M. The Halstead-Wepman aphasia screening test. *Journal of Speech and Hearing Disorders*, 1959, *14*, 9–15.

Hammeke, T. A., Golden, C. J., & Purisch, A. D. A standardized, short and comprehensive neuropsychological test battery based on the Luria neuropsychological evaluation. *International Journal of Neuroscience*, 1978, *8*, 135–141.

Hammond, G. R. Hemispheric differences in temporal resolution. *Brain and Cognition*, 1982, *1*, 95–118.

Hamsher, K. deS. & Benton, A. L. Interactive effects of age and cerebral disease on cognitive performances. *Journal of Neurology*, 1978, *217*, 195–200.

Hamsher, K. deS., Benton, A. L., & Digre, K. Serial digit learning: normative and clinical aspects. *Journal of Clinical Neuropsychology*, 1980, *2*, 39–50.

Hamsher, K. deS., Levin, H. S., & Benton, A. L. Facial recognition in patients with focal brain lesions. *Archives of Neurology*, 1979, *36*, 837–839.

Hane, M., Axelson, O., Blume, J., et al. Psychological function changes among house painters. *Scandinavian Journal of Work and Environmental Health*, 1977, *3*, 91–99.

Hanfmann, E. Concept Formation Test. In A. Weider (Ed.), *Contributions toward medical psychology.* New York: Ronald Press, 1953.

Hannay, H. J. Real or imagined incomplete lateralization of function in females? *Perception and Psychophysics*, 1976, *19*, 349–352.

Hansch, E. C. & Pirozzola, F. J. Task relevant effects on the assessment of cerebral specialization for facial emotion. *Brain and Language*, 1980, *10*, 51–59.

Hansch, E. C., Syndulko, K., Pirozzolo, F. J., et al. Electrophysiological measurement in aging and in death. In G. J. Maletta & F. J. Pirozzolo (Eds.), *The aging nervous system*. New York: Praeger Publishers, 1980.

Harasymiw, S. J. & Halper, A. Sex, age, and aphasia type. *Brain and Language*, 1981, *12*, 190–198.

Hardy, C. H., Rand, G., & Rittler, J. M. C. *H-R-R Pseudoisochromatic Plates*. Buffalo, New York: American Optical Co., 1955.

Hardyck, C. & Petrinovich, L. F. Left-handedness. *Psychological Bulletin*, 1977, *84*, 385–404.

Härkönen, H., Lindström, K., Seppäläinen, A. M., et al. Exposure-response relationship between styrene exposure and central nervous functions. *Scandinavian Journal of Work and Environmental Health*, 1978, *4*, 53–59.

Harley, J. P., Leuthold, C. A., Matthews, C. G., & Borge, I. F. *Wisconsin Neuropsychological Test Battery T-score norms for older Veterans Administration Medical Center patients.* Madison, Wis.: C. G. Matthews, May, 1980.

Harper, C. The neuropathology of blunt head injury. In G. A. Broe & R. L. Tate (Eds.), *Brain impairment. Proceedings of the Fifth Annual Brain Impairment Conference.* Sydney: Postgraduate Committee in Medicine of The University of Sydney, 1982.

Harris, A. J. *Harris Tests of Lateral Dominance. Manual of directions for administration and interpretation* (3rd ed.). New York: Psychological Corporation, 1958.

Harris, D. B. *Childrens drawings as measures of intellectual maturity.* New York: Harcourt Brace, 1963.

Harris, G. W., Michael, R. R., & Scott, P. Neurological site of action of stilbesterol in eliciting sexual behavior. In K. H. Pribram (Ed.), *Brain and behavior* (Vol. 1, *Mood, states and mind*). Baltimore: Penguin Books, 1969.

Harris, L. J. Sex differences in spatial ability: Possible environmental, genetic, and neurological factors. In M. Kinsbourne (Ed.), *Asymmetrical function of the brain*. Cambridge, England: Cambridge University Press, 1978.

Harrison, D. M. & Chagnon, J. G. The effect of age, sex, and language on the Minnesota Percepto-Diagnostic Test. *Journal of Clinical Psychology*, 1966, *22*, 302–303.

Harrison, M. J. G., Thomas, G. H., DuBoulay, G. H., & Marshall, J. Multi-infarct dementia. *Journal of Neurological Sciences*, 1979, *40*, 97–103.

Harrower, M. Differential diagnosis. In B. B. Wolman (Ed.), *Handbook of clinical psychology*. New York: McGraw-Hill, 1965.

Harrower-Erickson, M. R. Personality changes accompanying cerebral lesions. *Archives of Neurology and Psychiatry*, 1940, *43*, 859–890.

Hartlage, L. *Anticonvulsant medication as a determinant of neuropsychological test profiles.* Paper presented at the ninth annual meeting of the International Neuropsychological Society, Atlanta, February, 1981.

Harvey, M. T. & Crovitz, H. F. Television questionnaire techniques in assessing forgetting in long-term memory. *Cortex*, 1979, *15*, 609–618.

Hathaway, S. R. & McKinley, J. C. *The Minnesota Multiphasic Personality Inventory Manual* (Revised). New York: Psychological Corporation, 1951.

Hayslip, B., Jr. & Kennelly, K. J. *Short-term memory and crystallized-fluid intelligence in adulthood.* Paper presented at the American Psychological Association Convention, Montreal, Canada, September, 1980.

657

Hayslip, B., Jr. & Sterns, H. L. Age differences in relationships between crystallized and fluid intelligences and problem solving. *Journal of Gerontology*, 1979, *34*, 404–414.

Healey, J. M., Rosen, J. J., Gerstman, L., et al. *Differential effect of familial sinistrality on the cognitive abilities of males and females.* Paper presented at the tenth annual meeting of the International Neuropsychological Society, Pittsburgh, 1982.

Heath, H. A. & Orbach, J. Reversibility of the Necker cube: IV. Responses of elderly people. *Perceptual and Motor Skills*, 1963, *17*, 625–626.

Heaton, R. K., Baade, L. E., & Johnson, K. L. Neuropsychological test results associated with psychiatric disorders in adults. *Psychological Bulletin*, 1978, *85*, 141–162.

Heaton, R. K., Chelune, G. J., & Lehman, R. A. W. *Relation of neuropsychological and personality test results to patients' complaints of disability.* Unpublished manuscript. University of Colorado Health Sciences Center, 1981.

Heaton, R. K. & Crowley, T. J. Effects of psychiatric disorders and their somatic treatments on neuropsychological test results. In S. B. Filskov & T. J. Boll (Eds.), *Handbook of clinical neuropsychology.* New York: Wiley, 1981.

Heaton, R. K., Grant, I., Anthony, W. Z., & Lehman, R. A. W. A comparison of clinical and automated interpretations of the Halstead-Reitan Battery. *Journal of Clinical Neuropsychology*, 1981, *3*, 121–141.

Heaton, R. K. & Pendleton, M. G. Use of neuropsychological tests to predict adult patients' everyday functioning. *Journal of Consulting and Clinical Psychology*, 1981, *49*, 807–821.

Heaton, R. K., Smith, H. H., Jr., Lehman, R. A. W., & Vogt, A. T. Prospects for faking believable deficits on neuropsychological testing. *Journal of Consulting and Clinical Psychology*, 1978, *46*, 892–900.

Heaton, S. R. & Heaton, R. K. Testing the impaired patient. In S. B. Filskov & T. J. Boll (Eds.), *Handbook of clinical neuropsychology.* New York: Wiley-Interscience, 1981.

Hebb, D. O. The effect of early and late brain injury upon test scores, and the nature of normal adult intelligence. *Proceedings of the American Philosophical Society*, 1942, *85*, 275–292.

Hebb, D. O. *Organization of behavior.* New York: Wiley, 1949.

Hebb, D. O. & Morton, N. W. The McGill Adult Comprehension Examination: "Verbal Situation" & "Picture Anomaly" series. *Journal of Educational Psychology*, 1943, *34*, 16–25.

Hécaen, H. Clinical symptomatology in right and left hemisphere lesions. In V. B. Mountcastle (Ed.), *Interhemispheric relations and cerebral dominance in man.* Baltimore: John Hopkins University Press, 1962.

Hécaen, H. Mental symptoms associated with tumors of the frontal lobe. *The frontal granular cortex and behavior.* New York: McGraw-Hill, 1964.

Hécaen, H. Cerebral localization of mental functions and their disorders. In P. J. Vinken & G. W. Bruyn (Eds.), *Handbook of clinical neurology* (Vol. 3, *Disorders of higher nervous activity*). New York: Wiley, 1969.

Hécaen, H. Right hemisphere contribution to language functions. In P. A. Buser & A. Rougeul-Buser (Eds.), *Cerebral correlates of conscious experience. INSERM Symposium No. 6.* New York: Elsevier/North-Holland Biomedical Press, 1978.

Hécaen, H. Aphasia. In M. S. Gazzaniga (Ed.), *Handbook of behavioral neurobiology. Vol. 2. Neuropsychology.* New York: Plenum Press, 1979.

Hécaen, H. Apraxia. In S. B. Filskov & T. J. Boll (Ed.), *Handbook of clinical neuropsychology.* New York: Wiley-Interscience, 1981.

Hécaen, H. & Ajuriaguerra, J. de. *Left-handedness.* New York: Grune & Stratton, 1964.

Hécaen, H., Ajuriaguerra, J. de, & Massonnet, J. Les troubles visuo-constructifs par lesion pariéto-occipitale droite. *L'Encéphale*, 1951, *40*, 122–179.

REFERENCES

Hécaen, H. & Albert, M. L. Disorders of mental functioning related to frontal lobe pathology. In D. F. Benson & D. Blumer, *Psychiatric aspects of neurologic disease*. New York: Grune & Stratton, 1975.

Hécaen, H. & Albert, M. L. *Human neuropsychology*. New York: John Wiley & Sons, 1978.

Hécaen, H. & Angelergues, R. *La cécité psychique*. Paris: Masson et Cie., 1963.

Hécaen, H. & Assal, G. A comparison of constructive deficits following right and left hemispheric lesions. *Neuropsychologia*, 1970, *8*, 289-303.

Heilman, K. M. Apraxia. In K. M. Heilman & E. Valenstein (Eds.), *Clinical neuropsychology*. New York: Oxford University Press, 1979.

Heilman, K. M., Scholes, R., & Watson, R. T. Auditory affective agnosia. *Journal of Neurology, Neurosurgery, and Psychiatry*, 1975, *38*, 69-72.

Heilman, K. M. & Valenstein, E. Frontal lobe neglect in man. *Neurology*, 1972, *22*, 660-664.

Heilman, K. M. & Valenstein, E. (Eds.), *Clinical neuropsychology*. New York: Oxford University Press, 1979.

Heilman, K. M. & Van Den Abell, T. Right hemispheric dominance for mediating cerebral activation. *Neuropsychologia*, 1979, *17*, 315-321.

Heilman, K. M. & Van Den Abell, T. Right hemisphere dominance for attention: the mechanism underlying hemispheric asymmetries of inattention (neglect). *Neurology*, 1980, *30*, 327-330.

Heimburger, R. F. & Reitan, R. M. Easily administered written test for lateralizing brain lesions. *Journal of Neurosurgery*, 1961, *18*, 301-312.

Heiskanen, O. & Sipponen, P. Prognosis of severe brain injury. *Acta Neurologica Scandinavica*, 1970, *46*, 343-348.

Helmes, E., Holden, R. R., & Howe, M. G. An attempt at validation of the Minnesota Percepto-Diagnostic Test in a psychiatric setting. *Journal of Clinical Neuropsychology*, 1980, *2*, 231-236.

Henry, G. M., Weingartner, H., & Murphy, D. L. Influence of affective states and psychoactive drugs on verbal learning and memory. *American Journal of Psychiatry*. 1973, *130*, 966-971.

Henry, W. E. The Thematic Apperception Technique in the study of cultural personal relations. *Genetic Psychology Monographs*, 1974, *35*, 3-135.

Herbst, L. & Petersen, A. *Timing of maturation, brain lateralization and cognitive performance*. Paper presented at the American Psychological Association Convention, Montreal, September, 1980.

Herrmann, D. J. Know they memory: the use of questionnaires to assess and study memory. *Psychological Bulletin*, 1982, *92*, 434-462.

Herrmann, D. J. & Neisser, U. An inventory of everyday memory experiences. In M. M. Gruneberg, P. E. Morris, & R. N. Sykes (Eds.), *Practical aspects of memory*. New York: Academic Press, 1978.

Heston, L. L., Mastri, A. R., Anderson, E., & White, J. Dementia of the Alzheimer type. *Archives of General Psychiatry*, 1981, *38*, 1085-1090.

Hetherington, R. A neologism learning test. *British Journal of Psychiatry*, 1967, *113*, 1133-1137.

Hewson, L. The Wechsler-Bellevue Scale and the Substitution test as aids in neuropsychiatric diagnosis. *Journal of Nervous and Mental Disease*, 1949, *109*, (Part 1), 158-183; (Part 2), 246-266.

Hicks, L. H. & Birren, J. E. Aging, brain damage, and psychomotor slowing. *Psychological Bulletin*, 1970, *74*, 377-396.

Hicks, R. E. & Kinsbourne, M. Human handedness. In M. Kinsbourne (Ed.), *Asymmetrical function of the brain*. Cambridge: Cambridge University Press, 1978.

Hierons, R., Janota, I., & Corsellis, J. A. N. The late effects of necrotizing encephalitis of the temporal lobes and limbic areas: a clinico-pathological study of 10 cases. *Psychological Medicine*, 1978, *8*, 21–42.

Hilbert, N. M., Niederehe, G., & Kahn, R. L. Accuracy and speed of memory in depressed and organic aged. *Educational Gerontology*, 1976, *1*, 131–146.

Hillbom, E. After-effects of brain injuries. *Acta Psychiatrica et Neurologica Scandinavica* 1960, *35*, Suppl. 142.

Hines, T. M. & Posner, M. I. *Slow but sure: a chronometric analysis of the process of aging.* Department of Psychology, University of Oregon, Eugene, Oregon. Unpublished manuscript, undated.

Hirschenfang, S. A comparison of Bender Gestalt reproductions of right and left hemiplegic patients. *Journal of Clinical Psychology*, 1960a, *16*, 439.

Hirschenfang, S. A comparison of WAIS scores of hemiplegic patients with and without aphasia. *Journal of Clinical Psychology*, 1960b, *16*, 351.

Hirschenfang, S., Silber, M., & Benton, J. G. Psychosocial factors influencing the rehabilitation of the hemiplegic patient. *Disorders of the Nervous System*, 1968, *29*, 373–379.

Hirst, W. The amnesic syndrome: description and explanation. *Psychological Bulletin*, 1982, *91*, 435–460.

Hochla, N. A. N. & Parsons, O. A. Premature aging in female alcoholics. A neuropsychological study. *Journal of Nervous and Mental Disease*, 1982, *170*, 241–245.

Holland, A. L. *Communicative Abilities in Daily Living. A test of functional communication for aphasic adults*. Baltimore: University Park Press, 1980.

Holmes, J. S. Acute psychiatric patient performance on the WAIS. *Journal of Clinical Psychology*, 1968, *24*, 87–91.

Holroyd, R. G. A profile sheet to facilitate administration of the Vineland Social Maturity Scale. *Journal of Clinical Psychology*, 1966, *22*, 197–199.

Hooper, H. E. *The Hooper Visual Organization Test. Manual*. Los Angeles: Western Psychological Services, 1958.

Horan, M., Ashton, R., & Minto, J. Using ECT to study hemispheric specialization for sequential processes. *British Journal of Psychiatry*, 1980, *137*, 119–125.

Horenstein, S. Effects of cerebrovascular disease on personality and emotionality. Presentation 17. In A. L. Benton (Ed.), *Behavioral change in cerebrovascular disease*. New York: Harper & Row, 1970.

Horenstein, S. The clinical use of psychological testing in dementia. In C. E. Wells (Ed.), *Dementia* (2nd ed.). Philadelphia: F. A. Davis, 1977.

Horn, J. L. *Statistical weaknesses of a unitary construct of intelligence*. Paper presented at the American Psychological Association Convention, New York City, September, 1979.

Horn, J. L. & Donaldson, G. On the myth of intellectual decline in adulthood. *American Psychologist*, 1976, *31*, 701–719.

Horne, D. J. de L. Sensorimotor control in Parkinsonism. *Journal of Neurology, Neurosurgery, and Psychiatry*, 1973, *36*, 742–746.

Horowitz, M. J. & Cohen, F. M. Temporal lobe epilepsy: effect of lobectomy on psychosocial functioning. *Epilepsia*, 1968, *9*, 23–41.

Horowitz, M. J., Cohen, F. M., Skolnikoff, A. Z., & Saunders, F. A. Psychomotor epilepsy: rehabilitation after surgical treatment. *Journal of Nervous and Mental Disease*, 1970, *150*, 273–290.

Horvath, T. B. Clinical spectrum and epidemiological features of alcoholic dementia. In J. G.

Rankin (Ed.), *Alcohol, drugs, and brain damage*. Proceedings of Symposium. Toronto: Addiction Research Foundation, 1975.

Houlard, N., Fraisse, P., & Hécaen, H. Effects of unilateral hemispheric lesions on two types of optico-geometric illusions. *Coretx*, 1976, *12*, 232–239.

Hovey, H. B. Brain lesions and five MMPI items. *Journal of Consulting Psychology*, 1964, *28*, 78–79.

Hovey, H. B. & Kooi, K. A. Transient disturbances of thought processes and epilepsy. *A. M. A. Archives of Neurology and Psychiatry*, 1955, 74, 287–291.

Hovey, H. B., Kooi, K. A., & Thomas, M. H. MMPI profiles of epileptics. *Journal of Consulting Psychology*, 1959, *23*, 155–159.

Howieson, D. B. *Confabulation*. Paper presented at the meeting of the North Pacific Society of Neurology and Psychiatry, Bend, Oregon, March, 1980.

Howieson, D., Golper, L. A., Rau, M. T., & Christensen, A. -L. *A study of facial recognition in a patient with visual object agnosia*. Paper presented at the ninth annual meeting of the International Neuropsychological Society, Atlanta, February, 1981.

Hoyle, M. & Haaland, K. Y. The case for collaboration between the speech pathologist and the neuropsychologist. *Proceedings of the Clinical Aphasiology Conference*, Amalia Island, Florida, May, 1977.

Hsia, Y. & Graham, C. H. Color blindness. In C. H. Graham (Ed.), *Vision and visual perception*. New York: Wiley, 1965.

Hubel, D. H. The brain. *Scientific American*, 1979, *241*, 45–53.

Hubel, D. H. & Wiesel, T. N. Brain mechanisms of vision. *Scientific American*, 1979, *241*, 150–162.

Hughes, R. M. Rorschach signs for the diagnosis of organic pathology. *Rorschach Research Exchange and Journal of Projective Techniques*, 1948, *12*, 165–167.

Hulicka, I. M. Age differences in Wechsler Memory Scale scores. *Journal of Genetic Psychology*, 1966, *109*, 135–145.

Hulicka, I. M. & Wheeler, D. *Recall scores of old and young people as a function of registration intervals*. Paper presented at the American Psychological Association Convention, Chicago, September, 1975.

Humphrey, M. E. Consistency of hand usage: a preliminary inquiry. *British Journal of Psychology*, 1951, *21*, 214–224.

Humphrey, M. E. & Zangwill, O. L. Dysphasia in left-handed patients with unilateral brain lesions. *Journal of Neurology, Neurosurgery, and Psychiatry*, 1952, *15*, 184–193.

Hunt, H. F. A practical clinical test for organic brain damage. *Journal of Applied Psychology*, 1943, *27*, 375–386.

Hunt, W. L. The relative rates of decline of Wechsler-Bellevue "hold" and "don't hold" tests. *Journal of Consulting Psychology*, 1949, *13*, 440–443.

Huppert, F. A. & Piercy, M. Recognition memory in amnesic patients: effect of temporal context and familiarity of material. *Cortex*, 1976, *12*, 3–20.

Hutchinson, E. C. & Acheson, E. J. *Strokes. Natural history, pathology, and surgical treatment*. Philadelphia: W. B. Saunders, 1975.

Hutt, M. L. The Hutt adaptation of the Bender-Gestalt test (3rd ed.). New York: Grune & Stratton, 1977.

Hutt, M. L. and Gibby, R. G. *An atlas for the Hutt adaptation of the Bender-Gestalt test*. New York: Grune & Stratton, 1970.

Hutton, J. T. *Clinical nosology of the dementing illnesses*. In G. J. Maletta & F. J. Pirozzolo (Eds), New York: Praeger, 1980.

REFERENCES

Hydén, H. The question of a molecular basis for the memory trace. In K. H. Pribram & D. E. Broadbent (Eds.), *Biology of memory*. New York: Academic Press, 1970.

Ingham, J. G. Memory and intelligence. *British Journal of Psychiatry*, 1952, *43*, 20–32.

Inglis, J. An experimental study of learning and "memory function" in elderly psychiatric elders. *Journal of Mental Science*, 1957, *103*, 796–803.

Institute of Rehabilitation Medicine. *Rehabilitation Monograph No. 61. Working approaches to remediation of cognitive deficits in brain-damaged persons*. New York: New York University Medical Center, May, 1980.

Institute of Rehabilitation Medicine. *Rehabilitation Monograph No. 62. Working approaches to remediation of cognitive deficits in brain-damaged persons*. New York: New York University Medical Center, May, 1981.

Institute of Rehabilitation Medicine. *Rehabilitation Monograph No. 63. Working approaches to remediation of cognitive deficits in brain-damaged persons*. New York: New York University Medical Center, May, 1982.

Irigaray, L. *Le langage des dements*. The Hague: Mouton, 1973.

Irving, G. Psychometric assessment in a geriatric unit. In G. Stöcker, R. A. Kuhn, P. Hall, et al. (Eds.), *Assessment in cerebrovascular insufficiency*. Stuttgart: Georg Thieme Verlag, 1971.

Isaacs, B. & Kennie, A. T. The Set Test as an aid to the detection of dementia in old people. *British Journal of Psychiatry*, 1973, *123*, 467–470.

Iscoe, I. A profile for the Vineland Scale and some clinical applications. *Journal of Clinical Psychology*, 1960, *16*, 14–16.

Ishihara, S. *Tests for color-blindness* (11th ed.). Tokyo: Kanehara Shuppan, 1964.

Ivison, D. J. The Wechsler Memory Scale: preliminary findings toward an Australian standardization. *Australian Psychologist*, 1977, *12*, 303–312.

Ivnik, R. J. Neuropsychological stability in multiple sclerosis. *Journal of Consulting and Clinical Psychology*, 1978, *46*, 913–923.

Jacobs, L., Kinkel, W. R., & Heffner, R. R. Autopsy correlations of computerized tomography: experience with 6,000 CT scans. *Neurology*, 1976, *26*, 1111–1118.

James, W. E., Mefferd, R. B., & Kimbell, I., Jr. Early signs of Huntington's chorea. *Diseases of the Nervous System*, 1969, *30*, 556–559.

Jarvie, H. Problem solving deficits following wounds of the brain. *Journal of Mental Science*, 1960, *106*, 1377–1382.

Jarvik, L. F. Thoughts on the psychobiology of aging. *American Psychologist*, 1975, *30*, 576–583.

Jarvik, L. F & Blum, J. E. Cognitive decline as predictors of mortality in twin pairs: a 20-year longitudinal study of aging. In E. Palmore & F. C. Jeffers (Eds.), *Prediction of life span*. New York: D. C. Heath, 1971.

Jastak, J. F. A rigorous criterion of feeblemindedness. *Journal of Abnormal and Social Psychology*, 1949, *44*, 367–378.

Jastak, J. F. & Jastak, S. R. Short forms of the WAIS and WISC Vocabulary subtests. *Journal of Clinical Psychology* (Special Monograph Supplement), 1964, *20*, 167–199.

Jastak, J. F. & Jastak, S. R. *The Wide Range Achievement Test Manual*. Wilmington, Delaware: Guidance Associates, 1965; Chicago: Stoelting, no date.

Jefferson, J. W. Subtle neuropsychiatric sequelae of carbon monoxide intoxication. *American Journal of Psychiatry*, 1976, *133*, 961–964.

Jennett, B. Some aspects of prognosis after severe head injury. *Scandinavian Journal of Rehabilitation Medicine*, 1972, *4*, 16–20.

Jennett, B. Scale, scope and philosophy of the clinical problem. In Ciba Foundation Symposium, No. 34 (New Series). *Symposium on the outcome of severe damage to the central nervous system*. Amsterdam: Elsevier, Excerpta Medica, 1975.

Jennett, B. & Bond, M. Assessment of outcome after severe brain damage. A practical scale. *Lancet*, 1975, *i*, 480–484.

Jennett, B. & Teasdale, G. *Management of head injuries*. Philadelphia: F. A. Davis, 1981.

Jennett, B., Teasdale, G., & Knill-Jones, R. Prognosis after severe head injury. Ciba Foundation Symposium, No. 34 (New Series). *Symposium on the outcome of severe damage to the CNS*. Amsterdam: Elsevier, Excerpta Medica, 1975.

Jensen, A. R. The current status of the IQ controversy. *Australian Psychologist*, 1978, *13*, 7–27.

Jernigan, T., Zatz, I. M., Feinberg, K., & Fein, G. Measurement of cerebral atrophy in the aged. In L. W. Poon (Ed.), *Aging in the 1980's. Psychological Issues*. Washington, D.C.: American Psychological Association, 1980.

Jernigan, T. R., Zatz. L. M., Pfefferbaum, A., et al. CT abnormalities and cognitive deficits in alcoholic and non-alcoholic dementia. *Psychiatry Research*, in press.

John, E. R., Karmel, B. Z., Corning, W. C., et al. Neurometrics. *Science*, 1977, *196*, 1393–1410.

Johnstone, E. C., Crow, T. J., & Frith, C. D. Cerebral ventricular size and cognitive impairment in chronic schizophrenics. *Lancet*, 1976, *ii*, 924–926.

Johnstone, E. C., Crow, T. J., Frith, C. D., et al. The dementia of dementia praecox. *Acta Psychiatrica Scandinavica*, 1978, *57*, 305–324.

Jones, B. M. & Jones, M. K. Alcohol and memory impairment in male and female social drinkers. In I. M. Birnbaum & E. S. Parker (Eds.), *Alcohol and human memory*. Hillsdale, N.J.: Lawrence Erlbaum Associates, 1977.

Jones-Gotman, M. & Milner, B., Design fluency: the invention of nonsense drawings after focal cortical lesions. *Neuropsychologia*, 1977, *15*, 653–674.

Jones-Gotman, M. & Milner, B. Right temporal lobe contribution to image-mediated verbal learning. *Neuropsychologia*, 1978, *16*, 61–71.

Jonsson, C.-O., Cronholm, B., & Izikowitz, S. Intellectual changes in alcoholics. *Quarterly Journal of Studies on Alcoholism*, 1962, *23*, 221–242.

Jordan, E. J., Jr. MMPI profiles of epileptics. *Journal of Counsulting Psychology*, 1963, *27*, 267–269.

Jortner, S. A test of Hovey's MMPI Scale for CNS Disorders. *Journal of Clinical Psychology*, 1965, *21*, 285.

Josiassen, R. C., Curry, L., Roemer, R. A., et al. Patterns of intellectual deficit in Huntington's disease. *Journal of Clinical Neuropsychology*, 1982, *4*, 173–183.

Joslyn, D. & Hutzell, R. R. Temporal disorientation in schizophrenic and brain-damaged patients. *American Journal of Psychiatry*, 1979, *136*, 1220–1222.

Joynt, R. J. Language disturbances in cerebrovascular disease. Presentation 5. In A. L. Benton (Ed.), *Behavioral change in cerebrovascular disease*. New York: Harper & Row, 1970.

Joynt, R. J. Human memory. In D. B. Tower & T. N. Chase (Eds.), *The nervous system* (Vol. 2. *The clinical neurosciences*). New York: Raven Press, 1975.

Joynt, R. J., Benton, A. L., & Fogel, M. L. Behavioral and pathological correlates of motor impersistence. *Neurology*, 1962, *12*, 876–881.

Joynt, R. J. & Goldstein, M. N. Minor cerebral hemisphere. In W. J. Friedlander (Ed.), *Advances in neurology* (Vol. 7). New York: Raven Press, 1975.

Joynt, R. J. & Shoulson, I. Dementia. In K. M. Heilman & E. Valenstein (Eds.), *Clinical neuropsychology*. New York: Oxford University Press, 1979.

663

REFERENCES

Judd, L. L. & Grant, I. Brain dysfunction in chronic sedative users. *Journal of Psychedelic Drugs*, 1975, *7*, 143–149.

Judd, L. L., Hubbard, B., Janowsky, D. S., et al. The effect of lithium carbonate on the cognitive functions of normal subjects. *Archives of General Psychiatry*, 1977, *34*, 335–357.

Jurko, M. F. *The mechanics of head injury and some behavioral, psychological, and EEG test findings.* Paper presented at the seventh annual meeting of the International Neuropsychological Society, New York City, 1979.

Jurko, M. F. & Andy, O. J. Verbal learning dysfunction with combined centre median, and amygdala lesions. *Journal of Neurology, Neurosurgery, and Psychiatry*, 1977, *40*, 695–698.

Kahana, B. The use of projective techniques in personality assessment of the aged. In M. Storandt, I. Siegler, & M. Ellis (Eds.), *The clinical psychology of aging.* New York: Plenum Press, 1978.

Kahn, R. L., Goldfarb, A. L., Pollack, M., & Peck, A. Brief objective measures for the determination of mental status in the aged. *American Journal of Psychiatry*, 1960–61, *117*, 326–328.

Kahn, R. L. & Miller, N. E. Assessment of altered brain function in the aged. In M. Storandt, I. Siegler, & M. Ellis (eds.), *The clinical psychology of aging.* New York: Plenum Press, 1978.

Kahn, R. L., Zarit, S. H., Hilbert, N. M., & Niederehe, G. Memory complaint and impairment in the aged. *Archives of General Psychiatry*, 1975, *32*, 1569–1573.

Kalant, H. Direct effects of ethanol on the nervous system. *Proceedings of the American Societies for Experimental Biology*, 1975, *34*, 1930–1941.

Kane, R. L., Sweet, J. J., Golden, C. J., Parsons, O. A., & Moses, J. A., Jr. Comparative diagnostic accuracy of the Halstead-Reitan and Standardized Luria-Nebraska Neuropsychological Batteries in a mixed psychiatric and brain-damaged population. *Journal of Consulting and Clinical Psychology*, 1981, *49*, 484–485.

Kaplan, E. F., Goodglass, H., & Weintraub, S. *The Boston Naming Test.* Boston: E. Kaplan & H. Goodglass, 1978.

Kaplan, J. & Waltz, J. R. *The trial of Jack Ruby.* New York: Macmillan, 1965.

Kaplan, R. & Tsaros, L. *Is psychological deficit in multiple sclerosis related to neurological and functional disability?* Paper presented at the seventh annual meeting of the International Neuropsychological Society, New York City, 1979.

Kapur, N. & Butters, N. Visuoperceptive deficits in long-term alcoholics and alcoholics with Korsakoff's psychosis. *Journal of Studies on Alcohol*, 1977, *38*, 2025–2035.

Kaszniak, A. W., Fox, J., Gandell, D. L., Garron, D. C., Huckman, M. S., & Ramsey, R. S. Predictors of mortality in presenile and senile dementia. *Annals of Neurology*, 1978, *3*, 236–252.

Kaszniak, A. W., Garron, D. C., Fox, J. H., et al. Cerebral atrophy, EEG slowing, age, education, and cognitive functioning in suspected dementia. *Neurology*, 1979a, *29*, 1273–1279.

Kaszniak, A. W., Garron, D. C., & Fox, J. Differential effects of age and cerebral atrophy upon span of immediate recall and paired-associate learning in older patients suspected of dementia. *Cortex*, 1979b, *15*, 285–295.

Kaszniak, A. W., Wilson, R. S., Lazarus, L., et al. *Memory and depression in dementia.* Paper presented at the ninth annual meeting of the International Neuropsychological Society, Atlanta, 1981.

Katz, M. M. & Lyerly, S. B. Methods for measuring adjustment and social behavior in the community: I. Rationale, description, discriminative validity and scale development. *Psychological Reports*, 1963, *13*, 503–535.

Kaufman, A. The substitution test: a survey of studies on organic mental impairment and the role of learning and motor factors in test performance. *Cortex*, 1968, *4*, 47–63.

Kear-Colwell, J. J. The structure of the Wechsler Memory Scale and its relationship to brain damage. *Journal of Social and Clinical Psychology*, 1973, *12*, 384–392.

Keenan, J. S. & Brassell, E. G. *Aphasia Language Performance Scales (ALPS). Manual.* Murfreesboro, Tenn.: Pinnacle Press, 1975.

Kellogg, C. E. & Morton, N. W. *Revised Beta Examination.* New York: Psychological Corporation, 1935.

Kelly, M. P., Kaszniak, A. W., & Garron, D. C. *Neuropsychological test performance in carotid disease and Alzheimer disease.* Paper presented at the eight annual meeting of the International Neuropsychological Society, San Francisco, February, 1980.

Kempinsky, W. H. Experimental study of distant effects of acute focal brain injury. *A.M.A. Archives of Neurology and Psychiatry*, 1958, *79*, 376–389.

Kendall, B. S. Orientation errors in the Memory-for-Designs Test: tentative findings and recommendations. *Perceptual and Motor Skills*, 1966, *22*, 335–345.

Kertesz, A. *Aphasia and associated disorders.* New York: Grune & Stratton, 1979.

Kertesz, A. & Dobrowolski, S. Right-hemisphere deficits, lesion size and location. *Journal of Clinical Neuropsychology*, 1981, *3*, 283–299.

Kertesz, A. & McCabe, P. Recovery patterns and prognosis in aphasia. *Brain*, 1977, *100*, 1–18.

Kertesz, A. & Poole, E. The aphasia quotient: the taxonomic approach to measurement of aphasic disability. *Canadian Journal of Neurosciences*, 1974, *1*, 7–16.

Kessler, I. I. Parkinson's disease in epidemiologic perspective. In B. S. Schoenberg (Ed.), *Advances in neurology* (Vol. 19). New York: Raven Press, 1978.

Khantzian, E. J. & McKenna, G. J. Acute toxic and withdrawal reactions associated with drug use and abuse. *Annals of Internal Medicine*, 1979, *90*, 361–372.

Kiernan, R. & Matthews, C. G. Impairment index versus *T*-score averaging in neuropsychological assessment. *Journal of Consulting and Clinical Psychology*, 1976, *44*, 951–957.

Kimura, D. Right temporal lobe damage. *Archives of Neurology* (Chicago), 1963, *8*, 264–271.

Kimura, D. Functional asymmetry of the brain in dichotic listening. *Cortex*, 1967, *3*, 163–178.

Kimura, D. Neuromotor mechanisms in the evolution of human communication. In H. D. Steklis & M. H. Raleigh (Eds.), *Neurobiology of social communication in primates: an evolutionary perspective.* New York: Academic Press, 1979.

Kimura, D. & Archibald, Y. Motor functions of the left hemisphere. *Brain*, 1974, *97*, 337–350.

Kimura, D. & Durnford, M. Normal studies on the function of the right hemisphere in vision. In S. J. Dimond & J. G. Beaumont (Eds.), *Hemisphere function in the human brain.* New York: Halsted Press, 1974.

Kimura, D. & Vanderwolf, C. H. The relation between hand preference and the performance of individual finger movements by left and right hands. *Brain*, 1970, *93*, 769–774.

Kimura, S. D. A card form of the Reitan-Modified Halstead Category Test. *Journal of Consulting and Clinical Psychology*, 1981, *49*, 145–146.

King, F. L. & Kimura, D. Left-ear superiority in dichotic perception of vocal nonverbal sounds. *Canadian Journal of Psychiatry*, 1972, *26*, 111–116.

REFERENCES

King, G. D., Hannay, H. J., Masek, B. J., & Burns, J. W. Effects of anxiety and sex on neuropsychological tests. *Journal of Consulting and Clinical Psychology*, 1978, *46*, 375–376.

Kinsbourne, M. Lateral interactions in the brain. In M. Kinsbourne & W. L. Smith (Eds.), *Hemispheric disconnection and cerebral function*. Springfield, Ill.: C. C. Thomas, 1974a.

Kinsbourne, M. Mechanisms of hemispheric interaction in man. In M. Kinsbourne & W. L. Smith (Eds.), *Hemispheric disconnection and cerebral function*. Springfield, Ill.: C. C. Thomas, 1974b.

Kinsbourne, M. Biological determinants of functional bisymmetry and asymmetry. In M. Kinsbourne (Ed.), *Asymmetrical function of the brain*. Cambridge, England: Cambridge University Press, 1978.

Kinsbourne, M. Hemispheric specialization and the growth of human understanding. *American Psychologist*, 1982, 37, 411–420.

Kinsbourne, M. & Warrington, E. K. A study of finger agnosia. *Brain*, 1962, 85, 47–66.

Kirk, S. A., McCarthy, J. J., & Kirk, W. D. *Illinois Test of Psycholinguistic Abilities. Examiner's Manual* (Rev. ed.). Urbana, Ill.: University of Illinois Press, 1968.

Kish, G. B. Alcoholics' GATB and Shipley profiles and their interrelationships. *Journal of Clinical Psychology*, 1970, *26*, 482–484.

Klawans, H. L. & Weiner, W. J. *Testbook of clinical neuropharmacology*. New York: Raven Press, 1981.

Klebanoff, S. G. Psychological changes in organic brain lesions and ablations. *Psychological Bulletin*, 1945, *42*, 585–623.

Klebanoff, S. G., Singer, J. L., & Wilensky, H. Psychological consequences of brain lesions and ablations. *Psychological Bulletin*, 1954, *51*, 1–141.

Klisz, D. K. *Task modality and functional cerebral asymmetry in left handers*. Paper presented at the American Psychological Association Convention, Toronto, 1978.

Klonoff, H. & Kennedy, M. Memory and perceptual functioning in octogenarians and nonagenarians in the community. *Journal of Gerontology*, 1965, *20*, 328–333.

Klonoff, H. & Kennedy, M. A comparative study of cognitive functioning in old age. *Journal of Gerontology*, 1966, *21*, 239–243.

Klopfer, B., Ainsworth, M., Klopfer, W. G., & Holt, R. R. *Developments in the Rorschach technique* (Vol. 1. *Technique and theory*). Yonkers, N.Y.: World Book, 1954.

Klopfer, B. & Davidson H. H. *Rorschach technique: an introductory manual*. New York: Harcourt, 1962.

Kløve, H. Relationship of differential electroencephalographic patterns to distributions of Wechsler-Bellevue scores. *Neurology*, 1959, *9*, 871–876.

Kløve, H. Clinical neuropsychology. In F. M. Forster (Ed.), *The Medical Clinics of North America*. New York: Saunders, 1963.

Kløve, H. Validation studies in adult clinical neuropsychology. In R. M. Reitan & L. A. Davison (Eds.), *Clinical neuropsychology*. Washington, D.C.: Hemisphere, 1974.

Kløve, H. & Cleeland, C. S. The relationship of neuropsychological impairment to other indices of severity of head injury. *Scandinavian Journal of Rehabilitation Medicine*, 1972, *4*, 55–60.

Kløve, H. & Doehring, D. G. MMPI in epileptic groups with differential etiology. *Journal of Clinical Psychology*, 1962, *18*, 149–153.

Kløve, H. & Fitzhugh, K. B. The relationship of differential EEG patterns to the distribution of Wechsler-Bellvue scores in a chronic epileptic population. *Journal of Clinical Psychology* 1962, *18*, 334–337.

Kløve, H. & Matthews, C. G. Neuropsychological studies of patients with epilepsy. In R. M.

Reitan & L. A. Davison (Eds.), *Clinical neuropsychology*. Washington, D.C.: Hemisphere, 1974.

Knapp, M. E. Problems in rehabilitation of the hemiplegic patient. *Journal of the American Medical Association*, 1959, *169*, 224–229.

Knave, B., Olson, B. Q., Elofsson, S., et al. Long-term exposure to jet fuel. *Scandinavian Journal of Work Environment and Health*, 1978, *41*, 19–45.

Knehr, C. A. Revised approach to detection of cerebral damage: Progressive matrices revisited. *Psychological Reports*, 1965, *17*, 71–77.

Knights R. M. & Moule, A. D. Normative data on the Motor Steadiness Battery for children. *Perceptual and Motor Skills*, 1968, *26*, 643–650.

Kocel K. M. Age-related changes in cognitive abilities and hemispheric specialization. In J. Herron (Ed.), *Neuropsychology of left-handedness*. New York: Academic Press, 1980.

Kochansky, G. E. Psychiatric rating scales for assessing psychopathology in the elderly: a critical review. In A. Raskin & J. Jarvik (Eds.), *Psychiatric symptoms and cognitive loss in the elderly*. Washington, D.C.: Hemisphere, 1979.

Kolansky H. & Moore, W. T. Toxic effects of chronic marijuana use. *Journal of the American Medical Association*, 1972, *222*, 35–41.

Kolb, B. & Wishaw, I. Q. *Fundamentals of human neuropsychology*. San Francisco: W. H. Freeman, 1980.

Kooi, K. A. & Hovey, H. B. Alterations in mental function and paroxysmal cerebral activity. *A.M.A. Archives of Neurology and Psychiatry*, 1957, *78*, 264–271.

Koppitz, E. M. *The Bender Gestalt test for young children*. New York: Grune & Stratton, 1964.

Korman, M. & Blumberg, S. Comparative efficiency of some tests of cerebral damage. *Journal of Consulting Psychology*, 1963, *27*, 303–309.

Kostlan, A. & Van Couvering, N. Clinical indications of organic brain dysfunction. *Proceedings of the 80th Annual Convention of the American Psychological Association*, 1972, 7, 423–424. (Summary)

Kramer, N. A. & Jarvik, L. Assessment of intellectual changes in the elderly. In A. Raskin & L. Jarvik (Eds.), *Psychiatric symptoms and cognitive loss in the elderly*. Washington, D.C.: Hemisphere, 1979.

Krashen, S. D. The left hemisphere. In M. C. Wittrock (Ed.), *The human brain*. Englewood Clifs, N.J.: Prentice-Hall, 1977.

Kraus, J. F. Epidemiologic features of head and spinal cord injury. In B. S. Schoenberg (Eds.), *Advances in neurology* (Vol. 19). New York: Raven Press, 1978.

Krauss, I. K. *Assessing cognitive skills of older workers*. Paper presented at the American Psychological Association Convention, Montreal, 1980.

Krayenbühl, H., Siegfried, J., Kohenof, M., & Yasargil, M. G. Is there a dominant thalamus? Second International Symposium on Stereoencephalopathy, Copenhagen, 1965, *Confinia Neurologica*, 1965, *26*, 246–249.

Kroll, P., Seigel, R., O'Neill, B., & Edwards, R. P. Cerebral cortical atrophy in alcoholic men. *Journal of Clinical Psychiatry*, 1980, *41*, 417–421.

Kronfol, Z., Hamsher, K., Digre, K., & Waziri, R. Depression and hemispheric functions: changes associated with unilateral ECT. *British Journal of Psychiatry*, 1978, *132*, 560–567.

Krop, H., Cohen, E., & Block, A. J. Continuous oxygen therapy in chronic obstructive pulmonary disease: neuropsychological effects. *Proceedings of the 80th Annual Convention of the American Psychological Association*, 1972, 7, 663–664. (Summary)

Kuller, L. H. Epidemiology of stroke. In B. S. Schoenberg (Ed.) *Advances in neurology* (Vol. 19). New York: Raven Press, 1978.

Lachar, D., Lewis, R., & Kupke, T. MMPI in differentiation of temporal lobe and nontemporal lobe epilepsy: investigation of three levels of test performance. *Journal of Consulting and Clinical Psychology*, 1979, *47*, 186–188.

Lacks, P. B., Harrow, M., Colbert, J., & Levine, J. Further evidence concerning the diagnostic accuracy of the Halstead organic test battery. *Journal of Clinical Psychology*, 1970, *26*, 480–481.

Ladurner, G., Iliff, L. D., & Lechner, H. Clinical factors associated with dementia in ischaemic stroke. *Journal of Neurology, Neurosurgery, and Psychiatry*, 1982, *45*, 97–101.

Landis, C. Remarks on the psychological findings attendant on psychosurgery. In *The biology of mental health and disease*. New York: Paul B. Hoeber, 1952.

Lansdell, H. Effect of extent on temporal lobe ablations on two lateralized deficits. *Physiology and Behavior*, 1968, *3*, 271–273.

Lansdell, H. Relation of extent of temporal removals to closure and visuomotor factors. *Perceptual and Motor Skills*, 1970, *31*, 491–498.

Lansdell, H. A general intellectual factor affected by temporal lobe dysfunction. *Journal of Clinical Psychology*, 1971, *27*, 182–184.

Lansdell, H. & Donnelly, E. F. Factor analysis of the Wechsler Adult Intelligence Scale subtests and the Halstead-Reitan Category and Tapping tests. *Journal of Consulting and Clinical Psychology*, 1977, *45*, 412–416.

Lansdell, H. & Mirsky, A. F. Attention in focal and centrencephalic epilepsy. *Experimental Neurology*, 1964, *9*, 463–469.

Lansdell, H. & Smith, F. J. *Effect of focus of cerebral injury on WAIS factors and the course of their recovery*. Paper presented at the American Psychological Association Convention, Honolulu, September, 1972.

Lansdell, H. & Smith, F. J. Asymmetrical cerebral function for two WAIS factors and their recovery after brain injury. *Journal of Consulting and Clinical Psychology*, 1975, *43*, 923.

Larrabee, G. J. & Kane, R. L. *Reversed digit repetition involves visual and verbal processes*. Paper presented at the meeting of the Southwest Psychological Association, Dallas, Texas, April, 1982.

Larrabee, G. J. & Kane, R. L. Differential drawing size associated with unilateral brain damage. *Neuropsychologia*, 1983, *21*, 173–177.

Larrabee, G. J., Kane, R. L., & Schuck, J. R. Factor analysis of the WAIS and Wechsler Memory Scale: An analysis of the construct validity of the Wechsler Memory Scale. *Journal of Clinical Neuropsychology*, 1983, *5*, 159–168.

Larsen, B., Skinhj, E., & Lassen, N. A. Variations in regional cortical blood flow in the right and left hemispheres during automatic speech. *Brain*, 1978, *10*, 193–209.

Lashley, K. S. *Brain mechanisms and intelligence: a quantitative study of injuries to the brain*. Chicago: University of Chicago Press, 1929.

Lashley, K. S. Factors limiting recovery after central nervous lesions. *Journal of Nervous and Mental Disease*, 1938, *88*, 733–755.

Laurence, S. & Stein, D. G. Recovery after brain damage and the concept of localization of function. In S. Finger (Ed.), *Recovery from brain damage: research and theory*. New York: Plenum Press, 1978.

Lebrun, Y. & Hoops, R. *Intelligence and aphasia*. Amsterdam: Swets & Zeitlinger, B. V., 1974.

Lechelt, E. C. Laterality differences and shifts as a function of tactile temporal pattern complexity: implications for differential processing strategies of the cerebral hemispheres. *Psychological Research*, 1980, *41*, 319–333.

Leehey, S. C. & Cahn, A. Lateral asymmetries in the recognition of words, familiar faces and unfamiliar faces. *Neuropsychologia*, 1979, *17*, 619–635.

Legg, J. F. & Stiff, M. P. Drug-related test patterns of depressed patients. *Psychopharmacology*, 1976, *50*, 205–210.

Lehmann, H. E., Ban, T. A. & Kral, V. A. Psychological tests: practice effect in geriatric patients. *Geriatrics*, 1968, *23*, 160–163.

Lehmann, J. F., DeLateur, B. J., Fowler, R. S., Jr., Warren, C. G., et al. Stroke: does rehabilitation affect outcome? *Archives of Physical and Medical Rehabilitation*, 1975, *56*, 375–382.

Lehr, U., & Schmitz-Scherzer, R. XI. Survivors and nonsurvivors—two fundamental patterns of aging. In H. Thomas (Ed.), *Patterns of aging*. Basel: S. Karger, 1976.

Leiter, R. G. *Examiner's manual for the Leiter International Performance Scale*. Chicago: Stoelting, 1969a.

Leiter, R. G. *General instructions for the Leiter International Performance Scale*. Chicago: Stoelting Co., 1969b.

Lesser, R. Verbal and non-verbal memory components in the Token Test. *Neuropsychologia*, 1976, *14*, 79–85.

Levin, H. S., Benton, A. L., & Grossman, R. G. *Neurobehavioral consequences of closed head injury*. New York: Oxford University Press, 1982.

Levin, H. S., Hamsher, K. de S., & Benton, A. L. A short form of the Test of Facial Recognition for clinical use. *Journal of Psychology*, 1975, *91*, 223–228.

Levin, H. S. & Grossman, R. G. Behavioral sequelae of closed head injury. *Archives of Neurology*, 1978, *35*, 720–727.

Levin, H. S., Grossman, R. G., & Kelly, P. J. Aphasic disorder in patients with closed head injury. *Journal of Neurology, Neurosurgery, and Psychiatry*, 1976a, *39*, 1062–1070.

Levin, H. S., Grossman, R. G., & Kelly, P. J. Short-term recognition memory in relation to severity of head injury. *Cortex*, 1976b, *12*, 175–182.

Levin, H. S., Grossman, R. G., & Kelly, P. J. Assessment of long-term memory in brain-damaged patients. *Journal of Consulting and Clinical Psychology*, 1977, *45*, 684–688.

Levin, H. S., Grossman, R. G., Rose, J. E., Teasdale, G. Long-term neuropsychological outcome of closed head injury. *Journal of Neurosurgery*, 1979, *50*, 412–422.

Levin, H. S., Grossman, R. G., Sarwar, M., & Meyers, C. A. Linguistic recovery after closed head injury. *Brain and Language*, 1981, *12*, 360–374.

Levin, H. S., Meyers, C. A., Grossman, R. G., & Sarwar, M. Ventricular enlargement after closed head injury. *Archives of Neurology*, 1981, *38*, 623–629.

Levin, H. S., O'Donnell, V. M., & Grossman, R. G. The Galveston Orientation and Amnesia Test. A practical scale to assess cognition after head injury. *Journal of Nervous and Mental Diseases*, 1979, *167*, 675–684.

Levy, J. Lateral specialization of the brain: behavioral manifestations and possible evolutionary basis. In J. A. Kiger, Jr. (Ed.), *The biology of behavior*. Corvallis, Oregon: Oregon State University Press, 1972.

Levy, J. Psychobiological implications of bilateral asymmetry. In S. J. Dimond & J. G. Beaumont (Eds.), *Hemisphere function in the human brain*. New York: Halsted Press, 1974.

Levy, J. Handwriting posture and cerebral organization: How are they related? *Psychological Bulletin*, 1982, *91*, 589–608.

Levy, J. & Gur, R. C. Individual differences in psychoneurological organization. In J. Herron (Ed.), *Neuropsychology of left-handedness*. New York: Academic Press, 1980.

REFERENCES

Levy, J. & Reid, M. Variations in writing posture and cerebral organization. *Science*, 1976, *194*, 337–339.

Levy-Agresti, J. & Sperry, R. W. Differential perceptual capacities in major and minor hemispheres. *Proceedings of the National Academy of Science*, 1968, *61*, 1151.

Lewin, W. Rehabilitation after head injury. *British Medical Journal*, 1968, *1*, 465–470.

Lewinsohn, P. M. *Psychological assessment of patients with brain injury.* Unpublished manuscript, Eugene, Oregon, University of Oregon, 1973.

Lewinsohn, P. M., Danaher, B. G., & Kikel, S. Visual imagery as a mnemonic aid for brain-injured persons. *Journal of Consulting and Clinical Psychology*, 1977, *45*, 717–723.

Lewinsohn, P. M., Zieler, R. E., Libet, J., Eyeberg, S., & Nielsen, G. Short-term memory. *Journal of Comparative and Physiological Psychology*, 1972, *81*, 248–255.

Lewis, G. P., Golden, C. J., Moses, J. A., Jr., et al. Localization of cerebral dysfunction with a standardized version of Luria's neuropsychological battery. *Journal of Consulting and Clinical Psychology*, 1979, *47*, 1003–1019.

Lewis, R. & Kupke, T. *The Lafayette Clinic repeatable neuropsychological test battery: Its development and research applications.* Paper presented at the annual meeting of the Southeastern Psychological Association, Hollywood, Fla., May, 1977.

Ley, R. G. & Bryden, M. P. A dissociation of right and left hemispheric effects for recognizing emotional tone and verbal content. *Brain and Cognition*, 1982, *1*, 3–9.

Lezak, M. D. *The Personal History Inventory.* Paper presented at the American Psychological Association Convention, San Francisco, September, 1968.

Lezak, M. D. Living with the characterologically altered brain injured patient. *Journal of Clinical Psychiatry*, 1978a, *39*, 592–598.

Lezak, M. D. Subtle sequelae of brain damage: perplexity, distractibility, and fatigue. *American Journal of Physical Medicine*, 1978b, *57*, 9–15.

Lezak, M. D. *Behavioral concomitants of configurational disorganization.* Paper presented at the seventh annual meeting of the International Neuropsychological Society, New York City, 1979a.

Lezak, M. D. Recovery of memory and learning functions following traumatic brain injury. *Cortex*, 1979b, *15*, 63–70.

Lezak, M. D. Coping with head injury in the family. In G. A. Broe & R. L. Tate (Eds.), *Brain impairment. Proceedings of the Fifth Annual Brain Inpairment Conference.* Sydney: Postgraduate committee in Medicine of the University of Sydney, 1982a.

Lezak, M. D. The problem of assessing executive functions. *International Journal of Psychology*, 1982b, *17*, 281–297.

Lezak, M. D. Specialization and integration of the cerebral hemispheres. In *The brain: recent research and its implications.* Eugene, Ore.: University of Oregon College of Education, 1982c.

Lezak, M. D. *The test-retest stability and reliability of some tests commonly used in neuropsychological assessment.* Paper presented at the fifth European conference of the International Neuropsychological Society, Deauville, France, June, 1982d.

Lezak, M. D. An individualized approach to neuropsychological assessment. In P. E. Logue & J. M. Schear (Eds.), *Clinical neuropsychology: a multidisciplinary approach.* Springfield, Ill.: C. C. Thomas, in press.

Lezak, M. D., Cosgrove, J. N., O'Brien, K., & Wooster, N. *Relationship between personality disorders, social disturbance, and physical disability following traumatic brain injury.* Paper presented at the eighth annual meeting of the International Neuropsychological Society, San Francisco, 1980.

Lezak, M. D. & Glaudin, V. Differential effects of physical illness on MMPI profiles. *Newsletter for Research in Psychology*, 1969, *11*, 27–28.

Lezak, M. D., Howieson, D. B., & McGavin, J. *Temporal sequencing of the remote events task with Korsakoff patients*. Paper presented at the eleventh annual meeting of the International Neuropsychological Society, Mexico City, February, 1983.

Lezak, M. D. & Newman, S. P. *Verbosity and right hemisphere damage*. Paper presented at the second European conference of the International Neuropsychological Society, Noordvijkerhout, Holland, 1979.

Lezak, M. D. & O'Brien, K. *A comparison of traumatically brain injured and control subjects on verbal and pictorial presentations of a learning task*. Paper presented at the ninth annual meeting of the International Neuropsychological Society, Atlanta, February, 1981.

Lhermitte, F. & Signoret, J-L. Analyse neuropsychologique et différenciation des syndromes amnésiques. *Revue Neurologique*, 1972, *126*, 164–178.

Lhermitte, F, & Signoret, J-L. The amnesic syndromes and the hippocampal-mammillary system. In M. R. Rosenzweig & E. L. Bennett (Eds.), *Neural mechanisms of learning and memory*. Cambridge, Mass.: Massachusetts Institute of Technology Press, 1976.

Libow, L. S. Senile dementia and "pseudosenility": clinical diagnosis. In C. Eisdorfer, & R. O. Friedel (Eds.), *Cognitive and emotional disturbance in the elderly*. Chicago: Year Book Medical Publishers, 1977.

Lichtman, M. *REAL: Reading/Everyday Activities in Life*. New York: CAL Press, 1972.

Lieberman, A. & Benson, D. F. Control of emotional expression in pseudobulbar palsy. *Archives of Neurology*, 1977, *34*, 717–719.

Lifshitz, K. Problems in the quantitative evaluation of patients with psychoses of the senium. *Journal of Psychology*, 1960, *49*, 295–303.

Likert, R. & Quasha, W. H. *The revised Minnesota Paper Form Board Test. Manual*. New York: Psychological Corporation, 1970.

Lilliston, L. Schizophrenic symptomatology as a function of probability of cerebral damage. *Journal of Abnormal Psychology*, 1973, *82*, 377–381.

Lindsey, B. A. & Coppinger, N. W. Age-related deficits in simple capabilities and their consequences for Trail Making performance. *Journal of Clinical Psychology*, 1969, *25*, 156–159.

Lindström, K. Changes in psychological performances of solvent-poisoned and solvent-exposed workers. *American Journal of Industrial Medicine*, 1980, *1*, 69–84.

Lindström, K. Behavioral changes after long-term exposure to organic solvents and their mixtures. *Scandinavian Journal of Work and Environmental Health*, 1981, *7*, (Suppl. 4), 48–53.

Lindström, K., Härkönen, H., & Hernberg, S. Disturbances in psychological functions of workers occupationally exposed to styrene. *Scandinavian Journal of Work Environment and Health*, 1976, *3*, 129–139.

Lipowski, Z. J. Organic brain syndromes: overview and classification. In D. F. Benson & D. Blumer (Eds.), *Psychiatric aspects of neurologic disease*. New York: Grune & Stratton, 1975.

Lipowski, Z. J. Organic brain syndromes: a reformulation. *Comprehensive Psychiatry*, 1978, *19*, 309–322.

Lishman, W. A. Brain damage in relation to psychiatric disability after head injury. *British Journal of Psychiatry*, 1968, *114*, 373–410.

Lishman, W. A. Emotion consciousness and will after brain bisection in man. *Cortex*, 1971, *7*, 181–192.

REFERENCES

Lishman, W. A. The psychiatric sequelae of head injury: a review. *Psychological Medicine*, 1973, *3*, 304–318.

Lishman, W. A. *Organic psychiatry*. Oxford: Blackwell Scientific Publications, 1978.

Lishman, W. A. Cerebral disorder in alcoholism syndromes of impairment. *Brain*, 1981, *104*, 1–20.

Lishman, W. A., Ron, M., & Acker, W. Computed tomography of the brain and psychometric assessment of alcoholic patients—a British study. In D. Richter (Ed.), *Addiction and brain damage*. London: Croom Helm, 1980.

Liston, E. H. Occult presenile dementia. *Journal of Nervous and Mental Disease*, 1977, *164*, 263–267.

Liston, E. H. Diagnostic delay in presenile dementia. *Journal of Clinical Psychiatry*, 1978, *39*, 599–603.

Livingston, K. E. & Escobar, A. The continuing evolution of the limbic system concept. In E. Hitchcock, L. Laitinen, & K. Vaernet (Eds.), *Psychosurgery*. Springfield, Ill: C. C. Thomas. 1972.

Locascio, D. & Ley, R. Scaled-rated meaningfulness of 319 CVCVC words and paralogs previously assessed for associative reaction time. *Journal of Verbal Learning and Verbal Behavior*, 1972, *11*, 243–250.

Loehlin, J. D., Lindzey, G., & Spuhler, J. N. *Race differences in intelligence*. San Francisco: W. H. Freeman, 1975.

Loftus, G. R. & Loftus, E. T. *Human memory. The processing of information*. New York: Laurence Erlbaum Associates, 1976.

Logue, P. E. Psychological methods for detection of brain damage. In J. C. Davis & J. P. Foreyt (Eds.), *Mental examiner's source book*. Springfield, Ill.: C. C. Thomas, 1975.

Logue, P. & Wyrick, L. Initial validation of Russell's revised Wechsler Memory Scale: a comparison of normal aging versus dementia. *Journal of Consulting and Clinical Psychology*, 1979, *47*, 176–178.

Long, C. J. & Brown, D. A. *Analysis of temporal cortex dysfunction by neuropsychological techniques*. Paper presented at the American Psychological Association Convention, New York, 1979.

Loo, R. & Schneider, R. An evaluation of the Briggs-Nebes modified version of Annett's handedness inventory. *Cortex*, 1979, *15*, 683–686.

Loranger, A. W., Goodell, H., McDowell, F. H., et al. Intellectual impairment in Parkinson's syndrome. *Brain*, 1972, *95*, 405–412.

Lorge, I. The influence of the test upon the nature of mental decline as a function of age. *Journal of Educational Psychology*, 1936, *27*, 100–110.

Lubin, B. Adjective check lists for measurement of depression. *Archives of General Psychiatry*, 1965, *12*, 57–62.

Lubin, B., Wallis, R. R., & Paine, C. Patterns of psychological test usage in the United States: 1935–1969. *Professional Psychology*, 1971, *2*, 70–74.

Lund, R. D. *Development and plasticity of the brain*. New York: Oxford University Press, 1978.

Luria, A. R. Neuropsychological analysis of focal brain lesions. In B. B. Wolman (Ed.), *Handbook of clinical psychology*. New York: McGraw-Hill, 1965.

Luria, A. R. *Higher cortical functions in man*. (B. Haigh, trans.). New York: Basic Books, 1966.

Luria, A. R. The functional organization of the brain. *Scientific American*, 1970a, *222*, 2–9.

Luria, A. R. *Traumatic aphasia* (Translated from the Russian). The Hague/Paris: Mouton, 1970b.

REFERENCES

Luria, A. R. *The man with a shattered world.* New York: Basic Books, 1972.

Luria, A. R. The frontal lobes and the regulation of behavior. In K. H. Pribram & A. R. Luria (Eds.), *Psychophysiology of the frontal lobes.* New York: Academic Press, 1973a.

Luria, A. R. *The working brain: an introduction to neuropsychology.* (B. Haigh, trans.). New York: Basic Books, 1973b.

Luria, A. R. & Homskaya, E. D. Disturbances in the regulative role of speech with frontal lobe lesions. In J. M. Warren & K. Akert (Eds.), *The frontal granular cortex and behavior.* New York: McGraw-Hill, 1964.

Lusins, J., Zimberg, S., Smokler, H., & Gurley, K. Alcoholism and cerebral atrophy: a study of 50 patients with CT scan and psychologic testing. *Alcoholism,* 1980, *4,* 406–411.

Lyle, O. E. & Gottesman, I. I. Premorbid psychometric indicators of the gene for Huntington's disease. *Journal of Consulting and Clinical Psychology,* 1977, *45,* 1011–1022.

Lyle, O. E. & Gottesman, I. I. Psychometric indicators of the gene for Huntington's disease: clues to "ontopathogenesis." *Clinical Psychologist,* 1979, *32,* 14–15.

Lyle, O. E. & Quast, W. The Bender Gestalt: use of clinical judgment versus recall scores in prediction of Huntington's disease. *Journal of Consulting and Clinical Psychology,* 1976, *44,* 229–232.

Lyman, H. B. *Test scores and what they mean.* Englewood Cliffs, N.J.: Prentice-Hall, 1963.

Lynn, J. G., Levine, K. N., & Hewson, L. R. Psychologic tests for the clinical evaluation of late 'diffuse organic,' 'neurotic,' and 'normal' reactions after closed head injury. *Trauma of the central nervous system. Research Publication of the Association of Nervous and Mental Disease.* Baltimore: Williams & Wilkins, 1945.

Machover, K. *Personality projection in the drawing of the human figure.* Springfield, Ill.: C. C. Thomas, 1948.

Mack, J. L. The MMPI and neurological dysfunction. In C. S. Newmark (Ed.), *MMPI: Current clinical and research trends.* New York: Praeger, 1979.

Mack, J. L. & Boller, F. The role of the minor hemisphere in assigning meaning to visual perceptions. *Neuropsychologia,* 1977, *15,* 345–349.

Mack, J. L. & Levine, R. N. The basis of visual constructional disability in patients with unilateral cerebral lesions. *Cortex,* 1981, *17,* 512–532.

Mack, J. L. & Levine, R. N. *A comparison of the Form Assembly Task with other visual processing tasks in identifying performance asymmetries in patients with unilateral hemispheric lesions.* Unpublished manuscript. (Available from J. L. Mack, Dept. of Neurology, Case Western Reserve University, Cleveland, Ohio, 44106).

MacQuarrie, T. W. *MacQuarrie Test for Mechanical Ability.* Monterey, Calif.: CTB/McGraw-Hill, 1925, 1953.

Maher, B. A. Intelligence and brain damage. In R. E. Norman (Ed.), *Handbook of mental deficiency.* New York: McGraw-Hill, 1963.

Maier, L. R. & Abidin, R. R. Validation attempt of Hovey's five-item MMPI index for central nervous system disorders. *Journal of Consulting Psychology,* 1967, *31,* 542.

Malamud, N. Organic brain disease mistaken for psychiatric disorder: a clinicopathologic study. In D. F. Benson & D. Blumer (Eds.), *Psychiatric aspects of neurologic disease.* New York: Grune & Stratton, 1975.

Malerstein, A. J. & Belden, E. WAIS, SILS, and PPVT in Korsakoff's syndrome. *Archives of General Psychiatry,* 1968, *19,* 743–750.

Malmo, H. P. On frontal lobe functions: psychiatric patient controls. *Cortex,* 1974, *10,* 231–237.

Malone, R. L. Expressed attitudes of families of aphasics. In J. Stubbins (Ed.), *Social and*

673

psychological aspects of disability: a handbook for practitioners. Baltimore: University Park Press, 1977.

Mandleberg, I. A. Cognitive recovery after severe head injury. *Journal of Neurology, Neurosurgery, and Psychiatry,* 1976, *39,* 1001–1007.

Mandler, G. Organization and memory. *Psychology of Learning and Motivation,* 1967, *1,* 327–372.

Manzoor, M. & Runcie, J. Folate-responsive neuropathy: report of 10 cases. *British Medical Journal,* 1976, *1,* 1176–1178.

Marcie, P. & Hécaen, H. Agraphia: writing disorders associated with unilateral cortical lesions. In K. M. Heilman & E. Valenstein (Eds.), *Clinical neuropsychology.* New York: Oxford University Press, 1979.

Marin, O. S. & Gordon, B. Neuropsychologic aspects of aphasia. In H. R. Tyler & D. M. Dawson (Eds.), *Current neurology* (Vol. 2). Boston: Houghton-Mifflin, 1979.

Marin, O. S., Schwartz, M. F., & Saffran, E. M. The origins and distribution of language. In M. Gazzaniga (Ed.), *Handbook of behavioral neurobiology.* (Vol. 2, *Neuropsychology*). New York: Plenum Press, 1979.

Markson, E. W. & Levitz, G. A Guttman scale to assess memory loss among the elderly. *The Gerontologist,* 1973, *13,* 337–340.

Marsden, C. D. The mysterious motor function of the basal ganglia: The Robert Wartenberg Lecture. *Neurology,* 1982, *32,* 514–537.

Marsh, G. G. Satz-Mogel Abbreviated WAIS and CNS-damaged patients. *Journal of Clinical Psychology,* 1973, *29,* 451–455.

Marsh, G. G. & Hirsch, S. H. Effectiveness of two tests of visual retention. *Journal of Clinical Psychology,* 1982, *38,* 115–118.

Marsh. G. R. Asymmetry of electrophysiological phenomena and its relation to behavior in humans. In M. Kinsbourne (Ed.), *Asymmetrical function of the brain.* Cambridge: Cambridge University Press, 1978.

Martin, A. D. Aphasia testing. A second look at the Porch Index of Communicative Ability. *Journal of Speech and Hearing Disorders,* 1977, *42,* 547–562.

Masdeu, J. C., Azar-Kia, B., & Rubino, F. A. Evaluation of recent cerebral infarction by computerized tomography. *Archives of Neurology,* 1977, *34,* 417–421.

Massaro, D. W. *The dimensions of short-term memory.* Paper presented at the meeting of the Midwestern Psychological Association, Chicago, 1973.

Masure, M. C. & Tzavaras, A. Perception de figures entrecroisées par des sujets atteints de lésions corticales unilatérales. *Neuropsychologia,* 1976, *14,* 371–374.

Matarazzo, J. D. *Wechsler's measurement and appraisal of adult intelligence* (5th ed.). New York: Oxford University Press, 1972.

Matarazzo, J. D., Carmody, T. P., & Jacobs, L. D. Test-retest reliability and stability of the WAIS: A literature review with implications for clinical practice. *Journal of Clinical Neuropsychology,* 1980, *2,* 89–105.

Matarazzo, J. D., Wiens, A. N., Matarazzo, R. G., & Goldstein, S. G. Psychometric and clinical test-retest reliability of the Halstead Impairment Index in a sample of healthy, young, normal men. *Journal of Nervous and Mental Disease,* 1974, *158,* 37–49.

Matthews, B. *Multiple sclerosis. The facts.* Oxford: Oxford University Press, 1978.

Matthews, C. G., Guertin, W. H., & Reitan, R. M. Wechsler-Bellevue subtest mean rank orders in diverse diagnostic groups. *Psychological Reports,* 1962, *11,* 3–9.

Matthews, C. G. & Haaland, K. Y. The effect of symptom duration on cognitive and motor performance in Parkinsonism. *Neurology,* 1979, *29,* 951–956.

Matthews, C. G. & Harley, J. P. Cognitive and motor-sensory performances in toxic and non-toxic epileptic subjects. *Neurology*, 1975, *25*, 184–188.

Matthews, C. G. & Kløve, H. *Instruction manual for the Adult Neuropsychology Test Battery.* Madison, Wisconsin: University of Wisconsin Medical School, 1964.

Mattis, S. Mental status examination for organic mental syndrome in the elderly patient. In L. Bellak & T. B. Karasu (Eds.), *Geriatric psychiatry.* New York: Grune & Stratton, 1976.

Mattis, S., Kovner, R., & Goldmeier, E. Different patterns of mnemonic deficits in two organic amnestic syndromes. *Brain and Language*, 1978, *6*, 179–191.

Maxwell, A. E. Obtaining factor scores on the WAIS. *Journal of Mental Science*, 1960, *106*, 1060–1062.

Mayeux, R., Stern, Y., Rosen, J., & Leventhal, J. Depression, intellectual impairment, and Parkinson disease. *Neurology*, 1981, *31*, 645–650.

Mazziota, J. D., Phelps, M. E., Carson, R. E., & Kuhl, D. E. Tomographic mapping of human cerebral metabolism: Auditory stimulation. *Neurology*, 1982, *32*, 921–937

Mazzocchi, F. & Vignolo, L. A. Localization of lesions in aphasia: clinical CT scan correlations in stroke patients. *Cortex*, 1979, *15*, 627–654.

McAlpine, D., Lumsden, C. E., & Acheson, E. D. *Multiple sclerosis* (2nd ed.). Edinburgh, London: Churchill Livingstone, 1972.

McCarty, S. M., Siegler, I. C., & Logue, P. E. Cross-sectional and longitudinal patterns of three Wechsler Memory Scale subtests. *Journal of Gerontology*, 1982, 37, 169–175.

McCormack, P. D. Recognition memory: how complex a retrieval system? *Canadian Journal of Psychology*, 1972, *26*, 19–41.

McFarland, R. A. Anoxia: its effects on the physiology and biochemistry of the brain and on behavior. In *The biology of mental heatlh and disease.* New York: Hoeber, 1952.

McFarling, D., Rothi, L. J., & Heilman, K. M. Transcortical aphasia from ischaemic infarcts of the thalamus: a report of two cases. *Journal of Neurology, Neurosurgery, and Psychiatry*, 1982, *45*, 107–112.

McFie, J. Psychological testing in clinical neurology. *Journal of Nervous and Mental Disease*, 1960, *131*, 383–393.

McFie, J. Recent advances in phrenology. *Lancet*, Aug. 1961, *ii*, 360–363.

McFie, J. The diagnostic significance of disorders of higher nervous activity. Syndromes related to frontal, temporal, parietal, and occipital lesions. In P. J. Vinkin & G. W. Bruyn (Eds.), *Handbook of clinical neurology* (Vol. 4). New York: Wiley, 1969.

McFie, J. *Assessment of organic intellectual impairment.* London: Academic Press, 1975.

McFie, J. In M. Piercy (Director), Restitution of function following cerebral lesions. Presented at the Eighteenth International Symposium of Neuropsychology (Summary). *Neuropsychologia*, 1976, *14*, 265–268.

McFie, J. & Piercy, M. F. The relation of laterality of lesion to performance on Weigl's sorting test. *Journal of Mental Science*, 1952, *98*, 299–305.

McFie, J., Piercy, M. F., & Zangwill, O. L. Visual-spatial agnosia associated with lesions of the right cerebral hemisphere. *Brain*, 1950, *73*, 167–190.

McFie, J. & Zangwill, O. L. Visual constructive disabilities associated with lesion of the left cerebral hemisphere. *Brain*, 1960, *83*, 243–260.

McGee, M. G. *Human spatial abilities.* New York: Praeger, 1979.

McGhie, A. Psychological aspects of attention and its disorders. In P. J. Vinken & G. W. Bruyn (Eds.), *Handbook of clinical neurology* (Vol. 3, *Disorders of higher nervous activity.*). New York: Wiley, 1969.

REFERENCES

McGlone, J. Sex differences in functional brain asymmetry (Research Bulletin 378). London, Ontario: Unviersity of Western Ontario, July, 1976.

McHugh, P. R. & Folstein, M. F. Psychiatric syndromes of Huntington's chorea. In D. F. Benson & D. Blumer (Eds.), *Psychiatric aspects of neurologic disease*. New York: Grune & Stratton, 1975.

McKeever, W. F. Handwriting posture in left-handers: Sex, familial sinistrality and language laterality correlates. *Neuropsychologia*, 1979, *17*, 429–444.

McKeever, W. F. & VanDeventer, A. D. Inverted handwriting position, language laterality, and the Levy-Nagylaki genetic model of handedness and cerebral organization. *Neuropsychologia*, 1980, *18*, 99–102.

McKinlay, W. W., Brooks, D. N., Bond, M. R., et al. The short term outcome of severe blunt head injury as reported by relatives of the injured persons. *Journal of Neurology, Neurosurgery, and Psychiatry*, 1981, *44*, 527–533.

McNeil, M. R. Porch Index of Communicative Ability (PICA) (Review). In F. L. Darley (Ed.), *Evaluation of appraisal techniques in speech and language pathology*. Reading, Mass.: Addison-Wesley, 1979.

McNeil, M. R. & Prescott, T. E. *Revised Token Test*. Baltimore: University Park Press, 1978.

McReynolds, P. & Weide, M. Psychological measures as used to predict psychiatric improvement and to assess behavioral changes following prefrontal lobotomy. *Journal of Mental Science*, 1960, *106*, 256–280.

McSweeny, A. J., Grant, I., Heaton, R. K., et al. Life quality of patients with chronic obstructive pulmonary disease. *Archives of Internal Medicine*, 1982, *142*, 473–478.

Meehl, P. E. *Clinical versus statistical prediction*. Minnesota: University of Minnesota Press, 1954.

Meehl, P. E. & Rosen, A. Antecedent probability and the efficiency of psychometric signs, patterns, or cutting scores. In D. N. Jackson & S. Messick (Eds.), *Problems in human assessment*. New York: McGraw-Hill, 1967.

Meer, B. & Baker, J. A. The Stockton Geriatric Rating Scale. *Journal of Gerontology*, 1966, *21*, 392–403.

Meier, M. J. The regional localization hypothesis and personality changes associated with focal cerebral lesions and ablations. In J. N. Butcher (Ed.), *MMPI: research developments and clinical applications*. New York: McGraw-Hill, 1969.

Meier, M. J. *Neuropsychological predictors of motor recovery after cerebral infarction*. Paper presented at the American Psychological Association Convention. New Orleans, September, 1974.

Meier, M. J. *The personality issue in epilepsy*. Paper presented at the eighth annual meeting of the International Neuropsychological Society, San Francisco, February, 1980.

Meier, M. J., Ettinger, M. G., & Arthur, L. Recovery of neuropsychological functioning after cerebrovascular infarction. In R. N. Malatesha (Ed.), *Neuropsychology and cognition*. Netherlands: Martinus Nijhoff, 1982.

Meier, M. J. & French, L. A. Longitudinal assessment of intellectual functioning following unilateral temporal lobectomy. *Journal of Clinical Psychology*, 1966, *22*, 23–27.

Meier, M. J. & Story, J. L. Selective impairment of Porteus Maze Test performance after right subthalamotomy. *Neuropsychologia*, 1967, *5*, 181–189.

Mercer, B., Wapner, W., Gardner, H., & Benson, D. F. A study of confabulation. *Archives of Neurology*, 1977, *34*, 429–433.

Merskey, H. & Buhrich, N. A. Hysteria and organic brain disease. *British Journal of Medical Psychology*, 1975, *48*, 359–366.

Merskey, H. & Woodforde, J. M. Psychiatric sequelae of minor head injury. *Brain*, 1972, *95*, 521–528.

Messerli, P., Seron, X., & Tissot, R. Quelques aspects des troubles de la programmation dans le syndrome frontal. *Archives Suisse de Neurologie, Neurochirurgie et de Psychiatrie*, 1979, *125*, 23–35.

Meudell, P., Butters, N., & Montgomery, K. The role of rehearsal in the short-term memory performance of patients with Korsakoff's and Huntington's disease. *Neuropsychologia*, 1978, *16*, 507–510.

Meyer, J. S. & Shaw, T. (Eds.). *Diagnosis and management of stroke and TIA's*. Menlo Park, Calif.: Addison-Wesley, 1982.

Meyer, V. Psychological effects of brain damage. In H. J. Eysenck (Ed.), *Handbook of clinical psychology*. New York: Basic Books, 1961.

Meyer, V. & Falconer, M. A. Defects of learning ability with massive lesions of the temporal lobe. *Journal of Mental Science*, 1960, *106*, 472–477.

Meyer, V. & Jones, H. G. Patterns of cognitive test performance as functions of the lateral localization of cerebral abnormalities in the temporal lobe. *Journal of Mental Science*, 1957, *103*, 758–772.

Meyer, V. & Yates, A. J. Intellectual changes following temporal lobectomy for psychomotor epilepsy. *Journal of Neurology, Neurosurgery, and Psychiatry*, 1955, *18*, 44–52.

Miceli, G., Caltagirone, C., & Gainotti, G. Gangliosides in the treatment of mental deterioration. A double-blind comparison with placebo. *Acta Psychiatrica Scandinavica*, 1977, *55*, 102–110.

Miceli, G., Caltagirone, C., Gainotti, G., Masullo, C., & Silveri, M. C. Neuropsychological correlates of localized cerebral lesions in nonasphasic brain-damaged patients. *Journal of Clinical Neuropsychology*, 1981, *3*, 53–63.

Mignone, R. J., Donnelly, E. F., & Sadowsky, D. Psychological and neurological comparisons of psychomotor and non-psychomotor epileptic patients. *Epilepsia*, 1970, *11*, 345–359.

Mikkelsen, S. A cohort study of disability pension and death among painters with special regard to disabling presenile dementia as an occupational disease. *Scandinavian Journal of Social Medicine*, 1980, Supplement 16, 34–43.

Mikkelsen, S., Gregersen, P., Klausen, H., et al. (Presenile dementia as an occupational disease following industrial exposure to organic solvents. A review of the literature.) *Ugeskrift for Läeger*, 1978, *140*, 1633–1638.

Milberg, W., Cummings, J., Goodglass, H., & Kaplan, E. Case report: a global sequential processing disorder following head injury: a possible role for the right hemisphere in serial order behavior. *Journal of Clinical Neuropsychology*, 1979, *1*, 213–225.

Miller, E. *Clinical neuropsychology*. Harmondsworth, Middlesex: Penguin, 1972.

Miller, E. Short- & long-term memory in patients with presenile dementia. (Alzheimer's disease). *Psychological Medicine*, 1973, *3*, 221–224.

Miller, E. & Hague, F. Some characteristics of verbal behaviour in presenile dementia. *Psychological Medicine*, 1975, *5*, 255–259.

Miller, L. L. Marijuana and human cognition: a review of laboratory investigations. In S. Cohen & R. C. Stillman (Eds.), *The therapeutic potential of marijuana*. New York: Plenum Press, 1976.

Millham, J., Chilcutt, J., & Atkinson, B. *Criterion validity of the AAMD Adapative Behavior Scale*. Symposium presented at the American Psychological Association Convention, Washington, D. C., 1976.

Mills, L. & Burkhart, G. *Memory for prose material in neurological patients: a comparison of two scoring systems*. Research Bulletin #510. London, Canada: Department of Psychology, University of Western Ontario, July, 1980.

Milner, A. D. & Jeeves, M. A. A review of behavioural studies of agenesis of the corpus callosum. In I. S. Russell, M. W. van Hof, & G. Berlucchi (Eds.), *Structure and function of cerebral commissures*. London: Macmillan, 1979.

Milner, B. Intellectual function of the temporal lobes. *Psychological Bulletin*, 1954, *51*, 42–62.

Milner, B. Psychological defects with temporal lobe excision. In H. C. Solomon, S. Cobb, & W. Penfield (Eds.), *The brain and human behavior*. Baltimore: Williams & Wilkins, 1958.

Milner, B. Laterality effects in audition. In V. B. Mountcastle (Ed.), *Interhemispheric relations and cerebral dominance*. Baltimore: John Hopkins University Press, 1962.

Milner, B. Effects of different brain lesions on card sorting. *Archives of Neurology*, 1963, *9*, 90–100.

Milner, B. Some effects of frontal lobectomy in man. In J. M. Warren & K. Akert (Eds.), *The frontal granular cortex and behavior*. New York: McGraw-Hill, 1964.

Milner, B. Visually-guided maze learning in man: effects of bilateral hippocampal, bilateral frontal, and unilateral cerebral lesions. *Neuropsychologia*, 1965, *3*, 317–338.

Milner, B. Brain mechanisms suggested by studies of temporal lobes. In C. H. Millikan & F. L. Darley (Eds.), *Brain mechanisms underlying speech and language*. New York: Grune & Stratton, 1967.

Milner, B. Visual recognition and recall after right-temporal lobe excision in man. *Neuropsychologia*, 1968, *6*, 191–209.

Milner, B. Residual intellectual and memory deficits after head injury. In A. E. Walker, W. F. Caveness, & M. Critchley (Eds.), *The late effects of head injury*. Springfield, Ill.: C. C. Thomas, 1969.

Milner, B. Memory and the medial temporal regions of the brain. In K. H. Pribram & D. E. Broadbent (Eds.), *Biology of memory*. New York: Academic Press, 1970.

Milner, B. Interhemispheric differences in the localization of psychological processes in man. *British Medical Bulletin*, 1971, *27*, 272–277.

Milner, B. Disorders of learning and memory after temporal lobe lesions in man. *Clinical Neurosurgery*, 1972, *19*, 421–446.

Milner, B. Hemisphere specialization: scope and limits. In F. O. Schmitt & F. G. Worden (Eds.), *The neurosciences third study program*. Cambridge, Mass.: Massachusetts Institute of Technology Press, 1974.

Milner, B. Psychological aspects of focal epilepsy and its neurological management. In D. P. Purpura, J. K. Penry, & R. D. Walter (Eds.), *Advances in neurology* (Vol. 8). New York: Raven Press, 1975.

Milner, B. Clues to the cerebral organization of memory. In P. A. Buser & A. Rougeul-Buser (Eds.), *Cerebral correlates of conscious experience*. INSERM Symposium No. 6. Amsterdam: Elsevier/North Holland Biomedical Press, 1978.

Milner, B. & Taylor, L. Right hemisphere superiority in tactile pattern-recognition after cerebral commisurotomy. *Neuropsychologia*, 1972, *10*, 1–15.

Mirsky, A. F. Attention: a neuropsychological perspective. *Education and the brain*. Chicago: National Society for the Study of Education, 1978.

Mirsky, A. F. & Orren, M. M. The neuropsychology of attention and its impairment—human symptoms and animal models. Unpublished manuscript, undated.

Mirsky, A. F., Primac, D. W., Marson, C. A., Rosvold, H. E., & Stevens, J. R. A comparison of the psychological test performance of patients with focal and nonfocal epilepsy. *Experimental Neurology*, 1960, *2*, 75–89.

Mitchell, G. A. G. & Mayer, D. *Essentials of neuroanatomy* (3rd ed.). New York: Churchill Livingstone, 1977.

Mizusawa, K. *The cerebral hemispheric specialization in the magnitudes of optical illusion.* Paper presented at the American Psychological Association Convention, Toronto, 1978.

Mohr, J. P., Watters, W. C., & Duncan, G. W. Thalamic hemorrhage and aphasia. *Brain and Language*, 1975, *2*, 3–17.

Monakow, C. von. Diaschisis. In K. H. Pribram (Ed.), *Brain and behavior* 1. *Mood, states and mind*. Baltimore,: Penguin, 1969.

Money, J. *A Standardized Road Map Test of Direction Sense. Manual*. San Rafael, Calif.: Academic Therapy Publications, 1976; Chicago: Stoelting, no date.

Montague, E. K., Williams, H. L., Lubin, A., & Gieseking, C. F. Army tests for assessment of intellectual deficit. *U.S. Armed Forces Medical Journal*, 1957, *8*, 883–892.

Monti, J. *The neuropsychology of advanced multiple sclerosis.* Paper presented at the fourth European conference of the International Neuropsychological Society, Bergen, Norway, June, 1981.

Mooney, C. M. Age in the development of closure ability in children. *Canadian Journal of Psychology*, 1957, *2*, 219–226.

Mooney, C. M. & Ferguson, G. A. A new closure test. *Canadian Journal of Psychology*, 1951, *5*, 129–133.

Moran, L. J. & Mefferd, R. B., Jr. Repetitive psychometric measures. *Psychological Reports*, 1959, *5*, 269–275.

Morley, G. K., Lundgren, S., & Haxby, J. Comparison and clinical applicability of auditory comprehension scores on the Behavioral Neurology Deficit Evaluation, Boston Diagnostic Aphasia Examination, Porch Index of Communicative Ability and Token Test. *Journal of Clinical Neuropsychology*, 1979, *1*, 249–258.

Morrow, L., Vrtunski, P. B., Kim, Y., & Boller, F. Arousal responses to emotional stimuli and laterality of lesion. *Neuropsychologia*, 1981, *19*, 65–71.

Morrow, R. S. & Mark, J. C. The correlation of intelligence and neurological findings on 22 patients autopsied for brain damage. *Journal of Consulting Psychology*, 1955, *19*, 283–289.

Mortimer, J. A., Pirozzolo, F. J., Hansch, E. C., & Webster, D. D. Relationship of motor symptoms to intellectual deficits in Parkinson disease. *Neurology*, 1982, *32*, 133–137.

Moscovitch, M. Language and the cerebral hemisphere: reaction-time studies and their implications for models of cerebral dominance. *Communication and affect*. New York: Academic Press, 1973.

Moscovitch, M. *Differential effects of unilateral temporal and frontal lobe damage on memory performance.* Paper presented at the fourth annual meeting of the International Neuropsychological Society, Toronto, 1976.

Moscovitch, M. *Asymmetries in spontaneous facial expressions and their possible relation to hemispheric specialization.* Paper presented to the second European conference of the International Neuropsychological Society, Noordwijkerhout, Holland, 1979a.

Moscovitch, M. Information processing and the cerebral hemispheres. In M. S. Gazzaniga (Ed.), *Handbook of behavioral neurobiology*. II. *Neuropsychology*. New York: Plenum Press, 1979b.

Moses, J. A., Jr. & Golden, C. J. Cross-validation of the discriminative effectiveness of the standardized Luria Neuropsychological Battery. *International Journal of Neuroscience*, 1979, *9*, 149–155.

Mountcastle, V. B. Some neural mechanisms for directed attention. In P. A. Buser & A. Rougeul-Buser (Eds.), *Cerebral correlates of conscious experience*. INSERM Symposium No. 6. Amsterdam: Elsevier/North Holland Biomedical Press, 1978.

.Mueller, J. E. Test anxiety and the encoding and retrieval of information. In I. G. Sarason (Ed.), *Test anxiety: theory, research, and applications*. Hillsdale, N.J.: Lawrence Erlbaum Associates, 1979.

Mueller, J. H. & Overcast, T. D. Free recall as a function of test anxiety, concreteness, and instructions. *Bulletin of the Psychonomic Society*, 1976, *8*, 194–196.

Mulder, D. W. & Daly, D. Psychiatric symptoms associated with lesions of the temporal lobe. *Journal of the American Medical Association*, 1952, *150*, 173–176.

Munday, C. S. *Emotional characteristics associated with laterality of brain lesion*. Unpublished doctoral dissertation, California School of Professional Psychology, Berkeley, 1979.

Mungas, D. Interictal behavior abnormality in temporal lobe epilepsy. *Archives of General Psychiatry*, 1982, *39*, 108–111.

Muramoto, O., Kuru, Y., Sugishita, M., & Toyokura, Y. Pure memory loss with hippocampal lesions. A pneumoencephalographic study. *Archives of Neurology*, 1979, *36*, 54–56.

Murray, H. A. *Explorations in personality*. New York: Oxford University Press, 1938.

Murstein, B. I. *Theory and research in projective techniques, emphasizing the TAT*. New York: Wiley, 1963.

Murstein, B. I. & Leipold, W. D. The role of learning of motor abilities in the Wechsler-Bellevue Digit Symbol test. *Educational Psychological Measurement*, 1961, *21*, 103–112.

Myers, R. E. Cerebral connectionism and brain function. In *Brain mechanisms underlying speech and language*. New York: Grune & Stratton, 1967

Najenson, T. *Rehabilitation of the severely brain damaged adult—a comprehensive approach*. Invited address to the Medical College of Virginia's Fourth Annual Post-Graduate Course on the Rehabilitation of the Traumatic Brain-Injured Adult, Williamsburg, Virginia, June, 1980.

Najenson, T., Mendelson, L., Schechter, I., David, C., Mintz, N., & Grosswasser, Z. Rehabilitation after severe head injury. *Scandinavian Journal of Rehabilitation Medicine*, 1974, *6*, 5–14.

Naquet, R., Baurand, C., Benayoun, R., et al. Données EEG et psychologiques chez un groupe de traumatisés craniens adultes. *Medécine Légale et Dommage Corporel*, 1970, *3*, 32–38.

Nash, S. C. Sex role as a mediator of intellectual functioning. In M. A. Wittig & A. C. Petersen (Eds.), *Sex-related differences in cognitive functioning*. New York: Academic Press, 1979.

Natsoulas, T. Consciousness. *American Psychologist*, 1978, *33*, 906–914.

Nauta, W. J. H. Some brain structures and functions related to memory. *Neuroscience Research Progress Bulletin*, 1964, *2*, 1–20.

Nauta, W. J. H., in R. B. Livingston (Chairman), Brain mechanisms in conditioning and learning. *Neurosciences Research Progress Bulletin*, 1966, *4*, 235–347.

Nauta, W. J. H. The problem of the frontal lobe. *Journal of Psychiatric Research*, 1971, *8*, 167–187.

Nebes, R. D. Hemispheric specialization in commissurotomized man. *Psychological Bulletin*, 1974, *81*, 1–14.

Nebes, R. D. Direct examination of cognitive function in the right and left hemispheres. In M. Kinsbourne (Ed.), *Asymmetrical function of the brain*. Cambridge, England: Cambridge University Press, 1978.

REFERENCES

Nehemkis, A. M. & Lewinsohn, P. M. Effects of left and right cerebral lesions in the naming process. *Perceptual and Motor Skills*, 1972, *35*, 787–798.

Nelson, H. E. A modified card sorting test sensitive to frontal lobe defects. *Cortex*, 1976, *12*, 313–324.

Nelson, H. E. *The Nelson Adult Reading Test (NART) test manual*. Windsor, England: NFER-Nelson, no date.

Nelson, H. E. & O'Connell, A. Dementia: the estimation of premorbid intelligence levels using the New Adult Reading Test. *Cortex*, 1978, *14*, 234–244.

Nemec, R. E. Effects of controlled background interference on test performance by right and left hemiplegics. *Journal of Consulting and Clinical Psychology*, 1978, *46*, 294–297.

Neugarten, B. L., Havighurst, R. J., & Tobin, S. S. The measurement of life satisfaction. *Journal of Gerontology*, 1961, *16*, 134–143.

Neuger, G. J., O'Leary, D. S., Fishburne, F., et al. Order effects on the Halstead-Reitan Neuropsychological Test Battery and allied procedures. *Journal of Consulting and Clinical Psychology*, 1981, *49*, 122–730.

Newcombe, F. *Missile wounds of the brain*. London: Oxford University Press, 1969.

Newcombe, F. Selective deficits after focal cerebral injury. In S. Dimond & J. G. Beaumont (Eds.), *Hemisphere functions in the human brain*. New York: Halsted Press, 1974.

Newcombe, F., Artiola i Fortuny, L. Problems and perspectives in the evaluation of psychological deficits after cerebral lesions. *International Rehabilitation Medicine*, 1979, *1*, 182–192.

Newcombe, F., Marshall, J. C., Carrivick, P. J., & Hiorns, R. W. Recovery curves in acquired dyslexia. *Journal of the Neurological Sciences*, 1975, *24*, 127–133.

Newcombe, F., Oldfield, R. C., Ratcliff, G. G., & Wingfield, A. Recognition and naming of object-drawings by men with focal brain wounds. *Journal of Neurology, Neurosurgery, and Psychiatry*, 1971, *34*, 329–340.

Newcombe, F. & Russell, W. R. Dissociated visual perceptual and spatial deficits in focal lesions of the right hemisphere. *Journal of Neurology, Neurosurgery, and Psychiatry*, 1969, *32*, 73–81.

Newcombe, F. & Steinberg, B. Some aspects of learning and memory function in older psychiatric patients. *Journal of Gerontology*, 1964, *19*, 490–493.

Nihira, K. Factorial descriptions of the AAMD Adaptive Behavior Scale. In W. A. Coulter & H. W. Morrow (Eds.), *Adaptive behavior: concepts and measurements*. New York: Grune & Stratton, 1978.

Nihira, K., Foster, R., Shellhaas, M., & Leland, H. *AAMD Adaptive Behavior Scale, 1974 Revision*. Washington, D.C.: American Association on Mental Deficiency, 1975.

Noble, C. E. Measurements of association value (a), rated associations (a'), and scaled meaningfulness (m') for 2100 CVC combinations of the English alphabet. *Psychological Reports*, 1961, *8*, 487–521.

Norman, R. D. A revised deterioration formula for the Wechler Adult Intelligence Scale. *Journal of Clinical Psychology*, 1966, *22*, 287–294.

North, R. D. & Zubin, J. Complex mental functions. In N. D. C. Lewis, C. Landis, & H. E. King (Eds.), *Studies in topectomy*. New York: Grune & Stratton, 1956.

Norton, J. C. Patterns of neuropsychological test performance in Huntington's disease. *Journal of Nervous and Mental Disease*, 1975, *161*, 276–79.

Nottebohm, F. Origins and mechanisms in the establishment of cerebral dominance. In M. S. Gazzaniga (Ed.), *Handbook of behavioral neurobiology* (Vol. 2), *Neuropsychology*. New York: Plenum Press, 1979.

REFERENCES

Obler, L. K. & Albert, M. L. *Language and communication in the elderly*. Lexington, Mass.: Lexington Books, 1980.

O'Brien, K. & Lezak, M. D. *Long-term improvements in intellectual function following brain injury*. Paper presented at the fourth European conference of the International Neuropsychological Society, Bergen, Norway, July, 1981.

O'Brien, M. T. & Pallett, P. J. *Total care of the stroke patient*. Boston: Little, Brown, 1978.

Oddy, M. & Humphrey, M. Social recovery during the year following severe head injury. *Journal of Neurology, Neurosurgery, and Psychiatry*, 1980, *43*, 798–802.

Oddy, M., Humphrey, M., & Uttley, D. Stresses upon the relatives of head-injured patients. *British Journal of Psychiatry*, 1978a, *133*, 507–513.

Oddy, M., Humphrey, M., & Uttley, D. Subjective impairment and social recovery after closed head injury. *Journal of Neurology, Neurosurgery, and Psychiatry*, 1978b, *41*, 611–616.

Ojemann, G. A. Correlations between specific human brain lesions and memory changes. *Neurosciences Research Progress Bulletin*, 1966, *4* (Suppl.), 1–70.

Ojemann, G. A. Mental arithmetic during human thalamic stimulation. *Neuropsychologia*, 1974, *12*, 1–10.

Ojemann, G. A. Organization of short-term verbal memory in language areas of human cortex: evidence from electrical stimulation. *Brain and Language*, 1978, *5*, 331–340.

Ojemann, G. A. Individual variability in cortical localization of language. *Journal of Neurosurgery*, 1979, *50*, 164–169.

Ojemann, G. A. Brain mechanisms for language: observations during neurosurgery. In J. S. Lockard & A. A. Ward, Jr. (Eds.), *Epilepsy: A window to brain mechanisms*. New York: Raven Press, 1980.

Ojemann, G. A., Hoyenga, K. B., & Ward, A. A. Prediction of short-term verbal memory disturbance after ventrolateral thalamotomy. *Journal of Neurosurgery*, 1971, *35*, 20–210.

Ojemann, G. A. & Mateer, C. Human language cortex: localization of memory, syntax, and sequential motor-phoneme identification systems. *Science*, 1979, *205*, 1401–1403.

Ojemann, G. A. & Whitaker, H. A. Language localization and variability. *Brain and Language*, 1978, *6*, 239–260.

Okawa, M., Maeda, S., Nukui, H., & Kawafuchi, J. Psychiatric symptoms in ruptured anterior communicating aneurysms: social prognosis. *Acta Psychiatrica Scandinavica*, 1980, *61*, 306–312.

Oldfield, R. C. & Wingfield, A. Response latencies in naming objects. *The Quarterly Journal of Experimental Psychology*, 1965, *17*, 273–281.

Olsen, J., & Sabroe, S. A case-reference study of neuropsychiatric disorders among workers exposed to solvents in the Danish wood and furniture industry. *Scandinavian Journal of Social Medicine*, 1980, *16*, (Suppl.), 44–49.

Ommaya, A. K., Corrao, P., & Letcher, F. S. Head injury in the chimpanzee. *Journal of Neurosurgery*, 1973, *39*, 152–166.

Ommaya, A. K. & Gennarelli, T. A. Cerebral concussion and traumatic unconsciousness. *Brain*, 1974, *97*, 633–654.

Ommaya, A. K., Grubb, R. L., & Naumann, R. A. Coup and contre-coup injury: observations on the mechanics of visible brain injuries in the rhesus monkey. *Journal of Neurosurgery*, 1971, *35*, 503–516.

Oppenheimer, D. R. Microscopic lesions in the brain following head injury. *Journal of Neurology, Neurosurgery, and Psychiatry*, 1968, *31*, 299–306.

Orgogozo, J. M. Le syndrome de Gerstmann. *L'Encéphale*, 1976, *II*, 41–53.

REFERENCES

Orme, J. E., Lee, D., & Smith, M. P. Psychological assessment of brain damage and intellectual impairment in elderly psychiatric patients. *British Journal of Social and Clinical Psychology*, 1964, *3*, 161–167.

Ornstein, R., Herron, J., Johnstone, J., & Swencionis, C. Differential right hemisphere involvement in two reading tasks. *Psychophysiology*, 1979, *16*, 398–401.

Oscar-Berman, M. Neuropsychological consequences of long-term chronic alcoholism. *American Scientist*, 1980, *68*, 410–419.

Osgood, C. E. & Miron, M. S. *Approaches to the study of aphasia.* Urbana, Ill.: University of Illinois Press, 1963.

Osterrieth, P. A. Le test de copie d'une figure complexe. *Archives de Psychologie*, 1944, *30*, 206–356.

Ota, Y. Psychiatric studies on civilian head injuries. In A. E. Walker, W. F. Caveness, & M. Critchley (Eds.), *The late effects of head injury.* Springfield, Ill.: C. C. Thomas, 1969.

Overall, J. E. & Gorham, D. R. The Brief Psychiatric Rating Scale. *Psychological Reports*, 1962, *10*, 799–812.

Overall, J. E., Hoffmann, N. G., & Levin, H. Effects of aging, organicity, alcoholism, and functional psychopathology on WAIS subtest profiles. *Journal of Consulting and Clinical Psychology*, 1978, *46*, 1315–1322.

Oxbury, J. M., Campbell, D. C., & Oxbury, S. M. Unilateral spatial neglect and impairments of spatial analysis and visual perception. *Brain*, 1974, *97*, 551–564.

Oxbury, J. M. & Oxbury, S. M. Effects of temporal lobectomy on the report of dichotically presented digits. *Cortex*, 1969, *5*, 3–14.

Paivio, A., Yuille, J. C., & Madison, S. A. Concreteness, imagery, and meaningfulness values for 925 nouns. *Journal of Experimental Psychology. Monograph Supplement.* 1968, *76*, No. 1, Part 2.

Palermo, D. S. & Jenkins, J. J. *Word association norms.* Minneapolis: University of Minnesota Press, 1964.

Pankratz, L. Symptom validity testing and symptom retraining: procedures for the assessment and treatment of functional sensory deficits. *Journal of Consulting and Clinical Psychology*, 1979, *47*, 409–410.

Pankratz, L., Fausti, S. A., & Peed, S. A forced-choice technique to evaluate deafness in the hysterical or malingering patient. *Journal of Consulting and Clinical Psychology*, 1975, *43*, 421–422.

Pankratz, L. & Glaudin, V. Psychosomatic disorders. *Encyclopedia of clinical assessment.* San Francisco: Jossey-Bass, 1980.

Panse, F. Electrical lesions of the nervous system. In P. J. Vinken & G. W. Bruyn (Eds.), *Handbook of clinical neurology* (Vol. 7, *Diseases of nerves*). New York: American Elsevier, 1970.

Panting, A. & Merry, P. H. The long term rehabilitation of severe head injuries with particular reference to the need for social and medical support for the patient's family. *Rehabilitation*, 1972, *38*, 33–37.

Pardue, A. M. Bender-Gestalt test and Background Interference Procedure in discernment of organic brain damage. *Perceptual and Motor Skills*, 1975, *40*, 103–109.

Parker, E. S. & Noble, E. P. Alcohol consumption and cognitive functioning in social drinkers. *Journal of Studies on Alcohol*, 1977, *38*, 1224–1232.

Parker, J. W. The validity of some current tests for organicity. *Journal of Consulting Psychology*, 1957, *21*, 425–428.

Parsons, O. A. Brain damage in alcoholics: altered states of unconsciousness. In M. M. Gross

(Ed.), *Alcohol intoxication and withdrawal, experimental studies*, No. 2. New York: Plenum Press, 1975.

Parsons, O. A. Neuropsychological deficits in alcoholics: facts and fancies. *Alcoholism: Clinical and Experimental Research*, 1977, *1*, 51–56.

Parsons, O. A. & Farr, S. P. The neuropsychology of alcohol and drug use. In S. B. Filskov & T. J. Boll (Eds.), *Handbook of clinical neuropsychology*. New York: Wiley-Interscience, 1981.

Parsons, O. A., Vega, A. Jr., & Burn, J. Differential psychological effects of lateralized brain damage. *Journal of Consulting and Clinical Psychology*, 1969, *33*, 551–557.

Pascal, G. R. & Suttell, B. J. *The Bender-Gestalt Test: quantification and validity for adults*. New York: Grune & Stratton, 1951.

Pauker, J. D. *Adult norms for the Halstead-Reitan Neuropsychological Test Battery: preliminary data*. Paper presented at the fifth annual meeting of the International Neuropsychological Society, Santa Fe, 1977.

Paterson, A. & Zangwill, O. L. Disorders of visual space perception associated with lesions of the right cerebral hemisphere. *Brain*, 1944, *67*, 331–358.

Paulson, G. W. Diagnosis of Huntington's disease. In T. N. Chase, N. W. Wexler, & A. Barbeau (Eds.), *Advances in Neurology* (Vol. 23). New York: Raven Press, 1979.

Payne, D. A. & Lehmann, I. J. A brief WAIS item analysis. *Journal of Clinical Psychology*, 1966, *22*, 296–297.

Payne, R. W. Cognitive abnormalities. In H. J. Eysenck (Ed.), *Handbook of abnormal psychology*. New York: Basic Books, 1961.

Payne, R. W. Disorders of thinking. In C. G. Costello (Ed.), *Symptoms of psychopathology*. New York: Wiley, 1970.

Payne, R. W. & Hewlett, J. H. G. Thought disorder in psychotic patients. In H. J. Eysenck (Ed.), *Experiments in personality* (Vol. 2, *Psychodiagnostics and psychodynamics*). New York: The Humanities Press, 1960.

Payne, R. W. & Jones, H. G. Statistics for the investigation of individual cases. *Journal of Clinical Psychology*, 1957, *13*, 115–121.

Pear, B. L. The radiographic morphology of cerebral atrophy. In W. L. Smith & M. Kinsbourne (Eds.), *Aging and dementia*. New York: Spectrum, 1977.

Peck, D. F. The conversion of Progressive Matrices and Mill Hill vocabulary raw scores into deviation IQ's. *Journal of Clinical Psychology*, 1970, *26*, 67–70.

Pendleton, M. G. & Heaton, R. K. A comparison of the Wisconsin Card Sorting Test and the Category Test. *Journal of Clinical Psychology*, 1982, *38*, 392–396.

Penfield, W. Functional localization in temporal and deep sylvian areas. *Research Publication, Association of Nervous and Mental Disease*, 1958, *36*, 210–227.

Penfield, W. Engrams in the human brain. *Proceedings of the Royal Society of Medicine*, 1968, *61*, 831–840.

Penfield, W. & Perot, P. The brain's record of auditory and visual experience. *Brain*, 1963, *86*, 595–696.

Penfield, W. & Rasmussen, T. *The cerebral cortex of man*. New York: Macmillan, 1950.

Peoples, C. & Moll, R. P. Bender-Gestalt performance as a function of drawing ability, school performance, and intelligence. *Journal of Clinical Psychology*, 1962, *18*, 106–107.

Perlmutter, M. What is memory aging the aging of? *Developmental Psychology*, 1978, *14*, 330–345.

Perret, E. The left frontal lobe of man and the suppression of habitual responses in verbal categorical behaviour. *Neuropsychologia*, 1974, *12*, 323–330.

684

Petersen, A. C. *Physical androgyny and cognitive functioning.* Paper presented at the American Psychological Association Convention, Washington, D.C., 1976.

Petersen, A. C. & Wittig, M. A. Sex-related differences in cognitive functioning: an overview. In M. A. Wittig & A. C. Petersen (Eds.), *Sex-related differences in cognitive functioning.* New York: Academic Press, 1979.

Peterson, L. N. & Kirschner, H. S. Gestural impairment and gestural ability in aphasia: a review. *Brain and Language,* 1981, *14,* 333–348.

Peterson, L. R. Short-term memory. *Scientific American,* 1966, *215,* 90–95.

Peterson, L. R. & Peterson, M. J. Short-term retention of individual verbal items. *Journal of Experimental Psychology,* 1959, *58,* 193–198.

Peyser, J. M., Edwards, K. R., & Poser, C. M. Psychological profiles in patients with multiple sclerosis. *Archives of Neurology,* 1980, *37,* 437–440.

Pfeiffer, E. SPMSQ: Short Portable Mental Status Questionnaire. *Journal of the American Geriatric Society,* 1975, *20,* 100 111.

Piazza, D. M. The influence of sex and handedness in hemispheric specialization of verbal and nonverbal tasks. *Neuropsychologia,* 1980, *18,* 163–176.

Piercy, M. The effects of cerebral lesions on intellectual functions: a review of current research trends. *British Journal of Psychiatry,* 1964, *110,* 310–352.

Piercy, M., Hécaen, H., & de Ajuriaguerra, J. Constructional apraxia associated with unilateral cerebral lesions—left and right-sided cases compared. *Brain,* 1960, *83,* 225–242.

Piercy, M. & Smyth, V. Right hemisphere dominance for certain non-verbal intellectual skills. *Brain,* 1962, *85,* 775–790.

Pillon, B. Négligence de l'hemi-espace gauche dans des épreuves visuo-constructives. *Neuropsychologia,* 1981a, *19,* 317–320.

Pillon, B. Troubles visuo-constructifs et méthodes de compensation: resultats de 85 patients atteints de lésions cérébrales. *Neuropsychologia,* 1981b, *19,* 375–383.

Pillon, B., Signoret, J.-L., & Lhermitte, F. Troubles de la pensée spatiale et syndrome amnésique consécutifs à une encéphalopathie anoxique. *Annales de Medécine Interne* (Paris), 1977, *128,* 269–274.

Pincus, J. H. & Tucker, G. *Behavioral neurology* (2nd ed.). New York: Oxford University Press, 1978.

Piotrowski, Z. The Rorschach inkblot method in organic disturbances of the central nervous system. *Journal of Nervous and Mental Disease,* 1937, *86,* 525–537.

Piotrowski, Z. Positive and negative Rorschach organic reactions. *Rorschach Research Exchange,* 1940, *4,* 147–151.

Pirozzolo, F. J. Disorders of perceptual processing. In E. C. Carterette & M. P. Friedman (Eds.), *Handbook of perception* (Vol. 9). New York: Academic Press, 1978.

Pirozzolo, F. J., Hansch, E. C., Mortimer, J. A., et al. Dementia in Parkinson disease: a neuropsychological analysis. *Brain and Cognition,* 1982, *1,* 71–83.

Plum, F. Organic disturbances of consciousness. In M. Critchley & J. L. O'Leary (Eds.), *Scientific foundations of neurology.* Philadelphia: F. A. Davis, 1972.

Plum, F. Dementia. *Nature,* 1979, *279,* 372–37.

Plum, F. & Caronna, J. J. Can one predict outcome of medical coma? In Ciba Foundation Symposium 34 (New Series). *Symposium on the outcome of severe damage to the central nervous system.* Amsterdam: Elsevier, 1975.

Plum, F. & Posner, J. B. *Diagnosis of stupor and coma* (3rd ed.). Philadelphia: F. A. Davis, 1980.

Plutchik, R. Conceptual and practical issues in the assessment of the elderly. In A. Raskin &

REFERENCES

L. F. Jarvik (Eds.), *Psychiatric symptoms and cognitive loss in the elderly*. Washington, D.C.: Hemisphere, 1979.

Plutchik, R., Conte, H., Lieberman, M., et al. Reliability and validity of a scale for assessing the functioning of geriatric patients. *Journal of the American Geriatric Society*, 1970, *18*, 491–500.

Plutchik, R., Conte, H., & Lieberman, M. Development of a scale (GIES) for assessment of cognitive and perceptual functioning in geriatric patients. *Journal of the American Geriatric Society*, 1971, *19*, 614–623.

Poeck, K. Modern trends in neuropsychology. In A. L. Benton (Ed.), *Contribution to clinical neuropsychology*. Chicago: Aldine, 1969.

Poeck, K. & Pietron, H. P. The influence of stretched speech presentation on Token Test performance of aphasic and right brain damaged patients. *Neuropsychologia*, 1981, *19*, 133–136.

Pollack, B. The validity of the Shipley-Hartford Retreat Test for "deterioration." *Psychiatric Quarterly*, 1942, *16*, 119–131.

Pollen, D. A. Some perceptual effects of electrical stimulation of the visual cortex in man. In D. B. Tower (Ed.), *The nervous system*. II. *The clinical neurosciences*. New York: Raven Press, 1975.

Polyakov, G. I. Modern data on the structural organization of the cerebral cortex. In A. R. Luria (Ed.), *Higher cortical functions in man*. New York: Basic Books, 1966.

Pontius, A. A. & Yudowitz, B. S. Frontal lobe system dysfunction in some criminal actions as shown in the Narratives Test. *Journal of Nervous and Mental Disease*, 1980, *168*, 111–117.

Poon, L. W., Fozard, J. L., Cermak, L. S., et al. (Eds.), *New directions in memory and aging*. Hillsdale, N.J.: Lawrence Erlbaum Associates, 1980.

Poppelreuter, W. *Die psychischen Schädigungen durch Kopfschuss im Kriege 1914/16*. Leipzig: Verlag von Leopold Voss, 1917.

Porch, B. E. *Porch Index of Communicative Ability*. Palo Alto, Calif.: Consulting Psychologists Press, 1967.

Porch, B. E. Multidimensional scoring in aphasia testing. *Journal of Speech and Hearing Research*, 1971, *14*, 776–792.

Porch, B. E., Friden, T., & Porec, J. *Objective differentiation of aphasic vs. non-organic patients*. Paper presented at the fifth annual meeting of the International Neuropsychological Society, Santa Fe, 1977.

Porteus, S. D. *The Maze Test and clinical psychology*. Palo Alto, Calif.: Pacific Books, 1959.

Porteus, S. D. *Porteus Maze Test. Fifty years' application*. New York: Psychological Corporation, 1965.

Posner, M. I. & Boies, S. J. Components of attention. *Psychological Review*, 1971, *78*, 391–408.

Post, F. Dementia, depression, and pseudodementia. In D. F. Benson & D. Blumer (Eds.), *Psychiatric aspects of neurologic disease*. New York: Grune & Stratton, 1975.

Potkay, C. R. *The Rorschach clinician*. New York: Grune & Stratton, 1971.

Power, D. G., Logue, P. E., McCarty, S. M., et al. Inter-rater reliability of the Russell revision of the Wechsler Memory Scale: an attempt to clarify some ambiguities in scoring. *Journal of Clinical Neuropsychology*, 1979, *1*, 343–346.

Prado, W. M. & Taub, D. V. Accurate prediction of individual intellectual functioning by the Shipley-Hartford. *Journal of Clinical Psychology*, 1966, *22*, 294–296.

REFERENCES

Pribram, K. H. The amnestic syndromes: disturbances in coding? In G. A. Talland & N. C. Waugh (Eds.), *The pathology of memory*. New York: Academic Press, 1969.

Price, L. J., Fein, G., & Feinberg, I. *Cognitive and neuropsychological variables in the normal elderly.* Paper presented at the American Psychological Association convention, New York City, September, 1979.

Price, L. J., Fein, G., & Feinberg, I. Neuropsychological assessment of cognitive function in the elderly. In L. W. Poon (Ed.), *Aging in the 1980s*. Washington, D.C.: American Psychological Association, 1980.

Prigatano, G. P. Wechsler Memory Scale is a poor screening test for brain dysfunction. *Journal of Clinical Psychology*, 1977, *33*, 772–777.

Prigatano, G. P. Wechsler Memory Scale: a selective review of the literature. *Journal of Clinical Psychology*, 1978, *34*, 816–832.

Prigatano, G. P. & Parsons, O. A. Relationship of age and education to Halstead Test performance in different patient populations. *Journal of Consulting and Clinical Psychology*, 1976, *44*, 527–533.

Prigatano, G. P., Parsons, O., Wright, E., et al. Neuropsychological test performance in mildly hypoxemic COPD patients. *Journal of Consulting and Clinical Psychology*, 1983, *51*, 108–116.

Prigatano, G. P. & Pribram, K. H. Perception and memory of facial affect following brain injury. *Journal of Perceptual and Motor Skills*, 1982, *54*, 859–869.

Psychological Corporation. *Test Service Bulletin*. No. 48, 1955.

Purdue Research Foundation. *Examiner's manual for the Purdue Pegboard*. Chicago: Science Research Associates, 1948.

Purisch, A. D., Golden, C. J., & Hammeke, T. A. Discrimination of schizophrenic and brain-injured patients by a standardized version of Luria's neuropsychological tests. *Journal of Consulting and Clinical Psychology*, 1978, *46*, 1266–1273.

Pyke, S. & Agnew, N. McK. Digit Span performance as a function of noxious stimulation. *Journal of Consulting Psychology*, 1963, *27*, 281.

Quattlebaum, L. F. A brief note on the relationship between two psychomotor tests. *Journal of Clinical Psychology*, 1968, *24*, 198–199.

Quereshi, M. Y. The comparability of WAIS and WISC subtest scores and IQ estimates. *Journal of Psychology*, 1968, *68*, 73–82.

Query, W. T. & Megran, J. Age-related norms for AVLT in a male patient population. Unpublished manuscript, 1982. (Available from W. T. Query, Psychology Service, 116B, VA Medical Center, Fargo, ND).

Rabin, I. A. Diagnostic use of intelligent tests. In B. B. Wolman (Ed.), *Handbook of clinical psychology*. New York: McGraw-Hill, 1965.

Raczkowski, D., Kalat, J. W., & Nebes, R. Reliability and validity of some handedness questionnaire items. *Neuropsychologia*, 1974, *12*, 43–47.

Raghaven, S. *A comparison of the performance of right and left hemiplegics on verbal and nonverbal body image tasks*. Master's Thesis. Northampton, Mass.: Smith College, 1961.

Raichle, M. E., De Vivo, D. C., & Hanaway, J. Disorders of cerebral circulation. In S. G. Eliasson, A. L. Prensky, & W. B. Hardin, Jr. (Eds.), *Neurological pathophysiology* (2nd ed.). New York: Oxford University Press, 1978.

Ramier, A.-M. & Hécaen, H. Rôle respectif des atteintes frontales et de la latéralisation lésionnelle dans les déficits de la "fluence verbale." *Revue Neurologique*, Paris, 1970, *123*, 17–22.

Randt, C. T., Brown, E. R., & Osborne, D. J., Jr. A memory test for longitudinal measurement of mild to moderate deficits. *Clinical Neuropsychology*, 1980, *2*, 184–194.

REFERENCES

Randt, C. T., Brown, E. R., Osborne, D. P., Jr., et al. *Memory test*. Department of Neurology, N.Y.U. Medical Center, 550 First Ave., New York, N.Y., 10016, no date.

Rao, S. M., Hammeke, T. A., Huang, J. Y. S., et al. *Memory disturbance in chronic, progressive multiple sclerosis*. Paper presented at the tenth annual meeting of the International Neuropsychological Society, Pittsburgh, February, 1982.

Rapaport, D., Gill, M. M., & Schafer, R. *Diagnostic psychological testing* (Rev. ed.; R. R. Holt, Ed.). New York: International Universities Press, 1968.

Ratcliff, G. Spatial thought, mental rotation and the right cerebral hemisphere. *Neuropsychologia*, 1979, *17*, 49–54.

Rausch, R., Lieb, J. P., & Crandall, P. H. Neuropsychologic correlates of depth spike activity in epileptic patients. *Archives of Neurology*, 1978, *35*, 699–705.

Raven, J. C. *Mill-Hill Vocabulary Scale* (2nd ed.). London: H. K. Lewis, 1958.

Raven, J. C. *Guide to the Standard Progressive Matrices*. London: H. K. Lewis, 1960; New York: Psychological Corporation, no date.

Raven, J. C. *Guide to Using the Coloured Progressive Matrices*. London: H. K. Lewis, 1965; New York: Psychological Corporation, no date.

Redlich, F. C. & Dorsey, J. F. Denial of blindness by patients with cerebral disease. *Archives of Neurology and Psychiatry*, 1945, *53*, 407–417.

Reed, H. B. C., Jr. & Reitan, R. M. Intelligence test performance of brain-damaged subjects with lateralized motor deficits. *Journal of Consulting Psychology*, 1963, *27*, 102–106.

Rees, M. Symbol Digit Modalities Test (SDMT) (Review). In F. L. Darley (Ed.), *Evaluation of appraisal techniques in speech and language pathology*. Reading, Mass.: Addison-Wesley, 1979.

Reifler, B. V., Larson, E., & Hanley, R. Coexistence of cognitive impairment and depression in geriatric outpatients. *American Journal of Psychiatry*, 1982, *139*, 623–626.

Reisberg, B. & Ferris, S. H. Diagnosis and assessment of the older patient. *Hospital and Community Psychiatry*, 1982, *33*, 104–110.

Reitan, R. M. *Instructions and procedures for administering the Neuropsychological Test Battery used at the Neuropsychology Laboratory, Indiana University Medical Center*. Unpublished manuscript, undated.

Reitan, R. M. Certain differential effects of left and right cerebral lesions in human adults. *Journal of Comparative and Physiological Psychology*, 1955a, *48*, 474–477.

Reitan, R. M. Investigation of the validity of Halstead's measure of biological intelligence. *A.M.A. Archives of Neurology and Psychiatry*, 1955b, *73*, 28–35.

Reitan, R. M. Validity of the Trail Making Test as an indication of organic brain damage. *Perceptual and Motor Skills*, 1958, *8*, 271–276.

Reitan, R. M. Correlations between the Trail Making Test and the Wechsler-Bellevue Scale. *Perceptual and Motor Skills*, 1959, *9*, 127–130.

Reitan, R. M. Psychological deficits resulting from cerebral lesions in man. In J. M. Warren & K. Akert (Eds.), *The frontal granular cortex and behavior*. New York: McGraw-Hill, 1964.

Reitan, R. M. Problems and prospects in studying the psychological correlates of brain lesions. *Cortex*, 1966a, *2*, 127–154.

Reitan, R. M. A research program on the psychological effects of brain lesions in human beings. In N. R. Ellis (Ed.), *International review of research in mental retardation* (Vol. 1). New York: Academic Press, 1966b.

Reitan, R. M. Psychological changes associated with aging and cerebral damage. *Mayo Clinic Proceedings*, 1967, *42*, 653–673.

Reitan, R. M. Verbal problem solving as related to cerebral damage. *Perceptual and Motor Skills*, 1972, *34*, 515–524.

Reitan, R. M. *Behavioral manifestations of impaired brain functions in aging.* Paper presented at the American Psychological Association Convention, Montreal, September, 1973.

Reitan, R. M. Neurological and physiological bases of psychopathology. *Annual Review of Psychology*, 1976, *27*, 189–216.

Reitan, R. M. & Davison, L. A. *Clinical neuropsychology: current status and applications.* New York: Hemisphere, 1974.

Reitan, R. M. & Kløve, H. *Hypotheses supported by clinical evidence that are under current investigation.* Unpublished manuscript, 1959.

Reitan, R. M., Reed, J. C., & Dyken, M. I. Cognitive, psychomotor, and motor correlates of multiple sclerosis. *Journal of Nervous and Mental Disease*, 1971, *153*, 218–224.

Reitan, R. M. & Tarshes, E. L. Differential effects of lateralized brain lesions on the Trail Making Test. *Journal of Nervous and Mental Disease*, 1959, *129*, 257–262.

de Reuck, A. V. S. & O'Connor, M. (Eds.), *Disorders of language.* Ciba Foundation Symposium. Boston: Little, Brown, 1964.

Rey, A. L'examen psychologique dans les cas d'encéphalopathie traumatique. *Archives de Psychologie*, 1941, *28*, No. 112, 286–340.

Rey, A. Sollicitation de la mémoire de fixation par des mots et des objets présentés simultanément. *Archives de Psychologie*, 1959, *37*, 126–139.

Rey, A. *L'examen clinique en psychologie.* Paris: Presses Universitaires de France, 1964.

Reynolds, E. H. *Behavioral effects of anticonvulsants.* Paper presented at the first European conference of the International Neuropsychological Society, Oxford, England, 1977.

Reznikoff, M. & Tomblen, D. The use of human figure drawings in the diagnosis of organic pathology. *Journal of Consulting Psychology*, 1956, *20*, 467–470.

Richardson, F. C. & Woolfolk, R. L. Mathematics anxiety. In I. G. Sarason (Ed.), *Test anxiety: theory, research, and applications.* Hillsdale, N.J.: Lawrence Erlbaum Associates, 1980.

Richardson, J. T. E. The effects of closed head injury upon memory. In M. M. Gruneberg, P. E. Morris, & R. N. Sykes (Eds.), *Practical aspects of memory.* New York: Academic Press, 1978.

Riddell, S. A. The performance of elderly psychiatric patients on equivalent forms of tests of memory and learning. *British Journal of Social and Clinical Psychology*, 1962a, *1*, 70–71.

Riddell, S. A. The relationships between tests of organic involvement, memory impairment and diagnosis in elderly psychiatric patients. *British Journal of Social and Clinical Psychology*, 1962b, *1*, 228–231.

Riege, W. H. & Williams, M. V. *Modality and age comparisons in nonverbal memory.* Paper presented at the American Psychological Association Convention, Montreal, September, 1980.

Riese, W. Dynamics in brain lesions. *Journal of Nervous and Mental Disease*, 1960, *131*, 291–301.

Riklan, M. *L-Dopa and Parkinsonism. A psychological assessment.* Springfield, Ill.: C. C. Thomas, 1973.

Riklan, M. & Cooper, I. S. Psychometric studies of verbal functioning following thalamic lesions in humans. *Brain and Language*, 1975, *2*, 45–64.

Riklan, M. & Cooper, I. S. Thalamic lateralization of psychological functions: Psychometric studies. In S. Harnad, R. W. Doty, L. Goldstein, et al. (Eds.), *Lateralization in the central nervous system.* New York: Academic Press, 1977.

Riklan, M. & Diller, L. Visual motor performance before and after chemosurgery of the basal

REFERENCES

ganglia in Parkinsonism. *Journal of Nervous and Mental Disease*, 1961, *132*, 307–314.

Riklan, M. & Levita, E. *Subcortical correlates of human behavior*. Baltimore: Williams & Wilkins, 1969.

Riklan, M., Zahn, T. P., & Diller, L. Human figure drawings before and after chemosurgery of the basal ganglia in Parkinsonism. *Journal of Nervous and Mental Disease*, 1962, *135*, 500–506.

Rimel, R. W. *An assessment of recovery following head trauma*. Paper presented at the fourth annual Post-Graduate Course on the Rehabilitation of the Traumatic Brain-Injured Adult, Williamsburg, Virginia, 1980.

Rimel, R. W., Giordani, B., Barth, J. T., et al. Disability caused by minor head injury. *Neurosurgery*, 1981, *9*, 221–228.

Ritter, E. G. Aphasia Language Performance Scales (ALPS) (Review). In F. L. Darley (Ed.), *Evaluation of appraisal techniques in speech and language pathology*. Reading, Mass.: Addison-Wesley, 1979.

Rivers, D. L. & Love, R. J. Language performance on visual processing tasks in right hemisphere lesion cases. *Brain and Language*, 1980, *10*, 348–366.

Rizzolatti, G., Umilta, C., & Berlucchi, G. Opposite superiorities of the right and left cerebral hemispheres in discriminative reaction time to physiognomical and alphabetical material. *Brain*, 1971, *94*, 431–442.

Roberts, A. H. Long-term prognosis of severe accidental head injury. *Proceedings of the Royal Society of Medicine*, 1976, *69*, 137–140.

Roberts, J. K. A., Robertson, M. M., & Trimble, M. R. The lateralising significance of hypergraphia in temporal lobe epilepsy. *Journal of Neurology, Neurosurgery, and Psychiatry*, 1982, *45*, 131–138.

Robinson, A. L., Heaton, R. K., Lehman, R. A. W., & Stilson, D. W. The utility of the Wisconsin Card Sorting Test in detecting and localizing frontal lobe lesions. *Journal of Consulting and Clinical Psychology*, 1980, *48*, 605–614.

Robinson, D. J. & Leung, P. *Neuropsychological test differences between blinded and sighted adults*. Paper presented at the American Psychological Association Convention, Montreal, 1980.

Robinson, D. N. Cerebral plurality and the unity of self. *American Psychologist*, 1982, *37*, 904–910.

Robinson, J. H. & Alexander, J. *Ravens performance as a function of intelligence and memory load*. Paper presented at the American Psychological Association Convention, Toronto, 1978.

Robinson, R. G. & Benson, D. F. Depression in aphasia patients: frequency, severity, and clinical-pathological correlations. *Brain and Language*, 1981, *14*, 282–291.

Robinson, R. G. & Szetela, B. Mood changes following left hemispheric brain injury. *Annals of Neurology*, 1981, *9*, 447–453.

Rochford, J. M., Detre, T., Tucker, G. J., & Harrow, M. Neuropsychological impairments in functional psychiatric disease. *Archives of General Psychiatry*, 1970, *22*, 114–119.

Ron, M. A., Toone, B. K., Garralda, M. E., & Lishman, W. A. Diagnostic accuracy in presenile dementia. *British Journal of Psychiatry*, 1979, *134*, 161–168.

Rorschach, H. *(Psychodiagnostics: a diagnostic test based on perception)* (P. Lemkau & B. Kronenburg, trans.). Berne: Huber, 1942. (U.S. distributor, Grune & Stratton).

Rose, S. P. R., Hambley, J., & Haywood, J. Neurochemical approaches to developmental plasticity and learning. In M. R. Rosenzweig & E. L. Bennett (Eds.), *Neural mechanisms of learning and memory*. Cambridge, Mass.: Massachusetts Institute of Technology Press, 1976.

Rosen, H. & Swigar, M. E. Depression and normal pressure hydrocephalus. *Journal of Nervous and Mental Disease*, 1976, *163*, 35–40.

Rosen, W. G. Verbal fluency in aging and dementia. *Journal of Clinical Neuropsychology*, 1980, *2*, 135–146.

Rosenbaum, M. & Najenson, T. Changes in life patterns and symptoms of low mood as reported by wives of severely brain-injured soldiers. *Journal of Consulting and Clinical Psychology*, 1976, *44*, 881–888.

Rosenman, M. F. & Lucik, T. W. A failure to replicate an epilepsy scale of the MMPI. *Journal of Clinical Psychology*, 1970, *26*, 372.

Rosenzweig, M. R., Bennett, E. L., & Diamond, M. C. Brain changes in response to experience. *Scientific American*, 1972, *226*, 22–29.

Rosenzweig, M. R. & Leiman, A. L. Brain functions. *Annual Review of Psychology*, 1968, *19*, 55–98.

Rosner, B. S. Recovery of function and localization of function in historical perspective. In D. G. Stein, J. J. Rosen, & N. Butters (Eds.), *Plasticity and recovery of function in the central nervous system*. New York: Academic Press, 1974.

Ross, E. D. Functional-anatomic organization of the affective component of language in the right hemisphere. *Archives of Neurology*, 1981, *38*, 561–569.

Ross, E. D. Disorders of recent memory in humans. *Trends in Neurosciences*, 1982, *5*, 170–172.

Ross, E. D., Harney, J. H., de Lacoste-Utamsing, C., & Purdy, P. D. How the brain integrates effective and propositional language into a unified behavioral function. *Archives of Neurology*, 1981, *38*, 745–748.

Ross, E. D. & Mesulam, M.-M. Dominant language functions of the right hemisphere? Prosody and emotional gesturing. *Archives of Neurology*, 1979, *36*, 144–148.

Ross, E. D. & Rush, A. J. Diagnosis and neuroanatomical correlates of depression in brain-damaged patients. *Archives of General Psychiatry*, 1981, *38*, 1344–1354.

Ross, P. & Turkewitz, G. Individual differences in cerebral asymmetries for facial recognition. *Cortex*, 1981, *17*, 199–214.

Ross, W. D. & Ross, S. Some Rorschach ratings of clinical value. *Rorschach Research Exchange*, 1942, *8*, 1–9.

Rossi, G. F. & Rosadini, G. Experimental analysis of cerebral damage in man. In C. H. Millikan & F. L. Darley (Eds.), *Brain mechanisms underlying speech and language*. New York: Grune & Stratton, 1967.

Roth, M. Diagnosis of senile and related forms of dementia. In R. Katzman, R. D. Terry, & K. L. Bick (Eds.), *Alzheimer's disease: senile dementia and related disorders* (Aging, Vol. 7). New York: Raven Press, 1978.

Roth, M. Aging of the brain and dementia: an overview. In L. Amaducci, A. N. Davison, & P. Antuono (Eds.), *Aging of the brain and dementia*. New York: Raven Press, 1980.

Roth, M. & Hopkins, B. Psychological test performance in patients over 60. I. Senile psychoses and the affective disorders of old age. *Journal of Mental Science*, 1953, *99*, 439–450.

Rozin, P. The psychobiological approach to human memory. In M. R. Rosenzweig & E. L. Bennett (Eds.), *Neural mechanisms of learning and memory*. Cambridge, Mass.: Massachusetts Institute of Technology Press, 1976.

Rubens, A. B. Anatomic asymmetries of human cerebral cortex. In S. Harnad, R. W. Doty, L. Goldstein, et al. (Eds.), *Lateralization in the nervous system*. New York: Academic Press, 1977.

Rubens, A. B. Agnosia. In K. M. Heilman & E. Valenstein (Eds.), *Clinical neuropsychology*. New York: Oxford University Press, 1979.

REFERENCES

Ruch, F. L. & Ruch, M. *Employee Aptitude Survey (EAS)*. San Diego, Calif.: Educational and Industrial Testing Service, 1963.

Ruesch, J. The diagnostic value of disturbances of consciousness. *Diseases of the Nervous System*, 1944, *5*, 69–83.

Ruesch, J. & Moore, B. E. The measurement of intellectual functions in the acute stage of head injury. *Archives of Neurological Psychiatry*, 1943, *50*, 165–170.

Russell, E. W. Effect of acute lateralized brain damage on a factor analysis of the Wechsler-Bellevue intelligence test. *Proceedings of the 80th Annual Convention of the American Psychological Association*, 1972a, *7*, 421–422.

Russell, E. W. *The effect of acute lateralized brain damage on Halstead's biological intelligence factors*. Paper presented at the American Psychological Association Convention, Honolulu, August, 1972b.

Russell, E. W. WAIS factor analysis with brain-damaged subjects using criterion measures. *Journal of Consulting and Clinical Psychology*, 1972c, *39*, 133–139.

Russell, E. W. A multiple scoring method for the assessment of complex memory functions. *Journal of Consulting and Clinical Psychology*, 1975a, *43*, 800–809.

Russell, E. W. Validation of a brain-damage vs. schizophrenia MMPI key. *Journal of Clinical Psychology*, 1975b, *31*, 659–661.

Russell, E. W. MMPI profiles of brain-damaged and schizophrenic subjects. *Journal of Clinical Psychology*, 1977, *33*, 190–193.

Russell, E. W. Three patterns of brain damage on the WAIS. *Journal of Clinical Psychology*, 1979, *35*, 611–620.

Russell, E. W. *Memory testing: the next step*. Paper presented at the American Psychological Association Convention, Montreal, September, 1980a.

Russell, E. W. Tactile sensation, an all-or-none effect of cerebral damage. *Journal of Clinical Psychology*, 1980b, *36*, 858–864.

Russell, E. W. *Theoretical bases of Luria-Nebraska and Halstead-Reitan batteries*. Paper presented at the American Psychological Association Convention, Montreal, September, 1980c.

Russell, E. W. The chronicity effect. *Journal of Clinical Psychology*, 1981a, *37*, 246–253.

Russell, E. W. The pathology and clinical examination of memory. In S. B. Filskov & T. J. Boll (Eds.), *Handbook of clinical neuropsychology*, New York: Wiley-Interscience, 1981b.

Russell, E. W. Factor analysis of the Revised Wechsler Memory Scale tests in a neuropsychological battery. *Perceptual and Motor Skills*, 1982, *54*, 971–974.

Russell, E. W., Neuringer, C., & Goldstein, G. *Assessment of brain damage. A neuropsychological key approach*. New York: Wiley-Interscience, 1970.

Russell, P. N., & Rix-Trott, H. M. An exploratory study of some behavioural consequences of insulin induced hypoglycaemia. *New Zealand Medical Journal*, 1975, *81*, 337–340.

Russell, W. R. Cerebral involvement in head injury. *Brain*, 1932, *55*, 549–603.

Russell, W. R. Some anatomical aspects of aphasia. *The Lancet*, 1963, *i*, 1173–1177.

Russell, W. R. *Explaining the brain*. London: Oxford University Press, 1975.

Russell, W. R. & Espir, M. L. E. *Traumatic aphasia*. Oxford: Oxford University Press, 1961.

Russell, W. R. & Nathan, P. W. Traumatic amnesia. *Brain*, 1946, *69*, 280–300.

Russo, M. & Vignolo, L. A. Visual figure-ground discrimination in patients with unilateral cerebral disease. *Cortex*, 1967, *3*, 118–127.

Rutledge, L. T. Synaptogenesis: effects of synaptic use. In M. R. Rosenzweig & E. L. Bennett (Eds.), *Neural mechanisms of learning and memory*. Cambridge, Mass.: Massachusetts Institute of Technology Press, 1976.

Ryan, C. & Butters, N. Further evidence for a continuum-of-impairment encompassing alcoholic Korsakoff patients and chronic alcoholics. *Alcoholism: Clinical and Experimental Research*, 1980a, *4*, 190–198.

Ryan, C. & Butters, N. Learning and memory impairments in young and old alcoholics: evidence for the premature-aging hypothesis. *Alcoholism: Clinical and Experimental Research*, 1980b, *4*, 288–293.

Ryan, C. & Butters, N. Cognitive effects in alcohol abuse. In B. Kissin & H. Begleiter (Eds.), *Cognitive effects in alcohol abuse*. New York: Plenum Press, 1982.

Ryan, C., Butters, N., Montgomery, K., Adinolfi, A., & DiDario, B. Memory deficits in chronic alcoholics: continuities between the "intact" alcoholic and the alcoholic Korsakoff patient. In H. Begleiter & B. Kissin (Eds.), *Biological effects of alcohol*. New York: Plenum Press, 1980.

Ryan, C., DiDario, B., Butters, N., & Adinolfi, A. The relationship between abstinence and recovery of function in male alcoholics. *Journal of Clinical Neuropsychology*, 1980, *2*, 125–134.

Rylander, G. Personality changes after operations on the frontal lobes: a clinical study of 32 cases. *Acta Psychiatrica et Neurologica Scandinavica*, 1939, (Supplement No. 20), 1–327.

Rzechorzek, A. Cognitive dysfunctions resulting from unilateral frontal lobe lesions in man. In M. Molloy, G. V. Stanley, & K. W. Walsh (Eds.), *Brain Impairment: Proceedings of the 1978 Brain Impairment Workshop*. Melbourne: University of Melbourne, 1979.

Sackeim, H. A., Greenberg, M. S., Weiman, A. L., et al. Hemisphere asymmetry in the expression of positive and negative emotions. *Archives of Neurology*, 1982, *39*, 210–218.

Sackeim, H. A., Gur, R. C., & Saucy, M. C. Emotions are expressed more intensely on the left side of the face. *Science*, 1978, *202*, 434–436.

Safer, M. A. & Leventhal, H. Ear differences in evaluating emotional tones of voice and verbal content. *Journal of Experimental Psychology: Human Perception and Performance*, 1977, *3*, 75–82.

Salvatore, A., Strait, M., & Brookshire, R. *Effects of patient characteristics on delivery of the Token Test commands by experienced and inexperienced examiners*. Paper presented at the Fifth Conference of Clinical Aphasiology. Santa Fe, April, 1975.

Salzman, C. & Shader, R. I. Clinical evaluation of depression in the elderly. In A. Raskin & L. Jarvik (Eds.), *Psychiatric symptoms and cognitive loss in the elderly*. Washington, D. C.: Hemisphere Publishing Co,, 1979.

Samuels, I., Butters, N., & Fedio, P. Short-term memory disorders following temporal lobe removals in humans. *Cortex*, 1972, *8*, 283–298.

Sanchez-Craig, M. Drinking pattern as a determinant of alcoholics' performance on the Trail-Making Test. *Journal of Studies on Alcohol*, 1980, *41*, 1083–1089.

Sanders, H. The problems of measuring very long-term memory. *International Journal of Mental Health*, 1972, *1*, 98–102.

Sanderson, R. E. & Inglis, J. Learning and mortality in elderly psychiatric patients. *Journal of Gerontology*, 1961, *16*, 375–376.

Sands, E., Sarno, M. T., & Shankweiler, D. Long-term assessment of language function in aphasia due to stroke. *Archives of Physical Medicine and Rehabilitation*, 1969, *50*, 202–206.

Sarno, J. E., Sarno, M. T., & Levita, E. Evaluating language improvement after completed stroke. *Archives of Physical Medicine and Rehabilitation*, 1971, *52*, 73–78.

Sarno, M. T. *The Communication Profile: Manual of Directions*. New York: Institute of Rehabilitation Medicine, New York University Medical Center, 1969.

Sarno, M. T. The status of research in recovery from aphasia. In Y. Lebrun & R. Hoops (Eds.), *Recovery in aphasics*. Amsterdam: Swets & Zeitlinger B. V., 1976.

693

Sarno, M. T. The nature of verbal impairment after closed head injury. *Journal of Nervous and Mental Disease,* 1980, *168,* 685–692.

Sattler, J. M. Analysis of functions of the 1960 Stanford-Binet intelligence Scale, Form L-M. *Journal of Clinical Psychology,* 1965, *21,* 173–179.

Satz, P. Specific and nonspecific effects of brain lesions in man. *Journal of Abnormal Psychology,* 1966, *71,* 65–70.

Satz, P. Incidence of aphasia in left-handers: a test of some hypothetical models of speech organization. In J. Herron (Ed.), *Neuropsychology of left-handedness.* New York: Academic Press, 1980.

Satz, P., Fennell, E., & Reilly, C. Predictive validity of six neurodiagnostic tests. *Journal of Consulting and Clinical Psychology,* 1970, *34,* 375–381.

Satz, P., Fletcher, J. M., & Sutker, L. S. Neuropsychologic, intellectual, and personality correlates of chronic marijuana use in native Costa Ricans. *Annals of the New York Academy of Science,* 1976, *282,* 266–306.

Satz, P. & Mogel, S. An abbreviation of the WAIS for clinical use. *Journal of Clinical Psychology,* 1962, *18,* 77–79.

Saunders, D. R. A factor analysis of the Information and the Arithmetic items of the WAIS. *Psychological Reports,* 1960a, *6,* 367–383.

Saunders, D. R. A factor analysis of the Picture Completion items of the WAIS. *Journal of Clinical Psychology,* 1960b, *16,* 146–149.

Savage, R. D. Intellectual assessment. In P. Mittler (Ed.), *The psychological assessment of mental and physical handicaps.* London: Methuen, 1970.

Savage, R. D., Britton, P. G., Bolton, N., & Hall, E. H. *Intellectual functioning in the aged.* New York: Harper & Row, 1973.

Schachter, D. L., *Imagery mnemonics, retrieval mnemonics, and the closed head injury patient.* Paper presented at the eighth annnual meeting of the International Neuropsychological Society, San Francisco, 1980.

Schacter, D. L. & Crovitz, H. F. Memory function after closed head injury. A review of the quantitative research. *Cortex,* 1977, *13,* 150–176.

Schacter, D. L. & Tulving, E. Memory, amnesia, and the episodic/semantic distinction. In R. Isaacson & N. Spear (Eds.), *Expression of knowledge.* New York: Plenum Press, 1982.

Schaeffer, J., Andrysiak, T., & Ungerleider, J. T. Cognition and long-term use of Ganja (Cannabis). *Science,* 1981, *213,* 465–466.

Schafer, R. *The clinical application of psychological tests.* New York: International Universities Press, 1948.

Schaie, J. P. *Strategies differentiating chronic brain syndrome from depression in the elderly.* Paper presented at the American Psychological Association Convention, Washington, D.C., 1976.

Schaie, K. W. Rigidity-flexibility and intelligence: a cross-sectional study of the adult life span from 20 to 70 years. *Psychological Monographs,* 1958, *72* (9, Whole No. 462).

Schalling, D. Qualitative changes in vocabulary test performance after lobotomy and selective frontal operations. *Acta Psychologica,* 1957, *13,* 279–287.

Scheinberg, P. Multi-infarct dementia. In R. Katzman, R. D. Terry, & K. L. Bick (Eds.), *Alzheimer's disease: senile dementia and related disorders* (*Aging,* Vol. 7). New York: Raven Press, 1978.

Schenkenberg, T., Bradford, D. C., & Ajax, E. T. Line bisection and unilateral visual neglect in patients with neurologic impairment. *Neurology,* 1980, *30,* 509–517.

Scherer, I. W., Klett, C. J., & Winne, J. F. Psychological changes over a five year period following bilateral frontal lobotomy. *Journal of Consulting Psychology*, 1957, *21*, 291–295.

Scherer, I. W., Winne, J. F., & Baker, R. W. Psychological changes over a three year period following bilateral prefrontal lobotomy. *Journal of Consulting Psychology*, 1955, *19*, 291–298.

Schmitt, F. O. Introduction. In G. M. Edelman & V. B. Mountcastle (Eds.), *The mindful brain*. Cambridge, Mass.: Massachusetts Institute of Technology Press, 1978.

Schneck, M. K., Reisberg, B., & Ferris, S. H. An overview of current concepts of Alzheimer's disease. *American Journal of Psychiatry*, 1982, *139*, 165–173.

Schonen, S. de Déficit mnésique d'origine organique et niveaux d'organisation des taches a mémoriser. *Année Psychologique*, 1968, *68*, 97–114.

Schonfield, D. Translations in gerontology—from lab to life. *American Psychologist*, 1974, *29*, 796–815.

Schreiber, D. J., Goldman, H., Kleinman, K. M., et al. The relationship between independent neuropsychological and neurological detection and localization of cerebral impairment. *Journal of Nervous and Mental Disease*, 1976, *162*, 360–365.

Schuell, H. Diagnosis and prognosis in aphasia. *A.M.A. Archives of Neurological Psychiatry*, 1955, *74*, 308–315.

Schuell, H. *Differential diagnosis of aphasia with the Minnesota Test*. Minneapolis: University of Minnesota Press, (2nd ed., revised), 1972.

Schulman, J. C., Kaspar, J. C., & Throne, F. M. *Brain damage and behavior*. Springfield, Ill.: C. C. Thomas, 1965.

Schwartz, A. S., Marchok, P. L., & Flynn, R. E. A sensitive test for tactile extinction: results in patients with parietal and frontal lobe disease. *Journal of Neurology, Neurosurgery, and Psychiatry*, 1977, *40*, 228–233.

Schwartz, M. F., Marin, O. S. M., & Saffran, E. M. Dissociations of language function in dementia: a case study. *Brain and Language*, 1979, *7*, 277–306.

Schwartz, M. S. & Ivnik, R. J. *Wechsler Memory Scale I: toward a more objective and systematic scoring system for the Logical Memory and Visual Reproduction subtests*. Paper presented at Psychological Association Convention, Montreal, September, 1980.

Scientific American. The brain. San Francisco: W. H. Freeman, 1979.

Scott, D. F. *Understanding EEG*. Philadelphia: J. B. Lippincott, 1976.

Scott, D. F. Psychiatric aspects of epilepsy. *British Journal of Psychiatry*, 1978, *132*, 417–430.

Scott, L. H. Measuring intelligence with the Goodenough-Harris Drawing Test. *Psychological Bulletin*, 1981, *89*, 483–505.

Searleman, A. A review of right hemisphere linguistic capabilities. *Psychological Bulletin*, 1977, *84*, 503–528.

Searleman, A. A. Subject variables and cerebral organization for language. *Cortex*, 1980, *16*, 239–254.

Seashore, C. E., Lewis, D., & Saetveit, D. L. *Seashore measures of musical talents* (Rev. ed.). New York: Psychological Corporation, 1960.

Secrest, M. *Verbal fluency in normal elderly subjects*. Unpublished master's thesis, Portland State University, Portland, Ore., 1982.

Seitelberger, F. & Jellinger, K. Protracted post-traumatic encephalopathy. *International symposium on head injuries*. Edinburgh: Churchill Livingstone, 1971.

Selecki, B. R., Simpson, D. A., Vanderfield, G. K., et al. The epidemiology of head injury in New South Wales, 1977. In G. A. Broe & R. L. Tate (Eds.), *Brain impairment. Proceedings of the Fifth Annual Brain Impairment Conference.* Sydney: Postgraduate Committee in Medicine of the University of Sydney (1982).

Seltzer, B. & Sherwin, I. "Organic Brain Syndromes.": an empirical study and critical review. *American Journal of Psychiatry,* 1978, *135,* 13–21.

Semenza, C., Denes, G., D'Urso, V., et al. Analytic and global strategies in copying designs by unilaterally brain-damaged patients. *Cortex,* 1978, *14,* 404–410.

Semmes, J. Hemispheric specialization: a possible clue to mechanism. *Neuropsychologia,* 1968, *6,* 11–26.

Semmes, J., Weinstein, S., Ghent, L., & Teuber, H.-L. *Somatosensory changes after penetrating brain wounds in man.* Cambridge, Mass.: Harvard University Press, 1960.

Semmes, J., Weinstein, S., Ghent, L., & Teuber, H.-L. Correlates of impaired orientation in personal and extrapersonal space. *Brain,* 1963, *86,* 747–772.

Seppäläinen, A. M., Lindström, K., & Martelin, T. Neurophysiological and psychological picture of solvent poisoning. *American Journal of Industrial Medicine,* 1981, *1,* 31–42.

Serafetinides, E. A. Psychosocial aspects of neurosurgical management of epilepsy. In D. P. Purpura, J. K. Penry, & R. D. Walter (Eds.), *Advances in neurology* (Vol. 8). New York: Raven Press, 1975.

Seron, X. Analyse neuropsychologique des lésions préfrontales chez l'homme. *L'Année Psychologique,* 1978, *78,* 183–202.

Seron, X. *Aphasie et neuropsychologie.* Bruxelles: Pierre Mardaga, 1979.

Shader, R. I., Harmatz, J. S., & Salzman, C. A new scale for clinical assessment in geriatric populations: Sandoz Clinical Assessment—Geriatric (SCAG). *Journal of the American Geriatrics Society,* 1974, *22,* 107–113.

Shakhnovich, A. R., Serbinenko, F. A., Razumovsky, A. Y., Rodionov, I. M., & Oskolok, L. N. The dependence of cerebral blood flow on mental activity and on the emotional state in man. *Neuropsychologia,* 1980, *18,* 465–476.

Shallice, T. Neuropsychological research and the fractionation of memory systems. In L.-G. Nilsson (Ed.), *Perspectives on memory research.* Hillsdale, N.J.: Laurence Erlbaum Associates, 1979.

Shallice, T. & Evans, M. E. The involvement of the frontal lobes in cognitive estimation. *Cortex,* 1978, *14,* 294–303.

Shalman, D. C. The diagnostic use of the McGill Picture Anomalies Test in temporal lobe epilepsy. *Journal of Neurology, Neurosurgery, and Psychiatry,* 1961, *24,* 220–222.

Shankweiler, D. Effects of temporal lobe damage on perception of dichotically presented melodies. *Journal of Comparative and Physiological Psychology,* 1966, *62,* 115.

Shapiro, B. E., Grossman, M., & Gardner, H. *Selective deficits in processing music after brain damage.* Paper presented at the eighth annual meeting of the International Neuropsychological Society, San Francisco, 1980.

Shapiro, B. E., Grossman, M., & Gardner, H. Selective musical processing deficits in brain damaged populations. *Neuropsychologia,* 1981, *19,* 161–169.

Shapiro, M. B. An experimental approach to diagnostic psychological testing. *Journal of Mental Science,* 1951, *97,* 748–764.

Shatz, M. W. WAIS practice effects in clinical neuropsychology. *Journal of Clinical Neuropsychology,* 1981, *3,* 171–179.

Shaw, D. J. The reliability and validity of the Halstead Category Test. *Journal of Clinical Psychology,* 1966, *22,* 176–180.

Shaw, D. J., & Matthews, C. G. Differential MMPI performance of brain-damaged versus pseudo-neurologic groups. *Journal of Clinical Psychology,* 1965, *21,* 405–408.

REFERENCES

Sheer, D. E. Psychometric studies. In N. D. C. Lewis, C. Landis, & H. E. King (Eds.), *Studies in topectomy*. New York: Grune & Stratton, 1956.

Sherman, J. A. *Sex-related cognitive differences*. Springfield, Ill.: C. C. Thomas, 1978.

Sherman, J. A. Sex differences in brain function. In *The brain: recent research and its implications*. Eugene, Ore.: College of Education, University of Oregon, 1982.

Sherrington, C. *Man on his nature* (2nd ed.). Garden City, New York: Doubleday, 1955.

Sherwin, I. & Seltzer, B. Senile and pre-senile dementia: a clinical overview. In K. Nandy & I. Sherwin (Eds.), *The aging brain and senile dementia*. New York: Plenum Press, 1976.

Shiffrin, R. M. *Short-term store: organized active memory*. Paper presented at Midwestern Psychological Association, Chicago, 1973.

Shipley, W. C. A self-administered scale for measuring intellectual impairment and deterioration. *Journal of Psychology*, 1940, 9, 371–377.

Shipley, W. C. *Institute of Living Scale*. Los Angeles: Western Psychological Services, 1946.

Shipley, W. C. & Burlingame, C. C. A convenient self-administered scale for measuring intellectual impairment in psychotics. *American Journal of Psychiatry*, 1941, 97, 1310–1325.

Shneidman, E. S. *Manual for the Make a Picture Story Method*. New York: Psychological Corporation, 1952.

Shure, G. H. & Halstead, W. C. Cerebral localization of intellectual processes. *Psychological Monographs*, 1958, 72 (12, Whole No. 465).

Silverstein, A. B. Perceptual, motor, and memory functions in the Visual Retention Test. *American Journal of Mental Deficiency*, 1962, 66, 613–617.

Simon, S. H. Effect of tranquilizers on the Trail Making Test with chronic schizophrenics. *Journal of Consulting Psychology*, 1967, 31, 322–323.

Simpson, C. D. & Vega, A. Unilateral brain damage and patterns of age-corrected WAIS subtest scores. *Journal of Clinical Psychology*, 1971, 27, 204–208.

Sines, J. O. Actuarial methods and personality assessment. In B. A. Maher (Ed.), *Progress in experimental personality research*. New York: Academic Press, 1966.

Sjögren, T., Sjögren, H., & Lindgren, A. G. H. Morbus Alzheimer and morbus Pick. *Acta Psychiatrica et Neurologica Scandinavica*, 1952, Supp. 82.

Skilbeck, O. E., & Woods, R. T. The factorial structure of the Wechsler Memory Scale: samples of neurological and psychogeriatric patients. *Journal of Clinical Neuropsychology*, 1980, 2, 293–300.

Sklar, M. Relation of psychological and language test scores and autopsy findings in aphasia. *Journal of Speech and Hearing Research*, 1963, 6, 84–90.

Slaby, A. E. & Wyatt, R. J. *Dementia in the presenium*. Springfield, Ill.: C. C. Thomas, 1974.

Smith, A. Changes in Porteus Maze scores of brain-operated schizophrenics after an eight year interval. *Journal of Mental Science*, 1960, 106, 967–978.

Smith, A. Duration of impaired consciousness as an index of severity in closed head injuries. *Diseases of the Nervous System*, 1961, 22, 1–6.

Smith, A. Ambiguities in concepts and studies of "brain damage" and "organicity." *Journal of Nervous and Mental Disease*, 1962a, 135, 311–326.

Smith, A. Psychodiagnosis of patients with brain tumors. *Journal of Nervous and Mental Disease*, 1962b, 135, 513–533.

Smith, A. Changing effects of frontal lesions. *Journal of Neurology, Neurosurgery, and Psychiatry*, 1964, 27, 511–515.

Smith, A. Certain hypothesized hemispheric differences in languages and visual functions in human adults. *Cortex*, 1966a, 1, 109–126.

REFERENCES

Smith, A. Intellectual functions in patients with lateralized frontal tumors. *Journal of Neurology, Neurosurgery, and Psychiatry*, 1966b, *29*, 52–59.

Smith, A. Consistent sex differences in a specific (decoding) test performance. *Educational and Psychological Measurement*, 1967a, *27*, 1077–1083.

Smith, A. The serial sevens subtraction test. *Archives of Neurology*, 1967b, *17*, 78–80.

Smith, A. The Symbol Digit Modalities Test: a neuropsychologic test for economic screening of learning and other cerebral disorders. *Learning Disorders*, 1968, *3*, 83–91.

Smith, A. Objective indices of severity of chronic aphasia in stroke patients. *Journal of Speech and Hearing Disorders*, 1971, *36*, 167–207.

Smith, A. Dominant and nondominant hemispherectomy. In W. Smith (Ed.), *Drugs, development and cerebral function*. Springfield, Ill.: C. C. Thomas, 1972a.

Smith, A. Replies to two comments on "Objective indices of severity of chronic aphasia . . ." *Journal of Speech and Hearing Disorders*, 1972b, *37*, 274–278.

Smith, A. *Symbol Digit Modalities Test. Manual*. Los Angeles: Western Psychological Services, 1973.

Smith, A. Neuropsychological testing in neurological disorders. In W. J. Friedlander (Ed.), *Advances in neurology* (Vol. 7). New York: Raven Press, 1975.

Smith, A. Practices and principles of neuropsychology. *International Journal of Neuroscience*, 1979, *9*, 233–238.

Smith, A. Principles underlying human brain functions in neuropsychological sequelae of different neuropathological processes. In S. B. Filskov & T. J. Boll (Eds.), *Handbook of clinical neuropsychology*. New York: Wiley-Interscience, 1981.

Smith, A. & Kinder, E. Changes in psychological test performances of brain-operated subjects after eight years. *Science*, 1959, *129*, 149–150.

Smith, C. M. & Swash, M. Effects of cholinergic drugs on memory in Alzheimer's disease. In L. Amaducci, A. N. Davison, & P. Antuono (Eds.), *Aging of the brain and dementia*. New York: Raven Press, 1980.

Smith, E. Influence of site of impact on cognitive impairment persisting long after severe closed head injury. *Journal of Neurology, Neurosurgery, and Psychiatry*, 1974, *37*, 719–726.

Smith, L. C. & Moscovitch, M. Writing posture, hemispheric control of movement and cerebral dominance in individuals with inverted and noninverted hand postures during writing. *Neuropsychologia*, 1979, *17*, 637–644.

Snodgrass, J. G. & Vanderwart, M. A standardized set of 260 pictures: norms for name agreement, image agreement, familiarity, and visual complexity. *Journal of Experimental Psychology: Human Learning and Memory*, 1980, *6*, 174–215.

Snow, W. G. *The Rey-Osterrieth Complex Figure Test as a measure of visual recall*. Paper presented at the seventh annual meeting of the International Neuropsychological Society, New York, 1979.

Sokolov, E. N. Brain functions: neuronal mechanisms of learning and memory. *Annual Review of Psychology*, 1977, *28*, 85–112.

Sommerhoff, G. *Logic of the living brain*. New York: Wiley, 1974.

Spearman, C. *The abilities of man*. London: Macmillan, 1927.

Spearman, C. & Jones, L. L. *Human abilities*. London: Macmillan, 1950.

Spellacy, F. J. & Spreen, O. A short form of the Token Test. *Cortex*, 1969, *5*, 390–397.

Spence, J. T. Patterns of performance on WAIS Similarities in schizophrenic, brain-damaged, and normal subjects. *Psychological Reports*, 1963, *13*, 431–436.

Sperry, R. W. Cerebral dominance in perception. In F. A. Young & D. B. Lindsley (Eds.),

REFERENCES

Early experience and visual information processing in perceptual and reading disorders. Washington, D.C.: National Academy of Sciences, 1970.

Sperry, R. W. Lateral specialization in the surgically separated hemispheres. In F. O. Schmitt & F. G. Worden (Eds.), *The neurosciences. Third Study Program.* Cambridge, Mass.: Massachusetts Institute of Technology Press, 1974.

Sperry, R. W. Changing concepts of consciousness and free will. *Perspectives in Biology and Medicine,* 1976, *20,* 9–19.

Sperry, R. W., Gazzaniga, M. S., & Bogen, J. E. Interhemispheric relationships: the neocortical commissures, syndromes of hemisphere deconnection. In P. J. Vinken & G. W. Bruyn (Eds.), *Handbook of Clinical Neurology* (Vol. 4). Amsterdam: North Holland, 1969.

Sperry, R. W., Zaidel, E., & Zaidel, D. Self recognition and social awareness in the deconnected minor hemisphere. *Neuropsychologia,* 1979, *17,* 153–166.

Spiers, P. A. Have they come to praise Luria or to bury him? The Luria-Nebraska Battery controversy. *Journal of Consulting and Clinical Psychology,* 1981, *49,* 001–011.

Spiker, C. C. & McCandless, B. R. The concept of intelligence and the philosophy of science. *Psychological Review,* 1954, *61,* 255–266.

Spitz, H. H. Note on immediate memory for digits: invariance over the years. *Psychological Bulletin,* 1972, *78,* 183–185.

Spreen, O. & Benton, A. L. Simulation of mental deficiency on a visual memory test. *American Journal of Mental Deficiency,* 1963, *67,* 909–913.

Spreen, O. & Benton, A. L. Comparative studies of some psychological tests for cerebral damage. *Journal of Nervous and Mental Disease,* 1965, *140,* 323–333.

Spreen, O. & Benton, A. L. *Neurosensory Center Comprehensive Examination for Aphasia.* Victoria, B. C.: Neuropsychological Laboratory Dept. of Psychology, University of Victoria, 1969.

Squire, L. R. Remote memory as affected by aging. *Neuropsychologia,* 1974, *12,* 429–435.

Squire, L. R. Short-term memory as a biological entity. In D. Deutsch & J. A. Deutsch (Eds.), *Short-term memory.* New York: Academic Press, 1975.

Squire, L. R. & Slater, P. C. Forgetting in very long-term memory as assessed by an improved questionnaire taxonomy. *Journal of Experimental Psychology: Human Language and Memory,* 1975, *104,* 50–54.

Squire, L. R. & Slater, P. C. Bilateral and unilateral effect on verbal and nonverbal memory. *American Journal of Psychiatry,* 1978, *135,* 1316–1320.

Staples, D. & Lincoln, N. B. Intellectual impairment in multiple sclerosis and its relation to functional abilities. *Rheumatology and Rehabilitation,* 1979, *18,* 153–160.

Stein, M. I. *The Thematic Apperception Test. An introductory manual for its clinical use with adults* (Rev. ed.). Reading, Mass.: Addison-Wesley, 1955.

Sternberg, D. E. & Jarvik, M. E. Memory functions in depression. *Archives of General Psychiatry,* 1976, *33,* 219–224.

Sterne, D. M. The Knox Cubes as a test of memory and intelligence with male adults. *Journal of Clinical Psychology,* 1966, *22,* 191–193.

Sterne, D. M. The Purdue Pegboard and MacQuarrie Tapping and Dotting tasks as measures of motor functioning. *Perceptual and Motor Skills,* 1969, *28,* 556.

Sterne, D. M. The effect of age and intelligence on Minnesota Paper Form Board scores of VA Hospital patients. Unpublished manuscript, no date.

Stevens, C. F. The neuron. *Scientific American,* 1979, *241,* 54–65.

Stone, C. P., Girdner, J., & Albrecht, R. An alternate form of the Wechsler Memory Scale. *Journal of Psychology,* 1946, *22,* 199–206.

Storck, P. A. & Looft, W. R. Qualitative analysis of vocabulary responses from persons aged six to sixty-six plus. *Journal of Educational Psychology*, 1973, *65*, 192–197.

Strauss, E., Moscovitch, M., & Olds, J. *Functional hemispheric asymmetries and depression: preliminary findings of cognitive correlates of electro-convulsive therapy.* Paper presented to the seventh annual meeting of the International Neuropsychological Society, New York City; and to the American Psychiatric Association Convention, 1979.

Street, R. F. *A Gestalt Completion Test.* Contributions to Education, No. 481. New York: Bureau of Publications, Teachers College, Columbia University, 1931.

Street, R. F. In L. L. Thurstone (Ed.), A factorial study of perception. *Psychometric Monographs*, 1944, No. 4.

Strich, S. J. Shearing of nerve fibers as a cause of brain damage due to head injury. *Lancet*, 1961, *ii*, 446–448.

Strich, S. J. The pathology of brain damage due to blunt head injuries. In A. E. Walker, W. F. Caveness, & M. Critchley (Eds.), *The late effects of head injury.* Springfield, Ill.: C. C. Thomas, 1969.

Stroop, J. R. Studies of interference in serial verbal reactions. *Journal of Experimental Psychology*, 1935, *18*, 643–662.

Strub, R. L. & Black, F. W. *The mental status examination in neurology.* Philadelphia: F. A. Davis, 1977.

Strub, R. L. & Black, F. W. *Organic brain syndromes.* Philadelphia: F. A. Davis, 1981.

Sugarman, J., Ley, R., & Bryden, M. *A right hemisphere advantage for emotionally toned musical passages.* Paper presented at the eighth annual meeting of the International Neuropsychological Society, San Francisco, February, 1980.

Suinn, R. M. *The predictive validity of projective measures.* Springfield, Ill.: C. C. Thomas, 1969.

Sullivan, E. T., Clark, W. W., & Tiegs, E. W. *California Short-Form Test of Mental Maturity* (1963 revision). New York: McGraw-Hill, 1963.

Sullivan, E. V., Shedlack, K. J., Corkin, S., & Growden, J. H. Physostigmine and lecithin in Alzheimer's disease. In S. Corkin, K. L. Davis, J. H. Growdon, et al. (Eds.), *Alzheimer's disease: a report of progress in research.* New York: Raven Press, 1981.

Sundberg, N. D. *Assessment of persons.* Englewood Cliffs, N.J.: Prentice-Hall, 1977.

Surridge, D. An investigation into some psychiatric aspects of multiple sclerosis. *British Journal of Psychiatry*, 1969, *115*, 749–764.

Sweet, R. D., McDowell, F. H., Feigenson, J. S., et al. Mental symptoms in Parkinson's disease during chronic treatment with levodopa. *Neurology*, 1976, *26*, 305–310.

Swiercinsky, D. P. *Manual for the adult neuropsychological evaluation.* Springfield, Ill.: C. C. Thomas, 1978.

Swiercinsky, D. P. & Warnock, J. K. Comparison of the neuropsychological key and discriminant analysis approaches in predicting cerebral damage and localization. *Journal of Consulting and Clinical Psychology*, 1977, *45*, 808–814.

Swisher, L. Functional Communication Profile (FCP) (Review). In F. L. Darley (Ed.), *Evaluation of appraisal techniques in speech and language pathology.* Reading, Mass.: Addison-Wesley, 1979.

Symonds, C. P. Mental disorder following head injury. *Proceedings of the Royal Society of Medicine*, 1937, *30*, 1081–1092.

Symonds, C. P. & Russell, W. R. Accidental head injuries; prognosis in service patients. *Lancet*, 1943, *i*, 7–10.

Talland, G. A. Effect of aging on the formation of sequential and spatial concepts. *Perceptual and Motor Skills*, 1961, *13*, 210.

REFERENCES

Talland, G. A. Cognitive function in Parkinson's disease. *Journal of Nervous and Mental Disease*, 1962, *135*, 196–205.

Talland, G. A. Psychology's concern with brain damage. *Journal of Nervous and Mental Disease*, 1963, *136*, 344–351.

Talland, G. A. *Deranged memory*. New York: Academic Press, 1965a.

Talland, G. A. Three estimates of the word span and their stability over the adult years. *Journal of Experimental Psychology*, 1965b, *17*, 301–307.

Talland, G. A. Some observations on the psychological mechanisms impaired in the amnesic syndrome. *International Journal of Neurology*, 1968, 7, 21–30.

Talland, G. A. & Ekdahl, M. Psychological studies of Korsakoff's psychosis: IV. The rate and mode of forgetting narrative material. *Journal of Nervous and Mental Disease*, 1959, *129*, 391–404.

Talland, G. A. & Schwab, R. S. Performance with multiple sets in Parkinson's disease. *Neuropsychologia*, 1964, 2, 45 58.

Tartaglione, A., Benton, A. L., Cocito, L., et al. Point localization in patients with unilateral brain damage. *Journal of Neurology, Neurosurgery, and Psychiatry*, 1981, *44*, 935–941.

Tarter, R. E. Intellectual and adaptive functioning in epilepsy. *Diseases of the Nervous System*, 1972, *33*, 759–770.

Tarter, R. E. An analysis of cognitive deficits in chronic alcoholics. *Journal of Nervous & Mental Disease*, 1973, *157*, 138–147.

Tarter, R. E. Psychological deficit in chronic alcoholics: a review. *International Journal of Addiction*, 1975, *10*, 327–368.

Tarter, R. E. Neuropsychological investigations of alcoholism. In G. Goldstein & C. Neuringer (Eds.), *Empirical studies of alcoholism*. Cambridge, Mass.: Ballinger, 1976.

Tarter, R. E. & Jones, B. M. Absence of intellectual deterioration in chronic alcoholics. *Journal of Clinical Psychology*, 1971, *27*, 453–454.

Tarter, R. E. & Parsons, O. A. Conceptual shifting in chronic alcoholics. *Journal of Abnormal Psychology*, 1971, *77*, 71–75.

Taylor, E. M. *The appraisal of children with cerebral deficits*. Cambridge, Mass.: Harvard University Press, 1959.

Taylor, L. B. Localization of cerebral lesions by psychological testing. *Clinical Neurosurgery*, 1969, *16*, 269–287.

Taylor, L. B. Psychological assessment of neurosurgical patients. In T. Rasmussen & R. Marino (Eds.), *Functional neurosurgery*. New York: Raven Press, 1979.

Taylor, M. L. A measurement of functional communication in aphasia. *Archives of Physical Medicine and Rehabilitation*, 1965, *46*, 101–107.

Teasdale, G. & Jennett, B. Assessment of coma and impaired consciousness. *Lancet*, 1974, *ii*, 81–84.

Telford, R. & Worrall, E. P. Cognitive functions in manic-depressives: effects of lithium and physostigmine. *British Journal of Psychiatry*, 1978, *133*, 424–428.

Tellegen, A. The performance of chronic seizure patients on the General Aptitude Test Battery. *Journal of Clinical Psychology*, 1965, *21*, 180–184.

Teng, E. L. Dichotic ear effects with digits and tones: a within-subject comparison. *Perceptual and Motor Skills*, 1979, *49*, 391–399.

Teng, E. L. Dichotic ear difference is a poor index for the functional asymmetry between the cerebral hemispheres. *Neuropsychologia*, 1981, *19*, 235–240.

Terman, L. M. *The measurement of intelligence*. Boston: Houghton Mifflin, 1916.

Terman, L. M. & Merrill, M. A. *Measuring intelligence*. Boston: Houghton Mifflin, 1937.

REFERENCES

Terman, L. M. & Merrill, M. A. *Stanford-Binet Intelligence Scale. Manual for the Third Revision, Form L-M*. Boston: Houghton Mifflin, 1973.

Terry, R. D. Aging, senile dementia, and Alzheimer's disease. In R. Katzman, R. D. Terry & K. L. Bick (Eds.), *Alzheimer's disease: senile dementia and related disorders* (*Aging*, Vol. 7). New York: Raven Press, 1978.

Terry, R. D. Structural changes in senile dementia of the Alzheimer type. In L. Amaducci, A. N. Davison, & P. Antuono (Eds.), *Aging of the brain and dementia*. New York: Raven Press, 1980.

Teszner, A., Tzavaras, A., Gruner, J., & Hécaen, H. L'asymétrie droite-gauche du *planum temporale;* à propos de l'étude anatomique de 100 cerveaux. *Revue Neurologique*, 1972, *126*, 444–449.

Teuber, H.-L. Neuropsychology. In M. R. Harrower (Ed.), *Recent advances in diagnostic psychological testing*. Springfield, Ill.: C. C. Thomas, 1948.

Teuber, H.-L. Physiological psychology. *Annual Review of Psychology*, 1955, *6*, 267–296.

Teuber, H.-L. Some alterations in behavior after cerebral lesions in man. In A. D. Bass (Ed.), *Evolution of nervous control*. Washington, D.C.: American Association for the Advancement of Science, 1959.

Teuber, H.-L. Effects of brain wounds implicating right or left hemisphere in man. Discussion. In V. B. Mountcastle (Ed.), *Interhemispheric relations and cerebral dominance*. Baltimore: The John Hopkins Press, 1962.

Teuber, H.-L. The riddle of frontal lobe function in man. In J. M. Warren & K. Akert (Eds.), *The frontal granular cortex and behavior*. New York: McGraw-Hill, 1964.

Teuber, H.-L. Neglected aspects of the posttraumatic syndrome. In A. Walker, W. F. Caveness, & M. Critchley (Eds.), *The late effects of head injury*. Springfield, Ill.: C. C. Thomas, 1969.

Teuber, H.-L. Effects of focal brain injury on human behavior. In D. B. Tower (Ed.), *The nervous system* (Vol. 2, *The clinical neurosciences*). New York: Raven Press, 1975.

Teuber, H.-L., Battersby, W. S., & Bender, M. B. Performance of complex visual tasks after cerebral lesions. *Journal of Nervous and Mental Disease*, 1951, *114*, 413–429.

Teuber, H.-L., Battersby, W. S., & Bender, M. B. *Visual field defects after penetrating missile wounds of the brain*. Cambridge, Mass.: Published for the Commonwealth Fund by Harvard University Press, 1960.

Teuber, H.-L. & Weinstein, S. Performance on a formboard task after penetrating brain injury. *Journal of Psychology*, 1954, *38*, 177–190.

Thatcher, R. W. & John, E. R. *Foundations of cognitive processes*. Hillsdale, N.J.: Lawrence Erlbaum Associates, 1977.

Thomas, D. G. & Campos, J. J. The relationship of handedness to a "lateralized" task. *Neuropsychologia*, 1978, *16*, 511–515.

Thomas, J. C., Fozard, J. L., & Waugh, N. C. Age-related differences in naming latency. *American Journal of Psychology*, 1977, *90*, 499–509.

Thompson, R. F. The search for the engram. *American Psychologist*, 1976, *31*, 209–227.

Thompson, R. F., Patterson, M. M., & Teylor, T. J. The neurophysiology of learning. *Annual Review of Psychology*, 1972, *23*, 73–104.

Thorndike, E. L. & Lorge, I. *The teacher's book of 30,000 words*. New York: Columbia University Press, 1944.

Thorp, T. R. & Mahrer, A. R. Predicting potential intelligence. *Journal of Clinical Psychology*, 1959, *15*, 286–288.

Thurstone, L. L. *Primary mental abilities*. Chicago: University of Chicago Press, 1938.

REFERENCES

Thurstone, L. L. A *factorial study of perception*. Chicago: University of Chicago Press, 1944.

Thurstone, L. L. & Jeffrey, T. E. *Closure Flexibility (Concealed Figures)*. Chicago: Industrial Relations Center, University of Chicago, 1956; Park Ridge, Ill.: London House Press, 1982.

Thurstone, L. L. & Thurstone, T. G. *American Council on Education Psychological Examination (ACE)*. Princeton, N.J.: Educational Testing Service, 1953, 1954.

Thurstone, L. L. & Thurstone, T. G. *Primary Mental Abilities (Rev.)*. Chicago: Science Research Associates, 1962.

Tiffin, J. *Purdue Pegboard Examiner's Manual*. Chicago: Science Research Associates, 1968.

Tikofsky, R. S. Halstead Aphasia Test, Form M (Review). In F. L. Darley (Ed.), *Evaluation of appraisal techniques in speech and language pathology*. Reading, Mass.: Addison-Wesley, 1979

Tissot, R., Lhermitte, F., & B. Ducarne, Etat intellectual des ophasiques, *Encéphale*, 1963, 52, 286–320.

Todd, J., Coolidge, F., & Satz, P. Wechsler Adult Intelligence Scale discrepancy index: a neuropsychological evaluation. *Journal of Consulting Psychology*, 1962, 65, 387–394.

Toglia, M. P. & Battig, W. F. *Handbook of semantic word nouns*. Hillsdale, N.J.: Lawrence Erlbaum Associates, 1978.

Tognola, G. & Vignolo, L.A. Brain lesions associated with oral apraxia in stroke patients: a clinico-neuroradiological investigation with the CT scan. *Neuropsychologia*, 1980, 18, 257–272.

Tolor, A. A comparison of the Bender-Gestalt test and the Digit-Span test as measures of recall. *Journal of Consulting Psychology*, 1956, 20, 305–309.

Tolor, A. Further studies on the Bender-Gestalt test and the Digit-Span as measures of recall. *Journal of Clinical Psychology*, 1958, 14, 14–18.

Toole, J. F., Yuson, C. P., Janeway, R., et al. Transient ischemic attacks: a study of 225 patients. *Neurology*, 1978, 28, 746–753.

Torack, R. M. *The pathologic physiology of dementia*. New York: Springer-Verlag, 1978.

Tow, P. M. *Personality changes following frontal leucotomy*. London: Oxford University Press, 1955.

Tower, D. B. Alzheimer's disease—senile dementia and related disorders: neurobiological status. In R. Katzman, R. D. Terry, & K. L. Bick (Eds.), *Alzheimer's disease: senile dementia and related disorders* (Aging, Vol. 7). New York: Raven Press, 1978.

Traxler, A. J. Negative transfer effects in paired association learning in young and elderly adults. *Proceedings of the 80th annual convention of the American Psychological Association*, 1972, 7, 655–666. (Summary)

Trites, R. L. *Child norms on selected neuropsychological measures*. Unpublished manuscript, no date.

Tryon, W. W. The test-trait fallacy. *American Psychologist*, 1979, 34, 402–406.

Tsushima, W. T. & Bratton, J. C. Effects of geographic region upon Wechsler Adult Intelligence Scale results: a Hawaii-mainland United States comparison. *Journal of Consulting and Clinical Psychology*, 1977, 45, 501–502.

Tsushima, W. T. & Towne, W. S. Effects of paint sniffing on neuropsychological test performance. *Journal of Abnormal Psychology*, 1977, 86, 402–407.

Tsushima, W. T. & Wedding, D. A comparison of the Halstead-Reitan Neuropsychological Battery and computerized tomography in the identification of brain disorder. *Journal of Nervous and Mental Disease*, 1979, 167, 704–707.

Tucker, D. M., Watson, R. T., & Heilman, K. M. Affective discrimination and evocation in patients with right parietal disease. Abstract. *Neurology*, 1976, 26, 354.

REFERENCES

Tucker, D. M., Watson, R. T., & Heilman, K. M. Discrimination and evocation of affectively intoned speech in patients with right parietal disease. *Neurology*, 1977, *27*, 947–950.

Tulving, E. & Pearlstone, Z. Availability versus accessibility of information in memory for words. *Journal of Verbal Learning and Verbal Behavior*, 1966, *5*, 381–391.

Tunks, E. *Neuropsychiatric examination procedures: a criterion-sensitivity problem*. Paper presented at the fourth annual meeting of the International Neuropsychological Society, Toronto, February, 1976.

Tutko, T. A. & Spence, J. T. Performance of process and reactive schizophrenics and brain injured subjects on a conceptual task. *Journal of Abnormal and Social Psychology*, 1962, *65*, 387–394.

Tweedy, J. R., Lapinski, R. H., Hines, T., et al. *Cognitive correlates of arteriosclerotic and depressive symptoms in a series of suspected Alzheimer patients*. Paper presented at the tenth annual meeting of the International Neuropsychological Society, Pittsburgh, February, 1982.

Tzavaras, A., Hécaen, H., & Le Bras, H. Le problème de la spécificité du déficit de la reconnaissance du visage humain lors des lesions hémisphèriques unilaterales. *Neuropsychologia*, 1970, *8*, 403–416.

Urmer, A. H., Morris, A. B., & Wendland, L. U. The effect of brain damage on Raven's Progressive Matrices. *Journal of Clinical Psychology*, 1960, *16*, 182–185.

Uyeno, E. Differentiating psychotics from organics on the Minnesota Percepto-Diagnostic Test. *Journal of Consulting Psychology*, 1963, *27*, 462.

Vajda, F. J. E., Walsh, K. W., & Bladin, P. F. Brain impairment in association with anticonvulsant therapy. In M. Molloy, G. V. Stanley, & K. M. Walsh (Eds.), *Brain Impairment. Proceedings of the 1978 Brain Impairment Workshop*. Melbourne: University of Melbourne, 1979.

Valenstein, E. & Heilman, K. Emotional disorders resulting from lesions of the central nervous system. In K. Heilman & E. Valenstein (Eds.), *Clinical neuropsychology*. New York: Oxford University Press, 1979.

Valenstein, E. S. *Brain control*. New York: Wiley, 1973.

Vandenberg, S. G. & Kuse, A. R. Spatial ability: a critical review of the sex-linked major gene hypothesis. In M. A. Wittig & A. C. Petersen (Eds.), *Sex-related differences in cognitive functioning*. New York: Academic Press, 1979.

Vanderplas, J. M. & Garvin, E. A. The association value of random shapes. *Journal of Experimental Psychology*, 1959, *57*, 147–154.

Van der Vlugt, H. Aspects of normal and abnormal neuropsychological development. In M. S. Gazzaniga (Ed.), *Handbook of behavioral neurobiology* (Vol. 2, *Neuropsychology*). New York: Plenum Press, 1979.

Van Zomeren, A. H. & Deelman, B. G. Long-term recovery of visual reaction time after closed head injury. *Journal of Neurology, Neurosurgery, and Psychiatry*, 1978, *41*, 452–457.

Varney, N. R. Colour association and "colour amnesia" in aphasia. *Journal of Neurology, Neurosurgery, and Psychiatry*, 1982, *45*, 248–252.

Vaughan, H. G., Jr. & Costa, L. D. Performance of patients with lateralized cerebral lesions. II. Sensory and motor tests. *Journal of Mental Disease*, 1962, *134*, 237–243.

Vega, A., Jr. & Parsons. O. A. Cross-validation of the Halstead-Reitan tests for brain damage. *Journal of Consulting Psychology*, 1967, *31*, 619–623.

Vega, A., Jr. & Parsons, O. A. Relationship between sensory-motor deficits and WAIS verbal and performance scores in unilateral brain damage. *Cortex*, 1969, *5*, 229–241.

Verhoff, A. E., Kaplan, E., Albert, M. L., et al. *Aging and dementia in the Framingham*

Heart Study population: preliminary prevalence data and qualitative analysis of visual reproductions. Paper presented at the seventh annual meeting of the International Neuropsychological Society, New York, 1979.

Vernea, J. Considerations on certain tests of unilateral spatial neglect. In G. V. Stanley & K. W. Walsh (Eds.), *Brain impairment. Proceedings of the 1977 Brain Impairment Workshop.* Parkville, Victoria, Australia: Neuropsychology Group, Dept. of Psychology, University of Melbourne, 1978.

Vernon, P. E. *The structure of human abilities.* New York: Wiley, 1950

Vernon, P. E. *Intelligence: heredity and environment.* San Francisco: W. H. Freeman, 1979.

Victor, M., Adams, R. D., & Collins, G. H. *The Wernicke-Korsakoff syndrome.* Philadelphia: F. A. Davis, 1971.

Vignolo, L. A. Auditory agnosia: a review and report of recent evidence. In A. L. Benton (Ed.), *Contributions to clinical neuropsychology,* Chicago: Aldine, 1969.

Vigouroux, R. P., Daurand, C., Naquet, R., et al. A series of patients with cranio-cerebral injuries studies neurologically, psychometrically, electroencephalographically and socially. *International symposium on head injuries.* Edinburgh: Churchill Livingstone, 1971.

Vilkki, J. Effects of thalamic lesions on complex perception and memory. *Neuropsychologia,* 1978, *16,* 427–437.

Vilkki, J. & Laitinen, L. V. Effects of pulvinotomy and ventrolateral thalamotomy on some cognitive functions. *Neuropsychologia,* 1976, *14,* 67–78.

Visser, R. S. H. *Manual of the Complex Figure Test.* Amsterdam: Swets & Zeitlinger B. V., 1973.

Vivian, T.N., Goldstein, G., & Shelly, C. Reaction time and motor speed in chronic alcoholics. *Perceptual and Motor Skills,* 1973, *36,* 136–138.

Vogel, W. Some effects of brain lesions on MMPI profiles. *Journal of Consulting Psychology,* 1962, *26,* 412–415.

Volle, F. O. *Mental evaluation of the disability claimant.* Springfield, Ill.: C. C. Thomas, 1975.

Volpe, B. T., Sidtis, J. J., & Gazzaniga, M. S. Can left-handed writing posture predict cerebral language laterality? *Archives of Neurology,* 1981, *38,* 637–638.

Vowels, L. M. Memory impairment in multiple sclerosis. In M. Molloy, G. V. Stanley, & K. W. Walsh (Eds.), *Brain Impairment: Proceedings of the 1978 Brain Impairment Workshop.* Melbourne: University of Melbourne, 1979.

Wada, J. A., Clarke, R., & Hamm, A. Cerebral hemispheric asymmetry in humans. *Archives of Neurology,* 1975, *32,* 239–246.

Wada, J. & Rasmussen, T. Intra-carotid injection of sodium amytal for the lateralization of cerebral speech dominance. *Journal of Neurosurgery,* 1960, *17,* 266–282.

Wahl, C. W., Golden, J. S., Liston, E. H., et al. Toxic and functional psychoses. *Annals of Internal Medicine,* 1967, *66,* 989–1007.

Walker, A. E. & Blumer, D. Long term behavioral effects of temporal lobectomy for temporal lobe epilepsy. *McLean Hospital Journal,* 1977, Special Issue, 85–103.

Walker, A. E. & Jablon, S. A follow-up of head-injured men of World War II. *Journal of Neurosurgery,* 1959, *16,* 600–610.

Walker, A. E. & Jablon, S. *A follow-up study of head wounds in World War II.* Washington, D.C.: Veterans Administration Medical Monograph, 1961.

Walker, J. A., Posner, M. I., & Rafal, R. D. *Separation of effects on cognition versus motor performance due to the basal ganglia dysfunction of Parkinsonian patients.* Paper presented at the tenth annual meeting of the International Neuropsychological Society, Pittsburgh, February, 1982.

Walker, R. E., Hunt, W. A., & Schwartz, M. L. The difficulty of WAIS Comprehension scoring. *Journal of Clinical Psychology*, 1965, *21*, 427–429.

Walker, S., III. *Psychiatric signs and symptoms due to medical problems*. Springfield, Ill.: C. C. Thomas, 1967.

Wallack, E. Selective limbic deficits after encephalitis. *Southern Medical Journal*, 1976, *69*, 669–671.

Walsh, K. W. Frontal lobe problems. In G. V. Stanley & K. W. Walsh (Eds.), *Brain impairment: Proceedings of the 1976 Brain Impairment Workshop*. Parkville, Victoria, Australia: Neuropsychology Group, Dept. of Psychology, University of Melbourne, 1978a.

Walsh, K. W. *Neuropsychology*. New York: Churchill Livingston/Longman, 1978b.

Walton, D. & Black, D. A. The validity of a psychological test of brain damage. *British Journal of Medical Psychology*, 1957, *30*, 270–279.

Walton, D. & Mather, M. D. A further study of the predictive validity of a psychological test of brain damage. *British Journal of Medical Psychology*, 1961, *34*, 73–75.

Walton, D., White, J. G., Black, D. A. & Young, A. J. The Modified Word-Learning Test: a cross-validation study. *British Journal of Medical Psychology*, 1959, *32*, 213–220.

Walton, J. N. *Brain's diseases of the nervous system* (8th ed.). Oxford: Oxford University Press, 1977.

Wang, H. S. Cerebral correlates of intellectual function in senescence. In L. F. Jarvik, C. Eisdorfer, & J. E. Blum (Eds.), *Intellectual functioning in adults*. New York: Springer, 1973.

Wang, H. S. Dementia of old age. In W. L. Smith & M. Kinsbourne (Eds.), *Aging and dementia*. Jamaica, New York: Spectrum Publications, 1977.

Wang, P. L. & Uzzell, B. P. *Hemispheric function and temporal disorientation*. Paper presented at the American Psychological Association Convention, Toronto, 1978.

Wapner, W., Hamby, S., & Gardner, H. The role of the right hemisphere in the apprehension of complex linguistic materials. *Brain and Language*, 1981, *41*, 15–33.

Warrington, E. K. Neurological deficits. In P. Mittler (Ed.), *The psychological assessment of mental and physical handicaps*. London: Methuen & Co., 1970.

Warrington, E. K. The fractionation of arithmetical skills: a single case study. *Quarterly Journal of Experimental Psychology*, 1982, *34A*, 31–51.

Warrington, E. K. & James, M. Disorders of visual perception in patients with localized cerebral lesions. *Neuropsychologia*, 1967a, *5*, 253–266.

Warrington, E. K. & James, M. An experimental investigation of facial recognition in patients with unilateral cerebral lesions. *Cortex*, 1967b, *3*, 317–326.

Warrington, E. K., James, M., & Kinsbourne, M. Drawing disability in relation to laterality of cerebral lesion. *Brain*, 1966, *89*, 53–82.

Warrington, E. K. & Pratt, R. T. C. The significance of laterality effects. *Journal of Neurology, Neurosurgery, and Psychiatry*, 1981, *44*, 193–196.

Warrington, E. K. & Rabin, P. Perceptual matching in patients with cerebral lesions. *Neuropsychologia*, 1970, *8*, 475–487.

Warrington, E. K. & Sanders, H. I. The fate of old memories. *Quarterly Journal of Experimental Psychology*, 1971, *23*, 432–442.

Warrington, E. K. & Silberstein, M. A questionnaire technique for investigating very long term memory. *Quarterly Journal of Experimental Psychology*, 1970, *22*, 508–512.

Warrington, E. K. & Taylor, A. M. The contribution of the right parietal lobe to object recognition. *Cortex*, 1973, *9*, 152–164.

Warrington, E. K. & Weiskrantz, L. New method of testing long-term retention with special reference of amnesic patients. *Nature*, 1968, *217*, 972–974.

REFERENCES

Wasserstein, J. *Differentiation of perceptual closure: implications for right hemisphere functions*. Doctoral dissertation. New York: City University of New York, 1980.

Wasserstein, J., Weiss, E., Rosen, J., et al. *Reexamination of Gestalt Completion Tests: implications for right hemisphere assessment*. Paper presented at the eighth annual meeting of the International Neuropsychological Society, San Francisco, 1980.

Watkins, M. J. Concept and measurement of primary memory. *Psychological Bulletin*, 1974, *81*, 695–711.

Watson, C. G. An MMPI scale to separate brain-damaged from schizophrenics. *Journal of Consulting and Clinical Psychology*, 1971, *36*, 121–125.

Watson, C. G. & Plemel, D. An MMPI scale to separate brain-damaged from functional psychiatric patients in neuropsychiatric settings. *Journal of Consulting and Clinical Psychology*, 1978, *46*, 1127–1132.

Watson, C. G., Thomas, R. W., Anderson, D., & Felling, J. Differentiation of organics from schizophrenics at two chronicity levels by use of the Reitan-Halstead organic test battery. *Journal of Consulting and Clinical Psychology*, 1968, *32*, 679–684.

Watson, P. J. Nonmotor functions of the cerebellum. *Psychological Bulletin*, 1978, *85*, 944–967.

Watson, R. T. & Heilman, K. M. Thalamic neglect. *Neurology*, 1979, *29*, 690–694.

Watson, R.T., Valenstein, E., & Heilman, K.M. Thalamic neglect. *Archives of Neurology*, 1981, *38*, 501–506.

Watts, G. O. *Dynamic neuroscience: its application to brain disorders*. New York: Harper & Row, 1975.

Weber, A. M. & Bradshaw, J. L. Levy and Reid's neurological model in relation to writing hand/posture: an evaluation. *Psychological Bulletin*, 1981, *90*, 74–88.

Wechsler, D. *The measurement of adult intelligence* (3rd ed.). Baltimore: Williams & Wilkins, 1944.

Wechsler, D. A standardized memory scale for clinical use. *Journal of Psychology*, 1945, *19*, 87–95.

Wechsler, D. *Wechsler Intelligence Scale for Children. Manual*. New York: Psychological Corporation, 1949.

Wechsler, D. *Wechsler Adult Intelligence Scale. Manual*. New York: Psychological Corporation. 1955.

Wechsler, D. *The measurement and appraisal of adult intelligence* (4th ed.). Baltimore: Williams & Wilkins, 1958.

Wechsler, D. Psychological diagnosis. In I. S. Wechsler, *Clinical neurology*. Philadelphia: W. B. Saunders, 1963.

Wechsler, D. *Wechsler Preschool and Primary Scale of Intelligence*. New York: Psychological Corporation. 1967.

Wechsler, D. *WISC-R manual. Wechsler Intelligence Scale for Children—Revised*. New York: Psychological Corporation. 1974.

Wechsler, D. Intelligence defined and undefined. *American Psychologist*, 1975, *30*, 135–139.

Wechsler, D. *WAIS-R manual*. New York: Psychological Corporation, 1981.

Weddell, R., Oddy, M., & Jenkins, D. Social adjustment after rehabilitation: a two year follow-up of patients with severe head injury. *Psychological Medicine*, 1980, *10*, 257–263.

Wedding, D. *A comparison of statistical, actuarial, and clinical models used in predicting presence, lateralization, and type of brain damage in humans*. Unpublished doctoral dissertation, University of Hawaii, 1979.

Weigl, E. On the psychology of so-called processes of abstraction. *Journal of Abnormal & Social Psychology*, 1941, *36*, 3–33.

REFERENCES

Weinberg, J. & Diller, L. On reading newspapers by hemiplegics—denial of visual disability. *Proceedings of the 76th Annual Convention of the American Psychological Association,* 1968, *3,* 655–656.

Weinberg, J., Diller, L., Gerstman, L., & Schulman, P. Digit span in right and left hemiplegics. *Journal of Clinical Psychology,* 1972, *28,* 361.

Weinberg, J., Diller, L., Lakin, P., & Hodges, G. *Perceptual problems in right brain damage: the case for treatment.* Paper presented at the fourth annual meeting of the International Neuropsychological Society, Toronto, Canada, 1976.

Weiner, P. S. Peabody Picture Vocabulary Test (PPVT) (Review). In F. L. Darley (Ed.), *Evaluation of appraisal techniques in speech and language pathology.* Reading, Mass.: Addison-Wesley, 1979.

Weingartner, H. Verbal learning in patients with temporal lobe lesions. *Journal of Verbal Learning and Verbal Behavior,* 1968, *7,* 520–526.

Weingartner, H., Caine, E. D., & Ebert, M. H. Encoding processes, learning, and recall in Huntington's disease. In T. N. Chase, N. S. Wexler, & A. Barbeau (Eds.), *Advances in neurology* (Vol. 23). New York: Raven Press, 1979.

Weingartner, H., Faillace, L. A., & Markley, H. G. Verbal information retention in alcoholics. *Quarterly Journal of the Study of Alcoholism,* 1971, *32,* 293–303.

Weingold, H. P., Dawson, J. G., & Kael, H. C. Further examination of Hovey's "Index" for identification of brain lesions: Validation study. *Psychological Reports,* 1965, *16,* 1098.

Weinstein, E. A. & Cole, M. Concepts of anosognosia. In E. Halpern, (Ed.), *Problems of dynamic neurology.* Jerusalem: Hebrew University Hadassah Medical School, 1963.

Weinstein, E. A., Cole, M., Mitchell, M. S., & Lyerly, O. A. Anosognosia and aphasia. *Archives of Neurology,* 1964, *10,* 376–386.

Weinstein, E. A. & Kahn, R. L. *Denial of illness.* Springfield, Ill.: C. C. Thomas, 1955.

Weinstein, S. Deficits concomitant with aphasia or lesions of either cerebral hemisphere. *Cortex,* 1964, *1,* 154–169.

Weinstein, S. Functional cerebral hemispheric asymmetry. In M. Kinsbourne (Ed.), *Asymmetrical function of the brain.* Cambridge, England: Cambridge University Press, 1978.

Weinstein, S., Semmes, J., Ghent, L., & Teuber, H.-L. Spatial orientation in man after cerebral injury: II. Analysis according to concomittant defects. *Journal of Psychology,* 1956, *42,* 249–263.

Weinstein, S. & Teuber, H.-L. Effects of penetrating brain injury on intelligence test scores. *Science,* 1957, *125,* 1036–1037.

Weintraub, S., Mesulam, M.-M., & Kramer, L. Disturbances in prosody. A right-hemisphere contribution to language. *Archives of Neurology,* 1981, *38,* 742–744.

Weisberg, L. A. Computed tomography in the diagnosis of intracranial disease. *Annals of Internal Medicine,* 1979, *91,* 87–105.

Weiskrantz, L. Treatments, inferences, and brain function. In L. Weiskrantz (Ed.), *Analysis of behavioral change.* New York: Harper & Row, 1968.

Weiskrantz, L. The interaction between occipital and temporal cortex in vision: an overview. In F. O. Schmitt & F. G. Worden (Eds.), *The Neurosciences Third Study Program.* Cambridge, Mass.: Massachusetts Institute of Technology Press, 1974.

Weissman, M. M. The assessment of social adjustment. *Archives of General Psychiatry,* 1975, *32,* 357–365.

Welford, A. T. Motor performance. In J. E. Birren & K. W. Schaie (Eds.), *Handbook of the psychology of aging.* New York: Van Nostrand, 1977.

Wells, C. E. Symptoms and behavioral manifestations. In C. E. Wells (Ed.), *Dementia* (2nd ed.). Philadelphia: F. A. Davis, 1977.

REFERENCES

Wells, C. E. Chronic brain disease: an overview. *American Journal of Psychiatry*, 1978a, *135*, 1–12.

Wells, C. E. Geriatric organic psychoses. *Psychiatric Annals*, 1978b, *8*, 466–478.

Wells, C. E. Pseudodementia. *American Journal of Psychiatry*, 1979, *136*, 895–900.

Wells, C. E. Chronic brain disease: an update on alcoholism, Parkinson's disease, and dementia. *Hospital and Community Psychiatry*, 1982, *33*, 111–126.

Wells, F. L. & Ruesch, J. *Mental examiner's handbook* (Rev. ed.). New York: Psychological Corporation, 1969.

Welman, A.J. Right-sided unilateral visual spatial agnosia, asomatognosia and anosognosia with left hemisphere lesions. *Brain*, 1969, *92*, 571–580.

Welsh, G. S. & Dahlstrom, W. G. (Eds.), *Basic readings on the MMPI in psychology and medicine*. Minneapolis: University of Minnesota Press, 1956.

Wepman, J. M. Mental disorders: organic aspects. *International encyclopedia of the social sciences*. New York. Macmillan, 1968

Wepman, J. M. Aphasia: language without thought or thought without language? *Journal of the American Speech and Hearing Association*, 1976, *18*, 131–136.

Wepman, J. M. & Jones, L. V. Aphasia: diagnostic description and therapy. In W. S. Fields & W. A. Spencer (Eds.), *Stroke rehabilitation*. St. Louis: W. H. Green, 1967.

Wepman, J. M. & Turaids, D. *Spatial Orientation Memory Test. Manual of Directions*. Palm Springs, Calif.: Language Research Associates, 1975; Chicago: Stoelting, no date.

Wertheim, N. & Botez, M. I. Receptive amusia: a clinical analysis. *Brain*, 1961, *84*, 19–30.

Wertz, R. T. The Token Test (TT) (Review). In F. L. Darley (Ed.), *Evaluation of appraisal techniques in speech and language pathology*. Reading, Mass.: Addison-Wesley, 1979a.

Wertz, R. T. Review of Word Fluency Measure (WF). In F. L. Darley (Ed.), *Evaluation of appraisal techniques in speech and language pathology*. Reading, Mass.: Addison-Wesley, 1979b.

Wetzel, C. D. & Squire, R. L. R. Encoding in anterograde amnesia. *Neuropsychologia*, 1979, *17*, 177–184.

Whalley, L.J., Carothers, A.D., Collyer, S., et al. A study of familial factors in Alzheimer's disease. *British Journal of Psychiatry*, 1982, *140*, 249–256.

Wheeler, L., Burke, C. H., & Reitan, R. M. An application of discriminant functions to the problems of predicting brain damage using behavioral variables. *Perceptual and Motor Skills*, 1963, *16*, 681–701.

Wheeler, L. & Reitan, R. M. Discriminant functions applied to the problem of predicting cerebral damage from behavioral tests: a cross-validation study. *Perceptual and Motor Skills*, 1963, *16*, 681–701.

Whelan, T. B., Schteingart, D. E., Starkman, M. N., & Smith, A. Neuropsychological deficits in Cushing's syndrome. *Journal of Nervous and Mental Disease*, 1980, *168*, 753–757.

Whitaker, H. & Ojemann, G. A. Graded localization of naming from electrical stimulation mapping of left cerebral cortex. *Nature*, 1977, *270*, 50–51.

Whitlock, F. A. & Siskind, M. M. Depression as a major symptom of multiple sclerosis. *Journal of Neurology, Neurosurgery, and Psychiatry*, 1980, *43*, 861–865.

Whitty, C. W. M., Stores, G., & Lishman, W. A. Amnesia in cerebral disease. In C. W. M. Whitty & O. L. Zangwill (Eds.), *Amnesia* (2nd ed.). London: Butterworths, 1977.

Whitty, C. W. M. & Zangwill, O. L. Traumatic amnesia. In C. W. M. Whitty & O. L. Zangwill (Eds.), *Amnesia* (2nd ed.). London: Butterworths, 1977.

Wickelgren, W. A. The long and the short of memory. In D. Deutsch & J. A. Deutsch (Eds.), *Short-term memory*. New York: Academic Press, 1975a.

REFERENCES

Wickelgren, W. A. More on the long and short of memory . In D. Deutsch & J. A. Deutsch (Eds.), *Short-term memory*. New York: Academic Press, 1975b.

Wickelgren, W. A. Human learning and memory. *Annual Review of Psychology*, 1981, *32*, 21–52.

Wickens, D. D. Encoding categories of words: an empirical approach to meaning. *Psychological Review*, 1970, *77*, 1–15.

Wilkie, F. L., Eisdorfer, C., & Nowlin, J. B. Memory and blood pressure in the aged. *Experimental Aging Research*, 1976, *2*, 3–16.

Wilkinson, D.A. Examination of alcoholics by computed tomographic (CT) scans: A critical review. *Alcoholism, Clinical and Experimental Research*, 1982, *6*, 31–45.

Wilkus, R. J. & Dodrill, C. B. Neuropsychological correlates of the electroencephalogram in epileptics: I. Topographic distribution and average rate of epileptiform activity. *Epilepsia*, 1976, *17*, 89–100.

Williams, H. L. The development of a caudality scale for the MMPI. *Journal of Clinical Psychology*, 1952, *8*, 293–297.

Williams, H. L. Psychologic testing. In B. Baker (Ed.), *Clinical neurology* (2nd ed.). New York: Hoeber-Harper, 1962.

Williams, M. *Mental testing in clinical practice*. Oxford: Pergamon, 1965.

Williams, M. *Brain damage and the mind*. Baltimore: Penguin Books, 1970a.

Williams, M. Geriatric patients. In P. Mittler (Ed.), *The psychological assessment of mental and physical handicaps*. London: Methuen, 1970b.

Williams, M. Memory disorders associated with electroconvulsive therapy. In C. W. M. Whitty & O. L. Zangwill (Eds.), *Amnesia* (2nd ed.). London: Butterworths, 1977.

Williams, M. Clinical assessment of memory. In P. McReynolds (Ed.), *Advances in psychological assessment*. San Francisco: Jossey-Bass, 1978.

Williams, M. *Brain damage, behaviour, and the mind*. Chichester, England: Wiley, 1979.

Wilson, R. S., Bacon, L. D., Kaszniak, A. W., & Fox, J. H. The episodic-semantic memory distinction and paired associate learning. *Journal of Consulting and Clinical Psychology*, 1982, *50*, 154–155.

Wilson, R. S., Kaszniak, A. W., Bacon, L. D., et al. Facial recognition memory in dementia. *Cortex*, in press.

Wilson, R. S., Kasniak, A. W., & Fox, J. H. *Depth of processing in dementia*. Paper presented at the American Psychological Association Convention, Montreal, Canada, September, 1980.

Wilson, R. S., Kaszniak, A. W., & Fox, J. H. Remote memory in senile dementia. *Cortex*, 1981, *17*, 41–48.

Wilson, R. S., Kaszniak, A. W., Fox, J. H., et al. *Language deterioration in dementia*. Paper presented at the ninth annual meeting of the International Neuropsychological Society, Atlanta, 1981.

Wilson, R. S., Kaszniak, A. W., Klawans, H. L., Jr., & Garron, D. C. High speed memory scanning in Parkinsonism. *Cortex*, 1980, *16*, 67–72.

Wilson, R. S., Rosenbaum, G., & Brown, G. The problem of premorbid intelligence in neuropsychological assessment. *Journal of Clinical Neuropsychology*, 1979, *1*, 49–54.

Winick, M. *Malnutrition and brain development*. New York: Oxford University Press, 1976.

Wisotsky, M. & Friedman, J. H. Problems of psychological testing with aged patients in a geriatric mental hygiene clinic. *Journal of American Geriatrics Society*, 1965, *13*, 243–247.

Witelson, S. F. Sex and the single hemisphere: specialization of the right hemisphere for spatial processing. *Science*, 1976, *193*, 425–427.

REFERENCES

Witelson, S. F. Neuroanatomical asymmetry in left-handers: A review and implications for functional asymmetry. In J. Herron (Ed.), *Neuropsychology of left-handedness*. New York: Academic Press, 1980.

Woltman, H. W. Late neurologic complications of injury to the nervous system. *Wisconsin Medical Journal*, 1942, *41*, 385–391.

Wood, F. B., Ebert, V., & Kinsbourne, M. The episodic-semantic memory distinction in memory and amnesia: clinical and experimental observations. In L. Cermak (Ed.), *Memory and amnesia*. Hillsdale, N.J.: Lawrence Erlbaum Associates, 1982.

Wood, F. B., McHenry, L. C., & Stump, D. A. *Memory and related neurobehavioral deficits in TIA patients: behavioral, rCBF, and outcome measures* (NIH Research Protocol No. 188-18-8951). Unpublished manuscript, Bowman Gray School of Medicine, 1981.

Wood, L. & Shulman, E. The Ellis Visual Designs Test. *Journal of Educational Psychology*, 1940, *31*, 591–602.

Wood, M. M. & Jeffries, R. V. Cognitive changes in the treatment of adult hydrocephalus. In M. Malloy, G. V. Stanley, & K. W. Walsh (Eds.), *Brain Impairment. Proceedings of the 1978 Brain Impairment Workshop*. Melbourne: University of Melbourne, 1979.

Woodcock, R. L. *The Psycho-Educational Battery*. Boston: Teaching Resources, 1977.

Woody, R. H. Inter-judge reliability in clinical electroencephalography. *Journal of Clinical Psychology*, 1968, *24*, 251–256.

Woolf, B. B. The application of the Hewson Ratios to the WAIS as an aid in the differential diagnosis of cerebral pathology. *Journal of Nervous and Mental Disease*, 1960, *130*, 98–109.

Worden, F. G. Attention and auditory electrophysiology. In E. Stellar & J. M. Sprague (Eds.), *Progress in physiological psychology* (Vol. 1). New York: Academic Press, 1966.

World health statistics annual. Geneva: World Health Organization, 1980.

Wright, L. The meaning of IQ scores among professional groups. *Professional Psychology*, 1970, *1*, 265–269.

Wrightsman, L. S. The effects of anxiety, achievement motivation, and task importance on intelligence test performance. *Journal of Educational Psychology*, 1962, *53*, 150–156.

Yacorzynski, G. K. Organic mental disorders. In B. B. Wolman (Ed.), *Handbook of clinical psychology*. New York: McGraw-Hill, 1965.

Yager, J. Intellectual impairment in uremic patients. *American Journal of Psychiatry*, 1973, *130*, 1159–1160.

Yates, A. J. The validity of some psychological tests of brain damage. *Psychological Bulletin*, 1954, *51*, 359–379.

Yates, A. J. Psychological deficit. *Annual Review of Psychology*, 1966, *17*, 111–144.

Yntema, D. B. & Trask, F. P. Recall as a search process. *Journal of Verbal Learning and Verbal Behavior*, 1963, *2*, 65–74.

Zaidel, E. Concepts of cerebral dominance in the split brain. In P. A. Buser & A. Rougeul-Buser (Eds.), *Cerebral correlates of conscious experience*. INSERM Symposium No. 6. Amsterdam: Elsevier/North Holland Biomedical Press, 1978a.

Zaidel, E. Lexical organization in the right hemisphere. In P. A. Buser & A. Rougeul-Buser (Eds.), *Cerebral correlates of conscious experience*. INSERM Symposium No. 6. Amsterdam: Elsevier/North Holland Biomedical Press, 1978b.

Zaidel, E. Performance on the ITPA following cerebial commissurotomy and hemispherectomy. *Neuropsychologia*, 1979, *17*, 259–280.

Zaidel, E., Zaidel, D. W., & Sperry, R. W. Left and right intelligence: case studies of Raven's Progressive Matrices following brain bisection and hemidecortication. *Cortex*, 1981, *17*, 167–186.

REFERENCES

Zangwill, O. L. *Cerebral dominance and its relation to psychological function*. London: Oliver & Boyd, 1960.

Zangwill, O. L. Psychological deficits associated with frontal lobe lesions. *International Journal of Neurology*, 1966, *5*, 395–402.

Zangwill, O. L. Consciousness and the cerebral hemispheres. In S. J. Dimond & J. G. Beaumont (Eds.), *Hemisphere function in the human brain*. New York: Halsted Press, 1974.

Zatz, L. M., Jernigan, T. L., & Ahumada, A. J., Jr. Changes on computed cranial tomography with aging: intracranial fluid volume. *American Journal of Neuroradiology*, 1982a, *3*, 1–11.

Zatz, L. M., Jernigan, T. L., & Ahumada, A. J., Jr. White matter changes in cerebral computed tomography related to aging. *Journal of Computer Assisted Tomography*, 1982b, *6*, 19–23.

Ziegler, D. K. & Hassanien, R. S. Prognosis in patients with transient ischemic attacks. *Stroke*, 1973, *4*, 666–673.

Zimet, C. N. & Fishman, D. B. Psychological deficit in schizophrenia and brain damage. *Annual Review of Psychology*, 1970, *21*, 113–154.

Zimmerman, I. L. Residual effects of brain damage and five MMPI items. *Journal of Consulting Psychology*, 1965, *29*, 394.

Zimmerman, I. L. & Woo-Sam, J. M. *Clinical interpretation of the Wechsler Adult Intelligence Scale*. New York: Grune & Stratton, 1973.

Zubrick, A. & Smith, A. Minnesota Test for Differential Diagnosis of Aphasia (MTDDA) (Review). In F. L. Darley (Ed.), *Evaluation of appraisal techniques in speech and language pathology*. Reading, Mass.: Addison-Wesley, 1979.

Zubrick, S. & Smith, A. *Factors affecting BVRT performance in adults with acute focal cerebral lesions*. Paper presented at the sixth International Neuropsychological Society meeting, Minneapolis, 1978.

Zung, W. K. A self-rating depression scale. *Archives of General Psychiatry*, 1965, *12*, 63–70.

Zung, W. K. Factors influencing the self-rating depression scale. *Archives of General Psychiatry*, 1967, *16*, 543–547.

Zytowski, D. G. & Hudson, J. The validity of split-half abbreviations of the WAIS. *Journal of Clinical Psychology*, 1965, *21*, 292–294.

Name Index

Bolton, N., 118, 219, 254, 273
Bond, M., 170, 210, 212, 593
Bond, M. R., 170, 173, 595
Bondareff, W., 181
Bonin, G. von., 50, 53
Bonner, F., 82
Borg, S., 193
Borkowski, J. G., 330
Bornstein, R. A., 465
Borod, J. C., 315, 406
Bortner, M., 278
Botez, M. I., 75, 190, 203, 243, 375
Botez, T., 35, 47, 203, 407
Botez-Marquard, T., 190, 243
Botwinick, J., 117, 215–19, 244, 266, 269, 273, 418, 419, 472, 503
Bourke, R. S., 170, 171, 174, 211, 291, 559, 586
Bowen, D. M., 181
Bowen, F. P., 186, 187, 508, 538, 547
Bowers, D., 353
Bowles, J. W., 114
Boyd, J. L., 358
Boyd, R. D., 586, 588
Bradford, D. C., 344, 345
Bradshaw, J. L., 224
Braff, D. L., 198
Brain, W. R., 25, 28, 29, 75
Brandt, J., 28, 189, 195, 196, 470
Brassell, E. G., 314
Bratton, J. C., 243
Bray, G. P., 37
Brierly, J. B., 28
Briggs, G. G., 222, 223
Briggs, M., 593
Briggs, P. F., 125, 272, 512
Brilliant, P. J., 151, 392
Brion, S., 76, 193
Britton, P. G., 118, 254, 273
Brizzee, K. R., 216
Broadbent, D. E., 27, 58
Brocklehurst, 384
Brodal, A., 41, 46, 50, 76, 212, 339
Brody, B., 72, 409, 541
Broe, G. A., 169, 174, 213
Bromley, D. B., 477, 505
Brooks, D. N., 170, 172–74, 212, 216, 441, 445, 447, 471, 503, 595
Brookshire, R. H., 56, 312, 323, 324
Brown, D. A., 264, 283, 285
Brown, E. R., 468
Brown, G., 94, 186
Brown, J., 416
Brown, J. W., 46, 47, 177, 216
Brown, L., 246, 253, 271
Brown, R. E., 182, 183
Brown, S. J., 571
Bruce, P. R., 218
Bruhn, A. R., 616

Bruhn, P., 198, 199
Brussel, I. A., 361, 605
Brust, J. C. M., 178
Bryden, M. P., 55, 60, 220
Buck, J. N., 404, 607
Buck, M. W., 37, 61, 84, 212
Buffery, A. W. H., 53, 58, 220, 224
Buhrich, N. A., 233
Burch, P. R. J., 187, 188
Burke, C. H., 563
Burke, D. M., 218
Burke, H. R., 503
Burkhart, G., 435, 437
Burlingame, C. C., 92
Burn, J., 242, 271
Burns, J. W., 123, 529
Buros, O. K., 287, 306
Buschke, H., 196, 473, 474
Butcher, J. N., 608
Butler, J. M., 132
Butters, N., 18, 28, 29, 47, 72, 77, 189, 193–97, 200, 273, 352, 408, 409, 421, 422, 431, 458, 463, 470, 473, 541, 543, 555
Byrd, M., 218

Caddotte, M., 203
Cahn, A., 54
Caine, E. D., 188, 189, 235, 432, 483
Calsyn, D. A., 481
Caltagirone, C., 179, 183, 187–89, 235, 332, 341, 429, 572
Camp, B. W., 307
Campbell, D. C., 213, 343, 442, 501, 505
Campbell, R. J., 601
Campos, J. J., 221
Canter, A. H., 91, 393, 394
Canter, G. J., 316
Cany, E., 418, 456
Capitani, E., 70
Caramazza, A., 32, 433
Carey, S., 352
Carlen, P. L., 193, 194, 196
Carlin, A. S., 198
Carmody, T. P., 116
Carmon, A., 68
Caronna, J. J., 592
Carothers, A. D., 181
Carr, D., 529, 532
Carrivick, P. J., 209, 211
Carson, R. C., 598, 609
Carson, R. E., 74
Carter, J. W., Jr., 114
Carter-Saltzman, L., 222
Casey, V. A., 231, 612, 617
Cassel, R. H., 114
Castro-Caldas, A., 177, 528
Cauthen, N., 460
Centofanti, C. C., 555

Test Index

Subject Index

Norms *(Continued)*
   in deficit measurement, 87–88, 90, 91
   species-wide, 88–89, 90, 133
   test, 87–88, 90, 111, 142–43
Nucleus (nerve center), *45*, 46, 48
Nutritional disease, 193, 194, 196, 202–3, 204,
   209

Observational data, 129–30, 134–35, 576
   in estimating premorbid ability level, 92, 96,.
   154, 156
Observational methods, 3–4, 129–30, 599
Occipital lobe disorders, 65–67, 70, 77
   and test performance, 367, 461, 541
Occipital lobes, 63–64, 65–67
   role in recall, 75
   visual association areas, 65, 77
Occupation and test norms, 103
Oculomotor disorders, 72, 555
Omnibus test format, *239*–40, 288, 297
Optical illusions, 365–67, 523
   subjective contour, 355–56
Optimal versus standard testing conditions,
   120–24, 127
Ordering, organizing, and planning, 30, 64,
   330, 510–11, 600. *See also* Executive
   functions
   defects of, 11, 38, 47, 163
   defects with right hemisphere lesions, 56, 69,
   74, 511
"Organicity", 16–17
Organizing. *See* Ordering, organizing, and
   planning
Organic mental syndrome (OMS), 551–52
Organic solvents. *See* Industrial toxins
Orientation, 533
   body parts, 67, 71, 378–79, 538
   directional, 538, 539, 547, 574
   geographic, 545–46
   personal, 538
   place, 534
   space, 55, 458, 537, 541
   time, 83, 406, 534. *See also* Time sense
   topographic, 544–45
Orientation defects, 47, 65, 202, 509, 533
   in acute brain conditions, 210, 533, 593
   in alcohol-related disorders, 18, 194, 197
   body schema, 538–39
   with brain damage, 535, 581, 583
   in dementing conditions, 181–82, 189–90,
   215, 235, 533, 544, 581
   in depression, 235
   directional, 71, 541, 547
   place, 533, 581, 583
   route finding, 544, 547
   spatial, 56, 71, 72, 74, 75, 187, 382, 541, 543,
   544, 601

and thalamic lesions, 47
time, 234, 533, 535
topographic, 74, 544
Outcome, 212–14, 225
   evaluating, 212–13, 593, 595
Overachievers, 95, 96, 259
Overlap zones, cortical, 50, 64, 71
Overwriting. *See* Hypergraphia

Pain, impaired perception, 71
Paint sniffing, 199
Paper and pencil tests, 108–9, 240, 287, 299–
   307
Paralysis, 50, 61. *See also* Motor disabilities
Paranoid reactions, 61
Pareital lobe disorders, 65, 68, 70, 543, 547
Parietal lobe lesions
   left, effects of, 66, 71
   left and test performance, 71–72, 264, 279–
   80, 300, 442
   right, effects of, 66, 72–73, 206, 345, 377
   right and test performance, 279–80, 286, 352,
   393, 411, 441, 442, 541, 543
   and test performance, 378, 393, 498
   and visual field defects, 281
Parietal lobes, 63–64, 65, 67, 70, 181
Parieto-occipital region disorders, 399–400
Parieto-occipital region lesions
   right, effects of, 66, 74
   right and test performance, 413
Parieto-occipital sulcus, *64*
Parieto-temporo-occipital region association
   area, 67–73
Parieto-temporo-occipital region lesions, effects
   of. *See* Posterior cortex lesions
Parkinson's disease, 48, 185–86, 226, 508
   cognitive deficits, 186–87, 393, 404, 538, 544,
   547, 549–50
   neuropathology and course, 185–86
   neurotransmitters in, 185
   personality characteristics, 187, 508
Partial complex seizures. *See* Epilepsy,
   temporal lobe
Pathological crying or laughter, 36–37, 236
Pathological inertia, *81*, 82, 312, 518, 526. *See
   also* Apathy
Patient attitudes and expectations, 105, 123–24,
   127
Patient care, 8–13. *See also* Rehabilitation
Patients, brain damage. *See* Brain damaged
   patients
Pattern analysis, 147, 154–62
   with Wechsler tests, 156, 251–53
Patterns of impairment. *See* Impairment
   patterns; Pattern analysis
Percentile scores, 138, 139, 140–41, 144
   and ability classifications, 147

Thought or language see p 260